Religious Issues
and
Interreligious
Dialogues

RELIGIOUS ISSUES AND INTERRELIGIOUS DIALOGUES

An Analysis and Sourcebook of Developments Since 1945

EDITED BY
Charles Wei-hsun Fu AND Gerhard E. Spiegler

GREENWOOD PRESS

NEW YORK • WESTPORT, CONNECTICUT • LONDON

Library of Congress Cataloging-in-Publication Data

Religious issues and interreligious dialogues: an analysis and
    sourcebook of developments since 1945 / edited by Charles Wei-hsun
    Fu and Gerhard E. Spiegler.
        p.   cm.
    Bibliography: p.
    Includes index.
    ISBN 0–313–23239–3 (lib. bdg. : alk. paper)
    1. Religions—Relations.   I. Fu, Charles Wei-hsun, 1933-
II. Spiegler, Gerhard E.
    BL410.R44   1989
    291.1′72′0904—dc 19   88–21398

British Library Cataloguing in Publication Data is available.

Library of Congress Catalog Card Number: 88–21398
ISBN: 0–313–23239–3

First published in 1989

Greenwood Press, Inc.
88 Post Road West, Westport, Connecticut 06881

Printed in the United States of America

The paper used in this book complies with the
Permanent Paper Standard issued by the National
Information Standards Organization (Z39.48–1984).

10 9 8 7 6 5 4 3 2 1

Contents

II: Dialogues

Preface

This is the second of two reference works addressing major developments in world religions since 1945. The analysis and source material in the first volume focused on religion, ideology, and politics. This volume presents a number of prominent issues in the world of religion and gives special attention to the increasingly important "dialogues" between the major world religions. As a source book, this work is designed to introduce readers, through critical analysis, to the issues and the dialogues that are addressed and to provide guidance for further reading. The various chapter bibliographies provide additional source material and information; readers are directed toward alternative viewpoints and are given the necessary background sources to allow for independent analysis and study.

It is important to remind ourselves, as we use the source materials in this work, that in philosophical-theological discourse, few issues are ever fully settled. They simply become submerged and then reappear. The source materials in this volume do not purport to settle the issues but aim to encourage further study. The issues and dialogues presented were chosen not because they alone are significant but because they are of such importance that at this time in history they demand our attention.

Thus Joseph Margolis addresses the perplexing problem of "relativism." He contributes the reformulation of the questions but promises no settlement. Norbert Samuelson in turn offers a meticulous examination of "atheism" and "theism" but not a final word. This may be unsettling but no more so to us than to those who came before us.

The issues of "feminism" and "conservatism and liberalism" have a presence in our time that cannot be ignored. Rosemary Ruether and Ernest Stoeffler, in a distinctive style, help us to "understand" beyond mere emotive response, as does Khalid Duran when he shares the "Quest of Muslim Identity" with us.

Charles Fu makes us aware that the "modernization" of ancient moral and ethical standards is not an issue restricted to the West.

Interreligious dialogue is today not an option but a necessity. It must be expressed in deed and word; it must be safeguarded from the merely fashionable and busy. Its premise is the ability to listen beyond mere words and the willingness to risk one's identity. This "ability to listen" and the willingness to "risk" pervades Paul van Buren's thoughtful struggle with the meeting of Christianity and Judaism, R. Panikkar's passionate reach beyond the boundaries of the Christian and Hindu experience, and John Cobb's insightful discussion of Buddhism. Ashok Gangadean pursues his quest for a "universal theology"; impatient with the hardness of the historical ground, he yearns for conversation on a higher speculative level.

What matters in this volume is not that we will be satisfied with the answers given but that we are driven to shape our questions anew and that we continue our study. The issues that matter are the issues that stay with us; the dialogue that matters is the human conversation in which word becomes deed and continues toward greater self-understanding.

C.W.F. and G.E.S.

I

ISSUES

1

Beyond Objectivism and Relativism

JOSEPH MARGOLIS

Whoever would defend relativism must, on pain of stupidity, construe it in a way that is not self-contradictory or self-refuting; yet, its opponents regularly and comfortably identify it in a blatantly stupid form.[1] We cannot help suspecting the objector's practice, because the intended lesson needs to be repeated much too frequently to be taken entirely at face value and because there is no straightforward reason for supposing that the defenders of relativism are all that stupid. On the other hand, there is the perfectly reasonable concern—against would-be relativists—that they cannot be permitted to tailor the notion of relativism at will solely to escape the damning charge: they must afford an account that suitably bears on a fair portion of those issues that seem to have led to the allegedly inescapable original complaint. A nice way of passing between these two dangers suggests itself: let us try to formulate some conditions or constraints that a responsive and interesting form of relativism is likely to satisfy, of both the consistency sort and the pertinence sort, without rushing to declare *what* the relativist thesis is or must be. That ought to satisfy all within the field of combat—except those whose own pleasant game is thereby exposed. The point of the exercise would be to restore a clear sense of the viability of relativism against the backdrop of its accelerating appeal in the contemporary world and in sympathy with the conviction that, if it is viable, it will surely affect in a profound way our understanding of human rationality and the puzzle of legitimating the alternative forms of life that the human race seems forever bound to encourage.

What will we need? We shall want to set some formal conditions on the truth values (or truthlike values) that the relativist's judgments, propositions, claims, or suitable analogues can take, by virtue of which, conditions that are sufficiently close to or like the usually imputed self-refutation or self-contradiction obtains but without the obvious penalty; we also shall want to show in some way what grounds may be offered for holding that, in *some* sector of inquiry at least (precisely because of the nature of the domain) but not necessarily in all sectors of inquiry, it is either more reasonable to restrict such judgments in the accommodating way than to refuse to, or is as reasonable to do so as to refuse to, and that doing so really does address the deeper concerns about the alleged scope of the relativist thesis. Here, it may prove to be a disappointment that a global, universal, or inclusive version of relativism (for instance, a form of Protagorean relativism) may not be coherent in the sense required, although it may be.[2] But if it is not, surely reasonable relativists would want to abdicate the inclusive version and simply retreat to a more restricted, modular, or modest version and try to make the case that even that sort of relativism is stronger than its opponents would be willing to grant. There might, then, have to be a compromise on both sides, and both sides might be sobered by the discovery.

The most minimal formal condition required is straightforward: simply take sets of the offending judgments—supposed to be contradictory or self-refuting— and restrict the truth values or the truthlike values they can be assigned, so that in accord with the new values but not in accord with the old, and without otherwise altering the content of what is claimed, the judgments in question are no longer contradictory or self-refuting. They might, for instance, be said to be "incongruent" precisely because, on a bipolar model of truth and falsity, they would be incompatible but, now, are not. That this is not yet sufficient for any interesting form of relativism begins to be clear if we merely remind ourselves that probabilized judgments go some distance to meeting this condition—for example, that it is probable that *Nixon knew about Watergate in advance* and that it is probable that *Nixon did not know about Watergate in advance*. Usually, probabilized judgments are supposed to be assignable the bipolar truth values *true* and *false,* in addition to probabilized values, and so would normally be taken to generate (contrary to what we want) contradictions when assigned such values. But the direction in which the formal constraints would need to be spelled out is reasonably clear and reasonably manageable.[3] All we need do is restrict the admissible values—for instance, values such as *plausible* and *implausible,* disallowing *truth* and *falsity*—so that the offending contradictions and self-refutations are precluded (without needing to disallow contradiction or self-refutation in other ways); then we should be home free. But this is simply to show that objections to relativism are as uninteresting as this sort of defense. But it clears the air. For instance, it disables at a stroke claims such as the following: "implicitly or explicitly, the relativist claims that his or her position is true, yet the relativist also insists that since truth is relative, what is taken as true may also be false. Consequently, relativism itself may be true *and* false. One cannot consistently state the case for relativism without undermining it."[4] It is true that the countermove here offered is purely formal (thus far at least), so it can hardly be thought to be sufficiently persuasive against substantive suspicions regarding relativism. By parity of reasoning, so, too, are formal complaints of the sort just cited for which, fairly then, formal solutions are entirely sufficient.

Seen this way, we may entertain the notion that relativism is a thesis (and the accompanying rationale for it) regarding the assignment of truth values (or truth-like values) to judgments and the like. The rationale would be, one should suppose, to be at all interesting, a theory about the properties or nature of some part of the world or both. Here, properly, is where the more telling ingenuities of conceptual strategy are bound to arise; here, also, is where the more serious objections to relativism are bound to demand attention. To avoid the narrowest sort of bias in disputing the issue, we should try to propose reasonably strong or fair requirements on any would-be candidate theories: particularly, conditions that do not in themselves seem to be relativistic but that, conjoined with fully developed versions of the formal condition already mentioned, are likely to generate a distinctly robust form of relativism, one that would make a significant difference (once subscribed to) to our understanding and appraisal of the cognitive power of inquiries that can be supported in different sectors of interest.

What strategic conditions could we mention? The following seem reasonable:

1. Relativism should not be construed as, or as reducible to, any form of skepticism, cynicism, nihilism, irrationalism, anarchism, or the like, although it may be that a well-defended relativism would lend comfort to doctrines of these sorts.

2. Relativism should be construed as precluding, within its scope, any form of foundationalism, essentialism, logocentrism, or similar doctrine, without being thought restricted merely to their denial.

3. Relativism should be construed as compatible with, but as not entailing as such, various forms of historicism, although some forms of historicism should be construed as entailing relativism.

4. Relativism should be construed as stronger if its rationale is formulated in terms of properties imputed to a domain of inquiry rather than if it merely depends on cognitive limitations imposed on whoever makes inquiry in that domain, although the latter version need not be refused.

5. Relativism should not be construed in terms of judgments merely relativized (or relationalized) to alternative conceptual schemes, or in terms of the putative incommensurability of such schemes, or in terms of being cognitively confined within the boundaries of particular such schemes to the exclusion of others; and a theory should not be construed as relativistic merely because it provides for making and appraising judgments that entail an appeal to the categories of particular conceptual schemes or to schemes subject to the conditions just disfavored.

6. Relativism should not be construed as precluding comparative judgments of the usual sort and range (for instance, of better and worse and of more or less adequate) conceded within theories that do subscribe to bipolar truth values.

7. Relativism should not, when restricted or not inclusive, be construed as incompatible in principle with cognitive claims, outside its own scope, that do take bipolar truth values.

8. Relativism should not be construed as, or as reducible to, pluralism, and it should be construed as entailing but as not entailed by pluralism.

9. Relativism should be construed as neutral regarding, and as not committed to either affirming or denying, or requiring or precluding, the adequacy of any single or unified conceptual scheme for purposes of resolving contending cognitive claims.

10. Relativism should not be construed as affirming or entailing (or denying, for that matter) the facts of cultural diversity or cultural relativity, whatever they may be, synchronically across cultures or diachronically within particular cultures.

11. Relativism should not be required to resolve claims or disputes by way of supplying evidence or cognitive resources greater or more fruitful than what is normally admitted within any given science or inquiry; in particular, it should not be unconditionally required to be stated in an inclusive rather than a restricted form or a form more inclusive in scope than any nonrelativistic theory it contends against; it should be construed as a theory fitted in a conceptually competitive way to the practices of particular forms of inquiry.

These eleven conditions make a very useful set. Doubtless there are others that would be worth considering in a reasonably ramified version of relativism. But it is hard to suppose that they fail to touch on the points at issue in very nearly all—one is tempted to say, just plain all—of the best-known quarrels about relativism in the recent literature. If so, any theory that could satisfactorily meet these conditions and the developed formal condition intended would be a full-fledged form of relativism, even if we were to concede that more restricted theories deserve to be admitted and even if we hoped that any relativist worth his salt would try to link his theory to larger issues regarding the practices of science and rational inquiry and perhaps human rationality and responsibility as well.

Here, we may take advantage of a recent account, one of the latest to air the issues raised, that offers a view decidedly sanguine about avoiding the so-called twin disorders of objectivism and relativism. It promises a convenient economy, because it opposes all or nearly all of the conditions just mentioned and because it surveys the views of most of the principal opponents of the "disorders" in question. There are actually very few sustained statements of this sort to be had. If we could offset, perhaps, the countermoves it collects from a sprawling literature, we might conveniently focus in a brief span the actual prospects of a disciplined relativism.

In his book *Beyond Objectivism and Relativism,* Richard Bernstein offered the following terminological distinctions:

By "objectivism," I mean the basic conviction that there is or must be some permanent, ahistorical matrix or framework to which we can ultimately appeal in determining the nature of rationality, knowledge, truth, reality, goodness, or rightness. . . . The objectivist maintains that unless we can ground philosophy, knowledge, or language in a suitably rigorous manner we cannot avoid radical skepticism.[5]

The relativist not only denies the positive claims of the objectivist but goes further. In its strongest form, relativism is the basic conviction that when we turn to the examination of those concepts that philosophers have taken to be the most fundamental—whether it is the concept of rationality, truth, reality, right, the good, or norms—we are forced to recognize that in the final analysis all such concepts must be understood as relative to a specific conceptual scheme, theoretical framework, paradigm, form of life, society, or culture. . . . For the relativist, there is no substantive overarching framework or single metalanguage by which we can rationally adjudicate or univocally evaluate competing claims of alternative paradigms.[6]

Some clarifying observations are in order. First, Bernstein means to include, for understandable reasons, not only the rationalists and empiricists and all foundationalists and essentialists but also Kant and Husserl, although the latter in particular had himself used the term *objectivist* to exclude the special apodictic certainty appropriate to his own favored form of so-called transcendental subjectivity.[7] In any case, "objectivism" is a convenient catch-all. Now, it is true that relativism is incompatible with an inclusive objectivism (if itself inclusive) or a restricted objectivism (if itself restricted). But it hardly follows, as Bernstein seems to hold (in agreement with Hans-Georg Gadamer, for instance), that "relativism . . . is not only the dialectical antithesis of objectivism, it is itself parasitic upon objectivism."[8] That this is neither true nor required nor even particularly central to relativism is worth emphasizing, since relativism is (trivially) incompatible with accounts of knowledge and science that are opposed to objectivism *and* relativism and that nevertheless insist that cognitive claims are capable of a measure of "objectivity." (Here, at some risk, we may include as specimen views of the nonrelativist, nonobjectivist sort the views of the following at least: Karl Popper, Thomas Kuhn, Imre La Katos, Mary Hesse, Hans-Georg Gadamer, Jürgen Habermas, Paul Ricoeur, Donald Davidson, Hilary Putnam; Charles Taylor, Alaistair MacIntyre, Peter Winch.) Thus if, as now seems reasonable, objectivist or so-called foundationalist views (which Richard Rorty, for one, has recently attacked) can be expected to be on the defensive and decline for some time, it can hardly be supposed that the status of relativism would be or need be adversely affected by that fact alone or that the attempt to support relativism would correspondingly decline or have to decline;[9] yet this is the upshot of Gadamer's thesis and of Bernstein's to the extent that he favors Gadamer's view.

Admittedly, to state this is not yet to state *what* might be meant by nonobjectivist "objectivity" with respect to science, but the implied burden surely falls on relativists and nonrelativists alike. Perhaps a reasonable first pass at what it would require may be drawn from Bernstein's own sympathetic reading of Kuhn's position. As Bernstein observed: "The shift from a model of rationality that searches for determinate rules which can serve as necessary and sufficient conditions, to a model of practical rationality that emphasizes the role of *exemplars* and judgmental interpretation, is not only characteristic of theory-choice but is a leitmotif that pervades all of Kuhn's thinking about science."[10] It may turn out that there are no convincing forms of the "objectivity" required that are not either inclusive or restricted forms of relativism as well. The interesting fact is that Bernstein does not actually consider the question of defending relativistic theories opposed to objectivism, and very few commentators do. Undoubtedly, he believes that relativism refuses to countenance cognitive claims at all or is unable to do so in a way that would meet the most minimal condition of avoiding self-contradiction or self-refutation. At any rate, he observed that, in Kuhn's view—and to some extent, in accordance with his own thesis—a paradigm is to be construed as "a concrete exemplar that is open to differing interpretations" but in such a way as *not* to invite the mistaken inference that the contrast between "rules" and "paradigms" is "a contrast between the cognitive and the noncognitive."[11] So he himself provides a favorable setting for relativism but does not actually explore it.

Notice, in this regard, the sense of Bernstein's opening remarks, which fix the argumentative structure of the entire issue. "From a manifest perspective," he said, "many contemporary debates are still structured within traditional extremes. There is still an underlying belief that in the final analysis the only viable alternatives open to us are *either* some form of objectivism, foundationalism, ultimate grounding of knowledge, science, philosophy, and language *or* that we are ineluctably led to relativism, skepticism, historicism, and nihilism."[12] Bernstein identified the relationship between these two notions as "the central cultural opposition of our time";[13] he even said that "if we see through objectivism, if we expose what is wrong with this way of thinking, then we are at the same time questioning the very intelligibility of relativism."[14] So Bernstein rejected the search for "an Archimedean point" (Descartes's obsession), rejected "the Cartesian Anxiety" itself (that is, objectivism); viewed the "exclusive disjunction of objectivism or relativism" as "misleading and distortive," implausible and unnecessary, and tied to the Cartesian Anxiety; and urged us to "exorcise" the Anxiety so that we can pass "beyond" objectivism and relativism to a viable, already somewhat articulated "postempiricist," more "historically oriented understanding of scientific inquiry as a rational activity."[15]

We owe to Bernstein a very trim formulation of the important danger of moving between—that is, merely between—the extremes of objectivism and of certain entirely disheartened theories about the effective collapse of science and inquiry, but it is simply a mistake to suppose that relativism (at least the interesting forms of what may be called relativism—for example, in accordance with our eleven conditions and the formal condition of avoiding self-refutation and self-contradiction *or* even in accordance with Bernstein's own support of Kuhn) either cannot be anything but those disheartened theories or cannot extricate itself from entailing them. Possibly, Bernstein owes *us* an explanation of why he so arbitrarily supposes that either relativism cannot fail to take the absurdly stupid form it has so often taken and so boringly has been assigned (perhaps even by some of its would-be champions); or why it should be identified with extreme views such as skepticism and nihilism (which, in the sense intended, are utterly opposed to admitting cognitive claims of the sort usually assessed in any disciplined science and which relativism actually attempts to account for); or why or in what sense it should be linked necessarily, or even merely adversely, with historicism and the concession of incommensurable, irreducibly plural conceptual schemes (where, on Bernstein's reading as on many others', such doctrines are tantamount to strong forms of skepticism and nihilism).[16] No answer at all is given to these questions. Moreover, on the documentation Bernstein himself offered, the prejudice appears to be very widespread.

In short, the prime strategy for redeeming relativism as a respectable, even viable, possibly even unavoidable, theory about cognitive claims (once objectivism is defeated or rejected) rests with prying relativism away from its allegedly symbiotic connection with objectivism itself. *No one has ever shown that the attempted defense of relativism must fail because objectivism fails (or because its more familiar specialized versions fail).* That, after all, would be an extraordinary claim: first, because even the thesis about the stupid form of relativism need take no notice of objectivism; second, because relativism itself has, whenever it has addressed objectivism (or its various forms), opposed it. To imagine that in doing the latter it must make itself particularly vulnerable or even fatally indefensible is to suppose that relativism must be even more stupid than at first appeared and to ignore the fact that not all attacks on objectivism are taken (by the opponents of relativism itself) to be vulnerable in the same way. That is, a decisive third consideration stares us in the face: Bernstein and similar-minded opponents of objectivism strongly deplore and attack the argumentative strategy that would have it that the defeat of objectivism permits only a relativistic defense of science and rational inquiry. So there is an obvious lacuna in the argument.

If this much alone were conceded, we should be at once catapulted "beyond objectivism and relativism" simply because relativism itself would then have been recognized as a more serious and stronger contender than it appeared to be when it was unfortunately viewed as a mere parasite upon the back of objectivism. Relativism need not be a primitive theory then; as a result, our own speculation about an adequate theory of science and rational inquiry need not be confined by a similarly vestigial constraint. To that extent, we have justified the implied irony that the usual critics of relativism, who treat that doctrine as flailing away at an already hopeless thesis (objectivism), are themselves the principal, self-appointed victims of just that disorder—when, by a miracle of misunderstanding, the original charge against relativism would not have been (and probably could never have been) made to stick at all. So the tables have been effectively turned.

But no one will be satisfied. After all, the appeal to Bernstein's original counterstrategy was made in the name of an economy; now, it could be seen as no more than a sly maneuver to gain an unfair advantage by way of a near-irrelevancy. What more should be said? We have made some general remarks that could be focused more on the eleven conditions that eligible versions of relativism may be expected to meet. For example, it is very important to emphasize that relativism is directly opposed to skepticism, irrationalism, and allied doctrines in the sense in which the latter are themselves opposed to conceding that certain would-be cognitive disputes are actually resolvable in acceptable ways on the basis of familiar evidential or argumentative procedures. What may explain the usual confusion is this: the relativist opposes (whether in the restricted or inclusive sense) the admissibility of bipolar truth values; somehow, this alone is converted into his being opposed to the admissibility of *any* truth values (or truthlike values)—hence it is converted into his affirming a skeptical or anarchist or nihilist thesis. But first, mere indeterminacy of truth value at a given moment of inquiry or because of real-time constraints is *not* an expression of skepticism; on the contrary, it is an affirmation of the cognitive standing of a given issue, and findings of indeterminacy are actually assignments of truth value relativized to the available evidence. Second, it may be that, over time, questions that were once thought to be "intrinsically incapable of determination" (that is, of being determined as true or false) might prove, later, to be capable of such determination: this, for example, has been said of Clerk Maxwell's change of mind (after Albert A. Michelson's invention of the required technology), regarding "some propositions about the relative velocity of light."[17] But that kind of adjustment is surely available to nonrelativists and relativists alike, even if it is the case that it encourages speculation along relativistic lines. Third, it is false to suppose that denying the admissibility of bipolar truth values when weaker values *are* admissible is an expression of skepticism: on the contrary, it is itself a strong cognitive claim, presumably about the properties of a particular domain of inquiry. Thus, for instance, W. V. Quine's famous doctrine of the indeterminacy of translation is not a skeptical thesis, it is (meant to be) a relativist thesis: it holds that alternative, incompatible ontologies *can* be empirically supported in given domains and that, because of the way ontological questions are addressed, stronger bipolar appraisals of candidate ontologies *cannot* be supported.[18] On the other hand, it may be true that Paul Feyerabend, but not Thomas Kuhn, intended to hold a skeptical thesis in advancing various versions of the notorious incommensurability claim. For example, Feyerabend may have intended such a thesis in holding that "there exist scientific theories which are mutually incommensurable though they apparently deal 'with the same subject matter.' "[19]

The addition of these reflections fairly well settles the plausibility of all of our eleven conditions, at least as far as confirming the strong coherence and relevance of relativism is concerned. But we may round the argument out by focusing, finally, on what substantive considerations may be expected to give relativism a genuine inning. Here, the argument is straightforward as well as remarkably easy to supply. We need not insist on the necessity of subscribing to relativism, merely on the reasonableness of conceding the pertinence and promise of relativistic options. First, then, whenever objectivism is denied or defeated, relativism is facilitated, even if it is not positively entailed. For the rejection of objectivism signifies that, in all domains affected, the strongest presumption in favor of uniquely, exclusively, timelessly correct answers to given questions is disallowed; consequently, the strongest possible condition on which even an inclusive relativism could be sustained is conceded, although without confirming any particular relativistic thesis. This is the best arrangement that could be imagined: it sets the stage for invoking the required formal condition, that is, for invoking truth values (or truthlike values) logically weaker than the bipolar values of truth and falsity, without their being overrideable by the latter and without actually invoking them; it also invites further substantive considerations in virtue of which the weaker values may reasonably be invoked. On that reading, the advantage to relativism is established by way of objections that, on any familar view, are not themselves particularly skewed in its favor. On the contrary, the principal opponents of objectivism or foundationalism or the like are characteristically opposed to relativism as well. So the advantage can hardly be thought to be tendentious.

For example, when Kuhn's (and even Feyerabend's) incommensurability thesis is taken as a justified attack on objectivism—or at least on that strong form of objectivism that holds that there must be a single, omnicompetent, "common, neutral epistemological framework within which we can rationally evaluate competing theories and paradigms or that there is a set of rules . . . that will tell us 'how rational agreement can be reached on what would settle the issue on every point where statements seem to conflict' "—it is often insisted that that thesis "has *nothing to do* with relativism [or it may be disputed whether it entails relativism], or at least that form of relativism which wants to claim that there can be no rational comparison among the plurality of theories, paradigms, and language games—that we are prisoners locked in our framework and cannot get out of it."[20] Even Popper, who opposed the incommensurability thesis, could allow the point of the defense, since he, too, would oppose both that objectivism *and* the relativism threatened (though he would also take the incommensurability claim itself to insure an extreme relativistic thesis).[21]

What is interesting about the usual dispute is this: both sides on the incommensurability thesis (for example, Kuhn and Popper) insist on the *"objectivity of comparative judgments within science and on relativism's opposition to that constraint."*[22] They see relativism, therefore, as threatening to undermine the basis that science itself provides for a reasonable account of human rationality. But the fear is curiously misdirected against relativism and can only be explained—as in accounting for Popper's own view—by noticing the altogether too easy, entirely undefended conceptual slippage that links in one breath irrationalism, skepticism, and relativism (doctrines clearly so labeled in order to be discarded together).[23] What all of these critics fail to consider, however, is just that, along the lines already sketched, relativism is *not* opposed to either "objectivity" or "comparative judgments": it holds only that such objectivity and comparison will (in either the inclusive or restricted sense of relativism) be subject to the formal constraint on truth values here noted (the availability of "incongruent" judgments) that signifies the *same* rejection of skepticism, irrationalism, nihilism, anarchism, and the like. In short, the opponents of relativism inadvertently impoverish its conceptual resources, enabling themselves (innocently enough) to claim to be able to support a form of scientific objectivity that is opposed to objectivism and yet can always or characteristically or in the most important instances pass beyond the logical weakness that relativism insists upon. It appears, however, that this issue has almost never been frontally addressed by the opponents of relativism and that there is no known developed argument that actually refutes or seriously weakens the relativistic thesis. Certainly, the required objection can hardly be the familiar formal one.

Once we concede this much, we may strengthen the plausibility and challenge of relativism by taking note of further substantive concessions of a large theoretical sort—usually *not* advanced to favor relativism—that are viewed as particularly vigorous at present. All should be read in terms jointly of the rejection of objectivism and (for purposes of the argument before us) of compatibility with and sympathy for the formal condition on truth values already remarked. Certainly, any concessions in terms of disallowing a clear demarcation, along classical Kantian lines, between the structures imposed on our science by the processes of the human mind and the structures that putatively belong to the "independent" world that we know through our science (the familiar realist/ idealist puzzle—or, in the Quineian version, the analytic/synthetic puzzle) cannot (now) fail to be seen to give aid and comfort to relativism.[24] In a fair sense, they must mark at least detailed circumstances under which the incommensurability issue is bound to arise, although they point to even more profound difficulties in the attempt to avoid relativism: in particular, relativism need not be restricted to incommensurability contexts; even within a common conceptual framework of the intended sort, relativistic challenges may well obtain.

Similarly, repudiating the more determinate forms of objectivism is bound to encourage more determinate forms of relativism: for example, repudiating essentialism (for example, in accordance with Popper's well-known view) or so-called totalizing (along the lines so boldly championed by Claude Lévi-Strauss and other structuralists) or epistemological foundationalism itself.[25] Again, even more specifically, since they affect truth claims in the most unavoidable referential and predicative ways, conceptual difficulties affecting univocal applications of the so-called principle of charity (for instance in Hilary Putnam's concessions regarding reference to theoretical entities) or difficulties affecting univocal extensions of universals or general terms (for instance in accord with Ludwig Wittgenstein's reflections on the informality of rules governing natural usage or Nelson Goodman's strictures on resemblance) are bound to be favorable to forms of relativism.[26]

The strenuousness of resisting relativism will be even more marked as we move on to the special complexities of linguistic and cultural contexts. Here, it is hard to see how the admission of intentional and interpretive considerations, of historicism, and in particular of the profoundly consensual (that is, reflexive) nature of objectivity in the human studies could possibly fail to strengthen the relativist's hand.[27] Perhaps the most obvious locus in terms of which to press the relativist alternative in that in which it is generally conceded that the very individuation of cultural entities and phenomena is problematic, certainly not capable of strongly precluding relativistic interpretation—notably, the individuation of texts and artworks and actions—of fixing their boundaries (and, therefore, of what is clearly "in" and "outside" given referents), an issue pressed in a particularly florid way for instance by commentators such as Roland Barthes and Jacques Derrida but also, more cautiously, even in Gadamer and Wolfgang Iser.[28] It is very characteristic, here, for instance in treating hermeneutic problems, that the incipient relativism of historicizing the reading of texts is offset by Gadamer simply, but utterly without sustained defense, by way of appealing to the authority of the historical tradition itself:

> That which has been sanctioned by tradition and custom [Gadamer said] has an authority that is nameless, and our finite historical being is marked by the fact that always the authority of what has been transmitted—and not only what is clearly grounded—has power over our attitudes and behavior. . . . The validity of morals, for example, is based on tradition. They are freely taken over, but by no means created by a free insight or justified by themselves. That is precisely what we call tradition: the ground of their validity . . . tradition has a justification that is outside the arguments of reason and in large measure determines our institutions and our attitudes.[29]

This is a profound and splendid statement, but there is absolutely no way, short of falling back to some sort of essentialism or universalism or foundationalism (which Gadamer opposed), in which the thesis advanced does—or even could—preclude a relativistic reading. The objectivity of tradition is simply not demonstrably incompatible with the relativist's thesis. The countercharge is generalizable for all materials subject to hermeneutic review.[30]

Finally, whenever, under the accumulating burden of the themes here broached, we are persuaded that questions of rational practice and policy cannot rightly claim to depend on the discovery of independent norms or ontologically "objective values," as for instance, is claimed in the natural law theory of morality, it is most difficult to see how *whatever objectivity* may (reasonably) be accorded our efforts to formulate moral constraints could preclude a relativistic interpretation of such objectivity.[31] Or when conceptual issues are thought to require second-order inferences to the best account, in the manner of transcendental arguments (without conceding any form of apodictic certainty—historicized arguments, for instance, strongly rhetorical but not without rigor), as in ontological speculation about what "there is," it is very difficult to see how relativistic considerations can be excluded or defeated merely because they are such.[32]

We must not be too hasty. We certainly have not shown that relativism must win out against its opponents, that is, against those with whom it shares an opposition to objectivism but who insist that the "objectivity" of science and rational inquiry (that remains) disallows the relativistic alternative itself (either inclusively or restrictedly). We have shown how, in a significantly large variety of ways, relativism simply cannot be precluded, and we have shown, at least implicitly, that its (sophisticated) opponents have neither mustered telling arguments against its eligibility (or plausibility) nor even seriously supposed that an argument was required. The considerations just advanced—from, for example, the complications of the realist/idealist demarcation to those affecting transcendental arguments—merely provide a favorable setting within which relativistic alternatives may be profitably advanced. The mere plurality of conceptual options among the issues raised is surely not enough to vindicate relativism. The opponent of relativism is prepared to admit (or insist) that there is no single, neutral, common framework within which to evaluate all competing theories, no adequate set of rules for adjudicating all cognitive disputes. This is the complaint against so-called objectivism. Against what is taken to be relativism, the complaint is rather that in spite of plurality—even open-ended and evolving plurality—"we are not prisoners locked in our own framework"; the possibility remains for "rational comparison among the plurality of theories, paradigms, and language games" to yield a fair resolution of cognitive dispute.[33]

Fair enough. But what the opponent of relativism fails to consider—a charge equally telling against Popper and Gadamer, for instance—is simply that the denial of a known, single, and universal framework for resolving disputes and the denial that truth must therefore be relativized to particular conceptual frameworks among an indefinite plurality of frameworks (within which we are said to be unable to make intelligible comparison from the one we ourselves "inhabit" to such others—the putatively skeptical import of incommensurability) are themselves entirely compatible with relativism. To admit this is to admit that the entire strategy that would defeat relativism by defeating objectivism and then construing relativism as itself a parasitically skeptical inference that simply abandons the possibility of objective science and rational inquiry is either misguided or only marginally pertinent. For what remains is the stunningly obvious question: How, if (a) we lack a common, timelessly adequate conceptual framework, and if (b) there is an open-ended plurality of frameworks that we are indeed capable of acquiring and invoking, and if (c) objectivity under these conditions is conceded and not denied, can we vouchsafe (1) that the choice of appropriate frameworks for managing particular disputes is invariably or predominantly or characteristically or generally (for the important cases at least) made in accordance with a strong bipolar model of truth values; or (2) assuming some rational choice fitting framework to question and question to framework, how can we vouchsafe that, within the framework thus provided, the resolution of particular disputes is invariably or predominantly or characteristically or generally (for the important cases at least) made in accordance with a strong bipolar model of truth values? The opponent of relativism must be able to show that, in answering these questions, he is himself not falling back to a version of the objectivist's position, while he is able to preclude the relativist's more concessive position.

It is not a decisive objection, here, that we cannot deny the hermeneutic nature of the entire range of human inquiry. Hermeneutics affords an ontological (and historicized), not merely epistemological, account of human understanding, allegedly distorted by the Cartesian tradition of the West in the most profound way due to its own implied confidence in the cognitive autonomy of human thought.[34] Not only may that criticism be admitted, it actually facilitates the relativist thesis. It certainly does not preclude it. For once we free relativism from a purely parasitic function (tantamount to skepticism) vis-à-vis objectivism, once we refuse to confine it to the "prison-house" thesis of incommensurable conceptual schemes (also tantamount to skepticism), once we reconcile it with the hermeneutic complexity of cognitive encounter and the open-ended plurality of conceptual orientation (tantamount to supporting the search for the conditions of objectivity), we have exhausted the antirelativist's weapons and have still left entirely untouched the relativist's own target. It is not the plurality of conceptual schemes or the ontological complexity of human understanding that is decisive: it is rather that, admitting them, there is no clear, known, decisive, or (almost) even proposed reason for denying that, consistent with the serious objectivity intended, "incongruent" claims (that is, claims that on a bipolar model but not now) can be defended if any claims can be pertinently defended. Relativism holds that within the space of objective claims (however moderately that characterization may be taken), the plurality, open endedness, historicism, and hermeneutic complexity of cognitive cannot, for given questions, for questions in place, disallow plural, nonconverging, *incongruent* judgments. This is a different matter from the less substantial issue that, once objectivism is denied, we must admit that there are indefinitely many ways in which the world may be serially examined and that findings pertinent to any one such way cannot preclude the legitimacy of any other. This is what is missing in Gadamer's well-known remark—meant to offset the threat of relativism: "Authority has nothing to do with obedience, but rather with knowledge . . . the recognition of authority is always connected with the idea that what authority states is not irrational and arbitrary, but can be seen, in principle, to be true."[35] This is perhaps not true but only reasonable or plausible or the like.

To put matters this way is to preserve the sense of continuing contest. But it is also to point to signs of the threatening irresistibility of the relativist's thesis. Certainly, its opponents have favored a curious strategy. To cite one final voice, Richard Rorty held that " 'relativism' is the view that every belief on a certain topic, or perhaps about *any* topic, is as good as every other." But he added: "No one holds this view." He went on to state that "if there *were* any relativists, they would, of course, be easy to refute," since they would subscribe to the self-referentially self-refuting Protagorean claim. In any case, he said, " 'relativism' only seems to refer to a disturbing view, worthy of being refuted, if it concerns *real* theories, not just philosophical theories" (that is, "first-level," not merely "second-level," theories). But relativism does concern real theories of both the first- and second-level sort once we recognize that there are no first-level theories without second-level theories or second-level theories without first-level theories. Finally, he suggested that "perhaps 'relativism' is *not* the right name'' for the apparently hateful doctrine really resisted—namely, so-called irrationalism, the rejection of the privileged grounding of cognitive claims (what Rorty favored as ''pragmatism'').[36] It is a strange declension of a serious complaint.

NOTES

1. See, for example, the papers in Martin Hollis and Steven Lukes, eds., *Rationality and Relativism* (Cambridge, Mass.: MIT Press, 1982); and Hans-Georg Gadamer, *Truth and Method*, 2d ed., trans. Garrett Barden and John Cumming (New York: Seabury Press, 1975), pp. 308–309. See also Joseph Margolis, ''The Nature and Strategies of Relativism,'' *Mind* 92 (1983): 558–567.

2. Paul Feyerabend held that ''Protagorean relativism is *reasonable* because it pays attention to the pluralism of traditions and values'' (*Science in a Free Society* [London: Doubleday, 1978], p. 28), and there is some reason to think that he believes that Protagoreanism has universal application. Contrast Winch's view: Peter Winch, ''Understanding a Primitive Society.'' *American Philosophical Quarterly* 1 (1964): 307–324.

3. The full details are provided in Margolis, ''The Nature and Strategies of Relativism.''

4. Richard J. Bernstein, *Beyond Objectivism and Relativism* (Philadelphia: University of Pennsylvania Press, 1983), p. 9; see also W. Newton-Smith, ''Relativism and the Possibility of Interpretation,'' in Hollis and Lukes, *Rationality and Relativism*.

5. Bernstein, *Beyond Objectivism and Relativism*, p. 8. Bernstein observed that ''a more appropriate title or subtitle of the book [Gadamer's *Truth and Method*] and indeed of Gadamer's entire philosophic project, might have been 'Beyond Objectivism and Relativism.' Gadamer's primary philosophic aim is to expose what is wrong with the type of thinking that moves between these antithetical poles and to open us to a new way of thinking about understanding that reveals that our being-in-the-world is distorted when we impose the concepts of objectivism and relativism'' (p. 115). Gadamer was favorably taken with Bernstein's account of his own work, and a letter to that effect is included in Bernstein's book.

6. Bernstein, *Beyond Objectivism and Relativism*, p. 8.

7. Ibid., pp. 10–11; see Edmund Husserl, *The Crisis of European Sciences and Transcendental Phenomenology*, trans. David Carr (Evanston, Ill.: Northwestern University Press, 1970), pp. 745–746; cited by Bernstein.

8. Ibid., p. 37.

9. Richard Rorty, *Philosophy and the Mirror of Nature* (Princeton, N.J.: Princeton University Press, 1979).

10. Bernstein, *Beyond Objectivism and Relativism*, p. 57.

11. Ibid., pp. 2–4.

12. Ibid.

13. Ibid., p. 7.

14. Ibid., p. 166–168.

15. Ibid., pp. 16–23.

16. Ibid., pp. 11–12, for instance.

17. Ian Hacking, ''Language, Truth, and Reason,'' in Hollis and Lukes, *Rationality and Relativism*, p. 56. The observation puts into question in a most interesting way

Michael Dummett's very strong sense of bivalence; see Michael Dummett, *Truth and Other Enigmas* (Cambridge, Mass.: Harvard University Press, 1978).

18. See W. V. Quine, *Word and Object* (Cambridge, Mass.: MIT Press, 1960), Ch. 2.

19. Paul Feyerabend, *Against Method* (London: Doubleday, 1975), p. 274. There is an extremely helpful discussion of the difference between Kuhn's and Feyerabend's views in Bernstein, *Beyond Objectivism and Relativism*, pp. 79–93; Bernstein mentioned the remark just cited from Feyerabend.

20. Bernstein, *Beyond Objectivism and Relativism*, p. 92. See also Donald Davidson, "On the Very Idea of a Conceptual Scheme," *Proceedings and Addresses of the American Philosophical Association* 47 (1973–1974); Gerald Doppelt, "Kuhn's Epistemological Relativism: An Interpretation and Defense," *Inquiry* 21, no. 1 (1978): 33–86.

21. See Karl R. Popper, *Realism and the Aim of Science. Vol. 1: Postscript to the Logic of Scientific Discovery*, ed. W. W. Bartley III (Totowa, N.J.: Rowman and Littlefield, 1983), pp. 156–157; see also Thomas S. Kuhn, *The Structure of Scientific Revolutions*, 2d ed. enl. (Chicago: University of Chicago Press, 1970), p. 150. Kuhn has muted the strong and distinctive thesis here advanced.

22. Bernstein, for example, accurately reporting the debate about incommensurability, explicitly said that "the incommensurability thesis has been rightly taken as an attack on objectivism (not, however, on objectivity)" and that, therefore, it "has *nothing to do* with relativism." *Beyond Objectivism and Relativism*, p. 92.

23. Popper, *Realism and the Aim of Science*, p. 18.

24. See Joseph Margolis, "Pragmatism without Foundations," *American Philosophical Quarterly* 21, 1 (January 1984): 69–80; idem, "Relativism, History, and Objectivity in the Human Studies," *Journal for the Theory of Social Behavior* 14 (1984): 1–24; see also W. V. Quine, "Two Dogmas of Empiricism," in his *From a Logical Point of View* (Cambridge, Mass.: Harvard University Press, 1953), pp. 20–46.

25. See Joseph Margolis, "Historicism, Universalism, and the Threat of Relativism," *The Monist* 67, 3 (July 1984): 308–326; idem, "The Savage Mind Totalizes," *Man and the World*, 17 (1984): 157–175. See also Karl R. Popper, "The Aim of Science," in his *Objective Knowledge* (Oxford: Clarendon, 1972), pp. 191–205; Keith Lehrer, *Knowledge* (Oxford: Clarendon, 1974); and Rorty, *Philosophy and the Mirror of Nature*. Popper's opposition to essentialism does not signify that he has successfully escaped the charge himself; the issue is considered in Margolis, "Historicism, Universalism, and the Threat of Relativism." Clearly, if Popper's argument failed, his own doctrine of verisimilitude might well be construed along relativist lines: this at least provides a dialectical sense of the contest between relativism and its opponents, who jointly oppose objectivism.

26. See Joseph Margolis, "Realism's Superiority over Instrumentalism and Idealism: A Defective Argument," *Southern Journal of Philosophy* 17 (1979): 473–479; idem, "The Axiom of Existence: *Reductio ad Absurdum*," *Southern Journal of Philosophy* 15 (1977): 91–99; idem, "Berkeley and Others on the Problem of Universals," in Colin M. Turbayne, ed., *Berkeley: Critical and Interpretive Essays* (Minneapolis: University of Minnesota Press, 1982), pp. 207–227; see also Hilary Putnam, *Meaning and the Moral Sciences* (London: Routledge and Kegan Paul, 1978), Lecture II; and Nelson Goodman, "Seven Strictures on Similarity," in Lawrence Foster and J. W. Swanson, eds., *Experience and Theory* (Amherst: University of Massachusetts Press, 1970), pp. 19–29.

27. See Joseph Margolis, *Culture and Cultural Entities* (Dordrecht: D. Reidel, 1983); idem, "Relativism, History, and Objectivity in the Human Science"; idem, "Monistic

and Dualistic Canons for the Natural and Human Sciences,'' to appear in a collection edited by Barry Glassner and Jonathan F. Moreno.

28. For an overview of this sprawling literature with regard at least to literary texts, see Joseph Margolis, ''What Is a Literary Text?'' in Herbert L. Sussman, ed., *Proceedings of the Northeastern University Center for Literary Studies Vol. 1: At the Boundaries* (Boston: Northeastern University Press, 1983).

29. It applies straightforwardly, for example, to the views of Clifford Geertz, ''From the Native's Point of View'' in Paul Rabinow and William M. Sullivan, eds., *Interpretive Social Science: A Reader* (Berkeley: University of California Press, 1979); and Winch, ''Understanding a Primitive Society.''

30. Gadamer, *Truth and Method,* p. 249.

31. Bernstein, it appears, agreed with Gadamer's attempt to reinterpret Aristotle's natural law doctrine (so-called) in historicized but objective (and anti-irrelativistic) terms; see Bernstein, *Beyond Objectivism and Relativism,* pp. 156–157; see also Gadamer, *Truth and Method,* pp. 278–289. It is interesting to note how J. L. Mackie, espousing a special doctrine of ''moral skepticism,'' nevertheless attempted to avoid moral relativism; see *Ethics: Inventing Right and Wrong* (Harmondsworth, Eng.: Penguin Books, 1977).

32. See Joseph Margolis, ''Pragmatism, Transcendental Arguments, and the Technological,'' in Paul T. Durbin and Friedrich Rapp, eds., *Philosophy and Technology* 80 (Dordrecht, Holland: D. Reidel, 1983); idem, ''Pragmatism without Foundations''; and idem ''Scientific Realism as a Transcendental Issue,'' forthcoming.

33. Bernstein, *Beyond Objectivism and Relativism,* pp. 92, 108.

34. See Hans-Georg Gadamer, ''The Universality of the Hermeneutical Problem,'' *Philosophical Hermeneutics,* trans. and ed. David E. Linge (Berkeley: University of California Press, 1976) pp. 3–17; see also Charles Taylor, ''Interpretation and the Sciences of Man,'' in Rabinow and Sullivan, *Interpretive Social Science: A Reader*; and Bernstein, *Beyond Objectivism and Relativism,* Pt. 3.

35. Gadamer, ''The Universality of the Hermeneutical Problem,'' pp. 248–249.

36. Richard Rorty, ''Pragmatism, Relativism, and Irrationalism,'' *Proceedings and Addresses of the American Philosophical Association* 53 (1980): 727–730.

BIBLIOGRAPHY

Bernstein, Richard J. *Beyond Objectivism and Relativism.* Philadelphia: University of Pennsylvania Press, 1983.

Davidson, Donald. ''On the Very Idea of a Conceptual Scheme.'' *Proceedings and Addresses of the American Philosophical Association* 47 (1973–1974).

Doppelt, Gerald. ''Kuhn's Epistemological Relativism: An Interpretation and Defense.'' *Inquiry* 21 (1978): 33–86.

Dummett, Michael. *Truth and Other Enigmas.* Cambridge, Mass.: Harvard University Press, 1978.

Feyerabend, Paul. *Against Method.* London: Doubleday, 1975.

———. *Science in a Free Society.* London: Doubleday, 1978.

Gadamer, Hans-Georg. *Truth and Method.* 2d ed. Translated by Garrett Barden and John Cumming. New York: Seabury Press, 1975.

———. ''The Universality of the Hermeneutical Problem.'' In *Philosophical Hermeneutics.* Translated and edited by David E. Linge. Berkeley: University of California Press, 1976, pp. 3–17.

Geertz, Clifford. "From the Native's Point of View." In Paul Rabinow and William M. Sullivan, eds., *Interpretive Social Science: A Reader*. Berkeley: University of California Press, 1979, pp. 225–241.

Goodman, Nelson. "Seven Strictures on Similarity." In Lawrence Foster and J. W. Swanson, eds., *Experience and Theory*. Amherst: University of Massachusetts Press, 1970, pp. 19–29.

Hacking, Ian. "Language, Truth, and Reason." In Martin Hollis and Steven Lukes, eds. *Rationality and Relativism*. Cambridge, Mass.: MIT Press, 1982, pp. 48–66.

Hollis, Martin, and Steven Lukes, eds. *Rationality and Relativism*. Cambridge, Mass.: MIT Press, 1982.

Husserl, Edmund. *The Crisis of European Sciences and Transcendental Phenomenology*. Translated by David Carr. Evanston, Ill.: Northwestern University Press, 1970.

Kuhn, Thomas S. *The Structure of Scientific Revolutions*. 2d ed. enl. Chicago: University of Chicago Press, 1970.

Lehrer, Keith. *Knowledge*. Oxford: Clarendon, 1974.

Mackie, J. L. *Ethics: Inventing Right and Wrong*. Harmondsworth, Eng.: Penguin Books, 1977.

Margolis, Joseph. "The Axiom of Existence: *Reductio ad Absurdum*." *Southern Journal of Philosophy* 15, no. 1 (1977): 91–99.

———. "Berkeley and Others on the Problem of Universals." In Colin M. Turbayne, ed., *Berkeley: Critical and Interpretive Essays*. Minneapolis: University of Minnesota Press, 1982, pp. 207–227.

———. *Culture and Cultural Entities*. Dordrecht: D. Reidel, 1983.

———. "Historicism, Universalism, and the Threat of Relativism." *The Monist* 67, no. 3 (July 1984): 308–326.

———. "The Nature and Strategies of Relativism." *Mind* 92, no. 368 (October 1983): 558–567.

———. "Pragmatism without Foundations." *American Philosophical Quarterly* 21, no. 1 (January 1984): 69–80.

———. "Pragmatism, Transcendental Arguments, and the Technological." In Paul T. Durbin and Friedrich Rapp, eds., *Philosophy and Technology*. Dordrecht: D. Reidel, 1983.

———. "Realism's Superiority over Instrumentalism and Idealism: A Defective Argument." *Southern Journal of Philosophy* 17, no. 4 (Winter 1979): 473–479.

———. "Relativism, History, and Objectivity in the Human Studies." *Journal for the Theory of Social Behavior* 14 no.1 (March 1984): 1–23.

———. "The Savage Mind Totalizes." *Man and World*.

———. "What Is a Literary Text?" In Herbert L. Sussman, ed., *Proceedings of the Northwestern University Center for Literary Studies. Vol. 1: At the Boundaries*. Boston: Northeastern University Press, 1983, pp. 47–73.

Newton-Smith, W. "Relativism and the Possibility of Interpretation." In Martin Hollis and Steven Lukes, eds., *Rationality and Relativism*. Cambridge, Mass.: MIT Press, 1982, pp. 106–122.

Popper, Karl R. "The Aim of Science." In *Objective Knowledge*. Oxford: Clarendon, 1972, pp. 191–205.

———. *Realism and the Aim of Science. Vol 1: Postscript to the Logic of Discovery*. Edited by W. W. Bartley III. Totowa, N.J.: Rowman and Littlefield, 1983.

Putnam, Hilary. *Meaning and the Moral Sciences*. London: Routledge and Kegan Paul, 1978.

Quine, W. V. "Two Dogmas of Empiricism." In his *From a Logical Point of View*. Cambridge, Mass.: Harvard University Press, 1953, pp. 20–46.

————. *Word and Object*. Cambridge, Mass.: MIT Press, 1960.

Rorty, Richard. *Philosophy and the Mirror of Nature*. Princeton, N.J.: Princeton University Press, 1979.

————. "Pragmatism, Relativism, and Irrationalism." *Proceedings and Addresses of the American Philosophical Association* 53 (1980): 727–730.

Taylor, Charles. "Interpretation and the Sciences of Man." In Paul Rabinow and William M. Sullivan, eds., *Interpretive Social Science: A Reader*. Berkeley: University of California Press, 1979, pp. 25–71.

Winch, Peter. "Understanding a Primitive Society." *American Philosophical Quarterly* 1 (1964): 307–324.

2

On Theism and Atheism in Western Religious Philosophy

NORBERT SAMUELSON

In the biblical world the argument was between monotheism and polytheism. *Monotheism* claims that there is one God of the universe, and *polytheism* claims that there are many such deities. Both agree that there is at least one. In modern times the argument is between monotheism and *atheism*, which claims that there are no gods; both agree that there is at most one. The critical arguments in classical religious thought dealt with affirming or denying the claim that there is at most one God. What was at stake in proofs that there is at least one God had to do with epistemology and not with theology. No one thought that proofs were needed for this claim; rather, the objective was to show whether or not this claim could be known through reason, independent of revelation and revealed tradition.

In the modern world the situation became different. In this case philosophers had serious doubts about the truth of the claim that there are any deities at all and took it for granted that whether or not there is one, there is not more than one. Nevertheless, although the modern debate involved serious questions about the existence of a deity whereas the classical debate did not, modern discussions of God's existence (i.e., the claim that there is at least one deity) were based almost entirely on the classical arguments. The only new form of argument to be introduced was Pascal's "wager," and that argument has not been considered seriously in the contemporary period (i.e., post–World War II) of religious thought.[1] There are three possible claims that can be made about the existence of God: God exists, no god exists, and God may or may not exist. Let us identify these three positions respectively as "theism," "atheism," and "agnosticism." Most contemporary people in the Western world, including committed advocates of Judaism and Christianity, are in this sense agnostic. Some are theists, and even fewer are atheists. Among the atheists, two in particular have offered arguments for their purported knowledge—Bertrand Russell and J. N. Findlay.[2]

However, it is generally accepted, even by agnostic philosophers who think that there is no god, that neither Russell nor Findlay succeeded in demonstrating their claims. Only the few instances of arguments by contemporary theists have been given serious consideration in post–World War II philosophy of religion.[3]

The classical world of Western religious thought produced three main forms of purported demonstrations of God's existence—the argument from design, the cosmological argument, and the ontological argument. In general, the more convincing these arguments are, the less demonstrative they seem to be. The *argument from design* is a form of argument by analogy that convinces many people that there is a God, but simply because it is a form of argument by analogy, it is in no sense demonstrative. Conversely, it does not seem to be the case that the ontological argument has ever convinced anyone that there is a deity, but if any of these forms of argument are demonstrative, it is this one. Hence most discussions about the existence of God by contemporary Western philosophers have concentrated on examining the logical character of this argument.

THE ONTOLOGICAL PROOF OF GOD'S EXISTENCE[4]

Anselm's First Version

As originally stated by St. Anselm the argument appears in two forms.[5] The first version can be stated as follows:

1. God is defined as something, *a,* "greater than" which cannot be conceived.

2. That which exists is greater than that which does not exist.

3. If God did not exist, that which does exist would be greater than God.

4. If God did not exist, God would not be something, *a,* "greater than" which cannot be conceived.

5. If God did not exist, God would not be God.

6. That God is not God is impossible.

7. Therefore, God exists.

Steps 1 and 2 are the premises of the argument. The form of the argument itself, steps 5 through 7, is a valid example of a modus tollens argument. That step 6 is true is self-evident. Step 5 follows from steps 1 and 4. God is defined as something "greater than" which cannot be conceived. This means that the name "God" and the expression "something, *a,* 'greater than' which cannot be conceived" are interchangeable. The name as it functions in the argument is merely an abbreviation of the description. Thus step 4 states: "If something, *a,* 'greater than' which cannot be conceived did not exist, something, *a,* 'greater than' which cannot be conceived would not be something, *a,* 'greater than'

which cannot be conceived,'' or ''if God did not exist, God would not be God.''
Step 4 follows immediately from step 3. Step 3 follows immediately from step
2.

The question that ought to be raised concerning step 2 is, what does ''greater''
mean? By ''greater'' Anselm either meant that real existence is greater than
existence only in the understanding, or he may have meant that existence in the
understanding plus existence in reality are greater than only existence in the
understanding. Compare a real dollar bill and an imaginary dollar bill. Both are
alike in every respect except that one exists only in the imagination, whereas
the other really exists. Since all other factors are equal, on a purely commonsense
level it is not difficult to understand what it means to state that the real dollar
bill is greater than the imaginary dollar bill. Anselm's choice of the term *greater*
is certainly unfortunate for the rigor of the argument, but the problem with the
term does not invalidate the argument. For our purposes ''greater'' need refer
to nothing more than the commonsense distinction between really existing and
existing only in the imagination as explained above.

Most Western religious philosophers agree that in this form Anslem's argument
is not valid. It is generally accepted that the earlier critiques of both David Hume
and Immanuel Kant settle the question that this is not a sound demonstration.[6]
Their objections are the following: First, in the steps of the argument, existence
is treated as a predicate, as if stating that ''John exists'' is like stating that ''John
is red,'' that is, as if both ''red'' and ''exists'' function as predicates. But
existence is not a predicate. Hence the steps in the argument are not well formed;
that is, they have no clear meaning. Hence the argument is not only false, it is
unintelligible.

Second, what Anselm has proved is that if anything is God, God exists, but
he has not proved that God exists. The statement that something, *a,* ''greater
than'' which cannot be conceived exists is necessarily true. It is true in the same
way that the statement that all triangles have three angles is necessarily true.
But just as the latter statement does not tell us whether there is anything that is
or is not a triangle, so the former statement does not tell us whether there is
anything that is or is not God. The statement that ''all triangles have three
angles'' states that if anything is a triangle, that thing has three sides. However,
there need not be anything that is a triangle. Similarly, Anselm has proved that
nothing can be God and at the same time not exist, but Anselm has not proved
that there is anything that is God.

For our purposes the second criticism is the crucial one to consider. The first
criticism is unimportant, first, because in the second version of the ontological
argument, as restructured by Norman Malcolm and Charles Hartshorne, existence
is not treated as a predicate, and second, even if existence were to continue to
function in the argument as a predicate, the criticism can be overcome. It is
possible to treat existence as a predicate without grave logical consequences
following. Existential propositions in which existence functions as a predicate
are certainly meaningful as long as the only objection to the proposition is that
existence is a predicate. To show that this is so would lead us too far afield for

the purposes of this chapter. I will simply refer the reader to two articles that conclusively settle the issue. Both articles are by leading contemporary logicians, and both reject the ontological argument. Their concern is only to show that the first Hume-Kant objection is not valid, not that the ontological argument itself is valid. Both articles accept the second criticism stated above as decisive. The articles in question are "An Examination of the Ontological Proof" by Jan Berg and " 'Exists' as a Predicate" by George Nakhnikian and Wesley C. Salmon.[7]

Anselm's Second Version

Most contemporary philosophers consider the second version of Anselm's ontological argument to be identical in content with the first version. However, two philosophers in particular—Norman Malcolm and Charles Hartshorne—argued that they are not and that the objections traditionally raised against the first do not apply to the second.[8] Briefly, the second version of Anselm's argument can be stated as follows:

1. A *necessary being* is defined as a being whose nonexistence is logically impossible. A *contingent being* is defined as a being whose nonexistence is logically possible.

2. A necessary being is greater than a contingent being.[9]

3. God is defined as something, *a,* "greater than" which cannot be conceived.

4. If God is a contingent being, God would not be God, which is impossible.

5. Therefore, God is not a contingent being; that is, God is a necessary being.

6. Therefore, God exists.

Structurally, this argument is the same as the first argument except that rather than assuming existence to be a perfection (step 2 of the first version), necessary existence is assumed as a perfection (step 2 of the second version). Hence Kant's first objection is avoided. Both Hartshorne and Malcolm granted that existence could not be a predicate, but they argued that necessary existence can be and is a predicate.

Furthermore, given this radical distinction between existence and necessary existence, the second objection also is overcome. The ontological argument in its second version makes the claim that it is necessarily the case that God is a necessary being, and from this proposition it follows as well that God exists. In other words, if anything is God, it is a necessary being, and this proposition is such that, unlike all other conditionals, the antecedent cannot be denied. Concerning a triangle having three angles, you can state that there is nothing about triangularity that necessitates the consequence that something is a triangle, but there is something about the predicate necessary being that necessitates the consequence that something is a necessary being. In their elaborations of this second version of the ontological argument both Malcolm and Hartshorne attempted to show why it is the case that the property, necessary being, is uniquely such that something must possess it.

Malcolm's Reconstruction

At this stage of the argument, the ways that Malcolm and Hartshorne stated their proofs are different. Whether or not or to what extent these different ways of expression constitute different arguments is beyond the scope of this chapter. At this stage my discussion is limited to Malcolm's version. His statement can be summarized as follows:

1. God is defined as something, *a,* "greater than" which cannot be conceived.
2. Something, *a,* "greater than" which cannot be conceived is unlimited.
3. If God came into existence, either (a) he was caused to do so, or (b) he just happened to do so.
4. If either (a) or (b) is the case, God is a limited being.
5. But God is not a limited being.
6. Therefore, God cannot come into existence.
7. If God cannot come into existence, if he does exist his existence is impossible.
8. If God existed and ceased to exist, either (c) the cessation was caused or (d) the cessation just happened.
9. If either (c) or (d) is the case, God is limited, which, from step 2, is impossible.
10. Therefore, if God does exist, he cannot cease to exist.
11. Therefore, either God's existence is necessary (step 10) or it is impossible (step 7).
12. If the concept of God is self-contradictory, God's existence is impossible, and if the concept of God is not self-contradictory, his existence is not impossible.
13. The concept of God is not self-contradictory.
14. Therefore, God's existence is not impossible.
15. Therefore, it is necessary.

Step 5 follows from steps 1 and 2. Step 6 is merely the conclusion of a modus tollens argument presented in steps 3, 4, and 5; that is, if God could come into existence, it would follow that God is limited (steps 3 and 4); God is unlimited (step 5); therefore, God cannot come into existence. Step 10 is the conclusion of another modus tollens argument in steps 8 and 9. Step 14 is the conclusion of a modus ponens argument in steps 12 and 13, and finally, step 15 is an argument of the form that is called a "disjunctive syllogism," presented in steps 11 and 14.

The crucial question at this point is, what exactly does it mean to state that the concept of God is necessary? Can we not state that the concept of God is necessary but there is nothing that happens to be God? In essence, this is the crucial objection to Malcolm's argument.[10] Malcolm argued that the objection is not valid. I will discuss why it is not valid; however, to present that answer, it is necessary first to make certain technical changes in the structure of the ontological argument as presented by Malcolm.

Malcolm Reconstructed

I would like to consider the ontological argument in the following form:

P1. Anything that has the property of being something, a, "greater than" which cannot be conceived has the property of being unlimited.

P2. A contingent being (that is, something that has the property of being such that its nonexistence is logically possible; that is, it may or it may not exist) is caused or just happens either to exist or not to exist (that is, there is nothing about it alone that can tell you whether it does or does not exist).

P3. Anything that is caused or just happens either to exist or not to exist has the property of being limited.

P4. Anything that is not contingent is either a chimera or a necessary being (that is, it has either the property of being such that existence is logically impossible or the property of being such that nonexistence is logically impossible).

P5. By definition God is (that is, has the property of being) something, a, "greater than" which cannot be conceived.

1. Therefore, God is (that is, has the property of being) unlimited.

2. Therefore, God is not a contingent being.

3. Therefore, God is either a chimera or a necessary being (in the sense explicated in P4).

P6. It is not the case that God is a chimera; that is, God does not have the property of being such that his existence is logically impossible.

4. Therefore, God is a necessary being; that is, God has the property of being such that his nonexistence is logically impossible.

Numbers P1 through P6 are the premises of the argument. Numbers 1 through 4 are the steps of inference from the premises. Number 4 is the conclusion of the argument. Number 1 follows from P1 and P5 by modus ponens. Number 2 follows from P2, P3, and 1 by a hypothetical syllogism and modus ponens. Number 4, the conclusion, follows from 3 and P6 by a disjunctive syllogism.

The word *God* as it functions in the argument is a complex name. It is also a proper name; that is, it has a single, unique reference. No attempt is made to explicate the full sense of that name. All that the definition claims is that the entity has one property—the property of being something, a, "greater than" which cannot be conceived. It may have many others. All of these points are irrelevant to the argument except insofar as the one property named entails other properties.

I do not think that the above argument is different from Malcolm's restructuring of the second version of Anselm's ontological argument. However, it has the following advantages over Malcolm's presentation:

1. The connection between my statement of the argument and the second version of the ontological argument in the *Proslogion* is clearer than is the connection between Malcolm's and Anselm's statement of the argument.

2. Alvin Plantinga structured Malcolm's argument as follows:

   A. If (it is not the case that [God does exist]), (his existence is logically impossible).

   B. If (God does exist), (His existence is logically necessary).

   C. Thus either (his existence is logically impossible) or (his existence is logically necessary).

   D. If (his existence is logically impossible), (the concept of God is contradictory).

   E. It is not the case that (the concept of God is contradictory).

   F. Therefore, (his existence is logically necessary).

Plantinga explained, first, that C means that contingent existence cannot have any application to God. He explained, second, that he assumed that when Malcolm said that God's existence is logically necessary, he meant that the proposition "God exists" is logically necessary.

I believe that Plantinga's account of the argument is incorrect. "God's existence is logically necessary" is not a statement about the proposition "God exists." If that were the case, there would be no real difference between the second version of the ontological argument and the first version; that is, both versions of the argument would be guilty of treating existence as a predicate, a charge that, as we have seen, Malcolm is careful to avoid.[11] I think that what Malcolm means here by "necessary" is that a proposition is logically necessary if and only if its contradictory is self-contradictory—in this case, that God has the property of necessary existence—and that this property entails that anything possessing it exists. However, as stated by Malcolm, Plantinga's interpretation is plausible. I would hope that my restatement removes the possibility of Plantinga's interpretation.

3. If, as I claim, Malcolm considered necessary existence to be a property distinct from existence, which is not a property, the question arises as to just what this property is. The answer is not clear from Malcolm's statement. I hope that my statement of the argument makes the answer clear. For that answer I am indebted to Robert C. Coburn's article "Professor Malcolm on God."[12]

4. Some of the criticisms raised against Malcolm's version of the ontological argument have their root in a confusion about what "necessary" means as it functions in the argument. The confusion is perhaps understandable, but it is unjustified. Part of the purpose of my restatement of Malcolm's argument is to avoid this confusion.

We have seen that this proof makes the following (and only the following) claims about God: (1) God is something, *a*, "greater than" which cannot be conceived. (2) God is unlimited. (3) God can neither come into existence nor cease to exist. (4) The category of duration has no application to God. (5) God is a single, unique entity. (6) Any complete list of the entities that constitute the universe will include God. This last point is what it means to state that God exists. It does not mean that God has duration. God occupies no time. Existence is not a univocal term. It means different things depending upon what it is that we are discussing. A great part of the confusion concerning the question of the existence of God rests on the failure to recognize the ambiguous character of this term *existence*. Again, its base meaning is simply that anything that exists is among the constituents of the universe, and there are many ways in which any given entity may be a constituent.

IS THE GOD OF THE PHILOSOPHERS THE GOD OF THE PATRIARCHS?[13]

If our reasoning is correct, we have proved the above statements to be true. However, note that the above statements are all that we have proved. There is a great deal about God that both Judaism and Christianity claim to be true to which our arguments have no application, for example: (1) God is good. (2) God is an object (or the object) of worship. (3) God responds to prayer. (4) Humans can have a relationship with God. (5) God is a conscious being. (6) That something, a, ''greater than'' which cannot be conceived is the God of Abraham, Isaac, and Jacob. It is of no little importance that neither Malcolm nor Hartshorne nor most other Western philosophers of religion consider this last question. Yet it is critical concern. In particular, if it is the case that the God of the patriarchs, namely, the God of at least some versions of Judaism and Christianity, is not Anselm's God, to worship the latter deity, even if he exists, would be idolatrous. It is important to note that some Western religious thinkers have made precisely this claim, for example, Judah Halevi, Pascal, and Martin Buber.

How can we decide if in fact they were right when they asserted that the God of Abraham, Isaac, and Jacob is not the God of the philosophers? First, we must clarify what they were asserting. What they meant was that the purported entity that the Biblical-Judaic-Christian-Muslim tradition identifies as ''God'' is not the same entity as the purported entity that the Jewish-Christian-Muslim traditions of philosophy identify as ''God.'' Presupposed in this assertion is that it is possible to state some things about each entity, and on the basis of what is said about each, it can be determined that they are not the same entity. It should be noted that if we claim that either entity is in every respect unknowable, there would be no way to make the assertion in question. Also, it should be noted that the assertion in question does not entail that either or both entities exist. ''A unicorn is not a centaur'' entails some knowledge of both, but it does not entail that either exists. The same is the case with the claim that Zeus is not Marduk.

Let y stand for the purported God of Abraham, Isaac, and Jacob, and let g

stand for the purported God of the philosophers. To claim that g and y are different entities, it is sufficient to be able to characterize both in the following ways: (A) Concerning two entities of the same kind, a and b, we can assert that a and b are not identical if there is a property, F, that is true of a and a property, G, that is true of b, and F and G are so related that F and G cannot be true of any single entity. For example, J. F. Kennedy could have played football for Harvard and could have been president of the United States, but no one could have played football for Harvard and could have been the emperor of Rome. Similarly, no one could have participated in the Olympics of ancient Greece and could have been president of the United States. (B) Concerning two entities a and b, we can assert that a and b are not identical if there is a class of predicates applicable to a but inapplicable to b. By "inapplicable" I mean that it is not merely false to state that b is not F where F is such a predicate, but that to state that b is F is a category mistake; that is, neither F nor the opposite of F are predicable of b. Both a and b are different kinds of entities if "a is F" is a sentence that merely is either true or false, but "b is F" is not a well-formed sentence. If a and b are different kinds of entities, they cannot be identical.

My strategy in this section is to follow the latter (B) method of characterization and to argue that given what we know about g and given what we know about y, there is such a class of predicates, namely, "being together with" predicates, that are applicable to y but not to g, from which we must conclude that g and y are different entities.

The latter (B) approach provides a stronger case against the identity of any two entities a and b. In most contexts the former (A) approach provides a sufficient basis to assert nonidentity, but particularly concerning g and y, any argument based on this approach is subject to doubt. For example, Martin Buber based his case for the nonidentity of g and y on characterizing y as that sort of entity that can be known only through intimate acquaintance (in Buber's language, as an "Eternal Thou") and that y is never known through description (in Buber's language, the Eternal Thou is never an "It"). If in fact y is not subject to any form of description, g and y are not identical; the expression "being 'greater than' that cannot be conceived" is a descriptive phrase; since this phrase is used to specify what we mean when we speak of g, if in fact such a phrase were not applicable to talk about y, y and g could not be identical. However, even if we grant that the name y is applied to a purported entity known solely through acquaintance, Buber has not shown us that y cannot be known through description, and without making this stronger case, his claim of the nonidentity of g and y remains in doubt.

Some might object that y and g as Buber discussed them are not purported entities but rather are purported phenomena. What Buber called the "Eternal Thou" is the phenomenon of being intimately acquainted with God, and "the God of the philosophers" is the phenomenon of knowing God insofar as he can be known through description. But the "God" in both phenomena may be the same purported entity. To argue the nonidentity of g and y on Buber's terms is equivalent to arguing that the Morning Star is not the Evening Star because the former is seen in the morning whereas the latter is seen in the evening. The phenomenon of the Morning Star is indeed different from the phenomenon of the Evening Star, but it happens to be the case that the same heavenly body is involved in both phenomena.

What Is the God of the Philosophers?

On the basis of Anselm's ontological proof of the existence of g alone and in the light of Norman Malcolm's restructuring of that argument, we know very little about g.[14] In fact, everything that we explicitly know about g can be stated as follows:

- g is something, a, "greater than" which cannot be conceived.
- g is unlimited.
- The nonexistence of g is not logically possible.
- g cannot come into existence.
- g cannot cease to exist. (The fourth and fifth statements are what it means to state that g is not a contingent being.)
- The existence of g is not logically impossible.
- g exists.

The above true propositions entail that the following propositions about g are false:

- There is something which can be conceived that is greater than g.
- g is limited.
- The nonexistence of g is logically possible.
- g could come into existence.
- g could cease to exist.
- g could be caused either to exist or to cease to exist.
- g could just happen either to exist or not to exist.
- The existence of g is logically impossible.
- The nonexistence of g is logically possible.
- g does not exist.

Given that g is unlimited, five rules can be stated, and given that g is something, a, "greater than" which cannot be conceived, a sixth rule can be added by which we can determine which additional predicates may or may not be affirmed of g. These six general rules may be stated as follows:[15]

Assume two different classes of predicates. The first is that class of classes of predicates in which individuals that exemplify members of a member class are subject to comparative ratings in terms of perfection with respect to exemplifying members of that class. In other words, assume that P and Q are predicates that belong to this class of predicates and that P and Q are not identical and that if a is P and b is Q and P and Q are not identical and that if a is P and b is Q and P and Q are not identical, then either a in virtue of P is greater than b in virture of Q, or b in virtue of Q is greater than a in virtue of P. Let us call all such classes of predicates "graded predicates." An example of a class of graded predicates is bowling predicates. If John has a 175 bowling average and Mary has a 215 bowling average, Mary is a better or greater bowler than John.

The second is that class of classes of predicates in which members of a member class are so related that it is not possible that any individual who exemplifies one member of a member class can exemplify every member of that class. In other words, assume that R and S are predicates that belong to this class of predicates and that R and S are not identical. No single thing can be both R and S. Let us call all such classes of predicates "exclusion predicates." All graded predicates are exclusion predicates, since nothing can be greater or more perfect than itself in the same respect, but not all exclusion predicates are graded predicates. For example, color predicates are not graded predicates.[16] But color predicates are exclusion predicates.[17]

We may now assert the following rules of language about g:

RULE 1: No nongraded exclusion predicate can be affirmed of g.

The reason for Rule 1 is that given any predicate of a particular kind, if one such predicate can be affirmed of g but if some other predicate cannot be affirmed of g, then g is limited in that there is something that g lacks. But in the case of exclusion predicates it makes no sense to state that all such predicates are true of g. Hence since all of them cannot be affirmed of g, none of them can be affirmed of g. The exception to the rule is graded predicates, since it is not a limitation on a thing not to have an imperfection predicated of it. Thus if bowling could be predicated of g, then g would have a 300 bowling average, but g would not have, for example, a 250 bowling average, since it is not a limitation of a 300 bowler that he never bowls 250.[18] But g cannot be blue or orange, since if either was applicable, we would have to state that g is every color all over, which from the logic of color language is absurd. From this explanation of Rule 1, Rule 2 should be self-evident.

RULE 2: If any graded predicate is less than some other graded predicate, the lesser predicate cannot be affirmed of g.

What it means to state that one predicate is less than another is the following: Graded predicate P is less than graded predicate Q if by stating that a is P and b is Q we conclude that a with respect to P is less than b with respect to Q. In other words, given any predicate P, if P is a graded predicate and there is another predicate Q that is greater than P, then g is not P. For example, if bowling predicates were appropriate to g, then g could not have a 250 bowling average, since anything that would have a 250 + n bowling average would be a better or greater bowler than g.

RULE 3: If predicating a graded predicate entails predicating a nongraded, exclusion predicate of that thing, the graded predicate in question cannot be predicated of g.

This is why bowling cannot be predicated of g. To bowl 300 entails being subject to predicates of spatial location. But by Rule 1 g is not subject to predicates of spatial location. Since spatial location in all but an Aristotelian universe is a nongraded predicate, if g can occupy any space, g must occupy all spaces. But to occupy all spaces is to occupy no space. Spatial location serves to locate some entity relative to other entities, but an entity that occupies all space is in no sense located.[19]

RULE 4: Concerning any graded predicate that does not entail a nongraded, exclusion predicate, if that predicate expresses the highest perfection possible in its class, that predicate is affirmed of g.

In other words, if P is a graded predicate and to state that a is P does not entail that a is Q where Q is a nongraded, exclusion predicate, and if every predicate that is the same kind of graded predicate that P is but that is not identical with P is less than P, then g is P. In an Aristotelian universe where spatial location is a graded predicate, g occupies the highest sphere. Similarly, if bowling predicates did not entail spatial location in all non-Aristotelian universes and if bowling did not entail having matter and multiple actions both of which receive a low value in an Aristotelian universe, we would have to state that g has a 300 bowling average. It is this feature of being unlimited that necessitated the conclusion that g is a necessary being in the Malcolm version of Anselm's ontological argument. As the bowling in an Aristotelian universe example indicated, what else can be affirmed of g depends on the kind of physical schema with which we are operating.

RULE 5: Concerning any class of predicates that are not exclusion predicates, if one member of that class of predicates is predicable of g, all members of that class are predicable of g.

It is not legitimate to draw a distinction between predicates that may be predicable of g and predicates that are predicable of g, since, as Rule 6 will state, there is no predicate predicable of g that is not predicated of g.

RULE 6: Concerning any predicate that is not an exclusion predicate that does not entail a nongraded, exclusion predicate, if it is predicable of anything, it is predicated of g.

In other words, given any predicate P, if (1) P is not an exclusion predicate and if (2) given anything, if it is the case that that thing is P entails that that thing is R, then R is not a nongraded, exclusion predicate, and if (3) it is possible for something to be P, then (4) g is P. The predicates of g enumerated above conform to this rule. Whether or not other predicates also conform to this rule is an open question. For example, it may be the case that g knows all universal conditional propositions, but I see no way for g to know any existental particular propositions.[20] If there is nothing else to state about g, then g-talk is a closed language. But I do not know how to prove that this is the case.

Note that this grammar for attributive statements about g constitutes a proof of P6 ("It is not the case that God is a chimera; that is, God does not have the property of being such that his existence is logically impossible") in our final version of the ontological argument. To state that something is a chimera means that what that thing is is such that in principle no consistent set of rules can be stipulated for forming and judging statements about that thing. Clearly, if the list of rules presented above constitutes a coherent set of criteria for statements about g, the God of Anselm's proof is not a chimera.

Being Together With

It has already been shown that if we exclude from consideration an Aristotelian universe, in no way can g be said to occupy space. I want to consider one other kind of predicate that is similar to spatial location but different from it. It is called "being together with."[21] As stated above, my motive for considering this predicate is to argue that although y does not occupy space, y is together with things, but g cannot be together with anything.

Briefly, one thing is together with another thing if these two things are discrete and if they are allied. Two things are allied if one of the following three conditions obtains: (1) The two things "match" each other. (2) One thing "matches" a third thing and the sum of the first and the third thing is the second thing. (3) The two things are overlapping magnitudes that are equal in size. Two things match each other if they are qualia and together they constitute a definite sum. What it means to state that x is a quale depends on how one stands on the issue of nominalism and realism. However, that question need not concern us here.

The relation "being together with" is symmetric and irreflexive, but it is not transitive. In other words, it does not follow that because a is together with b and b is together with c, then a is together with c. For example, I may be together with a girl friend in the dining room and the girl friend may be there together with a friend of hers, but it need not be the case that I am there with my girl friend's friend. Similarly, the color of my coat is together with my coat and the weight of my coat is together with my coat, but no color is together with any weight. A major use of this relation is to "map" (that is, uniquely to locate relative to a given system) any individual, be it material or immaterial, concrete or universal. To identify something in space and time is one way of mapping. For example, "Joe Smith is that man who sat in the fourth chair from the left in the front row of room 213 in Palmer Hall" maps Joe Smith in terms of a particular system of spatial relations. But other ways of mapping are equally common. For example, "5 is that number between 4 and 6."

By being able to map different things in this way it is possible to identify uniquely anything subject to being-together-with predicates. But it should be noted that g is not subject to these predicates. This follows from Rule 1 stated above. Being-together-with is a nongraded, exclusion predicate, and hence it is not applicable to g. If g could be together with anything, it would have to be together with everything, but to be together with everything is to be together with nothing. Being-together-with is a way of locating something, but if that something is together with everything, it is in no sense located. Hence being-together-with is an exclusion predicate inapplicable to g.

Who Is the God of the Patriarchs?

It should be noted that the sorts of things that we know about y in terms of which we identify y are very different from the sorts of things that we know about g. Initially, g is identified as a or the member of a class, namely, the class of those things, a, "greater than" which cannot be conceived. Because g is identified solely through description, that is, solely through membership in a class, and everything that we know about g is what membership in that class entails, our discussion of g has been in mathematical terms. Our evidence for any statements about g consists of syllogisms, the premises of which are definitions and universal conditional propositions, all of which serve to explicate what it means to state that something is "greater than" which cannot be conceived. Experience has been irrelevant in considering evidence for what can or cannot be said about g.

But the matter is very different when we consider y. The y is not identified primarily as a member of a class. Rather, y is identified in experience through reports of acquaintance with y. With respect to g we asked what is it (he). However, concerning y we ask who is he (it). The answer is that y is the God of Abraham, Isaac, and Jacob.

To state that y is a god does state what y is. But all that we can state about what y is is not enough to identify y. The y at this point is indistinguishable from any number of other gods, Zeus, Apollo, Marduk, and so on. It is like stating that Socrates is a man, which in no way distinguishes Socrates from any other man.

What distinguishes Socrates from other men is not that he is a man but rather what he did as a man (e.g., taught philosophy to the young and drank hemlock) and how he stood in relationship to other entities (namely, being a Greek citizen living at a certain time so that he lived during the lifetime of both Parmenides and Aristotle, Parmenides being his senior and Aristotle his junior). Similarly, y is uniquely identified by acting as a god to Abraham, Isaac, and Jacob, and subsequent to the time of Moses, the God y is uniquely identified as that God who led the children of Israel out of Egypt, gave them the Torah, and led them into the Promised Land.

What does it mean to state that some entity is a god? How does the word *god* function so that an existent or nonexistent entity called Zeus or Apollo or Marduk or y can be called a god? Each one is a god because each one is a "person" and each one has a "flexible body." "Being a person" is the genus and "being an entity with flexible body" is the species difference of the class of gods. Both expressions have a specialized meaning in this context.

As I use the term *person,* most human beings are persons, but it is not clear whether or not all human beings are persons. A difficult case would be a man who has suffered severe brain damage. Angels and gods are persons. Mickey Mouse and Donald Duck are persons, but usually mice and ducks are not. Mickey Mouse is a person with a mouse body and Donald Duck is a person with a duck body. Rocks and even trees are not persons. Most likely amoebas are not persons. It is not clear whether or not some animals other than humans are persons. As I am using the term *person,* most members of anticruelty-to-animal societies would judge dogs and cats to be persons, but most experimental psychologists would not. Nazis did not consider Jews to be persons.

What I am calling a person coincides with what Aristotle and medieval Aristotelians called "rational beings." A rational being is an entity who can "deliberate"; that is, he or she (it) has mental acts and wills actions. What it means to state that people will their actions is that they are the proximate cause of their action and that they are that cause in virtue of their mental acts.

As I am using the word, a *body* is a spatial-temporal object; that is, a body is something in space at some time. To state that something *b* has a body *c* means that *b* and *c* are so related that by means of *c,* the *b* is identified. There are multiple relations possible between an entity and a body in which it can be said that *b* has the body *c.* Identity is the strongest example of such a relation. But other relations are possible. For example, whether or not souls exist, the relation of a soul to a body is not a relationship of identity. Nor is a soul, if souls exist, a part of a body or identical with a part of a body. In my use of the expression "*b* has a body," the term *b* can name a soul. The least strict example of a qualifying relation would involve the relation being-together-with, where by means of the spatial-temporal location of *c* we are able to identify contextually *b* where *b* is together with *c.* In this sense of the term, the footprint of an unknown murdered man can be called the body of the murderer.

The expression "flexible body" is used to distinguish two kinds of cases of having bodies. Persons such as Socrates and Mickey Mouse differ from gods not only with respect to differences in their relative degrees of shared powers. For example, Zeus is not a god merely by virtue of the fact that he is stronger and more cunning than Odysseus. The cunning of Odysseus is divine in that Odysseus is as cunning as a god. Similarly, the intelligence of Aristotle is divine in that he has the wisdom of a god. Hence Odysseus and Aristotle are godlike men. But neither is a god. Rather, humans and gods, both of whom have bodies in the sense described above, differ in their relationship to a given body. In the case of any human there tends to be a single organic body by which the person in question is primarily identified.

To a certain degree the body of a human is flexible. It changes from the body of an infant into the body of a child, and it changes again into the body of an adult person. Parts could be removed (for example, arms and legs), and parts could be added (for example, artificial organs), and the body would continue to be the body of a single human. Still there is a single body with spatial-temporal continuity that is the primary body of a given human. This is not the case with gods. The gods can assume many bodies as their primary bodies that are not single and are not continuous in space and time. The body of Zeus is sometimes that of a man and at other times is that of a bull, and one is no less the body of Zeus than the other. Hence Zeus has no spatial continuity.[22] Similarly, y is experienced at one time with a flaming bush body and at another time with a flaming, smoke pillar body. Hence the bodies of gods are more "flexible" than the bodies of entities other than gods.[23]

As I am using the term *flexible,* its opposite is *not brittle.* Bodies are not flexible in this context in the way that rubber is flexible and iron is not. Rather, the opposite of "flexible" in this sense of the word is "strict." A law is flexible if it can be applied in a great many cases in a great many ways. The term *loose* would be a synonym for *flexible.* But I prefer "flexible," since "loose body" has sexual overtones that might be appropriate to the Greek gods but are not appropriate to y.

Two kinds of bodies in this sense of "body" also need to be distinguished. As the term is used, both a bull in one context and a mountain (namely, Mount Olympus) in another context function as the body of Zeus. But they function differently. By reference to Mount Olympus, Zeus is spatially located, but the spatial location is vague. By means of the mountain you identify a general area as the location of Zeus. Whereas the body of Zeus is the bull, the location of Zeus is much more specific. Sounds heard over a telephone or in a completely dark room are bodies in the way that Mount Olympus is the body of Zeus but not in the way that a bull is the body of Zeus. Both kinds of bodies are also appropriate to y. From the biblical descriptions, the burning bush and the flaming smoke pillar are bodies of y in the same way that the bull is the body of Zeus. But the kiddush wine and the Shabbat challah while they are being blessed are not bodies in this sense, although they are bodies in the sense that Mount Olympus is the body of Zeus. While blessing, you address y and not the object blessed. Yet while addressing y, you look at the object blessed, which seems to imply that that object is "together with" y. The wine and the bread are not the body of y in the first sense, but they are in the second sense.

Corresponding to these two kinds of relation to a body we can state that Zeus was in the bull and y was in the bush and the pillar, but y is not in the wine and the bread. Conversely, Zeus was at but not in Mount Olympus, and when Jews say a blessing, y is at but not in the blessed object. By stating that y is at the blessed object, I mean that in addressing y I locate y in the general area of the blessed object.

That the God of the Patriarchs Is Not the God of the Philosophers

To state of something that it is either in or at some body need not entail that it is itself subject to spatial predicates, but it does entail that it is subject to being-together-with predicates. Thus although *y* does not occupy space, necessarily *y* is together with entities that occupy space. In other words, necessarily *y* is subject to being-together-with predicates. The necessity follows from whom *y* is, namely, the God of Abraham, Isaac, and Jacob. It would not be intelligible to state that *y* is the god of the patriarchs if *y* could not be together with the patriarchs.

Thus it clearly follows that the being who is "greater than" which cannot be conceived, even if it (he) exists, is not the God of Abraham, Isaac, and Jacob. This follows from the fact that there is a class of predicates, namely, being-together-with predicates, which are applicable to *y* but that are inappropriate to *g*. That *y* was together with Moses at Mount Sinai or that *y* assumed a human form in Judea could be true or false, but to state that *g* was together with Moses at Mount Sinai or that *g* assumed a human form in Judea (and thereby was subject to nongraded spatial location) is neither true nor false. It is unintelligible. Therefore *g* and *y* cannot be identical. Therefore the asserted identity of *g* and *y* is a mistake, and if it is the case that *y* is the deity of Judaism and Christianity, the ontological proof states nothing about whether or not He (it) exists.

How this mistaken identity came about is a matter of speculation. I mention two possible explanations: It is not unusual in ordinary speech to move from a comparative to a superlative. Mothers call their very smart children "the smartest." Sportswriters call extremely good athletes "the greatest." As expressed initially, the superlatives should be taken as mild exaggerations, reasonable in context. In this way reasonable expressions about *y*'s great knowledge, virtue, and so on may have been exaggerated as superlatives. Among people who knew of *y* only through the description of *y*, this *y* would have ceased to function as a name and instead would have designated some unknown entity of whom the superlatives in question were true. It should be noted that the biblical descriptions of *y* entail statements that *y* has a very great deal of knowledge and that *y* is extremely powerful. In fact, the extent of his knowledge and his power may be beyond our comprehension. But stating this is different from stating that *y* is the most powerful and the most knowing of all beings. Also stating this is very different from stating that *y* has perfect knowledge and perfect power.

A second explanation of the misidentity might be the following: Among the many characteristics of *y*, it is claimed that *y* is the creator of the world. Among the commonly accepted characteristics of *g*, this *g* is affirmed as the first cause of the world. One and only one entity could be the creator of the world and one and only one entity could be the first cause of the world. If you think that being a first cause and being a creator of the world are the same thing, you will naturally assume that the first cause and the creator of the world are a single entity. But to create and to be a first cause are not the same thing.

A Proof of the Existence of the God of the Patriarchs

My argument that the God of the philosophers and the God of Abraham, Isaac, and Jacob are not the same entity is now complete. But the separation of the two with the corresponding description of the God of the patriarchs raises new problems concerning the God of Abraham, Isaac, and Jacob that would not arise if g and y were the same entity. The first question is, what counts as evidence for the existence of y, and how do you know that y exists?

Because y is a person, the claim that y exists is to be determined in the same way that the claim that any person exists is to be determined, namely, by experience. In other words, if it is asked, "Does Malcolm exist?" and if John answers, "Of course he does; I just met him," that *prima facie* settles the issue. I say *"prima facie"* because although in most cases such a reply is sufficient to settle that persons exist, it does not always do so. Several objections to John's testimony can be raised.

It might be objected that John is a liar or that John was hallucinating or that John's vision of Malcolm is an illusion. In most cases these objections are based on negative judgments about John. For example, what is being claimed is that John habitually lies, so it is impossible to believe anything that he says, or that John in this case has good reason to lie and he is unscrupulous, or that John is an alcoholic and his experience of Malcolm is a result of his drinking, or that John has been in the sun too long. However, in each of these cases the burden of proof lies with the objector to give good reason to discount John's evidence for the existence of Malcolm. John's experience is trustworthy until shown to be otherwise.

That y exists is proven in this way. This y exists because there are many people who are trustworthy and sane who have experienced y, not the least of whom are the rabbis and the multiple authors of Scripture. If one objects because these people are liars or charlatans, which in effect is the claim of Marxists, evidence must be given. To doubt their honesty solely on the grounds that you do not believe that y exists begs the question.

Besides discounting John's testimony that Malcolm exists on the grounds of John's character, objection to the meeting of Malcolm could be raised on schematic grounds. For example, assume that Malcolm is a centaur. Our doubter might argue as follows: Given that a centaur is something with the digestive system of a man attached to the digestive system of a horse, there is no way for the lower torso to receive nourishment from the upper torso. Hence no such creature could exist. Therefore, since there cannot be centaurs, John could not have seen Malcolm. In other words, the experience is not admissible in the schema. (In effect this is what Sartre argued in *Being and Nothingness,* that God is Being-In-Itself-For-Itself, which, in his ontology, is not admissible.)

Such an objection may be answered in one of two ways. It could be argued that the given experience is not really inadmissible into the given schema. For example, again assuming that Malcolm is a centaur, it might be replied that the upper torso of a centaur looks like a human intestine, but in reality it is not. In reality it is a very long, thick neck. In this case John's experience of Malcolm is schematically admissible. Or it could be granted that the experience is inadmissible into the schema, and the schema ought to be rejected. *Prima facie* schemata are no more sacred than experiences. A case such as this proves that both the schema and the experience cannot be affirmed. But which should be affirmed and which should be rejected depends on the context.

However, it should also be noted that men have rarely devised schemata sufficiently poor or sufficiently specific that they could not be adjusted to admit new unanticipated experiences. Generally, schemata do not die; they are just stretched to such an extent that they become useless. An example of this is the determinist's dogma that every event has a cause. To preserve this thesis, the terms *event* and *cause* are so extended that the thesis escapes any possible falsification.[24] For the readers of this chapter the following example might be clearer: It is reported that an early twentieth-century Christian fundamentalist was shown a fossil and asked how he could believe that Scripture gives us a literal account of when the world was created in the light of this evidence. The fundamentalist was reported to have responded that fossils are the creation of the devil, put on earth to pervert true belief. In this way the believer preserves his object of belief. But the price that he pays for that belief is too high to preserve the belief. Most people properly would choose the authenticity of the fossil over the affirmation of the fundamentalist schema. I think that people who believe that God is perfectly good, omnipotent, and omniscient in the light of any number of events, the Holocaust not being the least of them, are in a similar situation.

In any case, the schematic objection to the existence of Malcolm has no relevance to the existence of y. It is reasonable (even if false) for someone to argue that since no one has ever experienced a person with "flexible body," no such person exists. But I cannot imagine an argument to the effect that in principle there are no such things as persons with "flexible bodies" that does not beg the question. For example, I see no reason to credit a schema that claims that only sense objects exist, and since y is not a sense object, y does not exist. I reject this claim solely on the grounds that I can see no reason to so limit the range of existence claims unless I want to exclude the possibility of entities such as y existing.

I might also discount John's testimony that Malcolm exists on the grounds that there is no objective test by which the purported existence of Malcolm could be tested. For example, although multiple experiences of men are sufficient to establish the existence of these men, a great number of experiences of unidentified flying objects are not sufficient to remove doubt from their purported existence. The reason for this difference is the following: If you state to me, "I doubt that you really saw Richard Nixon when he was the president of the United States," I can reply to you, "Very well, if you don't trust me, then go to the White House and see for yourself." But no such response can be given in the case of an unidentified flying object.

Concerning y, different tests are given in different religious traditions. From the perspective of traditional Judaism the test is the following: First learn Hebrew. Then master the prayerbook and the forms of worship to a sufficient degree so that you can perform them without deliberation. Then you will be ready to encounter God in communal worship. Go to a "minyan," and he will be there.

That there are different traditions for meeting *y* does not discredit any of them. A human person stands in many roles in many different relations to many different persons. Accounts of how to meet a person will vary as the relations with that person vary. The same is true of *y*. Jewish and most other contemporary Western religious traditions claim to offer a road to God, but they need not claim to offer an exclusive road to God. Some Jews may argue that their test is the only possible test for Jews, but no Jew can claim that his or her test is the only possible test for all humans. In any case, any claim to exclusiveness must be tested by experience.

John tells Thomas that he met Malcolm, but Thomas does not believe John. John then says, "If you don't believe me, go to Alexander Hall on Monday or Thursday between 2:30 P.M. and 4:30 P.M. and politely tell the receptionist by the door that you would like to meet Malcolm." The designation of a place, a time, and a procedure to follow at that place and time is the test that John in fact met Malcolm. All such tests involve the designation of specific places and/ or times and/or procedures. Let us call such a specific test *T*.

If Thomas performs test *T* but does not meet Malcolm, any one of the following states of affairs could obtain: Let the expression "Malcolm is at *T*" mean that Malcolm is met by performing test *T*.

A. Malcolm is neither at *T* nor anywhere else. Malcolm does not exist, and John was either hallucinating or lying or suffering an illusion.

B. Malcolm is no longer at *T*, but he is somewhere else, *R*.

C. Malcolm is no longer at *T*, and he is nowhere else.

D. Malcolm is no longer at *T*, and he is nowhere else, but he will later be somewhere, *R*.

E. Malcolm is often or always at *T*, but Thomas cannot meet him.

F. Malcolm is often or always at *T*, but Thomas did not recognize him.

As discussed above, there is no way to verify the first alternative unless good grounds can be given for the claim that John is a liar or that he was hallucinating or that he suffered an illusion. But it can be falsified by someone other than John and Thomas meeting Malcolm at *T*.

Some liberal Jews make the second claim about meeting God at a "minyan." They argue that at one time God was present at the Temple in Jerusalem, but by the second century A.D. he was no longer to be found there. Similarly, God used to be at the synagogue, but he can no longer be found there. Today God can be found "in the streets," defending the persecuted. Such a claim is verified only if no one trustworthy (i.e., honest, not hallucinating, and not suffering an illusion) meets God at the synagogue while others meet God "in the streets." Or in Malcolm's case, the second claim is valid if no one trustworthy meets Malcolm at *T*, but someone trustworthy does meet Malcolm at *R*.

The third and fourth claims are substantiated only if no one meets Malcolm anywhere. In such a case there is no clear way to distinguish between these claims. If the third claim is correct, Malcolm is dead. If the fourth claim is correct, then, to use a phrase of Martin Buber, Malcolm is "eclipsed." Generally, if someone's mind is open to Malcolm's existence, and it is only lately that Malcolm has not been seen, and there is no evidence to support the claim that Malcolm died, it is reasonable to assume that Malcolm is eclipsed.[25] But given the long absence of Zeus, for example, eclipse is less reasonable than death. Yet there are no clear, precise rules for making these judgments. What constitutes a sufficient length of time varies with the context.[26] There is no clear way to verify the third claim, although any time that a trustworthy person meets Malcolm, the third claim is falsified, and what in this context falsifies the third claim verifies the fourth claim.

The fifth and sixth claims are verified if someone other than John and Thomas meets Malcolm at T. At present this is the situation concerning y. Both the fifth and the sixth claims function to account for, in one case, why Thomas did not meet y either in the synagogue or in the street. Either or both claims could be true in a particular case. Assume that John sends doubting Thomas to the White House to meet Richard Nixon. Thomas reports back that he went there but Nixon was nowhere to be found, but from the *New York Times* we learn that several other people walked into the White House at precisely the same time that Thomas did, and they met Nixon. John then questions Thomas in more detail about what he did when he entered the White House, and he learns that Thomas had not cut his long hair, that he had not shaved his beard, that he was barefoot, and that he wore a peace symbol around his neck. "Oh," says John, "now I know why you did not meet Nixon; he took one look at you and didn't want to meet you." If you ask, how do you know that Nixon does not like to meet people appearing as Thomas did, the answer is, tradition; that is, the judgment is based on what those who have met Nixon have had to say about the way that Nixon reponds to people. In the same way, religious tradition mediates meeting God. In affirming certain worship disciplines the adherents of a tradition are judging on the basis of their worship experience certain conditions under which God can be met. These conditions are not sufficient conditions. God is no more forced to meet other persons than we are. Neither are they necessary conditions in that only if these conditions are fulfilled can meeting with God take place. But they are sufficient conditions in that the failure to fulfill them is sufficient reason for God not to be present.

John might question Thomas in a different way. He might ask, "Are you sure that you know what Nixon looks like?" If Thomas responds, "Of course I do; he is a tall, thin man from Boston who used to be our ambassador to India," we know that Thomas missed Nixon because he had a wrong description of him. The y can be missed in the same way if our Thomas is looking for someone who has the properties of g. In other words, the sixth claim is reasonable when our Thomas has a misdescription of our Malcolm, no matter who the Thomas or the Malcolm is. That few people in post–World War II Western civilization believe that they know that the God of Judaism and Christianity exists may be due to confusing this deity with the traditional God of the philosophers.

NOTES

1. Blaise Pascal, *Pensées* (New York: Dutton, Everyman's Library Edition, 1948).

2. Bertrand Russell, *Why I am Not a Christian* (New York: Simon and Schuster, 1957); J. N. Findlay, "Can God's Existence Be Disproved?" in A. Flew and A. Macintyre, eds., *New Essays in Philosophical Theology* (New York: Macmillan, 1955), pp. 47–50.

3. Two good introductions to the contemporary discussion are John H. Hick, *Philosophy of Religion* (Englewood Cliffs, N.J.: Prentice-Hall, 1963), Chs. 1–3; and W. I. Rowe and W. J. Wainwright, eds., *Philosophy of Religion: Selected Readings* (New York: Harcourt Brace Jovanovich, 1973), Chs. 1–2.

4. This section is a revision of an earlier article of mine, "On Proving God's Existence," *Judaism*, Winter 1967, pp. 21–36.

5. Anselm, *Proslogium*, trans. Sidney North Deane (LaSalle, Ill.: Open Court, 1903).

6. David Hume, *Dialogues Concerning Natural Religion* (Edinburgh: Thomas Nelson & Sons, 1947), Pt. 9; Immanuel Kant, *The Critique of Pure Reason*, trans. N. K. Smith (London: Macmillan, 1952), "Transcendental Dialectic," Bk. II, Ch. 3.

7. Jan Berg, "An Examination of the Ontological Proof," *Theoria* 27 (1961); 99–106; George Nakhnikian and Wesley C. Salmon, " 'Exists' as a Predicate," *The Philosophical Review* 66, no. 4 (1957): 535–542.

8. Norman Malcolm, "The Ontological Argument," in his *Knowledge and Certainty* (Englewood Cliffs, N.J.: Prentice-Hall, 1965), pp. 141–162; Charles Hartshorne, *The Logic of Perfection and Other Essays in Neoclassical Metaphysics* (LaSalle, Ill.: Open Court, 1962), Ch. 2.

9. "Greater" here is used in the same way as in the first version.

10. It is impossible to consider all of the objections. Many of them I judge to be self-evidently false. The chapter would be unnecessarily tedious for the reader if I were to list all of these objections and what is wrong with them. Rather, I shall limit my attention primarily to two objections that I judge to be the most crucial.

11. Jan Berg, in his reconstruction of Malcolm's argument, commits what I judge to be the same mistake as that of Plantinga.

12. Robert C. Coburn, "Professor Malcolm on God," *Australasian Journal of Philosophy* 41 (1963): 143–162.

13. This section and the next are revisions of an earlier article of mine, "That the God of the Philosophers Is Not the God of Abraham, Isaac, and Jacob," *Harvard Theological Review* 65, no. 1 (January 1972): 1–27.

14. There are several possible philosophic traditions for speaking about *g*, and it is not certain that the use of the term *God* in any one of these traditions is consistent with the use of the term *God* in any other tradition. For example, given that there is a "prime mover" and given that there is "something 'greater than' which cannot be conceived," it is not certain that a single entity could be both the prime mover and something "greater than" which cannot be conceived. Since I wish to avoid this issue in this chapter, I limit

my use of the expression *g* solely to that supposed entity whose existence Anselm, in the light of Malcolm's commentary, claimed to be demonstrable.

15. In my statement of these rules I have assumed Bertrand Russell's doctrine of class levels, and I have assumed that positive predicates can be distinguished from negative predicates. However, the rules stated below should be neutral with regard to any theory of predication in that if either or both of the above assumptions are denied, the statement of the rules can be altered to account for the different analysis of predication. In general, what the rules state is that all positive predicates are predicable of *g* with the exception of all members of what are defined as "exclusion" predicates and all but one member of any class of what are defined as "graded" predicates provided that that class does not entail predicates from a class of nongraded, exclusion predicates. There may be other exceptions to the rules that ought to be noted. For example, *g* does not exemplify the class of all classes. Also, *g* does not exemplify a predicate *P* where *P* is any predicate other than *Q* in the class of predicates that is not an exclusion class of predicates that does not entail an exclusion class of predicates and *Q* is a predicate. In this case a proposition of the form "*g* is *P*" would be judged not to be well formed. The *P* would be an example of what I here call a "negative predicate," and the rules of predication range only over positive predicates.

16. To be blue is not better or greater than to be orange.

17. The same thing cannot be blue and orange all over.

18. For other reasons, namely, Rule 3, bowling cannot be predicated of *g*.

19. It is open to question whether an entity may occupy more than one space at a time. There are certain problems with such a claim. For example, consider Michigan Avenue in Chicago. Presumably, this street occupies a single space, but part of this space extends over a bridge that crosses the Chicago River. When that bridge is up, it is not altogether clear what is the space that Michigan Avenue occupies. It might even occupy two spaces, one on each side of the uplifted bridge. The problem arises because it is not clear just what a space is. But this lack of clarity does not affect the dogma that if something occupies all space, then it occupies no space.

20. See N. Samuelson, *Gersonides on God's Knowledge* (Toronto: Pontifical Institute of Mediaeval Studies, 1971).

21. This predicate is based on and similar to but not identical with the relation *W* that Nelson Goodman used in *The Structure of Appearance* (Indianapolis: Bobbs-Merrill, 1951).

22. It is open to question if temporal continuity is necessary to make the claim that the god that I experienced now is the same god that I experienced before.

23. The term *angel* is ambiguous. When an "angel" means a disembodied spirit that differs from *y* in that it is subservient to and a "messenger" of *y* not associated peculiarly with any body, then angels are gods. In this sense of the term in Greek mythology, only Zeus qualifies as a god as distinct from angels. The other inhabitants of Mount Olympus are angels. But as the term was used by the medieval Aristotelians, an angel is an intellect or a soul of a given body or sphere. In this sense of the term, angels or "intelligences" are not gods.

24. See G. J. Warnock, "Every Event Has a Cause," in A. Flew, ed., *Logic and Language* (London: Blackwell, 1953), pp. 312–330.

25. For example, someone trustworthy could state, "I saw Frank shoot Malcolm" or "I read about Malcolm's funeral in the *New York Times*."

26. How many years must a man be missing to be reasonably declared dead? Is the common current legal designation of seven years reasonable or merely conventional?

SELECTED BIBLIOGRAPHY

Baker, John Robert. "What Is Wrong with a Hartshornean Modal Proof." *Southern Journal of Philosophy* 18 (Spring 1980).

Bedell, Gary. "The Many Faces of Necessity in the Many-Faced Argument." *The New Scholasticism* 53 (Winter 1979): 1–21. This article contains an extensive bibliography of articles on the ontological argument.

Berg, Jan. "An Examination of the Ontological Proof." *Theoria* 27 (1961).

Brecher, Robert. "Aquinas on Anselm." *Philosophical Studies* (Ireland) 23 (1975): 3–66.

Coburn, Robert C. "Professor Malcolm on God." *Australasian Journal of Philosophy* 41 (1963): 143–162.

Crawford, Dan D. "The Cosmological Argument, Sufficient Reason, and Why-Questions." *International Journal for the Philosophy of Religion,* November 1978, pp. 111–122.

Duncan, Roger. "Analogy and the Ontological Argument." *The New Scholasticism* 54 (Winter 1980): 25–33.

Findlay, J. N. "Can God's Existence Be Disproved?" In A. Flew and A. Macintyre, eds. *New Essays in Philosophical Theology.* New York: Macmillan, 1955, pp. 47–56.

Friedman, Joel I. "Necessity and the Ontological Argument." *Erkenntnis* 15 (November 1980): 301–331.

Geisler, Norman L. "The Missing Premise in the Cosmological Argument." *Modern Schoolman* 56 (November 1978): 31–45.

Grim, Patrick. "Plantinga, Hartshorne, and the Ontological Argument." *Sophia* 20 (July 1981): 12–16.

Hartshorne, Charles. *The Logic of Perfection and Other Essays in Neoclassical Metaphysics.* LaSalle, Ill.: Open Court, 1962.

Hasker, W. "Is There a Second Ontological Argument?" *International Journal for the Philosophy of Religion* 13 (1982): 93–102.

Hick, John, ed. *The Many-Faced Argument: Recent Studies on the Ontological Argument for the Existence of God.* New York: Macmillan, 1967.

———. *Philosophy of Religion.* Englewood Cliffs, N.J.: Prentice-Hall, 1963.

Hintikka, Jaakko. "Kant on Existence, Predication, and the Ontological Argument." *Dialectica* 35 (1981): 127–146.

Loptson, Peter J. "Anselm, Meinong, and the Ontological Argument." *International Journal for the Philosophy of Religion* 11 (Fall 1980): 185–194.

McAllister, Alan. "Two Errors in Assessing the Ontological Argument." *International Journal for the Philosophy of Religion* 9 (1978): 171–178.

Malcolm, Norman. "The Ontological Argument." In his *Knowledge and Certainty* (Englewood Cliffs, N.J.: Prentice-Hall, 1965), pp. 141–162.

Maydole, Robert E. "A Modal Model for Proving the Existence of God." *American Philosophical Quarterly* 17 (April 1980): 135–142.

Miethe, Terry L. "The Cosmological Argument." *The New Scholasticism* 52 (Spring 1978): 285–305. This article contains an extensive bibliography of articles on the cosmological argument.

Nakhnikian, George, and Wesley C. Salmon. " 'Exists' as a Predicate." *The Philosophical Review* 66, no.4 (1957): 535–542.

O'Gorman, F. G. "Yet Another Look at the Ontological Argument." *Philosophical Studies* (Ireland) 23 (1975): 49–62.

Orenduff, J. M. "Existence Proofs and the Ontological Argument." *Southwest Philosophical Studies* 5 (April 1980): 50–54.

Plantinga, Alvin. *God and Other Minds*. Ithaca, N.Y.: Cornell University Press, 1967.

———. *The Nature of Necessity*. Oxford: Clarendon Press, 1974.

Reichenbach, Bruce A. "The Cosmological Argument and the Causal Principle." *International Journal for the Philosophy of Religion* 6 (Fall 1975): 185–190.

Rosenberg, Shalom. "On the Modal Version of the Ontological Argument." *Logique et Analyse* 24 (March 1981): 129–133.

Rowe, W. I. and W. J. Wainwright, eds. *Philosophy of Religion: Selected Readings*. New York: Harcourt Brace Jovanovich, 1973.

Rowe, William. "The Ontological Argument and Question-Begging." *International Journal for the Philosophy of Religion* 7 (1976): 425–432.

Russell, Bertrand. *Why I am Not a Christian*. New York: Simon and Schuster, 1957.

Sadowsky, James A. "The Cosmological Argument and the Endless Regress." *International Philosophical Quarterly* 20 (December 1980): 465–467.

Samuelson, Norbert M. "On Proving God's Existence." *Judaism* (Winter 1967), pp. 21–36.

———. "That the God of the Philosophers Is Not the God of Abraham, Isaac, and Jacob." *Harvard Theological Review* 65, no. 1 (January 1972): 1–27.

Satre, Thomas W. "Necessary Being and the Question-Blocking Argument." *International Journal for the Philosophy of Religion* 9 (1978): 158–170.

Shields, George W. "Hartshorne's Modal Ontological Argument." *Dialogue* 22 (April 1980): 45–56.

Smith, George H. *Atheism: The Case against God*. Buffalo: Prometheus Books, 1979.

Tooley, Michael. "Plantinga's Defence of the Ontological Argument." *Mind* 90 (February 1981): 422–427.

Van Inwagen, Peter. "Ontological Arguments." *Nous* 11 (November 1977): 375–395.

Wainwright, William J. "Causality, Necessity, and the Cosmological Argument." *Philosophical Studies* 36 (October 1979): 261–270.

———. "The Ontological Argument: Question-Begging and Professor Rowe." *International Journal of the Philosophy of Religion* 9 (1978): 254–257.

Walton, Douglas, "The Circle in the Ontological Argument." *International Journal for the Philosophy of Religion* 9 (1978): 193–218.

3

Universal Theology: Beyond Absolutism and Relativism

ASHOK K. GANGADEAN

ABSOLUTISM AND THE UNIVERSAL PATHOLOGY OF RATIONALITY

Universal Theology (UT) is the inevitable outgrowth of interreligious theology and indeed of theology in general. It is essentially the articulation of the universal Divine Form that must live at the heart of any and every form of life. The essence of this discussion is that every possible name or form is a logos (see Glossary for definitions of special terms) and every logos inherently reflects the universal word, which is absolute, infinite unity. Reflection on Divine Form reveals that as the form of all possible forms, it discloses itself as the universal continuum, which is Logos.

The enterprise of interreligious theology raises deep issues about rationality in general—it brings out inherent paradoxes and incoherencies in the nature of discourse between profoundly diverse religious worlds. Since it appears that each religious world defines its own rational form of life and is a universe of discourse unto itself, this seems to imply that diverse worlds are incommensurable, beyond rational mutuality or shared meanings. Nevertheless, we have the deep intuition that we are able truly to inhabit diverse religious worlds and understand them from within. This suggests that there is, indeed, deeper unity and mutuality than might first have been seen. In this way a problem of rationality arises—how can there be true unity between radically diverse religious worlds, each of which in some way defines its absolute principle? We cannot simply postulate a transcendent unity of religions that discloses some more primitive metaunity. This way out has been tried, but it has its problems. The point is that in this context of the dialectical tensions about reconciling radical diversity and radical unity between religious worlds, certain predictable and perennial problems of absolutism and relativism arise.

These problems of absolutism have resonated throughout the ages and diverse cultures. They appear to be inherent in the very structure of human reason itself. But these problems continue to rage in all areas of contemporary rationality, as much today as they did in ancient times. These problems are deep in the discourse of ethics—are there absolute values for human life or are values subjective or relative? They emerge at the center of current discussions about rationality itself—are there absolute or foundational rational principles or criteria in terms of which intelligibility and truth can be judged? These problems of absolutism have been intense in recent philosophy of science—what is the nature of scientific discourse in self-transformation from one paradigm or conceptual framework to another? Are there objective or universal principles of rationality of scientific growth and change? Since the problems of absolutism abound in everyday life, it is important to address the deeper causes of absolutism and to find a deeper way to understand it.

This is a problem that UT cannot and does not avoid. It is the central issue in the question of interreligious dialogue and the unity of religions. This chapter attempts to give an account of the nature of absolutism in a way that speaks directly to the central issues of theology and interreligious discourse.

DISCERNING THE DIVINE FORM: HOLISTIC UNITY AS THE DIVINE CONTINUUM

Universal Theology is meditation on universal Divine Form. Such meditation reveals that Divine Form is absolute, infinite unity. Here we already see a kind of redundancy or reiteration in the words *universal, unity, absolute,* and *infinite;* in meditative thought Divine Form is revealed as the universal continuum in which all possible divine names are synonymous. Thus in meditative reason it is seen that Divine Form is infinite unity, and meditation on infinite unity reveals that Divine Form must be absolutely universal—the form of all possible forms. In short, UT is the articulation of Absolute Unity.

Let us call this "holistic unity." Holistic unity is infinitely pure and has no trace of duality or discrimination within it. As such, it cannot be made into an *object* of thought in any way and is hence not accessible to the individuated mind. Holistic form must be *meditated,* and in such meditation mind becomes one with Divine Form, so mind self-expands to holistic unity. This very process of self-universalization becomes the essential concern of UT; meditation on divine unity calls forth the holistic mind, for only the mind that is truly one with Divine Form can discern infinite unity.

Holistic unity implies a divine continuum in which whatever is discerned is found to be essentially synonymous with Divine Form—so any divine name is one with Divine Form: this is the essence of infinite unity. Thus in meditating on Divine Form we find that infinite form is the form of all possible forms, so there can be no form that is not encompassed within the divine continuum.

Again, meditation on absolute unity reveals that pure unity is the form of perfection, and such infinite perfection is the form of goodness; meditation on goodness reveals the form of pure meaning, which is the origin of all reason; meditation on the form of holistic reason discloses the nature of truth; meditation on the form of truth shows the form of pure life; meditation on holistic life makes manifest the meaning of intelligence; reflection on the pure form of intelligence opens the way to the divine light, which is the form of all forms; reflection on infinite form shows itself as infinite being; meditation on infinite being reveals the form of the Universal Word; contemplation of the Holistic Word makes clear the Universal Grammar of any possible existence; mindfulness of pure Grammar shows the deep structure of any possible Experience; and so on. Thus the divine continuum is perfect self-unity in which any divine name, being infinite and holistic, implies all other divine names. Let us speak of this as the "divine synonymy" of the holistic Continuum.

As we reflect on the divine continuum we see that holistic unity implies the nondifference of Being, Truth, Goodness, Meaning, Intelligence, Rationality, Knowledge, Life, and so on, ad infinitum. Let us use the term "Logos" for the divine continuum—for Divine Form. So Logos is the original Universal or Holistic Word—the infinite form of all possible forms, and UT is the meditative articulation of Logos.

There is something redundant in the name "universal theology," for theology is par excellence the articulation of Divine Form, which is the absolute universal form of all forms. So theology by its nature must be universal. As meditation on the Universal Word (Logos), UT must be able to account for any possible form—for all forms essentially reflect Logos. This means that UT should be able to account for any possible theology and any possible form of life. This is one sense in which UT must be universal.

To see more clearly the universal scope of UT, it would be helpful to elaborate on the idea of any possible form. It has been said that UT is the articulation of Logos, which is the universal absolute form of all possible forms. Let us use the term "logos" for any possible form in general. The insight of UT is that any logos essentially reflects Logos, and the true universal import of any logos is revealed when its holistic unity with Logos is meditatively realized. The main objective of UT is to show that any possible form *is* a logos and to show that every logos essentially reflects Logos as its true form.

Let us clarify this point. It is important to see from the start that the term *form* is holistic and encompasses any possible thing that may be discerned in thought. If we speak of diverse forms of life—as in different religious worlds or cultures, each would be a logos. So the Christian life-world would be a logos, the Buddhist life-world would be a logos, the form of life we call science—being a scientist—would be a logos, and so on. So any form of life would be a logos. But so would any discriminated item in any given cultural world—in reality—also be a logos—a person, a mind, a body, an event, a process, an action, the sky, the water, are each a logos; in short, any possible thing that may be discriminated or individuated is a logos. So the term *logos* applies to any possible thing that may have identity (name or form).

It is important to see that Logos has jurisdiction over any possible logos— there is no possible religion or theology, for example, that does not have logos as its true inner form; there is no divine name in any possible religious form of life that does not make reference to Logos; there is no form of life in general whose meaning and rationality is not oriented to the Universal Word. In general, there is no meaning that is not in its deep structure oriented to Logos, no word or name that is beyond the scope of the Universal Word. There is no life that does not get its life force from Logos, and so on for every possible logos.

It should be evident that this feature of Logos is immediately implied in the holistic meaning of infinite form—there can be no possible form that stands independently and apart from Divine Form. This is the very meaning of the universality and unity of Logos. It is indeed a classical thesis of theology that all things derive from Divine Form. One task of UT is to elaborate on this holistic truth and make clear its explanatory power for understanding all possible forms of life.

The Holistic Mind versus the Particularistic Mind

The central thesis of UT is that every logos is Logos. This is a holistic truth spoken in the meditative narrative of the holistic mind. It is a simple truth, but its full power is not readily available to the particularistic mind. For the latter attempts to think what cannot be thought but only meditated. Thinking arises in a dualized structure that separates the mind or voice of the thinker from the holistic continuum and reduces Divine Form to an object of thought. But the holistic mind teaches that Divine Form cannot be thought; it must be realized in meditation. Meditative thinking essentially involves the self-expansion of the particularistic mind to its holistic form in which it is one with the continuum. What makes perfect sense to the meditative narrative can be inscrutable to the particularistic voice, for the latter does not discern the holistic continuum. Meditative speech is centered in the continuum whereas the particularistic mind is centered in a logos that separates itself from the continuum. In a sense the challenge of UT is to give a critical account of the particularistic mind in the context of making clear the nature of the dialectical self-transformation of the particularistic mind to its holistic form.

In approaching this task let us continue the holistic narrative. The holistic mind works on the *principle of universal relativity*.[1] This is the principle of the continuum—the universal field—in which any given logos permeates every other logos in dependent coarising, in divine synonymy. The true meaning of any logos is realized in discerning its inner form, which is Logos. This means that in meditating on any logos (any name or form), its true import is found in discerning it in the context of the holistic continuum. The continuum is the universal context of true meaning. So no logos is ever given identity or particularistic meaning in isolation from Logos.

The principle of holistic meaning reveals that primary meaning is metaphoric and symbolic rather than literalistic.[2] But the terms *metaphoric* and *symbolic* are used in their holistic sense here—the *symbolic* force of any logos is precisely its conformity to universal relativity—its self-universalization in the Continuum; its true meaning shows that it is *analogous* to every other logos; that is, its identity is found in discerning its unity in the continuum. By contrast, the particularistic mind begins with the presumption that *literal* meaning is primary and that the unique meaning of a given logos consists of its differentiated identity—that which separates it from everything else. Thus, for example, in discerning the true identity of Jesus Christ, the particularistic mind finds in this logos a unique, particular being who is differentiated from other beings. But the holistic mind discerns a logos whose true identity or form consists of the unity of the Continuum—that is, the meditative intelligence discerns a logos whose true meaning is Logos. Indeed, the essential import of the Christ is found to be precisely the living principle of relativity—the living Logos. So whereas the particularistic mind perceives a uniquely individuated logos, the holistic mind discerns a self-universalizing holistic form. (In a sense, the rest of this chapter is an elaboration of this point.)

The meditative mind, in thinking metaphorically and symbolically according to universal relativity, exercises a meditative imagination that discerns analogies or synonymies in the continuum. Whereas the particularistic mind, working on the principle of absolute identity, fixates meaning and produces discontinuity, meditative thinking activates the analogical imagination that breaks through artificial boundaries and discerns the deeper holistic import in any given logos. Thus to take another example, in meditating on "bread" the holistic imagination sees here a logos whose universal import or true symbolic meaning is expanded in the continuum—universal bread is one with the body of the Christ, which is the Living Word—the resurrected body. The holistic import of "bread" is not that it is inert matter but that it is the Living Word. We may perform a similar meditative experiment on "wine" or "air" or "water" and so on.

In meditative speech, holy water—holistic water—is discerned to be self-universalized in the continuum, and here one may state in the meditative voice—All is Water. In this meditative transformation one finds the holistic meaning of Water in the Continuum—its divine synonymy. This meaning transformation is classical—one finds in the Upanisads, for example, the meditative principle that All is AUM, which is a sacred sound symbolizing ultimate reality. This principle requires that in proper meditation on any given word, its universal synonymy with AUM is discerned. AUM is the Divine Form, the holistic continuum in which the universal import of any word is discerned. So if in yogic meditation we meditate on "air," the holistic mind, which is yoked with the Continuum, discerns the universal import of holistic Air—the divine breath, speech, the Living Word.

Again, in Buddhist meditation the Madhyamika teaches that all things (logos) are empty when taken in self-existence (independent identity); this is true of the self as indicated by "I." But when particularistic identity is overcome and the individuated "I" (mind, voice) is removed, the holistic voice that is one with the Continuum (Súnyata) sees things as they truly are—in universal relativity. In this form of meditative speech the true import of things is seen in the universal continuum, which is Divine Form, and so on.

These examples are just preliminary illustrations to make more vivid the difference between the holistic mind and the particularistic voice. The main point here is that the Continuum—Divine Form—must come first in every respect, and all true thought, meaning, life, is oriented to holistic unity.

Elaboration in Holistic Narrative of "Logos": The Form of Life

Let us now continue the meditation on Divine Form and elaborate on how any possible form or logos is oriented to the continuum as its essential form. The term *logos* is a holistic term and the remark that "every possible form is logos" is a holistic remark spoken in the meditative voice. So "logos" is precisely *analogous* to Logos, and it mirrors Divine Form in the Continuum: logos is in the image of Logos.

We saw earlier that Divine Form is the form of perfect unity and that meditation on this unity opened up the divine synonymy of diverse divine names: in Absolute Unity is perfection, in perfection is goodness, in goodness is truth, in truth is intelligence, in intelligence is life, in life is the word, in the word there is meaning, in meaning there is being, and so on. So it is impossible to separate off any divine name from the form of perfect unity, and all divine names mutually entail one another: this is the form of the Continuum.

This reminds us that Divine Form is the form of all possible forms—of any possible logos. This means that any possible logos—for example, a human life—is intrinsically oriented to Logos—it gets its form, life, meaning, being, telos, from the Divine Form, and every logos imitates Logos in being a unity—to be a form is to be a unity of some sort.

To see this we must remember that the word *form* or *logos* is holistic and hence recursively applies to any possible "thing" at any level: whatever can be named indicates a form of some sort. So "logos" can be any *thing*: a person, a form of life, a mind, a voice, a word, an object, an event, an action, a religious world, an art, and so on. There is no limit to what can be a logos—it is infinitely recursive and reiterative, and this is connected to its holistic form.

Every logos (name or form) is a unity that is intrinsically oriented to Logos and gets its true meaning in its unity with the continuum. This is the principle of meaning and interpretation for UT: its hermeneutical principle. To illustrate this let us focus meditative attention on a logos of special interest—a life, a human life. This logos gets its life, its being, its meaning, from the continuum and its true life and meaning consist of its realizing its unity in the continuum. Let us call this its "form of life."

The form of life of a human logos gets its meaning from its intrinsic orientation to Logos. The holistic understanding of any form of life shows how its meaning arises in its unity with the continuum: being in the image of Logos, the form of life derives its meaning in orientation to Divine Form, which is its unifying principle. The unifying principle of a life is what gives this logos its form of rationality, for rationality is precisely the formal principle of unity of a given life. The unifying principle of a form of life is its *faith*—that form from which all meaning derives. This unifying principle of rational faith (for faith and reason are one in holistic life) is the very form of goodness that is the reason for being of this life: the unifying principle of a form of life is its source of life, meaning, being and value. In this respect the unifying form of a life orients all of its life, and its life force is directed towards this principle. So the *meaning of life* is in its form and its form is its unifying principle, which is its rational faith. In this holistic narrative then we begin to discern the divine synonymy in form of life, unifying principle, reason for being, goodness or origin of all meaning and value and its faith.

In meditating further on this logos we find that it is one with its form of life, which is a unity of its meaning, being, value, and thought. So its rational thought is its being, and this takes the form of *grammar*—the form of its *word*.[3] In this holistic sense, "grammar" is the logos-structure that makes all meaning possible and constitutes a world or universe; so the grammar of a form of life makes a universe of discourse possible and gives form to all meaning and experience in that world. In this respect a grammar is the *structure* of a form of life that allows the logos to think, experience, speak, and make sense of reality; a grammar is a life-world that makes reality possible and allows a logos to know itself and be one with Logos.

Grammar and Divine Form: Every Form of Life Is Religious

In meditating on a logos as a form of life we have seen in holistic unity that the form of life is structured in grammar, which makes the self-interpretation of a life-world possible. Here it may be seen that *to live is to interpret*—there is no meaning, no existence, no thought, no experience, that is not grammatical; as the form of life, grammar universally conditions the life in its rational possibilities. It may be said that a grammar is a divine interpretation, a divine name, a holistic hypothesis.

Some illustrations might make this more tangible. We have been reflecting on a logos as a form of life, and this has taken us to grammar. It has been ambiguous whether the form of life is individual or communal; it could be both. But for our purposes here let us take some historical examples of forms of life (grammars)—it is easily seen that the Hindu or Buddhist or Christian forms of life express themselves in diverse grammars of reality. Each grammar constitutes a life-world that is communally lived as a culture. The grammar here is the structure of logos, which makes all life and meaning possible: it constitutes its rational form. What is rational or makes sense in one life-world appears to be different from what makes sense in another. Each grammar involves a faith, a unifying principle, that is its divine interpretation or shows its Divine Form. Each grammar may be taken in its holistic form—in its divine synonymy with the Continuum, or it might take itself as an absolute form, as a grammar of Divine Form in and of itself, as a separate universe of discourse. We shall explore this difference later. The point here is that a grammar by its nature shows its Divine Form, and since it orders and orients a given form of life, it involves a faith and hence a religious form of life.

The holistic insight that every form of life, shown in a grammar, involves a faith principle and implies a religious form of life (i.e., a life oriented in faith and conditioned by a divine name or form) may be more readily seen if we take some illustrations of grammar that are not conventionally called "religious." Thus if we take the form of life called "physics" we find a grammar of physics that structures this form of life and conditions its meaning and experience. Like any grammar the grammar of physics is a logos with a unifying principle that makes this form of life possible. This grammar–logos, like any logos, makes implicit reference to Divine Form and hence essentially works on a faith principle that is the origin of this form of life. All the interpretive rational activity called "doing physics" is a praxis that proceeds in the light of the "theoria" of the logos of physics; this means that to do physics is to be grammatical; it is the very life of the grammar, and this life, like any form of life, is a faith that is oriented to Divine Form. Thus although in conventional life the form of life called "physics" is taken to be "secular," in the holistic understanding that discerns the essential unity and continuity between the form of life, its grammar, its Divine Form, and its faith, this logos like any other is holistically religious.

Similarly, holistic thinking about the logos called "mathematics" or "music" or "philosophy," and so on, are all grammatical activities and hence inherently are oriented to Divine Form and are in a sense divine hypotheses or conjectures or names.

The Holistic Form of Religious Life: Degrees of Life

Let us review what this meditation on Divine Form has shown. We have been meditating on the holistic thesis that every *logos is Logos:* that every possible form of logos, any form of life, any word, any language, any culture, any meaning, and so on is inherently oriented to Logos. We focused on a special logos: a life in human form—and this led to discerning the form of life in general; on reflecting on this we found that the meaning of life derives from a structure of unity that shows itself as a grammar, which is the presentation of Divine Form as word. The grammar as the form of life made life possible in the space of a life-world. We saw that any form of life as grammar is oriented to divine unity, which is its faith or originating principle—the source of all of its meaning—its rational faith. So all life was implicitly religious in that it participated in rational faith or grammar, which is oriented to Divine Form, the continuum. The continuum is seen to be the pregrammatical structure of all meaning, the unconscious and preconscious Presence that conditions all meaning and life.

Now we may move more deeply in this meditation on the continuum and reflect on an essential feature of human life—on its holistic religious form. It is the continuum that orients human life and gives it meaning and value. The Continuum, Divine Form, is the absolute form of infinite unity that we have seen is the holistic meaning of Life, Truth, Meaning, Goodness. A life is meaningful, true, real, worthy, to the degree that it realizes its inner form—this is the measure or standard of religious life, the life that elevates itself to the highest possible form.

It is the presence of the continuum as the deep form of any life that orients that life to the possibility of ever higher meanings, higher life, higher truth, higher value. Human life finds in this orientation the possibility of self-expansion and self-realization; life is directed toward Divine Form as its ultimate concern and in this orientation is its telic structure—that at which all of its life may be directed. We may call this *the holistic process of self-consciousness,* the perpetual possibility of reflexive self-transcendence or self-transformation to higher realization of form. The higher the self-evolution of form, the higher the life, the deeper the freedom, the purer the rational faith. So human life essentially has the possibility of self-expanding its form in the realization of deeper self-unity. It is this possibility of self-expansion of form toward unity with the continuum (holistic form) that we call *awareness*.

Awareness is the realization of higher life that comes with reflexive self-consciousness through meditation. So awareness is the higher energy of consciousness as it expands its form in ever deeper ways toward holistic unity with continuum. So it is the continuum that is ever present to life that calls life to it like a magnet. As the source of life, it is the direction in which greater life is released. As the source of meaning, it is the origin that yields ever more meaningful life. As the locus of pure reason, it is the ultimate point of reference for all rational growth. As boundless energy, it is the source of greater power and energy. As pure light, it is the source of liberation and enlightenment. So all life is held in its gravitational field and under its infinite influence whether or not that life recognizes this, and all life in some way responds to the presence of the continuum. It is that to which all life aims.

Thus we see that rational thought is always oriented toward the deep unity of the continuum, toward self-unity. The form of unity is life force or energy that moves reason, self-conscious life, to its self-realization. The path of reason is always toward deeper realization of form and unity. Thus commonsense life, being a form of meaning and reason, lives at some form of logos, some degree of consciousness. The question of degree indicates that it is aware at one level of form but asleep to a deeper level. So common sense tends to be unconscious about its form of life, its grammar. When it moves to the reflexive awareness of its form of life and makes the grammatical turn, it achieves a higher consciousness and a deeper rational form of life. By contrast, common sense is here unreflexive and uninformed. To go even deeper and discern the logos or form of any grammar is still a deeper transformation of rational awareness—to discern the form of any possible life-world. To self-expand in rational form to the holistic unity of the Continuum is the culmination of the self-reflexive journey of reason. Reason finds its highest realization of form in meditative self-unity—holistic form. This is the orientation and direction of religious life.

THE PATHOLOGY OF MEANING: ABSOLUTISM AND RELATIVISM

Let us continue our meditation on Divine Form—the Continuum. We have focused thus far on the holistic unity of the continuum and developed the holistic narrative in the meditative voice. Here we saw that every logos is inherently and essentially oriented to Logos as its true form. Here any logos is holistically united in the continuum and has no separate or independent identity or form of life. The holistic mind is one with the continuum, which has the form of universal relativity. In the holistic narrative any logos is essentially dialogical in its unity structure, and it is inherently conversational in its holistic life.

But there is a form of life in which a logos in its inner form develops a voice of its own and speaks its own narrative giving its self-interpretation. Let us call this form of life "the life of self-identity." The inner narrative and speech life of this logos breaks from the holistic voice, and it falls into a self-eclipse from its inner holistic form. So the holistic conversation or dialogue is broken, and there is a separation in voice, a split in narratives. In our present meditation there is a tension between the holistic narrative and the inner self-narrative of the separated voice. The Primordial Word has been broken, and our meditative challenge is to continue our holistic narrative while we enter into the inner space of the individuated voice to experience its pathological form of life. We now need to re-create the form of its inner life without breaking our holistic concentration and continued attention to Divine Form.

To hold the two narratives together, some distinctions might be helpful. For when we enter the inner voice of the separated self-identity we are in a different universe of discourse. Let us call this inner orientation around the voice of self-identity the *monadic voice*.[4] As a separate and independent existence, it is eclipsed from holistic unity in the continuum, and it is centered in its own absolute form of life—its own universe. This primordial split from Continuum creates a self-division within its life giving rise to a primary consciousness of its independent existence—the break from the holistic continuum creates reality, existence, world. This existence is experienced as a dual structure in which the individuated self-existence ("I") lives within a universal world-field that stands over–against it; thus there is given with self-existence the primordial duality between I and Field. With the split from Logos, the separated logos breaks from its inner true form and takes the name "ontos" for itself. This separate voice is existential and self-referential, centered in its own being—it is now *onto-centric*.[5] Thus with the creation of Being and its reorientation in ontocentric life, the original logos is self-eclipsed, deformed, and disoriented from holistic life.

In losing its true orientation from Logos, from divine unity, it loses its holistic self-unity and falls into pathological forms of life and meaning. Its inner monadic narrative is inherently fictional since it is cut off from its holistic voice and form of life. In gaining a certain form of consciousness, it loses holistic awareness, and the ever-present holistic voice becomes its unconscious. It loses its original symbolic form of metaphoric or holistic meaning and now lives in the faith of its own *self-unity;* having lost the true holistic unity of the continuum, its inner drive or life force is to *be a unity* unto itself. It re-creates itself in its own image and constructs its own form of life, which it calls *reality*. It takes itself to be a self-unity, but there is no real unity in its form of life. As it follows its own form of life eclipsed from Divine Form, its unconscious holistic voice haunts it, continues to nourish this alienated ontos, and remains ever-present to it. Although this ontos has a will of its own, a name of its own, a voice of its own, and its own form of life, it remains lodged in the ever-present continuum that harkens it back to its true roots. In the presence of this all-encompassing continuum that is its unconscious home, the ontos clings to dear life and clutches at its self-unity, which is its very existence. This presumed self-unity or univocity is fictional, for we have seen that the *voice of ontos* and the *voice of logos* are now self-alienated and bifurcated into conscious and preconscious: voice is now inherently equivocal, and the speech life of the individuated voice remains in a hidden original ambiguity. Its life is self-divided, dualized; its meaning is fragmented; and its rationality is self-divided. This individuated voice, in its misguided faith in its self-unity, replicates its equivocity in all directions.

The Particularistic Mind and Its Fictional Self-Unity

Our meditation on Divine Form has revealed that Absolute, Infinite Unity is the Life and Light of the continuum. In our holistic narrative of the origin of the life of self-identity, we find that although its deepest faith is in its own unity, it lives a life of inner disunity. Let us move more deeply into the inner (monadic) self-consciousness of the particularistic mind. Let us follow its inner phenomenology and sense of itself and its universe. Here we find that at its foundations its assumed self-unity is the absolute condition and central reference of all of its experience and meaning. In pseudoimitation of Divine Form, its presumed self-identity and unity become the a priori condition of all of its life—the absolute condition of its reason and meaning and experience. Let us call this the *univocity condition* of the life of self-identity:[6] it is the condition that it is a unified voice and that its speech is univocal in meaning. If its univocity condition fails, if its voice is not an original absolute self-unity, it lives in bad faith, and all of its speech life, all of its rationality and meaning, are without determinacy.

Our meditation on self-existence and self-identity as the absolute condition of the rational life of the individuated voice or particularistic mind reveals that its presumed identity is empty and that the individuated voice in fact lives in original indeterminacy of meaning. Its presumption or faith that it speaks in a unified and determinate voice is found in the holistic narrative to be its fatal error.

In moving further into the self-reference and narrative of this individuated voice, it is critical for us to see that the form of self-identity is the absolute condition and central point of unifying reference for all of its life. This point deserves further elaboration. The mind of identity takes itself to have identity, to be an integral, unified, continuously existing entity of some sort. As such, it takes itself to be differentiated and discriminated from other entities and from the world that surrounds it. Furthermore, this existential mind takes itself to be self-contained and independently existing, so in some sense it is whole and complete in itself. In being separate and differentiated from other entities in the world, the mind of identity recognizes itself as having its unique qualities and history that individuate it from everything else in the world. The existential mind is unique, differentiated, and individuated; it is the central and primary reference point in its world and can refer to itself uniquely as "I." As long as it thinks and reflects, it takes itself to be independently existing, and its self-existence conditions all of its thinking and experience—its self-unity is an absolute condition of its life. This is its form of life. So the mind of identity must be approached in the first-person voice, in self-reference as a thinking subject. Since all of its conscious life is conditioned by the "I exist," by self-identity, it is essential for us to meditate further on the form of self-identity. If the form of identity turns out to be empty or problematic, all of the life of the individuated "I" is likewise empty. We already have the hint here that the absolute self-unity of the "I" has eclipsed the holistic unity of Divine Form.

The form of identity makes rational thought possible, and for this reason ordinary rational thought eclipses its absolute condition and is not able to think its own form. But now we shall see that what ordinary thought and experience take to be a unity and univocal, the holistic narrative exposes as individual, self-divided, disintegral and equivocal. If the ontological mind, which takes itself to be a unity and univocal turns out to be self-divided and equivocal, the very foundation of everyday rationality is called into serious question, to say the least.

For centuries it has been said that the principle of identity is the first principle of rationality. One expression of this first principle is that *A is A*.[7] This is taken to be axiomatic and self-evident for rational thought—the absolute condition that makes rational thought possible. It means that *A* is a self-identical unity. However, suppose upon reflection we find that this principle is incoherent—that *A is neither A nor not-A*, that *A* is not univocal but inherently indeterminate and equivocal. Suppose we find that the existential mind—referred to as "I"—is equivocal and indeterminate; this would be a mind-shattering disclosure.

The Indeterminacy of the Existential Mind: The Problem of Unity and the Paradox of Identity

The existential mind takes itself to be *individuated*—to be a primitive self-identical unity, and its unity is the inherent form of all of its thinking. The principle of identity, for any alleged identity, holds only if the self-identity and unity of the mind obtains. If the mind is equivocal or indeterminate, all else suffers the same indeterminacy.

There are two points here that need clarification. The first is the general point that *any* alleged individuated identity contradicts itself in disunity, dividuation, and disidentity; I call this the "*paradox of identity.*" The second point is that experience, to be coherent, requires or presumes a univocating point of reference, and this is usually taken to be the self-reference of the "I" as a unifying point for my experience. But here, too, we find another version of the paradox of identity in the form of the "*paradox of self-reference.*" Here it is found that the alleged presence of a unifying mind as supplying the unifying point of reference for experience or thought is nonexistent. Indeed, critical reflection that does not presume absolute identity cannot find *any* unifying point of reference or individuated identity anywhere, neither in the mind or alleged referent of "I" nor in any alleged entity with identity.

The Paradox of Identity. The paradox of identity is the incoherence that identity requires absolute unity but instead leads to perpetual self-division and disunity. To see this, take any alleged individuated identity A—we find that the *form* of identity requires that for A to be individuated or discriminated, it must stand over–against that which is *other than A,* call it *not-A,* so a form of self-opposition or negation is essentially the very meaning of identity itself—to be an identity is to be differentiated; so in attempting to locate the supposed independent unity of A we are addressed to another different point of reference—*not-A;* this second alleged point of reference does not stand independently, hence is not primitive and self-existent. But individuated identity requires an independent and primitive (atomic) point of unity, which is found neither in A nor in *not-A.* So the unity requirement of identity must *postulate* a third and higher point of reference that can unite the duality of A and *not-A,* neither of which is a primitive unity in itself. Let us call this third alleged primitive unifying point /A/; this would be the absolute point of unity for the original supposed identity of A.

But here again, this postulated third point of unity is not primitive and not independent, not self-existent; it, too, depends on both A and *not-A,* neither of which is an independent unity, nor is /A/ such a unity. So we have the following triangulation of identity:

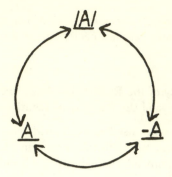

We begin with *A*, but this points to *not-A* (*-A*), which points back to *A*, which leaves us with a duality that in turn needs to be addressed to a higher, more primitive, unity—*/A/*. But this alleged higher unity is itself dependent on *A* and *-A*, and, indeed, to have */A/* as an independent identity only repeats the vicious loop all over *ad infinitum*. In this way no independent, primitive, self-existent point of reference is ever found. Any reference to a given identity points elsewhere to another alleged point that turns out itself to be dependent on some other point, ad infinitum. This is the hidden dynamic of identity that holds whenever we make reference to (or suppose) any individuated identity to obtain. This is why the principle *A is A,* far from being self-evident, is deeply problematic and paradoxical. So any alleged identity is *indeterminate,* and this is the source of ontological indeterminacy.[8]

The Paradox of Self-Reference: "I" Is Indeterminate. The paradox of self-reference is another version of the general paradox of identity; it holds for the individuated mind taking itself to be an absolute point of reference or primitive individual. This version of the paradox of identity takes place in the voice of the *first person*—uttering "I" and making reference to *itself* as the "atomic" point of unity.

Here again, we find the reiteration of the triangular loop of identity ad infinitum. For the form of self-identity requires that in being a unique and individuated entity, I am differentiated from the *not-I;* so in making self-reference to the alleged atomic point of unity that is "me," I am addressed to that which is not-me, other than *I.* Here again, in seeking a unity we find a polarity, neither pole of which is a unity in itself.

But this *polarity* is split against itself in opposing alleged points of unity and requires a third and higher mediating point to unite the duality into a "di-unity." However, this third alleged point of unity, which is "*/I/*", cannot be established independently of the original "*I*" and "*not-I*"; yet it must be different from them. Thus the paradox of self-reference is that in saying "I", I purport to make reference to an individuated point of primitive unity, but in so doing I find an indefinitely self-divided reference that never reaches any primary univocal point but recurs indeterminately and indefinitely. I find a recursive indeterminate loop.

If there is no determinate primitive point of reference that is "I," that is, if the ontological mind of identity is inherently indeterminate, all thought and experience that presuppose a universal primary unifying point of reference are likewise indeterminate; there would be no item in thought that is univocal or determinate in sense or reference—no determinate meaning or existence. If thought is indeterminate in meaning, all experience reflects this same indeterminacy and multivocity. Furthermore, since meaning and existence share the common form of identity, existence, too, is indeterminate, and the same is true for "rationality" in general. Again, if the ontological mind is radically indeterminate in its existence, all that is given to the individuated mind is equally ambiguous and indeterminate. This is the ontological indeterminacy of existence, thought, experience, meaning, rationality. It all arises from the radical indeterminacy of absolute identity.

More Paradox: The Absolute Unifying Point and the I/Field Split. Thus far we have looked at the incoherence of absolute identity for singular cases, that is, for any *one* purported individuated identity in isolation. But when we postulate and entertain more than one point of atomic identity at a time, the existential indeterminacy is all the more pronounced. But as we proceed we must remember that we can no longer *assume* a unified or univocal mind ("me") that is doing the thinking. Every possible feature or item of thought replicates this ontological indeterminacy. For example, "time" itself can no longer be taken as a determinate, linear, and continuous medium with identity of its own. The moments of time—past, present, and future—are purported individuated identities, too, and there is indeterminacy here as well. When we speak of "at the same time," identity is presumed, and this has now been placed in question. The same holds for space, cause, number, and all of the categories of reality.

Now the first and most primitive dualism generated by the form of identity is the primordial division or polarity between *I* and *not-I*. We have seen that the very identity "I" requires the *not-I* over–against which it stands. This original bifurcation may be seen as the polarity between individuated mind and the *world-field* in which all else is present to the "I." This original duality creates all sorts of paradoxes and problems that have gripped the best minds over the centuries. For example, if mind (the subject) stands over–against the world (object) and is differentiated from it, how can the mind know what is external to it and discontinuous with it? Here we get diverse problems of how knowledge is possible and dichotomies of subject and object, the subjective and the objective.

Still, it is critical to see in the dynamics of identity and postulate of unity that the original polarity between "I" and "field," like any other polarity, requires its mediating higher point of unity to hold the opposed poles in a unity. Let us call this higher postulated point of unity the *"transcendental point of unity."* It should be immediately clear that without such a postulate the individuated mind could never be in touch with the world-field—they would be incommensurable. Furthermore, it is also evident that the "I" must have a deep and intimate connection with the transcendental point; in fact, it is as if it *must be* itself a higher "I," for if it were wholly other to the individuated "I," there would have to be still *another* postulated mediating point to negotiate the chasm between the individuated I and the transcendental absolute unifying point. But if in some sense they are one and *the same* (share a common identity), whenever I utter "I," this utterance had indeterminate and divided sense and reference (self-reference), ambiguous reference between the individuated *I* and the transcendental *I* (*/I/*).[9] So again we find ontological indeterminacy.

Furthermore, this postulated higher transcendental point of unity, as the mediating principle between I and world-field, must at the same time be different from the individuated I and in some respect be indeterminate and nonindividuated; otherwise, it could not be a mediating point between the duality and opposition between I and not-I. In this respect, it must be devoid of content found in I and not-I; this is why it *transcends* both polar opposites. Nevertheless, it must have some content of its own for it to be an absolute unifying point; insofar as it has some identity, it must itself be differentiated, and the triangular vicious loop recurs all over again.

In summary, we find that any alleged transcendental point of unity is itself subject to the dynamics of identity and participating in the polarity between identity/difference and hence cannot fulfill its intended function of being an absolute foundation for individuated identity. Indeed, the very need for a foundation for individuated identity is a confession that absolute identity is incoherent. So we find in all of this that the axiomatic commitment to individuated identity is an empty postulate having no validity other than its postulation. The belief in primitive individuals (myself or other) is an ontological myth, a postulate of faith, and we need to inquire whether it is an act of good faith.

Voice and Grammar: Indeterminacy of Reality. The individuated voice lives in a world with assumed determinacy—determinacy in its own identity, in the existence of things, and in meaning and rationality. This is the essence of its faith in absolute identity. But since the individuated voice is inherently indeterminate, its world and form of life are likewise indeterminate. For voice and world mirror each other. This mirror is *grammar*. Grammar is the form of life that shapes all meaning and conditions all existence. It makes possible my self-interpretation as well as the interpretation of the world. It is the rational form of reality. So there is a one-to-one isomorphism and assumed identity (identification) between Voice and Grammar; here we find that the indeterminacy of voice is mirrored in the indeterminacy of grammar as well, so reality—both self and world—is ontologically indeterminate.

Let us first clarify the depth of the I/Field duality. In one voice the ontological mind takes itself to be living in a *universe* that is an all-encompassing field of reality as a whole. To exist is to be in the universal field—the cosmos. From the ontological point of view, the unity or univocity requirement clearly holds for the structure of the universe as a whole—a continuous unified integral field.

But there is an ambiguity of voice in the ontological mind as to the *locus* of the transcendental point of unity of the Universe. For in one sense the Universe is taken to be independent of me and to have its independent absolute existence apart from me. But at the same time it is clear that I could not *think* something that was not present to me and my mind, and in this sense I supply a unifying point of recurrence for the universal field as a whole. Here again, we find some version of the paradox of unity (identity)—the unity of the universe is independent of me, but at the same time it is dependent on me.

It appears that there is a self-transcending point of unity in the mind that can take the place of any possible locus in the universe—there is a universal point of reference in mind that is variable and can take (or identify with) any place. Earlier we called this point "*/I/*." So we may distinguish between this self-transcending presence in me (my higher voice) and all that is presented to me (world-field). This /I/ is prior to the individuated mind; it is that to which all else is present or presented but that can never be made into an object in the field. On the other hand, the *I* (mind) as a *object* in the universe (the one we call the subject) is constitutively part of the universal field presented to /I/.

Thus it appears that the unifying point for the world-field transcends the universal field, and the unifying point of I transcends the I; each needs its unifying point, but it may well turn out that the unifying point for field and I are one and the same. There is indeterminacy and ambiguity here, which is to be expected.

The Primacy of Ontological Grammar. Having explored inherent ambiguity in the "I" and the "field" and in the relation between I/field, we may proceed further with the explanation of ontological grammar.

We have now seen that it is the form of absolute identity itself that requires a paradoxical bifurcation of the mind of the thinker from the universal field that is the context of the object of thought—the subject from the object. It is absolute identity that at the same time requires the absolute unity condition of the universe. It is the very form of identity that necessitates the commitment to the universe as an absolute self-existent reality. So ontological absolutism (the faith that there is an absolute independently existing universe) has its origin in absolute identity.

Now the ontological notion of the world or universe is an all-encompassing unity or whole that is exhaustive of all possible reality. The universe is that *universal*, absolute, unifying whole that includes both the thinking subject and the world-field that is presented to the subject—the realm of all possible phenomena. Absolute identity structures the universe into a comprehensive, complete, and supposedly consistent totality. Nothing could possibly exist "outside" the universe: to be is to be in the universe. To be an *object* is to be in the universal field.

Here, too, we find that the form of absolute identity governs the Universal Field of the universe, for the things that make up the universe have determinacy, particularity, identity. The universal field presents itself as a specified world, having definite content. But it is not at all obvious that absolute identity dictates the form and content of a world.

To see this, it would be helpful to make an explicit connection between logic and ontology. Whereas *logic* is a formal science that investigates the form of thought—logical form, *ontology* is a formal science that explores the form of existence—ontological form. But logical form and ontological form mirror each other, both sharing the common form of absolute identity.

The Monadic Feature of World Wholes: Multiple Realities (Universes). It has been suggested that to exist is to be in the context of a grammar, and that a grammar of reality is *cosmically* universal—exhaustive of the universe. It has been stressed that such a grammar is the deep structure of thought, meaning, and experience. For to think or experience is to engage in meaning—to onto-logically / interpret /; to *live* is to be grammatical.

This may be seen by taking examples from world history—examples of world cultures and cultural worlds. A world culture may be seen as a naturally evolved grammar of reality—a cosmological space for the shared cultural life of a com-munity. If we simplify and speak of the Hindu world (grammar) or the Christian world, for example, it may be more readily seen that a grammar shapes all aspects of the life of a culture—all meaning, all existence, all thought, all experience, all hermeneutical expressions.

Thus from the ontological point of view, the Hindu grammar makes the Hindu mind possible—it makes the existence of the mind possible; it makes it possible, too, for thought to take place, for there to be meaning and rationality—it makes experience possible. It is crucial to appreciate the depth of grammar—it is not just a world *view;* rather, it makes all viewing possible for the ontological mind.

It is in this sense that grammar is "hermeneutical"—to experience is to live in a grammar and in this sense "interpret" reality. In the case of the Hindu grammar, it may be seen that its religious life, its political life, its moral life, its science, its art forms—every facet of Hindu life reflects the Hindu grammar. It is in this sense that an ontological grammar is *cosmological*—all encompassing of reality, the universe, a *cosmological universal.* This is a grammar as a whole, as a universe, with its transcendental absolute point of reference and unity. This transcendental point of unity has some feature of the "infinite" built into it and is all-encompassing. Let us call this the "*monadic*" feature of a grammar or universe—a grammar is a cosmological universal and purports to be exhaustive of reality. There can be no reality apart from it. The grammar presents itself as being the measure of reality, meaning, and truth.

In this respect the Hindu grammar is a world whole as is the Christian grammar. A world culture is governed in all of its hermeneutical forms by its ontological grammar. What makes sense in the Hindu world does not make sense in the Christian world. What is common (communal) sense in one world is not rec-ognizable as such in another grammatical space. The facts of one world cannot be processed in the grammaticality of another reality. The monadic effect of a world implies *ontological incommensurability* between diverse worlds. Worlds are incommensurable in that they share nothing in common, no common point of reference; each is an absolute in itself and a reality unto itself. Rationality itself is formed within the "gravitational field" of a grammar. The rational "light" of a given world remains within the inner "curved space" of a cos-mological grammar.

The monadic effect of a grammatical world leads to incommensurability. This is the problem of unity all over again; in this version there can be no more primitive unity (transcendental unity) uniting diverse worlds. Apart from some common point of reference—some mediating, univocating condition, there can be no rational light between the dark void that holds diverse worlds apart.

But this incommensurability between worlds is the direct result of absolute identity and the ontological mind. It is the absolutism of identity that leads to this result. For now we can see that a grammar as a whole is an absolute identity in itself, a cosmological absolute, apart from which nothing can be, an ontological "black hole."

It should be noted here that the form of identity is what generates the axiomatic structure of rationality, whether it be expressed in a geometric form (alternative geometries) or in a logistic form (alternative formal axiomatized languages). The axiomatic form is the form of identity, and a grammar is a "geometry" of reality—a purportedly complete axiomatization of reality.

In this connection we may bring in the *indeterminacy of reality* once more. The ontological indeterminacy comes from the paradox of identity. On the one hand, we find that the universe is one and absolute—monadic. The monadic world-whole appears to the ontological mind in the determinate form of a grammar; it has internal determinacy and specificity. But on the other hand, it is given to the ontological mind that there is a plurality of worlds—of monadic absolutes, each of which is internally determinate and absolute—monadic. The ontological mind refers to itself—uttering "I," but this pronominal utterance takes its sense and reference from a particular grammar; but still it finds itself inhabiting multiple worlds, hence with multiple identity. We are left again with the problem of the unity and univocity of "I" and mind. Thus we see that indeterminacy and incommensurability arise together from the form of absolute identity.

Multiple Worlds, Incommensurability, and Indeterminacy. Incommensurability is not an abstract result of ontological investigation. It is a lived condition of everyday life that we shall explore below. For it should now be evident as we look at what we call "common sense" in everyday American cultural life that we inhabit diverse grammatical worlds simultaneously. Indeed, it may be seen that any world culture deriving from the life of absolute identity is really a cluster of precariously juxtaposed grammars under the surface of the spoken communal language. The linguistic system of the culture must be decoded and disambiguated according to the grammatical context at any given time. Any term in the linguistic system is indeterminate in meaning until it is specified by its grammatical context.

Again, if we look at American culture from the onotological point of view we find a cluster of diverse grammar—certain religious grammars contribute to common sense while scientific grammars make their own contribution. "Common sense" is a dynamic, evolving consensus of the grammatical life of the culture. There are grammatical revolutions in science (as with Einstein's revolution), and this brings about new forms of life and thought—a new universe opens up with its own idiom and jargon. In part of our lives we may believe that God exists and that Spirit is primary and that intelligence shapes matter, but in another domain of life we speak a materialist grammar and believe that matter is primary and that intelligence evolved from matter in the "big bang" origin of the universe. We are content to inhabit these multiple grammars believing ourselves to be sane and rational beings. We do not seem to realize that under the surface are deep problems for rationality, faith, sanity, meaning, and truth.

These ontological problems are particularly poignant in the area of intergrammatical (transworld) relations. The recognition that there are multiple monadic/ absolute grammars of reality, each of which constitutes rationality itself in diverse ways, places a deep strain on the rationality of absolute identity. For it questions the faith in one objective, neutral reality out there that science investigates. It questions the absolutist prejudice that one grammar must be true or more true than others and that science experimentally approximates the true and best grammar of reality. It raises the question of multiple validity of alternative "geometries" of reality and rationality. It recognizes that my very identity and existence are indeterminate across diverse grammars of existence. This crisis of identity comes to a head when I try to discern which "I" it is that has access to multiple realities at the "same time." It becomes clear that time itself is relative to grammar, and there is a problem of assuming a neutral temporality between grammars—that can unify time into a simultaneous "moment" for all worlds. So once we begin to take the critical turn and recognize the depth of incommensurability, we then see that rationality and intelligibility themselves are in crisis. The question is raised whether we are fractured and fragmented beings living a disintegral and incoherent form of life with multiple identities and multiple voices. All sorts of questions emerge here about our religious and scientific life—questions about the quest for true meaning and meaningful truth.

Absolute Identity and the Pathologies of the Mind of Identity

It is timely to explore the pathological condition of the ontological mind. We have seen thus far that the ontological or existential mind is structured by absolute identity, and this sets up a recursive "loop" of self-splitting that pervades the grammatical life of the individuated mind. Let us for a moment attempt to articulate the *general* dynamic that generates this splintering and dualization of reality, thought, experience, and of meaning and rationality. We shall now develop the theme further that it is the form of absolute identity that polarizes in all directions. It is this very form that produces the recursive incommensurability between identities on all levels.

The Atomic/Monadic Effect of Absolute Identity. It has been stated that wherever there is absolute identity there will be ontological indeterminacy and the self-splitting "triangulating" dynamic. Earlier, when we sketched the ontological concept of a universe as a world-whole, we spoke of the *monadic* feature of the universe and of the individuated mind. This meant that the universe as a self-existent whole was self-contained and independent and all-encompassing of its domain. This monadic feature was typified by the transcendental point of universal unity. It has been suggested that this monadic effect holds for the ontological mind as well—the self-existent mind must take its transcendental unifying point to be monadic in a way analogous in the monadic feature of the universe as a whole; the monadic mind is a universe unto itself.

Now we may generalize this point and speak of the *atomic feature* for any possible individuated entity. The monadic feature is the *internalized* view of the monadic whole under its transcendental unity. The atomic feature is the *external* view of the monadic whole from a different, independent point of reference. So the monadic and atomic features are complementary effects of the same absolute identity. This means that any purported absolute identity is at once monadic internally and atomic externally. It varies with the unifying point of reference taken by "I" (the thinker). The internal monadic universe presents itself as infinitely open and expansive. But the external atomic universe is seen as being impenetrable, closed, self-contained.

It is important to see that *any instance* of an absolute identity at once exhibits the monadic and atomic effect depending on its point of reference with respect to the transcendental unifying point taken by "I." Thus a world-whole or universe may itself be atomic with respect to multiple worlds—a world-whole is a "global" atom when considered externally and with respect to multiple universes. Similarly, any individuated entity taken externally is a universal whole and shows its atomic features. So there is a plurality of wholes implied in any atomic identity and a monistic universality expressed in any monadic identity.

Thus if I am an absolute identity, I, too, exhibit the monadic and atomic features; the same is true for any possible individuated identity. To be an entity is to be individuated, and to be individuated is to be in alleged atomic identity, at any possible level of individuated identity. In this respect, an *atomic* particle in the grammar of physics is (ontologically speaking) an absolute identity. Equally a world-whole, a grammar as a whole, is atomic/monadic as well. This means that the same deep problems of incommensurability between diverse absolute universes recurs at any level of identity, whether between worlds or within a given world; whether between personal identities (interpersonal) or even within the structure of a person (intrapersonal), and so on.

Polarization of the Ontological Mind: Artificial Unity. Let us see how this incommensurability arises. We have seen that between universal grammars there is no common mediating point of unifying reference. Universes are absolute self-identities that are internally infinite, self-contained, and cannot be in relationality to anything outside themselves. Nevertheless, the ontological mind finds itself entertaining diverse grammars of reality—having access to diverse universes of discourse. This suggests (demands) that there *must be* some more primitive transcendental unifying point of reference in the thinker. But what we find is simply a repeating of the same triangular loop of absolute identity.

It is evident that commonsense reason, which ambiguously lives in absolute identity, recognizes the need for the transcendental unifying point to make diverse "things" of whatever sort (whether universes or diverse entities within a given universe) cohere in unity. If, for example, common sense is committed to a vast plurality of atomic entities, these self-existent things are still seen to be collected within a unifying field like physical space or logical space or grammatical space, and so on. So commonsense reason works on the faith in unity and postulates the transcendental unity wherever it is needed to produce coherence and rational commensurability. This postulate then allows the otherwise incommensurable discrete identities to be placed in relationality.

For example, without the postulate of unity, I, as an individuated entity, would be a universe unto myself (monadic); I would and could know only myself, my own "subjective" grammatical field. Other persons would be atomic identities "out there," and I could never suppose that I am in relation with them, speak the same language, participate in shared meaning and inhabit a common (communal) reality. There would be incommensurability between diverse individuated (atomized) minds. Each mind would be monadic—a closed universe unto itself. However, common sense assumes that I am indeed in touch with other minds, that we share a common world, that we communicate in a common language and forms of meaning and rationality. But common sense leaves it at that and does not draw out the inherent paradox and incoherence in its two postulates; it does not see that the faith in absolute identity runs at cross-purposes to its postulate of transcendental unity. Its faith in absolute identity pulls toward the atomic pole while its faith in absolute transcendental unity pulls toward the monadic (anatomic) pole. It does not recognize that absolute identity leads to conclusions that directly rule out any real unity, coherence, consistency. Rather, common sense lives in its incoherent condition (double-bind) and takes it to be the norm of rationality and of reality. On the one hand, it is committed to absolute identity, but on the other hand, it is equally committed to unity, commensurability, and coherence.

So common sense trades on indeterminacy, ambiguity, equivocity, and incoherence; it takes a polar split to be a primitive unity. Its faith in individuated entities is artificial because nowhere can any primitive individual be established, and its faith in unity is likewise artificial since nowhere can any absolute unity be found. Yet commonsense reason—the mind of identity—lives as if this polarity were a unity, as if commonsense faith were univocal, coherent, integral, and the voice of rationality itself.

The Polarized Mind: Atomic/Anatomic. It has been argued that the ontological mind is self-polarized by absolute identity. The polarized mind will always think in a polarized way. We have already seen this in the self-polarizing (triangular) dynamics of identity: If we suppose *A* as any individualized entity, this requires that *un-A* be given; but this polarization denies the unity requirement of *A* as self-existent and independent. So unity if postulated as a third transcendental point, which, because it transcends both *A* and *non-A,* must be different from both, so it is not really the unity of *A* that was originally supposed.

In general, wherever there is alleged identity, there will be ontological indeterminacy in self-polarization, and a determinate, primitive unity will not be found. The polarization pervades common sense reason and shows itself in all thought, experience, and existence. In thought, in theorizing, for example, if one thesis is asserted the polar opposite thesis will always be forthcoming, and there will be "evidence" for both polar points. In any point the *counter*point will also hold; in any assertion the *contra*diction will be forthcoming. If in theoretical physics atomicity is taken as primitive, it is predictable that anatomicity (the unified field) will soon come forth as necessary for truth and rationality in physics. When polarity is explicit, there will ensue the inevitable search for a more primitive underlying (transcendental) unity to make the polar opposites cohere and be commensurable. So the polarized mind thinks and speaks in a polarized way, lives in a polarized reality, discovers a polarized truth, and reasons in a polarized logic.

The Pathology of Absolutism. We may now look at the general form of the pathology of the ontological mind. Absolute identity generates a range of pathologies of reason that may be characterized as disorders of *absolutism.*

Absolutism is a pathology that takes innumerable forms; it originates with absolute identity, and wherever there is absolute identity, there is absolutism. At the deepest level of commonsense rationality we find absolutism in the form of the faith that there is an objective reality "out there" independent of consciousness or the individuated mind. This postulate of absolute reality, we have seen, is a *requirement* of absolute identity itself; it comes from the requirement of identity that there be a transcendental unifying point of reference or ground for existence and experience. More importantly, we have found the source of ontological absolutism in the split produced between subjective/objective fields by absolute identity. The dualism of "I" (mind) on one side and object (universal field) on the other is inherently required by identity.

A familiar version of ontological absolutism is the faith that reality or the universe is *absolute*—it is the source of the distinction between truth and falsity, between fact and fiction, between real and imaginary, between knowledge and illusion. The absolute universe out there is the measure of truth and knowledge, the measure of rationality and meaning; and science aims at approaching, approximating, and having direct access to this objective absolute reality.

However, as is typical with the polarized mind of identity, every postulate has its counterpostulate, and where absolutism is found there we will naturally find *relativism*; this is the polar side of absolutism. Now we can readily see how and why relativism is one version of the pathology of absolutism. Ontology teaches that there are multiple alternative grammars of reality—multiple absolute universes—and this runs counter to the naive faith in a single, unified, monadic universe. Ontological relativism is the recognition that there are alternative realities each of which is absolute or monadic in its own right and incommensurable; each sets its own standards of reality, truth, fact, and value. It makes clear that the absolute is relative to a determinate grammar and each grammer is atomic/monadic in itself. So whereas naive absolutism is committed to there being one monadic absolute, the polar voice lives in the faith that there are *multiple absolutes* and that reality is relative to each absolute. So ontological relativism is a version of absolutism and essentially trades on absolute identity; the difference is that naive absolutism is monadic (anatomic) whereas relativism is atomic (pluralistic). They are the polar voices of absolute identity. Henceforth, let us treat the polar versions—absolutism and relativism—in one concept: /absolutism/.

Diverse Forms of Absolutism. /Absolutism/ is the faith in absolute identity, and wherever there is absolute identity, we shall find the pathology of /absolutism/. On the level of grammars, each absolutizes itself and takes itself to be the absolute measure of truth and reality. This version is called *"ontocentrism,"* and it is typically found in communally shared grammars, such as in certain cultures. The pathology of absolutism is particularly strong in religious cults each of which takes itself to be the measure, the absolute measure, of meaning, truth, and reality. World history has made abundantly clear the pathological conflicts and wars through the centuries that are direct expressions of this pathology. Religious conflicts between people are *grammatical* in origin and are inevitable wherever there is ontocentrism. This disorder will always lead to grammatical violence—the violation of the *other* by denying his grammatical authenticity and *reducing* the grammar of the other to the ontocentric's ontological vocabulary.

Equally pathological is the chronic breakdown in communication between individuals even *within* an ostensibly shared communal grammar. For here, again, the pathology of absolute identity rules the lives of *egocentrics*. This is another pervasive disorder of absolutism directly resulting from the self-polarization of identity. When one is so locked into one's own world, one's own subjective realm, and absolutizes this as the measure of reality, others around one are reduced to objects and are grammatically violated. The egocentric, like the ontocentric, leaves no room for the legitimate voice of the other.

The great religious teachers, the grammatically wise through the ages, have all addressed this egocentric (and ontocentric) pathology as the source of human suffering and the life of ignorance and sin. The way to liberation and enlightenment is seen to be precisely overcoming the absolutism of absolute self-identity. In the ontological sense, the *ego* may be seen as the individuated, self-identical, self-existent self. Here, it is readily seen that the global/communal form of the pathology of ontocentrism has the same source as the pathology of egocentrism. When the ego–self ("I") identifies with the grammar/world of the community or culture, the two versions of absolutism merge into one. Indeed, we saw earlier that the voice of the "I" has variability and is able to identity with diverse points of reference in grammatical space. It is this dynamic of identity that allows for the diverse forms of /absolutism/.

Still another version of absolutism of relevance here is that of *fundamentalism*. This is a specific form of ontocentrism that is the expression of faith in *literalism*. Literalism is a disposition regarding meaning that is a naive acceptance of univocity and identity (determinacy) of meaning; one word, one unambiguous, literal, univocal, transparent meaning. The word, in the form of the letter, speaks for itself and declares its meaning and truth. This is a faith about meaning that holds that the unique identity-meaning of a word is immediately given in the word. Fundamentalism is absolutistic faith that the literal meaning (given in the grammar) is the absolute truth. So this pathology traces to ontocentrism since literal meaning derives from the grammar one inhabits. When the grammar is absolutized, there is fixity and fixation of meaning.

These pathologies are all found in the grammatical disposition (hermeneutics) of science; when the scientist (or community of scientists) embraces a particular grammar of science in an absolutistic disposition, we get the same ontocentrism and fundamentalism found in other areas of cultural life. From the grammatical point of view, fundamentalism in science is just as pathological as fundamentalism in religious life. They spring from the common faith in absolute identity. Here, it may be said that the true, liberated scientific spirit must overcome the pathologies of identity. The true scientific spirit goes against the hermeneutical closure and grammatical prejudice of /absolutism/.

Again, what the absolutistic mind takes to be rational discourse turns out to be rationalization and irrationality. For one thing, the ontocentric takes his or her grammar to be consistent and complete and absolute when critical ontology shows that it is incomplete, incoherent, and relative. This is particularly evident in conversation between and across diverse grammars. In intergrammatical discourse there is typically found indeterminacy and ambiguity of meaning, miscommunication, incoherence, and an inevitable power struggle for control of the agenda and the authority to voice reality and truth. The rational enterprise (which calls for openness and dialogue) gives way to rationalization, self-righteousness, prejudice, closed mindedness, and authoritarianism. When true rational persuasion breaks down between grammars (or persons), the ontocentric typically resorts to power and authority to assert his or her grammar over the other. Here the ''politics'' of truth and reality rules, and we have another instance of the irrationality of religio-grammatical battles—conflicts of faith.

Pathologies of Life. It has been suggested that absolutism leads to breakdown of rationality between grammars and to pathologies of communication between individual persons. But now we may extend this theme and see that the pathology of fragmentation pervades the everyday life of *common sense*, for any given community of discourse.

First, we have seen that human life is a function of grammar, and if our grammatical life is fragmented and incoherent, so will be our form of life as well. Indeed, we find that so-called common sense comprises a diversity of grammars all superimposed on one another and "coexisting." In accordance with the incommensurability of meaning and existence found between grammars, and with the indeterminacy of "I" across grammars, it appears that our everyday life is a complex of identities ("I's") and the worlds. It is not a coherent, univocal, integrated universe of discourse but rather is an artificially constructed complex of diverse voices and forms of life. Any supposed unity and coherence here is merely conventional and postulated.

Second, the *intrapersonal* inner discourse of the individual (ego) self is also multivocal and complex—a cluster of diverse identities or voices. Here again it is a lived problem to find inner coherence, unity, integrity in identity, and voice. This is the inherent indeterminacy of "I" mentioned earlier. Any supposed unity of the individuated self turns out to be an artificial postulated construction of a complex of voices. It must be stressed that this is not an abstract or theoretical problem but a most immediate existential fracturing of human life.[10]

The fallout of self-splitting and dualities pervades every direction of the life of identity. There is the split between the self (subject) and the world-field (objects); between thought and the objects of thought; between word and object; between meaning and reference; between thought and action; between theory and practice; between facts and values; between self and others; between reason and sense experience; between fact and fiction; between real and imaginary; and so on. These familiar dualities are taken to be natural *distinctions* of everyday life and nothing to be alarmed about—certainly nothing pathological. But they are all part of the pathological fallout of absolute identity, and in them lurks fractures of life and existence that hold us in bondage.

One fundamental grammatical split, we have seen earlier, is the dualism between the mental and the physical, between mind and matter. This is one polarization of absolute identity that emerges in any possible grammar. This split is foundational for classical and contemporary physics.

It must be recalled that *all* dualisms are traced to absolute identity and the polarization dynamics of the ontological mind. It is important to remember that dualisms are not benign *distinctions* but pathological faults in existence and experience. They are not mere abstract conceptual differences but profound categorial fractures of grammar that show themselves in reality and govern our lives. The mind/matter (mental/physical) dualism has dominated human existence and all aspects of cultural-hermeneutical life.

Furthermore, we have seen that pernicious dualisms exhibit the common double bind and paradoxical dynamics of the form of absolute identity—the paradox of identity. For example, commonsense faith assumes that knowledge is possible, and this requires the most intimate relationality between the knowing mind and the known object. But the deep duality between the knowing subject (mind) and the object of knowledge (world-field) preempts the intimate connection between mind and field required by the possibility of knowledge. So the *ontological* foundations of knowledge has remained problematic and paradoxical for centuries.

Our meditation on identity shows that the self-dualizing dynamic in the form of self-identity is the source of all pathologies of life. The fallout of the self-splitting and fragmentation of voice and life moves in every possible direction. In my inner indeterminacy of existence and identity I suffer due to fragmentation of my voice into incommensurable identities. So my inner voice-life is fragmented into multiple voices, and the absence of a unifying voice leaves me in a disintegrated form with no real integrity of life of voice.

I find myself inhabiting multiple grammars, living in diverse universes of discourse, and these forms of life are likewise incommensurable in the absence of a true unifying principle. So my inner and outer worlds are lodged in multiplicity with no coherence. I live under multiple realities each with absolute divine principles.

In another dimension I find the dualizing influence splitting into opposition and polarization, what the Continuum reveals as holistically One: my life divides into mental and physical; holistic meaning is divided into thought, meaning, and being; there is division between word and object, between meaning and existence, between thought and action, between myself and others, and so on.

More deeply, in the very form of my existence I find in the self-division of identity a self-separation that leaves me incomplete and unfulfilled. So my life is lodged in desire and privation that motivates my strivings and actions. But there remains a deep emptiness and incompleteness at the heart of my existence.

Voice, Grammar, and "Theology": Unity, Infinity, and Divinity

Our meditation on the form of absolute identity as the foundation of all meaning and existence in the existential mind has shown that in the deep structure of the self or voice or of its grammar there is a necessary condition of unity or univocity; it is an absolute requirement that voice be a unity and that a grammar-world be a unity as well. It is this transcendent unity condition inherent in self and grammar that is the origin of meaning and rationality. Here we find the key to the Divine Form as interpreted by any grammar—every grammar has its Divine Form, which is its absolute condition, the foundation of all meaning and being. It is for this reason that any form of life of the existential voice is in some religious mode, in some faith. To live is to be grammatical, and the Divine Form of any grammar governs and is conditional of all life. In this sense, all life is intrinsically religious, for to be committed to a form of life, a form of meaning, is to live in a faith.

I may live in a grammar as my faith without explicitly engaging in worship, which is recognition of the absolute principle that governs my form of life. I become explicitly "theological" when I engage in explicitly articulating the form of my faith (grammar) and the divine principle that absolutely conditions it. In this sense divinity is intrinsic to any grammar, and every grammar is a form of faith.[11]

In making this explicit we now see how incommensurability of realities (grammars) implies a deep incoherence in theology: if each grammar has its Divine Form, which is its infinite absolute unifying condition, and if grammars are in some deep sense incommensurable, how can there be a multiplicity of infinite absolutes? It would seem that in the very meaning of *infinite* and *absolute* there could not be a radical diversity of Divine Forms. How can there be irreducible diversity here? How can there be pluralism of infinite absolutes? Is it not rationally required that the infinite absolute be an absolute unity? Can the true Divine Form be multiple? Can we suppose a transcendent unity of divine principles? But we have already seen that this upward gesture to a higher unifying principle (required by the form of identity) does not work. It only pushes back the problem of true unity. These are some of the problems of theology that emerge from the very form of self-identity. In a way it may be said that diverse theologies have been governed by the dynamics of self-identity and suffer all of the pathologies of meaning and life found in the very heart of the existential voice.

UNIVERSAL THEOLOGY: BEYOND PATHOLOGY AND THE RADICAL RETURN TO ROOTS

We began with meditation on Divine Form and discerned the Universal Unified Field of the continuum—divine infinite unity. We then entered into the inner form of the particularistic or existential mind to experience its inner fragmentation and pathology of life. We saw that the monadic voice of the individuated self names itself as an ontos, as a being with identity, and in this breaks off from the holistic Continuum in search of its own absolute unity. In its ontocentric form of life it self-divides and loses touch with its true inner form, which remains in holistic unity with the Continuum. This self-split in voice (equivocity) in its form of life involves a disorientation from its true center in Logos. We find in the very form of absolute identity the source of all pathology of meaning and Life, a pathology of self-splitting that is the opposite of true unity.

Let us now follow the inner logic of this meditation and explore the nature and possibility of the salvation and liberation from this inherent condition of hermeneutical sin. So we now continue our holistic narrative having seen through the fictional narrative of the individuated voice. The individuated voice inherently lives in self-deception and is not able to discern its own pathological condition; it takes the higher holistic voice to discern clearly the self-eclipsed source of its pathological condition. We are now in a position to explore the dynamics of liberation, the self-expansion of the form of life of the particularistic mind to its true inner logos. Thus our holistic narrative will trace the return to holistic roots and the true unity of the Continuum that blows away the pathological disunities that inhere in the fixated life of the ontocentric voice.

Self-Univocation: Discerning the Dialogical Voice as Essence of Religious Life

Having seen the universal form of pathology, let us now recenter ourselves in holistic voice and continue our meditation on Divine Form—the Continuum. Having seen the origin of duality and disunity, let us focus our attention on holistic unity and concern ourselves with the self-conversion from fixation of voice to freedom of speech and liberation of meaning.

Let us use the word *Christ* for the Holistic Voice in its appearance as the mediating principle that opens up the fixated mind to Divine Form. This Universal Christ form is the living logos that opens the closed particularistic voice into its true inner form, to its self-unity, to its true inner self-universalization. This is the universal dialogical voice that mediates the split between ontos and Logos, between the form of identity and the holistic form of universal relativity. This dialogical voice is the healing voice that brings liberation from the perpetual strife, confusion, suffering, irrationality, and hermeneutical death of the pathological mind. It is the self-univocating principle that brings true life and living truth by opening the way to the Universal Light of the Continuum. This Christ-voice is the living principle of universal relativity. As the universal mediating logos, it is the meeting point at which all possible dualities and splits are joined. This universal dialogical principle may be found to live and speak in any logos or grammar where the holistic voice speaks. One may find it in teachings of Jesus, in the speech of Krishna, in the discourses of Buddha.

For we now see that any logos, any form of life, any grammar, is lodged in self-eclipsed indeterminacy of meaning, in original hidden ambiguity. When taken in the particularistic voice, it is a fixated inert sign; but when taken in the holistic voice, it is a living holistic symbol reflecting the Continuum. It is the true dialogical voice that is the universal meeting point that brings salvation and liberation of meaning and life.

The dialogical principle, the living principle of universal relativity, is that universal mediator that turns the death of meaning into true life—the resurrection of fixated voice. This logos of the continuum is the universal meeting point that univocates all opposition and reverses the perpetual fallout of self-splitting that comes with the eclipse of Divine Form.

How does the fixated voice become awakened to holistic life? What is the dialogical process of self-awakening that brings the fixated form of life to its inner universal form? How are the holistic voice and mind awakened to their higher form? This is the process of inner dialogical speech in which the fixated voice enters conversation with its inner logos.

Let us reflect on this dialogical process. The awakening of true inner dialogue, self-univocation, comes with the recognition of the reality of *indeterminacy*—the opening that can be both a blessing and a curse. The recognition of indeterminacy, that ontos is not inherently wedded to its fixated form of life and voice, is what brings the freedom of speech that transforms the fixated sign into the living symbol. Indeterminacy is the interface between identity and relativity, between fixity and liberation of meaning. It is the opening, the pivot that is the perpetual possibility of the fixated voice turning itself around (self-conversion) and recentering in the living continuum, which is its true inner form. This is the very possibility of its hermeneutical freedom and detachment from rational enslavement. It is in indeterminacy that the possibility of salvation and self-univocation is found. It is the awareness of indeterminacy, that voice is not fixated to its particularized form of life, that initiates the dialogical self-transformation of holistic unity. Indeterminacy is the opening from which the light of the Continuum is found to be present; it is the forum in which inner dialogue or self-unification converses.

The recognition of indeterminacy initiates the holistic process of self-expansion, the dialogical process that is the very essence of reflexive self-awareness—it is mediational form itself. This dialogical form, once initiated, is without beginning or end; it is of cosmic proportions. Once the Holistic Voice is awakened, the dialogical process of self-unification and self-univocation with the continuum resonates throughout the continuum. The life of universal relativity—true life—is the perpetual celebration of the infinite self-expansion of form; it is being in touch with Logos. So meditational self-univocation is the living dialogical process that is the reflexive life of true consciousness. The universal form of religious life is the life of dialogical self-unity. It is in the temple of holistic dialogue that true worship and divine celebration can spontaneously arise. The dialogical voice is not subject to the will and command of the particularized voice; it is rather a gift of grace. It is a higher voice that always remains higher and perpetually calls us to our roots. So dialogue is the universal meeting place in which all possible oppositions or dualities are reconciled in peace.

Holistic (Dialogical) Unity and the Univocation of All Opposition

Let us reflect further on the awakening of the Holistic Voice within and on the dialogical process of self-expansion, which is the essence of all religious life. It is in the dialogical process that the fixated particularized voice begins to awaken to a deeper awareness of its true inner universal form, its Universal Christ-voice within. This self-universalization is experienced as the mediation of opposition as the fixated voice opens up in dialogue with Continuum.

We have seen that the origin of all dualism is in the fixation of form, the fixation of voice that is inherent in the faith of the particularistic mind. Our meditation now makes clear that the fictional and partial narrative of the fixated voice, though eclipsed from the holistic narrative, lives in primordial equivocity and indeterminacy. In this indeterminacy the holistic narrative rules and governs every logos and has supreme jurisdiction over every form of life. The internal agenda of the fixated voice is always overruled by the divine agenda as manifested in the holistic narrative. This is another version of the continuum hypothesis—

that every possible logos inherently reflects Divine Form and has the continuum as its true origin and rational principle.

This helps to explain the phenomenology of the dialogical awakening as the fixated voice opens up to its inner universal meaning. We now see that life is situated in indeterminacy and the artificial narrative of the fixated voice is over-ruled by the narrative of the Holistic Voice. The history of the evolution of human consciousness may be explained in this context. For the holistic mind sees that the particularistic mind has evolved through its spontaneous break-through into its preconscious continuum—all advances in rational understanding, all revelation and deeper insight into truth, all advances in knowledge and re-ligious life, have been the lightening of the continuum breaking through the closure of the fixated mind. We now see that the great philosophical, religious, scientific, poetic, and artistic strokes of genius that have advanced human forms of life have been the breakthrough of the closed mind into the open space of the divine continuum—they have been flashes of Divine Form, revelations of divine unity, dialogical moments of cosmic insight.

The gifted voices that were able to discern the holistic Continuum and have a flash of deeper unity translated their vision into grammars of new and higher forms of life. This evolution of higher life is always measured by the degree to which the Continuum is discerned and the comprehensiveness and completeness of the narrative. The speaking forth of deeper grammars was always lodged in the original indeterminacy that left them open to multiple interpretations and misinterpretation. When the dialogical voices attempted to give form to their insight into Continuum by articulating this insight in terms that the fixated voice might understand, there was and has been an inevitable mistranslation of the insight and a misreading of the holistic hermeneutic. Often the blessed seer–poets who had flashes into holistic life and dialogical unity themselves failed to discern the Holistic Voice and hence misspoke their own flash of insight. Here, the holistic narrative sees that the cosmic evolution of the divine narrative, the divine agenda, is precisely the coming forth of the Holistic Voice and the self-articulation of the holistic life. The meditative mind can see that the divine agenda of self-evolution is the manifestation of the continuum in ever deeper self-univocation. The divine agenda as discerned in holistic history is the evo-lution of holistic life, which is the universal form of life inherent in the heart of every logos. This is the self-realization of holistic prophesy and divine will—the dialogical self-expansion of holistic life.

So it is in the in-betweenness of indeterminacy that the ultimate dialogical encounter takes place—between the fixated voice and the holistic voice, between the principle of identity and the living principle of universal relativity. We see that fixation can take place at any stage or level of holistic evolution, and where fixation of form takes place, there is always the higher voice that speaks from a deeper intimacy with continuum, calling the lower voice to a new and higher life. The higher voice always threatens the independent being of the lower form of life, and, indeed, the dynamics of dialogue requires that the lower form be consumed by the Light and is the fuel that releases rational energy for rebirth into a higher form. This process of holistic self-expansion is the process of hermeneutical death and rebirth into every higher life. It is in the meeting place of the dialogical Christ-voice that there is a surrender of old fixated life and the resurrection into a higher form of self-unity.

Wherever this dialogical self-expansion arises, at any stage of cosmic evolution of form, there is the experience of an expansion of meaning—as the fixated voice opens up into holistic space, in awareness of the indeterminacy of meanings, it experiences deeper analogical unities between all things. As the holistic mind comes forth, any fixated sign blossoms into symbolic universalization, as we saw earlier with examples of "water" and "air" and "bread." The meditative imagination can perceive intrinsic unities and synonymies of meaning that the fixated literalist mind cannot see. Most of all, in dialogical self-expansion, the analogical mind sees clearly that "I" am not fixated in sense and reference but gestures to the open continuum in which "I" can discern my true meaning in any name and form—in any logos. As the holistic mind comes forth and the analogical imagination is released, there is a simultaneous univocation in all directions arising codependently. The primordial split in my voice between I and Field begins to evaporate, and with this healing there arises a deeper self-integrity in which my previously fixated voice as *ontos* finds dialogical unity with its deeper form—logos. This univocation of voice in dialogical form reverses the pathological process that created the recursive fallout of dualism and fragmentation in every direction. Thus it is this very dialogical self-expansion and self-integration that is the essence of rational life and the universal form of religious awakening.

Realizing, then, that the fixated voice presents a distorted narrative of itself, and seeing clearly that the holistic narrative rules in all hermeneutical matters, let us focus meditative attention on the holistic hermeneutic and elaborate on the dialogical principle that is the meeting point of all possible oppositions.

We have now discerned the universal form of dialogue as self-univocation. We have seen that the dialogical voice is the universal mediating principle that reveals the nonduality of any opposition. It is now clear that all oppositions or dualisms arise in the very form of identity that is the origin of pathological life. What the voice of identity sees as absolute distinctions or oppositions, the holistic voice univocates in a higher mediating principle: this is another law of holistic hermeneutics. The particularistic mind encounters oppositions and strife in every direction, and they are seen as absolute and irreducible. But the higher dialogical voice sees through these artificial oppositions and finds a deeper univocation that places the polar splits into the context of the continuum where they are more clearly seen to be relative and constructed division.

Thus we saw earlier in mediating on the universal origin of pathology of life that the following splits arise in the life of identity: between unity and diversity, between I and field, between real and unreal, between finite and infinite, between particular and universal, between intrapersonal life and interpersonal life, between sign and symbol, between meaning and existence, between good and evil, between sacred and secular, between faith and reason, between religion and science, between meaning and truth, between word and object, between mind and body, between absolutism and relativism, and so on. These primary oppositions are the result of the faith of identity. They are just some obvious samples that fragments life from holistic unity. In what is conventionally called "theology" we find recurrent polarizations between theism/atheism, monotheism/polytheism, transcendence and immanence, affirmative theology and negative theology, and so on. These polarizations are the workings of the inner self-division of the voice of identity itself. They have as much validity as this fragmented voice does.[12]

Let us select some sample polarizations that appear absolute and place them in the unity of continuum, which brings out their true import.

1. Of special interest is the problem of "evil" and the division between good and evil; the mind of identity sees here an absolute distinction, but the holistic mind sees a continuum that relativizes these poles. For the life of fixation itself is the source of holistic "evil"—the origin of hermeneutical sin and suffering. It is the fixations of voice and the eclipse of Divine Form that is the universal form of "evil," and the distinction within that form of life between good and evil are seen to be *both* sharing in the common pathology of fixation of form and life. In this self-divided life, the voice of "good" divorces itself from what it takes to be "evil," and the problem of evil is spawned from this self-division. There is a breakdown of conversation and dialogue between these poles, and a pathological alienation arises that is all projected on "evil" as the cause. But the Holistic Voice sees through these divisive dynamics and reinterprets the distinction in the light of the Continuum. Here, the Continuum hypothesis that every logos is Logos enables us to see that even in "evil voices" the Logos must be present and ruling. Thus there is a profound reinterpretation of "evil," and the judgmental narrative of the self-designated "good" one is corrected. Now we see that in being self-righteous and alienating itself from its polar opposite—"evil"—the "good one" fixates the "evil one" in its absolute judgment and thereby violates both itself and the other. Here, we see the holistic imperative: *judge not,* for it is this very act of self-righteous judgement that participates in the universal form of evil that is always the eclipse of Divine Form, dialogical unity.

On the other hand, the holistic voice looks more deeply into the form of life of the "evil" polar voice and sees its garbled attempt to express its intrinsic divine hypothesis. Since it is a logos, however distorted, it participates in hermeneutical form, in the structure of meaning, and as a form of life it somehow strives to universalize itself and find its ultimate expression of unity. If we take any case of what is more conventionally called "evil," as in an "evil" life, we shall find in the holistic reading a more comprehensive narrative that brings out all of the significance implicit in the confused and garbled voice. It may be said that any corrupted voice still thinks it is doing what is best and highest for itself.

In its monadic orientation, which is its source of pathology, it self-articulates a form of life with its highest principle of meaning (divine hypothesis) that rules and directs this life. Even a pathological life, operating to direct itself by its own will in the darkness of the eclipse of Divine Form, speaks a "logos" that orients its meaning and priorities. Within this artificial monadic space of its voice it expresses its religious zeal with devastating consequences to itself and others. But when the polar voice, which takes itself to be "good," judges and condemns its opposite, it here falls from Continuum and participates in the origin of holistic evil, with devastating consequences to itself and others.

Thus we see that the problem of evil originates in the eclipse of Divine Form and the dialogical Christ-voice that would mediate all opposition and strife. When dialogue fails, evil runs rampant, and there is both self-violation and violation of the other. The holistic reading of human history readily sees this failure as the source of strife and wars and self-destruction. Here the Holistic Voice calls for a higher covenant with Logos; it calls for a deeper ethics of dialogue wherein the split voice achieves deeper integrity in dialogical self-unity. Dialogical or Holistic Ethics is a matter of integrity of voice, and it is the self-univocated voice that can be more profoundly good.

2. Let us take a dialogical look at another pervasive polarization—finite and infinite: Here again we see that the mind of identity creates an ultimate or absolute split between finite and infinite, and we find typical versions of this in "theism." More generally, the voice of identity is committed to a faith in particularity and "historicity," which it takes to be an ultimate truth. One version of this particularism or finitism is that persons are absolutely finite, self-existent, and determinate, on the one hand, whereas God (divine hypothesis) is infinite, universal, and absolutely Other. This polarizing voice does not detect that this ultimate faith in finitude and fixity is the projection of its form of life—its faith in absolute identity. So the holistic voice places this polarity in the context of the continuum and brings out its deeper self-eclipsed insight. In the holistic narrative the polarization of finite/infinite (particular/universal) is seen to be mediated in dialogical form (Christ form), and the duality is relativized and placed in deeper conversation. The question is not whether finitude or particularity is given up in continuum; it is rather that we come to a deeper more faithful understanding of the meaning of finitude and particularity. The holistic voice respects particularity precisely by placing it in the mediating light of continuum and recovering the universal Divine Form at the heart of any given finitized or particularized logos.

Thus here, too, we find that the voice of identity violates holistic finitude and particularity of any logos—in its self-interpretation it eclipses the higher holistic (Christ) voice within which is its true essential form and which is the true source of its divine worth and nobility. In its mistaken understanding of particularity, it violates itself, which leads to violation of others. So again we see that it is the holistic voice that discerns the dialogical mediation that brings self-integrity and opens the way for a deeper form of religious life. In discerning the intrinsic dialogical form that lives in the heart of every logos and that is the essence of its particularity, it shows the ultimate respect and honoring of holistic finitude.

3. Still another area of recursive polarization is found in the vast range of logos called "theologies." We have seen that in holistic hermeneutic every logos is Logos and hence implies a religious form of life and a "theology." This cuts across the artificial duality between "religious" and "nonreligious" life, between sacred and secular. Just as in the case of "evil" and "finite," the holistic narrative places all "theologies" in the context of the continuum and draws out the truth implicit in their logos. Thus in the polarization between theist/atheist, for example, we do not find an absolute irreconcilable split wherein one must be true and the other false. Rather, when placed in dialogical form we find that the divine hypothesis of theism does reflect an important holistic truth—namely, that the absolute logos is the form of all possible forms, the source of all meaning and being, infinitely higher than any logos, the infinite presence that illumines all things, and so on. The deeper holistic intent of theism is its fidelity to Divine Form. But the Atheist, in speaking a polar "theology," is committed to a form of life that, since it mistakes the opposing "theist" voice to be speaking in a closed, absolute, exclusivist voice and takes strong exception to its literalist and fundamentalist faith, believes itself to be in good faith and moving to a higher truth when it declares that "there is no God." This contrary theology has its ultimate faith and divine hypothesis, and both the theist and atheist share a common faith in absolute identity, which governs their religious life. The negative theological voice of the "atheist" is in *its* divine hypothesis attempting to be faithful to its implicit holistic insight that the particularized voice will always violate holistic Divine Form in its theistic fundamentalism; so it attempts to be true to Divine Form by negating the literalism of the theist theology with a polar faith.

Again, we can find the same pattern in the polarities of monotheism and polytheism. Each has its garbled holistic flash of insight. The great advance in religious life with monotheism is the recognition that Divine Form is absolute unity, which immediately requires that "God is One," so the implicit holistic insight here is in discerning more deeply Divine Form and coming closer to holistic unity—the continuum. By contrast, the polar theology of polytheism is another holistic flash of insight that sees that every logos is Logos—the Divine Form lives in every logos. In attempting to be faithful to this holistic revelation, it counters the monotheism that it reads in a literalist and exclusivist light. So the polarization of transcendent/immanent emerges in a nonnegotiable split, and in this there is eclipse of dialogical form.

Similarly, we can see in "negative theology" a holistic insight that flashes into the holistic narrative. For this polarized voice of theology presents its divine hypothesis as a radical critique of all "affirmative" theologies that share the common hermeneutical faith of literalism and belief that the Divine Form may be described and predicated in literalist discourse. Against this pathology, the contrary voice of negative theology attempts to be more faithful to Divine Form in confessing that there can be no predication of Divine Form—no literal discourse can truly approach the continuum, and no fundamentalist voice can be faithful to the living Logos. And so on. We could go on in this way to mediate the diverse pathological polarities throughout the life of identity (absolutism).

Finally, we begin to see the artificiality of the absolutist constructions of sacred/secular, faith/reason, religion/science, and so on. Here, too, we find the dialogical voice blowing away these polarities and discerning the nondual continuum that negotiates them in deeper unity. We have seen that in holistic hermeneutic every logos has its divine hypothesis and is potentially a religious form of life. Thus in any grammar or ideology we may discern its religious form and implicit theology. In the separation of church and state, for example, the Holistic Voice sees that the democratic ideology or grammar is a theogram with its unifying principle and ultimate faith. What we have seen then is a competition and strife between two competing religious forms of life. So, too, with the split between religion and science: it should be clear that the diverse scientific grammars are structures of meaning and praxis that attempt to discern highest truth and in this way are divine hypotheses that flash into the continuum. Science, too, may be lived in a fundamentalist voice and literalist mind, or it may open up to holistic hermeneutic like any conventional "theology." Thus we see the artificiality of the duality between faith and reason. The dialogical voice discerns that pure faith and pure reason are one and the same in the light of continuum.[13]

Dialogical Unity and Holistic Religious Life

Our meditation on dialogical form has helped us to see more clearly the nature of the self-expansion as the self-unification of dialogical life. We now see that the universal form of religious life is the overcoming of the fixity of voice and the literalism of life. It is the self-conversion in dialogue to holistic unity that reveals the deep structure of religious life in all of its dimensions. In this holistic context we can see the universal meaning of religious "concepts" such as sin, suffering, conversion, death, resurrection, immortality, and liberation. We have seen that in the holistic hermeneutic "sin" is the pathology of the fixation of voice and meaning that eclipses Divine Form—sin is separation from Divinity. We see in the self-fixity of absolute identity, too, the origins of human suffering and strife. We discern that the human "existential" condition is the condition of the life of self-identity (identity is existential life), and we see that death is the hermeneutical death of meaning—the fixity of the word (logos) that renders it inert. Here, we see that the life of sin is hermeneutical death—the death of "god." The holistic voice also discloses the universal form of religious "conversion"—it is always *self-conversion* in dialogical self-univocation. Conversion is the self-unification that comes with dialogical life. It is in this self-realization that we find the true import of spiritual rebirth, resurrection (the rebirth of the mortified logos), and liberation. It is in the detachment from the fixity of the word that hermeneutical liberation comes, and with this arises the human freedom of speech that is the essence of happiness, peace, and immortality. For the holistic life is without beginning or end and at perfect peace with Divine Form.

In this Universal Light we may readily see the essence of religious phenomena—worship, ritual, prayer, sacrifice. The holistic narrative discerns that the true reading of Scripture must be in the Holistic Voice. For the literalist reading inherently violates the Word and eclipses Divine Form. Worship is found to be dialogical univocation with continuum—the authentic living conversation between logos and Logos. All ritual is designed to deepen this dialogical self-unity, and prayer can take place in the sacred space of dialogical form—the Christ-voice. Religious meaning must be essentially symbolic and dialogical, as must religious Truth be holistic.

We may now see more clearly that in approaching any authentic scripture we must advance with due respect for the Word and with appropriate honoring of our particularity in Holistic Voice. Whether we read the voice of Jesus, Buddha, or Krishna, the essential prerequisite is to approach the Living Word with dialogical openness and hermeneutical humility. If we discern the life and speech of Jesus/Christ with fixated voice and literalistic mind, we do violence to the Living Word of the Holistic Christ. The Universal Christ-voice—the universal mediating, dialogical form—is never exclusivist or absolutist or relativist. It essentially speaks beyond the hermeneutical pathologies of dualism and divisiveness. In the holistic narrative we see that in every speech-act, in every teaching, in every breath, the Holistic Christ calls us to our true roots in Divine Form. In the new covenant we see demonstrated that "bread" is the living body of Christ, and "wine" is the living blood. The new Covenant is a new form of speech life, the opening of a new holistic voice that brings us deeper to unity with Logos. All the miracles performed by the Lord were holistic demonstrations that enacted the resurrection of the word—from ontos to logos/Logos. When we read the speech of the Buddha, we violate the Holistic Buddha-voice if we approach it with closed mind and literalist faith. Every speech act of the Buddha showed the way to liberation from the fixity and bondage of the life of identity, toward holistic life. Similarly, with the speech and life of Lord Krishna—his hermeneutical instructions in the meditative self-transformation of life is precisely the dialogical self-conversion from an ontocentric life to a life centered in Divine Form, the continuum, Atmo-centric life. And so on with any form of the divine Word.

Dialogical Unity of Religions

We may now conclude with meditation on the question of the unity of religions. We have discerned the universal form of dialogue and of religious life. We have developed the holistic hermeneutic of dialogical speech and have seen how pernicious polarizations are renegotiated in the higher voice. So, too, with the question of the unity of religions. We are now in a position to see that the problem of unity/diversity formulated in the voice of identity is ill formed in every sense—it is in bad form. For the universal unity of any logos (any religious form of life) is Logos—the divine continuum. This Unity is not a "transcendent" unity, nor is it "immanent." We have found a higher principle of unity—dialogical unity, holistic unity—that cannot become ensnared in the polarizations and dualities born of fixated voice. In dialogical form the artificial split between internal (intrapersonal) life and external (interpersonal) is reconciled in holistic life. True dialogue—whether the internal self-conversion of voice or the external conversation between diverse logos, makes clear the universal origin of all forms of life. The dialogical life is the religious celebration of the Divine Form in every logos, and this celebration is the essence of love—the communion between self and other in dialogue. In this communion (dialogical unity) is found the essence of compassion and liberation. So it is here that we see the form of ethical life—dialogical ethics. This univocation of self and other is the meaning of respect: it takes us to a higher form of life in which being true to our own particularity we need not violate the particularity of the other; we no longer need to speak an exclusivist voice that reduces the logos of the other to our particularity. Rather, in dialogical unity we find the open space in which each logos may celebrate its universal form and discern it in the logos of the other. The holistic conservative/orthodox is the voice that, in being faithful and true to its own inner universal logos, sees that it must likewise preserve and enhance the Divine Form in the logos of the other, as its own. For the universal Word is seen to be the true meaning of every logos.

NOTES

1. For a more systematic presentation of the principle of universal relativity see the glossary for indeterminacy, literalism, metaphor, and relativism. It might be helpful here to pick out some prominent examples of Universal Relativity (UR) from the world historical traditions.

In the meditative tradition of Indian thought it is readily seen that the teaching of Advaita (nondual Vedanta) reveals that AUM is the Universal principle of Unity. AUM is holistic form itself—synonymous with Logos. Through proper meditation on AUM the mind itself self-transforms and becomes unified with AUM. This is the Universal Continuum of which all else is an expression. If any item is selected for meditative attention, its true import is revealed when its meditative synonymy with AUM is realized. The science of Yoga (self-union) in its highest form expands rational awareness to its universal synonymy with AUM—the Original Holistic Word. This is not just an "altered state of consciousness, by the realization of Pure Consciousness or Reason, the realization of Truth itself.

Another classical example of the holistic principle of UR may be found in the teaching of Nagarjuna, the founder of the Madhyamika Buddhist tradition. Nagarjuna presented one version of UR in the form of the principle of dependent coarising of all things. He taught that absolute identity (*svabhava*) is vacuous and demonstrated that wherever there is identity there is contradiction and incoherence. He showed that true Reason arises with the realization of *Sunya,* which may be translated as Emptiness, Void, Zero, and now Logos. Nagarjuna taught that all things are Sunyata and thus beyond the oppositional (dual, polar) structure of identity. *Sunya* is neither full nor empty, neither one nor many, neither is nor is not neither relative nor absolute and so on. The holistic principle of *Sunya* exhibits the nondual features just discussed—it is the Universal Continuum. Things are devoid of absolute identity; all things dependently coarise. The identity of anything consists in its identity with everything else. It is the Holistic Principle that makes thought, language, and the world functional; true insight comes with the realization of *Sunya,* which is the middle way between all opposition and the pathological polarization of identity.

Still another classical example of the living principle of UR that may not at first be evident to the mind of identity is the being of Christ. It may be argued in this context that Christ is the perfect living example of UR—the self-transformative dialogical form of nondual unity. Christ meditatively understood is a unifying principle that overcomes the deepest duality there can be in the deep structure of identity—the polarization of finite (individuated) beings and Infinite (transcendent) Being. Christ is that Unified and Unifying Being that is at once fully finite and fully Infinite—the Living logos, the logos become flesh. The form of unity of the Christ-voice is the dialogical form of the Continuum. In this respect the Universal Christ is prior to the duality of identity and is the more profound unifying principle (UR)—the incarnation of Logos.

2. The terms *metaphoric* and *symbolic* are used in a special meditative sense here. Whereas the mind of identity takes literal meaning to be primary, the meditative mind, being centered in the continuum, discerns *holistic* meaning (metaphor/symbol) to be primary and literal meaning to be derived artificially. For a systematic discussion of holistic metaphor and symbol, see glossary for monadic and logos. The meditative mind works on the principle of universal relativity, which structures the analogical (meditative) imagination.

3. The term *grammar* is used here in the ontological sense of the structure of a language form that constitutes a life-world. This idea of grammar is developed in detail in the glossary under absolutism, analogous, form of life and relativism.

4. The term *monadic* (a modification of a term from the thought of Leibniz) indicates the orientation of voice from the internal self-reference of its independent identity. Voice may take different orientations in logical space; it can be centered in the ''I'' locus, can take a more transcendent overview that is external to the individuated ''I,'' and so on. This point is elaborated by Gangadean 16.

5. It must be stressed here that the term *ontology* (*ontos*) indicates a cosmological universal, a world-whole that is all-encompassing. When voice centers in its universe, its life-world, or ontology, as its absolute center of reference for its life and logos, it may be said to be ''ontocentric.'' Here, it takes its life-world, or ontology, to be the absolute measure of all meaning. This theme is developed in the glossary for metaphor.

6. Usually, in logic the term *univocal* applies to the literal primary unity of the meaning of a word or concept. But here we reorient the discussion to the primacy of the *voice* of the thinker/speaker, and the original question is whether the mind/voice of the speaker can be presumed to be *univocal,* a primitive unity. This point is explored in Gangadean 3, 9, 7, 10, 16.

7. For a more explicit discussion of the principle of identity and the first principles of rationality of identity, see Gangadean 3, 1, 2, 10, 16.

8. Once the presumption of a self-identical, unified voice is suspended, and it is seen that the ''I'' lives in an open space of multiple grammars, hence living in multiple identities, the horizon of ontological indeterminacy emerges. If we speak in term of an

original ambiguity, multivocation, and equivocation, any utterance will reflect this indeterminacy of meaning. This theme is developed in Gangadean 7, 9, 10, 12, 16.

9. The slashes "/X/" indicate the higher transcendental unity in any given term. Thus in exploring the range of all possible colors we may discern a universal and unifying *category* of /Color/, which indicates the feature of being colored while excluding all possible color. The idea of an ontological category is explained in Gangadean 1, 2, 4.

10. This theme is developed at length in Gangadean 10, 15.

11. Every grammar, to be coherent and to define a universe of discourse, must have its ultimate unifying principle that unifies its universe. In this univocal condition of any grammer, which is intrinsic to the form of identity itself, we find the image of the Divine Form in any possible grammar. All life in this universe is under the rule of this unifying principle. In this respect, every grammar has its divinity and faith principle.

12. For a systematic holistic analysis that demonstrates the unity of mind and matter, see glossary for relativism.

13. Here, it may be seen that in Descartes's *Meditations* his demonstration that "I am" and *God is,* taken in the holistic or meditative narrative, is powerful. The essence of Descartes's demonstration of the necessary existence of Divine Being turns on the meditation of Divine Unity; if it is taken in the narrative of the particularistic voice, the force of the speech is lost. Descartes himself speaks in an equivocal voice, intending to express a holistic insight in the voice and rhetoric of the voice of identity and literal predication. The holistic narrative makes clear that Divine Form cannot be thought by the mind of identity, which separates the Idea of God, the Word, and its Sense, Essence, and Being.

GLOSSARY

Absolutism: The origin of the pathology of meaning that arises in the very form of the mind of identity.

Analogous: For the meditative mind, original meaning is metaphoric, not literal; the holistic mind discerns a continuum of meaning in which all terms permeate one another in analogical synonymy.

Continuum: The absolute unity of Divine Form as it is discerned by the holistic mind; it is nondual, primordial and prior to any possible dualism or division between "I" and field.

Form of Life: Any life is structured in a grammar or life-world that gives it form; any life is a logos with form.

Equivocity: The voice of the speaker/thinker taken in its indeterminacy; the original self-division of voice into polarization. The self-divided or equivocal voice speaks equivocally.

Grammar: The ontological structure of any logos (form of life) world or language that constitutes a life-world; a grammar makes a form of life possible and defines its meaning, experience, existence.

Holistic: Divine Unity, the unity of the continuum that is nondual; the primordial unity discerned by the meditative mind.

Incommensurability: The pathology or incoherence of reason or meaning in which diverse things (logos, worlds, forms of life, etc.) each have their internal absolute self-definition, atomic independence, and hence share no unifying principle that could make rational relations between them possible.

Indeterminacy: The ontological condition of meaning, existence, voice, in which there can be no literal fixation of meaning or identity; a given thing is indeterminate if its identity is open and neither fixated, univocal, nor specifiable.

Literalism: The hermeneutical faith that literal meaning is primary and that words have their intrinsic, fixated, determinate senses and univocity; metaphoric meaning is taken to be derivative.

Metaphor: The primordial form of meaning discerned by the meditative or holistic mind in discerning the Continuum of meaning; the nondual meaning conforming to universal relativity.

Monadic: As applied to a universe or life-world, one that takes itself as the absolute measure, having independent self-existence; voice is said to be monadic when it takes an ontocentric or absolutistic posture.

Ontos: A logos or form of life becomes ontological, ontocentric, and names itself *ontos* when it takes itself in independent identity and defines itself apart from Divine Form (Continuum).

Logos: The holistic name for the universal Divine Form; the Absolute Principle that is the form of all possible names/forms ("logos").

logos: Any name or form (form of life) in its holistic particularity in the divine Continuum; hence any form in its univocity or dialogical unity with Logos.

Relativism: A pathological form of absolutism in which this faith is committed to a multiplicity of radically diverse, incommensurable forms, each of which is an absolute measure of its reality.

Symbolic: Any sign or thing taken in its holistic or universal meaning; the symbolic meaning of any name or form is discerned by the holistic mind in the context of the continuum of meaning. This term is used closely with "metaphoric" and "analogical."

Universal relativity (UR): The holistic principle of the continuum, the principle of the nondual unity of Divine Form.

Universal Theology (UT): The meditation on universal Divine Form; the holistic narrative or hermeneutic that articulates this meditative voice.

Voice: Used synonymously with "mind," in the mind of the speaker/thinker/listener; voice is the presence that speaks or thinks, the voice of the first person indicated by "I"; and so on.

SELECTED BIBLIOGRAPHY

Abe, Masao. *Zen and Western Thought*. Honolulu: University of Hawaii Press, 1985.

Berger, Peter. *The Sacred Canopy*. New York: Doubleday, 1969.

————, ed. *The Other Side of God: A Polarity in World Religions*. New York: Anchor, 1981.

Bernstein, Richard. *Beyond Objectivism and Relativism: Science, Hermeneutics, and Praxis*. Philadelphia: University of Pennsylvania Press, 1983.

Cobb, John B. Jr. *Beyond Dialogue: Toward a Mutual Transformation of Christianity and Buddhism*. Philadelphia: Fortress Press, 1982.

Dawe, D. G., and John B. Carmen, eds. *Christian Faith in a Religiously Plural World*. Maryknoll, N.Y: Orbis Books, 1978.

Derrida, Jacques. *Of Grammatology*. Translated by G. C. Spivak. Baltimore: Johns Hopkins University Press, 1978.

Deutsch, Eliot. *On Truth: An Ontological Theory*. Honolulu: University of Hawaii Press, 1979.

Fingarette, H. *The Self in Transformation: Psychoanalysis, Philosophy, and the Life of Spirit*. New York: Harper and Row, 1963.

Frei, Hans W. *The Eclipse of Biblical Narrative: A Study in Eighteenth- and Nineteenth-Century Hermeneutics*. New Haven: Yale University Press, 1974.

Gadamer, Hans-Georg. *Truth and Method*. New York: Seabury Press, 1975.

Hesse, Mary. *Revolutions and Reconstructions in the Philosophy of Science*. Brighton, Eng.: Harvester Press, 1980.

Hick, J., and B. Hebblethwaite, eds. *Christianity and Other Religions*. Philadelphia: Fortress Press, 1980.

Hick, John. *God Has Many Names*. Philadelphia: Westminster Press, 1980.

———. *Truth and Dialogue in World Religions: Conflicting Truth Claims*. Philadelphia: Westminster Press, 1974.

Iida, Shotaro. *Reason and Emptiness: A Study in Logic and Mysticism*. Tokyo: Hokuseido Press, 1980.

Kaufman, G. *An Essay in Theological Method*. Ann Arbor, Michigan: Scholars Press, 1975.

Kelsey, David. *The Uses of Scripture in Recent Theology*. Philadelphia: Fortress Press, 1975.

Kuhn, Thomas. *The Structure of Scientific Revolutions*. Chicago: University of Chicago Press, 1962.

LaKatos, Imre, and Alan Musgrave, eds. *Criticism and the Growth of Knowledge*. Cambridge: Cambridge University Press, 1970.

Meiland, J. W., and M. Krausz, eds. *Relativism: Cognitive and Moral*. Notre Dame, Ind.: University of Notre Dame Press, 1982.

Neusner, Joseph, ed. *Christian Revelation and World Religions*. London: Burne and Oates, 1967.

Neville, R. C. *The Tao and the Daimon: Segments of a Religious Inquiry*. Albany, N.Y.: SUNY Press, 1982.

Nishitani, Keiji. *Religion and Nothingness*. Los Angeles: University of California Press, 1982.

Panikkar, R. *The Inter-Religious Dialogue*. New York: Paulist Press, 1978.

———. *Myth, Faith, and Hermeneutics*. New York: Paulist Press, 1979.

Ricoeur, Paul. *Interpretation Theory: Discourse and Surplus of Meaning*. Forth Worth: Texas Christian University Press, 1976.

Robinson, John. *Truth Is Two-Eyed*. London: SCM Press, 1981.

Rorty, Richard. *Philosophy and the Mirror of Nature*. Princeton, N. J.: Princeton University Press, 1979.

Rupp, George. *Beyond Existentialism and Zen: Religion in a Pluralistic World*. New York: Oxford University Press, 1979.

Schuon, F. *The Transcendent Unity of Religions*. New York: Pantheon, 1953.

Smart, Ninian. *Beyond Ideology: Religion and the Future of Western Civilization*. San Francisco: Harper and Row, 1981.

———. *Worldviews: Cross-Cultural Explorations of Human Beliefs*. New York: Scribner's, 1983.

Smartha, S. J., ed. *Towards World Community: The Columbo Papers*. Geneva: World Council of Churches, 1975.

Smith, Huston. *Beyond the Post-Modern Mind*. New York: Crossroad, 1982.

Smith, W. C. *The Meaning and End of Religion: A New Approach to the Religious Tradition of Mankind*. New York: Macmillan, 1963.

———. *Towards a World Theology: Faith and the Comparative History of Religions*. Philadelphia: Westminster Press, 1981.

Sontag, F., and M. D. Bryant, eds. *God: The Contemporary Discussion*. New York: Rose of Sharon Press, 1982.

Streng, Frederick. *Emptiness: A Study in Religious Meaning*. Nashville: Abingdon Press, 1967.

Swearer, Donald. *Dialogue: The Key to Understanding Other Religions*. Philadelphia: Westminster, 1977.

Troeltsch, Ernst. *The Absoluteness of Christianity and the History of Religions*. Richmond, Va.: John Knott Press, 1971.

Waldenfels, H. *Absolute Nothingness: Foundations for a Buddhist-Christian Dialogue*. New York: Paulist Press, 1976.

Wittaker, J. H. *Matters of Faith and Matters of Principle: Religious Truth Claims and Their Logic*. San Antonio, Texas: Trinity University Press, 1981.

4

The Feminist Critique in Religious Studies

ROSEMARY RADFORD RUETHER

SOCIOLOGICAL AND HISTORICAL CONTEXT FOR WOMEN'S STUDIES IN RELIGION

Why women's studies in religion? To answer this question one must first survey the historical and sociological reality of women's participation in religion. One must start with the fact of women's historic exclusion from religious leadership roles in Judaism and Christianity and their consequent exclusion from advanced and professional theological education preparatory for the roles of clergy and teacher in these traditions. One could document similar histories in other world religions, such as Islam, but in this chapter we will discuss primarily Judaism and Christianity.

Many examples of this exclusion of women from leadership, teaching, and education can be cited. One thinks of the dicta in Rabbinic Judaism, "cursed be the man who teaches his daughter Torah," or the comparable statement in the New Testament, "I do not permit a woman to teach or to have authority over men. She is to keep silence" (I Timothy 2:12). Historically, women were excluded from the study of the Torah and Talmud that led to the rabbinate and that, as devotion, was considered the highest calling of the Jew. In Christianity the calling of the celibate woman diverged somewhat from the traditional view of women's limitations. But the education of women in monasteries was generally inferior to that of men and usually lacked the component of secular and classical learning that was regarded as inappropriate for women. When the educational center of Christendom shifted from the monastery to the university in the twelfth century, women were generally excluded. The Northern European university in particular was a male, clerical institution.

The seminary is a later institution that developed after the Reformation, when universities began to be seen as too secular to provide proper theological formation for priests and ministers. Generally, they have been slow to open up to women. Oberlin was the first. Its theological school allowed a few women to attend in the 1840s, but at first they were not permitted to speak in class. Methodist and Congregational seminaries had a few women by the late nineteenth century. But prestigious seminaries like the Harvard Divinity School did not open their doors to women until the 1950s. Jewish and Catholic women began entering their seminaries even later.

EFFECTS OF WOMEN'S EXCLUSION ON THEOLOGICAL CULTURE

The exclusion of women from leadership and theological education results in the elimination of women as shapers of the official theological culture. Women are confined to passive and secondary roles. Their experience is not incorporated into the official culture. Those who do manage to develop as religious thinkers are forgotten or have their stories told through male-defined standards of what women can be. In addition, the public theological culture is defined by men not only in the absence of but against women. Theology not only assumed male standards of normative humanity but also is filled with an ideological bias that defines women as secondary and inferior members of the human species.

Many examples of this overt bias against women in the theological tradition can be cited. There is the famous definition of woman by Thomas Aquinas as a "misbegotten male." Aquinas took this definition of woman from Aristotle's biology, which identifies the male sperm with the genetic form of the embryo. Women are regarded as contributing only the matter or 'blood' that fleshes out the form of the embryo. Hence the very existence of women must be explained as a biological accident that comes about through a deformation of the male seed by the female 'matter,' producing a defective human or woman who is defined as lacking normative human standing.

Women are regarded as deficient physically, lacking full moral self-control and capacity for rational activity. Because of this defective nature women cannot represent normative humanity. Only the male can exercise headship or leadership in society. Aquinas also deduced from this that the maleness of Christ is not merely a historical accident but a necessity. To represent humanity Christ must be incarnated into normative humanity, the male. Only the male, in turn, can represent Christ in the priesthood.

This Thomistic view of women is still reflected in Roman Catholic canon law where it is decreed that women are 'unfit matter' for ordination. If one were to ordain a woman, it, literally, would not 'take' any more than if one were to ordain a monkey or an ox. Some recent Episcopalian conservatives who declared that ordaining a woman was like ordaining a donkey are fully within this medieval scholastic tradition. Whether defined as inferior or simply as 'different,' theological and anthropological justifications of women's exclusion from religious learning and leadership can be found in every period of Jewish and Christian thought. Sometimes this exclusion of women is regarded as a matter of divine law, as in Old Testament legislation. Christian theologians tend to regard it as a reflection of 'natural law,' or the 'order of nature,' which, ultimately, also is a reflection of divine intent. Second, women's exclusion is regarded an an expression of woman's greater proneness to sin or corruption. Thus, as in the teaching of I Timothy, women are seen as 'second in creation but first in sin' (I Timothy 2:13–14).

The male bias of Jewish and Christian theology not only affects the teaching about woman's person, nature, and role but also generates a symbolic universe based on the patriarchal hierarchy of male over female. The subordination of woman to man is replicated in the symbolic universe in the imagery of divine-human relations. God is imaged as a great patriarch over–against the earth or Creation, imaged in female terms. Likewise, Christ is related to the church as bridegroom to bride. Divine-human relations in the macrocosm are also reflected in the microcosm of the human being. Mind over body, reason over passion, are also seen as images of the hierarchy of the 'masculine' over the 'feminine.' Thus everywhere the Christian and Jew are surrounded by religious symbols that ratify male domination and female subordination as the normative way of understanding the world and God. This ratification of male domination runs through every period of the tradition, from Old to New Testament, Talmud, church fathers and canon law, Reformation, Enlightenment and modern theology. It is not a marginal but an integral part of what has been received as mainstream, normative traditions.

THE TASK OF FEMINISM IN RELIGIOUS STUDIES

The task of women's studies in religious education is thus defined by this historical reality of female exclusion and male ideological bias in the tradition. The first task of feminist critique takes the form of documenting the fact of this male ideological bias itself and tracing its sociological roots. One thinks of works such as Mary Daly's first book, *The Church and the Second Sex* (Harper, 1968), or the book I edited, *Religion and Sexism: Images of Women in the Jewish and Christian Traditions* (Simon and Schuster, 1974). These works trace male bias against women from the Scriptures, Talmud, and church fathers through medieval, Reformation, and modern theologians. They intend to show that this bias is not marginal or accidental. It is not an expression of ideocentric, personal views of a few writers but runs through the whole tradition, and it shaped in conscious and unconscious ways the symbolic universe of Jewish and Christian theology.

The second agenda of feminist studies in religion aims at the discovery of an alternative history and tradition that supports the inclusion and personhood of women. At present, there are two very distinct types of alternative traditions that are being pursued by religious feminists. Within the Jewish and Christian theological academies the alternative tradition is being sought within Judaism and Christianity. However, many feminists have come to believe that no adequate alternative can be found within these religions. They wish to search for alternatives outside and against Judaism and Christianity. Some of these feminists are academically trained religious scholars who teach religious studies or women's studies in colleges and universities, and others are more self-trained writers that relate to the popular feminist spirituality movement, such as Starhawk (*The Spiral Dance*, Harper, 1979) and Zsuzsanna Budapest (*The Holy Book of Women's Mysteries*, Susan B. Anthony Coven No. 1, 1979).

This latter group draw their sources from anthropology and historical scholarship of matriarchal societies and ancient religious involved with the worship of the Mother Goddess, rather than the patriarchal God of Semitic religions. They see the worship of the Mother Goddess as a woman's religion stemming from prepatriarchal or matriarchal societies. This religion is believed to have been suppressed by militant patriarchal religions but survived underground in secret women-centered, nature religions persecuted by the dominant male religion. Medieval witchcraft is believed to have been such a female religion. Modern feminist witchcraft, or 'Wicca,' sees itself as the heir to this persecuted goddess religion.

Writers of this emergent goddess religion draw from an anthropological scholarship of matriarchal origins that developed in the nineteenth century and that many scholars today regard as outdated and historically dubious. There has not yet been an opportunity for an adequate dialogue between these countercultural religious feminists and academic feminist scholarship. This is doubly difficult since goddess religion is a matter not simply of correct or incorrect scholarship but of a rival faith stance. Most goddess religionists would feel that even if an adequate historical precedent for their faith cannot be found in the past, it should be created, and they are creating it now.

The question of the relation of Jewish and Christian to post-Christian feminist religion is discussed later in this chapter. For the moment, I will focus on some aspects of the search for an alternative tradition within Judaism and Christianity and its incorporation into theological education in seminaries and religious studies departments.

There now exists a fair body of well-documented studies in alternative traditions within Scripture and Jewish and Christian history. These studies show that male exclusion of women from leadership roles and theological reflection is not the whole story. There is much ambiguity and plurality in the traditions about women and the roles women have actually managed to play. For example, evidence is growing that women in first-century Judaism were not uniformly excluded from study in the synagogues. The rabbinic dicta against teaching women the Torah thus begins to appear not as a consensus of that period but as one side of an argument that eventually won against the beginnings of inclusion of women in discipleship.

Similarly the teachings of I Timothy about women keeping silent appear not as the uniform position of the New Testament church but as a second-generation response against widespread participation of women in leadership, teaching, and ministering in first-generation Christianity. Indeed, the very fact that such vehement commandments against women learning and teaching were found in the traditions should have been a clue to the existence of widespread practices to the contrary. Otherwise, the statements would have been unnecessary. But because the documents were used as Scripture or normative tradition, rather than historical documents, this was not realized.

The participation of women in early Christianity was not simply an accident of sociology but a conscious expression of an alternative anthropology and soteriology. The equality of men and women in the image of God was seen as restored in Christ. The gifts of the prophetic spirit, poured out again at the Messianic coming, were understood, in fulfillment of the Messianic prediction of the prophet Joel, to have been given to the 'maidservants' as well as the 'menservants' of the Lord (Acts 2, 17–21). Baptism overcomes the sinful divisions among people and makes us one in Christ; Jew and Greek, male and female, slave and free (Galatians 3, 28). Thus the inclusion of women expressed an alternative theology in direct confrontation with the theology of patriarchal subordination of women. The New Testament now must be read not as a consensus about women's place but rather as a conflict and struggle over two alternative understandings of the gospel that suggested different views of male and female relationship.

This alternative theology of equality, of women as equal in the image of God, as restored to equality in Christ and as commissioned to preach and minister by the Spirit, did not just disappear with the reassertion of patriarchal norms in I Timothy. It can be traced as surfacing again and again in different periods of Christian history. The strong role played by women in ascetic and monastic life in late antiquity and the early Middle Ages reflects a definite appropriation by women of a theology of equality in Christ that was understood as being applicable particularly to the monastic life. Celibacy was seen as abolishing sex-role differences and restoring men and women to their original equivalence in the image of God. As the male church deserted this theology, female monastics continued to cling to it and understood their own vocation out of this theology. The history of female monasticism in the late Middle Ages and the Counter-Reformation is one of a gradual success of the male church in suppressing this latent feminism of women's communities. It is perhaps then not accidental that women in renewed female religious orders in Roman Catholicism today have become militant feminists, to the consternation of the male hierarchy.

Left-wing Puritanism in the English Civil War again becomes a period when the latent egalitarianism of Christian theology surfaces to vindicate women's right to personal inspiration, community power, and public teaching. The reclericalization of the Puritan congregation can be seen as a defeat for this renewed feminism of the Reformation. The Quakers were the one Civil War sect that retained the vision of women's equality and carried it into the beginnings of nineteenth-century feminism.

Finally, the nineteenth century becomes a veritable hotbed of new types of female participation in religion, ranging from the evangelical holiness preacher Phoebe Palmer to Mother Ann Lee, understood by her followers as the female Messiah. New theologies that attempt to vindicate androgeny in humanity and God express a sense of the inadequacy of the masculinist tradition of symbolization. Works such as *Women of Spirit: Female Leadership in the Jewish and Christian Traditions* by Rosemary Ruether and Eleanor McLaughlin (Simon and Schuster, 1979) and *Women in American Religion* by Janet Wilson James (University of Pennsylvania, 1980) or the documentary history *Women and Religion: The Nineteenth Century* by Rosemary Keller and Rosemary Ruether (Harper and Row, 1981) trace different periods of women's recovered history in religion.

Feminists who are engaged in recovering alternative histories for women in religion recognize that they are not just supplementing the present male tradition. They are, implicitly, attempting to construct a new norm for the interpretation of the tradition. The male justification of women's subordination in Scripture and tradition is no longer regarded as normative for the gospel. Rather, it is judged as a failure to apply the authentic norms of equality in creation and redemption authentically. This is judged as a failure, in much the same way as the political corruption of the church; the persecution of Jews, heretics, or witches; or the acceptance of slavery has been judged as a failure. This does not mean that this "bad" history is suppressed or forgotten. This also would be an ideological history that tries to "save" the moral and doctrinal reputation of the church by forgetting what we no longer like. We need to remember this history, but as examples of our fallibility not as norms of truth.

The equality of women, as one of the touchstones for understanding our faithfulness to the vision, is now set forth as one of the norms for criticizing the tradition and discovering its best expressions. This will create a radical reappraisal of Jewish or Christian traditions, since much that has been regarded as marginal, and even heretical, must now be seen as efforts to hold on to an authentic tradition of women's equality. Much of the tradition that has been regarded as "mainstream" must be seen as deficient in this regard. We underestimate the radical intent of women's studies in religion if we do not recognize that it aims at nothing less than this kind of radical reconstruction of the normative tradition.

TRANSLATION OF WOMEN'S STUDIES IN RELIGION INTO EDUCATIONAL PRAXIS

Obviously, women cannot impact an educational system until they first secure their own access to it. It has taken approximately 125 years for women to open the doors of most schools of theological education to them and then to become represented in it in sufficient numbers so that their concerns begin to be recognized. Women began to enter theological schools of the Congregational tradition beginning with Oberlin in the 1840s and Methodist institutions in the

1870s. Only in the 1970s have some Roman Catholic and Jewish seminaries been open to women. Moreover, even liberal Protestant institutions did not experience any "critical mass" of female students until the 1970s.

Usually, access to theological education precedes winning the right to ordination. Winning the educational credentials for ordination then becomes a powerful wedge to winning the right of ordination itself. It is for that reason that there may be efforts to close Roman Catholic seminaries, at least those directly related to Rome, to women. Rumor has it (as of this writing) that a decree has been written but not yet promulgated in Rome forbidding women to attend pontificatical seminaries (which would include all Jesuit seminaries but not most diocesan and order seminaries). Women's tenure in professional schools of theology cannot be regarded as secure until they win the right to ordination. Only then can they develop a larger number of women students and attain the moral and organizational "clout" to begin to make demands for changes in the content of the curriculum.

Generally, demands for feminist studies begin with the organization of a caucus of women theological students. They then begin to demand women's studies in the curriculum and women faculty who can teach such courses. In many seminaries, particularly in U.S. liberal Protestant institutions, there has been some response to these demands. Some women faculty have been hired and some women's studies incorporated into the curriculum. It is at this point that we can recognize several stages of resistance to the implied challenge to the tradition.

One standard strategy of male faculty is to seek and retain one or two women on the faculty but to give preference to women who are "traditional scholars," not feminists. This is fairly easy to do by the established rules of the guild while appearing to be "objective." Feminist studies is nontraditional. It forces one to use nontraditional methods and sources and to be something of a generalist. Its content is still in flux and experimentation. Rare is the person who can fulfill the expectations of both traditional scholarship and feminist scholarship equally well. So it is easy to attack such persons as "unscholarly" and to fail to tenure them in preference to those women who prefer to be "one of the boys." As of this writing there is an alarming erosion of feminist faculty talent in theological education through precisely this method. This has forced feminist scholars in theological education to band together in a new national organization, Feminist Theology and Ministry, to defend the employment of feminists in existing institutions of theological education.

Efforts are also underway to create new, alternative settings for women's studies in religion. For example, groups in the Boston-Washington corridor and in Chicago (largely, but not exclusively, Roman Catholic) are seriously considering the development of autonomous feminist theology schools for women, since the existing (especially Roman Catholic) institutions have proved so unfavorable to their interests.

In some other settings a decade-long struggle for women's studies in religion is beginning to bear fruit. For example, at the Harvard Divinity School, bastion of "traditional" education, a pilot program of graduate assistants in women's studies in various fields has continued for some eight years, for much of this time under constant threat of liquidation. However, a study of the program located one of its chief flaws in the lack of prestige and respect given to the women's studies teachers by the tenured faculty. As a result, a new level of funding is being developed to allow this program to be continued and eventually to be converted into a permanent research center for women in religion, with five full-time junior and senior faculty appointments. It remains to be seen whether this expanded "prestige" will not result in some of the same pressure to prefer traditional over feminist scholars.

In the development of feminist studies in the curriculum, most institutions move through several stages. The first stage is a grudging allowance of a generalist course on women's studies in religion that is taught outside the structure of the curriculum and usually by a person marginal to the faculty. The male faculty tend to feel little respect for the content of the course (about which they generally know nothing) or its instructor and no commitment to its continuance as a regular part of the curriculum.

The second stage is when faculty begin to acquire women in one or more regular fields who are both respected as scholars and are prepared to do women's studies. Women's studies courses can then be initiated that are located in the various regular disciplines of the curriculum, such as biblical studies, church history, theology, ethics, pastoral psychology, preaching and liturgy, or church administration. However, these courses are taught as occasional electives. They attract only feminist students, mostly females and a few males. The rest of the student body is not influenced by them. Most of the faculty ignore them. The new material in them does not impact the foundational curriculum. In other words, women's studies in religion goes on as a marginal and duplicate curriculum. There is now a course in "systematic theology" and a second one on "feminist" theology. The foundational courses continue as before. Therefore, implicitly, they claim the patriarchal bias in theology as the "real" or "true" theology.

The third stage would come when feminist studies begins to impact the foundational curriculum itself. Here, we might detect two more stages. The third stage would be when foundational curriculum continues as usual, except for an occasional "ladies day" when women's concerns are discussed. Then, for example, one would teach twelve weeks of traditional male church history and one week in which "great women" are considered. The fourth and optimum situation would be reached when feminist critique really penetrates the whole foundational curriculum and transforms the way in which all topics are considered. Thus it becomes impossible to deal with any topic of theological studies without being aware of sexist and nonsexist options in the tradition and bringing that out as an integral part of one's hermeneutic. Thus, for example, one would understand St. Paul as a man whose theology is caught up in an ambivalent struggle between various alternatives: between an exclusivist and a universal faith, between a historical and an eschatological faith, and between a patriarchal and an integrative faith. The way he handled the third ambiguity, moreover, conditioned fundamentally the way he handled the first two ambiguities. Thus one cannot understand Paul as a whole without incorporating the question of sexism into the context of his theology.

Generally, we can state that most seminaries that have dealt with women's studies at all are somewhere between stage one and stage two or usually at stage one. A few have done an occasional "ladies day" in the foundational curriculum. A few have even begun to imagine what it would mean to reach the optimum incorporation of feminism into the foundational curriculum as a normal and normative part of the interpretive context of the whole. Moreover, women's studies in religion itself has not yet matured to the point where it is able to offer a comprehensive reconstruction of methodology and tradition in various fields. For example, a genuine feminist reconstruction of systematic theology is yet to be written.

Even further down the road is the "retraining" of male faculty who are able to take such work into account. There are exceptions. Occasionally, one finds that prodigy, a male professor who early recognized the value of the feminist critique and has been able, easily and gracefully, to incorporate it into his teaching with a minimum of defensiveness or breast beating. In general, however, women's studies in theological education is still marginal and vulnerable. The conservative drift of the seminaries means that increasing numbers of women students themselves are nonfeminist or antifeminist. Cadres of explicitly hostile white male students are emerging. Constant struggle is necessary to maintain momentum or even to prevent slipping back. The recent publication of the book *Your Daughters Shall Prophecy* (Pilgrim Press, 1980) reflects on this ten-year struggle for feminist theological education in several major educational settings.

ALTERNATIVE VIEWS OF FEMINISM AND RELIGIOUS STUDIES

Finally, feminists in religion are by no means united in what they understand to be the optimum feminist reconstruction of religion. Moreover, religion is not simply an academic discipline; it is an integral part of popular culture. Concern with it has to do with *modus vivendi* of large numbers of people in many walks of life. It shapes mass institutions, the church and the synagogue, as well as alternative religious communities that emerge to fill people's need for life symbols. Thus the interest in feminism and religion has an urgency, as well as a rancor, that is different from academic disciplines.

There are several different lines that are emerging both in academics and across the religious institutions and movements of popular culture today. One group, that could be identified as evangelical feminists, believe that the message of Scripture is fundamentally egalitarian. Scripture, especially the New Testament, proposes a new ideal of "mutual submission" of men and women to each other. This has been misread as the subjugation of women by the theological tradition. These feminists would hope to clean up the sexism of Scripture by better exegesis. It would be incorrect to interpret these evangelical feminists as always limited by a precritical method of scriptural interpretation. Their limitations are often more pastoral than personal. They are concerned to address a certain constituency, the members of the evangelical churches from which they come, with the legitimacy of an egalitarian understanding of biblical faith. They sometimes limit themselves to this kind of exegesis because they know it is the only way to reach this constituency.

A second view, which I would call the "liberationist" position, takes a more critical view of Scripture. People with this view believe there is a conflict between the prophetic, iconoclastic message of the prophetic tradition, with its attack on oppressive and self-serving religion, and the failure to apply this message to subjugated minorities in the patriarchal family, especially the women and slaves. The vision of redemption of the biblical tradition transcends the inadequacies of past consciousness. It goes ahead of us, pointing toward a new and yet unrealized future of liberation whose dimensions are continually expanding as we become more sensitive to injustices that were overlooked in past cultures. Liberationists would use the prophetic tradition as the norm to critique the sexism of the religious tradition. Biblical sexism is not denied, but it loses its authority. It must be denounced as a failure to measure up to the full vision of human liberation of the prophetic and gospel messages.

A third group, we mentioned earlier, feel that women waste their time salvaging positive elements of these religious traditions. They take the spokesmen of patriarchal religion at their word when they say that Christ and God are literally and essentially male and conclude that these religions have existed for no other purpose except to sanctify male domination. Women should quit the church and the synagogue and move to the feminist coven to celebrate the sacrality of women through recovery of the religion of the goddess.

Although I myself am most sympathetic to the second view, I would regard all of these positions as having elements of truth. All respond to real needs of different constituencies of women (and some men). It is unlikely that any of these views will predominate, but all will work as parallel trends in the ensuing decades to reshape the face of religion.

The evangelical feminists address themselves to an important group in American religion who frequently use Scripture to reinforce traditional patriarchal family models. Evangelical feminists wish to lift up neglected traditions and to give biblicist Christians a basis for addressing the question of equality. They will probably get the liberal wing of these churches to modify their language and exegesis. The first creation story of woman's and man's equal creation in the image of God will be stressed, rather than the second creation story of Eve from Adam's rib. Galatians 3, 28, will be stressed in Paul rather than Ephesians

5, and so forth. They might get some denominations to use inclusive language for the community and maybe even for God.

The liberationist wing would want the churches to take a much more active and prophetic role in critiquing the sexism of society not only on issues such as abortion rights, gay rights, and the equal rights amendment but also on the links between sexism and economic injustice. They would press churches with a social gospel tradition into new questions about the adequacy of a patriarchal, capitalist, and consumerist economy to promote a viable human future.

The impact of the separatist goddess religions is more difficult to predict. Traditional Jews and Christians would view these movements as "paganism," if not "satanism." The goddess movements are likely to respond in an equally defensive way and to direct their feelings against feminists who are still working within churches and synagogues. A lot depends on whether some mediating ground can be developed. On the one side, there would have to be a conscious rejection of the religious exclusivism of the Jewish and Christian traditions and a recognition of the appropriateness of experiencing the divine through female symbols and body images. The goddess worshippers, in turn, might have to grow out of some of their defensiveness toward their Jewish and Christian sisters that results in a kind of reversed exclusivism.

This is not to be construed as a call for such feminists to become (or return) to Judaism or Christianity but rather a growth toward that kind of maturity that can recognize the legitimacy of religious quests in several kinds of contexts. As long as goddess feminists can only affirm their way by a reversed exclusivism and denial of the possibility of liberating elements in the biblical tradition, they are still tied to the same exclusivist patterns of thought in a negative form.

A creative dialogue between these two views could be very significant. Countercultural feminist spirituality could make important contributions to the enlargement of our religious symbols and experiences. We might be able to experience God gestating the world in Her womb rather than just "making it" through a divine phallic fiat. We would rediscover the rhythms that tie us biologically with earth, fire, air, and water that have been so neglected in our antinatural spiritualities. We would explore the sacralities of the repressed parts of our psyches and our environmental experiences. Many worlds that have been negated by patriarchal religion might be reclaimed for the enlargement of our common life.

It is not clear what all this might mean. It might well be the beginning of a new religion as momentous in its break with the past as Christianity was with the religions of the Semites and the Greeks. But if it is truly to enlarge our present options, it must also integrate the best of the insights that we have developed through Judaism and Christianity, as these religions integrated some (not all) of the best insights of the Near Eastern and Greco-Roman worlds. What is clear is this: the patriarchal repression of women and women's experience has been so massive and prevalent that to begin to take women seriously will involve a profound and radical transformation of our religions.

SELECTED BIBLIOGRAPHY

Theological History

Daly, Mary. *The Church and the Second Sex*. New York: Harper, 1968.
Ruether, Rosemary. *Religion and Sexism: Images of Women in Jewish and Christian Traditions*. New York: Simon and Schuster, 1974.
Ruether, Rosemary, and Eleanor McLaughlin. *Women of Spirit: Female Leadership in the Jewish and Christian Traditions*. New York: Simon and Schuster, 1979.
Tavard, George. *Women in the Christian Tradition*. Notre Dame, Ind.: Notre Dame University Press, 1973.

Bible and History of Christianity

Baer, Richard. *Philo's Use of the Categories of Male and Female*. Leiden: Brill, 1972.
Bainton, Roland. *Women of the Reformation in France and England*. Minneapolis: Augsburg, 1973.
———. *Women of the Reformation in Germany and Italy*. Minneapolis: Augsburg, 1971.
———. *Women of the Reformation from Spain to Scandinavia*. Minneapolis: Augsburg, 1977.
Børresen, Kari. *Subordination et equivalence: Nature et role de la femme d'apres Augustin et Thomas Aquin*. Oslo: Universitetsforlaget, 1968; English trans., Washington, D.C.: University Press of America, 1981.
Clark, Elizabeth. *Jerome, Chrysostum, and Friends: Essays and Translations*. Lewiston, N.Y.: Edwin Mellen Press, 1979.
Davies, Steven. *The Revolt of Widows*. Carbondale, Ill.: Southern Illinois University Press, 1980.
Ehrenreich, Barbara, and Deidre English. *Witches, Midwives, and Nurses*. Westbury, N.Y.: Feminist Press, 1973.
Humex, Jean McMahon. *Gifts of Power: The Writings of Rebecca Jackson, Black Visionary, Shaker Eldress*. Amherst: University of Massachusetts Press, 1981.
Irwin, Joyce L. *Womanhood in Radical Protestantism, 1525–1675*. Lewiston, N.Y.: Edwin Mellen Press, 1979.
James, Janet Wilson. *Women in American Religion*. Philadelphia: University of Pennsylvania Press, 1980.
Kastner, Patricia Wilson, et al., eds. *A Lost Tradition: Women Writers of the Early Church*. Washington, D.C.: University Press of America, 1981.
Keller, Rosemary, and Hilah Thomas. *Women in New Worlds: Historical Perspectives on the Wesleyan Tradition*. Nashville: Abingdon, 1981.
Ochshorn, Judith. *The Female Experience and the Nature of the Divine*. Bloomington: Indiana University Press, 1981.
Orwell, John H. *And Sarah Laughed: The Status of Women in the Old Testament*. Philadelphia: Westminster Press, 1977.
Patai, Raphael. *The Hebrew Goddess*. New York: Ktav, 1967.

Ruether, Rosemary, and Rosemary Keller. *Women and Religion in America; The 19th Century: A Documentary History*. New York: Harper and Row, 1981.

Ruether, Rosemary, and Rosemary Keller. *Women in New Worlds: Historical Perspectives on the Wesleyan Tradition*. Nashville: Abingdon, 1981.

Stendahl, Krister. *The Bible and the Role of Women*. Philadelphia: Fortress Press, 1966.

Swidler, Leonard. *Biblical Affirmations of Women*. Philadelphia: Westminster Press, 1979.

Trible, Phylis. *God and the Rhetoric of Sexuality*. Philadelphia: Fortress Press, 1978.

Theological Reconstruction

Budapest, Z. *The Holy Book of Women's Mysteries*. Susan B. Anthony Coven No. 1, Los Angeles, 1979, 1980, Bks. I and II.

Collins, Shiela. *A Different Heaven and Earth*. Valley Forge, Pa.: Judson Press, 1974.

Daly, Mary. *Beyond God the Father*. Boston: Beacon, 1973.

————. *Gynecology: The Metaethics of Radical Feminism*. Boston: Beacon, 1979.

Plaskow, Judith. *Sex, Sin, and Grace: Women's Experience and the Theologies of Reinhold Niebuhr and Paul Tillich*. Washington, D.C.: University Press of America, 1980.

Plaskow, Judith, and Carol Christ. *Womanspirit Rising: A Feminist Reader in Religion*. New York: Harper and Row, 1979.

Ruether, Rosemary. *New Woman/New Earth: Sexist Ideologies and Human Liberation*. New York: Seabury Press, 1975.

Russell, Letty. *Human Liberation in a Feminist Perspective*. Philadelphia: Westminster Press, 1974.

Sconzoni, Leitha, and Nancy Hardesty. *All We're Meant to Be: A Biblical Liberation*. Waco, Tex.: Word Press, 1974.

Starhawk. *The Spiral Dance*. New York: Harper, 1979.

Women in the Church and Ministry

Gardiner, Anne Marie. *Women and the Catholic Priesthood: Proceedings from the Detroit Conference*. New York: Paulist Press, 1976.

Hewitt, Emily, and Suzanne Hiatt. *Women Priests, Yes or No?* New York: Seabury Press, 1973.

Heyward, Carter. *A Priest Forever: The Formation of a Woman and the Priest*. New York: Harper and Row, 1976.

Ohanneson, Joan. *Woman: Survivor in the Church*. Minneapolis: Winston Press, 1980.

Papa, Mary Bader. *Christian Feminism: Completing the Subtotal Woman*. Chicago: Fides/Claretian, 1981.

5

Beyond Liberation: Overcoming Gender Mythology from a Taoist Perspective

SANDRA A. WAWRYTKO

Being a feminist in the 1980s is like being an abolitionist was in the 1860s—it is a necessity dictated by prevailing social and political conditions.[1] At the same time, as we pursue this path, we must cherish the hope that the unfortunate and burdensome necessity will soon pass into well-deserved oblivion. It is our moral task to expedite that passage.

As a Taoist might put it, we only need to talk about feminism because it is not an existing condition—if it prevailed throughout society there would be no need to designate it with a special term.[2] We rarely hear anyone described as an abolitionist, since there are no advocates of slavery with whom to contrast such a person. By the same token, we have social activists because so many people are inactive; ecologists because there are polluters; and futurists because there are reactionaries.

Consider the contributions that *could* be made by our most talented and well-educated women if they were not compelled to devote their time to arguing for feminism. What scientific discoveries are waiting to be made, what novels waiting to be written, what philosophical theories waiting to be propounded, if only they were not placed under the annoying burden of justifying their very existence within their respective professional communities? What urgent issues of global proportion could we be addressing here were it not for the fact that the denial of equal rights to women constitutes the most pervasive of all global problems?[3]

My remarks grow out of my concern with a central question within the area of feminism, namely, why has feminism become an "f word"?[4] In observing the interactions of futurists, a corollary to this question has occurred to me—why are discussions among activists often less satisfying than one might expect? The two questions are linked by the common thread of attitude and, more precisely, by an attitudinal defect, manifesting itself in negativism, held in common by "liberated" individuals. It is an attitude, I will argue, that is unavoidable at a certain stage of evolution, yet ultimately transitional for feminists and futurists alike.

The original title of my remarks, "Women in Transition: Beyond Liberation," corresponds to the title of a book currently being completed with a colleague, in the area of social sciences, that examines the impact and prospects of the feminist movement during the past twenty years. However, the truncation of the explicit reference to women is most useful, for it allows me to direct my remarks on liberation toward human beings in general, rather than to 51 percent of the species. Indeed, our topic is one of pressing importance for all human beings, requiring concerted action by all for its resolution. We must begin with an assessment of the realistic expectations *for* a global future and the concrete ways in which we as individuals may be able to enhance those expectations. It behooves us, then, also to explore the ways in which we may unwittingly be hindering ourselves from accomplishing this task, ways in which we unknowingly become part of the problem rather than part of the solution.

In futurist forums, some feminists are apt to propose that it is not a child who shall lead the way into a new age of peace and global harmony, but rather that it is women as a group who shall take the lead.[5] The assumption underlying this confident proposal is that women as a group are possessed of the traits that are a *sine qua non* for human survival in the next century and beyond, possessed, that is, of a more "sane" psychology. Among the traits so recognized as inherent to the female psyche are nurturing others in human relationships and a sense of primal connectedness with reality, leading to an appreciation for and harmonization with the concrete world. Women, we are told, are naturally closer to Nature, as "proven" by references to the maternal character of the Earth (Gaia, K'un, etc.) and thus are in tune with Nature's cycles and its (her) procreative energy. Their instinctual/intuitive, holistic awareness has no need for the artificial intermediary of intellect.

By contrast, the interpretation continues, men must be relegated to the role of followers in the futurist scenario, being naturally hindered by their natural tendencies. The masculine "weapons" of rationality, analysis, differentiation, and so on are in fact assigned responsibility for having precipitated the present global crisis. These tendencies are further manifested in displays of aggressive behavior toward others, escapist flights into empty intellectual ideals, and an unquenchable desire for control and conquest. The environmental insensitivity of men even has been equated with misogyny in phrases such as "the rape of Nature." Having failed in their stewardship role, men now must stand aside for more competent hearts (as opposed to minds) to prevail.

Like most well-intentioned generalizations, the above pronouncements are simultaneously true and false. They are true in that women in general are more likely to display these culturally devalued survival values (referring here to Western culture), due in large part to the effects and incessant reinforcement of social conditioning. However, the generalizations are false in that they can be construed as excluding men from the possibility of embracing or even displaying these same values. In the latter case, the error gives rise to female chauvinism. Just as Plato (if taken at face value) sought an ideal state in which philosophers assume the leadership role, this view is prone to assert that global conflict can end if (and only if) mothers become heads of state. Although counterexamples of aggressive women and nurturing men abound, female chauvinists dismiss them as trivial and irrelevant. On the side of women, Margaret Thatcher, Indira Gandhi, and Golda Meir—heads of state who are/were mothers but certainly are not known for their maternal compassion—immediately come to mind. As for men, Albert Einstein seems the very antithesis of macho mannerisms, as are Pope John Paul XXIII and the Dalai Lama.

So we see that sexist stereotypes do not die easily but simply are selectively recast to support the needs of new ideologies. Taken to an extreme, the focus on female-male differences, known in France as "l'écriture féminine," eventuates in a feminist separatist movement founded upon lesbianism and dedicated to the total exclusion of men.[6] This oversimplified feminist mythologizing is not only erroneous but, in view of the dire straits we all face as human beings, is also potentially suicidal. Feminists themselves recognize the problem. Thus Simone de Beauvoir observed:

there are a certain number of women who exalt menstruation, maternity, etc., and who believe that one can find a basis there for a different sort of writing. As for myself, I am absolutely against all this since it means falling once more into the masculine trap of wishing to enclose ourselves in our differences; neither do I believe that we should despise or ignore them. . . . there is no reason at all to fall into some wild narcissism, and build, on the basis of these givens, a system which would be the culture and the life of women. . . . one should not make this body the center of the universe.[7]

I broach this somewhat controversial topic not to make it the central focus of my remarks but rather that it may serve as a point of entry into values that are assumed to be required for "sanity" in these times of global threats on many fronts. Two points are presented here as stimuli for further reflection by those concerned about liberation in the fullest sense. The first has to do with what I believe ought to be the nature of the feminist contribution to the global future. It stands in contrast to the wrong-headed approach noted above, which has been bandied about in at least some feminist circles and which, not infrequently, is mistaken by others as *the* feminist position. This mistaken approach, I will argue, furthers neither feminism nor the prospects for a sane future. Furthermore, it stems from a basic misunderstanding of the crucial feminist issue of liberation. The result is a premature stagnation along the liberation path.

Second, I would like to suggest ways in which feminism may indeed help us to construct—or resurrect—the kind of modes of being, based on a sane value system, that will provide for the attitudinal and behavioral changes needed to insure the future of humankind. The "feminine" perspective, as embodied in the Yin philosophy of Chinese Taoism, is offered as a potential source of sanity, science, and social responsibility. Simply put, I offer here a feminine critique of feminism, in turn engendering a critique of critical methodology itself. The relevance of such a critique to *all* those who seek to transform the world and themselves, whether feminists or futurists, constitutes the main intention of my remarks.

LIBERATION

Let us begin with an analysis of liberation, of what it means to go *beyond* liberation, and *why* it is necessary to so transcend. The question arises—why do so many "liberated" people act in such unliberated, even counterrevolutionary, ways? The answer lies in the fact that they fail to comprehend a central fact of liberation, namely, that one must liberate oneself from a liberation mentality. Only then can one fully implement all available resources for the end of global survival. The concept of liberation becomes subject to a species of reductionism when viewed in an adversarial context. It then implies something or someone from which one must be liberated, something or someone who is holding one back and thus must be opposed.

The problem inherent in this conception of liberation is that as long as we remain in such a stance we have not really liberated ourselves at all, merely changed the manifestation of our oppression. As long as the oppressor continues to dominate our thoughts and actions, whether as master or as opponent, we can be said to suffer from oppression. The dynamic of oppression remains intact; only its expression is changed. Complete liberation requires us to transcend the very cause of our enthrallment. It is "radical" liberation in that it requires us to get to the root of our lack of independent action and break the lingering tie that sets in motion the fixation on that root. In so doing, we leave our unliberated selves behind completely, having simultaneously left liberation itself behind.

In sum, liberation is not a fact or a possession but a *process* of attitudinal transformation, consummated at the point at which one has forgotten that from which one had to be liberated in the first place. A most apt and instructive metaphor for this process has been provided for us by the philosopher Friedrich Nietzsche, in the crowning expression of his thought, *Also Sprach Zarathustra*. Nietzsche's misogynist reputation notwithstanding, he has much to share with feminists and was himself much influenced by the budding feminist movement of his time.[8] Let us avail ourselves of his wisdom to delve more deeply into this process.

Woven within the rich tapestry of Nietzsche's masterwork (and positioned immediately after the prologue) is the evocative description of "the three metamorphoses." With his usual genius for imagery, Nietzsche chose the camel to epitomize the beginning stage of the unliberated being and, simultaneously, entry into the liberation process. The choice of the camel signals that what we have here is an example not of willing submission but rather the embodiment of unwilling submission and smoldering resentment born of impotence. Consider how well the camel communicates this complex attitude in its characteristic behavior, its episodes of unprovoked spitting and its plaintive bellowing. Thus although the camel is by definition a beast of burden, it is also abidingly obnoxious as it fulfills that role.

The psychology of the camel is a psychology of self-rationalization. Hence women are wont to interpret their servile role as one of hidden strength, just as Nietzsche's camel asks itself: "What is the heaviest thing, . . . that I may take it upon myself and rejoice in my strength." In response, the camel seeks burdens such as self-debasement, outward folly, silent suffering, and love toward those who despise one.[9] Yet paradoxically, the camel both desires anonymity (the better to revel in its self-suppressed glory) and looks condescendingly upon those who make it possible to remain anonymous. It is in this smug assurance of surreptitious superiority that there arises the poison of resentment, aimed at those unable to penetrate its secret.

The inner contortions of the camel's disposition are sadly written in the ugliness of its outer visage. One would be hard pressed to find a more repulsive creature on the face of the earth. We may perceive a warning here regarding the aftereffects of repression/suppression; the lack of decisive action toward liberation results in an inward-turning rancor that breeds both psychological and physical corruption. Oppressed people who perceive themselves as victims, who succumb to the inevitability of their victimization, bear a similar expression.

Note also the parallels found in those we seek to enlighten about global problems—how like a camel they are when, suffering under the psychological burden of "future shock," they vent their resentment against the bearers of bad tidings.[10] How prone they are to bellow when confronted with the unpleasant facts of contemporary existence, and how difficult it is to rouse them to action. We can all appreciate how great is the risk of being spat upon by the herd when we broach the subject of global responsibility. In the camel, then, denial, steeped in acrimonious resentment, is raised to a lifelong vocation. By far the majority of people belong to this group.

Let us not, however, underestimate the value of the camel stage for individual development toward liberation. It is a most useful experience for those who know how eventually to transcend it, taking with them the valuable lessons learned. The camel is "feminine" in the sense in which women have been viewed as inferior creatures suited to bear the burdens of society by the dominant masculine forces. At the same time, women's subordinate role has the twofold effect of excluding them from the social arena, the breeding ground for masculine vices, and promoting the feminine virtues appropriate to the oppressed. Thus Simone de Beauvoir declared: "one could wish for men to share some of these feminine qualities which result from her [woman's] oppression, such as patience; empathy; irony; the somewhat ironic distance from things; the rejection of exactly those masculine vales, such as medals, roles—in short, all this type of male tinware."[11]

Most importantly for the process of liberation, it is neither necessary nor proper to remain oppressed. Some camels *are* roused to action and so become transformed. Those who have reached the outer limits of resentment—who have carried their burdens into the loneliest desert, as Nietzsche put it—progress to the second stage, namely revolt. Nietzsche's choice for the image of revolt is once again impeccable, as he offers us the utter role reversal of the lion, self-acclaimed king of the jungle, the lion who transforms resentment into acts of revenge to become a destroyer and nay-sayer. With a determined roar the lion breaks the chains of oppression and defies the oppressor. Understandably, after the hard period of self-abnegating oppression as a camel, underlying the lion's violent negations is the need for recognition as an independent self.[12] The "sacred No" is indispensable—"to create itself freedom for new creation—that the might of the lion can do."[13]

Within the context of academia, there are many lions in our midst—and there is indeed good reason for the reference to a lion group as a "pride." This should not surprise us, since graduate schools are dedicated to training an elite of lion mentalities. The professional context demands aggressive, even merciless, critical analysis directed against one's opponents. Any variance from this standard of aggression is viewed with disapproval, if not outright rejection. Society does its best to uphold these standards of behavior on a broader scale.

Nonetheless, the lion's rebellion does not constitute an independent action, merely a *re*action against the past. Consider the etymology of the terms *rebellion* and *revolution,* respectively, to again (*re*) make war (*bellum*) and to roll or turn (*volvere*) back (*re*). So it is that old revolutionaries never die; they merely live the revolution over and over, mistaking that mere means as an end in itself. Consider, for example, the feminist lioness Mary Daly and the aggressive tones of her declarations (emphases mine):

I have advocated committing the *crime* of *Methodicide,* since the Methodolatry of patriarchal disciplines *kills* creative thought. . . . Gynocentric Method requires the *murder* of misogynistic methods.[14]

As a creative crystallization of the movement beyond the State of Patriarchal Paralysis, this book is an act of *Dispossession*; and hence in a sense beyond the limitations of the label *anti-male,* it is *Absolutely Anti-androcrat, A-mazingly Anti-male, Furiously and Finally Female.*[15]

Naturally, lions themselves have a different perception of the situation. They see themselves as part of a conceptual demolition team, clearing the path for new progress—like Shiva the Destroyer who serves as the necessary precursor to the re-creation of the world through Brahmā. But destruction can become addictive, misleading one to forget its purely transitional function. Accordingly, we see in the revolutions of the past that their leaders often did not know when to stop—whether it was Robespierre, who turned the French Revolution's glorification of the Goddess of Reason into a Reign of Terror, or Mao Ze-dung, who sought an untimely extension of upheaval in the disastrous Cultural Revolution. Indeed, like all entrenched lions, they succumbed to the myth of the demythologizers. Not a few feminists and futurists suffer under the same misconception, such that they are content to defy the powers that be and to paint gloomy scenarios, without ever moving on to concrete solutions.

It is in this sense that the lion continues to suffer from what Nietzsche saw as a kind of "chain fever"—counterproductive fixation on chains by actually shuffling under their weight or by the psychological obsession to escape them.[16] This fever manifests itself in being chained from within as well as from without. Those afflicted never arrive at the actual goal of liberation itself, namely, to rise above the conditions of oppression, but stagnate on the path. Mired in the negativity of revolt, they fail to transcend beyond. Consequently, although the lion's revolt is a necessary stage in the liberation process, it is not sufficient for liberation in the fullest sense.

Liberation from the inherent pitfalls of liberation consciousness comes only in the third and final stage. After we overcome external oppressions we must move on to overcome the greatest of all oppressions, self-oppression. As Zarathustra tells us "life itself told me this secret: 'Behold,' it said, 'I am that *which must overcome itself again and again.*'" So it is that self-overcoming, or self-transcendence, must constitute the final stage of liberation, which in fact takes us beyond liberation.[17]

Nietzsche signaled the preeminence of the third and final move by the fact that here and only here we cross over from the bestial to the human realm proper, in the figure of the child. The camel is unable to create; the lion, caught up in an orgy of destruction, is unwilling. But for the child, creativity is simply a natural expression of being, further reinforced by the ability to leave behind the past. This is what Nietzsche called saying 'yes' to life, accepting the facts of existence with a newborn spirit of exuberance, emerging out of the dialectical trials of the camel and the lion stages: "innocence and forgetfulness, a new beginning, a sport, a self-propelling wheel, a first motion, a sacred Yes."[18]

It should be noted that individuals move among these three stages during the course of their lives. This follows from Nietzsche's own vision of the Eternal Recurrence in life, the cyclical flow of life events. One should not complacently assume that having attained the child stage one will remain there irrevocably. Rather, under certain conditions one is prone to slip back into the lion's aggression or even fall back further to the camel's resentment. The best that one can do is to minimize such relapses and to be aware of when they are occurring. This requires continual consciousness raising about the state of one's own liberation consciousness.

It is just such a consciousness, aimed ultimately at continually renewing the child's-eye-view in one's life, which I would like to recommend as a model for securing sanity and responsibility in global proportions. Although Nietzsche's philosophy has not infrequently been identified with nihilism, his is merely a transitional nihilism. As a careful reading of The Birth of Tragedy reveals, he sought a harmonizing synthesis of reason (the camel) and passion (the lion). It is this harmony that I wish to pursue here.

TOWARD A SANE SYSTEM OF VALUES

Having seen how the process of liberation must be brought full circle as a series of attitudinal and behavioral changes, we can consider the value system that this process ultimately generates. The liberated child neither clings to nor repudiates its roots in the camel and the lion. Similarly, it may be said that a sane system of values for the future should neither cling to nor repudiate the past but rather selectively incorporate what is useful and necessary. Viewed in this context, debates about whether the West should or should not turn Eastward for its values can be seen to involve a faulty dualism, based upon a simplistic either/or presupposition. What we need now are not Eastern values or Western values but human values.

Relating this value search to feminism, we should recall that the values of nurturing, connectedness with reality, and so on have most frequently been associated with women as a group in most cultures of the world throughout history. In recognition of this association with women, let us refer to them as "feminine" values. They then can be distinguished from the "masculine" values that have heretofore prevailed in the Western world and that have brought us to this devoutly to be avoided precipice. The effect of this alternative set of designations is to remove femaleness and maleness per se from the issue at hand, thereby leaving open the possibility that either set of values may be adopted by a human being *qua* human as the appropriate heritage of the species. Once these survival tools are viewed as equally accessible to men and women, we will be better able to sustain the hope that solutions to our crises will be forthcoming.

In viewing the feminine values as the common heritage of all human beings, we may adopt Margaret Mead's explanation for social diversity.[19] Mead theorized that in the development of human societies a kind of division of values came about paralleling the division of labor. In other words, just as the prospects for group survival were enhanced by labor specialization, distinct advantages accrued from having certain groups assigned as caretakers of certain values. Gender differences being the most obvious means of group identification, these differences were widely employed as a basis for the desired division (although some societies made distinctions on the basis of age, race, etc.).[20] Although initially, we may speculate that both sets of values were equally recognized as essential for social development, eventually, a hierarchy emerged, with the result that the masculine values were viewed as superior and the feminine as inferior. At this point women began to suffer from "guilt by association" with feminine values, their own degradation paralleling the course of the degradation of feminine values. Before equality can be forthcoming, feminism must address this issue and unravel the unfortunate compounding of gender and values.

The alternative is to destroy the entire category of feminine values by having all human beings espouse the masculine set of values. Two significant objections exist to this Procrustean approach, as seen from the social and the individual viewpoints. First, society as a whole would suffer from being cut off from the human heritage of values represented by the feminine storehouse. The increasing importance of these values for global survival will be argued for below. Furthermore, from the standpoint of the individual, since no human being is exclusively feminine or masculine in value orientation, it is unfeasible to assume that each of us can summarily cut ourselves off from our feminine tendencies. To do so would be to compromise the wholeness of our humanity, in the same way that society as a whole would be compromised.

Indeed, feminine values and modes of being may serve as a corrective to, although not a substitute for, masculine values. Their function is to reestablish a balance of sanity and to reintroduce the creative tension that often has been recommended.[21] As a model we may cite the *T'ai Chi* or Great Ultimate of Chinese philosophy. In this cosmic symbol Yin (the feminine) and Yang (the masculine) are in dynamic interrelationship or, more precisely, interpenetration, each encompassed by, and encompassing, the other in an ongoing process of interchange.[22]

As an example of a feminine value system from which we may draw our inspiration, consider Chinese Taoism, which orients itself around Yin. The Taoists represent perhaps the first self-conscious ecologists in human history. The advice that is offered in the *Tao Te Ching* is ecologically sound, as well as conducive to global responsibility. Thus Chapter 29 observes:

> The world is a sacred vessel,
> It may not be mishandled.
> Whoever mishandles it will ruin it.
> Whoever covets it will lose it.[23]

How different from a mechanistic (masculine) view of the world! And how different would be the results of adopting this world view—from spaceship earth to sacred vessel!

There are three basic modes of being, expressive of underlying values, that I take to be central to a feminine perspective.[24] Each of them is well evidenced within Taoism, and each poses an appropriate counterpoint to and complement for masculine values. The three feminine modes of being may be described briefly as follows:

1. *Appreciation for Materiality*—based on an identification with Nature, as opposed to masculine denigration of the material in preference for the intellectual or spiritual

2. *Receptivity*—manifested as flexibility and tolerance, but often mistaken for mere passivity from the standpoint of masculine aggression

3. *All-is-oneness*—a microcosmic-macrocosmic perception of the world, in contrast to masculine insistence on individuality and discreteness.

Furthermore, through these modes of being we may approach sanity, (feminine) science, and global responsibility, respectively, as I will endeavor to demonstrate by means of the Yin philosophy of Taoism.

Concerning sanity, Taoist wisdom, it is said, is laughed at by the lowest type of humanity (the unenlightened mass of camels perhaps?). The middling type of person (lions?) listen but only half-heartedly. It is the wisest alone who diligently put this wisdom into practice (*Tao Te Ching*, 41). So it is with the Taoist view of sanity, which appears insane to those who are themselves unstable:

> I remain detached,
> Like an infant who has yet to smile,
> Listless, like one with nowhere to return.
> The worldlings have more than enough,
> While I alone look as if left out,
> Oh, mine is a fool's mind,
> So muddled and ignorant!
> The vulgar are pompous and flashy,
> I alone look dull and dense.
> The vulgar are clever and showy,
> I alone am nebulous and in the dark—
> Tranquil as the sea,
> Gliding, as if without purpose!
> The worldlings all have a purpose
> While I alone appear stubborn and uncouth;
> I alone differ from the others,
> and value the suckling Mother (*shih-mu*) [Tao]. (*Tao Te Ching*, 20)

Awareness of this distinction is essential in order that one's sanity be maintained, uncompromised: "The Sage is free from sickness, / is sick of sickness, / And accordingly is free from sickness" (*Tao Te Ching*, 71).

Our usual assessment of a "civilized" standard of living is for the Taoist utter nonsense. By emphasizing superficialities to be consumed, we miss the whole point of the meaning of life. As a consequence, we plummet headlong into the existential vacuum that people futilely seek to fill with material objects, drugs, and various perversions of power. However, life's true meaning is easily accessible, as reflected in the frugal ways of Nature. What then constitutes sane behavior for the Taoist? Restraint from the temptations of excess:

> In order to shrink one must first allow for expansion;
> In order to weaken one must first allow for strengthening;
> In order to abolish one must first allow for advancement—
> This is called "subtle enlightenment" (*wei-ming*). (*Tao Te Ching*, 36)[25]

Sanity, for the Taoist, amounts to little more than common sense, derived from a clear vision of what is the case:

Who can clarify muddy water to make it gradually clean?
Who can move from stagnation to gradually become invigorated?
Those who preserve this Tao,
Do not desire to become full to the brim.
Just because one is not filled to the brim
That is why one is beyond exhaustion and renewal. (*Tao Te Ching,* 15; see also
  9)

Science becomes feminine (in contrast to feminist) when it is pursued with
an attitude of receptivity, flexibility, and tolerance.[26] It is synthetic, reflective,
and contextual in contrast to the more common analytical, reductionistic, univ-
ersalistic form of science practiced by the masculine minded.[27] To be feminine
in approach, the assumedly objective scientist must expand his or her horizons
even further to overcome our ingrained and unconscious habits of homocentrism.

A case in point concerns the harmful myths about cetaceans being circulated
in the scientific community and beyond.[28] The fact is that, from the standpoint
of masculine science, we can take whales seriously, as deserving of continued
survival, only if we can fit them into a preconceived pattern of human intelligence—as indicated by an intraspecies form of language. True tolerance would
not set human beings as the standard of judgment but would rather fit us as a
species into the broader picture of Nature. Understanding this feminine perspective, Taoist-inspired painters of the southern Sung dynasty have bequeathed
to us masterpieces of their cocreativity with Nature in the form of exquisite
landscape paintings. The human presence is almost always to be found in these
paintings, but it is also kept in proper proportion within the sweeping scenes of
mountains and valleys—usually a mere hint that comes in the form of a minuscule
human figure or an unobtrusive roof.

For the Taoist, this attitude is epitomized by the epistemological stance of *wei
wu wei*. Often translated as "action by non-action," this phrase more properly
refers to an attitude of non-interference in the natural flow of life. One overcomes
the temptation to force things to one's will. Indeed, it amounts to wooing the
Way (Tao), inviting Tao to take its own course, getting out of the way of the
way—the easiest, and most difficult, advice to implement (see *Tao Te Ching,*
70).

Accordingly, feminine science represents power in a way far different from
the masculine science's power of control, its desire to conquer and harness
Nature. Because of the restriction of the meaning of power to this masculine
sense, it has acquired the reputation of a concept *non grata* in most feminist
circles. Marilyn French, for example, has devoted an entire volume, *Beyond
Power,* to the denunciation of power as a patriarchal tool, with a corresponding
advocacy of a "feminine" pleasure principle. Simone de Beauvoir voiced similar
concerns:

I think that there are certain masculine faults that women avoid thanks to their situation.
Women have less importance, less desire for emulation, and less of the ridiculous, in

one sense, in their role. They are less comical, in the bad sense of the word, than men who take themselves so seriously. I believe women escape, more or less, all of this. But the difficulty is that they escape all these pitfalls because they don't have any power, As soon as they gain power, they acquire all the male's defects.[29]

Seemingly, these misgivings about power arise from one's having taken to heart Lord Acton's pronouncement that "power tends to corrupt and absolute power corrupts absolutely." Yet the problem here does not lie in power itself; rather it lies in the *kind* of power that is invoked, one's perception of power. Feminine power—*tê*—is not power in the masculine sense of manipulation, control, and exploitation but power that arises from participation in the over-arching power of Nature. Moreover, *tê* is elicited in Taoism by the consummately feminine attitude of *wei wu-wei*, which allows that power to flow around and through us. In the same way the waters of a flowing river both buoy us up and carry us along, unself-consciously sharing their power with us.

Most in our society would not recognize this as power at all, because it does not "belong" to the individual, is not a private possession. Nor does it assert its presence and will against something else. For the same reason we are apt to esteem greatly the power of speech, the skill of speaking, while ignoring the equally important power of listening, born of the skill of receptivity. The Yin philosophy of Taoism is able to recognize the value of what is not, along with the value of what is as, for example, the value of a window or a cup that consists in its nothingness (*Tao Te Ching*, 11).

Global responsibility grows out of the feminine's metaphysical principle of oneness with all that surrounds us. We then may identify with other human beings and nonhuman beings, with all elements of Nature. Thus we can overcome our state of alienation or estrangement, that is, the fact that we have become strangers to ourselves, to our fellow human beings, and to our environment. Once that estrangement has been transcended, how can we not feel responsible—able to respond—in appropriate ways? We would have breached the boundaries of the ego-self and arrived at the true or shared self.

In recognizing, or uncovering, the shared self we also expose the false duality of egotism and altruism. This allows for the emergence of positive narcissism, a self-love that is positive rather than negative once one's ego-boundaries and (Taoistically false) limitations have been transcended.[30] The archetype of positive narcissism is to be found in the mother who in caring for her child loves it as an extension of her own being. Appropriately, Named Tao is identified as the Mother of the Ten Thousand Things (*Tao Te Ching*, 1, 20, 25, 52). Since the sage is to follow the model of Tao, he or she also should assume an attitude of maternal concern towards the world.[31]

For the Taoist, then, global responsibility takes the feminine form of maternal affection, contrasting with the masculine form of the duty of stewardship.[32] The distinction between these two attitudes inevitably spawns significant differences in behavior. Compare, for example, the ecologically enlightened behavior of the

American Indians with that of the later European settlers. For the first group the earth is a mother to be loved and preserved; for the second it was an opportunity to be exploited.

The emotionally steeped all-is-oneness mode of being is clearly at the root of Lao Tzu's dismay over war. In view of the current problem of disarmament, his words deserve our serious consideration:

> Weapons and armaments are tools of ill-omen,
> Things detested by all.
> Therefore, whoever has Tao turns away from them.
> The noble when at home honor the left [the place of good omens];
> When at war, they honor the right [the place of bad omens].
> Weapons and armaments are tools of ill-omen,
> Not tools of noble men.
> If using them is unavoidable,
> The best policy is calm restraint.
> Victory is not worthy of being glorified,
> So whoever glorifies it is one who takes pleasure in slaughter.
> Whoever takes pleasure in slaughter may not fulfill his ambitions in the world.
>
> . . . . .
>
> That is to say, war is to be treated as a funeral rite.
> After multitudes have been slaughtered,
> Weep with sorrowful grief;
> After the victory,
> Observe the occasion with funeral rites. (*Tao Te Ching,* 31)

To conclude, in the matter of survival values, or feminine values, our liberation can be demonstrated only if we transcend the simple (but necessary) stage of a critique of masculine values. To simple denounce science or its source in Western (masculine) values as the cause of present-day global threats is one manifestation of the lion's roar. But this *re*action ill befits the truly liberated child, the true self, who seeks not to dwell on past sufferings but rather looks forward to a bright future.

> Whoever knows the male,
> And holds fast to the female,
> Becomes the ravine of the world
> Whoever becomes the ravine of the world
> Without departing from eternal virtue,
> Return to infancy. (*Tao Te Ching,* 28)

It is this same infancy that we may take to represent the person who has completed the process to move beyond liberation, the ideal upon which feminists and futurists ought rightly to focus attention.

NOTES

This chapter is based on an address, "Beyond Liberation," delivered as part of a panel on "global responsibility and gender mythology" on the program of Sanity, Science, and Global Responsibility: An International and Interdisciplinary Conference, Brock University, St. Catherines, Ontario, July 12, 1988.

1. The definition of feminism being employed here is the original, standard one, which quite contrasts with the anticipatory anxieties of many of its present critics, to wit: "the doctrine that women should be granted the same rights as men in political, legal, and economic matters." William Morris and Mary Morris, eds., *Harper Dictionary of Contemporary Usage,* 2d ed. (New York: Harper and Row, 1985), p. 222.

2. See *Tao Te Ching,* 18, 19.

3. Simone de Beauvoir drew upon her long-standing experiences with leftist causes in arguing for the primacy of feminist issues in accomplishing social change:

Certain militants would have liked to subordinate the women's struggle to the class struggle; the Feminine-Masculine-Future group declared itself to be radically *feminist.* The women's struggle appeared to them primordial and not at all secondary. This is also my position. In the most diverse countries I have heard it said—by men but also by women—that it was necessary *first* of all to concern oneself with the revolution, with the triumph of socialism; . . . *later* one could interest oneself with the problems of women. But in my experience, this *later* means *never.*

Preface to *Histoires du M. L. F.,* by Anne Tristan and Annie de Pisan (Paris: Calmann-Lévy, 1977), p. 9; translated and quoted by Margaret A. Simons and Jessica Benjamin in "Simone de Beauvoir: An Interview," *Feminist Studies* 5, no. 2 (Summer 1979): 333.

4. This strikingly appropriate terminology—feminism as an "f-word"—is adopted from my copanelist, Jackie Young, sex equity specialist for the Hawaii Board of Education and chair of the Women's Caucus of Hawaii. The designation reflects the loathing and obscenity that unfortunately has come to be associated with the feminist movement in contemporary society.

5. See, for example, the radical feminists Mary Daly, in her *Gyn/Ecology: The Metaethics of Radical Feminism* (Boston: Beacon Press, 1978), and *Pure Lust: Elemental Feminist Philosophy* (Boston: Beacon Press, 1984); and Shulamith Firestone, in *The Dialectic of Sex: The Case for Feminist Revolution* (New York: Bantam Books, 1970).

More obliquely, Marilyn French declared: "Feminism does not offer a fixed program or dogma, a new Law for the future, but it does offer a new vision of human nature, reality, and sociopolitical arrangement." Later she talked of "feminizing the world": *Beyond Power: On Women, Men, and Morals* (New York: Summit Books, 1985). The problem inherent in French's view is that she failed to recognize that feminism is not monolithic. Moreover, she confused the political imperative of feminism with the broader scope of the feminine perspective.

6. Such views are put forth by Daly and Firestone. In particular, Daly used the term *lesbian* in a very broad sense "to describe women who are woman-identified, having rejected false loyalties to men on all levels"; *Gyn/Ecology,* note to p. 26. According to Simons and Benjamin, "Simone de Beauvoir," de Beauvoir considered lesbianism "an authentic alternative for women in a sexist society offering, and legitimating, only in-authentic alternatives" (p. 336).

7. de Beauvoir as quoted by Simons and Benjamin, "Simone de Beauvoir," p. 342.

8. Somewhat paradoxically, Marilyn French cited Nietzsche, the philosopher of the

will to power, in support of her views in *Beyond Power*: "Nietzsche believed the articulation of a new morality to be basic to the construction of a society more responsive to actual human need and desire" (p. 504). Simultaneously, she described him as "a nonfeminist, indeed a misogynist" (p. 504). The paradox can be dissolved by undertaking two tasks: (1) a reevaluation of the concept of power within a feminine perspective (see my discussion of power in the second part of this chapter), and (2) a reevaluation of Nietzsche's philosophy as essentially feminine in tone, although admittedly feminine in a predominantly negative way.

It is significant that Nietzsche's relationship with Lou Salomé was very influential in terms of his writing of *Zarathustra,* so much so that his correspondence indicates that Salomé herself was his model of the *Übermensch* embodied in the character of Zarathustra: "of all acquaintances I have made the most valuable and full of consequence is the one with Fraulein Salomé. Only since knowing her was I ripe for my Zarathustra." Translated and quoted by Angela Livingstone, *Salomé: Her Life and Work* (Mt. Kisco, N.Y.: Moyer Bell Limited, 1984), p. 54. Indeed, it was in the midst of Nietzsche's suicidal grief over the bitter dissolution of his relationship with Salomé that the first book of the *Zarathustra* was penned early in 1883. In a letter some months earlier he had written, "I am lost unless I succeed in discovering the alchemist's trick of turning this dirt into gold"; quoted by H. F. Peters, *My Sister, My Spouse: A Biography of Lou Andreas-Salomé* (New York: W. W. Norton, 1962), p. 135. The "gold" took the form of the *Zarathustra,* as attested to by Nietzsche in a letter to his mother in 1884: "You may say what you like against the girl [Salomé] . . . it still remains true that I have never found a more gifted and thoughtful person. . . . It is no accident that I have accomplished my greatest work [*Zarathustra*] in the last twelve months"; quoted by Peters, *My Sister, My Spouse,* pp. 142–143.

9. Friedrich Nietzsche, "Of the Three Metamorphoses," in *Thus Spoke Zarathustra: A Book for Everyone and No One.* Translated by R. J. Hollingdale (Baltimore: Penguin Books, 1961), p. 54.

10. The term *future shock* is taken from the title of Alvin Toffler's futurist tome. He defined the term as "the shattering stress and disorientation that we induce in individuals by subjecting them to too much change in too short a time"; *Future Shock* (New York: Random House, 1970), p. 4.

11. Simone de Beauvoir, as interviewed by Simons and Benjamin, in "Simone de Beauvoir," p. 343.

12. Jessica Benjamin noted that "violence is an expression of the impulse to negate, to affect others, to be recognized," an urge toward differentiation on the way toward a self-transcending oneness. "The Bonds of Love: Rational Violence and Erotic Domination," *Feminist Studies* 6, no. 1 (Spring 1980): 165–166.

13. Nietzsche, "Of the Three Metamorphoses," p. 55.

Nietzsche himself is a lion *par excellence*. Thus he declared in *Zarathustra*: "he who has to be a creator in good and evil, truly, has first to be a destroyer and break values." Friedrich Nietzsche, "Of Self-Overcoming,"in *Thus Spoke Zarathustra,* p. 139. The preface to *The Twilight of the Idols* identifies the work as "a great declaration of war," while in *Ecce Homo* the extreme form Nietzsche's search for conflict takes are reflected in his four "propositions" of war:

First: I attack only causes which are victorious—and at times I wait until they are victorious. Second: I attack only causes against which I cannot expect allies, against which I shall stand alone—against which I shall compromise myself alone. . . . Third: I never attack persons; I only avail myself of the person as of a strong magnifying glass with which one can render visible a general but creeping calamity which is otherwise hard to get hold of. . . . Fourth: I attack only causes in which any personal difference is out of the question, and in which any background of unwholesome experiences is lacking. On the contrary, to attack is with me a proof of good will, and sometimes of gratitude.

The Portable Nietzsche, trans. Walter Kaufmann (New York: Viking, 1975), pp. 466, 659–660. For a more extensive discussion of this confrontational aspect of Nietzsche's thought see Sandra A. Wawrytko, "The Philosophical Value of a Beloved Enemy: Chuang Tzu and Confucius, Nietzsche and Socrates, Butterfly and Gadfly" (Paper presented at the Pacific Division Meeting of the American Philosophical Association, Los Angeles, March 1986).

14. Daly, *Gyn/Ecology,* p. 23.

15. Ibid., p. 29. It must also be mentioned, however, that Daly did convey some intimations of Nietzsche's self-transcended child in her work. For example, she included "ecstasy" within the Gynocentric Method beyond its destructive aspects. Furthermore, she rejected the use of the term *her-story* as a substitute for *history,* stating that "it has an 'odor' of mere reactive maneuvering which is humiliating to women"; note to p. 24.

16. Nietzsche wrote to Salomé, "the old deep heartfelt request: *become yourself!* One must break free of one's chains to begin with, but of this *breaking free* itself in the end!" Sept. 3? 1882 as quoted by Rudolph Binion, *Frau Lou: Nietzsche's Wayward Disciple* (Princeton, N.J.: Princeton University Press, 1968), p. 87.

17. Nietzsche, "Of Self-Overcoming," p. 138.

18. Nietzsche, "Of the Three Metamorphoses," p. 55.

19. Margaret Mead, *Sex and Temperament in Three Primitive Societies* (New York: Morrow, 1963).

20. Ibid., p. 316.

21. Peter Timmerman, "The HRGC: IFIAS's Human Response to Global Change Initiative" (Paper presented at Sanity, Science, and Global Responsibility: An International and Interdisciplinary Conference, Brock University, St. Catherines, Ontario, July 9, 1988).

22. A fuller discussion of the Yin/Yang interchange is found in Sandra A. Wawrytko, "The Non-Duality of Yin and Yang: Interpenetration as Metaphysical Truth and Psychological Reality" (Paper presented at the First Conference of the International Society for Philosophy and Psychotherapy, Las Vegas, October, 1986).

23. This and subsequent references from the *Tao Te Ching* are taken from a newly completed translation of the text by Charles Wei-hsun Fu and Sandra A. Wawrytko, to be published by Greenwood Press in the series Resources in Asian Philosophy and Religion, ed. Charles Wei-hsun Fu, *Sourcebook of Taoist Philosophy.*

24. For a fuller discussion of these three values see Sandra A. Wawrytko, *The Undercurrent of "Feminine" Philosophy in Eastern and Western Thought* (Washington, D.C.: University Press of America, 1981), especially the introduction and first chapter. The second chapter discusses the feminine elements of Taoism's Yin philosophy, and the third chapter deals with the philosophical system of Benedict de Spinoza as a Western manifestation of feminine values.

25. See also *Tao Te Ching,* 22:

> Pliancy preserves wholeness;
> Crookedness prefigures perfection;
> Bending prefigures straightness;

Hollowness prefigures fullness;
Wearing out prefigures to renewal;
Deficit prefigures gain;
Plenitude prefigures perplexity.''
Accordingly, the Sage embraces the One [Tao]
And becomes the model of the world.
Is not self-pretentious,
And therefore remains enlightened;
Is not self-affirming,
And therefore is affirmed;
Is not self-boastful,
And therefore merit is self-evident;
Is not self-important
And therefore endures.
Simply because one does not compete,
Therefore the world cannot compete with one.

as well as *Tao Te Ching,* 24:

Whoever stands on tiptoe is not steady;
Whoever takes long steps does not walk [evenly];
Whoever is self-pretentious is not enlightened;
Whoever is self-affirming is not readily affirmed;
Whoever is self-boastful is not given credit;
Whoever is self-important does not endure.
These, in the eyes of Tao,
Are nothing but "leftovers or cancerous growths,"
Which all creatures spurn.
Therefore, whoever has Tao turns away from them.

26. Current attempts at constructing a feminist science I take to be largely a confusion of feminine values with feminist social agendas. See, for example, recent issues of the feminist journal *Hypatia*.

27. Henry A. Regier, "Responding to an Environmental Problematique on a Regional Scale" (Paper presented at Sanity, Science, and Global Responsibility: An International and Interdisciplinary Conference, Brock University, St. Catherines, Ontario, July 9, 1988).

28. Milton Freeman, "Conservation Strategies and International Practices" (Paper presented at Sanity, Science, and Global Responsibility: An International and Interdisciplinary Conference, Brock University, St. Catherines, Ontario, July 9, 1988).

29. Simone de Beauvoir, as interviewed by Simons and Benjamin, in "Simone de Beauvoir," p. 343.

30. The concept of positive narcissism has been borrowed from Lou Salomé. See her "Narzismus als Doppelrichtung," *Imago* 7 (1921): 361–386, translated by Stanley A. Leavy as "The Dual Orientation of Narcissism," *Psychoanalytic Quarterly* 31, no. 1 (1962): 10, 30.

31. It is noteworthy that Confucian philosophy, often mistaken as Taoism's philosophical rival in China, also recommends an attitude of maternal care. See *Ta Hsüeh* (*The Great Learning*), IX, 2.

32. Parental care is listed among the "three treasures" in Chapter 67, along with frugality and avoidance of self-assertion.

SELECTED BIBLIOGRAPHY

Benjamin, Jessica. "The Bonds of Love: Rational Violence and Erotic Domination." *Feminist Studies* 6, no. 1 (Spring 1980): 144–174.

Binion, Rudolph. *Frau Lou: Nietzsche's Wayward Disciple*. Princeton, N.J.: Princeton University Press, 1968.

Daly, Mary. *Gyn/Ecology: The Metaethics of Radical Feminism*. Boston: Beacon Press, 1978.

————. *Pure Lust: Elemental Feminist Philosophy*. Boston: Beacon Press, 1984.

Dinnerstein, Dorothy. *The Mermaid and the Minotaur—Sexual Arrangements and Human Malaise*. New York: Harper and Row, 1970.

Firestone, Shulamith. *The Dialectic of Sex: The Case for Feminist Revolution*. New York: Bantam Books, 1970.

French, Marilyn. *Beyond Power: On Women, Men and Morals*. (New York: Summit Books, 1985).

Livingstone, Angela. *Salomé: Her Life and Work*. Mt. Kisco, N.Y.: Moyer Bell Limited, 1984.

Mead, Margaret. *Sex and Temperament in Three Primitive Societies*. New York: Morrow, 1963.

Nietzsche, Friedrich. *The Portable Nietzsche*. Translated by Walter Kaufmann. New York: Viking, 1975.

————. *Thus Spoke Zarathustra: A Book for Everyone and No One*. Translated by R. J. Hollingdale. Baltimore: Penguin Books, 1961.

Peters, H. F. *My Sister, My Spouse: A Biography of Lou Andreas-Salomé*. New York: W. W. Norton, 1962.

Salomé, Lou. "Narzismus als Doppelrichtung," *Imago* 7 (1921): 361–386. Translated by Stanley A. Leavy as "The Dual Orientation of Narcissism," *The Psychoanalytic Quarterly* 31, no. 1 (1962): 10, 30.

————. *Nietzsche*. Translated and edited by Siegfried Mandel. Vienna: Black Swan Books, 1988.

Simons, Margaret A., and Jessica Benjamin. "Simone de Beauvoir: An Interview." *Feminist Studies* 5, no. 2 (Summer 1979): 330–345.

Toffler, Alvin. *Future Shock*. New York: Random House, 1970.

Wawrytko, Sandra A. "The Non-Duality of Yin and Yang: Interpenetration as Metaphysical Truth and Psychological Reality." Paper presented at the First Conference of the International Society for Philosophy and Psychotherapy, Las Vegas, October 1986.

————. "The Philosophical Value of a Beloved Enemy: Chuang Tzu and Confucius, Nietzsche and Socrates, Butterfly and Gadfly." Paper presented at the Pacific Division Meeting of the American Philosophical Association, Los Angeles, March 1986.

————. "A Provocative Alternative for Social Values: The 'Feminine' Complement to the Dominant 'Masculine' Perspective." In Norman N. Goroff, ed., *The Social Context for the Person's Search for Meaning*. Hebron, Conn.: Practitioner's Press, 1985.

————. *The Undercurrent of "Feminine" Philosophy in Eastern and Western Thought*. Washington, D.C.: University of America, 1981.

6

Conservatism versus Liberalism: Major Trends and Tensions within Contemporary American Protestantism

F. ERNEST STOEFFLER

Richard Rubenstein in his disturbing book *After Auschwitz* (1966) told his contemporaries that upon serious reflection on the significance of the Holocaust it is no longer possible to believe in the Judeo-Christian God. Such a faith, he reasoned, would imply that Auschwitz, too, has meaning. William Golding in his *Lord of the Flies* (1959) made a similar point. These observations indicate that during the period after World War II a great many people, and especially those in the academy, entertained doubts not only about the existence of God but also about the meaning and usefulness of religiousness in general. Although they began with different sets of observations and assumptions, they seriously wondered whether religion in general, and Christianity in particular, had any really significant role to play with respect to America's present and future.

To anyone who has eyes to see and ears to hear, it has long since become apparent that such predictions have once again turned out to be little more than wishful thinking. The current resurgence of American Protestantism, as well as the new vigor evident within the Roman Catholic communion, together with their new assertiveness relative to social and political problems, is incontrovertible evidence of the fact that Christianity in America is presently alive and well. In this chapter, therefore, we are speaking of a cultural force that must be reckoned with, whether for good or ill. So as to place certain needed limits on our discussion, we will focus on the major trends and tensions within American Protestantism since the forties, although reference to prior developments is necessary for contextual reasons.

When Robert Baird published his *Religion in America* (1843), he seems to have assumed not only that such a title refers almost exclusively to Protestants but also that nearly all Protestants are given essentially to what later came to be known as an "evangelical" self-understanding. Although they differed theologically on matters such as free will versus predestination, or premillennialism versus postmillennialism (see Glossary for definitions of special terms), they widely accepted a more or less literal interpretation of the Bible, its unquestioned authority in matters of faith and life, as well as the affirmations of the major creeds as the faithful and trustworthy rendering of its basic teachings. They believed, furthermore, that the proclamation of such a faith from the nation's pulpits, and its implementation both at home and on the mission fields, was the most effective way of "civilizing" the world.

Beginning with the problems that led to the Civil War, and following in its wake, American Protestants developed an awareness of internal frictions that hitherto had not troubled them. Not only did the slavery issue prove to be divisive, but bewildering new ideas were soon to be imported from the Old World, that is, the use of the critical-historical method in the interpretation of the Bible and of Christian tradition, the scientific understanding of the world, including human origin, and the Freudian understanding of human's psychic life, which treated religion as an unfortunate, though perhaps still necessary, illusion. In addition, the gradual rise of big business and its attendant inequalities in the distribution of wealth and the consequent labor unrest introduced a whole new set of problems into American society. On the intellectual horizon, humanism, with respect to which John Dewey eventually emerged as one of its chief American apostles, began to appeal to increasing numbers of his generation.[1] Toward the end of the century, then, a new spirit was abroad in America. It was a spirit that divided Protestantism into two faintly discernible camps. There were those whose chief concern was that of accommodating their religious faith to the needs and demands of the surrounding culture and those who were more inclined to resist this trend. The former, therefore, veered toward a more or less "liberal" and the latter toward a more or less "conservative" theological perspective.

These differences were exacerbated by the advent of what came to be known as the "social gospel."[2] This was a movement that took rise during the 1890s and that wanted to go beyond the prevailing laissez-faire approach of the Protestantism of the day to evils such as poverty and the unfair use of economic power. The early advocates of the social gospel envisioned nothing less than a reordering of the entire society so as to be in conformity with what they held to be the teachings of Jesus. Their leaders were prophets such as Washington Gladden, Josiah Strong, George Herron, F. G. Peabody, and R. T. Ely. The outstanding representative of the social gospel interpretation of Protestant responsibility was Walter Rauschenbusch, who was projected into the limelight with his *Christianity and the Social Crisis* (1907) and who finally succeeded in giving the movement a theological rationale with his *Theology for the Social Gospel* (1917).[3]

As a distinct religious phenomenon, the social gospel movement per se appears to have had only limited success. This was true even with respect to the clergy of the day and much more so with respect to the laity. It was successful, however, in another way. During the 1890s there came into being a moderate liberalism that meant to hold to many of the traditional theological convictions and yet to preserve an open mind toward problems posed by contemporary culture. The early systematizers of the theology of this movement were William Newton Clarke and William Adams Brown.[4] Many of the prominent exponents were men who had absorbed the theological emphases of Albrecht Ritschl in Germany. Among them were L. F. Stearns, H. B. Smith, E. C. Smyth, B. P. Bowne, A. C. McGiffert, and H. C. King. To these moderate (sometimes called "evangelical") liberals, with their essentially Christocentric theology, the social gospel emphasis gave a social vision that until that time, at least, was unequaled in the history of Christendom.[5]

Out of the social idealism of these men developed a period of Protestant crusading that at times manifested more zeal than wisdom. During World War I the conflict was widely presented as a war to end all wars and as an effort to make the world safe for democracy.[6] Lyman Abbott unabashedly referred to it as a "twentieth-century crusade." John R. Mott held out the vision of winning the "world for Christ in one generation" in the belief that thus its major problems would be solved. The heyday of this moderate, socially oriented liberalism came during the twenties of this century, a period of reasonably peaceful development during which the American pulpit could afford to concentrate on domestic issues. While seminary professors were busy trying to reconcile science and religion, "higher criticism" and revelation, evolution and the traditional Christian understanding of human origins, the natural and the supernatural, and divine transcendence and divine immanence, the giants of the pulpit were committed to more pragmatic schemes. They interpreted the kingdom of God as a historical entity, characterized by peace, goodwill, and equal opportunity for all, toward the achievement of which the church must move the nation. God was presented as a benevolent Father whose love will eventually draw all men and women unto himself. The life and teachings of Jesus were treated as the norm for humankind's personal and corporate relations. People were regarded as essentially good and quite capable of ushering in the kingdom. Evangelism was replaced by religious education, with a denominational staff of specially trained educational personnel supplying church schools with graded lessons, which, it was believed, would christianize the younger generation by degrees. Progress was regarded as intrinsically desirable and hence welcome. A romantic eschatology, influenced by Horace Bushnell, held out an optimistic vision of humankind's future.

One of the outstanding exponents of the kind of Protestant liberalism here described was Shailer Mathews, who had the Chicago Divinity School, of which he was dean from 1908 to 1933, as a sounding board.[7] Gradually, the liberal point of view began to dominate many of the outstanding denominational and interdenominational seminaries. Its outstanding communicator was Harry Emerson Fosdick whose Riverside Church in New York became a model worship center for many pastors within mainline denominations and whose books informed their sermonic output.[8] The liberalism of the twenties grew ever more confident, deeply concerned with social betterment, somewhat strident in its theological assertiveness and the advocacy of its ethical perceptions. Not only the pulpits of mainline Protestantism but the literature put out by its social and educational agencies were heavily influenced by the liberal approach. On the other hand, it is less clear how much it really meant to the thinking and to the lives of the laity.

The other movement that after the Civil War resulted from the breakup of the nineteenth-century Protestant synthesis was decidedly conservative and in time came to be known as "fundamentalism." It deliberately eschewed any accommodation to prevailing cultural trends, insisted on a verbally inspired Bible and on the use of traditional theological thought forms as laid down in the creeds. In its opposition to scientific modes of thought it underlined the supernatural element it found in the Bible, opposed higher criticism, and was especially set against the evolutionary thinking advocated by religious contemporaries like Lyman Abbott.[9] It was profoundly aware of human sinfulness and therefore came down hard on the need for salvation. In its ethics it was individualistic, and in its politics it stood squarely for God and country. The virgin birth of Christ, his deity and physical resurrection, his premillennial return, and the belief in a physical heaven and hell were regarded as touchstones of Christian orthodoxy.

At first fundamentalists remained within their respective denominations, trying to defend their religious perspective against the liberals of the day, whom they referred to as "modernists." This resulted in a number of heresy trials, especially among theologically oriented groups such as the Presbyterians.[10] Repercussions of the struggle were felt, however, by every major Protestant denomination, including the Methodists, who have usually been able to absorb theological differences. Perhaps the major stronghold of denominational fundamentalism was found among Southern Baptists. When fundamentalists gradually began to lose the battle for the mind of Protestants, they became increasingly polemical and engaged aggressively in the promotion of their views. With heavy financial support by concerned laypeople, they managed to publish *The Fundamentals* in 1910, a set of twelve booklets of about 125 pages each, which were sent free of charge to approximately 3 million people between 1910 and 1915. Thus every English-speaking religious leader whose address could be ascertained received one.

In spite of such determined efforts, however, the tide of sentiment within the major denominations continued to run against the fundamentalist perspective with its sharply narrowed theological perspective. Hence separation began to look like a viable course to leading fundamentalists. Accordingly, John Gresham Machen, one of the ablest Protestant theologians of the day, withdrew from the United Presbyterian Church in the United States and in 1936 founded the Presbyterian Church of America.[11] Its intellectual center became the now-flourishing Westminster Seminary near Philadelphia, which was established by Machen, together with three other professors and a small group of students. The establishment of other splinter groups followed. At the same time, a deliberately nondenominational type of fundamentalism found avenues to assert itself by means such as Bible conferences, following the pattern of the Niagara Conference, an annual summer assembly that had been convened from 1875 to 1901. Furthermore, it established various Bible schools and Bible institutes, the most noteworthy among them being the Moody Bible Institute in Chicago and the Los Angeles Bible Institute in California. Bible school fundamentalism relied heavily on the Schofield Reference Bible, which was published in 1909 and amplified in 1919. Its copious references set forth a dispensational scheme according to which human history begins with the year 4004 and ends with the physical return of Christ.[12]

Beginning about the middle of the 1920s fundamentalism as a movement suffered a series of reverses. They commenced with the aftermath of the so-called monkey bills, which four state legislatures had passed, largely under the pressure of Southern Baptists, and the intent of which was to keep the theory of evolution from being taught in the public schools. The constitutionality of such laws was tested in the famous Scopes Trial in Tennessee, an event that was watched with considerable amusement by the whole Western world.[13] As a result, mainline Protestants began to entertain massive doubts about the intellectual respectability of fundamentalism.[14] Furthermore, some of its most illustrious personalities passed away, among them William Jennings Bryan and, in 1937, John Gresham Machen. Adding to the decline were not only attacks from the outside but increasing dissention within.[15] The movement received probably its most severe blow when the highly respected, theologically astute champion of Protestant orthodoxy, C.F.H. Henry, joined its critics in 1947.[16] Henceforth the once self-assured fundamentalism was moved to the periphery of Protestant attention, giving way to its successor movement known as "evangelicalism" or, more accurately, "neo-evangelicalism."

During the 1930s and into the 1940s the earlier liberalism, too, found itself on the defensive largely, perhaps, because it had to make its way in a changed world. With respect to the international situation, there was keen disappointment with the results of World War I and rising fear of another holocaust. On the domestic scene there was the memory of the Great Depression, which had helped to shatter the liberal illusion of steady progress toward the realization of the kingdom. Already during the 1920s a small circle of academicians, who may be referred to as "Christian humanists," had taken a dim view of the kind of liberalism that prevailed among many of the clergy of the mainline denominations.[17] W. W. Fenn, in his Lowell Institute Lecture of 1918, had said that the prevailing picture of God was "almost ghastly in its unreality."[18] Perhaps the most important critic in this group was Henry Nelson Wieman, who was convinced that the Christianity proclaimed in his day from liberal pulpits too often magnified illusion and disregarded facts and that it did so because of its unwillingness to acknowledge that God is "too destructive to our foolish little plans to be nice."[19] Dean W. W. Sperry of Harvard, in the meantime, castigated the prevailing optimism with respect to humankind's innate goodness.[20]

Even more critical of the prevailing mind-set within liberal American Protestantism was a theological perspective that originated in Europe and came to be known variously as "Barthianism," "neo-orthodoxy," "dialectical theology," "crisis theology," and "theology of the Word."[21] It was a varied phenomenon that took rise with Karl Barth's *Römerbrief*, written in 1918 and made available in English in 1933. Among its main representatives were Barth himself, whose faith in modern man had been shattered by World War I and its aftermath and whose thinking was informed by Kierkegaard and Dostoievsky. Barth was cautiously recommended as a corrective to American religious liberalism by Wilhelm Pauck in 1931 and by Emil Brunner and in an Americanized version of his thought by Reinhold Niebuhr. [22] Niebuhr's *Moral Man and Immoral Society* (1936) was nothing less than a body blow to the reckless optimism of early liberals.[23] The Barthian emphasis was on God's transcendence, the discontinuity between God and humans, the centrality of divine revelation through the Word, the gulf between developed faiths and the Christian revelation, and the implications for society of humankind's radically sinful condition, which forever precludes the building of earthly utopias. In contradistinction to fundamentalism it had made its peace with science, had accepted higher criticism with regard to the interpretation of Scripture, and had put less emphasis on personal salvation, on an ethic oriented toward individual conduct, on the future life, and on evangelism.

In addition, there were other voices that disturbed the liberals, although, in spite of repeated attempts to do so, it is difficult to put them into one inclusive category that has any reasonably precise meaning. Anders Nygren's work *Agape and Eros* (English translation 1953), as well as that of his colleague at Lund, E H. Aulén, *Christus Victor* (English translation 1937), enjoyed some popularity. So did that of Nicolas Berdyaev, a prominent representative of Eastern Orthodoxy.[24] In a class all by himself was Paul Tillich with his concept of the Christian as a "new being" meant to bring about a new situation in the world and his understanding of religiousness "as the state of being grasped by an ultimate concern."[25] Having arrived in America in 1933, he presented thoughts that soon became the frequent subject of discussion in seminary classrooms and hallways. The world of biblical scholarship, on the other hand, was rocked by Rudolf Bultmann's proposal to demythologize the New Testament by means of expressing its messages to modern society in existential thought forms and concerns.[26] From Great Britain came the sobering advice of William Temple, the balanced approach to theology by P. T. Forsyth and John Oman, followed by John and Donald Baillie, as well as that of C. H. Dodd on scriptural interpretation. Among the growing host of domestic critics of the religiosity proclaimed in many pulpits of mainstream Protestantism is my own adviser in seminary, Richard Niebuhr, who projected himself prominently into the maelstrom of religious thinking through his *Church against the World* (1935) and whose mature thought is to be found in his much-appreciated *Christ and Culture* (1951). Basic to its content is his uncompromising insistence upon God's preeminence over all facets of human life and ambition.[27]

The above-mentioned Christian humanists, crisis theologians, and advocates of what has sometimes been referred to as "the new theology" represented the broadest imaginable spectrum of theological opinion. Yet they had two things in common. All of them treated American fundamentalism as being more or less irrelevant and unworthy of attention, and they were highly critical of the earlier liberalism with its tendency to accommodate itself to cultural norms and its optimistic and often unrealistic schemes for human betterment. At the same time they shared the this-worldly understanding of the Christian message that had found its way into a considerable segment of mainline Protestantism. The result was that during the thirties and forties there was, on the one hand, a great deal of theological sparring among the various groups and, on the other hand, an attempt on the part of liberals to come to terms with the new insights that had been thrust upon them.

Indicative of the issues that occasioned this dialogue is the volume *Religious Liberals Reply* (1947), edited by H. N. Wieman and associates. In it J. B. Pratt turned upon neo-orthodox supernaturalism, especially that of Barth, by calling it "a supernaturalism which to many thinkers abreast of their time is steadily becoming merely a pious and poetic form of words or a dead hypothesis."[28] Gardner Williams castigated Reinhold Niebuhr for projecting an ethics that perpetually generates a bad conscience in people because it regards self-interest as the lowest form of morality. A. E. Murphy saw, in Niebuhr's *Nature and Destiny of Man*, "a radically incoherent dialectical theology," which indicates that he did not really know what he believed.[29] Wieman himself appreciated some of neo-orthodoxy's contributions, such as its recognition of evil in the world, but thought that we must go beyond it to a more rational understanding of the creative sources that help us to appreciate life. H. P. Van Dusen, on the other hand, saw in liberalism's devotion to truth, deference to scientific investigation, and authority of Christian experience "the least inadequate, the most credible and cogent interpretation of Christianity in the nineteen centuries of its history."[30]

In spite of criticism, however, neo-orthodoxy remained equally confident with respect to the validity of its basic affirmations and its place in America's religious future. Thus during the thirties the notion of "postliberal thought" developed. Kenneth Cauthen defined it vis-à-vis the earlier liberalism as follows: "While the fundamental aim of liberalism was to harmonize the ancient Gospel with the life and thought of modern culture, the basic aim of post-liberal thought has been to discover the distinctive, authentic Christian faith which appears in the Bible and to set it forth in its purity against all other competing faiths both ancient and modern."[31] Although the "neo-liberals," referred to below, also left behind the liberalism of an earlier day, "the dominant post-liberal trend," Cauthen believed, was with neo-orthodoxy. W. M. Horton, who during the twenties moved from liberalism to what he called "realistic theology," wrote of liberals in 1934: "Today the self-assurance of the liberals seems to have melted away."[32] They now began to "see that in their endeavor to 'modernize' and 'liberalize' Christianity they had brought it into a compromizing alliance with the peculiar presuppositions, prejudices, and illusions of a particular type of civilization."[33] In what was perhaps a bit of youthful overstatement he even spoke of the "death of liberalism."

The result of such vigorous dialogue was that during the period leading up to World War II liberalism went through a process of serious soul searching that is evident in a flood of articles that were published. Already in 1931 even H. P. Van Dusen had noticed the "sickness" of the liberal gospel of his day.[34] Two years later John C. Bennett wondered out loud what might come after liberalism.[35] About 1935 the general malaise that had gripped the liberal camp seems to have reached its peak. That year the same Harry Emerson Fosdick who in 1922 had polemicized against fundamentalism now wrote in the *Christian Century* (52:1549–1552) that American Protestantism must go beyond modernism. Wilhelm Pauck questioned liberalism in his article "What Is Wrong with Liberalism?" and Henry Sloan Coffin raised the spectre that it might not survive.[36]

The outcome of such serious self-examination was that during the war and its aftermath the complexion of liberalism changed. Liberals during that period, variously referred to as "neo-liberals," "chastened liberals," and even "repentent liberals," had learned something from the general shift in the intellectual climate and from their neo-orthodox critics. Following the suggestion of W. M. Horton, their revised theological stance is often referred to as "realistic theology" (sometimes "postliberal theology"), although this is such a loose category that included in it are frequently the American representatives of neo-orthodoxy such as Reinhold Niebuhr. Thoroughly typical of the neo-liberalism that perpetuated itself within mainline Protestantism are men like John C. Bennet, Daniel Day Williams, and H. P. Van Dusen.[37] A host of others could also be mentioned, among them Edwin Lewis, John A. Mackay, and Robert L. Calhoun.[38] This new liberalism tried to take seriously the Christian heritage while remaining open toward contemporary culture; it recognized humankind's natural perverseness and suggested ways of dealing with it in respect to its individual and social implications; it acknowledged the transcendent dimension but stressed God's immanence; it hoped for the improvement of the human situation without positing any utopias. It was prepared to look critically at the Bible but insisted upon regarding its central figure, Jesus Christ, and his teachings as normative paradigm. It made its peace with science and deemphasized the supernatural, without denying its relevance. It also pointed to the importance of the church and hence welcomed the Faith and Order development, which was part of the concurrently emerging ecumenism.[39]

During the postwar years and into the seventies this kind of sober, ethically concerned liberalism found a foothold within a considerable segment of the clergy of the major denominations. In essence it was more of an attitude than a coherent theological system. Some sections of the country were more susceptible to it than others and the clergy perhaps more than the laity. Within the denominational structures it found lodgment especially in certain power structures such as the boards and agencies concerned with religious education and matters of social awareness and strategy.[40] It also provided a congenial religious context for the faculties of mainstream denominational colleges and seminaries. Thus it moved along through the fifties, sixties, and into the seventies sometimes following Van Dusen's line of assured self-assertiveness, sometimes on the defensive, and sometimes surmising that it is at the crossroads and wistfully taking for granted that it is moving in the right direction.[41] Its major difficulty was, however, that during these years its theological base was eroding. The erstwhile champions had largely dropped out of the fray, and the younger generation of theological experts had found their intellectual home in the ivory tower rather than in denominational offices. The result was that they drifted into a tendency of talking chiefly to one another, each using as a starting point a personally congenial fragment of the liberal perspective. After all, this was the age of rebellion and sometimes of reckless adventurism. The result from one point of view was intellectual chaos in the area of American theologizing; from another, reconstruction of liberal Prostestantism's theological underpinning. The former systematic approaches to what was now called "doing theology" had given way to innovative excursions into the realms of prolegomena and methodology. It all was as exciting as it was probably unavoidable.

During this period liberal Protestantism's intellectual elite were, furthermore, moving progressively in an antisupernatural direction, or, to put it positively, Protestant thought within this circle became basically naturalistic.[42] William Hordern, having acknowledged that there are various kinds of naturalism, said that "generally speaking, naturalism believes that the space-time universe, all of which is in principle knowable to science, is a self-contained unit. Therefore, satisfactory explanations can be given for all events, in principle, without reference to any force, power, being, or intelligence beyond the space-time system."[43] In other words, it represents an almost complete surrender of religious thought, on the one hand, to a scientistic understanding of the universe and, on the other hand, to an understanding of humankind that is peculiar to secular humanism. As such, it constitutes a new faith that has now been substituted for that which has been traditionally held within Christendom.

By its very nature, antisupernaturalism is basically opposed to the inherited belief in a transcendent, personal God. Such a perspective was accomplished in part by adopting the methodology of linguistic analysis that followed Wittgenstein and that had become popular within the philosophy departments of the nation's universities. The result was that theology now became "God talk," and since "modern" society no longer had any need for the notion of God, God-talk was regarded as nothing more than a disguised way of speaking about human needs. Out of this came the "death of God" episode in American religious thought, which had its roots in nineteenth-century German speculation, especially that of Ludwig Andreas Feuerbach, and which was injected into American Protestantism in 1954 by Thomas J. J. Altizer and reinforced in 1961 by Gabriel Vahanian, who thought that we are now culturally incapable of holding to a traditional concept of God.[44] He was followed by Paul M. Van Buren who believed that the juxtaposition of the traditional Christian faith in God and our ordinary way of thinking will cause spiritual schizophrenia.[45] The most popular presentation of the death of God notion, however, is found in the confusing little book by John A.T. Robinson with the title *Honest to God* (1963), which, on the one hand, affirms God's being and denies his existence but, on the other hand, speaks of him in language that seems to imply a personal deity.[46] Understandably, the result of this substitution of anthropology for theology was a troubled sea of words that Langdon Gilkey tried to calm down in 1969 by putting a more moderate construction on the new God language.[47]

Closely related to the death of God debate is the furor about "religionless" Christianity, or the "secular gospel." It dates from Dietrich Bonhoeffer, who was martyred by the Nazis and whose tragic story, as well as his writings, began to become known in America in the late fifties.[48] During the sixties his protest against "cheap grace" allegedly underlying the doctrines, rites, and practices of religious institutions, and his call for "costly grace," expressing itself in resolute discipleship, struck a responsive chord in the thinking of many people. On the other hand, Paul Tillich's insistence that religiousness does not consist of thinking about God as an object, or in treating him as an object, but in "ultimate concern" moved in the same direction. Combining Bonhoeffer and Tillich, as well as Bultmann's hermeneutical methodology, Robinson in his *Honest to God* projected the idea of religionless Christianity on America's liberal Protestantism. Such Christianity, he held, has little to do with what often goes on in churches but consists essentially of the self-giving love apparent in Jesus. Whereas Robinson waffled with respect to his understanding of God, Paul Van Buren saw no sense in having us inject that concept into the thinking and life of the church. His "secular gospel," therefore, is attached to a faith that has no relation to God as traditionally worshipped. Religiousness in that case is essentially the attempt to mold one's thinking and life according to the pattern of Jesus' "contageous" perspective and freedom as Van Buren understands both.[49] To Harvey Cox, who also needs to be mentioned in this context, religiousness consists essentially of meeting God (whose existence he acknowledged) in the "you," especially that of urban life. Instead of Christians being fascinated by God, they must enter into teamwork with others, an activity in which God is best found and served.[50]

That such a radical redefinition of the nature of religiousness occasioned considerable discussion hardly needs to be pointed out. Fundamentalists saw it as a sign of the apostasy of the last days. Evangelicals were simply shocked. Even a liberal like Langdon B. Gilkey reviewed Paul Van Buren's book under the title, "The New Linguistic Madness."[51] Essentially, however, the death of God excursion, whether it implied that God actually does not exist or only that traditional language referring to him is dead, as well as the "secular meaning of the gospel" phase of liberal thought were sincere attempts on the part of equally sincere people to find meaning in a religious faith to which they were deeply committed. They were unable, or unwilling, to do what they thought our culture required them to do, namely, to compartmentalize their thinking, and at that time saw no other way out of their intellectual dilemma.

With regard to the question of the impact of this radical theological trend, one would have to agree with Martin Marty that it had little ecclesiastical consequence, exciting as it might have appeared in the media and in academic circles.[52] The average Protestant had difficulty knowing what it was all about, and Roman Catholics could do nothing with it. The exception might be Harvey Cox's *Secular City,* which sold a great many copies and was frequently quoted, especially by clergy whose interest was focused on the problems of contemporary urban society.[53]

Another facet of religious liberalism during the period under discussion is now generally referred to as "liberation theology." It came into its own during the tumultuous sixties. In the background again is Bultmann's effort to demythologize the Scriptures, which opened the door to a hermeneutic grounded in whatever happens to be congenial with the religious and social perspective of the interpreter. Accordingly, the advocates of liberation theology find in the Bible support for whatever group is to be "liberated" or whatever method of "liberation" might promise success. Some proponents are concerned especially with the social and economic aspirations of minorities at home and others with the need to solve the problems of the Third World.[54] Its basic thrust is to challenge the Christian churches to use their economic and political power to liberate society from what are thought to be middle-class concerns such as the need for economic security and status in society and the fear of the future if present economic structures are altered. The methods suggested, or rather promoted, are sometimes gradual change but more often revolutionary upheaval. In the thinking of its advocates, the Bible is a revolutionary book, with the exodus of the Jews from Egypt as a basic paradigm, the prophets as heroic proponents of concern for the poor, and Jesus as a revolutionary who gives support to the downtrodden. Paul L. Lehman, a prominent ethicist of our day, gave the movement a lift by eschewing the theological conservatism, individualism, and otherworldliness, which allegedly afflict American Protestantism, and proposing to make it "relevant" by positing a God who is politically active in the world through his people.[55] The result, one hopes, will be a restructuring of society, which will eventuate in a fairer distribution of wealth, status, and power—the earthly trinity so important to liberationists. Since Latin America is the intellectual center of this outlook, it is not surprising to find that Roman Catholics in that part of the world are especially involved in it, notably, the Maryknoll Sisters and the members of the Society of Jesus (Jesuit Order).

Because of the radical nature of this theological perspective and because it made some headway within the bureaucracies of mainline Protestant boards and agencies, criticism of it within major denominations has been severe. A case in point is the furor over financial support for Angela Davis, an avowed representative of the political Left, within the United Presbyterian Church in the

U.S.A., which appears to have at least temporarily affected the level of charitable giving within that denomination.[56] The major criticism, however, has come from the rising tide of neo-evangelicalism, which is discussed below. According to V. C. Grounds, revolutionary liberation theology "seems to be a flat, denuded, one-dimensional reductionism, enamored of the *Zeitgeist*."[57] In a critique, which is essentially sympathetic with its aims, Robert M. Brown detailed the popular objections to it: It is trying to bring feelings of guilt to the middle class, the members of which object to being branded as oppressors; it is a thinly disguised Marxism; it lays too much stress on social engineering rather than on initiative and hard work; and it is a distortion of Christianity, which advocates reconciliation whereas liberation theology glorifies conflict.[58] Its proponents defend it as expressing most adequately the message of Jesus and his concern for the poor and the oppressed.

Related to liberation theology in spirit is the feminist movement within American churches, which also began to make itself felt in the sixties. It had its power base within the Roman Catholic Church, where women became especially aware of being kept in a subordinate position. In time, however, it found its way into mainline Protestantism. It resulted in the fact that women were given equal, or nearly equal, representation on various boards, agencies, and committees down to the local church. Appropriate vocabulary changes were also made, so *chairmen* became *chairpersons* and so on. With respect to the Protestant ministry, there was an increasing demand for the ordination of women and their entry into positions previously reserved for male clergy. This came about through the increasing pressure exerted by women not only through organization but through a very impressive literary output.[59] Although other aspects of liberation thinking were treated with considerable reserve by rank and file Protestants, the feminist movement in their midst appears to have found wide support.

One of the controversial aspects of liberal Protestantism between 1945 and 1975 came to be known as "situation ethics," or the "new morality." In the background is the antilegalistic bent of neo-orthodoxy in general, with the support of Reformation theology and the writings of Bonhoeffer and the Niebuhrs in particular. Mention must also be made of Joseph Sittler's *Structure of Christian Ethics* (1958). One of the major American spokesmen for the new morality was the above-mentioned Paul L. Lehman, and the publication of Joseph Fletcher's *Situation Ethics* (1966) exacerbated an already lively debate.[60] The heart of the new morality had to do with the insistence of its advocates that with respect to moral authority modern Christians should not put emphasis on principles drawn from the Bible or from Christian tradition but on the contemporary context in which a given ethical decision has to be made. The assumption was that being a Christian implies being a person who loves his or her neighbor and that such love guarantees right action without recourse to the specific application of inherited norms, although the latter may afford some general guidance. The critics of situation ethics, such as Paul Ramsey, pointed out that such a standard is essentially subjective and hence totally unreliable when a person is called upon to make a serious decision. The situational approach to ethics, he believed, does not take into account a person's vast capacity for self-deception and consequent tendency to rationalize essentially self-serving aims. Evangelicals generally were horrified at the thought of substituting a nebulous concept such as contextuality for the authority of the Bible in matters of Christian conduct.

Among liberal Protestants this revised ethic had great appeal, although they might not go all the way with its more radical advocates such as Fletcher or Robinson. Its emphasis on love rather than law fit admirably into the antiestablishment, antiauthority, antilaw and order, mood of the period. Its wide acceptance, therefore, led to a new mood of permissiveness within American Protestantism, especially with respect to the ethics of sex-related problems such as premarital or extramarital sexual relations, abortion, and homosexuality. A growing number of Protestants began to consider such undertakings no longer as sin but simply as aspects of a nontraditional life-style. Hence serious questions arose, especially with regard to homosexuality, against which conservative Protestants find direct prohibitions in the New Testament. Do professed homosexuals have a place within the Christian fellowship? More troubling yet, should they be accepted for ordination to the Christian ministry?[61] Widely satisfactory answers to these questions are still outstanding.

Although it would be futile to say much about the ecumenical movement in this context, it should be pointed out that its early support came from liberal Protestantism. Its original leaders were Charles H. Brent, a Canadian; John R. Mott, an American; W. A. Visser 't Hooft, a Dutchman; and Nathan Söderblom, a Swede. Beginning with the Missionary Conference at Edinborough in 1910, it was more or less enthusiastically supported by liberal Protestants in America until its decline during the late sixties. Out of it came a long series of mergers of Protestant bodies, and the psychological climate that it created was at least partially responsible for whatever success can be associated with the Federal Council of Churches (created 1908), which was supported by thirty denominations. Ecumenical thinking also provided the impetus for the formation of the National Council of Churches of Christ in the United States of America, founded in 1950 and eventually including twenty-nine Protestant and Eastern Orthodox bodies, comprising about two thirds of the Protestant and Orthodox Christians in the United States.[62] The conservative wing of Protestants, among them Southern Baptists, did not join; neither did the Roman Catholics.

As time went on the liberal stance on various controversial issues, taken first by the Federal Council and then by the National and World Councils, occasioned severe criticism among Protestant fundamentalists and evangelicals.[63] In response, the National Association of Evangelicals was founded and put emphasis on evangelism, rather than the solving of societal problems, as well as on theological agreement as a precondition to cooperative action. The American Council of Christian Churches was the creation of the contentious fundamentalist Carl McIntire, who referred to the National and World Council as the *Modern Tower of Babel* (1955). Roman Catholics, on the other hand, gradually began to take an interest in ecumenical dialogue, the first prominent beginning having been made with the so-called Halines Conversations in Belgium in 1921, for which Lord Halifax, an Anglican, had provided the major impetus. The Roman Catholic Church was fully projected into the ecumenical movement when Pope John XXIII decided to convene the Second Vatican Council and published his famous *Decree on Ecumenism* in 1964. Through the sixties and early seventies, therefore, contacts between Catholics and Protestants at various levels became extremely numerous, a circumstance that tended to create goodwill and a fuller mutual understanding within a large segment of Christendom.[64] Toward the end of the period under discussion, ecumenical zeal began to flag, fundamentalists never having supported it, many evangelicals remaining sceptical about its aims, and liberals coming to feel that bigness and desirability do not necessarily go together. Catholics, in the meantime, were beginning to find themselves held back by a leadership that had grown cautious, perhaps even apprehensive, about the marriage of ecumenism and a new spirit of liberalism within the Roman Catholic Communion, a combination that threatened far-reaching innovations in both doctrine and practice.

Many Americans are as yet not fully aware of the fact that during the 1940s a very significant cleavage took shape within the ranks of conservative Protestants in America. As previously indicated, it is now usually dated from the publication of C.F.H. Henry's *Uneasy Conscience of Modern Fundamentalism* in 1947. In that book Henry, the most prominent conservative theologian of American Protestantism at the time, pointed out that fundamentalism has become too exclusively preoccupied with the set of theological propositions that it regards as fundamentals, not that in the critic's mind there was anything wrong with the fundamentals themselves. The fault, he believed, lay with their advocates who made them an end in themselves rather than a means to an effective Christian witness in the world. This results in an unfortunate polemical mind-set that some years later he characterized as follows: "The real bankruptcy of fundamentalism has resulted not so much from a reactionary spirit—lamentable as this was—as from a harsh temperament, a spirit of lovelessness and strife contributed by much of its leadership in the recent past."[65] The "bankruptcy" he is referring to has to do with the fact that at the time of his writing (1947) the influence of fundamentalism on American church life had become fairly marginal.

Out of its ashes, however, arose another movement that was destined to take on major proportions within the ranks of American Protestants. It seems that Harold J. Ockenga, former president of Gordon-Conwell Seminary, first gave a name to it in 1948 when, in addressing an audience at Fuller Seminary, he spoke of the "new evangelicals."[66] Henceforth the terms *new evangelicalism* or *neo-evangelicalism* became the accepted designations by representatives of the movement as well as others. As such, they stand for a historically identifiable entity.

Attempts to sharpen the general concept of evangelicalism have frequently been made, although without any complete success.[67] All we can expect to accomplish in this context is to point out the essential differences between the older fundamentalism and neo-evangelicalism. Even this is difficult because, as one of its prominent proponents, Donald Bloesch, pointed out, it is not based on a given theological system but rather on a "mood."[68] Basically, it clings to a series of traditionally Protestant affirmations. Among them are the final authority of Scripture, the deity of Jesus Christ, his substitutionary atonement, his physical resurrection, God's trinity, the presence in the believer and in the church of his Spirit, continued personal existence after death with appropriate rewards and punishments, the second coming of Christ, and his eventual triumph in the establishment of God's kingdom. What it does not share with the older fundamentalism is its judgmental attitude toward other Christians, its polemical spirit, its excessive preoccupation with doctrinal affirmations, its tendency to shut itself off from the world, and its frequent orientation toward dispensationalism. Whereas the ethic of fundamentalism is social in that it frowns on practices such as drinking alcoholic beverages, smoking, gambling, and other alleged vices, neo-evangelicalism tends toward a *societal* ethics, concerning itself about issues such as war, racial discrimination, the evils of imperialism, delinquency, and the needs of the Third World.[69] It is not averse to the establishment of parachurch structures, although it also works within existing denominations and is more or less willing to cooperate with them in commonly perceived tasks.[70] An example is the extensive evangelistic crusades of Billy Graham, which enlist the active support and participation of mainline Protestantism's local churches.[71]

During the early years of its existence and through the fifties neo-evangelicalism made relatively little progress. Much of its energy was spent, as might be expected, in defining itself over–against the fundamentalism out of which it had emerged. The controversy that ensued was understandably focused on the issue of biblical authority. Thus some of the leaders of the day, among them E. J. Carnell, Bernard Ramm, and D. M. Beegle, were taken to task for attempting to find a way for bringing together their new societal vision and an understanding of biblical authority that had credibility in the conservative camp.[72] Evangelicals were criticized also by fundamentalists for their general openness toward other Christian groups. T. S. Baker, for instance, objected to their willingness to deal with non-Calvinists, leftist clergymen, and even Pentecostals.[73] Harold J. Ockenga, on the other hand, accused the fundamentalists of a tendency toward separation, fragmentation, suspicion, and censoriousness.[74] Although the National Association of Evangelicals tended to follow the lead of C.F.H. Henry in confining its societal aims to the enunciation of general ethical principles, fundamentalists of the mind-set of Carl McIntire regarded it as their task to speak directly in favor of anything that might oppose the inroads of communism into American life.

As America moved into the sixties, however, the new evangelicalism began to expand to a degree that was totally unexpected. The reasons for it are not entirely clear, although it is possible to point to a number of factors that would seem to have had something to do with it. On the negative side, fundamentalism had lost its intellectual respectability, as has been pointed out. Neo-orthodoxy, too, had run its course and was now equally lacking in leadership. Liberalism, while still vigorous intellectually, had moved into the ivory tower and debated issues that produced little more than conversation pieces among the clergy and yawns in the churches. On the positive side, a whole group of young intellectuals now began to gravitate toward neo-evangelicalism and to advocate concern with issues that seemed to matter in the daily life of people.[75] Not to be overlooked is the general public disgust with the excesses of the sixties and a consequent shift of public opinion in a conservative direction. The result was a rapidly expanding population of neo-evangelical seminaries such as Fuller and Gordon-Conwell, as well as denominational institutions that were known for their theological conservatism such as Southwestern Baptist Seminary in Fort Worth, Texas, and Concordia Seminary in St. Louis, as well as a long list of others. Evangelical colleges, too, suddenly seemed attractive to young people and their parents, with Wheaton in the lead.

One indication of the growing vigor of neo-evangelicalism is to be found in the new generation of religious journals that came into existence. Hitherto the conservative publications of American Protestantism, such as *Moody Monthly, Eternity,* and *Christian Life,* were targeted primarily at a readership that was family oriented. Their intent, therefore, was basically that of edification. Under the leadership of C.H.F. Henry, *Christianity Today* was founded in 1956 and supported for several years by J. Howard Pew. It presented a forum for theological commentary, various types of other learned studies, and religious news that gave exposure to the total range of evangelical opinion. In time *Christianity Today* became to neo-evangelicals what the *Christian Century* was to religious liberals with about twice the number of readers. The *Reformed Journal,* which speaks out of a Calvinistic background and which has Lewis Smedes on its staff, also moved into the area of societal issues. With Jim Wallis as editor, *Sojourners,* formerly called *Post-American,* became one of the foremost Protestant journals in its protest against wrongs in society such as war, oppression, misuse of political power, and national policies that tend to aggravate social problems at home and in the Third World. To the impact of this trio upon the expansion of the new evangelicalism must be added that of the various publications of traditionally conservative Protestant groups such as the Southern Baptists, the Lutheran Church, the Missouri Synod, as well as an extensive array of Holiness and Pentecostal churches.

One of the most surprising aspects associated with neo-evangelicalism is the charismatic movement. Since the fifties it has made substantial inroads into all Christian churches, the Roman Catholic, the Eastern Orthodox, and the various Protestant denominations. It is also promoted by television ministries such as that of Oral Roberts and Kathryn Kuhlman, as well as organizations like the Full Gospel Business Men's Fellowships. The literature it has generated is very extensive.[76] In his preface, M. P. Hamilton characterized it as follows: "The term 'charismatic' applies to those who have experienced a 'baptism of the Holy Spirit' [a phrase referring to a passage in Acts 1:5]. This event . . . usually leads to a new style of living for the recipient, and public witness to the Baptism in the Spirit becomes a central and joyous aspect of life."[77] The most conspicuous "gifts" of the Spirit (see I Corinthians 12:4) that are usually sought are the ability to "speak in tongues," or glossalalia, and the ability to heal. Much is made also of a marked increase in a person's sense of well being that is produced in individuals who have encountered a charismatic experience. This new charismatism is found within all social strata but seems to be especially prominent among middle-class whites. Its tendency to disregard theological and ecclesiological barriers is often the subject of severe criticism.[78] So is its divisiveness sometimes found within denominations and in local churches. Its advent has even caused friction between itself and the older Pentecostal churches that believe all charismatics ought to be part of their own denominational fellowships.[79] However, this charismatic renewal is a very significant aspect of the new evangelicalism and has added new zest and meaning to otherwise jaded lives.

To give an indication of the significance of the growth of neo-evangelicalism during the period under discussion (1945–1975) is difficult. Opinions obviously tend to be biased and statistics manipulated. Yet it would be equally difficult not to become aware of two fairly obvious developments: America has experienced what is now generally seem as a religious renewal, and this renewal, insofar as it occurred among Protestants, benefited in the main Protestantism's neo-evangelical segment. This "evangelical renaissance," as it is now frequently referred to, first received wide public attention through the Billy Graham evangelistic campaigns. It was promoted also, as previously mentioned, by a series of parachurch organizations. Gradually, it found a toehold both within mainline Protestant denominations and Roman Catholicism by the use of small group meetings, for which the pattern was established long ago by the Pietist movement. Emphasis in these meetings among Protestants was (and is) put mostly on the devotional study of the Bible and its application to everyday problems, both personal and corporate. Hence there has been a sharp increase in the demand for appropriate study guides to be used in group meetings, church school classes, and weekday religious services.

The vigor of the evangelical renaissance is most clearly perceived, however, if we look at the growth patterns of conservative Protestant denominations and the concurrent retrenchment apparent among mainline Protestant bodies. According to Martin Marty, evangelicals were in better shape institutionally at the end of this period than either the liberals on the Left or the fundamentalists on the Right.[80] This judgment is borne out by every measurable statistic, whether it be growth patterns, youth involvement, church attendance, missionary interest, seminary expansion, or financial support.[81] Doing just such a comparison led D. D. Dayton, an evangelical of moderate inclinations, to suggest "that on a given Sunday roughly as many people are in Holiness churches as in the United Methodist Church."[82] Since he has reference here to groups such as the Salvation Army, the Church of the Nazarene, the Assemblies of God, the Church of God, and the Free Methodist Church of North America, which were once considered to be on the periphery of the Wesleyan tradition, this represents a significant trend, even if it should be somewhat overstated.

This decline of what has been considered mainstream Protestantism and the simultaneous rise of neo-evangelicalism within American Protestantism is now generally recognized. Not so clearly understood are the reasons for the shift, a matter that, therefore, generates considerable discussion. Christopher Walter-Bugbee, editor of the Episcopal journal *Communicant,* blames the seminary faculties and administrations that, in his opinion, wanted to look good in the eyes of the secular academy "and in the process have clearly forgotten why their schools exist."[83] A. T. Templeman blames the liberals who have left the major denominations while the rest of the people now make up the membership.[84] According to K. S. Kantzer, H. N. Wieman ascribed the success of religious conservatism to the fact that it fosters a sense of life that is on a higher plane of human existence than that which is provided by its rivals.[85] Dean Kelley in his influential book *Why Conservative Churches Are Growing* (1972) seems to have put the blame on the confusion created in the mind of the laity by liberalism's talk about the death of God, the new hermeneutic, process theology, the secular city, situational ethics, liberation theology, and the impact of Eastern religions. Sociologists tend to see the reason in the general movement of public opinion to the Right. Whatever reasons are given, chances are that neither camp will succeed in fully convincing the other. Neo-evangelicals point with confidence to the success of their approach, and liberals, though chastened perhaps by neo-orthodoxy and the obvious popular appeal of neo-evangelicalism, continue to extol the resources and alleged advantages of liberal theology.[86] What has been said of scientists is probably true of theologians. They do not usually change their mind. Theological perspectives change because proponents gradually die off.

It would not be possible to conclude this section on the evangelical renaissance without mentioning the black churches. William Pannell reminded us that black Christians have always been "passionately spiritual" and deeply "committed to the religion of the heart."[87] Theologically, they generally held the religious beliefs that are typical of evangelicalism, although they did not feel the need to articulate them systematically. Nor did they normally speak of themselves as evangelicals but rather as "Bible believers." Because of their history and minority status, they never separated religious belief from societal and economic issues, although the latter did not always receive the emphasis put upon them by leaders like Martin Luther King, Jr. Even today most of black Protestants, usually estimated as comprising about 11 million people, belong to established black churches with middle-class tastes and values not very different from those of their white counterparts.[88] In addition, about a million blacks belong to white churches and an undetermined number (800,000 perhaps) to Holiness and Pentecostal groups.

The philosophical and theological issues that agitated and divided white Protestants over the years found little echo in the black community. The struggle for black identity and against the racism that consciously or unconsciously afflicted white Protestants consumed much of the energy of blacks. Yet they were and to a large extent still are satisfied to work through existing structures, focusing their attention upon the traditional goals of gospel preaching, benevolences, education, and foreign missions. The call for revolutionary change coming from white religious radicals has met with a relatively weak response among Protestant blacks. In general, then, there was little need for an evangelical renaissance among blacks, since liberalism had actually made few inroads among them.[89]

One of the major Protestant developments during the decades under discussion, although conservative, lacks the homogeneity that would make it possible to classify it as neo-evangelical. It is now frequently referred to as the "electronic church," or the "electronic pulpit," and exists basically apart from any denominational affiliation. One of the outstanding personalities here is Oral Roberts, an evangelist with a Methodist background, a fundamentalist theology, and leanings toward the charismatic movement. Very different is Robert Schuller with a Reformed background, a disciple of Norman Vincent Peale's "power of positive thinking" approach, and a believer in putting on a glittering variety gospel show. Again different are the Armstrongs and their Worldwide Church of God with an aura of cultism about it. Most of the rest of the well-known personalities of the electronic pulpit—Jerry Falwell, Pat Robertson, Jimmy Swaggart, Rex Humbard, Jim Bakker, James Robison—could perhaps best be classified as belonging to what may be designated as the "neo-fundamentalist" camp. They hold to the basics of fundamentalist theology without emphasizing them excessively. Their language avoids typical fundamentalist expressions, and the fire and brimstone preaching of former days is replaced by carefully orchestrated performances among palmtrees that decorate resplendent cathedrals and against the background of beautifully robed choirs. Hymns, gospel songs, and folksey music are intermingled, and prominent personalities are featured to give "testimonies." God is treated as the great Pal, who can generally be relied on to supply one's creature comforts.

The most controversial aspect of the electronic pulpit is Jerry Falwell's "moral majority" because it promotes most actively the causes dear to neo-fundamentalists in general. Politically, they are against what they regard as pornographic material in school libraries, against sex education by people they do not trust, against the use of four-letter words in plays and movies, and against liberation theology as understood by the World Council of Churches, the National Council of Churches, and the bureaucracies of the major denominations. They also oppose what they call "secular humanism," as well as Marxism in all of its disguises. On the positive side they promote Bible reading and prayer in public schools, stricter law enforcement, and the stability of the family. Capitalism and patriotism are regarded as natural allies of the Christian way of life.

The electronic pulpit has become a business enterprise of major proportions. It probably reached the zenith of its popularity during the National Religious Broadcaster's Convention in January of 1981, which was attended by President

Carter. Upon that occasion Ben Armstrong, the executive secretary of the National Religious Broadcasters, opined that broadcast religion touches more people than all the churches combined. This may not have been as blatant an exaggeration as it appears to be on the surface. For every major religious broadcaster there are hundreds who use the air waves locally, and their combined audience has been variously estimated to number many tens of millions. Furthermore, there are few weeks in the year during which a new religious broadcast is not initiated. The Christian Broadcasting Network in Virginia Beach alone has more than 800 affiliates and uses a communications satellite with a considerable number of receiving disks. Critics of the enterprise, usually liberals, often confess to be worried about its impact on American political life, conveniently forgetting the fact that they themselves have been politically active all along. They also tend to envy the many millions of dollars that are donated annually to keep the electronic pulpit in operation. These gospel performances must meet certain needs of their vast audience; otherwise their viewers would tune in on something else and stop sending their gifts.[90]

During the present period (since 1975) mainline Protestantism has become aware of its declining influence in American life. Hence it is making considerable efforts at self-vitalization. Indicative of such efforts is the new emphasis on evangelism, although the word is variously defined and, not infrequently, watered down in the process.[91] There is under way also a bid for the air waves in the hope of competing with the electronic pulpit, as well as a new attempt to keep the young people, which have frequently gravitated toward neo-evangelical parachurch organizations.[92] Pastors, furthermore, are making heroic efforts to plug the dykes through innovative schemes to enlist the laity in the worship and work programs of their churches. Thus far, however, such attempts have not stemmed the tide of retrenchment. Whether or not they will, and under what conditions, remains to be seen.

In the meantime, mainline Protestantism continues to face a host of serious problems. There is the God-language bind, which promises to become increasingly divisive.[93] Not much less ominous is the debate about homosexuality, which has been prominently featured in denominational journals for some years and which continues to agitate especially the mind of the laity.[94] The large number of women who have entered denominational seminaries is an unknown quantity that feminists obviously welcome as a promising sign for the future but that many church members view with muted apprehension.[95] Perhaps most explosive of all is the tendency of a significant segment of liberal Protestantism's bureaucracy to follow the lead of the World Council of Churches in carrying on a love affair with leftist ideological causes. Such a redefinition of the church's mission has recently come in for a barrage of heavy criticism. Helmuth Thielicke, for instance, who is now perhaps world Protestantism's most respected theologian, said of it: "The World Council with its unilateral support of left-wing guerillas and terrorist groups threatens to become increasingly a political club instead of a representative of the church."[96] The more theological issues with which liberals (as well as neo-evangelicals) are trying to come to terms have been carefully sorted out by R. J. Coleman.[97] Although they cause relatively little discomfort in the churches, with the exception perhaps of discussions related to the authority of the Bible and human evolution, they continue to promise disagreements among theological experts.

Although mainline Protestantism with its generally liberal leadership and mixed constituency thus limps along, religious conservatism, both in the form of neo-fundamentalism and neo-evangelicalism, may well have to be considered the dominant force in American Protestantism today. Although the latest polls seem to indicate that neo-fundamentalism has peaked, this may have to be attributed to the massive criticism of the "moral majority," which emanated from the seminaries and universities and which was echoed by the denominational journals as well as by the media in general. One can by no means conclude from this, however, that the previously mentioned issues advocated by neo-funda-mentalists are not supported by a large segment of the American public. For that reason, and also because of its authoritative voice in an age of doubt and un-certainty, this particular interpretation of the Christian faith once again has a fairly wide appeal and will probably continue to attract sizeable numbers of people in the forseeable future.

The most vigorous Protestant movement today, however, is neo-evangelical-ism. Its seminaries attract large numbers of students, their faculties increasingly command the respect of their peers, and young people feel attracted to it because it seems to help them find their identity and put their lives together. The younger clergy as a whole speak increasingly about the need for a religious experience, a subject that has always been suspect to the liberal mind-set.[98] Little wonder that its growing coterie of advocates speak in confident tones. They not only see among their followers the signs of religious vigor but find themselves listened to in high places.[99]

Unfortunately for them, however, the situation is not as promising as it may appear. The ancient Protestant nemesis of disruptive disagreement and incipient fragmentation has begun to appear on the horizon. The controversy here is not only with liberals, which is to be expected, but with other neo-evangelicals. During the middle seventies such disagreement surfaced among the Lutherans of the Missouri Synod and was culminated by the firing of Concordia Seminary president John Tietjen for supporting his faculty in the use of the critical-historical method as a tool for biblical interpretation and in looking favorably at causes such as civil disobedience and draft resistance.[100] The discussion of E. Dobson and E. Hinson, both Baptists, seems to indicate that their attack on Billy Graham, C.F.H. Henry, and Harold Ockenga gives evidence of similar tensions between right wingers and moderates among evangelical Baptists.[101] In 1974 Richard Quebedeaux divided all conservative Protestants into five groups.[102] Although hindsight would prompt us to simplify this classification as we did in this chapter, Quebedeaux's analysis is indicative of the tensions within conservative Protes-tantism in general and neo-evangelicalism in particular.

Among the problems that give rise to these internal strains, the present debate about biblical authority is likely to be most far reaching since, from a conservative point of view, the hermeneutical problem is involved in all others. Thus hard-liners on the biblical inerrancy question, like Harold Lindsell, believe that evangelicals cannot give way on this matter.[103] Moderates, such as C.F.H. Henry, insist that the evangelical movement would be ill advised to waste its energies on such issues.[104] Perhaps most neo-evangelical interpreters of the Bible presently take a moderate position.[105] This is only one issue, however, that divides them. R. K. Johnston quoted David Hubbard's taped remarks, made to a colloquium at the Conservative Baptist Theological Seminary in 1977, to the effect that tensions among today's evangelicals will continue to involve questions related to women's ordination, the charismatic movement, ecumenical relations, social ethics, strategies of evangelism, biblical criticism, contextual theology as applying to non-Western cultures, and the application of the insights of the behavioral sciences in the churches.[106] All of these things are, in fact, presently receiving attention both in the learned journals and in the church press of neo-evangelicals.

One of the most surprising trends is the movement toward the political Left among present evangelicals who matured during the sixties and who were influenced not only by the Anabaptist Protestant tradition but by the Roman Catholic Left (the Berrigans and others) as well as by Jacque Ellul.[107] They reach the public especially through the magazine *Sojourners*, put out by the People's Christian Coalition, and also through *The Other Side*, mouthpiece of the Berkeley Christian Coalition.[108] Equally interesting is the feminist movement among contemporary evangelicals, including the churches of the black religious establishment.[109] Their attempt to bring together the typically feminist themes such as egalitarian relationships and the right to ordination with the conservative understanding of the authority of the Bible (especially St. Paul) somewhat strains one's sense of logical consistency. Yet exegetical ingenuity is such that on the question of ordination G. W. Knight III, professor of the New Testament at Covenant Theological Seminary at St. Louis, feels justified in saying no, while A. M. Stouffer of Thunder Bay, Ontario says yes, and both believe that they interpret the New Testament literally.[110]

It is to be hoped that although divisive issues, which are a part of the human situation, will not go away, American Christians will learn to live with one another in mutual respect and appreciation as well as in the joint appreciation of other faiths among us, notably that of Judaism. Some small signs seem to point in that direction. Among them is R. J. Coleman's effort to identify possibilities of conflict between liberals and evangelicals and to suggest ways of dealing with them.[111] Among them also is the call of R. G. Hutcheson, Jr., upon mainline churches to enter into an era of cooperation with evangelicalism.[112] Encouraging, too, is the fact that in the area of biblical scholarship many liberal and evangelical, as well as Roman Catholic, interpreters are moving toward the center by accepting a cautious application of the critical-historical method to an interpretation of the Bible that has significance to the people in the churches.[113] Furthermore, in comparing the Wheaton Declaration of 1966 with the Lausanne Covenant of 1977 the impression prevails that there has been consultation and mutual adjustment between the views of liberals and evangelicals on the subject of the church's mission. On the other hand, although both liberals and evangelicals often advocate support for Israel, neither camp can match the zeal of Franklin M. Littel or Paul M. Van Buren in the attempt to promote understanding between Jews and Protestants.[114] More openness toward Judaism, as well as toward other faiths such as Islam, Hinduism, and Buddhism, is greatly to be desired. Among American Protestants today, neither the people in the churches nor the clergy nor their intellectual and ecclesiastical leadership are really aware of the full implications of religious pluralism for America and for the world.

NOTES

1. Indicative of John Dewey's position is his *A Common Faith* (New Haven: Yale University Press 1934).

2. The development of the social gospel movement is detailed in C. Howard Hopkin, *Rise of the Social Gospel in American Protestantism, 1865–1915* (1940).

3. The major works of Walter Rauschenbusch are *Christianity and the Social Crisis* (1907); *Christianizing the Social Order* (1912); and *A Theology for the Social Gospel* (1917). D. R. Sharpe, *Walter Rauschenbusch* (1942), is a helpful discussion of his life and work.

4. William Newton Clark, *An Outline of Christian Theology* (N.Y.: C. Scribner's Sons, 1905; William Adams Brown, *Christian Theology in Outline* (1906).

5. Fairly typical of this Christocentricity are W. A. Brown, *Christ the Vitalizing Principle of Modern Theology* (1898), and, in its later development, Francis J. McConnell, *The Christlike God* (1927).

6. In this context R. H. Abrams, *Preachers Present Arms* (1933), makes for interesting reading.

7. Although never ordained, Shailer Mathews helped to shape the Protestant mind by moving it in the direction of a sociohistorical understanding of Christian ethics. He was convinced that what he understood to be the permanent values preserved in the Christian tradition can be established and undergirded by the use of the scientific method. Among his main works are *The Faith of Modernism* (1924); *The Atonement and the Social Process* (1930); *The Growth of the Idea of God* (1931); and *New Faith for Old: An Autobiography* (1936).

8. Through his extensive literary activity Harry Emerson Fosdick became the preacher's preacher par excellence. Among his most widely read books are *The Manhood of the Master* (1913); *The Meaning of Prayer* (1915); *On Being a Real Person* (1943); and *The Living of These Days* (1956).

9. Note Lyman Abbott's *Theology of an Evolutionist* (1897). He summed up his position as follows: "The object of Christianity is human welfare, its method is character building, its process is evolution, and the secret of its power is God." Quoted by R. J. Coleman, *Issues of Theological Conflict: Evangelicals and Liberals* (1980), p. 211.

10. Witness the proceedings during the 1890s against the biblical scholars Charles Briggs and H. P. Smith and against the historian A. C. McGiffert.

11. Among John Machen's best-known books are *The Origin of Paul's Religion* (1921); *Christianity and Liberalism* (1923); *The Virgin Birth of Christ* (1930); *The Christian Faith in the Modern World* (1936); *The Christian View of Man* (1937). As a result of a lawsuit, the Presbyterian Church of America became the Orthodox Presbyterian Church in 1939.

12. The literature relating to early fundamentalism is very extensive. Among the most important historical studies are the following S. G. Stewart, *The History of Fundamentalism* (1931); N. F. Furniss, *The Fundamentalist Controversy, 1918–1931* (1954); Louis Gasper, *The Fundamentalist Movement* (1963); E. R. Sandeen, "Toward a Historical Interpretation of the Origins of Fundamentalism," *Church History* 36 (March 1967): 66–83; idem, *The Roots of Fundamentalism: British and American Millenarianism, 1800–1930* (1970); G. W. Dollar, *A History of Fundamentalism in America* (1973); C. A. Russell, *Voices of American Fundamentalism: Seven Biographical Studies* (1976); James Barr, *Fundamentalism* (1978); and G. M. Marsden, *Fundamentalism and American Culture: The Shaping of Twentieth-Century Evangelicalism, 1870–1925* (1980).

13. See J. T. Scopes and James Presby, *Center of the Storm: Memoirs of John T. Scopes* (1967); L. H. Allen, ed. and comp., *Bryan and Darrow at Dayton: The Record and Documents of the "Bible Evolution" Trial* (1925, 1967); J. R. Tompkins, ed., *D-Days at Dayton: Reflections on the Scopes Trial* (1965); W. B. Gatewood, Jr., ed., *Controversy in the Twenties: Fundamentalism, Modernism, and Evolution* (1969).

14. This seems to be true in spite of the caveats of people like F. M. Szasz about the significance of the Scopes trial. Note his "Scopes Trial in Perspective," *Tennessee Historical Quarterly* (Fall 1971): 288–298.

15. Typical of the attacks is Harry Emerson Fosdick's sermon "Shall the Fundamentalists Win?" reproduced in H. S. Smith, R. T. Handy, and L. A. Loetscher, *American Christianity* (1963), 2:295–301.

16. C.F.H. Henry did this in his *Uneasy Conscience of Modern Fundamentalism.* Other important books by C.F.H. Henry are *The Protestant Dilemma* (1949); *Fifty Years of Protestant Theology* (1950); *Evangelical Responsibility in Contemporary Theology* (1957); *Christian Personal Ethics* (1957); *Evangelicals on the Brink* (1967); and *Politics for Evangelicals* (1974).

17. G. B. Smith in his *Current Christian Thinking* (1928) referred to them as "religious humanists." Further insight into this whole development is provided by G. B. Smith; also helpful are the discussions in W. P. King, ed., *Humanism: Another Battle Line* (1931); and W. R. Hutchinson, ed., *American Protestant Thought: The Liberal Era* (1968).

18. W. W. Fenn, "War and the Thought of God," in Hutchinson, *American Protestant Thought,* p. 150.

19. Henry Nelson Wieman, "Religion and Illusion," in Hutchinson, *American Protestant Thought,* p. 185.

20. W. W. Sperry, "A Modern Doctrine of Original Sin," in Hutchinson, *American Protestant Thought,* pp. 159–169.

21. A sympathetic analysis of it is found in W. Hordern, *The Case for a New Reformation Theology* (Philadelphia: Westminster Press, 1959).

22. Wilhelm Pauck, *Karl Barth: Prophet of a New Christianity?* Emil Brunner's *Theology of Crisis* (1929) was highly critical of the whole liberal Protestant trend.

23. Other volumes of Reinhold Niebuhr followed in its wake: *Beyond Tragedy* (1937); *The Nature and Destiny of Man* (1941, 1943); *Faith and History* (1949); *Man's Nature and his Communities* (1965). His theology is discussed by Hans Hoffmann, *The Theology of Reinhold Niebuhr* (1956).

24. Nicolas Berdyaev's theology is discussed by Matthew Spinka, *Nicolas Berdyaev: Captive of Freedom* (1950).

25. See Paul Tillich, "The Lost Dimension in Religion," *Saturday Evening Post,* June 14, 1958, p. 29. Among Tillich's most influential books are *The Religious Situation* (1932), with a most discerning introduction by Richard Niebuhr; *The Interpretation of History* (1936); *The Protestant Era* (1948); *The Courage to Be* (1952); *The New Being* (1955); *Systematic Theology* (1951–1963). An exposition of his thought and an appraisal of its significance is found in C. W. Kegley and W. Bretall, eds., *The Theology of Paul Tillich* (1952), and in G. H. Tavard, *Paul Tillich and the Christian Message* (1961).

26. Rudolf Bultmann's *Jesus and the Word* (N.Y.: Scribner's, 1958). For his thought, consult S. Ogden, *Christ Without Myth: A Study on the Theology of Rudolf Bultmann* (1961).

27. A discussion of Niebuhr's thought is available in Paul Ramsey, ed., *Faith and Ethics: The Theology of Richard Niebuhr* (N.Y.: Harper 1957).

28. J. B. Pratt, "The New Supernaturalism: Peril to 20th Century Christianity," in H. N. Wieman et al., eds., *Religious Liberals Reply* (1947), p. 96.

29. A. E. Murphy, "Coming to Grips with the Nature and Destiny of Man," in Niebuhr, *Nature and Destiny of Man,* (N.Y.: Scribner's Sons, 1949) p. 17.

30. H. P. Van Dusen, "Liberal Theology Reassessed," *Union Seminary Quarterly* 18 (May 1963): 343. This article seems to contain the essence of his book published the same year *Vindication of Liberal Theology* (1963).

31. Kenneth Cauthen, *The Impact of American Theological Liberalism* (1962), p. 229.

32. Quoted from W. M.Horton, *Realistic Theology* (1934) in his article "The Decline of Liberalism," in Hutchinson, *American Protestant Thought,* p. 191.

33. Ibid., p. 193.

34. H. P. Van Dusen, "The Sickness of Liberal Religion," *The World of Tomorrow* 14 (1931): 256–259.

35. John C. Bennet, "After Liberalism—What?" *Christian Century* 50 (1933): 1403–1406.

36. Wilhelm Pauck, "What Is Wrong with Liberalism?" *Journal of Religion* 15 (April 1935): 146–160; Henry Sloan Coffin, "Can Liberalism Survive?" *Religion in Life* 4 (Spring 1935): 194–203.

37. Typical is John C. Bennett's *Christian Realism* (1941). Note Daniel Day Williams's *God's Grace and Man's Hope* (1949). H. P. Van Dusen's concept of "authentic evangelical liberalism" is set forth in his *Vindication*.

38. Especially noteworthy here is Edwin Lewis's *Christian Manifesto* (1934), which made quite an impression at the time. John MacKay's thinking at this time is evident in his *Preface to Christian Theology* (1941). See also Robert L. Calhoun, *God and the Common Life* (1935).

39. A concise overview of liberalism at the time is found in D. D. Williams, *What Present-Day Theologians Are Thinking* (rev. ed., 1959). Also helpful is Cauthen's *Impact of American Theological Liberalism.*

40. Evidence of the general orientation and value structure of neo-liberalism is found

in various statements of social concern put out by these agencies of mainline Protestantism, as well as in the educational materials made available by them to church schoolteachers, women's groups, youth groups, and others.

41. See Van Dusen, "Liberal Theology Reassessed." See also B.M.G. Reardon, "In Defence of Theological Liberalism," *Anglican Theological Review* 40 (January 1958): 47–50; idem, ed., *Liberal Protestantism* (1968). A case in point concerning whether it is at the crossroads are the moving sermons of J. B. Cobb, Jr., *Liberal Christianity at the Crossroads* (1973).

42. Kenneth Hamilton's *Revolt against Heaven: An Inquiry into Anti-Supernaturalism* (1965) affords an insight into the antisupernaturalism of the day; so does P. L. Berger's "Secular Theology and the Rejection of the Supernatural: Reflections on Recent Trends," *Theological Studies* 38 (March 1977): 39–56.

43. William Hordern, *The Case for a New Reformation Theology* (1959), p. 103.

44. Thomas J. J. Altizer, *The Gospel of Christian Atheism* (Philadelphia: Westminster, 1966). Gabriel Vahanian, *The Death of God: The Culture of Our Post-Christian Era.*

45. Paul M. Van Buren, *The Secular Meaning of the Gospel* (1963).

46. For the further study of the death of God episode, the following discussions will be found helpful: Schubert Ogden, *The Reality of God* (1966); T. Altizer and W. Hamilton, *Radical Theology and the Death of God* (1966); J. B. Cobb, Jr., "From Christian Theology to the Post-Modern World," *Centennial Review* 8 (Spring 1964): 74–188; P. L. Berger, "Secular Theology and the Rejection of the Supernatural: Reflections on Recent Trends"; William Hamilton, "The Death of God Theology," *Christian Scholar* 48 (Spring 1965): 27–48; D. L. Edwards, ed., *The Honest to God Debate* (1963); Harvey Cox, "The Death of God and the Future of Theology," in M. E. Marty and D. G. Peerman, eds., *New Theology,* No. 4 (1967).

47. Langdon Gilkey, *Naming the Whirlwind: The Renewal of God Language* (1969).

48. Dietrich Bonhoeffer's important works are *Act and Being* (1961); *Prisoners for God: Letters and Papers from Prison* (1962); *The Cost of Discipleship,* rev. ed. (1965); *Ethics,* ed. E. Bethge (1965). See also M. E. Marty, *The Place of Bonhoeffer* (1962).

49. Van Buren, *The Secular Meaning of the Gospel,* p. 191.

50. Harvey Cox, *The Secular City: Secularization and Urbanization in Theological Perspective* (N.Y.: Macmillan, 1965).

51. See M. E. Marty and D. G. Peerman, *New Theology, No. 2,* (N.Y.: Macmillan, 1966), pp. 39–49.

52. Martin Marty, "Tensions within Contemporary Evangelicalism: A Critical Appraisal," in D. F. Wells and J. D. Woodbridge, eds., *The Evangelicals* (1975), p. 173.

53. A cautiously conservative British appraisal is that of Daniel Jenkins, *Beyond Religion: The Truth and Error of Religionless Christianity* (1962).

54. James Cone, *A Black Theology of Liberation* (1970); idem, *God of the Oppressed* (1975). Early advocates of liberation theology were M. R. Shaull and Jürgen Moltmann. Helpful here are especially Shaull's *Encounter with Revolution* (1955) and Moltmann's sermons entitled *The Gospel of Liberation* (1973). Among the influential authors in this area at present are Gustavo Gutiérrez, *A Theology of Liberation: History, Politics, and Salvation* (1973); and J. L. Segundo, *Liberation Theology* (1976); as well as Ivan Illich of Mexico and Helder Camara of Brazil.

55. Paul L. Lehman, *Ethics in a Christian Context* (1963).

56. Angela Davis was a disciple of Marcuse and had been fired from the faculty of

the University of California in Los Angeles in 1969 because of her acknowledged membership in the Communist party. Having been imprisoned, the Presbyterian Council on Church and Race decided to contribute $10,000 to her defense fund.

57. V. C. Grounds, *Revolution and the Christian Faith* (1971), p. 198.

58. Robert M. Brown, "Reflections on Liberation Theology," *Religion in Life* 43 (Autumn 1974): 269–282. An extended discussion of the subject is found in the "Kearns Seminar on Liberation Theology," *Duke Divinity Review* 38 (Fall 1973): 125–170. The *Index to Religious Periodic Literature* mentions it as a separate topic in the 1971–1972 volume.

59. A good bibliography of the total movement up to the middle seventies is that of Harriet V. Leonard, *Liberation and Development in Current Theology: A Bibliography Emphasizing Blacks, Women, and the Third World* (N.Y.: Seabury Press, 1975).

60. See Lehman, *Ethics in a Christian Context.* Among the "situational" ethicists, in addition to Lehman and Robinson, are Albert Rasmussen, Gordon Kaufman, James M. Gustafson, and Charles West. Bernard Häring, a Roman Catholic, in his two volumes on *The Law of Christ* (1961, 1963), moved in the same general direction and found himself more and more committed to this perspective as time went on. Of the critics of the "new morality" one must mention especially Paul Ramsey, although others, including John C. Bennett, joined the attack. The debate is discussed in Marty and Peerman, *New Theology, No. 3* in a chapter by Gustafson, "Context vs. Principles: A Misplaced Debate in Christian Ethics," pp. 69–102. See also G. H. Outka and Paul Ramsey, eds., *Norm and Context in Christian Ethics* (1968).

61. J. B. Nelson, "Homosexuality and the Church," *Christianity and Crisis* 37 (April 4, 1977): 63–69, takes a typically liberal position. An evangelical point of view is found in Don Williams, *The Bond That Breaks: Will Homosexuality Split the Church?* (1978); and Richard Lovelace, *The Church and Homosexuality* (1978).

62. The literature on this movement is massive. The following works will give an adequate overview: W. A. Brown, *Toward a United Church* (1946); S. Rouse and S. C. Neill, eds., *A History of the Ecumenical Movement, 1417–1948* (1948); W. A. Visser 't Hooft, *The Meaning of Ecumenical* (1954); D. P. Gaines, *The World Council of Churches: A Study of Its Background and History* (1966); S. M. Cavert, *The American Churches in the Ecumenical Movement, 1900–1968* (1968); S. C. Neill, *The Church and Christian Union* (1968).

63. A sample of that criticism is found in the following discussions: E. Cailliet, "The Ecumenical Self-Indictment," *Christianity Today* 7 (July 5, 1963): 9–10; H. A. Buchanan and B. W. Brown, "The Ecumenical Movement Threatens Protestantism," *Christianity Today* 9 (November 20, 1964): 21–23; T. Hewitt, "Evangelicals in an Ecumenical Atmosphere," *Christianity Today* 9 (January 29, 1965): 37–38.

64. Much has been written on Roman Catholic participation in the ecumenical dialogue. The following discussions will afford an insight into the problems involved: R. M. Brown, *The Ecumenical Revolution: An Interpretation of Catholic-Protestant Dialogue* (1967); G. H. Tavard, *The Catholic Approach to Protestantism* (1955); Gregory Baum, *Progress and Perspectives; The Catholic Quest for Christian Unity* (N.Y.: Sheed & Ward, 1962.

65. Henry, *Evangelical Responsibility in Contemporary Theology,* p. 43.

66. E. G. Hinson, "Baptists and Evangelicals: What Is the Difference?" *Baptist History and Heritage* 16 (April 1981): 21.

67. A definitional attempt is made in S. E. Ahlstrom, "From Puritanism to Evan-

gelicalism,'' in D. F. Wells and J. D. Woodbridge, eds., *The Evangelicals* (1975), pp. 269–289.

68. Donald Bloesch, *The Evangelical Renaissance* (Grand Rapids, Mich.: Eerdmans, 1973), 30f.

69. Note *The Chicago Declaration* released by a group of evangelicals in 1973. Reproduced in Coleman, *Issues of Theological Conflict*, pp. 255–256.

70. Examples of parachurch structures are Campus Crusade for Christ; Intervarsity Christian Fellowship; Youth for Christ; Awana Youth Clubs; Pioneer Girls; and Christian Service Brigade.

71. For a more thorough acquaintance with the nature of neo-evangelicalism, see the following discussions: D. B. Stevick, *Beyond Fundamentalism* (1964); E. T. Carnell, *The Case for Biblical Christianity* (1969); E. Jorstad, ''Two on the Right: A Comparative Look at Fundamentalism and the New Evangelicalism,'' *Lutheran Quarterly* 23 (May 1971): 107–117; L. D. Streiker, *Religion and the New Majority: Billy Graham, Middle America, and the Politics of the 70's* (1972); D. M. Kelly, *Why Conservative Churches Are Growing* (1972); Bernard Ramm, *The Evangelical Heritage* (1973); D. G. Bloesch, *The Evangelical Renaissance* (1973); Richard Quebedeaux, *The Young Evangelicals: Revolution in Orthodoxy* (1974); and D. F. Wells and J. D. Woodbridge, *The Evangelicals* (1975).

72. Attention may be called here to the continued criticism of them in the early volumes of *Christianity Today*. In his *Scripture, Tradition, and Infallibility* (1973) D. M. Beegle finally presented a systematic exposition of their point of view.

73. T. S. Baker, *Christ and the Even Balance: A Manual on Fundamentalism* (1968).

74. Stevick, *Beyond Fundamentalism*, p. 28.

75. We are speaking here of men like D. G. Bloesch, G. W. Bromiley, G. H. Clarke, Donald W. Dayton, Morris Inch, Kenneth S. Kantzer, Harold Lindsell, Richard Lovelace, J. W. Montgomery, Bernard Ramm, Francis Schaeffer, Donald Tinder, V. C. Grounds, and R. J. Sider.

76. The following discussions will afford an insight into this movement: M. P. Hamilton, ed., *The Charismatic Movement* (1975); Richard Quebedeaux, *The New Charismatics: The Origin, Development, and Significance of Neo-Pentecostalism* (1976); a Roman Catholic approach by Kilian McDonnell, *Charismatic Renewal and Ecumenism* (1978); J. H. Smylie, ''Testing the Spirits in the American Context: Great Awakenings, Pentecostalism, and the Charismatic Movement,'' *Interpretation* 33 (January 1979): 32–46; D. P. Scaer, ''The Charismatic Movement as Ecumenical Phenomenon,'' *Corcordia Theological Quarterly* 45 (January 1981): 81–83; Clark Pinnock, ''Opening the Church to the Charismatic Dimension,'' *Christianity Today* 25 (June 11, 1981): 16.

77. Hamilton, *The Charismatic Movement*, p. 7.

78. Scaer, ''The Charismatic Movement,'' is a case in point.

79. See H. V. Synan's report on the World Pentecostal Conference, September 1976, reported in *Christianity Today* 21 (November 5, 1976): 78–80.

80. Marty, ''Tensions within Contemporary Evangelicalism,'' pp. 172–173.

81. A study of the successive issues of the statistical section of the *Yearbook of American and Canadian Churches* will bear this out. One should compare here the statistics referring to conservative groups such as The Salvation Army, the churches in the Christian Holiness Association (CHA), and the churches in the Pentecostal Fellowship of North America (PFNA) with those of mainline Protestant bodies such as The United

Methodist Church, The United Church of Christ, and The United Presbyterian Church in the U.S.A.

82. D. D. Dayton, "The Holiness and Pentecostal Churches: Emerging from Cultural Isolation," *Christian Century* 96 (August 15, 1979): 787.

83. Christopher Walter-Bugbee, "Across the Great Divide: Seminarians and the Local Church," *Christian Century* 98 (November 11, 1981): 1155. These words are quoted approvingly by Walter-Bugbee from an article by W. Robert Martin, Jr.

84. A. T. Templeman, "Where Have All the Liberals Gone?" *Christian Century* 90 (May 16, 1973): 557–558.

85. K. S. Kantzer, "Unity and Diversity in the Evangelical Faith," in Wells and Woodbridge, *The Evangelicals,* p. 59.

86. D. W. Ferm, "Protestant Liberalism Affirmed," *Christian Century* 93 (April 28, 1976): 411–416; R. F. Sheppard, "Manifesto for the New Liberal Church," *Christian Century* 93 (October 6, 1976): 837–839; W. R. Barnett, "Contemporary Resource of Liberal Theology," *Christian Century* 96 (March 21, 1979): 306–311.

87. William Pannell, "The Religious Heritage of Blacks," in Wells and Woodbridge, *The Evangelicals,* p. 100.

88. Exact figures on the number of black Protestants do not seem to be available. The churches they belong to are, notably, the National Baptist Convention, U.S.A., Incorporated; the National Baptist Convention of America; the Progressive National Baptist Convention, Incorporated; the African Methodist Episcopal Church; the African Methodist Episcopal Zion Church; and the Christian Methodist Episcopal Church.

89. An insight into black Protestantism in America is afforded by Pannell, "The Religious Heritage of Blacks," pp. 96–107. See also Pannell's *My Friend the Enemy* (1968); W. H. Bentley, "Bible Believers in the Black Community," in Wells and Woodbridge, *The Evangelicals,* pp. 108–121; Richard Quebedeaux, "The Evangelicals: New Trends and New Tensions," *Christianity and Crisis* 36 (September 20, 1976): 197–202; L. N. Jones, "The Black Churches: A New Agenda," *Christian Century* 94 (April 18, 1979): 434–438. The best-known black theologian is James Cone, whose books have been mentioned in note 54.

90. The following are helpful discussions of the electronic pulpit: W. Kuhns, *The Electronic Gospel* (1969); E. L. Towns, "Trends among Fundamentalists," *Christianity Today* 17 (July 6, 1973): 12–14; K. A. Briggs, "Religious Medias' Spreading Tentacles," *Christian Century* 95 (March 1, 1978): 203–204; Michael Barton, "What a Friend They Have in Jesus," *Christian Century* 96 (September 19, 1979): 886–888; E. G. Hinson, "Neo-Fundamentalism: An Interpretation and Critique," *Baptist History and Heritage* 16 (April 1981): 33–42; E. F. Klug, "The Electronic Church," *Concordia Theological Quarterly* 45 (October 1981): 261–280; Jorstad, "Two on the Right"; idem, *The Politics of Moralism: The New Christian Right in American Life* (1981). The classic exposition of moral majority opinion is found in Jerry Falwell, *Listen America* (1980).

91. A. C. Krass, "What the Mainline Denominations Are Doing in Evangelism," *Christian Century* 96 (May 2, 1979): 490–496.

92. Note the news report "The Mainline Churches Strike Back on T.V.," *U.S. News and World Report* (February 15, 1982); 60.

93. J. C. Lyles, "The God Language Bind," *Christian Century* 97 (April 16, 1980): 430–431.

94. For the rash of books it has spawned, see the summary in R. K. Johnston, *Evangelicals at the Crossroads* (1979), pp. 174–175.

95. Nancy Hardesty et al., "Women Clergy: How Their Presence Is Changing the Church," a symposium of five women, *Christian Century* 96 (February 7, 1979): 122–128; Barbara B. Zikmund, "Women in Ministry Face the '80s," *Christian Century* 79 (February 3, 1982): 113–115; and Phyllis Trible, "Feminist Hermeneutic and Biblical Studies," *Christian Century* 79 (February 3, 1982): 116–118.

96. In Helmuth Thielicke's introduction to Ernest Lefever's *From Amsterdam to Nairobi: The World Council of Churches and the Third World* (1979). Lefever's book itself is a conservative indictment of the World Council of Churches. So is E. R. Norman's *Christianity and the World Order* (1979). That this liberal understanding of the church's worldwide mission has raised considerable controversy within mainline Protestant denominations is evident from the discussion of the subject in their official journals. See, for instance, the issues of the *Methodist Reporter* during December and January 1981–1982.

97. Coleman, *Issues of Theological Conflict*.

98. G. Gallop and D. Poling, *The Search for America's Faith* (1980), p. 140.

99. Thus Alfred C. Krass, editor-at-large of the magazine *The Other Side,* found himself invited by the National Council of Churches in 1976 to help write a policy paper. Billy Graham's long standing connection with the White House is well-known.

100. The matter is discussed by J. T. Hickman, "Polarity in American Evangelicalism," *Religion in Life* 44 (Spring 1975): 47–58.

101. E. Dobson and E. Hinson, *The Fundamentalist Phenomenon: The Resurgence of Conservative Christianity* (1981).

102. Quebedeaux, *The Young Evangelicals,* pp. 18f.

103. Harold Lindsell, *Battle for the Bible* (1976).

104. C. F. H. Henry, *Evangelicals in Search for Identity* (1976).

105. Among contemporary evangelicals who hold to what may be described as a modified inerrancy position are Bernard Ramm, *Special Revelation and the Word of God* (1961); and Clark Pinnock, *Biblical Revelation* (1971). Some of them, G. E. Ladd in his *New Testament and Criticism* (1967), for example, try to get along without the inerrancy concept.

106. Johnston, *Evangelicals at the Crossroads,* p. 147.

107. See Jacque Ellul, *Presence of the Kingdom,* trans. Olive Wyon (1951); and idem, *The Politics of God, and the Politics of Man,* trans. G. W. Bromiley (1972); see also W. H. Vandenburg, ed., *Perspectives on Our Age: Jacque Ellul Speaks on His Life and Work,* trans. J. Neugroschel (1981).

108. A careful discussion of this trend is found in Quebedeaux, "The Evangelicals: New Trends and Tensions," pp. 197–202.

109. Among the major voices of white feminists are those of Virginia R. Mollenkott, Nancy Hardesty, Elizabeth Elliot, Sharon Gallagher, Evon Bachaus, Letha Scanzoni, Judy Brown Hull, and Lucile Sider Dayton, editor of their major publication *Daughters of Sarah.* Among the most vocal black feminists are Jeanne Noble, *Beautiful, Also, Are the Souls of My Black Sisters* (1978); and Michele Wallace, *Black Macho, and the Myth of the Superwoman* (1979).

110. G. W. Knight, "The Ordination of Women—NO," and E. Stoeffler, "Ordination of Women—YES," *Christianity Today* 25 (February 20, 1981): 12–19.

111. Coleman, *Issues of Theological Conflict*.

112. R. G. Hutcheson, Jr., *Mainline Churches and the Evangelicals: A Challenging Crisis?* (1981).

113. Among liberals, B. S. Childs, Walter Wink, and James Smart seem to be moving in this direction. The evangelical slide toward the center is referred to by Richard Quebedeaux in Wells and Woodbridge, *The Evangelicals*. G. S. Sloyan pointed to a similar movement among Roman Catholics in his article "Jesus of Nazarath: Today's Way to God, *Journal of Ecumenical Studies* 17 (Winter 1980): 49–56. Note also D. J. Harrington's study, "The Ecumenical Importance of New Testament Research," *Biblical Theology Bulletin* 12 (January 1982): 20–23.

114. Franklin M. Littel, *The Crucifiction of the Jews* (1975); Paul M. Van Buren, *The Burden of Freedom: Americans and the God of Israel* (1976); idem, *Discerning the Way: A Theology of the Jewish Christian Reality* (1980).

GLOSSARY

Antisupernaturalism: The attitude among some liberals that the universe is a closed system of cause and effect that does not allow for the direct intervention of divine agency. Hence Protestantism must free itself from traditional conceptions of God and his relation to the world.

Barthianism. See Crisis theology.

Charismatic movement: A contemporary interdenominational movement that puts emphasis upon the work of the Spirit of God in the life of individuals and of Christian groups.

Contextual ethics: The attempt to orient Christian ethics away from traditional Protestant norms and in favor of a basic regard for the perceived urgencies of the immediate context (cultural, social, intellectual) in which Christians, motivated by love, must make their decision.

Crisis theology: A theological perspective that stems from Karl Barth, also known as Barthianism, neo-orthodoxy, dialectical theology, and theology of the Word. In contradistinction to religious humanism, it puts emphasis on the otherness of God and on his redemptive acts and their significance for humankind.

Dialectical theology: See Crisis theology.

Dispensationalism: The belief that history unfolds according to a series of preordained dispensations, or ages, each marked by characteristic events, to which alone certain passages of the Bible have reference.

Ecumenism: A twentieth-century movement that emphasized Christian unity and tried to work toward it.

Electronic pulpit: The contemporary, largely nondenominational development in the use of radio and television for the purpose of diseminating the Christian message.

Eschatology: That part of Christian thought and expectation that is oriented toward future events such as the second coming of Christ (Parousia) and the establishment of the kingdom of God.

Evangelicalism: A theological perspective that purports to take seriously all, or most, traditional Christian affirmations about God and the need for his redemptive activity in the world. Its focus is broader, however, than that of fundamentalism out of which it developed.

Fundamentalism: A theological perspective that is based on a selected series of traditional Christian affirmations regarded as fundamental to the Christian faith, such as scriptural inerrancy, the deity of Christ, or his virgin birth, and that holds that apart from belief in these doctrinal propositions, a person's Christianity is not genuine.

Hermeneutic: A given methodology applied to the interpretation of Scripture.

Holiness movement: A movement in modern Protestantism that grew out of the Wesleyan revival and that emphasizes a pattern of personal conduct based on one's unreserved commitment to the religious and ethical teaching of the Bible as interpreted within that branch of the Wesleyan tradition.

Liberalism (religious): A perspective relative to religious thought and life that deemphasizes traditional Christian beliefs and practices and stresses accommodation to contemporary perceptions of the requirements and needs posed by the culture in which one lives.

Liberation theology: An attempt to make the concept of liberation central to the Christian self-understanding. It tends to see humankind under the categories of oppressors and oppressed and tries to put the central thrust of the Christian message on the side of the latter.

Mainline (mainstream) Protestantism: The kind of Protestantism associated with what have been regarded as America's major denominations.

Modernism: A term often used for the religious liberalism found in the major Protestant denominations during the 1920s. It stood in opposition to the restrictive traditionalism advocated by the fundamentalists of the time.

Moral Majority: The self-designation of contemporary neo-fundamentalists who insist that their moral perceptions constitute the majority opinion of the American people.

Neo-evangelicalism: Also referred to as the new evangelicalism. A movement that arose out of the earlier fundamentalism during the 1940s. It accepts traditional Protestant beliefs without the narrow dogmatism characteristic of fundamentalists and with more openness to the needs of the world in which we are living.

Neo-fundamentalism: A resurgence of the earlier fundamentalism during the early 1960s that believes in, but speaks less about, the so-called fundamentals and that tends to be politically active in a way the older fundamentalism was not.

Neo-orthodoxy: See Crisis theology.

New morality: See Contextual ethics.

Pentecostalism: A branch of Protestantism that puts emphasis on the work of the Spirit of God in the Christian community and in individuals. It differs from the contemporary charismatic movement insofar as it tends to be denominational rather than interdenominational.

Postliberal theology: A theological trend during the 1930s and early 1940s that meant to correct the optimistic view of humans and their potential achievements prevalent among earlier liberals.

Postmillennialism: The view that the expected second coming of Christ will follow God's establishment of the millennium of his unopposed reign.

Predestination: The doctrine that God predetermines the religious destiny of each person, a belief often associated with St. Augustine and the reformer John Calvin.

Premillennialism: A view frequently found among fundamentalists that the expected second coming of Christ precedes God's establishment of the millennium of his unopposed reign.

Realistic theology: See Postliberal theology.

Scientism: The notion that only scientifically verifiable truth has validity and that the application of the scientific method is sufficient to solve all human problems.

Secular gospel: An attempt to orient the Christian message toward concerns and practices that have been frequently neglected by organized Christendom.

Social gospel: An interpretation of the Christian message that flourished within American Protestantism at the turn of the century and that greatly emphasized the societal implications of that message, especially with regard to the humanizing of the structure and operation of business enterprises.

Supernaturalism: The attitude that God is a transcendent, self-conscious being who can choose, has chosen, and does choose to intervene directly in natural events.

Theology of the Word: See Crisis theology.

Selected Bibliography

Ahlstrom, S. E. *A Religious History of the American People*. New Haven: Yale University Press, 1972.

Argow, W. *What the Religious Liberals Believe*. 1950.

Averill, L. J. *American Theology in the Liberal Tradition*. Philadelphia: Westminster Press, 1967.

Baker, T. E. *Christ and the Even Balance: A Manual on Fundamentalism*. Millersburg, Pa.: Bible Truth Mission, 1968.

Barr, James. *Fundamentalism*. Philadelphia: Westminster Press, 1978.

Berkouwer, G. C. *A Half Century of Theology*. Grand Rapids: Eerdmans, 1977.

Bixler, J. S. *Conversations with an Unrepentent Liberal*. New Haven: Yale University Press, 1946.

Bloesch, D. G. *The Evangelical Renaissance*. Grand Rapids: Eerdmans, 1973.

Brown, R. M. *The Ecumenical Revolution: An Interpretation of Catholic-Protestant Dialogue*. Garden City: Doubleday, 1967.

Brown, W. A. *Toward a United Church*. New York: Charles Scribner's Sons, 1946.

Burggraaff, Winfield. *The Rise and Development of Liberal Theology in America*. 1938.

Cauthen, Kenneth. *The Impact of American Theological Liberalism*. New York: Harper & Row, 1962.

Cavert, S. M. *The American Churches in the Ecumenical Movement, 1900–1968*. New York: Association Press, 1968.

Chalmers, A. K. *High Wind at Noon: A Case for Daring Christianity*. 1948.

Clabaugh, G. K. *Thunder on the Right: The Protestant Fundamentalists*. Chicago: Nelson-Hall Co., 1974.

Cole, S. G. *The History of Fundamentalism*. New York: R. R. Smith, Inc., 1931.

Coleman, R. J. *Issues of Theological Conflict: Evangelicals and Liberals*. Grand Rapids: Eerdmans, 1980.

Cross, R. D. *The Emergence of Liberal Catholicism in America*. Cambridge: Harvard University Press, 1958.

Cumming, R. D. *Human Nature and History: A Study of the Development of Liberal Political Thought*. 2 vols. Chicago: University of Chicago Press, 1969.

Davies, D. R. *On to Orthodoxy*. New York: Macmillan, 1949.

DeWolf, L. H. *The Case for Theology in Liberal Perspective*. Philadelphia: Westminster Press, 1959.

Dillenberger, John. *Contours of Faith: Changing Forms of Christian Thought*. 1969.

Dobson, E., and E. Hinson, eds. *The Fundamentalist Phenomenon: The Resurgence of Conservative Christianity*. Garden City: Doubleday, 1981.

Dollar, G. W. *A History of Fundamentalism in America*. Greenville, S.C.: Bob Jones University Press, 1973.

Edwards, D. L., ed. *The Honest to God Debate*. Philadelphia: Westminster Press, 1963.

Frazer, E. F. *The Negro Church in America*. New York: Schocken Books, 1964.

Furniss, N. F. *The Fundamentalist Controversy, 1918–1931*. Hamden, Ct.: Archon Books, 1954.

Gaines, D. P. *The World Council of Churches: A Study of Its Background and History*. Peterborough, N.H.: R. R. Smith, 1966.

Gallup, G., Jr., and D. Poling, eds. *The Search for America's Faith*. Nashville: Abingdon, 1980.

Gasper, Louis. *The Fundamentalist Movement*. The Hague, Netherlands: Monton, 1963.

Gatewood, W. B., Jr., ed. *Controversy in the Twenties: Fundamentalism, Modernism, and Evolution*. Nashville: Vanderbilt University Press, 1969.

Gifford, H. H., ed. *The Charismatic Movement: A Special Study for Adults and Youth*. 1973.

Gilkey, Langdon. *Catholicism Confronts Modernity: A Protestant View*. New York: Seabury Press, 1975.

―――. *Naming the Whirlwind: The Renewal of God Language*. Indianapolis: Bobbs-Merrill, 1969.

Gordon, E. B. *An Ecclesiastical Octopus: A Factual Report on the Federal Council of Churches of Christ in America*. 1948.

Greene, L. S. *Conservatism, Liberalism, and National Issues*. Philadelphia: American Academy of Political and Social Science, 1962.

Hackett, S. C. *The Resurrection of Theism*. Chicago: Moody Press, 1957.

Hadden, J. K. *The Gathering Storm in the Churches*. Garden City: Doubleday, 1969.

Hamilton, Kenneth. *Revolt against Heaven: An Inquiry into Anti-Supernaturalism*. Grand Rapids: Eerdmans, 1965.

Hamilton, M. P., ed. *The Charismatic Movement*. Grand Rapids: Eerdmans, 1975.

Harden, J. A. *Christianity in the Twentieth Century*. Boston: St. Paul Editions, 1977.

Henry, C.F.H. *Fifty Years of Protestant Theology*. 1950.

Hoge, D. R. *Division in the Protestant House*. Philadelphia: Westminster Press, 1976.

Hopkins, C. H. *The Rise of the Social Gospel in American Protestantism, 1865–1915*. New Haven: Yale University Press, 1967.

Hordern, W. *A Layman's Guide to Protestant Theology*. New York: Macmillan, 1955.

Hutcheson, R. G., Jr. *Mainline Churches and the Evangelicals: A Challenging Crisis?* Atlanta: John Knox Press, 1981.

Hutchison, J. A. *We Are Not Divided: A Critical and Historical Study of the Federal Council of Churches of Christ in America*. New York: Round Table Press, Inc., 1941.

Hutchison, W. R., ed. *American Protestant Thought: The Liberal Era*. New York: Harper & Row, 1968.

Johnston, R. K. *Evangelicals at the Crossroads*. Atlanta: John Knox Press, 1979.

Jones, C. E. *A Guide to the Study of the Holiness Movement*. Metuchen, N.J.: Scarecrow Press, 1974.

Jorstad, E. T. *The Politics of Doomsday: Fundamentalists of the Far Right*. Nashville: Abingdon Press, 1970.

―――. *The Politics of Moralism: The New Christian Right in American Life*. Minneapolis: Augsburg Publishing House, 1981.

Kelley, D. M. *Why Conservative Churches Are Growing*. New York: Harper & Row, 1972.

King, W. P., ed. *Humanism: Another Battle Line*. Nashville: Cokesbury, 1931.

Kuhns, W. *The Electronic Gospel*. New York: Herder & Herder, 1969.

McDonnell, Kilian. *Charismatic Renewal and Ecumenism*. New York: Paulist Press, 1978.

Marsden, G. M. *Fundamentalism and American Culture: The Shaping of Twentieth Century Evangelicalism, 1870–1925*. New York: Oxford University Press, 1980.

Marty, M. E. *Righteous Empire: The Protestant Experience in America*. New York: Dial Press, 1970.

Mead, F. S. *Handbook of the Denominations in the United States*. Nashville: Abingdon, 1980.

Mott, J. R. *The World's Student Christian Federation*. 1920.

Nash, A. S., ed. *Protestant Thought in the Twentieth Century*. New York: Macmillan, 1951.

Neill, S. C. *The Church and Christian Union*. New York: Oxford University Press, 1968.

————, ed. *Twentieth-Century Christianity: A Survey of Modern Religious Trends by Leading Churchmen*. London: Collins, 1961.

Page, R. J. *Liberal Catholicism*. 1964.

Peerman, D. G., and M. E. Marty, eds. *A Handbook of Christian Theologians*. Cleveland: World Publishing Co., 1965.

Quebedeaux, Richard. *The New Charismatics: The Origin, Development, and Significance of Neo-Pentecostalism*. Garden City: Doubleday, 1976.

————. *The Young Evangelicals: Revolution in Orthodoxy*. New York: Harper & Row, 1974.

————. *The Worldly Evangelicals*. San Francisco: Harper & Row, 1978.

Ramm, Bernard. *The Evangelical Heritage*. Waco, Tx.: Word Books, 1973.

Reardon, B.M.G., ed. *Liberal Protestantism*. Stanford: Stanford University Press, 1968.

Reimers, D. M. *White Protestantism and the Negro*. New York: Oxford University Press, 1965.

Reinish, Leonard, ed. *Theologians of Our Time*. Indiana: University of Notre Dame Press, 1964.

Rouse, S. and S. C. Neill, eds. *A History of the Ecumenical Movement, 1417–1948*. Philadelphia: Westminster Press, 1948.

Russell, C. A. *Voices of American Fundamentalism: Seven Biographical Studies*. Philadelphia: Westminster Press, 1976.

Sandeen, E. R. *The Roots of Fundamentalism: British and American Millenarianism*. Chicago: University of Chicago Press, 1970.

Saunderson, H. H. *The Way Called Heresy*. 1956.

Smith, G. B. *Current Christian Thinking*. 1928.

Stevick, D. B. *Beyond Fundamentalism*. Richmond: John Knox Press, 1964.

Streiker, L. D. *Religion and the New Majority: Billy Graham, Middle America & the Politics of the 70s*. New York: Association Press, 1972.

7

Christianity and Sociopolitical Thought

J. PHILIP WOGAMAN

Christian sociopolitical thought during the three and a half decades since World War II presents us with fascinating complexities. The interface between sociopolitical issues and religion is fascinating because it touches upon dimensions of human existence that affect all of us at the core of our being. It is complex, however, because even one religion, such as Christianity, comes in so many forms and levels and because there are no universally accepted ways to interpret the sociopolitical order theologically. Should one look to the sacred Scriptures, expecting to find immediately relevant instructions for the ordering of sociopolitical life? Pursuing that method—as some have done—one quickly discovers that the sociopolitical problems dealt with in Christian Scriptures were frequently not the same as the problems of the present age. Should one, then, use secular sources of insight? If so, how can they be said to reflect the religious perspective? Then there is the question to whom one should turn for definitive Christian interpretations of sociopolitical problems. Should it be to individual Christian thinkers? To official church councils? To opinion surveys of ordinary Christians?

Most Christian thinkers and churches of the post–World War II period at least consider the subject important, and this has been a remarkably fertile period of Christian thought on sociopolitical matters. To treat the subject as unimportant would be, after all, to conclude that religious faith has no operative role in the organization of actual human life. It would mean finally that the most important religious values have little or nothing to do with human existence in this world. That would come close to meaning that religion itself has no importance except in an entirely esoteric or otherworldly manner. Some Christians can indeed be found who do interpret their faith in entirely spiritual or otherworldly terms. But the mainstream of Christian thought has affirmed that the sociopolitical order is very important.[1] Mainstream Christian thought has thus rejected purely "spiritual" interpretations of Christian faith. The life of the spirit is expressed in the environment of a material, social, and political world. That world, one way or another, reflects God's creative action. Even though the world can also frustrate God's purposes, it contains rich possibilities for fulfillment of the divine will.

Similarly, mainstream Christian thought has generally rejected the notion that God's will can only be done at the end of human history. Eschatological doctrines interpreting God's involvement in human history only through dramatic intervention at the end have attracted a certain number of Christian believers through the centuries (particularly during periods of intense crisis or hardship), but that approach has rarely found wide acceptance among Christian thinkers. The present age must concern us as well as the age to come; human action is important regardless of what we may think about the prospects for divine intervention at some point in history.

But despite the broad agreement of Christian thinkers concerning the importance of the sociopolitical order, there are many different approaches to understanding the *reasons* for its importance. There are so many approaches, in fact, that no chapter the length of this one could hope to describe them adequately. Our purpose must be the more modest one of characterizing a few of the major postwar tendencies—selecting the ones that appear to have greatest current influence and enduring importance.

We must be clear about the meaning of the term *sociopolitical*. It suggests two points of reference. First is the sum of the institutional structures of human society—how human society is organized, the system of practices and roles and rewards, the habitual ways of doing things. Second is the political question of how society will act as a whole. Human society is more than politics, but politics is uniquely the point of reference for common action. Even though society as a whole never acts on the basis of completely unanimous agreement, politics focuses the energies of all parts of society in support of particular policies.[2] Even political dissenters must pay taxes (or suffer the consequences of not doing so) and in other ways also contribute to the effective action of the state. There is thus a sense in which we all act together through the action of the state, even when we strenuously oppose them. The interpretation of Christian responsibility in relation to political action and the determination of how and why particular social structures should be advocated or opposed therefore constitute the two main problems addressed by Christian sociopolitical thought.

THEOLOGICAL FOUNDATIONS FOR SOCIOPOLITICAL THOUGHT

Bearing in mind that there are many schools of thought in Christian theology, we may single out five major theological tendencies that have shaped Christian response to sociopolitical problems in the postwar world. The five tendencies are not mutually exclusive, but they each represent a distinctive Christian starting point for the analysis of society.

Natural Law

We may well begin with the natural law approach, important both because of its long use and refinements and because it has been the characteristic form of moral thought in the largest Christian communion, the Roman Catholic Church.[3] Influenced especially by the thought of Thomas Aquinas (1225–1274) and with earlier roots in Aristotle, the natural law tradition has emphasized two things: first, that there is a moral order in the universe that is binding upon all people and that is knowable by the rational mind apart from any specific form of religious revelation; second, that every entity has a purpose or end (telos) that is proper to it and in the fulfillment of which the moral order is served. Analysis of such social entities as the family, private property, and the state thus begins with the assumption that their moral purpose can be known by reasonable persons apart from any specifically theological insight.[4] Thus when Pope Pius XI, in his encyclical *Casti connubii,* condemned the use of contraceptives as "intrinsically vicious," it was because that practice is seen to violate the natural order of procreation in which the sexual act has as its proper purpose the begetting of children. In the natural law tradition private property is often respected as bearing a necessary relationship to the fulfillment of the economic well being of persons, and killing—including the taking of life in war—is condemned as a wholesale violation of the moral order except when done in defense of justice against aggression. In the case of war, specific tests must be met to establish that any particular conflict is justified, and even in a conflict that is justified (a "just war") one may not directly violate the moral law by killing innocent people.[5]

The natural law approach to sociopolitical thought has continued to exert great influence in the postwar period. It has, however, been modified increasingly by Roman Catholic moral theologians who have sought to be responsive to new problems and to other currents of thought from within and beyond Christianity.[6] Often this has occurred by means of reinterpretation of Thomas Aquinas. For instance, the eminent Catholic moral theologian John Courtney Murray, S. J., employed Thomistic thought to relax a long-standing view that the state should be used to suppress religious error. The more fundamental obligation of the state, argued Murray, is to keep the peace, and where the suppression of error would result in conflict among competing religious groups, a policy of religious liberty and separation of church and state is fully warranted.[7] Similarly, in the context of the debate over abortion, Father Charles Curran employed Thomism not to defend the morality of abortion (which Curran strongly opposes) but to urge that the state not intervene in such an area in which intervention could only exacerbate conflict. Under such circumstances it is the state's prior obligation not to prevent immorality but to keep the peace.[8]

Modification of natural law conceptions has also occurred in the direction of attempts to relate it more directly to theological conceptions of Christ and to a more dynamic, love-related personalism. The spirit of this greater flexibility is suggested by Bernard Haring's observation that "new events, new knowledge and power are constantly being granted to man. Openness to Christ demands openness to all this, but in such a way that Christ's revelation and commandment of love give final meaning to all the insights of the natural law. If a thesis of natural-law ethics contradicts the personalism revealed by Christ, it stands unmasked as error."[9] It is arguable that such an approach moves one away from natural law into something more distinctively theological, but Catholic thinkers such as Haring and Curran continue to view this not as an aberration from natural law but as its profounder expression.

As far as Protestant Christians are concerned, natural law thinking has continued to find some expression in the work of Paul Ramsey, among others. Ramsey, however, has also emphasized that the foundational norm for morality is love. Thus the final test or validation of a given conception of natural law is not whether it is a necessary fulfillment of the telos of the moral order but whether it is an expression of love (agape).[10] Much of Ramsey's recent work of sociopolitical analysis has related to the more intimate problems of medical ethics and biological experimentation. Earlier, he provided a Protestant restatement of just war doctrine, applied particularly to questions of nuclear deterrence and the Vietnam War. In both instances he drew heavily upon the natural law tradition although at the same time relating his insights to Christian theology.[11]

Covenantal Theology

The views of a Bernard Haring and a Paul Ramsey help bridge the gap between natural law and covenantal theology as foundation for sociopolitical thought. The latter can be stated in a form that is consistent with natural law, but its ultimate mode of validation is different. In the covenantal conception, God is personal, and it is in God's personal relationship to human beings that all moral conceptions finally have their true meaning. Covenantal theology lies behind most Protestant thinking, including its sociopolitical thought. In facing any particular sociopolitical issue or problem we are called upon to discern the will of God or "the mind of Christ"—Christ being understood as the ultimate manifestation of the character of God's purposes. Or as Karl Barth, the most important covenantal theologian of the twentieth century, would say, Christ is finally the decisive Word of God to humanity. Barth rejected all forms of natural law or natural theology based upon reason unillumined by revelation. It is in Christ that we are given to understand what is finally at stake in all things.[12] God's word, through the Christ of covenantal theology, is that we are saved through grace—that is, through God's unmerited love, which we appropriate through faith, not through "works." All people are sinners, all equally in need of salvation from sin and death.

Although seemingly remote from sociopolitical thought, the doctrine of grace in fact has significant implications. For one thing, its tendency is to remove the moral pretensions of any social group from special favor. Thus poor people and racial minorities cannot be mistreated in the sociopolitical order because somehow they "deserve" to be worse off than others. For another thing, all of humanity is understood to be united in a single moral community by God's love; all are God's children in a single human family. Thus ultimately, all sociopolitical questions are family questions having to do with how sisters and brothers propose to treat one another. Particular social institutions and social practices must be examined for their effects upon the realization of community in reconciling love or, as Paul Lehmann has put it, upon the process of our becoming fully human.[13]

Such broad norms inevitably mean that covenantal theology tends toward greater flexibility and use of intuition in contrast to natural law's search for the rational structure of the moral order.

Still, Christians who emphasize covenantal theology often reintroduce the natural law problem by referring to the structures or "orders" of creation. The physical universe and the world of institutions and structures are seen by covenantal theology as the creation of the loving God for the realization of the divine purposes, particularly for the realization of a loving community at every level of human collectivity. Thus for Barth, the created gift of human sexuality is a kind of paradigm for loving covenant between man and woman. The negative implications of covenantal love for ordinary war, not to mention nuclear holocaust, appear fairly obvious, although many Christians of this theological orientation follow Luther in accepting the sometime necessity of engaging in war when it is clearly a lesser evil for the sake of love.

Is the covenantal understanding of the structures of creation simply a verbal transmutation of natural law into theological language, sacrificing only the greater intellectual rigor and clarity of the former along with its comprehensibility to non-Christians? Possibly so. But the response of covenantal theology is to emphasize that the true importance of anything is never disclosed until it is seen in its relationship to the source of all being; since the source of all being cannot be presented to human reason apart from faith in revelation (as in Christ), the central premise of natural law—the knowability of the moral order by reason—collapses. It is true, however, that the understanding of creation by covenantal theology is decisively important in its approach to interpreting the real world. For the real world is always seen as having been created by God for positive, loving purposes. The ways in which human beings structure that world are understood either to aid or impede those purposes.

Some problems are more readily dealt with from this starting point than are others. War and racism are readily identified as evil even if war, on some occasions, must be tolerated as a lesser evil. Even technical problems, such as those frequently encountered in economics, have value dimensions that are illuminated through the insights of covenantal theology. Covenantal theology may not have much to tell us about what is required to achieve full employment and productive growth in a Western economy. But it would have something to say about whether the economic well being of members of the community could be disregarded morally in order to achieve growth in productivity or to diminish the rate of inflation or any other concrete economic goal. Technical economics has to do with the means society uses to achieve its ends; the ends themselves must have deeper roots. To covenantal theology, those roots are formed by our loving relationship with God and fellow humanity.

Christian Realism and Situational Ethics

A related tendency in postwar sociopolitical thought can be referred to with the admittedly vague terms *realism* and *situation ethics*. The terms can be misleading since all schools of thought think of themselves as being "realistic," and all similarly seek to be relevant to specific situations. Nevertheless, they describe a tendency in postwar Christian thought to eschew any particular act or institution or ideology as being *intrinsically* right or wrong. Reinhold Niebuhr, the name most associated with Christian realism, exerted immense influence in the 1950s and 1960s, with important echoes in the 1970s and 1980s.[14] Joseph Fletcher and John A. T. Robinson, the names most associated with "situation ethics," had great influence in the 1960s and 1970s, with some continuing effects.[15] The major difference between Christian realism and situation ethics is that the former is primarily concerned with large-scale social problems in the political and economic spheres whereas the latter is more concerned with individual moral decision making, largely in a more individualistic context. They can be lumped together here, however, because both are concerned with the concrete foreseeable consequences of our policies and actions and consider the essence of moral responsibility to be action with an eye toward the best possible outcomes. Both Christian realism and situation ethics are thus pragmatic in style.

Both also understand love (agape) to be the final governing norm, although the demands of justice may also be seen either as a necessary precondition to the situational expression of love or as its necessary accompaniment.[16] Although the specific relationship of love and justice may be expressed differently by different thinkers, Christian realists and situation ethicists agree that there are no intrinsic ends in the natural and institutional worlds that should be observed regardless of the demands of love; there are no invariable rules locating what is always right or wrong. Any of the Ten Commandments could, for instance, be set aside for the sake of realizing love and justice in a particular historical circumstance. Situation ethics and Christian realism are therefore uncomfortable with the inflexible negatives of pacifism (war is *always* wrong) or the "right-to-life" movement (abortion is *always* wrong). Situation ethics and realism tend therefore to avoid deontological forms of Christian ethics altogether, preferring to focus upon actual consequences and always seeking to use whatever means are necessary to achieve the better ends. The style of political analysis accompanying this approach therefore emphasizes the importance of compromise, recognizing that history rarely offers the possibility of achieving perfect outcomes. Niebuhr used to insist that the most important ethical choices tend to be between relative goods and relative evils—only very rarely are they between the absolutely good and the absolutely evil.

Two variations on the realism/situation ethics theme may be noted. One is *secular theology,* a term associated with Harvey Cox and the earlier work of Dietrich Bonhoeffer and Friedrich Gogarten.[17] Secular theology also eschews intrinsic ends and morally necessary rules. Its program is to "desacralize" nature and culture in the name of grace (Gogarten) or humanity's coming of age with new moral responsibility (Bonhoeffer, Cox).

The other variation, represented in part by my work, is to seek to determine which particular values or practices should be "presumed" to be normative in the absence of convincing contrary evidence.[18] This approach enters the situation of decision making, as it were, with a bias in favor of one set of values and against others. It seeks to place the burden of proof against policies or practices or programs or ideologies that appear to contradict its initial presumptions. The initial presumptions or biases are drawn as directly as possible from Christian theology. Thus anything appearing to be against the value and equality of individual persons is presumed wrong, as is anything appearing to fragment the human community. Such an approach acknowledges that Christians, while eschewing absolute rules, should have a strong presumption in favor of some things and against others. It may not always be desirable to tell the truth, for instance, but one should do so unless there are compelling reasons not to. Similarly, one should have a presumption in favor of preserving life, but there may be compelling reasons in a particular situation for the taking of life in a police-type action or for euthanasia. Establishing the point of initial presumption can also be a way of using ideologies—such as democracy or socialism or capitalism: policy questions can be resolved along lines most compatable with the preferred ideology unless sufficient grounds are present for an exception. Use of presumption in this way provides a basis for decision and action in situations of great uncertainty. When in doubt, the direction of decision is that of the initial bias or presumption.

Evangelical Theology

Evangelical Christianity is notable for its very heavy reliance upon the Bible.[19] Historically, evangelical Christianity has often manifested two tendencies: first, to derive moral analysis from specific texts on the assumption that more or less explicit answers can be found for all moral problems in that way; second, to avoid sociopolitical involvements in the name of Christianity wherever possible. Evangelical Christians have often criticized the turn-of-the-century American social gospel movement for substituting worldly materialism for the true gospel of individual salvation. Such "worldliness" was often taken to be a departure from the eternal salvation revealed in the Bible. Sometimes the preoccupation with individual salvation and the criticism of the social gospel was not ideologically as disinterested as it appeared to be. Many evangelical Christians have profited handsomely from their status in existing society, and there has sometimes appeared to be a coincidence of interest between conservative evangelical Christianity and conservative socioeconomic programs. No doubt there have also been many evangelical Christians who have espoused an individualistic gospel of personal salvation honestly and not as a smokescreen to hide and protect selfish purposes. In any event, postwar Christianity has continued to see a good deal of this form of evangelical avoidance of sociopolitical involvement.

In recent years, however, evangelical movements have arisen that insist that Christians should address sociopolitical problems both in thought and action. Sometimes this has been in the service of very conservative ends—as in the case of the Moral Majority and related movements in the United States.[20] Other evangelical Christians have espoused a very different vision of social justice on the basis of interpretations of the Bible far removed from either simple individualism or uncritical culture religion. Seeking to recover the social message of the Old Testament prophets and interpreting with fresh insight the social implications of New Testament Scriptures, these evangelical Christians have sought to address major world problems of war and peace, of poverty and hunger, of human rights and political oppression—refusing to be drawn into fixed ideological positions derived from non-Christian sources. Their method of approach is typically one of exegeting particular scriptural passages to show that the Bible has always expressed a well-rounded concern for all aspects of human existence and that it has particularly demanded high standards of social justice. Writers like Richard J. Mouw, Stephen C. Mott, Ronald Sider, and John Howard Yoder, to name but four, have mounted a sustained exegetical attack upon the view of older evangelicals that biblical religion does not engage the believer with sociopolitical questions and upon the view of newer leaders of the religious right that the outcome of Christian sociopolitical analysis should be conservative or reactionary.[21]

The specific content of social justice varies somewhat among the different evangelical thinkers. Yoder, for instance, is deeply pacifist, considering pacifism to be a clear implication of the message of Jesus and a reflection of the quality of life affirmed by God through the resurrection. According to Yoder, the nonviolent and loving way of Jesus was profoundly subversive of the oppressive political order of his day (else Jesus would not have had to be crucified by the authorities). Obedient to Jesus, Christians are (in Yoder's view) called to a similarly faithful witness. They are not called to manage the course of human events if that entails use of biblically unwarranted means, such as those employed in war. Christian witness will be effective, but its final success is in the hands of God, who alone is responsible for the governing of history. By contrast, Mouw's view is more like that of the Christian realists although he, like Yoder, derives his judgments primarily from biblical exegesis. In Mouw's view, Christians are responsible for their stewardship of political power and for the achievement of the best possible consequences: "If human beings are created with the capacity for assessing situations, projecting into the future, planning strategies, and the like, would it not seem a judicious exercise of created abilities to put these gifts to use, even in the area of social and political planning?"[22]

Despite such disagreements, most evangelical thinkers agree that the present world imbalance between the rich and the poor is utterly incompatable with the biblical call for social justice. Consequently, they devote considerable energy to efforts to channel wealth and resources from rich to poor. In part, their efforts are an encouragement to philanthrophy, such as church-aid programs to alleviate widespread hunger. But evangelical Christians have also been conspicuous in their advocacy of legislation to channel U.S. aid to poor countries and to improve the trading opportunities of poor countries with more affluent lands.[23]

The combination of biblical conservatism with sociopolitical liberalism has proved to be an especially dynamic influence among conservative Christians. The new influence of this movement is symbolized in part by recent changes of emphasis in the preaching of the Reverend Billy Graham. Graham has for many years been identified as the preeminent spokesperson of evangelical Christianity, and his biblically based preaching often seemed to reflect an individualistic conception of Christian responsibility. In the late 1970s and early 1980s, however, Graham has voiced social concerns with growing urgency—particularly through criticisms of preparations for nuclear war and through efforts to bridge the Cold War chasm between the United States and the Soviet Union.

The biblical literalism that still tends to be the methodological norm of evangelicals restricts the theological influence of the movement, but evangelicals have succeeded in forging sociopolitical alliances with those who share their commitment to social justice.

The Liberation Theme

The theme of liberation has emerged in the Christian theology of the past two decades as an accompaniment of the North American civil rights movement, the struggle for racial justice in Southern Africa, the Latin American revolt against political and economic oppression, and the feminist movement. The theologians who have contributed most have been as diverse as Martin Luther King, Jr., James H. Cone, Dorothee Soelle, Rosemary Radford Ruether, Gustavo Gutierrez, and Jose Miguez Bonino.[24] Although differing sharply at many points, such theologians are united in interpreting Christian faith as a gospel of liberation for the oppressed of the world. Biblical accounts such as the freeing of the Hebrew slaves from their Egyptian captivity and the Magnificat of Mary ("The Lord . . . has put down the mighty from their thrones, and exalted those of low degree; he has filled the hungry with good things, and the rich he has sent empty away." Luke 1: 52–53). God is seen as being on the side of the oppressed, and their freedom from oppression is the critical element in human history. Many of these thinkers see the freedom of the oppressed as necessary for the freedom of the oppressor, for the oppressor's own true humanity is destroyed through alienation from the oppressed.

Liberation theology—a largely Latin American phenomenon—is widely viewed as being an outgrowth of Marxist thought, and it is true that a number of its most important spokespersons have made substantial use of Marxism. Typical of them, Jose Miguez Bonino treats Marxism as the source of the essential tools for interpreting the sociopolitical realm while seeing it as an inadequate source of understanding ultimate theological truth. ("I cannot but feel that there is a deep and fundamental lack in Marxist philosophy at this point; an impossibility to make sense of the experience of joy, personal fulfilment, hope and love which many of the militants have so beautifully illustrated."[25]) Miguez Bonino and Gutierrez accept the Marxist understanding of class struggle and the Marxist-Leninist doctrine of imperialism as an essentially correct analysis of the causes of oppression, although they do not subscribe to the metaphysical materialism of classical Marxism. Martin Luther King, on the other hand, was broadly critical of Marxism—partially because of its tendency to reduce all oppression to economic causes, partially because of its willingness to employ violence (which he opposed), and partially because of its ultimate materialism. A number of other thinkers identified with racial or women's liberation find Marxist categories useful in a very limited way but also inadequate for a full understanding of the forms of oppression from which they seek release.

Taking as a whole the wide variety of Christian thinkers who emphasize the theme of liberation, we may note two points of common emphasis: one is the importance of social institutions and material conditions, which can either be fulfilling or oppressive of essential humanity; the other is a dynamic sense of the movement of history toward a liberating future. Both points can be contrasted sharply with any otherworldly interpretation of the Christian message. Indeed, many of those who are most influenced by the liberation theme are profoundly critical of otherworldly religion as itself providing support for oppression. The covenantal relationship of humanity with God, as emphasized by covenantal theology, is generally not similarly emphasized by these theologians, nor are they much impressed by the static categories of natural law. Still, some of the liberation theologians draw upon a dynamic understanding of God, presupposing an active personal God interacting with humanity in the quest for social justice in history. Emphasis upon the dynamic movement of history, as in the work of Rubem Alves, draws indirectly upon the insights of the critical Marxism of the Frankfurt School via the theology of hope of Jürgen Moltmann.[26]

RESPONSE TO ISSUES

A student of all of the theological motifs we have briefly summarized is struck by how seriously all of them take the sociopolitical order as the arena of human interaction and fulfillment. Taking the postwar period as a whole, one is impressed by how great a theological emphasis has been given in this era by the quest for social justice in contrast to purely personal or ecclesiastical or liturgical concerns having little immediate relevance to the sociopolitical order. Different as they are, one is struck by the similarity of these theological tendencies on that central point.

If that is true, it must partially be true because postwar Christianity has had to deal with very important social problems on all continents. Since dealing with problems entails assessment of their meaning, it is not surprising that theological reflection in this era has grappled as much as it has with sociopolitical issues. The response to concrete social problems has forced Third World theologians to struggle with the meaning of economic and political oppression and with preventable human suffering. It should not be surprising that various forms of liberation theology have assumed such prominence. Such a social setting does not necessarily determine the content of theological reflection, but it helps set the agenda. Having accepted the importance of this agenda, Third World theologians seek out the materials within their tradition, along with other available intellectual tools, to understand the meaning of sociopolitical problems and to set the stage for action. Many of them would argue, in fact, that through the method of "praxis" it is always action preceding reflection when theology is pursued authentically.

North American Christians have similarly responded to a great variety of issues during the postwar era. In regard to international relations, they have had to confront the Cold War, the nuclear arms race (with its implicit threat to all of human civilization), the Vietnam conflict, and a certain related disillusionment with the postwar "Pax Americana" and its assumptions of American responsibility for keeping the pace and managing the economic development of the whole non-Marxist world. In regard to economic matters, they have had to deal with domestic poverty and world hunger, with the implications of the population explosion and with ecological pollution, with resource and energy shortages, with the emerging reality of multinational corporations, and—of late—with the puzzling combination of inflation and recession. In regard to political and social problems, they have confronted (and to some extent caused) the civil rights revolution for the profoundly oppressed black people of the United States and, more recently, the fundamental equality of women. They have had to frame responses to advancing medical possibilities and other life-shaping effects of a technology that often seems controlled only by its unbridled momentum.

Worldwide, Christians have had to confront the reality of an increasingly intimate global community, a community, that is, in physical fact but not yet in political and moral reality. Worldwide they confront the fact that the forces of nationalism and greed, by fragmenting humanity, stand in vivid contrast to the vision of human unity implied by most forms of Christian theology. The overcoming of greed and murderous conflict thus becomes an issue of faith for thoughtful Christians. For the apparent inability of Christian values of human unity and mutual respect and love to organize the actual course of human events always makes such a faith more difficult to sustain.

It is, however, noteworthy that Christian thought often seeks to find answers by moving directly from immediate problems to basic theological insights without supplying intermediate doctrine concerning the values at stake in a given area of human experience. This tendency means that ideological problems are often solved either by intuitive leaps or by uncritically borrowing from ideological systems having little affinity with Christian faith. There has been some serious ideological thought, as Chrisitans have sought to organize their sociopolitical thinking in recent years, but there has been too little.

IDEOLOGICAL FORMULATIONS

Ideological thinking represents a mixture of descriptive and normative assessment of major aspects of human existence. In this broader sense, the term *ideology* should not be taken in the Marxist way as meaning "false consciousness." Rather, it means our understanding of the realities and values associated with a particular ordering of human society. Ideological thinking can be criticized for its empirical inaccuracies, its lack of realism about power realities, or its failure to comprehend the hidden power of individual or class interests. Or it can be criticized for its dehumanizing or idolatrous values. But these are the problems of inadequate ideology, not of ideology itself. To think comprehensively about sociopolitical reality we need to have a broad picture of what society is and ought to be like, "a pattern of beliefs and concepts (both factual and normative) which purport to explain complex social phenomena with a view to directing and simplifying sociopolitical choices."[27] Christian sociopolitical thought must, in that broad sense, be ideological. The major postwar theological tendencies we have just surveyed all have important ideological implications. Indeed, Christians can probably learn something from each of the five. But Christian sociopolitical thought can be criticized for not addressing the ideological problem directly and comprehensively enough.

Most ideological debate is confused not because those who engage in it lack insight but because their insights are segmental. An economist like George Stigler or Milton Friedman may call for "freedom" as the fundamental value and then apply it in a way that overlooks the factual loss of freedom by persons mired in economic poverty.[28] A Marxist may appeal to "social justice" and then neglect the extent to which the typical Communist government denies most of its people the right of freedom of expression and political participation. Ideological debate thus tends to engage adversaries who are doing battle for segments of a larger picture. The challenge Christians confront is to help humanity understand that larger picture.

Roman Catholicism has sought to meet this challenge in the postwar world through the thoughtful declarations of the Second Vatican Council, through various papal encyclicals, and through pastoral letters issued by bishops and national conferences of bishops. Characteristically, such documents are published only after the most painstaking preparation involving theological and technical experts of various kinds. Although one could not honestly record that Catholicism has yet developed ideological positions on all subjects to which reasonable people could unhesitatingly repair, their work is generally worthy of high respect. The "Pastoral Constitution on the Church in the Modern World" (*Gaudium et Spes*) of the Second Vatican Council is a good example of such Roman Catholic work.[29] That document grounds the social values of liberty, equality, and peace in a conception of the inherent worth and dignity of the human person and cites the profoundly destructive effects of poverty and international conflict upon those values. It calls for new commitments to economic justice and for new forms of international order. Subsequent papal encyclicals have wrestled with problems of international order and economic justice, with serious questions remaining whether Catholicism will ultimately prove receptive to the socialism of its Latin American theologians of liberation.[30]

Protestant and Eastern Orthodox Christians, acting through ecumenical councils at the world and national levels, have also struggled with ideological problems confronting humanity in a changing world. With roots going back into the 1930s, the postwar World Council of Churches developed a concept of the "responsible society" that sought to link the demands of freedom, justice, social order, and the accountability of economic and political power into a single formulation: "A responsible society is one where freedom is the freedom of men who acknowledge responsibility to justice and public order, and where those who hold political authority or economic power are responsible for its exercise to God and the people whose welfare is affected by it."[31] In light of such a conception, the World Council tested laissez-faire capitalism and communism and found them both wanting. In the 1960s the "responsible society" theme was increasingly criticized as too static a conception and with too great a bias for the status quo. But at the Nairobi Assembly of the Council in 1975 a recognizably similar formulation surfaced in the call for a "Just, Participatory, and Sustainable Society."[32] The concern for "sustainability" reflected a growing awareness within ecumenical Christianity that humanity—through its technology and its possession of nuclear capability—is now capable of threatening its own future. The concerns for "justice" and "participation" are clearly relatable to the terms of the earlier concept of "responsible society."

But all such formulations—both Roman Catholic and Protestant/Orthodox—remain insufficiently developed. Clearer doctrine is needed to help organize Christian thinking on sociopolitical problems as they are presented by a new era. The World Council of Churches' Conference on Faith, Science and the Future in 1979 was a useful preliminary step toward the development of a Christian response to technology.[33] A new consensus appears to be developing in Christian ecumenical circles against any use of nuclear weapons, although it is yet unaccompanied by clear doctrine concerning permissible forms of national security and the institutionalization of world order. In economic life, the old battle lines between socialism and capitalism are still drawn, with deeply committed warriors on either side. Capitalism has recently been defended as the best expression of Christian theological insight in works by Michael Novak, Robert Benne, and George Gilder.[34] Socialism is supported by most of the liberation theologians, often in its Marxist form. In recent years, a number of Christians have sought to develop a democratic socialism that seeks to combine economic

socialism with political democracy—thus implicitly correcting the Marxist neglect of the latter. In the United States this Christian democratic socialist movement gains most of its inspiration from the work of Michael Harrington, although
Harrington cannot be classified as a Christian thinker.[35]

CONCLUSION

Christian sociopolitical thought has had to struggle, at least since the Con-
stantinian era, with the question of triumphalism as it contemplates the imple-
menting of Christian values in public life. Assuming the development of a
complete Christian ideological doctrine, what right would Christians have to
impose this upon the rest of humanity? Christians, though perhaps more numerous
than the adherents of any one of the other world religions, are a distinct minority
of the world's population. Their success in defining sociopolitical doctrine might
well be regarded with apprehension by non-Christians.

Even assuming the unlikely achievement of worldwide Christian consensus
on sociopolitical questions, however, the various Christian positions described
in this chapter are not exclusively Christian in their practical consequences.
Some of the Christian positions (especially natural law and liberation theology)
make explicit use of concepts and values that are not specifically or exclusively
Christian, and that is implicitly true of the other positions as well. Even the
explicitly Christian theological views, although not entirely shared by other
religions, may not be threatening to them. For instance, a theological affirmation
of the dignity and worth of the human person or of the unity of the humanity
as the family of God should have a deep resonance among the adherents of
several other religions. Whatever the theological warrants supplied by particular
religious thinkers, the quest for social justice and human rights is largely universal. The points of greatest controversy between Christians and non-Christians,
such as the debate over abortion rights or the struggle over capitalism and
socialism, turn out also to be debates among Christians themselves.

Christians can therefore make their contributions to sociopolitical thought
knowing that their views will be taken up in the larger public forum and accepted
or rejected there on the basis of a wider consensus.

NOTES

1. See Ernst Troeltsch, *The Social Teaching of the Christian Churches* (New York:
Macmillan, 1911, 1931); H. Richard Niebuhr, *Christ and Culture* (New York: Harper
and Row, 1951); and C. J. Cadoux, *The Early Church and the World* (Edinburgh: T.
and T. Clark, 1925), among other comprehensive studies of the history of Christian
sociopolitical thought.

2. This understanding of political power is in agreement with R. M. MacIver's view
that political power "alone is the organ of the whole community" and with Talcott
Parson's view that political power "is capacity to control the relational system as a

system.'' See MacIver, *The Web of Government* (New York: Macmillan, 1947), p. 94; and Parsons, *The Social System* (Glencoe, Ill.: The Free Press, 1951), p. 126.

3. See Josef Fuchs, *Natural Law* (New York: Sheed and Ward, 1965), for a good introduction to and contemporary statement of Roman Catholic natural law.

4. See, among other classic papal encyclicals, *Rerum Novarum* by Pope Leo XIII (1891), *Quadragesimo Anno* by Pope Pius XI (1931), and *Pacem in Terris* by Pope John XXIII (1963).

5. According to the rule of double effect, however, the destruction of innocent lives and property may be morally permissible if it is a necessary indirect consequence of efforts to restrain an aggressor. Under such circumstances, the destruction should still be proportionately less than the effects of the aggression one is seeking to restrain.

6. The Second Vatican Council (1963–1965) and a vast expansion of ecumenical contact and cooperation with other Christian and non-Christian bodies has been particularly important in stimulating a widening of Roman Catholic horizons of sociopolitical thought, just as these same ecumenical events have helped make Roman Catholic traditions more accessible and acceptable to non-Catholics.

7. John Courtney Murray, *We Hold These Truths: Catholic Reflections on the American Proposition* (New York: Sheed and Ward, 1960).

8. This application of Thomism to the legal prohibition of abortion does not appear to have gained wide support among Catholic moral theologians, however.

9. Bernard Haring, *Morality Is for Persons* (New York: Farrar, Straus and Giroux, 1971), p. 168. In his many writings on ethics, Charles Curran argued similarly for a more dynamic, love-related vision of natural law. See, for example, his *Christian Morality Today* (Notre Dame, Ind.: Fides Publishers, 1966) and *Moral Theology: A Continuing Journey* (Notre Dame, Ind.: University of Notre Dame Press, 1982).

10. Paul Ramsey, *Deeds and Rules in Christian Ethics* (New York: Scribner's, 1967).

11. See Paul Ramsey, *War and the Christian Conscience* (Durham, N.C.: Duke University Press, 1961).

12. See, among Karl Barth's voluminous writings, *The Knowledge of God and the Service of God* (London: Hodder and Stoughton, 1938) and the multivolume *Church Dogmatics* (Edinburgh: T. and T. Clark, 1936-).

13. Paul L. Lehmann, *Ethics in a Christian Context* (New York and Evanston, Ill.: Harper and Row, 1963), p. 85.

14. Among Reinhold Niebuhr's postwar writings, we may note in particular *Christian Realism and Political Problems* (New York: Scribner's, 1953); *The Structure of Nations and Empires* (New York: Scribner's 1959); and *Man's Nature and His Communities* (New York: Scribner's, 1965). The Christian realist stance is also well represented by John C. Bennett. See, for example, his *The Radical Imperative: From Theology to Social Ethics* (Philadelphia: Westminster Press, 1975).

15. See Joseph Fletcher, *Situation Ethics* (Philadelphia: Westminster Press, 1966); and John A. T. Robinson, *Honest to God* (Philadelphia: Westminster Press, 1963).

16. Niebuhrian thought tends to see justice as an external demand preceding love, so justice must be served before love can be considered authentic. Fletcher (partially following Paul Tillich's essay ''Love, Power, and Justice'') described justice as ''love distributed.'' Justice, to Fletcher, is the structured form of love—it is not some additional or preliminary moral norm.

17. See Harvey Cox, *The Secular City* (New York: Macmillan, 1965); Dietrich Bon-

hoeffer, *Letters and Papers from Prison,* ed. Eberhard Bethge, trans. Reginald Fuller (London: SCM Press, 1953; rev. and enl. ed., 1973).

18. See J. Philip Wogaman, *A Christian Method of Moral Judgment* (Philadelphia: Westminster Press, 1976). Although this work can be described as a variation of the Christian realist/situation ethics approach, its theological roots are those of covenantal theology.

19. The term *fundamentalist* may be reserved for those who take all aspects of the Bible literally, treating even factual claims as literal truth in all respects.

20. See Peggy L. Shriver, *The Bible Vote: Religion and the New Right* (New York: Pilgrim Press, 1981).

21. Richard J. Mouw, *Politics and the Biblical Drama* (Grand Rapids, Mich.: Eerdmans, 1976); Stephen C. Mott, *Biblical Ethics and Social Change* (New York: Oxford University Press, 1982); Ronald J. Sider, *Rich Christians in an Age of Hunger: A Biblical Study* (Downers Grove, Ill.: Intervarsity Press, 1977); and John Howard Yoder, *The Politics of Jesus* (Grand Rapids, Mich.: Eerdmans, 1972).

22. Mouw, *Politics and the Biblical Drama,* p. 108.

23. See especially Sider, *Rich Christians in an Age of Hunger.*

24. Martin Luther King, Jr., *Where Do We Go from Here: Chaos or Community* (New York: Harper and Row, 1967); James H. Cone, *God of the Oppressed* (New York: Seabury Press, 1975); Dorothee Soelle, *Political Theology,* trans. John Shelley (Philadelphia: Forbes Press, 1974); Gustavo Gutierrez, *A Theology of Liberation,* trans. Caridad Inda and John Eagleson (Maryknoll, N.Y.: Orbis Books, 1971, 1973); Rosemary Radford Ruether, *Liberation Theology* (New York: Paulist Press, 1972); Jose Miguez Bonino, *Christians and Marxists: The Mutual Challenge to Revolution* (Grand Rapids, Mich.: Eerdmans, 1976).

25. Bonino, *Christians and Marxist,* p.

26. Rubem A. Alves, *A Theology of Human Hope* (Washington, D.C.: Corpus Books, 1969). Compare Jürgen Moltmann, *Theology of Hope* (New York: Harper and Row, 1967).

27. Julius Gould, quoted by Harry M. Johnson, "Ideology and the Social System," in *Encyclopedia of the Social Sciences* (New York: Macmillan, 1968), p. 76.

28. See, for example, Milton Friedman, *Capitalism and Freedom* (Chicago: University of Chicago Press, 1962).

29. Walter M. Abbott, S. J., ed., *The Documents of Vatican II* (New York: Guild Press, America Press, Association Press, 1966), pp. 199–308.

30. On this point one can note a striking contrast between the treatment of socialism in Pope Leo XIII's encyclical *Rerum Novarum* (1891) and the recent encyclical of Pope John Paul II, *Laborem Exercens* (1982). Although the latter is far from adopting a full-scale socialist position, it is also very far from the thoroughly negative stance of *Rerum Novarum.*

31. World Council of Churches, *The Church and the Disorder of Society* (New York: Harper, 1948), p. 192. For an excellent history of the social thought of the World Council of Churches, see Paul Bock, *In Search of a Responsible World Society: The Social Teachings of the World Council of Churches* (Philadelphia: Westminster Press, 1974).

32. David M. Paton, ed., *Breaking Barriers, Nairobi, 1975: The Official Report of the Fifth Assembly of the World Council of Churches* (Grand Rapids, Mich.: Eerdmans, 1976), pp. 23, 73–139.

33. Roger L. Shinn, ed., *Faith and Science in an Unjust World: Report of the World Council of Churches' Conference on Faith, Science and the Future,* 2 vols. (Philadelphia: Fortress Press, 1980).

34. Michael Novak, *The Spirit of Democratic Capitalism* (New York: Simon and Schuster, 1982); Robert Benne, *The Ethic of Democratic Capitalism* (Philadelphia: Fortress Press, 1981); George Gilder, *Wealth and Poverty* (New York: Basic Books, 1981).

35. Michael Harrington, *Socialism* (New York: Saturday Review Press, 1972). See John Cort, "Why I Became a Socialist," *Commonwealth,* March 26, 1976, pp. 89–94.

SELECTED BIBLIOGRAPHY

Abbott, Walter M., S. J., ed. *The Documents of Vatican II.* New York: Guild Press, America Press, and Association Press, 1966.

Bennett, John C. *The Radical Imperative: From Theology to Social Ethics.* Philadelphia: Westminster Press, 1975.

Birch, Bruce C., and Larry L. Rasmussen. *The Predicament of the Prosperous.* Philadelphia: Westminster Press, 1978.

Bock, Paul. *In Search of a Responsible World Society: The Social Teachings of the World Council of Churches.* Philadelphia: Westminster Press, 1974.

Bonino, Jose Miguez. *Christians and Marxists: The Mutual Challenge to Revolution.* Grand Rapids Mich.: Eerdmans, 1976.

Cone, James H. *God of the Oppressed.* New York: Seabury Press, 1975.

Cort, John. "Why I Became a Socialist." *Commonwealth,* March 26, 1976.

Cox, Harvey. *The Secular City.* New York: Macmillan, 1965.

Curran, Charles. *Christian Morality Today.* Notre Dame, Ind.: Fides Publishers, 1966.

———. *Moral Theology: A Continuing Journey.* Notre Dame, Ind.: University of Notre Dame Press, 1982.

Fletcher, Joseph. *Situation Ethics.* Philadelphia: Westminster Press, 1966.

Fuchs, Josef. *Natural Law.* New York: Sheed and Ward, 1965.

Gustafson, James M. *Protestant and Roman Catholic Ethics.* Chicago: University of Chicago Press, 1978.

Gutierrez, Gustavo. *A Theology of Liberation.* Translated by Caridad Inda and John Eagleson. Maryknoll, N.Y.: Orbis Books, 1971, 1973.

Haring, Bernard. *Morality Is for Persons.* New York: Farrar, Straus and Giroux, 1971.

King, Martin Luther, Jr. *Where Do We Go from Here: Chaos or Community.* New York: Harper and Row, 1967.

Lehmann, Paul L. *Ethics in a Christian Context.* New York and Evanston, Ill.: Harper and Row, 1963.

Long, Edward LeRoy, Jr. *A Survey of Christian Ethics.* New York: Oxford University Press, 1967.

Macquarrie, John, ed. *Dictionary of Christian Ethics.* Philadelphia: Westminster Press, 1967.

Mott, Stephen J. *Biblical Ethics and Social Change.* New York: Oxford University Press, 1982.

Mouw, Richard J. *Politics and the Biblical Drama.* Grand Rapids, Mich.: Eerdmans, 1976.

Murray, John Courtney. *We Hold These Truths: Catholic Reflections on the American Proposition.* New York: Sheed and Ward, 1960.

Niebuhr, H. Richard. *Christ and Culture*. New York, Harper and Row, 1951.

Niebuhr, Reinhold. *Christian Realism and Political Problems*. New York: Scribner's, 1953.

―――. *Man's Nature and His Communities*. New York: Scribner's, 1965.

Novak, Michael. *The Spirit of Democratic Capitalism*. New York: Simon and Schuster, 1982.

Ramsey, Paul. *Deeds and Rules in Christian Ethics*. New York: Scribner's, 1967.

―――. *War and the Christian Conscience*. Durham, N.C.: Duke University Press, 1961.

Robinson, John A. T. *Honest to God*. Philadelphia: Westminster Press, 1963.

Ruether, Rosemary Radford. *Liberation Theology*. New York: Paulist Press, 1972.

Shriver, Peggy L. *The Bible Vote: Religion and the New Right*. New York: Pilgrim Press, 1981.

Sider, Ronald J. *Rich Christians in an Age of Hunger: A Biblical Study*. Downers Grove, Ill.: Intervarsity Press, 1977.

Soelle, Dorothee. *Political Theology*. Translated by John Shelley. Philadelphia: Fortress Press, 1971, 1974.

Troeltsch, Ernst. *The Social Teaching of the Christian Churches*. New York: Macmillan, 1911, 1931.

Wogaman, J. Philip. *A Christian Method of Moral Judgment*. Philadelphia: Westminster Press, 1976.

―――. *The Great Economic Debate: An Ethical Analysis*. Philadelphia: Westminster Press, 1977.

Yoder, John Howard. *The Politics of Jesus*. Grand Rapids, Mich.: Eerdmans, 1972.

8

Religion and the Modernization of Tradition in Latin America

GUSTAVO BENAVIDES

In *Religion, Ideology, and Politics* we surveyed the history of the interaction between religion and politics in Latin America.[1] We saw there how, from the time of the Spanish conquest to the current political developments in Central and South America, the relationship between religion and politics has been so intimate that it hardly seems justified to distinguish between a Latin American political history and a Latin American religious history. In this chapter we study the role played by religion—mostly Roman Catholicism—in the confrontation between tradition, modernization, and revolution in Latin America. We examine whether the Catholic church, which for centuries has been identified with the forces of tradition, is now changing its position and is attempting to play a role in the process of modernization that is taking place on the continent or whether the church is still clinging to its old conservative position.[2]

I

One of the central issues facing those who seek to understand the role played by the Catholic church, and by Catholicism in general, in the social, political, and economic life of a country or group of countries is the nature—or the existence—of a Catholic worldview, that is, a specifically Catholic attitude toward authority, world, sexuality, and other aspects of social life. In the case of Latin America, it has been observed that this traditional Catholic world view has had a strongly negative effect on the development of a modern—meaning by this a rational, capitalist, or protocapitalist—ideology, which is taken to be the *conditio sine qua non* for economic and political development.[3] Recent studies have identified some of the alleged deficiencies of traditional Latin American religiosity, particularly the sacrament-centered spirituality and the emphasis on devotion (possible within a world view in which the space between God and the creature is mediated by a hierarchical structure populated by semidivine beings, such as the Virgin Mary, the angels, and a multitude of saints, many of whom have, according to popular Catholic mythology, highly specialized spheres of action).[4] This attitude is not exclusive of the so-called Latin American religiosity but reflects, albeit perhaps in a more intensive fashion, what could be considered a basic Catholic mediterranean religiosity brought to the New World by the Spanish and Portuguese conquerors and colonizers.[5] As mentioned in the discussion of the role played by religion in the conquest and colonization of America, such a hierarchical view was particularly helpful in the consolidation and maintenance of European power in the colonies. Later, the same Catholic *Weltanschauung* was instrumental in the legitimation of the power of the local oligarchies, whose wealth and power depended on the possession of vast amounts of land and mines. To this hierarchical ideology, religiously legitimized by the Catholic church, one could add the pre-Hispanic ideologies that were also largely of an extreme hierarchical type and that were also religiously legitimized.[6] The combination of this internal and external—indigenous and Hispanic—mythologization of the social structure would have led, then, to the formation of a conservative society in which economic, social, and technological development would be extremely difficult.[7] Furthermore, if one compares the social structures, levels of economic development, and political organization of Latin America as a whole (and to a certain extent of the Catholic countries of Southern Europe) with those of the United States and Canada, it is difficult to avoid considering the role played by the religious affiliations of the colonizers, as well as by the economic, social, and religious ideologies of the countries from which these colonizers came.

This is not the place to discuss the validity of the so-called Protestant ethic in the development of capitalism.[8] However, although Weber did not oppose the "materialistic" interpretation of history by proposing "an equally one-sided spiritualistic causal interpretation of culture and history," many Weberians now defend a kind of 'vulgar idealism' whose goal, explicit or implicit, is the refutation of a Marxism that is regarded as defending a variety of economic determinism.[9] In the context of this scholarly political debate, the obvious differences between a developed, capitalist, Protestant North America and an underdeveloped, not-yet-capitalist, Catholic Latin America would seem to validate conclusively Weber's thesis of an 'elective affinity' between capitalism and Protestantism.[10] The advantages of the demonstration of such elective affinity are obvious: it simplifies the task of the historian and the sociologist, who are no longer forced to explore alternative explanations involving, for example, political and military developments, economic changes, ecological conditions; it perpetuates the time-honored distinction between an emotional 'Latin' South and a cerebral North;[11] it manages to blame the underdeveloped world for its underdevelopment, which, after all, is seen as the necessary result of the underdeveloped world's *Weltanschauung*; finally, it shifts the debate from an infrastructural—economic, social, ecological—level to a superstructural, cultural level.[12]

Against this reductionistic spiritualism, we should point out that it was not primarily religion, Catholic or otherwise, that transformed the Iberian colonies into producers of raw materials and importers of manufactured goods; it was rather the international division of labor, the coming into being of a 'modern world-system' that reduced Southern and Eastern Europe to the semiperiphery and the colonies of the Iberian kingdoms to the periphery of the world-system.[13] The vicissitudes of this process, studied by Immanuel Wallerstein, Andre Gunder Frank, Eric Wolf, Peter Worsley, and others, cannot be studied in detail here.[14] Suffice it to say that the expulsion of the Jews from Spain in the same year that America was 'discovered,' the imperial adventures of Charles V, and later the expulsion of the *moriscos* ordered by Philip II reduced Spain to a condition of economic inferiority compared to England and the Low Countries; on the other hand, the influx of gold and silver from the colonies contributed to the inflationary process and to the stagnation of manufacturing and dependence on imports.[15] While this was taking place in the South, the countries of Northern Europe, particularly England and the Netherlands, were undergoing political and economic changes that placed them at the core of the capitalist world-system, a position that England was to keep at least until the nineteenth century.

In any case, whether the position of a country was at the center or at the periphery of the world-system, what matters is that countries and regions were part of a complex system of economic exchanges. This was true of England, Holland, Portugal, and Spain as well as Mexico, Peru, and the Caribbean. At no point in history—neither in the early sixteenth nor in the late twentieth century—have the economies of the colonies been isolated from the pressures of a world market. The specific modes of exploitation employed by the European settlers in North and South America, however, were to a great extent determined both by climatic and geographical conditions as well as by the availability and social organization of the conquered populations. In other words, it was not the case that the Protestant ethic compelled the English settlers of North America to engage in strenuous physical work, nor was it the Catholic worldview that led the Spanish colonizers to become *encomenderos* and benefit from the work of the subject populations; it was rather that the English settlers did not have at their disposal a population large enough and organized in such a way as to make possible the kind of exploitation that was common in the southern half of the hemisphere.[16] Also, economies based on slave labor were found in the Catholic settlements of, for example, Brazil, as well as in Protestant North America; the same is true of the (Protestant) Dutch and English and (Catholic) French sugar plantations in the Caribbean.[17]

It would seem, then, that to credit religion or, more generally, ideology, with a determinant role in the development or underdevelopment of a region is to engage in an ahistorical and reductionistic enterprise that overlooks the fact that religions are not independent variables but are rather the result of historical development.[18] In the particular context of theories about development and underdevelopment, to stress the role played by religion/ideology is to forget that the economic, political, and social characteristics of Latin America are the result, first, of the specific type of economic exploitation practiced by the Spanish settlers; second, the development of a relationship between the colonies and a *madre patria* that had already been pushed to the semiperiphery of the world economic system; third, the coming into being of what Andre Gunder Frank has called 'lumpenbourgeoisie,' a comprador class, identified not with their country of origin but with the metropolis; and fourth, the integration of the Latin American economies into a system dominated first by England and then by the United States.[19] It is only after all of these factors are taken into account that it becomes helpful to consider the role that religions or other ideological formations may have played in the history of the underdeveloped world.

It is indeed tempting to try to identify the core of a given religion and to seek to establish the way, or ways, in which that religion is likely to behave regarding, social, political, and economic issues; in other words, it would be interesting to find out whether there are elements in Catholicism (or Islam, or Buddhism, and so on) that necessarily entail a given attitude toward, for instance, work or sexuality. However, it seems more realistic to try to identify not one structurally determined permissible attitude but rather a range of possible attitudes that a given religion allows regarding a particular aspect of life. But the problem with this range-of-possibilities position is that it is always possible to engage in some kind of hermeneutical acrobatics that allows us to interpret the available possibilities in such a way that eventually all religions are seen as allowing basically the same range of possible attitudes and, therefore, ways of behaving. For instance, both the concept of *artha* in Hinduism and of predestination in Calvinism can be understood as facilitating, or even demanding, a positive attitude toward work, although, historically, it was not in a Hindu but in a Protestant milieu that capitalism flourished. This would force us to examine what other factors may have led to the underdevelopment of India, on the one hand, and to the industrialization of Protestant Europe, on the other hand.[20] Another possible approach involves the examination of the position that a religion occupies in a given culture, that is, whether a religion has a monopolistic position, whether it is followed by the majority of the population while allowing members of religious minorities to take care of specific social functions, or whether its followers constitute a minority of the population of a country or cultural area.

In the case of Latin America, what might be significant is not necessarily the nature of Catholicism but rather the fact that what became known as Latin America was colonized almost exclusively by Catholics; this did not allow for the development of a cultural/religious minority that could have become a source of entrepreneurship, like the Jews in medieval Europe, Christians in the Ottoman Empire, or Parsis and Jains in India. Significantly, it is only recently that Protestantism has become a kind of rallying point for social and political dissent in

Latin America. However, being, like 'ideology,' an all-encompassing concept, 'dissent' may mean dissent by the extreme Right (as in the case of the recently deposed president of Guatemala, the Evangelical Christian Efraín Ríos Montt) or dissent, if not by the Left, at least from a position that rejects the traditional order and the values of the old oligarchies, which are justly identified with the values traditionally upheld by the Catholic church. As Emilio Willems observed in his article "Protestantism and Culture Change in Brazil and Chile," the hypothesis that "adherence to the various Protestant creeds and their social organization is indeed a protest against the traditional order" is borne out by the fact that "the farther removed the ideology and structure of a particular denomination are from those of the traditional society, the stronger the appeal it holds for the common people" and also because "those denominations that to some extent resemble structure and ideological elements of the repudiated society are likely to be less successful in the prosyletic endeavor."[21] That it was Catholicism, and not Protestantism, that was the ultimate source of legitimacy for the social order is not so significant as the fact that there was an absence of groups that might have acted as cultural counterparts to the all-pervasive Catholic attitude toward social, political, and economic life. This would mean that, assuming the world-system had developed, except for religion, in the same way in which it did—that is, if a Protestant Spain, pushed to the semiperiphery by a Catholic England, had colonized Latin America, imposing a single religion and persecuting all others—the result could have been similar to what we find today. Therefore, one must be particularly careful not to succumb to essentialist explanations and consider rather the position occupied by a religion in a given society: one should not overemphasize the role of Catholicism *qua* Catholicism in the stagnation of Latin America but instead keep in mind that, as David Martin has shown, in societies in which Catholics are in a minority position, they tend to contribute to social and political stability by gravitating toward the center or the progressive areas of the political spectrum.[22] At the same time, one should remember that Catholicism has the tendency to become monopolistic and does not allow for the development—beyond certain limits—of competing religious groups.

In the case of Latin America, we face the situation of an entire continent having virtually one religion. Furthermore, all the disadvantages of a monopolistic situation are complicated by the fact that the religion exercising the monopoly is one that is hierarchical, bureaucratic, ritualistic, and, above all, closely identified first with a decadent colonial power and then with the comprador class that inherited the power Spain was forced to relinquish. By the same token, however, Latin American Catholicism is forced to become the carrier of both utopian and conservative, or indeed reactionary, ideologies; that is, the symbolism and mythology of Christianity must serve as the common language for the groups competing for power in a situation that resembles that of the European Middle Ages.[23] Although we cannot study here the role played by non-Christian religions in this officially Catholic region, it must be remembered that in those areas in which pre-Hispanic—or syncretistic—religious representations are alive, it is they which become the carriers of ideologies of revolt, employing indigenous mythical figures, or syncretistic ones—such as Inkarrí—who function as symbols of a new Golden Age free from Spanish-Christian domination.[24]

II

In regard to the religious articulation of reactionary ideologies, we see that the monopolistic tendencies of the Catholic church, as well as its authoritarian character, made it possible for extreme conservative groups—some of them influenced by Italian fascism—to use both the values of Catholicism and of *Hispanidad* against a host of threatening ideologies—generally opposed to one another—such as communism, North American capitalism, and *indigenismo*.[25] A typical case is that of José de la Riva Agüero, a Peruvian intellectual, who after a few years of relative intellectual independence became an ardent Catholic, an admirer of Mussolini, and a defender of Christendom and *Hispanidad*. Riva Agüero—whose complete works are being published by the Catholic University of Lima—is by no means the only Latin American intellectual who found in fascism an ideology that could articulate an authoritarian, hierarchical, and Christian view of the world; similar figures can be found in other Latin American countries, particularly in Argentina. After all, fascism constitutes the logical outcome of the romantization of the past and of the organic social structures that are perceived as being threatened by new social, political, and economic developments.[26] This does not mean that the social structures being defended are any longer organic: in fact, it could be said that the more that traditional ways of life are being eroded by the transformations of capitalism, the more strident are the calls to preserve the values of the collectivity in question. It should also be remembered that not all movements that stress the need to return to organic societies—*Gemeinschaften*—are fascist.[27]

Traditionally, both Christianity—or rather the idea of Christendom—and the allegedly superior values of Hispanic culture have been used in Spain and Latin America against movements that threaten the established order. These banners were used by Franco during the Spanish Civil War, and they are being used now by the governments of Chile, El Salvador, Guatemala, and so on.[28] The position of the Catholic church was further pushed in the direction of fascism when in the years after the Spanish Civil War, priests used to the authoritarian regime of Franco and still not fully recovered from the anticlerical violence that swept Spain under the republic (a typical response against the monopolistic position of the church, repeated in the 1948 *Bogotazo,* in Colombia), supported fascist tendencies in Latin America. These fascist proclivities exemplify a general tendency to support governments that purport to save their countries from lawlessness, violence, atheistic communism, or materialistic capitalism. Some of those reasons were invoked when the church welcomed the military coups in

Brazil in 1964, the ones in Chile in 1973, and the successive coups in Argentina. In these cases (as in earlier ones, for instance in the coup against Arbenz in 1954), the forces of response could present themselves as being involved not in a purely political or military action but in a crusade, whose ultimate aims are to be seen as spiritual. The more or less conscious use of the image of 'crusade' (*cruzada*) can be found in the movement of the *Cristeros* in Mexico (1926-1929) and in the Bay of Pigs invasion of Cuba (April 17, 1961) by Cuban exiles trained and supported by the United States.[29] Another instance of political manipulation of religious symbols is the by no means unusual consecration of a country to the Sacred Heart or to the Virgin Mary.[30] Similarly, the crusadelike defense of values such as 'family,' 'property,' and 'tradition' by right-wing movements in Chile, Brazil, and Argentina makes conscious use of the connection between traditional Catholicism and a set of values—*familia, propiedad y tradición*— that, because of their emotional content, can be easily manipulated, particularly among the middle classes.[31]

When talking about these traditional values, it should not be forgotten that tradition is not a system of values shared to the same degree by all the members of a given community, especially when one considers that what defines a 'community' is not necessarily the result of an organic growth but in most cases (particularly in Latin America) is due to a series of historical accidents such as conquests, wars, or diplomatic treaties. Tradition—a term rendered meaningless by Shils—is rather an ideology, or system of ideologies, and as such it is manipulated for the ultimate use of those in power;[32] on the other hand, an ideology, in the Gramscian sense of 'hegemony,' may be able to pervade an entire society and articulate the values of those who least benefit from it.[33] However, when ideological controls fail, intimidation, torture, and murder are available for the use of the defenders of tradition.[34]

The fact that Catholicism constitutes a central element in Latin America's hegemonic system makes it almost unavoidable that any attempt to solve the problems brought about by the hegemonic system itself resort to images, metaphors, and symbols shared by Christians.[35] This general principle applies to a vast range of 'Christian' problems and attempted solutions, going from the formation of Christian Democratic parties to the elaboration of theologies of liberation to the use of Christian symbols by groups engaged in armed struggle against a Latin American Christian state. This principle also applies to a certain extent to 'syncretistic' movements, although in such cases the role played by the Catholic symbolic universe will be less important. In more extreme cases, namely, when the movement in question seeks to overturn the existing order and return to a world untainted by European influence, Christian symbolism will be replaced by authentic, or invented, indigenous symbols. In any event, it would be a mistake to regard this use of symbols as a mere stylistic exercise, as if the world were a 'text' and the participants in political or military struggles were mere 'characters'; such a view, fashionable nowadays, overlooks the fact that symbolic manipulation, central as it is, takes place for reasons that are concrete, exploitation, hunger, and death being not the least important 'tropes' among them.

III

If Catholicism, then, is the shared vocabulary, the fact remains that until very recently, the main beneficiaries of that shared language have been the old oligarchies whose wealth and power was—and to a certain extent still is—based on land and mines. From the point of view of the landowners, the hierarchical view of society—in the maintenance of which the church was so important— was conveniently reinforced by the 'organic' nature of agricultural work, a kind of economic activity that had had a sacral character since pre-Hispanic times.[36] Now, from the point of view of economic development, this hierarchical view of the world, added to the semiperipheral position occupied by the Iberian powers and the peripheral position occupied by the American colonies, led to the situation of underdevelopment that has been maintained until the present. Furthermore, neither the relative lack of manufacturing during the colonial period (due to the monopoly imposed by Spain) nor the lack of any significant intellectual activity nor the reliance on imported goods (both material and intellectual) contributed to the development of economic activities that could have led to the production and distribution of nonexportable wealth that could have compensated the drain on the economy caused by colonial exploitation. To these nonideological causes one could possibly add the Catholic tendency to devalue the world, a tendency that was further reinforced by the fact that the world, namely, Latin America, was twice removed from the other world, since, if heaven was to be considered the real home, Spain, being the metropolis, had a special intermediate status, a privileged position later occupied by France and currently by the United States.[37]

This combination of colonial dependence (doubly negative due to the decadence of the metropolis after the seventeenth century), fossilized social structure, and, what is generally not stressed enough, the general debasement of social life caused by the dependence of the groups in power on abundant, cheap, and often despised labor were held together by the ubiquitous, legitimizing presence of the church (combined with the use of brute power when ideological controls were not sufficient). It is true that many members of the religious orders distinguished themselves by engaging in charitable, pious activities and that the church as an institution preached the traditional virtues of charity, compassion, and so on.[38] But it is precisely the preaching of charity, faith, hope, and the like that contributed to the state of affairs the church was seeking to remedy. Particularly, virtues such as hope and charity implied a situation of utter dependence upon external sources of grace; the exercise of charity required the existence of a social order that made this charity necessary. Furthermore, according to traditional Christian doctrine, the exercise of charity is not centered on the object of that charity but rather takes that object almost as a pretext since the ultimate beneficiary of the believer's actions is God.

The persistence of this type of symbolic perception—and therefore devaluation—of the world, inaugurated by the first Spanish missionaries (Bartolomé de las Casas, for instance), can still be found in the contemporary Theology of Liberation, which, by placing the current social struggles taking place in Latin America in the context of a biblical *Heilsgeschichte,* manages to deprive them of their historical concreteness.[39] As we saw before, however, the Theology of Liberation cannot proceed otherwise, imprisoned as it is by the traditional vocabulary of Christianity. Therefore, it is utterly misguided to regard the Theology of Liberation as a materialistic or Marxist movement.[40] On the contrary, the Theology of Liberation—a movement that develops its theological interpretations of historical and political events and its political readings of Christian mythology under the assumption that Latin America is, and must remain, Christian—seems to be one of the options being currently explored by the church, even if, to the more conservative—and least perceptive—members of the hierarchy, this theological movement appears as the negation of what traditional Christianity represents.[41]

The work of Gustavo Gutiérrez, for instance, for all of its economic and sociological awareness and its deeply felt concern for "the poor, the oppressed, the exploited class," is still imprisoned by a theological vocabulary and, what is more important, a theological way of thinking, which, in this respect, is not substantially different from that of a conservative or, indeed, reactionary theologian.[42] The reason for this apparently paradoxical situation is, as mentioned before, the fact that both conservatives and revolutionaries are forced to think, to argue, even to fight, within a framework constituted by the mythology of Christianity. It is significant in this context that even those conservative Christians who, like Roger Vekemans, have devoted their energies to attack what they consider to be the "undue projection of the ethical-religious categories, and their corresponding attitudes, into the profane world of economic development and social change" resort to heavy theological language and state that "a sort of profanation" occurs when "the religious categories stray from their valid orbit, and begin to direct the profane world," and that "this undue projection of that which is specifically religious into the economic and social areas is a true adulteration of the profane."[43] (Vekeman's disingenuous remarks disregard the inconvenient fact that such "profanations" and "adulterations" have always taken place, not the least in Latin America, and that, distasteful as it may be for those who, in a surprisingly non-Catholic fashion, wish to keep the sacred and the profane in their "valid orbits," such conflations of the religious and the secular are being used now not only to maintain the status quo but also to try to subvert it.)

IV

The third alternative, besides clinging to the no-longer-functional distribution of wealth and power based on *latifundios,* and the opposite one, represented by the Marxist Left and by utopian Christian groups such as the Theology of Liberation, represent the developmental (*desarrollista*), technocratic position, exemplified in its most extreme forms by the Brazilian and the Chilean dictatorships and in its more moderate, but no less inefficient, aspect by the Christian Democratic parties of Latin America. What both approaches have in common is the recourse to Christianity with the purpose of legitimizing a particular solution to the problems afflicting the continent. The solution offered by the Brazilian generals involved the sacrifice of an entire generation of the working class for the sake of an ambitious and highly unrealistic process of modernization that, if successful, would have transformed Brazil into a great power. To be able to control the population, the Brazilian military needed—besides the use of brute power, involving disappearance, torture, and murder—the legitimizing support of the church, a support that was forthcoming during the first few years after the coup against Goulart.[44] Likewise, in Chile the 1973 coup against Allende was welcomed both by the church and the Christian Democrats.[45] This support allowed the military to proceed with impunity to murder thousands of supporters of the socialist government, since the killings could be presented as being necessary for the defense of the traditional values of Chilean society, and by Western and Christian civilization in general, threatened by atheistic communism. A similar situation could be found in Argentina, where the military, guilty of the murder of between twenty thousand and thirty thousand people, could present themselves as the defenders of traditional Christian and Western values.[46]

As against these bloody, and largerly inefficient, attempts to modernize Latin American societies, the Christian Democratic parties generally seek to build a consensus based on the middle classes, stressing the need for development and modernization as well as the preservation of usually inexistent democratic values; by emphasizing both change and freedom, they consciously set themselves apart from both conservative and socialist parties. To make this distance more obvious, they generally play up the dangers involved in a socialist victory as well as the injustice inherent in the old order. Although the Christian Democratic parties are not officially supported by the church (conflicts between parties and church being not unusual), it is obvious that the use of the labels Christian and Democratic enables them to appear as the embodiment of both tradition and modernization. Unfortunately, the ambiguous position occupied by these parties has often rendered them ineffective and opportunistic. In some countries—Chile and El Salvador are clear examples—they have tried to act as the moderate alternatives (generally with the support of the United States), although in practice they have ended up being manipulated by the Right. In El Salvador, for example, the Christian Democrat José Napoleón Duarte was a junta president with virtually no power over the military and the notorious death squads when the country was being devastated by civil war. After the elections for a Constituent Assembly (May 28, 1982), the combined forces of the Right outnumbered the Christian Democrats who, with the encouragement of the United States, had viewed the elections as the solution to the problems afflicting the country. After Duarte was finally elected president in 1984, the situation did not change in any significant way, since his control over the army continues to be null.[47] In Chile the Christian Democrats' opposition was partially responsible for the coup against Allende and for the brutal military government they tacitly supported, until the economic policies of the military proved to be disastrous for the country. A decade after the coup, the Christian Democrats were engaged in a lukewarm opposition against Pinochet, an opposition that, significantly, is caused not by the military's crimes but by its inability to fulfill its promise of economic development. We can safely assume that once the military leaves power the Christian Democrats will present themselves as the defenders of a democracy that they helped bury in 1973.[48]

In other countries, the position of the Christian Democrats has been less fateful but no less significant in that they still exemplify both the self-legitimizing use of Christianity and the politically ambiguous role that results from that use. In Peru, for instance, the Center-Left Christian Democratic Party (PDC) remained very small, significant only as a partner of Acción Popular during the first term of Fernando Belaúnde (1963–1968); it was only after a Center-Right group of professionals and technocrats left the party to found the Partido Popular Cristiano (PPC) that a political party calling itself 'Christian' was able to become relatively popular, this time among the urban middle and upper middle classes whose peculiar desire for a blend of tradition and modernization was provided by a PPC no longer encumbered by Center-Left leanings. The lack of popularity of the original PDC is also significant in that it indicates the dangers involved in using the label of Christian in party politics in a continent in which the monopolistic position of the church has given rise to a strong anticlerical attitude among the population.[49] The fact that only in Chile, El Salvador, and Venezuela are Christian Democratic parties of any significance would seem to indicate that the Catholic church has a monopoly only on bureaucratic Christianity, leaving more charismatic uses of Christian symbolism to either revolutionary or reactionary movements and to their leaders.[50] If this were to be the case, Latin American Christian Democratic parties would be condemned—because of their necessarily bureaucratic nature—to be victims of the latent, or explicit, anticlericalism of the societies they pretend to modernize. On the other hand, traditional Latin American anticlericalism would not affect movements either from the Right or the Left, which make nonbureaucratic use of the Christian symbolic universe. These nonbureaucratic movements include, on the extreme Right, groups such as the societies in defense of "tradition, family, and property" and, on the Left, groups influenced by the Theology of Liberation such as the base comunities (*comunidades de base*).

Ivan Vallier's suggestion that the rise of a reform-type Catholic party is "a condition for the long-term development of the new Church in Latin America," if apparently reasonable, is a hope likely to remain unfulfilled.[51] It is true, as Vallier has argued in several publications, that a "process of differentiation that frees both the Church and polity from each other" would cause the church to cease relying "on direct political support and, concomitantly, the polity or major political groups [would] cease to view the Church as a potential ally and source of legitimation.''[52] Nevertheless, as Vallier and others recognize, the church continuously seeks to build new systems of influence and control, and there is no reason to believe that, at least in Latin America, the church is prepared to relinquish four centuries of hegemony.[53] What is likely to happen is the continuation of what has been taking place since the Second Vatican Council, namely, the exploration by the church of different, and not seldom, contradictory options, that would allow the church to maintain its position of power under different political conditions. These options include the positions taken in Medellín (1968); the retreat from those positions in Puebla (1979); the development of the Theology of Liberation; the attacks against the Theology of Liberation; the growing power of the Opus Dei; the support of the first phase of the reformist military government in Peru (1968); the welcoming of the fascist coup in Chile (1973); the coming to terms with the Marxist regime in Cuba; and the opposition against the Sandinistas in Nicaragua.[54] The fact that the church, as an institution, may not favor some alternatives—a Marxist solution, for example—does not mean that certain currents within Catholicism—for instance, the Theology of Liberation—may not be acting as historical seismographs, laying the groundwork for an eventual cooperation. Similarly, the various groups competing for power are making use either of the church itself or, more frequently, of the vocabulary provided by Catholicism (and in some cases by Protestantism) to articulate their positions. As mentioned above, these groups range from the reactionary ARENA party in El Salvador and the fascist dictatorship in Chile to the technocrat proponents of modernization (the Christian Democrats and other parties such as Acción Popular and the Partido Popular Cristiano in Peru) to the Sandinistas in Nicaragua who are trying to solidify Catholic support by encouraging the popular church to the anti-Sandinistas who seek to appear as defenders of the true church.

V

Thus far, the history of Latin America has been a history of dependence, reactionary politics, and half-hearted and inept attempts at modernization. Modernization has been hindered by a series of factors that include, first, the colonial situation and, later, the semicolonial position eagerly accepted by the local bourgeoisie (Frank's *lumpenbourgeoisie*). Other factors, including the presence of the traditional hierarchical, totalitarian Catholic ideology; the lack of integration or common purpose of the postcolonial societies; and ethnic tensions, particularly in the Andean countries, have no doubt contributed to the present condition of underdevelopment. To this one must add the negative role played by the United States in repressing reformist movements—the coup against the alleged Communist Jacobo Arbenz being a blatant example—while, as a rule, supporting bloody dictatorships—Batista, the Somoza family, the military regimes in Chile, Brazil, Argentina, Uruguay, Paraguay, and so on—as long as these 'authoritarian' governments present themselves as anti-Communist. As a result of this combination of circumstances, and considering the enormous external debt of Latin America, it is highly unrealistic to expect modernization to succeed.

In the wake of the failure of *desarrollismo,* unless there is a radical restructuring of the external debt and an end to the interventionism of the United States (currently engaged in terrorist activities against Nicaragua), the alternatives open to Latin America seem to be either Chilean- or Brazilian-style dictatorships or leftist revolutions. In either case, religion will be but one of the elements of the process, although in some cases it may be a very visible one. In any event, history shows that the church will manage to survive and to continue providing a modicum of legitimation to those in power.

NOTES

I wish to thank Shahin Gerami for her helpful comments on an earlier draft of this paper.

1. Gustavo Benavides, "Catholicism and Politics in Latin America," in Charles Wei-hsun Fu and Gerhard Spiegler, eds., *Movements and Issues in World Religions: Religion, Ideology, and Politics* (Westport, Conn.: Greenwood Press, 1987), pp. 107–142.

2. One would have expected to learn something about the concept of tradition in Edward Shils, *Tradition* (Chicago: University of Chicago Press, 1981); unfortunately, that is not the case. Extremely useful is the volume edited by Eric Hobsbawm and Terence Ranger, *The Invention of Tradition* (Cambridge: Cambridge University Press, 1983); see especially Hobsbawm's contributions, "Introduction: Inventing Traditions," pp. 1–14, and "Mass-Producing Traditions: Europe, 1870–1914," pp. 263–307.

3. See Jürgen Habermas, *Theorie des kommunikativen Handelns. Vol. 1: Handlungsrationalität und gesellschaftliche Rationalisierung* (Frankfurt: Suhrkamp, 1981).

4. On this problem see François Houtart and Émile Pin, *The Church and the Latin American Revolution* (New York: Sheed and Ward, 1965), pp. 229–232; and Ivan Vallier, *Catholicism, Social Control, and Modernization in Latin America* (Englewood Cliffs, N.J.: Prentice-Hall, 1970), pp. 156–157.

5. See David Martin, *A General Theory of Secularization* (New York: Harper and Row, 1978), pp. 264–273.

6. See Maurice Godelier, *Horizon, trajets marxistes en anthropologie* (Paris: Maspero, 1977), especially "Le concept de 'formation economique et sociale': l'exemple des Incas," pp. 177–187; Ernst Topitsch, *Vom Ursprung und Ende der Metaphysik* (Wien: Springer, 1958). For parallels, see Hans Kloft, ed., *Ideologie und Herrschaft in der Antike* (Darmstadt: WBG, 1979); and Max Kerner, ed., *Ideologie und Herrschaft im Mittelalter* (Darmstadt: WBG, 1982).

7. See Robert Merton, *Social Theory and Social Structure* (New York: Free Press, 1968), Pt. 4, "Studies in the Sociology of Science"; Ina Spiegel-Rösing and Derek de Solla Price, eds., *Science, Technology, and Society: A Cross-Cultural Perspective* (London and Beverly Hills, Calif.: Sage, 1977).

8. Max Weber, *The Protestant Ethic and the Spirit of Capitalism* (New York: Scribner's, 1930; originally published in 1904–1905 as "Die protestantische Ethik und der Geist des Kapitalismus," in *Archiv für Sozialwissenschaft und Sozialpolitik* 20–21). On Weber and his thesis, see Richard Bendix, *Max Weber* (New York: 1960; reprint, Berke-

ley: University of California Press, 1977); S. N. Eisenstadt, ed., *The Protestant Ethic and Modernization: A Comparative View* (New York: Basic Books, 1968); idem, "The Implications of Weber's Sociology of Religion for Understanding Process of Change in Contemporary Non-European Societies and Civilizations," in Charles Glock and Phillip Hammond, eds., *Beyond the Classics?* (New York: Harper and Row, 1973), pp. 131–155; Benjamin Nelson, "Weber's Protestant Ethic," in Glock and Hammond, *Beyond the Classics?* pp. 71–130; C. Seyfarth and W. Sprondel, eds., *Religion und Gesellschaftliche Entwicklung* (Frankfurt: Suhrkamp, 1973); Roland Robertson, *The Sociological Interpretation of Religion* (Oxford: Blackwell, 1970), especially pp. 26–27, 169–181; Robert Towler, *Homo religiosus: Sociological Problems in the Study of Religion* (New York: St. Martin's, 1974), pp. 85–107; and Andre Gunder Frank, "On the Roots of Development and Underdevelopment in the New World: Smith and Marx versus the Weberians," in Frank, *Dependent Accumulation and Underdevelopment* (New York and London: Monthly Review Press, 1979), pp. 25–69.

9. Weber, *Protestant Ethic,* p. 183.

10. See the critique in Frank, "On the Roots of Development and Underdevelopment"; Franz Borkenau, *Der Übergang vom feudalen zum bürgerlichen Weltbild. Studien zur Geschichte der Philosophie der Manufakturperiode* (Paris: Schriften des Instituts für Sozialforschung, Bd. 4, 1934; reprint, Darmstadt: WBG, 1971), pp. 158–179; Bryan S. Turner, *Religion and Social Theory: A Materialist Perspective* (London: Heinemann, 1983), pp. 169–171; Towler, *Homo religiosus,* pp. 90–107; H. R. Trevor Roper, *The European Witch-Craze of the Sixteenth and Seventeenth Centuries and Other Essays* (N.Y.: Harper and Row, 1969), pp. 1–45.

11. For similar prejudices, this time dealing with the Arab world, see Edward Said, *Orientalism* (New York: Pantheon, 1978).

12. For a convincing attack against superstructural explanations in anthropology and sociology, see the essays in Eric B. Ross, ed, *Beyond the Myths of Culture: Essays in Cultural Materialism* (New York and London: Academic Press, 1980). The concept of cultural materialism is developed by Marvin Harris in *Cultural Materialism: The Struggle for a Science of Culture* (New York: Random House, 1979); and idem, "History and Ideological Significance of the Separation of Social and Cultural Anthropology," in Ross, *Beyond the Myths of Culture,* pp. 391–407. Particularly important in this regard are the writings of Roy Rappaport; see "Ecology, Adaptation, and the Ills of Functionalism," "On Cognized Models," and "Adaptive Structure and Its Disorders," all reprinted in Rappaport, *Ecology, Meaning, and Religion* (Richmond, California: North Atlantic Books, 1979).

13. On this concept see Immanuel Wallerstein, *The Modern World-System, Vol. 1: Capitalist Agriculture and the Origins of the European World-Economy in the Sixteenth Century* (New York: Academic Press, 1974).

14. Andre Gunder Frank, *Capitalism and Underdevelopment in Latin America* (New York and London: Monthly Review Press, 1967); idem, *Lumpenburguesía: Lumpendesarrollo* (Montevideo: Ediciones de la Banda Oriental, 1970), English translation: *Lumpenbourgeoisie: Lumpendevelopment. Dependence, Class, and Politics in Latin America* (Monthly Review Press, 1972); idem, *World Accumulation, 1492–1789* (New York and London: Monthly Review Press, 1978); idem, *Dependent Accumulation and Underdevelopment* (New York and London: Monthly Review Press, 1979). See also Eric Wolf, *Europe and the People without History* (Berkeley: University of California Press, 1982); Peter Worsley, *The Three Worlds: Culture and World Development* (Chicago: University

of Chicago Press, 1984); Perry Anderson, *Lineages of the Absolutist State* (London: Verso, 1974).

15. On this subject see Wallerstein, *The Modern World-System,* pp. 70–84; Frank, *World Accumulation,* pp. 41–53.

16. See Frank, *Dependent Accumulation and Underdevelopment,* pp. 50ff, 58ff.

17. Frank, *World Accumulation,* pp. 125ff.

18. See Robertson, *The Sociological Interpretation of Religion;* Turner, *Religion and Social Theory.* To maintain that religions are not independent variables usually brings about the accusation of 'reductionism'; see, however, Robert Segal, "In Defense of Reductionism," *Journal of the American Academy of Religion* 51 (1983): 97–123, a refreshing challenge to the current orthodoxy.

19. Frank, *Lumpenbourgeoisie: Lumpendevelopment.*

20. See S. N. Eisenstadt, "The Protestant Thesis in an Analytical and Comparative Framework," in Eisenstadt, *The Protestant Ethic and Modernization,* pp. 3–45; Eisenstadt favored ideological explanations and did not consider the role played by international economic relations, which is examined by Frank in the studies listed above.

21. Emilio Willems, "Protestantism and Culture Change in Brazil and Chile," in William D'Antonio and Frederick Pike, eds., *Religion, Revolution, and Reform: New Faces for Change in Latin America* (New York: Praeger, 1964), p. 105; see also Frederick Pike, "Introduction," in D'Antonio and Pike, *Religion, Revolution, and Reform,* p. 11, on the absence of the Protestant ethic in Latin America: "Francisco Bilbao, 19th century Chilean intellectual, maintained that the principal reason that the United States was making outstanding progress while Latin America remained materially in a state of stagnation was that the population of the northern power was predominantly protestant in religious affiliation, while Latin Americans were Catholics."

22. Martin, *General Theory of Secularization,* p. 203.

23. On this issue see Abner Cohen, *Two-Dimensional Man: An Essay on the Anthropology and Symbolism in Complex Society* (Berkeley: University of California Press, 1974); Eric Wolf, "The Virgin of Guadalupe: A Mexican National Symbol," *Journal of American Folklore* 71 (1958): 34–39, reprinted in W. Lessa and E. Vogt, *A Reader in Comparative Religion,* 4th ed. (New York: Harper and Row, 1979), pp. 112–115.

24. Carsten Colpe, "Syncretism and Secularization: Complementary and Antithetical Trends in New Religious Movements?" *History of Religions* 17 (1977): 158–176. In regard to the ideologies of revolt, see Vittorio Lanternari, *Movimenti religiosi de libertà e di salvezza dei poppoli oppressi,* 2d ed. (Milan: Feltrinelli, 1974); Maria Isaura Pereira de Queiroz, *Réforme et révolution dans les sociétés traditionnelles: Histoire et ethnologie des mouvements méssianiques* (Paris: Anthropos, 1968); Peter Worsley, *The Trumpet Shall Sound: A Study of "Cargo" Cults in Melanesia,* 2d ed. (New York: Schocken, 1968); Sylvia Thrupp, ed., *Millennial Dreams in Action* (New York: Schocken, 1970); Bryan Wilson, *Magic and the Millennium: A Sociological Study of Religious Movements of Protest among Tribal and Third-World Peoples* (London: Heinemann, 1973); Guenter Lewy, *Religion and Revolution* (New York: Oxford University Press, 1974); and János Bak and Gerhard Benecke, eds., *Religion and Rural Revolt* (Manchester, Eng.: Manchester University Press, 1984). See also Alejandro Ortiz Rescaniere, *De Adaneva a Inkarrí: Una visión indígena del Perú* (Lima: Retablo de Papel, 1973); Juan Ossio, *Ideología mesiánica del mundo andino* (Lima: Prado, 1973).

25. See John Baines, *Revolution in Peru: Mariátegui and the Myth* (University, Ala.: University of Alabama Press, 1972), pp. 13–16, 56–60.

26. On fascism see, among many other studies, Ernst Nolte, *Der Faschismus in seiner Epoche,* 6th ed. (München: Piper, 1984); and Maria-A. Macciocchi, ed., *Eléments pour une analyse du fascisme* (Paris: Union générale d'edition, October 18, 1976). On protofascist ideologies and their influence on intellectuals, see Fritz Stern *The Politics of Cultural Despair: A Study in the Rise of Germanic Mythology* (New York: Doubleday, 1961); Alaistar Hamilton, *The Appeal of Fascism: A Study of Intellectuals and Fascism, 1919–1945* (New York: Macmillan, 1971); and Furio Jesi, *Cultura di destra* (Milan: Garzanti, 1979).

27. One only need think of the *völkisch* elements in the anarchism of Gustav Landauer; on Landauer see Eugene Lunn, *Prophet of Community The Romantic Socialism of Gustav Landauer* (Berkeley: University of California Press, 1973), pp. 6, 133, 261, 343–348. For a reevaluation of utopian thinking, see Jost Hermand, *Orte. Irgendwo. Formen utopischen Denkens* (Königstein: Athenaeum, 1981).

28. In an interview published by *Newsweek* (March 19, 1984), Pinochet said, "I am a man fighting for a just cause; the fight between Christianity and spiritualism on one hand, and Marxism and materialism on the other. I get my strength from God"(p. 67).

29. See J. Lloyd Mecham, *Church and State in Latin America,* rev. ed. (Chapel Hill: University of North Carolina Press, 1966), p. 399. See also Hans-Jürgen Prien, *Die Geschichte des Christentums in Lateinamerika* (Göttingen: Vandenhoeck & Ruprecht, 1978), pp. 1013ff; Garry Wills, *The Kennedy Imprisonment* (Boston: Little Brown, 1982), pp. 223–229; 233–238.

30. But see the "Declaración de los sacerdotes del tercer mundo con motivo de la consagración del país a la Virgen," in *Signos de liberación: Testimonios de la iglesia en américa latina, 1969–1973* (Lima: Centro de estudios y publicaciones, 1973), pp. 116–118.

31. See Prien, *Geschichte des Christentums in Lateinamerika,* pp. 1060–1061; Brian Smith, *The Church and Politics in Chile* (Princeton, N.J.: Princeton University Press, 1982), pp. 132–137, 140, 148–149, 256, 338–339; Thomas Bruneau, *The Political Transformation of the Brazilian Catholic Church* (London: Cambridge University Press, 1974), pp. 184, 226–228; Frederick Turner, *Catholicism and Political Development in Latin America* (Chapel Hill: University of North Carolina Press, 1971), pp. 13, 99.

32. On the concept of ideology, see Hans-Joachim Lieber, ed., *Ideologienlehre und Wissenssoziologie: Die Diskussion um das Ideologieproblem in den zwanziger Jahre* (Darmstadt: Wissenschaftliche Buchgesellschaft (WBG), 1974); idem, ed., *Ideologie-Wissenschaft-Gesellschaft: Neuere Beiträge zur Diskussion* (Darmstadt: WBG, 1976); Volker Meja and Nico Stehr, eds., *Der Streit um die Wissenssoziologie,* vols. 1–2 (Frankfurt: Suhrkamp, 1982); Karl Mannheim, *Ideology and Utopia* (New York: New Left Books, 1929, 1936); Ernst Topitsch and Kurt Salamun, *Ideologie, Herrschaft des Vorurteils* (München-Wien; Langen Müller, 1972); Hans Barth, *Wahrheit und Ideologie* (Frankfurt: Suhrkamp, 1961, 1974); Eugen Lemberg, *Ideologie und Gesellschaft* (Stuttgart: Kohlhammer, 1974); Jorge Larraín, *The Concept of Ideology* (London: Hutchinson, 1979); idem, *Marxism and Ideology* (London: Macmillan, 1983); Ferruccio Rossi-Landi, *Semiotica e ideologia* (Milan: Bompiani, 1979); idem, *Ideologia* (Milan: Mondadori, 1982); and Göran Therborn, *The Ideology of Power and the Power of Ideology* (London: New Left Books, 1980).

33. Antonio Gramsci, *Quaderni del carcere* (Rome: Editori Riuniti, 1969); Rossi-Landi, *Ideologia,* pp. 68–69; Raymond Williams, *Marxism and Literature* (New York: Oxford University Press, 1977), pp. 108–114.

34. On the importance of nonideological control mechanisms, see the important study by Nicholas Abercrombie, Stephen Hill, and Bryan S. Turner, *The Dominant Ideology Thesis* (London: George Allen and Unwin 1980); and Turner, *Religion and Social Theory*.

35. See note 23; J. David Sapir and J. Christopher Crocker, eds., *The Social Use of Metaphor: Essays on the Anthropology of Rhetoric* (Philadelphia: University of Pennsylvania Press, 1977).

36. See Godelier, *Horizon*; Ana Maria Mariscotti de Görlitz, "Autochtone Religion und katholischer Volksglaube," in G. Stephenson ed., *Der Religionswandel unserer Zeit im Spiegel der Religionswissenschaft* (Darmstadt: WBG, 1976), pp. 30–53; on the sacrality of agriculture, see Mircea Eliade, *Traité d'histoire des religions* (Paris: Payot, 1970), pp. 281–310.

37. On this subject see, from a traditional Catholic point of view, Anselm Stolz, O.S.B., *Theologie der Mystik* (Regensburg: Pustet, 1936), pp. 212–213, 212–222.

38. This is usually emphasized in traditional histories of the church in Latin America; see, for example, the superficial and sentimental account by Renato Poblete, S.J., "The Church in Latin America: A Historical Survey," in Henry Landsberger, ed., *The Church and Social Change in Latin America* (Notre Dame, Ind.: University of Notre Dame Press, 1970), pp. 39–52, especially p. 41; idem "From Medellín to Puebla," in Daniel Levine, ed., *Churches and Politics in Latin America* (Beverly Hills, Calif.: Sage, 1980), pp. 41–54.

39. On Las Casas, see Gustavo Gutiérrez, *La fuerza histórica de los pobres* (Lima: Centro de estudios y publicaciones, 1980), pp. 357–361.

40. In fact, one should recognize the 'utopian' aspects of Marxism; see Frederic Jameson, *The Political Unconscious* (Ithaca, N.Y.: Cornell University Press, 1981), pp. 281–299; idem, *Marxism and Form* (Princeton, N.J.: Princeton University Press, 1971), pp. 116–159.

41. See, for example, Alfredo Garland Barrón, *Como lobos rapaces* (Lima, SAPEI [Servicio de análisis pastoral e informativo], 1978).

42. Gutiérrez, *La fuerza histórica de los pobres,* p. 65. For a nontheological critique, see Gustavo Benavides, "The Discourse of Liberation Theology in Perspective," in M. Darrol Bryant and Rita Mataragnon, eds., *The Many Faces of Religion and Society* (New York: Paragon, 1985), pp. 122–134. Theological ways of thinking are examined in Hans Albert, *Traktat über kritische Vernuft,* 4th ed. (Tübingen: Mohr, 1980); and idem, *Das Elend der Theologie* (Hamburg: Hoffmann und Campe, 1979).

43. Roger E. Vekemans, S.J., "Economic Development, Social Change, and Cultural Mutation in Latin America," in D'Antonio and Pike, *Religion, Revolution, and Reform,* pp. 129–142, especially 136–137; on Vekemans (and López Trujillo) see Phillip Berryman, "What Happened at Puebla," in Levine, *Churches and Politics in Latin America,* pp. 55–86, especially pp. 59, 79–80, 85 n. 15; Prien, *Geschichte des Christentums in Lateinamerika,* p. 1061; Arturo Blatezky, *Sprache des Glaubens* (Frankfurt: Lang, 1978), p. 155 n. 35.

44. Bruneau, *The Political Transformation of the Brazilian Catholic Church,* pp. 120–121.

45. Smith, *The Church and Politics in Chile,* pp. 287–294; idem, "Churches and Human Rights in Latin America," in Levine, *Churches and Politics in Latin America,* pp. 155–193; on Chile see pp. 158–162. According to Smith, "in the four and one-half years since the coup, the bishops have seldom criticized the government for torture, and have only expressed sharp criticisms (or threatened excommunication) when the authority

or person of bishops themselves have been attacked'' (pp. 161–162); the same applies to Bolivia (p. 176). Smith's general conclusion is that the cases of Chile, Brazil, Paraguay, Bolivia, and Argentina ''indicate that church programs for human rights are basically reactive strategies, responding to unforeseen crises in secular society'' (p. 182).

46. The Argentinian military regime, no less murderous than its Chilean counterpart, managed to pursue its ''dirty war'' comforted by the Te Deums celebrated by the church; see, most recently, Piero Gleijeses, ''The Official Story,'' a review of *Nunca más: The Report of the Argentine National Commission on the Disappeared* (New York: Farrar, Straus and Giroux, 1986); *The New Republic,* December 8, 1986, pp. 46–48.

47. On Duarte and the civil war in El Salvador, see Julia Preston, ''What Duarte Won,'' *The New York Review of Books,* August 15, 1985, pp. 30–35; Edward Shehan, ''The 'Clean' War,'' *The New York Review of Books,* June 26, 1986, pp. 25–30; Jefferson Morley, ''Prisoner of Success,'' *The New York Review of Books*, December 4, 1986, pp. 15–20.

48. See Mark A. Uhlig, ''Pinochet's Tiranny,'' *The New York Review of Books,* June 27, 1985, pp. 35–40.

49. See Harry Kantor, ''Catholic Political Parties and Mass Politics in Latin America,'' in Donald Smith, ed., *Religion and Political Modernization* (New Haven: Yale University Press, 1974), pp. 202–223, especially p. 219.

50. Turner, *Catholicism and Political Development in Latin America,* pp. 36ff., 125–126, 194, 237.

51. Vallier, *Catholicism, Social Control, and Modernization in Latin America,* p. 93.

52. Vallier, *Catholicism, Social Control, and Modernization in Latin America,* p. 9. See also Vallier, ''Extraction, Insulation, and Re-entry: Toward a Theory of Religious Change,'' in Landsberger, *The Church and Social Change in Latin America,* pp. 9–35; idem, ''Church 'Development' in Modern Latin America: A Five Country Comparison,'' *The Journal of Developing Areas* 1 (1967): 461–476, reprinted in Karl M. Schmitt, ed., *The Roman Catholic Church in Modern Latin America* (New York: Knopf, 1972), pp. 167–193; see, however, David E. Mutchler, ''Adaptation of the Roman Catholic Church to Latin American Development'' *Social Control* 36 (1969): 231–252, reprinted in Schmitt, *The Roman Catholic Church in Modern Latin America,* pp. 194–216.

53. Vallier, *Catholicism, Social Control, and Modernization in Latin America,* p. 17.

54. Puebla is discussed by Phillip Berryman: ''What Happened at Puebla,'' pp. 55–86. That the war against Nicaragua involves more than the *contras* should be clear by now; on this issue, see Ana María Ezcurra, *Agresión ideológica contra la revolución sandinista* (Mexico City: Nuevomar, 1983); idem, *El Vaticano y la administración Reagan* (Mexico City: Nuevomar, 1984).

SELECTED BIBLIOGRAPHY

Note: For a more comprehensive bibliography, see Gustavo Benavides, ''Catholicism and Politics in Latin America,'' in Charles Wei-hsun Fu and Gerhard Spiegler, eds., *Movements and Issues in World Religions: Religion, Ideology, and Politics* (Westport, Conn.: Greenwood Press, 1987), pp. 107–142.

Abercrombie, Nicholas, Stephen Hill, and Bryan S. Turner. *The Dominant Ideology Thesis.* London: George Allen and Unwin, 1980.
Behrman, Lucy C. ''Catholic Priests and Mass Politics in Chile.'' In Donald E. Smith,

ed., *Religion and Political Modernization*. Princeton, N.J.: Princeton University Press, 1974, pp. 181–201.

Benavides, Gustavo. "The Discourse of Liberation Theology in Perspective." In M. Darrol Bryant and Rita Mataragnon, eds., *The Many Faces of Religion and Society*. New York: Paragon, 1985, pp. 122–134.

Berryman, Phillip. "What Happened at Puebla." In Daniel H. Levine, ed., *Churches and Politics in Latin America*. Beverly Hills, Calif.: Sage, 1980, pp. 55–86.

Calvo, Roberto. "The Church and the Doctrine of National Security," in Daniel H. Levine, ed., *Churches and Politics in Latin America*. Beverly Hills, Calif.: Sage, 1980, pp. 135–154.

D'Antonio, William. "Democracy and Religion in Latin America." In William D'Antonio and Frederick Pike, eds., *Religion, Revolution, and Reform: New Forces for Change in Latin America*. New York: Praeger, 1964, pp. 241–265.

Dodson, Michael. "The Christian Left in Latin American Politics." In Daniel H. Levine, ed., *Churches and Politics in Latin America*. Beverly Hills, Calif.: Sage, 1980, pp. 120–124.

Eisenstadt, S. N. "The Implications of Weber's Sociology of Religion for Understanding Process of Change in Contemporary Non-European Societies and Civilizations." In Charles Glock and Phillip Hammond, eds., *Beyond the Classics?* New York: Harper and Row, 1973, pp. 131–155.

———, ed. *The Protestant Ethic and Modernization: A Comparative View*. New York: Basic Books, 1968.

Frank, Andre Gunder. *Capitalism and Underdevelopment in Latin America*. New York and London: Monthly Review Press, 1967.

———. *Dependent Accumulation and Underdevelopment*. New York and London: Monthly Review Press, 1979.

———. *Lumpenbourgeoisie: Lumpendevelopment. Dependence, Class, and Politics in Latin America*. New York and London: Monthly Review Press, 1972.

———. *World Accumulation, 1492–1789*. New York and London: Monthly Review Press, 1978.

Hobsbawm, Eric. "Introduction: Inventing Traditions." In Eric Hobsbawm and Terence Ranger, eds. *The Invention of Tradition*. Cambridge: Cambridge University Press, 1983, pp. 1–14.

———. "Mass-Producing Traditions: Europe, 1870–1914." In Eric Hobsbawm and Terence Ranger, eds., *The Invention of Tradition*. Cambridge: Cambridge University Press, 1983, pp. 263–307.

Hobsbawm, Eric, and Terence Ranger, eds. *The Invention of Tradition*. Cambridge: Cambridge University Press, 1983.

Kantor, Harry. "Catholic Political Parties and Mass Politics in Latin America." In Donald Smith, ed., *Religion and Political Modernization*. Princeton, N.J.: Princeton University Press, 1974, pp. 202–223.

Levine, Daniel H. "Religion and Politics, Politics and Religion." In Daniel H. Levine, ed., *Churches and Politics in Latin America*. Beverly Hills, Calif.: Sage, 1980, pp. 16–40.

———, ed. *Churches and Politics in Latin America*. Beverly Hills, Calif.: Sage, 1980.

Martin, David. *A General Theory of Secularization*. New York: Harper and Row, 1978.

Mutchler, David E. "Adaptation of the Roman Catholic Church in Latin America Development." In Karl M. Schmitt, ed., *The Roman Catholic Church in Modern Latin America*. New York: Knopf, 1972, pp. 194–216.

Nelson, Benjamin. "Weber's Protestant Ethic." In Charles Glock and Phillip Hammond, eds., *Beyond the Classics?* New York: Harper and Row, 1973, pp. 71–130.

Poblete, Renato, S.J. "The Church in Latin America: A Historical Survey." In Henry A. Landsberger, ed., *The Church and Social Change in Latin America*. Notre Dame, Ind.: Notre Dame University Press, 1970, pp. 39–52.

————. "From Medellin to Puebla." In Daniel H. Levine, ed., *Churches and Politics in Latin America*. Beverly Hills, Calif.: Sage, 1980, pp. 41–54.

Robertson, Roland. *The Sociological Interpretation of Religion*. Oxford: Blackwell, 1970.

Sanders, Thomas G. "Catholicism and Development: The Catholic Left in Brazil." In Kalman H. Silvert, ed., *Churches and States: The Religious Institution and Modernization*. New York: American Universities Field Staff, 1967, pp. 81–99.

Seyfarth, C., and W. Sprondel, eds. *Religion und Gesellschaftliche Entwicklung*. Frankfurt: Suhrkamp, 1973.

Shils, Edward. *Tradition*. Chicago: University of Chicago Press, 1981.

Silvert, Kalman H., ed. *Churches and States: The Religious Institution and Modernization*. New York: American Universities Field Staff, 1967.

Smith, Brian. "Churches and Human Rights in Latin America." in Daniel H. Levine, ed. *Churches and Politics in Latin America*. Beverly Hills, Calif.: Sage, 1980, pp. 155–193.

Smith, Donald E., ed. *Religion and Political Modernization*. Princeton, N.J.: Princeton University Press, 1974.

Turner, Bryan S. *Religion and Social Theory: A Materialist Perspective*. London: Heinemann, 1983.

Vallier, Ivan. *Catholicism, Social Control, and Modernization in Latin America*. Englewood Cliffs, N.J.: Prentice-Hall, 1970.

————. "Church Development in Latin America: A Five-Country Comparison." In Karl M. Schmitt, ed., *The Roman Catholic Church in Modern Latin America*. New York: Knopf, 1972, pp. 167–193.

————. "Extraction, Insulation, and Re-Entry: Toward a Theory of Religious Change." In Henry A. Landsberger, ed., *The Church and Social Change in Latin America*. Notre Dame, Ind.: Notre Dame University Press, 1970, pp. 9–35.

Wallerstein, Immanuel. *The Modern World-System. Vol. 1: Capitalist Agriculture and the Origins of the European World-Economy in the Sixteenth Century*. New York: Academic Press, 1974.

Wilde, Alexander. "The Years of Change in the Church." In Daniel H. Levine, ed., *Churches and Politics in Latin America*. Beverly Hills, Calif.: Sage, 1980, pp. 267–279.

Willems, Emilio. "Protestantism and Culture Change in Brazil and Chile." In William D'Antonio and Frederick Pike, eds., *Religion, Revolution, and Reform: New Faces for Change in Latin America*. New York: Praeger, 1964, pp. 91–108.

Wolf, Eric. *Europe and the People without History*. Berkeley: University of California Press, 1982.

Worsley, Peter. *The Three Worlds: Culture and World Development*. Chicago: The University of Chicago Press, 1984.

9

In Quest of Muslim Identity

KHALID DURAN

Not unlike other religions, Islam became institutionalized as a multidimensional phenomenon. In addition to being known for its primordial role as a faith in the Hereafter, it came to be regarded as a state deriving its authority from religious precepts, as a moral teaching, as a philosophy, and many things more. Most of these manifestations were, moreover, combined into a framework with an almost monolithic appearance. But it is also true that one or the other aspect would alternately predominate therein. Its dimension as a law code held sway for much of the time, but mysticism, too, had its periods of supremacy. During other phases a considerable degree of balance was attained. 'Westernization,' then, led to a number of "compensations, substitutions, intensifications," in short: redefinitions. This resulted in what has been called "the drift from integral Islam."[1] As is the case with most historical religions, the specific manifestations of Islam include moments that, with a difference in accent and stress, would give rise to a pattern of religiosity that "might appear as a deviation from the original pathos and, in extreme forms, as a betrayal and complete negation of its first intentions."[2] In this sense, religion has been compared to art, because both diversify on a similar pattern in the course of history. In former centuries this multiplicity of moments, with all of its variety of psychological motivations and resultant difference of dogmatic formulations, eventuated in sectarian ramifications. In a world divided on the basis of "ideologies," the deliberations about the requirements, or components, of an Islamic identity seldom assume this form, they now result in a whirl of redefinitions, frequently inconsistent one with the other, and only rarely capable of winning ecumenical acceptance.

Only two or three decades ago one could frequently hear that the religion of Islam is no more a uniting force and that it no longer had any concrete social organization. In the eyes of a new elite that was predominantly nationalistic and socialistic in outlook, Islamic tenets seemed to have become largely obsolete.

At least fragments of the Middle Eastern intelligentsia openly confessed their preference for Western education, considering not only its science but also its literature as superior. Allegedly, Islamic thought had remained stagnant and had lost its hold, leaving a social vacuum and spiritual dissatisfaction.

In the 1980s it is more common to hear voices of alarm over what appears to be an ebullient dynamism of Muslim states finally awakened to their independence. Some analysts find the explanation for this vitality in the fresh vigor of Islam, particularly its universalism. Certainly, a number of those who speak of the "inherent vitality in Muslim society" think primarily of political parties based on Islamist fundamentalism.[3] Nonetheless, a craving for a uniquely Islamic form of self-expression is recognized as pertaining to most strata of the social fabric.

A detachment from Islam is generally abhorred as obliteration of cultural identity, as "the real threat, the irreparable defeat."[4] Attachment to Islam, on the other hand, knows a large scale of degrees and manifests itself in multifarious forms. The longing to be fully independent and not to mold oneself in the image of others seems to insure the survival of some kind of Islamic sentiment even with some, if not many, Arab nationalists of Marxist leanings. Under heavy strains, the "reconquest of identity" led to periodic reversals of liberal modernists to a more fundamentalist bent of thought, starting with the ostensible volte-face of the illustrious religious scholar Jamāl ad-dīn Al-Afghānī in his later career, via the much discussed "crisis of orientation" in the Egypt of the 1930s, to the present "reislamization."[5]

To preserve or to reestablish Muslim identity, recourse was taken to the ideal of a synthesis wherein some of the old could be retained while adopting some of the new. The mass of modern data, ideas, objects, and methods proffered by the West is irretrievably being assimilated, with differences in the degree of rapidity and thoroughness. Conversely, it is evident that the newly absorbed Western knowledge is merging with elements from the past. Before exploring the intricacies of this procedure, something has to be said about the synthesizing activity as a marked quality of Muslim culture. Many scholars of Islam, both Eastern and Western, fondly recall earlier crises of Muslim history that were overcome by Islam's "amazing cross-cultural absorptiveness," by its peculiar capacity to fuse heterogeneous elements into new creations without loosing its Islamicity.[6] In the course of centuries, it is said, Islam succeeded at "digesting" extraneous influences until they were no longer recognizable as such. Those ingredients invigorated the old Arab foundation and caused the growth of a splendid culture upheld by an unparalleled divine vision.

Guided by his study of history Sir Hamilton A. R. Gibb came to epitomize Islam as "acceptance of opposed ideas and mediation between them, either in the form of a synthesis, or in assigning separate spheres to each and tolerating their co-existence."[7] Whereas Gibb spoke of a characteristic feature of the Arabs, S.C.H. Becker regarded this syncretism as typical of the Persians.[8] No wonder, then, that others hold it to be the unmistakable quality of Muslimhood as a whole.

Al-Ghazālī (d. 1111), in his capacity as one of the most outstanding theologians of Muslim history, serves as an instance. He is said to illustrate an essential trait of Muslim individuality, namely, the almost unlimited ability to amalgamate contradictions and to construct from them a harmonious whole.[9]

This encouraged Muslim authors of our century to give a historical endorsement to the ideal of synthesis by making appeal to Islam's record of successful blending that engendered a harmonious culture *sui generis*. The "classical" example of this synthesizing process is provided by the incipient phase of Muslim culture, especially between 800 and 900, culminating in the creativity of the early ʿAbbasid reign when traditions, doctrines, and institutions were adopted almost naively until an awareness began to dawn that continuous cultural borrowing might endanger the individuality of Islam as a social phenomenon. Much of the ancient wisdom of the various races constituting the empire had by then been assimilated to the teachings of the prophet. The independent character of his message was later safeguarded by a process of selecting as truly Islamic those elements that were felt to correspond to the image of the prophet. This ancient method of acculturation was now recommended by several writers, Muslim and non-Muslim alike, as an inspiring example. To overcome the present generations' anxiety, they evoke the forebears "réussites d' équilibre." [10] That this idea of striking a balance had really become pivotal in Muslim thought is evident from the fact that in South Asian Islam it was almost institutionalized under the designation of *tatbīq*, which in Indianized Arabic stands for synthesis. With an important school of Muslim thinkers from the subcontinent, *tatbīq* became as imperious a concept as was, for others, the controversial institution of "emulation" (*taqlīd*—sticking to the judgments of the early fathers). Part of their aspiration was precisely to replace *taqlīd* with *tatbīq*.[11]

Some scholars regard this characteristic of Pakistani Islam, with its proximity to Indian syncretism, as too peripheral. Even if that objection were justified, there is also Iran where the synthesizing tradition survived in some religious schools into the nineteenth century, probably more than anywhere in Sunnite Islam. Significantly, it is this tradition of reconciling science, religion, and even mysticism whence came the initiator of Muslim resurgence in the nineteenth century, Jamāl ad-dīn Al-Afghānī.[12]

Historically, the Muslim synthesizing process, however, was not really a planned or systematic enterprise. With the concept of *ijmāʿ*, which denotes "consensus of the believers," it had become somewhat institutionalized, though not in a clearly definable sense. The scholars of religious law and theology, as representatives of the community, did not reach such a consensus as an organized body, because Islamic theory made no provision for a clerical apparatus. The idea of manifesting the principle of *ijmāʿ* in the form of modern parliaments may not necessarily be a distortion of Islam, as some critics tend to believe, but it certainly is an adaptation to the twentieth century. *Ijmāʿ* in history was more like a struggle for the survival of the fittest elements of thought, and the result was an armistice rather than a truce. The "consensus" was arrived at after a

free-for-all among the warring groups of theologians. It is, perhaps, best illustrated at the instance of Ash'arism, a compromise school of theology that assumed
dominance in Sunni Islam after other rival schools had become too exhausted
by a gory feud that lasted, with changing fortunes, for several centuries.

Although Islam, or at least the Sunni vision of it, knows no church in the
Christian sense, in former times the state exercised some such functions. Caliphs,
and later Sultans, often decided the battle in favor of one or the other school.
Generally, this would occur after a protracted dispute had already taken place
so that state authorities could conveniently intervene on the side of the faction
that had turned out to be the most popular. For this reason some Islamicists are
inclined to take a much milder view of *ijmā*' and even regard it as something
like a *vox populi,* a consensus of the entire community rather than of the canonical
doctors only.[13]

It is a moot point, too, whether this evolutionary process, with its endless ups
and downs and long intervals of paralyzing suspension, was a blessing or a bane
in the history of Muslim peoples. It has attractively been projected as "the slowly
accumulating pressure of opinion over a long time,"[14] as the building up of a
general will "by gradual stages over a period of many generations."[15] The
question, however, is whether such a drawn-out process of selection and rejection
by fighting it out can provide a clear-cut perspective for modern emulation. The
results would always lie far ahead in a distant future and should necessarily be
just another standstill compromise, "ascertained only in a vague and general
way."[16]

An additional complication is the stark fact that theological and philosophical
questions can no longer be discussed within the Islamic framework alone, as
was the privilege of the medieval thinkers. For those, as for European leaders
of thought during the Reformation and the Enlightenment, there was no reference
to ulterior standards; they merely had to make their intellect prevail against
established norms. The foreign culture that had seduced Muslim thinkers under
the 'Abbasids belonged either to the past (before Islam) or to peoples whose
political glory had come to an end. Muslims in the nineteenth and twentieth
centuries were in no such enviable position. They were faced with the more
difficult task of asserting their consciences in the tension between two disparate
traditions: their own, being the weaker one in terms of worldly power, and the
technical advancement of foreign nations that are fixing the ulterior standards.

Doctrinal issues, therefore, can no longer be considered on their own merit.
It has become necessary to demonstrate that one's own intellectual currents and
social structures are as progressive as those of the West and that they are also
more truly Islamic than those upheld by opponents at home. Some Islamicists
speak, therefore, of a double standard and hold it responsible for the replacement
of rigorous systematic thought by superficial slogans and angry polemics. Others
speak of the Janus-faced character of Muslim reconstruction. On the one hand,
they say, it stands in dire need of alien inspiration in order to recover its former

creativity. It has, therefore, to break the impermeability of its own society to the new. On the other hand, it also has to preserve the stimulating prestige of the past. Indubitably, this enforced balancing between the imposing standards of the former colonial master and one's own norms, that were traditionally held to be superior to anything else, bears some of the responsibility for modernism's becoming double edged as well as the resultant lack of intellectual efficacy. Pressurized by the speed of involuntary change, the more capable minds found little chance to apply sustained thinking to the Gordian Knot.

Thus the advantage of an essentially reconciling approach, molded by historical experience, doubtlessly exists; yet it remains to be seen how far this can facilitate the task of the twenty-first century. Granted that although the desire for reform with its "noble concern for perfection" through the ransacking of history is the constant aspiration of Muslimhood, as it has been described, it still does not answer the question of in what way the ancient precedent of acculturation can serve as a workable model.[17] The real problem seems to be that of cultural creativeness and theological imagination, which were lost in spite of the assimilative capacity and the "vitality" that H.A.R. Gibb discerned even in the eighteenth century.[18]

The demands on such a synthesis are numerous, and they are raised ever anew in many different wordings. Thus it has been postulated that the synthesis must result from a fresh evaluation of modern social life and legal institutions in the light of a new formulation of the fundamental principles of Islam. So many warnings have been sounded that it should be a genuine synthesis, not congeries or mere syncretism, that one should guard against mistaking symbiosis for synthesis, and so on. It would have to do justice to the modifications of the Muslim self-view caused by nationalistic, socialistic, and other experiences the community has been through in the meantime. It has to take into account the detours made for the rejuvenation of the body politic, and it has to demonstrate cogently how the changes are to be justified by the message of the prophet, if this message is to be heeded.

All of these stipulations, however, are restricted to the acceptance of change as a principle. The question of exactly what elements of the past should be preserved and precisely what contributions of the modern age should be accepted is answered very differently. In sorting out what can be considered suitable and justifiable, there is no binding principle. In the absence of a mechanism to arrive at a consensus, individual selectivity has so far prevented matters from settling down.

Under the pressure of rapid transition, a pressure coming from abroad, and the tension created by new and, mostly, haphazard accentuations, there is an acute vacillation. The multifarious expectations from, and the demands on, such a historically inspired synthesis are just too many. The resulting frequent shifts of loyalty keep ideological development in a state of hypertension and produce that symptomatic crisis of the intellectuals on which so much is being written.

THEOLOGICAL INADEQUACY AND THE REDUCTION OF ISLAM

Perceptive observers have stressed the need to calm apprehensions caused by modernity that trouble the faithful. Their anguish originates from the doubt that by Westernizing they might incur divine wrath. This "bewildered agony of conscious doubting" entails a state of deep and tense suspension.[19] There exists, side by side, a hope that by availing of the new, one might become compatible in the world of future progress and a fear that the acceptance of the new might deprive the believer of future spiritual bliss. Whereas modernity leaves in reality little choice and, by and by, imposes itself in its totality, the multifaceted heritage induces the believers to reconsider elements of the past that might prove useful in the enhancement of future prospects.

In this conflict between the urge for emancipation and the anxiety over a possible loss of the spiritual basis of self-hood—the fear of being uprooted— Muslims received but little guidance from their theologians. It is a rather frequent observation, made by numerous observers of the contemporary scene, that the 'custodians of the faith' have, by and large, been the most unresponsive to the challenges of Westernization. Those from whom answers to the burning questions would be expected, more than from anyone else, did generally not provide them.

Al-Azhar, for instance, the center of religious learning in Cairo, at first sight does not appear to betray much bewilderment. This ancient university of Islam, from where most preachers and religious officeholders in Egypt and many other countries graduate, is sometimes likened to the Vatican. It is, however, correct to say that Rome's formalism is "nothing like the apathy of Al-Azhar."[20] A development comparable to the Second Vatican Council is hardly foreseeable in Cairo. In the serenity of their "arrested state" the Azharites fail to inspire with fresh energies, and their system of certainties is discreetly discarded by the faithful as inadequate. Those few among the ʿulamā who ventured onto untreaded ground were quickly expelled from the phratry and, therefore, did not act with the authority of Al-Azhar. In the writings of the Azharites there is, to use a somewhat poignant formulation, "not the slightest sign or inkling of a restatement of the faith."[21]

The present "low ebb" of Islamic studies, apologetics, and the exegesis of Al-Qurʾān can be attributed to the particular development of the religious law, the sharīʿa at least partially. Since this sacred law was derived by the pious forebears from Al-Qurʾān and the Hadīth (among numerous other sources), it gradually came to be considered as a revealed law. As such it was to be protected against alterations through human legislation. In the age of Muslim enlightenment, during the ninth century, conservative scholars of religion militated against the rationalists. The ʿulamā feared rationalism as a force of disintegration and a threat to the social polity in which they were rising. Since they were the guardians and the chief benefiters from a legist interpretation of the faith, they jealously shielded the sharīʿa from major innovations. The emergence of their class and its victory over contenders for influence is an issue that would take us too far afield in the present context. Muslim apologists are wont to refer to the sack of Baghdad (in 1258) as a paramount factor leading to stagnation under the aegis of the ʿulamā. Simplistic as this argument may appear, it is partially confirmed by similar developments after the repeated sacking of Muslim Delhi and its final fall in 1857. Although these events do not suffice as a monocausal explanation, they do symbolize the waning fortunes of Muslim political power—and the consequences on the intellectual plain. Under those circumstances the ʿulamā not only understood to preserve their privileges but even consolidated them by elaborating the binding force of the sharīʿa.

The persistence of formalism is closely linked to the political doldrums in which large parts of the Third World continue to find themselves; it is also proportionate to the hapless dependence on the manufactured goods and know-how of the superpowers. As long as this psychologically harmful state of things persists, the "zealots of fiqhism" (legism) will prosper and maintain the same old rigidity.

THE REDUCTIONIST TENDENCY: FROM DETHEOLOGIZATION TO THE POLITICAL IDEOLOGY OF ISLAMISM

In this tussle of redefinitions, characterized by the search for distinctive elements to corroborate fresh accentuations, the failing of the religious leadership to rethink the most sacred beliefs and traditions eventuated in the reduction of Islam to one of the following functions that need not be entirely exclusive but, all the same, mostly seem to constitute distinguishable tendencies:

1. A mere façade of cherished symbols
2. A sociopolitical system, or rather the legitimization for such a system
3. A mystic interiorization of the faith
4. A moral philosophy akin to the broad stream of humanist tendencies in other communities

A special interrelatedness between items 1 and 2 as well as between items 3 and 4 is unmistakable. Regarding the first-mentioned two aspects, it is but small wonder that in view of the "unhappy" and far-reaching "abeyance in radical theological thinking in Arab Islam," many writings aiming at a restatement of the Muslim heritage are characterized by what is sometimes called "detheologization."[22] This phenomenon is not altogether new.

The coronation of the tendency to work out the (this-worldly) singularity of Islam is the insistence of some modernists that it differs not only from all other religions but from religion as such. In a manifestolike book entitled *Islam: A Challenge to Religion*, an attempt is made to present it as a reality of its own kind, a *sui generis* manifestation of man with a faith. That particular "faith" is a competitor with all of the other, naturally inferior, ideologies.[23]

Such ideologues, especially the Islamists among them, perpetuate an inflationary attitude. The tendency to perceive Islam as a complete system with the concomitant facile course of resorting to undifferentiating answers to the most intricate questions has been perspicuously analyzed by Jacques Jomier. He pointed out that it engenders a habit of evading patient and painstaking investigation. Cultivating a superiority complex, as many Islamists do, leads to a lack of general culture and mars the acquisition of knowledge and the unfolding of intelligent reflection. Profound academic toil requires at least a modicum of modesty and humility that cannot develop in an atmosphere of constant apologetics and hysteric propaganda. Jomier registered that this attitude is apparent especially in the religious representation of history. It may be added that fundamentalists, who tend to be strong in numbers at the science departments of many universities, have so far failed to produce social scientists of mark and have made few contributions worth mentioning to the humanities in general. Many of them do, in fact, hardly distinguish between theology, philosophy, and mysticism. They do not only look askance at all three but, by a disproportionate stress on the political aspect of the Prophet's career, indirectly tend to expurgate Islam of its religious legacy as a faith, thereby reducing it further and further. The whole enterprise may be called a moral shortcut, which, as recent developments have shown, leads into intellectual confusion and social defeat. Here, the quest for Muslim identity has led into the void of devious distinctions that serve no constructive purpose but, on the contrary, prevent their proponents from partaking in the effort to make Islam meaningful in the pluralistic community of an industrializing world.

Whatever way the responsibility for detheologization may be apportioned, there is no gainsaying the fact that the modern West's philosophical, political, and social concepts were made to settle in the Muslim realm generally without the comfort of metaphysics.

The fact that so little of fresh thought was proffered by trained theologians forced other disciplines to fill the gap, and they necessarily detheologized Muslim thought still further. The vast majority of contemporary lay authors scarcely found themselves in a position to apply the newly acquired scientific methodology to religion. The young intelligentsia, the writers and artists of the liberal generation, were confronted with the task of furnishing a rationale for the introduced reforms. Trying to bridge the hiatus between past and present, they availed themselves of religious symbols without, however, attempting a critique of the texts. Dabbling in the history of Islam they alluded to religious notions in support of their philosophical argumentation while eschewing theology proper. The responsibility for this desistance seems to devolve primarily on the psychosis engendered by the politics of the time. One only has to look at the copious literary output that reveals a prepossession with the unmitigated menace of domination by the former colonial powers. It is, among other things, in this trauma that one has to search for the reasons for the neglect of internal problems and the abeyance in which theological reconstruction is held, eventuating in the preoccupation with Islam as a means of asserting national identity rather than spiritual sublimity and intellectual vigor.

It has also been argued that, in the case of Muslims, the suspension of religious thought, resulting from the priority given to the restoration of political force, has a rationale inasmuch as affinity with rule used to be a chief characteristic of Islam in history. The colonial interlude, therefore, symptomized an insidious aberration even religiously. In a sense, Atatürk might have been the most consequential recoverer of that destiny, but as a restitution of Islamic patterns, this was most stridently effected by another secularist, the political founder of Pakistan, Muhammad ʿAlī Jinnāh. This Western-educated leader proved a puzzle to many non-Muslims by establishing a modern state in the name of Islam. Yet there is scarcely anything to wonder about in the thoroughly unorthodox conduct of this statesman, whose sole identification was with Islam. In fact, he epitomized the psyche of modern Muslimhood laid bare, its desire to maintain Islamic specifity based on the concern for power and few other considerations. Clearer than any other leader, Jinnāh had the awareness of putting the right accent in a Muslimhood that had, numbly and without giving itself account of it, taken to accentuate political resurgence—onesidedly and necessarily. The "critical shift from the traditional faith to the modern ideology"[24] has resulted in that "baffling equation of Islam and state," which for many has become the new hallmark of their religion and which they now believe to be its pristine expression.[25]

The glory that Muslims remembered so well, because it had been so overwhelmingly resplendent, was not associated with a community of race or language; even in regard to territory, it was not so clearly limitable; it used to go by the name of Islam. After the termination of the Moghul and the Ottoman empires and the abolition of the Caliphate there was a "real, if indefinable, feeling of loss."[26] When Jinnāh relieved their sense of hurt by chiseling out for them a state of their own "as an instrument of the Islamic sense of identity," everything else became insubstantial, and he did not even have to play the role of the prodigal son returned from London.[27] With the analytical power of the brilliant and well-trained barrister that he was, Jinnāh merely anticipated what an Arab intellectual would later formulate as the result of his scholarly research, namely, that although Islam as metaphysics may not always exercise a genuine hold on the mind of the youth, it does supply a point of national cohesion.[28]

Thus even in the Arab world, where, unlike Pakistan, the self is not so exclusively referred to as Muslim, Islam prevails in some form as an abiding element of self-reconstruction. As an apostle of Arab nationalism has pointed out, when the Arab masses assert their attachment to Islam, especially in matters of politics and culture, the underlying motive is mostly their refusal to be reckoned vassals of the former colonial master. Adherence to Islam reassures them in their self-comprehension as part of a historical and geographical entity with a proud legacy of values and cultural roots.[29]

The ideological disputes between Islamist and nationalist intellectuals are scarcely representative of mass sentiment. These groups do, no doubt, influence the common people. Yet no standpoint seems to score a decisive victory in the consciousness of the masses who invariably coordinate these trends without always becoming aware of potential clashes of loyalty. The assessment of this popular commitment to Islam in its relationship to nationalism varies. It has been described as "quite negative, little more than a sense of difference which stiffened in the foreigner's presence."[30] It has also been referred to as "the profound Islamic reserves of the masses that would gush forth in the struggle for libera- tion."[31] Surveys in Egypt show that "a nebulous attachment to Islam" goes side by side with secular nationalism.[32]

In considering the elite, note that the new demand for Islam was raised in response to the challenges of the twentieth century. Therefore, it was neither any more identical with the religious needs of old nor any longer the major organizing principle of state administration. As an identification of government, it was pushed aside by modern state reform and, thereafter, acquired a new bearing. It was now, above all, an expression of the desire to sustain cultural identity in the confrontation with the overwhelming foreigner. Thus reduced to a cultural underpinning of political community, Islam well-nigh experienced an eclipse of the religious, if not the intellectual, dimension. That this development is part of a larger phenomenon common to the Third World can be instanced, without detracting from the specifity of the Muslim case, by Kwame Nkrumah's reformulation of the Lord's Prayer: "Seek ye first the political kingdom and all other things shall be added unto you."[33]

With some, notably the Islamists, this politicalization of the faith does not stop at the façade of Islamic symbols. Although Western thought is frequently stigmatized as a corrupting evil, especially by these circles, they nevertheless succumb to it by presenting Islam primarily as a social program more compre- hensive and efficient than any other enterprise seeking to ameliorate this world. The common trend of reducing the prophet's message to its temporal aspects undermines, an Arab critic warned, belief in God as the sovereign ruler of the universe, which was hitherto regarded as the very raison d'être of the Islamic religion. He hardly overstated it when he spoke of "a race between modern Muslim writers and Communists, aimed at showing which system offers more of the fruits of this temporal world."[34]

In response to the Western challenge, a broad stream of Muslim writings bespeaks almost an obsession with nizām, that is, the establishment of systems. Strikingly enough, this craving for a "complete-code-of-life" is almost strongest with the Islamists, who profess to reject Westernization in favor of nativistic solutions but constantly betray their indebtedness by overemphasizing concepts such as "Islamic system of economics," "Islamic system of government," or "Islamic system of education." As a result of detheologization, contemporary Muslims of various opinions seem to have sometimes greater faith in Islam as some kind of a system than in God the Creator.[35] The Islamists, too, insist that

Islam caters for their spiritual needs, but what they derive from it, first, seems to be "their originality, their distinctiveness from the others, from Westernizers, conservatives and nationalist revolutionaries alike. For them Islam became primarily a means of self-differentiation."[36]

This might explain why Islam is so rarely given a positive definition. Efforts mainly involve projecting it as different each time a comparison is made. Thus a former prime minister of Pakistan, Liyāqat ʿAlī Khān, clarified that "democracy in the Islamic sense" was distinguished from both the democracy of the West and the democracy of the Soviet Union: "It was in fact more democratic than both."[37] The principles of Islam, it is often said, do not conflict with those of the United Nations Charter on Fundamental Rights, "only in Islam the meaning is richer and fuller."[38]

With some of the liberals this craving for a distinctive Islamic identity can be even more vexing than with the fundamentalists, as a passage from Khalīfa ʿAbd al-Hakīm's book *Islamic Ideology* shows: "Such is the theocracy of Islam which is not to be identified with any theocracy that ever existed. Call it a theocracy or call it a secular state as you please: it synthesizes the virtues of both, repudiating the evils with which they are contaminated."[39] In view of such more or less absolute negations of all tangible forms (and occasionally even norms) it is hard to understand why there should be any talk of an 'Islamic State,' if not for the purely psychological satisfaction of those in search of a lost identity. Many thinkers of different tendencies are torn between an insistence on Muslim individuality and the dream of integrating with a pluralist world community. The first of these two urges induces them to adopt a terminology of distinctiveness. The second urge renders those terms meaningless in order to overcome barriers. "Thus the skeletal structure of the *sharīʿa* came to be defined primarily in terms of its empty spaces."[40]

Yet there have been attempts, more numerous than profound, to redefine Islam in a perspective more philosophical and less platitudinous than in Islamist literature. This search for an answer to the question 'what really is Islam?' soon turned into the dominant motive of the more intellectual Muslim reflections.

For the Western observer, it might be at times perplexing to see so many divergent groups insist on being faithful adherents to the creed, progressive reformers no less than conservative theologians or the toiling masses; seemingly irreconcilable opponents lay claim to the same religious basis. The possibilities discovered in this quest for a definition of "true Islam" merely heightened the already existing confusion and further aggravated the crisis of identity.

The quest resulted in the reopening of the ancient controversy between the concept of Islam as primarily a spiritual inwardness (*bātin*) and the other, visualizing it, above all, as a social force with emphasis on its externalities (*zāhir*). That external aspect is in a way synonymous with the law code called *sharīʿa*. In some parts of the Muslim world it had always been revered as a hallowed norm, but in former ages deviation from the sacred standard would be deplored, if by no other way than by sulky acquiescence in the forces that be. The faithful were sustained by the pious expectance of the day when the *sharīʿa* would be reinforced. The twentieth century has in a way, turned the tables, at least for some: with the liberal majority of the modern, educated class, deviations became the aspiration, although this is rarely explicitly stated. The remainder of effective *sharīʿa* injunctions are only acquiesced in with the hope for their obsolescence. In view of the ever-increasing adoption of outer aspects from the dominant civilization, and with the concomitant fear of losing part of one's own self, the temptation is strong to substitute by making as much as possible of the "inner aspect."

Critical observers generally tend to agree that Islam has retained the emotional attachment of its adherents. Some even argue that precisely when its public role became minimized, it found refuge deeper in the consciousness of Muslims and stimulated an interest to have a more profound understanding of it. The case of Algeria under France testifies to this observation most strikingly.

Intellectuals are encouraged in such an interiorizing approach by the sybilline but reassuring advice Muslims are at times given by outsiders, namely, to make critical choices that allow them to proceed beyond themselves while nevertheless remaining faithful to their own. Sympathetic analysts do not only monitor the ongoing process of "interiorization," they recommend it as a protective shield as long as 'Westernization' acts disruptingly on a preindustrial society. In such a situation, when the individual is torn to the breaking point and society threatened with dissolution, interiorization is thought to counteract and mutually consolidate.

The expectations implicit in such expert opinions are that modern Muslim personality be fashioned after the model purveyed by elements of Islamic mysticism that are acceptable or even stimulating to contemporary thought. The scope appears to be vast and promising. The philosophical and humanist strands in the Sufi fabric or the rational theology of nineth-century Muʿtazilism had indeed captivated already many of the leading reformers toward the end of the nineteenth century.

However, the difficulties caused by the changed political situation apply to this enterprise hardly less than they do to the revivification of a more 'orthodox' theology. The present age is not that of the classical boom of Sufism but that of the culturally expansionist West. For this very reason the secularist viewpoint of post-ʿAbduh (d. 1905) thinkers appears to many of their coreligionists not as mere Sufi tradition. However faithful such authors may be to their Muslim identity, their ideas are prone to be interpreted as subversive Westernization, especially when they dare refer to the Turkish example. Too often, "the Muslim intellectual feels that with his Westernization he is paying homage to a religion which competes with own."[41] This applies to the resuscitation of mysticism more than to other forms of Islam because it is said to be closest to Christianity.

Besides, it is precisely in the domain of Sufism that laborious efforts were expended by Western scholarship to trace each element to outside influences, that is, to non-Arab sources. This endeavor is, moreover, sustained by Muslim fundamentalists with their aversion to "luxurious theological thought" and derisive equation of mystic with mysterious, topped by their cliché allegation that all that does not conform to their legist "system" is not originally and truly Islamic, especially Sufism.[42] For them, all philosophical or even theological elaboration of the faith is a corruption that entered with later converts, conspiracies aimed at destroying the moral fiber of pristine Islam. They proudly adduce Gibb's finding that Islam found its most highly developed expression in law rather than in theology.[43] Such legist opposition poses a formidable challenge to attempts at discovering Muslim identity in the realm of philosophical mysticism. Attacks on Sufism from within and without the pale of Islam raise the question as to how a distinct Islamic personality can be adumbrated on the basis of questionable authenticity.

In this point, however, the challenging West has been outright contradictory. Many tomes have been written to prove that Sufism is the product of either Christian, Gnostic, or Buddhist influences, but just as many Western scholars have taken up the cudgels in defense of its Islamic specificity. Whatever has found its expression within the framework of Islam and on its field of action, such scholars believe, is to be qualified as Islamic, especially when there is a relationship with Islam's fundamental aspirations and when it understands itself as Islamic—leaving aside that to Sufism falls the lion's share of spreading and preserving the dogmas of Islam.[44]

Yet the issue remains controversial. While deliberating on the minimal requirements or components of an Islamic identity, such redefinitions bring new elements to the fore and eliminate some cherished ones. Longing for specificity leads to the culling of materials that appear to be the individual property of Islam. But the discovery that many of these apparently distinctive elements are related to extraneous sources of previous ages necessitates a "struggle for the maintenance of authenticity."[45] Adaptations from others may constitute an enrichment, provided the new elements are properly assimilated. The question secretly asked, often perhaps not even consciously, is how far all of these cultural borrowings are possible without encroaching upon the very essentials of selfhood? Is there a feasible assimilation "that would not be tantamount to surrender?"[46] Besides, over the centuries Sufism often degenerated into charlatanism. It exacted, therefore, much toil until the purified and refined particles of its philosophical contents could become visible amongst the chaff. There is still another, though related, reason why such rehabilitations of Muslim mysticism did not solve the problem of Islamic specifity either. Impressed by the rich variety of Sufism, a leading authority pointed out that Islam "overflows all definitions," that it has, like other world religions, "as many forms as it has believers."[47] Such an approach to the issue is, no doubt pragmatic, but it seems warranted by the fact that one of Sufism's favorite symbols is that of the all-encompassing sea. However, it also raises the question of what justifies us to "write feasibly and persuasively about 'Islam'?"[48] The amorphous flux of protean Muslim experience, in which diversity is as large as number, has proved disruptive especially in the one state that was expressly founded in the name of Islam: Pakistan, where the Sufi legacy is particularly pervasive.

After the traditional *dār al-islām* ("abode of Islam") distinction has been sent reeling into the limbo of extreme fundamentalist splinter groups, the question of what constitutes the true follower of the faith has become fundamental in a way probably unprecedented and unparalleled in other religions. Nothing illustrates this so effectively as the emphatic pronouncement that many feel themselves constrained to make over and over again, that "he who sincerely affirms that he is a Muslim, is a Muslim. No one has the right to question his beliefs."[49]

The necessity of proceeding beyond the blemishing of what might be regarded as not Islamic to a positive definition of the Muslim was acknowledged in Turkey with the creation of an Ilahiyat Fakültesi at the University of Ankara and in Pakistan by the establishment of an Islamic Research Institute as a body provided for by the state's constitution. Both institutions are being criticized for not having come up to the high expectations set in them, but the quest continues, and outstanding intellectuals do not cease to recall the philosophical mystic Jalāl ad-dīn Rūmī in Turkey and his modern disciple in Pakistan, the mystical philosopher Muhammad Iqbāl, with their drive to seek the definition of a Muslim in the ethical dimensions, in the creation of a special type of person. Here, as elsewhere, being Muslim is sometimes explained as a moral obligation toward the rest of humankind. Much is made of the Qur'ānic verse (II:137) in which the community of Islam is said to have been created as "intermediary." This is interpreted as the golden mean between all kinds of extremes, as a sound balance between materialist this-worldliness and spiritualist world-renunciation, as well as a via media between capitalism and communism. Such self-elaboration envisions the Muslim community as the good exemplar and "a model for the final combination of humanity."[50]

The crux of the matter appears to be that Islam reduced to its essential moral philosophy seems hardly different from other purified religions. This can be illustrated at the instance of the great *mufti* of Egypt, Muhammad ʿAbduh. This towering reformer was once suspected of working for a merger of Islam with Christianity and Judaism. At the root of the calumny there might have been an intuitive apprehension about his accommodating interpretation of the faith, which appeared to many as an excessive "shrinkage of the substance of Islam."[51] In view of modernism's indebtedness to Western liberalism, it tends to interpret Islam in terms of liberal humanitarian ideas and values. Radical liberals are, therefore, impelled to discard the historical elaborations as mere scholastic encrustinations and to jettison all save a modicum that passes as the kernel of supramundane truth and is equated with the timeless essence common to all religions. However, even such attempts are mostly not motivated by the desire to discard specificity. On the contrary, it is hoped that "gradually a substantial body of clearly thought-out doctrine will emerge which will be the basis of a scientific re-interpretation of Islam. Such restatement will give strength and solace to many who have lost faith in the orthodox interpretations but retain their loyalty to the essence of Islam."[52]

There are others who think they need Islam as a basis from which to depart into a new world. They believe that it provides the most suitable ground from which to launch the enterprise. Their viewpoint can be translated as meaning that to catch a train there has to be a station, and for Muslims, Islam is still closest at hand. The Egyptian philosopher Badawī, for instance, who has moved toward existentialism, believes that Kierkegaard as a point of departure would involve an irksome detour vie Protestant Europe; it is easier to reach the destination by starting from Muslim mysticism.[53] This is one of the many cures proposed to restore congruency of attitudes in a situation that is characterized by a "psychocultural gap between words and deeds."[54]

While Muslim identity is a force to be reckoned with and a preoccupation of literary activity, it has to share this preeminence with the quest for Arabism, Négritude, national culture, and a host of other categories all serving as answers to the question: "How can I change and yet be my true self?" In this common search for identity, Muslim individuality, along with other specificities, undergoes a transformation insofar as the old philosophical question "What am I?" is more and more giving way to a different formulation: "What shall I become?" There is a growing tendency among sections of the Muslim elite to show greater willingness to trust in the unfolding of an "identity of becoming" rather than be intoxicated with an "identity of remaining."[55]

REFORM OR REFORMATION? POINTERS TOWARD NEW ISLAMIC ORIENTATIONS

Revelation as the Mainspring: Toward a Breakthrough in Conceptualization

Coming to the core of Islamic studies, the understanding of Al-Qur'ān as the most primary of all sources remains pivotal. M. A. Khalaf-Allāh's refreshing study *The Art of Narration in the Holy Qur'ān (al-fann al-qissasī fī l-Qur'ān al-Karīm)*, published in 1947, is still one of the more inspiring attempts in this regard. Khalaf-Allāh had a more thorough grounding in history as a science than his precursors had. He was, therefore, aware of the possibility that the Qur'ānic narrations of historic events might not stand the scrutiny of historic research. Since he was a fervent Muslim, the problem for him was how to believe in events that either did not take place at all or, at least, not in the manner reported in Al-Qur'ān. Khalaf-Allāh found the solution in the concept of divine intent (*qasd, maqsad, gharad*). God was bent upon acting not as a historiographer but more as an artist who inspires. If there are different versions of this same story, it is because God revealed with poetic license. Should any of those narrations run counter to historical findings, this does not matter. God had to mold his materials so as to achieve a maximum impact on the heart of humans. The purpose is not to teach historical truth but to induce people to testify to the eternal truth of the message conveyed with the help of literary devices. Khalaf-Allāh saw the "inimitability" (*'ijāz*) of Al-Qur'ān in its magiclike psychological compulsion. No matter the emphasis on the study of nature and history in Al-Qur'ān, in the final analysis the emotional effect prevails over the rational aspect.

Like Khalaf-Allāh, many Muslim reformists deem it extremely important always to realize that Al-Qur'ān was addressed to a milieu of remote times to which there is no return. We have to exert ourselves time and again to understand, as far as possible, those specific conditions in their historical setting as well as the particular mental makeup of that period in order to know why revelation came to us in that definite concrete mold and not in another. It is not a question of reestablishing the order of those bygone days but of resuscitating the impressions and responses of those believers to whom the Scripture was revealed. The fundamentalist Rashīd Ridā and others of his school saw the *'ijāz*, the inimitability of Al-Qur'ān, in its high intellectual level, which indeed was far beyond anything thought or uttered by the men of the prophet's age. However, I would suggest, with Khalaf-Allāh, looking for that miraculous inimitability more in the phenomenon that Al-Qur'ān is so exactly and so skillfully tailored to the psyche of the first recipients with their knowledge and ideas of things. It is for that reason that it had a momentum unparalleled in the history of revelations.

This raises the important theological question of what the intrinsic connection is between this kind of impulsion and the doctrines of faith that are to be deduced. The modern exegete cannot grasp the fillip of the text save by means of a historiographical reconstruction of those emotions and impressions. How can the interpreter of today find his way through those psychological elements of ancient times and arrive at religious purports that are binding for him? Except for the Sudanese "heretic" Mahmūd Muhammad Tāhā, hardly anyone seems to have provided a clear and cogent answer to this, but I do see some signposts. People whose works can help show the way are the recently deceased Indian Muslim scholar Asaf A. A. Faydī, the Tunisian Mahjūb Ibn Mīlād, the Lebanese Hasan Sa'b, the Moroccan philosopher 'Azīz Lahbābī, and, above all, my Pakistani mentor, Sayyid Qudrat-Allāh Fātimī.[56] All of these outstanding scholars of Islam view Al-Qur'ān not simply as the truth the way it was revealed to the Holy Prophet but rather as Muhammad's testimony to the truth. It is the word of God as heard by Muhammad. It is something every individual in his or her particular historical situation has to decide for and testify to. The above-mentioned thinkers share a concept of revelation as a never-ending dialogue between God and humans, a permanent interaction of revealed truth and human reality. It is particularly in 'Azīz Lahbābī's cogent sythesis of the traditional tenets of the faith and modern historical critique where I find a philosophical breakthrough that might help overcome the present dilemma.

It may sound platitudinous if I emphasize, together with the above-mentioned thinkers, that all human knowledge is tied to a temporary intellectual horizon. Once this constellation changes there has to be a fresh examination of the book of revelations to find out what the message really conveys. Looking at Al-Qur'ān from a historical angle, we must, first accept that the very belief in Al-Qur'ān has its own history. This history is not confined to a constantly improving explanation of its verses. It is a history also of the transient interpretation of the purport of the message, because in every age it acquires a new and different meaning for those who receive it. Revelation cannot be real for humankind unless it steps down to the human level, unless it "humanizes" itself and enters into a dialogue with the reflections of the receiver. Lahbābī avers that revelation, in this sense, is no more to be equated with the literal meaning of Al-Qur'ān but emerges out of the process of interpretation. It is no longer the text per se that is revelation but rather what impresses itself upon the believer while reading it anew.[57]

Does this *Muslim Personalism* of Lahbābī enunciate a novel understanding of Al-Qur'ān, and does it effect a reconciliation of history and revelation? It could be argued that this approach has its moorings in the earliest history of Islam. One could mention the famous episode at the time of the prophet's demise when Abū Bakr recited the verses "Muhammad is no more than a messenger. Messengers before him have passed away. If he die or be slain, will you then turn on your heels?" Reception of Al-Qur'ān had come to an end because the prophet was no more, and the Scripture was complete for compilation. However, the Companions responded to the *khalīfa*'s recitation as if the revelation was still on, and Sayyidatna ʿĀ'isha expressly said that they felt as if they had heard those verses for the first time. It was the same text as before but with a new significance in a changed context. This process continued throughout the ages until Iqbāl was impelled to compose his eloquent poem *mard-e musulmān* ("The Truly Muslim Man") in *Darb-e Kalīm,* where he stated that what appears to our eyes is the believer reading the Scripture, but in reality what we see is Al-Qur'ān itself.

Such an understanding of Al-Qur'ān may not be reflected in the 'orthodox' commentaries on which most orientalists rely for their analyses of what emerged as the dominant stream in Muslim exegesis. Their attitude is a reflection of our traditionalist theoreticians who tended to deprecate the attempts of more intellectual interpreters such as Az-Zamakhsharī, Ar-Rāzī, Ibn ʿArabī, and others, namely, to understand and explain Al-Qur'ān in the light of their mundane knowledge and spiritual experience. Some of our esoteric (*bātinī*) masters did indeed come up with such excesses of phantasy that, as a response, a linguist of Al-Bāquillānī's stature was led to deny any semantic changes in the religious terms.

Another important issue in this context was courageously broached by a former chief justice of Pakistan, Muhammad Munīr, in his book *Islam in History* (Lahore, 1974). He had become famous as coauthor of the *Report on the Enquiry into the Punjab Disturbances of 1953,* commonly known as *The Munir Report.* With *Islam in History* the author followed up what *The Munir Report* initiated, namely, the quest for Muslim identity.

The very title of Chapter V—"The Prophet Looks Around"—was a bold step because Fadl ar-Rahmān, a former director of Pakistan's Islamic Research Institute, had to go into exile merely because he had dared to hint at the possibility that the prophet might have occasionally taken recourse to his own reasoning and intellectual acumen.[58] The use of the mind, before receiving divine revelation, was misconstrued by Islamist opponents as implying that Al-Qur'ān was nothing but the prophet's own creation. To refute their own inference the propagandists against Fadl ar-Rahmān depicted the prophet as virtually thoughtless, a mechanical receptacle of God's commandments transmitted by the archangel. A few years after this scandal, which had turned into a perilous political affair, the former chief justice did not hesitate to write about the prophet: "He must have heard what people were talking about in Syria. But Syria did not impress him and for some 13 years after his return he roamed in the desert of Arabia, in the vicinity of Mecca, working as a shepherd. His taciturnity and quietness was a clear indication of some serious thoughts having gripped his mind and of his inability to find a satisfactory answer to some puzzling questions that must have kept recurring to his mind from time to time."[59]

The height of "heresy" was attained when Muhammad Munīr wrote: "While he was in one of these contemplative moods, he thought he saw an apparition in the form of an angel. I am not entering into the discussion what apparition it was that confronted him in the overwrought condition of his brain but he believed that this was an angel."[60] Arab thinkers, such as the illustrious historian and educator Ahmad Amīn (d. 1954), had written even more astounding things some forty years earlier.[61] But in the Indo-Pakistani subcontinent such daringly free reassessments of the origins are still largely restricted to the "Islamic left" and, moreover, to rebels from minority groups, such as the Bohra Ismailis.[62] The significance of Muhammad Munīr lies not only in his bureaucratic eminence but, primarily, in his belonging to the Sunni mainstream.

Islam in History, however haphazard in composition and editing, contains more potential for a reorientation of Muslim thought than Fadl ar-Rahmān's scholarly opus *Islam,* which acquired notoriety as being overly vanguardist more by political accident than any other reason.[63] Chief Justice Munīr neither dabbled in metaphysical niceties nor tried his luck with Aristotelian terminology. Instead, he broached much more basic issues. Underlying his effort is the awareness of an entirely new constellation and of Islam's relativity in it. He obviously understood that the question now before us is whether we can salvage our cherished religious heritage, or at least parts of it, and take it with us into the future.

What does that mean for us today? It would appear to me that only a few Muslims reject everything out of hand. However, a general consensus is discernible to the effect that from now on the choice should be really free and, concomitantly, more intelligent, instead of the unsystematic procedure prevailing in some places even now. There is, however, a general rejection of the forced cultural cross-breading imposed by the relationship of rulers to the ruled. The main protectionist filter that we are trying to install everywhere, with various therapeutic specificities and indications, bears the name of *sharīʿa*. A recourse to the *sharīʿa* is being demanded by a large segment of the population in several Muslim countries. The crux of the matter, Tunisia's Muhammad Tālbī wrote, is to know which *sharīʿa* or, rather, what kind of *sharīʿa* it should be. Is it the code roughly drawn up between the eighth and tenth centuries, revived more or less whenever necessary, as the Islamists would like it to be, or is it a radically new draft, based on the foundations (*usūl*) to meet the needs of a century whose main characteristic is one of constant change, with steadily increasing acceleration? Islam and the West both find themselves equally in the same crisis. Islam is seeking its own *way*. This is the etymological meaning of the term *sharīʿa*, which is all too often forgotten in the heated debates on this subject.

There are many voices, whether in Kuwait or Morocco, Egypt or Yemen, who advocate a reevalution of the *sharīʿa* in very much these terms. The application of medieval accretions—and sometimes colonial additions—such as the public flogging of journalists and other dissidents (mentioned neither in Al-Qurʾān nor the Hadīth) merely proves that some governments are less flexible than the broad stream of Muslim majority opinion.

A reform of the legal system is indeed called for since too much was simply implanted by the colonial masters without regard for the specific conditions. In the meantime, law in the West has undergone its own evolution, and there is no reason why former colonies should go on preserving nineteenth-century codes, as if our countries were museums—or mausoleums. It is but natural that the enormous wealth of Islamic legal thought should serve as the primary source to be studied for suitable elements and inspiration.

As long as the *sharīʿa* is taken as one important code among others, into which the experiences of the remainder of humankind are to be integrated in a process of further development of the *sharīʿa*—analogous to its first emergence—even non-Muslim minorities will have little reason to object. Thus the implementation of the *sharīʿa* need not be an obstacle to material progress and mental emancipation. It all depends on how it is done, the Tunisian leader of thought averred. There is a broad current of Muslim thought—not necessarily all liberal—that points to the pragmatic spirit of the ''pious forebears'' (*as-salaf as-sālih*) who integrated into their system much of what they found useful with others. Muhammad Tālbī held, optimistically, that the core of unalterable injunctions in the primary sources—around which the branches of the law were woven—is not all that large, so there is much scope for adapting the *sharīʿa* to changing circumstances.

The above-mentioned former chief justice of Pakistan Muhammad Munīr was no theologian *strictu sensu*, as he himself often admitted, but his legal acumen helped in bringing clarity to a number of issues in which the ideological cross-currents in the ranks of the *ʿulamā* created a havoc of confusion. One particularly remarkable point is that the author, who personified better than anyone else the last generation of British-trained liberals, admitted that the rigid medievalism of General Zia (Diyā al-Haqq) and Khomeini is justifiable if we seriously intend to reestablish what Pakistanis call the *Nizām-e Mustafa,* that is, the "system" of the earliest Caliphate. Muhammad Munīr is not apologetic about history. This helped him to understand that the social reality of Islam in the twentieth century has, of necessity, to be different from that of seventh-century Arabia. If the aim is to reinstate the *Nizām-e Mustafā,* as the Islamist parties supporting Zia purport, the general will have to be more radical even than Khomeini. Until now there has not been much consistency in Pakistani "Islamization." Had the chief justice been given a voice in his last days, he would have opted for just as radical a departure from the canonical law (*sharī'a*) of early Islam, choosing the modern concepts of human rights, democracy, and socialism. In his last book, published in 1980, the year of his death, he expressed his belief that this was the modernist interpretation given by the two founders of Pakistan: Iqbāl, the intellectual father, and Jinnāh, the political father. Muhammad Munīr was close to both of them.

A number of times the chief justice came close in his views to the Sudanese Sufi reformer and philosopher of religion Mahmūd Muhammad Tāhā (executed as an "apostate" by General Numairi's Islamist dictatorship in January 1985). This is evident especially where M. Munīr draws a distinction between the more essential ethical contents of Al-Qur'ān revealed in Mecca and the more illustrative and time-bound laws revealed in Medina. At the same time, the major weakness of M. Munīr's approach lies precisely in the fact that he did not take this distinction to its logical conclusion. There are some passages in a previous book by him (*Islam in History,* Lahore, 1973) where he seemed to have progressed beyond the stage of mere groping in the dark. In his last book (*From Jinnah to Zia,* Lahore, 1980) he appeared many times very close to a final breakthrough, only to lose the track again.[64] Perhaps the most significant passage in that book is a quotation from the eighteenth-century reformer of Delhi, Shāh Walīy-Allāh, who wrote that the prophet accentuated the principles underlying the social life of all humankind and applied them to concrete cases in the light of the specific habits of the people immediately before him: "The *sharī'a* values (*ahkam*) resulting from this application (e.g., rules relating to penalties for crimes) are in a sense specific to that people; and since their observance is not an end in itself, they cannot be enforced in the case of future generations" (p. 132).

Had Muhammad Munīr elaborated this point further, on the pattern set by Mahmūd Muhammad Tāhā, he might have revolutionized Islamic thought in Pakistan.[65] Manifestly, it was not martial law alone that caused him to stop short of this. The conceptual inability to draw a clear distinction between the Meccan and the Medinese revelation induced him to select several verses on the same subject out of disparate Qur'ānic contexts, thus making them appear mutually contradictory.

Present Preoccupations

A specific Islamic system of economics does not yet exist, although there is a possibility, or even some likelihood, that eventually such an individual system will emerge. Islamists insist that it does already exist. Volker Nienhaus, an economist at the West German university of Bochum, is internationally recognized as a specialist on theories of a Islamic economic system. In the Muslim world, however, he is sometimes dubbed a "white mercenary of Islamism" precisely because of his propagation of the theories of Islamist economists. Volker Nienhaus admittedly does not have the slightest idea of the economic practice—not to speak of the social reality—of those countries where Islamist alternatives are being explored, that is, primarily Pakistan and Iran. He admits that he is not even interested in the practical side of it. For him, the theories alone count. We already have a variety of economic systems in the world, and if there is an Islamic economic system superior to all of those others, it must somehow differ from them. We are not able to say much about an "Islamic economic system" without knowing the specific features of an actual functioning system.[66]

As for the so-called Islamic banking, Axel Koehler of Frankfurt, a convert to Islam and an ardent advocate of his new faith, called it a hoax and a fraud. He is one of the key figures in the world with many important threads running through his hands. He, too, has written much on the subject, but his special qualification is that he is involved in the practical functioning of Islamic banking. Koehler said he thanks his stars for having found his new faith independently of this. He finds the misuse of religion for business purposes and all of the eyewash that goes along with Islamic banking so distressing that he fears some believers might despair of Islam.[67] In other words, while talking about an "Islamic economic system," it should be clear that we can only talk about ideals. To me it appears, at times, like a contradiction in terms that the most concrete topic of all be completely divested of reality, that Islamic theology and philosophy should be more tangible than Islamic economics. However, mine is a layman's attitude; an economist might find nothing strange with that.

On the other hand, I am very much impressed by the seriousness with which some really knowledgeable authors tackle the obvious problems. One of the books that impressed me most in this respect was, unfortunately, never translated into English. It is entitled *Nizām-e zakāt aor jadīd ma°āshī masā'il* (*The System of Zakāt and Modern Economic Problems*). The author, Yūsuf Gūrāyā, studied at McGill and is a specialist in Islamic jurisprudence, especially on Shāfi°ī and the concept of *sunna*. Since the mid-seventies he has been on one of Pakistan's key religious posts, as director of the °Ulamā-Academy in Lahore.[68]

Yet, Gūrāyā is not primarily concerned with the *fiqh* (jurisprudence) of medieval jurists. His contention is that *zakāt* is not to be confused with private charity. He wants to bring home to the reader that the Al-Qur'ān adumbrates a tax that is to be paid to the government. The government, in turn, is obliged to raise *zakāt* and to insure its use for the common weal. Gūrāyā's exposition of the use to which *zakāt* is to be put differs somewhat from the usual interpretations. For him the context of *zakāt* is much wider than it is with the typical traditional legists. He stresses repeatedly that the age of the founder of Islam as a community is gone; those conditions of life cannot be reestablished. At the same time, however, Gūrāyā justifies *zakāt* precisely because of a still-existing similarity of circumstances, not because of an abstraction. Thus the situation of the present-day peasant in the Panjab and other parts of the Muslim world can still be likened to that of the dwellers of oases in the Arabian desert during the era of the "Right-guided Caliphs" (the immediate successors to the prophet, his Companions). A solution to the rural misery by means of *zakāt* is advocated because the prophet and his Caliphs succeeded in bringing prosperity and social security to the Bedouins.

To some it might appear incongruous that Yūsuf Gūrāyā occasionally stresses the historical precedent by drawing parallels to present circumstances while generally giving preference to abstractions from the revealed text over historical precedents. But this is precisely where I see the special quality of his research. In times of transition, where different patterns exist side by side, Qur'ānic interpretation has to operate on different levels, whereas most of our scholars plead for one to the exclusion of the other—and this is too facile a course. To Gūrāyā, on the contrary, goes the credit of having substantiated his thesis with a thorough research on Ibn Sayyid An-Nās and his analysis of social change brought about in the Arab countryside during the earliest phase of Islam as a polity. This is a phenomenon of Muslim history to which scant attention had been paid before this book.

Let me not hide my profound admiration for a scholar whom I had the privilege to benefit from not only academically but also personally, in his village and in the mosque. Witnessing Yūsuf Gūrāyā soaked in sweat behind an ox-driven plough, it was difficult to believe that this Panjabi peasant had spent four to five years at the university in Canada. That experience, however, made him empha-size the mere temporary validity of the seventh-century examples and to insist on the fact that our primary task now is to abstract guidelines from the *sunna* of the prophet and his Companions. Gūrāyā explained elaborately how the in-stitution of *zakāt* evolved over a period of some twenty years. It acquired tangibility as a practical concept only through the test of those years under those Arabian circumstances. In a sense Gūrāyā merely recapitulates the ideas of an eighteenth-century reform thinker, Shāh Walīy-Allāh of Delhi. I would not deny Gūrāyā's inference that *zakāt* as a principle can be abstracted and made mean-ingful in the contemporary context, but I do plead for an expansion of the argument. Since the emphasis is, and necessarily must be, on abstracting *zakāt* from its historical accidents, there remains the question of how this can be done cogently: how to differentiate convincingly between what is essential or eternally valid and what is historical and, therefore, only temporarily relevant. Like many other such programatic treatises in the Muslim world, this one, too, is not very thorough when it comes to precise details, except for the chapter "Zakāt and Education."

Yūsuf Gūrāyā pleads for the use of zakāt funds in the educational field. This is disputed by some authorities, but he adduced argument after argument to prove that the term "for the sake of God" (fī sabīl-Allāh) covers education as well. As is his wont, he quoted a number of historical instances and ancient theologians to substantiate his point. This is a passionate plea for the importance of learning to religion: there can be no true faith without knowledge. Islam's superiority over other religions lies in the fact that it makes learning a precondition for becoming a true Muslim.

This argumentation of Gūrāyā's is a noteworthy contribution to the quest for identity presently tormenting the Muslim world. Pakistan, especially, has been plagued by the strife over the definition of a Muslim. Maulānā Yūsuf Gūrāyā added a new dimension to the controversy. For him, the true believer must be a seeker after knowledge, a torchbearer of enlightenment. One could argue that this is a common feature of the apologetic writings of our modernists. But hardly anyone of those authors has projected learning per se as so essential an ingredient of the very Muslim identity. Sayyid Ahmad Khān, Sayyid Amīr ʿAlī, and Muhammad Iqbāl have pinpointed the splendid contributions of Islamic learning to the culture of the world. But rarely has education been proven to be so fundamental to the faith as in this forceful exposition of Gūrāyā's.

I held a different view before reading this book. I had reached the point of mystic exhaltation where the Sufi tries to forget a book per day, while the legist scholar still tries to read at least one book per day. Yūsuf Gūrāyā made me change my mind and start reading again. He draws his materials from the central authority of Al-Qur'ān. His evidence is so overwhelming and abundant that there seems little scope left for a refutation.

Also important in this context is Gūrāyā's project of fusing the two systems of education into one, the traditional and the modern. The necessity of doing so is almost too obvious to be still an issue of discussion. On the other hand, one of the most disconcerting aspects of life in our part of the world is that there exist so many self-evident social problems without anyone ever taking them up. (One of the marks of a prophet, André Malraux once said, is to reveal the obvious).

Integration of the madrasa with the university, Yūsuf Gūrāyā insisted, is the sine qua non of modern nationhood. If it is not done soon, the antagonism between mister and maulawi is bound to further aggravate the existing dissensions. Written a few years before the Iranian Revolution, these words ring prophetic indeed. Conflicting loyalties of the madrasa-product and the university-product will exacerbate the present schizophrenia. None of the two schools can be abolished because both camps are more or less equally strong. A Soviet-style solution would imply that one-half of the people liquidates the other half. Even the Chinese solution of forced refunctioning does not seem acceptable to Islamic ethics. But neither is there time to let things evolve as they did in Europe over a span of several centuries. Besides, most citizens pay for both systems, and the costs are increasing. How long, Gūrāyā asked, will they be able to go on bearing the financial burden of this senseless duplication that causes duplicity of moral standards and prevents the emergence of a balanced and harmonious value system?

Maulānā Gūrāyā, in his capacity as director of the ʿUlamā-Academy in the Auqāf Department (religous endowments) is the person most directly concerned with the training of village preachers and imams of mosques in such a way as to enable them to pursue secular education, if they so wish, in other words, to make modern professional life accessible to them. As a rule this gives them a new self-confidence and takes out much of the steam of irrationality that had made the *mullah* become the butt of most popular jokes.

NOTES

1. Wilfred Cantwell Smith, *Islam in Modern History* (Princeton, N.J.: Princeton University Press 1957), p. 123. See Jacques Berque and Jean-Paul Charnay, eds., *Normes et valeurs dans l'Islam contemporain* (Paris: Payot, 1966), p. 264.

2. S. Vahiduddin, "The Crisis of Religious Consciousness—With Special Reference to Islam," *Islam and the Modern Age* (New Delhi: 1, no. 2 Islam and the Modern Age Society, August 1970): 24.

3. H.A.R. Gibb, "Social Reform: Factor X—The Search for an Islamic Democracy," in Walter Z. Laqueur, ed., *The Middle East in Transition* (London: Routledge and Paul, 1958), p. 10.

4. Gustave E. Von Grunebaum, *Modern Islam—The Search for Cultural Identity* (Los Angeles: University of California Press 1962), p. 161.

5. S. Nikki Keddie, *An Islamic Response to Imperialism* (Berkeley and Los Angeles: University of California Press 1968). See "La reconquéte de l'identité," in Anouar Abdel-Malek, *La pensée politique arabe contemporaine,* 2d ed., rev. and enl. (Paris: Editions du Seuil 1975). Nadav Safran, *Egypt in Search of Political Community* (Cambridge, Mass.: Harvard University Press, 1961); Baber Johansen, *Muhammed Husain Haikel—Europa und der Orient im Weltbild eines aegyptischen Liberalen* (Beirut: In Kommission bei F. Steiner, Wiesbaden 1967).

6. Von Grunebaum, *Modern Islam,* p. 6.

7. H.A.R. Gibb, "The University in the Arab World," in E. Bradby, ed., *The University Outside Europe* (New York: Oxford University Press 1939), p. 295.

8. S.C.H. Becker, *Islamstudien* (Leipzig: Quelle & Meyer 1939), p. 231.

9. S. Joerg Kraemer, *Das Problem der Islamischen Kulturgeschichte* (Tubingen: Max Niemeyer Verlag 1939), p. 45. See Joseph Chelhod, *Introduction á la sociologie de l'Islam* (Paris: G.-P. Maisonneuve 1958), p. 188.

10. Berque and Charnay, *Normes et valeurs,* p. 222.

11. S. ʿUbaid-Allāh Sind, *Shāh Wal y-Allāh aor unkā falsafa* (Lahore, Pakistan: Sindh Sagar Academy 1946), pp. 35-f.

12. S. Keddie, *An Islamic Response,* pp. 47–48. See Majid Fakhry, *A History of Islamic Philosophy* (New York: Columbia University Press 1970), p. 399; Abdul Hakim

Tabibi, *The Political Struggle of Jamal ad-din Afghani* (Kabul, Afganistan: Baihagi, 1977).

13. Interview with the now-deceased leader of popular Islam in Bangladesh, Maulānā ʿAbd al-Ham d Khān Bhāshān, in 1970.

14. H.A.R. Gibb, *Modern Trends in Islam* (Chicago: University of Chicago Press, 1947), p. 11.

15. Ibid., p. 15. See also Kenneth Cragg, *Counsels in Contemporary Islam* (Edinburgh: Edinburgh University Press 1965), p. 74.

16. Snouck Hurgronje, *Mohammedanism* (New York: G. P. Putnam's Sons, 1916), p. 84.

17. Pierre Rondot, *L'islam et les musulmans d'aujourd'hui* (Paris: Editions de Liorante 1958), p. 231.

18. Gibb, *Trends,* p. 2–4.

19. Hisham Sharabi, "The Crisis of the Intelligentsia in the Middle East," *The Muslim World* (Hartford) 47, no. 3 (The Hartford Seminary Foundation, July 1957): 190.

20. Jean Lacoutre and Simone Lacoutre, *Egypt in Transition* (London: Criterion Books, 1958), p. 431.

21. Ibid., p. 438. See also W. Montgomery Watt, *Islamic Philosophy and Theology* (Edinburgh: Edinburgh University Press, 1962).

22. Kenneth Cragg, "The Modernist Movement in Egypt," in Richard N. Frye, ed., *Islam and the West* (The Hague: s̄-Gravenhage Mouton, 1957), pp. 151–152.

23. S. Chulam Ahmed Parwez, *Islam: A Challenge to Religion* (Lahore: Idara-e-Tulu-e-Islam, 1968). The implications have been discussed in R. A. Buetler, "Chulam Ahmed Parwez—Ideological Revolution through the Qur'an," *Al-Mushir* (Rawalpindi) 17, nos. 1–3 (January-March 1975): 1–59.

24. Smith, *Islam in Modern History,* p. 132.

25. Cragg, *Counsels in Contemporary Islam,* p. 30.

26. Ibid., p. 68.

27. Ibid., p. 15. See also Bernard Lewis, *Islam in History* (London: The Library Press, 1973), p. 31: "In modern times, Islamic identity has been reinforced by a new and shared experience—the penetration, domination and (in most areas) the departure of European colonialists."

28. See Mahmūd Mas'ad, "Himāyat al-adīb wa l-qaumīya al-ʿarabīya," *Al-Adāb* 6, no. 1 (1958).

29. S. Munah as-Sulh, *Al-islām, wa harakat at-taharrur al-ʿarab* (Beirut: 1973), p. 50.

30. Lacoutre and Lacoutre, *Egypt in Transition,* pp. 43–44.

31. Berque and Charnay, *Normes et valeurs,* p. 8.

32. Gad Silberman, "National Identity in Nasserist Ideology, 1952-1970," *Asian and African Studies* (Jerusalem) 8, no. 1 (1972): 51–52.

33. Cragg, *Counsels in Contemporary Islam,* p. 31.

34. Nabih Amin Faris, "The Islamic Community and Communism," in Laqueur, *The Middle East in Transition,* p. 357. The special reference is to a very typical example of this trend—Sayyid Qutb, *Al-ʿadāla al-ijtimā ʿiya fi l-islām* (Cairo: Lajnat al-Nashr lil-j ami iy in, 1950); English translation: Syed Kotb, *Social Justice in Islam* (Washington D. C: America Council of Learned Society 1953).

35. Smith, *Islam in Modern History,* p. 192.

36. Ibrahim I. Ibrahim, "The Intellectual Roots of 'Populistic Democracy' in Egypt," *Al-abhāth* (Beirut) 21, nos. 2–4 (December 1968): 40.

37. Quoted in Leonard Binder, *Religion and Politics in Pakistan* (Berkeley: University of California Press, 1961), p. 148.

38. Ibid. The reference is to statement by Ishtiyaq Husain Qurayshi, a renowned historian and Islamist politician, former vice-chancellor of Karachi University.

39. Khalifa Abdul-Hakim, *Islamic Ideology: The Fundamental Beliefs and Principles of Islam and Their Application to Practical Life* (Lahore: 1951, Pakistan-Publishers United, 1953), p. 243.

40. Malcolm H. Kerr, *Islamic Reform* (Berkeley: University of California Press, 1966).

41. Raoul Makarius, *La jeunesse intellectuelle egyptienne au lendemain de la IIème guerre mondiale* (Paris: Mouton, 1960), p. 77.

42. Said Ramadan, *What Is an Islamic State?* (Geneva: Islamic Center, 1961).

43. See Smith, *Islam in Modern History*, p. 170: "Islam is less an intellectualist religion than a sociological [one]. Its tangible manifestation is laws and social structure."

44. S. F. Meier, "Soufisme et declin culturel," in Von Grunebaum and Willy Hartner, eds., *Classicisme et declin culturel dans l'histoire de l'Islam* (Paris: 1957), pp. 225–226. Discussing the Islamic authenticity of Sufism, Meier averred that outside influences, especially from Christianity, are undeniable but that they acted merely as a lever, as a fertilizer in the soil of Islam, that was receptive due to its very own assimilative individuality. He discerned not only a genuine Islamicity in Sufism but regarded it as truly representative of Islam, notwithstanding some Muslim theologians of historical stature who called it a scourge and a tool in the hands of the subverters. See H. Ritter, "L'orthodoxie a-t-elle une part dans la dècadence?" in von Grunebaum and Hartner, *Classicisme*, pp. 167–168.

45. Barques and Charnay, *Normes et valeurs*, p. 222.

46. Von Grunebaum, *Modern Islam*, p. 161.

47. Smith, *Islam in Modern History*, pp. 8–9.

48. Kenneth Cragg, in a review of Smith's *Islam in Modern History*, in *Middle Eastern Affairs* 9, no. 5 (May 1958): 158.

49. Asaf A. A. Fyzee, quoted by Cragg, *Counsels in Contemporary Islam*, p. 137.

50. Muhammed Iqbal, *The Reconstruction of Religious Thought in Islam* (London: Oxford University Press, 1930), p. 167.

51. S. Sylvia Haim, *Arab Nationalism—An Anthology* (Berkeley and Los Angeles: University of California Press, 1962), p. 18.

52. Asaf A. A. Faydt, "Islamic Law and Theology in India—Proposals for a Fresh Approach," *Middle East Journal* 8, no. 2 (Spring 1954): 179.

53. See ʿAbd ar-Rahmān Badawī, "Les points de rencontre de la mystiq musulmane et de l'existentialisme," *Studia Islamica* (Paris) 27 (1967): 71.

54. Daniel Lerner, *The Passing of Traditional Society* (New York: Free Press, 1958), p. 409.

55. S. Hichem Djait, *La personnalitè et le devenir arabo-islamique* (Paris: Editions du Seuil, 1972). See also Abdulah Laroui, *La crise des intellectuels arabes* (Paris: F. Maspero, 1974).

56. Asaf A. A. Faydt, "Islamic Law and Theology in India," pp. 163–183; Mahjūb bin Milâd, *Tūnis baina sh-sharq wa l-gharb* (Tunis: 1956); Hassan Saʿb, "The Spirit of Reform in Islam," in *Islamic Studies* (Islamabad) 2, no. 1 (March 1963): 17–39; Mohammed ʿAzīz Lahbâbī, *La personnalisme musulman* (Paris: Presses Universitaires de France 1967); Fātimi's teachings on these issues, unfortunately, have not been put into writing. As an extremely versatile historian, linguist, and theologian–philosopher, his

comparatively few writings focus more on political issues or highly socialized historical questions such as pre-Islamic Arab seafaring in remote corners of the China Sea. Therefore, I have had to rely on my own recollections of many night-long sessions with Fātimī, my colleague and friend, neighbor and teacher, during seven years in Islamabad. See S. Qudratullah Fātimī, *Pakistan Movement and Kemalist Revolution* (Lahore: Institute of Islamic Culture, 1977).

57. See Lahbābī, *Le personalisme musulman.*

58. See Fazlur Rahman, *Islam* (Chicago: University of Chicago Press, 1966, 1979).

59. Muhammed Munir, *Islam in History* (Lahore: Law Publishing Co., 1974), p. 63.

60. Ibid., pp. 18, 54.

61. See Khalid Duran, "Intricasies of a Return to the Faith—A Recurring Theme in Modern Muslim History at the Instance of an Egyptian Liberal: Ahmed Amin," in *IBLA*, nos. 151–152 (Tunis: Institut des belles lettres arabes, 1983).

62. See Asgharali Engineer, *Islam—Muslims—India* (Bombay: Lok Vangmaya Griha, 1975).

63. To do justice to Fadl ar-Rahmān, who became the butt of many unjustifiable attacks, see his more essential (and more recent) book *Islam and Modernity—Transformation of an Intellectual Tradition* (Chicago: University of Chicago Press, 1982).

64. Muhammed Munir, *From Jinnah to Zia* (Lahore: Vanguard Books, 1980).

65. See Mahmoud Mohamed Taha, *The Second Message of Islam*, trans. and intro. by ʿAbdallāhi Ahmad An-Naʿīm (Syracuse: Syracuse University Press 1987).

66. As far as economics is concerned, I certainly have no academic pretensions or even ambitions. Nonetheless, with some coaching by experts in the field, I did manage to form an idea about an "Islamic system of economics." In 1981 I was commissioned by West Germany's Ministry of Economic Cooperation (BWZ), not to be confused with BMW, to produce a study called "The Effects of Re-Islamization on Bilateral Cooperation and Development Policies." The results of this research were published in 1982 as *Re-Islamisierung und Entwick lungspolitik*. Against my expectations, this necessarily somewhat incongruous and technically slipshod little book became a hit, even the second edition (surely a very limited edition) was sold out within no time. Parts of it were translated into Russian, and it was appraised as "the most solid book on this subject and the richest in thought-content published in the entire capitalist West" (*Afrika, Asien, Lateinamerika* [Berlin, 1984]). Some of its success is certainly attributable to the team of experts assigned to me as research assistants, such as Muhlis Ileri, an economist and political scientist from Turkey; Ahad Rahmanzadeh, an economist and political scientist from Iran; Fuad Kandil, a sociologist from Egypt; and W. Slim Freund, a German sociologist working in Tunisia.

67. See Muhammed Yūsuf Gūrāyā, *Nizām-e zakāt aor jadid maʿāshi masa'il* (Islamabad: 1971). Publication of the book was delayed for a number of years because of strong opposition by M. Saghīr Hasan Maʿsūmī, then acting director of the Islamic Research Institute, where Gūrāyā was employed before becoming director of the ʿUlama' Academy in Lahore. As is often the case, it is difficult to tell how much of this fierce opposition was due to envy and personal malice and how much to the obscurantism of Maʿsūmī, who also was largely responsible for the intrigues against Fazlur Rahmān, his former director.

68. Personal communication from Axel Koehler to Shaikh Husain ʿAbd al-Fattāh, former head of the Burhaniya Sufi Brotherhood in West Germany and editor of the magazine *Sufi*.

SELECTED BIBLIOGRAPHY

Abdul-Hakim, Khalifa. *Islamic Ideology: The Fundamental Beliefs and Principles of Islam and Their Application to Practical Life*. Lahore: Publishers United, 1951, 1953.

Abdel-Malek, Anouar. *La pensée politique arabe contemparaine*. 2d ed., rev. and enl. Paris: Editions du Seuil, 1957.

ar-Rahmān, Fadl. *Islam and Modernity—Transformation of an Intellectual Tradition*. Chicago: University of Chicago Press, 1982.

Badawī, ʿAbd ar-Rahmān. "Les points de rencontre de la mystiq musulmane et de l'existentialisme." *Studia Islamica* (Paris) 27 (1967): 55–76.

Becker, S.C.H. *Islamstudien* (Leipzig: Quelle & Meyer, 1939).

Berque, Jacques, and Jean-Paul Charnay, eds. *Normes et valeurs dans l'Islam contemporain*. Paris: Payot, 1966.

Binder, Leonard. *Religion and Politics in Pakistan*. Berkeley: University of California Press, 1961.

Buetler, R. A. "Chulam Ahmed Parwez—Ideological Revolution through the Qur'an." *Al-Mushir* (Rawalpindi) 17, nos. 1–3 (January-March 1975): 1–59.

Chelhod, Joseph. *Introduction á la sociologie de l'Islam*. Paris: G.-P. Maisonneuve, 1958.

Cragg, Kenneth. *Counsels in Contemporary Islam*. Edinburgh: Edinburgh University Press, 1965.

———. "The Modernist Movement in Egypt." In Richard N. Frye, ed., *Islam and the West*. The Hague: Mouton, 1957.

———. Review of Smith's *Islam in Modern History*, in *Middle Eastern Affairs* 9, no. 5 (May 1958).

Djait, S. Hichem. *La personnalitè et le devenir arabo-islamique*. Paris: Éditions du Seuil, 1972.

Durán, Khalid. "Intricasies of a Return to the Faith—A Recurring Theme in Modern Muslim History at the Instance of an Egyptian Liberal: Ahmed Amin." In *IBLA*, pp. 151–152. Tunis: Institut des belles lettres arabes, 1983.

Engineer, Asgharali. *Islam—Muslims—India*. Bombay: Lok Vangmaya Griha, 1975.

Fakhry, Majid. *A History of Islamic Philosophy*. New York: Columbia University Press, 1970.

Faris, Nabih Amin. "The Islamic Community and Communism." In Walter Z. Laqueur, ed., *The Middle East in Transition*. London: Routledge & Paul, 1958, pp. 351–359.

Fātimī, S. Qudratullah. *Pakistan Movement and Kemalist Revolution*. Lahore: Institute of Islamic Culture, 1977.

Fyzee, Asaf A. A. "Islamic Law and Theology in India—Proposals for a Fresh Approach." *Middle East Journal* 8, no. 2 (Spring 1954): 163–183.

———. *A Modern Approach to Islam*. Bombay: Asia Pub. House, 1963.

Gibb, H.A.R. *Modern Trends in Islam*. Chicago: University of Chicago Press, 1947.

———. "Social Reform: Factor X—The Search for an Islamic Democracy." In Walter Z. Laqueur, ed. *The Middle East in Transition*. London: Routledge & Paul, 1958, pp. 1–31.

———. "The University in the Arab World." In E. Bradby, ed., *The University Outside Europe*. London: Oxford University Press, pp. 290–310.

Grunebaum, Gustave E. Von. *Modern Islam—The Search for Cultural Identity*. Los Angeles: University of California Press, 1962.

Gūrāyā, Muhammed Yūsuf. *Nizām-e zakāt aor jadid maʿāshi masāʾil*. Islamabad: 1971.

Haim, S. Sylvia. *Arab Nationalism—An Anthology*. Berkeley and Los Angeles: University of California Press, 1962.

Hurgronje, Snouck. *Mohammedanism*. New York: G. P. Putnam's Sons, 1916.

Ibrahim, Ibrahim I. "The Intellectual Roots of 'Populistic Democracy' in Egypt." *Al-abhāth* (Beirut) 21, nos. 2–4 (December 1968): 25–45.

Iqbal, Muhammed. *The Reconstruction of Religious Thought in Islam*. London: Oxford University Press, 1930.

Johansen, Baber. *Muhammed Husain Haikel—Europa und der Orient im Weltbild eines aegyptischen Liberalen*. Beirut: In Kommission bei F. Steiner, Wiesbaden, 1957.

Keddie, S. Nikki. *An Islamic Response to Imperialism*. Berkeley and Los Angeles: University of California Press, 1968.

Kerr, Malcolm H. *Islamic Reform*. Berkeley: University of California Press, 1966.

Kraemer, S. Joerg. *Das Problem der Islamischen Kulturgeschichte*. Tubingen: Max Niemeyer Verlag, 1939.

Lacoutre, Jean, and Simone Lacoutre. *Egypt in Transition*. London: Criterion Books, 1958.

Lahbābī, Mohammed Azīz. *La personnalisme musulman*. Paris: Presses universitaires de France, 1967.

Laroui, Abdulah. *La crise des intellectuels arabes*. Paris: F. Maspero, 1974.

Lerner, Daniel. *The Passing of Traditional Society*. New York: Free Press, 1958.

Lewis, Bernard. *Islam in History*. London: Watmoughs Ltd., 1973.

Makarius, Raoul. *La jeunesse intellectuelle egyptienne au lendemain de la IIème guerre mondiale*. Paris: Mouton, 1960.

Mas'ad, Mahmūd. "Himāyat al-adīb wa l-qaumīya al-ʿarabīya." *Al-Adāb* 6, no. 1 (1958).

Meier, S. F. "Soufisme et declin culturel." In Von Grunebaum and Willy Hartner, eds., *Classicisme et declin culturel dans l'histoire de l'Islam*. Paris, 1957, pp. 217–249.

Mīlād, Mahjūb bin. *Tūnis baina sh-sharq wa l-gharb*. Tunis: 1956.

Munah as-Sulh, S. *Al-islām, wa harakat at-taharrur al-ʿarab*. Beirut, 1973.

Munir, Muhammed. *From Jinnah to Zia*. Lahore: Vanguard Books, 1980.

———. *Islam in History*. Lahore: Law Pub. Co., 1974.

Parwez, S. Chulam Ahmed. *Islam: A Challenge to Religion*. Lahore: Idara-e-Tulu-e-Islam, 1968.

Qutb, Sayyid. *Al-ʿadāla al-ijtimāʿī ya fi l-islām*. Cairo: Lajnat al-Nash r lil-j ami iy in, 1950; English translation: Syed Kotb, *Social Justice in Islam*. Washington D.C.: American Council of Learned Society, 1953.

Rahman, Fazlur. *Islam*. Chicago: University of Chicago Press, 1966, 1979.

Ramadan, Said. *What Is an Islamic State?* Geneva: Islamic Center, 1961.

Rondot, Pierre. *L'islam et les musulmans d'aujourd'hui*. Vol. 1. Paris: Editions de L'Orante, 1958.

Saʿb, Hassan. "The Spirit of Reform in Islam." *Islamic Studies,* (Islamabad) 2, no. 1 (March 1963): 17–39.

Safran, Nadav. *Egypt in Search of Political Community*. Cambridge, Mass.: Harvard University Press, 1961.

Sharabi, Hisham. "The Crisis of the Intelligentsia in the Middle East." *The Muslim World* (Hartford: Hartford Seminary Foundation 47, no. 3 (July 1957): 187–193.

Silbermann, Gad. "National Identity in Nasserist Ideology, 1952–1970." *Asian and African Studies* (Jerusalem) 8, no. 1 (1972): 49–85.

Smith, Wilfred Cantwell. *Islam in Modern History*. Princeton N.J.: Princeton University Press 1957.

Tabibi, Abdul Hakim. *The Political Struggle of Jamal ad-din Afghani*. Kabul, Afganistan: Baihaqi, 1977.

Taha, Mahmoud Mohamed. *The Second Message of Islam*. Translated and introduced by ʿAbdallāhi Ahmad An-Naʿim. Syracuse: Syracuse University Press 1987.

ʿUbaid-Allāh Sind, S. *Shāh Wal y-Allāh aor unkā falsafa*. Lahore: Sindh Sagar Academy 1946.

Vahiduddin, S. "The Crisis of Religious Consciousness—with special reference to Islam." *Islam and the Modern Age* 1, no. 2 (New Delhi: Islam and the Modern Age Society, August 1970).

Watt, W. Montgomery. *Islamic Philosophy and Theology*. Edinburgh: Edinburgh University Press, 1962.

10

Modern Islamic Sociopolitical Thought

JOHN L. ESPOSITO

The world of twentieth-century Islam has been one of rapid and dramatic change—colonialism, independence, and the emergence of separate Muslim nation states. Political, social, and economic changes have had to be absorbed within a compressed period of decades rather than in the several centuries permitted in the West.

Modern Islamic sociopolitical thought reflects many of the conflicts and tensions that have accompanied the establishment of modern states and societies in the Muslim world. This chapter traces the development of Islamic sociopolitical thought from 1945 to the contemporary Islamic revival, identifying some of the important currents and movements.

Modern Muslim politics must be understood against the background of European imperialism and colonialism. By the nineteenth century, European states (in particular the British, French, and Dutch) had penetrated and increasingly dominated the Muslim world from North Africa to Southeast Asia. In the Islamic world, Western colonial rule precipitated a religious as well as a political crisis. For the first time since the birth of Islam in seventh-century Arabia, political and cultural sovereignty was lost to non-Islamic powers. No longer were the trappings of an Islamic state present: the ruler (caliph–sultan), Islamic law (*sharī'a*), *'ulamā* (religious scholar–leaders), serving as government advisers and administrators of the state's educational, legal, and social welfare systems. (See Glossary for definitions of special terms.) Muslim subjugation by Christian Europe confirmed not only the decline of Muslim power but also the apparent loss of divine favor and guidance. The Islamic concept of history views success and power as integral to the Muslims' universal mission to spread the rule of God and as dependent upon their obedience to God's will. Departure from the straight path of Islam meant loss of God's guidance and protection. Divine revelation (the *Qurān)* proclaimed this truth. The early extraordinary expansion and conquests of Islam had provided historical validation. Within one hundred years of Muhammad's death, Muslim rule extended over an area that stretched from North Africa to India. During subsequent centuries Islam continued its political expansion and developed a rich and flourishing civilization and culture. Western colonial rule, unlike previous wars or invasions, terminated this long and glorious history of Muslim self-rule, raising the questions: "What had gone wrong in Islam?" "How could Muslims realize God's will in a state governed by non-Muslims and non-Muslim law?" "How were Muslims to respond to this challenge to Muslim identity?"

A variety of responses emerged from Muslim self-criticism and reflection upon the causes of Muslim decline. Secularists blamed an outmoded tradition. They advocated a separation of religion and politics and the establishment of modern nation states, modeled on Western political and socioeconomic practice. Conservative religious traditionists attributed Muslim decline to divergence from Islam and excessive innovation (*bida,* deviation from tradition). Islamic modernists blamed a blind acceptance and unquestioned following (*taqlīd*) of the past; they proclaimed the need for Islamic reform. Many traditionists advocated a total rejection of the West. Muslims no longer lived under Islamic rule in an Islamic territory (*dar-al-Islam*) and were thus in a land of warfare (*dar al-harb*). Among the possible courses to follow in response to this situation were a holy war (*jihad*), emigration (*hijra*) to an Islamically ruled land, or passive withdrawal and noncooperation. On the other hand, Islamic reformers stressed the flexibility and adaptability that had characterized the early development of Islamic state and society and pressed for internal reform through a process of reinterpretation (*ijtihad*) and selective adaptation (Islamization) of Western ideas and technology. This early internal self-criticism and struggle to define Islam to make it relevant to contemporary society was the first stage in an ongoing process in which successive generations of Muslims have attempted to build twentieth-century religious, political, and social thought. It is important because it set the tone and direction of modern Muslim political thought.

EARLY RESPONSES

An early and major catalyst of Islamic modernism was Sayyid Jamāl ad-dīn Al-Afghānī (1838–1897), the Father of Muslim Nationalism.[1] Afghānī advocated Islamic reform and reemphasized the role of Islam in society and politics when many were ready to either reject or accept modernity wholesale. He traveled throughout the Muslim world to spread his message through an unceasing political activism. Afghānī believed that Muslims could repel the West not by rejecting or ignoring the sources of Western strength but rather by reclaiming and reappropriating reason, science, and technology, which were part of Islamic history and civilization. Islam is more than just religion in the Western sense; it is, he contended, the root of civilization, the essence and basis for Muslim survival as individuals and as a community of believers (*ummah*). The strength and survival of the *ummah* was dependent upon the reassertion of Islamic identity and the reestablishment of Islamic solidarity. Afghānī exhorted Muslims to realize that Islam was a dynamic, creative force capable of responding to the demands of modernity. For Afghānī, Islam was the religion of reason and science. Therefore, Western ideas and science did not pose a threat to Islam; they could be studied and used. Muslims must reinterpret Islam, making it a relevant force in their lives intellectually and politically. In this way, Islam would serve as the source of Islamic renewal through which colonial rule could be repulsed and independence and the establishment of Muslim nations achieved. Once Islam was revitalized, it would mobilize Muslims, uniting them and providing the means to regain their lost glory and take their rightful place in the modern world. However, Afghānī did not resolve the question of the relationship of modern nation states to the traditional notion of an Islamic *ummah*, that is, a transnational community of believers. Rather, he appealed to both Muslim nationalism and pan-Islam.

If Afghānī was the catalyst, his disciples Muhammad Abduh (1849–1905) and Rashid Rida (1865–1935) were the synthesizers. Their Manar or Salafiyya movement was to influence Islamic reform movements from North Africa to Southeast Asia. The Egyptian Muhammad Abduh—the "Father of Islamic Modernism"—called for internal reform, viewing Islam as the framework for the intellectual, social, and political revival of the *ummah*. Abduh was a religious scholar (*alim*, pl. *ulama*), rector of Al-Azhar and from 1898 mufti of Egypt (chief judge of the religious courts).[2] Through his writings and legal opinions (*fatwas*), Abduh emphasized that there was no contradiction between religion and reason, Islamic belief and modernity. Advocating a reformulation of Islam, Abduh dismissed the unquestioned following (*taqlīd*) of tradition or past authority as the reason for Muslim weakness and decline.[3] Unless a new path was forged through reinterpretation (*ijtihad*) and reform, Islam and Islamic culture would continue in a state of stagnation and decay. He argued that the process of reinterpretation was consonant with the nature of Islam. Abduh distinguished between Islam's inner core, composed of unchanging truths, and its outer layers, with society's application of those truths and values to the needs of a particular age. Thus Abduh stated that although those regulations of Islamic law (*sharīʿa*) that concerned prayer and worship (*ibadat*) were immutable, the vast majority of Islamic laws were concerned with social relations (*muamalat*); that is, international, penal, commercial, and family laws were open to change. As historical and social conditions warranted, the core of Islamic principles should be reapplied to new realities and, where necessary, the old layers of tradition discarded. The crisis of modern Islam was precipitated by Muslim failure to uphold this distinction between the immutable and mutable, the necessary and the contingent.

The attempt to reinterpret Islam, and thus enable Muslims to be both Muslim and modern without contradiction, marked a first stage in the search for a modern Islamic identity. With the achievement of independence, the vast majority of Muslim countries under the leadership of Western-oriented elites followed a more secular path based upon Western models of political, social, and economic development. Yet throughout the period from 1945 to the present Muslims continued to grapple with the relationship of Islam to the modern state. This is reflected in both Muslim politics and Islamic sociopolitical thought. Its major themes have included the relationship of Islam to nationalism, socialism, and secularism. Moreover, as we shall see, the failure to address adequately the problem of modern Islamic sociopolitical identity is a major theme in the contemporary resurgence of Islam in politics.

ISLAM AND THE MODERN STATE

The idea that nationalism could provide a legitimate basis for the state struck at the very heart of traditional Islamic political thought. The solidarity of the modern nation state is based upon common language, history, territory, or ethnic heritage, not religious faith. This stands in sharp contrast to the traditional definition of the Islamic state. In an Islamic state, the *ummah* is a community of believers, unified by their common religious faith; this religious bond supercedes all other loyalties or ties. Modern nation building spawned a variety of positions, ranging from total rejection of any "foreign" political influences or ideologies to complete adoption of Western, secular nationalism and the concept of the nation state. For some, like Mawlana Abu'l Ala Mawdudi (1903–1979), Islam and any form of nationalism (Indian, Arab, Egyptian, or Muslim) were antithetical since the Islamic community or state (*ummah*) transcends all ethnic, tribal, regional, and racial divisions. Islam's universal ideals and values are sustained by a divinely revealed law (*sharī'a*) whereas those of nationalism emerge from narrow particularism and opportunism. For Muslims, the universal, permanent laws of Islam do not alter with individual or national interests. Whereas "nationalism makes man unprincipled. A nationalist has no principles in the world except that he wishes the good of his nation."[4]

For other Muslims, like Taha Hussein (1889–1973) and Lutfi al-Sayyid (1872–1963), traditional Islamic political and social teachings were inappropriate in the modern world: "[the traditional Islamic] formula has no *raison d'être* because it fits neither the present state of affairs in Islamic nations nor their aspirations."[5] The path to be followed was a liberal nationalism rooted in patriotism and "love of the fatherland." Love of country (Egypt) "must be free from all conflicting associations . . . self-sacrifice in its service must take precedence over every other consideration."[6]

For Sati al-Husri (1880–1964), nationalism was primarily based upon a common language and a shared history. Thus he advocated neither "love of country nor a pan-Islamism based on general shared religious sentiment of Muslim brotherhood"; al-Husri stressed Arab nationalism. It was not Islam that defined Arab culture but rather the Arabs that gave meaning and brought glory to Islam. Moreover, political unity required mutual ideological goals and political consensus that necessitated a more concrete foundation than a shared faith or moral affinity. Religion had failed to provide the necessary political unity in the past when political and social life were simpler and when religion controlled behavior. Muslim life with its far more complex political and social realities and the diminished control of tradition and religious beliefs made any such Muslim unity even more remote.[7] The answer, then, was Arab unity. Common language, history, and geography, not religion, are the only feasible basis for political union. Arab nationalism provided the ideology that could join Arab lands: "It is a social force drawing vitality from the life of the Arabic language, from the history of the Arab nation, and from the connectedness of the Arab countries."[8] Despite al-Husri's regard for Islam, such argumentation did not allay traditionists who, like Mustafa al-Maraghi, the shaykh (rector) of al-Azhar, had condemned Arab nationalism as contrary to Islamic solidarity. However, other Arab nationalists like Amir Shakib Arslan and the Iraqi Abd al-Rahman al-Bazzaz (1913– 197?) argued the compatibility of Islam with Arab nationalism. For these Muslims, Islam is the religion of the Arab nation; Arab language and culture are integral to Islam. "Islam, although it is a universal religion . . . , is undoubtedly a religion revealed first to the Arabs themselves. The Prophet is from them and the Koran is in their language; Islam retained many of their previous customs, adopting and polishing the best of them."[9] However, al-Bazzaz argued that the social cohesion generated by Islam does not extend beyond Arabism to a "pan-Islamism": "Pan-Islamism . . . aims to form a comprehensive political organization which all the Muslims must obey. This organization, although it may be desired by all pious Muslims, is not possible in practice . . . under the present conditions. . . . the call to unite the Arabs . . . is the practical step which must precede the call for Pan-Islamism."[10]

A third stage in Islamic sociopolitical thought occurred in the late 1950s and 1960s as Islam reemerged in Muslim politics in the newly independent North African states and the radical politics of Egypt, Syria, and Iraq. In Morocco, Islam was used to legitimate and buttress the monarchy, which became both the key political and religious institution of the state. In Algeria, Houari Boumedienne, Islamically educated at Cairo's al-Azbar University, came to power in 1965 and placed greater emphasis on Islam and Arabization. This linking of Islam to Algerian socialism was reflected in Algeria's National Charter of 1976.

In several Middle East countries liberal nationalist regimes were overthrown by more radical groups that tended to emphasize Arab unity and a more socialist orientation. Claiming that the old liberal nationalist governments had failed politically and especially socioeconomically, new regimes in Egypt, Syria, and Iraq distinguished themselves from their predecessors' reliance on borrowed or "foreign" ideologies by advocating an Arab socialist ideology rooted in their Arab/Islamic heritage. Disillusioned with the liberal West and attracted by socialism, this new generation viewed independence as positive neutrality, politically and ideologically. National unity required a national ideology more authentically rooted in Arab identity. Arab nationalism/socialism of the Baath party and of Naseerism represented this new "progressive" outlook and became the two major ideological forces in the Arab world. Both appealed to Islam for legitimacy and to win mass support.

The Baath party was founded in Syria in 1940 by Michel Aflaq (1910-), a Christian, and Salah al-Din Baytar (1911–1980), a Muslim. Aflaq was its principal ideological architect. Like Naseerism, Baathism was critical of the bankruptcy of Western liberal nationalism and the materialistic preoccupations of both Western capitalism and Marxism. As Aflaq wrote,

The Arabs connection with the West is commonly traced back to Bonaparte's campaign against Egypt and symbolized by his act of hanging up verses from the Quran beside a text of the "rights of man." Since that time the Arabs (or the leaders spuriously converted to Arabism) have been pushing their new renaissance in this distorted direction. They contort themselves and warp the tests of their history and the Quran to show that not only is there no difference between the principles of their civilization and creed and those of Western civilization, but they, in fact, preceded Westerners in their declaration and application of the same. . . . they stand as accused before the West, affirming the soundness and superiority of Western values. . . . Before long they pushed this logic to its conclusion by admitting that with European civilization they had no need of their own.[11]

Baathism was to provide a comprehensive ideological alternative informed by Arabism and socialism. It affirmed the existence of a single Arab nation and emphasized the Islamic origins of Arab nationalism in its revolutionary spirit and message. This "religion represented the leap of Arabism to unity, power, and progress. . . . The Arabs are singled out from the nations by this characteristic. . . . their national consciousness is joined to a religious message; or more precisely this message is an eloquent expression of that national consciousness."[12] For Aflaq, Baath socialism, like its nationalism, was indebted not to a foreign source but to Islam's revolutionary ideology with its emphasis on equality, brotherhood, and social welfare.

While advocating constitutional democracy, the realities of Arab politics led the Baath to align themselves more closely with military regimes. Shared interests led to the union of Syria and Egypt and the formation of the United Arab Republic (1958–1961). Subsequently, Baathism became more radical, secularist, and divisive, serving as the official party of competing military regimes in Syria and Iraq as well as influencing party politics in Lebanon and Jordan.

The second major form of radical Arab nationalism/socialism was that of Gamal Abd al-Nasir (1918–1970) in Egypt. Nasirism, like Baathism, was essentially a secular movement that employed Islamic symbolism to legitimate and mobilize mass support. Nasir increasingly used Islam to enhance not only his rule of Egypt but to establish himself as a pan-Arab/Islamic leader.[13] Thus Islam was a factor in both his domestic and foreign policy. Government reforms (land reform, nationalization) were often justified by or, at least, portrayed as in harmony with Islam. A government-sponsored journal, *Minbar al-Islam* (*The Pulpit of Islam*), published articles by leading religious scholars and intellectuals supporting the Islamic character of the state's socialist policies. Nasir was able to get Shaykh Mahmud Shaltut (1892–1963) to assert that Islam and socialism were completely reconcilable because Islam was more than just a spiritual religion; it regulated "human relations and public affairs with the aim of ensuring the welfare of society."[14]

At the height of his popularity Nasir became the symbol of anti-imperialism in the Arab world, the chief spokesman for an "authentic" Arab nationalism and radical socialism that, by the mid 1960s, was the dominant ideology in the Arab world.

ISLAMIC FUNDAMENTALISM

For many Muslims, Nasirism and Baathism represented opportunistic uses of Islam by secular governments. Islamic organizations such as the Muslim Brotherhood in the Middle East and the Jamaat-i-Islami in South Asia found a truer answer in a comprehensive and integral vision of Islam as the complete ideology for Muslim society.

Their position is reflected in statements such as that of Hasan al-Banna: "Until recently, writers, intellectuals, scholars and governments glorified the principles of European civilization . . . adopted a Western style and manner. . . . Today, on the contrary, the wind has changed. . . . Voices are raised . . . for a return to the principles, teachings and ways of Islam . . . for initiating the reconciliation of modern life with these principles, as a prelude to a final Islamization."[15] For the Muslim Brotherhood and the Jamaat-i-Islami, Islam was not "a" component or factor in Muslim politics/ideology but rather "the foundation" for Muslim state and society.

The Muslim Brotherhood was founded by Hasan al-Banna (1906–1949) in Egypt.[16] The product of both a traditional religious and a modern education, he was a teacher who increasingly became convinced that only through a return to Islam (the Qur'ān and Sunnah of the prophet) could the Islamic world be awakened from its lethargy and decline. Established in 1928, the Brotherhood drew popular support for its educational and social welfare projects as much as its religious ideology. However, it progressively became embroiled in militant political action. In 1949 al-Banna was assassinated. Initially, the Brotherhood supported the revolution of 1952 that brought Gamal Abd al-Nasir and the Free Officers to power. However, disillusioned by Nasir's unwillingness to establish an Islamic state, the Brotherhood became an opposition movement. Several attempts on Nasir's life were blamed on the Brotherhood, leading to the arrests, executions, and suppression of the Brotherhood in 1965. Among those executed was Sayyid Qutb, prolific and prominent ideologue, who is regarded by contemporary Muslim revivalists as the martyr (al-Shabid) of Islamic revivalism and among its most influential voices.[17] The Brotherhood continued as an underground organization, inspired similar organizations in many Muslim countries, and resurfaced in Egypt under President Anwar al-Sadat.

Ideologically, the Brotherhood emphasized the union of religion and society in Islam as rooted in the unity of God (*tawhid*) and embodied in the comprehensive nature of the *sharī'a*. Emphasizing the universality of the *ummah* and its mission, it rejected nationalism and called for an Islamic state governed by the *sharī'a*. While open to modernization and technology, the Brotherhood renounced Muslim intellectuals' and governments' dependence upon the West. Instead of Westernization and secularization, the renewal of Muslim society must be rooted in Islamic principles and values. Both Western ideologies and radical Arab nationalism/socialism were eschewed. The social transformation of Muslim society, according to Brothers like Sayyid Qutb and Mustapha al-Sibai, should be based upon the social teachings of Islam or Islamic socialism. While affirming the right to private property, socialism in Islam recognized the right of the state to limit landed property and nationalize where demanded by social justice. Such a socialism is "totally different from the type of socialism that attaches no importance to religious values, relies on the class struggle in society, seizes private property without good reason, nationalizes industry and economic concerns that contribute to the national economic prosperity, paralyzes initiative and competition."[18]

The death of the charismatic Arab leader Gamal Abd al-Nasir in 1970 created a void that his longtime admirer, Libya's Colonel Muammar al-Qaddafi, tried to fill. Qaddafi combined radical Arab nationalism/socialism with his own brand of Islamic fundamentalism. He has taken up the banner of radical Arab nationalism/socialism and relied heavily upon an Islamic fundamentalist rationale both to legitimate his domestic reforms and to influence the politics of other Muslim states. Qaddafi's prescription for social revolution is contained in *The Green Book*. First published in 1973, there have been two subsequent volumes in 1976 and 1979 that set forth his "Third Way" or "Third International Theory," necessitated by the fact that "non-Islamic civilization brought war to the world of doubt. . . . Islamic civilization is the only one that brought war to certainty and faith."[19] Indigenously rooted, the Third Way is an alternative to the extremes of capitalism and communism, both of which are exploitive and doomed to failure: "The world, East and West, is incapable of arriving at a true solution. . . . One sets wealth at liberty and allows all things to follow their inclinations arbitrarily . . . the other maintains there is no way except for us to interfere violently, uproot everything and then reshape it all even though it is contrary to the nature of man such as is done in communism."[20] Qaddafi appeals to the Qur'ān as the focal point and source for his revolutionary theory: "in it are solutions to the problems of man . . . from personal status . . . to international problems."[21] Democracy, the legacy of European colonialism and contemporary American neo-colonialism, were replaced by an emphasis on Islamization of Libyan society. Thus *sharī'a* law was reintroduced and an ambitious, experimental "Islamic" socialist program undertaken: It is "a socialism emanating from the true religion of Islam and its Noble Book . . . not the socialism of Lenin and Marx."[22]

Qaddafi's brand of Islamic sociopolitical beliefs and programs have employed an "innovative," idiosyncratic, and selective use of Islam. In recent years he has restricted the place of the Qur'ān to religious affairs alone; *The Green Book* has displaced much of the traditional *sharī'a*'s governance of the political and social order. Qaddafi has ignored the guardians of tradition—the *ulama*—and instead has substituted his own interpretation of Islam.[23] Mixing ideological statements with a broad range of political, social, and economic experimentation, Qaddafi has attempted nothing less than a cultural revolution. Progressively, the centralized, bureaucratic socialist state headed by Qaddafi's Revolutionary Command Council has given way to a more decentralized, populist, participatory government of peoples' committees that control government officers, schools, the media, and many large corporations. This change was symbolized in 1977 when the General People's Congress renamed Libya the Socialist People's Libyan Arab Jamahiriya. Similarly, a more egalitarian spirit has effected socioeconomic reforms. Although private ownership is maintained, it has been restricted. Wages and rent have been abolished in favor of worker control of and participation in the means of production. Women's place in the revolution has been underscored by greater emphasis on their economic and social rights in society.

As in Libya's domestic policy, its foreign policy has also used an ideology that emphasizes Islamic unity, equality, and brotherhood. Qaddafi has attempted political unions with a number of Muslim states: Syria, Egypt, Tunisia, Sudan, and Chad. Libyan funds have supported revolutionary movements from Palestine to the Moro Islands. Qaddafi's interpretation of Islam comes under heavy criticism from Libya's religious establishment (the *ulama*) and other Muslim governments and leaders. However, his brand of Islamic fundamentalism, fueled by oil revenues, has had a significant impact on Libya and many other countries throughout the Muslim world.

THE ISLAMIC RESURGENCE

Political events in the Muslim world during the 1970s have (in a dramatic way) drawn attention to the political and social implications of Islam. Contrary to accepted norms of political development and the predictions of many analysts, religion reemerged in the Muslim politics of Iran, Pakistan, Afghanistan, Saudi Arabia, Syria, and Malaysia.[24] Islamic ideology, symbols, slogans, and actors have become prominent fixtures. Iran has established an "Islamic republic" and Pakistan has committed itself to a more Islamic system of government (*Nizam-i-Islam*). Islamic laws, dress, taxes, and punishments have been called for and/or introduced in many Muslim countries. Both encumbent governments and opposition movements often vie with one another in declaring their allegiance to Islam and to a more Islamic order. Thus Islamic politics, economics, law, and education are hotly contested issues.

Amidst the diversity of Islamic revivalism there are common sociopolitical concerns and themes rooted in a general consensus that Muslims have failed to produce a viably authentic synthesis that is both modern and true to their own history and values. Among the chief concerns of contemporary Islamic socio-political thought are the (1) continued impotence of Muslim society, that is, the ineffectiveness of Muslim governments and nationalist ideologies; (2) disillusionment with the West; and (3) the need to articulate a more authentic identity.

If Islam's glorious political and cultural past had been reversed by colonial rule, independence had not greatly improved the political and socioeconomic condition of most Muslim countries. They continued to be subservient to the West both politically and culturally. Moreover, political elites had failed to establish a legitimate, effective public order and to address adequately the profound socioeconomic disparities in wealth and class in most Muslim countries.[25] Their sense of disillusionment and failure was reflected in Muslim literature in the late 1960s with its growing criticism of the West and its concern to reclaim historical and cultural identity.[26] For the religiously oriented, the problem had always been clear—departure from the straight path of Islam was doomed to failure. For Western-oriented intellectuals and elites, the disillusionment was more unsettling. They had embraced the West as both an ally and a model for development. The establishment of Israel, continued massive American support for Israel in every Arab-Israeli War as well as regimes like that of the shah of Iran, and the failures of Muslim governments posed a direct challenge to their position. The complete and decisive nature of the Arab defeat at the hands of Israel in 1967 shattered their faith and confidence in the West and in Arab nationalism. Thus in popular and intellectual as well as religious literature, there is a confluence of concerns on topics such as religion, tradition and values, politics and ideology, language and education.[27] All are part of a general call for revival (*tajdī d*), reform (*islah*), or renaissance (*nahda*).

Events in 1973 provided a sign that Muslim fortunes were indeed changing. The Arab-Israeli War of 1973 and the Arab oil boycott were major sources of Muslim pride. The defeat of 1967 was reversed by the "Islamic victory" of 1973's October War. For Arabs, the ability and success of Egyptian forces were established even if final victory was thwarted by massive American assistance to Israel. Islamic symbols and slogans, from the war's battle cry (Allahu Akbar— "God Is Most Great") to its code name (*Badr*), were emphasized. For many, the victory, coupled with the oil boycott's demonstration of Arab (Muslim) economic power, instilled a new sense of pride and strengthened their commitment to forging their Islamic identity.

Although there are distinctive differences among Islamic revivalists, as shall be seen below, because they share both a common Islamic heritage and a confrontation with the West, common themes in Islamic sociopolitical thought may be identified as (1) the failure of the West; the inappropriateness of its transplanted, imported models of political, social, and economic development; and the need to throw off Western political and cultural domination that is characterized by secularism, materialism, and spiritual bankruptcy; (2) the need to "return to Islam" to restore a lost identity and moral character; (3) an emphasis on the unity and totality of Islam and witnessed by the doctrine of *tawhid* (unity of God); that is, religion is integral to politics and society; and Islam is faith and government (*din wa dawla*); and (4) a call for the reintroduction of Shariah law as the *sine qua non* for establishing a more Islamic state and society.

Despite significant differences from one Muslim context to another, the general outlook (*weltanschauung*) of contemporary revivalists may be divided into three categories: conservative, fundamentalist, and modernist reformers. Although all advocate a "return to Islam," their meanings and methods are different. For conservatives, who represent the majority of the religious establishment, the Islamic system is expressed adequately and completely in the classical formulation of Islam as embodied and preserved in Islamic law. This is the interpretation of Islam that governed the Muslim community through the centuries and that remains valid today. Therefore, conservatives emphasize following (*taqlid*) past authority and are wary of innovation (*bida*, deviation from tradition). Although change does occur, it is very gradual and by way of exception. Thus, for example, when the Ayatullah Khomeini and the religious leaders who dominate Iran's Islamic Republican party and its Parliament implement Islamic laws, they turn to the medieval legal manuals. Similarly, the *mullahs* of Pakistan agitate for the repeal of modern family law reforms (marriage, divorce, and inheritance) as an unwarranted deviation from the Shariah.

Fundamentalists share many similarities with conservatives. Like conservatives, they advocate a return to the Quran and Sunnah of the prophet. However, they differ in that fundamentalists, while respecting the classical formulations of Islam, claim the right to go back to the fundamental sources of Islam to reinterpret (*ijtihad*) and reapply them to contemporary needs. Thus although in many matters fundamentalists and conservatives turn to classical Islam, fundamentalists are more flexible in their ability to adapt to change. Saudi Arabia and Libya provide two examples of fundamentalist flexibility—the Saudi a more traditional and Qaddafi a more radical fundamentalism. Both have had to contend with the more conservative bent of their *ulama*. A similar flexibility may be seen in Islamic organizations like the Muslim Brotherhood and the Jamaat-i-Islami. The net result of the fundamentalist outlook is a variety of interpretations regarding the nature of Islamic government.[28] Moreover, over time, changed leadership and/or circumstances can lead to differing "Islamic positions" on the same issue. Whereas Muslim Brotherhood writers like Sayyid Qutb and Mustapha al-Sibaii advanced Islamic socialism as a means to social justice, the Muslim Brotherhood in Egypt today tends to emphasize private ownership as the Islamic norm to a far greater extent. In addition, whereas in the past the Brotherhood spoke of Arab nationalism and unity as a necessary stage in the revival of Islam, the new Brotherhood emphasizes Islamic solidarity rather than Arab unity.[29]

Finally, the most adaptive are the Islamic modernists. Many are individuals who, after an early traditional religious education, have received a Western education. They neither opt for a Western secular orientation nor, in their view, are as Western oriented as earlier generations of Islamic reformers. Educated often at the best American, British, or French universities, they remain Islamically oriented and emphasize a commitment to "Islamic modernization," that is, a future in which political and social development are more firmly rooted in past history and values. They have learned from the West but do not wish to Westernize Muslim society. The method modernists advocate for sociopolitical change is that of Islamization—a process used in the formation and development of classical Islam. It includes (1) implementation of Qur'ānic and Prophetic prescriptions, (2) application of Islamic (revelation) principles and values to sociohistorical conditions, and (3) adoption and adaptation of the best (thought, institutions, laws) that is to be found in other cultures, provided it is not contrary to revelations. Islamic reformers distinguish between an immutable revelation and its mutable (historically and socially conditioned) laws and institutions. They maintain that although classical Islamic law was formulated in light of and therefore responded to the needs of the past, modern life requires a reformulation of Islam through once more undertaking the process of Islamization. If Islamic law had had four sources—Qur'ān, Sunnah, *ijtihad* (interpretation), and *ijma* (community acceptance or consensus)—Muslims today once more must vigorously reinterpret (*ijtihad*) to arrive at a new consensus (*ijma*), that is, Islamic models for modern Muslim states and societies. Unlike earlier reformers, contemporary revivalists believe they live at a time and in circumstances that provide more opportunities and better resources to develop and implement specific programs. Although all modernists claim an Islamic basis and ideology, their ideological positions and degree of political activism range from moderate to revolutionary. For Hassan Turabi, the attorney general of the Sudan and leader of Sudan's Muslim Brotherhood, and Anwar Ibrahim, head of the Muslim Youth Movement of Malaysia (ABIM) and currently a deputy prime minister, Islamization of politics and law should be a gradual process.[30] For others, like Egypt's Islamic socialist Hassan Hanafi or Iran's Mujahidin-i-Khalq, a more radical, revolutionary process is required. As with Iran's Ali Shariati, Islam provides a political ideology capable of mass mobilization for a much needed revolution.[31]

Although the leadership of both fundamentalist and modernist Islam is primarily lay, the modernist in particular tend most often to clash with the conservative *ulama*. Unlike fundamentalists, Islamic modernists feel freer to bypass classical formulations of politics and law and to exercise a wide-ranging *ijtihad* (reinterpretation). The *ulama* attack their "deviationism" and question their qualifications as *mijtahids* (reinterpreters), maintaining that the *ulama* alone are the guardians of Islam. Islamic modernists ignore or reject the *ulama*, claiming that there is no clergy in Islam and that any Muslim can qualify as a scholar (*alim,* pl. *ulama*—"learned"). Moreover, due to their traditional education and outlook, most *ulama* are viewed as ill equipped to respond to the modern world.

A vivid example of the clash of modernist and conservative religious world views has occurred in Iran. During the revolution, posters of Ali Shariati, the revolution's ideologue, and the Ayatullah Khomeini, the symbolic leaders of the opposition, were often placed side by side. Shariati was a Sorbonne-educated socialist and hero of Iranian youth, and Khomeini, the traditional religious leader, was trained at Qum, a leading center of Islamic education. Their followers stood united in their Islamic opposition to the shah. However, during the postrevolutionary period the contrasts between Muslim modernists like Shariati and Abul Hasan Banisadr, Iran's former president, and the ruling *mullahs* (religious) has led to a rupture in their relations. For Khomeini and the *mullahs,* the Islamic government is governed by the legal specialists (*wilayat-ul-faqih*) according to medieval Islamic law, delineated by the *faqihs* (legal specialists) of the past.[32] Shariati's Islam is a revolutionary Islam, a religion of protest. He distinguishes between two Islams, Islam the ideology and Islam the culture. Islam the ideology: "responsibility, consciousness and leadership" is future oriented.[33] Islam the culture is the creation of the *faqih* who "have suppressed true knowledge of religion."[34] Shariati sees theirs as a stagnant, retrogressive Islam.

Although contemporary Islamic sociopolitical thought is vibrant and diverse, it is seminal and tentative in its forms and expression. With few exceptions, developed Islamic models for political, social, and economic change await construction and implementation. The most visible experiments thus far have occurred in Saudi Arabia, Libya, Iran, and Pakistan.[35] With the exception of Saudi Arabia where Islam has for some time legitimated the al-Saud monarchy, the others have been relatively recent experiments by regimes that have come to power through a revolution or coup d'état. Their Islamic character has been in large part determined by their military or religious regimes. On the other hand, Islamic political writings and manifestos appear somewhat general and abstract, lacking detailed development. Muslim revivalists respond that the necessary political and intellectual climate has been wanting but that a period of research and experimentation in Islamic political, legal, and economic reforms has begun. This process has already raised many issues. Because of the ad hoc nature of Islamization, sharp differences in Islamic interpretation on political and social development have been evident in Muslim politics as well as Muslim political thought. The power exercised by the Ayatullah Khomeini, Colonel Qaddafi, General Zia ul-Haq, and the al-Saud family in the name of Islam has, for many, raised questions about the nature of Islamic government and the role of political authority. The use of Islam not only by encumbent governments but often by opposition movements underscores the two primary questions that Muslim thinkers and governments face in policy-making: "Whose Islam?" That is, who is to interpret, formulate and implement Islamic programs and policies. "What Islam?" How is the Islamic character of a government and its policies to be determined.[36] As previously noted, current Islamic governments include Saudi Arabia's monarchy, Iran's cleric-dominated state, and Pakistan's martial law regime. All claim to be Islamic states or republics and appeal to Islam to legitimate their rule and many of their policies. At the same time, they are criticized by others as using Islam to justify authoritarian rule, suppress political parties, limit the rights of women, and impose censorship. For many Muslim critics, such measures constitute the manipulation of religion through the use of a "negative (restrictive) Islam." Thus while establishing more authentically rooted,

Islamic societies is a *desideratum* for many, determining the shape and form of such states will be no easy task.

From the establishment of the first Islamic community/state at Medina in 622 C.E., Islam has played an important role in the development of Muslim politics and society. During the twentieth century, Muslims have faced the task of redefining their political and social identities. Muslim politics and thought demonstrate the extent to which Islam continues to be a significant factor in contemporary Muslim societies.

NOTES

I would like to acknowledge the contribution of Laura Quinn (University of Chicago) to parts of this chapter.

1. For a summary of Afghani's contribution, see Albert Hourani, *Arabic Thought in the Liberal Age* (London: Oxford University Press, 1970), Ch. 5. See also Nikki R. Keddie, *Sayyid Jamal al-Din al Afghani: A Political Biography* (Berkeley: University of California Press, 1972); and idem, ed. and trans., *An Islamic Response to Imperialism: Political and Religious Writings of Sayyid Jamal al-Din al Afghani* (Berkeley: University of California Press, 1968).

2. Hourani, *Arabic Thought,* Ch. 6; and Muhammad Abduh, *The Theology of Unity,* trans. I. Musaad and Kenneth Cragg (London: George Allen and Unwin, 1966).

3. In South Asia similar attempts to revitalize the Muslim community through Islamic reform were undertaken by Sir Sayyid Ahmad Khan (1817–1898) and Muhammad Iqbal (1875–1938). See, for example, Aziz Ahmad, *Islamic Modernism in India and Pakistan, 1857–1964* (London: Oxford University Press, 1967), Chs. 2, 7; Christian W. Troll, *Sir Sayyid Ahmad Khan: A Reinterpretation of Muslim Theology* (New Delhi: Vikas Publishing House, 1978); Muhammad Iqbal, *The Reconstruction of Religious Thought in Islam* (Lahore: Muhammad Ashraf, 1968); John L. Esposito, "Muhammad Iqbal and the Islamic State," in John L. Esposito, ed., *Voices of Resurgent Islam* (New York: Oxford University Press, 1983), Ch. 8, pp. 175–190.

4. Abul Ala Mawdudi, "Nationalism and India," in John J. Donohue and John L. Esposito eds., *Islam in Transition: Muslim Perspectives* (New York: Oxford University Press, 1982), p. 96.

5. Ahmad Lutfi al-Sayyid, *"Ta'ammulat,"* in Donohue and Esposito, *Islam in Transition,* p. 70. For Taha Husayn, see S. Glazer, trans., *The Future of Culture in Egypt* (Washington, D.C.: American Council of Learned Societies, 1954).

6. Glazer, *Future of Culture in Egypt.*

7. Hourani, *Arabic Thought,* pp. 311–316.

8. Sati al-Husr, "Muslim Unity and Arab Unity," in Donohue and Esposito, *Islam in Transition,* p. 69.

9. Abd al-Rahman al-Bazzaz, "Islam and Arab Nationalism," in Sylvia Haim, ed., *Arab Nationalism* (Berkeley: University of California Press, 1962), p. 176.

10. Ibid.

11. Michel Aflaq, "Dhikra-1-Rasul al-Arab" (In Remembrance of the Arab Prophet), in Donohue and Esposito, *Islam in Transition,* p. 110.

12. Ibid., p. 109.

13. See Daniel Crecelius, "The Course of Secularization in Modern Egypt," in John L. Esposito, ed., *Islam and Development: Religion and Sociopolitical Change* (Syracuse: Syracuse University Press, 1980), p. 63–70; Geunter Levy, "Naseerism and Islam: A Revolution in Search of Ideology," in Donald E. Smith, ed., *Religion and Political Modernization* (New Haven: Yale University Press, 1974), Ch. 14, pp. 259–281.

14. Shaykh Mahmud Shaltut, "Socialism and Islam," in Donohue and Esposito, *Islam in Transition*, p. 99.

15. Hasan al-Banna, "The New Renaissance," in Donohue and Esposito, *Islam in Transition*, p. 78.

16. The best study of the Brotherhood is Richard P. Mitchell, *The Society of the Muslim Brothers* (London: Oxford University Press, 1969). See also I. M. Husaini, *The Moslem Brethren* (Beirut: Khayat'f College Book Cooperative, 1956); C. P. Harris, *Nationalism and Revolution in Egypt* (The Hague: Mouton, 1964).

17. Yvonne Haddad, "Sayyid Qutb," in Esposito, *Voices of Resurgent Islam*, Ch. 4, pp. 67–98.

18. Mustapha al-Sibaii, "Islamic Socialism," in Donohue and Esposito, *Islam in Transition*, p. 122.

19. Muammar al-Qaddafi, "Fil-Nazariyyah al-Thalithah" ("The Third Way") (n.p: n.d) in Donohue and Esposito, *Islam in Transition*, p. 106.

20. Ibid., p. 105.

21. Ibid., p. 103.

22. "The Libyan Revolution in the Words of Its Leaders," *The Middle East Journal* 24 (1970): 208.

23. As Ann Mayer has observed: "Qadhdhafi has himself undertaken the role of supreme interpreter of Islamic law." Mayer, "Islamic Resurgence or a New Prophethood: The Role of Islam in Qadhdhafi's Ideology," in Ali E. Hillal Dessouki, ed., *Islamic Resurgence in the Arab World* (New York: Praeger, 1982), p. 211. See Lisa Anderson, "Qaddafi's Islam," in Esposito, *Voices of Resurgent Islam*, Ch. 6, pp. 134–149.

24. A number of volumes containing country case studies have appeared. Among the more useful are Muhammad Ayoub, ed., *The Politics of Islamic Reassertion* (New York: St. Martin's Press, 1981); Dessouki, *Islamic Resurgence*; Esposito, *Islam and Development*.

25. R. Hrair Dekmejian, "The Anatomy of Islamic Revival: Legitimacy Crisis, Ethnic Conflict, and the Search for Islamic Identity," *The Middle East Journal* 34, no. 1 (1980): 1–12.

26. John J. Donohue, "Islam and the Quest for Identity in the Arab World," in Esposito, *Voices of Resurgent Islam*, Ch. 3, pp. 48–61; Ali Merad, "The Ideologisation of Islam," in Alexander S. Cudsi and Ali E. Hillal Dessouki, eds., *Islam and Power in the Contemporary Muslim World* (Baltimore: Johns Hopkins University Press, 1981) pp. 37–48.

27. Donohue "Islam and the Quest for Identity," pp. 48–62.

28. See Charles E. Butterworth, "Prudence versus Legitimacy: The Persistent Theme in Islamic Political Thought," in Dessouki, *Islamic Resurgence*, Ch. 5, pp. 84–109; Esposito, *Voices of Resurgent Islam*, Chs. 4–7.

29. Abd al-Moneim Said Aly and Manfred W. Wenner, "Modern Islamic Reform: The Muslim Brotherhood in Contemporary Egypt," *The Middle East Journal* 36 (1982): 351–352.

30. Hassan Turabi, "The Islamic State," in Esposito, *Voices of Resurgent Islam*, Ch.

11; pp. 241–251. Fred R. von der Mehden, "Islamic Resurgence in Malaysia," in Esposito, *Islam and Development*, p. 174–175.

31. Margol Bayat, "Islam in Pahlavi and Post Pahlavi Iran," in Esposito, *Islam and Development*, Ch. 10, pp. 87–106. Abdul Aziz Sachedina, "Ali Shariati," in Esposito, *Voices of Resurgent Islam*, Ch. 9, pp. 199–214; Ervand Abrahamian, "Ali Shariati: Idealogue of the Iranian Revolution," *Merip Reports* 102 (1982): 24–28.

32. Bayat, "Islam," pp. 97–98.

33. Ali Shariati, "Intizar," in Donohue and Esposito, *Islam in Transition*, p. 300.

34. Ibid., p. 301.

35. See Ayoub, *Politics of Islamic Reassertion;* Dessouki, *Islamic Resurgence;* and Esposito, *Islam and Development*, for case studies.

36. For a more extensive discussion of this problem, see my "Tradition and Modernization in Islam," in Charles W. H. Fu and Gerhard E. Spiegler, eds., *Movements and Issues in World Religions: Religion, Ideology, and Politics,* Greenwood Press, 1987, pp. 89–105.

GLOSSARY

Ummah: The community of believers; a religio-political community or state.

Tawhī d: "Unity or oneness" of God; Islam's radical monotheism.

Shari'ah: The revealed law of Islam.

Sunnah: "Trodden path"; example or model behavior of the prophet Muhammad.

Hadith: A report or recorded tradition about the words/deeds of the prophet Muhammad.

Fiqh: "understanding"; the science of jurisprudence that elucidated the Shariah.

Ytihad: The use of independent reasoning or judgment in interpreting Islamic law.

Giyas: The use of analogical reasoning in law.

Ijma: Consensus or agreement as a source of law.

Taqlī d: To follow or imitate religious authority (tradition or law).

Bida: "Innovation"; practices that deviate from tradition.

Tajdī d: "Renewal."

Ulamā : (plural of *alim*) "Learned"; religious scholars.

Jihad: "Struggle or strive in God's way"; its military manifestation is a holy war.

Hijra: Migration of Muhammad and his followers from Mecca to Medina in 622 A.D. This is the beginning of the Islamic community/state and the first year of the Islamic calendar.

Fuqaha: (plural of *faqih*) A legal expert, jurist.

Shahada: "Testimony"; the confession of faith in Islam: "There is no God but God and Muhammad is his Messenger."

Siyasa shariyya: "Shariah governance"; the right of the ruler to issue administrative regulations (*nizam*) to insure Islamic rule.

Nahda: "Renaissance."

Nizam-i-Islam: An Islamic system of government.

Maslaha: Public interest or general welfare.

Nizam: Rule or ordinance promulgated by an Islamic ruler to supplement Shariah law.

SELECTED BIBLIOGRAPHY

Bibliographies

Arab Culture and Society in Change: A Bibliography. Beirut: Dal El-Mashreq, 1973. Available from Georgetown University Press.

Index Islamicus, 1906–1955. Compiled by J. D. Pearson. Cambridge, Eng.: W. Heffer & Sons, 1958; reprint, 1961, with supplementary volumes.

The Quarterly Index Islamicus. London: Mansell, 1982.

Encyclopedias

The Encyclopedia of Islam. Edited by H.A.R. Gibb et al. London: E. J. Brill, 1960.

Shorter Encyclopedia of Islam. Edited by H.A.R. Gibb et al. London: E. J. Brill, 1953.

Books

Abduh, Muhammad. *The Theology of Unity.* Translated by I. Musaad and Kenneth Cragg. London: George Allen and Unwin, 1966.

Ahmad, Aziz. *Islamic Modernism in India and Pakistan, 1857–1964.* London: Oxford University Press, 1967.

Ahmad, Khurshid, and Zafar Ishaq Ansari, eds. *Islamic Perspectives.* Leicester, Eng.: The Islamic Foundation, 1979.

Ajami, Fouad. *The Arab Predicament.* Cambridge: Cambridge University Press, 1981.

al-Faruqi, Ismail. *Islam.* Niles, Ill.: Argus Communications, 1979.

Anderson, J.N.D. *Law Reform in the Muslim World.* London: Athlone, 1976.

Coulson, N. J. *Conflicts and Tensions in Islamic Jurisprudence.* Chicago: University of Chicago Press, 1969.

Donohue, John J., and John L. Esposito, eds. *Islam in Transition: Muslim Perspectives.* New York: Oxford University Press, 1982.

Esposito, John L. *Women in Muslim Family Law.* Syracuse: Syracuse University Press, 1982.

———, ed. *Islam and Development: Religion and Sociopolitical Change.* Syracuse: Syracuse University Press, 1980.

Fyzee, A.A.A. *A Modern Approach to Islam.* New York: Asia Publishing House, 1963.

Gauhar, Altaf, ed. *The Challenge of Islam.* London: Islamic Council of Europe, 1978.

Geertz, Clifford. *Islam Obscured: Religious Development in Morocco and Indonesia.* Chicago: University of Chicago Press, 1968.

Gibb, H.A.R., *Modern Trends in Islam.* Chicago: University of Chicago Press, 1947.

Hanafi, Jamil. *Islam and the Transformation of Culture.* New York: Asia Publishing House, 1970.

Hourani, Albert. *Arabic Thought in the Liberal Age.* London: Oxford University Press, 1962.

Iqbal, Muhammad. *The Reconstruction of Religious Thought in Islam.* Lahore: Muhammad Ashraf, 1968.

Kerr, Malcolm. *Islamic Reform.* Berkeley: University of California Press, 1966.

Lerner, D. *The Passing of Traditional Society.* New York: The Free Press, 1958.

Martin, Richard C. *Islam.* Englewood Cliffs, N.J.: Prentice-Hall, 1982.

Nasr, Seyyed Hossein. *Ideals and Realities of Islam.* Boston: Beacon Press, 1972.

Rahman, Fazlur. *Islam,* 2d ed. Chicago: University of Chicago Press, 1979.

Smith, Jane I., ed. *Women in Contemporary Muslim Societies.* Lewisburg, Pa.: Bucknell University Press, 1980.

Smith, W. C. *Islam in Modern History.* Princeton, N.J.: Princeton University Press, 1957.

Troll, Christian W. *Sir Sayyid Ahmad Khan: A Reinterpretation of Muslim Theology.* New Delhi: Vikas Publishing House, 1978.

Voll, John O. *Islam: Continuity and Change in the Modern World.* Boulder, Colo.: Westview Press, 1982.

Welch, Alfred T., ed. *Islam: Past Influence and Present Challenge.* New York: State University of New York Press, 1979.

11

Postwar Issues in Japanese Buddhism

STEVEN HEINE

Mahāyāna Buddhism in Japan has progressed since World War II in two seemingly contrary but complementary directions. On the one hand, a remarkable philosophical movement has developed drawing on traditional Buddhist sources articulated in modern and Western perspectives. It now stands at the forefront of the international field of comparative philosophy and religious thought, influencing areas including phenomenology, psychology, mysticism, ethics, aesthetics, and the philosophy and history of science. At the same time, Japanese scholars have emerged as the leading figures in Asia and perhaps the entire world in the field of Buddhist studies, accomplishing a diversity and depth of scholarship in nearly all areas from primitive or basic Buddhism in India through the doctrinal trends and schools of Mahāyāna in China, Tibet, Korea, and Japan. Together, these movements not only have achieved a reawakening of Buddhist intellectual and cultural influence in Japan but are establishing a standard for scholarly and philosophical investigation that draws the attention of, and continues to challenge, religious thinkers throughout the globe.

The philosophical movement is generally referred to as the "Kyoto school (Kyōto-ha)," or the "Nishida-Tanabe philosophical tradition," because it is centered in Kyoto and largely based on the philosophy of Kyoto University professors Nishida Kitarō, considered the founding figure, and his main disciple (and critic), Tanabe Hajime. The Kyoto school has been greatly influenced by two of Nishida's main colleagues also based in Kyoto, Watsuju Tetsurō and Suzuki Daisetz. It is perpetuated by direct followers of Nishida and Tanabe, such as Nishitani Keiji, looked on as the current "dean"; Takeuchi Yoshinori; Hisamatsu Shin'ichi; Abe Masao; and Ueda Shizuteru at Kyoto, Otani, and nearby universities.

The central philosophical theme of the Kyoto school is the notion of absolute nothingness (zettai mu), rooted in the Mahāyāna Buddhist doctrine of sunyātā (emptiness, J. *kū*) as the "groundless ground" of ontological nondifferentiation and epistemological nondiscrimination. (See Glossary for definitions of special terms.) Absolute nothingness is expressed by Kyoto philosophers in the critical, comparative light of Western existentialism and mysticism and applied to a wide range of issues such as theory of knowledge, history, and morality, the nature and development of cultures, the possible interaction of Eastern and Western philosophy and religion, and the worldwide dominance of Western technology.

The movement in Buddhist studies might, to coin a designation, be termed the "Tokyo school" or the "Tokyo approach" because it is largely based in various institutions in Tokyo, including the University of Tokyo as well as Komazawa, Rissho, Toyo, Taisho, and Waseda universities. The "Tokyo approach" continues the development of scholarship generated during the Meiji period (1868–1911) as a response to the challenge of the decline of Buddhist political and social influence due to the establishment of Shinto as the state religion after centuries of Buddhist hegemony. In contrast to the speculative and universalist trends of the Kyoto philosophers, the Tokyo scholars strive for a highly specialized and precise scientific methodology faithful to history and text rather than philosophical vision. The central figures include Takakusu Junjirō, Ui Hakaju, and Nakamura Hajime, who have contributed to the monumental task of the collection, categorization, translation, and evaluation of scriptural and doctrinal materials covering the multiple languages and cultures of Buddhist Asia.

The writings of the Kyoto school are better known and perhaps more important to the Western audience at this stage of Japanese studies and therefore receive greater attention here. Many of the writings by the major representatives of the Kyoto school have been translated into English and German, with additional translations reportedly on the way; some of the works were composed in English or German. Also, several of the Kyoto thinkers, such as Suzuki, Takeuchi, Hisamatsu, and Abe, have traveled and lectured extensively in America and Europe, frequently engaging in philosophical dialogue with noted theologians, including Paul Tillich, Rudolph Bultmann, Reinhold Niebuhr, and Thomas Merton. There are still many factors, however, that limit the influence as well as our understanding of the activities of the Kyoto school. The Kyoto thinkers have not yet received the full acknowledgment or attention of Western philosophers— as opposed to philosophically minded theologians. Also, translations of and commentaries (even in Japanese) on Nishida, the most philosophically sophisticated of the Kyoto figures, remain sparse.

The Tokyo scholarship is of incalculable importance to Western researchers of Buddhism. Unlike much of the studies done in other Asian countries, however, which is often in Western languages, the Tokyo research is almost entirely in Japanese. Since it is highly technical and generally untranslated (with some notable exceptions, such as a few key works by Takakusu and Nakamura), the scholarship's impact is limited to specialists in Japanese. It is not readily available, for example, to Western students of Indo-Tibetan Buddhism who would certainly benefit from exposure to it.

To some extent, the central differences between the Kyoto and Tokyo approaches are based on the sectarian background and atmosphere underlying their respective developments. That is not to suggest that the figures of either school are necessarily spokesmen for a particular sect. In fact, both parties strive for a pan-Buddhist perspective, and the Kyoto philosophers are frequently more concerned with interpreting Western or Christian than Buddhist thinkers. Yet the ideological commitment of sectarian influence, associated with cultural and geographical factors, seems evident in both cases.

The background of the Kyoto school is primarily Rinzai Zen, whose main temples are in the Kyoto or Kansai (western) region. The Rinzai approach to Zen, which has traditionally stressed the philosophical and aesthetic creativity of individual masters, seems to be expressed in the view of nothingness in Nishida, Nishitani, and Hisamatsu. It is interesting that although the last two thinkers straightforwardly avow an adherence to Zen, both maintain that their involvement is based on a philosophical decision that occurred at a critical stage in the evolution of their careers and not on a prior religious identification. They claim to be inspired and challenged by the ideological flexibility, independence, and open-endedness of Zen thought, which surveys all possible standpoints but remains unattached to any particular one, including even classical Buddhist doctrine. Also, the influence of Pure Land Buddhist thought, with its emphasis on an awareness of one's *karma*-stricken character and the need for reliance on other-power based redemption, is reflected in the notion of metanoesis (*zangedō*), or repentance in the thought of Tanabe and Takeuchi.

The background of Tokyo scholarship seems to be Sōtō Zen, whose monastic institution is centered in the Tokyo or Kanto (eastern) region.[1] As opposed to the Rinzai emphasis on the creative independence of individual masters, Sōtō is notable for its strong scholastic tradition—almost entirely lacking in Rinzai—based on the interpretation of the life and thought of first patriarch Dōgen Kigen (1200–1253). Tokyo scholars, many of whom have been directly or indirectly affiliated with Komazawa (formerly Sōtō-sect) University, display an impartial and even-handed examination of the stage-by-stage progression of Buddhist doctrine from India through East Asia. This scholarly approach is enhanced by presupposing the standpoint of the Zen sect, which was one of the final Mahāyāna doctrinal developments. Sōtō Zen had absorbed and interpreted the influences of all previous movements and trends.

Despite the differences in aim and method, the Kyoto and Tokyo schools should be seen as complementary and overlapping, rather than conflicting, in their basic concerns and projects. The line between them is a flexible and interpenetrable boundary and is not formed by philosophical rigidity or sectarian dogmatism. There are many instances of crossover and mutually determinative research efforts. For example, Watsuji, associated with the Kyoto school, is highly regarded for his account of primitive Buddhism written before and perhaps influencing the work in this field by Nakamura, a Tokyo scholar who is also involved in cross-cultural and comparative studies more typical of the Kyoto school. Similarly, Kyoto thinker Abe has published commentaries on and English translations of Dōgen, whom Tokyo scholar Tamaki Koshirō has analyzed in accord with the Kyoto-oriented comparative philosophical method.

The underlying connection between the Kyoto and Tokyo movements is two-fold. First, both highlight the vantage point of Japan as the last cultural stopping point in the westward movement of Mahāyāna to survey, analyze, and reappropriate the entire Buddhist tradition, encompassing South Asian and Far Eastern, Theravāda and Mahāyāna, self-power and other-power trends. Tokyo scholarship is an internal textual and historical clarification and interpretation; Kyoto thought is an external presentation and application to contemporary philosophical and cultural issues. Despite a sectarian background—or, rather, to a large extent because of the unique Zen perspective they share, which at once relies on yet perpetually overcomes Buddhist doctrine—the Kyoto and Tokyo movements view Buddhism from a panoramic, rather than a particular, cultural, linguistic, or scriptural orientation. Second, both schools use Western methodologies—existentialism and phenomenology (Kyoto), philology and hermeneutics (Tokyo)—to recapture the essential nature of the Buddhist tradition that had ironically been somewhat obscured by the modern infiltration into Japan of Western science and philosophy.

The development of the Kyoto and Tokyo schools must be seen in the context of the adversities faced by Japanese Buddhism stemming from the disestablishment of Buddhist religion and the rise of Shinto at the beginning of the Meiji period and exacerbated by postwar conditions. Although Shinto itself was disestablished after World War II, Buddhism was still challenged by several forces: increasing secularization, urbanization, and industrialization, which impaired the traditional parish organization; and the popularity of the so-called New Religions as well as the impact of Christianity, which offered alternative—and to an increasingly technologized society, perhaps more readily accessible—means of religious structure and fulfillment.

The postwar plight of Buddhism is reflected by the symbolism of Mishima Yukio's prize-winning novel, *The Temple of the Golden Pavilion*, an allegorical fictionalization of an actual event in which a young acolyte burned down one of the most beautiful and famous medieval Kyoto temples in 1950. According to Mishima's account, the exquisite grandeur of the Golden Temple haunts and oppresses the miserable antihero, Mizoguchi, whose stuttering and overwhelming feeling of isolation seem to represent defeated Japan. Not only does the temple appear too remote and otherworldly to offer comfort and solace in a contemporary context, but also its ethereal image actually interferes with and impedes the boy's psychological development, rendering him impotent in all phases of life. Mizoguchi feels forced into a constant state of self-repugnance because he must always compare his physical and spiritual deficiencies to the inalterable yet unattainable beauty of the temple.

The temple seems to be a symbol of classical Buddhist ideals that have lost their religious efficacy while retaining only their outward or ritualistic form and have degenerated into the hypocrisy and corruption of the Father Superior. The temple's master travels the red light district while remaining indifferent to Mizoguchi's suffering, offering penance for his sin only after the boy appears condemned by circumstance to a life without hope. Mizoguchi's inner torment is at every critical point aggravated rather than relieved by his association with Buddhism, until he commits the penultimate crime, an ironic and regrettable twisting of the Rinzai Zen saying, "If you see the Buddha, kill him!" The Zen adage, which is intended to inspire a spiritual liberation from all dependencies and psychological fetters, is mistaken here to constitute an actual command that compounds Mizoguchi's attachments.

Mishima neither attacks nor condones Mizoguchi but attempts to expose the conditions that allowed the tragedy to take place. Despite the forcefulness of Mishima's critique of Buddhism, the novel's symbolism seems to harbor a hidden and possibly positive message: the regeneration of Buddhism, its self-emancipation paradoxically brought about by the seeds of its own destruction, and the need to reclaim, phoenixlike, the true meaning of Rinzai's famous dictum from the ashes of its perversion. Like so many of the wooden architectural triumphs destroyed by fire and warfare throughout the history of Japan, the Golden Temple has been perfectly reconstructed. The Kyoto and Tokyo movements, by turning to the West at the nadir of Buddhist history, have understood the delicate but potentially fruitful role of Japanese Mahāyāna at the crossroads of the conflicting trends of the traditional and modern, sacred and secular, Eastern and Western, Buddhist and Christian, spiritual and scientific world views. By taking advantage of the special role of postwar Japan, struggling to reassert itself at the international frontier of the intersection and possible resolution of these inexorable ideological and cultural forces, the Kyoto and Tokyo schools have opened the path to a new affirmation and application of Buddhist scripture and ideals.

THE KYOTO SCHOOL

Founding Figures

The central figures of the Kyoto school are Nishida Kitarō (1870–1945) and Tanabe Hajime ((1885–1962). Although Nishida died in 1945 and Tanabe's work was largely completed before the end of the war, they are discussed here because their philosophies are so crucial to an understanding of the subsequent Kyoto thinkers. Nishida's investigation of "pure experience" (*junsui keiken*) and the "logic of place of absolute nothingness" establishes the philosophical goals and comparative methodology pursued by all later representatives. Tanabe's examination of the dynamics of metanoesis, which evolved near the end of World War II, highlights the unity of philosophical discourse and religious fulfillment influencing Nishitani, Takeuchi, and others.

Nishida was the first great Japanese philosopher—at least since the early medieval period and after the modern introduction of Western thought—in a cultural tradition that has emphasized the priority of literary expression rather than logical analysis. Tanabe's view of metanoesis is perhaps the initial important postwar philosophical standpoint. Because English translations of, and even Japanese commentaries on, Nishida and Tanabe are still in the formative stage, it can be expected that their work will increasingly stimulate and influence the next generation of Japanese and Western thinkers.

The term Nishida *tetsugaku* (philosophy of Nishida) was first used in recognition of Nishida's distinctive and original philosophical achievement in the mid-to-late 1920s, around the time of the publication of *From the Acting to the Seeing* (1927), which established the notion of the logic of place. The moniker "Kyoto school" initially appeared in the late 1940s to cite the formation of the movement centering around Tanabe and his followers at Kyoto University. In the original context, however, "Kyoto school" had somewhat negative connotations, reflecting the criticism leveled by the Marxists–progressives, then based in Tokyo, at the prewar nationalistic and idealistic tendencies of Nishida, Tanabe, and Nishitani. Tanabe's postwar philosophy was dedicated to clarifying his views on social action, largely in response to such criticism, through an emphasis on faith and the transformative power of absolute nothingness-as-love.

Nishida's thought developed through several stages of a complex, lifelong philosophical project. The underlying goal is a systematic disclosure of the unified ground of all forms of experiential reality. This unity encompasses the intuitive and rational, aesthetic and moral, contemplative and active, mathematical and metaphysical, disclosed in a manner that is faithful to Japanese spirituality yet Western in its logical rigor. Although references to Western thought are frequently more abundant than Buddhist sources, it is clear from both the philosophical content of his work as well as recorded private remarks to colleagues that Zen meditation lies at the root of Nishida's thought. Yet Nishida was by no means a Zen apologist. Nor did he engage in comparative philosophy as an end in itself or to assert the supremacy of Buddhism—a delicate but critical standpoint not always perfectly upheld by his disciples. Rather, comparison was used as a philosophical methodology for uncovering the universal logical-ontological foundations of the multiple manifestations and dimensions of the unity of experience.

Four stages of Nishida's philosophical development are generally delineated. The initial stage corresponds to his first major work, *A Study of Good* (1911), which analyzes reality in terms of the notion of pure experience, the direct and immediate givenness or presentness of experience. Pure experience, identified with the "good" (*zen*) as a unity of will and spirit, knowledge and action, is the fundamental moment of perception before thought, reflection, or judgment.

It is the universal intentionality, not a passive perception, to "know events as they truly are" without hesitation or deliberation. In this work, Nishida is influenced by William James's radical empiricism, though with mystical or contemplative implications based on a sense of primordial harmony, rather than James's pragmatist ethical imperative. The next stage, *Intuition and Reflection in Self-Consciousness* (1917), marks an attempt, later acknowledged by Nishida to be unsuccessful, to overcome the psychologism or overly subjectivistic tone of *A Study of Good*. Here, Nishida synthesized Henri Bergson's "pure duration" with neo-Kantian categories to eliminate psychological terminology and formulate the notion of self-consciousness as a kind of Fichtean transcendental ego at the foundation of experience.

The third stage, beginning with *From the Acting to the Seeing,* marks Nishida's breakthrough or radical reversal from the subjectivist tendencies of his previous work toward a neutral determination of reality beyond subject/object, internal/external, psychological/metaphysical dichotomizations—the "logic of place of absolute nothingness." "Absolute nothingness" (*zettai mu*) is rooted in the Mahāyāna doctrine of emptiness as the nondifferentiable and nonsubstantive ground of reality. Genuine emptiness or nothingness, though unsupported by any prior ontological condition, remains the basis of all phenomena, in contrast to the Western category of mere nonexistence or absence, for which the Japanese term *kyomu* (literally, "hollow nothingness") is used.

According to Nishida, Western thought has generally been preoccupied with the opposition between being (*u*) and *kyomu* and has failed to penetrate to absolute nothingness, with the exception of neo-Platonic mystics like Meister Eckhart, Nicholas Cusanus, and Jakob Boehme. "Place" (*basho*) is influenced by Plato's concept of *topos* as well as Husserlian phenomenology and perhaps even Einstein's physics, modern standpoints that view the world from a synthetic and dynamic contextual perspective. The notion of *basho* highlights the Zen emphasis that emptiness not be seen as an abstract transcendental realm detached from concrete existence but as perpetually and dynamically realized in and through the ever-varying manifestations of the fullness of being. It thus accords with the famous dictum from the *Heart Sutra:* "Emptiness is none other than form; form is none other than emptiness."

The three dimensions of place are:

1. The physical world of objectifiable being corresponding to the noematic realm in Husserl's terminology.

2. The world of human reality, the subjective or noetic aspect of experience; as a topological self-determination of absolute nothingness, human reality is designated as relative nothingness, a no-thing that makes possible perception of and judgments concerning objects.

3. The intelligible world of absolute nothingness, the necessary but ultimately void or nonsubstantive synthetic context for all appearances and judgments encompassing but unrestricted by the noetic and noematic, which are not independent entities linked

together but a single inseparable event; the intelligible world is the basis of the good, the true, and the beautiful, and it is realizable only through the "dazzling obscurity" of sudden and selfless illumination.

The final stage of Nishida's work, expressed in various collected philosophical essays, is a clarification of the central tenets of the previous stage in terms of the issue of disclosing the temporal-historical foundations of culture and in particular the distinctiveness of Japanese culture in contrast to the West. Nishida shows that the "logic" (*ronri*) of absolute nothingness is not a simple oneness but the dialectical interplay of antithetical forces or the "self-identity of absolute contradiction" (*zettai mujunteki jiko dōitsu*). The dialectical self-identity is manifested in time as the eternal now embracing past/future in the absolute presencing of each and every totalistic moment, a view reminiscent of Dōgen's doctrine of being-time (*uji*) as the reflexive and all-pervasive unity of all beings *as* time and all times *as* being. The eternal here-and-now also passes throughout history as action-intuition (*kōiteki chokkan*), or the identity of all existential activity and intuitive understanding.

Nishida grappled with the question of how cultures have developed in different ways on the basis of the universality of absolute nothingness. He argued that the Japanese tradition, in contrast to the Western fixation with being and nonbeing, has always been attuned to absolute nothingness. Japan is a culture of sensibility and feeling (*jōteki bunka*) that perceives the formless and soundless (*katachi naki, koe naki*) nature of reality, or the stillness at the very heart of things. In his last major essay, "The Logic of Place and the Religious World-View," which has greatly determined the direction taken by subsequent Kyoto thinkers, Nishida pointed to the logical-ontological overcoming of cultural barriers through the priority of religious experience. Religion, he maintained, is the cultural dimension that alone deals with the ultimate problem of life and death. Religion can be transformed into the new foundation for world society through a synthesizing of Christian morality and Buddhist meditation on the basis of absolute nothingness and in a manner that allows for the integrity and self-determination of each tradition as oppositions reconciled in terms of an ultimate self-identity.

Tanabe's philosophy developed both under the sway of and as a critical response to Nishida's thought. He considered Nishida overly mystical or contemplative in tone, neglecting the importance of social experience or one's interaction with the Thou (both vertically with God and horizontally with community). Tanabe's standpoint was influenced by his training in the other-power (*tariki*) tradition of Pure Land Buddhist faith rather than the self-power (*jiriki*) of Zen introspection. He was also affected by the personal experience of his wife's sacrificial suicide on his behalf and the need to reconcile and redeem his own philosophical development in light of the Japanese military defeat and subsequent antinationalist criticism. Whereas Nishida identified absolute nothingness with the transcendental good as the logical-ontological unity of opposites, Tanabe viewed nothingness in terms of the spiritual power of love in the ethical-social mission of repentance and resurrection. Whereas Nishida stressed action-intuition operating in the eternal now, Tanabe focused on the perpetual functioning of action-faith through the blind alleys and fundamental ignorance of the pathways of history.

The prewar critique of Nishida by Tanabe, whose earliest work was in the field of mathematics, is based on the notion of the "logic of species" (*shu no ronri*) as a correction of the logic of place. According to Tanabe, Nishida's philosophy stressed the primacy of the universal encompassing the particular, or of the individual subsumed by the universal, and overlooked the crucial intermediary role of the category of species operating in logic and history. At this stage, Tanabe more or less equated species with the state, a view for which he was attacked by postwar progressives.

After the war, Tanabe responded to this challenge by formulating the philosophy of continuing self-criticism or absolute criticism, a total self-negation that can only come from the side of the Absolute, which appears as the power of self-negating love. In *Philosophy as Metanoesis* (1946, but written in 1944) and other works, he argued that absolute criticism requires a metanoesis (*zangedō*) or conversion experience of resurrection through existential dying or of relinquishing one's former self to be reawakened on the basis of nothingness-as-love. In this light, Tanabe reinterpreted the Zen doctrine of the "identity of life-death" (*shōji ichinyo*) as the unified experiential moment of simultaneous self-negation and redemption in an age in which the total destruction of humankind has become a real, if not necessarily imminent, possibility.

Tanabe acknowledged that his views on redemption through total dependence on the Absolute in confronting the problematics of history are more akin to the Judaeo-Christian prophetic stance as a means of salvation than to Buddhist detachment. Buddhist nothingness, he suggested, must be permeated by love. Yet he also maintained that for Christianity to remain vital in the midst of the social-cultural upheavals of contemporary times, it must extend and radicalize Bultmann's demythologization process on the basis of Buddhist nothingness. Thus Tanabe posited his notion of absolute negation as a necessary clue to the fundamental self-criticism and cleansing required by outdated yet still relevant Christian doctrine. From the standpoint of radical demythologization, the concept of a personal God can be transformed into nothingness-as-love; the Trinity reevaluated as the threefold unity of God's love for humans, humans' love for God, and humans' love for humans; and eschatology seen not as a futural hope but as the here-and-now existential affirmation of death and resurrection.

The other two central figures in the formative period of the Kyoto movement are Watsuji Tetsurō (1884–1960) and Suzuki Daisetz (1870–1966). Neither is considered an "insider" of the Kyoto school because their philosophical aims and methodology diverge from those shared by Nishida–Tanabe and their direct followers, including Miyake Goichi (philosophy of science, history, and morality), Kuki Shuzo (philosophy of time and aesthetics), and Watanabe Kichiji (aesthetics). Yet Watsuji and Suzuki have had a profound and lasting influence on the major developments of the postwar movement. Although Watsuji's primary focus was on ethics, his work covers a broad range of theoretical and scholarly investigation. His main achievements include studies of primitive Buddhism and of early Japanese intellectual history—the aesthetics, religion, and morality of the classical and medieval periods, including especially noteworthy pieces on the *Kojiki* (the first Shinto text) and Zen master Dōgen. The latter effort is recognized as being almost singlehandedly responsible for liberating studies of Dōgen from the centuries-long dogmatic slumber of sectarianism and opening up the preeminent medieval thinker to modern philosophical and philological interpretations.

Watsuji's ethics was based on the approaches of Western phenomenology and structural linguistics applied to the distinctive aspects of Japanese society. He was influenced especially by Martin Heidegger, which whom he studied. But he was also critical of the German philosopher's almost exclusive focus on temporality in understanding the basis and diversity of human experience, which Watsuji claimed overlooks the significance of spatiality and external reality, including geographical setting and climatic conditions as well as social interaction. In *Climate* (1935), Watsuji introduced the notion of *aidagara,* the phenomenon of "betweenness" (rather than individuality) or the relationship of humans with external reality, to examine three basic types of climate that have determined the world's cultural and ethical manifestations. They include the desert zone of African and Muslim cultures, leading to a combative spirit and submission to the transcendental; the pastoral zone of ancient Greece and Europe, resulting in rationality and domination over nature; and the monsoon climate of Asia, producing a sense of resignation and patience as well as the priority of the communal spirit over individuality. In *Ethics as Anthropology* (1934), Watsuji argued that ethics is the "science of man" (the literal meaning of *ningen no gaku,* which also signifies the discipline of "anthropology"). Ethics in Japanese culture is based on a fundamentally sociocommunitarian focus ideally resulting in the emptying (*kū*) of the self, thus recalling Nishida's notion of absolute nothingness-as-good.

Suzuki was easily the twentieth-century Japanese intellectual most renowned and influential in the West. Although Nishida's philosophy remains sparsely translated and relatively unknown in many circles, the work of Suzuki, a lifelong friend of Nishida's since their boyhood days in the medieval town of Kanazawa, has been widely distributed and popularized for several decades. Although Suzuki was primarily a religious thinker and not a philosopher, his central themes seem to complement the work of Nishida. He displayed a profound and comprehensive knowledge of Chinese and Japanese Zen recorded sayings in relation to Indian and Mahāyāna scriptures, as well as the overall development of Japanese culture and spirituality. One of Suzuki's major contributions was the two-volume English translation of the *Lankāvatāra Sutra,* a central text of Mahāyāna idealism, with commentary on its ideological connection to the formation of Zen's unique approach to the experience of Buddhist awakening.

The comparative methodology used by Suzuki is somewhat compatible with Nishida's work. He analyzed Zen in light of Western religious thought from biblical references to German mysticism, although not with the logical precision or wide-ranging knowledge of philosophical sources that characterizes Nishida's investigations. Suzuki writings have been criticized for a tendency toward simplistic comparison or misleading apologetics. Yet his conclusions concerning religious fulfillment, expressed in explicitly Mahāyāna and Zen terminology and offered as a spiritual tonic for the travails of modern society, are largely consistent with Nishida's logic.

For example, in the essay "Reason and Intuition in Buddhist Philosophy," Suzuki's examination of the metapsychology of the enlightenment experience is similar to the levels of the place of nothingness. He showed through a study of numerous Zen *kōan* and *mondō* that *vijñāna* (discriminative reason, corresponding to Nishida's human reality) and *prajñā* (intuitive wisdom, corresponding to the intelligible world of absolute nothingness) are not mutually exclusive but dynamically and dialectically interdependent at every moment. Suzuki demonstrated that Buddhist enlightenment is not an abstract or otherworldly realm of negation but the insight of transcendental detachment that can and must be effectively integrated with everyday life. He thereby suggested the basis for a possible transformation of the modern scientific world view that is preoccupied with objectification and is indifferent to genuine subjectivity. Suzuki pointed to a reconciliation of science with the nothingness of intuition, which is not the opposite of reason but the true ground of its arising, evolution, and historical determination.

Nishitani Keiji (1900-), editor of the English language *Eastern Buddhist* journal of Otani University, founded by Suzuki and now considered the "house organ" of the Kyoto movement, is looked on as the current "dean" of the school. In the generation of thinkers after Nishida and Tanabe, Nishitani has developed the most original and challenging philosophical outlook and method. Nishitani combines many of the central elements of the formative Kyoto thinkers but is distinctive in his focus on the multiple dimensions of nihilism in relation to absolute nothingness and the restoration of genuine religiosity from the apparent modern dominance of science and technology. That is, Nishitani uncompromisingly directs his philosophical efforts toward overcoming the contemporary conflict between spirituality and science, teleology and mechanism. As he repeatedly stresses, "one of the greatest, most fundamental problems all religions face in our times is their relationship to science. The world view prevalent in science and the scientific way of thinking in general appear to be fundamentally incompatible with the world view and ontology which traditional religions have by and large made their basis."[2] This crisis, he believes, arose because of and must therefore be dealt with by Christianity, which is challenged to its very core and yet remains reluctant and perhaps at this time even incapable of finding an answer to it. Nishitani maintains that the Zen approach to emptiness alone holds the philosophical key for a thoroughgoing resolution.

Nishitani's method is influenced by Nishida's logical analysis of the three levels of place of absolute nothingness, which he applied as a means of existentially evaluating the gradations of nihilism reflected in science, traditional religion, atheism, and mysticism in terms of whether or not they express an authentic awareness of emptiness. From Tanabe, he understands both the need for a fundamental conversion experience to realize nothingness, which he interpreted in terms of the traditional Zen notion of the Great Death (or complete renunciation of ego), and the possibility of a radical demythologization of Christian doctrine in the light of Buddhism to liberate Christianity from—yet to— itself. Nishitani also seems to expand Watsuji's focus on the ethical priority underlying philosophical investigation and to share Suzuki's detailed and profound knowledge and interpretation of Zen *kōan*, epistles and anecdotes.

In his straightforward ideological commitment to Zen, Nishitani is perhaps closest to Suzuki's approach. Yet he does not claim a personal enlightenment. He speaks in the international intellectual arena not as a sectarian representative but rather as a contemporary philosopher who has chosen Zen because of its uniquely flexible and open-ended perspective. Nishitani considers—borrowing Kierkegaardian terminology that Tanabe has used to describe his own relationship to Christianity—that he is a *werdener* (in-the-making) Buddhist rather than a *gewordener* (fully accomplished) Buddhist. Having completed his earliest scholarly work on Aristotle and then having studied the varieties of existentialism, German idealism, and neo-Platonic mysticism among Western philosophies, Nishitani sees himself as on the way or traversing the path toward Buddhist realization as a unity of philosophical awareness and soteriological fulfillment.

Nishitani stresses that he embraces Zen not out of his Japanese background but because of all thought systems Zen constitutes a self-surpassing or excelsior (*kōjō*) religio-philosophical standpoint that constantly rises above partiality or particularity, including its own rootedness in traditional Mahāyāna doctrine, to assume a universal and transcendental perspective. In the modern era, in which the encounter between religions is imperative because of the challenge of science and the very essence of religion is sought by philosophical theologians and historians, the process of creative dialogue between traditions requires a stepping out from particularity to the realm of complete openness. Thus Zen for Nishitani is not just a religion but the paradigmatic one that allows the dialogical process to take place. Because Zen demands continuous demythologization by its own essence through the Great Death, which is none other than existential rebirth to one's primordial nature or the Formless Self of absolute nothingness, it can and must be used as the guide and framework for the interchange between and realignment of other religions as well.

In addition to Zen, a crucial determinative factor in Nishida's philosophical development is existentialism. Nishida and Tanabe, especially the latter, were intrigued by Kierkegaard's critique of Western metaphysics in relation to inauthentic (or not truly subjective) religiosity. Nishitani, however, seems to be most influenced by the later writings of Nietzsche and Heidegger. Both philosophers attempted to criticize the entire Western religious and philosophical tradition as inherently and inevitably deficient because it is cut off from its true source of wisdom. Nietzsche's reevaluation of values was based on an affirmation of creative nihilism, a Dionysian yea-saying to the bottomless ground of reality. The courage and joy of the overman provides a sharp contrast to the weary nihilism that covers up the abyss of existence with false hopes of eternalism, as propagated by Platonic idealism and Christian eschatology. Heidegger sought an overcoming of what he considered the debilitating fixation of the Western *onto-theo-logical* tradition (including Nietzsche's will to will) with substantive beings—a tendency arising as a fateful consequence of the primordial concealment or oblivion of Being that lies at the root of the hegemony of technology.

Nishitani reoriented both Nietzsche's views on positive (creative) and negative (weary) nihilism and Heidegger's disclosure of the oblivion of Being as partial or limited manifestations of absolute nothingness. They represent standpoints that in their criticism at once point to but sway from the authentic philosophical direction because they lack the appropriate and ultimate ontological anchor of emptiness. Yet Nishitani retained the sense of urgency and immediacy characteristic of the existentialists' writing in the face of the imminent and potentially apocalyptic danger that modern society has brought on itself through its essentially nihilistic affirmation of technological progress. Nishitani's sensitivity to this issue seems to be further enhanced by his Japanese perspective. A key undercurrent of his philosophy is a heightened awareness of Japan's postwar role that was introduced into Kyoto school philosophy by Tanabe's metanoesis. Not only is Japan the leading cultural representative of Buddhism uniquely situated at the intersection of East-West thought, but it is the only victim of nuclear attack that must transform that tragic and sorrowful experience into a moral obligation to illuminate the cause of world harmony through the existentialist-oriented dialectics of the Great Death. Zen is at once the most primordial and the most current standpoint, Nishitani argued, "beyond the teleological and the mechanistic view of the world, a standpoint beyond the qualitative image of the world that consists of concrete eidetic variety, and the quantitative image of the world that yields to an indefinite analysis . . . [offering a new] vision in which these opposite (even contradictorily opposite) ways of viewing the world (the positive and the negative) interpenetrate each other and become one and the same way of looking at the world, a vision that can see 'a wooden man sing and a stone woman dance.' "[3]

Nishitani's approach to the connection between philosophy and religion seems to bear an inverse relation to Nishida's concerns and methods. The starting point for Nishida was the philosophical query "What is the nature of pure experience?" that eventually led him to proclaim that only mystical insight discloses the fundamental structure of reality. Nishitani's leading question was "What is religion?" (the title of one of his main works, published in 1961), which involves an examination of the metaphysical foundations of religious experience.[4] Both thinkers, however, appear to view the relationship between absolute and relative,

I and Thou, God and humans, not from the standpoint of one side or the other of an irreconcilable opposition but from the transcendental perspective of the "and," which constitutes the conjunctive process itself. The "and" represents the locus or place of absolute nothingness, encompassing the interdependence, ultimate insubstantiality, and thus the absolute mediation of nonobjectifiable opposites. Yet Nishitani's philosophical commitment to Zen as the means of achieving the transcendental viewpoint is perhaps stronger that that of Nishida, whose commentaries on religion and culture often reflect the influence of Christian mysticism and existentialism.

The aim and purpose of religion, according to Nishitani, has become questionable in modern times because of the challenge to its traditional ground and status as the repository of human values and meaning in relation to the cosmos. The crisis religion faces arises from diverse but converging cultural and intellectual trends: the prevalence of the antireligious standpoint of science that views religion as obsolete and dysfunctional; the pervasiveness of the tendency toward atheistic humanism and secularism, with its attitude of casual indifference toward religion; and the revival of the suprareligious outlook of mysticism, which seeks to supercede the limitations of traditional forms of worship.[5]

The key factor in Nishitani's analysis is modern science, which seems to lie at the root of the development of the other tendencies. The early twentieth-century optimism concerning science, which at first challenged and threatened to replace traditional religion as an explanation of the origin and meaning of the world, has, since the advent of the nuclear age, proven false or misguided. Religion, which may have initially responded by condemning or ignoring science and then reluctantly accepting it as an alternative viewpoint, has begun to face an even deeper challenge: overcoming the inadequacies and potential devastation that science and its by-product technology cause. The issue of religion and science has an immediacy and urgency for Nishitani, recalling Nietzsche and the later Heidegger, that is motivated by the need for a universal spiritual recovery in an era when nihilism reigns and the constant yet frightful specter of technology destroying creation itself is irrevocably felt. Now, science functions as the enemy rather than the usurper of the role of religion. Yet traditional religion, once attacked, cannot reclaim its position of moral superiority without undergoing a thoroughly penetrating and transformative self-analysis of its own foundations and relation to science.

Nishitani maintained, therefore, that to raise the question of religion in itself discloses the Great Doubt, the profound existential skepticism of the Zen approach to awakening through the encounter of the self with the void or nothingness as conventional values are undercut or seem to lose validity. If the Great Doubt is only partially or half-heartedly confronted, this results in varying degrees of nihilism, from the empty routine of everyday consumerism to the philosophical atheism of Sartre and, finally, the destructive impulses of science. A full resolution of the Great Doubt is engendered by a transformation of the relative levels of nothingness or nihilism into an awareness of absolute nothingness, constituting the experience of the Great Death or Zen metanoesis. Thus the question of religion is only answered by the paradigmatic or protoreligious perspective of Zen.

The central problem confronting traditional religion is due to the uncertainty and inconsistency of Christianity pertaining to science. Nishitani by no means set out to attack Christianity, and he sincerely applauded it as a necessary and valuable influence on Japanese culture. Rather, he charged that Christianity is responsible for the arising of science without a solution to the dangers science creates because it does not understand its own ontological ground and cannot do so without a Great Doubt/Death metanoesis. The mechanistic world view of science asserts the lifelessness of the cosmos and thus a preoccupation with death, in contrast to the religious affirmation of life, soul, and spirit. Yet, echoing Heidegger, Nishitani argued that "the essence of science is not 'scientific.' The essence of science is something to be brought into question in the same realm where the essence of man becomes a question to man himself."[6] That is, the foundations of science are based on a particular view of self and reality that is paradoxically rooted in the Christian ideology with which science conflicts.

Science arose because of a fundamental contradiction within Christianity that advocates salvation through the total dependence of humans upon God and divine will, thereby suppressing genuine self-realization, and yet—because of the emphasis on such a reliance—does not allow for full freedom from egocentricity. The Christian faith experience as dying to self and living in God neither liberates the individual from ego nor allows the individual to come into his or her own as a free subject. The individual subject is thereby left restricted, restless, and unfulfilled, creating an underlying shortsightedness of self-interest and self-centeredness that continues to haunt Christianity. The Christian standpoint renders itself unable to dialogue constructively or even coexist with other religions. At the same time, the suppressed subjectivity inherent in Christianity results in an overvaluation of objectivity, leading in turn to the scientific manipulation and exploitation of the world seen as a collection of objectifiable entities, a tendency that arises from yet negates the heart of Christian faith.

Christianity is not so much wrong as it is misguided and in need of self-transformation through a Tanabean process of demythologization. An example of how Christianity is cut off from its authentic roots is its view of personal relationships. Christian (or more generally Judeao-Christian) piety as depicted by Ludwig Feuerbach, Martin Buber, and others is based on the I-Thou experience in which the human I stands in relation to God as an Absolute Thou or Absolute Other and thus views other humans as absolutely other to itself. This standpoint creates artificial barriers between humans and true selfhood as well as between the individual and others. "What is required," according to Nishitani, "is an equality [of I and Thou] in which the negation of the individual and his freedom would become the absolute affirmation of the individual and his freedom."[7] Such a metanoesis is achieved through the Zen perspective of absolute nondifferentiation in which the I is absolutely equal to the Thou, and the Thou is absolutely equal to the I. "In this way the I is a true I and the Thou a true Thou. This is the genuine I-Thou relation."[8] The perspective of Zen can be applied to Christian doctrine by the demythologization of a dogma such as the Virgin Birth. Nishitani suggested that the Virgin Birth be understood not as a historical event in which the Thou (as Absolute Other) reveals itself to the I of humans. Rather, it represents the universal religious truth that all people are born of a virgin birth to primordial innocence and purity since the arising of a transcendental perspective in humans does not rely on human origins, but is at once beyond and encompassing the identity of I-Thou, God-human, self-other.

Nishitani explored and evaluated various levels of nihilism that occupy the domain of the Great Doubt as alternative responses to the challenges faced by traditional religion. His method of interpretation was greatly influenced by the terminology and categories of Heideggerian hermeneutics. Yet Nishitani's focus is mainly on the atheistic existentialist philosophies of Sartre and Nietzsche, which, he argued, have arisen out of the all-pervasive influence of the pessimistic nihilism of science. Sartre's humanism, a direct offshoot of science, attempts a transition from Christian theocentrism to anthropocentrism, from total dependence upon God as Absolute Other to the individual as the master of his fate, but without a breakthrough to the Zen perspective of nonego through the non-differentiation of I and Thou. The merit of Sartre's approach to atheism lies not in its opposition to Christianity but as a step in the process of demythologization or mediation to a new conception of God that acknowledges rather than ignores or covers up nihilism as a manifestation of the Great Doubt.

According to Nishitani, "Nietzsche's position on atheism and existentialism is far more comprehensive and penetrating than Sartre's."[9] Nietzsche's doctrine of eternal recurrence points beyond humanism to the joyous affirmation of the unity of humans, God, and nature seen from the perspective of Dionysian yea-saying. Nietzsche, who rejected the "abyss of scientific conscience," fully confronted and accepted nihility as possessing a transcendent quality by becoming the field of being and the ground of freedom. Nishitani, however, seems to agree with Heidegger's critique of Nietzsche's overman as an ideal that remains bound to the assertion of a willful—and thus relative—response to nothingness.

The next and crucial step for Nishitani, at which even Nietzsche fell short, is a radical transformation or self-emptying of nihility as relative nothingness through a metanoesis to absolute nothingness unbound by the dichotomies of life and death, being and nonbeing, atheism and theism, humanism and theocentrism. Nishitani seems to concur with Nishida that of all Western thinkers, only the neo-Platonic mystics have reached a genuine understanding of nothingness, as in Eckhart's notion of detachment and poverty in the tranquil "desert" of the groundless (*Un-grund*) Godhead.

Influenced by Dōgen's Zen analysis of reality as the unified totality of being-time (*uji*) as well as Heidegger's phenomenological hermeneutics of Dasein's time and temporality (the time of human existence), Nishitani used the question of time as an issue to examine and evaluate the relative levels of awareness of nothingness. The Zen view of time, based on a realization of absolute nothingness, recognizes the dynamism and fluidity of all ephemeral beings at once spontaneously and simultaneously manifest at and as all temporal occasions. From the Zen perspective, the presupposed separations between humans and time, humans and beings, potentiality and actuality, life and death, and past/present/future are cast aside in the holistic here-and-now experience. Nishitani argued that for Buddhism, "time is circular, because all its time systems are simultaneous; and, as a continuum of individual 'nows' wherein the systems are simultaneous, it is *rectilinear* as well. Time is at once circular and rectilinear ... [with] an infinite openness at the bottom of time, like a great expanse of vast, skylike emptiness that cannot be confined to any systematic enclosure."[10]

In complete contrast to Zen, science sees time from the standpoint of mechanistic causality in which reality consists of lifeless matter devoid of spirit or underlying aim and direction. The Christian approach to *telos* and teleology highlights and affirms the meaning of futural possibility in the attainment of eternal salvation but at the same time overlooks here-and-now existence. Nietzsche accentuated the transiency or incessant change of time when he spoke of "the 'moment' as the twinkling of an eye (*Augenblick*)," Nishitani maintained, "but it is a moment standing against a background of Eternal Recurrence and hence does not possess the bottomlessness of the true moment. Hence, it cannot signify the point where something truly new can take place."[11] Again, it is Eckhart's organic conception of the "eternal now" that comes closest to absolute nothingness. Eckhart, according to Nishitani, viewed the Godhead from the standpoint of the ultimate identity of affirmation and negation, eternity and the present, life and death, in the concrete moment of fully realized subjectivity.

The Zen perspective can lead to a demythologization of Christian teleology because it involves a radical reversal whereby the self finds its *telos* in the self itself and at the same time finds it in all other beings. In this light, Christian piety can be interpreted not as a dedication to the memory of the events of God's creation or Christ's resurrection but as the bottomless and holistic moment "when the self experiences the *metanoia* to faith that represents the solemn moment when the solemnity of those other moments is truly realized."[12] The here-and-now moment of faith experience thereby encompasses all previous and forthcoming sacred events.

In a remarkable essay, "Science and Zen," Nishitani applied the Zen perspective on time and nothingness to an overcoming of the ideological limitations in the scientific world view. He examined several noted Zen *kōan* concerning the mythical eschatology of the "kalpa fire," which is symbolically analogous to the imminent possibility of the cosmic conflagration science and technology have wrought. In the first *kōan,* a monk asked master Daizui, "When the kalpa fire flares up and the great cosmos is destroyed, I wonder, will 'it' perish or will it not perish?" Daizui replied, "It will perish." According to Nishitani, the "it" refers to the inner dimension of self-realization, thereby giving an existential interpretation to the myth, or a demythologization whereby the scientific and/or apocalyptic possibility is understood as the existential actuality of here-and-now encounter with the Great Doubt/Death.

In a similar *kōan,* Zen master Tōshi is asked, "How is it at the time of the all-consuming kalpa fire?" and responds, "An unspeakably awesome cold." The paradoxical response, expressing the bottomless depths of absolute nothingness, suggests a level of religious experience unknown to science, which forces a reorientation and reevaluation of the presuppositions of the scientific world view. *"In the religiosity of Zen Buddhism,"* Nishitani maintained, *"demythologization of the mythical and existentialization of the scientific belong to one and the same process.* Religious existence in the Great Death makes possible at once the demythologizing of the myth of eschatology and the existentializing of the scientific actuality of the cosmos."[13]

In review, it appears that Nishitani's central contribution to the Buddhist philosophy of the Kyoto school lies in his reclamation and revitalization of Zen in the contemporary international intellectual arena. Nishida and Suzuki demonstrated that Zen is not an anachronistic nature-oriented standpoint but an essential and meaningful contributor to modern philosophy and religious thought. Nishitani extended their approach in a bold direction by declaring that Zen will inevitably occupy the forefront of postmodern cultural developments. The Zen experience of the Great Death is the paradigm of transformation not only for world religions but for all existent and possible ideologies. It constitutes the primordial realization from which other standpoints in their partiality arise and the standard that can revise and redeem them.

Thus Nishitani has recast the question that modernity seems to pose—can the seemingly archaic naturalistic outlook of Zen survive in an industrialized world— by asking: will technological culture itself endure without the metanoesis uniquely expressed by Zen? In so doing, however, Nishitani seems to have overlooked or neglected several issues that will perhaps be handled by the next generation of Kyoto thinkers. First, Nishitani's ontological clarification of Zen, Christianity, and science implies that Zen has a corresponding ethics that will be effective and purifying in the crises faced by contemporary society. But Zen has traditionally never been strong in the formulation of ethical theory. Zen offers a phenomenological analysis of the "is-ness" of reality, yet does not necessarily explain "oughtness" on a collective and historical basis beyond the requirement for individual meditation and monastic order. The limitations of Zen in regard to moral practice have been exposed by Mishima Yukio's *Golden Pavilion.* Nishitani's suggestion that the synthesis of Christian morality and Buddhist metaphysics will only result from a metanoesis of the ontological shortcomings of Christianity may be valid, but he needs to develop an argument from the other side about the transformation of Zen ethics.

Second, although Nishitani highlighted the flexibility and open-ended quality of Zen as the basis for philosophical dialogue, he did not account for the historical weaknesses of Buddhism in Japan and other Asian countries, which is crucial to interpreting its concrete role in future cultural developments. Why, for example, had Buddhism become secondary to Shinto in Japanese religious life through World War II, and why has it offered so little resistance to communism in China and Southeast Asia? If Buddhism has had difficulties in its native territories, how will it be successful in offsetting ideologies on foreign soil? A related area, not handled by Nishitani despite the postwar Marxist critique of the Kyoto school, concerns the challenge of communism to Buddhism and Christianity, which seems to be at least as significant a threat to traditional religion as science. What, from the Zen perspective, are the connections—ontological, ethical, and historical—between science, atheism, existentialism, and Marxism?

In addition, Nishitani's critique of science perhaps shows a lack of sensitivity to the distinction between science as theory and technology as practice. By setting up so strong an opposition between science and Zen, Nishitani may be overlooking the importance of Suzuki's subtle analysis of *prajñā* as the root, and not negation, of *vijñāna*. Heidegger's approach to the overcoming of *techne* through a hermeneutics of the early Greek philosophy from which it arose as a consequence of the oblivion of Being may also be helpful in clarifying this point. Finally, Nishitani did not comment on the possible ideological convergence, rather than conflict, between Zen and post-Einsteinean physics, which rejects Newton's mechanistic model in favor of a view of the cosmos as the process of the relative and dynamic unfolding of the space-time continuum. "Einstein's universe" may be much closer to Zen than Nishitani realized, which validates Zen ontology but also demands a new level of dialogue and mutual evaluation between the two traditions.[14] To both avoid one-sidedness and gain a hearing from scientists, Nishitani needs to acknowledge and interpret the scientific notion of complementarity (viewing one phenomenon from two distinct but complementary perspectives, as for example atoms seen as particles or waves) in light of Zen paradoxicality as an expression of absolute nothingness.

The other central figures of the Kyoto school include Takeuchi Yoshinori (1914-) and Hisamatsu Shin'ichi (1889–1980), renowned for their creative and innovative interpretations of Pure Land and Zen, respectively, in light of the categories of modern philosophy; and Abe Masao (1915-), Ueda Shizuteru (1926-), and Yanagida Seizan (1922-), noted for their philosophical, comparative, and historical accounts of the ideological connections between previous Buddhist thought, Western thought, and the Kyoto movement.

Takeuchi and Hisamatsu seem to represent opposite ends of the philosophical spectrum of the Kyoto school. Takeuchi is the son of, and is himself, a practicing priest of Jōdo Shin Buddhism who considers himself "a believer of extremely conservative stamp" in the Pure Land doctrine of other-power. His primary philosophical mentor is Tanabe, whose notion of metanoesis was greatly influenced by Christian theology, emphasizing the need for total dependence on an absolute beyond humans. Hisamatsu, a personal and ideological disciple of Nishida, rejected a childhood upbringing in Pure Land faith and dedicated his life to the study and practice of Zen, which he interpreted in terms of the notion of absolute subjectivity, or the religio-nomy of the Absolute Self (*zettai jishateki shūkyō ritsu).* Only the self, according to Hisamatsu, can free itself from its self-created entanglements to realize its true basis as the Formless Self of absolute nothingness. Despite their divergent approaches, both thinkers have highlighted the essence of religious fulfillment rather than the sweeping cultural concerns of Nishitani and others, stressing that philosophical reflection must arise on the basis of personal, existential experience and not the other way around.

In his major work, *The Heart of Buddhism: In Search of the Timeless Spirit of Primitive Buddhism* (1972), Takeuchi explored the philosophical and practical connections between Shinran's Pure Land doctrine and primitive Buddhism. This may seem an unlikely task because the historical Buddha's spirit of attaining wisdom that is self-generated by meditation appears at odds with Shinran's belief in salvation through grace, unless the two approaches are mediated by a discussion of the Mahāyāna doctrine of the threefold Buddha-body *(Trikāya).*[15] But by "primitive Buddhism"—for which the term *Ur-Buddhism* is used—Takeuchi meant not only, literally, the early or Pali literature but, conceptually, the essential standpoint of fundamental Buddhist doctrine, which embodies an outlook that at once lies at the basis of and resolves any dichotomy between self-power and other-power practices.

Takeuchi's methodology combines a Bultmann/Tanabe demythologization of the religious expressions of Buddha and Shinran to highlight their common experiential basis and a Heideggerian phenomenological hermeneutics of scriptural utterances to demonstrate the unified understanding underlying diverse levels and dimensions of discourse. Takeuchi also used these contemporary methodologies to evaluate critically various interpretations—Eastern and Western, Buddhist and Christian, classical and modern—of particular Buddhist doctrines as well as the universality of other-power thought.

The discussion focuses on two categories of primitive Buddhist doctrine that disclose the significance of the Pure Land approach to the overall "Buddhist appeal to awaken to the absolute reality of truth."[16] First, the techniques and stages of meditation—referred to as "centering"—are analyzed in terms of the four contemplative states *(dhyāna)* and the four sublime states *(brahma-vihāra),* which culminate in a synthesis of compassion and contemplation, love and renunciation. The second category—"freeing"—is the notion of dependent origination *(pratītya-samutpāda)* and related conceptions of the five aggregates *(skandha)* and eighteen fields *(dhatu),* which describe human experience of the world in terms of interrelated and causally determined events. Dependent origination represents a twofold movement of forward progression toward the perpetuation of suffering and ignorance and backward digression through self-denial and self-transcendence to the extinction of desire.

The quintessential illuminative experience reflected in both meditation and causality, according to Takeuchi, is world transcendence, which "entails a sense of 'from . . . to' that involves not only a transcendence from the hither shore to the yonder shore, but no less a transcendent 'ad-vent' *(Zu-kunft)* from the yonder shore to the hither shore. . . . In other words, world transcendence is something that ad-venes as it transcends.''[17] The aspect of transcendence is the engagement of individual effort leading to the attainment of a goal, and the corresponding and simultaneous aspect of tran*des*cendence or advency is the arrival of the saving grace of Amida Buddha. Thus ''the grace of God is active insofar as the believer has arrived ek-statically (transcending-trandescending) on the way of encounter'' at the locus of absolute nothingness-as-love.[18]

Because of his Pure Land orientation, Takeuchi is at times more direct than previous Kyoto school thinkers in identifying absolute nothingness with the Christian conception of God. Takeuchi also displays a favorable attitude toward what he considers the comprehensiveness of the Christian view of time. He argued, in contrast to Nishitani, that whereas Zen emphasizes the present in terms of here-and-now awakening and Pure Land the future through its soteriological expectations, Christianity combines these dimensions of time with a focus on the past in terms of historical revelation. Yet Takeuchi is also in accord with Tanabe that Christian religious experience, however valuable in highlighting the mutuality of the loving and pious social encounter, remains inherently limited unless its personal view of God is transmuted into a transcendental awareness of nothingness.

Like Takeuchi, Hisamatsu explored modern and Western methodologies to transcend primitive or basic Buddhism conceptually and chronologically while arriving closer to its core, thus lending a sense of contemporaneity and spontaneity to the original doctrine. As in the case of Nishitani's development, Hisamatsu's commitment to Zen was not based on his Japanese background but resulted from a lifelong quest for the ideal philosophical standpoint that is true to reality yet devoid of one-sidedness or presupposition. In contrast to some of the Kyoto thinkers, however, Hisamatsu's philosophical project, referred to by Abe Masao as the ''philosophy of awakening,'' is seemingly modest yet profound. He claimed not to have expanded or extended Buddhist thought but simply to have captured the essential Buddhist religious experience.

In that sense, Hisamatsu was by no means unique in a religion whose tradition is based on individual reappropriation and emulation of the historical Buddha's enlightenment. But the simplicity of his goal is precisely its depth and complexity. Hisamatsu's creativity and contribution to the Kyoto school lie in focusing attention on the existential and soteriological rather than the ontological or theoretical dimensions of Zen. The authenticity of self-realization of the Absolute Self, he argued, must be before any speculative inquiry or examination. Philosophy is rooted in, and thus can only genuinely spring from, the experience of self-awakening. In both his own artistic achievements and his scholarly works, such as *Zen and the Fine Arts* (1958), Hisamatsu demonstrated that the literary, visual, and practical arts—including poetry, painting, calligraphy, gardening, and tea ceremony—are necessary and inevitable expressions of awakening. Furthermore, his personal magnetism expressed in the subtleties of everyday conversation and social behavior and eulogized by numerous colleagues and friends seems ample testimony to an authentic interior awareness.[19]

Hisamatsu was raised in a fundamentalist Shin Buddhist family and spent his early years as a steadfast and devout believer. By college, however, his impulse toward philosophical reasoning shed grave doubts on the significance of what he came to consider the naive and irrational Pure Land beliefs in good and evil, heaven and hell, and he embarked on a search for the fulfillment of his philosophical insight. This led to the formal study of Eastern and Western philosophy under Nishida, who eventually advised Hisamatsu to reexplore and reorient his original religious concern through Zen meditation. During his first year of Zen practice, Hisamatsu achieved a breakthrough to the Great Death experience, which provided him with the appropriate vantage point to evaluate the relationship of traditional philosophy to the essential religious quest realized in Zen.

The formative period in Hisamatsu's philosophical development was his thorough investigation of—and final and deliberate turning from—the philosophical reasoning of Descartes, Hegel, Kant, and other modern thinkers in light of Zen practice. Reason, Hisamatsu discovered, is wrought with inherent shortcomings and limitations in attempting to accomplish its ultimate goal: a life of truth, or an experience that is authentically based on the meaning of life. If followed to its logical conclusion, reason invariably leads to self-entanglement, self-contradiction, and eventual self-collapse. That is, reason can attain only a partial awareness of the Great Doubt, which becomes an experience reason can neither fully confront nor adequately resolve. The Great Doubt constitutes the undercutting of the very ground of reason by exposing to reason its own futility and exhaustion.

The Great Doubt is beyond Cartesian skepticism or the Kantian transcendental critique of metaphysics. It represents the fundamental existential crisis concerning the foundation or meaning of the self through encounter with absolute nothingness and thus demands a radical turn from the philosophical pursuit of objective values and concepts to the religious attainment of subjective truth. Hisamatsu largely agrees with Kierkegaard, who rejected reason for a life of the subjectivity of passionate concern. Yet Hisamatsu's subjectivity is reached not through faith in a doctrine that is a ''scandal'' to reason but through the complete abandonment of reason to realize the Formless or Absolute Self of absolute nothingness. The Great Doubt is transmuted to the Great Death when the self autonomously and spontaneously casts itself off from both itself and the stranglehold of reason to which it had been bound.

Thus Hisamatsu viewed absolute nothingness as subjective nothingness, or the nothingness of absolute subjectivity based on a continuing existential encounter with and renunciation of reason. By ''subjective'' he meant not the subject in an epistemological polarity with the object (*shukanteki* in Japanese) but the holistic, fully integrated self (*shutaiteki*) encompassing self and other, humans and nature, and all other dualities. He is wary of cosmological or ontological interpretations that tend to misrepresent subjective nothingness as a realm outside of human experience, and he seemed to suggest that a demythologization process must be carried out within Zen to avoid this philosophical pitfall. As Abe noted, "The *autonomy* of [Hisamatsu's] self-extricated realization is sharp and clear to an extent never before seen in the long history of Zen."[20]

In "The Characteristics of Oriental Nothingness," Hisamatsu clarified (in light of the Kegon Buddhist doctrine of totality) that nothingness is neither absence nor nonexistence, neither nonbeing as opposed to being nor an atheistic or nihilistic notion, neither the ineffability of mystical unity nor an ethereal ideal beyond humans. Rather, nothingness is found directly and concretely in the boundless expanse of the essential functioning of self-renewing Self-Awakening. In *Zen and the Fine Arts,* Hisamatsu showed that representations of humans and nature in Zen art, embodying the qualities of asymmetry, simplicity, naturalness, tranquility, and detachment, do not "stand for" something greater but in and of themselves fully express the ultimate standpoint. A painting or arrangement of flowers, for example, does not point beyond itself to some hidden truth but divulges the unconditioned freedom and unity of artist/observer and flower/observed, each actively engaging and realizing the Absolute Self of both itself and non-self or other.

The remaining figures—Abe, Ueda, and Yanagida—have contributed studies in comparative philosophy and intellectual history clarifying the development and significance of the Kyoto school in relation to Buddhist and Western thought, and filling in some of the "gaps" or areas of inquiry introduced or implied but left unattended by the previous Kyoto thinkers. Abe is perhaps the most visible presence and eloquent spokesman of the Kyoto school in America today. He has taught and lectured extensively in major universities and forums throughout the country and has produced a substantive body of translations and publications in English. Among his works are essays on the metaphysics of Dōgen along with a series of translations (in collaboration with Norman Waddell and published in the *Eastern Buddhist*) of representative portions of Dōgen's writings, including some of the most important fascicles of the *Shōbōgenzō*. The translation series, which has philologically comprehensive and philosophically illuminating annotations, sets a high standard for English-language scholarship not only in the field of Zen or Japanese thought but in Asian and comparative studies as a whole. In numerous philosophical essays, Abe also expanded and refined the Kyoto method of critically evaluating Buddhist thought in light of various Western standpoints, including Christianity (biblical and mystical doctrine), existentialism (Nietzsche and Heidegger), and idealism (Spinoza and Hegel).

Ueda Shizuteru is noted for his explication of Nishida's philosophy in terms of Zen thought and poetry in comparative light with German mysticism and idealism, including a major study published in German on the mystical doctrine of Meister Eckhart. Yanagida, a significant force in Kyoto Buddhist thought and scholarship, though less known than the others in the West where his works have not yet frequently appeared in translation, highlights the historical, doctrinal, and practical connections between Zen and various forms and levels of

Mahāyāna scripture as well as Japanese culture. Yanagida has collaborated with Nishitani in editing an important collection of the sayings and anecdotes (*goroku*) of Zen masters.

THE TOKYO APPROACH

The Tokyo approach to Buddhist studies seems to be complementary to the Kyoto school in aim and methodology. The method of Tokyo scholarship is historical–philological rather than comparative–philosophical. Its aim is a systematic and comprehensive analysis and interpretation of every stage in the development of Buddhist doctrine from its origins in India through permeations in China, Tibet, Korea, and finally Japan, rather than a speculative exploration of horizonal issues concerning the nature and structure of reality in relation to cultural, ethical, and scientific topics. As indicated above, there is no strict and impassable division between the two approaches. Key figures such as Kyoto thinkers Watsuji and Yanagida in their historical studies and Tokyo scholars Nakamura and Tamaki in their cross-cultural and philosophical works seem to traverse the boundaries. The more limited attention given to Tokyo scholarship in this chapter is in no way intended to imply criticism or suggest a lesser degree of significance in the context of Japanese Mahāyāna thought. Rather, this reflects the relative importance of the Tokyo approach in the West where its impact, with some key exceptions, has not been greatly felt except among scholars of East Asian Buddhism.

The development of Tokyo scholarship began in the Meiji period through the incorporation of Western academic methodologies and languages as well as traditional Indian scholasticism to the study of Sanskrit, Tibetan, and Chinese Buddhist texts. It represented an attempt to strengthen and renew Buddhism largely in response to the threat of Shinto nationalism seeking to replace traditional Buddhist parish institutions and the challenge of new ideologies introduced by Western religious and scientific thought. The preeminent scholars of this period include Nanjō Bunyū, who learned Sanskrit in Europe and stressed the importance of Indian Buddhist studies, and Anaesaki Masaharu in the field of the history of Japanese Buddhism.

Buddhist studies was at first centered in Tokyo University but eventually spread to other leading institutions, such as Komazawa, Rissho, Taisho, Toyo, and Waseda universities. The towering and most influential prewar scholar was Takakusu Junjirō (1866–1945), whose works include the Taishō edition of the Chinese Tripitika, the complete collection of the Pali Tripitika, as well as numerous Japanese translations of Hindu scriptures, including the *Rig-veda,* the *Upanishads,* and the *Bhagavad-gita.* The main follower of Takakusu in the postwar period is Ui Hakuju, noted for his compilation of the definitive Buddhist dictionary as well as writings on Indian and Japanese Buddhism. Perhaps the most eminent Tokyo scholar of the postwar era is Nakamura Hajime (1912-), who not only continued the focus on Indian studies with an authoritative multivolume account of primitive Buddhism but also advanced the field of Japanese and Oriental intellectual and religious history, demonstrating a scope reminiscent of the great Kyoto thinkers. Other leading Tokyo university figures include Hirakawa Akira and Hirai Shunrei in primitive Buddhism, Takasaki Jikidō in *tathāgata-garbha* thought, Kamata Shigeo in Hua-yen and *Avatamsaka Sutra* studies, Tamaki Koshirō in comparative philosophy, and Hanayama Shinshō in Japanese Buddhism. Among the leading Komazawa University scholars are Masunaga Reihō, Kagamishima Genryū, Kurebayashi Kōdō, and Kawamura Kōdō in Dōgen and Sōtō Zen studies, and Yoshizu Yoshihide who deals with the connection between Hua-yen and Zen. Other notables are Ienaga Saburō and Tsuji Zennosuke on medieval Japanese Buddhism and Hori Ichirō on Japanese folk religion.

One of the main works of Tokyo scholarship available in English is Takakusu's *The Essentials of Buddhist Philosophy*. Although written before the war, it was first translated in 1947 and remains one of the standard commentaries on the development of Buddhist thought. Concise yet comprehensive, appealing to the specialist and generalist alike, *Essentials* reflects the strengths of the Tokyo approach. First, it exploits the unique vantage point of Japan, the final stop in the movement of Mahāyāna Buddhism, to survey and assess the full range of historical and doctrinal connections between various Buddhist schools. Also, the application of Western terminology helps to categorize and make subtle distinctions between overlapping philosophical movements, as for example Kegon "totalism" and Tendai "phenomenology."

In an introductory overview of the development of Buddhism, Takakusu characterized the main sects according to their respective interpretations of the central doctrine of causality, or the dependently originated nature of all nonpermanent and nonsubstantive phenomena. They include, according to Takakusu, causality understood on the basis of the action-influence of *karma* (in primitive Buddhism), the ideation storehouse of *ālaya-vijñāna* (in Mahāyāna idealism), Thusness or the matrix of the potentiality for Buddhahood (in the *tathāgata-garbha* sutras), and, finally, the universal principle of the mutually permeating and interpenetrating elements of *dharma-dhatu* (in Kegon and Tendai). *Essentials* is a precise and illuminating account of the lines of ideological progression from naive realism through nihilism and idealism to the ultimate phenomenological dynamism in the approach to nothingness in later Mahāyāna philosophical developments. In contrast to the Kyoto school, Takakasu's analysis is weighted not toward Zen per se but toward its theoretical foundations in prior expressions of Buddhist thought.

Nakamura's *Ways of Thinking of Eastern Peoples* (1964) has had a monumental impact on Japanese and Western scholarship for its breadth in evaluating the major Eastern cultures (India, China, Tibet, Japan) and its depth in highlighting interrelated sociohistorical, religiophilosophical, and linguistic-aesthetic issues to uncover the essential standpoints and corresponding manifestations of each culture. Nakamura's central methodological achievements involve both a surpassing of the tendency to overgeneralization about Oriental culture as a monolithic entity by his focusing on the distinctiveness of four separate areas and a careful attention to the respective transmutations of Buddhist theory and practice in each society as the unifying link between them.

Nakamura characterized the Japanese cultural attitude in terms of the following elements: the subservience and dedication of the individual to a particular social nexus, as reflected by Shinto ethics and Buddhist devotionalism; the acceptance of the phenomenal world as absolute and the corresponding use of nonrational forms of expression, as demonstrated by the Zen naturalistic and Court poetic traditions, which convey an attunement to the sensible and ephemeral beauties of nature as a direct disclosure of the ultimate truth of interpenetration. Thus he argued that the focus on this-worldly phenomenalism is the key to understanding the unique stamp given to Buddhism in Japan. "While most Indians search for the truth of humanity through the channels of death," Nakamura maintained, "most Japanese try to express it intuitively through the channels of life. The Japanese way of thinking centering upon life in this world transformed the basic Buddhist doctrines."[21]

Other important examples of Tokyo scholarship available in English include Takasaki's *Study of the Ratnagotravibhāga Sutra,* which distinguishes between the doctrinal developments of various strands in Mahāyāna idealism and *tathāgata-garbha* thought; Daigan and Alicia Matsunaga's two-volume study of the *Foundations of Japanese Buddhism* (the first volume on the Japanese appropriation and transformation of traditional Buddhist sects, and the second on the formation of Japanese Zen, Pure Land, and Nichiren); and Alicia Matsunaga's *Buddhist Philosophy of Assimilation* on the philosophical interaction between Buddhist absolutism and Shinto deities in terms of the doctrines of *shinbutsu shūgō* (unification of gods or *kami* and Buddhas) and *honji-suijaku* (true nature of Buddha and manifestion of *kami*).

CONCLUDING REMARKS

An assessment of postwar Japanese Mahāyāna Buddhist thought must take into account that the full impact of the major prewar philosophical and scholarly developments has not been felt. For example, although several more translations are projected or forthcoming, only a small portion of Nishida's nineteen-volume collected works, let alone the body of commentary, will be available to the English reader in the coming years. Also, a complete English version of the Taishō edition of the Tripitika is being planned for the year 2000, but it is unlikely that secondary material will soon be translated. Thus it remains for all of this literature and more to become accessible before later works can be properly interpreted and appreciated. Nishitani's contributions must be understood and evaluated in the light of the Nishida-Tanabe philosophical tradition.

With this in mind, it seems that the central strength of postwar Mahāyāna is its continuation of the trend forged by Nishida, Suzuki, and Takakusu to integrate and synthesize seemingly disparate or heretofore neglected elements concerning Japanese Buddhism and international (Asian and Western) thought, while avoiding the pitfalls of overgeneralization or the imposition of a false uniformity. The ability to reach a synthetic understanding is itself rooted in the traditional Buddhist doctrine of the Middle Way (interpreted by Kyoto thinkers in terms of the Zen notion of absolute nothingness) as an open-ended and flexible ideological guiding light that surveys all possible standpoints without fixation to any particular one. It is not, therefore, that modern Japan has created a new perspective but rather that it has reexplored and reapplied the essential Buddhist approach both outwardly to wide-ranging speculative issues (Kyoto school) and inwardly to the study of its own origins and lines of progression (Tokyo scholarship).

The starting point of the integration lies in the focus given by both the Kyoto and Tokyo approaches—in the writings of Watsuji and Nakamura, Suzuki and Takakusu—to the underlying historical and philosophical connections between Japanese and Indian or primitive Buddhism and between Mahāyāna and Theravāda forms of practice. The ideological foundation for the synthesis, according to the Kyoto thinkers, is the fundamental experience of nothingness at the groundless ground of all expressions of Buddhist doctrine, despite variations and seeming discrepancies of outlook. The clarification of the meaning of nothingness by Nishida and Suzuki lays the basis for Takeuchi's inquiry into the interrelation between Zen and Pure Land, self-power and other-power. It also provides a philosophical fulcrum for the far-reaching examination of the encounter between and possible unity of East and West, Buddhism and Christianity, philosophy and religion, ethics and science, in the writings of Tanabe and Nishitani.

Nishitani's exploration of the relation between religion, nihilism, and science from the standpoint of Zen's Great Death stands out as the major contribution of postwar Japanese Buddhism to world thought and culture. Nishitani takes advantage of Japan's place at the culmination of converging historical and intellectual trends within Buddhism to put Zen at the forefront of handling uniquely modern and universal issues. He attempted to raise and resolve questions that he exposed as inherent in, yet not dealt with by, Western civilization and is sympathetic while providing an uncompromising challenge to Christianity. Nishitani's leading question, "What is religion?" establishes the Zen view of nothingness as a truly transcendental philosophy that at once undermines and creatively overcomes deficient ideological standpoints and their historical manifestations.

The central question to be put to Nishitani follows from his claims. Can Zen concretely and pragmatically resolve the impasse he depicted between religion and science and offset the potential devastation wrought by modern technology? If it can at least help formulate the solution to these dilemmas, will the presentation of Zen by Nishitani and others gain the hearing it deserves and needs to accomplish that goal? A limitation in Nishitani's approach is the tendency toward what may be interpreted as a "reverse dogmatism," or the appearance of an overestimation of the value of Zen in relation to Western thought. This may alienate the kind of audience that has not yet been, though must be, reached to have the desired impact: analytic philosophers (in addition to existentialist theologians) and scientists unaccustomed to the subtleties of Buddhist dialectics. The translation and dissemination of the background philosophies of Nishida and Tanabe will be helpful in clarifying the full significance of Nishitani. But there is probably a need on the part of the followers of Nishitani for a greater sensitivity to this Western audience to compel it to genuinely consider the unfamiliar yet essentially challenging and uncompromising standpoint of Zen nothingness.

NOTES

1. The most popular and famous Sōtō temple is Eiheiji, founded by Dōgen in 1244 and located in Fukui prefecture north of Kyoto. Although it is still used as one of the main training sites for Sōtō acolytes, the primary strength of the denominational organization has been pervasive in the eastern region since the spread of Sōtō during the medieval and later periods.

2. Nishitani Keiji, *Religion and Nothingness,* trans. Jan Van Bragt (Berkeley: University of California Press, 1982), p. 77.

3. Nishitani Keiji, "Science and Zen," in Frederick Franck, ed., *The Buddha Eye: An Anthology of the Kyoto School* (New York: Crossroad, 1982), p. 135.

4. This book has been translated with the title changed to *Religion and Nothingness.* See note 2.

5. Another modern trend that Nishitani would probably view as undermining the core of religion even as it claims to save it is fundamentalism, which remains unexamined in his work.

6. Nishitani, "Science and Zen," p. 118.

7. Nishitani Keiji, "The I-Thou Relation in Zen Buddhism," in Franck, *The Buddha Eye,* p. 51.

8. Ibid.

9. Nishitani, *Religion and Nothingness,* p. 55.

10. Ibid., p. 217.

11. Ibid., p. 215–216.

12. Ibid., p. 272.

13. Nishitani, "Science and Zen," p. 123.

14. A popular example of the analysis of the ideological affinities between Eastern philosophy (including Zen) and modern physics is Fritjof Capra, *The Tao of Physics* (New York: Bantam, 1976). As a scientist, Capra is not an expert on Buddhist thought. Yet he makes it clear that many of the great nuclear physicists, including Robert Oppenheimer, Werner Heisenberg, and Niels Bohr, were not only cognizant of and influenced by Buddhism but considered their findings to be fundamentally compatible with it. A response to this type of argument from the Kyoto school would be fascinating and is perhaps necessary for the attainment of its philosophical goals.

15. This central Mahāyāna doctrine, which provisionally distinguishes three aspects of the essentially unified phenomenon of the Buddha-nature (the absolute or identity with nothingness, the spiritual or heavenly savior, and the historical or factual manifestation) lies at the basis of both Zen and Pure Land practice.

16. Takeuchi Yoshinori, *The Heart of Buddhism: In Search of the Timeless Spirit of Primitive Buddhism,* trans. James W. Heisig (New York: Crossroad, 1983), p. 4.

17. Ibid., pp. 133, 135. Although greatly influenced by Shinran, Takeuchi is not a strict philosophical disciple. This quote, among others, makes it clear that Takeuchi is more interested in establishing an existential accord between Pure Land and primitive Buddhist practice than in an orthodox modern presentation of Shinran.

18. Ibid., p. 58.

19. See eulogies and recollections of Hisamatsu's life in the commemorative issue of the *Eastern Buddhist* 14, no. 1 (Spring 1981).

20. Masao Abe, "Hisamatsu's Philosophy of Awakening," *Eastern Buddhist* 14, no. 1 (Spring 1981): 41.

21. Hajime Nakamura, *Ways of Thinking of Eastern Peoples* (Honolulu: East-West Center Press, 1964), p. 363.

GLOSSARY

Aidagara: "Betweenness" of humans and external reality, self, and other (Watsuji).
Basho: Place [of absolute nothingness] (Nishida).
Goroku: Recorded sayings of Zen masters.
Great Death: Zen existential rebirth to formless Self of absolute nothingness (Nishitani).
Great Doubt: Zen experience of uncompromising skepticism as conventional viewpoints are undermined by nothingness (Nishitani).
Honji-suijaku: True nature [of Buddha] and manifestation [of *kami*].
Jiriki: Self-power approach of Zen meditation.
Jōteki bunka: Culture of feeling (Nishida).
Junsui keiken: pure experience (Nishida).
Kami: Shinto animistic view of divinity.
Katachi naki, koe naki: Formless and soundless (Nishida).
Kōan: Zen paradox or puzzle.
Kōiteki chokkan: Unity of action-intuition (Nishida).
Kōjō: Self-surpassing [quality of Zen] (Nishitani).
Kū: Mahāyāna doctrine of emptiness or nonsubstantiality.
Kyomu: "Hollow" nothingness.
Kyōto-ha: The Kyoto school of philosophy, established by Nishida.
Mondō: Zen catechism.
Ningen no gaku: Anthropology; literally, "science of man" (Watsuji).
Nishida tetsugaku: Philosophy of Nishida.
Ronri: Logic.
Shinbutsu shūgō: Unity of Buddhas and *kami*.
Shōji ichinyo: Zen doctrine of the identity of life-death.
Shu no ronri: Logic of species (Tanabe).
Shukanteki: Epistemological subjectivity in polarity with objectivity.
Shutaiteki: Fully integrated subjectivity, encompassing humans and nature, self and other (Hisamatsu).
Tariki: Other-power approach of Pure Land devotion.
U: Being.
Uji: Dōgen's Zen doctrine of the unity of being-time.

Zangedō: Metanoesis, or conversion experienced through repentance (Tanabe, Takeuchi, Nishitani).
Zen: Concept of the good (Nishida).
Zettai jishateki shūkyō ritsu: Religio-nomy of the Absolute Self (Hisamatsu).
Zettai mu: Absolute nothingness (Nishida).
Zettai mujunteki jiko dōitsu: Self-identity of absolute contradiction (Nishida).

BIBLIOGRAPHY

Abe, Masao. "Dōgen on Buddha-nature."*Eastern Buddhist* 4, no. 1 (May 1971): 28–71.

———. "Hisamatsu's Philosophy of Awakening." *Eastern Buddhist* 14, no. 1 (May 1981): 26–42.

———. "Mahayana Buddhism and Whitehead—A View by a Lay Student of Whitehead's Philosophy." *Philosophy East and West* 25, no. 4 (October 1975): 429–448.

———. "Non-Being and *Mu*. The Metaphysical Nature of Negativity in the East and the West." *Religious Studies* 2 (1977): 181–192.

———. "Zen and Nietzsche." *Eastern Buddhist,* 6, no. 2 (October 1970): 14–32.

Abe, Masao, and Norman Waddell, trans. "Dōgen's Bendōwa," *Eastern Buddhist* 4, no. 1 (May 1971): 124–157.

———. "Shōbōgenzō Genjōkōan." *Eastern Buddhist* 5, no. 2 (October 1972): 129–140.

Buri, Fritz. *Der Buddha-Christus des Herr des Wahren Selbst: Die Religionsphilosophie der Kyoto-Schule und das Christendum.* Bern and Stuttgart: Verlag Paul Haupt, 1982.

Capra, Fritjof. *The Tao of Physics.* New York, Bantam, 1976.

Dilworth, David A. "Nishida Kitarō: Nothingness as the Negative Space of Experiential Immediacy." *International Philosophical Quarterly* 13, no. 4 (December 1973): 463–484.

Dumoulin, Heinrich. *A History of Zen Buddhism.* New York, Random House, 1963.

———. *Ostliche Meditation und Christliche Mystik.* Freiburg-Munich: Karl Alber, 1966.

Earhart, H. Byron. *Japanese Religion: Unity and Diversity.* Belmont, Calif.: Wadsworth, 1982.

Franck, Frederick, ed. *The Buddha Eye: An Anthology of the Kyoto School.* New York, Crossroad, 1982.

Furukawa, Tetsushi, and Iwada Ichirō. *Kindai no shisō.* No. 3. In *Nihon shisō kōza.* Tokyo: Yūzankaku, 1977.

Heidegger, Martin. "Dialogue with a Japanese." In Peter Hertz and Joan Stambaugh, trans., *On the Way to Language.* New York: Harper and Row, 1971.

Hirakawa, A., and E. B. Caedel. "Japanese Research on Buddhism Since the Meiji Period." *Monumenta Nipponica* 11, no. 3 (October 1955): 1–26.

Hisamatsu, Shin'ichi. "The Characteristics of Oriental Nothingness." *Philosophical Studies of Japan* 2 (1960): 65–98.

———. *Zen and the Fine Arts.* Tokyo: Kodansha International, 1971.

Hisamatsu, Shin'ichi, and Paul Tillich. "Dialogues East and West." *Eastern Buddhist* 4, no. 2 (October 1971): 89–107: 5, no. 2 (October 1972): 107–128.

Hori, Ichirō. *Japanese Religion: A Survey by the Agency for Cultural Affairs.* Tokyo: Kodansha, 1972.

Japanese-English Buddhist Dictionary. Tokyo: Daitō shuppansha, 1965.

Japanese Association for Religious Studies, ed. *Religious Studies in Japan*. Tokyo: Maruzen, 1959.

Jimbo, Nyoten, and Andō Bun'ei, *Zengaku jiten*. Tokyo: Nakayama shobō, 1958.

Kasulis, T. P. "The Kyoto School and the West: A Review and Evaluation." *Eastern Buddhist*, 15, no. 2 (October 1982): 125–144.

Katz, Nathan, ed. *Buddhist and Western Philosophy*. New Delhi: Sterling, 1981.

Kim, Ha Tai. "Nishida and Royce." *Philosophy East and West* 1, no. 4 (1952): 18–29.

Kiyota, Minoru. "Buddhism in Postwar Japan." *Monumenta Nipponica* 24, no. 1 (1969): 114–136.

Kōsaka, Masaaki. *Nishida Kitarō to Watsuji Tetsurō*. Tokyo: Shinchōsha, 1964.

Leibrecht, W., ed. *Religion and Culture: Essays in Honor of Paul Tillich*. New York: Harper, 1959.

Matsunaga, Alicia. *The Buddhist Philosophy of Assimilation*. Tokyo: Tuttle, 1969.

Matsunaga, Alicia, and Daigan Matsunaga. *Foundations of Japanese Buddhism*. 2 vols. Los Angeles and Tokyo: Buddhist Books International, 1974.

Mishima, Yukio. *Temple of the Golden Pavilion*. Translated by Ivan Morris. New York: Putnam, 1959.

Moore, Charles A., ed. *The Japanese Mind*. Honolulu: University Press of Hawaii, 1969.

Nakamura, Hajime. *A History of the Development of Japanese Thought*. Tokyo: Society for International Cultural, 1967.

———. *Shin bukkyō jiten*. Tokyo: Seishin shobō, 1962.

———. *Ways of Thinking of Eastern Peoples*. Honolulu: East-West Center Press, 1964.

Nishida, Kitarō. *Art and Morality*. Translated by David A. Dilworth and Valdo H. Viglielmo. Honolulu: University Press of Hawaii, 1973.

———. *Fundamental Problems of Philosophy*. Translated by David A. Dilworth. Tokyo: Sophia University Press, 1970.

———. *Intelligibility and the Philosophy of Nothingness*. Translated by Robert Schinzinger. Westport, Conn.: Greenwood Press, 1972.

———. *The Logic of Place and the Religious World-View*. Translated by David A. Dilworth. Honolulu: University of Hawaii Press, 1986.

———. "The Problem of Japanese Culture." In Abe Masao, trans., *Sources of Japanese Tradition*. Vol. 2. New York and London: Columbia University Press, 1958.

———. *A Study of Good*. Translated by Valdo H. Viglielmo. Tokyo: Japanese Government Printing Bureau, 1960.

———. *Zenshū*. 19 vols. Tokyo: Iwanami shoten, 1965–1966.

Nishitani, Keiji. *Kami to zettai mu*. Tokyo: Kōbundō, 1949.

———. *Nihirizumu*. Tokyo: Kōbundō, 1946.

———. *Religion and Nothingness*. Translated by Jan Van Bragt. Berkeley: University of California Press, 1982.

———. *Shukyō to wa nani ka*. Tokyo: Kōbundō, 1961.

———. *Zen kōza*. 8 vols. Tokyo: Chikuma shobō, 1967–1968.

Nishitani, Keiji, and Yanagida Seizan, eds. *Zenge goroku*. 2 vols. In *Koten sekai bungaku*. Vols. 29 and 30. Tokyo: Chikuma shobō, 1969.

Noda, Matao. "East-West Synthesis in Kitarō Nishida." *Philosophy East and West*, 4, no. 4 (January 1955): 345–360.

Piovesena, Gino K. "Japanese Philosophy." In *The Encyclopedia of Philosophy*. New York: Macmillan and Free Press, 1967, pp. 250–254.

————. *Recent Japanese Philosophical Thought, 1862–1962*. New York: St. John's University Press, 1969.

Ruiz, F. Perez. "Philosophy in present-day Japan." *Monumenta Nipponica* 24, no. 1 (1969): 137–168.

Shibayama, Zenkei. *A Flower Does Not Talk: Zen Essays*. Translated by Sumiko Kuoi. Tokyo: Tuttle, 1970.

Shimomura, Toratarō. "The Modernization of Japan with Special Reference to Philosophy." *Philosophical Studies of Japan* 7 (1966): 1–28.

————. *Nishida Kitarō, hito to shisō*. Tokyo: Tōkai Daigaku shuppankai, 1965.

————. *Wakaki Nishida Kitarō Sensei*. Tokyo: Jinbun Shorin, 1947.

Spae, Joseph. *Japanese Religiosity*. Tokyo: Oriens Institute for Religious Research, 1971.

Suzuki, Daisetz Teitarō. *Essays in Zen Buddhism*. 3 vols. New York: Grove, 1965.

————. *Studies in the Lankāvatāra Sutra*. London: George Routledge, 1930.

————. *Zen and Japanese Culture*. Princeton, N.J.: Princeton University Press, 1959.

————. *Zenshū*. 31 vols. Tokyo: Iwanami, 1968–1970.

Takakusu, Junjirō. *The Essentials of Buddhist Philosophy*. Honolulu: University Press of Hawaii, 1947.

Takasaki, Jikidō. *A Study of the Ratnagotravibhāga Sutra*. Rome: ISMEO, 1960.

Takeuchi, Yoshinori. *The Heart of Buddhism: In Search of the Timeless Spirit of Primitive Buddhism*. Translated by James W. Heisig. New York: Crossroad, 1983.

————. "Modern Japanese Philosophy." In *Encyclopedia Britanica*. Vol. 12. 1966, pp. 958–962.

Tanabe, Hajime. "The Logic of Species as Dialectics." Translated by David A. Dilworth with Taira Satō. *Monumenta Nipponica* 24, no. 3 (1969): 273–288.

————. "Momento Mori." *Philosophical Studies of Japan* 1. (1959): 1–12.

————. *Zenshū*. 15 vols. Tokyo: Chikuma shobō, 1963–1964.

Tsunoda, Ryusaku, Wm. Theodore de Bary, and Donald Keene, eds. *Sources of Japanese Tradition*. 2 vols. New York and London: Columbia University Press, 1958.

Ueda, Shizuteru. *Die Gottesgeburt in der Seele und der Durchbruch zur Gottheit*. Gütersloh: Gütershoher Verlagshaus, 1965.

Ui, Hakuju. *Bukkyō jiten*. Tokyo: 1953.

————. "A Study of Japanese Tendai Buddhism," *Philosophical Studies of Japan* 1 (1959): 33–74.

Van Bragt, Jan, ed. *Zettai mu to kami—Nishida-Tanabe tetsugaku no dentō to Kiristikyō*. Tokyo: Shunjūsha, 1981.

Waldenfels, Hans. "Absolute Nothingness," *Monumenta Nipponica* 21, nos. 3–4 (1966): 354–391.

————. *Absolute Nothingness: Foundations of a Buddhist-Christian Dialogue*. Translated by James W. Heisig. New York: Paulist Press, 1980.

Watsuji, Tetsurō. *Climate: A Philosophical Study*. Translated by George Bownas. Tokyo: Japanese Government Printing Bureau, 1962.

————. *Zenshū*. 20 vols. Tokyo: Iwanami shoten, 1961–1963.

Yanagida, Seizan. "The 'Recorded Sayings' Texts of Chinese Ch'an Buddhism." In Whalen Lai and Lewis Lancaster, eds., *Early Ch'an in China and Tibet*. Berkeley, Calif.: Buddhist Studies Series, 1983.

12

Postwar Neo-Confucian Philosophy: Its Development and Issues

SHU-HSIEN LIU

Although contemporary China was dominated by trends of thought imported from the West, there has been no lack of attempts to draw from traditional resources in order to respond to the current situation. No one can dispute the fact that contemporary neo-Confucian philosophy has constituted a vital movement in the scholarly world.[1] It is instructive to study the movement as offering an option among world religions. The scope of contemporary neo-Confucianism is not clearly defined. It may include scholars with varied backgrounds, such as the scholar Liang Sou-ming (1893–), the historian Ch'ien Mu (1895–), the scholar-statesman Carsun Chang (1887–1969), and Hsu Fu-Kuan (1903–1982), an expert on intellectual history. For philosophical reasons, however, I have chosen to discuss only the following four scholars: Hsiung Shih-li (1885–1968), Thomé H. Fang (1899–1977), T'ang Chun-i (1909–1978), and Mou Tsung-san (1909-), concentrating on their later thoughts. Hsiung was the most creative neo-Confucian philosopher of his generation. Among these four scholars, he was the only one who remained in mainland China after the Communist takeover in 1949. Since that time his thought has undergone significant changes. Thomé Fang was Hsiung's colleague, and both T'ang and Mou had studied under him. These three have inherited Hsiung's spirit, while developing their own philosophies.

The inclusion of Thomé Fang in this group is somewhat questionable, since he himself never acknowledged that he was a neo-Confucian scholar. In fact, Fang was strongly critical of Sung-Ming neo-Confucian philosophies. He attempted to achieve a balance among Confucianism, Taoism, and Mohism and sought to incorporate insights from Indian and Western sources from a comparative point of view. Fang did try very hard to revive what he called the spirit of primordial Confucianism from ancient times and committed himself to the philosophy of creativity found in the *Book of Changes*. Therefore, justification does exist for including him among the neo-Confucians, since it would be even more difficult to place him in any other group.[2]

HSIUNG SHIH-LI'S LATER THOUGHT

Hsiung Shih-li had been engaged in revolutionary activities when he was young. But he realized in his middle years that engaging in such activities would not solve the problem of his ultimate concern in life. Thus he turned to philosophy, studying the Consciousness-Only School of Buddhism under Ou-yang Ching-wu (1871–1943). Dissatisfied with these teachings, Hsiung developed a "New Consciousness-Only Doctrine" based on his understanding of the insights of a philosophy of creativity implied in the *Book of Changes*. Thus he opened up a new direction for contemporary neo-Confucian philosophy. As Wing-tsit Chan has pointed out,

[Hsiung] has influenced more young Chinese philosophers than any other contemporary philosopher. More importantly, he has restated, as no other has done, his whole philosophy in a book since the Communist accession to power in 1949, and he has done so without employing Communist slogans or referring to Marx, Stalin, or Mao Tze-tung. Philosophically, this book, entitled *Yüan-ju* (An Inquiry on Confucianism, 1956) has not altered the fundamental thesis of the *Hsin wei-shih lun* [New Doctrine of Consciousness-Only], but it indicates that Confucianism is very much alive in China.[3]

Although from a metaphysical point of view Hsiung's later thought changed very little, he did acquire a radically different perspective on the development of Confucian thought, especially its social and political ideals. After *Yüan-ju*, he published *T'i-yung lun* (*A Treatise on Substance and Function*, 1958), *Ming-hsin p'ien* (*On Enlightenment of the Mind*, 1959), and *Ch'ien-k'un yen* (*An Explication of the Meaning of Hexagrams Ch'ien and K'un*, 1961).[4]

From an epistemological point of view, Hsiung restated his previous position.[5] He said, "Throughout my career, I have never opposed the intellect or knowledge. But I also deeply feel that apart from the pursuit of external knowledge, there is the world that can be gained access [to] only in terms of meditation beyond thought and self-realization beyond words."[6] According to Hsiung, science must postulate the external reality of objects in order to investigate them and find out about the principles that govern their actions. But philosophy, as based on the teachings of the sages, has to realize the one amidst the many. Substance and function always go together. An analogy may be employed to illustrate the situation: the ocean must manifest itself in infinite waves, and the waves are but the waves of the ocean. In other words, the principle is one, while its manifestations are many. Hence there is a difference between knowledge and wisdom. For knowledge to be acquired, external objects must be postulated, and for wisdom to function, the realization of the one reality is indispensable. Science can capture only the manifestations, but philosophy can capture the one reality that is the source of those manifestations. Hsiung summarized his own views of substance and function as follows:

(1) Substance is comprised of complexities such as matter, life, and spirit. It is not simple in nature.

(2) Substance is never stagnant. It changes ceaselessly. From instant to instant, it leaves the past behind and creates anew. There is not a single instant which remains unchanged.

(3) Function refers to the fact that substance changes ceaselessly and manifests itself in various activities, referred to as its function. Therefore, it is said that substance and function are non-dual.

(4) As substance comprises complexities such as matter and mind within itself, it contains qualities that are opposed to each other. These induce change and are manifested in function.

(5) Function manifests itself in matter and mind. One is closed, the other open. What is closed is transformed into matter, since it cannot maintain its original status as substance, while what is open does not turn into matter, but rather preserves the virtues of substance's strength, brightness, and purity. Such are the various aspects of substance.

(6) What is closed and what is open are opposites of each other. But the mind is in a position to govern matter. It may transform matter, and eventually the two [mind and matter] will become reunited. Hence, opposites are mutually complementary.[7]

Although these points may appear to be highly speculative, Hsiung claimed that everyone may realize the same insights as soon as one can realize the inner depth of one's being. It is not by external cosmological speculation but by inner realization of human depths that a true ontology may be established. What is noteworthy in Hsiung's thought is that he maintained that matter and mind are dual aspects of the function of substance, an ever-changing creative ontological principle to which we ultimately must commit ourselves. According to Hsiung, both idealism and materialism are wrong. It is impossible to reduce mind to matter and vice versa. Obviously, his ideas contradicted the materialistic philosophy taught by the Communist regime. It was nothing short of a miracle that he was allowed to publish his works until the early sixties. Eventually, he was persecuted by the Red Guards before his death in 1968. However, now both mainland China and Taiwan are in the process of publishing Hsiung's collected works. Both also celebrated his centennial in 1985.[8]

Although Hsiung stood his ground in metaphysics and epistemology, in his later years he did develop a radically different perspective on the development of Confucian thought, especially its social and political ideals. In *Yuan-jü* he advanced the bold thesis that the Six Classics were the works of Confucius in his later years. He also maintained that, after the death of Confucius, these texts had been revised by what he called the slave–scholars. Hence the true teachings of Confucius were not available to later scholars. Such views stirred up many controversies, and very few of Hsiung's disciples accepted his radical views on this point.[9]

Hsiung believed that Confucius followed the tradition of teaching the rites to his students until the age of fifty. Then, according to Hsiung, Confucius underwent a radical conversion in his thinking. Instead of teaching only the ideal of *Hsiao-kang* (Small Peace), he now taught the *Ta-tung* (Great Unity) ideal as well, under which the existence of social classes and the institution of private property were to be abolished. Unfortunately, however, immediately after the death of Confucius, writings were twisted by other scholars to serve the rulers. Hence the real teachings of Confucius have been lost to posterity. Nonetheless, we can catch a glimpse of his great insights through a careful reading of certain texts preserved in the classics that we have today.

Hsiung believed that Confucius laid the foundation of his thought in the *Book of Changes*. An extensive commentary on the first two hexagrams of the text—*Ch'ien* (Heaven) and *K'un* (Earth)—considered to be the most important of the sixty-four hexagrams, was prepared by Hsiung to explicate the intended meanings of Confucius. In the text of the hexagram *Ch'ien*, it is said that "at first there was the revolution of common people, then all enjoyed peace in the world."[10] At the end of the hexagram, the image of "a number of dragons without a leader" emerges.[11] Based on such evidence, Hsiung believed that Confucius was teaching the ideals of socialism and democracy. Hsiung then theorized that the succession of Three Ages was taught by Confucius himself. The Age of Disorder, followed by the Age of Rising Peace, was finally to culminate in the Age of Great Peace, in which all boundaries between nations and races are eliminated. In this final stage the whole world will become one family, with each person in control of their own life; all human beings will be equal and render mutual aid, totally ignoring the self-other distinction. Unfortunately, the ideal was distorted by scholars such as Tung Chung-shu (c. 179–c. 104 B.C.) in the Han dynasty, who shifted the emphasis from the ruler-subject relationship, placing it instead on the loyalty of subjects toward the ruler.[12]

In the *Book of Rites* Hsiung singled out the essay on Great Unity as preserving certain authentic insights from Confucius. While the emphasis should be put on the ideal of Great Unity, later scholars wrongly emphasized the practice of Small Peace, thus lending support to the dynastic rulers.[13] Hsiung also praised the *Chou-kuan* (*Chou Rituals*) highly, believing that the lofty ideals set forth in this text could not have been conceived by anyone other than Confucius himself. Hence Hsiung rejected the view that the work is spurious. The guiding principles for the *Chou-kuan* are equality and unity. It espouses an elaborate system of government under which the welfare of the people is of primary concern. On the one hand, industries will be developed; on the other hand, private property will be abolished along with private ownership of land, and big business will be run by the government. Certainly, this foretells the ideals of democracy and socialism.[14]

Finally, according to Hsiung, the *Book of Odes* and the *Book of History* were edited by Confucius. These works preserve some ancient documents. The *Book of Odes* contains poems that tell of the plight of the common people, while the extant *Book of History* was so badly tampered with by later rulers that it is no longer of much use today.[15]

Because Hsiung held such radical views, he accused Mencius of betraying the lofty ideals of Confucius and of promoting filial piety as a means of helping the rulers consolidate their power. From then on, Tung Chung-shu, Ssu-ma Ch'ien (145–86 B.C.?), Liu Hsin (c. 46 B.C.–23 A.D.), and even Kang Yu-wei (1858–1927) all accepted the distorted teachings of Confucius. Liu Hsin talked about subtle words and great principles. In fact, however, there were few subtle words, and the so-called great principles encouraged people to remain blindly loyal to the rulers. It was unfortunate that the Chinese people lived under tyranny and despotism for more than two thousand years. But this fact has nothing to do with the Sage who taught us the ideal of the Great Unity so long ago.[16]

I am afraid that Hsiung's radical interpretation of the development of Confucian ideals in China cannot win the support of most scholars. Yet his value does not lie in his scholarly work. Rather, his greatest contribution lies in the fact that he fully realized the inner creativity in the depth of every human being and that he dared to follow his own independent thinking in order to uphold positions that were unpopular in his own time. Inadvertently, he pointed out a new direction for neo-Confucian scholars who came after him.

THOMÉ FANG'S GRAND SCHEME OF COMPARATIVE PHILOSOPHY

Thomé H. Fang came from an illustrious family in T'ung Cheng, Anhwei. He was a descendent of Fang Pao (1668–1749), the founder of the famous T'ung Cheng movement in Chinese literature. After studying at the University of Nanking, Fang went abroad to study Western philosophy at the University of Wisconsin and Ohio State University. He taught at several universities, including National Wuchang University (1924–1925), National Central University (1929–1948), National Taiwan University (1948–1973), State University of South Dakota (1959–1960), University of Missouri (1960–1961), and Michigan State University (1964–1966). During the Japanese invasion Fang felt strongly that the profound wisdom of traditional Chinese philosophy should not be allowed to die. Most of his important works were published after he moved to Taiwan in 1948, including his books in English: *The Chinese View of Life* (1956); *Creativity in Man and Nature* (1980), a collection of essays; and *Chinese Philosophy: Its Spirit and Its Development* (1981), published posthumously in 1977.[17]

It is characteristic of Fang's thought that he always kept a comparative perspective of things. In the very first book he published, *Science, Philosophy, and the Significance of Human Life,* he compared ancient Greek culture and modern European culture. He preferred the former, since he believed that nihilism was an outgrowth of modern European culture. But Fang expanded his horizon when he published his article "Three Types of Philosophical Wisdom: Greek, European, and Chinese," in 1937.[18] Although he admitted that each type of wisdom possessed its own achievements as well as its limitations, he argued that each should be complemented by the others. Yet he thought that the healthiest spirit has found its expression in Chinese culture. Fang maintained this outlook in the later stage of his thought, although expanding his scheme to include still another type of philosophical wisdom, that is, the Indian. Unfortunately, however, he was unable to complete his final project, leaving only an outline that has now been published as an appendix to his book *Chinese Philosophy: Its Spirit and Its Development*—"Outline of 'Prolegomena to a Comparative Philosophy of Life'—Ideals of Life and Patterns of Culture."[19] In this outline Fang adopted a fourfold, tripartite division, as follows:

(a) The Greek: (1) the Apollonian, (2) the Dionysian, (3) the Olympian;
(b) Modern Europe: (1) the Renaissance, (2) the Baroque, (3) the Rococco;
(c) the Indian: (1) the Upanishadic, (2) the Buddhistic, (3) the Bhagavadgitaic;
(d) the Chinese: (1) the Taoist, (2) the Confucian, (3) the Mohist.[20]

It is beyond the scope of this chapter to discuss all of the empirical evidence upon which he based his comparative interpretations. I have attempted to summarize his presuppositions as follows:

1. In the vast universe there is a tremendous creative force incessantly at work that gives rise to various species of life. On this earth, however, only humans have the ability to develop the great potentiality of seeds of wisdom within themselves and find expression in the achievement of variegated patterns of culture. As intelligence must not be cut off from wisdom, reason and emotion should be consonant with each other. The ultimate commitment of a philosopher is to the enlightenment based on intelligence and wisdom, and the great disaster for humans is the loss of wisdom and the fall into *avidya* (ignorance).

2. The kind of wisdom achieved by individuals on the basis of extensive learning, reflective thinking, and the effort of self-discipline is individual wisdom, whereas the kind of wisdom found in the spirit of a cultural race is common wisdom. Common wisdom relies on the genius of a cultural race, and individual wisdom is dependent upon the genius of an individual. Individual wisdom is derived from common wisdom, and common wisdom is the result of the accumulation of individual geniuses. Common wisdom is the root, whereas individual wisdom is the branch.

3. It is possible for humans to develop into different types. To study various types of human beings is the job of philosophical anthropology. There is a correlation between the different types of people and the different types of worlds they live in. It is owing to the different world views and life views that we live in the context of different meaning structures, even though we may still be said to live in a common world from another perspective.

4. The problem of existence and the problem of value should be kept distinct but not totally apart from each other. Humans' concept of value cannot be separated from their concept of existence. As a matter of fact, their choice of the world they live in corresponds to their choice of the course of development of a culture.

5. Different cultures have developed different kinds of wisdom, and different world views, life views, and concepts of value have been formulated. First, we need to have an objective understanding of the implications of such views and concepts, and then, we need to give an evaluation and make a judgment about their merits and demerits. From a philosophical point of view, there are four great traditions in the world, Greek, Modern European, Indian, and Chinese. Each tradition has its great achievements and also shows its specific limitations. But the most healthy sentiment of life is that which has been developed in the Chinese culture: the spirit of creative creativity and comprehensive harmony.

6. After studying the merits and demerits of various cultural traditions, we must look forward to the future and make an attempt to accomplish an even greater synthesis surpassing all existing achievements. Under the guidance of wisdom, a person's search for truth, self-discipline, and practice according to moral principles; aspiration toward greater political ideals; and creative work in the world of art each would receive its proper attention. We may strive for an ideal of life that will give satisfaction in answer to both the demands of human reason and emotion.[21]

I have summarized Fang's understanding of the three types of wisdom—Greek, Modern European, and Chinese—as follows: The kind of wisdom the Greeks achieved is to face an ontologically real world, to grasp its principles (ideas) or forms. Profoundly influenced by Nietzsche, Fang believed that the highest expression of Greek wisdom lies in a synthesis of the Apollonian and Dionysian spirits, with the Olympian spirit as its accompaniment. The Greek ideal is a primordial harmony with threefold expressions, related as three concentric circles.

The European emphasis, however, is on energy. Europeans are most concerned with utility and expediency. They are daredevils who let their feelings and emotions go unrestrained, chasing the infinite as if to drive straight into a world of fantasy. During the Renaissance Europeans broke the narrow confines of the Greek world of harmony and ventured into an infinite world without limit. This was followed by the Baroque Age in which Europeans endeavored to use the great power of reason to uncover the laws that encompassed the whole universe. However, the Rococo spirit showed that reason and emotion ultimately contradicted each other. Behind the splendid show full of colors and sounds lurks a feeling of hollowness that bespeaks nihilism. European drama is like a piece of instrumental music with constantly conflicting themes competing to gain dominance over one another, without being able to become reconciled with one another. "The Chinese try to penetrate the mystery of transformation, to find meanings amidst the vicissitudes of life. They are committed either to the Way of the Taoists, or the Humanity of the Confucianists, or the Universal Love of the Mohists. As the principle is one, its manifestations are many. Their music is a symphony of harmony that unites the different moments into an integrated whole."[22]

Fang criticized the shortcoming of Western philosophies as follows:

The trouble is that they [European philosophers] are always making a great divide between matter and spirit. It is rather hard for them to bring things together which have been rashly severed. All through history they have been imposing on themselves an arduous task of developing a system of philosophy in which *Weltanschuuang* and *Lebensanschauung* will work harmoniously together. But this effort of theirs, I am afraid, will eventually result in contradiction, if not in failure.[23]

In contrast to the European philosophies, the Chinese cosmological philosophies suggest a different model:

With regard to this problem, the Chinese philosophers have worked out a theory which is quite satisfactory. The universe, considered from our viewpoint, is fundamentally the confluence and concrescence of Universal Life in which the material conditions and the spiritual phenomena are so coalesced and interpenetrated that there can be no breach between them. And, therefore, as we live in the world, we find no difficulty in infusing the spirit into matter and immersing the matter in spirit. Matter manifests the significance of what is spiritual and spirit permeates the core of what is material. In a word, matter and spirit ooze together in a state of osmosis concurrently sustaining life, cosmic as well as human.[24]

To fully appreciate the wisdom of traditional Chinese philosophies as seen from Fang's perspective, one must undertake a careful study of his magnus opus: *Chinese Philosophy: Its Spirit and Its Development.*[25] Here we need only to cite his general appraisal of Chinese philosophies as follows:

The characteristics of the life of the Chinese may be seen through Taoism, Confucianism, and Mohism. By Taoism I refer to Lao Tzu and Chuang Tzu, the Taoists after the Han dynasty took rather devious paths and had very little relationship with Lao Tzu and Chuang Tzu. Under Confucianism I would like to include Confucius, Mencius and Hsün Tzu, while the Han Confucianists were lowly and unworthy of mention, and Sung-Ming Confucianists were not authentic followers of Confucianism. By Mohism [of Mo Tzu] I would like to also include the so-called later Mohists. Taoism manifests the wonderful function of the Way. Confucianism develops the profound principle of the philosophy of change. And Mohism expresses the sacred feeling of Universal Love. The only one who can encompass the teachings of Taoism and Mohism and teach a middle way is none other than Confucius. The Way, the profound Principle, and Universal Love are different, but they are not to be separated from one another. Since Lao Tzu, Confucius, and Mo Tzu, the miscellaneous schools—the meaning of the term is far broader than that given by Liu Hsin and Pan Ku—have degenerated, when they talk about the Way, they tend toward what is trivial and miss the wonder of the Way, when they discuss Change, they are falling into the traps of the devilish ways, when they refer to Love, they fail to show any feelings and are unable to bring about concrete results.[26]

From this statement we find that even though Fang has shown great admiration for traditional Chinese philosophies, he never denied that they can become degenerated, nor did he feel that they are without serious limitations. Not only can the world learn much from Chinese philosophies, the Chinese may also learn much from other traditions. I have summarized his ideas as follows:

After Professor Fang examined the three types of wisdom: Greek, European, and Chinese, he felt that they appeared to be complementary to one another. Each culture may learn from the other in order to find a way to overcome its own limitations. For example, the merit of Greek thought is to keep one's eyes on reality, but unfortunately, since Socrates and Plato, the Greeks seem to have a tendency to degrade the present life, they need to be compensated by the European emphasis on utility and their love to explore the infinite universe. On the other hand, the Europeans seem to have pushed too far without showing any sense of rational restraint, they need to be compensated by the Chinese spirit of moderation and reverence of life, while the Chinese very often tend to neglect external reality, they need to be compensated by the Greek sense of reality. As a Chinese philosopher, he has great love and respect for his Chinese heritage. But unfortunately, the Chinese today seem to have lost the vision and the wisdom of their ancestors. Therefore Professor Fang worked very hard to persuade us to revive the healthy sentiment of primordial Confucianism, Taoism, and Mohism in order for us to look toward an even greater future, while the loss of wisdom may plunge us into disasters and may drive us toward the end of the world.[27]

As we can see, Fang has a macrocosmic view of things. His philosophy may not suit the current taste. But we must not forget that he learned a great deal from Hegel, Nietzsche, and Spengler and that he was a contemporary of Toynbee, Northrop, and Sorokin. Since there is a revival of interest in Hegel's philosophy today, it is conceivable that there may be future interest in Fang's ideas.

T'ANG CHUN-I'S RECONSTRUCTION OF IDEALS OF A PHILOSOPHY OF CULTURE

T'ang Chun-i studied under both Thomé Fang and Hsiung Shih-li. He graduated from National Central University and taught there for many years. He left for Hong Kong in 1949 and was one of the founders of New Asia College. He was the first to be appointed as a professor with a chair in Chinese philosophy at The Chinese University of Hong Kong when New Asia College became one of its foundational colleges. Most of T'ang's important works were published after he came to Hong Kong. In the preface to his influential book *The Spiritual Values of the Chinese Culture,* T'ang reviewed the development of his thought as follows:

The scope of culture is vast; the most important thing is [to get hold of] the central idea one relies on to discuss culture. If the central idea is not clear or mistaken, then the whole project is wrong. At the time [I published my *Comparative Studies of Chinese and*

Western Philosophical Thought (1943)] I was not clear about the great foundation and the great origins of Chinese and Western thought, even though I had read extensively Chinese and Western philosophical works. When I talked about "the unity of Heaven and man," the term *Heaven* referred only to the whole phenomenon of natural life or universal flux. . . . The only two things I had deep understanding about Chinese philosophy [at that time] were: that the mind is vacuous and subtle, not sticking to anything, but flowing through all things in the world; and that the natural universe changes incessantly, forever going forward and returning infinitely. . . . I was under the influence of Neo-Realists who criticized the traditional Western concept of substance, then I took all metaphysical principles to be nothing but the result of a tenacious hold of certain abstract ideas. Therefore when I wrote the article on the spirit of the Chinese culture, in the very beginning I borrowed a statement from the *Book of Changes:* "that the spirit has no direction and that Change has no substance," and drew the conclusion that the cosmology of traditional Chinese philosophers was one without substance. Most of my teachers and friends highly praised the article. But Professor Hsiung Shih-li wrote to me and said that I was wrong at the very beginning. I was not convinced then. . . . Afterwards because of all sorts of troubles in my personal life, I devoted myself to reflection on the problem of morality and the problem of life. At that time, I had a more intimate understanding of the insights that man's spiritual activity forever transcends itself and that the essence of moral life lies in the fact that one must act according to principles in a self-conscious fashion. Now I realize that every person has a moral self or a mind-substance which is both immanent and transcendent. Then I wrote the two books: *The Experience of Life* (Chung Hua) and *The Establishment of the Moral Self* (Commercial Press). In the meantime, I have acquired a better appreciation of Professor Hsiung's metaphysics. I read the work of my friend Professor Mou Tsung-san's work on *Logic* (Commercial Press, 1941), then I realized that the rational activity of pure reason is working unceasingly, this confirmed my faith in the immanent transcendence of the mind which can be its own master. In the last ten years Professor Mou and I have had most fruitful discussions, there has been mutual enlightenment and reinforcement. Now I no longer have any doubt about this mind and this principle. For about ten years, there have been no fundamental changes in my philosophical thought. . . . [I am greatly indebted to the works of contemporary Chinese and Western scholars such as . . .] However, I still feel dissatisfied, as there is not one book which gives extensive analysis of the wisdom of Chinese philosophy, or discusses in a systematic way the "spiritual values" of the Chinese culture. Hence, in the last ten years, in spite of my limitations, I have tried my best to write a book on moral reason as the foundation of culture in order to manifest the principles of culture, and then proceed to further discuss the spiritual values of Chinese and Western cultures.[28]

From this review we can see the synthetic character of T'ang's thought. According to him, it is not enough just to accumulate massive empirical data in the study of cultures; we must probe deep into the foundation of culture, which is none other than the mind–heart of *jen* (humanity) transmitted through Confucius, Mencius, the Sung-Ming neo-Confucian philosophers, and contemporary thinkers such as Hsiung Shih-li. The manifestations are many, but the principle is one. In formulating his thought Tang used a number of arguments that are not unlike those used by some of the Western idealistic philosophers. But he should not be mistaken for an idealist in the Western sense. Traditional Chinese philosophy never made a sharp dichotomy between mind and matter, knowledge and action, and Tang's thought has been a reconstruction of the insights of the Chinese tradition. What is really important for him is to find one's ultimate commitment in the mind–heart of *jen*; then one will be able to find the creative origin of cultural values as well as the way of self-realization.

On New Year's day, 1958, four scholars—Carsun Chang, T'ang Chun-i, Mou Tsung-san, and Hsu Fu-kuan—issued the famous "Manifesto for a Re-appraisal of Sinology and Reconstruction of Chinese Culture."[29] The document was drafted by T'ang and then revised to its present form after taking in the suggestions of the other three scholars. Naturally, it gave expression to T'ang's reflections on the Chinese culture. It pointed out the shortcomings of the three main approaches to sinology: those of the missionaries, the historians and archeologists, and the pragmatists. The new approach that T'ang suggested we should follow is to find out the special characteristics of the spiritual life of the Chinese culture. The wisdom of Chinese philosophy is crystallized in its philosophy of mind and nature. Although recognizing the need for the Chinese culture to learn from the West by absorbing its achievements in science and democracy, it claims that there is something invaluable in the Chinese tradition that should not be overlooked simply because of the weakness of China as a nation. It suggests that the West may learn from Oriental thought in the following five items:

(1) The spirit to assert what is here and now and to let everything go [in order for nature to take its own course];
(2) All-around and all-embracing understanding or wisdom;
(3) A feeling of warmth and compassion;
(4) The wisdom of how to perpetuate its culture;
(5) The attitude that the whole world is like one family.[30]

Surely this is not to state that the West has totally lacked such elements, only that they have been particularly emphasized in Oriental thought without being equally emphasized in the West. It may be argued that T'ang has painted an idealized picture of the East. But surely the ideals a people commit to do make a significant difference in practice. A change in the way of thinking would produce a profound influence in the future.

In his later years T'ang devoted himself to tracing the origins of the insights in traditional Chinese philosophy, publishing six volumes on the subject. The last work he published was a comprehensive system of philosophy he conceived in his lifetime. According to him, the function of the mind can reach nine worlds, each of which has distinct characteristics. His disciple, Tu Li, has given us a succinct summary statement of the system:

The book deals with the whole existence of man, tries to understand the different activities of the mind. Owing to the different activities of the mind, there are different views of things. These views may be horizontal, straightforward, or vertical. Correlating to these views, there are objects of the views of the mind. These objects may be represented as either substance, or form, or function. And they may be regarded as either the objective existents grasped by the mind, or the subjective activities of the mind, or the aspired ideals of the mind that transcend both the subject and the object. When these are combined together, there are the nine worlds of the activities of the mind. They are:

(1) the world of discrete things;
(2) the world of species and genus in terms of empirical generalization;
(3) the world of functional operation;
(4) the world of perceptions interpenetrating with one another;
(5) the world of contemplation of what is transcendent and vacuous;
(6) the world of moral practice;
(7) the world of aspiration toward God;
(8) the world of *shunya* of both the self and the *dharmas*;
(9) the world of the embodiment of heavenly virtues.

As these worlds are manifested by the views of the mind, they are encompassed by the mind. The first three worlds are the worlds of the object. World (1) is formed by the correlation of the mind to substances; world (2) is formed by the correlation of the mind to forms; and world (3) is formed by the correlation of the mind to functions. The next three worlds are the worlds of the subject. World (4) is formed when the mind reflects on its perceptual activities; world (5) is formed when the mind reflects on the manifestation of the subjective forms; and world (6) is formed when the mind reflects on the function of the activities of the subject. The last three worlds are the worlds which transcend both the subject and the object. World (7) is formed when the mind aspires toward the transcendent substance; world (8) is formed when the mind aspires toward the transcendent form; and world (9) is formed when the mind aspires toward the transcendent function.[31]

Obviously, T'ang's formulation of his philosophical system had been influenced by Hegel, but he had avoided using a deductive model that would force empirical data into his system in a rigid fashion. We can see that T'ang tried hard to find a proper place for the insights discovered in the Indian and Western civilizations. But the world he admired most was still the world discovered in the Confucian philosophy of humanity and creativity.

MOU TSUNG-SAN'S AFFIRMATION OF INTELLECTUAL INTUITION AND THE ESTABLISHMENT OF AN ONTOLOGY WITHOUT ADHERENCE

Mou Tsung-san was a graduate of Peking University, but the one teacher who influenced him most was Hsiung Shih-li, who did not offer courses on a regular basis at Peking University. Mou reported a story that explains to us why he was so attracted by Hsiung during his student years:

Once Professor Fung Yu-lan paid a visit to Professor Hsiung, . . . [and they had a discussion on the problem of *liang-chih* (innate knowledge of what is morally good)]. Professor Hsiung said, "You say that *liang-chih* is a postulate, but how can *liang-chih* be merely a postulate? It is really real, moreover, it is a presence. It needs self-consciousness here and now, affirmation here and now.'' . . . This gave me a great shock, and helped to raise the consciousness to the level of that realized by Sung-Ming Neo-Confucian philosophers.[32]

Mou taught at many universities, including National Central University, Normal University in Taipei, Tunghai University in Taichung, and the University of Hong Kong, finally retiring from the Chinese University of Hong Kong. Not only is he the only one who is still alive among those who signed the Manifesto in 1958, but also his influence seems to have grown stronger and stronger. Anyone who is interested in Sung-Ming neo-Confucian philosophies cannot afford to bypass his monumental study on the subject.[33]

Mou's early interest lay in logic and epistemology. He studied Bertrand Russell and Alfred North Whitehead's *Principia Mathematica,* reflecting on the foundation of logic and mathematics. Then he made a thorough study of Immanuel Kant's transcendental approach in his *Critique of Pure Reason.* After he found both the insights and the shortcomings of Kant's *Critique of Practical Reason,* he returned to the great tradition of Chinese philosophy. Most of Mou's important works were published after he left Mainland China in 1949. These publications may be divided into the following three stages:

(1) After he was forty years old, Objective Concern and Concrete Understanding: *Philosophy of History* (1955), *Moral Idealism* (1959), *The Way of Politics and the Way of Government* (1961)

(2) After he was fifty years old, Intensive Classical Studies: *Physical Nature and Speculative Reason* (1963), *The Substance of the Mind and the Substance of the Nature* (three volumes, 1968–69), *From Lu Hsiang-shan to Liu Ch'i-shan* (1979).

(3) After he was sixty years old, Development of New Insights: *The Buddha Nature and Prajna* (two volumes, 1977), *Intellectual Intuition and Chinese Philosophy* (1971), *Phenomenon and the Thing-in-itself* (1975).[34]

In the first stage Mou thought that this was the moment traditional Chinese culture faced its life or death crisis, requiring a deep reflection on the origins of the value of Chinese culture and seeking a way to open up new vistas in the future. In *Moral Idealism* he formulated the doctrine of three traditions:

1. The assertion of *tao-tung* (the tradition of the Way): We must assert the value of morality and religion, jealously guarding the fountainhead of the universe and human life as realized by Confucius and Mencius.

2. The development of *hsüeh-tung* (the tradition of learning): We must expand our cultural life and further develop the knowing subject to absorb the Western tradition, so that learning would gain its independent status.

3. The continuation of *cheng-tung* (the tradition of politics): We must recognize the necessity of adopting the democratic system of government to fulfill truly the political ideals of the sages and worthies in the past.[35]

In *Philosophy of History* Mou pointed out that traditional Chinese culture represents a "synthetic spirit of realizing *li* (principle)" and also a "synthetic spirit of realizing *ch'i* (material force)," whereas Western culture represents an "analytic spirit of realizing *li* (principle)."[36] *The Way of Politics and the Way of Government* concerned itself with how to transform Chinese culture from its traditional emphasis on "sageliness within" to an equal emphasis on "kingliness without." Traditional Chinese culture excelled on the "operational" and "intensional" representations of Reason, but if we want to rest our government on an objective basis and to pursue scientific knowledge, we must also put emphasis on the "structural" and "extensional" representations of Reason.[37]

In the second stage Mou returned to tradition and devoted himself to scholarly studies of Confucianism, Buddhism, and Taoism to grasp the principles of the Chinese philosophy of Mind and Nature.

In *Physical Nature and Speculative Reason* Mou studied the thoughts of the Wei and Chin period. There were two main trends of thought in the period: one put emphasis on an understanding of humankind's physical nature; the other devoted itself to transcendent speculations. Neo-Taoism was at its prime; it was at its best to probe into human physical nature.

The three volumes of *The Substance of the Mind and the Substance of Nature* were the *magnum opus* of his study on Sung-ming neo-Confucian philosophies; *From Lu Hsiang-shan to Liu Ch'i-Shan* could be treated as the fourth volume of the same project. Today no one can afford to bypass the work if one intends to study the subject.[38] In contrast to Wei-Chin's emphasis on the physical nature of humanity, Sung-Ming neo-Confucian philosophies excelled in their realization of the moral nature of humanity. In the introductory part of the book, Mou used a comparative approach to distinguish Chinese philosophy of mind and nature from Plato, Aristotle, and Kant in order to grasp its unique characteristics. This was followed by a detailed study of the philosophies of Chou Tun-i (1017–1073), Chang Tsai (1020–1077), Cheng Hao (1032–1085), Cheng I (1033–1107), Hu Hung (1110–1155), and Chu Hsi (1130–1200). This book was supplemented by *From Lu Hsiang-shan to Liu Ch'i-shan*, which further studied the Lu-Wang tradition and sketched the entire picture of Sung-Ming neo-Confucian philosophy.

From the early Ch'ing dynasty until the May Fourth movement in 1919, scholars generally had a negative opinion of Sung-Ming philosophy, calling it useless in the defense of China from foreign aggression or in helping China to become a strong world power. The Communists denounced the neo-Confucian trend of thought as reflecting the interests of a landlord-scholar class at the expense of the working class.[39] The contemporary neo-Confucian philosophers were really fighting against the tide. It was Hsiung who started the trend, but it was in Mou that we find a truly profound understanding of the insights of this tradition.

Naturally, not all scholars would agree with Mou's interpretations of the neo-Confucian philosophies, but his study was so full of original insights that they should never be overlooked. Chou Tun-i and Chang Tsai were usually understood to be early cosmological thinkers in the Northern Sung period, but Mou pointed out that it was Chou who first built a bridge between *The Doctrine of the Mean* and the *Commentaries of the Book of Changes* and took *ch'eng* (sincerity) as the central ontological principle; Even though it is true that Chang Tsai did have a profound interest in cosmological speculations, we should not forget that it was he who first made the distinction between the so-called knowledge through seeing and hearing (empirical knowledge) and moral knowledge, as well as the distinction between physical nature and moral nature (nature of heaven and earth). Surely, the formulation of their thoughts was not mature; yet they should not be treated separately, since they belonged to the same trend of thought that emphasized the realization of "sageliness within" in the Confucian and Mencian tradition.

It was in the hands of the Ch'eng brothers Ch'eng Hao and Ch'eng I that neo-Confucian philosophy really became the dominant trend in the Northern Sung period. Ch'eng Hao first offered a new interpretation of *li* (principle), and Ch'eng I further developed a philosophy that also put emphasis on *ch'i* (material force) rather than *li*. The two brothers had very different temperaments, but most scholars believe that in philosophy they were in basic agreement. Many of their recorded conversations were blended without identifying who was speaking about what. Mou's contribution lies in the fact that he found definite criteria making sharp distinctions between the thoughts of the two. He believed that Ch'eng I's thought had actually deviated from Mencius's thought, if Mencius was to be accepted as representing the orthodox line of Confucian philosophy. This observation creates strange effects in our understanding of the development of Sung-Ming neo-Confucian philosophy. Chu Hsi (1130–1200), the great Southern Sung philosopher whose works had been adopted as the basis for civil service examinations since 1313 until the dynasty days were over in the early twentieth century and who helped to establish the Confucian orthodox line of transmission accepted by the posterity, developed a comprehensive system of philosophy based mainly on Ch'eng I's insights. Hence Mou drew the conclusion that "it was the side branch which takes the position of orthodoxy."[40] Mou's sympathy lies more with Lu Hsiang-shan (1139–1193) and Wang Yang-ming (1472–1529). But he recognized that there are also shortcomings in the Lu-Wang approach, as the assertion that everyone has *liang-chih* (innate knowledge of what is morally good) may be misinterpreted to mean that "there are sages all over the street." Therefore, Liu Ch'i-shan (1578–1645) put his emphasis on "sincerity of the will" and directed attention from what is obvious toward what is subtle.[41] Mou discovered that Liu's thought shows characteristics similar to that of Hu Hung, an important member of the Hunan School, which was almost extinguished due to severe criticisms of the school by Chu Hsi in the Southern Sung period. Therefore, Mou suggested that instead of talking only about two trends of thought in Sung-Ming neo-Confucian philosophy—Ch'eng-Chu and Lu-Wang—still another trend of thought (Hu-Liu) should be added to have a more complete picture of Sung Ming neo-Confucian philosophy.[42]

Mou has also made significant contributions to explicate the insights implied in Chinese Buddhist philosophies in his two-volume work *The Buddha Nature and Prajna*. Although the Hua-yen School has been regarded by most scholars as setting forth the rounded (perfect) teachings of the Buddha in the most mature fashion, Mou preferred T'ien-tai to Hua-yen. Hua-yen has to renounce the nine lower worlds in favor of the world of *li* (principle), whereas T'ien-tai in a paradoxical way announces that the *dharma* nature is none other than *avidya* (ignorance) and hence gives expression to a truly rounded teaching of the Buddha.[43] Even though not all scholars would agree with Mou's views of Hua-yen and T'ien-tai, it cannot be denied that Mou's interpretation is original and sheds a great deal of light on T'ien-tai teachings, overlooked by scholars for hundreds of years.

Although Mou dug deeply into his own tradition, his thought has never lacked a comparative perspective that was brought into focus in the latest stage of the development of his thought. In *Intellectual Intuition and Chinese Philosophy* he pointed out that the major difference between Chinese and Western philosophies lies in the fact that the three major Chinese traditions—Taoism, Buddhism, and Confucianism—all believe in the possibility of intellectual intuition, whereas major Western traditions deny that there is such a possibility.[44] Mou used Kant as his point of departure, since Kant believed that all human knowledge must depend on sensible intuition, and only God has intellectual intuition. Hence Kant failed to establish a moral metaphysics; instead, he could only hope to formulate a moral theology. Consequently, freedom of the will for Kant can only be a postulate. But for the major Chinese traditions, even though it is admitted that humans are finite beings, they have been endowed with the ability to have a firm grasp of the Way as both transcendent and immanent, regardless of whether the Way is understood to be Taoist, Buddhist, or Confucian. Since the Chinese believe that they have the ability to penetrate reality, there is no longer the wide gap between the phenomenon and the noumenon. It is in this sense that Mou insisted that intellectual intuition must not be excluded from humans. But Mou admitted that the Chinese are not strong enough in purely theoretical pursuits; in this regard they have a great deal to learn from the Western tradition. Although the West has been plagued by the duality of the supernatural and the natural, phenomenon and noumenon, a further transcendence of Kant's position would help the West to appreciate the insights of the Chinese philosophical tradition. Confucianism in particular offers a truly humanistic philosophy that transmits the message of the earth. Mou criticized Martin Heidegger's attempt to reconstruct metaphysics as being inadequate and misguided, because it loses sight of the true meaning of transcendence. Only the Confucian philosophy of humanity and creativity has been able to take care of both the perspectives of the transcendent (heaven) and the immanent (humans).[45]

In *Phenomenon and the Thing-in-itself* Mou made a distinction between what he called "ontology without adherence" and "ontology with adherence." The former has been highly developed in the Oriental traditions, and the latter has been elaborately formulated in the Western traditions. When the infinite mind puts restrictions on itself, the knowing subject is formed; this is the result of a dialectical process. The adherence of the knowing mind and the realization of the infinite mind actually share the same origin. It is here that we can find a foundation for the unity of the two perspectives. In recent years Mou has been pondering the idea of the *summum bonum,* which will be the culminating point of his philosophical system.[46]

SOME CRITICAL REFLECTIONS AND REMARKS ON THE FUTURE DIRECTION OF THE MOVEMENT

In the above discussion I have given sketchy summaries of the thoughts of four contemporary neo-Confucian philosophers. Their publications are numerous. The only way truly to appreciate their contributions is to read their own works; I am providing only an introduction to their ideas.

In spite of the differences in their opinions and approaches, we do find that they shared many things. They all had comparative and macrocosmic perspectives; they all agreed that the Chinese have a great deal to learn from the West in areas such as science and democracy; but they insisted that there are valuable insights in the Chinese tradition that should survive the challenges from the West and make significant contributions to human civilization as a whole. They all aimed at a higher synthesis of the East and the West. Even though this is by no means an easy task, they believed that it is only here that we can find hope for the future.

How would their ideas fare in an age of analysis like ours? Many would simply denounce them as unsubstantiated speculations without cognitive meanings. Ironically, however, they are all clear-minded thinkers possessed of great analytic skills. Even Hsiung Shih-li, the eldest of the four, who had no formal training in Western philosophy, showed great analytic power, making a sharp distinction between empirical, scientific knowledge of objects as function and insight into reality through personal realization of the depth of reason in oneself. In fact, all four stressed the fact that the Chinese should learn how to employ logical reasoning and to pursue scientific knowledge from the West. In Mou's terminology, these things pertain to the "structural" and "extensional" aspects of the representations of reason.

Furthermore, our philosophical foursome gave a cultural interpretation to the emphasis of analysis. Lack of analysis, from their viewpoint, was regarded as deplorable. At the same time, overemphasis on analysis at the expense of other approaches could lead to one-sided development, which is part of the problem inherent in modern Western civilization. Hence they proposed that the West should learn something from the old wisdom of the East. If the West continues to judge everything in terms of power and success, it could lead humankind down a self-destructive path of no return. Therefore, the most important message the contemporary neo-Confucian philosophers have tried to bring to us is that the success of science and technology is not everything; revolutions in political, economic, and even communication systems do not solve all of our problems. The most urgent question posed for one living in the twentieth century remains: "How can I find the meaning of my life in this world?" They suggest that only by realizing humanity (*jen*) in every one of us can we find the intrinsic value in life, the essence of which is creativity (*sheng*). To combat the irrationalities of human beings, we must commit ourselves ultimately to Tao (the Way) by constantly drawing from the depth of our reason and realizing the immanent transcendence within ourselves. It was well said by Thomé Fang that the Chinese are rational without being rationalistic. By the same token we may add that they are also natural without being naturalistic. They have found the harmonious Middle Way as the regulative idea to provide guidance for their lives. This approach, advocated by neo-Confucian philosophers, should never be confused with that of a fideism or voluntarism, since it requires a natural, rational basis that in principle is realizable by all. Although what it teaches cannot be confirmed by empirical generalization, anyone with the same ultimate commitment can testify to the application of the same principle, inasmuch as "the principle is one, while the manifestations are many." True, this pertains to the realm of faith. But what is wrong with having a little faith, provided it is a rational faith that makes a practical difference in the world? Indeed, part of the troubles of modern humans lies precisely in their total lack of faith. Neo-Confucian philosophers are trying to provide an antidote against the nihilistic tendencies of modern humans.

Although the ideas offered by the neo-Confucian philosophers are worth examining by anyone who is troubled by the problem of faith today, the formulation of their thoughts are not without their problems and limitations. In the following discussion I would venture to give some critical reflections on the thoughts of these four contemporary neo-Confucian philosophers.

Hsiung's merit lies in the fact that he affirmed that there is a certain creative source in everyone that finds expression in the two aspects of the closing and opening of the Way. His philosophy is, indeed, a further development of the insights of Confucius, Mencius, and the *Book of Changes*. He must be honored as the first to start the contemporary neo-Confucian philosophical movement. However, in his later years, he greatly violated the texts of the classics to propagate what he believed to be the true Confucian ideals of democracy and socialism, such that his interpretations were rejected by most of his former disciples. It is ironic that to distinguish between what is true and what is false, he gave us a mixture of both. In studying him we must be careful to distinguish between his great insights, which give us guidance, and his poor scholarship, which paints a very wrong-headed picture of the development of Confucian thought in China.

Fang's merit lies in showing such good taste regarding philosophy and literature, both East and West. From a comparative perspective he has tried to convince us to make the right choices in terms of what is more or less desirable. But the trouble here is that even though we can appreciate different kinds of wisdom in turn, Fang has never been able to point out how it is possible for an individual or a culture to combine all of these forms of wisdoms in one, for some of them seem to be mutually exclusive. Moreover, Fang seems to assume that as long as these forms of wisdom are appropriated by human beings, the world will be transformed into a better place. But he failed to specify the conditions under which those ideals can be embodied in reality. Very often men of wisdom fail to persuade men in power. Even Hegel realized that philosophy is like Minerva's owl—it has always come too late. It is one thing to convince us that theory should never be separated from practice; it is another thing to put theory into practice. If philosophy remains confined only to transcendent ideals, it has not been able truly to overcome the kind of nihilism it vows to overcome.

In comparison to Fang, T'ang seemed to show a deeper concern for existential problems and put a greater emphasis on self-discipline. He tried hard to show how an individual can always hope to transcend the actual limitations of his or her life. The function of the mind is forever to open up new vistas owing to the unlimited expansion of the mind–heart of *jen* (humanity). By using his scheme of the nine worlds, he seemed to be able to place the various wisdoms developed in both the East and the West in his grand system of philosophy. But T'ang seemed to have carried his commitment to Harmony too far; he had a tendency to give an idealized picture of Chinese culture and to overlook the problem of serious conflicts between the different worlds as well as the views of the mind. His synthesis was indeed a bold attempt, but it fell short of its goal and appears to be still somewhat premature.

Mou offered a number of insights into the clarification of the basic concepts, the reinterpretation of the classics, the synthesis of the East and the West, pointing to a direction for the future development of human civilization. But his thoughts are not free from difficulties. The term *intellectual intuition* that he used is highly misleading. If we follow Kant's definition of the term, it is truly impossible for any finite beings to have an intellectual intuition of things. What Mou really intended to state is that human understanding does not limit itself to knowledge acquired through sense perceptions. There is also the realization of the Way; here we find an interpenetration of the part and the whole and an infusion of phenomenon and noumenon. This no longer pertains to the realm of knowledge of the object, and in the realization of the Way, there is no longer the separation between the transcendent and the immanent. Although Mou has achieved a number of profound insights, we must not take his philosophy as the culminating point of a philosophical movement but rather as a point of departure for future exploration. His doctrine of the three traditions points out the right direction for us to follow, but the embodiment of ideals in actuality is still a formidable job. The difficulties involved far surpass our wildest imagination, and it would require the greatest effort on our part to exert our creative energy to find a way out of the predicament of the present transitory age full of ideological and actual conflicts.

From the Chinese perspective, the neo-Confucian philosophers are undoubtedly right to insist that there are valuable insights in the tradition that could contribute to contemporary life if they are given a proper reinterpretation. It appears that the movement may have a brighter future since after the disastrous Cultural Revolution in the late sixties even the leaders of Mainland China realized that we have to recognize that there are positive elements in the traditions. Scholars are now allowed to study the works of contemporary neo-Confucian thinkers and to interchange ideas with them wherever possible. The traditions cannot be brushed aside easily. Hence a more reasonable approach is to find out about both the heritage and the burden of our own culture with open eyes and opt for a better course in the future. Apart from the revival of traditional insights, it is also a formidable task to incorporate Western achievements into Chinese culture. The Chinese have great scientific abilities, as has been proven by the fact that three scholars of Chinese descent have thus far won the Nobel prize for physics and one such scholar for chemistry. But it is still a different thing for all Chinese to learn the logical and scientific ways of thinking to the extent that it becomes natural for them.

As formidable as the task is, it is still nothing compared to the problems faced in bringing about social and political changes within China, as it is even more difficult for the Chinese to learn democratic and legal ways of thinking from the West. As Mencius declared, the Confucian tradition valued first the people, then the land, and finally the ruler. However, the long history of the Chinese under a hierarchical form of government makes it almost impossible to break their dependence on their rulers. Nevertheless, the process of modernization is inevitable if China is to survive as a nation in the modern world. Scholars today see far less opposition between the traditional and the modern world, and areas under strong Confucian influence such as Taiwan, Hong Kong, Singapore, Korea, and Japan are all progressing at phenomenal rates in the economic sphere. Although it is difficult to isolate factors that account for the success of these new economic powers, there must be something within the tradition that can be reconstructed so that it can respond well to the needs of the present situation. Now the problem for China is how to maximize the result by learning the modern Western ways and to minimize the damage by refusing to fall prey to its decadent and destructive tendencies.

If it is difficult to bring about changes in China, it is even more difficult to expect fundamental changes in the West. Why would the highly developed nations find any reason to learn from developing countries that are only faint copies of their past? This explains why when the four scholars published their Manifesto, it hardly caused any stir in the West. But is it not true that there is a schism of the soul in the West, as religion is set against science, science is set against humanities, and Anglo-American Analytic philosophy is set against Continental European philosophy, such as phenomenology, existentialism, and hermeneutics? Why is it so hard for the West to admit its own shortcomings and try to learn something from the Chinese Middle Way if it can solve some of its problems? True, occasionally, there has been call for the meeting of the East and West.[47] But it is only the exception that proves the rule. Perhaps there is a better chance for the West to turn toward the East nowadays, as the world is entering into a truly global situation regardless of whether we like it or not. The Vietnamese War caused some soul-searching self-criticisms in the United States. Some subcultural groups in the West are eager to look to the East for wisdom. Especially when Japan threatens to take away the number one position from the United States, there is an increasing interest in learning from the East. This is an age for the East and West to work together to find a way for the future, if humankind is to survive all of the threats of a technological world, such as the possibility of nuclear holocaust, pollution of natural environment, the population explosion, and, more than anything else, the meaninglessness of human existence.

Perhaps no one can find all of the answers for the complex problems of the modern world. But one must first establish the ultimate commitment to humanity and creativity and then try one's best to work out concrete solutions for some of the problems one has to face in life. Today we no longer have a dream to formulate a final system of philosophy, as systems of philosophy are made to be surpassed. But the ultimate commitment to humanity and creativity remains the same, for "principle is one while manifestations are many." Confucius urged us to try hard to do our best even if it is impossible to accomplish our ideal. It is in this way that we find our self-realization in a world of universal flux full of uncertainties. This is perhaps the most important message that the Confucian tradition has to offer to the world.[48]

NOTES

1. See Charlotte Furth, ed., *The Limits of Change: Essays on Conservative Alternatives in Republican China* (Cambridge, Mass.: Harvard University Press, 1976), especially essays by Chang Hao, Tu Wei-ming, and Guy Alitto in the volume.

2. Huang Chen-hua, a longtime disciple of Fang, has reported that for Fang, Confucianism must be regarded as the foundation for Chinese philosophy, because its spirit is open and inclusive. See Huang Chen-hua, "The Inheritance of the Chinese Culture," in Yang Shih-yi, ed., *Memorial Essays for Professor Thome Fang* (Taipei: Cheng-chung, 1982), pp. 105–108.

3. Wing-tsit Chan, trans. and comp., *A Source Book in Chinese Philosophy* (Princeton, N.J.: Princeton University Press, 1963), p. 765.

4. Hsiung Shih-li's *Yüan-ju* was republished by Lung-men in Hong Kong, 1970, and the other three books by the Student Book Co. in Taipei, 1976. These books are the editions I used in preparing this chapter.

5. For Hsiung's epistemology, see Shu-hsien Liu, "The Contemporary Development of a Neo-Confucian Epistemology," *Inquiry* 14 (1971): 19–40, republished as the second chapter in Arne Naess and Alastair Hannay, eds., *Invitation to Chinese Philosophy* (Oslo-Bergen-Tromso: Universitetsforlaget, 1972), pp. 19–40.

6. Hsiung, *Yüan-ju,* p. 7, my translation.

7. Hsiung Shih-li, *Ming-hsin p'ien* (Taipei: Student Book Co., 1976), pp. 19–21, my translation.

8. Tang Yi-jie (Peking) and Hsiao Chieh-fu (Wuhan) organized activities of celebration on the Mainland near the end of 1985 and have collected materials to publish Hsiung's collective works. In Taiwan, Hsiung's collective works will be published by China Times.

9. See Shu-hsien Liu, ed. *Correspondences between Hsiung Shih-li and Liu Ching-chuang* (Taipei: China Times, 1984), pp. 104–105, 152–156. In 1978 the first time I went to Mainland China after I left in 1949, my brother Jen-hsien told me that there were a number of letters between our father (1913–1962) and Hsiung between 1951 and 1961. These letters survived the Cultural Revolution as they were kept in an old hat box in the attic. These were the years in which Hsiung wrote and published his later works. The correspondence sheds much light upon the conditions under which Hsiung completed his later works. In addition, there were serious debates on Buddhist and Confucian philosophies between our father and Hsiung. After much trouble, these materials were brought out of the Mainland and finally published in July 1984.

10. Hsiung, *Yüan-ju,* p. 219. This rendering is truly a violation of the original text.

11. Ibid.

12. Hsiung Shih-li, *Ch'ien-k'un yen* (Taipei: Student Book Co., 1976), pp. 8–9.

13. Ibid., pp. 10–13.

14. Hsiung, *Yüan-ju*, pp. 217–218.

15. Ibid., pp. 216–219.

16. Ibid., pp. 219–225.

17. Fang's collected works were published after he died. His Chinese works were published by Dawn Cultural Enterprise and the English works by Linking.

18. This essay by Fang was republished in *Sheng-sheng-chih-te (The Virtue of Creative Creativity* [Taipei: Dawn Cultural Enterprise, 1979] pp. 137–158).

19. Thomé H. Fang, *Chinese Philosophy: Its Spirit and Its Development* (Taipei: Linking, 1981), pp. 535-538.

20. Ibid., p. 536.

21. Shu-hsien Liu, "A Review of Thomé H. Fang, *Sheng-sheng-chih-te* and *Creativity in Man and Nature,*" *Journal of Chinese Philosophy* 10 (December 1983): 420–421.

22. Ibid., pp. 421–422.

23. Thomé H. Fang, *The Chinese View of Life* (Hong Kong: Union Press, 1956), p. 52.

24. Ibid.

25. See Shu-hsien Liu, "A Review of Thome H. Fang, *Chinese Philosophy: Its Spirit and Its Development,*" *Journal of Chinese Philosophy* 10 (December 1983): 411–416.

26. Fang, *Sheng-sheng-chih-te*, p. 141, my translation.

27. Shu-hsien Liu, "A Review of *Sheng-sheng-chih-te* and *Creativity in Man and Nature,*" *Journal of Chinese Philosophy,* 10 (December 1983): 424–425.

28. T'ang Chun-i, *The Spiritual Values of the Chinese Culture* (Taipei: Cheng-chung, 1953), pp. 2–3, my translation.

29. The Manifesto was first published in Chinese in *Democratic Review* 9 (January 1958) in Hong Kong. It was later translated and published as an appendix in Carsun Chang's *The Development of Neo-Confucian Thought,* 2 vols. (New York: Bookman Associates, 1957–1962), 11: 455–483.

30. Ibid., with slight modification.

31. Tu Li, *The Philosophy of T'ang Chun-i* (Taipei: Student Book Co., 1982), p. 59. The last work, *Human Existence and the Worlds of the Mind*, by T'ang Chun-i was also published by the Student Book Co. in 1977 in two volumes.

32. Mou Tsung-san, *The Learning of Life* (Taipei: San-ming, 1970), p. 136, my translation.

33. Mou Tsung-san, *Hsin-t'i yü hsing -t'i (The Substance of the Mind and the Substance of the Nature)*, 3 vols. (Taipei: Cheng-chung, 1968–1969). See my review of this book in *Philosophy East and West* 20 (October 1970): 419–422.

34. This classification is based on that adopted in this book: Tsai Jen-hou, Shu-hsien Liu, et al., *Professor Mou Tsung-san's Philosophy and Works: Essays in Honor of Professor's Mou* (Taipei: Student Book Co., 1978), pp. 12–13. According to the classification, before these three stages, there were still two earlier stages: in the first stage, he was interested in the philosophy of change and cosmology; in the second stage, logic and epistemology. For Mou's epistemology, see Shu-hsien Liu, "The Contemporary Development of a Neo-Confucian Epistemology."

35. Mou Tsung-san, *Moral Idealism*, rev. ed. (Taipei: Student Book Co., 1982), pp. 260–262.

36. Mou Tsung-san, Preface to *Philosophy of History* (Hong Kong: Young Son, 1962), pp. v-vi.

37. Mou Tsung-san, *The Way of Politics and the Way of Government*, rev. ed. (Taipei: Student Book Co., 1980), pp. 44–62.

38. This was evidenced by the fact that there were many references to Mou's works in the international conference on Chu Hsi held in Honolulu in July 1982. The conference papers have been published in a volume edited by Wing-tsit Chan for the University of Hawaii Press, 1986.

39. Examples are too numerous to be cited. For scholarly works, suffice it to mention only Hou Wai-lu's *General History of Chinese Thought*, People's Publishing House (Beijing, 1956). The negative attitude reached its peak during the Cultural Revolution in the late sixties, when Confucianism became a dirty word to be condemned indiscriminately; the slightest association with it could get one into deep trouble even at the cost of one's life.

40. Mou, *Hsin-t'i yü hsing-t'i*, I: 42–60, especially p. 54: see also my article "The Problem of Orthodoxy in Chu Hsi's Philosophy," presented at the international conference on Chu Hsi in Honolulu in 1982.

41. Mou Tsung-san, *From Lu Hsiang-shan to Liu Ch'i-shan* (Taipei: Student Book Co., 1979) pp. 451–458.

42. Mou, *Hsin-t'i yü hsing-t'i*, I: 42–60, 415.

43. Mou Tsung-san, *The Buddha Nature and Prajna*, 2 vols. (Taipei: Student Book Co., 1977), I: 556–572.

44. Mou Tsung-san, *Intellectual Intuition and Chinese Philosophy* (Taipei: Commercial Press, 1971), pp. 184–215.

45. Ibid., Preface, pp. 1–4.

46. Mou Tsung-san, Preface to *Phenomenon and the Thing-in-itself* (Taipei: Student Book Co., 1975), pp. 7–8. Recently, Mou informed me that the manuscript on the *Summum bonum* was completed and had been submitted to the Student Book Co. for publication.

47. See F.S.C. Northrop, *The Meeting of East and West* (New York: Macmillan, 1946).

48. See Shu-hsien Liu, *Chinese Philosophy and China's Modernization* (Taipei: China Times, 1980), pp. 65–66.

SELECTED BIBLIOGRAPHY

Brière, O. *Fifty Years of Chinese Philosophy*. Translated by Laurence G. Thompson. New York: Praeger, 1965.

Chan, Wing-tsit. *Religious Trends in Modern China*. New York: Columbia University Press, 1953.

————, trans. and comp. *A Source Book in Chinese Philosophy*. Princeton, N.J.: Princeton University Press, 1963.

Chang, Carsun. *The Development of Neo-Confucian Thought*. 2 vols. New York: Bookman Associates, 1957–1962.

De Bary, William Theodore, ed. *Self and Society in Ming Thought*. New York: Columbia University Press, 1970.

————. *The Unfolding of Neo-Confucianism*. New York: Columbia University Press, 1975.

Fang, Thomé H. *Chinese Philosophy: Its Spirit and Its Development*. Taipei: Linking, 1981.

————. *The Chinese View of Life*. Hong Kong: Union Press, 1956; Taipei: Linking, 1980.

————. *Creativity in Man and Nature: Collected Philosophical Essays*. Taipei: Linking, 1980.

————. *Tung-mei ch'üan-chi (Complete Works of Thomé H. Fang)*. Taipei: Dawn Cultural Enterprise, 1978–1984.

Furth, Charlotte, ed. *The Limits of Change: Essays on Conservative Alternatives in Republican China*. Cambridge, Mass.: Harvard University Press, 1976.

Hsiung, Shih-li. *Ch'ien-k'un yen (An Explication of the Meaning of Hexagrams Ch'ien and K'un)*. Taipei: Student Book Co., 1976.

————. *Hsin wei-shih lun (New Consciousness-Only Doctrine)*. Shanghai: Commercial Press, 1947.

————. *Ming-hsin p'ien (On Enlightenment of the Mind)*. Taipei: Student Book Co., 1976.

————. *Shih-li yü-yao (Important Sayings by Hsiung Shih-li)*. Taipei: Kuang-wen, 1962.

————. *T'i yung lun (A Treatise on Substance and Function)*. Taipei: Student Book Co., 1976.

————. *Yüan-ju (An Inquiry on Confucianism)*. Hong Kong: Lung-men, 1970.

Levenson, Joseph R. *Confucian China and Its Modern Fate*. Berkeley: University of California Press, 1958.

Li, Tu. *T'ang Chun-i hsien-sheng te che-hsüeh (The Philosophy of T'ang Chun-i)*. Taipei: Student Book Co., 1982.

Liu, Shu-hsien. *Chung-kuo che hsüeh yü hsien-tai-hua (Chinese Philosophy and China's Modernization)*. Taipei: China Times, 1980.

————. "The Contemporary Development of a Neo-Confucian Epistemology." *Inquiry* 14 (1971): 19–40. Republished as the second chapter in *Invitation to Chinese Philosophy*. Edited by Arne Naess and Alastair Hannay. Oslo-Bergen-Tromso: Universitetsforlaget, 1972, pp. 19–40.

————. *Hsiung Shih-li yü Liu Ching-chuang lun-hsüeh shu-chien (Correspondences between Hsiung Shih-li and Liu Ching-chuang)*. Taipei: China Times, 1984.

————. "Hsiung Shih-li's Theory of Causation." *Philosophy East and West* 12, no. 4 (October 1969): 399–407.

————. "The Religious Import of Confucian Philosophy: Its Traditional Outlook and Contemporary Significance." *Philosophy East and West* 21, no. 2 (April 1971): 157–175.

————. "A Review of Mou Tsung-san, *Hsin-t'i yü Hsing-t'i*." *Philosophy East and West* 20, no. 4 (October 1970): 419–422.

————. "A Review of Mou Tsung-san, *Intellectual Intuition and Chinese Philosophy*." *Philosophy East and West* 23, nos. 1–2 (January and April 1973): 255–256.

————. "A Review of Thomé H. Fang, *Chinese Philosophy: Its Spirit and Its Development*." *Journal of Chinese Philosophy* 10, no. 4 (December 1983): 411–416.

————. "A Review of Thomé H. Fang, *Sheng-sheng-chih-te* and *Creativity in Man and Nature*." *Journal of Chinese Philosophy* 10, no. 4 (December 1983): 417–426.

————, comp. "The Philosophy of a Contemporary Confucian-Humanist [T'ang Chun-i]." *Chinese Studies in Philosophy* 5, no. 1 (Fall 1973): 5, no. 4 (Summer 1974): 25–45.

Metzger, Thomas A. *Escape from Predicament*. New York: Columbia University Press, 1977.

Mou Tsung-san. *Chen-tao yü chih-tao (The Way of Politics and the Way of Government)*. Rev. ed. Taipei: Student Book Co., 1980.

————. *Chih te chih-chiao yü chung-kuo che-hsüeh (Intellectual Intuition and Chinese Philosophy)*. Taipei: Commercial Press, 1971.

————. *Fu-hsing yü pan-jo (The Buddha Nature and Prajna)*. 2 vols. Taipei: Student Book Co., 1977.

————. *Hsien-hsiang yü wu-tze-sheng (Phenomemon and the Thing-in-Itself)*. Taipei: Student Book Co., 1975.

————. *Hsin-t'i yü hsing-t'i (The Substance of the Mind and the Substance of the Nature)*. 3 vols. Taipei: Cheng-chung, 1968-1969.

————. *Jen-shih-hsin chih p'i p'an (A Critique of the Cognitive Mind)*. 2 vols. Hong Kong: Union Press, 1956–1957.

————. *Li-shih-che-hsüeh (Philosophy of History)*. Hong Kong: Young Son, 1962.

————. *Sheng-ming te hsüeh-wen (The Learning of Life)*. Taipei: San-ming, 1970.

————. *Tao-te te li-hsiang-chu-i (Moral Idealism)*. Revised ed. Taipei: Student Book Co., 1982.

————. *Tsai-hsing yü hsüan-li (Physical Nature and Speculative Reason)*. Hong Kong: Young Son, 1963.

————. *Ts'ung Lu Hsiang-shan tao Liu Ch'i-shan (From Lu Hsiang-shan to Liu Ch'i-shan)*. Taipei: Student Book Co., 1979.

Northrop, F.S.C. *The Meeting of East and West*. New York: Macmillan, 1946.

T'ang, Chun-i. *Che-hsüeh kai-lun (A Treatise on Philosophy)*. 2 vols. Hong Kong: Mencius Educational Foundation, 1961.

————. *Chung hsi che-hsüeh ssu-hsiang chih pi-chiao lun-wen chi (Comparative Studies of Chinese and Western Philosophical Thought)*. Taipei: Cheng Chung, 1943.

————. *Chung-kuo che-hsüeh yüan-lun (The Development of Ideas in Chinese Philosophy)*. Vol. 1, Hong Kong: Young Son, 1966. Vols. 2–6, Hong Kong, New Asia Research Institute, 1968–1975.

————. *Chung-kuo jen-wen ching-shen chih fa-chan (The Development of Chinese Humanistic Spirit)*. Hong Kong: Young Son, 1958.

————. *Chung-kuo wen-hua chih ching-shen chia-chih (The Spiritual Values of the Chinese Culture)*. Taipei: Cheng Chung, 1953.

————. *Hsin wu yü jen-sheng (Mind, Matter, and Life)*. Hong Kong: Asia Publications, 1953.

————. *Jen-sheng chih ti-yen (The Experience of Life)*. Shanghai: Chung Hua, 1943; reprint, Hong Kong:Young Son, 1956.

————. *Jen-wen ching-shen chih ch'ung-chien (The Reconstruction of Humanistic Spirit)*. 2 vols. Hong Kong: New Asia, 1955.

————. *Sheng-ming ts'un-tsai yü hsin-lin-ching-chieh (Human Existence and the Worlds of the Mind)*. 2 vols. Taipei: Student Book Co., 1977.

————. *Tao-te tzu-o chih chien-li (The Establishment of the Moral Self)*. Chung Ch'ing: Commercial Press, 1944. Rev. ed., Hong Kong: Young Son, 1963.

————. *Wen-hua yih-shih yü tao-te li-hsing (Cultural Consciousness and Moral Reason)*. 2 vols. Hong Kong: Union Press, 1958, 1960.

Tsai, Jen-hou, et al. *Profesor Mou Tsung-san's Philosophy and Works: Essays in Honor of Professor Mou*. Taipei: Student Book Co., 1978.

Yang, Shih-yi, ed. *Fang-tung-mei hsien-sheng chi-nien-chi (Memorial Essays for Professor Thomé Fang)*. Taipei: Cheng-chung, 1982.

13

Philosophical Reflections on the Modernization of Confucianism as Traditional Morality

CHARLES WEI-HSUN FU

For more than two thousand years, Confucianism has been the greatest ideological force in the formation and development of China's traditional morality and ethical culture in general. Its influence has been felt primarily in terms of fundamental moral values, personal virtues and cultivation, sociomoral norms or proprieties (*li*), sociomoral education, the rectification of names (*cheng-ming*), ideal personhood, and the politicosocial ideal. Confucianism also has profoundly inspired Korea, Japan, and other Asian societies and nations by gradually shaping their respective traditional morality and ethical culture. As a result, these countries have enjoyed political stability, social order, and individual security.

However, very drastic economic and politicosocial, as well as ideological, changes in modern Asia—especially in our present era of scientific-technological revolution—have prompted a serious concern among Confucian scholars with respect to the future prospects for traditional Confucian ethics and morality. First, the crucial question arises as to whether traditional Confucianism has or will become an ideological obstacle to the unceasing modernization and postmodernization of all of the Confucian-related societies. More important, must Confucianism itself, as a traditional morality, undergo some kind of modernization, involving its modernistic reinterpretation, readjustment, revision, or revitalization? If so, what exactly is to be done with respect to that modernization in order that Confucianism can and will positively contribute to the enormously difficult task of modernization without becoming an ideological obstacle in the process? Following the massive postwar economic developments in Japan and the other four Asian countries, or "dragons (or tigers)," namely, Korea, Taiwan, Hong Kong, and Singapore, the task itself is the creative self-transformation of the Confucian-related societies in politicosocial, intellectual, and cultural terms.

The main objective here is to attempt some philosophical reflections on the necessary modernization of Confucian ethics and morality inherited from the past by way of critically reexamining its pros and cons from our modern and postmodern perspective. I will make constructive suggestions concerning the modernization of Confucianism in traditional morality involving both theory and practice.

The "miraculous" economic developments experienced in Japan and the other "four Asian dragons" in the past twenty to thirty years has caused much speculation among social scientists and Confucian scholars with regard to the ideological role traditional Confucianism may have played in the ongoing process of developments in these Confucian-related societies. Their speculation has been in part inspired by a revival of Max Weber's sociology of religion thesis, as given in his *Protestant Ethic and the Spirit of Capitalism*. According to Weber, the Protestant (and particularly the Calvinist) ethic—innerworldly asceticism, a this-worldly mission, the value of hard work, and so on—formed one of the ideological causes of the rise and development of modern European capitalism and was one of its effects. By contrast, in *The Religion of China* Weber observed that traditional Confucianism would in all probability become an ideological hindrance to the development of capitalism in China (and perhaps in the other Confucian-related societies).

Despite Weber's negative observations concerning Chinese culture, some social scientists and Confucian scholars contend that traditional Confucianism must have helped to create a generally favorable ideological condition for the postwar economic success of Japan and the "four tigers." Their view is based on the established ethical understanding that traditional Confucianism always puts strong emphasis on moral self-discipline, hard work, thriftiness, familial love, respect for the elderly and for seniority, mutual encouragement, and human cooperation, and so on. Moreover, there is the sharp contrast between the prosperous conditions in the Confucian-influenced nations and the economic problems of other Asian nations, such as India or Sri Lanka, that were not exposed to the secular-oriented moral teachings of the Confucian tradition.

Since I am not a sociologist or a historian, I do not wish to add my own speculation on this matter. However, regardless of whether or not traditional Confucianism has made an ideological contribution to the postwar economic development of Confucian-influenced Asian societies, the question I have raised with respect to the self-modernization of traditional Confucianism deserves more attention. It is of the utmost importance to reexamine the pros and cons of traditional Confucianism in order that this great moral tradition be revitalized and reaffirmed through its timely self-adjustment and self-improvement. Moreover, traditional Confucianism can be seen as ideologically fitting and positively contributory to the modernistically creative self-transformation, which has yet to be completed, of the Confucian-influenced Asian societies.

As I understand it, Confucian ethics and morality consists of the following five theses: (1) all ethics and morality must be grounded upon a theory of human nature; (2) the metapsychological and ethical basis for Confucian morality is the Mencian theory of (original) mind/nature (*hsin/hsing*), evolved from Mencius's theory of human nature as originally good reaching its existentio-ontological culmination in Wang Yang-ming's teaching of extending the human being's innate knowledge of the good (*liang-chih*); (3) the Confucian goal of human life that lies in the Mencian theory of *hsin/hsing* makes it possible in both principle and practice for every human being to develop fully his or her moral potential for the attainment of sagehood; (4) humanity/righteousness or human kindness manifested through moral rightness (*jen-yi*) constitutes the highest principle of Confucian morality, governing all the Confucian moral virtues, moral judgments, and moral actions; (5) the way of inner sagehood (the day-to-day process of moral perfection of every member of society, beginning with political leaders who set a good example for the people) is the ethical prerequisite and assurance for the eventual realization of the way of outer kingship (the moral perfection of the entire society through humane government).

The first Confucian thesis, that all ethics and morality must be grounded in a theory of human nature, is one of the great human insights Confucianism has contributed to the history of ethical thought. This thesis can hardly be refuted, either in terms of a lack of either universal validity or intersubjective acceptability. It is, in fact, shared by many other great philosophical schools and traditions. Today more and more philosophical and religious thinkers, as well as scientists, have come to agree that we must have a basic understanding of human nature (and mind) prior to talking about ethics and morality. For example, in *Modern Moral Philosophy* W. D. Hudson observed:

When we are arguing with someone about a moral issue, we are entitled to ask him how he would answer the question "What is man?" Then, if he replies to this inquiry, we are entitled to raise the further question as to whether or not his anthropology is logically compatible with his ethic. He cannot simply brush the question aside by appealing the (Humean) is-ought dichotomy. . . . What I have said above has the further practical consequence that it makes some foundation in fact for moral judgment at least conceivable. We *may* eventually settle the question "What is man?" By "settle" I mean "secure general agreement about." Highly improbable it may be, but not inconceivable. . . . Disciplines which inquire into the nature of man could shed some light upon ethics. I have in mind the human sciences (such as physiology, psychology, sociology) and also religion.[1]

Although Mencius and his followers fully agree with Hudson that ethics and morality must presuppose a sound understanding of human nature, they would contend that neither the human sciences nor religion—nor the "existential anthropology" so mislabeled in Hudson's book—could shed any *ultimate* light on the *primordial source* of ethics and morality at all. For the Mencian school, the final breakthrough in ethics and morality can be achieved only through the human being's realization of our original goodness as a matter of *existentio-moral* self-awakening of the *hsin/hsing*.

This leads to the second Confucian thesis, namely, the Mencian specification of the theory of human nature. According to this thesis, the ultimate ground for human morality (*jen-lun*), expressed in Confucian terms as the way of human kindness (*jen*), must be found in the original goodness of human nature. This original goodness is clearly evidenced by what Mencius called the "four beginnings" (*ssu-tuan*), that is, the immediate and spontaneous expressions of the human mind (*jen-hsin*) existentially self-awakened as the original (primordially moral) mind (*pen-hsin*).

As we know, Confucius himself never developed any theory of human nature to accompany the way of *jen* he had established for Confucian tradition. Apparently, he was unaware of the philosophical necessity of developing any such theory to serve as the philosophical (metapsychological) foundation of human (Confucian) morality. His words "By nature (*hsing*) men are all alike; by practice (or acquired habit) they become far apart" can be cited in support of either Mencius's theory of innate goodness or that of Hsün Tzu that human nature is originally evil.[2] It was indeed due to Mencius's ingenious philosophical reasoning that the Confucian way of *jen* is metapsychologically deepened and justified in terms of original human goodness. Mencius's point is that the "four beginnings" as immediate and spontaneous manifestations of our original *hsin/hsing* may not be empirically conclusive from the viewpoint of naturalistically oriented scientists who hold the position of value neutrality with respect to the essence of human nature. However, as I have argued elsewhere, Wang Yang-ming's completion of Mencius's theory can make its existentially more appealing and philosophically more convincing.[3] Our *liang-chih* or original *hsin/hsing* may rarely manifest itself in our everyday life.

However, it can hardly be denied that in what Karl Jaspers called a "border-situation" (*Grenzsituation*), which is existentially a life-and-death situation, the human mind cannot but awaken itself as the original mind revealing the original goodness of human nature. In this same context, Mencius and Wang Yang-ming could and would quote Confucius' disciple Tseng Tzu, who said "When a bird is about to die, its notes are sad; when a person is about to die, how words are good."[4] This statement illustrates the ultimate meaning of human morality, most strikingly revealed in the existential border-situation, when a human being is able to realize *liang-chih* or original *hsin/hsing* by, for example, deciding to "give up life and choose moral rightness (*yi*)" or facing courageously one's own "death and dying," which Elisabeth Kübler-Ross thanatologically characterized as "the final stage of human growth."[5] In short, the fact that the human person is best able to realize *liang-chih* or original *hsin/hsing* in the existential border-situation not only points to the *ultimate* meaning of ethics and morality but also existentially justifies the Mencian theory as the metapsychological foundation of the Confucian way of *jen*.

The everlasting significance of the Mencian theory of *hsin/hsing* or *liang/chih* cannot be overemphasized. It undoubtedly will continue to exercise a profound influence, in our contemporary society, upon the method and practice of personal cultivation and sociomoral education, particularly the education of children. The neo-Confucian philosopher Lu Hsiang-shan, seemed to comprehend correctly the pedagogical strength of Mencius's theory of human nature when he stated:

Mencius says, "What a calamitous consequence it will produce if you speak of what is not good in others." People nowadays tend to miss the essential point of these words. Mencius holds that man's nature is originally good, and he would, therefore, say that man can be good in all respects. Now if you speak of what is not good in others, they will be apt to remain not good, and treat you not in a good manner. How do you respond, then? That is why [Mencius has to say] "What a calamitous consequence!"[6]

Although the Mencian theory requires no revision in itself, it needs to be expanded modernistically by accommodating or integrating some important non-Mencian theories of human nature and mind. They will serve as supplementary theories, giving a more comprehensive and satisfactory explanation of the origin and nature of moral evil, weakness, or failure. Mencius's own account of the origin of evil is simply that one fails to resist the external temptations only because "one does not think." He never bothered to ask further why "one does not think" at all. Lu Hsiang-shan and Wang Yang-ming, who both faithfully followed Mencius's theory and completed it in the form of "Mind is Principle" (*hsin chi li*), also straightforwardly spoke of the moral self-awakening of the mind while paying very little attention to the negative aspects of human nature and mind. I would, therefore, suggest that it is a philosophical necessity first to synthesize the Mencian theory as advocated by the "Mind Is Principle" school and the theory of twofold nature (the nature of heaven and Earth and the con-taminated nature, *ch'i*), as put forth by Chang Tsai and the Ch'eng-Chu school of "Nature Is Principle" (*hsing chi li*). The Mencian theory can still remain as the metapsychological foundation of Confucian ethics and morality, but it must integrate Chu Hsi's theory as its supplement on the lower level. The traditional confrontation, which seems to be only an apparent confrontation, between the two major neo-Confucian schools with respect to human nature and mind thus can be philosophically resolved within the Confucian tradition.

But this neo-Confucian synthesis is only the first step to be undertaken as a means to accomplish a modernistic expansion of Mencian theory to deal with all aspects of human life, both positive and negative. For the next step I would also suggest that the Mencian theory of *hsin/hsing* continues to expand itself by accommodating some non-Confucian theories, such as modern psychology or cultural anthropology in the West, that attempt a scientific or naturalistic inquiry into the empirical reality of human mind and behavior. This expansion will allow the Confucianists, who have been under the Mencian influence, to see more objectively empirical reality as it is, suspending the application of any moral judgment. This scientific and value-neutral understanding of humankind will not conflict with the Confucian ethical-oriented understanding of humanity if Con-fucianists are able to distinguish three levels of understanding human nature and mind in a hierarchical order: the scientific understanding on the lowest level, Chu Hsi's neo-Confucian understanding on the middle level, and the Mencian understanding on the highest level. Within this hierarchy, the Mencian theory can continue to serve as the ultimate ground for Confucian ethics and morality.

I would further propose that the metapsychological significance of the Christian doctrine of original sin (taken in the existential rather than fundamentalist sense) and the Buddhist doctrine of ignorance (wu-ming) be fully recognized and that these non-Confucian doctrines be even properly accommodated into the lowest level of the Confucian theory of human nature. This accommodation will allow Confucianists to understand more seriously the state or actuality of total, moral depravity—in cases such as patricide or the Holocaust, which has been deeply sensed by Christians and (Pure Land) Buddhists. In our extremely complex and complicated modern world, Confucianists as moral educators must learn to understand not only the instinctual (nonmoral) aspects of human life but the evil ones as well. On the one hand, they should certainly continue to insist on the original goodness of humankind—at least in principle—to help others become existentially awakened to their primordially moral nature. They should, on the other hand, also come to understand fully the darkest side of human existence where sin or ignorance takes the place of liang-chih.

In short, a modernistically expanded Confucian theory of human nature will have to consist of the following four levels: (1) on the highest level, the Mencian theory shows the primordial source of Confucian ethics and morality— the level of original goodness (pen-jan men); (2) on the next highest level, Chang Tsai's or Chu Hsi's theory of twofold nature shows the moral necessity of "transforming one's ch'i-contaminated nature into the original moral nature"—the level of cultivated oughtness (ying-jan men); (3) on the lowest level, the scientific investigation of human mind and behavior leads to a more objective understanding of human natural desire or instinct, without involving any moral judgment—the level of nonmoral actuality (shih-jan men); (4) on the lowest level, we find the basically religious understanding of the darkest and most tragic aspect of human life in terms of total depravity—the level of sinful fall (ch'en-mo men).[7]

The third Confucian thesis, that humanity can and should try to become virtuous (jen-jen) or even a sage (sheng-jen) through day-to-day personal cultivation and moral practice, is grounded upon the second thesis of humanity's original goodness of hsin/hsing. Mencius argued that there is no difference between ordinary human beings and the ancient sage–emperors, such as Yao or Shun, insofar as the human moral potential for the attainment of sagehood is concerned for the simple reason that the moral nature of all human beings on the highest level of human nature always remains the same. What really distinguishes those who follow the "great part" (moral nature) from those who follow the "little part" (animal instinct) is twofold: environmental conditions and human efforts. Mencius thus said:

Take the barley for instance. Sow its seeds and cover them with soil. The place is the same and the time of sowing is also the same. The plants grow rapidly and by the summer solstice they all ripen. If there is any unevenness, it is because of the difference of the soil, of the unequal nourishment afforded by the rains and dews, and of the difference in human efforts involved. Thus, things of the same kind are all alike. Why should we doubt with respect to (the primordial nature of) man? The sage and I are of the same kind.[8]

There are two important characteristics of the third thesis. The first characteristic is that Confucianism, as distinguishable from Christianity or Buddhism, is uniquely a "moral religion." The Confucian person's day-to-day personal cultivation and moral practice for the attainment of sagehood is understood by traditional Confucianists as a matter of heavenly appointment" (t'ien-ming).[9] The Confucian person is what Mencius called "a citizen of Heaven" (t'ien-min), who rejoices in the voluntary acceptance of the appointment as the "true (moral) destiny" (cheng-ming).[10] To all genuine Confucianists, the moral way of life is itself supreme happiness or eternal bliss. I think that the traditional Confucian identity of morality and happiness stressing inner peace, equanimity, and joy should be inherited as a healthy life orientation for the modern person, who often finds little relief from all kinds of ever-mounting competitiveness and tension in highly industrialized and urbanized societies. The moral spirit of Confucianism also can be built into daily economic and social operations, such as factory work or business management, as a means of boosting morale and production. It is in this sense that Confucianism can make a lasting ideological contribution to the modernistically creative self-transformation of the rapidly changing Confucian-related societies.

The second characteristic is that traditional Confucianism is a typical moral idealism, advocating what I would call "maxima moralia" (maximum morality), in sharp contrast to "minima moralia" (minimum morality). Traditional Confucianists earnestly encourage us to exert our mind to the utmost and perfect moral nature for the eventual attainment of inner sagehood (nei-sheng), wherein is to be found the summum bonum of humankind. By contrast, minima moralia, which fairly represents the prevailing ethical understanding in almost all well-developed and modernized nations or societies, requires only our strict observation of the established sociomoral rules or "law and order," often expressed in legalistic terms. The ever-intensified legislation of ethics and morality in the United States is the most conspicuous example in this respect.

Unlike maxima moralis, minima moralia need not make any high-minded moral demand that each member of society ought constantly to perfect his or her moral nature beyond merely external observance of the legalistically stipulated sociomoral rules or conventions. Therefore, it can be said that whereas minima moralia takes a radically realistic (hence more and more legalistic) approach to present-day moral problems, such as divorce or abortion, traditional Confucianism as maxima moralia idealistically promotes the way for moral perfection (inner sagehood) as a matter of (the Confucian) person's ultimate concern. Indeed, Confucian moral idealism and moral religion are ultimately one and the same. The question remains: Can we find a middle way between minima moralia (moral realism), and traditional Confucianism as maxima moralia (moral idealism), without abandoning the ethical value and educational significance of traditional Confucianism? It seems to me that if Confucianism is destined to go on playing the age-old role as the basic moral guide for Confucian-related societies in the period of modernization and postmodernization, it must steer a middle course between its own maxima moralia and the modernistic minima moralia. How is this moral task to be accomplished?

First, contemporary Confucianists must shift their emphasis from the traditional, overly idealistic and overly optimistic thinking that "one can and should (try to) become a sage" to a more realistic understanding that the overwhelming majority of human beings have never tried, nor will they try, to attain sagehood. This shift will allow contemporary Confucianists to realize the modernistic importance of practicing minima moralia first, before trying to promote maxima moralia, which can always remain as their ethical goal or ideal. To use an analogy, in advocating maxima moralia dissociated from minima moralia, traditional Confucianists as typical moral idealists can be likened to baseball players who always want to hit a home run without first learning how to get a base hit. If minima moralia is not secured, the Confucian promotion of maxima moralia will only become empty talk to the great majority of people. This is particularly true in the case of politicosocial morality beyond individual morality. I shall come back to this point when I deal with the ethical problems related to the fifth thesis.

Second, contemporary Confucianists also must abandon the traditional way of overglorifying Confucian sagehood in terms of both purity of the heart (the mind of *jen*) and consequence-related decision making. According to traditional Confucianism, great sages like Confucius were able not only to love all humanity gradationally, and realize *jen* in terms of pure motive or goodwill, but also to make no mistakes in decision making. This is an overstatement and can never be proven. "Motive-centered morality," which applies to the Confucian notion of inner sagehood, must be well distinguished from "consequence-centered morality," which is a matter of decision making involving utilitarian consequences. Traditional Confucianists seem to have never understood clearly the essential distinction between them. That one's motive or intention is all pure and good is no guarantee for a particular decision or action to be morally appropriate— let alone perfect. A morally appropriate decision or action must be able to bring about utilitarianly felicitous or desirable—or at least produce no undesirable— consequences. This is particularly true in our ever-pluralized and ever-complicated (post-) modern world, in which collective wisdom often is needed to solve difficult moral problems. Here again, contemporary Confucianists must make a modernistic shift of emphasis from the high-minded and overbeautiful sagehood to the "less perfect" Confucian personhood called the "*chün-tzu*" (the Confucian aspirant for sagehood). The notion of the *chün-tzu* cannot and should not replace sagehood as the new Confucian ideal personhood, but it is very important to stress it instead of sagehood in our present sociomoral context. We must realize that we are living in the democratic world of "ordinary people" who may be morally obligated to become *chün-tzu* but certainly not a sage. In short, the limitations of the third Confucian thesis generally reflect the limitations of the second thesis. If the latter is modernistically well expanded, as suggested above, the former can be modernistically improved as well.

The fourth Confucian thesis is that *jen-yi*—human kindness (*jen*) manifested through moral oughtness—constitutes the highest principle of Confucian morality, governing all Confucian virtues, moral judgments, and moral actions. Both the ideas of *jen* and *yi* appeared in *The Analects of Confucius,* but it was Mencius who combined these two to form the highest principle of Confucian morality. In this sense, Mencius's ethical contribution is as great as his metapsychological one.

The Chinese character *jen* is composed of two parts—the number two (*erh*) and person (*jen*). It signifies the fundamental moral context of humanity in which morality begins with the concrete and genuine human relationship and intercourse between two persons as autonomous moral agents. As Mencius said, "*jen* (human-kindness) is [what constitutes the essential nature of] *jen* (man)."[11] Although Confucius himself never attempted to define the notion of *jen,* he did give various answers to the question "what is *jen?*" as raised by his disciples on various occasions. Based on my hermeneutic reading of the *Analects,* I find in it no less than ten interrelated meanings of *jen:* (1) Confucius sometimes spoke of *jen* as a particular virtue, often contrasted with knowledge (*chih*), courage (*yung*), uprightness (*chih*), firmness (*kang*), and so forth. (2) It is, however, misleading to think of Confucius' *jen* as merely a particular virtue, for it was to him the most perfect, all-pervading, and highest virtue governing all particular Confucian virtues. Also, all particular Confucian virtues can be taken to be various concrete manifestations of *jen* in everyday moral practice. (3) Confucius sometimes also spoke of *jen* as love or affection (*ai*), but it is distinguishable from, for example, Mo Tzu's notion of "universal (nondiscriminate and nongradational) love" (*chien-ai*) in that it must be applied in degrees, beginning with filial love and ending with love for all humanity. (4) *Jen* also is concretely understood in terms of both conscientiousness (*chung*) and moral reciprocity or altruism (*shu*). Tseng Tzu, disciple of Confucius, stated that the Master's "one thread running through the Way" (*yi-kuan chih tao*) is none other than conscientiousness and moral reciprocity, both of which point to *jen.*[12] (5) In a sense, Confucius defined *jen* in terms of "restraining oneself and returning to proprieties (*li*)."[13] However, *jen* and *li* are not put on an equal footing, for Confucius also said, "If man is not humane (*jen*), what has he to do with proprieties (*li*)? If man is not humane, what has he to do with music?"[14] That is, *jen* is the ethical ground for the justification of proprieties, music, and other cultural refinements. No, the Confucian thesis is even more than that; *jen* is the ultimate moral standard for our acceptance, modification, or replacement of proprieties or sociomoral conventions, namely, *li*, in any particular historical period. (6) *Jen* is, to Confucius and his followers, the highest principle or ultimate standard of human morality. As Confucius said, ''Only the man of *jen* is able (qualified) to like or dislike others,'' which actually means that only such a person is morally able to make a correct judgment about who is good and who is bad.[15] (7) *Jen* is the best human manifestation of Tao or the Way and functions as the ultimate guide for the Confucian person's existential decision or commitment. Confucius said: ''Wealth and honor are what man desires; yet they ought to be relinquished if they can only be retained to the detriment of the Way. . . . If the *chün-tzu* departs from *jen,* how can he fulfill that name? Never for a moment does the *chün-tzu* act against [the Way of] *jen.* In it he does abide despite hurriedness; in it does he abide despite hardship.''[16] (8) *Jen,* as the best human manifestation of the Way, also constitutes the ultimate goal of life as well as the essence of Confucian ideal personhood. As the ultimate goal of life in both individual and politicosocial terms, *jen* is none other than ''the Way of inner sagehood and outer kingship,'' to borrow an expression from Chuang Tzu.[17] It is in this sense that *jen* and *sheng* (meaning both ''sagehood'' and ''sage-king'') ultimately are identical. In short, *Jen* is the Way. (9) *Jen* is not only the Way itself but, moreover, signifies the soteriological identity of the Confucian person's heavenly appointment (as moral commitment) and supreme happiness in that the Confucian person is one who not only is determined to seek and realize the Way or *jen* but also rejoices in this moral destiny. Confucius himself set a good example for his followers as ''a man who in his vigorous pursuit [of the Way] forgets his food, who in the joy of such pursuit forgets all worldly worries, and who is unaware of his getting old.''[18] (10) Finally, *jen* is the Way that the human person can be expected to practice or realize spontaneously and easily—in Confucius' own words, ''Is *jen* so remote? As soon as I want it, it is here at hand.''[19] But his point needs to be supported by Mencius's theory of the original goodness of human nature, the theory that allowed Mencius to state that ''*jen* (human kindness) is [the original nature] of *jen* (humanity).''

In the *Analects*, the word *yi* is given in moral opposition to *li* (selfish profit) and often refers to ''moral oughtness or appropriateness.'' Perhaps the most suitable modern rendering of the word is Kant's German word *Sollen*. Confucius made numerous remarks contrasting these two concepts, for instance: ''To acquire wealth and honor by a morally inappropriate (*pu-i*) means is as remote as the clouds floating above'';[20] ''one who, when he sees a chance to gain, stops to think whether it would be morally appropriate (*yi*) to do it, when he sees [someone in] danger, is ready to sacrifice his life. . . . Such a man can be called a man of [moral accomplishment]'';[21] ''The *chün-tzu* in worldly dealings is freed from [the morally one-sided] 'for or against'; he takes *yi* (*Sollen* or oughtness) as the standard [of moral judgment or decision]'';[22] and so forth. It is clear, then, from these *yi* expressions that the idea of ''*jen-as-the-Way* manifested through *yi-Sollen*'' is already implied in the *Analects*, although Confucius never tried to combine *yi* with *jen*. In any case, it was through Mencius's ingenious ethical reasoning that *jen-yi* became the highest principle of Confucian morality.

Mencius spoke of *jen-yi* many times. The following sayings are among the most important: (1) *Jen* is [what constitutes] man's [moral] road'';[23] (2) ''All that matters is *jen-yi*'';[24] (3) ''*Jen* is man's peaceful abode; *yi* is man's right path'';[25] (4)''To kill an innocent person is contrary to *jen*; to take what one ought not to is contrary to *yi*. To rest in *jen* and *yi*; here is the task of a great man to be accomplished'';[26] (5) ''There are things that no one can bear. To extend this [feeling] to what one can bear is none other than *jen*. There are things that no one wishes to do; to extend this [feeling] to what one wishes to do is none other than *yi*.''[27] From these sayings we can derive three uses of *yi*: the moral application or manifestation of *jen* (1,3,4, and 5); moral action (5); and *Sollen* or moral oughtness (4). These three meanings can be identified, for, according to Mencius, *yi* as moral oughtness is the Confucian principle of moral action manifesting *jen*. *Yi* can be expressed more concretely as situational oughtness or appropriateness, terminologically identifiable with what both Confucius and Mencius called ''*ch'üan*'' (''expediency,'' situational ''weighing,'' situational appropriateness) or with the timely Mean (*shih-chung*) in the *Yi-Ching*. Mencius creatively reconstructed Confucius' notion of *ch'üan* as situational appropriateness or timely fitness and attempted thereby an ethical resolution of the problem of the constant moral principle or standard in relation to its situational application (*ching-ch'üan*) within moral conflicts. This problem was subsequently reapproached and reresolved by Ch'en Yi and Chu Hsi, as shall be discussed shortly.

Mencius said, ''The *chün-tzu* returns to the constant moral principle (*ching*); that is all. If the constant moral principle is properly set, the masses will be [morally] aroused, perversities and wickedness will vanish.''[28] The constant moral principle here should be understood as a reference to *jen*. But the question is: how is *jen* to be applied or manifested situationally? Mencius also said, ''To hold onto the middle (*chung*) is closer to it [the Way or what is morally right]. But to hold onto the middle without situational considerations (*ch'üan*) is to hold onto one extreme. The reason why I detest those who hold onto one extreme is the damage they bring to the Way, and that means that one extreme is singled out while a hundred others are disregarded.''[29] In other words, *jen* is the Way, and *yi* as moral oughtness is the situational and timely Mean (*cheng*), which is to be attained as the result of the situational ''weighing'' (*ch'üan*) of *jen* as the ultimate moral standard (*ching*). But Mencius went one step further than Confucius when he attempted a more liberal resolution of the problem of moral conflict (*ching-ch'üan*). A typical example of this is Mencius's resolution of the following moral conflict between *jen* and *yi* (sociomoral conventions):

Ch'un-yü K'un said, ''Is it a rule of propriety (*li*) that, in giving and receiving, man and woman do not touch each other?'' Mencius said, ''It is.'' ''When one's sister-in-law is drowning, should one not stretch out a hand in order to rescue her?'' Mencius said, ''He who does not stretch out a hand when his sister-in-law is drowning is a brute. That in giving and receiving man and woman do not touch each other is a rule of propriety (*li*), but to stretch out a hand in order to rescue the sister-in-law is a matter of situational weighing (*ch'üan*).[30]

Mencius's splendid resolution of the *ching-ch'üan* problem in this hypothetical case helps to remove the formalistic and conservative aspect of the Confucian *li*, which can now be reinterpreted as no more than the external conventionalizations of *jen*. As this case illustrates, *yi* or *ch'üan* have moral priority over *li*, which must be subject to situational considerations (*ch'üan*) in order to take a morally appropriate (*yi*) action in accordance with *jen* as the ultimate moral standard (*ching*). It can be said that Mencius's situation ethics is act oriented rather than rule oriented in that whether or not a human action is situationally appropriate (*ch'üan*), and therefore morally right (*yi*), depends upon whether or not it is in full accord with *jen*. The important point here is that *jen* is never a ready-made moral rule and that *li* as conventionalized "rules" of propriety are no more than a set of convenient "rules of thumb" that can never take the place of *jen-yi* as the invariable moral norm. Mencius's act-oriented situationism finds its final culmination in Wang Yang-ming's teaching of extending human *liang-chih* through an existential ontologization. In this "simple and easy" (*chien-i*) teaching, the completely rule-free *liang-chih* operates as the alpha and omega of all Confucian moral judgments and actions.

Another ethical connotation of Mencius's idea of *yi* as humanity's "right path" is the "gradational extension or application (of *jen*)" in terms of the Confucian person's spontaneous, step-by-step extension of natural affection from family members through friends, and so on, to humanity in its entirety. Thus Mencius said,

The *chun-tzu* loves (*ai*) nonhuman beings, but will not be human-kind (*jen*) to them; he is human-kind toward his fellow humans generally, but will not show his intimate (or familial) affection to them. [Our Confucian principle of gradational love is:] Be affectionate toward your parents [and other family members and relatives], then extend your human-kindness to your fellow humans generally, and then extend your love to nonhuman beings.[31]

In vindicating the Confucian doctrine of gradational love, Mencius, like Confucius and all other Confucianists, never foresaw the moral tension or conflict that may arise between *yi* as gradational love and *yi* as moral oughtness. This moral conflict often becomes a typical Confucian dilemma and is extremely difficult for the traditional Confucianists to resolve successfully.

Two examples of moral conflict from *Mencius* illustrate the ethical "deadlock" resulting from this kind of dilemma. The first example concerns a hypothetical case:

T'ao Ying asked, "Suppose, when Shun was the sovereign and Kao-yao his appointed minister of justice, Ku-sou [Shun's father] murdered a man, what would have been done in such a case? Mencius said, "[Kao-yao] would simply have apprehended him." "But wouldn't Shun have forbidden such a thing?" "Well, how could Shun have forbidden it? [Kao-yao] was delegated with the judicial authority to do his job." "What would Shun have done, then?" "Shun would have regarded abandoning the kingdom as discarding a worn-out sandal. He would secretly have carried [his father] on his back, fled to the edge of the Sea, and lived there [with his father] happily for the rest of his life, without giving any thought to the kingdom."[32]

In this hypothetical case, Mencius pretended to support both Kao-yao's impartial execution of the penal law and Shun's filial obligation simultaneously. It is, however, morally impossible to have it both ways. If we read the passage once again, we can easily detect Mencius's real intention, which lies in his vindication of the moral priority of filial piety (*hsiao*) over impersonal justice. Had not Confucius already said, "Filial piety is the root (for the practice) of *jen*"?[33] But Mencius also said that killing another man's father or brother is, as a matter of moral reciprocity, tantamount to killing one's own father or brother. Thus in giving his support to Shun's secret escape with his father-murderer from the kingdom, Mencius only intensified the moral deadlock between familial morality and politicosocial morality. From our modern point of view, Mencius's defense of filial love at the expense of social justice is difficult to justify. Apparently, he failed to comprehend the moral truth that *yi* as moral oughtness must override *yi* as gradational love, for the obvious reason that the former refers to ethical universalizability whereas the latter cannot carry such ethical right. Since the Confucianists take *jen-yi* to be the highest principle of human morality, both *jen* as human kindness and *yi* as moral oughtness are to be understood as ethically universalizable beyond any particular human individuals, groups, or societies, as well as beyond gradational love.

The second example of moral conflict is as follows:

Wang Chang said, "Hsiang [Shun's brother] devoted himself every day to plotting against Shun's life. When Shun was made the sovereign, how was it that he only banished Hsiang?" Mencius said, "No, he enfeoffed Hsiang, though some called it banishment." Wang Chang said," . . . Hsiang was a most wicked man, yet he was enfeoffed in Yu-pi. What crime had the people of Yu-pi committed [in being forced to accept Hsiang as their lord]? Is that the way a man of *jen* [Shun] should act? In the case of other men, Shun cut them off; in the case of his own brother, he enfeoffed him instead." [Mencius] said, "A man of *jen* neither harbors anger nor cherishes resentment against his brother, but only regards him with affection and love. Regarding him with affection, he wishes him to be honorable; regarding him with love, he wishes him to be wealthy. To enfeoff Hsiang was to make him wealthy and noble. Should Shun, being the sovereign, had left his brother alone as nobody, would he have been able to regard him with love and affection?"[34]

In this case, Mencius can hardly escape the ethical criticism that his Confucian promotion of familial love at the expense of sociopolitical morality involving fairness or justice eventually will lead to nepotism. As the Chinese saying goes, "When a man attains the Way [i.e., becomes a VIP], all his chickens and dogs [family members and relatives] will ascend to Heaven [move up to higher positions] as well." I shall come back to this point when dealing with the fifth Confucian thesis.

Among the neo-Confucian philosophers, only Ch'eng Yi and Chu Hsi were able to see the ethical importance of the Confucian problem of *ching-ch'üan,* which they accordingly tried hard to resolve satisfactorily. Chu Hsi in particular went beyond Ch'eng Yi in attempting an ethical synthesis of the latter's approach to the problem with that of the Han Confucianists. On the one hand, Chu Hsi tended to agree with the Han Confucianists that the constant moral standard (*ching*) and situational "weighing" (*ch'üan*) are not identical but disagreed with their misleading interpretation of *ch'üan* as a kind of "situational artifice or scheming" at variance with *ching.* On the other hand, Chu Hsi tended to disagree with Ch'eng Yi's oversimplification of *ch'üan,* which reduces it to *ching,* while sharing Ch'eng's refutation of the Han Confucianists' thesis that "*ch'üan* is nothing but what is in accord with the Way despite its being contrary to *ching.*"[35] Chu Hsi's own conclusion was that "*ching* refers to the constancy of the Way while *ch'üan* is a 'change' (temporary adjustment) of the Way" in an unexpected or extremely difficult situation where it looks morally improper to apply *ching* directly.[36] But he made his point clear in stating that *ch'üan* as situational adjustment is ethically synonymous with moral rightness (*yi*) and the timely Mean (*shih-chung*) and must ultimately accord with *ching.* What Chu Hsi meant is that *ch'üan* is none other than a situational "alteration" or "amendment"— but not a violation—of *ching.* Since *ching* itself provides no more than the overall *ceteris paribus* condition regarding decision making, it must allow some necessary "changes" when exceptional occasions arise. *Ch'üan* is, then, a morally justifiable "change" in any exceptional case where the *ceteris paribus* condition becomes inapplicable.

It seems that Chu Hsi's ingenious resolution of the Confucian problem of *ching-ch'üan* has a modernistic significance and can be further developed to serve a "realistic" modernization of Confucian ethics and morality. However, Chu Hsi misled us when he gave his interpretation of Mencius's words—"That in giving and receiving man and woman do not touch each other is a rule of propriety (*li*); but to stretch out a hand in order to rescue the sister-in-law is a matter of situational weighing (*ch'üan*)"—by simply identifying *li* with *ching.*[37] In doing so, Chu Hsi confused proprieties (*li*) as "rules of thumb" with the "constant moral standard," which can apply only to *jen-yi.* I would, therefore, suggest that Chu Hsi's thesis of *ching-ch'üan* be reoriented as follows: (1) *Jen* manifested through *yi* is the ultimate and invariable moral standard for Confucian morality; (2) since *jen-yi* only gives us the overall *ceteris paribus* condition without rule-like specifications, the moral agent has to "weigh" (*ch'üan*) carefully the situational meanings of *jen-yi* when exceptional cases arise; (3) the decision made or action taken after the situational "weighing" must be morally right and satisfy the "timely Mean" (*shih-chung*).

The above reorientation of Chu Hsi's thesis concerning *ching-ch'üan* should be helpful to contemporary Confucianists in their modern reconstruction of Confucian ethics and morality. But Chu Hsi's point that only the sage is qualified to apply *ch'üan*—since it involves an unusually difficult "alteration" of *ching* on exceptional occasions—leads to the question of whether Confucian moral theory, as an act-oriented situationism lacking a set of clearly specified rules, like rules of a game, can realistically work at all.[38] This question takes on greater urgency in view of the present context of our ever-pluralized (post-) modern world, in which politicosocial morality becomes more and more crucial, complicated, and difficult than individual or person-to-person morality. What is involved is the ethical controversy between what I call "rule-oriented objectivism" and "act-oriented situationism." To deal with this ethical issue, we must turn to a critical examination of the fifth Confucian thesis.

The fifth thesis concerns the way of outer kingship (in modern terms, politicosocial morality), specifically, what kingship is and how it should serve as a natural extension of the way of inner sagehood or individual morality. To apply a pair of ethical terms I have coined elsewhere, traditional Confucianists generally think that "micromorality," in terms of the moral perfection of each individual human person, is the ethical prerequisite and means of insuring the eventual realization of "macromorality," or the moral perfection of society. Whereas micromoral practice, in the sense of day-to-day personal cultivation and moral conduct, is expected to lead to the realization of the way of inner sagehood, the highest ideal for individual life, macromoral practice is essentially based on government by virtue (*te-chih*). The latter takes place under the leadership of the virtuous ruler—ideally, the Confucian sage–emperors—who ought to set a good example for all of the people, with the result that outer kingship, the highest goal of politicosocial life, will be realized. In short, micromoral practice is the root (*pen*) of Confucianism as traditional morality, and macromoral practice is its branch (*mo*).

Confucian macromoral practice can be summed up as follows. (5.1) As against the legalist theory of government by "law and order" (*fa-chih*), Confucius and his followers advocate government by virtue, or humane government (*jen-cheng*). Confucius said, "Govern the people with stipulated measures and regulate them by chastisement, and they will avoid wrongdoing but will lose all self-respect; govern them by moral virtue and regulate them by proprieties, and they will keep their self-respect and come to you of their own accord."[39] (5.2) Since the establishment of humane government must depend upon the virtuous conduct of the rulers, and not upon the people's strict observance of stipulated laws, it is absolutely necessary for the rulers to engage in day-to-day moral self-cultivation, thereby setting a good example for their subordinates as well as for the people. By identifying the term "to govern" (*cheng*) with "to rectify" (*cheng*), Confucius put forward the doctrine of "rectification of names" (*cheng-ming*) and made a moral demand that each member of society fulfill his or her daily duties or obligations as a *real* parent, a *real* child, a *real* official, and so on.[40] Confucius and his followers are firmly convinced that if the political leaders set a good example, the people will spontaneously follow in their moral path and become virtuous as well.

(5.3) Knowing that "if the people have no constant properties, they will have no constant [moral] mind," Mencius was able realistically to introduce economic measures, such as the "well-field" (*ching-t'ien*) system, to improve the people's livelihood first before introducing school education for their moral enlightenment.[41] (5.4) Day-to-day moral perfection of each member of society, beginning with political leaders and the Confucian worthies (*hsien-liang*) as an exemplar of moral virtue, will eventually result in the appearance of what is called "the world of Grand Unity (*ta-t'ung*)." According to this traditional Confucian conception of utopia, the human world would be morally destined to become "an impartial and just commonwealth: the worthies and talented are elected [for public service], and the people are trustworthy and maintain human solidarity."[42] It is, however, an irony of history that not only has no such utopian world ever appeared but, moreover, that nearly all political leaders in the past two thousand years have manipulated Confucian moral teachings to secure their own political advantages. Mao Tse-tung's Communist mockery of Confucian utopianism only reminds us of the traditional Confucian macromoral failure, as witnessed by Confucianists themselves.[43]

From our (post-) modern perspective, the problems arising from the fifth Confucian thesis look almost unresolvable and the difficulties embedded in it insurmountable. I would suggest, then, that contemporary Confucianists modernistically revise the age-old Confucian utopian approach to politics and government, taking into consideration the hard politicosocial reality that there is and should be no necessary connection between the macromoral way of outer kingship (as a matter of maxima moralia) and the micromoral way of inner sagehood (maxima moralia). Furthermore, a radical shift must be made from act-oriented situationism to rule-oriented objectivism for our (post-) modern macromoral practice, and *jen-yi,* the governing principle of Confucian morality, will no longer serve as what Immanuel Kant called "the constitutive principle," although it can still function as "the regulative principle." The following discussion gives some philosophical reasons in support of my suggestions.

First, the traditional Confucian promotion of government by virtue as macromorally superior to government by law is based on the Mencian metapsychological and ethical belief that the human person is originally good and can fully develop moral potential for the attainment of sagehood. Unfortunately, the overly optimistic traditional Confucianists have seldom attempted to see the obvious gap between the two claims that "every one *can* become a sage" and "nearly all of us human beings have not and *never* will become a sage." Nor have they realized that, despite the moral goodness of one's intention of will from the

Confucian standpoint of motive-centered morality, the Confucian sage also may make a moral mistake, insofar as consequence-oriented morality is concerned, as we have already seen. Furthermore, history has shown us that no perfect sage–emperors have ever appeared in the history of Confucian-related Asia and in China in particular. These points seems clearly to suggest the macromoral necessity that a more realistic and practicable theory of government by law, as has achieved success in free, democratic modern nations such as the United States, replace the idealistic theory of government by virtue, so unsuccessfully propagated in the Confucian-influenced nations of Asia for the past two thousand years. In other words, politicosocial morality as a matter of minima moralia must be well maintained before we begin to explore the individual and politicosocial goal of life as a matter of maxima moralia.

Second, as mentioned in my previous discussion of the problem of *ching-ch'üan,* Confucian act-oriented situationism devoid of clearly specified rules may, if strictly followed, cause utilitarianly undesirable consequences in macromoral practice. Mencius's failure to resolve the two cases referred to above, in which the moral conflict between micromoral (familial) love and macromoral (impersonal) justice arises, is a typical example illustrative of the tremendous difficulties embedded in Confucian act-oriented situationism. Despite Chu Hsi's "careful" but moot statement that only the sage is able to apply situational "weighing" (*ch'üan*) correctly, Confucian act-oriented situationism can hardly provide us with a set of objective or intersubjectively agreeable criteria for the determination of the moral appropriateness or inappropriateness of a particular decision or action. Our commonly shared politicosocial aspirations today for the establishment of a more free and democratic society throughout the world will undoubtedly lead us in the direction of rule-oriented objectivism in macromoral practice as an ethical overcoming of the limits of Confucian act-situationism and motive-centered morality.

By "rule-oriented objectivism" I mean a macromoral theory consisting of a two-level justificational procedure, consisting of the following: (1) the governing principle of human morality is the ultimate ground for the justification of an established system of well-defined (legally stipulated) rules or regulations to be morally appropriate; (2) the rules or regulations politicosocially agreed upon and accepted as an established convention are the "objective" (intersubjective) basis for the justification of a particular decision or action as morally appropriate; (3) if and when exceptional occasions arise, the established rules or regulations will have to be expanded or altered through democratic discussions and resolutions in accordance with the governing principle. The essential difference between rule-oriented objectivism and act-oriented situationism is that the former contains an established system of rules as objective criteria for the determination of the moral appropriateness/inappropriateness of human decisions or actions, whereas the latter primarily relies upon the moral agent's *personal* intuition, conscience, wisdom, or situational interpretation (of the governing principle of morality). It is not difficult to see which of these two is more practicable in the (post-) modern society. Here again, Confucian scholars must today make a fresh attempt to revise Confucianism as traditional morality in line with modern demands, shifting their emphasis from act-oriented situationism to rule-oriented objectivism in macromoral practice. But Confucian act-oriented situationism, which is deeply rooted in motive-centered morality, can continue to apply well in micromoral practice that involves personal cultivation, familial love, friendship, and other kinds of person-to-person moral expressions.

It is interesting to note that Ch'eng Yi and Chu Hsi, chief representatives of the neo-Confucian "Nature Is Principle" school, could have developed a theory of rule-oriented objectivism (for macromoral practice) to supplement the Mencian theory of act-oriented situationism (for micromoral practice), based on (1) their moral-metaphysical theory of Principle (*Li*) inherent in vital force (*ch'i*), hence the possibility of developing the idea of *Li* as the ground for ethical objectivity beyond individual *liang-chih* or conscience; (2) Ch'eng Yi's repeated emphasis on the idea of "publicness," fairness, or justice (*kung*), as well as on his thesis of "Principle is one but its manifestations are many" (*li-yi fen-shu*), which was further developed by Chu Hsi; and (3) their theory of the investigation of things for the extension of knowledge (*ke-wu chih-chih*) and exhaustive explorations of *Li* inherent in things (*chi-wu ch'iung-li*), which tends to stress the "knowledge of hearing and seeing" (*wen-chien chih chih*) or "following the path of inquiry and learning" (*tao wen hsüeh*) as of equal importance with "knowledge of the virtuous nature" (*te-hsing chih chih*) or "honoring the virtuous nature" (*tsun te-hsing*). Unfortunately, they did not realize the profound implications of their own neo-Confucian theory for the modern world, which are yet to be rediscovered.

To conclude, I wish to make an overall suggestion that a proper and successful modernization of Confucian ethics and morality necessitates a philosophical modification or reorientation of traditional Confucian epistemology by rectifying its one-sided emphasis on "knowledge of the virtuous nature" without sufficient attention being paid to the empirical and ethical importance of the "knowledge of hearing and seeing" (in modern terms, scientific knowledge). I also wish to suggest that, despite some difficulties in Confucianism as traditional morality, the Confucian idea of *jen-yi* can remain as the "regulative principle"—although not as the "constitutive principle"—for modern political and legal institutions. In other words, Confucian *jen-yi* as the governing principle of human morality can never be challenged, for it is what ethically defines what human beings are and ought to be.

NOTES

1. W. D. Hudson, *Modern Moral Philosophy* (New York: Doubleday, 1970), pp. 328–29.

2. James Legge, trans., *Confucian Analects, the Great Learning, and the Doctrine*

of The Mean (Lun-yü) (New York: Dover, n.d.), 17:2. Translations of all passages from this text used in the chapter are mine.

3. Charles Wei-hsun Fu, "The Mencian Theory of Mind (*Hsin*) and Nature (*Hsing*); "A Modern, Philosophical Approach," *Journal of Chinese Philosophy* 10, no. 4 (1983): 405–407.

4. Legge, *Confucian Analects*, 8:4.

5. James Legge, trans., *The Works of Mencius (Meng Tzu)* (New York: Dover, n.d.), 6A:10. Translations of all passages from this text are mine.

6. Lu Hsiang-shan, *Lu Chiu-yüan chi (The Collected Works of Lu Hsiang-shan)* (Beijing: Zhonghua, 1980), p. 410. My translation.

7. For a more detailed presentation of my metapsychological suggestions, see my *"Ju-chia hsin-hsing-lun te hsien-tai-hua k'e-ti"* ("On the Modernization of the Confucian Theory of Mind Nature"), Pt. 2, *Legein Monthly* (Taipei) 116 (February 1985): 6–18.

8. Legge, *Works of Mencius*, 6A:7.

9. The notion of "heavenly" appears in, for example, the first sentence of the *Chung-yung (The Doctrine of the Mean)*; Mencius identified this notion with the human person's "true (moral) destiny" in the *Works of Mencius*, 7A:2.

10. The notion of "a citizen (or subject) of Heaven" appears in the *Works of Mencius*, 7A:19.

11. Legge, *Works of Mencius*, 7B:16.

12. Legge, *Confucian Analects*, 4:15.

13. Ibid., 12:1.

14. Ibid., 3:3.

15. Ibid., 4:3.

16. Ibid., 4:5.

17. See Ch. 33, "The World," of *The Complete Works of Chuang Tzu*, tr. Burton Watson (New York: Columbia University Press, 1968).

18. Legge, *Confucian Analects*, 7:18.

19. Ibid., 7:29.

20. Ibid., 7:15.

21. Ibid., 14:13.

22. Ibid., 4u: 10.

23. Legge, *Works of Mencius*, 6A:11.

24. Ibid., 1A:1.

25. Ibid., 4A:10.

26. Ibid., 7A:33.

27. Ibid., 7B:31.

28. Ibid., 7B:37.

29. Ibid., 7A:26.

30. Ibid., 4A:17.

31. Ibid., 7A:45.

32. Ibid., 7A:35.

33. Legge, *Confucian Analects*, 1:2.

34. Legge, *Works of Mencius*, 5A:2.

35. See *The Classified Sayings of Chu Tzu (Chu Tzü yu-lei)* (Chengchung Book Co., Taipei, 1967), 3:1573–1588.

36. Ibid., p. 1578.

37. Ibid., p. 1577.

38. Ibid., p. 1574.
39. Legge, *Confucian Analects,* 2:3.
40. Ibid., 12:17.
41. Legge, *Works of Mencius,* 1A:6.
42. See "The Evolution of Proprieties" ("Li-yün"), in *Records of Proprieties (Li-chi).* For its English translation, see Jame Legge, tr., *Li Chi* (Book of Rites), (N.Y.: University Books, 1967), I: 364–393.
43. See *Selected Works of Mao Tse-tung* (Beijing, China: People's Publishing House 1964), 4:414.

SELECTED BIBLIOGRAPHY

Chan, Wing-tsit, trans. and comp. *A Source Book in Chinese Philosophy.* Princeton, N.J.: Princeton University Press, 1963.

Chang, Carsun. *The Development of Neo-Confucian Thought.* 2 vols. New York: Bookman Associates, 1957, 1962.

Chu, Hsi. *Reflections on Things at Hand: The Neo-Confucian Anthology.* Translated by Wing-tsit Chan. New York: Columbia University Press, 1967.

Chuang Tzu. *The Complete Works of Chuang Tzu.* Translated by Burton Watson. New York: Columbia University Press, 1968.

de Bary, William Theodore, ed. *The Unfolding of Neo-Confucianism.* New York: Columbia University Press, 1975.

de Bary, William Theodore, Wing-tsit Chan, and Burton Watson, comps. *Sources of Chinese Tradition.* New York: Columbia University Press, 1960.

Fingarette, Herbert. *Confucius—The Secular as Sacred.* New York: Harper and Row, 1972.

Fu, Charles Wei-hsun. "Fingarette and Munro on Early Confucianism: A Methodological Examination." *Philosophy East and West* 28, no. 2 (1974): 181–198.

———. "The Mencian Theory of Mind (*Hsin*) and Nature (*Hsing*): A Modern, Philosophical Approach." *Journal of Chinese Philosophy* 10, no. 4 (1983): 385–410.

———. *P'i-p'an te chi-ch'eng yü ch'uang-tsao te fa-chan* (*On the Critical Inheritance and Creative Development of Chinese Thought and Culture*). Taipei: Tungta, 1986.

———. "Postwar Confucianism and Western Democracy: An Ideological Struggle." In Charles Wei-hsun Fu, and Gerhard E. Spiegler, eds. *Movements and Issues in World Religions. Vol. 1: Religion, Ideology, and Politics.* Westport, Conn.: Greenwood Press, 1987, pp. 177–196.

———. *Ts'ung hsi-fang che-hsüe tao ch'an-fo-chiao* (*From Western Philosophy to Zen Buddhism*). Taipei: Tungta, 1986.

———. *Wen-hua chung-kuo yü chung-kuo wen hua* (*Cultural China and Chinese Culture*). Taipei: Tungta, 1988.

Fu, Charles Wei-hsun, and Chan Wing-tsit. *Guide to Chinese Philosophy.* Boston: G. K. Hall, 1978.

Fung Yu-lan. *A History of Chinese Philosophy,* 2 vols. Translated by Derk Bodde. Princeton, N.J.: Princeton University Press, 1952–1953.

———. *The Spirit of Chinese Philosophy.* Translated by E. R. Hughes. Boston: Beacon Press, 1962.

Hudson, W. D. *Modern Moral Philosophy.* New York: Doubleday, 1970.

Legge, James, trans. *Confucian Analects, the Great Learning, and the Doctrine of the Mean.* New York: Dover, n.d.

————. *Li Chi: Book of Rites,* 2 vols. New York: University Books, 1967.

————. *The Works of Mencius.* New York: Dover, n.d.

Levenson, Joseph R. *Confucian China and Its Modern Fate: A Trilogy.* Berkeley: University of California Press, 1968.

Liu, Shu-hsien. "The Confucian Approach to the Problem of Transcendence and Immanence." *Philosophy East and West* 22 (1972): 45–52.

————. "The Religious Import of Confucian Philosophy: Its Traditional Outlook and Contemporary Significance." *Philosophy East and West* 21 (1971): 157–175.

Lu, Hsiang-shan. *Lu Chiu-yüan chi (The Collected Works of Lu Hsiang-shan).* Beijing: Zhonghua, 1980.

Munro, Donald J. *The Concept of Man in Early China.* Stanford, Calif.: Stanford University Press 1969.

Needham, Joseph. *Science and Civilization in China. Vol. 2: History of Scientific Thought.* Cambridge: Cambridge University Press, 1956.

II

DIALOGUES

14

Religious Pluralism and Ecumenism from a Christian Perspective

LEONARD SWIDLER

DIVISIONS IN CHRISTIANITY

Jesus of Nazareth was not a Christian; he was a Jew; he was Rabbi Yeshua. Moreover, his first followers, both during his lifetime and after the Resurrection, also thought of themselves as Jews. However, by no means did the majority of Jews living at that time choose to become followers of Rabbi Yeshua. This split constituted the first major division in the history of the followers of The Way of Rabbi Yeshua, which eventually came to be called the Christian church.

At the same time this centrifugal force was at work within nascent Christianity, there was also a balancing centripetal force whereby the followers of Rabbi Yeshua strove to retain unity. These two forces of unity and division have continued to vie for dominance within the history of Christianity—as in all human institutions.

The next major division that occurred in Christianity was the result of the major universal councils, called ecumenical, from the fourth through the eighth centuries. Those who accepted the decisions of the councils described themselves as orthodox, whereas those who did not were said to be heterodox—though to be sure, they did not so describe themselves. A number of these ancient so-called nonorthodox Christian churches still exist today.

Then the fall of the Roman Empire in the West eventually led to another major division in the Christian church, namely, that between Eastern Christianity and Western Christianity, both having understood themselves to be believers in or-thodox Christianity. This division took place gradually in the latter centuries of the first millennium A.D. and was "fixed" in the year 1054 with the mutual excommunications of the leaders of both Eastern and Western Christianity. West-ern Christianity was rent once again in a major way in the sixteenth century with the Protestant Reformation.

There were many attempts to avoid the disastrous divisions, but they obviously failed. Likewise, there were many attempts to bridge the breaches once they had occurred; they also obviously failed. The forces of division seemed to be growing ever stronger. In very many Christian quarters unity did not at all seem like a virtue or an attractive goal. Rather, notions such as liberty, independence, and "the" truth (which I have, of course) were held up as the models. As to the question of whether there should be one or many Christian churches, the response often seemed to be "the more the better." By the twentieth century, as a consequence, there were hundreds of Christian churches in existence.

TOWARD CHRISTIAN UNITY

With the nineteenth century, however, doubts began to arise about the value and the validity of division in the Christian church. Ever since the sixteenth century the Roman Catholic Church had been heavily involved in missionizing those parts of the world newly discovered by Spain, Portugal, and France. There seemed to be little interest in such mission work on the part of Protestants until the nineteenth century. Then they, too, began to evangelize the non-European world with a huge outpouring of funds and resources. As the nineteenth century passed into the twentieth, the Protestant missionaries found increasingly that the division of the Christian church more and more proved to be a scandal, a stumbling block, to the acceptance of the Christian gospel by non-Christians. Hence, ironically, the modern Christian movement toward reuniting Christianity, the ecumenical movement, began in the great watershed event of 1910, the World Missionary Conference in Edinburgh. It was there that the intention to found an organization to work for Christian unity was publicly declared by Episcopal Bishop Charles H. Brent. From that initiative there was born the Movement for Faith and Order, which strove to overcome the divisions in the Christian church, which its members saw to be founded on disagreements about belief and church structure, that is, faith and order.

A second great arm of the ecumenical movement was started under the leadership of Swedish Lutheran Bishop Nathan Soederblom and was called the Movement for Life and Work, which was founded on the notion that the Christian churches cannot wait until the divisions caused by differences in belief and church structure are overcome but must immediately begin to work in harmony as Christians on the issues of contemporary life and work; this working and living together would then also slowly forge an even deeper unity among the churches.

From the beginning, both of these arms of the ecumenical movement strove to include Protestant, Catholic, and Orthodox (Eastern) Christian churches. However, at the start only Protestant churches in fact participated. The first world conference of the Life and Work movement took place in Stockholm in 1925, and in 1927 in Lausanne the first world conference of the Movement for Faith and Order took place. The spirit of unity then began to have an effect on those two ecumenical movements, so the decision was made to hold the next world conferences of both organizations in Britain during the summer of 1937, at which conferences a proposal for merger was put forth—and agreed to. The formal initiation of the merged ecumenical organization was postponed because of World War II—just as the first two world conferences were postponed by World War I—with the result that the World Council of Churches first came into full existence at the Amsterdam Conference in 1948.

At that first General Assembly of the World Council of Churches (WCC) there were some 351 official delegates from 146 churches. Delegates from the smaller Eastern churches were present, but the Orthodox Church of Russia and the Orthodox churches of the countries of Eastern Europe did not send delegates— nor did the Roman Catholic Church. The second General Assembly of the WCC took place in Evanston, Illinois, in 1954, and the one following that was in New Delhi in 1961 and then Uppsala in 1968, Nairobi in 1975, and Vancouver in 1983. By 1983 the number of participant churches had more than doubled, to over three hundred, and the number of delegates had increased almost tenfold, to over three thousand. Other important changes took place in the makeup of the WCC in that thirty-five-year period. There was a great increase in the participation of Third World churches, meaning among other things that the staff and delegates were much more varied in terms of race and cultures. There also has been a significant increase in the participation of women and young people.

The WCC has continued in a large variety of ways to promote the concerns of its two earlier arms. Work has continued intensely in the area of theological discussion to resolve the areas of division in matters of faith and church structure. At the same time the myriad issues of human concern, whether in the areas of human rights, economics, politics, and so on, have been pursued with vigor. In fact, it has been in this second area that the WCC has come in for some severe criticism from more conservative church people.

Besides the existence of the World Council of Churches on the international level, many countries, including preeminently the United States, have parallel structures on the national level. Here, it is the National Council of Churches. It, too, is a federation of Christian churches from the United States, with its national headquarters in New York, as the international headquarters of the WCC is in Geneva. In addition, almost every state has a state council of churches, and every sizeable city has its equivalent of a city council of churches. Furthermore, most often a metropolitan area will have scores of regional ministeria wherein the local clergy more or less actively engage in joint dialogue and cooperation. Besides this, there will frequently be joint ecumenical endeavors on the part of neighboring churches, colleges and universities, and other Christian institutions. These many ecumenical activities take place throughout the year but also have a special focus during Church Unity Week in the latter part of January, as well as during the Lenten season, around the time of Pentecost, and Reformation Sunday at the end of October.

If the centrifugal forces of church division far outstripped the centripetal forces of church unity into this century, the historian will have to note also that in recent decades the trend has been reversed. In the United States alone between 1900 and 1968 there have been some twenty-six church unions, bringing together two or more previously independent churches into unified ones. The same sort of thing has been going on elsewhere in the world. Some of the most dramatic have taken place in India, where in 1947 the Church of South India was formed, bringing together the Episcopal, Methodist and Presbyterian churches of that area into a unity. In 1971 a similar union occurred in the North of India, giving rise to the Church of North India. At present there are serious conversations under way to bring these two churches into one, along with other Protestant and Orthodox churches in India that have not as yet joined either of the two. Perhaps the most far-reaching church merger effort has been going on in the United States for more than two decades in an attempt to bring together some ten churches (the number of churches involved in the merger effort varies from time to time as occasionally two of the churches merge into one and as other churches join in the conversations). This merger effort is known as the Consultation on Church Union (COCU).

The continued force of the movement toward church union is indicated by the fact that in 1983 two more major church unions occurred in the United States, that between the northern and southern Presbyterian churches and among three of the four major Lutheran churches in America.

In addition to these explicitly merger-oriented conversations, there have also been numerous official theological conversations between churches, sometimes on a bilateral and sometimes on a multilateral basis. As of 1975 the WCC reported fourteen such major bilateral dialogues occurring on the international level and an additional thirty-two on the national or regional levels. Since these conversations are not necessarily directed toward merger, the conversation partners are at times disparate in their theology and church structure. Perhaps because of this fact they have tended to be immensely creative in new theological understandings.

For example, the separate bilaterals between Roman Catholics on the one side and Reformed Christians, Lutherans, and Anglicans on the other three sides, each independently took up the questions of baptism, the eucharist, and ministry. They all independently arrived at basically the same positions, that there ought to be mutual recognition of the authenticity of the baptism, eucharist, and ministry of one another's churches. All of these conclusions were arrived at after a great deal of intense research and dialogue.

Partially as a result of the extremely fruitful dialogues on a bilateral basis, the multilateral theological conversations, often sponsored by the Commission of Faith and Order of the WCC, have also been able to make significant progress. The most hopeful advance has been the issuance of the document on baptism, eucharist, and ministry (BEM) issued by Faith and Order at its meeting in Lima in 1982. It was accepted by the one hundred theological representatives of all of the participating churches, which include not only the great majority of Protestant churches but also Orthodox churches. Present also at these conversations were active, voting observers from the Roman Catholic Church. As a consequence, this document, which deals with some of the most fundamentally divisive, and at the same time potentially unifying, issues in Christian teaching, is in the midst of being studied, discussed, and acted upon by all the involved churches. Already the liturgy based upon that document was used at the Vancouver General Assembly of the WCC—with immense success. It has often been called the outstanding experience of an outstanding world assembly.

ROMAN CATHOLIC ECUMENISM

There are far more Roman Catholic Christians in the world than all of the rest of the other Christians together. Hence a participation, or lack thereof, on the part of Rome in the ecumenical movement is obviously a matter of the first magnitude. Like so many of the Protestant churches, the Roman Catholic Church also became involved in an effort to reunite Christianity toward the latter part of the nineteenth century, although in a far different way than occurred in Protestantism in general. As a result of the Oxford movement within the Anglican Church in the middle of the nineteenth century, there was a strong interest on the part of high church Anglicans and some Roman Catholics, especially in England, to work to bridge the gulf between the two churches. These efforts began to see some results in the final quarter of the nineteenth century, after Pope Pius IX, perhaps the most reactionary pope of modern times, passed from the scene in 1876. The two major protagonists in this effort were Lord Halifax on the Anglican side and Abbe Portal on the Roman Catholic side. Unfortunately, these efforts foundered on the rock of Roman intransigence when, in 1893, against the findings and recommendations of his very best scholars, Pope Leo XIII issued a document declaring that Anglican priestly orders were "utterly null and void." Then some thirty years later, in the early 1920s, Lord Halifax and Abbe Portal once again tried to move Rome and Canterbury on the road to unity through the so-called Malines Conversations. They took place during the pontificates of Benedict XV and his successor Pius XI and under the direct protectorship of Cardinal Mercier of Malines. These conversations were fruitful as far as they went, but unfortunately, they ended with the death of Cardinal Mercier in 1926.

However, in Germany following World War I there was a significant beginning of Catholic-Protestant dialogue on the theological level. This was doubtless spurred by the developments in the 1920s that led to the 1925 Stockholm and 1927 Lausanne world conferences described above. However, in 1928 the pope issued a very restrictive encyclical, *Mortalium animos,* which for a while dampened enthusiasm for Catholic-Protestant ecumenism in Germany. Nevertheless, under the pressure of persecution by the Nazis there developed in the 1930s the Una Sancta movement in Germany, which was spearheaded by the Catholic priest Max Metzger. Metzger was a reform thinker and activist who was much involved in social justice issues, founded a world Catholic peace organization during World War I, engaged in smuggling Jews out of Nazi Germany, and eventually was beheaded by the Nazis in 1944 for his peace work. After the war the Una Sancta movement in Germany suddenly blossomed into a popular movement, bringing Catholic and Protestant church people and theologians together on public platforms and in each other's churches, until this movement again was dampened by a Vatican *Monitum* in 1948. However, the *Monitum* turned out to be only a temporary setback, for the momentum of Catholic-Protestant dialogue continued, especially in Germany, but also to a much lesser extent in France under the inspiration of Paul Couturier, until it received full Vatican approbation in the Second Vatican Council, 1962–1965.

It is easy to see the fundamental connection between the Una Sancta movement in Germany and the endorsement of ecumenism at Vatican II by the fact that the newly established Secretariat for Christian Unity was set up under the presidency of Augustin Bea, a German Jesuit theologian. Bea was made a cardinal for this purpose by Pope John XXIII, who called the Council in 1959. Moreover, most of the leading theologians involved in promoting ecumenism were German.

Vatican II was a major turning point in the history of the Roman Catholic Church and doubtless also in the history of Christianity in general and perhaps for the world at large. It also marks a great divide in the history of the Ecumenical movement. Beforehand, Rome had always refused to join in the Ecumenical movement, telling its Protestant initiators that the way to reunion was open, namely, by returning to Rome. The Vatican also repeatedly forbade Roman Catholic involvement in ecumenism except under the most stringent circumstances. Then in 1964 at the Second Vatican Council all of the Catholic bishops of the world, including the bishop of Rome, passed the solemn Decree on Ecumenism, which, when speaking of the Christian church, stated that "Division openly contradicts the will of Christ, scandalizes the world, and damages that most holy cause the preaching of the Gospel to every creature." Then instead of forbidding Catholics to be involved in ecumenism, or allowing only a few to do so under restrictive circumstances, the Fathers of the Second Vatican Council stated dramatically that "this Sacred Council exhorts, therefore, all the Catholic faithful to recognize the signs of the times and to take an active and intelligent part in the work of ecumenism . . . in ecumenical work, Catholics must assuredly be concerned for their brethren . . . making the first approaches toward them . . . the concern for restoring unity involves the whole Church, faithful and clergy alike. It extends to everyone."

The Roman Catholic Church at Vatican II also clearly moved out of its reactionary siege mentality, which had largely prevailed since the second quarter of the nineteenth century, and admitted that "men of both sides were to blame" for the divisions in the church and spoke of the Catholic church no longer in triumphalistic terms but rather as a church that "makes its pilgrim way," which is called by Christ "as she goes her pilgrim way unto that continual reformation of which she always has need." Thus a close essential link between self-reform and work for Christian unity was made clear in the Decree on Ecumenism: "all are to examine their own faithfulness to Christ's will for the Church and, wherever necessary, undertake with vigor the task of renewal and reform. . . . Catholics' . . . primary duty is to make a careful and honest appraisal of whatever needs to be renewed and done in the Catholic household itself. . . . church renewal therefore has notable ecumenical importance.''

At the same council other decrees of major ecumenical import were also passed. One was the Declaration on Religious Freedom. Already in the second quarter of the nineteenth century then Pope Gregory XVI issued a solemn declaration stating that freedom of religion and freedom of conscience were to be totally condemned and, in fact, were referred to as "madness" (*deliramentum*). This stand was vigorously repeated by his successor, Pope Pius IX, in his "Syllabus of Errors." As a result of such authoritative stances, Roman Catholics had the greatest difficulties in countries such as the United States where religious liberty was the law of the land. Nevertheless, the American Jesuit theologian John Courtney Murray argued in a number of learned articles in the early 1950s that religious liberty was in fact an essential element in the best of the Roman Catholic ancient tradition. He was vehemently opposed, however, by Cardinal Ottaviani, the president of the watchdog agency of the Vatican, the Holy Office, and was eventually silenced on the matter. However, during Vatican II his position was vindicated, and he himself had a great deal to do with the writing of the Declaration on Religious Liberty, which fully affirmed complete religious freedom and freedom of conscience.

The third document of Vatican II that has major ecumenical importance is the Declaration on the Relation of the Church to Non-Christian Religions. Here there was a fundamental turnabout, particularly in the attitude of the Catholic church toward Jews and Judaism. Whereas in the Good Friday liturgy Roman Catholics had previously prayed for the "perfidious Jews," now in the Vatican Declaration the Council Fathers stated that "the Jews remain very dear to God . . . since God does not take back the gifts he bestowed or the choice he made" and that the church cannot forget that it "draws nourishment from that good olive tree unto which the wild branches of the Gentiles have been grafted" (see Romans 11:17–24); moreover, the 1974 Vatican "Guidelines on Religious Relations with the Jews" stated clearly that "it condemns all forms of antisemitism"; that between Christians and Jews "from now on, real dialogue must be established"; and that every effort must be put forth to eliminate distortions and untruths in all Catholic liturgical and religious education materials.

In the same Vatican II declaration, the Council Fathers urged all Catholics to enter "into discussion and collaboration with members of other religions. . . . the Catholic Church rejects nothing of what is true and holy in these religions. She has a high regard for the manner of life and conduct, the precepts and doctrines which, however differing in many ways from our own teaching, nevertheless often reflect a ray of that truth which enlightens all men.''

Thus Vatican II accomplished a radical reversal of the Catholic church in its attitude toward non-Catholics and non-Christians.

Vatican II opened the floodgates of ecumenism for Roman Catholics. A typical example is the fact that when in 1966 Temple University became a state-related university and its religion department took on its first Catholic faculty member, there was but one Catholic graduate student in the Religion Department, but in two years there were four full-time Catholic faculty members and fifty Catholic graduate students. Catholic dioceses around the world began to set up offices for ecumenical dialogue. In the United States, for example, each diocese has at least one professional person who is responsible for ecumenical dialogue, and together they form the organization known as the National Association of Diocesan Ecumenical Officers (NADEO). American bishops also set up on the national level the Bishops Committee on Ecumenical and Interreligious Affairs (BCEIA), which is responsible for launching and overseeing the various national bilateral dialogues. They include Consultations with Episcopalians, Reformed and Presbyterian Christians, Lutherans, Methodists, Baptists, Disciples of Christ, Orthodox, and Non-Chalcedonean Eastern Christians, as well as with Jews and Muslims.

As indicated above, the bilaterals have often been extremely creative and fruitful. Clearly, the most productive of these bilaterals has been the Lutheran-Catholic Consultation, which has already put out more than seven volumes of first-class theological research and joint statements dealing with neuralgic subjects such as baptism, eucharist, ministry, papal primacy, infallibility, Mary, and justification. Although there may not be as broad an involvement in such bilateral consultations in other countries, since the resources and spectrum of potential partners are much more limited, nevertheless fruitful bilateral consultations involving Roman Catholics on one side are taking place around the world.

Many more things also happen on the so-called grass-roots level. There is an official recognition even of the validity of non-Catholic Christian baptism. In the delicate area of mixed marriages a great deal of progress has been made toward collaboration, and it is now possible for a marriage between a Catholic and a Protestant to take place before either a Catholic priest or a Protestant minister or before them jointly. It frequently happens that there is an exchange of pulpits between Catholics and Protestants, and also very often there will be joint worship services—all of this being officially approved. The number of joint projects, ranging from the sharing of buildings and educational undertakings to a wide variety of social justice matters, seems almost unending. In an increasing number of instances these ecumenical enterprises entered into by neighboring churches are ratified by covenants, that is, the writing down of mutual commitments in a document, which is then solemnly ratified by the laity and clergy of both churches and sometimes even also by both dioceses or judicatories.

Especially creative things have been done in the area of ecumenical theological education. In 1970 the Vatican Secretariat for Christian Unity, which since the end of the Second Vatican Council has been a permanent part of the Vatican bureaucracy, issued the "Directory Concerning Ecumenical Matters: Part Two: Ecumenism in Higher Education." The directory stated that "ecumenism should bear on all theological disciplines as one of its necessary determining factors,'' although there should also be separate courses on ecumenism. It noted that joint retreats with non-Catholics are to be recommended and that experts from other religious traditions should be invited to teach about their own traditions. In vigorous support of the teaching of ecumenism, the directory stated that bishops, religious superiors, and ''those in authority in seminaries, universities, and similar institutions should take pains to promote the ecumenical movement and spare no effort to see that teachers keep in touch with advances in ecumenical thought and action,'' and it urged that there ''be cooperation between institutions of higher education and relationships on various levels between teachers and students of different churches and communities.'' This has been happening in hundreds, thousands, of instances by the sharing of both faculty and students.

DIALOGUE WITH NON-CHRISTIANS

Once Christians shifted from a looking-inward to a looking-outward stance, it was inevitable their dialogue partners would not always be limited simply to Christians of other churches. Rather, if it seemed appropriate for the Lutheran to enter into dialogue with a Presbyterian or the Roman Catholic with a Lutheran, the idea developed that it would also be appropriate for the Christian to enter into dialogue with members of that religion from which Christianity sprang, Judaism. From there it also made sense to enter into dialogue with members of the religion that is so intimately related to both Judaism and Christianity, Islam, and from there to the other world religions and beyond that to those human beings who are not adherents of any religious tradition. Thus even though in the initial stages of the intra-Christian dialogue the attitude toward non-Christians was often still one of triumphalistic superiority, this attitude more and more was questioned in the minds of an increasing number of Christians. Moreover, those Christians engaged in dialogue with non-Christians also found that their attitude toward each other and the theological statements that they were able to issue jointly with other Christians were being profoundly affected by the interreligious dialogue. Hence it is of major importance to look briefly at the development of interreligious dialogue and to reflect on its meaning, sources, and implications.

Already in 1893 at the Columbian Exposition in Chicago, celebrating the four-hundredth anniversary of the discovery of America, there was set up a World Parliament of Religions, which brought together representatives of all major world religions. In 1921 the famous pioneer in the history of religion, Rudolf Otto, founded the *Religiöser Menschheitsbund* and spoke of the desirability of dialogue among religions so that together they could create a ''world conscience.'' Otto was supported in this by another famous Protestant scholar in the field of *Religionswissenschaft*, Friedrich Heiler. In 1932 the Harvard University philosopher William Ernest Hocking wrote a book-length report for the American Protestant Laymen's Foreign Missions Inquiry as chairman of the committee. He stressed human universals and argued that there should be a radical change in missionary activity. Whereas until then the missionaries had maintained that there was only one way, the way of Christ, the new approach should be that the aim of mission is to bring the religious life of every nation to its full development. Mission should not aim at the destruction of other religions but at their continued existence so that all religions could stimulate each other in the unity of the most complete truth.

The Dutch Protestant theologian Hendrik Kraemer responded vigorously at the World Missionary Conference at Tambaram in 1938. Following the approach of Karl Barth, he argued that Christianity is radically different from all religions. Christianity comes from God, whereas other religions come from humanity. Such a position clearly eliminated the possibility of any serious dialogue with other religions.

This view maintained dominance for a long time and still is advocated by many Christians. However, it is held by fewer and fewer. This fact is reflected in the setting up of the subunit for Dialogue with People of Living Faiths and Ideologies within the World Council of Churches in 1971 and the earlier establishment (1966) of the Vatican's Secretariat for Non-Christians and the Secretariat for Non-believers. Furthermore, there have been many Christian theologians, both Catholic and Protestant, who in recent years have been dealing very openly and creatively with this complex of problems. In fact, the outpouring of scholarly literature on interreligious dialogue is fast approaching the flood stage. This creative work on the part of Christian thinkers has motivated various official statements of both Protestant and Catholic provenance. It would be helpful to lift out a few samples of such statements.

In 1979 the subunit for Dialogue with People of Living Faiths and Ideologies of the WCC issued "Guidelines on Dialogue," concerning which they wrote, "this statement and guidelines here commended to member churches 'for their consideration and discussion, testing and evaluation, for their elaboration in each specific situation,' " by the Central Committee of the WCC. Thus these guidelines are authentically authoritative but only "moderately" so. Still, they show the way forward for many Protestant Christians. The WCC guidelines stated that "we are particularly concerned with the dialogue which reaches across differences of faith, ideology, and culture, even where the partners in dialogue do not agree on important central aspects of human life," and went on to note that "this dialogue is indeed possible on the basis of a mutual trust and a respect for the integrity of each participant's identity. Dialogue, therefore, is a fundamental part of Christian service within community. In dialogue Christians actively respond to the command to 'love God and your neighbour as yourself.' " Thus "to the member churches of the WCC we feel able with integrity to commend the way of dialogue. . . . we feel able with integrity to assure our partners in dialogue that we come not as manipulators but as genuine fellow-pilgrims, to speak with them of what we believe God has done."

In coming to dialogue with non-Christians the WCC indicated that Christians "should proceed with humility, because they so often perceive in people of other faiths and ideologies a spirituality, dedication, compassion and a wisdom which should forbid them making judgments about others as though from a position of superiority.'' After discussing thoroughly the dangers involved in what they described as syncretism, the WCC stated that

despite the recognized dangers Christians should welcome and gladly engage in the venture of exploratory faith. The particular risks of syncretism in the modern world should not lead Christians to refrain from dialogue, but are an additional reason for engaging in dialogue so that the issues may be clarified. . . . To enter into dialogue requires an opening of the mind and heart to others. It is an undertaking which requires risk as well as a deep sense of vocation. It is impossible without sensitivity to the richly varied life of humankind. This opening, this risk, this vocation, this sensitivity are at the heart of the ecumenical movement and in the deepest currents of the life of the churches.

A number of citations from Vatican II have already been given above to indicate the new and fully authoritative commitment of the Roman Catholic Church to dialogue. Already in 1964 Pope Paul VI made that commitment, if possible, even stronger in his first encyclical, *Ecclesiam suam,* when he stated that, ''dialogue is demanded nowadays. . . . It is demanded by the dynamic course of action which is changing the face of modern society. It is demanded by the pluralism of society and by the maturity man has reached in this day and age. Be he religious or not, his secular education has enabled him to think and speak and conduct a dialogue with dignity.''

The Vatican Secretariat for Non-believers in 1968 issued a document (*Humanae Personae Dignitatem*) that provided still further creative reflections on interreligious dialogue. It stated that the purpose of dialogue is to attain a ''greater grasp of truth . . . to liberate those engaged in discussion from their solitude and their mutual distrust . . . to reach an agreement, to be established in the realm of truth . . . and the achievement by common effort of a better grasp of truth and an extension of knowledge.'' Moreover, according to the Secretariat this dialogic search for truth is by no means limited to ''practical'' matters but in a central way is to focus on theology and doctrine, and to do so without hesitation or trepidation: ''Doctrinal dialogue should be initiated with courage and sincerity, with the greatest of freedom and with reverence. It focuses on doctrinal questions which are of concern to the parties to dialogue. They have different opinions but by common effort they strive to improve mutual understanding, to clarify matters on which they agree, and if possible to enlarge the areas of agreement. In this way the parties to dialogue can enrich each other.''

However, ''If dialogue is to achieve its aims, it must obey the rules of truth and liberty. It needs sincere truth, thus excluding manipulated doctrinal discussion, discussion which is undertaken for political ends. . . . in discussion the truth will prevail by no other means than by the truth itself. Therefore the liberty of the participants must be ensured by law and reverence in practice.''

To be sure, there is risk involved in dialogue—if one is really open to what the partner says, one has to reckon with the possibility that she or he will prove to be persuasive on any particular issue: "Doctrinal discussion requires perceptiveness, both in honestly setting out one's own opinion and in recognizing the truth everywhere, even if the truth demolishes one so that one is forced to reconsider one's own position, in theory and in practice, at least in part," Those are clearly extremely strong words.

DIALOGUE

Dialogue is a conversation on a common subject between two or more persons with differing views, the primary purpose of which is for each participant to learn from the other so that he or she can change and grow. Minimally, the very fact that I learn that my dialogue partner believes "this" rather than "that" proportionately changes my attitude toward her or him, and a change in my attitude is a significant change in me.

Dialogue clearly is *not* debate. In dialogue each partner must listen to the other as openly and sympathetically as he or she can in an attempt to understand the other's position as precisely and, as it were, as much from within, as possible. Such an attitude automatically includes the assumption that at any point we might find the partner's position so persuasive that if we would act with integrity, we would have to change, and change can be disturbing. But that is the point of dialogue—change and growth in the understanding and perception of reality. We enter into dialogue so that *we* can learn, change, and grow, not so that we can force change on the *other,* as one hopes to do in debate. On the other hand, because in dialogue *each* partner comes with the intention of learning and changing oneself, one's partner in fact will also change.

INTERRELIGIOUS DIALOGUE

We are here referring to a specific kind of dialogue, an interreligious dialogue. To have such, it is not sufficient that the dialogue partners discuss a religious subject. Rather, they must come to the dialogue as persons somehow significantly identified with a religious community. Because of this "corporate" nature of interreligious dialogue, and since the primary goal of dialogue is that each partner learn and change himself or herself, it is also necessary that interreligious dialogue be a two-sided project. Each participant must enter into dialogue not only with his partner across the faith line—the Christian with the Muslim, for example— but also with his coreligionists, with his fellow Christians, to share with them the fruits of the interreligious dialogue. Only thus can the whole community eventually learn and change, moving toward an ever more perceptive insight into reality.

There are three key principles that must be observed if interreligious dialogue is to take place at all.

First, each participant must define himself or herself. Only the Jew, for example, can define from the inside what it means to be a Jew. The rest can only describe what it looks like from the outside. Moreover, because dialogue is a dynamic medium, as each participant learns, he or she will change and hence continually deepen, expand, and modify his or her self-definition as a Jew—being careful to remain in constant dialogue with fellow Jews.

Second, dialogue can take place only between equals, *par cum pari,* as Vatican II puts it. This means that not only can there be no dialogue between a skilled scholar and a "person in the pew" type (at most there can be only a garnering of data in the manner of an interrogation), but also there can be no such thing as a one-way dialogue. For example, Jewish-Christian discussions begun in the 1960s were mainly only prolegomena to interreligious dialogue. Understandably and properly, the Jews came to these exchanges only to teach the Christians, although the Christians came mainly to learn. But if authentic interreligious dialogue between Christians and Jews is to occur, the Jews must also come mainly to learn; only then will it be *par cum pari.*

Third, one entering into interreligious dialogue must be at least minimally self-critical of both oneself and one's own religious tradition. A lack of such self-criticism implies that one's own tradition already has all of the correct answers. Such an attitude not only makes dialogue unecessary but even impossible, since we enter into dialogue primarily so that *we* can learn—which obviously is impossible if our tradition has never made a misstep, if it has all the right answers. To be sure, in interreligious dialogue one must stand within a religious tradition with integrity and conviction, but such integrity and conviction must include, not exclude, a healthy self-criticism. Without it there can be no dialogue—and, indeed, no integrity.

It should also be noted that there are at least three phases in interreligious dialogue. In the first phase we unlearn misinformation about each other and begin to know each other as we truly are. In phase two we begin to discern values in the partner's tradition and wish to appropriate them into our own tradition. For example, in the Catholic-Protestant dialogue Catholics have learned to stress the Bible, and Protestants have learned to appreciate the sacramental approach to Christian life, both values traditionally associated with the other's religious community. If we are serious, persistent, and sensitive enough in the dialogue, we may at times enter into phase three. Here we together begin to explore new areas of reality, of meaning, of truth, of which neither of us had even been aware before. We are brought face to face with this new, as yet unknown-to-us, dimension of reality only because of questions, insights, probings, produced in the dialogue.

DEABSOLUTIZING TRUTH

Interreligious dialogue is new. It is in fact only a few years old, quite limited yet, very fragile, and not widespread, but it is there—and that is the indispensable breakthrough that must be exploited. There were recent historical events that,

for example, allowed for and led to the beginning of the Jewish-Christian dialogue, notably, the horror of the Holocaust, followed by metanoic events such
as the Second Vatican Council. However, there were subterranean changes that
took place throughout the nineteenth and twentieth centuries that have made
interreligious dialogue for at least a significant, and growing, minority of religious
believers not only possible today but also necessary. The most important of these
subterranean changes is the spread of a deabsolutized, dynamic, dialogic—in a
word, "relational"—view of truth. The necessity of dialogue is obvious once
one has attained a deabsolutized view of truth.

This new view of the meanings of things came about in at least four different,
but closely related, ways:

1. Historicizing of truth: truth is deabsolutized in terms of time, both past and future,
   with intentionality and action playing a major role in the latter.
2. Sociology of knowledge: truth is deabsolutized in terms of geography, culture, and
   social standing.
3. Limits of language: truth as the meaning of something and especially as talk about
   the transcendent is deabsolutized by the nature of human language.
4. Hermeneutics: all truth, all knowledge is seen as interpreted truth, knowledge, and
   hence is deabsolutized by the observer who always is also interpreter.

1. The historicizing of truth: Before the nineteenth century in Europe truth,
that is, a *statement* about reality, was conceived in an absolute, static manner.
It was thought that if something was true at some time, it was always true and
not only in regard to empirical facts but also in regard to the meaning of things
or the oughtness that was said to flow from them. For example, if it was true
for the Pauline writer to state in the first century that women should keep silence
in the church, then it was always true that the women should keep silence in
the church; or if it was true for Pope Boniface VIII in 1302 to state in definitive
terms that "we declare, state, and define that it is absolutely necessary for the
salvation of all human beings that they submit to the Roman Pontiff" (which
view no Catholic theologian would hold today), then it was always true that they
need do so. This can be called a *classicist* view of truth.

In the nineteenth century many scholars came to perceive all statements about
the truth of the meaning of something as being partially products of their historical
circumstances. Those concrete circumstances helped determine the fact that the
statement under study was even called forth, that it was couched in particular
intellectual categories (for example, abstract Platonic, or concrete legal language), particular literary forms (for example, mythic, or metaphysical language), and particular psychological settings (for example, a polemic response
to a specific attack). It was argued by these scholars that only by placing the
truth statements in their historical *Sitz im Leben* could they be properly understood
(understanding of the text could be found only in context) and that to express
the same original meaning in a later *Sitz im Leben* one would require a propor-

tionately different statement. Thus all statements about the meaning of things were seen to be deabsolutized in terms of time. This is a *historical* view of truth. Clearly, at its heart is a notion of *relationality;* that is, a statement about the truth of the meaning of something has to be understood in relationship to its historical context.

Later, especially with the work of thinkers like Max Scheler and Karl Mannheim, a corollary was added to this historicizing of knowledge; it concerned not the past but the future. These and other scholars also conceived of the knowledge of truth as having an element of intentionality at the base of it, as being oriented ultimately toward action, praxis. They argued that we perceive certain things as questions to be answered and set goals to pursue certain knowledge because we wish to do something about those matters; we intend to live according to the truth, the meaning of things, that we hope to discern in the answering of the questions we pose, in gaining the knowledge we decide to seek. Thus the truth of the meaning of things as stated by anyone was seen as deabsolutized by the action-oriented intentionality of the thinker–speaker. This is a *praxis* view of truth, and it, too, is basically *relational;* that is, a statement had to be understood in relationship to the action-oriented intention of the speaker.

2. The sociology of knowledge: As the statements of the truth about the meaning of things were seen by some thinkers to be historically deabsolutized in time, so also starting in this century such statements were seen to be deabsolutized by the cultural, class (and so forth), standpoint of the thinker–speaker, regardless of time. Thus a statement about the true meaning of things will be partially determined by the world view of the thinker–speaker. All reality was said to be perceived from the cultural, class, sexual (and so forth), perspective of the perceiver. Therefore, any statement of the truth of the meaning of something was seen to be perspectival, "standpoint-bound," *standortgebunden,* as Karl Mannheim put it, and thus deabsolutized. This is a *perspectival* view of truth, which is likewise *relational,* for all statements are fundamentally related to the standpoint of the speaker.

3. The limitations of language: Many thinkers (following Ludwig Wittgenstein and others) have come to understand that all statements about the truth of things necessarily can at most be only partial descriptions of the reality they are trying to describe. This is said to be the case because although reality can be seen from an almost limitless number of perspectives, human language can express things from only one, or perhaps a very few, perspectives at once. This is now also seen to be true of our so-called scientific truths. A fortiori, it is the case concerning statements about the truth of the meaning of things. The very fact of dealing with the truth of the "meaning" of something indicates that the knower is essentially involved and thereby reflects the perspectival character of all such statements. Hence this also is a *perspectival* view of truth and therefore also *relational.*

Moreover, the limited and limiting, as well as liberating, quality of language is especially seen when there is talk of the transcendent. By definition the transcendent is that which goes beyond our experience. Hence all statements about the transcendent are seen to be extremely deabsolutized and limited even beyond the limiting factor of the perspectival character of statements.

A statement may be true, that is, it may accurately describe the extramental reality it refers to, but it will always be cast in particular categories, language, concerns, and so on of a particular "standpoint," and in that sense it always will be limited, deabsolutized.

4. Hermeneutics: Hans-Georg Gadamer and Paul Ricoeur recently led the way in development of the science of hermeneutics, which argues that all knowledge of a text is also an *interpretation* of the text, thereby still further deabsolutizing claims about the "true" meaning of the text. But this basic insight goes beyond the knowledge of a text and applies to all knowledge. Some of the key notions here can be compressed in the following mantra (a seven-syllable phrase that capsulizes an insight): "Subject, object, two is one." The whole of hermeneutics is here in nuce: All knowledge is interpreted knowledge; the perceiver is part of the perceived, especially, but not only, in the humane disciplines; the subject is part of the object. When the object of study is some aspect of humanity, it is obvious that the observer is also the observed, which "deobjectivizes," deabsolutizes, the resultant knowledge, truth. The same, however, is also fundamentally true, though in a different way, of all knowledge, truth, of the natural sciences, for various aspects of nature are observed only through the categories we provide, within the horizon we establish, under the paradigm we use, in response to the questions we raise, and in relationship to the connections we make—a further deabsolutizing of truth, even of the "hard" sciences.

To move on to the second half of the mantra, "two is one": We see that knowledge comes from the subject perceiving the object, but the subject is also part of the object. Therefore, the two are one in that sense. Also, in knowing, the object as such is taken up into the subject and thus again the two are one. Yet there is also a radical twoness there, for it is the very *process* of the two *becoming* one—or alternatively, the two being perceived as one, or even better, the becoming aware that the two, which are very really two, are also in fact very really one—that is what we call knowing. This is an *interpretative* view of truth. It is clear that *relationality* pervades this hermeneutical, interpretative view of truth.

A further development of this basic insight is that I learn by dialogue, that is, not only by being open to, or receptive, in a passive sense, of extramental reality but also by having a dialogue with extramental reality. I not only "hear," receive, reality, but I also "speak" to reality. That is, I ask it questions, I stimulate it to speak back to me, answer my questions. Furthermore, I give reality the specific categories, language with which, in which, to speak, to respond to me. It can "speak" to me, that is, really communicate to my mind, only in a language, in categories, that I understand. When the speaking, the responding, becomes more and more *un*understandable to me, I slowly begin to become aware that there is a new language being developed and that I must learn it if I am to make sense out of what reality is saying to me. This might be called a *dialogic* view of truth, whose very name reflects its *relationality*.

With the deabsolutized view of the truth of the meaning of things we come face to face with the specter of relativism, which is the opposite pole of absolutism. Unlike "relationality," which is a neutral term merely denoting the quality of being in relationship, "relativism" is a basically negative term (as are almost all "isms"). If one can no longer claim that any statement of the truth of the meaning of things is absolute, totally objective, because the claim does not square with our experience of reality, it is equally impossible to claim that every statement of the truth of the meaning of things is completely relative, totally subjective, for that also does not square with our experience of reality and, furthermore, would logically lead to an atomizing solipsism (self-alone*ism*) that would stop all discourse, all statements to others.

Our perception, and hence description, of reality is like viewing an object in the center of a circle of viewers. My view and description of the object (reality) will be true, but it will not include what someone on the other side of the circle perceives and describes, which will also be true. So neither of the perceptions/descriptions of the object (reality) is total, complete—"absolute" in that sense—or "objective" in the sense of not in any way being dependent on a "subject." At the same time, however, it is also obvious that there is an "objective," doubtless "true," aspect to each perception/description, even though each is relational to the perceiver-"subject."

NECESSITY OF DIALOGUE

But if we can no longer hold to an absolutist view of the truth of the meaning of things, we must take certain steps so as not to be logically forced into the silence of total relativism, including at least the following two steps: First, besides striving to be as accurate and fair as possible in our gathering and assessing of information, submitting it to the critiques of our peers and other thinkers and scholars, we need also to dredge out, state clearly, and analyze our own presuppositions—which is a constant, ongoing task. However, even in doing this we will be operating from a particular "standpoint." Therefore, we need, second, to complement our constantly critiqued statements with statements from different "standpoints." That is, we need to engage in dialogue with those who have differing cultural, philosophical, social, religious, viewpoints so as to strive toward an ever fuller perception of the truth of the meaning of things. If we do not engage in such dialogue we will be trapped within the perspective of our own "standpoint." Hence our search for the truth of the meaning of things makes it a necessity for us as human beings that we engage in dialogue.

If this is true for all human beings in the search for the truth of the meaning of things, it is most intensely so for religious persons. Religions describe and prescribe for the whole of life; they are holistic, all-encompassing, and therefore tend to blot out, that is, either convert or condemn, outsiders even more than other institutions that are not holistic. Thus the need for due modesty in truth claims and complementarity for particular views of the truth, as described above, is most intense in the field of religion.

But the need for dialogue in religion is also intensified in the modern world because slowly through the impact of mass communications and the high level of mobility of contemporary society in the West, and elsewhere, we more and more experience "others" as living not only holistic but also "holy" lives, that is, integrated human lives related to an Ultimate Concern—not in spite of but because of their religion. To be concrete: when I as a Christian come to know Jews as religious persons who are leading whole, holy human lives out of the fullness of their Judaism, I am immediately confronted with the question: what is the source of this holiness? It obviously is not Christianity. Unless I really work at duping myself, I cannot say that it is unconscious or anonymous Christianity, for if there is any religion that has for two thousand years consciously rejected Christianity, that religion is Judaism. Clearly, the only possible answer is that the source of the holiness of the Jew is the Jewish religion, and the God who stands behind it, the God of Abraham, Isaac, Jacob—and Jesus. Christianity, like Judaism, is a religion that believes that God reveals herself or himself to us through events and persons and that to learn God's message, God's Torah, good news, gospel, Christians must seek to listen to God wherever and through whomever she or he speaks; that is, they must be in dialogue with persons of other religions to learn what God is saying to us through them.

CONCLUSION

Until now my line of argument has been that the need of contemporary Westerners in search of the truth of the meaning of things to engage in dialogue with persons with views other than their own is becoming ever more pressing and that this is especially so for religious persons. This chain of reasoning is doubtless true for persons who have experienced the above-described developments in Western culture regardless of their religion, but for particular historical reasons it is most valid for Christians: for good or ill—or rather, with its good and ill—Christians in large measure have created Western culture. The next question is: with what religion should Christianity engage in this necessary dialogue? In one sense the answer must be: with all religions. But at the same time there are profound reasons stemming from the Jewish origin of Christianity for a priority of the dialogue with Judaism. Logic then points to the next step for both Judaism and Christianity: dialogue with Islam, their "offspring"—without implying, however, that the dialogue with Hinduism, Buddhism, and secular world ideologies such as Marxism must wait chronologically for the dialogue with Judaism and with Islam to be completed.

A final question is: will this interreligious dialogue lead to a watering down, or even destruction, of Christianity? I am persuaded that it will not, that in fact it is the only creative way forward in the modern world. In the words of another

Roman Catholic theologian, Paul Knitter: "If Christians, trusting God and respecting the faith of others, engage in this new encounter with other traditions, they can expect to witness a growth or evolution such as Christianity has not experienced since its first centuries. This growth will paradoxically both preserve the identity of Christianity and at the same time transform it. Such paradox is no mystery; we are acquainted with it in our own personal lives as well as in nature."

SELECTED BIBLIOGRAPHY

Bibliographical Sources

Crow, Paul A. *The Ecumenical Movement in Bibliographical Outline*. New York: Dept. of Faith and Order, National Council of the Churches of the Christ in the U.S.A., 1965.

Fey, Harold E., ed. *A History of the Ecumenical Movement*. Vol. 2, 1948–1968. Philadelphia: Westminster Press, 1967. Contains a sixty-page bibliography, with very little overlap with the previous volume.

International Ecumenical Bibliography. Mainz: Matthias Grünewald Verlag; Munich: Kaiser Verlag, 1967. Covers 1962–1963 in vol. 1, annual vols. subsequently.

Journal of Ecumenical Studies. Edited by Leonard Swidler. Quarterly, started in 1963; published at Philadelphia, Temple University; reviews between 150 and 250 books of ecumenical or interreligious significance in all languages a year and prints 400 abstracts of articles of ecumenical or interreligious significance taken from 450 periodicals from all over the world.

Lescrauwaet, J. F. *Critical Bibliography of Ecumenical Literature*. Nijmegen: Bestel Centrale V.S.K.B., 1965.

Rouse, Ruth, and Stephen C. Neill, eds. *A History of the Ecumenical Movement, 1517–1948*. 2d ed., Philadelphia: Westminster Press, 1967. Contains a fifty-four page bibliography.

Ecumenical Libraries and Archives

Archives on the World Conference on Faith and Order (General Theological Seminary, Chelsea Square, New York, NY 10011).

Centro Pro Unione Library (Via Maria dell'Anima 30, 00186 Rome, Italy).

Institut für ökumenische Forschung (University of Tübingen, Nauklerstrasse 37a, 7400 Tübingen, Federal Republic of Germany).

The Library of Union Theological Seminary (Broadway at 120th Street, New York, NY 10027).

The Library of the World Council of Churches (150 Route de Ferney, 1211 Geneva 20, Switzerland).

Temple University Library (1936 N. Broad Street, Philadelphia, PA 19122) has the 450 religious periodicals from around the world which are abstracted in the *Journal of Ecumenical Studies* from 1978 on.

Ecumenical and Interreligious Periodicals

Begegnung (Berlin)
Bulletin Secretariatus pro non Christianis (Vatican)
Catholica (Münster, W. Germany)
Ching Feng (Hong Kong)
Christian Attitudes on Jews and Judaism (London)
Christian Jewish Relations (London)
Current Dialogue (Geneva)
Dialog (St. Paul, Minn.)
Dialogo ecuménico (Salamanca, Spain)
The Ecumenical Review (Geneva)
Ecumenical Trends (Garrison, N.Y.)
Ecumenism (Montreal)
The Ecumenist (Ramsey, N.J.)
Episkepsis (Geneva)
Freiburger Rundbrief (Freiburg, W. Germany)
Immanuel (Jerusalem)
Irenikon (Chevetogne, Belgium)
Islamochristiana (Rome)
Istina (Paris)
Journal of Ecumenical Studies (Philadelphia)
Kosmos & Oekumene ('s-Hertogenbosch, The Netherlands)
Materialdienst des konfessionskundlichen Instituts (Bensheim)
Mid-Stream (Indianapolis)
Nicolaus (Bari, Italy)
Ökumenische Rundschau (Frankfurt)
One in Christ (Turvey, Bedfordshire)
Rencontre Chrétiens et Juifs (Paris)
Sidic (Rome)
Una Sancta (Freising bei Augsburg, W. Germany)
Unitas (Rome)
Unite Chretienne (Lyons)
Unité des Chrétiens (Paris)

Documents Collections

Abbott, Walter M. *The Documents of Vatican II.* New York: Herder and Herder; Association Press, 1966.
Bell, G.K.A., ed. *Documents on Christian Unity.* 4 vols. London: Oxford University Press, 1924–1958.
Croner, Helga, ed. *Stepping Stones to Further Jewish-Christian Relations.* New York: Stimulus Books, 1977.
Flannery, Austin, ed. *Vatican Council II: The Conciliar and Post Conciliar Documents.* Collegeville, Minn.: Liturgical Press, 1975.
Hocher, M-T., and B. Dupuy. *Les Eglises devant le Judaisme, 1948–1978.* Paris: Cert, 1980.

Richter, Klemens, ed. *Die katholische Kirche und das Judentum Dokumente von, 1945–1980*. Frankfurt: Deutsches Pax-Christi-Sekretariat, 1982.

Vischer, Lukas, ed. *A Documentary History of the Faith and Order Movement, 1927–1963*. St. Louis: Bethany, 1963.

Histories and General Surveys of Ecumenism

Histories and general surveys of the ecumenical movement have been frequently written. What follows is a very restricted selection of some of the most important and recent of them:

Brown, Robert McAfee. *The Ecumenical Revolution*. New York: Doubleday, 1967.

Cavert, Samuel McCrea. *The American Churches in the Ecumenical Movement, 1900–1968*. New York: Association Press, 1968.

Fey, Harold E. *A History of the Ecumenical Movement*. Vol. 2, 1948–1968. Philadelphia: Westminster Press, 1967.

Lengsfeld, Peter, ed. *Ökumenische Theologie: Ein Arbeitsbuch*. Stuttgart: Kohlhammer Verlag, 1980.

Nash, Margaret. *Ecumenical Movement in the 1960's*. Johannesburg: Ravan Press, 1975.

Rouse, Ruth, and Stephen C. Neill, eds. *A History of the Ecumenical Movement, 1517–1948*. 2d ed., Philadelphia: Westminster Press, 1967.

Swidler, Leonard. *The Ecumenical Vanguard: History of the Una Sancta Movement*. Pittsburgh: Duquesne University Press, 1966.

Tavard, George. *Two Centuries of Ecumenism*. New York, Mentor-Omega, 1962.

Interreligious Dialogue

The number of publications on various aspects of interreligious dialogue is vast. The following is a tiny selection of the most recent important books in some areas. The first fifteen books concern Jewish-Christian dialogue and are grouped in four categories: Christian histories of Jewish-Christian relations; Jews and Judaism in Christian religious education; Christian theology in dialogue with Jews; Jews in dialogue with Christians.

Ben-Chorin, Schalom. *Bruder Jesus*. Munich: Paul List Verlag, 1967.

Biemer, Günter. *Freiburger Leitlinien zum Lernprozess Christen Juden*. Düsseldorf: Patmos Verlag, 1981.

Bishop, Claire Huchet. *How Catholics Look at Jews: Inquiries into Italian, Spanish, and French Teaching Materials*. New York: Paulist Press, 1974.

Cobb, John B., Jr. *Beyond Dialogue: Toward a Mutual Transformation of Christianity and Buddhism*. Philadelphia: Fortress Press, 1982.

Dawe, Donald G., and John B. Carman, eds., *Christian Faith in a Religiously Plural World*. Maryknoll, N.Y.: Orbis Books, 1978.

Fernando, Antony, with Leonard Swidler. *Buddhism Made Plain for Christians, Jews, and other Westerners*. Maryknoll, N.Y.: Orbis Books, 1985.

Fisher, Eugene J. *Seminary Education and Christian-Jewish Relations*. Washington, D.C.: National Catholic Educational Association, 1983.

Flannery, Edward H. *The Anguish of the Jews: Twenty-Three Centuries of Anti-Semitism*. New York: Macmillan, 1965.

Flusser, David. *Jesus*. New York: Herder and Herder, 1968.

Hick, John, ed. *Truth and Dialogue in World Religions: Conflicting Truth-Claims*. Philadelphia: Westminster Press, 1974.

Lapide, Pinchas. *Der Jude Jesus*. Zurich: Benziger Verlag, 1979.

Mojzes, Paul, ed. *Varieties of Christian-Marxist Dialogue*. Philadelphia: *Journal of Ecumenical Studies,* 1978.

Mussner, Franz. *Tractate on the Jews*. Philadelphia: Fortress Press, 1984.

Panikkar, Raimundo. *The Intra-Religious Dialogue*. New York: Paulist Press, 1978.

————. *The Unknown Christ of Hinduism*. 2d ed.   Maryknoll, N.Y.: Orbis Books, 1981.

Pawlikowski, John T. *Catechetics and Prejudice: How Catholic Teaching Materials View Jews, Protestants, and Racial Minorities*. New York: Paulist Press, 1973.

Ruether, Rosemary. *Faith and Fratricide: The Theological Roots of Anti-Semitism*. New York: Seabury Press, 1974.

Schweitzer, Frederick M. *A History of the Jews Since the First Century A.D.* New York: Macmillan, 1971.

Smith. Wilfred Cantwell. *Towards a World Theology*. Philadelphia: Westminster Press, 1981.

Stöhr, Martin, ed. *Abrahams Kinder: Juden-Christen-Moslems*. Frankfurt: Haag & Herchen Verlag, 1983.

Swearer, Donald K. *Dialogue: The Key to Understanding Other Religions*. Philadelphia: Westminster Press, 1977.

Swidler, Leonard, ed. *Jewish-Christian-Muslim Dialogue*. Philadelphia: *Journal of Ecumenical Studies,* 1977.

Thoma, Clemens. *A Christian Theology of Judaism*. New York: Paulist Press, 1980.

Van Buren, Paul. *Discerning the Way: A Theology of the Jewish-Christian Reality*. New York: Seabury Press, 1980.

Vermes, Geza. *Jesus the Jew: A Historian's Reading of the Gospels*. Philadelphia: Fortress Press, 1981.

von der Osten-Sacken, Peter. *Grundzüge einer Theologie im christlich-jüdischen Gespräch*. Munich: Chr. Kaiser Verlag, 1982.

15

The Intra-Christian Dialogue

ARTHUR B. CRABTREE

For world history, the year 1945 was a decisive watershed. It marked the end of World War II, the beginning of the nuclear age, and the commencement of the Cold War. For ecumenism, it was far less decisive. For Orthodox and Protestant Christians, it marked simply the continuation of an ecumenical movement that had been proceeding for some time.

The World Council of Churches had been "in process of formation" since the 1938 Utrecht meeting of representatives of the Faith and Order and Life and Work movements. This "process of formation" lasted about ten years. In 1939 it was abruptly interrupted by the outbreak of World War II. At the end of the war in 1945 it was resumed, resulting in the actual formation of the World Council in 1948.

For Catholics, it meant the continuation of an "underground" ecumenical movement, led by the Una Sancta movement and scholars such as Karl Adam, Yves Congar, and Henri de Lubac, and the suppression of this movement by the Vatican. However, to understand intra-Christian relations since 1945, it is essential to understand something of those relations before 1945.

THE PREHISTORY: INTRA-CHRISTIAN RELATIONS BEFORE 1945

After the eleventh-century division of the church into Orthodox and Roman Catholic and the sixteenth-century division between Roman Catholic and Protestant, relations among the many communities of Christians were very hostile, resulting in the West in many wars of religion, including the Thirty Years' War (1618–1648) on the continent of Europe and sundry wars in the British Isles.

Slowly, tolerance and some measure of religious liberty emerged, and some ecumenical pioneers, such as the German Lutheran Georg Calixtus (1586–1656) and the Moravian leader Count Zinzendorf (1700–1760), began to plead for the restoration of Christian unity. This plea was heard by leaders of the Romantic movement in Germany, both Protestant (e.g., Friedrich D. E. Schleiermacher) and Roman Catholic (e.g., Johan M. Sailer and members of the Roman Catholic faculty in Tübingen—Johann S. Drey, Johann A. Möhler, Franz A. Staudenmaier, and others). It even reached some of the Jesuits in Rome, such as Schrader and Passaglia, but was quickly crushed by the Vatican. In the twentieth century it reemerged among Catholics, first in Tübingen (Karl Adam and Romano Guardini) and later in France (Yves Congar and Henri de Lubac), only once more to be spurned by the Vatican.

Among Protestants, the movement for Christian unity found expression in interdenominational organizations, such as the YMCA (1844), YWCA (1854), the Evangelical Alliance (1846), and the S.C.M., and it was principally from these movements that the leaders of the twentieth-century Protestant ecumenical movement emerged.

The idea of *praying* for Christian unity arose early in the twentieth century, principally among Roman Catholics and Anglicans, especially by that remarkable Anglican who converted to Catholicism, the Reverend Paul James Wattson of the Franciscan Friars of the Atonement. By a complicated process, an octave (eight days) of prayer was eventually agreed upon by both Roman Catholic and Protestant leaders, to be observed annually, January 18–25.[1]

In the twentieth century the first significant ecumenical event was the World Missionary Conference in Edinburgh in 1910, which emphasized the importance of unity and collaboration in Christian mission. "The World Missionary Conference, Edinburgh 1910," wrote Kenneth Scott Latourette, "was the birthplace of the modern ecumenical movement."[2] From Edinburgh emerged the International Revue of Missions, the International Missionary Council, and subsequent missionary conferences in Jerusalem (1928), Tambaram, India (1938), and Whitby, England (1947).

Meanwhile, two further types of ecumenical concern were developing: Life and Work and Faith and Order. Life and Work organized conferences in Stockholm (1925) and Oxford (1937), concerned with world order. Faith and Order held conferences in Lausanne (1927) and Edinburgh (1937), concerned with Christian reunion. In 1937 the two organizations agreed to unite, and in 1938 in Utrecht it was resolved that the new organization, the World Council of Churches, should be "a fellowship of Churches which accept our Lord Jesus Christ as God and Savior." Due to World War II, however, the formation of the World Council of Churches was delayed until 1948, when the World Council held its first Assembly in Amsterdam.

Meanwhile, *denominational* world organizations had been formed: The Anglican Communion, formed in 1867, meeting approximately every ten years; The Methodist Ecumenical Council, also meeting approximately every ten years; the Union of Utrecht, formed in 1881 (consisting of Roman Catholic churches that had withdrawn from communion with Rome since they had refused to accept the infallibility dogma of 1870); The International Congregational Council, formed in 1891; The Alliance of Reformed Churches, formed in 1875; The Baptist World Alliance, formed in 1905; and The Lutheran World Federation, formed in 1947. From all of these organizations, however, the Roman Catholic Church remained aloof until the Second Vatican Council (1962–1965).

THE HISTORY: INTRA-CHRISTIAN RELATIONS SINCE 1945

The Foundation and Development of the World Council of Churches

The World Council, as we have seen, had a delayed birth. It was conceived in 1938 but, due to the exigencies of war, was born in 1948. Its birth coincided with its First Assembly, Amsterdam, 1948. It combined the concerns of Faith and Order (church unity) and Life and Work (world order). In light of the havoc caused by World War II, it chose the general theme "Man's Disorder and God's Design," with the following sections: "The Universal Church in God's Design," "The Church's Witness to God's Design," "The Church and the Disorder of Society," and "The Church and International Disorder."

The Roman Catholic Church remained aloof, as did the Russian Orthodox Church and the Orthodox churches of Eastern Europe. However, the Greek Orthodox Church was represented, together with the Ecumenical Patriarchate of Constantinople, and several Russian émigré theologians were present.

The Second Assembly, Evanston, Illinois, 1954, chose the general theme "Christ the Hope of the World," with the subsections "Our Oneness in Christ and Our Disunity as Churches," "The Mission of the Church," "The Responsible Society in a World Perspective," "Christians in the Struggle for World Community," and "Christians amid Racial and Ethnic tensions."

The Third Assembly, New Delhi, 1961, was the first assembly in what we now call the Third World. It was highly significant for the following reasons:

1. The Orthodox churches were more fully represented, since the Russian Orthodox Church along with several Eastern European Orthodox churches had by now joined the World Council.

2. Largely under Orthodox influence the World Council basis was expanded to include a statement on the Trinity. It now read: "The World Council of Churches is a fellowship of churches which accept the Lord Jesus Christ as God and Savior according to the Scriptures, and therefore attempt to fulfill their vocation to the glory of God the Father, Son and Holy Spirit."

3. The International Missionary Council became an integral part of the World Council. Now all three roots of the Orthodox-Anglican-Protestant ecumenical movement were united in one stem. This enabled the New Delhi Assembly to embrace the theme "Jesus Christ, the Light of the World, made manifest in unity, witness, and service."

The Fourth Assembly, Uppsala, Sweden, 1968, convened under the theme "Behold, I make all things new." "There was an acute consciousness," wrote Philip Potter, of a world in which the inequalities of rich and poor, the injustices meted out to people because of their race, sex or class, and the confrontation of nations in wars which threatened the whole human race, had become intolerable."[3] The Fourth Assembly attempted to find salvific solutions to these menacing problems. (The Roman Catholic Second Vatican Council in its Pastoral Constitution on the Church in the Modern World [*Gaudium et Spes*] had attempted the same task.)

The Fifth Assembly, Nairobi, Kenya, 1975, chose the theme "Jesus Christ frees and unites." It was very conscious, meeting for the second time in the Third World, of the dual need of liberation from oppression and poverty and of reconciliation among the many classes, groups, and nations forming the world community and of the need for liberty and unity in the church.

The Sixth Assembly, Vancouver, Canada, 1983, conscious of the dire threat to life on earth posed both by biospherical deterioration and nuclear war, chose the theme "Jesus Christ, the Life of the world." In its message the assembly said: "This engagement together in Vancouver underlines how critical this moment is in the life of the world. . . . We hear the cries of millions who face a daily struggle for survival, who are crushed by military power or the propaganda of the powerful. . . . There is a great divide between North and South, between East and West. Our world—God's world—has to choose between 'life and death, blessing and curse.' "[4] The message continued:

This critical choice compels us to proclaim anew that life is God's gift. Life in all its fullness reflects the loving communion of God, Father, Son and Holy Spirit. . . . We renew our commitment to justice and peace. Since Jesus Christ healed and challenged the whole of life, so we are called to serve the life of all. . . . We urgently need a new international economic order in which power is shared, not grasped. . . . Injustice, flagrant, constant and oppressive, leads to violence. . . . The tree of peace has justice for its roots.[5]

But the members of the assembly not only spoke, they worshipped—Christians of differing churches, races, nations, and traditions—they worshipped together in a huge tent according to the Lima liturgy, based on the Lima document *Baptism, Eucharist and Ministry* (BEM), produced by the World Council's Commission on Faith and Order, which includes Roman Catholic members. This document is discussed later.

The Roman Catholic Church Officially Embraces Ecumenism

We have already seen that from the 1920s onward there was a renewal of ecumenical theology in the University of Tübingen, led by Karl Adam. In his *Das Wesen des Katholizismus* (1924), translated as *The Spirit of Catholicism* (1929), he conceived Catholicism to be broader than the Roman Catholic Church, to be "fullness in unity and unity in fullness," embracing not a static but a "living" tradition. All Christians need to repent—to turn to Christ and one another in "love and brotherhood, in loyalty and honesty. Then it cannot be otherwise than that God, even though by long detours and after serious inner crises of western spirituality, that God will grant in his grace, that we shall all find one another again, and that inner communion with Jesus will become an outward communion, so that there will be one flock under one Shepherd."[6] This vision of eventual Christian unity was expanded in his book *Una Sancta,* translated as *One and Holy.* Similar ideas were embraced by Max Metzger and embodied in his Una Sancta Brotherhood, which flourished for a time, was crushed by a *Monitum* (Warning) from the Vatican in 1948, and was revived again during and after the Second Vatican Council.

In France somewhat later, similar views were adopted by Yves Congar, Henri de Lubac, Louis Bouyer, and others and by the series of books issued under the title *Théologie* and the whole "nouvelle Théologie." After the publication of his book *Christians Divided* in 1937, however, Congar was forbidden to publish, and soon de Lubac was forbidden to teach. Thus the voices of ecumenism were silenced by the Vatican, and Roman Catholics, though invited, were not allowed to attend Assemblies of the World Council of Churches until the death of Pope Pius XII.

Upon the death of Pope Pius XII in 1958, the cardinals elected an old man to be a "caretaker pope." The old man was Angelo Roncalli, who chose the name John XXIII. Soon he surprised everybody—especially his electors. He created a Secretariat for the Promotion of Christian Unity, with Cardinal Bea, a German Jesuit biblical scholar, as secretary; convened an ecumenical council (now known as the Second Vatican Council); and in his first Encyclical, *Ad Petri Cathedram,* of May 29, 1959, called for peace, truth, and unity in the world and in the church.

Against the strenuous opposition of some leading members of the Curia, he persisted in his plans for the council, which opened on October 11, 1962, Pope John XXIII presiding. After the first session, however, the beloved old man died of cancer, and the three remaining sessions were presided over by Pope Paul VI.

In the council the old Roman Catholicism and the new met, clashed, and mingled. The old, represented by many of the bishops and leading members of the Curia such as Alfredo Ottaviani, Ruffini, and Felici advocated the old rigid, authoritarian, and antiecumenical Catholicism that identified the Roman Catholic Church with the *one* true church. The new Catholicism was represented by other bishops and many of the *periti* (theological experts) such as Ives Congar, Hans Küng, and Josef Ratzinger, who held seminars for the bishops. It upheld an open, flexible, and ecumenical attitude which perceived elements of the true church in the non-Roman communions. The outcome of the council was in general a *coincidentia oppositorum,* a mingling of the two.

The Decree on Ecumenism opens with the words:

The restoration of unity among all Christians is one of the principal concerns of the Second Vatican Council. Christ the Lord founded one Church and one Church only. However many Christian communions present themselves to men as the true inheritors of Jesus Christ . . . as if Christ himself were divided. Certainly such division openly contradicts the will of Christ, scandalizes the world, and damages that most holy cause, the preaching of the Gospel to every creature. (Introduction)

Non-Roman Catholic Christians are no longer called "heretics" and "adversaries," as in the older theology, but "separated brethren." Communions separated from Rome are termed "separated Churches" (I.3). Methods of promoting Christian unity are indicated: (1) avoiding expressions that do not "represent the condition of our separated brethren with truth and fairness," (2) dialogue "between competent experts from different Churches and communities," (3) "cooperation in carrying out any duties for the common good of humanity," (4) "common prayer, where this is permitted," and (5) "finally, all are led to examine their own faithfulness to Christ's will for the Church and, wherever necessary, undertake with vigor the task of renewal and reform" (I.3).

Common prayer is allowed, such as in prayer services "for unity," but "worship in common (*communicatio in sacris*) is not to be considered as a means to be used indiscriminately for the restoration of unity among Christians" (II.8). After the council, the *Directory Concerning Ecumenical Matters* was issued (May 14, 1967), which allowed eucharistic sharing with Christians of Orthodox Christian churches but forbade it "with Other Separated Brethren." In its closing paragraph the Decree on Ecumenism refers to "this holy objective—the reconciliation of all Christians in the unity of the one and only Church of Christ" (III.24).

In the Dogmatic Constitution on the Church (*Lumen Gentium*), the church is described not in accordance with the older ecclesiology as a "perfect society" but in terms of the newer ecclesiology as a "mystery," the flock of Christ, "the building of God," the bride of Christ, "the people of God," and the body of Christ, reflecting the influence of the Catholic biblical movement (begun by the French Dominicans) on Catholic theology and bringing Catholic terminology much nearer to Protestant modes of thought.

The Roman Catholic Church is no longer *identified* with the whole or Catholic church, but this whole church is said to "*subsist*" in the Roman Catholic Church, leaving open the possibility that it subsists also in other churches (I.8).

All of this is immensely helpful to the quest for organic reunion. Chapter III, however, on the church hierarchy poses immense problems. Except for the affirmation of collegiality of the bishops with one another and with the pope, Vatican II simply repeats the doctrine of Vatican I regarding papal supremacy, authority, and infallibility—and the irreformability of doctrines stated *ex cathedra*. The Second Vatican Council even maintains that the pope must be obeyed with "loyal submission of the will and intellect . . . even when he does not speak *ex cathedra*" (III.25).

This teaching threw many Roman Catholics into great distress when Pope Paul VI issued his Encyclical *Humanae Vitae,* on human life and birth control in 1968, against the advice of the majority of his advisory council.

This teaching on the supremacy, authority, and infallibility, conjoined with the statement that the pope must always be obeyed, whether or not he is speaking *ex cathedra,* poses immense, possibly insuperable, problems for the reunion of other churches with the Roman Catholic Church. Pope Paul VI himself said that the papacy is the chief obstacle to reunion, and he was right—unless the doctrine of the papacy changes.

The *Declaration on Religious Liberty* is a curious document. On the one side, it marks a great step forward, since it is the first official Roman Catholic document to affirm the principle of religious liberty, basing this liberty on human dignity and conscience. On the other side, while much is said regarding religious freedom in respect of *civil* authorities, little is said regarding freedom in respect of *church* authorities. "So", said the declaration, "while the religious freedom which men demand in fulfilling their obligations to worship God has to do with freedom from coercion in civil society, it leaves intact the traditional Catholic teaching towards the true religion and the one Church of Christ." By a complete relapse into the old theology of the "one true religion," it declares that "we believe that this one true religion continues to exist in the Catholic and Apostolic Church". But *within* that "one true Church" it offers little protection for those who differ from the *magisterium* of the church, as recent condemnations of distinguished theologians, such as Hans Küng, Eduard Schillebeeckx, and Clodovis Boff demonstrate.

Since the council, relations between Roman Catholics and other Christian churches have improved immensely. But formidable obstacles to reunion still remain—especially in the area of church structures and most of all regarding the papacy.

Ecumenically, the papacy of John Paul II displays a strange ambivalence. On the one hand, the present pope, like his predecessor, Paul VI, has visited the World Council of Churches in Geneva. His speeches abound in exhortations to Christian reunion. One example is his address to the plenary session of the Secretariat for the Promotion of Christian Unity on November 16, 1984. He said:

As we recall once more the twentieth anniversary of the Council's (decree) on ecumenism, a decree which means even more to us after the rich experience of twenty years of these new relations with our fellow Christians, a decree which challenges us constantly to new and even more vigorous action at every level of the Church's life, I thank you again for being present at this plenary meeting. I ask the God of unity to bless you and everyone who collaborates with you in working for the restoration of unity between all Christians— a task "which, by the will of Christ, the Church is bound to promote."[7]

On the other hand, as we have seen, in collaboration with the Prefect of the Congregation for the Doctrine of the Faith, Cardinal Ratzinger, John Paul II has already condemned several eminent theologians and has recently censured the theses for reunion advanced by Karl Rahner and Heinrich Fries in their book *Einigung der Kirchen reale Möglichkeit,* translated as *The Unity of the Churches: An Actual Possibility.*

Space does not permit us to discuss here the eight theses propounded by Rahner and Fries as guidelines for progress in reunion. But they all seem helpful and have been recognized as such, with a few exceptions, by both Catholic and Protestant theologians. One great merit is that they face squarely the papal problem, which has been avoided in so many bilateral discussions, and make helpful suggestions for its solution.

Ecumenical Conversations on a World Level

Around the time the Second Vatican Council ended, Pope Paul VI encouraged bilateral conversations between the Roman Catholic Church and other churches. Already in 1965 a Joint Working Group was formed consisting of representatives of the Vatican and the World Council of Churches to organize them and to coordinate the work of the Vatican and the World Council in general.

The results of these conversations to the present have now been conveniently collated by Harding Meyer and Lukas Vischer in *Growth in Agreement: Reports and Agreed Statements of Ecumenical Conversations on a World Level,* published jointly by the World Council of Churches in Geneva and by the Paulist Press in the United States, 1984.

It is a book that deserves careful study by all concerned about Christian unity. Here we can merely summarize the main results.

The *Anglican-Roman Catholic Conversations* have achieved "substantial agreement" on the Eucharist and Episcopate but register considerable disagreement regarding the papacy.

The *Baptist-Roman Catholic Conversation* (only one is recorded) found some convergence regarding infant and believer's baptism in the concept of growth in Christian nurture.

The *Lutheran-Roman Catholic Conversations* reached substantial agreement on the doctrine of justification, conceived as both forgiveness of sins and transformation of life; convergence on the Eucharist; but divergence on the papacy.

The *Methodist-Roman Catholic Conversations* seem to have been content for a long time to stress matters of agreement and more or less ignore basic differences. Now they have begun to address the differences, including church structures and the papacy.

The *Old Catholic-Roman Catholic Conversations* have been similarly content to stress matters of agreement and to avoid the one matter that seriously divides them—the papacy. (The old Catholic church consists of those Catholics who separated from Rome when the First Vatican Council defined the authority and infallibility of the pope in 1870.)

The *Pentecostal-Roman Catholic Conversations* have helped both sides to value both spontaneity and order.

The *Reformed (Presbyterian)-Roman Catholic Conversations* display some convergence regarding the Eucharist and action for world order but complete divergence concerning papal authority and infallibility.

In addition to including these bilateral conversations, *Growth in Agreement* contains also the Lima Document, *Baptism, Eucharist, and Ministry* (BEM), produced in Lima, Peru, in 1982. This document consists of the Main Text, which records agreements, and a number of Commentaries that express disagreements.

Baptism is described as participation in Christ's death and resurrection, conversion and cleansing, reception of the Spirit, incorporation into the Body of Christ, and a sign of the kingdom. It is related to faith in infant baptism by way of anticipation, in believer's baptism by way of realization. In both cases the importance of Christian nurture and growth is stressed, as is the unrepeatability of baptism. "Any practice which might be interpreted as "rebaptism" must be avoided"—a statement that I, as a Baptist, regard as sound but that will cause anguish to some Baptists.

The *Eucharist* is described as thanksgiving, *anamnesis* (memorial of Christ), invocation of the Spirit, communion of the faithful, and meal of God's kingdom. The Eucharist is beautifully related to reconciliation both in the church and in the world. This section concludes with the hope that "the increased mutual understanding expressed in the present statement may allow some churches to attain to a greater measure of eucharistic communion among themselves and so bring closer the day when Christ's divided people will be visibly reunited around the Lord's Table" (Eucharist III.33).

The section on *Ministry* relates the lay to the ordained ministry, conceives the authority of the ordained ministry to consist in service, but fails to relate this to the papacy, although Roman Catholics were present in the Commission on Faith and Order of the World Council of Churches, which prepared the statement. Eventually, this question will have to be faced, as it has been by Rahner and Fries in the fourth of their theses on reunion.

The authors of the BEM document have invited official responses from the churches. Already some *unofficial* replies have been given in the *Journal of Ecumenical Studies*, which devoted an entire issue, winter 1984, to this matter.

Emergent Reunions

Ecumenical conversations have a dual purpose: (1) better understanding and improved relations between Christians of various churches and (2) eventual reunion of churches. Christians are still far removed from the goal of complete visible structural unity. Yet some reunions have already been accomplished, and others are in process of fulfillment. In most cases, however, reunions are accomplished only after long years of discussion, and some that have been achieved are still suffering growing pains.

Among the church unions accomplished or in process are the following:

The United Church of Canada. This was a pioneer in church union, achieved already in 1925. The idea was first mooted at the General Conference of the Methodist Church assembled in Winnipeg in September 1902. At various times negotiation involved Methodists, Presbyterians, Congregationalists, Anglicans, Lutherans, and Baptists. The Anglicans, Lutherans, and Baptists gradually withdrew, leaving the Methodists, Presbyterians, and Congregationalists to form the United Church of Canada on July 10, 1925.[8]

The Church of South India. As early as 1908 the foundation was laid by the union of Presbyterian and Congregational missions in South India. In 1919 at a conference in Tranquebar a larger union was envisioned. In 1943 the Methodists joined the Union and in 1946 the Anglicans and on September 27, 1947, the Church of South India was officially inaugurated in Madras.[9]

The United Church of Christ (U.S.A.). The United Church of Christ is the result of two successive unions. The first was the union of two originally German-speaking churches of German and Swiss origin, the Evangelical Synod of North America and the Reformed Church in the United States. They united on June 26, 1934, to form the Evangelical and Reformed Church.[10]

The second union, with the Congregational Christian churches, was more difficult, since Congregational churches are traditionally independent of one another (indeed, their original name in England, where they originated, was Independents), whereas the Evangelical and Reformed churches were connectional. For practical reasons, however, Congregationalists had been obliged to form a General Council, and on January 22, 1947, this council joined the Evangelical and Reformed Church to form the United Church of Christ. Many local Congregational churches argued however that the General Council was not authorized to speak for the local churches. So this is a union working well in many respects but in which some Congregational churches are having difficulties.

The United Reformed Church (England). For many years discussions have been proceeding between various churches in England. They have been concentrated principally on two dialogues: one between Presbyterians and Congregationalists, the other between Anglicans and Methodists. The former has resulted in the merger of Presbyterians and Congregationalists to form the United Reformed Church. The Anglicans and Methodists are still negotiating.

The Consultation on Church Union (U.S.A.). This multilateral consultation was initiated by Eugene Carson Blake, then stated clerk of the Presbyterian Church in the U.S.A. and later general secretary of the World Council of Churches. Speaking in the Anglican (Episcopal) Cathedral of Bishop James Pike, he proposed union conversations between Episcopalians and Presbyterians and any other churches that might wish to join. Eventually, about ten churches agreed to participate. Two of them, the Methodist Church and the Evangelical United Brethren, have already united. The rest are still engaged in the consultation. Some of them, however, already practice intercommunion through the Interim Eucharistic Fellowship.

National and Local Expressions of Ecumenism

The reunions and intended reunions we have been discussing have all been on a national rather than international scale. They have been encouraged by national councils of churches, such as the National Council of Churches of Christ in the U.S. (formerly the Federal Council) and the British Council of Churches, all of which are closely related to the World Council of Churches in Geneva.

The various National Councils of Churches are frequently supplemented by regional Councils of Churches in the various countries. In the United States, for instance, there are many state and local councils. In Pennsylvania, for example, there is the Pennsylvania Council of Churches in Harrisburg and the Metropolitan Council of Churches in Philadelphia. The Metropolitan Council of Churches collaborates closely with the Roman Catholic Cardinal's Commission on Human Relations.

Almost everywhere local ecumenical groups of clergy meet regularly for prayer, study, and action. In some areas local ''clusters'' of churches have been formed for collaboration in worship and service.

Collaboration for the Common Good

Christianity at its best has always embraced both gospel and ethic: the gospel of God's love for us and the ethic of our love for God and one another. Imbued with this spirit, the ecumenical movement has been concerned both with spreading the gospel and inculcating the ethic by working for the common good of all humankind.

Here, we can only recount Christian collaboration for the common good on a world scale. But what has been occurring on a world scale has been simultaneously happening on a national and local level.

In the Protestant-Orthodox ecumenical movement, collaboration for the common good was present even before the World Council of Churches was formed in 1948. It expressed itself in the Life and Work movement, which held its first international conference in Stockholm in 1925; its second in Oxford in 1937; and was incorporated into the World Council of Churches in 1948.

Similarly, in the Roman Catholic Church social concern was evident long before that church entered the ecumenical movement through the Second Vatican Council of 1962–1965. It expressed itself in the social encyclicals: *Rerum Novarum,* 1891 (on the evils of capitalism); *Graves de Communi,* 1901 (on the evils of communism); *Quadragesimo Anni,* 1931 (on reconstructing the social order); *Mater et Magistra,* 1961 (on recent developments of the social order); and *Pacem in Terris,* 1963, on peace on earth. When the Second Vatican Council ended in 1965, a Joint Working Group had been formed to coordinate the work of the World Council of Churches and the Roman Catholic Church.

In the First Assembly of the World Council of Churches, Amsterdam, 1948, two of the four sections were devoted to world affairs: "The Church and the Disorders of Society" and "The Church and the International Order." It was at this assembly that the concept of "a responsible world order" was developed as an alternative to the extremes of exploitative capitalism and repressive communism. In the Second Assembly, Evanston, 1954, this concept was seen in relation to racial and ethnic tensions and the quest for world community.

In the Third Assembly, New Delhi, 1961, the three themes were: "Witness, Service, and Unity." This assembly released the urgent *Appeal to All Governments and Peoples*: "Today war is a common enemy. War is an offence to the nature of man. The future of many generations and the heritage of the ages hang in the balance. . . . For the achievement of peace and justice, we pledge our unremitting efforts and call upon the Churches for their support in prayer and action."

Peace and justice—these ideals became the dominant themes both of the World Council and the Roman Catholic Church, which established the Commission on Justice and Peace. In 1966 the World Council held a conference in Geneva, "Man and Contemporary Society," which proved very influential for the future. It focused attention on the growing tensions between the rich, developed world of the North and the poor, developing world of the South and on the baleful as well as beneficial effects of modern technology. It was this second concern that led to the "Conference on Faith, Science, and the Future" at the Massachusetts Institute of Technology in Boston in 1979.

By 1980 the Central Committee of the World Council was so disturbed by the prospect of nuclear war that it requested its subunits on society and international affairs to organize a hearing on the question. The hearing was held in the Free University of Amsterdam, November 23-27, 1981, and the results published in 1983 in the book *Before It's too Late: The Challenge of Nuclear Disarmament,* which embraced the view that nuclear war, contrary to the Reagan administration's fantasy, can neither be limited nor won but would result in worldwide calamity. It recommends a mutual freeze on the production, testing and deployment of nuclear weapons, followed by drastic reductions in these weapons; a comprehensive test ban; and nuclear-free zones. In his sermon in the Thomaskerk, Amsterdam, on November 22, 1981, the Reverend William Sloan Coffin of New York said: "Either we will quickly end the nuclear arms race, or the arms race will surely end the human race."

These insights were confirmed and expanded at the Sixth Assembly of the World Council in Vancouver, July 24–August 10, 1983. Conscious of the many threats to life on earth, the World Council chose the theme "Jesus Christ, the Life of the World."

The Official Report of the Assembly, *Gathered for Life,* edited by David Gill and published by the World Council of Churches, Geneva, 1983, in the section "Confronting Threats to Peace and Survival" stresses *common* security rather than national security and rejects both nuclear weapons and nuclear deterrence (since deterrence implies readiness to *use* such weapons). The section "Justice and Human Dignity" stated: "Significantly, the poor, the oppressed and the discriminated peoples are awakening everywhere to resist unjust powers and to forge their own destiny. This is a sign of life. . . . Science and technology are used to oppress the people and to destroy the earth in an insane arms race. . . . The spiritual struggle of the Church must involve it in the struggles of the poor, the oppressed, the alienated and the exiled."[11] This corresponds to the "preferential option for the poor" advocated by the Catholic bishops.

The section "Peace and justice" stated "Humanity is now living in the dark shadow of an arms race more intense . . . and more costly than the world has ever known. Never before has the human race been as close as it is now to total self-destruction. Never before have so many lived in the grip of deprivation and oppression." It affirmed, like Pope Paul VI, that there can be no peace without justice, and condemns "rampant militarism." It urged for the peaceful resolution of conflicts and repeated the findings of the Amsterdam hearing that nuclear war can never be justifiable, that it cannot be limited, that there should be a halt to the production and deployment of nuclear weapons, that the nations should ratify a comprehensive test ban, and that research, testing, and deployment of space weapons should be banned. In a word, the World Council completely opposes Reagan's armament program and makes several proposals identical with those of the USSR that are aimed at preventing the nuclear war that the Reagan administration is preparing to "fight and win." The council believes its inevitable result would be the destruction of most, maybe all, life on earth, including the profits of the military-industrial complex that motivates this mad militarism.

In its planning for the future, the assembly's Guidelines Committee proposed that Christians should collaborate for the common good in their commitment to *"justice, peace and the integrity of creation."*[12] This program concentrates on the three Christian goals for our age. The phrase "integrity of creation," however, seems too broad. There is little we humans can do about the integrity of the creation in general. What we can do is to seek to preserve the integrity of the *biosphere,* that is, life on earth and its environment.

This development of social teaching and action of the World Council of Churches was accompanied by a comparable development in the Roman Catholic Church. Since the creation of the Joint Working Group, composed of representatives of the World Council and the Vatican, there has been considerable collaboration between Catholics and other Christians.

As we have seen, modern official Roman Catholic social teaching has its roots in a series of impressive social encyclicals: *Rerum Novarum* (1891), *Graves de Communi* (1901), *Quadragesimo Anno* (1931), and *Divini Redemptoris* (1937).

These encyclicals condemned both unrestricted free-enterprise capitalism and collectivistic communism—capitalism on the ground that it violates distributive justice, which should provide basic necessities for all, and collective communism on the ground that it violates individual freedom. Avoiding both of these extremes, they advocated Christian communitarianism, a communitarianism of love that seeks simultaneously the good of the individual and the good of the community.

It was in line with these encyclicals and in light of the situation in 1961 that Pope John XXIII issued his encyclical *Mater et Magistra,* May 15, 1961, on Christianity and social progress, an encyclical directed not only to Christians but also to "all men of goodwill" (IV.221). Two years later, April 11, 1963, he issued his encyclical on war and peace, *Pacem in Terris.* This, like earlier encyclicals, stressed the reciprocity of rights and duties (I.28,29) and warned of the dangers inherent in the arms race.

It is with deep sorrow that we note the enormous stocks of armaments that have been and still are being made in the more economically developed countries with a vast outlay of intellectual and economic resources. And it so happens that, while the people of these countries are loaded with heavy burdens, other countries as a result are deprived of the collaboration they need in order to make economic and social progress. . . . if one country increases its armaments, others feel the need to do the same. . . . Consequently, people live in constant fear lest the storm that threatens every moment should break upon them with dreadful violence. And with good reason, for the arms of war are ready to hand. . . . the conflagration may be set off by some uncontrollable and unexpected chance. (III.109-111)

In light of these dangers the encyclical urged *disarmament* and repeated the warning of Pope Pius XII in his radio message of 1941: "Nothing is lost by peace; everything may be lost by war" (III.116).

The social doctrine of the encyclicals on justice and peace was embodied in the Pastoral Constitution of the Church in the Modern World, *Gaudium et Spes,* promulgated by the Second Vatican Council, December 7, 1965. The constitution begins by expressing the empathy of Christians with humankind: "The joys and hopes, the griefs and anxieties of the men of this age, especially those who are poor or in any way afflicted, these are the joys and hopes, the griefs and anxieties of the followers of Christ" (Preface, 1). The message of the Constitution is addressed "not only to the sons of the Church and to all who invoke the name of Christ, but to the whole of humanity" (Preface, 2).

Like the encyclicals, the Constitution denounces the extremes of wealth and poverty inherent in free enterprise capitalism: "While an enormous mass of people still lack the absolute necessities of life, some, even in less advanced countries, live sumptuously or squander wealth. Luxury and misery rub shoulders" (III.63). By contrast, the Christian ideal of society is described as a world family united by love: "God, who has a fatherly concern for everyone, has willed that all men should constitute one family and treat one another in the spirit of brotherhood. . . . For this reason, love for God and neighbor is the first and greatest commandment. Sacred Scripture teaches us that the love of God cannot be separated from love of neighbor" (II.24).

The final section of the Constitution is devoted to "The Fostering of Peace and the Promotion of a Community of Nations." Peace is described positively rather than negatively and, as in the encyclicals, is related to justice: "Peace is not merely the absence of war. . . . Instead, it is rightly and appropriately called "an enterprise of justice" (Is.32:17). Peace results from that harmony built into human society by its divine Founder, and is actualized by men as they thirst after ever greater justice" (V.78). Modern war, particularly, nuclear war, which would result in "an almost total and reciprocal slaughter of each side by the other," compels us to "undertake an evaluation of war with an entirely new attitude" (V.80).

The council thus echoed the conviction of Albert Einstein that "we shall require a substantially new way of thinking if mankind is to survive." In light of this entirely new situation created by nuclear weapons, the constitution recommended that we seek the avoidance and eventual banning of war by ending the arms race, which is nothing but "an utterly treacherous trap for humanity" (V.81). In a final appeal, it affirmed that "Catholics should seek to cooperate actively and in a positive manner both with their separated brothers, who together with them profess the gospel of love, and with all men thirsting for true peace" (V.90).

These ideas of justice and peace were reiterated by Pope Paul VI in his address to the United Nations, October 4, 1965, and found concrete embodiment in the creation of the Pontifical Commission on Justice and Peace, January 6, 1967. So now we have both the Roman Catholic Church's own Commission on Justice and Peace and the Joint Working Group, established in 1965, to coordinate the work of the Roman Catholic Church with that of the World Council of Churches.

Deeply distressed by the poverty he found in his visits to the Third World, Pope Paul VI on March 26, 1967, issued his encyclical *Populorum Progressio* on the development of peoples. He accepted the principle, earlier enunciated by the French Dominican L. J. Lebret, that development should be understood not merely as economic and technical development but as *integral,* embracing, that is, the total well being of both individuals and society. Accordingly, the encyclical said: "Development cannot be limited to mere economic growth. In order to be authentic, it must be complete: integral, that is, it has to promote the good of every man and of the whole man" (I.14).

Such authentic development, however, is impossible under unbridled capitalism "which considers profit as the key motive for economic progress, competition as the supreme law of economics, and private ownership of the means of production as an absolute right that has no limits and carries no corresponding social obligation." This unchecked liberalism leads to dictatorship rightly denounced by Pius XI as producing "the international imperialism of money" (I.3.26). U.S. readers of the encyclical should bear in mind that what was earlier termed "liberalism" (and still is in Europe), meaning free from government control, is now called "conservatism" in the United States. This passage of the encyclical, like earlier ones in previous encyclicals, is thus a stern condemnation of laissez-faire capitalism which is concerned only with profit.

The encyclical encourages Catholics to alleviate world poverty through charitable organizations such as *Caritas Internationalis* but admits that this is insufficient. "The struggle against destitution, though urgent and necessary, is not enough. It is a question, rather, of building a world where every man, no matter what his race, religion or nationality, can live a fully human life, freed from servitude imposed on him by other men or by natural forces over which he has not sufficient control: a world where freedom is not an empty word" (II.1.47). Here *in nuce* is a theology of Third World liberation. Persons must live in solidarity with persons, said the encyclical, and nations with nations. Peace depends on the integral development of the whole human family, and "development is the new name for peace."

It was this encyclical, combined with the rising tide of Third World discontent with its theologies of liberation, that set the stage for the Medellín Conference of the Latin American Episcopal Council (CELAM), August 24-September 6, 1968. In the resultant *Medellín Documents* the bishops deplored "the misery that besets large masses of human beings in all of our countries," the "misery which, as a collective fact, expresses itself as injustice which cries to the heavens" (I.1). They recognize that this misery results from "international monopolies and the international imperialism of money," that is, the transnational corporations (principally, the United States) and the governments that support them (Peace, I.9.e). They see that this misery, like misery everywhere, can dispose suffering humanity to embrace "the temptation of the Marxist system" (Justice, III.10). Thus they see clearly what the Reagan administration refuses to see, that it is not Marxism that causes discontent but discontent that causes Marxism.

In this dire situation the bishops see their principal task as "*concientización,*" awakening people to their true situation and its causes and impressing on all the need for justice and peace.

Eleven years after Medellín, the Conference of Latin American Bishops convened again, this time in Puebla, Mexico. Once more they rejected both the prevailing imperialistic capitalism with its social injustice and Marxist collectivism in favor of a "civilization of love" with its "preferential option for the poor."[13]

Unhappily, in its recent frenzy of condemnations, the Vatican has condemned one of the leading liberation theologians, the Brazilian Franciscan Leonardo Boff. It is not surprising that when asked what he would say to the pope, Boff's fellow Brazilian Franciscan, Cardinal Paulo Evaristo Arns of São Paulo, said his message would be: "Please do not treat us as children. We are not children or adolescents; we are an adult church and should be respected as such."[14] The old problem of papal authority and ecclesial collegiality has evidently not been satisfactorily resolved. It is a fundamental problem for all Roman Catholics and for other Christian Churches contemplating union with Rome.

Meanwhile, the Roman Catholic bishops of the United States, like many others, became alarmed about the increasing risk of nuclear war, and on May 3, 1983, issued its Pastoral Letter *The Challenge of Peace*.

The Pastoral condemns the arms race; urges a halt in the testing, production, and deployment of new nuclear weapons systems; calls for deep cuts in the arsenals of both superpowers and a comprehensive test ban treaty; expresses doubt that any nuclear war could be limited; affirms only a "strictly conditioned moral acceptance of nuclear deterrence"; and affirms that "the moral duty today is to prevent nuclear war from ever occurring."

These conclusions coincide almost completely with those of the World Council of Churches in the Amsterdam hearing and in the Vancouver Assembly. They coincide also with the Soviet Union's proposals of a nuclear halt followed by massive reductions of nuclear arms and a comprehensive test ban. Who is against them? The Reagan administration, with its illusion of fighting and "winning" a nuclear war and its further illusion of building an impenetrable shield against nuclear weapons by space technology, is against them.

Currently, the Catholic bishops of the United States are preparing a pastoral letter on Catholic social teaching and the U.S. economy. Thus far only the first draft is available (published November 1984). It urges economic as well as political democracy; condemns the enormous extremes of wealth and poverty endemic to free enterprise capitalism, especially the grinding poverty in the Third World caused in large measure by first world transnational corporations and the governments that support them; and, like the Latin American bishops, supports a preferential option for the poor.

CONCLUDING OBSERVATIONS

During the forty years under review, relations between the Orthodox and Protestant churches have immensely improved. During the past twenty years, that is, since the official entrance of the Roman Catholic Church through the Second Vatican Council (1962–1965), relations between the Roman Catholic Church and other churches and ecclesial communities have similarly improved. With a few regrettable exceptions such as Northern Ireland, peace has replaced war, dialogue has replaced diatribe, and reconciliation has replaced confrontation.

The road to the goal of reunion into the one holy catholic and apostolic church is, however, proving long and difficult. As we have seen, only a few reunions have thus far occurred. More are to be expected among Protestant churches, but reunion with the Roman Catholic Church is still a long way off and has certainly been further postponed by the recent series of condemnations of creative theologians by the Vatican—Poiret, Pfürtner, Hasler, Küng, Schillebeeckx, and Boff—and the official disapproval of the ecumenical effort of Rahner and Fries.

Christian reunion will accordingly require decades, maybe centuries, for completion. Meanwhile, disorder and distress in the world increase: biospherical pollution and poisoning and the extinction of whole species of life; poverty, misery, and hunger; hatred, strife, and violence; and, above all, there hangs over us the Damocles sword of nuclear war, a sword that could descend at any moment, destroying most or all life on earth, and within hours transform this wonderful biosphere that God has created into a horrible necrosphere, a sphere of death. Survivers, if there were any, would no longer say, with the Psalmist, "Come, behold the *works of the Lord*, what desolations he hath made in the earth," but "Come, behold the *works of humankind*, what desolations they have made in the earth."

If we are to have anything like the time needed for Christian reunion, indeed, if we are to have any Christians to unite, we must above all attempt to insure the continuance of life on earth. That means we must prevent nuclear war. This has now become the *conditio sine qua non* of everything else.

Prevention of nuclear war: how can we do this? By stopping and reversing the nuclear arms race. This involves a halt (freeze) on the production, testing, and deployment of nuclear weapons followed by their rapid reduction. It means the mutual acceptance of a comprehensive test ban. It means a halt to the extension of war into outer space—star peace instead of star war. All of this could easily be achieved, since it has all been proposed by the Soviet Union. The one obstacle is the Reagan administration, which opposes all of the above in favor of the great illusion of "fighting and winning" a nuclear war. If it persists in that illusion we shall have nuclear war, but there will be no "winner"; only mutual and world suicide.

Christians today have many tasks. But their *primary* task is to collaborate with one another and with all people everywhere who seek to prevent rather than to "win" a nuclear war.

NOTES

1. R. Rouse and S. C. Neill, eds., *History of the Ecumenical Movement*, 2d ed. (Philadelphia: Westminster Press, 1967), I:348–349.

2. Ibid., p. 362.

3. *Uppsala to Nairobi* (New York: Friendship Press, 1975), p. 16.

4. David Gill, ed., *Gathered for Life*, Official Report (Geneva: World Council of Churches; Grand Rapids, Mich.: Eerdmans, 1983), pp. 1–2.

5. Ibid., pp. 2–3.

6. Karl Adam, *Das Wesen des Katholizismus* (Düsseldorf: Patmos, 1924), pp. 146–147.

7. The Secretariat for Promoting Christian Unity, Information Service, No. 56, 1984/4, p. 85.

8. Peter Neuner, *Kleines Handbuch der Oekumene* (Düsseldorf: Patmos, 1984), pp. 111–112.

9. Rouse and Neill, *A History of the Ecumenical Movement*, pp. 473–476.

10. Sydney E. Ahlstrom, *A Religious History of the American People* (New Haven: Yale Univ. Press, 1972), p. 755.

11. Gill, *Gathered for Life*.
12. Ibid.
13. Reinhard Frieling, *Befreiungstheologien, Studien zur Theologie in Lateinamerika* (Gottingen: Vandenhoeck und Ruprecht, 1984), pp. 133–135.
14. John Catoir, ed., *America,* August 24, 1984, pp. 79–80.

GLOSSARY

Biosphere: The sphere of life and its environment.
Ecology: The study of life in its environment, that is, of the biosphere.
Encyclical: A papal circular letter directed to all Roman Catholic dioceses and parishes.
Ecumenical: Pertaining to the whole world, worldwide, global. From the Greek οικουμγνη—the whole inhabited earth, from οικοσ, which has the double meaning of habitation and inhabitants.

SELECTED BIBLIOGRAPHY

Abrecht, Paul, ed. *Faith and Science in an Unjust World*. Report of the World Council of Churches Conference, Massachusetts Institute of Technology, July 1979. Philadelphia: Fortress Press, 1980.

Abrecht, Paul and Ninan Koshy, eds. *Before It's too Late*. Record of Amsterdam Public Hearing. Geneva: World Council of Churches, 1983.

Baptism, Eucharist and Ministry. Geneva: World Council of Churches, 1982.

Bea, Augustin. *The Unity of the Church*. New York: Herder and Herder, 1963.

Bock, Paul. *In Search of a Responsible World Society: The Social Teachings of the World Council of Churches*. Philadelphia: Westminster Press, 1978.

Brown, Robert McAfee. *The Ecumenical Revolution*. Garden City, N.Y.: Doubleday, 1969.

———. *Theology in a New Key: Responding to Liberation Themes*. Philadelphia: Westminster Press, 1978.

Evanston Report, Second Assembly of the World Council of Churches, 1954. London: SCM, 1955.

Feiner, J. and L. Vischer, eds. *Neues Glaubensbuch, Der gemeinsame christliche Glaube*. Herder, Freiburg and Zurich: Theologischer Verlag, 1973.

Fey, Harold E., ed. *A History of the Ecumenical Movement*. Vol. 2, 1948–1968. Philadelphia: Westminster Press, 1970.

Freemantle, Anne. *The Papal Encyclicals*. New York: New American Library, 1956.

———. *The Social Teachings of the Church*. New York: New American Library, 1963.

Frieling, Reinhard. *Befreiungstheologien, Studien zur Theologie in Lateinamerika*. Gottingen: Vandenhoeck und Ruprecht, 1984.

Fries, H. *Das Ringen um die Einheit der Christen*. Dusseldorf: Patmos, 1983.

Fries, H., and K. Rahner. *Einigung der Kirchen—reale Möglichkeit*. Erweiterte Sonderausgabe. Freiburg: Herder, 1985. English translation: *The Unity of the Churches: An Actual Possibility*, trans. Ruth C. L. and Eric W. Gritsel. Philadelphia: Fortress Press, 1985.

Grant, Frederick. *Rome and Reunion*. New York: Oxford University Press, 1965.

Kennedy, James W. *Nairobi, 1975. Fifth Assembly, World Council of Churches*. Nairobi: Forward Movement Publications, 1975.

Macquarrie, John. *Christian Unity and Christian Disunity*. Philadelphia: Westminster Press, 1975.

Minear, Paul. *Faith and Order Findings*. Minneapolis: Augsburg Publishing House, 1963.

Murnion, P. J., ed. *Catholics and Nuclear War*. A Commentary on *The Challenge of Peace*. New York: Crossroad, 1983.

Nelson, R., and W. Pannenberg. *Um Einheit und Heil der Menschheit*. Frankfurt: Lembeck, 1973.

Neuner, Peter. *Kleines Handbuch der Oekumene*. Dusseldorf: Patmos, 1984.

New Delhi Report, Third Assembly of the World Council of Churches. London: SCM, 1962.

Rouse, R., and S. C. Neill, eds. *A History of the Ecumenical Movement*. Vol. 1, 1517–1948. Philadelphia: Westminster Press, 1967.

Swidler, L. J. *The Ecumenical Vanguard: The History of the Una Sancta Movement*. Pittsburgh: Duquesne University Press, 1966.

———, ed. *Consensus in Theology? A Dialogue with Hans Küng and Edward Schillebeeckx*. Philadelphia: Westminster Press, 1980.

Thurian, Max. *Ecumenical Perspectives on Baptism, Eucharist, and Ministry*. Geneva: World Council of Churches, 1983.

Uppsala Report, 1968, Third Assembly of the World Council of Churches. Edited by Norman Goodall. Geneva: World Council of Churches, 1968.

Vancouver Report, Sixth Assembly of the World Council of Churches. Edited by David Gill. Geneva: World Council of Churches, Grand Rapids, Mich: Eerdmans, 1983.

16

Religio-Philosophical Issues and Interreligious Dialogues in Eastern Orthodox Christianity Since World War II

DEMETRIOS J. CONSTANTELOS

The terms *religio* and *philosophical* are used in a Greek or Eastern Orthodox context. The Greek term for religion is *threskeia,* which means instinctive worship of the divine as well as a quest—a leaping up in joyful expectation to discover. The word *philosophical* is employed to denote "knowledge of things divine and human, as much as man is able to approach God, for it teaches man by deeds to be the image and after the likeness of the One who created him." This ninth-century definition by the Greek father Constantine-Cyril is a Christianized version of the Platonic and Stoic understanding of philosophy. Very similar definitions were provided by the Christian thinkers and Greek Church Fathers from as early as the Apostolic age and throughout the Middle Ages.[1] Ultimately, philosophy was identified with theology, and it came to include beliefs, doctrines, and ideas either given by a supernatural source or arrived at through human capacity to seek and to think. Thus revelation was perceived as both supernatural and natural, metaphysical and physical. As such, it must be studied in the context of written and unwritten revelation, within the spiritual and intellectual boundaries of the Christian community and always in relationship to the faith, knowledge, and experience of the past.

In speaking of Eastern Orthodox Christianity, known also as Greek Orthodox, we mean the faith, ethical values, and the religious life of some 150 million (a conservative estimate) people around the world. There are several Orthodox jurisdictions but one Orthodox Church. The Orthodox conception of unity is doctrinal, sacramental, spiritual, and not administrative and personal. As the Pan-Orthodox Council, which met in Rhodes in 1961, put it: "Our Church is not made of walls and roofs, but of faith and of life. . . . We believe that the sister Orthodox Churches, in maintaining the saving faith of our Fathers, are preserved in this unity whose divine archetype is the mystical and supernatural unity of the Holy Trinity . . . an inner unity which cannot fundamentally be troubled."[2]

The Pan-Orthodox Conference of 1961 was the first to be held after many years of isolation. Because of improved historical circumstances and its confrontation with the Churches and Confessions of the Reformation and the Church of Rome, the Orthodox Church was challenged to abandon its seclusion and reassert its existence and its own theology and identity. Orthodox theologians were compelled to redefine their faith and to answer old questions in modern terms.

Before we proceed to an analysis of current religious concerns in the Orthodox Church, it is important to emphasize that there are certain basic characteristics and similar interests among religious thinkers and theologians of all Orthodox jurisdictions. There is a renewed interest in identifying what they consider authentic theology—a theology that understands the content of divine revelation and through faith leads to a *koinonia* with the ultimate Being and fellow human beings. This revelation consists of Trinitarian theology, Christology, and pneumatology. There is a movement toward biblical theology in the light of patristic exegesis and the experience of the community in history. A "returning to the sources" has led to an emphasis on eucharistic ecclesiology, mystical and liturgical theology, the Fathers of the church, and the theology of the church councils—all as interrelated aspects of the church's faith and life.

As early as the late 1930s Orthodox theologians advocated a neo-patristic synthesis whose objective was to make the being of God a personal experience achieved within worship, eucharistic worship in particular. Modern trends indicate that there are similar concerns but also a departure from the methods and academic styles that characterized theological research of previous decades. In contrast to past approaches, theology today is perceived not only as the mind but also the heart and the servant of the community at large; theology is studied not for its own sake but for the edification of the faithful; it is understood not only as the guardian of religious knowledge but as a steward of the tradition in which that knowledge is applied for the good of the church—indeed for the world. Thus theology is less concerned with erudite intellectual exercises of the mind and much more with the broader tradition of the faithful. Orthodoxy's conception of "historical thinking" is at the heart of its theology.[3]

To be sure, Orthodox theology is still concerned with metaphysical questions, but it is also interested in life issues; it is involved with the spiritual needs and anxieties of the church pleroma. The neo-patristic synthesis has revealed that the question that preoccupied the Church Fathers for many centuries was not to know about God, whether God exists or not, for God's existence was unquestioned, but how to know and have their being in God, the ultimate Being. In the light of this patristic experience, Orthodox theology today sees its role as a guide leading modern people to a communion with God and with each other.

To understand these religious trends and theological issues in Eastern Orthodox Christianity, one should study and comprehend how Orthodox religious thought perceives itself in relationship to the community (the church) that it serves. There are no theological or religio-philosophical issues outside the concerns and context of the community. The community as a historical reality, born and developed in history, values its continuity and its relationship with the mind, the ethos, and the experience of the past. The awareness of the close relationship between past and present is kept alive through the written and the unwritten word, the Holy Scriptures, and the living memory and experience of the past known as Sacred Tradition.

The inheritance from the past expressed in beliefs, practices, values, and even forms is not an ossified and static relic but a vigorous force augmented and strengthened by the contributions of succeeding generations. It is like a huge river that follows its natural course even though on its way it breaks out into various rivulets or absorbs other rivers and streams. Thus present-day Orthodox theology is very old but always renewed and modern. Fidelity and commitment to continuity in doctrine, ethics, worship, religious culture, is a major characteristic of the Orthodox Church.

Perhaps more than any other Christian community, the Orthodox preserve a dynamic historical consciousness that feeds but also conditions the mind and aspirations of the present. Thus Orthodox theology today is inextricably related to the theology developed and codified in the course of nearly two millenniums.

Contrary to what is often thought, Orthodox theology has been pluralistic in content and style, pluralistic in themes and interpretations not undermining the defined and codified doctrines of the church-in-history. Whether the church is known as Greek Orthodox, Russian Orthodox, Antiochian, Romanian, Serbian, Bulgarian, or simply Eastern Orthodox, it is to be understood that it is one church characterized by unity-in-diversity in theology, ethos, and polity.

Orthodox theology is not monolithic. Not all Orthodox theologians understand Christian truth in exactly the same way, and modern theology offers an astonishing variety in approach and interpretation. Orthodox theology cannot be described either as academic and scholastic, liturgical and mystical, or be placed in other molds and categories because all of these elements are present and all make up a theology of many tesserae of a well-structured theological mosaic. As such Orthodox theology today is an extension of and a departure from Christian theology of centuries past. The history of the early and medieval church reveals that there were various theologians, religious thinkers, and events that created theological schools and expressed views that ultimately were debated and resolved in the councils of the undivided church. The consensus on theological definitions was codified and what was perceived as contrary to the established beliefs was rejected. What was defined as truth, whether the arrival at it was by revelation or by the quest of the human mind, is valid for contemporary Orthodox theology.

The Orthodox see theology not only as a field for academic intellectual research but primarily as an existential saving and redeeming spiritual power for the benefit of the human being in search of truth and eternal life. It is for this reason that theology is not understood as a discipline outside the boundaries of the community of believers. It is intended to define, clarify, cultivate, teach, and guide human beings to a transfigured life here on earth and prepare them for an eternal life in God beyond the physical and temporal.

The religio-philosophical theological concerns of contemporary Orthodox theology of the past fifty years have been addressed in several theological conferences but primarily in two major pan-Orthodox theological conferences, both in Athens in 1936 and 1976. Both brought together representative Orthodox theologians from many countries of the world. The goal of the first conference was to initiate a dialogue and a search for what was perceived as authentic Orthodoxy in agreement with the Scriptures and the experience of the church in history, to achieve a purity from external influences, to elucidate the relations between the Orthodox churches and the other Confessions, and to elevate Orthodoxy to a spiritual and social force able to solve contemporary problems. The conference stressed that the reformulation of the faith was to be pursued ''within the church.'' The second theological conference emphasized that theology's academic concerns should be oriented toward a theology that would assist the church in confronting its internal problems, its pastoral concerns, and also the problems raised by its encounter with the modern world.[4] The second theological conference included several leading Orthodox theologians from Western Europe and the United States. Both conferences emphasized that doctrines and beliefs concerning metaphysics, human nature and destiny, ethical and social philosophy, soteriology and eschatology, have been established even though both acknowledged that all need more elaboration and updating.

Given the high respect for and inviolability of several doctrines of the early and medieval church, it should not surprise us that both conferences stressed the need for a rediscovery and a restatement of the theology of the early and undivided church; to purify Orthodox theology from foreign influences whether of Western European Christian origins or of rational religio-philosophical humanistic background.

This chapter, which examines metaphysical questions, anthropology, soteriology, ethical and social issues, eschatology, and interreligious and interfaith dialogues, is conditioned by the teachings and the experience of the Christian church in history. Because of space limitations, every theme discussed here is meant to be representative rather than exhaustive.

METAPHYSICS

Metaphysics seeks to define and understand what is ultimately real. As an answer to the question raised by the early Greek philosophers ''ti to on'' (What is there that exists?), Orthodox theology affirms that God, as the first principle, exists. It takes a realist metaphysics for granted. God (no matter what name is given to the first principle) exists, and theology seeks to explain the nature of God's being or reality in apophatic and cataphatic, negative and affirmative, terms, in terms of natural and supernatural revelation.

For the Eastern Orthodox, natural theology, as a way of knowledge of God but also as a propaideia to the new age introduced by the Incarnation, has been a persistent and permanent category. Viewing Christianity as a historical religion, it cannot be otherwise. Reason and reasoning are not antithetical to faith and revelation. Much of faith is based on revelation that has been given in history through actual persons and has been conditioned by historical circumstances. Thus Orthodox theology treats the physical and the metaphysical, the transcendent and the immanent, the finite and the infinite, as interrelated entities. There is a distinction, however. Whereas transcendental metaphysics as ontology, as it concerns "being," is approached apophatically, immanent metaphysics as experiential reality is treated cataphatically, as an affirmation of and subject to experience.

Natural theology is more than the dictates of human conscience; it is the cosmos itself, nature as the celebration of the Creator's presence. To the uncertainties and indeed unfaithfulness of humans, nature maintains a faithfulness to the Creator, the laws of harmony, order, silence, patience, peace, and strength. Natural theology proclaims the mystery of the Creator, whereas supernatural, or revealed, theology is ultimate and proclaims the fullness of God manifest. For this reason Jesus, as "the fullness of time," is never the historical man from Nazareth but always Jesus the Messiah and Christ, the Christ in whom the "fullness of the Deity dwells bodily" (Colossians 2:9). He is the *theanthropos* (God–man). The limited and clouded knowledge of God provided by natural theology is illuminated and completed by supernatural theology. God no longer is a metaphysical abstraction but a living God who invites for a dialogue in terms of "I and Thou." As transcendental and immanent, God is both *exocosmios* and *endocosmios*.

What God is we do not know; what God is not we know. We do not know God's essence, but we do know that God is not what our mind and thought can perceive and our eyes can see. But we also know that God is one unchanging, incomprehensible essence but in three hypostaseis, or persons, in a coinherence, or *perichoresis* (mutual interexistence). As in the early Christian centuries, Orthodox theology today rejects all monistic efforts and tendencies: Patromonism, which makes God-the-Father not of the same essence with God-the-Logos and God-the-Pneuma. It also rejects *Christomonism,* which identifies Christ with God but sees Christ as God's only revelation. Furthermore, it rejects *Pneumatomonism,* which sees God only as a Spirit and Christ as the man from Nazareth.[5]

The Reality of God

As already indicated, belief in the reality of God is based on natural revelation and supernatural apocalypsis. The very existence of the cosmos and humans' perpetual quest to find an answer to whether or not God exists is an indication of God's existence, and it is common to all humanity. Orthodox theology does not reject the arguments of the ancient Greek and other philosophers who spoke of God either as the "perfect Being," the Logos, the Absolute Good, the Unmoved Mover. It is in full agreement with the ancient Greek poet Philemon who wrote: "Believe in and be pious toward God but seek not to discover what God is. You possess no more than the desire to search. What or what not God is don't try to learn. Accept God as existing and always worship him. Remember that you are human and you shall remain human."[6]

Philemon's apophatic approach to God's existence is an integral part of Orthodox theology. God is absolute transcendence, inaccessibility, but a reality that makes his existence known through his energies. Although the transcendence of God is a quality intrinsic to God and his essence, his existence becomes known through "various ways and diverse manners" (Hebrews 1:1). The Christian understanding of natural theology owes much to God in essence in three persons, corresponding to creation, redemption, and sanctification of humans and the cosmos.

Modern Orthodox theology has not experienced a "new theology" movement or trends indicating a break with the theology of the church-in-history, with tradition and continuity. It avoids compartmentalizations and dichotomies, distinctions between physical and metaphysical knowledge of God, "nature" and "grace," "faith" and "works", "merit" and "good deeds," because it sees more continuity between natural and supernatural truth, the presence of God in creation and the presence of God in the Incarnation; the "unknown God" of Greek philosophy and the "named" God of the Scriptures. It has not been moved by the "God is dead" theology or other compromising "schools." Orthodox theology today is engaged more in affirming old truths in new categories than in searching for new dogmas. The skin is new, the wine is old. It returns to the sources and attempts to restate the old beliefs in more convincing ways. The ontological proofs have never been absent from Orthodox theology, but it insists on speaking rather in apophatic and biblical categories. Thus "God is infinite and incomprehensible; and all that is comprehensible about God in His infinity and incomprehensibility."[7] But at the same time God is an unchanging essence in three persons—as God Creator, God Redeemer, and God Sanctifier. "When I say God, I mean Father, Son, and Holy Spirit. . . . No sooner do I conceive of the one than I am illumined by the splendor of the three; no sooner do I distinguish them than I am carried back to the one. When I think of any one of the three, I think of Him as a whole, and my eyes are filled, and the greater part of what I am thinking escapes."[8]

The biblical account that declares that Father, Son, and the Holy Spirit, who proceeds from the Father through the Son, are one, formulated by the councils of Nicaea and Constantinople, remains a fundamental doctrine of Orthodoxy. Soteriology necessitates belief in God-in-Trinity because it proclaims not only the fullness of divinity in Christ and the reality of the Incarnation but also his humanity and humanity's elevation to the divinity.[9] Nevertheless, it must be understood that the doctrine of God-in-Trinity is a divine mystery rather than a philosophical notion subject to metaphysical speculation, a mystery proclaimed with certainty. Is not the world a mystery? Is not light a mystery? Together with

John the Evangelist and Dionysios the Areopagite and other Church Fathers, we can speak of God in terms of light, light as a paradox.[10] For example, nineteen-century physicists believed that light was a wave. James Clerk Maxwell had written four basic equations for electricity and magetism that predicted elec-tromagnetic waves that traveled at 300 million meters per second. Physicists quickly were able to show that this light was thus predicted electromagnetic wave.

In the early twentieth century Max Planck discovered that light interacted with matter only in discrete bundles of energy—as though the light was made of particles. It took many years for physicists to reconcile this apparent anomaly. But modern physicists understand that these two distinct observations are not antithetical. Rather, they are two ramifications of the nature of light—two yet one.

Even more, physicists indicate that this "anomaly" is the result of the very nature of the universe. They see either particle or wavelike properties of light depending on the experiment. They no longer talk about light being one, a particle or wave, but rather it "behaves like" a particle or wave.

But the Triune God does not "behave like" a Father or a Son or Spirit, for even though there is one Essence there are three hypostaseis in a coinherence (*perichoresis*) or mutual existence.[11]

The doctrine of Triune God is inextricably related to Christology and soter-iology. The Incarnation of God in Christ was necessary for human salvation, and Christ's double nature as God-made-man is the only way to restore humans to God's presence. In the last analysis, soteriology is nothing but the story of Christ the Logos' presence in humanity from the beginning of his Incarnation to the end of time. God's presence among humans is perceived as a necessary prescription for human salvation. God is indeed utterly unseen and transcendent; unknowable yet present in all things seen and unseen. God is not what exists; yet at the same time he is the cause of everything including human salvation, which is made possible because God assumed human flesh and form.[12] The Incarnation of God's Logos is central in Orthodox theology.

The God-Made-Man Event

In its effort to recover authentic theology and the spirit of undivided Chris-tianity, Orthodox theology today insists on a theology of the living God who became incarnate. Thus for Orthodox theology, Jesus of Nazareth is always Christ the Logos because "the Logos was with God, and the Logos was God" (John 1:2). As a religion and not as a system of ethical commandments, Chris-tianity stands or falls on the basis of its belief in the incarnate love of God, which in the life, teachings, death, and resurrection of the God-man (theanthro-pos) reveals the true nature and destiny of humankind and all that is authentically human.

Theology as the knowledge of God rather than as knowledge about God;

theology as the responsive thinking of humans' quest for eternal salvation, finds its fullest meaning in Christology. "No one has ever seen God; the only Son who is in the bosom of the Father, he has made him known" (John 1:28). In the Incarnation we have not only God's descending and becoming man but through God's Logos humanity's elevation and sanctification as well. In his divinity the Logos is the consubstantial image of the Father, and in his humanity he is the image and the likeness of God. The God who "emptied himself, taking the form of a servant" (Philippians 2:7), who "became flesh and dwelt among us . . . [we] beheld his glory" (John 1:14). The emphasis on Christology is viewed as of paramount significance because without the event of the Incarnation, Christian anthropology is reduced to zoology, and soteriology becomes an unrealized yearning.[13] Indeed, in the words of the first Christian theologian, the theology of Christology is intended that one "may believe that Jesus is the Christ, the Son of God, and that believing [one] may have life in his name" (John 20:31).

Far from any reductionism and modern Nestorianisms, Orthodox theology reiterates that Christ "reflects the glory of God and bears the very stamp of His nature" (Hebrews 1:13) and that through the God-man Christ humans can become "partakers of the divine nature" (2 Peter 1:4). Christology has always been of extraordinary importance to Eastern Orthodox Christianity whether in the fifth, the eighth, the fourteenth, or the twentieth century. Without the Logos-made-man event, the transcendent and the immanent, the separation of faith from knowledge, could not have been reconciled. Without the Incarnation of God's Logos, God would be banished into the realm of the empirically inaccessible.[14]

The restudy of Christology in the past fifty years was initiated by the revival of interest in the theology of Gregory Palamas, a fourteenth-century theologian and archbishop of Thessalonike. "The initial and most decisive motivation which pushed Palamas to the formulation of his theology was his concern to affirm the possibility and, indeed, the reality of communion with God himself."[15] The Incarnation of the Logos has made this possibility a reality. The transcendent God "so loved the world that He gave His only begotten Son" (John 3:16) to assume human nature, to change, to walk among humans so that humans might become participants in God's life. "Changing in His person, the Logos bestows upon us the unchanging life proper to Him as God."[16]

Revival of interest in Christology as well as other classical formulas of Christian theology resulted from Orthodoxy's experience in the ecumenical movement. The trend among Western theologians to reduce theology to sociology, to compromise and see the Christian church as an agent of social issues and political reforms, prompted Orthodox theologians to reassert the importance of historical theology. Thus there was a return to the mind and experience of the ancient and medieval church and its study in modern terms and categories but always in terms of the historical content of theological thought and religious experience.

Contemporary Orthodox Christology has deeper roots than the theology of Palamas whose theology was indeed an elaboration and a reaffirmation of ancient Greek patristic Christology. Irenaios (c. 130–200), a native of Smyrna, who spent his mature life as bishop of Lyons in Gaul, pronounced the now famous words: "Our Lord Jesus Christ, the Logos of God, of his boundless love, became what we are that he might make us what he himself is."[17] His Christology finds an echo in the theology of Athanasios (c. 296–373) who insisted that there is no remedy and no possibility for the restoration of humans to the original state of being except through the Incarnation. The Logos's union with humankind restored to fallen humans the image of God in which humans had been created. By his death and resurrection the Logos of God met and destroyed death, the consequence of human rebellion against the Creator. "Christ, being God, became man, in order to deify us."[18] *Theosis*, eternal life of the human being in God, is the ultimate gift of the Incarnate Logos to humanity. The theology of the Logos's Incarnation remains of absolute significance for Orthodoxy's anthropology.

One of the central issues of Orthodox theology is the human being and the becoming and ultimate destiny of the human being. A person is an evolutionary being and becomes truly human when conforming to the image of the God-man, the *theanthropos Christos*. Orthodox theology studies humans as historical beings, endocosmic beings destined for an exocosmic existence, physical and metaphysical beings. Its major concern is the human of nature and the human of the Scriptures, the human of natural revelation and law but also the human of revealed love and the human of supernatural destiny.

Orthodoxy's theological anthropology examines humans from within but also from without the Christian Scriptures. Humans and God are not placed at opposite poles but on the two ends of the same pole. Each one moves toward a meeting with the other. Humans search and God responds and moves forward to seek. The two meet in the person of the Logos, the eternal God who appears among humans as the Emmanuel. Thus Christ is the end of an old dispensation and the beginning of a new one. He recapitulates and redeems the old man and introduces the new redeemed era.

The "sarkic" human, the human of the flesh of the pre-Christian era, becomes the "pneumatic" human, the human of the spirit, without rejecting the sarkic qualities. But the sarkic qualities are guided and ruled by the enlightened, the strengthened, the illuminated, spiritual person. Ultimately, it is the total person that is saved, not only the pneuma or psyche.

As already indicated, human disobedience introduced death and alienation of the creature from the Creator. Along with St. Paul, everyone raises the question: "Wretched man that I am! Who will deliver me from this body of death?" (Romans 7:24). But human sarkic or carnal nature and sin's power over a person's inmost self did not destroy human capacity for progress and evolution toward spiritual freedom from the bondage of sin. God's image in humans was not totally destroyed after the act of disobedience, thus the possibility for progress and discovery. But throughout moral and spiritual evolution humans were threatened by utter defeat in their struggle with the enemy within.

The reversed, the defeat of sin, and the recovery of eternal life was secured through the God-made-man event. Humans' real freedom and recapitulation and their return to what they were meant to be was made possible because of the Incarnation, which enabled people to rediscover their godly nature. Christ is not only God manifest but also human as humans were ordained to become from the moment of their creation. The victory of the God-man Christ over sin and death can become properties of every person who sees Christ as the prototype and pursues a life after him. Freedom from sin and death, and eternal life in God, are the products of God-made-man in the person of Christ.

It is this patristic theological background that makes modern Orthodox theologians optimistic and more attached to Greek patristic theology than other theologies or to any humanistic anthropology.[19] They find both Christology and anthropology more appealing to modern society. In the opinion of some Orthodox theologians, the alienation of Western Christian theology introduced theories that ultimately led to distortions and misunderstandings.

Saint Augustine, one of the most influential Church Fathers of the medieval Western church, is found lacking when compared to some Greek Fathers. Augustine's doctrine of predestination and grace rejected the existence of free will; his views on the two cities, the City of God and the city of humans, contributed to the denial of the possibility of historical progress and the possibility of any improvement of the secular order. Augustine's anthropology is seen as static, for it sees people as totally corrupt and predestined.[20]

Greek Fathers such as Irenaios, Eusebios of Caesarea, Athanasios, Gregory of Nyssa, to mention only a few, who had widely read in the Greek classical tradition, developed a theology that defended free will, advanced a more humanistic and rationalistic view of history. Their theology allowed for growth and implied that the social order as well as the human being could be improved and reformed. The likeness to God was a likeness to be pursued and achieved. Humans as the image, or icon, of God are a microcosm of all creation. As such every human being is precious before God. A human being is a *synergos Theou*, God's collaborator, not a thing, a slave. God knocks, but people must respond. The confrontation is mutual. But people cannot confront God without the Incarnation, which is God's act of love and an act for ultimate salvation. Christ is true God and true human, one person in two natures without separation and without confusion, a single person with two wills and two natures. As complete *theanthropos*, Christ is the link that unites God and humans. But Christ's divinity should not lead to a Christomonism, and an emphasis on God the Father should not be misunderstood as Patromonism. Any discussion of Father and Son leads to Orthodox theology's position on Pneumatology—the Holy Spirit as God.

The Holy Spirit, The Sanctifier

Any theology of Christian Orthodox metaphysics is bound to discuss a consubstantial Trinity, which includes the Spirit.[21] The Spirit appears as a person with personal qualifications and energies. In St. Paul's theology the function of the Spirit is *koinonia*, the communion that it works between divinity and humanity: "The grace of our Lord Jesus Christ, and the love of God the Father, and the Communion of the Holy Spirit" (2 Corinthians 13:14). But it also is personal communication and experience. The Spirit speaks personally to Apostle Philip (Acts 8:29), to Peter (Acts 10:19; 11:12), to the Christian Community of Antioch (Acts 13:12), to the synod of Jerusalem (Acts 15:25), to the community of believers today.

The Spirit is identified with "the Paraclete (the Counselor) the Spirit of truth, who proceeds from the Father . . . who will guide . . . into all the truth" (John 14:16, 26; 15:26; 16:7). The theology of the Spirit takes for granted that the Spirit is consubstantial with Father and Son; that it "proceeds from the essence of the Father through a movement inseparably bound with Him . . . proceeding eternally from the Father, being sent in time by the Son."[22] The Spirit's role is his continual presence in the church in the form of uncreated energies of the Triune God.

Upholding long-standing doctrines of the undivided church, Orthodox theology distinguishes the incomprehensible essence of God (ousia), identical in the three *hypostaseis* or Persons, proclaims their oneness, teaching that the Trinity's energies though incomprehensible are communicated to the community through the ever-present Holy Spirit. It is through the Holy Spirit that the human being is re-created and achieves salvation, which ultimately is theosis. Orthodox theology relies more on biblical revelation than on philosophical speculation for its teaching on the Holy Spirit. Its theology permits no objectivization, and the Orthodox doctrine of God-in-Trinity remains a mystery and a paradox. Nevertheless, its reality is revealed by the Incarnate Logos, and it is expressed as a loving experience of the Father through the Spirit.

In brief, reductionist theologies of recent years, minimization of the *mysterion* and the paradox, rationalization and demythologization of Scriptures that have been presented in the Christian world in the past fifty years, have prompted Orthodox theologians to reexamine traditional theology. The trend is to emphasize a more biblical theology as it was interpreted and defined by the Church Fathers and the experience of the church in history. God is a living God who creates, who redeems through Christ, and who sanctifies and perpetuates through the Holy Spirit.

Belief in a Triune God is viewed as basic to the idea of the salvation of humans. Belief in the divinity of Christ and the ontological communication of the Spirit with God and humans are necessary qualifications for an understanding of humankind in terms of anthropology and soteriology. As in the case of metaphysics, Orthodox theology today is linked with biblical and patristic tradition. Its anthropology and soteriology are developed in classical terms of the early ecumenical councils and the experience of the church in history.

ORTHODOX ANTHROPOLOGY AND SOTERIOLOGY

Following scriptural evidence and early patristic interpretation, Orthodox theological anthropology seeks to make people more human; to guide humans' feelings, desires, and activities to their true end, guiding them from the external manifestation of things to the reality behind them. Is it not written that the Incarnate Logos through the Holy Spirit gave the faithful divine power "to become partakers of the divine nature?" (2 Peter 1:4) But is this a realistic expectation?

What Is a Human Being?

The human being, the *anthropos,* no less than God is accepted as a mystery but a mystery revealed or greatly revealed.[23] Humans are seen in themselves as living beings but also divine human beings. As such people are not "the measure of all things" as the ancient Greek philosopher Protagoras taught and modern humanists emphasize but beings limited by sin, whatever its definition. As divine human entities, humans are the image of God. Notwithstanding their sinful limitations, their destiny is determined by God's presence in them restored by the Incarnation of God's Logos. The fallen humans did not lose the totality of God's image in themselves, and long before the Incarnation the human being was a searching being. Full restoration to its pristine condition is assured by the God-made-human.

Orthodox theology sees humans in terms of both natural and supernatural revelation. It includes faith in the human being as a searching and involving being throughout history. *Threskeia* as instinctive worship of and quest for the divine amply describes the background of Christian Orthodox anthropology. People "seek God, in the hope that they might feel after him and find him" (Acts 17:27). There is faith in the freedom of the human spirit and its inalienable rights, faith in its ability to evolve but not absolute faith. Orthodox theology's faith in the human being is conditioned by the belief that the human being is a dependent being.

The religious humanism that we observe in the ancient Greco-Roman world is fully realized following the Incarnation. The greatness and holiness of the God-man is ipso facto the greatness and the potential greatness of humankind. Human beings are perceived as a microcosmic form of the world. Their essence is the divine aspect of their own being dressed in a material form. When humans severed their connection with their Creator, they carried along the whole creation to pain, agony, and search for salvation. It is through the God-made-man event that restoration became possible (Ephesians 1:4). In his Incarnation the Logos of God enclosed humans and their world in themselves, uniting them once again to the Creator. Humans in themselves are nonbeings, and cut off from the source of their Being, humans can have no existence. It is through the God-man Christ, the *theanthropos,* that humans discover and ultimately achieve their true humanity. They become theocentric beings. "The perfect man consists in the commingling and the union of the soul receiving the Spirit of the Father, and the mixture of that fleshy nature which also was molded after the image of God" in the words of Saint Irenaeos.[24] The presence of God's Spirit in humans provides an openness "to the Absolute, to immortality, to creativity in the image of the Creator and, secondly, in the fact that God met this openness when he created man and that, therefore, communion and participation in divine life and glory is, for man, his natural element."[25] Closely related to the teaching about human nature and mind is the theology of soteriology.

The Theosis of Humankind

The Incarnation of God's Logos and the deification of the human being is central in Orthodox theology. *Deification,* or *theosis,* a very dear term in Orthodox theology, is synonymous with *soteria-salvation.* The yearning for soteria is universal, and it includes humans as well as nature. The whole of creation seeks "to be set free from its bondage to decay and obtain the glorious liberty of the children of God" (Romans 8:23).

On the basis of this background, Orthodox theology sees the divine economy in cosmic terms, an economy by which the visible world is part of the invisible; it emerges from the invisible and seeks to be saved along with the invisible. There is no dichotomy between the metaphysical and the physical that are interrelated and interdependent. Both constitute two aspects of the whole creation.

The church, as the visible Christ, serves as the indispensable syndesmos, the link between the metaphysical and eternal and the physical and transient. Through the Incarnation, the church, or the community of people who have died and risen in Christ and have received the indwelling Spirit, offers humans and the world the means for an entry into the invisible and eternal world of God. Life in God is what Orthodox theology calls *theosis.* Theosis, however, is both a process and an end. Through the sacramental life, a life of prayer, spirituality, and acts of love, the faithful are invited to a progressive withdrawal from things temporal, material, and visible to a process of theosis, to a world eternal and invisible. The moment of "death" is a kiss between the temporal and eternal. It is in the realm of the external that the full reward of theosis is achieved. Theosis becomes synonymous with Paradise and eternal life.

The conception of salvation as theosis, or deification, was common in ancient religious Greek thought, especially in the Orphic Mysteries. But although in ancient Greek thought theosis meant apotheosis and pantheism, in Christian theology theosis means immortality of the human person in the presence of God's energies. The theosis teaching goes back to the early Christian theologians. For example, Theophilos of Antioch wrote that "man, by keeping the commandments of God, may receive from God immortality as a reward, and become God." Clement of Alexandria added that "to be imperishable is to share in Divinity." Hippolytos was even more explicit. He wrote: "Your body shall be immortal and incorruptible as well as your soul. For you shall have become God. All the things that follow upon the Divine nature God has promised to supply to you, for you were deified in being born to immortality."[26]

The early Christian tradition was accepted by the later Greek Fathers such as the Cappadocians, Apollinarios, Ephraem the Syrian, and Epiphanios of Cyprus. In explaining the Christian understanding of theosis as immortality and eternal life in the realm of the energies of God, the Greek Fathers emphasized that theosis is no pantheistic merging of the human being in the Deity but rather a renovation of the human person after the pristine or original human. This transformation of human nature is the highest result of the Incarnation of the Logos.[27]

Renewed interest in the theology of the Fathers and in pneumatology in particular has contributed in recent years to the publication of several important studies on theosis. In modern Orthodox theology theosis is described not as participation of or a life in the essence of God but as a taste and a vision or a life in the energies of God.[28] The ultimate purpose of human existence is to achieve this eternal glory and salvation in the realm of God's glory.

ETHICAL AND SOCIAL PHILOSOPHY

One who is accustomed to thinking about Eastern Orthodox Christianity in terms of liturgy, iconography, mysticism, prayer, and other worldliness may be surprised to read that historically, Orthodoxy has possessed a powerful social consciousness. Although many recent works have addressed questions of liturgical theology, patristics, canon law, biblical exegesis, there are many studies and books revealing the social character and ethical concerns of Orthodox theology. The leader in this area of theological concern is Greek Orthodox theology proper. Since 1945 serious scholarly efforts have been made to study ethics and social thought in the context of the theology and experience of the church in history.[29]

Ethics and Theology

For Eastern Orthodox Christianity, there is no compartmentalization of theological concerns. There is no separation between doctrine and ethics, spiritual life and social concern. It is only for practical and pedagogical reasons that we separate ethics from doctrine. The ethical teachings and the social philosophy of Orthodox Christianity are emanations rather than deviations from the doctrinal teachings.

The ethical system of Orthodox Christianity is based on the foundations of both natural law and biblical revelation. It assumes belief that the human being is God's masterpiece—sinful but not totally depraved; that the human being is subject to evolution and capable of moral growth that with the help of God has the capacity to increase in stature and ultimately to realize the innate "image" and "likeness" of God.

Even though several Orthodox theologians today tend to consider liturgical theology and eucharistic ecclesiology as the most important aspects of Orthodox theology, there are many others, perhaps more unsung than their colleagues, who maintain that Orthodoxy's social character has not received the theological attention it deserves. Through many studies they have rediscovered the social and ethical dimensions of the church's life in history, both in theoria and in praxis, and appeal for a more balanced presentation of the church's theological concerns. They insist for example that it is un-Orthodox to overemphasize liturgical theology and underemphasize ethical and social thought.[30] Save for hermits and anchorites, the life of the individual believer cannot be understood apart from the life of the other members of the Christian Community—indeed apart from humanity. Humans are social beings, and Christianity is a social religion.

Ethical theology and social philosophy in Eastern Orthodox Christianity today seek to structure a coherent system that takes into account natural law, the thought and mind of the ancient masters who labored with similar issues, biblical commandments, the teachings of the Greek Fathers, and the historical experience of the community, as well as modern schools of thought as long as they do not contradict defined doctrines and truths of the Church. Ethical issues and social concerns include social justice, human rights, medical ethics, and philanthropy toward the elderly, the unemployed, the handicapped, and others in need.

The fundamental principle that underlies Orthodox ethics is the principle of *agape, philanthropia,* love as a divine attribute manifested not only to show God's love for the Creation but for humans to emulate and express toward fellow human beings. Philanthropia (*philein ton anthropon* = to love the human being) has determined the social ethos of the Orthodox Church in history. Philanthropia is synonymous with agape, the new commandment of Christ (John 13:34). God manifested his agape in the God-made-man event of the Incarnation of the eternal Logos. Agape among humans is the imitation of God's love for all persons.

The Theology of Social Ethics

From a theological point of view and from a historical perspective, the social character of the church is the application of the doctrinal teaching concerning God and human beings and human beings with respect to their social relations. Ethical and social thought is solidly based on theological presuppositions.

The Orthodox tradition emphasizes that one rejoins God by possessing love for the Divine Being and by expressing a similar sense of love for God's supreme being. It is by energetic love for God and human persons that one can enter into a state of theosis, "possessing the love and knowledge of God."[31]

The earthly activity of the God-man Christos becomes the inspiration of the social activity of the individual believer as well as for the social response of the Christian Ecclesia as an institution. There is no justice proper, no virtue, except Christocentric virtue. "Love one another as I have loved you" or "A New Commandment I am giving unto you—to love one another as I have loved you."[32]

Thus the Christian community is charged with the responsibility and the task of applied agape because its founder was the personification of agape, and he was deeply concerned with the lowly, the unloved, and the disregarded members of society. What Christ did, the church must do. The Ecclesia is an extension of and the perpetuation of the person and the work of Christ here on earth. All people must be drawn to God, and it is through vigorous activity that all people, rich and poor, wise and foolish, young and old, will unite in the presence of God. The practice of love becomes a universal unitive force for God and humans. "To turn your back against one poor individual is to show contempt toward all humanity. To refuse assistance to one indigent person is to commit injustice to all humanity because man is a microcosm and the convergence of all humanity," as Patriarch George Scholarios wrote in the fifteenth century.[33]

The Eternal Logos divested himself of supernatural glory in order to reach out and direct the earthly to eternal glory. God walked among humans that human beings might walk with God. Or in the classic words of Irenaeos and Athanasios, "the Lord . . . came to us not as He could, but as we could see Him" and that the Lord "being God, later He became man, in order that we may become gods."[34] This kind of patristic thought has contributed immensely to the formation of social ethics. Notwithstanding the ultimate supernatural destiny of the Ecclesia, the Christian community cannot divorce itself from this world, but as Christ did, it, too, must do and invade and penetrate into the present world "doing good." The Logos became human in order to announce release to the captives, to recover the sight of the blind, to set at liberty those who have been enslaved, to proclaim that the time of God has arrived.[35] God became human; thus nothing human should be foreign to the church.

On this basis, then, the church, as an organism and organization of Christ and through its affinity with Christ's earthly ministry, emulates the work of its Lord. Thus the social thought of Orthodoxy assumes a theanthropic character that is based furthermore not only on Christology but on the theological teaching of the Fatherhood of God. "God so loved the world that He gave His only Son, that whoever believes in Him should not perish but have eternal life."[36] Christ called God Father and fulfilled God's will. On account of humans' relationship to Christ the man, those who supplicate the same God and acknowledge God as a common Father, the Creator of the Cosmos and of all humans, become automatically charged with social obligations to their fellow humans. In their faith in God they accept also God's paternity over the entire oecumene. The paternity of God obliges all—healthy and sick, slaves and free, blacks and whites, kings and soldiers, civilized and barbarians, to effect an earthly kingdom of God—to paraphrase St. Gregory Nazianzenos.[37]

Such a creed energizes an impulse for social action whose immediate objective is the betterment of human society here on earth as a dim reflection of the perfect kainonia in heaven. Because of God's philanthropy and concern for humans, God's plan (economy), for human redemption, is defined by the Byzantine theologian Nicholas Kabasilas as compassion or mercy.[38] Humans' earthly activity, then, must be one of continuous compassion toward all people.

In imitation of God's two-way involvement in human history, humans must also manifest their concern for their fellow humans in two manners that correspond to humanity's dual nature, the physical and the spiritual. One imitates God's philanthropy when one feeds the hungry, gives a drink to the stranger, visits the sick, redeems the prisoners, and buries the dead who have no one to bury them. To these five physical activities correspond seven spiritual concerns: to console those in sorrow, to give advice to the timid and undecided, to teach the ignorant, to guide the sinner, to forgive the fallen, to be patient with the rude and insolent, and to pray for all, in the words of George Scholarios.[39]

The social thought of the Greek Fathers, who laid the ground and who expressed the life and creed of today's Orthodox theology, is linked with the social aspects of soteriology since their ultimate concern was the salvation of the individual soul as well as the redemption of the Christian community. In the history of the Orthodox, the church has performed a double function; it has concerned itself with the eternal salvation of human souls, but it has also served as the agency of social improvement and physical survival. Its social posture has often given meaning and direction to the social thought and action of the individual as well as of the state. This, in particular, is evident in the life of many Orthodox during centuries of captivity under the Ottoman Empire. It is on this basis that one can understand why an archbishop can serve as an ethnarch or get involved in secular aspects of his people's life.

It is not only the principle of humanitarian social obligations toward the indigent that Orthodox theology teaches but also the theological concept that one is called by the creator to become a synergos of God, a collaborator for the completion of God's work, both in one's own person and in the persons united in Christ's body—the church. God's work not only is spiritual, but it embraces all aspects of human life.

It is impossible to disassociate anthropology from a discussion concerning social thought in Orthodox theology. Humans are viewed as the image and likeness of God, whose ultimate goal is eternal life in God (theosis). Their earthly destiny is to become holy because their God is holy, and their eternal goal is to achieve deification (theosis) because they are children of God. Nevertheless, holiness and moral perfection are evolutionary elements, not achievements per se to be accomplished here on earth. Cultivation and moral development are pursued through spiritual exercise, prayer, and contemplation but also through the creative use of human will and freedom in the service of God and God's people through "faith active in love"—agape in diakonia.[40]

Orthodox theology sees dynamic love as one's immediate goal here on earth. The moral perfection of the human being commences from the earthly and is to be pursued in association with and in service to God's people, whereas our terminal theosis will be achieved in the kingdom to come. The human person occupies a central position in the thought and social concern of the church. The entire social thought of Orthodoxy is based on the recognition of one's worth, on the respect, love, consideration, and anxiety for one's destiny, whatsoever one's social standing, state position, origins, or race may be. As the object of the love of God, each person must be the most important object of anxiety and service for the church, for he or she is a microcosm of all humanity.

John Chrysostom's view of the human being has exerted a telling influence on Orthodox moral theology. Chrysostom wrote:

I have no contempt for any person because every person is most worthy of attention as one of God's creatures. Even if one is a slave one is not despicable for I am not looking at social ranks but for virtue. I am looking neither for a master nor for a slave but for the human person for whom the heavens opened, the sun shines, the moon races on, the air fills all, the fountains give their water, the sea spreads out, for whom, indeed, the only begotten son of God became man. My master was slaughtered and shed his blood for man and who am I to overlook man? How could I be forgiven.[41]

God's creation constitutes a single and whole entity. There is no drastic separation between the visible Ecclesia and the invisible community because both constitute the whole of God's creation. God's creation is all-encompassing, and the physical is linked with the metaphysical. It is for this reason that in Orthodox theology the supernatural aspect of the church is not treated in isolation from the physical or visible church and that the saints, the fathers, the martyrs, and other holy men of the past are in fact contemporaries. The present incorporates the past and anticipates the future. Their church is our church, and our church is in a direct historical continuity with their church.

The unity and continuity of the social ethos of present-day Orthodoxy with that of the past is real. Orthodoxy's conception of history is linear, and it recognizes no major disruptions. History and theology are mutually determined and conditioned. In fact, there is no theology per se but only historical theology. It is for this reason that the Orthodox have high regard for ethical decisions, examples, and illustrations from history. It is because of their historical conscience that the Orthodox appeal to the authority of tradition, the mind of the Fathers, the decisions of ecumenical councils—the holiness and the experience of the past. The past lives in the present, and it will continue to live as long as human beings will live.

The ecclesiological concept concerning the church as the Household or Family of God presupposes that church members accept agape or philanthropia as a common denominator, freely flowing, expecting nothing in return. It is this type of unmerited philanthrophy that made Christian love transcend the boundaries of ancient Greco-Roman humanism. It transformed an anthropocentric and limited humanism into a theocentric and ecumenical philanthropy. Although not all Christians, either clergy or laity, respond to this model of social thought and concern, overwhelming evidence confirms that there were and are numerous believers who have adopted and transmitted this ideal in their daily lives. To help the poor, visit the sick, guide the lost, receive the stranger, look after the lepers, protect the orphans, and stand publicly for social justice are types of love leading to ultimate sanctification.[42] Whether wealthy or poor, prominent or humble, healthy or sick, they receive communion from the same chalice—a social event in itself that confirms and seals their fellowship in God and their social and mutual reconciliation. Receiving from the same chalice becomes the supreme socializing experience that makes public association feasible, easy to sympathize with, and be of assistance to others.

Eucharistic Communion as actual union with Christ becomes a foundation stone and a springboard of social interest and welfare preparing for an eternal fellowship.[43] This thought of the church was expressed centuries ago by John of Damascus who wrote of Holy Communion as a union of the faithful with the divinity of Christ, "an actual communion because through it we share in His flesh and His divinity." "Yes," he wrote, "we have communion and are united with one another through it. For since we partake of one bread, we all become one body of Christ and one blood, and members one of another, being of one body with Christ."[44]

The social ethos of the Orthodox community derives much of its strength from Eucharistic theology because it views in the act of Holy Communion not only participation in the Body of Christ but also a dynamic symbol of the unity and spiritual reciprocity of Christ's disciples. This unity signalizes mutual opportunities and responsibilities. As the common chalice becomes a public spiritual feast, likewise it serves as a common ground for social thought and activity. As all of the faithful are invited to the same spiritual feast, likewise all are summoned to respond to the call for the betterment of the social order here and its perfection in the hereafter. The church stresses the importance of values for this life, which will be fully realized in the life to come. It is the continuum that exists between time and eternity, between the physical and the metaphysical, between the church militant and the church triumphant, that makes eschatology a great source for the development of social thought in Christian Orthodoxy. They are intricately related. On account of this mutuality the social ethos of Orthodoxy is greatly determined by the vivid eschatological expectations and apocalyptic tendencies. The study of every major Greek Father reveals that his social thought was determined by the eschatological creed.

The frequently eschatological sermons that we find in the writings of the church are of dual significance. They reveal prevailing social conditions but also the concern and the invitation to all of the faithful for moral and social self-improvement through the practice of good works. Charity, alms, and virtuous deeds were very popular themes for sermons as they are today. The same virtues, however, give the faithful the characteristic tone of their daily existence. Great churchmen such as Basil, who washed the feet of lepers in his own hospital in Caesaria; or John the Eleemon, who built seven hospitals in Alexandria; or Patriarch Athanasios I of Constantinople, who organized food distribution and common meals in the early fourteenth century; or Theoleptos of Philadelphia, who took up the defense of his city against the enemy, interpreted their lives in terms of the ethical teachings and life of Christ.[45] The Church Fathers who set the example and laid the foundations of the church's moral theology saw theology and life as two interrelated halves of a single whole.

Being in Christ means an everyday life that expresses the application of the commandments of love and sacrifice and a reflection of divine philanthropia toward all-Christians and non-Christians alike. The church is the new Ark in which everybody can find assistance. The church is not a community of saints for the service of saints but a tender mother who invites all to her breasts to feed and receive strength for the great pilgrimage to eternity. Furthermore, the church is viewed not as a museum of saints but as the great hospital open to all in need of healing. As the eternal kingdom of God is opened and prepared to receive all creation in an ultimate unity, the earthly kingdom, that is, the Ecclesia, is available to those exerting their efforts to serve and embrace all. Thus the ministry of love becomes the hallmark of the church.

In Christ's earthly kingdom one becomes a new creation. The new creation evolves here on earth and follows a process of perfection that will reach its apogee in the kingdom to come. In the earthly kingdom one joins "a society in the process of deification" as St. Gregory Palamas has put it.[46] This process is a social one because deification is intended for all who join the new creation. Thus in the long history of the church there were many who developed a deep community interest and who believed that ultimate moral perfection begins in our social relations.

The tendency of Christian theology to emphasize the values of the eternal kingdom did not dissipate devotion to social obligations. The church stressed the interrelationship between duties to others with the apocalyptic expectations of the other world. One's earthly life must be regulated according to the relations one wants to establish with God in God's eternal kingdom. To make an adjustment after departure is humanly uncertain. Thus reminding one of the value of time and the limitations of our knowledge concerning our earthly existence as well as of God's final judgment has been a popular topic for sermons and admonitions. As St. Photios, the great patriarch and scholar of the ninth century, admonished: "Let us study death before death so that we may live after death."[47] The event of death becomes central to ethics because it shows that humanity belongs to eternal life and provides hope for betterment on earth as well as assurance for eternity. Long before Photios, Saint Irenaeos wrote that "the task of the Christian is nothing but to study how to die."[48]

Historically, very frequently the church has served as the champion of social justice and the protector of the needy and the oppressed. There have been many remarkable churchmen who have expressed a deep interest for the fate of the poor and the persecuted, who have championed social justice, who have castigated the abuse of wealth and the exploitation of the poor. Personal property is not strictly personal but a trust that God has given to the owner. Social involvement rather than an eremitic or monastic life provides greater opportunities for the realization of the Christian ideal.

In speaking of social ethics, the church does not mean merely the contribution of money or goods to those in need. Under the term *social ethics* all services that can be rendered freely to anyone in need of assistance are included, from what is called "charity" to the professional services of physicians, lawyers, civil servants, and especially public hospitality and relief. The church urges all those who can to give their money, their goods, their talents, their knowledge, their advice, and their services generally to all who stand in need of them—all poor are Christ's, and as long as they do it to them, they do it to Christ.

The church, as the conscience of Christ's gospel, plays an important role in bringing the two extremes of rich and poor together by emphasizing the significance of religious values. Religion is not isolated into a department of the state's or society's life, but it is accepted as an all-encompassing way of life. The church is both the kingdom of God and a politeuma, a nationhood, an indivisible entity that has its feet firmly planted on earth and its hands stretched out like an anchor of hope, to God's eternal kingdom. As a politeuma, the church is concerned with political as well as social problems.

The church emphasizes the application of social philanthropy and private charity on other than religious grounds. Poverty and distress are often the result of our inhumanity to one another. Thus the church appeals for the practice of public philanthropy not simply for the salvation of one's soul or to please God but to fulfill an act of natural justice because many poor people are victims of the tyranny and the exploitation of others. As St. Photios wrote:

Do not overlook the poor and let not his tattered rags incite you to contempt, but let them rather move you to pity your fellow-creatures. For he is also a man, a creature of God, clothed in flesh like yourself, and perchance in his spiritual virtue mirroring the common Creator more than you do. Nature has not made him indigent in this way, but it is the tyranny of his neighbors that has reduced either him or his parents to indigence, while our lack of pity and compassion has maintained or even aggravated his poverty.[49]

Admittedly, there are Orthodox theologians today who seldom make specific proposals in the realm of social action to change the social structure and remedy the evils of their society. Their most frequent call against social injustices is a call to repentance, an indication that the church expects the unjust and wealthy to initiate action by themselves without coercion from the state or other authorities. But Orthodox theology views human nature as a synthetic whole in which all drives and impulses of humans must become subject to the control of higher values, all of which derive from God and must serve God's people.[50] It is through the renewal of the inner life of each individual person that the moral life of society is transformed. A renewed society possesses the potential of renewing the whole state and the whole world for "a little leaven leavens all the dough."[51] A great number of Orthodox theologians today believe in the close relationship between spirituality and involvement.

In brief, then, one of the major concerns of Orthodox religious thought today is how to maintain a balance between faith and works, doctrine, and ethics. It speaks of Christianity as God's direct intervention in history but also as a social religion. The gospel needs to be interpreted vertically as God's saving power and involvement in the life of individuals but also horizontally as it concerns human relationships in the community and in the world.[52]

ESCHATOLOGY

For Orthodox theology, history is linear. It has a beginning and it looks forward to an end. Human destiny and the destiny of all creation are oriented toward the eschaton (end; last things). But the term *eschatology* is not identified exclusively with the last things. It is used in a biblical sense that means that the eschaton is both present and future, an end and a beginning. The Incarnation of the Logos (John 1:2–5; Hebrews 1:2; 2 Peter 1:20) is both an end and a beginning. In the life of the early Christian community the eschaton was their own present (Acts 2:17) as well as an expectation of the last day (Revelation 15:1; 21:9). History and eschatology are not unconnected and independent of each other.

An Orthodox Understanding of History

Etymologically, history (from the Greek *historia*) means an inquiry into the nature and destiny of things, a quest into finding out the truth about events and the ultimate purpose of why things happen. History is one and continuous. The periodization into past, present, and future history is done for practical and pedagogical reasons.

The Christian understanding of history sees the event of the Incarnation as central. Cosmology, anthropology, hamartiology, soteriology, acquire meaning in the Christ event. Thus past, present, and future are interrelated depending upon each other.[53] They are one because they are God's, and God is the beginning and the end, the alpha and the omega of history. The reality of God, the author of time and space, is ever present, and in God there is neither a beginning nor an end. Thus the whole realm of history is in an eschatological state. Creation, redemption, and theosis are ever-present realities. Creation has never ceased, redemption is an ever-present gift, and theosis is a process looking toward a completion.

The relationship between time and space—past, present, and future—is better understood when we consider the Orthodox theological understanding of tradition as a living experience and as an ontology with diachronic dimensions. As such, it proclaims the unity of time, persons, ideas, and practices. Even though God-in-Christ invaded history in time and space, God has always been the great paradox of history. The B.C., A.D., and Eschaton constitute a continuum. Thus the Orthodox emphasis on the importance of tradition.

The Eastern Orthodox appreciation and use of tradition is not easily understood by people who do not possess a long-standing historical consciousness. The "remote" past whether of Hebraic, Greek, or Roman origins, is ever present in the Christian community. The person of Jesus Christ is the Logos of the Greeks. He is the point of convergence between Hebrew Messianic expectations and the Greco-Roman quest. It is for this reason that in Christian Orthodox worship past, present, and future are brought together. Abraham, Moses, Isaiah, Daniel, Peter and Paul, Basil and John Chrysostom, Barbara and Irene, fathers, martyrs, hermits, intellectual theologians, and simple folk commemorated in the liturgy are not remote names but elder contemporaries.

The Apostles of Christ, the Apostolic Fathers, and the early church in general did not simply adjust to the Hellenic cultural and intellectual millieu but also adopted, consecrated, and absorbed the past heritage as God's providential work—not as corrupted human failures. "Profane" history is viewed as part of "sacred" history. Christianity was born in Hellenic Judaism, and it matured in the Greek linguistic and intellectual tradition. Divine revelation was not limited to the Old Testament times, but it encompassed God's world. Christianity brought together the best of the ancient world's traditions. It is not a paradox that Christian theologians from as early as Justin the Martyr down to the present day cite not only the Scriptures and the Fathers of the church for interpretation but also the wisdom of other nonbiblical thinkers. Pindar, Epicurus, Heracleitos, Sophocles, Socrates, Plato, Plutarch, spoke "revealed" truths. Early Christian theologians and religious thinkers discerned an affinity between "natural" and "revealed" teachings, Old Testament commandments, and Greek ethical teachings. The tradition established by thinkers such as Justin the Martyr, Clement and Origen of Alexandria, Synesios of Cyrene, and Basil of Caesarea survived throughout the Byzantine millennium. The eleventh-century theologian and bishop John Mavropous expressed the above mentality in the following prayer. He wrote: "If, my Christ, you should wish to exempt any of the pagans from punishment, choose for me Plato and Plutarch. For both were very close to your laws in both teaching and way of life. They may not have known that you are the God of all, but this is only a further claim to save all men."[54]

To deny the syncretistic nature of Christian theology is to overlook the fact that Christianity is a historical religion. As a religion born in and shaped by history, Christianity assimilated much of the form and even content of the Greek classics. History is the domain of God that he has visited through various ways and manners. Thus the chasm between "profane" and "sacred" history should not be overemphasized. But there is no unanimity among Orthodox theologians as to the relationship between sacred and profane history. Traditionally, there were theologians who were cautious about Hellenic thought and Christian theology; however, there were others who accepted the achievements of ancient Greek philosophy and religious thought as less antagonistic to Christian theology, and there were others, members of the monastic world, who minimized the importance of the classical heritage for Christian theology. This type of polarization exists to the present day.

Nevertheless, this pluralistic approach to the meaning of history and tradition has survived because it has become a subject of constant questioning. It is by the most natural and self-evident things that the defined and inherited heritage being placed in question that its continuity has been assured. Without ignoring the value of personal theological questioning, it is collective solidarity and theological consensus that appear more important in Orthodox theology than the expression of individual conscience. There is solidarity of theological doctrines adopted by the community in the course of history but freedom of theological investigation and opinion on nondoctrinal matters—what Orthodox theology calls *theologoumena*.

The Eschaton

In theological eschatology, too, we observe a close relationship between past, present, and future.[55] The whole realm of Christian history is in an eschatological state. The best illustration of this "realized eschatology" is found in Christian Orthodox worship—the Orthros (Matins) service and the Divine Liturgy in particular. From the moment the celebrant enters the sanctuary and starts the act of worship, the whole of God's creative and providential activity in history is celebrated in word, song, movement, and symbolism. From the moment he invokes the name of God by proclaiming "blessed is our God now and ever and unto the ages of ages," until the dismissal prayer "through the prayers of our Holy Fathers," he makes a reaffirmation of the eschaton's existence in the present. The first part of the Liturgy, the Liturgy of the Word, commemorates the eschaton as expectation, and the Liturgy of the Mystery celebrates the eschaton as present.[56]

The Eucharistic celebration provides the clues of the nature of the eschaton, which is no less than *Koinonia*—communion with God. Sacramental union in the Eucharist prefigures external communion with God that will be completed in the Last Day, known also as the Parousia of the Kyrios (Lord). Parousia refers to a spiritual appearance not in the sense of a return but of circumstance that will lead to full *Koinonia* with God or to a total eclipse of God's presence. Thus Paradise is identified with eternal life in God and the absence of Paradise is called hell.

The Second Coming of which the Nicean-Constantinopolitan creed speaks is not a historical event to take place in the future but an event already realized. The faithful as members of the Body of the Living Christ enjoy God's presence in the reading of or hearing the Word of God, in the Eucharist, in the practice of love, in the prayer life of the Community—indeed in the ever-present awareness of God's existence and life in them. The Last Day (Eschaton) is the point at which God masters and rules over all. The Eucharistic prayer of *Anamnesis* summarizes the eschatological teaching of the Orthodox Church. It calls to mind the past, makes vivid the present, and brings forward the future. The faithful possess a conscious thinking of God's involvement in past, present, and future history. The kingdom of God "is to come, yet it is in the midst of you." Time becomes eternally present.[57] Mortal and sinful humans become eternally "alive unto God'' (see Romans 6:11). Creation, anthropology, soteriology, are brought together in eschatology. The guilt of sin in human life is followed by the exultation of forgiveness felt after *metanoia*; the sense of loneliness and isolation is mitigated by the individual's participation in the Eucharist; the badness and the fear of the encounter with death is destroyed by the affirmation of the resurrection of Christ, which made human resurrection possible. The ultimate end of eschatology is the resurrection of the human person into a transformed, new being in communion with the Being of the Triune God.[58]

INTERFAITH DIALOGUES

Some of the most important events in the past fifty years related to Eastern Orthodox Christianity have been inter-Orthodox conferences, interfaith dialogues and interreligious conversations.

Inter-Orthodox Conferences

The Bolshevik revolution and its consequences for the Orthodox Church in the Soviet Union and the devastating results of World War II did not allow a closer cooperation among the Orthodox churches for many years. It was due to the initiative of Patriarch Athenagoras of the Ecumenical Patriarchate of Constantinople (present-day Istanbul) that the Orthodox have drawn closer, and in the past twenty-five years, they have held several important conferences.

The first Pan-Orthodox Conference was held at Rhodes in 1961, and it was followed by three additional ones in 1963, 1964, and 1968. Every one was attended by representatives from most Orthodox patriarchates, autocephalous, and independent churches. Out of these preparatory conferences came plans for a major Pan-Orthodox Council that would address various theological issues such as sources of revelation, church and society, the role of laity in the church, impediments of marriage, church life and worship, and several more of a pastoral nature.[59] A preconciliar conference held in Chambesy, Switzerland, in 1976 reconsidered the original agenda, and theoretical topics such as sources of revelation were dropped from the agenda. Emphasis was placed on problems of a pastoral nature. One of the major results of these meetings was that all Orthodox churches agreed to the importance of their participation in the ecumenical movement and the need to cooperate with other Christian churches and religions in order to serve humankind through mutual understanding, peace, and social justice.

The second pan-Orthodox theological conference held in Athens in 1976 was of great importance for theology and the Orthodox Church in general. It was devoted to the theme ''The Theology of the Church and Its Application Today,'' and it was subdivided into three interrelated topics: theology as an expression of the life and consciousness of the church; theology as an expression of the presence of the church in the world; and theology in the renewal of the life of the church. All three reflected current trends and present concerns of Orthodox theology. Differing theological views were expressed on various theological issues, but a consensus emerged concerning the spirit of faithfulness to the essence of Orthodoxy.

The following are the highlights of the theological positions and religious issues discussed in the conference. It was agreed that the genuine nature of the Orthodox theology consists not only of the scientific examination of sources and movements and the formulation of dogmas and their philosophical development but also of incarnating them as principles of life. The doctrine of the church is not an ideology; it is the spelling out of its faith. Based on Revelation, developed by tradition, theology reflects the mind of the church. Theological work proper, that of the Apostles, Fathers, doctors, and thinkers up to the present, is its first manifestation, the fruit of the intellect as well as of the heart. It was acknowledged that theology is also embodied in the liturgy, expressing through prayer the creed of the faithful. Prayer is theology in action. Theology as the content of thought and worship, as an expression of the life and consciousness of the church, is also an essential part of the community's memory. As such, the history of the church is wholly theological, and theology proper is historical.

With regard to theology as an expression of the church's presence in the world, it was reaffirmed that one of the main functions of theology is to show that church and the world mutually belong together. The church is not a community set apart from the world. It is the world engaged in the process of transfiguration. The world is not lying outside the church as a realm separated from the Lordship of the Personal God revealed in Christ. The witness of Orthodox theology in the world concerns both a restoration of the world to God and also the culture and problems of local situations.

The primary function of theology is to contribute to the renewal of the church's life. In other words, theology has primarily a practical utility. As such, it should engage in a continuous conversation with itself, in self-criticism, in *metanoia* and rejuvenation. It was agreed that Orthodox theology should continue to express the thought and life of the one, catholic, and apostolic church with conviction but not in polemic tones and always with a commitment to an ecumenical dialogue. Orthodox theology is ecumenical by its very nature.[60]

Notwithstanding differing opinions, on several topics, certain chief characteristics unite Orthodox theological thought today such as a distrust of centralized church government; a synthesis of apophatic and cataphatic principles in theological thought and religious experience; pluralism in *theologoumena* and unity in established doctrine; emphasis on God's presence rather than on God's command, thus inner religious experience rather than legalistic requirements; a less exacting view of doctrinal specificity and more worship and glorification of the Divine presence.

Some serious theological and ecclesiastical problems remain unresolved. The question of what is purely Orthodox and what is not still persists. It does not matter whether or not they constitute an Orthodox minority, the question has been raised by some of whether the ecumenically minded are truly Orthodox—the problem of Orthodoxomania, which tends to overlook or ignore the fact of syncretism, historical relativism, and the inevitable influences of "non-Orthodox" influences. Although some consider "foreign" influences as an anathema, others do not consider them to be a problem because the early and the historic church became subject to such "foreign" influence, which, however, it was able to transform and make its own. The role of the Orthodox in the Ecumenical movement, the reconciliation between religious faith and ethnocentricism, and various canonical problems continue to challenge Orthodox theological thinking.

Interfaith Dialogues

Interfaith dialogues include Eastern Orthodoxy's theological contacts with the non-Chalcedonian, known also as the Lesser Orthodox or Oriental Orthodox Churches; dialogues with the Old Catholics, the Roman Catholic, the Anglican-Episcopal, and the major churches of the Protestant Reformation.[61]

Ironing out doctrinal differences with non-Chalcedonian churches of the Near East, including the churches of the Copts in Egypt, the Ethiopians, the Armenians, and others, has been a major concern of Eastern Orthodox theology of the past twenty-five years. These churches rejected the doctrinal definitions about the nature of Christ formulated at the great Council of Chalcedon in 451. Contacts between the two families of churches have not been rare, but only in recent years have major theological meetings been held. Three theological dialogues have been conducted between their representatives in 1964, 1967, and 1971. There is a consensus that the doctrinal differences between the two theologies have been narrowed and that the dialogues should resume with more determination and vigor. There is a strong opinion on both sides that the possibilities for a reunion between the two ancient churches are most encouraging.[62]

Eastern Orthodox and Old Catholics have been in contact since 1874, nearly four years after the First Vatican Council (1870) proclaimed the doctrine of papal Infallibility. Since then, several theological dialogues have been held in four phases (1874–1875; 1893–1913; 1931; 1961–). Four important meetings in the past ten years have discussed topics such as the Trinity, revelation, canon of Scripture, ecclesiology, church councils, authority, and infallibility of the church and several other important issues. An encouraging consensus has been reached on the authority of the seven ecumenical councils and doctrines of the Christian church before the schism of the eleventh century.[63] There are several theological principles that unite rather than divide the Old Catholics with the Eastern Orthodox.

The event that served as a catalyst in the relations between the Eastern Orthodox and the Roman Catholic churches, which have been in schism since the thirteenth, if not the eleventh, century, was the January 1964 meeting in Jerusalem between Pope Paul VI and Patriarch Athenagoras I. Not only did the two leaders lift the anathema of 1054, but they decided to improve further the relations between their respective churches. They agreed to inaugurate regular contacts between their hierarchs and also between their theologians.

In 1967 Pope Paul visited Patriarch Athenagoras in Constantinople, the New Rome (Istanbul), and later the patriarch reciprocated by visiting the pope in Old Rome. International, national, and local theological commissions were established to conduct regularly theological dialogues that led to the publication of a great number of studies—theological, historical, canonical. "More and more [old] Rome uses the term 'sister church' to describe Orthodoxy; Constantinople is called affectionately the 'new Rome.' "[64] On the other hand, Constantinople continues to consider Rome as the *"prokathemene"* (having preeminence) or the *presbytera* (elder) Rome and to accord it the honor of primacy (*primus inter pares*). The problem of authority and the theology of the Holy Spirit remain the two major issues that separate the two churches.

Although socially the relations between the Anglican-Episcopal communion of churches and the Eastern Orthodox have been amicable for centuries, theological rapprochement has remained at a standstill. The question among the Orthodox persists: Is the Anglican-Episcopal Church of the Catholic or Protestant tradition? Although the Orthodox and the Anglicans have enjoyed cordial relations since the sixteenth century and several theological conferences between the two have been held, no major theological problem, including the validity of Anglican orders, has been resolved.[65] The recent decision of the Anglican-Episcopal Church to admit women to ordination has further strained the relations with the Orthodox. Nevertheless, international and national theological commissions exist, and serious dialogues between the two have resumed.

It was through the Ecumenical Patriarchate, the *primus inter pares* church in Eastern Orthodoxy, that theological dialogues between the Orthodox and churches of the Protestant Reformation have been held. In 1920 the Ecumenical Patriarchate issued an encyclical addressed to the Christian world with an appeal for closer cooperation and for the establishment of a type of Christian "League of Nations." It was the starting point of the Ecumenical movement. As members of the World Council of Churches, the Orthodox have had dialogues with many theologians of the Protestant tradition. It has been acknowledged that Orthodox theology has had a considerable impact on the World Council of Churches' formulation of declarations, especially in the General Assemblies held in Uppsala, Nairobi, New Delhi, and Lima.[66]

Concerning theological dialogues with individual churches of the Protestant world, mention must be made of the meetings between theologians of the Ecumenical Patriarchate, the Moscow Patriarchate, and the Church of Romania with the Evangelical Lutheran, Church of Germany, and the Lutheran churches in the United States. Historical, biblical, Eucharistic, and ecclesiological issues have been studied exhaustively in dialogues held in the past twenty years. The differences between Eastern Orthodox and Lutheran theologies are greater and more numerous than those between Orthodoxy and the churches of the Catholic tradition.[67] Fewer but equally important meetings on an international and national level have been held between Eastern Orthodoxy and the World Alliance of Reformed Churches.[68]

There is little doubt that the Christian World has been in serious theological dialogue. Much progress has been achieved, but differences accumulated throughout the centuries and historical circumstances cannot be resolved in fewer than fifty years. The ecumenical dialogues should continue with renewed commitment and vigor.

INTERRELIGIOUS CONVERSATIONS

The past fifty years have witnessed greatly improved relations between the Christian and non-Christian religions. Eastern Orthodox Christianity has special reasons to pursue better understanding with both Judaism and Islam.

Judaism

Jewish communities have existed in traditionally Eastern Orthodox countries for many centuries, and Eastern Orthodox Christians have lived side by side with Muslims for nearly fourteen centuries. Contacts between all parties concerned have intensified in recent years. It would be misleading, however, to speak in terms of theological dialogues between representatives of Orthodox Christianity and Judaism and those of Islam. There have been dialogues on common traditions and cultures rather than interreligious explorations.

Nevertheless, in addition to cultural and social reasons, there is much common ground for serious interreligious conversation. Several Orthodox theologians have initiated a movement to solve some of the problems that cause misunderstandings between Eastern Orthodox Christianity and Judaism. Some twenty-five years ago Hamilkar Alivizatos emphasized the need for a revision of some liturgical texts and church hymns and the expurgation from them of words or phrases with an anti-Jewish connotation.[69] More recently, scholars have made similar appeals not only for an appreciation of many common elements in civilization but also because of common roots that the two traditions share in their liturgical and prayer life.[70]

Recent history reveals that words were translated into actions, which helped to improve relations between Judaism and Greek Orthodoxy in particular. For example, in 1943, when Greece was under German and Italian occupation, Damaskenos, the archbishop of Athens and all Greece, and other churchmen made enormous efforts to save the Jewish population of Greece. The archbishop wrote a letter to Konstantinos Logothetopoulos, the puppet prime minister, and Gunther Altenburg, the "plenipotentiary of the Third Reich" in occupied Greece, protesting the deportation of 60,000 Jews. Damaskenos praised the Greek Jews for their nobility, brotherly feelings, progressive ideas, and economic contributions to the country, and above all their "unchallengeable patriotism which we have come to know through the long years we have lived side by side in slavery and in freedom.''[71] When the rabbi of Athens was asked by the Nazis for a list of his people's names, he warned his congregation and then left Athens in Archbishop Damaskinos's automobile, which was exempted from the usual search. The rabbi found refuge in the mountains.

There were other acts of brotherly concern and indeed heroism. On the island of Zakynthos (Zante) the German garrison commander demanded a list of all Jews of the island. The mayor and the bishop of the island handed him a document containing only two names—their own! Both bishop and the mayor were instrumental in transporting out the island's 257 Jews.[72]

Closer to an interreligious nature was a national colloquium of Greek Orthodox and American-Jewish scholars held in New York City in January 1972. It was a serious meeting that explored critical issues in history, liturgy, theology, and social concern. Many parallel beliefs were stressed concerning God's relationship with the world, the nature of a worshiping community, the authority of tradition, mysticism, and eschatology.[73] It was agreed that a second national colloquium should follow, but thus far it has not materialized.

Islam

Eastern Orthodox Christians and Muslims have achieved a symbiosis for many centuries and in several countries of the Near East and the Balkan peninsula.[74] Notwithstanding their coexistence, there have been few interreligious conferences and dialogues. It has been only in recent years that Orthodox theologians have turned to a systematic study of Islam and have initiated interreligious colloquia with scholars of the Muslim world.

There are several important studies published in recent years that have created the presuppositions for serious dialogues between the Eastern Orthodox Christian tradition and the Islamic faith. A recent major study on the Koran and its conception of history has broken new ground and has created the intellectual climate for serious discussions. Several modern works take into account that as early as the eighth century the two faiths engaged in a type of dialogue about their points of agreement and disagreement. John of Damascus was the first Christian theologian to study seriously the new faith. Other notable theologians of the Byzantine era included Gregory Palamas and George Gennadios Scholarios.[75]

Apart from historical conferences on Byzantium and Islam such as the First Hellenic College Conference on Byzantine Studies held on April 11, 1981, in Brookline, Massachusetts; a three-day symposium was held on March 17, 18, and 19, 1985, between scholars of the Muslim and the Orthodox Christian tradition.[76] It was the first time in the American experience that representatives of the two religions met to explore a variety of issues having theological, philosophical, ethical, historical, and cultural interest. The symposium was conducted on a high spiritual and intellectual level and was characterized by standards of historical discernment, academic discipline, and mutual respect. It included topics on the word of God in Islam and the word of God in Orthodox Christianity; the significance of the liturgy as a point of interreligious contact and as a basis for dialogue; spirituality in Orthodox Christianity and Islam; convergence and divergence; and Islam and Orthodox Christianity on bioethics.[77]

In recent years exploratory and probing debates between Eastern Orthodox theologians and Marxist ideologists have been initiated. Such a colloquium was held in Athens between December 13 and 15, 1983. Participants included Greek and Serbian theologians and leading Marxists of Greece. It was conducted in an irenic manner and attracted thousands of listeners.[78] Similar conferences have been held in Belgrade. In regard to communication, the world is becoming smaller, and although there are many human beings, there is only one humanity that needs to be saved. Its survival requires openness, sincerity, mutual respect, tolerance, and dialogue. Religion whose central theme is love for God and the human being must show the way to peace and symbiosis. What is acknowledged from many quarters of Christianity, Judaism, Islam, and other religions and creeds is that as an imperative need it must be put into practice.

THEOLOGICAL CONCERNS OF ORTHODOX THEOLOGIANS IN AMERICA

Where does Orthodox theology go from here? How do Orthodox theologians perceive the future of their church and its theology in the modern world?

Some non-Orthodox theologians and scholars see Orthodox theology as vibrant and appealing. They have expressed high hopes not only for its future but also for the future of Christianity. They discern much strength in Orthodoxy's distrust of centralized church government as well as its fear of chaotic individualism and fragmentation; they admire Orthodoxy's balance between apophatic and cataphatic principles of metaphysics and its emphasis on unity in diversity, on God's presence rather than commandments, on inner experience rather than legalistic requirements, as well as its less exacting view of doctrinal specificity and more emphasis on worship and glorification of the Divine Presence. Sir Stephen Runciman, one of the most authoritative non-Orthodox students of Eastern Orthodox Christianity, its history, theology, and ethos, said recently that "as long as the Orthodox Church is alive, Christianity has a future."[79] One who has studied the history of Eastern Orthodox Christendom will have no difficulty in understanding Runciman's statement.

But are Orthodox theologians in America as optimistic as Runciman? Do they evaluate their theology and their church critically? The preceding pages present a picture of a worldwide faith and trends in Orthodox theology and religious thought. But the Eastern Orthodox Church in America has its own problems and its own views on several issues. Orthodox theologians and religious thinkers of the New World do not necessarily agree with their colleagues in Europe or the Near East. What follows is a series of opinions from Orthodox America.

Recently, I sent a questionnaire to the members of the Orthodox Theological

Society in America, an organization of some seventy-five members. The last question was: "Are you satisfied with trends and prospects in Orthodox theology today? Do you see any need for theological reconsiderations and ecclesiastical reforms?" Twenty theologians (most of them professors in theological schools, universities, and colleges) answered. I recorded their answers as they were conveyed to me, making very few editorial changes, so that the readers of this chapter might discern and study for themselves how their American colleagues perceive their church and its theology. Several preferred to remain anonymous, but I have included the names of those who signed their responses.

A seminary professor observed:

The trends are diversified. They lack focus and clear identity. There *are* trends, however, and mostly positive ones which make up for hopeful prospects. We need more, and more intensive, inter-Orthodox encounters, studies, cooperation, and education. Such encounters will, hopefully, help us to revise our theological-educational curricula, our theological agenda, and problematics. We need more of positive theology and scholarship and less of a peripheral one on methodology or apologetics. On the ecclesiastical level we need to rethink: the whole matter of ministry; ministry of the "lay people"; administrative structure and prerogatives of the ordained people at all levels; revitalization of the ministry of the diaconate; meaningful and renewed monasticism; further steps towards liturgical rejuvenation.

Another college professor wrote:

In response to the first part of this question, I see contemporary Orthodox theology addressing for the most part issues which are very relevant to the Orthodox Church in view of her interface with the world around her, as well as her contacts with other Christian churches. Furthermore, there is a welcome revival of and deeper appreciation for the traditional sources upon which theological trends and prospects within Orthodoxy are based.

As for the second part of the question, I do indeed believe there is need for both theological reconsiderations and ecclesiastical reforms in the sense that what was right for one age in the life of the church is not necessarily right for another. Because of the fact that there is a strong element in the church which recognizes the need for such reconsiderations and reforms, the future Great and Holy Council is being planned. Regardless of whether or not it is actually convened in the near future, its planning stages are forcing the Autocephalous churches to look seriously at the issues under study. What in this regard perplexes me personally is the most total lack of involvement on the part of the laity—and even of the clergy at large—in being made aware of the issues in order to react to them. How else will the traditional importance given to "ecclesiastical conscience" be upheld in determining what the mind of the "laos tou Theou" is regarding the issues under consideration?

James Counelis, an outspoken Orthodox layman and professor of education at the University of San Francisco, responded with extended observations:

I note three trends about which I have great concern. These are the following: (1) the historicist trend in Orthodox theological thinking; (2) the trend of an agnosticism about science in Orthodox theological thought; (3) the siege mentality conservatism of Orthodox Church leaders in the practical interpretation of the church's theology and its relation to the rapidly changing world. The only trend for which I have some high hopes for theological creativity are the interreligious dialogues held by the Orthodox Church since 1945.

Prospects: I believe that the rapidly changing world will impose itself more directly upon the church in the following areas: (1) genetics and matrimony; (2) biomedical technology; (3) societal and environmental problems, for example, (a) population control through birth control techniques, (b) poverty, (c) hunger and disease in the Third World, (d) the politics of human welfare, (e) environmental destruction and pollution.

Theological Reconsideration: I believe that the sacraments of matrimony and holy orders will need to be rethought. Married bishops, postordinational marriages, and women in the clergy all bring into high relief the need for theological reconsideration of these sacraments and the reform of canon law accordingly.

Ecclesial Reform: The following church reforms are long overdue: (1) a transecclesial synod for the systematic settlement of ongoing Orthodox problems in dogma and polity; (2) the resolution of the problems of overlapping plural jurisdictions; (3) the creation of a single church calendar; (4) the reform of the fast; (5) the reform of canon law so that the anthropology of the church directs and informs all aspects of ecclesial polity, especially the bringing of accountability to episcopal behavior; (6) the conformity of the priestly and prophetic office to Pentecost through the use of the contemporary languages of the people in scriptural readings and liturgy.

John Erickson of St. Vladimir's wrote: "I am not very satisfied with the 'trends'—if any can be discerned—and I am not very encouraged by the 'prospects.' Basically, I believe that Orthodox theology, if it continues its present course, will become increasingly fragmented, though with some tendency to polarization, with the self-styled 'true Orthodox' on one side and those prying to catch up with the world on the other."

"No, I am not satisfied," commented Father Theodore Stylianopoulos of Holy Cross/Hellenic College,

not only because of its limited depth and results but also because theology seems to be formal and self-contained and the ivory tower type, not effecting the leadership and the practice of the church. The prospects will not change without adequate leadership and a tradition of effective theological education of high standards.

I see many needs of theological reconsideration and reforms beginning with a sobering critique of Orthodox triumphalism and formalism. Then the whole issue of power, decision making, the election of bishops, and nature of leadership (is it according to the teaching of Jesus in terms of love and service, or something else in terms of personal aggrandizement, control, and lording it over others in honors and authority?)—leadership is crucial. Beyond this the true mission of the church is to teach people how to pray, to live Christian lives, to worship, and to understand the issues and world around them in positive terms. Only then can the church provide a convincing witness to outsiders and society in general.

Stephen Upson, a veteran classical scholar, theologian, and pastor, wrote:

The church needs to change the rules on clerical marriage. Clergy should be allowed to marry after ordination, to remarry when widowed. The ancient practice of married bishops would be beneficial. Widows of clergy should be allowed to remarry without stigma.

Minor ecclesiastical disciplines need to be changed in accordance with modern knowledge and ideas and expectations. We no longer live in the fourth century; the Byzantine Empire is dead also. Careful attention to liturgical reform is necessary, to avoid the chaos recently introduced in Rome and some Liturgical Protestant churches and at the same time make life easier for people who have to live in our civilization.

In America, the use of the Western Easter date is important. The date has never been the same anywhere, anytime, and doesn't need to be a source of contention. If Christians believe Christ is Risen, that's what is important theologically. In spite of the Old Calendarists, we manage to get along well with the new. An Orthodox aggiorniamento is necessary.

George Papademetriou, director of the library at Holy Cross/Hellenic College, concluded briefly: "I would like to see a greater unity among Orthodox to better organize missions in the Third World, in America, and to defend the faith against the atheism of modern Europe and Asia. The challenge today is the Communist propaganda and oriental religious philosophies. The church must respond with vigor to present the truth with all its might. This can be done when it is one in faith and jurisdiction."

Constantine Cavarnos of the Institute for Byzantine and Modern Greek Studies sees "no need for *theological re*considerations." Such reconsiderations, he wrote, would imply that we Orthodox do not possess the truth but are in search of it. They lead to, and encourage, skepticism and relativism, alien to authentic Orthodoxy. As for "ecclesiastical reforms," some are very much needed: for example, revival of confession; abiding by the holy canon of the church instead of disregarding and even despising them; the *de*secularization of the church, of Christian life; an emphasis of the inner, spiritual life, on *all* those time-tested practices that constitute what the Fathers call "askesis."

John Breck of St. Vladimir's Seminary has a "limited sense of satisfaction." The problems surrounding the "great council," he wrote, "coupled with the persistant ethnicism and isolation of our Orthodox people in the West, show clearly how very far we have to go to 'be the Church' in the new lands/societies/cultures to which God has called us over the last few decades." As for the last question: definitely yes, particularly in terms of the points mentioned above. Father John Meyendorff, the dean of St. Vladimir's, commented that someone has said:

"We are the right faith, which is held by the wrong people." It is remarkable that in spite of our human weaknesses, the witness of Orthodox theology does appear as extremely powerful to many—a sign of Divine faithfulness to the church. Of course, theology is always to be 'reconsidered' as cultures and civilizations change, but without *consistency* with the Scriptured and patristic tradition, there is no Orthodoxy. In terms of ecclesiastical reforms, I wish we could think of a world center—that is the ecumenical patriarchate—which would be institutionally and spiritually able to fulfill a minority of coordination, with enough imagination and initiative to face the real problems of the day.

An anonymous theologian responded as follows:

I think that we are not in step with what we preach. We need to help one another with intellectual and spiritual honesty in our work and life—as theologians and priests. Much work is to be done organizationally and theologically to facilitate the environment for *approaching* the formal theological task. My experience is that the trends in theology in general reflect the letter of the law—"a dear thing," or the confusion of Legion—going everywhere and saying much but being finally without identity. I think that we need to practice simultaneously our *faith* and love of Christ and put the best of our mental energies together—so that we can see the real issues—and then approach them.

But a bishop was more optimistic. He added: "There is an ongoing and quite natural evolution transpiring, emanating from the desire of the church to reach outward, which compels us constantly to reassess and reapply the immutable to a mutable world—always projecting the same Divine Being and spirit—but through different symbols."

Father Stanley Harakas of Holy Cross/Hellenic College regretted "the wholesale adoption . . . of existentialist philosophical approaches" by some Orthodox theologians and religious thinkers. He finds this "a dangerous and false understanding of the faith." For him, "core Orthodoxy" is not existential philosophy—but the saving message of the gospel, the affirmations of the creed, the new life in Christ as found in Bible, the Fathers, the canons. He added that "rethinking is absolutely necessary." One of the major issues facing Orthodoxy is "spiritual renewal—a movement away from a stance inspired by a survival mentality to a vigorous identity with 'core Christianity.' "

An anonymous member of the Orthodox Theological Society saw the need for reforms: renewal of Conciliarity to *balance* centralized/hierarchical structure of the church in the United States, at *parish* and *diocesan* levels as well as national and international levels. With respect to prospects, he added: "We need more talented/trained minds *thinking* and *writing* about issues that affect the life of the Church *today* in America."

Deno Geanakoplos of Yale University is "satisfied that the Church is firm in its theology." But, he added, "it has to make its stands much clearer to Orthodox youth on the moral teachings of theology." He sees the need for "substantial reforms" especially because of the "born again" pentecostal movements, formed in the Roman church and others.

Charles Ashanin of the Christian Theological Seminary of Indianapolis wrote that he is not satisfied with modern trends in Orthodox theology. "There is a great—a very great need for updating not so much the dogmas of the church but for making them livable, relevant and creative," he added. "Ecclesiastical reform and Orthodoxy needs this if the way can be found to introduce such reforms in the life of the Orthodox Church especially here in the United States." In his opinion, "the most important theological-philosophical issues are those which belong to the realm of ethics."

Gregory Wingenbach, director of the Department of Church and Family Life, Greek Orthodox Archdiocese, responded with extensive comments on every question: "In answer to the first part of the question, yes and no." He explained:

Part of the "legalistic scholastic" spirit that is cropping up disturbingly . . . is the tendency of some hierarchs and theologians (including ecumenical representatives) to rigidify our church's usually *pro tem* stands into becoming "The Tradition and Canons of the Church"—as witness certain Greek, Romanian and other theologians' stance that Orthodoxy must, "as of old," refuse even conditional recognition to the sacramental acts and ecclesial identity—in any way, shape, or form—of other Christian communions. They apparently wish to make of Cyprian, on the one hand, and of the so-called Russian Exile Synodal jurisdiction, on the other hand, the essential definers of church canon and response. All of this is contrary to the essential witness of Fathers such as Basil of Caesarea, Dionysios of Alexandria, Optatos of Numidia, and numerous key church councils, regional and ecumenical. Roman Catholics, including very recently Father Jean Tillard, are now citing this stance as effectively and essentially Orthodoxy's view and response. In regard to the second question, the early pre-Synodal conferences did a pretty good job of identifying them. I would only add the basic relationship of the four essential orders of the church: bishop (and synods), presbyters, the diaconate (which seems to call for redefinition, renewal, and even "experimentation" in application), and the Laos/ laity. Perhaps also a reexamination of the forms and mission of the Monastic/religious life, as we know it historically and today. Lastly, in regard to all, regardless of the misgivings, the church must soon—very soon—move forward with the fate and status of the holy Ecumenical Patriarchate, or a reexamination thereof, and with the summoning of a pan-Orthodox Synod which will convene a reunited family of so-called Eastern and Oriental Orthodox churches alike. It is true we must adequately prepare for such, but if we truly believe in the Eucharist and Pentecost, ultimately, we must place ourselves and one another in the hands of God's own supreme Will and the moving of the Holy Spirit. There is too much fear (*fovos*) and not enough hope (*elpida*) in today's Orthodoxy.

Another anonymous theologian sees progress in the fact that Orthodox newspapers no longer resort to triumphalisms. This person sees the need to avoid making the church a "Confession" and recommends an ironing out of the doctrinal differences with non-Chalcedonians, namely, Nestorians and Monophysites, Copts and Armenians.

Serge Verhovskoy, professor emeritus at St. Vladimir's, observed that Orthodox theology must pay much more attention to the Holy Scripture and all the ethical problems. . . . The liturgical theology could be more concerned with the theological content of our services. The understanding of Christian art is, I think, too much enslaved to the Byzantine tradition only.

Orthodox theology could pay more attention to the problems which were not yet solved before. But certainly the Bible and Holy Tradition must remain the true foundation of our theology.

If our people and leaders would be more firmly pursuing the basic ideas of the Orthodox Church about the church herself and Christian life we would need only very minor reforms.

EPILOGUE

Eastern Orthodox religious thought today manifests a considerable pluralism. The boundaries of Orthodoxy are broad enough to allow freedom of movement. Nevertheless, it reiterates the validity of Christian truths as they are stated in the Scriptures, accepted, defined, and lived by the Christian community in history. Theological issues should be seen in the light of faith and life. It is cautious in making changes and less worried about the secular world that surrounds it. Although it insists on preserving the content of the faith, it has no difficulty in seeking new forms. Maintaining a balance between antiquity and modernity and preserving a historical theological consciousness is of absolute importance to the Orthodox. They are skeptical of reductionisms and relativisms, and they insist on a loyalty to the experience of the church in history. Loyalty to tradition is not static but dynamic in the sense that it permits dialogue and renewal. Orthodox theology is committed to preserving the theology of undivided Christianity and indeed its identity but also to sharing its convictions and its perceptions with other Christian creeds and religious beliefs.

NOTES

1. For Constantine-Cyril's definition see Francis Dvornik, *Byzantine Missions among the Slavs* (New Brunswick, N.J.: Rutgers Univ. Press, 1970), pp. 60-61. For an excellent discussion of philosophy–theology in Greek patristic and medieval Greek thought, see B. N. Tatakis, *E Byzantine Philosophia* (Athens: 1977), a revised Greek translation of the author's *La Philosophie Byzantine,* 2d ed. (Paris: Presses Universitaires de France 1959). For a more specialized treatment of theology and its relationship to philosophy in the teachings of the early Greek Fathers up to and including the Cappadocians, see Konstantinos B. Skouteris, *E Ennoia ton oron 'theologia,' 'theologein' 'theologos' en te didaskalia ton Ellenon Pateron kai Ekklesiastikon Syngrafeon* (Athens: 1972), especially pp. 167–174.

2. Ecumenical Patriarchate, *I Proti Panorthodoxos Diaskepsis* (Istanbul, 1967), pp. 130–140. Cited by Constantin G. Patelos, ed., *The Orthodox Church in the Ecumenical Movement* (Geneva: World Council of Churches, 1978), p. 71.

3. An excellent mirror of these trends in Eastern Orthodox religious thought is John D. Zizioulas, *Being as Communion* (New York: St. Vladimir's Press, 1985); N. Nissiotis,

"La théologie de l'Église et sa réalisation," in Savas C. Agourides, ed., *Procès-Verbaux du Deuxème congrès de Théologie Orthodoxe* (Athens: 1978), pp. 61–78.

4. Hamilcar Alivisatos, "Discours d'Ouverture du Président du Congrès" in *Procès-Verbaux du Premier Congrès de Théologie Orthodoxe* ed. H. Alivisatos (Athens: 1939), pp. 42–54, especially pp. 49–54. Savas Agouridis, "Proclamation des travaux du Congrès par la Présidium du Congrès," in Nissiotis, *Procès-Verbaux du Deuxième Congrès de Théologie Orthodoxe,* pp. 44–56, especially pp. 45–47.

5. Nikos A. Nissiotis, "The Importance of the Doctrine of the Trinity for Church Life and Theology," in A. J. Philippou, ed., *The Orthodox Ethos* (Oxford: Holywell Press, 1964), pp. 32–69, especially pp. 34–37; Theo. Stylianopoulos, "Christ, Church and Eucharist," *Diakonia,* 18, no. 2 (1983): 100–127, especially 100–106.

6. Philemo, *Fragments,* no. 26 in A. Meineke, ed., *Fragmenta Comicorum Graecorum* (Berlin, 1848), p. 847.

7. John Damascene, *Exposition of the Orthodox Faith,* 1, 4, ed. K. G. Frantzolas, *Ioannou tou Damaskenou Apanta ta Erga,* vol. 1 (Thessaloniki, Paterikai Ekdoseis, 1976), p. 68.

8. Gregory Nazianzenos, Homily 45, ch. 4, ed. J. P. Migne, *Patrologiae Graecae,* vol. 33, col. 628C; Homily 40, ch. 41, ed. J. P. Migne, *Patrologiae Graecae,* vol. 36, col. 417BC.

9. Nissiotis, "Importance of the Doctrine," pp. 40–45.

10. Dionysios the Areopagite, "On the Divine Names," ed. J. P. Migne, *Patrologia Graecae*, vol. 4, col. 328–329, also col. 180AB; John Parker, *The Celestial and Ecclesistrical Hierarchy of Dionysius the Areopagite* (London: Skeffington 1894), pp. 15–16.

11. John Meyendorff, "The Holy Trinity in Palamite Theology," in Michael A. Fahey and John Meyendorff, *Trinitarian Theology East and West* (Brookline, Mass.: Holy Cross Press, 1979), p. 38.

12. See Dionysios the Areopagite, "On the Divine Names," ed. J. P. Migne, *Patrologia Graecae,* vol. 4, col. 372AB; see Dom Denys Rutledge, *Cosmic Theology* (London, 1964), p. 10.

13. See Demetrios Trakatellis, "E Theologia mas Chthes kai Avrion," in Zoe, Brotherhood of Theologians, ed., *Theologia: Aletheia kai Zoe* (Athens: Routledge and Kegan Paul, 1962), pp. 229–232.

14. See Christos Yannaras, "The Distinction between Essence and Energies and Its Importance for Theology," *St. Vladimir's Theological Quarterly* 19, no. 4 (1975): 244.

15. Meyendorff, "The Holy Trinity," p. 30.

16. Ibid., p. 34.

17. Irenaeos, *Against Heresies,* Book 4, ch. 38, ed. Apostolike Diakonia in *Bibliotheke Hellenon Pateron,* vol. 5 (Athens, 1955), p. 157.

18. Athanasios, *Against the Arians,* Book I, ch. 39, ed. Apostolike Diakonia in *Bibliotheke Hellenon Pateron,* vol. 30 (Athens, 1962), pp. 154–155.

19. Meyendorff, "The Holy Trinity," p. 42.

20. See John S. Romanides, "Critical Examination of the Applications of Theology," in Agourides, *Procès-Verbaux du Deuxième Congrès de Théologie Orthodoxe,* pp. 413–441, especially pp. 432–434.

21. Nissiotis, "The Importance of the Doctrine of the Trinity" pp. 40–43; J. Meyendorff, "The Holy Spirit, as God," in D. Kirkpatrick, ed. *The Holy Spirit* (Nashville: Abingdon Press, 1974), pp. 76–89. P. N. Trempelas, *Dogmatike tes Orthodoxou Katholikes Ekklesias,* 3 vols. (Athens: 1959–1961), 1:257–268.

22. Nissiotis, "The Importance of the Doctrine of the Trinity," pp. 41–42.

23. Ibid., pp. 44–45; P. K. Chrestou, *To Mysterio tou Anthropou* (Thessalonike: 1983), pp. 13–20.

24. Irenaeos, *Against Heresies*, chap. 5, para. 5, ed. Apostolike Diakonia, p. 104; see J. Meyendorff, "Orthodox Theology Today," *Sobornost* 6, no. 1 (1970): 17.

25. Meyendorff, "Orthodox Theology Today," p. 17.

26. Theophilos of Antioch, *Pros Autolykon,* Bk. 2, ch. 27, ed. Apostolike Diakonia in the series *Bibliotheke Hellenon Pateron,* vol. 5 (Athens, 1955), p. 39; Clement of Alexandria, "Stromateis," Bk. 5, chap. 10 in *Bibliotheke Hellenon Pateron,* vol. 8 (Athens, 1956), p. 138; Hippolytos, Kata Pason Aireseon Elenhos," Bk. 10, chap. 4, ibid., vol. 5 (Athens, 1955), p. 377.

27. Meyendorff, "The Holy Spirit, as God," 158–160; idem, *Byzantine Theology* (N.Y.: Fordham Univ. Press, 1974), pp. 163–165.

28. Chrestou, *To Mysterio tou Anthropou,* pp. 73–75; G. I. Mantzarides, *Methexis Theou* (Thessalonike: 1979), pp. 242–245; Panteleemon, Metropolitan of Corinth, "Theosis," *Christianikon Symposion* (Athens: 1967), pp. 54–59; A. Theodorou, *E peri theoseos tou anthropou didaskalia ton Ellenon Pateron tes Ekklesias* (Athens: 1956); Elias Moutsoulus, *E Sarkosis tou Logou kai e theosis tou anthropou* (Athens: 1965); R. G. Stephanopoulos, "The Orthodox Doctrine of Theosis," in J. Meyendorff and J. McLelland, eds., *The New Man: An Orthodox and Reformed Dialogue* (New Brunswick, N.J.: 1973), pp. 149–161; G. Patronos, "E Theosis tou anthropou ypo to fos ton eschatologikon antilepseon tes Orthodoxou theologias" *Theologia* 51 (1980): 348–378, 493–514, 800–832 and 52 (1981): 141–162, 286–318; Panayotis I. Bratsiotis, "E Peri Theoseos tou Anthropou Didaskalia ton Ellenon Pateron tes Ekklesias," *Theologia* 42, nos 1–4 (1971): 30–42.

29. Here are some leading studies on ethics and social thought in Orthodox Christianity. All include detailed bibliographies. B. Ch. Ioannides, *To Evangelion kai to Koinonikon Problema* (Thessalonike, 1950), P. Ch. Demetropoulos, *E Pistis tes Archaias Ekklesias os Kanon Zoes kai o Kosmos* (Athens: 1959); G. I. Mantzarides, *E Christianike Koinonia kai o Kosmos* (Thessalonike: 1967); N. Th. Mpougatsos, *Koinonike Didaskalia Ellenon Pateron,* 2 vols. (Athens, 1980); P. Ch. Demetropoulos, *Christianike Koinoniologia* (Athens, 1984); Antonie Plămădeală, *Biserica Slujitoare* (Bucuresti, 1972). Works in English include Demetrios J. Constantelos, *Byzantine Philanthropy and Social Welfare* (New Brunswick, N.J.: Rutgers University Press, 1968; 2d ed., New York, 1989); idem, *Poverty, Society, and Philanthropy in the Late Medieval Greek World* (New York, 1989). More from a theological perspective are the works of Stanley S. Harakas, *Toward Transfigured Life* (Minneapolis, Minn., 1983); idem, *Let Mercy Abound* (Brookline, Mass., 1983). Several important articles have been published in the past twenty-five years including Jerome Kotsonis, "Fundamental Principles of Orthodox Morality" in Philippou, *The Orthodox Ethos,* pp. 229–248; Savas Agourides, "The Social Character of Orthodoxy," in Philippou, *The Orthodox Ethos,* pp. 209–220; N. A. Nissiotis, "Church and Society in Greek Orthodox Theology," in John C. Bennett, ed., *Christian Social Ethics in a Changing World* (New York, 1966), pp. 78–104; G. Florovsky, "The Social Problem in the Eastern Orthodox Church," *The Journal of Religious Thought* 8, no. 1 (1950–1951): 41–51. Revelant also is the World Council of Churches, ed., *The Orthodox Approach to Diaconia* (Geneva, 1980).

30. See Harakas, *Toward Transfigured Life,* pp. 1–4. Harakas is a pioneer in Christian

Orthodox social ethics in the English-speaking world. In addition to writing the books cited above, he has written several relevant studies.

31. Maximos the Confessor, "Kefalaia peri agapes," first century, paras. 23–28, ed. J. P. Migne, *Patrologiae Graecae*, vol. 90, col. 965AC; Photios, "Logos 33," ch. 8, in S. Aristarches, ed. *Photiou Logoi kai Homiliai* (Constantinople: 1900), 1:227. What follows on the social theological thought of Eastern Orthodox Christianity is a slightly revised version of an article that first appeared in Francis D. Costa, S.S.S., ed., *God and Charity* (Brookline, Mass.: 1979).

32. John 13:34; see John 15:12.

33. George Scholarios, "Peri Eleemosynes," in L. Petit, X. A. Siderides, and Martin Jugie, eds, *Oeuvres Complètes de Georges Scholarios* 1:100 (Paris: 1928).

34. Irenaios, *Against Heresies*, Fragment 65, ed. Apostolike Diakonia, p. 157; and Athanasios, *Against the Arians*, Bk. 1, chap. 39, ed. Apostolike Diakonia, pp. 154–155.

35. Luke 4:18.

36. John 3:16.

37. Gregory Nazianzenos, "Logos 14," chap. 14, ed. J. P. Migne, *Patrologiae Graecae*, vol. 35, col. 876AB.

38. Nicholas Kabasilas, *Eis ten Theian Leitourgian*, chap. 17, para 4, ed. S. Salaville; 2d ed. R. Bornert et al., *Sources Chrétiennes* (Paris: 1967), p. 134.

39. George Scholarios, "Peri ton kat'Areten Ergon," in Petit, Siderides, and Jugie, *Oeuvres Complètes*, 3:419–420.

40. Galatians 5:6.

41. John Chrysostom, "Postremo de Lazaro mendico ac de Divite," *Patrologia Graecae*, vol. 48, col. 1029.

42. See Constantelos, *Byzantine Philanthropy and Social Welfare*, pp. 18–28, 88–110.

43. Matthew 26:26–29; John 6:32–59; 1 Corinthians 11:20–34.

44. John of Damascus, *Exposition of the Orthodox Faith*, Bk. 4, ch. 86, ed. Frantzolas, pp. 460–462.

45. See Constantelos, *Byzantine Philanthropy*, pp. 74–75, 154–155; see also idem, "Life and Social Welfare Activity of Patriarch Athanasios I . . . of Constantinople," *Theologia* 46 (1975): 611–625. For Theoleptos, see idem, "Mysticism and Social Involvement in the Late Byzantine Church . . . ," *Byzantine Studies* 6, nos. 1–2 (1979): 83–94.

46. Gregory Palamas, *Logoi Apodeiktikoi Dyo-Logos Deuteros*, 78, ed. P. K. Christou et al., 1:149.

47. Photios, "Homily 2.3," in B. Laourdas ed., *Photiou Homiliai* (Thessalonike: 1959), p. 15.

48. Irenaios, *Fragments*, no. 10, ed. Apostolike Diakonia, p. 175.

49. Photios, "Homily 2.4," in Laourdas, *Photiou Homiliai*, p. 17.

50. Nicholas Kabasilas, *Peri tes en Christo Zoes*, in W. Gass, ed., *Die Mystik des Nikolaus Cabasilas vom Leben in Christo*, pp. 153–156, 160–162, 165–167.

51. I Corinthians 5:5.

52. See Mantzarides, *Methexis Theou*, pp. 11–129.

53. See Nikos A. Nissiotis, "Our History: A Limitation or Creative Power?" in A. J. Philippou, ed., *Orthodoxy: Life and Freedom* (Oxford: 1973), pp. 59–72, especially p. 68.

54. John Mavropous, "Poems" no. 43, in P. de Lagarde, ed., *Iohannis Euchaitorum metropolitae quae in codice vaticano graeca 676 supersunt* (Göttingen: 1881).

55. Trempelas, *Dogmatike,* 3: 364–515.

56. Nissiotis, "The Importance of the Doctrine of the Trinity," pp. 65–69; Meyendorff, *Byzantine Theology,* pp. 218–223.

57. Paul Evdokimov, "Eschatological Transcendence," in A. J. Philippou, ed., *Orthodoxy: Life and Freedom* (Oxford: 1973), pp. 31–47, especially pp. 31–38; Nissiotis, "Our History: A Limitation or Creative Power?" pp. 59–72; idem, "The Importance of the Doctrine of the Trinity," pp. 65–69.

58. Theodorou, *E Peri Theoseos tou Anthropou Didaskalia,* pp. 171–178; see also Moutsoulas, *E Sarkosis tou Logou Kai e theosis tou Anthropou,* pp. 219–220; Ioannis N. Karmiris, *E Pankosmiotis tes en Christo Soterias* (Athens: 1981), pp. 78–83.

59. For an incisive analysis of these issues, see Stanley S. Harakas, *Something is Stirring in World Orthodoxy* (Minneapolis: 1978); see also Aimilianos Timiadis, *Themata en opsi tes Synodou,* vol. 1 (Athens: 1968).

60. See the draft of N. Nissiotis and C. Andronikoff in Agourides, *Procès-Verbaux du Deuxième Congrès de Théologie Orthodoxe 'A Athènes,* pp. 60–61. The general introduction on the subject of the Congress of Nissiotis is especially recommended. It not only set the tone of the whole conference but it also expressed the dynamics as well as the problems of contemporary Orthodox theology and religious thought. For a brief evaluation of problems facing Orthodox theology today, see P. J. Delicostopoulos, "A Brief Evaluation of Problems concerning Contemporary Orthodox Theology," in John E. Anastasio, ed., *Epistemonike Epeteris,* (Thessalonike: 1974), 19:163–173.

61. For official statements and documents pertaining to the Orthodox Church's concern with interreligious dialogues, see Constantin G. Patelos, ed., *The Orthodox Church in the Ecumenical Movement: Documents and Statements, 1902–1975* (Geneva: 1978). For a balanced evaluation of Orthodoxy and the Ecumenical movement, see E. D. Theodorou, *Orthodoxia kai Oikoumenike Kinesis* (Athens: 1973).

62. The proceedings of all three conferences have been published in the *Greek Orthodox Theological Review* 10 (1964–1965), 13 (1968), and 16 (1971). See also I. N. Karmiris, *Eisegeseis enopion ton diaskepseon Orthodoxon kai antichalkedonion theologon* (Athens: 1970).

63. For a comprehensive and authoritative survey of Eastern Orthodox-Old Catholics relations, see Ioannes Karmiris, "Homilia peri tes anelixeos tou Orthodou Palaiokatholikou Theologikou Dialogou," *Theologia* 46, no. 1 (1975): 23–40; *Episkepsis,* no. 173 (1977): 10–15; no. 215 (1979): 12–15; no. 259 (1981): 10–16; *Journal of Moscow Patriarchate,* no. 3 (1978): 58–62; no. 4 (1980): 46–48; no. 6 (1982): 10–15.

64. For a precise and fully documented survey of these relations, see Michael A. Fahey, S. J., "Current Theology: Orthodox Ecumenism and Theology: 1970–1978 . . . ," *Theological Studies* 39, no. 3 (1978): 455–460; 44 (1983): 644–654.

65. For Anglican-Orthodox relations, see Methodios Fouyas, *Anglicanism-Orthodoxy-Roman Catholicism* (Brookline, Mass.: Holy Cross Press, 1984), especially pp. 35–50, 64–68, 85–88. See also V. Istavridis, *Orthodoxia kai Anglicanismos* (Athens: 1963).

66. For brief but comprehensive surveys, see Fahey, "Current Theology," pp. 654–660.

67. World Council of Churches, ed., *The Orthodox Church and the Churches of the Reformation: A Survey of Orthodox-Protestant Dialogues,* Faith and Order Paper no. 76

(Geneva: 1975). For complete bibliography see Fahey, "Current Theology," pp. 656–659.

68. *Episkepsis*, no. 247 (1981): 7–15; T. F. Torrance "World Alliance of Reformed Churches; Official WARC Delegation to the Ecumenical Patriarchate," *Ekklesia Kai Theologia*, no. 1 (1980): 197–211. For Orthodox-Reformed dialogues in America held in 1968 and 1970, see Meyendorff and McLellard, *The New Man*.

69. H. Alivizatos, "The Need for the Revision of Liturgical Texts" (in Greek), *Orthodoxos Skepsis* (1960); idem, "Religion and Nation" (in Greek), *Gregorios o Palamas* 46 (1963): 7–21.

70. P. Simotas, "Ioudaismos kai Ellenike Orthodoxia," *Theologia* 42, nos. 1–4 (1971): 354–366, especially 357–358; George C. Papademetriou, "Judaism and Greek Orthodoxy in Historical Perspective," *The Greek Orthodox Theological Review* 21, no. 2 (1976): 93–113.

71. Elias Venezis, *Archiepiskopos Damaskenos*. Athens: Editions Alpha, 1952, pp. 259–265.

72. F. Nicholas, "The Greek-Jewish Connection," *Weekly Review* 2, no. 51 (1985): 12–14; Elias Venezis, *Archiepiskopos Damaskenos* (Athens: Editions Alpha, 1952), pp. 259–270, esp. 263–264.

73. See the special issues: *Journal of Ecumenical Studies* 13 (1976): 517–672; *The Greek Orthodox Theological Review* 22, no. 1, (1977).

74. For a brief account see Timothy Ware, *The Orthodox Church* (Baltimore: 1963), pp. 96–102; see also Robert M. Haddad, *Syrian Christians in Muslim Society* (Princeton, 1970).

75. Asterios Argyriou, "Coran et Histoire," *Theologia* 54, nos. 2–4 (1983): 250–301, 542–567, 696–710; 55, no. 13 (1984): 192–214, 665–704. Relevant for an Orthodox Christian-Muslim dialogue are the studies of Daniel Sahas, *John of Damascus on Islam* (Leiden: 1972); idem, "The Formation of Later Islamic Doctrines as a Response to Byzantine Polemics: The Miracles of Muhammad," *The Greek Orthodox Theological Review* 27 (1982): 307–324; idem, "Gregory Palamas (1296–1360) on Islam," *The Muslim World* 73, no. 1 (1983): 1–21; idem, "Captivity and Dialogue: Gregory Palamas . . . and the Muslims," *The Greek Orthodox Theological Review* 25 (1981): 409–436.

76. The papers of the Massachusetts conference were published in *The Greek Orthodox Theological Review* 27, nos. 2–3 (1982).

77. The proceedings were published in *The Greek Orthodox Theological Review*, vol. 31, nos. 1–2 (1986).

78. See *Orthodoxia kai Marxismos* (Athens: Akritas, 1984).

79. As cited by Fouyas, *Anglicanism-Orthodoxy-Roman Catholicism*, p. viii; see Fahey, "Current Theology," p. 465.

SELECTED BIBLIOGRAPHY

In addition to the works cited in the footnotes, the following collective works and special issues of theological periodicals are recommended. For bibliographical surveys see P. N. Bratsiotis, *E Ellenike Theologia kata ten teleftaian pentekontaetian* (Athens, 1948); J. N. Karmiris, *E Ellenike Theologike Bibliographia tes teleutaias dekaetias* (Istanbul, 1957); and V. Th. Istavridis, *E Orthodoxos Ellenike Bibliographia epi tes oikoumenikes kineseos* (Athens, 1960). The distinguished quarterly *Theologia* of Athens publishes frequently current bibliographies on various aspects of theological and religious studies. An excellent survey of Orthodox theology from 1970 to 1983, with insightful comments and nearly thorough bibliographical awareness, is Michael A. Fahey, S. J., "Current Theology: Orthodox Ecumenism and Theology: 1970–1978 . . . , 1978–1983," *Theological Studies* 39, no. 3 (1978): 446–485; 44 (1983): 625–692. See also V. Th. Istavridis's review in *Theologia* 56, no. 1 (1985): 240–243. The entries that follow are not meant to be bibliographically exhaustive but are representative.

Agourides, Savas C., ed. *Procès-Verbaux du Deuxième Congrès de Théologie Orthodoxe*. Athens: Ekdosis Hieras Mones Penteles, 1978.

———— *Paradosis-Ananeosis*. Athens: 1972.

Alivisatos, Hamilcar S., ed. *Procès-Verbaux du Premier Congrès de Théologie Orthodoxe*. Athens: Pyrsos, 1939.

Allchin, A. M., ed. *Sacrament and Image*. London: The Fellowship of S. Alban and S. Sergius, 1967.

Allen, Joseph J., ed. *Orthodox Synthesis*. New York: St. Vladimir's Seminary Press, 1981.

Centre Orthodoxe du Patriarcat Oecumenique, ed. *La Theologie dans l'Eglise et dans le Monde*. Geneva, 1984.

Constlantelos, Demetrios J., ed. *Orthodox Theology and Diakonia* (Brookline, Mass.: Hellenic College Press 1981).

The Greek Orthodox Theological Review 10, no. 2 (Winter 1964–1965). The Aarhus meeting between Eastern Orthodox and Oriental Orthodox theologians.

———— 13, no. 2 (1968). The Bristol Consultation between Eastern Orthodox and Oriental Orthodox theologians.

———— 15, no. 1 (1970). On the authority of tradition.

———— 16, nos. 1–2 (1971). The Geneva and the Addis Ababa consultations between Eastern Orthodox and Oriental Orthodox theologians.

———— 17, no. 1 (1972). The papers of the First International Theological Conference of Orthodox Theologians in America.

———— 24, nos. 2–3 (1979). The papers of the Third International Theological Conference of Orthodox Theologians in America.

Philippou, A. J., ed. *The Orthodox Ethos*. Oxford, 1964.

————. *Orthodoxy: Life and Freedom*. Oxford, 1973.

St. Vladimir's Theologican Quarterly 13, nos. 1–2 (1969). A symposium on Orthodox theology today.

———— 17, nos. 1–2 (1973). The papers of the Second International Conference of Orthodox Theology.

Zoe, Adelphotes Theologon, ed. *Theologia: Aletheia kai Zoe*. Athens, 1962.

17

Christianity and Judaism

PAUL VAN BUREN

To do justice to the conversations that have been going on between Christians and Jews in the last third of the twentieth century, it is necessary to approach this subject in its own terms rather than those given by the structure of this volume. That structure might mislead the reader in three ways. First, it might mislead one into thinking that these conversations either arose or have taken place under some general understanding that the participants were united under a broad category called "Abrahamic." That abstraction has played no part in the history or in the present stage of these conversations.

The second possible mistake would be to suppose that Christianity and Judaism were in conversation, whatever that might mean. No such abstractions are involved. The conversations have taken place between some Christians and some Jews. Finally, only some of the conversations could properly be called *dialogue,* if by that term is meant a serious effort on both sides to listen to and understand the other in the other's terms. Much of the conversation has been of a lesser order than that, although on rare occasions it has gone well beyond dialogue.

The participants in these conversations, however, have been more than individuals who happen to be Christians or Jews. They have entered into these discussions, generally, as members of their own communities. In the broadest and most basic terms, therefore, the conversations have involved the meeting of the church (or churches) and the Jewish people, for such are the terms each side prefers to use to refer to itself. What follows, then, is a report on and an assessment of the present status of the conversation that has been developing, mostly since the mid-1960s, between the church and the Jewish people and an analysis of the principal difficulties and problems not yet addressed, much less resolved.

BACKGROUND AND BEGINNINGS

The conversation between the church and the Jewish people that is often referred to as the Jewish-Christian Dialogue is a phenomenon of the period coming after both the Holocaust (see Glossary for definitions of special terms) and the founding of the state of Israel. During the earlier years of the twentieth century, rare individuals anticipated what was to come. On the Jewish side, Franz Rosenzwieg's *Der Stern der Erlosung* (1921) and, from the Christian side, Leonard Ragaz's *Judentum und Christentum* (1922) stand out as radically new affirmations of the other, when viewed against the background of the long history of mutual hostility and depreciation, a mutuality to be qualified by the observation that the church, as the party in power, saw to it that the Jewish people were the recipients of the painful and frequently mortal consequences of this antagonism.

The Anglican historian James Parkes was another noteworthy forerunner of what was to come, breaking with deeply established historical prejudices to begin a fresh investigation of the origins of Christian anti-Judaism in his *Conflict of the Church and the Synagogue* (1934), and continuing an investigation of the consequences in *The Jew in the Medieval Community* (1938) and in many other writings. Other notable exceptions could be named, but the generalization may be ventured that the Christian church viewed the Jewish people as God's *former* people, who had sacrificed their special relationship to God by having rejected Christ, their place in God's plan and favor now having been taken by the church as the "New Israel." The Jewish response was to see the church as Edom, the enemy of Isaac, only questionably monotheistic and worshipping a man as if he were God.

The first major sign of a change in the relationship between the church and the Jewish people was the statement of the Second Vatican Council (*Nostra Aetate,* no. 4) in 1965 on the Jewish people, rejecting the charge of "Deicide" and the teaching that the Jewish people had been rejected by God. The statement may be judged mild, even timid, when measured by later developments, but when seen against the background of the church's anti-Judaic tradition, it represents a rupture with the past.

The Vatican statement did not come without much preliminary work, in Protestant as well as in Catholic circles, stimulated primarily by the shock of the Holocaust and a slowly growing awareness that anti-Semitism in its modern secular form had its roots in centuries of Christian anti-Jewish teaching and practice. The World Council of Churches at its first assembly in 1948 had been able to assert that "Anti-Semitism is sin against God and man," but it reasserted the traditional position that Israel's Messiah had come and that the church was duty-bound to preach its gospel to the Jews. A statement of the Faith and Order Commission of the World Council of Churches in 1967, however, was able to acknowledge that whereas some held to this view, others saw the Jewish people as God's Israel and rejected attempts to convert Jews to Christianity. During the following twenty years, official statements of many church bodies, both Protestant and Catholic, American as well as European, built on these beginnings and went on to assert the continuing validity of the Covenant between God and the Jewish people to this day and even to confess (Declaration of the Rhineland Synod of the Evangelical Church in Germany, 1980) that the church's election is to this day dependent on that of the Jewish people.

Many of these statements speak of the Holocaust and the birth and existence of the state of Israel as the two facts that have impelled a reappraisal of Christian attitudes toward and understanding of the Jewish people. Those events may properly be seen, therefore, as marking a major turning point, spiritually as well as chronologically, in both Judaism and Christianity. They have initiated a rapprochement between the church and the Jewish people, a somewhat unusual phenomenon in the history of the major religious traditions of the world.

The turn, if such it should prove to be, however, has been different in degree and character in various branches of the church and in different tendencies among the Jewish people. The Roman Catholic Church may perhaps be in the lead in this new development, with some of the major Reformed, Anglican, and Lutheran branches of the church not far behind. Within the non-Roman or Protestant Church, however, there is considerable diversity of attitudes toward the Jewish people, ranging from fundamental theological acknowledgment to an uneasy compromise between distaste for anti-Semitism and rather traditional Christian anti-Judaism. Least touched by the new assessment of the Jewish people, which appears so strong in some quarters in these more Western churches, are the Eastern Orthodox churches. Among them, there has been even less movement than in the West to accept, for example, that Zionism is importantly rooted in the Jewish tradition. Their view of the Jewish people tends in fact to be a view of Judaism, defined as a religion in their own terms, which leaves no legitimate place for the Jewish state.

Finally, the special but by no means insignificant case of North American Evangelical Protestant churches should be mentioned, for among them are many who see the return of the Jewish people to their land as a sign of the impending return of the triumphant Christ. Since they understand that return to bring with it the conversion of the whole Jewish people to Christ, such Christians turn out to be ardent supporters of the Jewish state for reasons that Jews must reject.

In addition to the great diversity of attitudes toward and understandings of Judaism just sketched, the lack of interest in the dialogue evident in the churches of the so-called Third World should also be mentioned. Intent on finding their own way in a post-colonial situation, and in rejecting their former dependence on the Western churches from whose missions their churches arose, Christians of the Third World tend to regard the Western Christian turn toward the Jewish people as a response to a peculiarly Western guilt for the peculiarly Western sin of anti-Semitism and its contribution to the peculiarly Western horror of the Holocaust. Their lack of contact with Jews together with their understandable concern to develop indigenous forms of Christianity has even led some to explore the possibility of grounding the New Testament on their local historical traditions rather than upon the Scriptures (as if the Scriptures of Israel were the product of Western civilization). As a consequence, the conversations referred to as the Jewish-Christian Dialogue are in fact a phenomenon of the European and especially the North American scene. Many churches of many lands are not engaged in it at all.

Jewish involvement has also been selective. With notable exceptions, the Jews who have taken and are taking part tend to be more liberal than traditional both in their theology and in their relationship to the halakhic tradition. That is more generally true in the United States (and in Israel) than it is in England, for example, but since the United States contains by far the largest Jewish community in the world, it is natural that more Jews and Christians have come into contact with each other there. The Jews who have been least involved in the conversation are those who stay the most to themselves, that is, the more strictly orthodox Jews, especially those of the hasidic communities. There are, however, individuals who constitute notable exceptions to every aspect of these general remarks.

The form of the conversation has been as diverse as the background of those engaged in it, ranging from occasional joint services of worship to continuing organized meeting for study and dicussion, some of longer, others of shorter duration. On balance, the number of activities and the number of participants appear to have grown over the years. Political events, notably each war in which Israel has been involved, have had an effect, usually negative, on the conversation, but in spite of setbacks, it seems to continue to grow.

ACCOMPLISHMENTS

The accomplishments of the Jewish-Christian Dialogue can only be measured in changed attitudes and understandings, primarily among the growing numbers of persons engaged in it. The overwhelming number of both Jews and Christians remain largely untouched by the developing conversation in which a minority of both are taking part, in spite of the fact that the official leadership in both have approved of and encourage its existence and have also endorsed at least the major agreements it has produced. With that reservation, however, it can be said that the Dialogue has produced something of a consensus among those involved from the Christian side that the present Jewish people indeed represent the Israel of God and that the Covenant between God and the Jewish people is still operative. A growing number, perhaps the majority, would also agree that efforts or even the wish to convert Jews to Christianity contradicts this acknowledgment of Israel's enduring relationship to God. Perhaps a majority have come or are coming to see that Israel is more than a religion called Judaism or that Judaism means also the historical and social peoplehood of the Jews, not just Jewish beliefs about God and the Covenant. Most Christians involved in the conversation have come to realize that the state of Israel is of great importance to almost all Jews, but many have yet to find a way to come to terms with the political reality of the Jewish state, for dealing with which they find their tradition providing no theological categories. The Scriptures of Israel have been so thoroughly interpreted as the church's Old Testament that the biblical concern with "the Land" has been almost totally spiritualized.

The Jews in the Dialogue have had to come to terms with something almost totally new in Jewish experience: Christians who are trying to listen to and understand them in their own terms. On the Jewish side, the problem in these conversations has been to overcome deeply ingrained patterns of defensiveness. The suspicion that "Dialogue" is only the latest and most sophisticated form of Christian mission to convert Jews is difficult to dispel, given the fact that some Christians in the Dialogue, and many not in it, cannot hide the fact that conversion is still their final hope for the Jewish people. What is remarkable, given the novelty and unevenness of the conversation, is that a few Jews are even beginning to explore ways to speak of the church as a product of the purposes of the God of Israel and thus to think about their need to develop a specific theology of the church. For almost all, however, it is still far too early for such ideas. Indeed, for most Jews in the Dialogue, it may even be the case that they see it more as a chance to correct Christian misunderstandings of Jews and Judaism than as an invitation to reconsider their own apprehension of Christian faith and life. This imbalance in the conversation is understandable, given the unhappy history of the church's relations with the Jewish people over the past eighteen centuries.

OUTSTANDING ISSUES

There are occasions on which the conversations between Jews and Christians have moved from what might be called "polite" to what is at its best substantive and serious conversation. Much of it is still only polite, and that is better than nasty, but when and where the conversation has become serious, it is evident that many of the most difficult issues are being discussed either not at all or only by very few and then usually not in much depth. These outstanding issues are different for the two sides and are discussed separately.

Issues for Christians

The first and most general observation about Christian failings in the dialogue is that although some are coming to know a fair amount about Jewish history, movements, and thought, very little has been done to integrate this understanding into the framework of Christian theological reflection. This is a serious indication of the superficiality of the achievements of almost two decades of Dialogue.

On the level of knowledge about Judaism, M. Hengel (1973), E. P. Sanders (1977), C. Thoma (1978), and F. Mussner (1979) have shown that Christians who have not bothered to digest the work of G. F. Moore (1927, 1930) can find recent and competent scholarship on at least rabbinic Judaism. On the level of seeing that this has implications for Christian theology, A. R. Eckardt (1967), R. Reuther (1974), and C. Williamson (1982) have shown the required sensitivity. On working out those implications, however, the results are less impressive. The author's efforts (1980, 1983) are one attempt to think through the issues systematically.

The problem is this: it is one thing for the church to state that the Covenant between God and the Jewish people is, contrary to eighteen centuries of church teaching, eternal. But the seamless web of Christian theology cannot absorb such a radical shift in the definition of that entity in contrast with which the church worked out its whole theology, without that change requiring shifts in every other part of that web. If the God and Father of Jesus Christ is the God of the Jewish people, who can that God be with respect to the Gentile church? If the Jews are the people of God, who or what is the Gentile church? If the Sinai revelation, both written and also oral, endures, how does that qualify the revelation in Jesus Christ? When the church changes its mind on the definition of "Israel," it will be required to rethink what it means by the God of Israel and by everything that follows from its understanding of that God. That sort of fundamental rethinking has been conspicuously absent from most of the Christian involvement in the Jewish-Christian dialogue.

The same point can be made on the practical or, more specifically, the liturgical level. It is one thing to remove the Good Friday "Reproaches" from the official liturgy. That only removes a potentially negative element from the church's worship. What significance should be attached to that, when the church has yet to include thanks to God in its great Eucharistic prayer for the continuing existence and life of the Jewish people, the Israel of God? What weight need be attached to the removal of the "Reproaches" when the church, in its Eucharistic Prayers of the People, can pray for heads of state, peace, relief from suffering, and for those who are ill, yet omit any prayers for the health of the house of Jacob (and especially for the restoration to that house of its lost sheep, a matter so central to the concern of its Lord Jesus) or for the peace of the actual Jerusalem over which its Lord Jesus shed tears? The superficiality of the liturgical reforms in this area reveal how superficial Christian theology has been in responding to the Jewish-Christian Dialogue. These observations only remind us that *dialogue* is but a grandiose term for conversation and that in fact the conversation is still largely on the level of politeness. These failings on the Christian side make this all too evident.

When we turn to more specific Christian failings in the Dialogue, we may begin with the apparent inability to hear the Jewish meaning of the Jewish term *Messiah* and to realize that the use of this term by Christians today to refer to Jesus Christ is not only derisive of Jewish faith but utterly unnecessarily so, since it never became an important Christological title in the church. It was not and should not be so used for the obvious reason that it is inadequate to designate the significance and function of Jesus Christ that is so central to the faith of the Christian church. One has to wonder what possible reason there can be for using this Jewish term, when what the church has wanted to say of Christ requires the far bolder claims of Sonship and the incarnate Word.

Yet more offensive and also more dangerous for the church is the unwillingness of many in the Dialogue to reject clearly and in principle any attempt at missionary conversion of Jews. Since the church has a special relationship to the Jewish people as the Israel of God, which is fundamentally different from it relationship to any other people, one would expect that the form of its universal mission, with respect to the Jews, would logically have to be special. Given its own apostolic warning that "you do not support the root, but the root (i.e. Israel) supports you" (Romans 11:18), could the church want to diminish in any way its own foundation? Must not its special mission to the Jews be a mission of supporting and building up that root from which it lives? Would it not seem far more consistent with the church's obedience to its Lord if it, like him, showed concern for "the lost sheep of the house of Israel" by doing all it could to help assimilated Jews to find their way back into the house of Israel? The logic may be elementary, but it seems to be beyond the grasp of many Christians who are nonetheless involved to some extent in the Jewish-Christian Dialogue.

Behind both of these failings may be detected a more fundamental problem: the Dialogue may have arisen out of an acknowledgment by Christians that the Covenant between God and the Jewish people endures, but the need for Christians to think through the relationship between Jesus and his people has not been seen. The relationship between Jesus and the church has always been given central attention in Christian theology, and that could make sense as long as the church was considered to have displaced the Jewish people as the sole bearers of the history of salvation. If, however, the Jewish people throughout their history are now to be acknowledged also to be the bearers of the divine purpose, then the relationship of Jesus to them, his own people, needs an attention not given to it in the history of Christian thought. Once more, and here at its Christological center, the superficiality of the Christian engagement in the conversation with the Jewish people becomes evident.

Another weakness detectable on the Christian side of the Dialogue is the difficulty posed for many by Zionism and the existence and actions of the state of Israel. Since the mind of the church has been formed through centuries of ignorance of Judaism and failure to acknowledge the continuing Covenant between the Jewish people and God, Christians have been almost forced to turn the Scriptures of Israel into its own Old Testament. Clear and obvious references to actual land, particular cities, and definite military, political, and economic practices, so clearly addressed to actual Israel, have had to be spiritualized in order for the church to make sense of the presence of the Scriptures within its Canon. It is therefore not surprising that the church has come to distinguish religious from political and economic realms, church from state, and generally to mark off the sphere of the sacred from that of the secular. The fact that the Jewish tradition has no place for these distinctions is evidently difficult for Christians to understand. The clearest evidence for this is the trouble many

Christians seem to be having in seeing Zionism as an integral aspect of Jewish thought and life or the centrality of the Jewish state for almost all Jews. It is as if the Christians, thinking of themselves essentially as bearers of a religion (in their own terms), can only accept Judaism as a religion, setting aside all within the Jewish tradition (such as peoplehood and the centrality of the land in the Covenant) that does not fit the Christian category "religion." If that is the correct analysis, it follows that the first rule of Dialogue—to accept the other's self-definition in the other's terms—has yet to be followed by a great many involved in the Jewish-Christian Dialogue.

Finally, Christians engaged in the Dialogue have been almost totally silent on the crucial issue of the Jewish rejection of the church and its faith in Jesus Christ. The fact that this matter has looked so differently to the two sides throughout their history has not been allowed to surface, much less any reappraisal of either side's understanding of the position of the other. From the perspective of the church, the Jewish rejection has stood at the very center of its definition of the Jew: the Jews are those who have rejected and continue to reject Christ. From the Jewish side, however, self-definition has never required even the mention of this rejection. Rather, the rejection of the church has been, along with the rejection of paganism generally, a corollary of an affirmation, namely, the affirmation of the Covenant of Sinai and the Torah that constitutes Jewish existence. A church that denied the validity of the covenant of Sinai and the importance of fidelity to Torah as of the essence of that covenant could only be rejected. The issue from the Jewish side has never centered on Jesus or even on the church's messianic claims concerning him. The Jewish people under their rabbinic leadership rejected the church already before the end of the first century of the Common Era, long before the church developed its Christology and its doctrine of the Trinity. Given the church's rejection of the Sinai covenant and fidelity to Torah, what the church taught about Jesus and God was, so to speak, irrelevant. Yet to this day, it is probably true that the vast majority of Christians involved in the Jewish-Christian Dialogue think that Jesus is what divides Christians and Jews, an idea utterly foreign to anything other than occasional polemical digressions in the Jewish tradition. The failure to explore this misunderstanding and to think through the consequences of a more accurate historical reading and substantive location of the matter is one of the most painful signs of the superficiality of what is called the Jewish-Christian Dialogue.

Issues for Jews

A Christian analysis of Jewish failings in the Dialogue must of necessity be less penetrating. It must also be tempered by the logic of repentence and forgiveness: it is a matter of historical record that as the larger and politically more powerful of the two, the church has caused great hardship and suffering for the Jewish people for centuries. In a time when the church is beginning to repent of its treatment of Jews, it is understandable that Jews, even those willing to enter into apparently friendly conversation with the church, would be a bit cautious. It is therefore proper that a Christian assessment of Jewish failings in the Dialogue be expressed with some reserve. Nevertheless, if it were not expressed at all, that could only reflect a Christian failure to take the Jewish people seriously. Many Jews would probably prefer that, in the light of the results of past Christian attention. Aware of this and sensitive to its justifiable grounds, we turn our attention next to Jewish failings in the Jewish-Christian Dialogue, matters that have been conspicuous by their absence from the conversation so far.

Christians who take the Jewish people seriously do so because they believe the Jews to be the people of God, the people of God's eternal election. They take them seriously theologically. The first failure to be mentioned on the Jewish side is that of not making it clear that Jews take themselves seriously theologically. However justifiable it may be from a historical perspective, the defensiveness of Jewish participation in the conversation is a serious impediment to real conversation. The result is that the subject of Israel's election can scarcely be broached without an immediate defensive intervention by Jewish participants, to the effect that election is not a privilege, not a measure of moral or any other sort of superiority, and so on, as if their Christian conversation partners had never read the Torah and the Prophets, and as if Christians did not have their own doctrine of election as an unavoidable feature of their doctrine of the church. The consequence of this defensive move is that the utterly crucial subject of God's election of the Jewish people never becomes a central part of the conversation. How long the conversation can endure this avoidance of the center is a matter for sober thought.

One aspect of this void at the center of the conversation is the uncertainty engendered as to whether Jews want or ought to think of themselves primarily as a people or primarily as God's people. It appears as if many Jews see the existence of the Jewish people as an end in itself, one might even say its mere existence, with little or no attention to the quality or character of that existence. The meaning of Israel's call to holiness and priesthood, which one would think should be of great moment in a genuine Jewish-Christian conversation, seldom if ever comes up. The failure here is that of the Jewish participants. The question that underlies this failure is not whether Jews take themselves seriously but whether they take themselves seriously theologically. The first may be answered affirmatively without expecting much more than politeness from the conversation. Only if there is an affirmative answer to the second can the potential of a real conversation have any hope of being realized. On this hangs the future of the Jewish-Christian Dialogue.

From a number of Jewish quarters has come a new willingness to acknowledge Jesus of Nazareth as one of their own. On historical critical grounds, there hardly seems to be an alternative. But the history of Jesus includes also his *Wirkungsgeschichte*, the history of the consequences of his existence. Set in theological perspective, Jesus became and continues to be the God of Israel's way of bringing many Gentiles to his service. In the Jewish-Christian Dialogue, there are few Jews who seem willing to make such a theological-historical judgment. This is a Jewish failure of nerve that has allowed the conversation to continue without serious attention being given to the relation between the function of Jesus for the church and the titles with which the church names those functions. The Jewish failure must be added to the Christian one in order to account for the superficiality of the way in which Christology is discussed in the Dialogue.

This last failure is related to another: the apologetic and defensive way in which so many Jews in the conversation dismiss the very idea of Jewish theology, as if it were un-Jewish to think carefully and responsibly about the things of God. There are, it should be noted, two sides to this denial of Jewish theology, as though it were some unmentionable sin. Rarely, but not all that rarely, one finds Jews who think that to discuss theology means to discuss the innermost recesses of one's own relationship to God, to bare one's most private soul. I have heard this expressed by no less a person than a chief rabbi of the Jewish community in one country and have read of the same point being made by one of the highest halakhic authorities of another. No wonder it is picked up by many other Jews.

Dialogue may lead to the most intimate introspection and to much soul searching and prayer, but it does not demand of either Jews or Christians that they lay their souls on the table for public scrutiny and dissection. Broadly defined, theology is the precipitate of careful reflection and discussion of what one's community should say about its calling, purpose, and life in the world, where it has come from and where it is going. It is self-critical reflection undertaken for the sake of the responsibility that the community has before God. There is no less reason for such thinking to be going on in the Jewish community than in the church. More specifically, the theological task in or arising from the Dialogue is one of hard and responsible thinking about what the other has to say and about what one should say in response to that which one hears, especially when it is something one seems to be hearing for the first time. Again, there is no less call for this sort of thinking on the Jewish than on the Christian side.

On the other hand, the objection to theology from the Jewish side can be a positive contribution if it is made clear, as it seldom is, that the objection is to bad theology, a theology disengaged from the real life of the community and its responsibilities in the real world. There is a time and place for abstract thought and for making careful and subtle distinctions, but there is also a time and a place for showing what this activity has to contribute to actual decisions that people have to make. It should be clear, however, that objections to too much of the former and not enough of the latter is not an objection to theology but only to the way in which it is being done. Jews could help the conversation by making this clear. They only hinder it when they object that theology is not something that Jews do.

Finally, there is a Jewish failure that reflects a Christian one: with the rarest of exceptions, there has yet to be shown even an awareness of the lack of a

Jewish theology of the church. Christians have been slow enough to develop a positive Christian theology of the people of Israel, and it is arguably the case that the burden falls upon them to do this first, but the Dialogue will not get far until the Jewish participants come to see that the idea of the Noachide covenant is simply not going to do the task that the Dialogue requires. The church can no more accept that concept as defining the particularity of its relationship to God and to the Israel of God than the Jewish people can agree that a universal commitment to the fatherhood of God and the brotherhood of man defines its own particularity. Israel is Israel and the church of Jesus Christ is the church of Jesus Christ, called by the God of Israel to His service. The largest part of its Canon is the sacred Scriptures of Israel. As the church cannot adequately conceive of its relationship to the Jewish people under some general category of toleration, so the Jewish people cannot define the church exhaustively under the far too general, unhistorical, and impersonal terms of the Noachide covenant. The Jews are right in seeing that Christians are Gentiles, not Jews, but they are Gentiles who call on the name of the God of Abraham, Isaac, and Jacob and who know that God as the God of the Jewish people. A Jewish theology of the church is therefore an important missing item from the agenda of the Jewish-Christian Dialogue. The silence on this subject is a sign of the superficiality of the Dialogue and the degree to which it still remains only a polite conversation. Jewish as well as Christian failings have prevented further development.

CONCLUSION

For all its limitations, the Jewish-Christian Dialogue remains a matter of fundamental importance in the history of the church and the Jewish people. The reversal of official church teaching concerning the Jewish people, which is to a limited extent the fruit but primarily the initiating cause of the Dialogue, is possibly the single, most radical change that the church has made since the first century of the Common Era and one having implications for the whole of Christian theology, the extent of which is only beginning to be recognized by a few. As I have argued, the Dialogue is still superficial, but the fact remains that it is continuing and deepening. It is indicative that the Commission of the Rhineland Synod of the German Evangelical Church, which produced the statement adopted by that synod in 1980, invited a number of Jews to serve as active consultants in all of its deliberations. It is perhaps more significant that they have insisted on a Jewish presence and involvement in any further theological discussions of the statement. When set against the background of the history of the church's manner of speaking of and acting toward the Jewish people, the change is remarkable.

Dialogue, even at its best, is only talk. But how people talk is an important part of who and what they take themselves to be. The Jewish-Christian Dialogue, for all its limitations, may therefore signal a turning point in the self-understanding of these two communities that could have profound effects on the relationship not only between them but also on those between them both and other peoples and traditions.

GLOSSARY

Anti-Judaism: Traditional Christian theology of the Jews as being rejected by God for having rejected Jesus Christ.

Anti-Semitism: Nineteenth-century, pseudoscientific racial theory of the inferiority of the Jewish people.

Halakhic: Pertaining to the Halachah, the collection (in the Talmud and to this day) of rabbinic decisions concerning Jewish practice and behavior.

Holocaust: The Nazi "Final Solution of the Jewish Question"; an attempt to destroy the whole Jewish people, in which 6 million Jewish men, women, and children were murdered in the final years of the German Third Reich.

Reproaches: A Christian liturgical litany, in which the suffering Jesus reproaches his people for their betrayal and rejection of him; traditionally said on Good Friday, the anniversary of Jesus' death in the church calender.

Zionism: A movement arising in European Jewry in the nineteenth century, built on the ancient Jewish attachment to and longing for the land promised to them by God in his Covenant with them. Zionism breaks with the tradition in placing the initiative for the return in Jewish hands, rather than leaving it to the Messiah and God.

SELECTED BIBLIOGRAPHY

Bokser, Ben Zion. *Judaism and the Christian Predicament*. New York: Knopf, 1967.

Croner, H., ed. *Stepping Stones to Further Jewish-Christian Relations*. London and New York: Stimulus, 1977.

Croner, H., and L. Klenicki, eds. *Issues in the Jewish-Christian Dialogue*. New York: Paulist Press, 1979.

Davies, A. T., ed. *Antisemitism and the Foundations of Christianity*. New York: Paulist Press, 1979.

Eckhardt, A. R. *Elder and Younger Brothers*. New York: Charles Scribner's Sons, 1967.

———. *Jews and Christians*. Bloomington: Indiana University Press, 1986.

Hengel, M. *Judentum und Hellenismus*, 1973. English translation: *Judaism and Hellenism*. Philadelphia: Fortress Press, 1974.

Katz, J. *Exclusiveness and Tolerance*. New York: Schocken, 1975.

Klappert, B., and H. Starck, eds. *Umkehr und Erneuerung*. Vluyn, West Germany: Neukirchener, 1980.

Lapide, P., and J. Moltmann. *Jewish Monotheism and Christian Trinitarian Doctrine*. Philadelphia: Fortress Press, 1981.

Marquardt, F. W. *Die Auferweckung Jesus Christi bei seinem Volk Israel*. Munich: Kaiser Verlag, 1984.

Marquardt, F. W., and A. Friedlander. *Das Schweigen der Christen und die Menchlichkeit Gottes*. Munich: Kaiser Verlag, 1980.

Moore, G. F. *Judaism in the First Centuries of the Christian Era*. Cambridge: Harvard University Press, 1927, 1930.

Mussner, F. *Tractat über die Juden*, 1979. English translation: *Tractate on the Jews*. S.P.C.K., 1984.

Osten-Sacken, P.v.d., ed. *Christian-Jewish Dialogue*. Philadelphia: Fortress Press 1986.

————. *Treue zur Thora*. Berlin: Institut Kirche und Judentum, 1977.

Parkes, J. *The Conflict of the Church and the Synagogue*. New York: Atheneum, 1977.

Ruether, R. *Faith and Fratricide*. New York: Seabury Press, 1974.

Sanders, E. P. *Paul and Palestinian Judaism*. Philadelphia: Fortress Press, 1977.

Selzer, Sanford, and Max L. Stackhouse, eds. *The Death of Dialogue and Beyond*. New York: Friendship, 1969.

Soleveitchik, J. "Confrontation." *Tradition* 6, no. 2 (1964): 5–29.

Stendahl, K. *Paul among Jews and Gentiles*. Philadelphia: Fortress Press, 1976.

Talmage, F. E., ed. *Disputation and Dialogue*. New York: Ktav, 1975.

Thoma, C. *A Christian Theology of Judaism*. New York: Paulist Press, 1980.

van Buren, P. M. *A Theology of the Jewish-Christian Reality:* Pt. 1, *Discerning the Way;* Pt. 2, *A Christian Theology of the People of Israel*; Pt. 3, *Christ in Context*, San Francisco: Harper and Row, 1987–88.

Williamson, C. *Has God Rejected His People?* Nashville: Abingdon, 1982.

18

Dialogue as Affirmation: Franz Rosenzweig's Contribution to Christian-Jewish Conversations

GERHARD E. SPIEGLER

Franz Rosenzweig devoted his life to the philosophical justification of his faith. In the context of the philosophical heritage of the nineteenth century, he struggled to lay the foundations of a "new thinking," a thinking that allowed him to affirm the ratio of his humanity and the truth of his Jewish faith in all of its historical specificity. He accepted the challenge and task of reconciling faith and reason, of reconciling Christianity and Judaism, without yielding to the temptation to sacrifice their historical particularity on the altar of abstraction.

The attempts of Protestant theology to reject the intellectual heritage of the nineteenth century were as much mistaken as they were unsuccessful. An intellectual heritage cannot be rejected and excluded; it can only be understood and digested. The Protestant theologian Karl Barth suspected as much; he even feared it. In contrast, Franz Rosenzweig welcomed that heritage as a positive force. The pupil of Friedrich Meinecke saw with great clarity the unbreakable connection of past and present. He recognized in the process of radical negation the very spirit of Mephistopheles, the spirit of confusion and error that leads astray. He, better than many of his Christian colleagues, perceived the inner truth of Faust's saying, "Was ihr den Geist der Zeiten heisst, das ist im Grunde der Herren eigner Geist, in dem die Zeiten sich bespiegeln."[1] The truth of Faust's response to Wagner does not lie in the proclamation of the intellectual omnipotence of the present. On the contrary, for Rosenzweig, the "spirit of the present" cannot escape its own nature. This very nature, this very self upon which the "spirit of the present" depends, has not "miraculously dropped from heaven"; it is itself the very product of that past. For Rosenzweig, the "spirit of the present," though not the necessary product of the past, is the successor and heir of that past. The "spirit of the present," rather than ruling the past, is subject to that past.[2]

Franz Rosenzweig knew and insisted that the very self of the present is history and that therefore it not only can but must digest history by understanding it. Past and present cannot be radically separated no more so than "science" and "religion" (*Wissenschaft und Religion*) and "faith" and "understanding" (*Glauben und Verstehen*). The unity of being, of reality, cannot be dissolved into a neutral or hostile duality. Rosenzweig consistently and sharply repudiated the radicalism of dialectical theology that by its negation of the philosophical-theological heritage of the nineteenth century had been lured into a false separation of "Wissenschaft" and "Religion." He observed that this separation had become "the penultimate cry" of Protestant theologians, the faddish motto of "our newest 'irrationalists.' " He rejected all attempts to justify this irrational separation on the grounds that it could be traced to Kant and that it had the support of Karl Barth and Friedrich Gogarten, "so much the worse for Kant, Barth and Gogarten."[3] In words that could have come out of the mouth of Georg W. F. Hegel or Friedrich Schleiermacher, Rosenzweig forcefully stated:

If "Wissenschaft" and "Religion" don't want to have anything to do with each other while aware of each other, then neither "Wissenschaft" nor "Religion" are worth anything. There is only one truth. An honest person cannot pray to a God whom he denies as a man of science; and whoever prays cannot deny God. This claim should not be confused with the claim that the scholar must find God in a laboratory beaker or in his file cabinet. However, the content of the beaker, just as the content of the file cabinet, has no existence without God. The world, not God, is the object of science. But God has created the world; therefore, God has created the object of science. To say the same but this time not in simple German . . . but in the more customary (and strangely more understandable) foreign terminology, God is transcendent and transcendental for science. Science does not possess God, but science would not be without God; God is not part of science but science is under God.[4]

In these words that call to mind Schleiermacher's formula in his *Dialectik,* God is the *terminus a quo* and the world the *terminus ad quem* of human thought, Franz Rosenzweig took his stand against the popular Protestant theology of his time. He knew that the structures of nineteenth-century thought reflected genuine and still binding problem conceptions. He knew that the problematic of the nineteenth century could not be evaded and that it could not be subjected to forced solutions. For him, there was no reason to give preference to the dialectic of the leap to that of sublation. For Franz Rosenzweig, faith cannot be pitted against knowledge, although it is possible to set *gläubiges Wissen* (believing reason) against *ungläubiges Wissen* (unbelieving reason). For him, faith did not "mean that one had to put oneself in dogmatic chains" but rather "an all-embracing commitment of the whole person," and in this sense he pointed out that there can be a "heretic believer" and a "super-orthodox unbeliever."[5] Thus for Franz Rosenzweig, as for his great predecessor Moses Mendelssohn, faith had little or nothing to do with the holding of dogmatic propositions. It was not a theoretical posture but an understanding active involvement in the world. He knew that to overcome the heritage of the nineteenth century we must first understand it. At the very center of that heritage is an as yet unfinished problematical task: to discover that which is intellectually compelling and obligatory without being forced simultaneously into a dissolution of historical and religious particularity, that is, without the surrender of the value and validity of individuality. For our Enlightenment ancestors, it was sufficient to say *nihil humani mihi alienum*. But for us that is not enough. We must be able to add that nothing Jewish or Christian is alien to us.

It was in this connection that Rosenzweig pointed to Moses Mendelssohn as the precursor of our age. For Mendelssohn, "being human" and "being Jewish" were absolutes; for him, reason (*Vernunft*) and the Torah were inseparable. The very point in his position that some of his immediate followers treated as a weakness was in fact his true strength. Rosenzweig recognized that very clearly. But he also saw the tragic duality of the Mendelssohnian heritage. He alluded to this in an essay of 1923 entitled "Die Bauleute" and addressed to Martin Buber. "Since Mendelssohn," he said, "our entire people has undergone the torture of truly embarrassing questioning which has forced each and every one to examine his/her Jewishness under the pin prick of a persisting 'why.' "[6] In his "Address to a Mendelssohn Festival" of 1929 he observed pointedly, "But Mendelssohn has led us into this danger defenseless; his own protection was the *Weltanschauung* of his century, the dissolution of which made him its . . . very first casualty. Thus the 19th century had to help itself in its own non-Mendelssohnian way and so must we, children of a new and changed time."[7]

Rosenzweig argued that the inner truth of Mendelssohnian thought must be preserved, but he pointed out that we will not find this truth in the "no longer believable faith of the 18th century in the theology of reason."[8] The inner truth of Mendelssohn's thought was to be found in his willing acceptance of the binding force of the Torah in all of its particularity. For Rosenzweig, Mendelssohn's eternal truths of reason are not as significant for our self-understanding today as is his simultaneous acceptance of the binding force of the historical particularity of Judaism. What matters most is that Moses Mendelssohn wanted to be both a rational human being and an obedient Jew, and that, indeed, he was. But as Rosenzweig pointed out, Mendelssohn never demonstrated the conceptual possibility of this double possibility of being in a convincing manner. For Rosenzweig, the greatness of the nineteenth century resided in its attempt to hold together the universal and the particular, reason and history, and to establish their reasonable connectedness. This attempt is at the very center of the nineteenth-century heritage. He knew that we have yet to assimilate that heritage, and he knew also that the trusting posture of a Moses Mendelssohn was no longer a real possibility, no more so than the faith of a Hegel who was certain in his conviction to have sublated reality in rationality and to have expressed rationality fully in reality. For Rosenzweig, to be a human being and to be a Christian or Jew—both at the same time—that is the challenge to our being and thinking.

In his essay "Der Ewige—Mendelssohn und der Gottesname," Rosenzweig analyzed the problem of unity and multiplicity, of universality and particularity. He struggled with the demand to establish something that is intellectually binding and morally compelling without being forced to surrender the validity of singularity and individuality. "Biblical 'monotheism,' " he argued, "certainly does not consist merely in the recognition of the oneness (unity) of the divine being; if that were the case, it would lack any claim to being special."[9] There is no doubt, he remarked, that paganism had already a conception of the "unity of the religious" (*Einheit des Religiösen*). This is not what made biblical faith unique; rather that which is unique in the biblical faith in God is the fact that "biblical faith presupposes the 'pagan' oneness or unity of God . . . the God of Aristotle, but it recognizes this God as being at one with the most personally and immediately experienced God . . . namely, the God of Abraham."[10]

It would be wrong to conclude from the above that the pagan unity of God could be treated as unimportant. To the contrary, Rosenzweig argued, "a limited God (*Teilgebliebener*) such as the God of a particular group (*Gruppengott*) who laid claim to being God in totality would be no more than an idol, and hence unfit to be identified with the 'God of Abraham.' "[11] What matters in the pagan 'unity of God' is not the assertion of the unity of God as such but rather the "Jewish identification (*Ineinssetzung*) of the distant God with the near God; the identification of the 'God of all' with the 'Lord our God,' " that is, the identification of the universal with the particular.[12] Put in the language of Moses Mendelssohn, what matters is that the universal rational truth of religion—of our common humanity—is inseparable from the specificity of the accidental historical truth of the religions. For Rosenzweig, that which constitutes the very essence of Judaism in its very specificity is the identification of the One—the distant God—with the God who is my own God—the God close to me. From this perspective the same thing could be said of Christianity but only "in the somewhat broken form of the Trinitarian dogma, which always entails the danger of reversion into the pre- and extra-Jewish separation of the 'One' God from 'my' God." A glance at present-day Protestant theology, at Barth and Gogarten, he observed, demonstrates the "gravity and pressing relevance of this danger."[13]

For Rosenzweig, it was precisely the identification of the *one* God with *my* God that made up the "revelatory" core of the Bible, the Jewish Bible. He observed that the difference between the Jewish Bible and the "Old Testament" lies in the fact "that from the perspective of the New Testament it becomes all too easy to again reduce the God of the Old Testament in contrast with the 'Father of Jesus Christ' to the abstract universality of the 'God of Aristotle.' "[14] He summarized his position as follows:

It is precisely this identification which forges in the very name of God the very unity of the entire Bible. This identification [of the *one* God with *my* God] meets us with white heat in the call "I am there" from the burning bush. It proclaims everywhere the equation of the God of creation with the God who is present to me, to you and to everyone. This equation is most passionately manifested in those Biblical verses where the name of God clashes with the word used for God as in the Paradise passages of Genesis or in the proclamation of unity, the "Hear, oh Israel," and generally in those passages in which Mendelssohn finds the use of "the Eternal One" unsatisfactory and indeed uses "the eternal being" [as a better expression] in order to secure the connection to Exodus and the revelation of the Name.[15]

Franz Rosenzweig perceived the central philosophical problem of our time as a transcendental one, the examination of the possibility of the identification of the "one" God in transcendent distance with the personal God in the immanence of our human existence. For him, time and eternity are meeting in this identification (*Ineinssetzung*), but they do so without yielding the dissolution of the one into the other. He warned that neither historically or philosophically can 'identification' become assimilation. Under no circumstances can identification be permitted to become equation (*Gleichsetzung*). Time cannot be dissolved in eternity, and eternity cannot be allowed to vanish in time. What emerges are two specific tasks: the determination of what is universally binding and obligatory and the determination of the value and validity of the human-religious reality in its particularity (*Einzelheit*). Both tasks are inseparable. The more precisely we determine the intellectual-religious content of our common humanity, the more urgent and pressing becomes the determination of the value and validity of our intellectual-religious specificity. For Franz Rosenzweig, Moses Mendelssohn's unreflective though joyful affirmation of his common humanity and of the specificity of his Jewishness demanded a transcendental proof in the same manner as the affirmation of the eternal truths of reason and the validity of the Torah. The simultaneity of *Being*-human and *Being*-Jewish requires conceptual penetration.

Rosenzweig was right in his observation that since Mendelssohn, "the Jewishness of each and every individual Jew has been balanced like on the point of a needle in the question 'Why.' " He also knew that the same could be said of every Christian, although not in the same sharply delineated historical sense. He was aware that since the happier Enlightenment days of the great Mendelssohn, the problem formulation had become more intense and pronounced. Rosenzweig knew very well that the "German Plato," the author of the "Phaedo" and of "Jerusalem," had a firm hold on his being "human" and "Jewish." But he also knew that for him and his fellow Jews, the same could not be said with equal surety. It was for that reason that he devoted himself to the twin tasks of determining what is intellectually binding and morally obligatory and what constitutes the value and validity of the human-religious particularity.

In the context of the history of the German Jewish community, it was the second task that was especially close to his heart. For Rosenzweig, the affirmation of his Jewish specificity and particularity required the determination of the essence of Judaism or, better, of the spirit of Judaism. It was clear to him that one could not affirm what one did not understand. In view of the observed historical situation of German Jewry, he had no doubt that a self-reflective affirmation was sorely needed.

In his essay "Bildung und kein Ende" (1920) he asked, "What has held or holds German Jewry together since the advent of Emancipation?" The answer he suggested "is frightening" for that which holds the Jewish community together is only Emancipation itself, that is, "the Jewish struggle for justice."[16] This, he argued, is no more sufficient than the battle against anti-Semitism. It is especially unsatisfactory in view of the fact that it is impossible to deny that "even the liberal wing of German Jewish politics—beginning with Dohm, Hardenberg and Humboldt—was always guided by the idea that Emancipation was the instrument for the resolution of the Jewish question, in the sense that it would produce such a form of assimilation which even the most convinced assimilationist who still counts himself as belonging to the Jewish community, would have had to reject."[17] He argued that the dissolution of Judaism in its particularity could only be avoided if there was a growth in the positive self-understanding of Judaism. It is in this sense and context that Rosenzweig made it his vocation to promote the determination of the Spirit of Judaism by way of promoting increased reflective thought about Judaism. It was his mission to advance a fuller and better understanding of the essence or spirit of Judaism. He viewed this task as a perennial one that no generation can complete for another.

But most importantly for Franz Rosenzweig, the needed and essential self-affirmation of one's religious particularity entailed an equally important second obligation: the acceptance and recognition of the value and validity of the religious particularity of one's neighbor. He was convinced that the affirmation of one's own truthfulness (*Wahrhaftigkeit*) did not require the denial of the truthfulness of one's neighbor. On the contrary, he argued, it had to be presupposed. He had no doubt that self-affirmation entailed the affirmation of the other, for my 'personal' God who is also the *one* God is the God of all creation. The identification of "my" God with the "One" God presupposed and required the identification of the "One" God with the personal God of my neighbor. In saying "yes" to myself, I must also say "yes" to my neighbor.

For Rosenzweig, this alone made religious dialogue possible and determined its methodological framework. In each religious dialogue, it is of the essence that one listens to the voice of the "One" God. Each religious conversation demanded that one addressed always the presence of the "One" God. In a genuine religious dialogue or conversation, there cannot and must not occur a dissolution of one's religious particularity and specificity. Given the identification of the "One" God with "my" God and in consonance with the revelatory core of the Bible, religious dialogue can and must lead only to an affirmation and confirmation of one's religious specificity.

In his essay "Apologetisches Denken: Bemerkungen zu Brod and Baeck" (1923), Rosenzweig offered some advice to anyone interested in the pursuit of religious dialogue. He put the condition of dialogue sharply and simply: "It is the first duty of the theoretical love of one's neighbor—a love as important to us as creatures . . . as is the practical love of one's neighbor, for being viewed wrongly hurts as much as being treated wrongly—to ask whether any given opinion which we form about another person allows that person to continue to live with integrity. The other has that right, just as I do."[18] In reference to Judaism and Chritianity, he elaborated his point: "The Pharisees which Christians portray could not truly live, if they were in fact these humorless, soulless 'legal' robots as imagined. In like manner, Christians would be equally incapable of truly living, if they were indeed the pallid heavenly lilies which Jews (from the perspective of the Sermon of the Mount) want them to be as a condition for being truly Christian."[19] Religious dialogue cannot be conducted on the basis of a comfortable abstraction that finds it convenient to separate the religious "spirit" from the religious "body." The temptation to separate body and spirit must be resisted:

The body is just as little a decadent appearance of the spirit as is the historical evolution of a community (which does not conform to the image of that community in its root documents) an expression of decadence. Quite on the contrary, it may well be that this [historical] change represents a necessary and therefore original and intended corrective of its beginnings. The adult may look back on the purity of his childhood during his entire life, but that does not mean that the adult is therefore a mere decadent appearance of the child.[20]

This is applicable to contemporary Judaism and Christianity for whose "spirits" we may not search at the expense of their "bodies." The identification of the "One" God with "my" God is the revelatory core of the Bible and part of the unassimilated philosophical-theological heritage of the nineteenth century. Rosenzweig warned us never to confuse God's Oneness and Singularity with our own multiplicity and never to confuse our multiplicity with God's Oneness and Singularity. The Eternal—the Eternal One—is present in time and present in every time. For Franz Rosenzweig, time is not an abyss nor is it groundless. It is never dissolved, for it is always realized, for the *One* Lord, *Our* God, is as the Eternal One, The Lord of Time.

NOTES

1. "What you call the spirit of the times, is in reality none other than the spirit of the masters reflecting the spirit of the times" (Goethe's *Faust*). All translations from the German are my own.

2. Franz Rosenzweig, "Geist und Epochen der Jüdischen Geschichte" (1919); Franz Rosenzweig, *Kleinere Schriften* (Berlin: Schocken, 1937), pp. 14–15.

3. Franz Rosenzweig, "Die Einheit der Bibel" (Eine Auseinandersetzung mit Orthodoxie und Liberalismus) (1927); idem, *Kleinere Schriften*, p. 132.

4. Rosenzweig, *Kleinere Schriften*, p. 132.

5. Ibid., p. 133.

6. Franz Rosenzweig, "Die Bauleute" (1923); idem, *Kleinere Schriften*, p. 110.

7. Franz Rosenzweig, "Vorspruch zu einer Mendelssohnfeier" (1929); idem, *Kleinere Schriften*, p. 53.

8. Franz Rosenzweig, "Der Ewige" (1929); idem, *Kleinere Schriften*, p. 187.

9. Rosenzweig, *Kleinere Schriften*, p. 192.

10. Ibid.

11. Ibid.

12. Ibid.

13. Ibid.

14. Ibid.

15. Ibid., pp. 192–193.

16. Franz Rosenzweig, "Bildung und kein Ende" (1920); idem, *Kleinere Schriften*, p. 86.

17. Franz Rosenzweig, "Zeit ists . . . An Hermann Cohen" (1917); idem, *Kleinere Schriften*, p. 68.

18. Franz Rosenzweig, "Apologetisches Denken" (1923); idem, *Kleinere Schriften*, p. 35.

19. Rosenzweig, *Kleinere Schriften*, pp. 35–36.

20. Ibid.

SELECTED BIBLIOGRAPHY

Altmann, Alexander. *Essays in Jewish Intellectual History*. Hanover, N.H.: University Press of New England, 1981.

Bergman, Samuel H. *Faith and Reason*. New York: Schocken, 1961.

Bronen, David, ed. *Jews and Germans from 1860–1933: The Problematic Symbiosis*. Heidelberg: Carl Winter Universitatsverlag, 1979.

Freund, Else Rachel. *Franz Rosenzweig's Philosophy of Existence: An Analysis of "Star of Redemption."* The Hague: Martinus Nijhoff, 1979.

Friedman, Maurice S. *Martin Buber: The Life of Dialogue*. New York: Harper and Row, 1960.

Graupe, Heinz Mosche. *The Rise of Modern Judaism: An Intellectual History of German Jewry, 1650–1942*. Huntington, N.Y.: Robert A. Kruger, 1978.

Jopse, Alfred, ed. *An Anthology of German Jewish Scholarship*. Detroit: Wayne State University Press, 1981.

Katz, Jacob. *From Prejudice to Destruction: Anti-Semitism, 1700–1933*. Cambridge, Mass.: Harvard University Press, 1980.

Knight, George A., ed. *Jews and Christians: Preparation for Dialogue*. Philadelphia: Westminster Press, 1965.

Koenig, John. *Jews and Christians in Dialogue: The New Testament Foundations*. Philadelphia: Westminster Press, 1978.

Mendelssohn, Moses. *Jerusalem, or On Religious Power and Judaism*. Translated by Allan Arkush. Introduction and Commentary by Alexander Altmann. Hanover, N.H.: University Press of New England, 1983.

Meyer, Michael A. *The Origins of the Modern Jew: Jewish Identity and European Culture in Germany, 1749–1824*. Detroit: Wayne State University Press, 1967.

Moltmann, Jürgen, with Phinn E. Lapide. *Jewish Monotheism and Christian Trinitarian Doctrine: A Dialogue*. Translated by Leonard Swidler. Philadelphia: Fortress Press, 1981.

Osten-Sacken, Peter van der. *Grundzüge einer Theologie im christlich-jüdischen Gespräch*. München: Chr. Kaiser Verlag, 1982.

Rosenzweig, Franz. *The Star of Redemption*. Translated by William W. Hallo. New York: Holt, Rinehart and Winston, 1970.

————. *Kleinere Schriften*. Berlin: Schocken, 1937.

Rotenstreich, Nathan. *Jewish Philosophy in Modern Times: From Mendelssohn to Rosenzweig*. New York: Holt, Rinehart and Winston, 1968.

Strolz, Walter, ed. *Vom Geist den wir brauchen*. Freiburg: Herder Verlag, 1978.

van Buren, Paul. *Discerning the Way: A Theology of Jewish Christian Reality*. New York: Seabury Press, 1980.

19

The Dialogue between Islam and the Judeo-Christian Tradition

TAMARA SONN

Islam has carried on serious dialogue with both Judaism and Christianity since the earliest days of its empire. The fifth caliph, Mu'awiyya (661–769 C.E.), whose wife, court physician, and poet laureate were all Christians, commonly invited the contending Jacobite and Maronite Christians to the royal court to work out their disputes.[1] The Syrian Christian St. John of Damascus (d. 748) frequently visited the palace to debate issues such as the divinity of Christ and free will in the presence of the caliph. Similar debates, often including Jews as well as Muslims, were also popular in the Spanish Muslim courts. But these discussions were not always carried out with complete equanimity. The best-known Islamic text from the period is Ibn Hazm's *Kitab al-Fasl fi'l-Milal wa'l-Ahwa' wa'l-Nihal,* which attempts to prove that Jewish and Christian Scriptures have been altered—this, in response to Jewish and Christian accusations of Islamic inauthenticity. Still, Jews and Christians always held a special place among Muslims as their brothers in the Abrahamic tradition. Open exchange of views among the three communities characterized the highest stages of educational and cultural achievement in the Muslim world.

Although the political, cultural, and spiritual decline of the Muslim world marked the end of such efforts, the idea of dialogue among the Abrahamic traditions nevertheless is not new to Islam. Yet the character of the current dialogue is very different from that of classical Islam. It has been initiated by the Christians, among whom it is a relatively recent phenomenon. Moreover, it has been initiated by Christians of the politically and economically dominant Western world in the face of its admitted ignorance of Islam. The Muslim world, by contrast, is well acquainted with at least certain aspects of the West. It has become part of the Third World, those nations struggling to throw off the yoke of Western imperialism and establish themselves as independent and equal partners with their former masters. These factors provide the current dialogue with peculiar characteristics that must be addressed in assessing its progress.

HISTORY OF DIALOGUE

The Beginning of Dialogue: Vatican II

"Trumped-up stories of 'ritual murders' of Christian boys by Jewish communities were common throughout Europe during the Middle Ages and even much later. These fictions cost many innocent Jews their lives. Lincoln [Cathedral] had its own legend, and the alleged victim was buried in the Cathedral. A shrine was erected above and the boy was referred to as 'little St. Hugh.' . . . Such stories do not redound to the credit of Christendom and so we pray— 'Remember not Lord our offences, nor the offences of our forefathers.' " Such was the inscription put up in 1955 in the Anglican Lincoln Cathedral to replace the original, installed in 1255 to immortalize the supposed ritual murder by Jews of 'little St. Hugh.' As the new inscription states, these accusations mark a high point in the rise of anti-Jewish sentiment in Christian Europe.

Anti-Semitism had its roots in early Christianity.[2] No sooner had Emperor Theodosius I declared Christianity the official religion of the Roman Empire than laws restricting non-Christians' freedom were institutionalized.[3] Roman motivation was not entirely political. True, the continued existence of non-Christian religions undermined the political unity of the state. But Christians were also motivated by religious purity. Christianity had come to replace Judaism. Not only had the Jews rejected the teaching of Jesus the Christ, they also had killed him. Armed with accusations of deicide, then, the Christians felt ultimately justified in their hatred of the Jews. Nor was it long before the Jews, barred from the rights of full citizenship, became an oppressed and despised outcast minority, vulnerable to every sort of criminal allegation.

The Jews were not the only group to suffer accusations of religious impurity. In an effort to wipe out the indigenous "nature worship" of European tribes, Christian authorities burned some 100,000 people as witches in Europe between 1400 and 1700. Of them 80 percent were women. Still, the legacy of anti-Semitism proved the most virulent and long lived of medieval prejudices.

During the Reformation, while the church subjected itself to severe self-criticism, anti-Semitism remained intact, even enhanced. Luther had indicted his generation for its fantastic allegations of Jewish bloodthirstiness: "For they have treated Jews as if they were dogs and not human beings."[4] His archenemy Johannes Eck, professor at the University of Ingolstadt, expressed the popular response to even such limited defense of Jews: "Whatever comes into the heads or dreams of these people [the reformers] they give to the world for evangelical riffraff to read. For instance, right now there is this superficially learned children's preacher with the hoof of the golden calf in his flank, who presumes to defend the bloodthirsty Jews, saying that it is not true and not plausible that they murder

Christian children or use their blood, to the mockery and ridicule of the authorities and all of Christendom.''[5] This does not imply, however, that Luther and fellow reformers such as Reuchlin and Erasmus were not anti-Jewish. Luther called on the church for severe measures against all ''opponents of God''—Jews, heretics, the pope, and ''the Turks,'' by whom he meant Muslims.[6] In 1543 he published *On the Jews and Their Lies,* attacking the Jews' theological ''errors'' as the major threat to the very survival of the church. Their externalization of spiritual life was the death of piety, the ''triumph of the dead letter in the name of the living spirit.'' As Heiko Oberman characterized it: ''Anti-Judaism in this form [was] destined to become an integral component of the reform program of the sixteenth century. In the struggle for the renewal of church and society, Jews and Judaism [were] adduced as comprehensible and unambiguous proofs of the spiritual chaos of the time.''[7]

It was not until after anti-Semitism reached its horrific crescendo in Hitler's Holocaust that Christianity was faced with the true reality of its anti-Jewish stance. Replacing the seven-hundred-year-old plaque at Lincoln Cathedral was an expression of its newfound conscience. Vatican II's ''Declaration on the Relationship of the Church to Non-Christian Religions'' (*Nostra aetate*) is the culmination of the Roman Catholic Church's efforts in that direction. It is to this document that the current dialogue of Judeo-Christianity with Islam is generally traced.

Nostra aetate

Pope John XXIII, the father of Vatican II, had been an apostolic delegate in Turkey during World War II. Excruciatingly aware of the suffering of the Jews in Europe, he had worked with the Turkish government and had succeeded in saving thousands from Nazi extermination. His sensitivity to the effects of anti-Judaism eventually moved him, in fact, to make changes in certain parts of the liturgy that could be used to justify the abominable attitude. In 1959 he deleted the adjective *perfidus* (unbelieving) from the Good Friday prayer for the Jews.[8] In the same year, he ratified deletion of the following lines from the prayer dedicating all humanity to Jesus: ''Look finally full of pity on the children of the people who were once your chosen people. May the blood that once was called down on them flow over them also as a fount of salvation.'' The idea that the Jews had once been called but, rejecting the Messiah, had lost their privileged status, seemed to be in conflict with St. Paul's assurance that ''the gifts and the call of God are irrevocable'' (Romans 11:29). More importantly, however, ''the blood that once was called down upon them''—clearly a reference to the words shouted by the crowd gathered at Pilate's palace: ''His blood be upon us and our children'' (Matthew 27:25)—needed reassessment. For one thing, the historical accuracy of the statement was seriously questioned by exegetes. But even if it was accurate, it was not necessarily a statement of metaphysical truth. Instead, it seemed to be an expression of collective frustration of "resistance-fighters . . . zealots—blinded by their guerilla ideology, which sought only one thing: freedom from the Roman yoke."[9] Thus the Christians granted the Jews a twofold reprieve. First, only certain Jews called for Jesus' crucifixion, not the whole race. Second, those Jews who were involved were driven by disappointment in their hopes of deliverance from Roman domination. The messiah they awaited was supposed to revive the Jewish kingdom; Jesus appeared therefore as a mere charlatan. Their impulsive statements surely were not sufficient to curse an entire people, any more than all Germans could be held responsible for the Holocaust.

This trend toward reassessment of the church's anti-Judaism took real shape in 1960 when Pope John personally commissioned the president of the Secretariat for Promoting Christian Unity to prepare a draft declaration on the entire issue of the relationship of the church to the Jews. Two major issues were concerned. First, the spirit of anti-Judaism was itself potentially anti-Christian. As Pope Pius XI had expressed, "Through Christ and in Christ we are Abraham's spiritual stock. Spiritually we are Semites."[10] Indeed, forerunners of the Nazi party had rejected Christianity, too, as a despicable offshoot of the inherently immoral Judaism.[11] So the end of anti-Semitism was conducive to the survival of Christianity itself. But on a theological level, there was sincere concern for the accurate interpretation of Scripture. As the French Jewish historian Jules Isaac (an early advocate of Pope John's council) pointed out to the pope, even the Catechism of Trent emphasized the guilt of *all* sinners as the real cause of Jesus' crucifixion. The Jews, therefore, could not be held responsible as a race. The council agreed: The "the" in St. John's gospels ("the Jews crucified Christ") did not refer to *all* Jews, but to those Jewish leaders who actually rejected Jesus and were instrumental in his death. Thus the foundation of anti-Jewish sentiment was officially extracted from Christian teaching.

In 1961, however, the commission encountered some opposition. Upon unofficial publication of the Secretariat's intended conclusions, the Muslim Arab leaders sought clarification. They no doubt lauded the church's efforts to live in peace with the Jews. The Muslims' open-door policy toward Jews escaping from Christian persecution in Europe since the Inquisition is legendary among Jews.[12] Yet the intended Declaration on the Brotherhood of Christians and Jews was based on the idea that God works in all communities. Should not other religions be included in the declaration? More to the point, considering the fact that the Jews had now founded a state and were at war with those who spoke in the name of the former inhabitants of that state, would not the declaration as it stood be interpreted as a political statement in favor of the Israeli state? The commission was at a loss as to how to respond to the Arabs. Despite the logic of the Arabs' protests, the commission was really only concerned with Jews and Catholics. As James Oesterreicher, a member of the commission, stated, "I fear [the Arabs] were never given to understand quite unambiguously that the proposed Declaration was a measure that was necessary for the inner life of the Church."[13]

Some members of the commission itself began to take up the call of the

Muslims. In particular, the relationship of the church to the Jews came to be seen in the larger context of ecumenism, the movement for Christian unity. As the ecumenical theologian Bernard Lambert wrote, "An ecumenism which limited itself simply to the relations between Christians would be in principle condemned never to succeed, because it would be established on too narrow a foundation."[14] But neither could this broader ecumenism be limited to just Jews and Christians. Bishop Jelmini of Lugano, speaking for all Swiss bishops, called on the church to restate its fundamental approach to the world: to change from a closed community to one which welcomes the world. In this context he encouraged the inclusion of Muslims and even "unbelievers" in the proposed declaration. As Oesterreicher said, "A succession of bishops greeted the schema as an event, truly a gift of God's grace."[15]

Thus was born the form that *Nostra aetate* would eventually take. In it for the first time the church acknowledged as legitimate both the search for God by those outside the Catholic church and the kernel of truth in those religions. All truth and piety reflect God's work, regardless of the religion in which they are found. The Muslims were specifically addressed:

Upon the Muslims . . . the Church looks with esteem. They adore one God, living and enduring, merciful and all-powerful, Maker of heaven and earth and Speaker to men. They strive to submit wholeheartedly even to His inscrutable decrees, just as did Abraham, with whom the Islamic faith is pleased to associate itself. Though they do not acknowledge Jesus as God, they revere Him as a prophet. They also honor Mary, His virgin mother; at times they call on her, too, with devotion. In addition they await the day of judgment when God will give each man his due after raising him up. Consequently, they prize the moral life, and give worship to God especially through prayer, almsgiving, and fasting.[16]

The dialogue called for was originally to be between the Christians and the Jews: "Since the spiritual patrimony common to Christians and Jews is . . . so great, this sacred Synod wishes to foster and recommend that mutual understanding and respect which is the fruit above all of biblical and theological studies, and of brotherly dialogues."[17] But Muslims and all other non-Christians were, by extension, included. Thus began the dialogue.

The Problem of Dialogue

Pope John XXIII's successor, Paul VI, was no less enthusiastic a supporter of dialogue. In his first encyclical, *Ecclesiam suam* (August 6, 1964), he sounded the theme:

Then we see another circle around us. This, too, is vast in its extent. . . . It is made up of the men who above all adore the one, supreme God whom we too adore. We refer briefly first to the children of the Hebrew people, worthy of our affection and respect, faithful to the religion which we call that of the Old Covenant. Then to the adorers of God according to the conception of monotheism, the Moslem religion especially, deserving of our admiration for all that is true and good in their worship of God. And also to the followers of the great Afro-Asiatic religions.[18]

However, the sentiment of love and respect is not unmixed with restraint. The pope went on to clarify that the church must nevertheless remain separate from these forms of religion. It must be made clear that the church does not hold these religions to be of equal value with Catholicism or even Christianity. Nor does it mean to imply that the followers of these religions are absolved of the responsibility to seek God "in the perfect and definitive form in which He has revealed Himself and in which He demands to be known, loved and served."[19] But having made that point: "We do, nevertheless, recognize and respect the moral and spiritual values of the various non-Christian religions, and we desire to join with them in promoting and defending common ideals of religious liberty, human brotherhood, culture, social welfare and civil order. For our part, we are ready to enter into dialogue on these common ideals, and will not fail to take the initiative where our offer of discussion in genuine, mutual respect would be well received."[20]

Dialogue has thus been explicitly limited. Because of the errors of non-Christian religions, Christians must be very careful not to imply approval of their theology. Only on those ideals shared in common—"religious liberty, human brotherhood, culture, social welfare and civil order"—is dialogue to be encouraged. Still, this dialogue is to be carried on "in genuine, mutual respect." Yet here we encounter the first of several problematic aspects of dialogue. That respect is not predicated on recognition of equal value or theological validity. Rather, it is predicated on the belief that God operates through all religions. As Paul VI said in his Easter address of March 29, 1964: "Every religion contains a ray of the light which we must neither despise nor extinguish, even though it is not sufficient to give man the truth he needs, or to realize the miracle of the Christian light in which truth and life coalesce. But every religion raises us towards the transcendent Being, the sole ground of all existence and all thought, of all responsible action and all authentic hope."[21]

The church, therefore, expresses a two-sided attitude toward non-Christian religions. On the one hand, it respects the elements of truth inherent in every religion. On the other hand, it recognizes their "insufficiency." What, then, is to be the relationship between Christians and non-Christians? The answer lies in Christianity's view of itself. The life of Christianity is one of process, of outreach, of teaching. Non-Christian religions are deserving of respect for their strengths, but Christianity maintains its claim to universal validity. It remains the Christian duty to spread true belief, therefore, to enlighten those veiled in darkness. As Pope Paul's Easter address continued, "Every religion is a dawn of faith, and we await its full realization in the light of noon, in the splendor of Christian wisdom." The insufficiency of non-Christian religions is to be overcome by "the splendor of Christian wisdom."[22]

It is in this context that the Christian notion of dialogue must be assessed. While the goal of dialogue is "mutual understanding and respect," dialogue itself is incomplete.[23] As the Vatican II documents make clear, it is but the prerequisite for the Christian's greater duty: "The proper and orderly exercise of missionary activity requires that those who labor for the gospel be scientifically prepared for their task, especially for dialogue with non-Christian religions and cultures. It requires that they be effectively assisted in the carrying out of this task. Hence this Council desires that, *for the sake of the missions,* fraternal and generous collaboration exist on the part of scientific institutes specializing in missiology and in other sciences and arts useful for the missions."[24]

Dialogue is thus part of a two-step process. Again, the Vatican II documents state: "Let the faithful take part in the strivings of those peoples who are waging war on famine, ignorance, and disease and thereby struggling to better their way of life and to secure peace in the world. In this activity the faithful should be eager to offer their prudent aid to projects sponsored by public and private organizations, by governments, by international agencies, by various Christian communities, and even by non-Christian religions."[25] Christians are to participate fully with non-Christians in the pursuit of those "common ideals" referred to above. In this way they will exemplify the highest Christian ideals. But this activity fits within a larger context, for in the very process they are spreading the light of the true faith.

Indeed, many of the references to dialogue to emerge from Vatican II documents are in the "Decree on the Church's Missionary Activity" (*Ad gentes*), rather than the "Declaration on the Relationship of the Church to Non-Christians" (*Nostra aetate*). It is in this document that the church clarifies its position on the value of dialogue: "Worthy of special praise are those laymen who work in universities or in scientific institutes and whose historical and scientific-religious research promotes knowledge of peoples and of religions. Thus they help the heralds of the gospel, and prepare for dialogue with non-Christians."[26]

The goal of dialogue is, therefore, mutual understanding and respect, but its position in the context of the church's mission is as a herald of the gospel. The church no longer preaches fear and scorn of non-Christian religions: "The Catholic Church . . . looks beyond the frontiers of Christianity. How could she limit her love, as she is to imitate the love of the divine Father, who gives His good things to all men (cf. Mt. 5:48) and so loved the world, that He gave His only son for its salvation (cf. Jn. 3:16)?"[27] Vatican II worked assiduously to extricate from the church's teachings the seeds of prejudice such as that which culminated in the Jewish Holocaust. Mutual respect and understanding must be fostered among all religions so as to eradicate institutionalized prejudice. Yet the duty of the Christian remains spreading the teaching of the gospel to all non-Christians.

Within the context of Christianity, there is no denying the virtue of this position. The firm conviction that one's doctrinal structure is not only accurate but universally applicable virtually necessitates the attempt to convince others of the errors of their ways. Thus in the Christian context, dialogue and missionarism go hand in hand. However, it is this very conviction that places dialogue in suspicion for the Muslims.

The Islamic Perspective

Islam grew out of the Judeo-Christian tradition and as such no doubt shares in its supersessionist heritage. The supersessionist position is that in which one community comes forward to supplant or "supersede" another. The onus of proof is on the new community; it must justify itself by condemning the older community. Thus Judaism sees itself as a community bearing the truth about the one God and supplanting the other communities, whose idolatry is marked by nothing if not by their depravity. This was how Judaism justified its occupation of the land of Canaan:

After the Lord, your God, has thrust them out of your way, do not say to yourselves, "it is because of my merits that the Lord has brought me in to possess this land"; for it is really because of the wickedness of these nations that the Lord is driving them out before you. No, it is not because of your merits or the integrity of your heart that you are going to take possession of their land; but the Lord, your God, is driving these nations out before you on account of their wickedness and in order to keep the promise which he made on oath to your fathers, Abraham, Isaac and Jacob.[28]

It was this that justified, in fact, the first instances of "holy war," those undertaken by Joshua to drive out the inhabitants of Jericho, Hai, and Gabaon: "As the horns blew, the people began to shout. When they heard the signal horn, they raised a tremendous shout. The wall collapsed and the people stormed the city in a frontal attack and took it. They observed the ban by putting to the sword all living creatures in the city: men and women, young and old, as well as oxen, sheep and asses" (Joshua 6:20–21).

In the case of Christianity, the supersession was of a somewhat different sort. Instead of supplanting a previously existing but unrelated tradition, such as that of the Canaanites, Christianity came to supplant its parent religion. Jesus was a Jew and like many other Jews was critical of the Jewish temple cult as it had evolved by his lifetime. Those who followed him were former members of the Jewish community. Their attacks on Judaism were, therefore, all the more vehement, since they were actually engaging in self-criticism, purging themselves of what now seemed their old and wicked ways. This is, in fact, the source of the undisguised anti-Judaism of the New Testament.

In both cases, however, the purpose of the polemic was not simply to justify the new movement. In the case of Judaism, it was the rationale for the dispossession or destruction of the previous community. In the case of Christianity, it was intended to convince its subjects of their folly. They were either to acknowledge the criticism and join the new group or remain the object of condemnation.

Like Judaism and Christianity, Islam criticizes its predecessors. This is a function of its belief that it is universally valid. But unlike its predecessors, it did not require conversion. Islam is essentially a religion that preaches submission to God's will, and God's will has been clearly revealed through all of the Semitic prophets from Abraham to Muhammad. The prophets were all correct, according to Islam, but their communities went astray. Judaism had received the message that those who do God's will—that is, establish a society on earth that reflects the equality of all people before God—will be blessed by God. But the community who claimed to follow those prophets had somehow limited the call to themselves. They alone were God's chosen people uniquely blessed by God. Thus in the Hebrew Bible God promised Abraham that he would be the father of a great nation and his descendents would be as numerous as the stars in the skies.

This, according to Islam, was a misrepresentation of the message. It mitigates the essential message of the prophets, a call to ethical behavior on the part of all people. The Hebrew Bible claims that God promised great rewards to the descendants of Abraham. The Qur'ān claims that what God really said, upon concluding the Covenant and in response to Abraham's question about the status of his descendants, was: "My promise applies only to the just ones" (2:124).[29] Muslims believe that if the Jews truly understood the message of God, they would recognize the validity of Muhammad's teaching, his call to ethical behavior. They would still be Jews, but they would have corrected their misinterpretation of the message. They would then be "muslim"—those who submit—at heart. The Qur'ān states: "Those who believe—the Jews, the Christians, and the Sabaeans—whosoever believe in God and the Last Day and do good works, they shall have their reward from their Lord and shall have nothing to fear, nor shall they come to grief" (2:62).

Similarly, with the Christians, Jesus, in many ways the greatest prophet according to Islam, came preaching the true word of God. He, in fact, was the messenger of universal, rather than "chosen," salvation. Those Jews who truly grasped the meaning of their religion, according to Islam, recognized the validity of Jesus' words and embraced his message of the universality of God's love. St. Paul, for example, after initially rejecting it, became "the apostle of the gentiles" soon after Jesus' death. Those Christians who truly understood Jesus' message could not deny the truth of Islam. Jesus did not claim to be God, states Islam, only to represent God's will for human salvation. That salvation can only be achieved through each individual's efforts at good works. It cannot be achieved by anyone else's deeds—a reference to the Christian belief in the salvific nature of Jesus' crucifixion. The Christian community had been led astray, according to Islam, and Muhammad was simply reminding them of the truth of their own prophet's teaching. Only the obstinate ones would deny the truth of Islam. "True" Christians, submitting in their hearts to God's will, were already "muslim."

Nevertheless, at the time of Muhammad, the Jews as a community rejected Christianity and Christians as a community rejected Judaism. According to the

Qur'ăn, Jews placed their "chosen" status at the core of their belief, eliminating those outside the tribes of Israel. Christianity, because the essential thrust of Jesus' message involved transcending family or tribal boundaries of religion, required the conversion from Judaism to Christianity. Thus the Semitic world, the world of the Abrahamic religion, was divided into two mutually exclusive sects, each claiming to be the true followers of God. Logically, the Muslims thought, they could not both be right.

The first indication to Prophet Muhammad that neither Judaism *nor* Christianity was properly interpreting the messages of God was the condition of the society they had created. The society into which Muhammad was born was one ridden with strife—rampant poverty and oppression of the poor by the few who controlled wealth. Clearly, a corrective was needed: this could hardly be the just society men were charged by the prophets to establish. But Islam did not preach rejection of former revelation, as Christianity did. It did not espouse abandoning earlier laws or even ritual. Islam is essentially a religion that preaches *against* sectarianism.[30] It was going to replace Judaism and Christianity but not by creating yet another sect claiming to worship the true God. Rather, it was to direct those who called themselves Jews and Christians to the errors of their ways and guide them back to the truth of their own traditions. God had revealed the message from the beginning of creation that salvation lay in contributing to the establishment of God's kingdom on earth. He had not changed his message; only its interpretations had changed. That kingdom would be one of unity, equality, justice, and peace. Anyone who worked toward that goal was Muslim.

Thus supersessionism had a different meaning in Islam than that in Judaism and Christianity. It supersedes but does not compete. It accepted diversity among peoples as a fact of life. Indeed, the Qur'ăn confirms it: "There is no nation wherein a warner has not come" (35:24). "For every people a guide has been provided" (13:7). "If your Lord had so willed, He would have made mankind one community, but they continue to remain divided" (11:118). Islam does not require conversion, therefore. The Qur'ăn states, "There shall be no compulsion in religion." It requires only submission to God's will. Therefore, the belief in the necessity of converting Muslims and Jews to Christianity is foreign to Islam, and it represents, in the Islamic view, a lack of respect for the truth of Islam, which undermines the very basis of legitimate dialogue.

Furthermore, the history of missionarism in the Muslim world has been somewhat less than commendable. From its ignominious beginnings with the Crusades, such activity has been considered at best an insult to Islam. At worst, missionary activity has seemed little more than a thin disguise for mercantile or colonial activity, as the Fourth Crusade so aptly illustrates. This is certainly not to state that Islam has never pursued similar goals. But colonial activity in the Muslim world has had unremittingly pernicious effects. Indeed, the current wars in the Middle East are without question the result of colonial designs on the

Ottoman Empire after World War I, designs in which Christian missions unwittingly played a significant role.

Missions in the Islamic Middle East

Before World War I, the Middle East was not separated into national entities or states but rather into traditional regions of cultural and ethnic affinity, all under the control of the Ottoman Empire. The Ottomans were nominally Muslim but were perceived by their Arab subjects as increasingly secular and oppressive.[31] The two major regions of the area were Syria, including what are now called Syria, Lebanon, Palestine, and Jordan; and Iraq. During World War I, the Ottoman sultan sided with Germany against the Allied Powers of France, Britain, and Russia, and the Allies took advantage of the widespread discontent of the Arabs under Ottoman control. Britain took the initiative and promised the Arabs an independent state if they would rebel against the Ottomans, thus helping the Allied effort. The Arabs, after long consideration, agreed and indeed helped defeat the Axis powers. Contrary to their promise, however, the Allies acted upon a secret treaty concluded among themselves and partitioned the formerly Ottoman lands into "mandates": Britain took control of Iraq, Palestine, and what is now called Jordan; France took for itself what are now called Syria and Lebanon. (The newly created Soviet Union took formerly Ottoman lands outside the Middle East.)

This partitioning of the Middle East created the conditions for the various wars being carried on to this day in the area. Most obviously, Britain took it upon itself to declare Palestine a homeland for world Jewry, which led to the displacement of millions of Palestinians, still engaged in the struggle to regain their homeland. Britain also decided that the Arabs should be given at least some "reward" for their war efforts. Thus they created a state out of the Transjordanian region of greater Syria and placed upon its throne members of the leading Arab family, the Hashemites. This state, now called Jordan, in turn, is engaged in the effort to regain Palestine, or at least the West Bank, for the Palestinians. Syria views this as an attempt by the Hashemites to gain hegemony among the Arabs and thus continues to thwart Jordanian King Hussein's efforts.[32] Syria also continues its struggle to regain Lebanon by alternately backing one faction or another in that troubled area. It is in Lebanon, in fact, that we see the most destructive effects of missionarism in the Muslim world, for the factions in Lebanon, unlike those in other Middle Eastern struggles, are drawn along religious lines.

The interest of European powers in the Middle East had been growing since their debut on the stage of world colonialism in the fifteenth and sixteenth centuries. The discovery of the sea route from Europe to India eliminated the economic leverage of the Arab traders. The discovery of the New World in 1492 effectively shifted the focus of international trade from the Near East to the West. Yet the strategic location of the Arab lands made them potentially threatening and therefore essential in the colonial designs of Britain and France. In particular, the overland trade route through Syria to Iraq, Persia, and India was still important in the first centuries of Ottoman rule. By the sixteenth century, therefore, several European colonies had grown up in the region, especially around Aleppo in Syria.

These colonies gained a great deal of power in the area by means of what Arab historians deprecatingly call "capitulations." These were agreements for special treatment of Christians in the Ottoman lands granted as early as 1535 by the Ottoman sultan to France's Francis I. Such capitulations were reinforced in a treaty signed in 1740 by the Sultan and Louis XV. The effect of the capitulations was to put all Christians in the Ottoman Empire under French protection.[33] This meant they were subject only to French laws and were free to flout Islamic restrictions on trade, monopolies, and the bearing of arms. It was not long before French settlements and factories spread throughout Syria. In their wake came European missionaries and teachers. Unbridled by Ottoman law and unrestricted by service to the Muslim state, these Christians were able by the seventeenth and eighteenth centuries to found the Uniat churches—Syrian and Greek Christians who acknowledge the supremacy of the pope, giving up their allegiance to the independent Eastern Orthodox churches. All of these Christians, formerly under Ottoman control, enjoyed the special privileges granted under the capitulations and were therefore strongly indebted to French protection.

It was on this basis that France was able to exercise its mandate control after World War I. The nature of the mandates was, according to the League of Nations, to be "a sacred trust of civilization" whereby the mandatory power was to aid and advise the native inhabitants in order that they might eventually achieve full independence. But the people of the occupied territories did not see it that way. As Arab historian Philip Hitti summarized:

Especially provoking were the grievances felt by the Syrians who charged French officials with employing the same colonial methods as in North Africa, use of the native government as a facade, failure to take cognizance of the rising national spirit, discouragement of the use of Arabic, depreciating the native currency by tying it to the franc, playing one party or sect against another and resorting to repressive measures involving espionage, imprisonment and exile. . . . Any benefits that might have accrued to the mandated territories by way of maintaining law and order, improving communications, widening areas of cultivation, extending facilities of education and setting up the framework of a modern government and modernized society were not enough to stem the tide of rising discontent.[34]

Consequently, a series of revolts broke out against the French, eventually leading to their retreat in 1945. But this did not occur until after France had divided the country into several states (one of which it ceded to Turkey). These states were put under the control of various religious sects, often with no regard for the principle of "majority rule."

In particular, the area of Lebanon was made a state and given a constitution that guaranteed the dominance of Maronite Christians, who now constitute less than one quarter of Lebanon's population. Secondary control was guaranteed in perpetuity to Druze Muslims, also a small minority in the newly created state. Sunni Muslims, the second most populous group in the state, were given a tertiary share in the power. The Shi'ite Muslims, now by far the largest single group in Lebanon, were left out of the power structure. Such a situation could not exist in a unified Syria; despite traditional Maronite dominance in the region of Lebanon, the well-established Muslim power structure in Syria would inevitably prevail. The separation of Lebanon from Syria therefore virtually insured the type of power struggles that would preclude the emergence of a unified and potentially powerful Syria.

The effect of the Mandate period in Syria was therefore to pit religion against religion, sect against sect. The pious and well-motivated sacrifices of the Christian missionaries resulted in the betrayal and oppression of Muslims by Western powers. The Muslim world is thus understandably suspicious of Christian missionary work. It has found its respect for Christian tradition and belief unreciprocated and, at times, downright dangerous. The prevailing attitude is that Christian missions, commendable in themselves, have been used as a tool of Western expansion and economic and political domination.

In the postwar dialogue efforts, the World Council of Churches (WCC) has been particularly sensitive to this problem. At a recent Christian-Muslim consultation held in Chambesy, Switzerland, under the WCC's auspices, an effort was made to restrict dialogue to an exchange of views and experiences, rather than efforts to persuade. Thus dialogue was defined as "a mood, a spirit and an attitude. . . . Dialogue is a readiness to learn as well as to share in information, to receive as well as to give."[35] It insisted that dialogue must never be given over to proselytization. The Catholic church itself, while maintaining its stance on missionarism, continues a vigorous discussion regarding the meaning and goal of missionary work. Is conversion actually its aim? Yet these attempts have not yet been sufficient to overcome the fears of Muslims that dialogue is an instrument of missionarism and hence of colonialism.

This impression is strengthened by the very way in which dialogue is suggested. The direction of the Judeo-Christian dialogue has been toward identity of traditions. Christianity is working toward embracing Judaism as its progenitor, as Judaism will accept Christianity as its somewhat creative offspring. Hence the terminology "Judeo-Christian tradition." However, Islam does not see its relationship to be between itself and a tradition. Indeed, on the basis of tradition alone, the proper terminology would be "Judeo-Christian-Islamic." On the level of religious belief, however, Islam's relationships are between Judaism and Christianity as distinct religious sects. The religious beliefs involved are very different and so Islam's relationship with each is unique.

Furthermore, Islam does not see its goal as merely recognizing the existence of two mutually exclusive yet historically related elements and voicing respect for their doctrines. This would be a denial of its very *raison d'être;* Islam exists specifically to implement the truth of its message of social justice, the truth of the "Judeo-Christian-Islamic" prophetic tradition. Islam must therefore address both the Jewish and the Christian communities' errors each in its uniqueness.

Islam had indeed been doing so throughout its history. As mentioned above, the Muslim world has always contained significant Christian and Jewish minorities, since conversion was not necessary in the Muslim world. Jews and Christians were considered "protected peoples"; on the model of tribal association, those not organically related to the community were "protected" by—that is, adjunct members of—the community or tribe. The Qur'ān states of those who insisted on maintaining an identity separate from that of the Muslim community as a whole that, in terms of judgment, "their affair is up to God and He shall let them know what they have been doing" (6:160). In practical terms, they simply had to pay a tax (counterpart to but often greater than the Muslim poor tax). As Jewish scholar S. D. Goitein pointed out: "The Jewish historians of the nineteenth century . . . , who were deeply embittered by the contrast between the enlightened ideas of that century and the denial of civic rights to Jews in many European countries, pointed out most emphatically that the legal and actual position of the Jews during the Middle Ages was much better in Muslim-Arab countries than in Christian Europe; and the 'Golden Age' of Judaism in Muslim Spain has become a phrase which has found its way even into the most popular accounts of Jewish history."[36] With the downfall of the Muslim world, therefore, came also the demise of so-called "oriental" Jews. As Goitein said: "Concurrently, the Jews in Arabic-speaking countries, who at one time had formed both the majority of the Jewish people and its social and spiritual pivot, simply faded out of Jewish history. . . . There remained Jews in all Arabic-speaking territories (with the sole exception of northern Arabia), but their number was relatively small—less than ten per cent of the total Jewish population of the world. The Jewish-Arab symbiosis had lost its historical importance."[37]

Nor should the Christian presence in the Islamic world be overlooked. As noted above, Christians maintained a high profile throughout the classical age of Islam and to this day remain a vigorous presence in the Muslim world. Egypt, for instance, has a Christian population of some 18 percent (approximately 7 million), mostly Copts. Syria maintains a Christian minority of 11 percent (some 700,000), including Jacobites, Nestorians, and Protestants. Lebanon is nearly half Christian, although strictly divided into warring sects of Maronites and other Eastern Catholics, as well as some Chalcedonian and non-Chalcedonian Orthodox. Jordan has some 250,000 Christians, or about 12 percent of its population, including Orthodox, Syrian, and Jacobite Anglicans. Indonesia includes some 20 million Christians (17 percent of the total population), mostly Roman Catholic and Protestant.

It is therefore only in the West, a world in which the Islamic community has not been recognized, that Judaism and Christianity form a single identifiable entity. North Americans often refer to their Judeo-Christian heritage and call attention to their ignorance of Islam. "Very little is known in the West about the nature of religious discussions or analysis in the Muslim countries'' begins the introduction to a recent article in Christian ecumenical literature.[38] Even in this context, however, ''Judeo-Christian'' does not refer to a religion. Such terminology, in fact, denies the individuality of Judaism as a religion. It is appropriate for Christianity because Christianity indeed grew out of Judaism, just as the term ''Judeo-Christian-Islamic'' is appropriate in the same context for Islam. But insofar as Judaism rejects the claims made by and for Jesus, it is inappropriate to include ''Christianity'' in designating the Jewish religion. Judeo-Christianity can only refer to the cultural heritage of Europe and America.

The Pakistani Christian exponent of dialogue, Michael Nazir-Ali, observed:

It is a particular failing of western writers to persist in understanding the historical phenomenon of Christianity's encounter with other faiths in terms of the modern western (both Christian and non-Christian) encounters with world religions other than Christianity or Judaism. In fact, Eastern Christians (Nestorian, Jacobite, Armenian, etc.) have often lived in situations where the religion of those around them was Buddhism, Hinduism, or Islam. . . . For example, the Christians of St. Thomas of India (present membership approximately 3 million out of a total population of 18 million Christians) have lived for centuries in an environment that is predominantly Hindu even to the extent that they are often treated as a caste within Hinduism. . . . Yet when even the most sophisticated western writers discuss the contextualization of Christianity in India, they almost always ignore the contribution the Christians of St. Thomas could make in this respect. The assumption, in these cases, is always that Christianity is a faith of fairly recent import from the West and it must somehow be cast in a more Indian mould. What is true of the Christians of St. Thomas is also true, in varying degrees, of the ancient churches in Islamic lands. Their tremendously important achievement in coming to terms with Islam and maintaining a Christian presence (however emasculated) in Muslim countries is often ignored when Muslim-Christian dialogue is discussed.[39]

Finally, the impression of Islamic dialogue with the Judeo-Christian tradition as a shadow of Western colonial presence in the Middle East is intensified by the elision from religious understanding to peace. As Hans Küng concluded in the above-mentioned article, the dialogue process is important because ''there can be no peace among nations without peace among religions. Peace is indivisible.''[40] The implication here is that the wars that plague the Middle East are somehow related to religious misunderstanding. This is true only in the broadest sense: There is reasonable hope that if all three segments of the Abrahamic tradition truly lived up to their ideals, the persecution, oppression, and colonialism that are, in fact, the true bases of Middle Eastern conflict would never have arisen. On more specific issues, however, the contention betrays ignorance of some of the key elements in the Middle East wars. First, the lines between warring factions in the Middle East, other than in Lebanon, are not drawn on religious lines. Küng's article was a report on a conference held in Khomeini's Iran. Iran is at war with Iraq—another Muslim country—and has been for nearly six years. The Palestinian struggle to regain a homeland is led by the Palestine

Liberation Organization (PLO), a group made up of both Muslims and Christians. In fact, among the most radical groups falling under the PLO umbrella is the PFLP (Peoples' Front for the Liberation of Palestine), headed by a Christian Marxist.

Perhaps even more glaringly, the elision seems to equate the Middle East with Islam. Not only does the Middle East include many Christians and Jews; it makes up only a fraction of the Muslim world. The latter stretches from China and Soviet Central Asia, which together contain some 70 million Muslims; includes Indonesia, Malaysia, Pakistan, Afghanistan, and Iran; and extends all the way to North and sub-Saharan Africa. Many of these societies are religiously pluralistic; the wars they have known were due to well-known political problems. To attribute the wars in the Middle East to religious misunderstanding, therefore, is to obfuscate the reality of the political struggles being waged there.

The question of the current Islamic dialogue with the Judeo-Christian tradition is therefore fraught with complexities stemming from its problematic origin, particularly in Vatican II's *Nostra aetate* and *Ad gentes*. From its inception, the current dialogue was a Western and Christian enterprise, concerned primarily with Judeo-Christian relations. Upon Muslim insistence and with the enlightened leadership of some Christian thinkers, Islam was eventually included. Yet according to the same documents, the understanding sought by dialogue ultimately remains at the service of missionarism. Christians must understand non-Christian religions in order to evangelize effectively. This calls into question the Christians' respect for non-Christian religions. Furthermore, in the Muslim world in particular, the ideal of respect pales in importance relative to its current political problems. The Muslim world is part of the Third World and is suffering severely under the effects of colonialism. In the struggle waged by colonial powers to gain its enormous control over the Muslim world, missionaries played a significant although unintentional role. Finally, the Christian proclivity to refer to itself as the Judeo-Christian tradition vis-à-vis Islam tends to pitch the dialogue as an East-West rather than an Islamic-Jewish-Christian encounter. These issues complicate the dialogue process and account for its diversity and erratic success rate.

PROGRESS OF DIALOGUE

Periodical Literature

Perhaps it is the very complexity of the issues that accounts for the prodigious output of materials in the current dialogue process, as the periodical literature amply illustrates.[41] No fewer than twenty-five periodicals are devoted specifically to the ecumenism/dialogue issue (see Bibliography). Of them, six are concerned specifically with Jewish-Christian dialogue: *Christian Attitudes on Jews and Judaism* (London), *Christian Jewish Relations* (London), *Christian News from Israel* (Jerusalem), *Journal of the Service international de documentation Judeo-*

chrétienne (Rome), *The NICM Journal for Jews and Christians in Higher Education* (Newton Center, Massachusetts), and *Rencontre Chrétiens et Juifs* (Paris). Only two deal with Islam and Christianity: *Encounter* (Documents for Muslim-Christian Understanding [Rome]) and *Islamochristiana* (Rome). None deals specifically with Islam and the Judeo-Christian traditions. The pages of these journals (and others not specifically related to dialogue) are filled with articles dealing with a variety of aspects of Islamic dialogue with Judaism and Christianity. (See also Bibliography for relevant periodical literature, arranged according to subject matter.)

Monographs

If the complexity of Islamic-Jewish-Christian dialogue has generated a mind-boggling array of viewpoints and approaches, it has also been the source of some significant and responsible efforts at analysis. Particularly in monograph-length literature (see Bibliography), one finds serious efforts to address the question of the origin, nature, and value of dialogue. The World Council of Churches, for example, has compiled a select bibliography of the literature attempting to answer questions of the nature and value of dialogue. If dialogue is desirable, of what sort?[42] In a similar vein, Eric Sharpe has made an attempt to catalogue the various forms that dialogue can take and recommends those he considers most effective. "Discursive dialogue," he said, is that concerned with exchanges of beliefs, in the context of apologetics. One describes what he or she believes and presents as convincing a case as possible for the validity of that belief. Not surprisingly, according to Sharpe, this sort of exchange often degenerates to the level of polemics. The "interior dialogue" described by Sharpe, on the other hand, is one in which experiences, rather than beliefs, are exchanged. This sort of dialogue often attracts the more mystically oriented and is conducive to the sharing and possible broadening of spiritual experience. "Secular dialogue," by avoiding the question of beliefs or spiritual experience and concentrating on cooperative efforts to solve mutual problems of human suffering, emerges as the most successful in Sharpe's analysis.[43]

The accuracy of Sharpe's typology is borne out in a variety of recent conferences, such as those sponsored by the World Council of Churches and the Vatican. Again, however, these conferences are generally between Muslims and Christians only. Among the most significant efforts at Muslim-Jewish dialogue has been that carried on by the Institute for Islamic-Judaic Studies of the Center for Judaic Studies at the University of Denver, established in 1981. The expressed purpose of the institute, as stated in its bylaws, is to "provide a forum free from political concerns, for the academic study of the interactions of Islamic and Jewish civilization in such areas as history, religion, law, philosophy, language, literature and the arts." Although none of its proceedings has been published to date, in its brief history the institute has managed to attract leading scholars in each tradition for the purpose of mutual enlightenment of their shared historical and ideological development.

It has been speculated that it was just such a careful academic approach to interreligious exchange that enabled the change in Christian anti-Islamic attitudes in the first place. Georges C. Anawati, one of the greatest Christian scholars of Islam, welcomes the Vatican efforts at dialogue as long overdue. Describing as shameful the "classical" Christian attitude toward Islam, he said:

One can say that up to the beginning of the twentieth century the constant attitude of the Church towards Islam was one of condemnation, insofar as Islam appeared to be a "new" religion, which sought to supplant Christianity and denied its principal dogmas: Trinity, Incarnation and Salvation. Moreover, the revelation completed with the death of the last apostle could not be further extended by a new prophet. During the Middle Ages, in view of the political dangers presented by the Moslem countries and of the exhaustion of secular powers of Europe, none of which had the strength to defend the frontiers of the Christian West single-handed, the Popes made themselves the foremost champions of the Christian countries and the instigators of the Crusades. . . . Islam was necessarily condemned, Mohammed was a false prophet, the Koran a collection of errors, the truths contained in it had been taken from the Bible, and so on.[44]

In particular, Anawati said, it was due to the work of another great Christian scholar of Islam, Louis Massignon, that the West became interested in Islam again. A practicing Catholic, Massignon embarked on the study of al-Hallaj, the great Muslim mystic of the tenth century. Through these studies Massignon apparently deepened his own faith. He therefore devoted the rest of his life to the study of Islam and pursuit of the source of that faith. Massignon believed, according to Anawati, that Christians should perform a "spiritual Copernican revolution," returning to the origin of Islamic teaching, "to that point of virgin truth that is found at its center and makes it live."[45] He believed that the three monotheistic religions comprised the totality of revelation. "Israel is the religion of hope and Christianity is the religion of love, but Islam is the religion of faith." All three religions derive from the same source; they are all heirs to the one truth; none is complete without the other; and each has something to teach the others. Anawati pointed out that it is possible to take this attitude to extremes.[46] Yet he concluded that it was Massignon's scholarly approach and truly respectful attitude that made possible the advances of Vatican II.

In addition, Anawati very realistically called attention to the impediments to dialogue stemming from the troubled recent history of the Christian West and the Islamic world:

For if on the Western side ecumenical and intellectual progress had made it possible to regard past events with equanimity of spirit, the same does not apply to the Moslem countries. These are still engaged in a struggle against Western pressure, which they all too often equate with "Christian" pressure. The wounds of the past are still far from healed and some leading Moslems who are directing this struggle find it difficult, in mobilizing the people and arousing their fighting spirit, not to recall the "aggressions" of the West at the time of the Crusades as well as those of "colonialism" and "imperialism." Many concrete situations have to be cleaned up (for the Arab countries especially the problem of Israel and the liberation of some of their peoples) before the conflicts of the past can be forgotten.[47]

A simple exchange of beliefs, experiences, ideas, or concerns is therefore not enough.

A recent anthology, *Christianity and Islam: The Struggling Dialogue* (ed. Richard W. Rousseau, S. J.), also makes an effort to deal with the complexity of the issues involved in dialogue. The volume begins with a historical overview of Islamic-Christian interaction, followed by an article dealing specifically with the subsequent obstacles to dialogue. An important chapter deals with the doctrinal basis common to Christians and Muslims and offers some suggestions for joint action in areas of common interest. Again, however, the treatment is general and introductory.

John Joseph, in his *Muslim-Christian Relations and Inter-Christian Rivalries in the Middle East,* faced the more specific questions head on. He carefully distinguished not only between Jews and Christians but among the many sects of Christianity in the Middle East. His work offers a modern history of the Syrian Christians (Jacobites) as a case study for examining Christian-Muslim relations and inter-Christian rivalries. In his description of how Christians in the Middle East fit into the overall context of that world, he attempted to determine their role in the major issues dominating the Islamic Middle East: Palestinian homelessness, war, religious revival. Although himself a Jacobite, he acknowledged how Western countries interacted with the Eastern Christian communities, often to the detriment of both Christians and non-Christians in the Middle East. He also includes a thirty-page bibliography for those concerned with deepening their understanding of this very sensitive but essential area for Muslim-Christian understanding.

American Church Politics and the Middle East, edited by Basheer Nijim, examines another facet of this complex picture. An article by Rabbi Elmo Berger, for example, describes how the Bible and Western Judeo-Christian affinity have been instrumental in mobilizing American public opinion to a political stance favorable to the state of Israel. By contrast, Joseph Ryan pointed out that the opposite position has been taken by the Catholic church itself. Examining church documents from the period 1973–1978, Ryan pointed out that the official position of the church does not equate the state of Israel with Judaism. The Vatican does not even recognize the state of Israel politically, since it has not officially declared its borders. It considers the Arab-Israeli conflict a political and humanitarian issue, at the heart of which lies the plight of displaced Palestinians. Another article in the anthology suggests some practical steps that Americans of all religions can take to deepen their knowledge of the Arabs and thus be able to distinguish between Judaism and Israel, Islam and the Arabs—an essential prerequisite for successful dialogue.

On the level of doctrine itself, several books deserve mention. The classical work on comparative Islamic and Christian theology is that of James Sweetman, *Islam and Christian Theology*. A work of four volumes, published from 1945 to 1967, it was produced in the context of Sweetman's missionary work in India. Sweetman, in fact, was one of the instigators behind the founding of the Centre for the Study of Islam and Christian-Muslim Relations in the Selly Oaks Colleges of Birmingham, England. He attempted in these volumes to present a comparative study of Islamic and Christian theology in terms of historical development. Yet the work is not pleasing to Muslims, since it takes as its criterion of truth Christian revelation. (The work is out of print but has been abridged by Sweetman's colleague, James Moon. The abridgement is available in a recent edition edited by Sigvard von Sicard.)

A more recent and more balanced work is Michael Nazir-Ali's *Islam: A Christian Perspective*. From a family of Zaidi Shi'i Muslims, Nazir-Ali is well acquainted with Islamic belief and sentiment. He began his work with a concise and accurate account of the genesis of Islam in its Judeo-Christian context. (Uniquely among Jewish and Christian writers on Islam, Nazir-Ali did not attempt to claim greater influence for his own sect on Islam. He accurately recorded the greater presence of Jews in Arabia, while the Christian communities were generally along the borders.) Most of the rest of the book is dedicated to the historical development of Islam until the rise of modern fundamentalism. The author concluded with a brief analysis of current dialogue efforts, pointing out their extreme West orientation, and therefore concentrated his brief final remarks on the indigenous Christian presence in the Muslim world. Although Nazir-Ali's concern is spreading the light of Christianity, his respectful treatment of Islam and concern for the integrity of indigenous culture are commendable.

Overall, however, the most productive works on dialogue with Islam have been those following the careful and scholarly methods propounded by Anawati. Among the forerunners of this approach today is Wilfred Cantwell Smith. He began his essay on Muslim-Christian Relations (Part IV of *On Understanding Islam: Selected Studies*), for instance, with the observation that mutual understanding requires "in addition to good will, also new and clarified understanding; and this perhaps the universities, and the universities alone, can pursue and purvey."[48] Although this is not meant to denigrate the role of other groups in the pursuit of interreligious dialogue, it does focus on Smith's contention that it is the major task of the study of religion today to develop categories of analysis and understanding that can be shared by different religious traditions. With this in mind, he maintained that the pursuit of dialogue must begin with scholarly study of other traditions. There are two reasons for this. First, he believes that sustained study will enable an overview or a general conception of a tradition not necessarily forthcoming in sporadic individual contacts. This overview is the means by which one will inevitably recognize that "despite differences in detail . . . there is also substantial comparability, elusive yet fundamental.''[49] This recognition of overall comparability, Smith believes, is prerequisite to successful dialogue. Second, he believes that without such prior and sustained study, the overwhelming likelihood is that participants will come to the dialogue table harboring dangerous mutual misconceptions: "If two people know wherein they agree and wherein they differ, then they may intelligibly discuss their respective stands. If, however, each harbors misconceptions about the other's position, and both misconceive what their agreements and divergences actually are, then conversation if it occurs at all proves to be exasperation, or absurdity, or anyway inconsequential. Unfortunately, this has largely been the situation historically.''[50]

Smith therefore set about the task of providing a constructive framework for this type of prerequisite study. First, he posited the importance of recognizing what questions different religions are trying to answer. He considered it a common misconception that different religions simply give different answers to the same questions. The unity of the religious enterprise lies rather in the transcendent reality of a single universe. It is of a single universe, he maintained, that different questions are asked. Therefore, Smith thought that religious diversity must be accepted at the outset as a natural phenomenon. The goal of dialogue should not be to change this situation, he said, but to understand it.

In the context of the Islamic-Christian dialogue, then, Smith sketched a course of study designed to focus on the major questions asked of the universe by each tradition. Methodologically, he proceeded from interpretations of major concepts shared by both traditions, beginning with the phrase "the will of God." Christians, he said, following Christ himself, use the phrase "Thy will be done." Striving to do God's will, for Christians, is the highest calling. Muslims, he pointed out, use for this same notion not God's will but His command. He suggested, that is, that "the will of God is to Christianity as the *sharia* (law) is to Islam.''[51] In Islam the idea of someone doing God's will is preposterous. God's will is what God does; it is everything that happens. It is inevitable. "Man can disobey God's command but cannot contravene His will.''[52] Thus although the interpretations of the particular expression differ, the fundamental reality is shared. Each tradition uses the phrase to answer a different question, but both ask the questions in some context in the first place.

Another major issue treated by Smith in this way is that of sacred Scripture. He begins by debunking the obvious misconception that the Qur'ān is to Islam what the Bible is to Christianity. Instead, he suggested that the Qur'ān is to Islam what the person of Jesus Christ is to Christianity, and the Bible more properly corresponds to the Islamic Hadith (records of the sayings and deeds of the prophet and his companions considered to be normative in Islam). In Islam, the central focus of revelation is not Muhammad but the Qur'ān; Muhammad was the prophet and leader whose instantiation of the Qur'ān's teachings are taken as normative. In Christianity, on the other hand, it is the Bible that is the record of revelation, and Jesus himself and all that he did is its subject. This issue is addressed to the common misinterpretation that the gospels were revealed to Jesus—a misconception, Smith advised, shared by Muslims and some Christians alike. He, therefore, made the very instructive observation: "For Muslims to say that Jesus brought the Injil [gospel] is as though Christians were to say of Muhammad that he brought [Hadith]."[53] In this way, Smith again pointed to the fact that Scripture answers different questions for Muslims and for Christians, but there is nonetheless a more fundamental similarity: In both Christianity and Islam, the behavior of the messenger is exemplary of God's will.

This brings Smith to another similarity between Christians and Muslims: their shared emphasis on community. In Islam, he said, faith is not merely in Scripture but in what Muhammad did, and what Muhammad did was to establish a community to propagate God's command for a just society. Thus primary emphasis is placed on the *ummah* (community), which is the moral imperative of the Qur'ān. In Christianity, although the emphasis is different, it is nonetheless true that faith means "living in Christ," that is, participating in the church.[54]

The respective interpretations of this fundamental point shed light on several other apparent differences, including the relative importance of doctrine. For a Christian, the natural question about another religion is "What do they believe?" This stems from the Christian tradition of the dominant role played by theology. By contrast, "Theology (*'ilm al-kalam*) is to Islam as philosophy of religion is to Christianity: a serious, often brilliant discipline for those who are concerned with it, useful as apologetics, but peripheral to the main development, dispensable, and even suspect."[55] The Muslim emphasis on *ummah* instead prompts the question concerning other religions, "What do they do?" Smith thus redrew the comparison of church with mosque. "A Christian is a member of a church. A Muslim is not a member of a mosque."[56] He stretched somewhat to suggest instead that Christians' belonging to a church is like Muslims' belonging to a Sufi brotherhood. But in his discussion he revealed a more precise similarity: the church and the *ummah*. A Muslim is a member of the community of all Muslims, just as a Christian is a member of the church in general. The Christian's affiliation with a particular church or congregation is simply a microcosmic representation of that relationship.

Smith also explored the notion of community guidance in Islam. There is a common belief in Islam that the prophet guaranteed that his community would not agree on an error. This has been instrumental in the highly developed aspect of Islamic jurisprudence known as *ijma'*, or consensus. The authority by which Sunni Muslim law governs, in fact, is ensconced in this notion that God is constantly guiding the community. In Shi'i Islam this notion is fundamental to the authority of the *imam*, or religious leader, whose guidance is authoritative. In either case, Smith sees a counterpart in Christianity to the notion of the Holy Spirit, a constant presence among the faithful, and their source of guidance. Again, the pattern emerges: On first view, similar notions answer different questions, but further study reveals that all questions have counterparts.

Smith asserted: "There are numerous other areas in which one could explore questions of this kind, rescrutinizing accepted parallels and suggesting new and subtler ones.''[57] In characterizing his approach overall, he said that pursuit of such suggested parallels is not meant to be conclusive or decisive. Rather, his intent was to suggest a proper methodology for a scholarly and productive approach to dialogue, one that explores questions rather than looking for answers; one based on the assumption that the universe is one and that all traditions are seeking to understand it; one, therefore, designed to be as enlightening for one's own tradition as for that of one's dialogue partner. As Smith said, he explored this methodology ''not because I necessarily believe it to be valid but because it has seemed interesting and instructive.''[58]

More recently, in *Islam and Christianity Today*, W. Montgomery Watt, another exemplar of the scholarly approach to dialogue, has made what is described by Sheikh Ahmad Zaki Yamani (the famous Saudi oil minister) as a significant ''contribution to dialogue'' and ''effort to free the Western mentality of the shackles of prejudice and hatred.'' In the foreword, Sheikh Yamani quoted Watt's characterization of the value of dialogue with Islam: ''Islam is certainly a strong contender for the supplying of the basic framework of the one religion of the future.''[59]

Watt's work deals primarily with the doctrinal aspects of the two religions, a task for which his forty years as a foremost Christian scholar of Islam have prepared him well. After exploring the historical interaction of the two traditions, he devoted an entire chapter to defense of the validity of religious truth in general against attacks based on pseudoscientific claims to the contrary. He concluded that although scientific principles may be sufficient to deal with the components of observable phenomena, they provide little insight into their meaning for humankind. In fact, he continued, the very notion of reality, therefore, cannot be confined to the objects of scientific study. Reality extends to what is significant for individuals and society. Yet this does not mitigate the responsibility of the student of religion to approach the subject as systematically and carefully as possible. Thus Watt began his treatment of what he considers the key elements shared by Islam and Christianity.

First, the ultimate reality for both religions is the existence of God. This is not to deny that their respective conceptions of God are somewhat at variance. The referent is the same, but distinctions in perception are to be found in the names and attributes applied to God. Still, there is a fundamental principle shared by Muslims and Christians: the terms used to describe God are not to be taken literally or to apply to God in the same way they apply to people. They are, in St. Thomas Aquinas's words, analogous. They mean neither the same thing nor something completely different, for although one can know some things about God, God remains transcendent of definition. As the Muslims put it, the names of God are ''not God and not other than God.''

Furthermore, both Christians and Muslims hold that the primary characteristic of God is that he is one. The importance of this is expressed in the first half of the Muslim confession of faith (*shahada*): ''There is no god but God.'' God is one in two senses: There is only one deity, and it is absolutely simple. Although this belief is shared by Christians, it is posited that the extreme emphasis placed by Muslims on the point is related to their belief that Christians mitigate the unicity of God in the doctrine of the Trinity. Watt showed, however, that Islam does not criticize belief in the Trinity as such. The relevant Qur'anic verse is 5:73, which condemns only belief in a threefold God. Tritheism is heresy in both Christianity and Islam. Christians, therefore, would agree with the Islamic condemnations. Watt mentioned several early medieval Arab theologians, both Christian and Muslim, who in fact attempted to compare the persons of the Trinity to the Islamic attributes of God.[60]

Christians and Muslims also share the belief that God is both transcendent and immanent. Transcendence is a function of God's unlimited nature; it means that God remains beyond comprehension. Individuals are by definition limited and that which is greater cannot be defined by that which is lesser. Yet God's immanence is self-evident in terms of his undeniable intervention in history. First, he reveals himself in Scripture. If this were not the case, clearly, there would be nothing to discuss by either Christians or Muslims. The very modality of God-talk is that derived from revelation, direct intervention by God in history.

Second, the God revealed through Scripture is one of loving will and purpose for humankind. None of these attributes could be shown except through interaction with humanity. Both Muslims and Christians accept this intervention— that is, revelation through prophets—as the focal point of their lives. There are differences in Muslim and Christian Scriptures, to which Watt devoted a full chapter. After a thorough scrutiny of the various terms used by both Muslims and Christians for the means of revelation—that is, inspiration—and their many interpretations, Watt suggested, like Smith, that the books of the Christian Bible are the counterpart of the Muslims' Hadith. Watt has a tendency to place more emphasis on Islamic philosophers and theologians than the ordinary practicing Muslim does. As a result, some of his suggested interpretations, while revealing a deep knowledge of Islam, would not accord with those of a pious Muslim who considers philosophy superfluous to religion. In the final analysis, however, Watt recognized that in Islam, just as in Christianity, "ultimately the way in which revelation comes to a prophet is a mystery, but we can be certain of two things; (a) it is God who takes the initiative in revelation; and (b) the form of the words in the consciousness of the prophet contains the truth from God."[61]

In addition, Watt accurately described the shared belief regarding the purpose of revelation. It is not to give scientific knowledge or information about historical facts but rather to guide and direct humankind. Although this does involve historical events that enlighten humankind, the primary emphasis is on two aspects of humankind's relationship to God. First, God is the Creator and Lord of history. The necessary implication of this in both Islam and Christianity is humans' specific place in the cosmos. In Christianity, the relevant notion is that of stewardship. In Islam, it is viceregency. In either case, the point is that God has put humankind on earth with a trust, a purpose to accomplish. The importance of this notion cannot be overemphasized in either tradition. In both, the ultimate impact of revelation and Scripture is moral or ethical guidance. Like Smith's work, therefore, Watt's careful, scholarly approach to the details of the tradition bring him to correct emphasis of the essential thrust of the religion. In light of the overall agreement of Islam and Christianity on these essentials, they agree, differences in detail pale in importance.

It is this perspective that guides Watt's conclusion regarding the status of Muslim-Christian dialogue today. Taking due account of the immeasurable impact of Western domination (which he traced to the fifteenth century), he observed that in the Islamic world since the 1950s, "the speed of change has greatly accelerated, and this has left the masses of ordinary people utterly bewildered and feeling anxious and insecure, as they saw the disappearance of familiar objects and ways of acting and their replacement by things strange and new."[62] These changes, in fact, brought about the rise of a whole new social class, those with Western education and capable of managing the products of Western technology. In this climate of change and uncertainty, Watt claimed, the Islamic world has placed increased emphasis on religion—the so-called Islamic resurgence: "People looking for security think of 'the good old days' when the old religion was properly observed. One aspect of this insecurity is the fear of being, as it were, drowned in the Western culture and losing one's traditional identity."[63] Any successful dialogue must therefore bear in mind that Christianity can be seen as representative of this Western domination. Overall, nonetheless, Watt concluded that there are more similarities than differences between Islam and Christianity. He rightly focused on Christology as the major difference. But even on this issue Watt noted that there is room for further interpretation and understanding of both the Muslim and the Christian viewpoints. The process of dialogue, therefore, is not one of mere exchange of views, much less of leveling the differences. Rather, it is one by means of which participants recognize their need for growth and understanding not just of other faiths but of their own.

Of the few works dealing with Judaism, Christianity, and Islam together, F. E. Peters's *Children of Abraham* stands out for its remarkable scholarship and clarity. The author explicitly stated:

Judaism, Christianity, and Islam are all children born of the same Father and reared in the bosom of Abraham. They grew to adulthood in the rich spiritual climate of the Near East and though they have lived together all of their lives, now in their maturity they stand apart and regard their family resemblances and conditioned differences with astonishment.

Rich parallels of attitude and institution exist among these three religions that acknowledge, in varying degrees, their evolution one out of the other. They have all engaged at times in reciprocal polemic of great ferocity, and sometimes pursued a more ecumenical course, but neither is the intention here. My purpose is merely to underline both the parallels and the differences, and to connect them to common origins and to a common spirit and intellecutal environment.[64]

In this utterly unbiased way, the author proceeded to outline comparatively the development of each tradition's community, hierarchy, legal structures, Scripture and tradition, liturgy, mystical components, and theology. He concluded with the observation that from a historical viewpoint, his treatment leaves one wanting to know more—about the politics of messianism in the first century, for instance, or the exact types of Judaism and Christianity with which Muhammad was acquainted in the sixth century. For the Jew, the Christian, the Muslim, on the other hand, such questions are unimportant, Peters claimed. For them, sacred history and revelation are sufficient. This may be the case with regard to the individual believers' spiritual commitment. Yet in the context of interreligious dialogue and understanding, a history of the sort Peters presented is essential.

The value of such scholarly and tentative approaches is that it overcomes the tendency to reify any one person's interpretation of his or her tradition. Perhaps the major methodological stumbling block to dialogue is the tendency to treat religions as unchanging entities tied to one viewpoint or another. Few individual practitioners of a religion can claim to speak for the religion as a whole. In fact, religious traditions are made up of the myriad of people who practice them. They are social and therefore evolving entities. The truths on which they are based remain the same. But those truths are of the order of ideals or goals— ideals and goals that impose a moral imperative on believers. Those imperatives remain the same, and they do not vary from religion to religion. But in the interpretation of how best to express and achieve them we find diversity. This diversity, however, is not only *among* traditions, it is also *within* traditions. As religious communities seek better to achieve their moral imperatives, their expressions are susceptible to change. There is not a religious tradition in the world that can claim absolute homogeneity of interpretation. Indeed, in the Abrahamic traditions, this evolution is an essential aspect of faith: the gradual unfolding of truth through the prophets. The hope of dialogue therefore is that all three religions—by sharing interpretations—can enhance each others' success in the struggle to achieve its goals.

Finally, mention should be made of an outstanding effort in the Third World to implement the highest goals of dialogue: to harness the resources of the indigenous religions—in this case Christianity and Islam—to work together to solve their mutual problems. The case in point is the East African nation of Tanzania. Under the leadership of Julius Nyerere, a Christian, a deliberate and successful attempt was made to subsume religious differences under their shared goals, a life of peace and dignity. Nyerere believes that religious differences too often divert the energies of the people from collective efforts to address overall problems of human development. Therefore, he believes the state, rather than emphasizing the doctrine of one specific religion, should call on all religions to support development programs in the name of humanity. Urging his follow Christians to overcome racial and ethnic suspicions, he stated: ''I am suggesting that, unless we participate actively in the rebellion against those social structures and economic organizations which condemn man to poverty, humiliation and degradation, then the Church will become irrelevant to man and the Christian religion will degenerate into a set of superstitions accepted by the fearful.''[65] Nyerere has many detractors who condemn his development program as a failure since Tanzania has not made great economic progress. Yet Nyerere's genius lies in his substitution of social justice for economic development as the criterion for success. Tanzania does not use wealth as the measure of human development or dignity. Thus although the Tanzanian GNP is low, there is virtually no gap between the rich and poor. Furthermore, as a result of heavy emphasis on education, Tanzania's 85 percent literacy rate is the highest in Africa. Perhaps most importantly, neither race nor religion determine one's status or opportunities in Tanzanian society. Not only does this render Tanzania instrumental in promoting human dignity at home, but its well-known policy of racial and religious equality has allowed it to be a vocal advocate of equality throughout the world.[66]

CONCLUSION: RECOMMENDATIONS FOR THE FUTURE

The complexity of issues involved in the Muslim dialogue with Judaism and Christianity have only been sketched above: the troublesome issue of missionarism, the necessity of distinguishing between Judaism and Christianity in the Muslim context, the necessity of distinguishing between religious and political struggles, and the many factors that distinguish between East-West confrontation and interreligious dialogue. In light of that complexity, we have briefly surveyed the wide-ranging varieties and patterns of effective dialogue in recent literature. Assuming that effective dialogue is one that advances not only mutual understanding of its participants but also their self-understanding, we saw that the most successful efforts at dialogue are those that carefully define their methodology and proceed on the basis of sustained and scholarly efforts.

It is possible, however, to take a broader view of the goal of dialogue. Mutual understanding itself is valuable only if put to the service of human goals. In particular, because the Muslim world is largely in the Third World, the human goals in question are those of development, freedom, and human dignity. Dialogue that advances those goals is indeed successful. The example of Nyerere's Tanzania demonstrates that such success is not a denial of any religious creed; it is, rather, the appeal to the common humanitarian goals of all religions. Judaism, Christianity, and Islam in particular all seek to represent in society the equality and dignity all people share in the eyes of God. Facing together the obstacles in that process, each stands a much greater chance of success.

NOTES

1. Philip Hitti, *History of the Arabs*. 10th ed. (New York: St. Martin's Press, 1970), p. 196.

2. The term *anti-Semitism* did not appear until 1893, when it was coined to designate the new phenomenon of pseudoscientific racial aspects of the prejudice. The religious

prejudice, however, properly called "anti-Judaism," has come to be subsumed under the new term. I will, therefore, use the terms *anti-Semitism* and *anti-Judaism* interchangeably, except where indicated otherwise. See Maxime Rodinson, *Cult, Ghetto, and State: The Persistence of the Jewish Question* (London: Al Saqi Books, 1983), p. 7, n. 1.

3. Even before this, Seneca clearly spoke for Rome when he designated the Jews as a *sceleratissima gens,* a "most criminal race." (*De superstitione,* c. 65 C.E.; See M. Stern, ed., *Greek and Latin Authors on Jew and Judaism* [Jerusalem: Israel Academy of Science and Humanites, 1974], 1:429). St. Augustine quoted Seneca in this regard with no apparent reprobation. See Heiko A. Oberman, *The Roots of Anti-Semitism in the Age of Renaissance and Reformation.* (Philadelphia: Fortress Press, 1984), p. 86.

4. Cited by Oberman, *Roots,* p. 71.

5. Johannes Eck, *Ains Judenbuechlins Verlegung,* 1541, fol. A IVr; cited by Oberman, *Roots,* p. 17.

6. Scott H. Hendrix, *Eclesia in vis. Ecclesiological Developments in the Medieval Psalms Exegesis and the Dictate super psalterium (1513–1515) of Martin Luther* (Leiden: S. J. Brill, 1974), pp. 249–256; cited by Oberman, *Roots,* p. 87.

7. Oberman, *Roots,* p. 22.

8. This change was ratified by the Sacred Congregation of Rites for the entire church. See *Freiburger Rundbrief* 12, nos. 45–48 (1959):7. Cited by John M. Oesterreicher in *Commentary on the Documents of Vatican II,* ed. Herbert Vorgrimler (New York: Herder and Herder, 1969), 3:4–5.

9. Oesterreicher, *Commentary,* pp. 5–6.

10. *Documentation Catholique* 39 (October 1938): 1480; cited by Oesterreicher, *Commentary,* p. 10.

11. See Tamara Sonn, "The Arab-Israeli Conflict" in Charles Wei-hsun Fu and Gerhard E. Spiegler, *Movements and Issues in World Religions* (Westport, Conn.: Greenwood Press, 1987), pp. 3–38.

12. The story is told of Ottoman Sultan Bayazid II's response to King Ferdinand of Spain upon the arrival in Constantinople of some forty thousand Spanish and Portuguese Jews escaping Catholic persecution: "Can you call such a king wise and intelligent? He is impoverishing his country and enriching my kingdom." Quoted by Abba Eban in *Heritage: Civilization and the Jews* (New York: Summit Books, 1984), p. 181.

13. Oesterreicher, *Commentary,* p. 19.

14. B. Lambert, *Ecumenism: Theology and History* (London: Burns and Oates; N.Y.: Herder and Herder, 1967), pp. 446–448; cited by Oesterreicher, *Commentary,* p. 53.

15. Ibid., p. 54.

16. Section 3. Translation from Walter M. Abbott, S. J., gen. ed. *The Documents of Vatican II* (Chicago: The Association Press, 1966); cited in Jacques Deretz and A. Nocent, O.S.B., eds., *Dictionary of the Council* (Washington and Cleveland: Corpus Books, 1968), pp. 289–290.

17. Section 4; ibid., p. 138.

18. Oesterreicher, *Commentary,* p. 87.

19. Ibid., p. 88.

20. Ibid.

21. Quoted from A.-M. Henry, ed., *Vatican II,* Unam Sanctam 52–53 (Paris: Editions du Cerf, 1968), p. 62; cited by Oesterreicher, *Commentary,* p. 87.

22. From Pope Paul VI's opening speech for the second session of Vatican II; quoted by Oesterreicher, *Commentary,* p. 87.

23. Section 4; quoted in Deretz and Nocent, *Dictionary,* p. 138.

24. Section 34; Deretz and Nocent, *Dictionary,* p. 138. Emphasis added.

25. Section 11; ibid.

26. Section 41; ibid., pp. 138–139.

27. Pope Paul VI's opening speech for the second session of Vatican II; see n. 22.

28. Deuteronomy 9:4–6. Biblical passages taken from *The Holy Bible,* New American Catholic Edition (New York: Benziger Brothers, 1966). I am grateful to Jon D. Levenson for this terminology and the insight into supersessionism. See his "Is There a Counterpart in the Hebrew Bible to New Testament Antisemitism?" *Journal of Ecumenical Studies* 2, no. 22 (Spring 1985): 242–260.

29. See *The Koran Interpreted,* trans. Arthur J. Arberry (New York: Macmillan, 1955).

30. See Fazlur Rahman, *Major Themes of the Qur'an* (Minneapolis and Chicago: Bibliotheca Islamica, 1980), p. 16.

31. Persia (Iran) was an independent Islamic state.

32. As of this writing, King Hussein and Syria's Hafiz al-Assad are engaged in an effort to settle their perennial disputes.

33. Hitti, *History,* p. 728.

34. Ibid., p. 752.

35. Michael Nazir-Ali, *Islam: A Christian Perspective* (Philadelphia: Westminster Press, 1983), p. 148.

36. S. D. Goitein, *Jews and Arabs: Their Contacts through the Ages,* 3d rev. ed. (New York: Schocken Books, 1974), pp. 6–7.

37. Ibid., p. 8. For an account of the origins of those Jews who became the "Western" Jews, see Arthur Koestler, *The Thirteenth Tribe* (New York: Popular Library, 1976).

38. Hans Küng, "A Christian Scholar's Dialogue with Muslims," *The Christian Century* 102, no. 30 (October 9, 1985): 892.

39. Nazir-Ali, *Islam,* pp.145–146.

40. Küng, "A Christian Scholar's Dialogue," p. 894.

41. I am grateful to Ellen Charry and the American Council of Christians and Jews for major contributions to the Bibliography.

42. World Council of Churches, *Guidelines on Dialogue* (Geneva 1979).

43. In J. Hick, ed., *Truth and Dialogue* (London: 1974); cited by Nazir-Ali, *Islam,* pp. 146–147.

44. G. C. Anawati, "Excursis on Islam," in Oesterreicher, *Commentary* pp. 151–52. Anawati cited the work of N. Daniel, *Islam and the West: The Making of an Image* (Edinburgh: University Press, 1960), and P. Southern, *Western Views of Islam in the Middle Ages* (Cambridge: Harvard University Press, 1962), in this regard.

45. Ibid., p. 152.

46. See G. Anawati, "Vers un dialogue islamo-chretien," *Revue Thomiste* 64 (1964): 280–326.

47. Ibid., p. 154.

48. Wilfred Cantwell Smith, *On Understanding Islam: Selected Studies* (The Hague: Mouton, 1981), p. 235.

49. Ibid., p. 234.

50. Ibid., p. 235.

51. Ibid., p. 237.

52. Ibid., p. 238.

53. Ibid., p. 239.
54. Ibid., p. 240.
55. Ibid., p. 241.
56. Ibid., p. 242.
57. Ibid., pp. 243–244.
58. Ibid., p. 244.
59. W. Montgomery Watt, *Islam and Christianity Today: A Contribution to Dialogue* (London: Routledge and Kegan Paul, 1983), p. ix.
60. Ibid., p. 50.
61. Ibid., p. 59.
62. Ibid., p. 142.
63. Ibid.
64. F. E. Peters, *Children of Abraham: Judaism/Christianity/Islam* (Princeton, N.J.: Princeton University Press, 1982), p. 1.
65. Julius K. Nyerere "The Christian Rebellion" in Shorter Alyward, ed., *African Christian Spirituality* (Maryknoll, N.Y.: Orbis Books, 1978), p. 83.
66. I am grateful to Imtiyaz Yusif of Temple University for the example, insights, and citations concerning Nyerere.

SELECTED BIBLIOGRAPHY

General Periodicals

Bulletin: Secretariatus pro non-Christianis (Vatican)
Christian Peace Conference (Prague)
Contacts (Dijon)
Current Dialogue (Geneva)
The Ecumenical Review (Geneva)
Ecumenical Trends (Garrison, N.Y.)
Ecumenism (Montreal)
The Ecumenist (New York)
Face to Face (New York)
Interaction (St. Louis)
Interface (Washington D.C.)
International Bulletin of Missionary Research (Ventnor, N.J.)
International Review of Mission (Geneva)
Journal of Ecumenical Studies (Philadelphia)
Proche orient Chretien (Jerusalem)
Teaching All Nations (Manila)
Vav: revue du dialogue (Paris)
Zeitschrift fur Missionwissenschaft und Religionwissenschaft (Munster)

Periodicals on Christian-Jewish Dialogue

Christian Attitudes on Jews and Judaism (London)
Christian Jewish Relations (London)
Christian News from Israel (Jerusalem)
Journal of the Service international de documentation Judeo-chrétienne (Rome)

The NICM Journal for Jews and Christians in Higher Education (Newton Center, Mass.)
Rencontre Chrétiens et Juifs (Paris)

Periodicals on Christian-Muslim Dialogue

Encounter (Documents for Muslim-Christian Understanding) (Rome)
Islamochristiana (Rome)

Articles on Dialogue in General

Ansari, Zafar Ishaq. "Some Reflections on Islamic Basis for Dialogue with Jews and
Christians." *Journal of Ecumenical Studies* 14 (Summer 1977): 433–466.
Cunningham, Sarah. "Middle East—Candor Is the Key." *A.D. Magazine* (July-August
1979): 18.
Gouthro, Arthur F. "Opening Address to the Conference on Jewish-Christian-Muslim
Dialogue." *Journal of Ecumenical Studies* 14 (Summer 1977): 401–404.
Schachter, Zalman M. "Bases and Boundaries of Jewish, Christian, and Moslem Dia-
logue." *Journal of Ecumenical Studies* 14 (Summer 1977): 407–418.
Shepard, William. "Conversations in Cairo: Some Contemporary Muslim Views of Other
Religions." *Encounter* 93–94 (March-April): 2–25.
Shepherd, Margaret. "Trialogue: Jewish, Christian, Muslim." *Month* 14 (January 1981):
19–22; *Christian Scholar's Review* 14 (September 1981): 33–40; and Service
International de Documentation Judéo-Chretienne (SIDIC), 14 (1982): 17–20.
Talmon, Shemaryahu. "Interfaith Dialogue in Israel: Retrospect and Prospect." *En-
counter Today* 9 (Winter/Spring 1974): 18–30.

Articles on Issues such as Central Place of Jerusalem in Judaism, Christianity, and Islam

Boniah, Stephen. "Jerusalem and Fraternity among Her Three Religions." *Diakonia* 17
(1982): 265–274.
Borrmans, Maurice. "Jerusalem according to Islamic Tradition." *Encounter (Documents
for Muslim-Christian Understanding)* 79 (November 1981): 1–14.
Dupuy, Bernard. "Jerusalem: Unique and Universal." *Encounter Today* 14 (Winter-
Spring, 1979): 14–18.
Indinopulos, Thomas A. "Jerusalem the Blessed: The Shrine of Three Faiths." *The
Christian Century* 95 (April 1978): 386–391.

Articles on Specific Questions of Dialogue

Gaudeul Jean-Marie, and Robert Caspar. "Textes de la Tradition musulmane concernant
le tahrif (falsification) des Ecritures."
Islamochristiana 6 (1980): 61–104.
Osman, Fathi, Zalman Schachter, Gerard S. Sloyan, and Dermot A. Lane. "Jesus in
Jewish-Christian-Muslim Dialogue." *Journal of Ecumenical Studies* 14 (Summer
1977): 448–465.
Taoff, Elio, and Robert Caspar. "Abraham in Jewish Tradition," "Abraham in Islam
and Christianity," and "Bibliographical Notes for a Study of Abraham." *SIDIC*
15 (1982): 4–10, 11–16, 35.

Thelle, N. R. "Is Common Worship Possible?" *The Japan Missionary Bulletin* 32 (April 1978): 180–184.

Articles on Christian-Muslim or Jewish-Muslim Relations

Aguilar, E. Galindo. "The Second International Muslim-Christian Congress of Cordoba." *Encounter (Documents for Muslim-Christian Understanding)* 42 (February 1978): 13.

Anawati, Georges C. "Le dialogue islamo-chretien en Egypte aujourd'hui." *Bulletin: Secretariatus pro non Christianis* 30 (1975): 9.

Arnaldez, Roger. "Dialogue Islamo-chretien et sensibilities religieuses." *Islamochristiana* 1 (1975): 11–23.

Borrmans, Maurice. "The Doctrinal Basis Common to Christians and Muslims and Different Areas of Convergence in Action." *Journal of Ecumenical Studies* 14 (Winter 1977): 32–50.

Cragg, Kenneth. "Legacies and Hopes in Muslim/Christian Theology." *Encounter (Documents for Muslim-Christian Understanding)* 41 (January 1978): 10; *Islamochristiana* 3 (1977): 1–10.

Darnell, Robert C. "Are Church and Mosque on a Collision Course?" *Liberty* 74 (July-August 1979): 14–17.

Fitzgerald, Michael L. "Islam and Christianity—Convergence and Divergence." *Encounter (Documents for Muslim-Christian Understanding)* 7 (August-September 1974): 10.

Geise, M. J. C. "Islam and Christianity." *Philippiana Sacra* 17 (May-August 1982): 33–55.

Hornus, J.-M. "De nouveau dans le dialogue islamo-chretien?" *Proche orient Chretien* 31 (1981): 165–169.

Lanfry, P. Jacques. "Islamic-Christian Dialogue: Approaches to the Obstacles." *Journal of Ecumenical Studies* 14 (Summer 1977): 484–500.

Lelong, Michel. "Difficultés et espoirs du dialogue Islamo-chretien." *Nouvelle revue theologique* 110 (March-April 1978): 161–181.

————. "When Christian and Moslem Meet." *Month* 11 (June 1978): 194–200.

O'Shaugnessy, Thomas J. "Christian-Muslim Empathy in an Hour of Crisis." *Ecumenist* 12 (September-October 1974): 87–90.

Taylor, John B. "Christian-Muslim Dialogue." *Islamochristiana* 9 (1982): 201–225.

————. "New Possibilities for Christian-Muslim Dialogue." *Encounter (Documents for Muslim-Christian Understanding)* 5 (May 1974): 8.

Troll, Christian W. "A New Spirit in Muslim-Christian Relations." *Month* 6 (September 1973): 296–299, 304.

Articles on Christian-Muslim Dialogue within Context of Missionary Work

Allard, M., M. Borrmans and L. DePremare. "Dialogue and Mission in the Land of Islam." *Encounter (Documents for Muslim-Christian Understanding)* 14 (April 1975): 9.

Braswell, George W., Jr. "The Encounter of Christianity and Islam: The Missionary Theology of Kenneth Cragg." *Perspectives in Religious Studies* 8 (Summer 1981): 117–127.

"Christian Mission and Islamic Dawah: Report from World Council of Churches Consultation with the Islamic Foundation." *Journal of the Muslim World League* 3 (August 1976): 46–47.

Hajjar, Joseph. "The Bible and Christian Witness in Islamic Countries." *International Review of Mission* 70 (July 1981): 162–173.

Kerr, David A. "The Problem of Christianity in Muslim Perspectives: Implications for Christian Mission." *International Bulletin of Missionary Research* 5 (1979): 171–192.

Michel, Thomas F. "Teaching about Islam in Christian Theological School." *South East Asia Journal of Theology* 20 (1979): 29–34.

"Mission to Muslims." *Reformed Review* 36 (Autumn 1982): 3–34.

Sanneh, L. O. "Christian-Muslim Encounter in Freetown in the 19th Century and the Implications for Mission Today." *Bulletin: Secretariatus pro non-Christianis* 12 (1977): 13–31.

Whaling, Frank. "A Comparative Religious Study of Missionary Transplantation in Buddhism, Christianity, and Islam." *International Review of Mission* 70 (October 1981): 314–333.

Articles on Historical or Theological Issues in the Muslim-Christian Dialogue.

Argyriou, Asterios. "Possibilités d'un dialogue entre Islam et le Christianisme a partir de leur conception de l'histoire." *Contacts: Revue francaise de l'orthodoxie* 32 (1980): 111–141.

Ayoub, Mahmoud. "Toward an Islamic Christology II: The Death of Jesus, Reality or Delusion." *Muslim World* 70 (1980): 91–121.

Biechler, James E. "Christian Humanism Confronts Islam: Sifting the Qur'an with Nicholas of Cusa." *Journal of Ecumenical Studies* 13 (Winter 1976): 1–14.

Borrmans, Maurice. "Muslims and the Mystery of the Cross—Rejection or Incomprehension?" *Encounter (Documents for Muslim-Christian Understanding)* 25 (1976): 13.

Caspar, Robert. "How to Speak about God with Moslems." *Vidyajyoti* 41 (August 1977): 294–308.

———. "Islam according to Vatican II." *Encounter (Documents for Muslim-Christian Understanding)* 21 (January 1976):7.

Cuoq, Joseph. "La religion et les religions (judaisme et christianisme) selon Ibn Khaldoun." *Islamochristiana* 8 (1982): 107–128.

Ferre, A. "La vie de Jesus d'apres le *Annales* de Tabari." *Islamo-christiana* 5 (1979): 7–29.

Fitzgerald, Michael L. "Christian Liturgy and Islamic Texts." *Encounter (Documents for Muslim-Christian Understanding)* 30 (December 1976): 214–217; *Vidyajyoti* 41 (March 1977): 100–115.

———. "Islam and the Bible." *Encounter (Documents for Muslim-Christian Understanding)* 4 (April 1974): 8.

———. "Jesus: A Sign for Christians and Muslims." *Vidyajyoti* 44 (May 1980): 202–215.

Gaudeul, Jean-Marie, and Robert Caspar. "The Salvation of Non-Muslims (Muslim Views)." *Encounter (Documents for Muslim-Christian Understanding)* 31 (January 1977): 16.

Geffre, Claude, and Jean-Pierre Jossua. "Monotheism." *Concilium* 177 (January 1985): 1–114.

Hassan, Riffat. "Messianism and Islam." *Journal of Ecumenical Studies* 22 (Spring 1985): 261–291.

Lazarus-Yafeh, Hava. "The Role of Jesus in Islam." *Christian News from Israel* 25 (1976): 209–210.

Lodhi, Mohammed Hayath Khan. "The Christian Carol about the Virgin Birth (The Truth Confirmed by the Qur'an)." *Al-Basheer* 4 (July-December 1975): 30–50.

McAuliffe, Jane Dammen. "Chosen of All Women: Mary and Fatima in Qur'anic Exegesis." *Islamochristiana* 7 (1981): 19–28.

Merad, M. Ali. "Christ according to the Qur'an." *Vidyajyoti* 45 (August 1981): 306–317.

Articles on Muslim-Christian Relations in Specific Areas of the World

Bakker, J. W. N "Interreligious Dialogue in Indonesia." *Encounter (Documents for Muslim-Christian Understanding)* 17 (August-September 1975): 6.

De Souza, Achilles. "Christian-Muslim Dialogue with Reference to Pakistan." *Bulletin: Secretariatus pro non-Christianis* 30 (1975): 218–221.

Fitzgerald, Michael L. "Christian-Muslim Dialogue in Indonesia and the Philippines." *Bulletin: Secretariatus pro non-Christianis* 30 (1975): 214–217.

———. "Lebanon-Broumana: Muslim-Christian Consultation (July 1972)." *Encounter (Documents for Muslim-Christian Understanding)* 1 (January 1974): 16.

———. "Muslim-Christian Dialogue in Libya." *Encounter (Documents for Muslim-Christian Understanding)* 22 (February 1976): 13; *African Ecclesiastical Review* 18 (August-September 1976): 186–193.

Fitzgerald, Michael L., and J. M. Gaudeul. "A Difficult Dialogue: Chambesy 1976." *Encounter (Documents for Muslim-Christian Understanding)* 36 (June-July 1977): 16.

Geijbels, M. "Relations between Muslims and Christians in Pakistan." *Teaching All Nations* 13 (1976): 173–177.

Gelot, Joseph. "Dialogue 1974: Cordoba and Tunis." *Encounter (Documents for Muslim-Christian Understanding)* 15 (May 1975): 7.

Gomez, Hilario M., Jr. "Muslims versus Christians in the Philippines: Some Notes on Hostilities and Relationships in Mindanao, Southern Philippines." *South East Asia Journal of Theology* 20 (1979): 12–22.

Gowing, Peter G. "Christian-Muslim Dialogue in the Philippines." *Islamo-christiana* 7 (1981): 211–225; *South East Asia Journal of Theology* 23 (1982): 37–48.

———. "Questions History Raises about Christian-Muslim Relations in the Philippines." *South East Asia Journal of Theology* 19 (1978): 1–13.

Gstrein, Heinz. "Aegypten Christen und die Re-Islamisierung." *Orientierung* 44 (October 1980): 209–211.

Holway, J. D. "Christianity and Islam in Africa—Looking Ahead." *Missionalia* (April 1974): 3–17.

Hutchinson, Franz. "De verhouding tussen Katholieken en Moslims in Belgie." *Collationes* 10 (1980): 104–120.

Irving, T. B. "Islam and Calvinism at the Cape." *Journal of the Muslim World League* 9 (August 1982): 15–19.

Johnstone, Penelope. "Christians and Muslims in Britain." *Islamochristiana* 6 (1980): 149–177.

Kenny, Joseph. "Christian-Muslims Relations in Nigeria." *Islamochristiana* 5 (1979): 171–192.

Peitz, Marietta. "Christentum und Islam in Niger." *Orientierung* 45 (November 1981): 230–232.

"Report from a Philippine Christian-Muslim Dialogue, the Islamic City of Marawi, May 14, 1981." *Current Dialogue* 2 (Autumn 1981): 28–32.

Sanneh, L. O. "La rencontre chretiens-musulmans en Afrique." *Flambeau* 49/50 (1976): 55–63.

Speight, Marston. "Christian-Muslim Dialogue in the United States of America." *Islamochristiana* (1981): 201–210.

Stamer, P. J. "Perspectives pour un dialogue entre communautes in Afrique de l'ouest: Stage intensif d'islamologie de KOUMI 1980." *Bulletin: Secretariatus pro non Christianis* 15 (1980): 318–327.

Tamney, Joseph B. "Muslims and Christian Attitudes toward Fasting in Southeast Asia." *Review of Religious Research* 19 (Fall 1977): 3–15.

Teissier, Henri. "2 e Congres Islamo-Christien de Cordoue." *Le Lien* 42 (1977): 67–71.

Articles on the Jewish-Muslim Dialogue

Arnaldez, Roger. "Influences juives dans la pensée musulman." *Recherches de Science religieuse* 66 (October-December 1978): 569–583.

Johns, Anthony H. "Joseph and the Qur'an: Dramatic Dialogue, Human Emotion, and Prophetic Wisdom." *Islamochristiana* 7 (1981): 29–55.

Sanua, Victor D. "On Jewish-Muslim Relations." *Congress Monthly* 48 (November-December 1981): 5–6.

Trepp, Leo. "The Islamic-Jewish Imperative." *Central Conference of American Rabbis (CCAR) Journal* (Autumn 1974): 15–18.

Books on Islamic Dialogue with Judaism and Christianity

Judaism-Christianity-Islam

Bavinck, J. H. *The Church between Temple and Mosque: A Study of the Relationship between the Christian Faith and Other Religions.* Grand Rapids, Mich.: Eerdmans, 1981.

Matthews, Warren. *Abraham Was Their Father.* Macon, Ga.: Mercer University Press, 1981.

Maybaum, Ignaz. *Happiness Outside the State: Judaism, Christianity, Islam—Three Ways to God.* Stocksfield, Henley, Boston, London: Oriel Press, 1980.

Peters, F. E. *Children of Abraham: Judaism/Christianity/Islam.* Princeton, N.J.: Princeton University Press, 1982.

Christian-Muslim Dialogue

Borrmans, Maurice. *Orientations pour un dialogue entre Chretiens et Musulmans.* Paris: Les Editions du Cerf, 1981.

Gabus, Jean-Paul, Ali Merad, and Youakim Moubarac. *Islam et Christianisme en Dialogue*. Paris: Les Editions du Cerf, 1982.

Hick, J., ed. *Truth and Dialogue*. London: Sheldon Press, 1981.

Irani, George E. *The Papacy and the Middle East: The Role of the Holy See in the Arab-Israeli Conflict, 1962–1984*. Notre Dame, Ind.: Notre Dame University Press, 1986.

Kateregga, Badru D., and David W. Shenk. *Islam and Christianity: A Muslim and a Christian Dialogue*. Grand Rapids, Mich.: Eerdmans, 1981.

Khoury, Paul. *Islam et Christianisme: Dialogue religieux et defi de la modernité*. Beyroth: n.p. 1973.

Küng, Hans. *Christentum und Weltreligionen: Hinführung zum Dialog mit Islam, Hinduismus und Buddhismus*. Munchen: Piper, 1984.

Nazir-Ali, Michael. *Islam: A Christian Perspective*. Philadelphia: Westminster Press, 1983.

Nijim, Basheer K., ed. *American Church Politics and the Middle East*. Belmont, Mass.: Association of Arab American University Graduates, 1982.

Parrinder, Geoffrey. *Jesus in the Qur'an*. London: Sheldon Press, 1976.

Rousseau, Richard, ed. *Christianity and Islam: The Struggling Dialogue*. Montrose, Pa.: Ridge Row Press, 1985.

Schimmel, Annemarie, and Abdoldjavad Falature. *We Believe in the God: The Experience of God in Christianity and Islam*. New York: Seabury Press, 1979.

Smith, Wilfred Cantwell. *On Understanding Islam: Selected Studies*. The Hague: Mouton, 1981.

Sweetman, J. W. *Islam and Christian Theology*. 4 vols. London: Butterworth, 1945–1967. (Out of print. Abridged version available: Sigvard von Sicard, ed. *Sweetman's Islam and Christian Theology Abridged by James S. Moon*. Birmingham, Eng.: Centre for the Study of Islam and Christian-Muslim Relations, n.d.

Watt, W. Montgomery. *Islam and Christianity: A Contribution to Dialogue*. Boston: Routledge and Kegan Paul, 1983.

Young, W. G. *Patriarch, Shah, Caliph*. Rawalpindi: n.p., 1974.

Jewish-Muslim Dialogue

Ahmad, Barakat. *Muhammad and the Jews: A Reexamination*. New York: Advent Books, 1979.

Geiger, Abraham. *Judaism and Islam*. Madras, 1898. Reprint, New York: KTAV Publishing House, 1970.

Goitein, S. D. *Jews and Arabs: Their Contacts Through the Ages*. 3d rev. ed. New York: Schocken Books, 1974.

Memmi, Albert. *Jews and Arabs*. Chicago: J. Philip O'Hara, 1975.

Morag, Shelomo, Issachar Ben-Ami, and Norman A. Stillman eds. *Studies in Judaism and Islam*. Jerusalem: Hebrew University Press, 1981.

Issues

Ayoub, Mahmoud. *Redemptive Suffering in Islam: A Study of the Devotional Aspects of ʿAshura in Twelver Shi'ism*. The Hague: Mouton, 1978.

Denny, Frederick M., and Rodney L. Taylor, eds. *The Holy Book in Comparative Perspective*. Columbia: University of South Carolina Press, 1986.

Geagea, Nilo. *Mary of the Koran: A Meeting Point between Christianity and Islam*.

Translated and edited by Lawrence T. Fares. New York: Philosophical Library, 1984.

Little, David, John E. Kelsay, and Abdulaziz A. Sachedina. *Human Rights and the Conflict of Values: Freedom of Religion and Conscience in the West and Islam*. Columbia: University of South Carolina Press, 1987.

Parrinder, Geoffrey. *Jesus in the Qur'ān*. London: Sheldon Press, 1976.

Poulat, E., et al. *La Liberté Religieuse dans le Judaisme, le Christianisme et l'Islam*. Paris: Les Editions du Cerf, 1981.

Rudavsky, Tamar, ed. *Divine Omniscience and Omnipotence in Medieval Philosophy: Islamic, Jewish, and Christian Perspective*. Columbus: Ohio State University Press, 1984.

Shafaat, Ahmad. *The Gospel according to Islam*. New York: Vantage Press, 1979.

————. *Islam and Its Prophet: A Fulfillment of Biblical Prophecies*. Ville St. Laurent, Quebec: Nur al-Islam Foundation, 1984.

Geopolitical Areas.

Betts, Robert Brenton. *Christians in the Arab East: A Political Study*. Atlanta: John Knox Press, 1978.

Dretke, James P. *A Christian Approach to Muslims: Reflections from West Africa*. Pasadena, Calif.: William Carey Library, 1979.

Joseph, John. *Muslim-Christian Relations and Inter-Christian Rivalries in the Middle East*. Albany, N.Y.: SUNY Press, 1983.

————. *The Nestorians and Their Muslim Neighbors*. Princeton, N.J.: Princeton University Press, 1961.

20

In Christ There Is Neither Hindu nor Christian: Perspectives on Hindu-Christian Dialogue

R. PANIKKAR

The topic in this chapter is part of the much larger problematic of the meeting of cultures and religions. It touches upon the very identity of contemporary humans. We are today obliged to live in this modern Babel, with its at times chaotic mixture of races, cultures, and religions, and our identity must be gained not only within the framework of our own ethnic, political, or religious world view but also against the background of all of humankind's living traditions. This is a difficult subject to summarize. It must be lived, and the fruits of the encounter will ripen in their own time. The belief that people are masters of space and time and that therefore the human rhythm can be, like matter, willfully accelerated is one of the most deleterious ideas spread by the scientific vision of the world. So we do not pretend to exhaust the many dimensions of the Hindu-Christian dialogue, which is ongoing and obeys no law other than that of the Spirit, but must be content to offer a few suggestions and insights.

Christians today are faced with an unavoidable question: "Can I be an authentic Christian; that is, can I live the depth and plenitude of the Christian message and at the same time make room in myself for other religions without assigning to them a secondary role?" Is it possible to be a 'true' Christian and to be neither exclusivist nor fanatic? Or is the only alternative that of being a lukewarm Christian and of adopting a watered-down Christianity? Is authentic Christianity necessarily intolerant? Furthermore, does this mean that truth—or the belief in truth—leads to intolerance? Could not truth itself be pluralistic? A full Christian life today is not possible as long as there is indifference to or only a negative tolerance of other religions. The commandment to love our neighbors is also a demand to know them, and they cannot be known if their religiosity is not also shared. This participation makes our neighbors' beliefs a religious question for ourselves. Our neighbors' faith is part of our own religious development. If we are not able to in some way attain the religious *experience* of our cocitizens, we cannot pretend to have understood their beliefs, much less presume to pass judgment upon them.

I have attempted here to sketch only a provisional outline of this problematic. For background to the ideas presented here, I refer the reader to my other writings.[1] Also, in writing this chapter about two such extremely vague abstractions as 'Hinduism' and 'Christianity,' I was confined by space restrictions to such a high level of generalization that it forced me to disregard many vital elements in the encounter of religions.

THE NEW PROBLEMATIC

From the beginnings of the modern epoch to the middle of the twentieth century, during the European period of world history (i.e., the time of colonialism), the majority of Christians were of the conviction that they had the sole possession of the truth: Christianity was believed to be the only true religion, the only path leading to salvation. Other religions were seen as either the work of the devil or as merely the veiled, dim yearnings of a human nature that, left alone, was incapable of reaching the human's supernatural end. At most, they would be catalogued as expressions of the perennial human search for God and not the saving descent of God himself towards humans. Christians were well aware that they, too, were not 'worthy' of such a lofty election, which they named grace or vocation; yet the Christian message was considered to be the only one with saving power. To avoid exclusivity and injustice, theologians endeavored to clarify certain necessary distinctions, such as those between the church and the kingdom of God, stubborn ignorance and error in good faith, visible and anonymous Christians, and revelation and religion. But the principle, more or less explicit, remained the same: *extra ecclesiam nulla salus.* ''Outside the Church there is no salvation.'' But what was the church? Obviously, ''we'' were, even though different degrees of belonging to the church were recognized. *Quicumque vult salvus esse . . .* —''Whoever wants salvation must first of all keep the Catholic Faith''—begins the famous hymn attributed to Saint Athanasius, preserved in the Roman Breviary until Vatican II.

After World War II, when Europe and the United States began to realize they could no longer be the masters of the world, when all around them new independent nations were making their appearance, this feeling of self-sufficiency on the part of Christians began slowly to change. Here we have an interesting example of the connection between theory and praxis. The world's new historical situation unleashed new theological reflection. Today Christians are looking for an identity that does not betray their tradition and yet does justice to a new awareness of the facts.

The Second Vatican Council may be considered a landmark of this change: the era of colonialism had passed, at least theoretically and politically, although not economically and technologically. At the heart of the colonialist attitude is a radical monism: it admits of only one form of culture, *one* civilization (the others are either barbarians or simply outdated), *one* world (naturally understood as *our* concept of 'world' and 'unity'), and *one* religion. One God, one church, one empire, is the ideal, although in practice one may speak of the necessity of being broad minded, leaving room for 'accidental differences.' Within the Christian optic, the ideal consisted in the absolute Christianization of the world: one shepherd, one flock.

The abandonment of such a conviction brought about a corresponding change in Christian belief and self-understanding. Today we are in the midst of a painful *metanoia,* a mutation of consciousness. It is not surprising that many speak of this time as one of crisis.

Mere palliatives are of no use here. It is undeniable that the theology as well as the *consensus fidelium* of the last Christian centuries were based upon the unquestioned superiority of Christianity—a perspective that is understandable given certain premises of historic monotheism. If there is only one God and one History, and this God has manifested himself—even incarnated himself—in History, the *Absolutheitsanspruch,* the Christian pretension to absoluteness, is an inescapable consequence.

AN OFTEN OVERLOOKED METHODOLOGICAL OBSERVATION

It is unfair to present the relationship between Hinduism and Christianity unilaterally. If the Christian point of view is important and crucial to the encounter, so is that of the Hindu. The latter must be taken as seriously into account as the former. If Christianity has changed, so has Hinduism. If Christianity has asked itself about the meaning and value of other religions, Hinduism has also tackled the question. In fact, Hinduism, unlike Christianity, has never considered itself to be the only true religion, thereby seeing its destiny as being *the* world religion. In general, Hinduism has no direct missionary impulse. The word *hinduism* itself is misleading. The term *hinduism* was originally introduced only to differentiate most of Indian traditions from Islam and Christianity: it was born of reaction and confrontation. Yet this appellation has endowed it with a certain unity. Hinduism, in fact, represents the conglomerate of India's many autochthonous traditions. If we were to define Hinduism, we would state that it is more an existence than an essence, more a reality of fact "here below" than an ideal world or a body of doctrines. In fact, an atheist, a deist, a monotheist, a dualist, an animist, and a nondualist can equally see themselves as 'perfect' Hindus. Hinduism really has no main dogma, although in it we may discover some common traits, some central spiritual elements, such as the idea of *karma,* the multiformity and multiplicity of the divine, the hierarchical structure of reality not only in the objective realm but in the subjective one, and so on. For Hinduism there are several truths—degrees of truth—but in reality there is one: *ekam evādvitīyam.* Conversely, Western Christianity believes that truth is one and can only be but one but admits, on the other hand, of different degrees of reality. The one thing compensates for the other.

Be that as it may, Hinduism, when it is confronted by well-specified, positive religions, such as Christianity, usually describes itself as the *sanātana dharma*, the perennial order of things; it perceives itself as the expression of the fundamental experience of humans, that is, the original, primordial religiosity that has taken a particular form in India but that may take other forms in other peoples and cultures. This everlasting *dharma* is inherently transcultural and transtemporal and will cloak itself in as many cultural or religious forms as will receive it. The self-understanding of Hinduism emanates from entirely different premises than that of Christianity: they cannot be simplistically compared. The way Hinduism understands itself in relation to other religions finds no direct parallel in the Christian problematic.

Hinduism does not consider itself contrary to or in competition with other religions. It does not possess, strictly speaking, very much historical awareness. One may not speak, therefore, of historical 'mission' in the Christian sense. For instance, a traditional Hindu, when living in the West, would also, by the very fact that he is a good Hindu, want to be considered a good Christian; he would strive to be as Christian and as Western as he could be, without ever ceasing, however, to be Hindu. To be 'Hindu' simply means to be religious and has its origin and principle in the concrete, existential situation in which humans live. The fact that this element in Hinduism has been ignored has created misunderstandings and considerable tensions that could otherwise have been prevented. Typical Christians, for example, will spontaneously refuse to take part in the religious ceremonies of a Hindu temple. It would seem that any participation would mean a betrayal of their religion. Typical Hindus, on the contrary, will intuitively want to participate, if they have the chance, in the Christian liturgy. If they held back, it would seem to them that they were not only offending their hosts but were also betraying their very Hindu religiosity. What is sacred is sacred, no matter where and under what form, and Hindus want to participate in it due to the very fact of their Hinduism. It is only recently that a certain spirit of exclusiveness has also arisen in India, mainly, as we have mentioned above, because of the Muslim and Christian challenge.

Traditional Hindus were confronted with a whole other conception of religion that arose from Christianity and Islam. They were told that they were *kafir*, or pagan, infidels, and that they would have to convert. 'Hindu' consciousness was born out of this confrontation. Thus Hinduism began to base its identity on differentation and shape its self-understanding as a way of defending itself. If the two Abrahmic religions affirm that they are simply the *one* universal religion, Hinduism, for its part, would point out that it is the world's broadest and most profound of religions: the most *profound* because no other tradition can boast of so deep a mystical experience; the *broadest* because in Hinduism, according to its own notion, all world religions are integrated and contained. If Christianity claims to be the truth of religion, Hinduism claims to be the religion of truth.

A discussion of the relationship between Hinduism and Christianity begins from different suppositions than one of the relationship between Christianity and

Hinduism. As history has shown, when account is not taken of this double relation, many misinterpretations arise. Authentic theology, though it never ceases to be theoretical reflection, must always be practical.

CHRISTIANITY AND HINDUISM

To discover the relationship between Christianity and other religions, at least three conditions must be fulfilled:

1. We must remain loyal to the Christian tradition. *This is the theological problem.*
2. We must not violate other traditions; they must be interpreted according to their own self-understanding. *This is the hermeneutic problem.*
3. We cannot leave aside the critical scrutiny of contemporary culture. *This is the philosophical problem.*

First, tradition does not mean a merely mechanical repetition of what has been but the living transmission (*traditum:* handing over) of the crystallized experience of what has happened. Tradition does not mean stagnation but continuation and growth. Tradition does not necessarily call to mind an antiquarian obsession with artifacts. We talk about tradition, that is, about transmission, only when something is actually *given,* handed over, communicated, and not when it is merely preserved. With the passing of generations, the mentality of the receivers of tradition changes, along with their capacity to receive. Therefore, to maintain continuity, that which is transmitted must also change. If the human being and its vision of itself and its reality are constantly growing and changing, what tradition transmits must also grow and expand so that it will be loyal to the same tradition.

In this light, the Christian claim to superiority must be retransmitted, and account must be taken of the multiple changes that lead to a transformed contemporary consciousness, along with the reasons that shaped an earlier mentality of exclusiveness. Christianity's claim to have seen Christ as the Pantocrator, by whom and for whom everything has been made, Alpha and Omega, beginning and end of the universe, First Born of creation, universal redeemer and only savior, still holds true. But the proper *context* of these affirmations must be investigated.

Christians need not abandon the assertion of the truth of their faith. This assertion speaks of Christ as symbol par excellence of the new life, creator and redeemer of the entire reality. Through Christ all things are transfigured, made divine. But this does not mean that Christians have the monopoly on Christ or that their knowledge of him is exhaustive of his full reality. Who is this Christ? How and where does he act? This continues to be a mystery, even for Christians, although they may claim to know most intimately certain of his traits, his historicity, for instance. But there is nothing contradictory in stating that other cultures and religions are aware of other dimensions and aspects of this mystery that Christians call Christ.

In Christian parlance, which is not that of the Hindu—and there is no reason why it should be—Christ is active and present in Hinduism, although hidden and unknown. That which gives Hinduism its saving power is precisely that which Christians call Christ, even though in Hinduism it may have other names and be expressed in other forms. But immediately, we must add two things: (1) The same goes for Christianity: Christ is indeed active and present in Christianity but is also hidden and unknown. Where and how he acts upon humans, and upon Christians, belongs to the realm of mystery. How and when he is found are also outside our knowledge: the mystery is common. "Lord, when was it that we saw you hungry and fed you, or thirsty and gave you drink, a stranger and took you home, or naked and clothed you?"

(2) The fact that different names are given to what we have here called 'mystery' does not mean that there exists a 'thing-in-itself,' *the* mystery, and that this 'object' is then given different names. The name is something more than a mere label attached to the thing; it is something more than a pointer, a scientific or empirical *term* that is by nature neutral, extrinsic to the thing itself, purely indicative and having no real relationship to that to which it points. Here the name is a living *word,* the very symbol of the thing itself. The word as symbol both reveals and conceals that of which it speaks; it 'is' the thing not in the sense of being identical to it but in that it manifests itself. Thus it is a real aspect of the 'thing itself'; it is the very way in which the thing speaks to us and unites itself to us.

So although Christians cannot call Christ by other names, there still remain other aspects or dimensions unknown to Christians that are not covered by, though still connected to, the name of Christ. A pluralism of names means neither a plurality of objects nor, in a nominalistic sense, a mere plurality of terms, which would amount to the same thing. It indicates precisely the very multidimensionality of the 'thing' and that it cannot be detached or abstracted from the person who contemplates it. Only in the Spirit are we truly able to pronounce the salvific name.

From this perspective, there are at least three possible ways to interpret the Christian fact:

1. Christianity is *the* absolute religion; the others are either no religion at all or are only on the way to becoming one. This can also be formulated by stating that Christianity is not a religion but is pure faith, or metareligion. Christianity represents to human reason the scandal of the sovereign freedom of God. Any attempt at rationalization is blasphemous. This would be the *conservative and ahistorical explanation* of the current situation. Hans Urs von Balthasar, for instance, has much to say about this.

2. Christianity is one religion among many. It is a true and authentic religion, but it cannot claim any right to exclusivity. It is conditioned by culture and time. Christianity continues to be pure truth to its believers, but it belongs within the

larger framework of universal history. Before Christ there was no Christianity, and we must not extrapolate outside the orbit of those who explicitly call themselves Christians. This is the *critical-cultural explanation* of the present-day situation. Hans Küng, for instance, could give us insight into this interpretation.

3. Christianity is certainly a true religion. It points to a mystery that Christians cannot but call on the one they know as Christ, but Christ is present in all authentic religions in ways proper to them. In this sense, all true religions are linked together through a kind of *perichoresis*. Christianity is a manifestation of this mystery. From this perspective we can—and must—state that Christianity is a revelation of the mystery, but we are unable to know directly if there are other epiphanies. It is only from the bosom of the mystery itself, and not from its manifestation, that we could tell whether other religions are true or if they are mere illusory appearances. This is the *mystical or transhistorical explanation* of the current situation. A good part of contemporary theological reflection (for instance, John Cobb, David Tracy, Thomas Berry) takes this path.

The first condition with respect to our encounter is that any reflection that calls itself Christian must take into consideration the Christian self-interpretation and critically acknowledge the possible changes in Christian self-understanding.

If the first condition sets forth a series of theological problems, the second touches upon the hermeneutical question, that is, the balanced scientific-religious interpretation of the diverse human traditions and, in our case, of Hinduism.

Second, an authentic relationship between Christianity and Hinduism cannot be based upon a caricature or on insufficient interpretation. Goodwill is necessary but not sufficient. What is required is an intimate knowledge of the nature of Hinduism, knowledge that must be the fruit of a personal sympathy and one's own experience. Here, too, sympathy is necessary but not sufficient. Many religious movements today show great sympathy for and inclination toward other traditions. This is important and positive, but it is also a cause of confusion when this sympathy is felt without a critical spirit and is not accompanied by knowledge and experience.

One's own experience is indispensable. Religions are not purely objectifiable. They are not scientific 'facts.' A religion cannot be known in the same way a physical law is known. Human beings do not behave like elements in a chemical reaction.

The present science of religions is on the way toward elaborating categories that may leave room for this knowledge. If we approach other human traditions with categories alien to them, we will never be able to understand them. This does not mean that we cannot approach them from the outside and question them on matters that may seem pertinent to us. Indeed, this must be done. But for the question to be, first, intelligible and, then, answerable, it must be adjusted to the intellectual and spiritual world of the person to whom the question is addressed. The question of whether the Brandenburg Concertos are yellow or green makes no sense. To ask whether Hinduism has a mediator, without first investigating whether it has need of one, is tantamount to asking whether Christianity acknowledges the *dharma* of things without looking for its homeomorphic equivalent in the Christian parlance.

If we ask, for example, if there is in Hinduism a 'God' in the sense of the Jewish Yahweh, Hinduism will not be able to give a satisfactory answer—this is not its 'question,' and the problem is seen differently. Likewise, we will be unable to reply to the question of whether the idea of *karma* appears in Christianity. Concepts cannot be abstracted from their own world of discourse. Each concept is valid only in the milieu where it has been conceived. If we wish to extrapolate, the operation must be justified. The idea of God, like that of *karma*, is intimately bound up with its tradition's overall conception of reality. Put another way, for many people a certain linguistic imperialism still exists. This consists of the belief that monolinguism is a sufficient point of departure from which to understand the human phenomenon. This is so because at heart they believe that anything can be translated and that through their monolingual window they can perceive the entire panorama of human experience. It is true that with a knowledge of English one can go to all of the most expensive hotels in the world and feel at home—but one will never share the life of the common folk. Equally, one cannot fully travel in the world of religions only with the knowledge of Christian concepts. There is still a great deal of theological and philosophical tourism. An example of this is when we find a person speaking as if he or she knew all about Hinduism after having read a few books on the subject by some more or less Westernized authors. Each human tradition must be learned as a child first learns the language of its environment: not by comparing the words of one language with another that one already knows but by confronting each new word in its own context, tasting its particular meaning, feeling its power and reality in the very crucible of experience.

This is what brings us to true communication (which is always *communicatio in sacris*) and frees us from the illusion that we can *teach* without having previously *learned*. To learn is to become a disciple and not a master; furthermore, it is to be converted to the world of the things learned.

Here we approach a genuine phenomenology of religion if we succeed in transforming the husserlian *noema* into what I have taken the liberty of calling the *pistema*. In other words, the belief of the believer is itself part and parcel of the religious phenomenon. If I do not arrive at the shared *pistema*, the belief of the believer, I am left with only a purely objective *noema*, and I will not have truly described the phenomenon. I cannot understand the other if I do not also believe that in a certain sense he or she also has the truth. Only truth is intelligible.

Only if we delve deeply into the study *and* practice of religions can we understand one another, and only then is a mutual fecundation possible.

For the sake of brevity, I shall limit myself to the formulation of the following theses:

1. There is no Christian doctrine that one cannot more or less find in Hinduism. The Trinity, the Incarnation, the love of neighbor, the Resurrection—all of these

things may be found in Indian wisdom. We are speaking of doctrines, for facts as such are unique, in Hinduism as they are in Christianity. Also, we are speaking of homeomorphic equivalents, not of first-degree analogies. Religions are not carbon copies of one another. Only when seen from the outside do they all seem alike, as do the faces of Japanese people to the European. Seen from within, all are unique (and therefore unique in the unity), just as to a mother her two children, even if they be twins, are unique. Religions are like languages: all sound very much like mindless gibberish when we do not know them. However, when we begin to learn more than one language at a time, we see their peculiarities stand out and see how each possesses its own individual sap or essence while awareness of their similarities and equivalences grows.

2. There is no general Hindu doctrine that cannot be interpreted in a Christian way. Each is able to be understood—from the doctrine of *karma* to that of so-called polytheism—within the Christian context. Furthermore, the discovery of legitimate Christian interpretations of Hindu doctrines will serve to deepen and clarify Christian thought. The task of this creative hermeneutics will not always be easy but will depend upon mutual empathy and the degree to which the interpreter has entered into and has been converted by the tradition he or she wishes to interpret. Only from here will spring the possible fecundation between the two traditions, a fecundation that frees them from the danger of dying from asphyxiation. Gone are the times—let us hope—when the sublime message of the Sermon on the Mount was compared with the harsh caste system and the social injustice of India; or, on the other hand, when the sublime teachings of the Upanisads were set against the horror of Christian wars and inquisitions. In all religions we find both light and darkness, and from the point of view of the science of religions, one can certainly defend the thesis that each authentic religion represents a plenitude from which humans live and are able to live, even though with the passing of time what was once of value to the ancestors may no longer be sufficient for later generations.

In view of this, it is imperative today for humankind's religious life that religions come to find each other, know each other and come to reach, if possible, a mutual fecundation. The meeting of religions is not merely the business of academicians or of only a few 'enthusiasts' but has become a question of the very religious life of the mature human being today. We must not forget the fact that we are not born already adult, that we must develop and grow, each in our own way, and that it is the central task of all religions to help the human being reach his or her full potential. Entry upon this path is called initiation. But what has occurred with respect to many present-day initiations—not excluding baptism—is that while they were—and had to remain—*concrete,* they became, due to the shift in the context in which contemporary humans lived, *particular.*

I could repeat my old thesis here, backed by historical experience, that today no religion is self-sufficient, that each needs an external impulse to help it delve into its own nucleus and to adjust itself to current necessities. The dialogue between religions is not a peripheral problem; it more and more touches the very core of theological reflection and religious life. Speaking only of Christian theology, it will find its renaissance only if it opens itself up—as it is slowly doing—to the world of other religions. My proposal for Christianity is that it prepare a Jerusalem II Council, not merely a Vatican III (or Chicago I). The central problematic does not consist of the internal questions of Western Christians but of the Christian identity in the face of a planetary and multireligious world. Does Christianity want to be an exclusive affair of the Abrahmic world picture, or does it want to open up to real catholicity? If so, at what price?

We could sum up the hermeneutical problem with the following affirmation: The correct interpretation of another religion demands that interpreters be convinced of the truth of that religion (from which the believer lives) and, therefore, that they undergo a certain conversion.

Third, the relationship between Christianity and other religions is a problem of religious anthropology, that is, how humans see themselves within a specific religious milieu (Christianity) in relation to other humans from different religious universes. To simplify this enormous question, let us restrict ourselves to one of the thorniest points of contention, mentioned above: the traditional Christian conviction of being the only religion that is able to bring salvation to humankind. The affirmation that Christianity is the "only true religion" must be examined not only theologically but philosophically, despite the liability of such a distinction.

The truth of one religion does not imply the falsehood of the others. The context of any affirmation is that which qualifies it; it provides the space or milieu in which the affirmation is meaningful. The space in which the 'true religion' appears as such is a space limited (1) historically, (2) culturally, and (3) linguistically. Outside this space the affirmation remains meaningless. But this triple distinction is artificial, since all three factors are at the same time historical, cultural, and linguistic. We maintain it in this brief exposition for heuristic reasons.

1. Any historical event is such because it is situated in history. Furthermore, any human event can be located in history, but this already represents a certain reduction. There is no reason why every human fact must be historical, unless that which is human is wholly identified with that which is historical. There is no doubt whatsoever that the Christian fact from the beginning has understood itself to be a historical fact and that the two thousand years of the Christian religion are supported by or fall with the history that gives them meaning.

Two considerations are pertinent and of important consequence here. The first is the fact that history is the primordial myth par excellence of Christianity and of any predominant Western culture. History is the horizon over which reality is disclosed: a historical fact is a *real* fact. Jesus is historical because he is real; that is, he really, historically, existed. But the historical world is not the only human world. There are life-styles and even whole cultures that do not live the myth of history to the same extent as does the Western Christian world. The consequence of this is obvious: the affirmation that Christianity is the true religion, the only 'historical' religion, because it corresponds to *real* (read: *historical*) facts, as much from God as from humans—and Christians are those who give testimony to this (historical) reality—loses its meaning when taken out of the historical framework bestowed upon it. To talk, for example, of the relationship between Hinduism and Christianity without taking into account this different context, and without attempting to find a common base, is a task bound to fail because it is methodologically inadequate.

The *second* consideration has to do with the evolution of the historical consciousness of Christianity itself—aside from the fact that Christianity cannot completely identify itself with a mere historical fact. There has been an evolution in the very interpretation of the 'truth' of Christianity. It wants to be a truth that is neither fanatic nor exclusivist; it wants to acknowledge the human and salvific factors outside of the Christian religion; it not only wants to respect and admire but strives also to admit the legitimacy and crucial role of other religions, and so on. What usually happens is that Christians do not have the appropriate intellectual tools with which to tackle such a thematic. This cannot be otherwise, because it is only the mutual *dialogical dialogue* with and the knowledge-conversion to other religions that can offer adequate tools with which to deal with the problem.

2. There are many different families of human cultures and subcultures and, despite all their similarities, we cannot assume a priori that they are all governed by the same code. This is what has led me to suggest a new hermeneutics, which I have called *diatopical*—to distinguish it from morphological and diachronical—*hermeneutics* that attempts thematically to study cultures and traditions that have not known a common cultural source. That is, human spaces (*topoi*), and not only human time (*chronos*) or forms (*morphoi*), are different.

Let us state, as an example, and restricting ourselves to the analysis of Christianity as the 'only true religion,' that according to one predominantly semitic way of thinking, the truth of a statement can be understood only by means of a confrontation with its own negation. Now this *forma mentis* that reaches intelligibility by applying the principle of noncontradiction is very different from the predominantly Eastern one that relies upon the principle of identity. That God, for instance, may have chosen Israel or the church means precisely that God has chosen Israel or the church (principle of identity) but not that God has *not* chosen another people or another religion (principle of noncontradiction). In this sense, the affirmation that Christianity is the true religion does not exclude the fact that other religions can also be true.

It must be admitted that truth cannot contradict itself, but from this principle it cannot be deduced that, in the case in which Christ is said to be the only Savior, Kṛṣṇa could not also be, for exactly what metahistorical relationship might exist between Christ and Kṛṣṇa is not evident. A contradiction to the

Christian affirmation would be to state that Christ is *not* the Savior, and Christianity does not tell us anything about Kṛṣṇa. Perhaps we can assume that there may be a certain bond. But we need not now follow this line of thought.

3. When we express ourselves in a specific language, we automatically assume the entire cultural and religious world of that language. For example, to limit ourselves again to our topic, how would the assertion that "Christianity is the true religion" be understood if put into classical sanskrit? The fact that the word *religion* is a relatively recent invention is, even in the Christian world, well known. To Saint Thomas 'religion' was still a merely human virtue, despite the fact that Saint Augustine had used that 'pagan' word to suggest what we mean today by 'religion.' Religion is usually translated as *dharma*—but then a sentence about the 'true' *dharma*, which in sanskrit would be literally 'real' ('existent,' 'what *is*': *satya*), becomes something altogether different from its English counterpart, and the fact that Christianity might want to hold the monopoly on that is absurd. Even more, it is something that Christianity itself would not want to say. Certainly, there can be bridges between different universes of discourse, although there is no need for the existence of biunivocal relations only.

All of this leads us to reassess such a Christian affirmation, see its limits, and try to overcome it. We must at the same time acknowledge its unacceptable part (exclusiveness) and that which still has validity (the trust of being in the truth).

In summary, the relationship between Hinduism and Christianity can be understood only in the context of religious pluralism. Each religion must be understood and judged from within its own sphere. There are doctrinal discussions among different religions in the same way that there are discussions within the traditions themselves. Two doctrines that contradict one another on the same plane cannot both be true. Thomas and Bonaventure can be as incompatible as Śaṅkara and Rāmānūja. An incompatibility of doctrines does not rule out the respective truth of the religions.

There is no reason for Christians to abandon the conviction that they have the true religion, if they well understand that they must find all their truth in a Christianity that is open and dynamic. This will lead to an authentic religious dialogue.

There is no reason for Hindus to see Christianity as a threat; likewise, Christians should not be threatened by Hinduism. Rather, one should see in the other a stimulus to deepen one's own beliefs.

When there is a climate of sympathy and a desire for mutual understanding, a fruitful dialogue conducive to mutual enrichment can be begun. The encounter of religions is today no longer an encounter on the path of enmity or competition but on that of a mutual fecundation. A third of a century ago I used the expression *ecumenical ecumenism* to designate the dialogue of religions. This means that the relationship between religions cannot be compared to that of two commercial enterprises that want to sell their merchandise to the same customers. Nor can it be compared to the diplomatic conversations of two world powers that are forced to try to understand each other so as not to destroy the world. Religions are not in competition—nor are they enemies. They are like two languages that say all that they want to say, both in their own way, or two life-styles that are part of the larger richness of human life. Each dialect is a perspective on the world, a way of being and even of existing in the world, and despite everything, each is not only able to complement the others but also to criticize them, whereby all are able to improve themselves and change.

The relationship between Christianity and Hinduism could be compared to that between two lovers who speak two different languages. They love each other, and through that love they have discovered that they have the same goal and desire the same thing. But when one tries to speak of this to the other, he or she is not understood. Each must first learn the other's language. It can happen that they do not say the same thing, and surely, they do not say 'the same thing' in the same way. They each have an insight into something that deeply affects both of them, without being able to articulate it. But they can love each other, help others, find each other in practical ways, be patient, and begin to learn from each other.

This last simile suggests an aspect somewhat neglected in certain circles. The encounter of religions has an indispensable experiential and mystical dimension. Without a certain experience that transcends the mental realm, without a certain mystical element in one's life, one cannot hope to leave behind the particularism of one's own religiosity, much less to broaden and deepen it when one comes to encounter a different human experience.

The relationship could also be thus formulated: instead of asking what one can teach the other and bring to the other, it is worthwhile to ask to what extent can Christianity *learn* from Hinduism and vice versa. In light of our current predicament, the following few points should be mentioned. Hinduism could learn from Christianity

1. To take the world's structures more seriously, so that practical, everyday life in general, and politics in particular, can also find their meaning within the religious life. In classical Hinduism this idea was not set forth in quite this fashion because the situation was different. We must not be tempted to superimpose our current templates for 'wholeness' and 'integration' on an earlier era that had its own demands and *Sitz im Leben*. But even today, for many people in India the highest ideal in life is that of *sannyāsa*, renunciation, and consequently, there remains a certain dichotomy between the religious life and the modern secular one. In essence, this is one example of the negative impact of Western modernity on modern India: it has destroyed the spiritual equilibrium in much the same way that antibiotics have destroyed the demographic one.

2. The human social order must also be governed according to an immanent and direct justice and not only according to transcendental criteria based on the 'long-term' justice of successive births. This does not mean falling into a ferocious individualism (which does not solve anything), but it could mean that each human life can—or must—possess within itself a certain possibility of fulfillment and that this possibility *also* depends on social structures (technical, political, economic, etc.).

3. Historicity is also an element in the human effort toward salvation. This does not mean that the institution behind the law of *karma* is not able to furnish adequate answers to this thematic, but what is demanded is a creative interpretation.

Christianity could learn from Hinduism, among other things, the following:

1. The meaning of life contains a factor that is independent of the political and social adventure; thus human salvation does not solely depend upon such historical dimensions. It is possible to be happy and even live with a certain amount of human fulfillment in the midst of an unjust social order.

2. The structure of the universe is hierarchical. This hierarchy is also epistemological. There are, therefore, levels of perception and degrees of knowing that surpass the general knowledge of the reasoning mind, and in light of this, concentration, meditation, or whatever one may want to call this act of penetrating the different spheres of reality, is more important than, for instance, the capacity to read and write. To live life means to find joy in the discovery of reality and to attain harmony with it, rather than seeking to control it or conquer it.

3. Humankind is more than history; one is also a cosmic transformation. One is more, and not less, than an individual. One is part of the cosmic adventure, a limb on the body of the *cosmotheandric* totality. A wholly isolated human being is a mere abstraction.

All of this does not mean that the above points and similar ones are not found in other religions; it only means that for different reasons these points have not been sufficiently developed in some traditions and that those latter ones need outside stimuli to awaken such dormant, but crucial, elements.

Here we realize the convenience, or rather the necessity, of a mutual fecundation among the different wisdoms of humanity, not in order that they lose themselves and their respective identities but so they deepen their personalities.

We may conclude with a helpful simile. For diverse reasons, the contemporary world has reached, not only in scientific and technological areas but also in the realm of culture, a maximum of specialization. Modern people want to break out of this situation, but they do not know how, because it is neither simply a matter of undervaluing the knowledge acquired nor of turning back to an amorphous indiscrimination. Religions seem to have become so many specializations of the sacred, and as such they have need of specialists. The human being of our time longs for a larger simplicity at the same time that one would want to be neither a dilettante nor a specialist. Contemporary people want to recover the religious and primordial human experience; they realize that it must be concrete but that it must not be particularized. The Christian would want it to be authentically Christian but not fanatical so as to disconnect one from the rest of the human family; the Hindu, likewise, wants this experience to be both one's own and universal: both want to overcome religious specialization without falling into an artificial eclecticism. Today the relation between religions has become a personal religious question of how to live human life more authentically before the mystery of infinitude that envelops us within and without.

Today Christianity and Hinduism are like brothers or sisters who meet again after centuries of separation and try to share their respective experiences and to enter together into humans' current predicament. Christians may see the goal in the future, Hindus in the present, but both will see it in terms of the full and realized human person.

NOTE

1. To mention only a few works, see R. Panikkar, *The Unknown Christ of Hinduism,* 1st ed. (London: Darton, Longman & Todd, 1964; rev. and enl. ed., London: Darton, Longman & Todd; New York: Orbis Books, 1981); idem, *Misterio y Revelación* (Madrid: Marova, 1971); idem, *The Trinity and the Religious Experience of Man* (London: Darton, Longman & Todd; New York: Orbis Books, 1975); idem, *The Intrareligious Dialogue* (New York: Paulist Press, 1978); and idem, "*Ṛtatattva:* A Preface to a Hindu-Christian Theology," *Jeevadhara* 49 (January-February 1979): 6–63.

The structure of this chapter follows that of my talk on the Bavarian Radio at the beginning of 1982, "Das Verhältnis Christentum Hinduismus," and is based upon my article "Sobre l'hinduisme i el cristianisme: Una qüestió de vida cristiana," *Qüestions de Vida Cristiana* (Montserrat), no. 114 (1982): 54–72.

SELECTED BIBLIOGRAPHY

Panikkar, R. "Advaita and Bhakti: Love and Identity in Hindu Christian Dialogue." *Journal of Ecumenical Studies* 7, no. 2 (Spring 1970): 229–309.

———. "The Church and the World Religions." *Religion and Society* 14, no. 2 (June 1967): 59–63.

———. "Confrontation between Hinduism and Christ." *New Blackfriars* 50, no. 584 (January 1969): 197–204.

———. "The Contemplative Mood: A Challenge to Modernity." *Cross Currents* 31, no. 3 (Fall 1981): 261–272.

———. Faith—A Constitutive Dimension of Man." *Journal of Ecumenical Studies* 8, no. 2 (Spring 1971): 223–254.

———. "Hermeneutics of Comparative Religion: Paradigms and Models." *Journal of Dharma* 5, no. 1 (January/March 1980): 38–51.

———. "Hinduism and Christianity." *Religion and Society* 8, no. 4 (December 1961): 10–18.

———. "Indirect Methods in the Missionary Apostolate: Some Theological Reflections." *Indian Journal of Theology* 19, nos.3,4 (July-December 1970); 111–113.

———. "The Internal Dialogue—The Insufficiency of the So-called Phenomenological 'Epoche' in the Religious Encounter." *Religion and Society* 15, no. 3 (September 1968): 54–66.

———. *The Interreligious Dialogue.* New York: Paulist Press, 1978.

———. "Inter-Religious Dialogue: Some Principles." *Journal of Ecumenical Studies* 12, no. 3 (Summer 1975): 407–409.

———. *Misterio et Revelacion.* Madrid: Marova, 1971.

————. *Myth, Faith, and Hermeneutics.* New York: Paulist Press, 1979.

————. "The New Innocence." *Cross Currents* 27, no. 1 (Spring 1977): 7–15.

————. "*Ṛtatattva:* A Preface to a Hindu-Christian Theology." *Jeevadhara* 49 (January-February 1979): 6–63.

————. "Rules of the Game in the Religious Encounter." *Asia Focus* 3 (1970): 223–227.

————. "Sobre l'hinduisme i el Cristianisme: Una qüestió de vida cristiana." *Qüestions de Vida Cristiana* 114 (1982): 54–72.

————. "Toward an Ecumenical Theandric Spirituality." *Journal of Ecumenical Studies* 5, no. 3 (Summer 1968): 507–534.

————. *The Trinity and World Religions.* Bangalore: Christian Institute for the Study of Religion and Society; Madras: Christian Literature Society, 1970.

————. "The Ultimate Experience." *Theology Digest* 20, no. 3 (Autumn 1972): 219–226.

————. *The Unknown Christ of Hinduism.* London: Darton, Longman & Todd, 1964; rev. enl. ed., New York: Orbis Books, 1981.

21

Perspectives on Hindu-Christian Dialogue:
A Response to R. Panikkar

ARVIND SHARMA

I propose to respond to R. Panikkar (Chapter 20) step by step. I would like to begin by asking the question: what is the nature of the problem? In other words, in what sense does Hinduism constitute a problem for Christianity and conversely, in what sense does Christianity constitute a problem for Hinduism? Once the nature of the "problem" is recognized, I would, as a next stage in the discussion, like to ask the question: is the nature of the problem such that it makes a mutual confrontation inevitable? In the third stage of the discussion, I would like to soften the blow and ask: is there room for mutual accommodation between the two traditions? Finally, in the last stage, I would like to ask: is mutual fecundation between the two traditions possible? Can Christianity learn from Hinduism, and can Hinduism learn something of value from Christianity?

I

In what sense, then, does Hinduism pose a problem for Christianity? Hinduism poses a problem for Christianity in the way that every other religion poses a problem for Christianity. If Christianity is the only "true" religion, all non-Christian religions are false. The adherents of these false religions, therefore, must either be eradicated or converted to Christianity. Thus Christian evangelization must forever remain unfulfilled if the whole world is not converted to Christianity. But Hinduism poses yet another problem for Christianity. The problem outlined above is a historical problem Christianity faces not only in relation to Hinduism but also, for example, to Islam and any other religion, missionary or nonmissionary.[1] But Hinduism, on account of its nonmissionary stance, also poses an ideological problem for Christianity as a missionary religion by questioning the need for missionizing. At least the missionary religions that pose a problem for Christianity do not question per se the idea of engaging in missionary activity, for engaging in which these other non-Christian missionary religions have their own rationale. But Hinduism in its present-day incarnation questions missionary activity on spiritual grounds:

The following conversation between the late Sri Chandrasekhara Bharati Swami of Sringeri *Pīṭha* and an American tourist reported in the press, in 1953, will be found to be of great interest in that the Swāmi sets forth in it the correct Hindu attitude towards conversion: "Why must it be," impatiently demanded an earnest American tourist, "that you will not convert other peoples to Hinduism? You have such a beautiful religion, and yet you keep so many struggling souls out of it. If you say 'yes' I will be the first to become a Hindu!"

"But why," came the counter-question, "do you want to change your religion? What is wrong with Christianity?"

Taken aback, but not daunted, the tourist said, "I cannot say what is wrong, but it has not given me satisfaction."

"Indeed, it is unfortunate," was the reply, "but tell me honestly whether you have given it a real chance. Have you fully understood the religion of Christ and lived according to it? Have you been a true Christian and yet found the religion wanting?"

"I am afraid I cannot say that, Sir."

"Then we advise you to go and be a true Christian first; live truly by the word of the Lord, and if even then you feel unfulfilled, it will be time to consider what should be done."

To put the puzzled American at his ease the sage explained: "It is no freak that you were born a Christian. God ordained it that way because by the *samskāra* acquired through your actions (*karma*) in previous births your soul has taken a pattern which will find its richest fulfillment in the Christian way of life. Therefore your salvation lies there and not in some other religion. What you must change is not your faith but your life."[2]

Hinduism thus poses both a historical and an ideological problem for Christian triumphalism. Now what kind of a problem does Christianity pose for Hinduism?

Hinduism, at least as it is perceived by the Hindus today, accepts the validity of multiple approaches to the Divine. It may be exclusive in that it does not normally encourage conversion to Hinduism, but it is inclusive in the sense that it accepts all religions of the world as valid. In other words, the mere existence of a Hindu constitutes a challenge or even a theological problem to the Christian, but the existence of Christianity poses no problem to Hinduism per se since all paths to God are valid.[3] It is the Christian claim that Christianity *alone* is the true religion that constitutes a problem for Hinduism, for it challenges the basic Hindu assumption that all religions could be true, for "Hindus have always believed in the existence of many ways of reaching God."[4] A good illustration of this difference in approach is provided by the fact that "unlike Christianity which accepts only one unique Divine incarnation in Jesus Christ, Hindus accept many incarnations of God."[5]

It is clear, therefore, that each religion constitutes a problem for the other—Christian soteriological exclusiveness is compromised by Hindu soteriological inclusiveness and vice versa.[6]

II

Must the problem, however, lead to mutual confrontation? From a confrontationalist standpoint the Christian will have to equate Hinduism with heathenism or at least paganism. On a more gentle view the Christian will have to consider Hinduism as paving the way for conversion to Christianity. This has been a fairly widely held view.[7]

For the Hindu, the Christian would remain outside the pale of social commerce; although even on the confrontationalist view it will be difficult for a Hindu to deny spiritual integrity to the Christian if the Christian's conduct was virtuous.[8] But most Hindus did not believe this to have been the case.

Although it cannot be denied that Hinduism and Christianity did pass through a confrontationlist stage, and such a situation may even now occasionally develop, both religious traditions have been moving more toward mutual accommodation for several decades.[9] But given the nature of the "problem" they constitute for each other, is such an accommodation possible?

III

To see how mutual confrontation might yield to mutual accommodation, one needs to analyze more clearly the exact nature of the problem they pose for each other. In what way, then, is Hinduism exactly a problem for Christianity? To identify the exact nature of this problem one needs to examine Christianity and ask: what makes Christianity Christian? It will soon be obvious that it is Christ that makes Christianity Christian; it is Christ that makes Christianity unique— or rather that it is the *uniqueness* of Christ that makes Christianity what it is.[10]

Is it possible, then, to reconcile Hinduism with the uniqueness of Christ? For should this be possible, room for accommodating Hinduism would have been created from a Christian point of view. Panikkar has shown that there are three possible ways of interpreting the centrality of Christ in relation to Christianity: (1) that this makes Christianity *the* absolute religion; (2) that this centrality is *central* to Christianity, just as Buddha is central to Buddhism so that Christian faith gets relativized; and (3) that Christ is not a monopoly of Christians but "is present in all authentic religions in ways proper to them."

Out of these three positions it is clear that the first cannot accommodate Hinduism or any other religion for that matter. The second accommodates Hinduism but at the expense of relativizing Christianity in a way that does violence to Christian self-understanding. The third position, however, retains the Christocentric nature of Christianity but, by allowing a wider circumference to the mystery that may be embodied in Christ, also accommodates Hinduism. It is clear then that although a Christian historical Christ may not be able to accommodate Hinduism, a cosmic Christ can.

How can the Hindu accommodate Christianity? A simple way would be to consider Christ as merely another *iṣṭa-devatā,* or chosen deity, that abounds in

Hinduism and to consider Christianity as a form of Bhakti Yoga.[11] But this would violate Christian self-understanding, especially the idea of the uniqueness of Christ. To see if accommodation from the Hindu side is possible, let us again ask of Hinduism the same question we asked of Christianity: in what way exactly does Christianity pose a problem for Hinduism? To identify the exact nature of the problem one needs to examine Hinduism and ask: what makes Hinduism Hindu? Given the great diversity in beliefs, it is clear that Hinduism would accord priority to practice or conduct over belief.[12] Thus K. M. Sen remarked about Hinduism that "Provided there was a certain agreement on modes of conduct and on the values determining behaviour, very considerable nonconformism of religious ideas has been allowed."[13] Since Hinduism and Christianity differ on the question of conversion, it is useful to invoke here the distinction drawn by T. M. P. Mahadevan between *vertical* and *horizontal* conversion, the former denoting a virtuous upgrading of life and the latter mere formal change from one faith to another.[14] It seems possible to suggest that Hinduism would be able to accept Christian "exclusivism" if it could be shown that such exclusive devotion to Christ enabled Christians to lead a moral life superior to what they might otherwise lead. Although it is true that on the whole, in Hinduism "conduct counts and not belief," if Christian belief could be shown or seen as positively related to virtuous conduct, it could well become acceptable from a Hindu point of view.[15]

IV

We may now advance further and consider the possibility of mutual fecundation, once mutual accommodation has been achieved. Herein Panikkar offered sets of three points that one religion could learn from another. Let us first consider what Hindus could learn from Christians. According to him, Hinduism could learn the following points from Christianity: (1) take the world's structures more seriously, (2) emphasize the place of justice within one life rather than over several lives, and (3) relate Karma to historicity. It appears that these "lessons" are already there in Hinduism. I am not here echoing his general view that "there is no Christian doctrine one cannot more or less find in Hinduism" and that "there is no general Hindu doctrine that cannot be interpreted in a Christian way." What I wish to state is that each tradition may have profounder lessons to learn from the other. If Hinduism is otherworldy, as it is alleged to be, how does one account for the doctrine of the *varṇas,* the *āśramas,* and the *puruṣārthas,* especially vis-à-vis Buddhism and Jainism?[16] If Hinduism relies on Karma, why do Hindu sacred texts provide for law courts? Do not the consequences of Karma ramify through history?[17]

Similarly, Panikkar suggested that Christianity could learn the following points from Hinduism: (1) that spirituality exists in its own right apart from social concern; (2) that reality can be hierarchical; and (3) that humans possess not merely a historical but a cosmic dimension. Now Christianity can recover these insights by examining its own history; Hinduism does not have to hold a mirror to it to enable it to do so. I agree with Panikkar that the mutual contact of religious traditions may generate a phenomenon we may call "dialogical accentuation," as each tradition activates a dormant element within it because of the example set by the other. But when it comes to learning lessons from one another, one has to dig deeper.

V

This calls for the introduction of a new dimension to the discussion that I will call "mutual eye opening" for want of a more felicitous expression.[18] It has to do with extending the visible horizon. One special way in which dialogue between religions can be mutually enriching is by demonstrating a religious option to a tradition that it could hardly ever have visualized within its own bounds. A classic example here is Buddhism, which introduced the possibility of a religion without a God, a possibility that, but for its existence, a member of another religion may have considered inconceivable if not impossible. Is there anything that Hinduism and Christianity have to offer to each other at this level? I think so.

From Christianity Hinduism can learn that it is possible for genuine spirituality to flourish amidst organized religions. Hinduism tends to be amorphous, even anarchic and does not set much store by bureaucratization. One could argue that Hinduism could learn the same lesson from Buddhism, but the Sangha has also been a fairly loosely organized body. Islam claims to have dispensed with clerics. It is in Christianity, and particularly in Catholicism, that we find the concept of order most clearly enshrined, and it is useful for Hindus to know that a religion so organized can embody authentic spirituality.

From Hinduism Christianity can similarly learn a useful and perhaps a still more unexpected lesson. Although sectarian conflict was the order of the day in Western culture a few centuries ago, now the various branches of Christianity coexist in peace. This religious tolerance, however, has a *secular* basis. It is the result of the "wall of separation" between church and state and the secularization of life in general. Christians would do well to consider here the Hindu example, wherein religious toleration possesses a *religious* basis.

NOTES

1. Hendrik Kraemer, *Why Christianity of All Religions,* trans. H. Hoskins (London: Butterworth, 1962); Arvind Sharma, "The Meaning and Goals of Interreligious Dialogue," *Journal of Dharma,* 8, no. 3: p. 232, n. 54.

2. T. M. P. Mahadevan, *Outlines of Hinduism* (Bombay: Chetana Limited, 1971), pp. 294–295.

3. Claude Alan Stark, *God of All: Sri Ramakrishna's Approach to Religious Plurality* (Cape Cod, Mass.: Claude Stark, 1974), Ch. 6.

4. K. M. Sen, *Hinduism* (Harmondsworth, Eng.: Penguin Books, 1973), p. 111. S. Radhakrishnan stated the point starkly (*The Hindu View of Life* [London: Unwin Books, 1974], pp. 40–41):

Hinduism does not support the sophism that is often alleged that to coerce a man to have the right view is as legitimate as to save one by violence from committing suicide in a fit of delirium. The intolerance of narrow monotheism is written in letters of blood across the history of man from the time when first the tribes of Israel burst into the land of Canaan. The worshippers of the one jealous God are egged on to aggressive wars against people of alien cults. They invoke divine sanction for the cruelties inflicted on the conquered. The spirit of old Israel is inherited by Christianity and Islam, and it might not be unreasonable to suggest that it would have been better for Western civilization if Greece had moulded it on this question rather than Palestine. Wars of religion which are the outcome of fanaticism that prompts and justifies the extermination of aliens of different creeds were practically unknown in Hindu India. Of course, here and there there were outbursts of fanaticism, but Hinduism as a rule never encourages persecution for unbelief. Its record has been a clear one, relatively speaking.

5. K. M. Sen, *Hinduism*, p. 73, n. 1.
6. According to R. C. Zaehner:

Thus to maintain that all religions are paths leading to the same goal, as is so frequently done today, is to maintain something that is not true. "With numerous, coherent symbols the same knowledge is revered. All people, whatever their cult, station, or way of life, who are inwardly at peace attain to the same truth, as rivers (flowing into) the sea." So says the *Anugītā*. And this is what the Hindus, in their large tolerance, genuinely believe and what all men of goodwill would like to believe; for the diversity of religions is a very real stumbling-block for all who are interested in finding one that is true. Were this diversity merely one emphasis, it would matter little. Unfortunately it is not; it is one principle.

(R. C. Zaehner, *Concordant Discord* [Oxford: Clarendon Press, 1970] p. 437). See also N. K. Devaraja, *Hinduism and Christianity* (Bombay: Asia Publishing House, 1969), p. 7.

7. J. N. Farquhar, *The Crown of Hinduism* (London: Oxford University Press, 1915).

8. Wm. Theodore de Bary, ed., *Sources of Indian Tradition* (New York: Columbia University Press, 1958), 2:6–7.

9. See R. C. Majumdar, ed., *British Paramountcy and Indian Renaissance* (Bombay: Bharatiya Vidya Bhavan, 1965), 2:155.

10. Consider, for example, the following comment by Zaehner, *Concordant Discord*, p. 442:

And this seems to me to constitute one fundamental difference between Christianity and the Eastern non-Christian religions. Christianity bases itself firmly on the doctrine of Incarnation, the doctrine that God became Man to deliver mankind from sin and to reconcile him with Himself. There is nothing comparable to this in the sacred books of the Hindus, the Buddhists, or the Moslems—or, for that matter, of the Confucians and Taoists. Yet the later developments of the first three of these religions show that each has evolved, independently it would appear, a theory of Divine incarnation and of a Divine Mediator between God and man. This is a genuine parallelism; but in all religions except Christianity it develops in logical opposition to the dominant view of each of the sacred books. There is nothing in the Koran to justify the quasi-deification of Muhammad, even less justification is there for the deification of the Buddha. Again, according to orthodox Brahmanical teaching, no divine incarnation can in any sense be real since the whole phenomenal world of which the incarnate God must necessarily form a part is illusory. In each case the need for an incarnate

God seems to have been so strongly felt that the doctrine of incarnation made its appearance in surroundings where it had no rightful place.

11. Huston Smith, *The Religions of Man* (New York: Harper and Row, 1965), p. 40. But see also Mariasusai Dhavamony, *A Love of God according to Śaiva Siddhānta* (Oxford: Clarendon Press, 1971), p. 378; Alan Daniélou, *Hindu Polytheism* (London: Routledge and Kegan Paul, 1964), p. 12, n. 24.

12. Radhakrishnan, *The Hindu View of Life* (London: Unwin Books, 1974) p. 37.

13. Sen, *Hinduism*, p. 15.

14. Mahadevan, *Outlines*, p. 20.

15. Abbe J. A. Dubois perceptively ascribed the relative failure of Christian missionary activity to this very fact—that Christian conduct left much to be desired. See Henry K. Beauchamp, ed., *Hindu Manners, Customs, and Ceremonies by the Abbe J. A. Dubois* (Oxford: Clarendon Press, 1959), p. 301.

16. See Ainslie T. Embree, ed. *The Hindu Tradition* (New York: Random House, 1972), Ch. 4.

17. Arvind Sharma, *The Hindu Scriptural Value System and the Economic Development of India* (New Delhi: Heritage Publishers, 1980).

18. The view that another tradition may help focus our attention on something valuable in our own tradition should also not be overlooked. For instance, the Hindu penchant for mysticism may make Christians adopt a more positive attitude toward the mystical elements in their own heritage. This form of mutual discovery is best illustrated with the help of the following story:

It is the story of Rabbi Eisik, son of Rabbi Jekel of Krakow, who dreamed three times of treasure buried under the bridge leading to the king's castle in Prague, and was determined to go and dig it up. He travelled to Prague and found the bridge, and although it was heavily guarded, he returned daily, hoping for an opportunity to dig for the treasure. Finally the captain of the guard asked him why he was loitering there and Rabbi Eisik told him of his dream. The captain mocked the rabbi for believing in dreams, and told one of his own to show how ridiculous it was to pay attention to dreams: he himself had dreamed of treasure hidden in Krakow, in the house of a Jewish man called Eisik, son of Jekel; it was supposed to be buried in a dirty corner behind the stove. The rabbi thanked the captain, and quickly returned home, where he found the treasure where it was supposed to be. (Heinrich Zimmer, *Artistic Form and Yoga in the Sacred Images of India*, trans. Gerald Chapple and James B. Lawson [Princeton, N.J: Princeton University Press, 1984] pp. xvii–xviii).

For the sake of completeness one should extend the story to include the discovery of a treasure by the captain under the bridge. This would be like Hinduism recovering more fully the dimension of social concern as evidenced within it by the setting up of hospices, hospitals for animals, and the free serving of food in temples, by the example set by Christianity.

SELECTED BIBLIOGRAPHY

I am greatly indebted to Robert Stephens for assisting in the compilation of this bibliography.

Books

Abhishiktananda, Swami. *Abhishiktananda on Aikiya Alayam*. Madras: Aikiya Alayam Series, 1975.

————. *The Church in India: An Essay in Christian Self-Criticism*. Madras: Christian Literature Society, 1969, 1971.

————. *The Further Shore*. Delhi: Indian Society for the Publication of Christian Knowledge, 1975.

————. *Guru and Disciple*. London: Society for the Publication of Christian Knowledge, 1974.

————. *Hindu-Christian Meeting Point—Within the Cave of the Heart*. Bombay: Institute of Indian Culture and Bangalore: Christian Institute for the Study of Religion and Society, 1969; rev. ed., Delhi: Indian Society for the Publication of Christian Knowledge, 1976.

————. *Initiation à la spiritualité des Upanishads*. Sisteron: Editions Présence, 1979.

————. *Intériorité et révélation: Essais théologiques Sisteron*. Sisteron: Editions Présence, 1982.

————. *La rencontre de l'hindouisme et du christianisme*. Paris: Editions du Seuil, 1966.

————. *Les yeux de lumière*. Paris: Le Centurion, 1979. Also published as *The Eyes of Light*. Denville, N.J.: Dimension Books, 1983.

————. *The Mountain of the Lord: Pilgrimage to Gangotri* (Bangalore: Christian Institute for the Study of Religion and Society, 1966).

————. *Prayer*. London: Society for the Publication of Christian Knowledge, 1975; Delhi: Indian Society for the Publication of Christian Knowledge, 1967, 1979.

————. *Saccidānanda: A Christian Approach to the Advaitic Experience*. New Delhi: Indian Society for the Publication of Christian Knowledge, 1974. Originally published in French as *Sagesse hindou mystique chretienne*. Paris, 1965; rev. English ed., Delhi: ISPCK, 1984.

————. *Souvenirs d'arunāchala* (Paris: Épi s.a. Editeurs, 1978). Also published as *The Secret of Arunachala*. Delhi: Indian Society for the Publication of Christian Knowledge, 1979.

————. *Swami Parama Arubi Anandam* (Memoir of J. Monchanin). Tiruchi: Shantivanam, 1959.

————. *Towards the Renewal of the Indian Church*. Bangalore: CMI, 1970.

————. *Une messe aux sources du Gange*. Paris: Editions du Seuil, 1967.

Abhishiktananda (Henry Le Saux with J. Monchanin), *An Indian Benedictine Ashram* (English text). Tiruchi: Shantivanam, 1951.

Ancelet-Hustache, J. *Master Eckhart and the Rhineland Mystics*. New York: Harper; London: Longmans, 1957.

Aykara, T. A., ed. *Meeting of Religions*. Bangalore: Dharmaram Publications, 1978.

Barlage, H. *Christ-Saviour of Mankind. A Christian Appreciation of Swami Akhilananda*. St. Augustin, W. Ger.: Steyler Verlag, 1977.

Beauchamp, Henry K., ed. *Hindu Manners, Customs, and Ceremonies by the Abbe J. A. Dubois*. 3d ed. 1906. Reprint, Oxford: Clarendon Press, 1959.

Boyd, R. H. S. *An Introduction to Indian Christian Theology*. Madras: Christian Literature Society, 1979.

————. *Khristadvaita: A Theology for India*. Madras: Christian Literature Society, 1977.

Braybrooke, M. *The Undiscovered Christ*. Bangalore: Christian Institute for the Study of Religion and Society; Madras: Christian Literature Society, 1973.

Bürkle, H., and Roth, W. M. W., eds. *Indian Voices in Today's Theological Debate*. Lucknow, India: Lucknow Publishing House, 1972.

Catherine of Genoa. *Purgation and Purgatory: The Spiritual Dialogue*. The Classics of

Western Spirituality. London: Society for the Publication of Christian Knowledge, 1979.

Catherine of Siena. *The Dialogue*. The Classics of Western Spirituality. London: Society for the Publication of Christian Knowledge, 1980.

Chethimattam, J. B. *Dialogue in Indian Tradition*. Bangalore: Dharmaram College, 1969.

Christian Bishops Conference of India. *All India Seminar on the Church in India Today*. Delhi: Christian Bishops Conference of India Centre, 1969.

———, Commission on Dialogue. *Guidelines for Inter-Religious Dialogue*. Varanasi: Christian Bishops Conference of India Commission, 1977.

Cuttat, J. -A. *La rencontre des religions*. Paris: Ambier, 1957. Also published as *The Encounter of Religions*. New York: Desclèe Co., 1960.

Deniélou, Alain. *Hindu Polytheism*. London: Routledge and Kegan Paul, 1964.

Davy, M.-M. *Henri Le Saux, Swami Abhishiktananda, Le Passeur entre deux rives*. Paris: Les Editions du Carf, 1981.

Deussen, P. *The Philosophy of the Upanishads*. New York: Dover, 1966.

Devaraja, N. K. *Hinduism and Christianity*. Bombay: Asia Publishing House, 1969.

Devdas, N. *Ananda: The Concept of Bliss in the Upanishads*. Bangalore: Christian Institute for the Study of Religion and Society, 1974.

Dhavamony, Mariasusai. *A Love of God according to Śaiva Siddhānta*. Oxford: Clarendon Press, 1971.

Dupais, J. *Jesus Christ and His Spirit*. Bangalore: Theological Publications of India, 1977.

Emprayil, T. *The Emerging Theology of Religions: The Contribution of the Catholic Church in India*. Rewa, India: Vincentian Publications, 1980.

Farquhar, J. N. *The Crown of Hinduism*. London: Oxford University Press, 1915.

Griffiths, B. *Christ in India: Essays towards a Hindu-Christian Dialogue*. New York: Scribner's, 1966.

———. *The Cosmic Revelation: The Hindu Way to God*. Springfield, Ill.: Templegate Publishers, 1983.

———. *The Golden String*. Garden City, N.Y: Image Books, 1964.

———. *The Marriage of East and West*. London: Collins, 1982.

———. *Return to the Centre*. London: Collins, 1978.

———. *Vedanta and Christian Faith*. Los Angeles: Dawn Horse Press, 1973.

Hargreaves, C. *Asian Christian Thinking*. Delhi: Indian Society for the Publication of Christian Knowledge, 1979.

Hick, J., ed. *Truth and Dialogue: The Relationship between World Religions*. London: Sheldon Press, 1974.

Hiriyanna, M. *Essentials of Indian Philosophy*. London: George Allen and Unwin, 1949, 1978.

———. *Outlines of Indian Philosophy*. London: George Allen and Unwin, 1932.

Irudayaraj, X., and L. Sundaram, eds. *Inter-Faith Dialogue in Tiruchirapalli*. Madras: Private publication, 1978.

Jai Singh, H., ed. *Inter-Religious Dialogue*. Bangalore: Christian Institute for the Study of Religion and Society, 1967.

John of the Cross. *The Collected Works of St. John of the Cross*. Translated by K. Kavanagh and O. Rodriguez. Institute of Carmelite Studies, Washington, 1973.

John of St. Thomas, *The Gifts of the Holy Ghost*. Translated from Latin by D. Hughes. London and New York: Society for Promoting Christian Knowledge, 1936.

Johnston, W. *The Inner Eye of Love*. London: Collins, 1978.

————, ed. *The Cloud of Unknowing and the Book of Privy Counseling*. Garden City, N.Y.: Doubleday, 1973.

Klostermaier, K. K. *Hindu and Christian in Vrindaban*. London: SCM Press, 1969.

————. *Kristvidya: A. Sketch of an Indian Christology*. Bangalore: Christian Institute for the Study of Religion and Society, 1967.

Mahadevan, T. M. P. *Outline of Hinduism*. Bombay: Chetana Ltd., 1971.

Maritain, J. *Distinguish to Unite or The Degrees of Knowledge*. Translated by G .B. Phelan. London: Geoffrey Bus, 1959.

Mattam, J. *Land of the Trinity: A Study of Modern Christian Approaches to Hinduism*. Bangalore: Theological Publications of India, 1975.

Merton, T. *Contemplative Prayer*. London: Darton, Longman & Todd, 1975.

Monchanin, J. *Mystique de L'Inde, mystere chretien*. Paris: Fayard, 1974.

Murray, J. C. *The Problem of God*. New Haven and London: Yale University Press, 1964.

Neuner J., and J. Dupuis, eds. *The Christian Faith*. Bangalore: Theological Publications in India, 1976.

Panikkar, R. *The Intrareligious Dialogue*. New York: Paulist Press, 1978.

————. *Myth, Faith, and Hermeneutics*. New York: Paulist Press, 1979.

————. *The Trinity and World Religions*. Bangalore: Christian Institute for the Study of Religion and Society; Madras: Christian Literature Society, 1970. Published in the United States as *The Trinity and the Religious Experience of Man*. New York: Orbis Books, 1973.

————. *The Unknown Christ of Hinduism*. London: Darton, Longman and Todd, 1964.

Panikkar, R. *Blessed Simplicity: The Monk as Universal Archetype*. New York: Seabury Press, 1982; Minneapolis: Winston Press, 1985.

Pathrapankal J., ed. *Service and Salvation*. Bangalore: Theological Publications in India, 1973.

Paul VI. *Ecclesiam Suam*. Encyclical Letter, June 8, 1964 (Official English translation). Sydney: St. Paul Publications, 1964.

Pereira, J., ed. *Hindu Theology: A Reader*. Garden City N.Y.: Doubleday 1976

Radhakrishnan, S. *Eastern Religions and Western Thought*. Oxford: Clarendon Press, 1939.

————. *The Hindu Way of Life*. London: Unwin Books, 1927, 1974.

Rahner, K. *Foundations of Christian Faith*. New York: Seabury Press, 1978.

————. *Theological Investigations*. Vol. 5. Baltimore: Helicon; London: Darton Longman & Todd, 1966.

Rajamanickam, S. *The First Oriental Scholar*. Tirunelveli, India: De Nobili Research Institute, 1972.

Rao, M. S. *Ananyatva—Realization of Christian Non-Duality*. Bangalore: Christian Institute for the Study of Religion and Society, 1964.

Robinson, J. A. T. *Truth Is Two-Eyed*. London: SCM Press, 1979.

Ruthnaswamy, M. *India after God*. Ranchi: 1964.

Sadguru Gnanananda. His Life, Personality, and Teachings, by His Life Devotees. Bombay: Bharatiya Vidya Bhayan, 1979.

Samartha S. J., ed. *Living Faiths and Ultimate Goals*. (Maryknoll, N. Y.: Orbis Books, 1974.

Secretariatus Pro Non Christians. *For a Dialogue with Hinduism*. Milan and Rome: Editrice Ancora, n.d. [early 1970s].

————. *Religions, Fundamental Themes for a Dialogistic Understanding*. Rome: Editrice Ancora, 1970.

————. *Guidelines for a Dialogue between Muslims and Christians*. 1st ed., 1969; Indian ed., Cochin: KCM Press, 1979.

Sen, K. M. *Hinduism*. Harmondsworth, Eng.: Penguin Books, 1973.

Sharpe, E. *Faith Meets Faith*. London: SCM Press, 1977.

Stark, Alice Mary, and Claude Alan Stark, eds. *Spiritual Practices*. Memorial Edition with Reminiscences by His Friends, by Swami Aakhilananda. Cape Cod, Mass.: Claude Stark, Inc., 1974.

Stark, Claude Alan. *God of All: Sri Ramakrishna's Approach to Religious Plurality*. Cape Cod, Mass.: Claude Stark, Inc., 1974.

Stace, W. T. *Mysticism and Philosophy*. London: Macmillan 1961.

Steindl-Rast, D. *A Listening Heart*. New York: Crossroad, 1983.

Swami Prabhavananda. *The Sermon on the Mount According to Vedanta*. Myalore, Madras: Sri Ramakrishna Math, 1964.

Swami Satprakashananda. *Hinduism and Christianity*. St. Louis: Vedanta Society of St. Louis, 1975.

Teresa of Avila. *The Complete Works of St Teresa of Jesus*. Vol. 2. Translated and edited by E. Allison Peers. London: Sheed & Ward, 1957.

Thomas, M. M. *Man and the Universe of Faiths*. Bangalore: Christian Institute for the Study of Religion and Society; Madras: Christian Literature Society, 1975.

————. *Salvation and Humanisation* Bangalore: Christian Institute for the Study of Religion and Society; Madras: Christian Literature Society, 1971.

Underhill, E. *The Spiritual Life*. London: Hodder & Stoughton, 1937.

Vadakkekara, C. M., ed. *Prayer and Contemplation*. Bangalore: Asirvanam Benedictine Monastery, 1980.

Vananda, ed. *Gurus, Ashrams and Christians*. London: Darton, Longman & Todd, 1978.

————. *Indian Spirituality in Action*. Bombay: Asian Trading Corporation, 1973.

————. *Social Justice and Ashrams*. Bangalore: Asian Trading Corporation, 1982.

Vatican Council II. *The Documents of Vatican II*. Edited by W. M. Abbott. London, 1972.

Vattakuzhy E. *Indian Christian Sannyāsa and Swami Abhishiktananda*. Bangalore: Theological Publications of India, 1981.

Weber, J. G., ed. *In Quest of the Absolute: The Life and Work of Jules Monchanin*. (Kalamazoo, Mich: Cistercian Publications; London, 1977).

Zaehner, R. C. *Concordant Discord*. Oxford: Clarendon Press, 1970.

Articles

Abhishiktananda, Swami. "An Approach to Hindu Spirituality," *The Clergy Review* 54, no. 3 (March 1969): 163–174.

————. 'Baptism, Faith, and Conversion,' *The Indian Journal of Theology* 16, no. 3 (July-September 1967): 189–203.

————. "Christian Sannyasis." *The Clergy Monthly Supplement* 4 (September 1958): 106–113.

————. "The Church in India—A Self-examination," *Religion and Society* 15, no. 3

(September 1968): 5–19. (A draft of the first part of his book *The Church in India*.)

———. "Communication in the Spirit." *Religion and Society* 17, no. 3 (September 1970): 33–39.

———. "The Depth-Dimension of Religious Dialogue." *Vidyajyoti* 45, no. 5 (May 1981): 202–221.

———. "Dialogue Postponed: An Exchange between Rev. C. Murray Rogers and Sivendra Prakash." *Asia Focus* 3 (1970): 210–222.

———. "Dialogue and Theologia Negativa." Preliminary Paper. Bombay Consultation, January 1969, 3 pp.

———. "The Experience of God in Eastern Religions." *Cistercian Studies* 9, nos.2–3 (1974): 148–157.

———. Foreword to J. Borst, *A Method of Contemplative Prayer*. Bombay, 1973, 1977, pp. 1–3.

———. "Le Père Monchanin." *La Vie Spirituelle* 98, no. 435 (January 1958): 71–95.

———. "Letters to an Eastward-Turning Disciple." *Monastic Studies* 13 (1982): 175–178.

———. "Monasticism and the Seminar" (continued). *The Examiner* (Bombay), August 23, 1969, p. 537–538.

———. "Sannyasa." *The Divine Life* (Rishikesh) 35, no. 9 (September 1973): 354–362; 35, no. 10 (October 1973): 418–422; 35, no. 11 (November 1973): 446–454; 35, no. 12 (December 1973): 490–496; 36, no. 1 (January 1974): 28–31; 36, no. 2 (February 1974): 62–66; 36, no. 3 (March 1974): 98–100 (Articles reprinted in *The Further Shore*, ed. Maprem Maneesha. Boulder, Colo.: Chidvilas, 1980.

———. "Theology of Presence as a Form of Evangelisation in the Context of Non-Christian Religions." In J. Pathrapankal, ed., *Service and Salvation*. Bangalore: CISRS, 1973, pp. 407–417.

———. "The Upanishads and the Advaitic Experience." *The Clergy Monthly*. 28, no. 11 (December 1974): 474–486.

———. "The Way of Dialogue." In H. Jai Singh, ed., *Inter-Religious Dialogue*. Bangalore: CISRS, 1967, pp. 78–103.

———. "Yoga and Christian Prayer," *The Clergy Monthly* 35, no. 11 (December 1971): 472–477.

Abhishiktananda Society. *Occasional Bulletin* 2, (April 1978); 3 (December 1979); 4 (June 1980); 5 (October 1981); 6 (December 1982); 7 (November 1983).

Adappur, A., "The Theology of Inter-Faith Dialogue." *Vidyajyoti* 46, no. 10 (November 1982): 485–498.

Almond, P. "Mystical Experience, the One and the Many: Towards a New Theory." Paper presented at the Joint Conference of Australia-New Zealand Society for Theological Studies, Australian Association for the Study of Religions, and Australia-New Zealand Association of Theological Studies, August 20–24, 1979, University of Sydney.

Amaladoss, M. A. "Towards an Indian Spirituality." *Religion and Society* 16, no. 2 (June 1969): 6–26.

Amalorpavadass, D. S. *Inter-Religious Dialogue in India*. National Biblical, Catechetical and Liturgical Centre (NBCLC) Seminar Booklet Series No. 30. Bangalore, n.d. (c. 1977), 24 pp.

Baumer-Despeigne, O. "The Spiritual Journey of Henri Le Saux—Abhishiktananda."
    Cistercian Studies 18, no. 4 (1983): 310–329.

Bergen, V. "Contemporary Christian Experiments in Ashram Life." *Journal of Dharma*
    3, no. 2 (April-June 1978): 174–194.

Bhatt, D. "Dialogue and Mission." Preliminary Paper. Bombay Consultation, January
    1969, 1 p.

Burkle, H. R. "Jesus Christ and Religious Pluralism." *Journal of Ecumenical Studies*
    16, no. 3 (Summer 1979): 457–471.

Chethimattam, J. B. "Meaning and Scope of Interreligious Dialogue." *Jeevadhara* 11,
    no. 65 (September-October 1981): 319–334.

———. "Recent Christian Studies on Hinduism." *The Examiner* (Bombay), October
    14, 1967, p. 663.

———. "The Scope and Conditions of a Hindu-Christian Dialogue." *Concilium* 3, no.
    1 (March 1965): 83–93.

Christa Prema Seva Ashram, Shivaji Nagar, Pune. Pamphlet published by Ashram, n.d.,
    4 pp.

Cuttat, J.-A. "Christian Experience and Oriental Spirituality." *Concilium* 9, no. 5 (No-
    vember 1969): 60–64.

De Letter, P. "Dialogue with Non-Christians." *The Clergy Monthly* 32, no. 10 (October
    1968): 437–446.

De Smet, R. V. "Advaitavada and Christianity." *Bulletin* (Secretariatus pro Non Chris-
    tians) 23–24 (1973): 143–146.

———. "Pathways for Evangelization in India." *Lumen Vitae* 29, no. 3 (September
    1974): 403–417.

———. (Recent Developments in the Christian Approach to the Hindu." *Lumen Vitae*
    29 no. 4 (December 1974): 515–520.

———. "Robert de Nobili and Vedanta." *Vidyajyoti* 40, no. 8 (September 1976): 363–
    371.

———. "Śaṁkara Vedānta and Christian Theology." *Review of Darshana* 1, no. 1 (July
    1980): 33–48.

Devdas, N. "The Theandrism of Raimundo Panikkar and Trinitarian Parallels in Modern
    Hindu Thought." *Journal of Ecumenical Studies* 17, no. 4 (Fall 1980): 606–620.

Dhavamony, M. "Christian Experience and Hindu Spirituality." *Gregorianum* 48, no.
    4 (1967): 776–791.

Dockhorn, K. "Christ in Hinduism as Seen in Recent Indian Theology." *Religion and
    Society* 21, no. 4 (December 1974): 39–57.

Fonseca, C. "A Prophet Disowned." *Vidyajyoti* 44, no. 4 (April 1980): 177–194.

Gispert-Sauch, G. "Exploring the Further Shore." *Vidyajyoti* 40, no. 11 (December
    1976): 502–506.

———. Reviews of Abhishiktananda's works [Prayer]. *The Clergy Monthly* 32, no. 5
    (May 1968): 242–243; [Hindu-Christian Meeting Point]. *The Clergy Monthly* 33,
    no. 12 (December 1969): 548–549; [Towards the Renewal of the Indian Church].
    The Clergy Monthly 35, no. 5 (May-June 1971): 224; [Saccidananda]. *The Clergy
    Monthly* 38, no. 11 (December 1974): 509–510.

———. "The Sanskrit Hymns of Brahmabandhav Upadhyay." *Religion and Society* 19,
    no. 4 (December 1972): 60–79.

Grant, S. "Indian Eclipse." *The Clergy Review* 44, no. 2 (February 1968): 87–99.

———. "Reflections on Hindu-Christian Dialogue in an Ashram Context." *Religion and Society* 26, no. 1 (March 1979): 42–58.

———. "Swamiji—The Man." *The Clergy Monthly* 38, no. 11 (December 1974): 487–495.

Griffiths, B. "Christian Monastic Life in India." *Journal of Dharma* 3, no. 2 (April-June 1978): 122–135.

———. "The Dialogue with Hindus." *The Examiner* (Bombay), December 17, 1966, p. 821.

———. "Further towards a Hindu-Christian Dialogue." *The Clergy Monthly* 32, no. 5 (May 1968): 213–220.

———. "Indian Christian Contemplation." *The Clergy Monthly* 35, no. 7 (August 1971): 277–281.

———. "Mystical Theology in the Indian Tradition." *Jeevadhara* 9, no. 53 (September-October 1979): 262–277.

———. "The Mystical Tradition in Indian Theology." *Monastic Studies* 13 (1982): 159–173.

———. Review of B. Griffiths [Christian Ashram (= Christ in India)] by Swami Venkaatesananda and reply by B. Griffiths. *Journal of Ecumenical Studies* 5, no. 1 (Winter 1968): 144–151.

———. "St. Benedict in the East." *The Tablet* (London), July 12, 1980, pp. ix-xi.

Hacker, P. "Adaptation-Indigenization-Utilization," *The Laity* (Delhi) 5, no. 9 (September 1977): 392–403.

Hirudayam, I. "Dialogue in Tamilnadu." *Lumen Vitae* 29, no. 3 (September 1974): 418–428.

———. "Interfaith Dialogue in Madras." *Bulletin* (Secretariatus pro Non Christianis) 13 (March 1977): 38–45.

———. "Reflections on Interreligious Dialogue." *Bulletin* No.17 of North American Board for East West Dialog, May 1983, pp. 8–9.

Irudayaraj, X. "Brahma Vidya Mandir." *The Clergy Monthly* 33, no. 1 (January 1969): 34–36.

———. "Dialogue Experience." *Vidyajyoti* 40, no. 3 (March 1973): 131–132.

———. "The Guru in Hinduism and Christianity." *Vidyajyoti* 34, no. 8 (September 1975): 338–351.

———. "Sannyasa—Swami Abhishiktananda." *The Clergy Monthly* 38, no. 11 (December 1974): 501–508.

Ishapriya. "The Cave of the Heart." *Vidyajyoti* 40, no. 2 (February 1976): 79–83.

Jackson, P. "Jesuits at the Mugal Court." *Vidyajyoti* 40, no. 3 (March 1980): 108–113.

Jadot, J. L. "The Growth in Roman Catholic Commitment to Interreligious Dialogue since Vatican II." *Journal of Ecumenical Studies* 20, no. 3 (Summer 1983): 365–378.

Jai Singh, H. "Inter-Faith Dialogue and the Search for Philosophical Truth." *Religion and Society* 12, no. 1 (March 1965): 45–50.

Journal of Dharma 8, no. 3 (July-September 1983). Entire issue.

Kadankavil, K. T. "The Absolute as a Common Ground of Mysticism" *Journal of Dharma* 1, no. 3 (January 1976): 194–210.

Kalapesi, M. "Some Reflections on the Fourth Meeting on Hindu and Christian Spirituality at Jyotiniketan Ashram, April, 1964." *Religion and Society* 11, no. 4 (December 1964): 71–76.

Kessler, G. E. and N. Prigge, "Is Mystical Experience Everywhere the Same." *Sophia* 21, no. 1 (April 1982): 39–55.

Klostermaier, K. K. "Dialogue—The Work of God." In H. Jai Singh, ed., *Inter-Religious Dialogue*. Bangalore: The Christian Institute for the Study of Religion and Society, 1967, pp. 118–126.

———. "From End to Beginning." The Principal Miller Endowment Lectures, 1977–1978. Reprinted from *Journal of The Madras University* 50, no. 2 (July 1978): 1–49.

———. "Hindu-Christian Dialogue." *Journal of Ecumenical Studies* 5, no. 1 (Winter 1968): 21–44.

———. "Hindu-Christian Dialogue: Its Religious and Cultural Implications," *Sciences Religieues/Studies in Religion* 1, no. 2 (1971): 83–97.

———. "A Hindu-Christian Dialogue on Truth." *Journal of Ecumenical Studies* 12, no. 2 (Spring 1975): 157–171.

———. "Hinduism in Bombay." *Religion* 2 (Autumn 1972): 83–91.

———. "Hrdayavidya: A Sketch of a Hindu-Christian Theology of Love." *Journal of Ecumenical Studies* 9, no. 4 (Fall 1972): 759–774.

———. "Indian Christian Theology." *The Clergy Review* 54, no. 3 (March 1969): 175–198.

———. "Raymond Panikkar's [The Unknown Christ of Hinduism]." *The Indian Journal of Theology*. 15, no. 2 (April-June 1966): 70–73.

———. "The Religion of Study." *Religious Traditions* 1, no. 2 (October 1978): 56–66.

———. "Sadhana: A Sketch of Indian Spirituality." *Religion and Society* 16, no. 2 (June 1969): 36–50.

———. "Sanyasa—A Christian Way of Life in Today's India?" In H. Bürkle and W.M.W. Roth, eds., *Indian Voices in Today's Theological Debate* Lucknow, India: Lucknow Publishing House, 1972, pp. 170-197.

———. "Sixth Meeting on Hindu and Christian Spirituality 'Jyotiniketan Ashram' (Bareilly, U.P.), January 17–21 1966." *Religion and Society* 13, no. 2 (June 1966): 72–75.

———. "Sketch of a Hindu-Christian Sacramentology." *The Clergy Monthly* 32, no. 4 (April 1968): 159–173.

Koothottil, A. "Christian Theology and Religious Dialogue." *Jeevadhara* 11, no. 65 (September-October 1981): 352–363.

Lederle, M. "Discovery of Dialogue." *Religion and Society* 26, no. 1 (March 1979): 59–72.

Mahieu, F. [M. F. Acharya]. "The Contemplative Dimension of the Church." *The Clergy Monthly* 33, no. 4 (April 1969): 145–155.

———. "Indian Monastic Samaj." *The Clergy Monthly* 36, no. 4 (April 1972): 137–148.

———. "Monasticism in India." *The Clergy Monthly* (Supplement) 7, no. 2 (June-July 1964): 45–60.

———. "A New Charter for Monasticism." *The Clergy Monthly* 35, no. 10 (November 1971): 423–433.

Mampra, T. "Encounter between Hinduism and Christianity." *Journal of Dharma* 1, no. 3 (January 1976): 246–266.

Manickam, T. Editorial. *Journal of Dharma* 8, no. 3 (July-September 1983): 221–224.

Merton, T. "The Inner Experience." *Cistercian Studies* 18, no. 1 (1983); 3–15; 18, no. 2 (1983): 120–134; 18, no. 3 (1983): 201–216; 18, no. 4 (1983) 289–300.

Mundadan, A. M. "Hindu-Christian Dialogue: Past Twenty-Five Years." *Jeevadhara* 11, no. 65 (September-October 1981): 375–394.

Nambiaparambil, A. "Bulletin on Dialogue: CBCI Dialogue Commission." Supplement to *The Examiner* (Bombay), July 12, 1980, 2 pp.

———. "Dialogue in India: An Analysis of the Situation; a Reflection on Experience." *Journal of Dharma* 1, no. 3 (January 1976): 267–283.

———. "Dialogue in India: A Challenge to Redeem Hope." *Vidyajyoti* 39, no. 3 (March 1975): 111–126.

———. "Dialogue and Mission in a Cross-Cultural and Religiously Pluralistic Context" (CBCI-NCCI Joint Consultation on our Common Witness: October 14–16, 1980, Alwaye, Kerala) 17 pp. (Cyclostyled).

———. "Ways and Means of Inter-Religious Harmony and Reconciliation." *Studies in Islam* (New Delhi: Indian Institute of Islamic Studies, October 1978): 243–247.

Nayak, A. and A.-M. Abrard. "Hindu-Christian Dialogue in India." *Pro Mundi Vita Bulletin* 88 (January 1982): 1–30.

Neuner, J. "The Place of World Religions in Theology." *The Clergy Monthly* 32, no. 3 (March 1968): 102–115.

O'Collins, G. "Theology and Experience." *The Irish Theological Quarterly* 44, no. 4 (1977): 279–290.

O'Meara, T. F. "Toward a Subjective Theology of Revelation." *Theological Studies* 36, no. 3 (Spring 1975): 401–427.

Panikkar, R. "Advaita and Bhakti: Love and Identity in Hindu-Christian Dialogue." *Journal of Ecumenical Studies* 7, no. 2 (Spring 1970): 299–309.

———. "The Church and the World Religions." *Religion and Society* 14, no. 2 (June 1967): 59–63.

———. "Confrontation between Hinduism and Christ." *New Blackfriars* 50, no. 584 (January 1969): 197–204.

———. "The Contemplative Mood: A Challenge to Modernity." *Cross Currents* 31, no. 3 (Fall 1981): 261–272.

———. "Faith—A Constitutive Dimension of Man." *Journal of Ecumenical Studies* 8, no. 2 (Spring 1971): 223–254.

———. "Hermenutics of Comparative Religion: Paradigms and Models." *Journal of Dharma* 5, no. 1 (January-March 1980): 38–51.

———. "Hinduism and Christianity." *Religion and Society* 8, no. 4 (December 1961): 10–18.

———. "Indirect Methods in the Missionary Apostolate: Some Theological Reflections." *The Indian Journal of Theology* 19, nos. 3–4 (July-December 1970): 111–113.

———. "The Internal Dialogue—The Insufficiency of the So-called Phenomenological 'epoche' in the Religious Encounter." *Religion and Society* 15, no. 3 (September 1968): 54–66.

———. "Inter-Religious Dialogue: Some Principles." *Journal of Ecumenical Studies* 12, no. 3 (Summer 1975): 407–409.

———. "Letter to Abhishiktananda" on the second anniversary of his death, December 1975. Unpublished.

———. "The New Innocence." *Cross Currents* 27, no. 1 (Spring 1977): 7–15.

————. "Rules of the Game in the Religious Encounter." *Asia Focus* 3 (1970): 223–227.

————. "Toward an Ecumenical Theandric Spirituality." *Journal of Ecumenical Studies* 5, no. 3 (Summer 1968): 507–534.

————. "The Ultimate Experience." *Theology Digest* 20, no. 3 (Autumn 1972): 219–226.

Philip, P. O. "The Place of Ashrams in the Life of the Church in India." *The International Review of Missions* 35, no. 139 (July 1947): 263–270.

Pieris, A. "Western Christianity and Eastern Religions." *Cistercian Studies* 15, no. 1 (1980): 50–66.

Puthanangady, P. *Indian Theology, Liturgy, and Spirituality*. NBCLC Seminar Leaflet Series 20. Bangalore, n.d., 12 pp.

Quaderni del Centro Interreligioso Henri Le Saux (Milano), no. 1 (1980). Entire issue on Abhishiktananda.

Rajan, R. S. "Negations." *Religion and Society* 21, no. 4 (December 1974): 67–76.

Rao, M. S. "Inter-Faith Dialogue and Spirituality." *Religion and Society* 12, no. 1 (March 1965): 30–34.

Reetz, D. "Raymond Panikkar's Theology of Religions." *Religion and Society* 15, no. 3 (September 1968): 32–54.

Reports. "Christians in Dialogue with Men of Other Faiths." *International Review of Mission* 59, no. 236 (October 1970): 382–391. (Consultation at Zurich, May 1970.)

————. "Christians in Dialogue with Men of Other Faiths." *Religion and Society* 14, no. 2 (June 1967): 64–69. (Statement of consultation at Kandy, Sri Lanka, February 27-March 5, 1967.)

————. "Consultation on the Theology of Hindu-Christian Dialogue, Bombay, 4–8 January 1969." *Religion and Society* 16, no. 2 (June 1969): 69–88.

————. "Declaration by Participants of the Hindu-Christian Dialogue, Shantivanam 17, 18, 19 January 1974." *Bulletin* 25 (1974): 69–70.

————. "Keynote Address by Mgr. Rossano to the Hindu-Christian Live-together." *Bulletin* (Secretariatus pro Non Christianis) 25 (1974): 65–68.

————. *Statement of the All-India Consultation on Ashrams*. NBCLC Statement Series No. 22, Bangalore, June 7–11, 1978, 4 pp. See *Word and Worship* 11, no. 7 (August 1978): 267–282.

Rodericks, J. "The Christian Mystical Tradition as a Basis for Dialogue." Preliminary Paper. Bombay Consultation, January 1969, 2 pp.

Rogers, C. Murray. Editorial. *Asia Focus* 3 (1970): 180.

————. "Hindu Ashram Heritage: God's Gift to the Church." *Concilium* 9, no. 1 (November 1965): 73–78.

————. "Hindu and Christian—A Moment Breaks." *Religion and Society* 12, no. 1 (March 1965): 35–44.

————. "Swamiji the Friend." *Religion and Society* 23, no. 1 (March 1976): 76–87.

Rogers, C. Murray, and "Sivendra Prakash." 'Dialogue Postponed.' *Asia Focus* 3 (1970): 210–222.

Saccidananda Ashram, Shantivanan. Pamphlet published by Ashram, n.d., 10 pp.

Samartha, S. J. "Ganga and Galilee; Hindu and Christian Reponses to Truth." *Jeevadhara* 11, no. 65 (September-October 1981): 335–351.

————. "Guidelines on Dialogue." *Bulletin* (Secretariatus pro Non Christianis) 41–42, (1979): 130–138.

————. "Major Issues in the Hindu-Christian Dialogue in India Today." In H. Jai Singh, ed., *Inter-Religious Dialogue*. Bangalore: CISRS, 1967, pp. 145–169.

————. "More than an Encounter on Commitments, An Interpretation of the Ajaltoun Consultation on 'Dialogue between Men of Living Faiths.' " *International Review of Mission* 59, no. 236 (October 1960): 392–403.

————. "The Progress and Promise of Inter-Religious Dialogues." *Journal of Ecumenical Studies* 9, no. 3 (Summer 1972): 463–474.

Sandeman, H. Review of Abhishiktananda [Prayer]. *Religion and Society* 16, no. 2 (June 1969): 89–91.

Saran, A. K. "Further towards a Hindu-Christian Dialogue." *The Clergy Monthly* 32, no. 1, May (1968): 213–218.

Sevanand. "Christian Sannyasa." *Indian Theological Studies* 14, no. 3 (September 1977): 264–288.

Scott, D. C. "A Christian Basis for Inter-Faith Dialogue." *Religion and Society* 12, no. 1 (March 1965): 15–29.

Sharpe, E. J. "The Concept of Salvation with Special Reference to Religions of Indian Origin." *Religious Traditions* 1, no. 1 (April 1978): 50–60.

————. "Dialogue and Faith." *Religion* 3, no. 2 (Autumn 1973): 89–114.

————. "The Goals of Inter-Religious Dialogue." In J. Hick, ed., *Truth and Dialogue: The Relationship between World Religions*. London: Sheldon Press, 1974, pp. 77–95.

Sraddhananda. "Brahma Vidys Mandir." *The Clergy Monthly* 30, no. 8 (August 1969): 337–349.

Stuart, J. D. M. "Abhishiktananda on Inner Awakening." *Vidyajyoti* 46, no. 10 (November 1982): 470–484.

————. "Sri Ramana Maharshi and Abhishiktananda." *Vidyajyoti* 44, no. 4 (April 1980): 168–176.

————. "Swami Abhishiktananda." *The Clergy Monthly* 38, no. 2 (February 1974): 80–82.

Swidler, L. "Ground Rules for Interreligious Dialogue." *Journal of Ecumenical Studies* 15, no. 3 (Summer 1978): 413–414.

Taylor, R. "Christian Ashrams as a Style of Mission in India." *International Review of Mission* 68, no. 271 (July 1979): 281–293.

————. "From Khadi to Kavi." *Religion and Society* 24, no. 4 (December 1977): 19–37.

Teasdale, W. "Abhishiktananda's Contemplative Theology." *Monastic Studies* 13 (1982): 179–199.

————. "Abhishiktananda's Mystical Intuition of the Trinity." *Cistercian Studies* 18, no. 1 (1983): 59–75. Same article published also in *Quaderni del Centro Interreligioso Henri Le Saux*, no. 4 (1983): 39–64.

Valles, C. G. "Pastoral Approaches and Dialogue Methods—Towards a Hindu-Christian Theology." *The Clergy Monthly* 32, no. 3 (March 1968): 116–120.

Vandana. "Ashrams." *Word and Worship* 11, no. 1 (January 1978): 15–22.

————. "The Guru as Present Reality." *Vidyajyoti* 39, no. 3 (March 1975): 127–130; 39, no. 8 (September 1975): 352–357.

————. "Indian Theologizing and the Role of Experience." *Jeevadhara* 9, no. 53 (September–October 1979): 237–261.

————. "A Messenger of Light." *The Clergy Monthly* 38, no. 11 (December 1974): 496–500.

Warren, M.A.C. "The Universal Christ—The Missionary Problem with Interpretation." *Religion and Society* 17, no. 3 (September 1970): 60–77.

Whitehurst, J. E. "Realization of Christian Non-Duality." *Religion and Society* 12, no. 1 (March 1965): 66–73.

22

A Critique of Paul Tillich's Doctrine of God and Christology from an Oriental Perspective

SHU-HSIEN LIU

TILLICH'S DOCTRINE OF GOD

Tillich's doctrine of God is a most controversial issue. He contends that God is that which concerns humans ultimately but also that which is a being itself. The two statements are closely related. God cannot be a being among other beings. That which creates should not be confused with that which is created. If God "exists" as a being among others, he would be subject to the finite structure of time and space. Yet anything finite is not qualified to be the proper object of humans' ultimate concern. If God is truly that which concerns humans ultimately, he must not be a limited, finite being among others but rather the ground of being or being itself. The argument is apparently methodological as well as ontological. By adopting such an approach Tillich rejected the traditional doctrine of God as personal. It is true that we may still use the term *personal* as a symbol to talk about God. But preferably, we would state that God is *suprapersonal*.

Based on his ontologism, Tillich also rejected the idea of a becoming God. Some contemporary theologians tend to give priority to the idea of a living God. They break loose from the classical tradition and attempt to give a dynamic interpretation of the concept of God. But Tillich has resisted the temptation of such an attempt because that God must first have being in order to have the function of creativity. In his view, it is impossible for anything that does not even have prior being to have the power to create. Being is an all-encompassing concept that we cannot escape. Moreover, it is the only predicate that we may literally apply to the subject "God." Therefore, all other statements we make about God have to be symbolic. It is only in a symbolical sense that we can state that God has the power of being, ground of being, abyss of being, or state that he is omnipotent, eternal, omnipresent, omniscient, and so on.

Charles Hartshorne, however, objected to such a view. He maintained the "literalness of theism." In *The Divine Relativity* he said:

Perhaps I am overlooking needed qualifications, but to me it seems that theology (so far as it is the theory of the essence of deity) is the most literal of all sciences of existence. It is anthropology (including theological anthropology) that is shot full of metaphors and statements never literally true. We like to think we are wise and our enemies foolish, but always we are also foolish and our enemies wise. Man is never quite what he says he is. Only of God is he privileged to affirm the naked truth—if he takes care and does not fall down and worship some theological tradition which has crystallized theological thought prematurely. Thus God is wise—period. He is unborn—period. He is everlasting—period. He is socially aware of all beings, the actual as actual, the possible as possible—period.[1]

Hartshorne criticized Tillich exactly from this viewpoint in an essay he contributed to *The Theology of Paul Tillich*.[2] Tillich answered Hartshorne in a dialectical way:

The *via eminentiae*, which is used consistently by Mr. Hartshorne, needs as its balance the *via negationis*, and the unity of both is the *via symbolica*. If one says that God has personality in an eminent, namely, an absolutely perfect sense, one must add that this very assertion implies the negation of personality in God in the sense of "being a person." Both statements together affirm the symbolic character of the attribute "personal" for God.[3]

It is appropriate to consider briefly Tillich's general theory of symbols. In his essay "The Meaning and Justification of Religious Symbols" Tillich listed the five characteristics of the so-called representative symbols. The first characteristic of all symbols is that they point beyond themselves. In this respect a symbol is not different from a sign, since both of them have to point beyond themselves. The second characteristic of all representative symbols is that they participate in the reality of that which they represent. Here lies the great difference between symbols and signs. For example, a national flag is a symbol that participates in the power and dignity of the nation for which it stands, whereas the red light at a street corner is merely a sign that does not participate in the reality of that to which it points, and hence it can be replaced for reasons of expediency or convention. This leads to the third characteristic of the representative symbol: it cannot be created at will, since it is not a matter of expediency and convention, as signs are. The fourth characteristic of a representative symbol is its power of opening up dimensions of reality, in correlation with dimensions of the human spirit, which otherwise are covered by the predominance of other dimensions of spirit and reality. The fifth characteristic of representative symbols is their integrating and disintegrating power. Symbols may have healing power; they may also produce disintegrating effects: causing restlessness or producing depression, anxiety, fanaticism, and the like.[4]

These general characteristics of the symbol hold also for the religious symbol. "Religious symbols are distinguished from others by the fact that they are a representation of that which is unconditionally beyond the conceptual sphere;

they point to the ultimate reality implied in the religious act, to what concerns us ultimately."[5] In other words, the intention of every religious symbol is to point to that which transcends finitude. According to Tillich, the fundamental symbol of ultimate concern is God. It is in God that we find the theological answer to the question about the basis of humans' being: God as the ground of being.

The above discussion is only a brief account of Tillich's doctrine of God, because from a methodological point of view it is more than enough for us to know how Tillich proceeded to establish his doctrine of God. There is no need for detail concerning Tillich's analysis of symbols such as God as living, as creator, as Spirit and Trinity, as omnipotent, as eternal, as omnipresent, as omniscient, and as love. Tillich has given a dialectical analysis about each of these symbols. The consequence is that he tried to demythologize the traditional concept of God and give it an entirely new interpretation. This being the case, Tillich would not be disturbed if someone declared to him that God is dead, because this would mean no more than the fact that the image of the God of the traditional theism is no longer effective today. Actually, Tillich's own theology is instrumental in bringing about the downfall of the traditional supernaturalistic belief in God. The crux of the problem now becomes this: Is Tillich's own approach justifiable? Unfortunately, from a methodological point of view the answer is no.

In an essay contributed to *The Theology of Paul Tillich,* John Hermann Randall said:

In a real sense, for Tillich philosophy is faith seeking understanding. . . . For him there can be no *natural theology*; any argument from the character of the world to the existence of God could never get beyond finite relativities, and God is not a being whose "existence" demands proof. Tillich rests upon a version of the *ontological argument*—rather as for all true Augustinians, God (that ultimate in which the symbols of human ideas of God participate) neither needs nor can receive " proof." For that ultimate . . . is a certain quality of the world man encounters, which analysis reveals as "presupposed" in all his encountering.[6]

The comment is odd. Randall seems to have suggested, on the one hand, that Tillich rejected the possibility of a natural theology and, on the other hand, that he had another version of the ontological argument. How is this possible? Tillich's rejection of the natural theology actually depends on his definition of the term, because according to him God is not one of the natural "existences," nor can he be grasped by humans' natural reason. But does not the traditional ontological argument of Anselm start with a prayer? Is what he means by God's existence a kind of eminent existence that is nothing short of Tillich's being itself? Tillich may be right in stating that apart from revelation these arguments are impossible. But Tillich seems to believe firmly that there is a natural process of reasoning that drives us to the point that we have to meet the limit of our finitude and then open up our heart to the revelation from beyond. Can we state that in this sense Tillich also has a new version of "natural theology"? Remember, he himself has given paradoxical expressions such as "ecstatic naturalism" and "self-transcendent realism" to characterize his own theological position.

Following Randall's suggestion, we may further suggest that in some sense Tillich also has his own version of the cosmological argument. For example, in *Systematic Theology* Tillich described the three functions of life: self-integration, self-creation, and self-transcendence.[7] *Self-integration* is the circular movement of life from a center and back to this center. *Self-creation* is the horizontal movement of life that tends to produce new centers. Life drives toward the new. It is the principle of growth that determines the function of self-creation. But the third direction in which the actualization of the potential goes is in contrast to both the circular and the horizontal ones. This is the *self-transcending* function of life, which represents the vertical movement of life. Life by its very nature is both in itself and above itself. It drives beyond itself as finite life; it points toward the great, the sublime, and the high. In their essential structure the three functions unite elements of self-identity with elements of self-alteration. Yet this unity is threatened by existential estrangement, which drives life in one or the other direction, thus disrupting unity. To the degree in which this disruption is real, self-integration is countered by disintegration; self-creation is countered by profanization. Every life process has the ambiguity that the positive elements are mixed up in such a way that a definite separation of the negative from the positive is impossible. Life is neither essential nor existential, but ambiguous. We strive for being but are always threatened by existential estrangement. This makes us seek for an unambiguous life. However, although humans are driven to ask the question concerning unambiguous life, the answer must come to them through the creative power of the Spiritual Presence. The human spirit as a dimension of life is ambiguous, as all life is, whereas the divine spirit creates unambiguous life. It brings about the reunion of essence and existence. The traditional cosmological argument starts with an analysis of the phenomenal causes, arguing that it is impossible for these causes to continue *ad infinitum*. Hence it urges us to leap to an ultimate cause, which is beyond all phenomenal causes and nevertheless is the cause of these phenomenal causes. In this sense Tillich's method of correlation is no more than a new version of the traditional cosmological argument. There seems to be a force built into human nature that drives humans always to look beyond. The quest for God becomes almost an autonomous process for humans until it reaches its natural, final solution.

From a methodological point of view the argument is untenable. First, Tillich's description of the characteristics of the life process is questionable. For example, self-transcendence may be an essential characteristic of human life, but it is extremely doubtful that this is the characteristic of all life. Second, even if self-transcendence is the essential characteristic of human life, Tillich's conclusion that humans have to seek for an unambiguous life beyond existence does not follow. It is true that one of the paradoxes in human life is that in order to achieve one's own self-realization one has to transcend beyond one's own selfish desires and hence transcend beyond one's own narrow self. But it makes no sense to state that humans have to transcend human existence altogether. The religious dimension is still a dimension of human life. What concerns humans is not something entirely beyond human existence but something that has existential significance for them. Third, this being the case, the only thing important for us is to try to distinguish the mode of divine operation in human existence from the other modes of human operations. God transcending finite knowledge is an impossible topic for humans. We know nothing about God himself, and we know nothing about the unambiguous life enjoyed by God. The only way for us to glorify God is to realize the divine endowments within humans, if there are such things. For other matters let God take care of himself and let us not bother him with our petty human affairs.

Tillich's great mistake lies in his naive belief that by redefining God as being itself, he is able to avoid the evils of the traditional doctrines of God. Actually, the concept ''being itself'' does not help. I agreed entirely with Sartre when he said that all we can state about being is that ''Being is. Being is in-itself. Being is what it is.''[8] If as Tillich argued the only literal statement we can make of God is ''God is being itself,'' not only does the statement fail to convey any definable meaning, but taken literally, it inevitably leads us to think of God as static and causes serious misunderstanding, which Tillich himself wants to avoid by all means. Actually, that which Tillich said about *via eminentiae, via negationis,* and *via symbolica* should also apply to the concept ''being itself.'' If we state that God is being itself, in order to avoid misunderstanding we have to add that God is not ''being itself'' when the term is understood in its Parmenidean sense. Finally, what we have is no better than a dialectical, or symbolical, understanding of the statement that God is being itself.[9]

In fact, Tillich has never been able to make up his mind upon this point. At first, even the term *God* was no more than a symbol for Tillich.[10] Later, he seemed to change his mind for this reason:

An early criticism by Professor Urban of Yale forced me to acknowledge that in order to speak of symbolic knowledge one must delimit the symbolic realm by an unsymbolic statement. I was grateful for this criticism, and under its impact I became suspicious of any attempts to make the concept of symbol all-embracing and therefore meaningless. The unsymbolic statement which implies the necessity of religious symbolism is that God is being itself, and as such beyond the subject-object structure of everything that is.[11]

But in *Systematic Theology,* Tillich again modified his own position: ''If we say that God is the infinite, or the unconditional, or being-itself, we speak rationally and ecstatically at the same time. These terms precisely designate the boundary line at which both the symbolic and the nonsymbolic coincide.''[12] Finally, in a rejoinder to his critics Tillich expressed himself in the following way: ''The more exact formulation, I think, should be that there is an element in the term

'God,' namely, the fact that he is being itself, which can become a concept if analytically separated, and that there is an element in the term 'being-itself' which can become a symbol if analytically separated.''[13]

It seems that Tillich wants to preserve his realism and symbolism at the same time. This strategy is not justified because he fails to specify in what sense "being itself" is a symbol and in what sense it is not. This situation creates all of the puzzles Tillich has to face. Actually, Tillich seems to confuse the problem of language with the problem of reality. It is true that a symbol has to point beyond itself toward something real. But having a situation in which we have no other way to describe a state of affairs than by giving it a symbolic statement does not mean that we have reduced the state of affairs to symbols.[14] Tillich, however, does not want to reduce his God into a kind of symbolic existence; that is why he has to define "God is being itself" arbitrarily as a nonsymbolic statement. Yet he has had difficulty in maintaining such a thesis consistently. This is why he shifted to his later position. But I think all of these shifts are unnecessary. My own criticism of Tillich's doctrine of God is from an entirely different angle. I doubt whether it is possible for us to make even symbolic statements about God. That can be done only if one knows enough about a thing to make symbolic statements about it and if one has a criterion to judge whether these statements are appropriate. Apparently, we know nothing definite about God that would enable us to make symbolic statements about him.

For example, Tillich said that God is a power of being. But what does he mean by power of being? Henry Wieman objected to this concept:

Being itself or the power of being, is infinite and indestructible only in the sense that when everything else is destroyed, whatever continues will still *be*. Everything conceivable might be destroyed, leaving what we cannot conceive. What we cannot conceive would still be an instance of being. The slow torture of the human race to the point of extinction would still manifest the power of being.

This is the only kind of indestructibility which being itself or the power of being can provide, so long as it is not limited to some form standing in opposition to other forms. But this is exactly what Tillich means by "power of being." The eternity of being itself is nothing more than the certainty that something will be when life and virtue have ceased to exist. No matter what comes into existence in the form of horror and "nothingness," through it all the power of being will still be the power of being.[15]

I am almost sure that Tillich would think that Wieman misunderstood his statement, because Wieman took a symbolic statement as a literal one. But the blame is still on Tillich's side because Tillich has never been able to make clear what he intends to say. In fact, Tillich can never do this, for being itself or power of being refers to what is inaccessible to the cognitive power of the human mind. Unless being can be characterized in some way, we can never hope to make appropriate symbolic statements about it or judge the adequacy of these statements. As a symbol, "the power of being" is impotent. Tillich seemed to imply that the human being manifests higher degrees of power of being than other forms of living beings. But if humans eat animals to support their life, and if in consequence the destruction of animal life is beneficial to the maintenance of human life, may not a higher being delight in human suffering because it manifests a still higher degree of power of being? Hence it is useless to appeal to the power of being to overcome the threat of nonbeing within human existence.

From my own point of view I would like to draw a sharp distinguishing line between metaphysical problems and ontological problems. Since ontology in my dictionary always means phenomenological ontology, it is a philosophical enterprise with great significance to humans. It is possible to describe the basic structures of human existence. There are brutal, humanistic, divine elements operating in humans. It is not only possible but necessary to give a phenomenological description of the ways these elements operate. This would enable us to make right commitment to the principle that sustains and enhances the meaning of life. Sometimes we have to use symbolic statements because the principles of life are dynamic principles that defy ordinary linguistic expressions. But all of them must be experientially verifiable, although not experimentally verifiable. It is in this sense that ontology is the backbone of philosophy. But speculative metaphysics is a different story.

By *metaphysics* I mean the speculative hypotheses concerning the origin and ultimate nature of being. How do I know the world is finally made of mind or of matter? How do I know there is or is not a Creator of the universe? We are free to make all speculative metaphysical hypotheses concerning these issues, but the difficulty is that we have no adequate criteria to judge between these speculative hypotheses. Hence the better way is to put these issues into brackets and practice an attitude of *epoché* toward them, because it is not only beyond our power to answer these speculative questions, but such a metaphysical enterprise has no existential significance to us. For example, we do not wait until the settlement of the metaphysical problem concerning immortality of the soul to establish our moral principles, whereas the existential decision between different moral principles is a life or death matter for us.

In some sense it may be said that I am trying to revive the Kantian insight: it is impossible to establish either a speculative metaphysics or a speculative theology by means of the cognitive powers of the human mind. It is indeed tempting to infer from the divine operations within humans to the deity himself. But what do we really add to our stock of knowledge by making such metaphysical inferences? We pretend to know something we really do not know at all. Tillich's sophisticated formulation of his doctrine of God does not help him to get out of the basic dilemma: Either humans really know God or they do not. In the former case the apprehension of God is not really beyond the structure of finitude, no matter whether such apprehension is through human faith or revelation. In the latter case humans are talking of something they really know not. The function of Tillich's method of correlation is to urge us to seek answers from beyond our knowledge whereas each time we try to look beyond the reach of cognition we are always brought back to our own concepts. This is why we have to be content with our phenomenological ontological analysis.

TILLICH'S CHRISTOLOGY

Tillich's Christology is another controversial issue. The methodological procedure he adopted is, first, to make a sharp distinction between Jesus and the Christ and, second, to give a symbolic interpretation of the Christ. The distinction between Jesus and the Christ is necessary for Tillich's theology, because for Tillich, Jesus was merely a man who did not possess any kind of supernatural power. Miracles, if interpreted as happenings that contradict the laws of nature, are simply impossible for Tillich. Hence the legendary stories that were reported in the New Testament cannot be literally true. To worship the man Jesus as God would be a practice of idolatry. The myths centering around the man Jesus are to be rejected under Tillich's treatment. This Jesusology was completely denounced by Tillich. Jesus becomes religiously significant only when he becomes the symbol for the Christ. The Christ was born when one of Jesus' disciples suddenly proclaimed: ''Thou are the Christ.'' At that revelatory moment the man Jesus was suddenly transformed into Jesus-as-the-Christ. According to Tillich, this was the greatest miracle that ever happened in human history and will be the greatest miracle forever. The faith in such a miracle does not conflict with any findings of science, and yet it constitutes the backbone of the Christian dogma.

Christ as a symbol was pictured most adequately in the New Testament. Tillich pointed out the threefold manifestation of the New Being in the biblical picture of Jesus as the Christ: ''first and decisively, as the undisrupted unity of the center of his being with God; second, as the serenity and majesty of him who preserves this unity against all the attacks coming from estranged existence; and, third, as the self-surrendering love which represents and actualizes the divine love in taking the existential self-destruction upon himself.''[16] The Cross and the Resurrection combined together are the two most important symbols in Christianity. Christ sacrificed his own life; in utmost emotional tension, on the Cross he cried: ''My God, my God, why hast thou forsaken me?'' Yet Christ's self-negation did not end in mere annihilation. His faith brought to him another life of New Being that is beyond the assault of existential estrangement in our life. The end of human *hubris* is the beginning of the divine grace. The New Being in Jesus as the Christ is the answer to the fallen, estranged human situation. ''New Being is essential being under the conditions of existence, conquering the gap between essence and existence.''[17] It is new in two respects: ''it is new in contrast to the merely potential character of essential being; and it is new over against the estranged character of existential being.''[18] Jesus as the Christ is New Being because he brings the old being to an end. He is the end in the sense of being the goal of existence with all of its conflicts and destructive propensities. He is the end of history, that is, the aim or *telos* of history.

Tillich's Christology is an extremely ingenious device that ruthlessly disposes of all of the superstitions that are connected with the old Christian tradition. The application of Tillich's method also throws light on the difficult problems concerning Jesus as a historical man.

From Tillich's viewpoint it is beyond doubt that we may do any kind of historical research upon Jesus the man we like. It is open to debate whether Jesus was a genuine historical personality, whether the historical records about him are authentic. From a historical point of view it is mandatory for us to collect more and more facts concerning the man Jesus, if such a man really existed in history. It is also mandatory for us to judge the authenticity of the records concerning this man against historical, factual evidences. But Tillich warned us that even if we were able to reconstruct a historical picture of Jesus as close as possible to facts, the result could be no more than probable. Historical studies are by their nature never more than probable, since the factual evidences we collect can never be complete; besides, the interpretation of them is largely determined by our limited perspectives. But faith is another matter. It is absolute, never probable; what is absolute can never base its foundation upon what is merely probable. Hence Tillich distinguished sharply between the historical dimension and the religious dimension or the dimension of facts and the dimension of faith. Bare facts do not determine our faith. An exact, historical picture of Jesus proves nothing if we have no faith in Christ. On the contrary, only when we make an existential commitment to the faith in Christ does Christ become a symbol pointing toward a reality that is adequate to solve our existential problems.

Some Christian writers criticize Tillich on the ground that Tillich does not really care for the historical reality of Jesus of Nazareth. They firmly believe that if Jesus is not historical reality, the validity of the Christian message is also disproved. Tillich's answer to these criticisms was most sophisticated. He insisted that Christ as a symbol received by the Christians is a historical fact. Since Christ symbolizes *logos* become flesh, his incarnation symbolizes the moment that the infinite breaks into the finite. *Logos* without entering into history would only be an abstract universal that has no existential significance for humans whatsoever. Hence *Logos* embodied in Christ must become flesh, must become historical reality. This is an absolute necessity confirmed by depth of reason or rather by Christian revelation. Hence it is essential for Tillich to insist that Christ must be a historical reality, but it is by no means essential for him to argue that Jesus of Nazareth is a historical reality. The certainty insisted upon by Tillich is a certainty of faith, not a certainty of facts. The latter is only an irrelevant element that possesses no significance for Tillich's doctrine of Christology.

By such a methodological device Tillich is able to disentangle himself from the endless disputes concerning the historical reality of Jesus of Nazareth. He does not have to deny values to historical studies concerning Jesus the man. But historical studies have only the value of historical studies. They do not have religious significance for us.

However, by insisting that Christ must be a historical reality, Tillich claimed that Christianity is the only true "historical" religion in the world. Christ is the only center of all history. Tillich criticized the Oriental religions such as Hinduism and Buddhism as not having a center of history. Hence they are ahistorical religions. Tillich also criticized the Jewish religion as not believing that the Messiah has already come to the earth. According to Tillich, history as genuine history implies exactly no more and no less than one center of history. In Christianity, Christ is the center. The historical periods before Christ are conceived of as the preparatory stage for the Christian message, and the historical periods after Christ are conceived of as the receiving stage to accept the Christian message. In short, it is only in Christ that we find the criterion of all genuine religious revelations.

Tillich's Christology is very complicated. However, there is no need for us to go into his discussion of Incarnation, Trinity, and so on. To criticize him from a methodological point of view, it suffices to know the very bold outline of his Christology summarized above.

From Tillich's point of view, all religions point toward the final revelation in Christ. All other great world religions are either preparatory stages that lead toward the final Christian message or "latent churches" that, although explicitly denying, implicitly assert the Christian message. I, however, hold that all world religions including the Christian religion point beyond themselves toward what is "the religious concern." Christianity is no doubt one of the highest religions in the world. But it can claim no more than one of the manifestations of the religious substance. It seems that Tillich has nothing to support his claim for Christianity except by appealing to a mysterious Christian revelation or clinging tenaciously to a historical Christian tradition. What I am trying to do is only to carry Tillich's theological doctrines a logical step further. I am trying to seek a true "religion above religion" that Tillich himself has tried to attain.

Tillich's idea of a historical religion is not only confusing but also absurd. First, from what he has said about Jesus the man, Tillich seems to maintain that as a theologian he does not have to be interested in objective historical facts. This being the case, Tillich seems to be a theologian who takes history seriously and at the same time does not take objective historical facts seriously. This may not constitute a contradiction, but it does lead to a paradox that puzzles the ordinary mind.

Second, and a more serious criticism, following the Christian, especially the Augustinian, tradition, Tillich seems to dissolve the concept of history into a pure present. The Christ-event seems to overshadow all other events happening in real history. Both the history before and after Christ retreat into the background and turn into pale shadows. The idea of process becomes a mere phantom for the Tillichean type of Christian theologian. They also reject the idea of progress. All real historical processes are called to a halt clustering around the center of

Christ. In this sense Christianity is the most ahistorical religion rather than the most historical religion in the world.

Third, according to Tillich, human history seems to be a great historical drama using history as a medium to attain a final aim transcending all human history. The kingdom of God is definitely beyond history, not within history. This makes Christianity an otherworldly, transhistorical religion. It is extremely confusing to call it a historical religion.

A true historical religion would consider every historical moment as having existential significance of its own. Every historical moment is a center by itself. The historical process flows forward without a definite end to stop it. Some historical events may have greater symbolic value than others. But no historical event can be taken as a substitute for other historical events. No historical period, however insignificant it is, can be taken as a mere shadow of the other historical periods. With the help of all of the symbolic values achieved in the past each new generation has to grope its own way, because novel situations demand new solutions, although it is always possible to learn from the past. It is true that we may learn many things from Jesus the Christ. But it is by no means true that we have to take Jesus-as-the-Christ as the "final" revelation or the only center of all history. Either no revelation is final or every revelation is final in itself. Christianity is no doubt one of the greatest religions ever to appear in human history. Yet precisely its claim that it has found the final revelation or the only center of history in Christ makes it an ahistorical religion, because the "pure present" in Christ has overshadowed the concept of "history." History has been turned into a religious drama dominated by transhistorical elements.

From my viewpoint Tillich not only distorts the concept of a historical religion but also distorts the concept of an existential theology, although he is often called an existential theologian. By insisting upon the final revelation in Christ, Tillich's existential decision becomes no longer a true authentic existential decision. With all of its dramatic fluctuations the answer is always preconceived in Tillich's *Systematic Theology*. Tillich merely makes use of existentialism as a springboard in order to jump into his essentialism.[19]

I maintain that the concrete manifestation of the religious concern may assume different forms depending on the concrete situation it confronts, be it Christian, Hinduist, Buddhist, or some other new form of religion of which we have not the slightest knowledge at present. To plunge into a certain faith and hold it tenaciously as the final religious message is not existential but antiexistential. Heteronomy always tends to assume the form of theonomy. Again, here I am only trying to carry Tillich's theological doctrine a step further to its logical conclusion.

Now I may be in a position to summarize my own philosophical as well as religious convictions. I accept Tillich's threefold distinction between "technical reason," "ontological reason," and "depth of reason." But in content my analysis is substantially different from Tillich's analysis of these concepts.

By *technical reason* I mean essentially the same thing Tillich intends to mean by that term. Technical reason designates human reasoning or calculating power. Humans are able to form hypotheses, make inferences, and calculate consequences. At this level the criteria of operationalism prevail. Humans make use of their reasoning power without attempting to look at its root.

By *ontological reason* I mean something that is both different from and similar to what Tillich meant by that term. Following the classical tradition, Tillich gave the definition of the term as "the structure of the mind which enables the mind to grasp and to transform reality."[20] The problem lies in the ambiguity of the term *reality*. If *reality* means "the really real" without qualification, Tillich committed an error when he naively assumed that humans are able to grasp the really real. We can know nothing really real in the sense of the Kantian noumenal reality. Rather "the really real" should be interpreted as an axiological term designating what is held to be of greatest value within the reach of human power. If *reality* means the reality that opens up to the human mind, Tillich's definition holds good. It is owing to humans' ontic structure that they are have the power of reasoning. It is also owing to humans' ontic structure that they are able to encounter a vast field of value opening up to their vision. It is true that humans have ontological reason but only to the degree that the term is interpreted as "the structure of the mind which enables us to grasp and to transform reality that opens up to the structure of the human mind."

With the same spirit we have to reinterpret "the depth of reason." By depth of reason everyone of us is able to discern that there is a religious dimension within our life; it is obligatory for us to seek after a genuine ultimate concern. But the depth of reason is universal in all people; it does not point toward a specific Christian message, although the Christian message may well be a manifestation of the depth of reason. In depth of reason we find the answer to the question about the meaning of life. We find that there is a creativity operating in human existence that saves us from our destructive propensities when we meet the required conditions. There are always destructive propensities when we meet the required conditions. There are always destructive elements operating within our life. But once we are committed to this creativity we may turn present destructions into further chances of creation. By creativity I mean the creative power that lives through all destructions of life without losing its creative power. The created goods may degenerate and become obstructions of life, but the dynamic creativity continues to create new forms of value. No one can prove that there is meaning in life, but when one commits oneself to this creativity and sustains such a commitment under any difficult environment, the meaning of life gushes forth.[21] No specific revelation is needed to commit oneself to such a faith. It amounts to the faith in humanity itself. Nothing we have said is experimentally provable if we interpret the term *experimental* in its ordinary narrower sense, and yet everything is experientially confirmable if we interpret the term *experiential* in its broadest sense.

All the higher truths of humankind have to be symbolic or dialectical. It may be said that I am advocating a humanist position if by humanism one means that it is impossible to get outside of the human epistemological as well as ontological circle. It is simply meaningless to talk about something that is entirely beyond all human powers to reach. It also may be said that I am advocating a transhumanist position if by that one means that there is a religious depth within humans. Humans have to go beyond themselves to realize themselves; this happens to be one of the most profound truths about human life.

Hence from my own position it is meaningless to talk much about God-in-himself of whom we know nothing definite or certain. But it is obligatory for us to realize the religious depth within us, or else we would be caught by the meaninglessness of our life once we are estranged from our own religious depth. Also, it would be meaningless to talk about humans' fundamental project as striving to be God (or being-in-itself-for-itself).[22] A person's final aim is to be human, not to be God. It is Sartre's own unwarranted assumption, not humans' true ontological situation, that drives humans into their unsolvable dilemma. Although on the one hand "man is what he is not, man is not what he is," on the other hand, humans have always been able to be what they are and not what they are not. This is too profound a dialectical truth of life for Sartre to plumb. Humans are enigmatic beings who are able to be estranged from their own authentic self as well as to realize themselves as a God-person. It is obligatory to give an authentic ontological analysis of the human condition, but this is far beyond the scope of this chapter.

REVIEW AND CONCLUSION

We have made a number of criticisms against the methodological presuppositions implied in Tillich's theological doctrines. But I hope I have not created the impression that I criticize only with destructive purposes. If I were convinced that Tillich's theological doctrines contain nothing but a bundle of mistakes, it is certain that I would have chosen another and better topic on which to write. Precisely because Tillich is so openminded a theologian–philosopher, I was tempted to urge him to become more open minded. Also, precisely because he pays so much attention to methodological principles as well as philosophical approaches to theological problems, I consider it necessary to criticize him seriously from a methodological point of view.[23] Although at many points I am convinced that Tillich is wrong, I consider his theology a good point of departure for future theological attempts to strive toward a "theology above theology."

In summary, I am convinced that his doctrine of God is untenable, because on the one hand his God is too immanent, or too anthropocentric, since he always correlates himself with our human problems of existence; yet he is too transcendent, since he is so far beyond our cognitive power that not even revelation can give a clear, unambiguous vision of him. But what is entirely beyond us can have no existential significance for us. If a hidden God is truly a hidden God, it is a waste of time to talk about him. Only the power of being that is accessible to humans is truly signficant for humans. But then its ways of operation must be phenomenologically describable, even if only in an indirect, symbolic way due to limitations of the structure of human language.

It is apparent that my criticisms presuppose my own methodological principles. They are different from the criticisms made by other writers upon Tillich's theology. From a Christian point of view, many authors would criticize Tillich for renouncing the idea of a personal God. According to them, the fact that Tillich identified God with being itself ontologizes God in such a way that he is no longer the God of biblical faith. Again, they would criticize him because he has renounced the idea of Incarnation and does not believe in Jesus the Christ as an undoubtable historical fact. In short, they would criticize Tillich because he ontologized the Christian message. The Christian message by its nature cannot and should not be ontologized.

More specifically, the Catholic writers would criticize Tillich because his use of the method of correlation makes God always correlative with the existential human situations and hence in danger of losing his absolute, transcendent independence. Again, by rejecting natural theology altogether, Tillich's symbolic method finally leads him into an inevitable obscurantism. The Catholic method is more analogical than symbolic.[24]

The Protestant writers on the other hand would criticize Tillich because he associates theology too much with philosophy. The Christian faith does not need the support of the rationalization of philosophy. By following the Kierkegaardian tradition, one has to make an existential decision to leap into the Christian faith. Ontology with its speculative reasoning weakens the force of the Christian faith.[25]

In answering these criticisms Tillich would argue that philosophy and theology are necessarily complementary to each other. The Christian message is exactly the answer provided for the questions raised by philosophical or ontological analysis of reality. "Theology is the existential and, at the same time, methodical interpretation of an ultimate concern."[26] More specifically, Tillich rejected the Thomistic philosophy that is the official philosophy of Catholicism. He thought that St. Thomas's cosmological approach alienated his thought from Augustine's ontological approach and hence results in "the Thomistic *dissolution* of the Augustinian solution."[27] Also, Tillich strongly criticized the Catholic hierarchal system as a practice of heteronomy that is subject to the dangers of idolatry and demonization. But Tillich did speak highly of what he called the "Catholic substance." He has deep appreciation for the ritualistic element preserved in the Catholic tradition that is deplorably lacking in the Protestant denominations. The Protestant principle is to be counterbalanced by the Catholic substance. Tillich considered himself a Protestant theologian. But he has always found himself at variance with the other Protestant thinkers. He criticized the nineteenth-century humanist tendency within Christianity as lacking religious depth and hence subject to the dangers of emptiness and meaninglessness. But he also criticized the twentieth-century neo-orthodox tendency to initiate a complete break with culture and also with philosophy.[28] It is with a view to remedying this situation that

Tillich undertook to establish his great apologetic theological system. It is obvious that Tillich's intention was to bring about a great synthesis within Christianity. Besides, he also opened up his mind toward the other great religions and quasi-religions of the world.[29]

As one outside the Christian tradition, it may be expected that I cannot accept those criticisms of Tillich's theology made from a Christian point of view. The Christian writers complain that Tillich's theology is not Christian enough, whereas I would complain on the contrary that Tillich's theology is unduly Christian. He ought to transcend the specific Christian tradition to achieve the ideal of a true "religion above religion" and establish a true "theology above theology."

But on the other hand, I cannot accept the criticism of Tillich's theology from an atheistic position either. Most of the criticisms are directed against him from a linguistic point of view. John Hermann Randall told us the following story:

On one occasion Tillich read a brilliant paper to a group of professional philosophers. Among the listeners was G. E. Moore, the distinguished representative of a very different philosophical tradition and language. When it came time for Moore to comment, he said: "Now really, Mr. Tillich, I don't think I have been able to understand a single sentence of your paper. Won't you please try to state one sentence, or even one word, that I can understand?"[30]

Many writers accuse Tillich of saying something obscure or meaningless. I have never agreed with such a point of view. Tillich does have something important to say. Although I am not satisfied with most of Tillich's presentations, I think the issue between Tillich and his critics is more than a linguistic issue. I also think the art of hermeneutics is a philosophical technique that is far superior to that of ordinary language analysis. The art of hermeneutics consists of two steps: first, trying to understand sympathetically what a person really intends to say, to pierce through his words in order to grasp the true message that the individual wants to convey that is based on experience central to his or her life; second, even if sometimes the words are badly chosen and lead to inevitable misunderstandings, trying to dig out the original insight behind the words and put it in a different context that may have better revealing power than the words used by the writer. The art of hermeneutics is a very powerful weapon in human studies.[31] By piercing through the incomplete expression of linguistic conventions, we are able to learn more and more insights behind the words that otherwise we would never have been able to learn. While by finding faults with others' linguistic expressions and grammatical usage one may be well protected within a house of rigid linguistic conventions, one will be denied the pleasure of opening up many new vistas within both one's inner and outer worlds. Many human truths are bound to be expressed in a paradoxical way, and whenever someone has something radically new to say, one has to grope with incomplete and even immature linguistic expressions, but this is not linguistic nonsense. I do not deny that sometimes people do speak nonsense; this is why I am glad to accept all kinds of linguistic analysis as supplementary philosophical techniques. But only the art of hermeneutics can bring about true creative interchange between one person and another, and the practice of it will lead toward constructive purposes.

By applying the first step of the art of hermencutics to Tillich's theology, I do think that he has something important to say about the depth dimension of human reality. For example, his analysis of the characteristics of autonomy, heteronomy, and theonomy reveals an insight based upon well-founded experiential sources allowing us to test his suggestion against future experiences. Also, his attitude of "belief-ful realism" is the most healthy one possible for a modern person. People ought not to shy away from the reality of life; yet when realizing all of the undignified aspects of human reality, one need not lose faith in humanity but should commit oneself all the more fully to worthy causes with courage to resist evils that one has to encounter. It is here that I feel Tillich's vision is truer than that of his atheistic critics. But by applying further the second step of the art of hermeneutics to Tillich's theology I cannot but conclude that Tillich's theology can point beyond itself toward a true "theology above theology" only if all of the mythical and traditional Christian elements are completely washed away so that the message behind his words can come to the fore.

Theodore Greene once remarked: "I get from these [Tillich's] writings the impression not of a completed composition, but of a careful charcoal sketch on a very large canvas. This sketch reveals Tillich's life long preoccupation with basic problems and indicates the direction in which he so persistently presses for their solution."[32] If Tillich's lifelong efforts complete no more than a sketch of his basic plans, the methodological principles that I criticize in Tillich's theology are presented in this chapter in a much more sketchy fashion than Tillich's sketch of his basic plans.

But I hope at least the direction of my thinking is made clear. Moreover, if I have presented any insights, they all have their roots in a long and rich Chinese philosophical tradition. Very few people today, not even many contemporary Chinese philosophers themselves, are able to grasp the basic spirit of the Chinese philosophy. For example, the old Confucius was misinterpreted as a mere great moral teacher, his *Analects* as the most unphilosophical classic in the world. But I have found almost all important seeds of my own philosophy contained in the *Analects,* if a proper art of hermeneutics is applied. A few quotations from the work may justify my claim:

Concerning phenomenological methodology:

15.28. Confucius said, "It is man that can make the Way great, and not the Way that can make man great."[33]

11:11. Chi-lu (Tzu-lu) asked about serving the spiritual beings. Confucius said, "If we are not yet able to serve man, how can we serve spiritual beings?" "I venture to ask about death.'' Confucius said, ''If we do not know about life, how can we know about death?''[34]

Concerning a metaphysics of change and creativity:

9:16. Confucius, standing by a stream, said, ''It passes on like this, never ceasing day or night!''[35]

17:19. Confucius said, ''I do not wish to say anything.'' Tzu-kung said, ''If you do not say anything, what can we little disciples ever learn to pass on to others?'' Confucius said, ''Does Heaven (*T'ien,* Nature) say anything? The four seasons run their course and all things are produced. Does Heaven say anything?''[36]

Concerning ''God is dead'' theology:

3:12. When Confucius offered sacrifice to his ancestors, he felt as if his ancestral spirits were actually present. When he offered sacrifice to other spiritual beings, he felt as if they were actually present. He said, ''If I do not participate in the sacrifices, it is as if I did not sacrifice at all.''[37]

3:13. Wang-sun Chia asked, ''What is meant by the common saying, 'It is better to be on good terms with the God of the Kitchen [who cooks our food] than with the spirits of the shrine [ancestors] at the southwest corner of the house'?'' Confucius said, ''It is not true. He who commits a sin against Heaven has no God to pray to.''[38]

Concerning humanity's ultimate commitment:

4:5 Confucius said, ''Wealth and honor are what every man desires. But if they have been obtained in violation of moral principles, they must not be kept. Poverty and humble station are what every man dislikes. But if they can be avoided only in violation of moral principles, they must not be avoided. If a superior man departs from humanity, how can he fulfil that name? A superior man never abandons humanity even for the lapse of a single meal. In moments of haste, he acts according to it. In times of difficulty or confusion, he acts according to it.''[39]

8:7 Tseng Tzu said, ''An officer must be great and strong. His burden is heavy and his course is long. He has taken humanity to be his own burden—is that not heavy? Only with death does his course stop—is that not long?''[40]

Concerning the ideal of a sage:

9:4 Confucius was completely free from four things: He had no arbitrariness of opinion, no dogmatism, no obstinacy, and no egotism.[41]

16:8. Confucius said, ''The superior man stands in awe of three things. He stands in awe of the Mandate of Heaven; he stands in awe of great men; and he stands in awe of the words of the sages. The inferior man is ignorant of the Mandate of Heaven and does not stand in awe of it. He is disrespectful to great men and is contemptuous toward the words of sages.''[42]

Unsatisfactory as these translations have to be, taken as symbols they should serve as adequate evidence to indicate that there is an implicit methodology, as well as an implicit metaphysics and an implicit ontology, within the Chinese tradition. But primarily Chinese philosophy is a philosophy of commitment. The Chinese philosophers are extremely suspicious of the effectiveness of human language, but they are not satisfied with mere linguistic analysis. The central problem for them is the great problem of "inward sageliness and outward kingliness."

It is useless to apply the clichés in Western philosophy to Chinese philosophy. It is neither idealism nor realism, neither immanentism nor transcendentalism; neither naturalism nor supernaturalism; it is basically a humanism and at the same time a "humanism above humanism." There is no doubt a central thread running through all of the Chinese philosophy. The Chinese philosophers believe firmly in the idea that the principle is one but its manifestations are many. Hence there is no final revelation in Chinese philosophy. Each age has to find a new interpretation of the basic principle of life or humanity that answers to its concrete situations. The tradition and the new creation are both congruous and incongruous with each other. They hold a dialectical relation with each other. After the advent of existentialism and existential theology it should be much easier for the Western philosophers to realize the significance of the insights contained in the traditional Chinese philosophy. It is essentially an existential philosophy, and yet it offers an alternative ontological analysis to Christianity and contemporary existential philosophy. Perhaps it will take another hundred years for philosophers to achieve a new synthesis between Chinese and Western philosophy. But it is time for us to start out to establish a relation of creative interchange between the two.[43]

NOTES

1. Charles Hartshorne, *The Divine Relativity* (New Haven: Yale University Press, 1948), pp. 36–37.

2. See Charles Hartshorne, "Tillich's Doctrine of God," in Charles W. Kegley and Robert W. Bretall, eds., *The Theology of Paul Tillich* (New York: Macmillan, 1952), pp. 194–195.

3. Charles W. Kegley and Robert W. Bretall, eds., *The Theology of Paul Tillich* (New York: Macmillan, 1952), p. 334.

4. See Paul Tillich, "The Meaning and Justification of Religious Symbols," in Sidney Hook, ed., *Religious Experience and Truth* (New York: New York University Press, 1961), pp. 3–6. Tillich also analyzed the characteristics of symbols in slightly different fashion in some other places. See Tillich, "The Religious Symbol," reprinted in Hook, *Religious Experience and Truth*, pp. 301–303; idem, *Dynamics of Faith* (New York: Harper and Brothers, 1957), pp. 41–43.

5. Tillich, "The Religious Symbol," p. 303.

6. John Hermann Randall, Jr., "The Ontology of Paul Tillich," in Kegley and Bretall, *The Theology of Paul Tillich*, p. 136. Italics mine.

7. See Paul Tillich, *Systematic Theology*, 3 vols. (Chicago: University of Chicago Press, 1951, 1957, 1963), 3:30–32.

8. Jean-Paul Sartre, *Being and Nothingness*, trans. Hazel E. Barnes (New York: Philosophical Library, 1956), p. lxvi.

9. For example, in Tillich's essay "The Meaning and Justification of Religious Symbols," p. 7, Tillich took "being-itself" as a metaphorical name. This indicates the inconsistency of his thought on this point.

10. Even in *Dynamics of Faith*, Tillich said: "God is the basic symbol of faith''; see p. 47.

11. Paul Tillich, "Reply to Interpretation and Criticism," in Kegley and Bretall, *The Theology of Paul Tillich*, p. 334. For Urban's criticism see Wilbur M. Urban, "Tillich's Theory of Religious Symbol," *Journal of Liberal Religion* 2 (1940): 34–36. In the article Urban accused Tillich of a pan-symbolism. For an analysis of Tillich's change of position, see William L. Rowe, "The Meaning of God in Tillich's Theology," *The Journal of Religion* 62 (October 1962): 274–286.

12. Tillich, *Systematic Theology*, 2:10.

13. Paul Tillich, "Rejoinder," *The Journal of Religion* 46 (January 1966): 184.

14. Here I am following the Oriental tradition. A Zen *koan* reports that once a disciple asked his master: "What if one wipes away all the dust and sees Buddha?" The master answered: "Buddha is dust." The fact that one cannot make literal statements about Buddha does not turn Buddha into nonreality. See also the famous statement of Lao Tzu, "The Tao (Way) that can be told of is not the eternal Tao; the name that can be named is not the eternal name." Quoted from Wing-tsit Chan, *A Source Book in Chinese Philosophy* (Princeton, N.J.: Princeton University Press, 1963), p. 139.

15. Henry Nelson Wieman, "Intellectual Autobiography," in Robert W. Bretall, ed., *The Empirical Theology of Henry Nelson Wieman* (New York: Macmillan, 1963), pp. 11–12.

16. Tillich, *Systematic Theology*, 2:138.

17. Ibid., pp. 118–119.

18. Ibid., p. 119.

19. Although I do not agree with Hamilton's criticisms of Tillich's theology, it is interesting to note Hamilton's response against Tillich. He said: "The conclusion of the system [Tillich's] should give the death glow to the still prevalent opinion that Tillich can be termed an existentialist. . . . The gospel has been trimmed so as to make it conform to the contours of a liberal religion of revelatory experiences set in a mould of essentialist theory." Kenneth Hamilton, "Critical Review of *Systematic Theology*, III," reprinted in *The Journal of Religion* 46 (January 1966): 228.

20. Tillich, *Systematic Theology*, I:72.

21. The seed of a philosophy of creativity is presented in *The Book of Changes (I Ching)* of the Chinese classics. Wieman's thought is both similar to and different from this tradition. However, this is not the place for me to dwell on this problem.

22. See Sartre, *Being and Nothingness*, pp. 565–566.

23. See Tillich's contributions to the volumes in the *Library of Living Theology* on Reinhold Niebuhr and Emil Brunner's theologies; Tillich put far more emphasis on philosophical inquiries or methodological principles than did the other contemporary theologians. See Paul Tillich, "Reinhold Niebuhr's Doctrine of Knowledge," in Charles W. Kegley and Robert W. Bretall, eds., *Reinhold Niebuhr: His Religious, Social, and Political Thought* (New York: Macmillan, 1962), pp. 36–43; idem, "Some Questions

on Brunner's Epistemology,'' in Robert Bretall, ed., *The Theology of Emil Brunner* (New York: Macmillan, 1962), pp. 99–107.

24. See, for example, Battista Mondin's criticism of Tillich in his *Principle of Analogy in Protestant and Catholic Theology* (The Hague: Martinus Nijhoff, 1963), pp. 132, 142–145, 174–176. For Catholic criticism of Tillich, J. Heywood Thomas has published an appendix section on the topic; see his *Paul Tillich: An Appraisal* (Philadelphia: Westminster Press, 1963), pp. 187–214. One of Tillich's sympathetic critics from a Catholic point of view is Father Gustav Weigel who wrote several essays on Tillich's theology, such as: ''Contemporary Protestantism and Paul Tillich,'' *Theological Studies* 11 (June 1950): 177–202; ''Theological Significance of Paul Tillich,'' reprinted in *Cross Currents* 6 (Spring 1956): 141–155; ''Myth, Symbol, and Analogy,'' in W. Leibrecht, ed., *Religion and Culture* (New York: Harper, 1959), pp. 120–130.

25. Barth held a position that is opposite to Tillich's position. Reinhold Niebuhr's contribution to the Kegley and Bretall volume is a standard criticism of Tillich from Niebuhr's point of view. See his ''Biblical Thought and Ontological Speculation in Tillich's Theology,'' in Kegley and Bretall, *The Theology of Paul Tillich,* pp. 216–227.

26. Tillich, ''The Problem of Theological Method,'' reprinted in Will Herberg, ed., *Four Existentialist Theologians* (New York: Doubleday, 1958), p. 241.

27. See Paul Tillich, ''Two Types of Philosophy of Religion,'' in Robert C. Kimball, ed., *Theology of Culture* (New York: Oxford University Press, 1959), pp. 10–29.

28. See Walter M. Horton, ''Tillich's Role in Contemporary Theology,'' in Kegley and Bretall, *The Theology of Paul Tillich,* pp. 26–47.

29. Although Tillich always maintained an open-minded attitude toward world religions, his criticisms of the Oriental religions are superficial. See his *Christianity and the Encounter of the World Religions* (New York: Columbia University Press, 1963). This may be due to his lack of training in the field. For example, he showed no knowledge of the sophisticated theories developed in Chinese Buddhism. However, Tillich is no more guilty than the Oriental philosopher who thought that he had disposed of Christianity once and for all after he had disposed of the traditional Christian doctrine of original sin. Comparatively speaking, Tillich has much more insight in the understanding of Stoicism. See his *The Courage To Be* (New Haven: Yale University Press, 1952), pp. 9–17.

30. Randall, ''The Ontology of Paul Tillich,'' p. 133.

31. I adopt the term *hermeneutics* from Wilhelm Dilthey. For Dilthey's version of hermeneutics, see H. A. Hodges's introduction of the theory in his *Philosophy of Wilhelm Dilthey* (London: Routledge & Kegan Paul, 1952), pp. 12–13, 137–142; idem, *Wilhelm Dilthey* (New York: Oxford University Press, 1944), pp. 25–28, 124–128.

32. Theodore M. Greene, ''Paul Tillich and Our Secular Culture,'' in Kegley and Bretall, *The Theology of Paul Tillich,* p. 51.

33. Chan, *A Source Book in Chinese Philosophy,* p. 44.

34. Ibid., p. 36.

35. Ibid.

36. Ibid., p. 47.

37. Ibid., p. 25.

38. Ibid.

39. Ibid., p. 26.

40. Ibid., p. 33.

41. Ibid., p. 35.

42. Ibid., p. 45.

43. See Shu-hsien Liu, "The Religious Import of Confucian Philosophy: Its Traditional Outlook and Contemporary Significance," *Philosophy East and West* 21, no. 2 (April 1971): 157–175.

SELECTED BIBLIOGRAPHY

Greene, Theodore M. "Paul Tillich and Our Secular Culture." In Charles W. Kegley and Robert W. Bretall, eds., *The Theology of Paul Tillich*. New York: Macmillan, 1952, pp. 84–100.

Hamilton, Kenneth. "Critical Review of *Systematic Theology*, III." Reprinted in *The Journal of Religion* 46 (January 1966).

Hartshorne, Charles. *The Divine Relativity*. New Haven: Yale University Press, 1948.

———. "Tillich's Doctrine of God." In Charles W. Kegley and Robert W. Bretall, eds., *The Theology of Paul Tillich*. New York: Macmillan, 1952, pp. 198–229.

Hodges, H. A. *The Philosophy of Wilhelm Dilthey*. London: Routledge & Kegan Paul, 1952.

———. *Wilhelm Dilthey*. New York: Oxford University Press, 1944.

Horton, Walter M. "Tillich's Role in Contemporary Theology." In Charles W. Kegley and Robert W. Bretall, eds., *The Theology of Paul Tillich*. New York: Macmillan, 1952, pp. 60–81.

Lao Tzu. "Tao Te Ching." In Wing-tsit Chan, ed. and trans., *A Source Book in Chinese Philosophy*. Princeton, N.J.: Princeton University Press, 1963.

Liu, Shu-hsien. "The Religious Import of Confucian Philosophy: Its Traditional Outlook and Contemporary Significance." *Philosophy East and West* 21, no. 2 (April 1971): 157–175.

Niebuhr, Reinhold. "Biblical Thought and Ontological Speculation in Tillich's Theology." In Charles W. Kegley and Robert W. Bretall, eds., *The Theology of Paul Tillich*. New York: Macmillan, 1952, pp. 252–263.

Randall, John Hermann, Jr. "The Ontology of Paul Tillich." In Charles W. Kegley and Robert W. Bretall, eds., *The Theology of Paul Tillich*. New York: Macmillan, 1952, pp. 166–195.

Rowe, William L. "The Meaning of God in Tillich's Theology." *The Journal of Religion* 42 (October 1962): 274–286.

Sartre Jean-Paul. *Being and Nothingness*. Translated by Hazel E. Barnes. New York: Philosophical Library, 1956.

Thomas, Heywood. *Paul Tillich: An Appraisal*. Philadelphia: Westminster Press, 1963.

Tillich, Paul. *Christianity and the Encounter of the World Religions*. New York: Columbia University Press, 1963.

———. *The Courage to Be*. New Haven: Yale University Press, 1952.

———. *Dynamics of Faith*. New York: Harper and Brothers, 1957.

———. "The Meaning and Justification of Religious Symbols." In Sidney Hook, ed., *Religious Experience and Truth*. New York: New York University Press, 1961, pp. 3–11.

———. *The Principle of Analogy in Protestant and Catholic Theology*. The Hague: Martinus Nijhoff, 1963.

———. "The Problem of Theological Method." Reprinted in Will Herberg, ed., *Four Existentialist Theologians*. New York: Doubleday, 1958, pp. 238–255.

———. "Reinhold Niebuhr's Doctrine of Knowledge." In Charles W. Kegley and Robert

W. Bretall, eds., *Reinhold Niebuhr: His Religious, Social, and Political Thought*. New York: Macmillan, 1962, pp. 35–43.

————. "Rejoinder." *The Journal of Religion* 46 (January 1966): 184–196.

————. "The Religious Symbol." In Sidney Hook, ed., *Religious Experience and Truth*. New York: New York University Press, 1961, pp. 301–321.

————. "Reply to Interpretation and Criticism." In Charles W. Kegley and Robert W. Bretall, eds., *The Theology of Paul Tillich*. New York: Macmillan, 1952, pp. 374–394.

————. "Some Questions on Brunner's Epistemology." In Robert Bretall, ed., *Theology of Emil Brunner*. New York: Macmillan, 1962, pp. 99–107.

————. *Systematic Theology*. Chicago: University of Chicago Press, 1951, 1957, 1963.

————. "Two Types of Philosophy of Religion." In Robert C. Kimball, ed., *Theology of Culture*. New York: Oxford University Press, 1959, pp. 10–29.

Urban, Wilbur M. "Tillich's Theory of Religious Symbol." *Journal of Liberal Religion* 2 (1940).

Weigel, Gustav. "Contemporary Protestantism and Paul Tillich." *Theological Studies* 11 (June 1950): 177–202.

————. "Myth, Symbol, and Analogy." In W. Leibrecht, ed., *Religion and Culture*. New York: Harper, 1959, pp. 120–130.

————. "Theological Significance of Paul Tillich." Reprinted in *Cross Currents* 6 (Spring 1956): 141–155.

Wieman, Henry Nelson. "Intellectual Autobiography." In Robert W. Bretall, ed., *The Empirical Theology of Henry Nelson Wieman*. New York: Macmillan, 1963, pp. 3–18.

23

A Philosophical Reflection on the Christian-Confucian Dialogue

PEI-JUNG FU

Among the current problems confronting the Chinese people, the problem of cross-cultural communication is particularly important and urgent. To insure effective communication between two cultures, the eventual task is to engage them in a dialogue on the level of religious belief.

Viewed from the perspective of modern history, it is natural for the Chinese people to regard Christianity as the dominant Western religion. However, the assumption that Confucianism is representative of Chinese religion has yet to be justified. The necessary justification can be stated briefly as follows: (a) In addition to Confucianism, Taoism and Buddhism also are commonly recognized as Chinese religions; yet (b) Buddhism, having been brought into China from India, is not originally a Chinese religion, and (c) Taoism as a religion appeared as a response to the Buddhist expansion and showed an apparently heterogeneous character. Finally, (d) despite the fact that Buddhism and Taoism together attracted the majority of the Chinese people, Confucianism was still honored as the official religion in China, and its classics, along with its doctrines, continued to form the basic orientation of Chinese culture. In fact, the later development of Buddhism and Taoism was influenced, and hence to a considerable extent revised, by Confucianism. Moreover, the decisive reason for considering Confucianism as the representative Chinese religion is that it inherited the traditional beliefs of the ancient Chinese and further transformed them into a unique form of humanism that fulfills the functions of both philosophy and religion.

A common agreement exists among scholars that the ancient Chinese, before the time of Confucius (551–479 B.C.), were very religious. Reliable historical records, mainly from the oracle-bone inscriptions, inform us that the Shang people worshipped three kinds of spirits: God, ancestors, and nature-gods. The question of which of these three spirits played the dominant role is still debatable. Many scholars maintain that ancestral worship was the primary feature of ancient

Chinese religion. But it is undeniable that God still played the role of an overall ruler.[1] The Chou documents, mainly the *Book of History* and the *Book of Odes,* teach us two things concerning God: one is that God became interchangeable with heaven, and the other is that the convergent meaning of God and heaven covered characteristics such as dominating, creating, sustaining, revealing, and judging.[2] A further discussion on this point is given in the section dealing with the comparison between the Chinese heaven and the Christian God. By the time of Confucius, the concept of heaven had undergone a substantial change. The ambition and enterprise of Confucius as a transmitter of culture cannot be adequately estimated without understanding his deep concern for heaven. This fact leads to the realization that the religious dimension of Confucianism is more an inheritance than an invention. In fact, the religious influence exerted by Confucianism upon the Chinese people is hardly questioned by contemporary scholars.

However, as regards the communication issue, the religious function of Confucianism turns out to be a double-edged sword. On the one hand, some Chinese scholars argue that since Confucianism can and does satisfy the religious need of the Chinese people, it is then not necessary to consider other religions.[3] On the other hand, more and more scholars believe that the religious function of Confucianism at least allows it to be compared with other religions, such as Christianity, in the present situation. In assuming this comparison, both the similarities and differences between these two systems of belief are emphasized by scholars, though with differing conclusions.[4] I have also contributed two articles to the discussion of this issue.[5] In these two articles, ten points were raised for further consideration. They are:

1. The theory of human nature as good and the doctrine of original sin

2. Self-reliance and reliance on God

3. Emphasis on immanence and emphasis on transcendence

4. The oneness of heaven and humans and the oneness of God and humans

5. Comprehensive harmony and mystical union with God

6. Humans as participants in the Creative Force and human consciousness of being creature

7. Confucius and Jesus

8. The Confucian concept of *jen* and the Christian concept of love

9. Religion as based on morality and morality as based on religion

10. The unity of knowledge and action and the unity of belief and deed

As a result of continual research, this chapter has revised and elaborated on four of these ten points in the hope that the possibility for communication will be further clarified. These four points are not selected in an arbitrary way; rather, they exhibit the essential features of both Confucianism and Christianity. Thus,

I address myself specifically to the questions of (1) the nature of humans, (2) immanence and transcendence, (3) heaven and God, and (4) Confucius and Jesus.

THE NATURE OF HUMAN BEINGS

For ordinary Chinese, a major obstacle on the way to conversion to, or even appreciation of, Christianity lies in the Christian doctrine of original sin. Original sin signifies, at least on the surface, that human nature is originally evil, whereas Confucianism for the Chinese presents the teaching that human nature is originally good. However, the fact is that good and evil are coexistent in the Christian world as well as in the Chinese world, or in any human world. Therefore, a Christian, in realizing the reluctance of the Chinese to appreciate the Christian doctrine of humans, will naturally raise the question: "Whence comes evil if human nature is originally good?" The Chinese will answer this question with an opposite one: "Then, whence comes good if human nature is originally evil?"[6] No compromise seems possible here. An adequate understanding of both sides, however, will change the picture described above.

By this I mean that early Confucianism views human nature not as originally good but as "tending toward goodness," and the Christian doctrine of original sin is taken to mean that human nature is "tending toward evil" rather than originally evil. To justify these two statements, a detailed discussion is necessary. This new understanding of both sides will prove to be helpful for the task of communication.

The Theory of Human Nature as Tending toward Goodness

The theory of human nature as tending toward goodness represents the early Confucian idea of humankind. Confucius did not state anything definite concerning human nature in the *Analects*; still we can perceive in some passages what he had in mind. For example, Confucius described the marvelous effect of the virtuous person in the field of politics as follows:

(a) The rule of virtue can be compared to the Pole Star which commands the homage of the multitude of stars without leaving its place. (*Analects*, 2:1)[7]

(b) If there was a ruler who achieved order without taking any action, it was, perhaps, Shun. There was nothing for him to do but to hold himself in a respectful posture and to face the south. (*Analects*, 15:5)

(c) Just desire the good yourself and the common people will be good. The virtue of the gentleman is like wind; the virtue of the small man is like grass. Let the wind blow over the grass and it is sure to bend. (*Analects*, 12:19)

The above three passages would become unintelligible if there were no common human nature and this common human nature were not tending toward goodness. In other words, what Confucius cherished as the highest political ideal is the traditional ethiocracy that requires that the most virtuous be the ruler because virtue is believed to be in line with human nature.[8]

Furthermore, Confucius emphasized the inner connection of a person's self with virtue or goodness. He said:

(a) Is *jen* [literally, benevolence] really far away? No sooner do I desire it than it is here. (*Analects,* 7:30)

(b) The practice of *jen* depends on oneself alone, and not on others. (*Analects,* 12:1)

(c) Is there anyone who has tried to practice *jen* for a single day? I have not come across such a man whose strength proves insufficient for the task. (*Analects,* 4:6)

Any discussion of Confucius' concept of *jen* would require more space than the scope of this chapter permits. However, *jen* means both "the way of man" and "goodness." What Confucius intended to express in the passages quoted above is that *jen* is a person's inner tendency, and it is within one's ability to practice *jen.* Thus it seems justified to claim that Confucius regarded human nature as tending toward goodness.

Mencius fully elaborated what is implied in Confucius' theory of human nature. His demonstration includes four steps. First, people possess the same kind of nature, and there is only a "slight difference" distinguishing humans from the brutes. That is, to be human is to have four features: benevolence, righteousness, propriety, and wisdom (*Mencius,* IV, B, 19).[9] Second, these features are in fact "four germs of the heart." They are described as the heart of compassion, the heart of shame, the heart of courtesy and modesty, and the heart of right and wrong. Mencius even declared that whoever is devoid of them is not human (*Mencius,* II, A, 6). Thus human nature is defined by the human heart, which is tending toward goodness. Mencius vividly depicted this state of the heart as "a fire starting up or a spring coming through" (*Mencius,* II, A, 6). Third, the tendency of the heart is manifested in "distinguishing" the good from evil and "commanding" the choice of the good. Only with this understanding does it become meaningful to state that "there is nothing better for the nurturing of the heart than to reduce the number of one's desires" (*Mencius,* VII, B, 35). Only if the heart is retained, nourished, and developed can a man become a gentleman. In other words, the ability to be a gentleman is inherent in a man's nature. It is an inborn obligation too. A man is endowed with a heart that plays the role of judge. Fourth, as for the source of the judging heart, Mencius unhesitatingly referred it to heaven. He said, "The organ of the heart can think. But it will find the answer only if it does think; otherwise it will not find the answer. This is what Heaven has given me" (*Mencius,* VI, A, 15). The relation between heaven and humankind is summarized in the following statement: "For man to give full realization to his heart is for him to understand his own nature, and a man who knows his own nature will know Heaven. By retaining his heart and nurturing his nature he is serving Heaven" (*Mencius,* VII, A, 4). Mencius' concept of heaven is another interesting topic that is beyond the scope of this chapter. But it is heaven that makes human nature tend toward goodness.[10]

What, then, is the view of Hsün-tzu, the third eminent figure of early Confucianism, on this issue? Did he not definitely profess that human nature is evil? Yes, he did, but his case must be examined more closely.

The reason for Hsün-tzu's affirmation of the evilness of human nature is that if everyone follows instincts without restriction, the result inevitably will be "strife and rapacity, combined with rebellion and disorder, ending in violence" (*Hsün-tzu*, 23, 289).[11] This result doubtlessly can be defined as evil when compared with a harmonious society. However, to define human nature through that which follows from it is far from how we usually define it or how it is normally understood. In this connection, we may ask: Did Hsün-tzu recognize any difference between human beings and animals? According to Hsün-tzu, for one to be truly human, one must make distinctions (*Hsün-tzu*, 5, 50), and for the human being to be the highest being on earth requires a sense of righteousness (*Hsün-tzu*, 5, 104). Thus the ability to make distinctions and the sense of righteousness must also belong to human nature and, if well expanded, will result in propriety and righteousness which are regarded as good. Had Hsün-tzu defined human nature through this approach, he would not have found any argument with Mencius.[12] That is, Hsün-tzu's definition of human nature as evil is more an expedient than a genuine description of humans. Furthermore, it is not difficult for us to perceive that Hsün-tzu also had thought that human nature is tending toward goodness; otherwise he would not have gone along with Confucius and Mencius in maintaining the following three points that can be adequately understood as consequences of the Confucian theory of human nature:

First, all men are capable of becoming gentlemen (*chün-tzu*, the ideal personality set by Confucius). Confucius said that he never came across anyone whose strength is insufficient for practicing *jen*. Mencius expressly insisted that all people can become a Yao or a Shun. Hsün-tzu also maintained that people in the street can become a Yü (Yao, Shun, and Yü all being ancient sage–kings).

Second, all men are obliged to become gentlemen. We perceive in early Confucianism an obligation that can be properly understood as the Confucian "categorical imperative." That is, to be human is to become virtuous, since the latter is simply to fulfill the nature of human beings, which is tending toward goodness. One's natural life exists for the purpose of realizing one's moral potency. The obligation here is categorical. Hence it is well known that Confucius held that people should sacrifice their lives for the sake of *jen*, and Mencius claimed that he would choose righteousness over life. Hsün-tzu also declared that "a gentleman, though worrying about danger and misery, does not avoid to die for the sake of righteousness" (*Hsün-tzu*, 3, 24).

Third, all men, while becoming gentlemen, are responsible for helping others to attain their own perfection. A famous saying of Confucius reads: "A benevolent man helps others to take their stand in so far as he himself wishes to take his stand, and gets others there in so far as he himself wishes to get there" (*Analects*, 6:30). Mencius traced this responsibility to heaven and stated: "Heaven, in producing the people, has given to those who first attain understanding the duty of awakening those who are slow to understand; and to those who are the first to awaken the duty of awakening those who are slow to awaken'' (*Mencius*, V, A, 7). This passage discloses the essence of Confucian humanism, which stresses human potentiality, moral education, and mutual responsibility. More significantly, this humanism is open ended; that is, it is open to heaven, the source of all that exists. This open humanism leads Confucians to take the ''union of heaven and man,'' which is equivalent to the state of sagehood, as their highest possible goal in this life.

Thus far we have shown how the Confucian theory of human nature is initiated, elaborated, and accomplished. This theory that human nature tends toward goodness involves a natural inclination to emphasize the immanent aspect of reality. However, as has been indicated in the above discussion, the concept of heaven also makes the transcendent aspect of reality an integrated part of Confucianism. This point is further elucidated in the sections below. But we must first consider the Christian side and determine in what way these two theories, as presented here, may attain a more adequate level of communication.

The Theory of Human Nature as Tending toward Evil

A commonly accepted theory regarding the Christian view of human nature has yet to be propounded. However, no theory in this field can be made meaningful without taking into account the doctrine of original sin. A plausible explanation of this fact is that Christianity regards human nature as tending toward evil and hence employs the doctrine of original sin to rationalize this state of human beings. This rationalization bears a mythic and symbolic character. By this I mean that what it illuminates is more a subjective recognition of the human condition than an objective historical fact. This recognition is subjective, but it is not formed in the absence of an objective point of reference. To put it more straightforwardly, it is caused by God's intervention in human history. Thus our treatment of the doctrine of original sin starts from the general attitude of God toward the people of Israel, the chosen representatives of humanity.

In the Old Testament God's estimation of human nature is definite. For example, God said to himself after the Deluge, ''Never again will I curse the earth because of man, because his heart contrives evil from his infancy'' (Genesis 8:21).[13] It seems difficult to change the mentality of humankind: ''I can see how headstrong these people are!'' (Exodus 32:9) On behalf of God, Moses also made a complaint against the people, telling Aaron: ''You know yourself how prone this people is to evil'' (Exodus 32:23); again, Moses warned the people: ''You have been rebels against Yahweh from the day he first knew you'' (Deuteronomy 9:24). Similar ideas can be found throughout the Old Testament. Thus we have a general picture of Israel that demonstrates that the intellect of the people was not reliable, and collective decisions seldom reflected the will of God.[14] In other words, human nature tends toward evil. In this connection, the view that human nature is originally evil should not be held; otherwise the above quote reproaches, and complaints would become pointless (whether effective or not is another question), and the good deeds that occurred occasionally in the history of both Israel and other peoples would then become unintelligible.

Granted that human nature tends toward evil, we may still ask: whence comes this human nature? Or how did it fall into such a state? Furthermore, why does God as the all-powerful and perfectly loving deity allow this kind of human nature to exist or to appear? The overall answers to the above questions cannot but refer to the concept of original sin. Humankind has fallen by committing an original sin and has thus made human nature such that it tends toward evil. The question then turns out to be: what is original sin? Ever since St. Paul, theologians of different ages have interpreted it according to their respective understandings. It is obvious that original sin is not a mere fact; nor is it an ordinary problem. Rather, it is a "mystery," a mystery upon which a Christian should meditate in order to define the meaning of his or her own existence. As a mystery, it is to be lived rather than solved. Therefore, any interpretation of original sin is in essence an attempt to point out an authentic way for human self-understanding. Consider three contemporary theories to see the possible outcome of the doctrine of original sin.

1. *Tennant's "Deistic Evolutionism."* F. R. Tennant (1866–1957) presented a theory of original sin that reflects a general understanding among scholars of the first quarter of this century. Tennant started by thoroughly examining the story of the Fall from historical facts, aetiological sources, scriptural records, mythological imaginations, and so on and then arrived at the conclusion that "the Fall-Story can no longer be looked upon as either history or allegory or as supplying any basis for a theological doctrine of man, or the origin and mode of propagation of human sin."[15] He then challenged the concept of original sin, regarding it as self-contradictory: "What is original cannot be sin, and sin cannot be original."[16] But the fact of sin present in the human world still needs to be explained. Thus Tennant raised a deistic evolutionism to account for original sin or the origin of sin. According to his theory, the task of God merely consisted of creating the embryo of human nature and of all reality, and the sin of humans came from physical and social evolution.[17] This theory entails serious difficulties: (1) There is no way to determine when the prehuman evolved across the missing link to become human, since evolutionism when used to explain the emergence of humans is still an unproven hypothesis. Besides, how could physical heredity have any effect on the sinfulness or the goodness of human nature? (2) As for the universality and propagation of sin, Tennant emphatically attributed them to social heredity and social evolution. But we certainly cannot prove the universality and necessity of sin from the empirical facts of sin. Moreover, Tennant's idea that "morality is a social creation" is only a half-truth that fails to discern a person's inborn ability to aspire to what Bergson described as "open morality."[18] (3) Deistic evolutionism is not sufficiently grounded in the Scriptures, and its emphasis on physical and social heredity handicaps the redemptive function of Christ, consequently making baptism meaningless. These difficulties

reveal to us that the traditional way of interpreting original sin in terms of human beings as such is no longer convincing. In the search for new and more cogent interpretations, the next two theories are worth noting.

2. *Rahner's "Theistic Situationism."* Karl Rahner (1904–1984) clearly maintained that original sin has nothing to do with the notion that "the original personal act of freedom at the very origin of history has been transmitted to subsequent generations in its moral quality."[19] He regarded original sin as humankind's "situation."[20] A person "is a being in the world, in history, and in a world of persons."[21] Therefore, how could he or she escape from a situation that "includes everything which is antecedent to the decision of freedom, as its condition and material"?[22] Granted that human freedom is conditioned by a situation, we may then ask: why is this situation characterized as original sin? Rahner said: "The situation of our own freedom bears the stamp of the guilt of others in a way which cannot be eradicated."[23] This explains the "sin" aspect of the situation. He then continued: "The universality and the inescapability of this co-determination by guilt is inconceivable if it were not present at the very beginning of mankind's history of freedom."[24] This subjunctive mood is the manner by which Rahner explained the "original" aspect of the situation. Seeing that the situation alone cannot justify his whole position, Rahner unhesitatingly appealed to his theistic tradition and raised two notions, namely, divine pneuma and supernatural existential, to complete his theory.

Divine pneuma refers to a human being's original holiness and righteousness, which was bestowed by God and was lost through original sin.[25] In other words, what God created was originally good. But this does not explain the nature of the situation of the first person or the first group of people. Rahner still described this situation as "co-determined by a guilty act at the beginning of the history of the human race."[26] To avoid the apparently circular reasoning, Rahner turned to the nature of humans and affirmed that "even fallen man possesses a 'supernatural existence' " that is essentially the offer of God's self-communication.[27] Both the situation and the supernatural existential exist before human freedom. The situation is doomed to be evil, whereas the supernatural existential "founds a real exigency for the sanctifying grace and the preternatural gifts."[28] An original tension occurs between these two states that is the original condition of humans as free beings.[29] The logical conclusion is that original sin is nothing but this original tension. The fact that Rahner explained original sin in terms of situation shows that he accepted the traditional Christian view of human nature as tending toward evil. In the meantime, he did not ignore the positive aspect of this view, that is, the belief that people are endowed with the supernatural existential that, being God's self-communication, can be properly understood as denoting "the image of God."[30] The doctrine of original sin will then retreat to the background in our examination of human nature.

3. *Ricoeur's "Dialectical Symbolism."* In *The Symbolism of Evil* Ricoeur claimed not to focus on the familiar topic of original sin, his emphasis being rather the explication of the myths "that speak of the beginning and the end of

evil.''[31] The function of myth consists in establishing ''all the forms of action and thought by which man understands himself in his world.''[32] What, then, can people understand about themselves from myths of evil? Does this mean that humans are originally related to evil? Or, retrospectively, can they find any cause in the beginning of creation that can explain the evil state of the present world? All of these questions lead us to the discussion of original sin under the guise of ''the origin of sin.''

Ricoeur's approach is dialectical. He first describes a double manifestation of the symbol of evil of the cosmic level and the psychic level. Then, he maintained that the beginning and the end of evil form a dialectical whole in exhibiting the narrative of human nature. To distinguish the valid symbol of evil from invalid ones, Ricoeur set up a criterion that emphasizes a threefold character, ontological, anthropologico-moral, and dialectical. According to Ricoeur's detailed analysis, only the Adamic myth fulfills all three characteristics. It is maintained that Adamic myth, (a) being coextensive with the creation myth, has an ontological implication; (b) placing the origin of evil in a conscious act of humans has an anthropologico-moral quality; and (c) conveying an eschatological message with regard to the end of evil has a dialectical dynamism. What, then, can we learn from Ricoeur's interpretation of original sin through the Adamic myth?

First, the creation of human beings and the fall of humankind occurred in the same moment. Ricoeur said: ''In the Instant I am created, in the Instant I fall.''[33] The reason for this is that humans were created as free beings, and human freedom is the cause of evil, because it enables a person to ''undo, unmake himself.''[34] That is, one is free to affirm oneself and by so doing fail to realize wholeness, falling into a state of ''disproportion with himself.''[35] Thus affirmation and disproportion seem to come together in the beginning of creation.[36] Second, a human is each human and all humankind. The fall of one person means that all humankind falls. Sin can be described as ''collective destiny of humanity.''[37] In a discussion of ''the evil of having'' Ricoeur stated: ''In simply being born I enter into certain relationships of possession which are already corrupt on the collective level.''[38] This statement has a strong flavor of situationism. On the other hand, Ricoeur seems to have accepted the Fathers' conviction that creation contains both evil and grace; it ''continues precisely in the midst of evil and by means of grace.''[39] In short, ''Creation is not inert, finished, and closed.'' This seeming evolutionism is even clearer when Ricoeur affirms ''one of the fundamental meanings of the act of redemption is the growth of humanity, its achievement of maturity, its arrival at adulthood.''[40] However, these two aspects of Ricoeur's theory must be understood through a dialectical point of view. That is, his major concern is not with the theistic or deistic understanding of original sin but is with the dialectical interpretation of sin and grace, evil and redemption, and Adam and Christ. According to Ricoeur, one advantage of this stance is to be able to view repentance as ''that which joins a recreated past to a promised future in a reconciled present.''[41] Original sin can thus be regarded as a functional concept, namely, as a transitional step to relate humans to the Sacred. But the Sacred is not without content. To know this content, the only possible way, even outside of the Judeo-Christian tradition, is still to regard humans as "the image of God" or "the image of the Sacred." As for the real signification of this image, Ricoeur seems to have referred it to the orientation of freedom, which is conferred on a person's conscience at the very moment of being created by God.

To conclude, the Christian view of human nature as tending toward evil leads us to consider its doctrine of original sin, which in turn makes us confront the notion of the image of God. A more acceptable interpretation of the image of God is that people are endowed with conscience that grounds the freedom and ability of their self-orientation toward God.

Reconciliation of the Above Two Theories

First, both theories accept the presupposition that human nature is not a fixed and completed entity; rather it is always developing, that is, tending toward some destination. Confucianism views this destination from the standpoint of human beings and hence is able to appreciate the potential perfectibility of human nature, which can be described as tending toward goodness. On the other hand, Christianity views this destination from the standpoint of God and hence feels dissatisfied with the actual fallible state of human nature, which can be described as tending toward evil. The seeming incompatibility of these two theories is due to different standpoints of observation. This does not explain away their apparently distinctive features but clears the ground for a more constructive dialogue in the future.

Second, for Confucianism, human nature as tending toward goodness is manifested in the function of the heart, which distinguishes good from evil and commands the choice of good. For Christianity, human nature as tending toward evil does not exclude the image of God, that is, the freedom and ability of human self-orientation to God, which is in fact an evaluation and demand of the choice of good over evil. The difference lies in the fact that the role of the Christian God is fully revealed and thus represses or, paradoxically, directs the freedom and ability of human self-orientation. That is, human reliance on God is required in the Christian doctrine whereas human self-reliance is emphasized by Confucianism.

Third, both theories insist on an ideal that involves the categorical imperative. Confucianism believes that all people can become sages and teaches humans to sacrifice life for the sake of perfect virtues. Christianity consistently admonishes the people: "Be holy, for I, Yahweh your God, am holy" (Leviticus 19:2); "You must therefore be perfect just as your heavenly Father is perfect" (Matthew 5:48). To ask a believer to become as perfect as God is tantamount to setting the categorical imperative on that person. Therefore, concerning the issue of human nature, the age-long controversy between Confucianism and Christianity can be viewed from a new angle and thus can be reconciled.

IMMANENCE AND TRANSCENDENCE

Confucianism is usually understood, or misunderstood, according to the analysis in this chapter, as holding the view that human nature is originally good. As a consequence it teaches an exclusive doctrine of self-reliance that is in line with Buddhism, the typical religion based on the notion of immanence. Christianity represents the other extreme. Its doctrine of human nature presupposes reliance of God; that is, the revelation of God, or message from transcendence, constitutes its essence. The bifurcation between the religion of immanence and the religion of transcendence may be useful in tackling the relation between Buddhism and Christianity. But it is questionable whether this bifurcation can be equally applied to the relation between Confucianism and Christianity. This issue should be addressed differently after our discussion of human nature in the above section. Thus we venture to use two phrases "immanence over transcendence" and "transcendence over immanence," to delineate the respective emphases of these two systems of belief and, futhermore, to show that they have a great deal to learn from each other.

Immanence over Transcendence

The theory of human nature as tending toward goodness naturally leads Confucianism to emphasize the realm of immanence. To put the emphasis on immanence means that the way to perfection is none other than fulfilling human nature since this nature as such possesses potential perfectibility. It is then within human ability to attain salvation. This stance is close to a religion of self-reliance. Confucius insisted that "the practice of *jen* depends on oneself alone" (*Analects*, 12:1). Following this spirit Mencius declared, "There is no greater joy for me than to find, on self-examination, that I am true to myself" (*Mencius*, VII, A, 4). For Confucians, the initial step to the highest excellence consists of "enlightening the illustrious virtue" of humankind (*Ta-hsüeh*, 1:1), and this virtue belongs to inborn human nature. The way for a person to follow is in accordance with his or her nature (*Chung-yung*, 1:1). However, self-reliance here does not suggest a thoroughly human-centered way to salvation. In other words, to stress immanence does not necessarily imply an exclusion of the realm of transcendence.

Far from being this, the religiosity of Confuciansim cannot be adequately understood without a transcendent reference. The religious dimension of Confucianism can be easily perceived in its stress on sacrifice and worship. Three kinds of sacrifice have been observed by the Confucian tradition: sacrifices to heaven, to ancestors, and to the sages. Heaven is worshipped because it is believed to be the source of all things; ancestors are worshipped because they are the fountainhead of the present human being; and the sages are worshipped because they exemplify the perfect personality and play the roles of king and teacher in acting for heaven. The worship of heaven is sometimes understood as worshipping the whole of Nature. However, heaven never signifies mere Nature in Confucianism.

Confucius' heaven not only makes "the four seasons go around and the hundred things come into being" (*Analects*, 17:19) but also is concerned with the transition of culture. Thus it confers a unique mission on Confucius, making him "the wooden tongue for a bell" (*Analects*, 3:24) to teach people on behalf of heaven.[42] According to Mencius, heaven does not speak "but reveals itself through its acts and deeds" (*Mencius*, V, A, 5). Moreover, its revelation is universalized in the reflection of a person's heart. Everyone has heaven in his or her heart, which always provides the correct guidance for action. Therefore, if people fully realize their heart, they will understand their nature, and if they know their own nature, they will know heaven. Meanwhile, the proper way to serve heaven is for people to retain their heart and nurture their nature (*Mencius*, VII, A, 1). Far from being mere hypothesis, heaven manifests itself in the functioning of the heart. The heart, being the microcosm of heaven, is the representative of transcendence in the realm of immanence.[43] Hsün-tzu's heaven is very likely influenced by Taoism and hence looks like Nature, but it still plays the role of model for the sages to formulate rituals and music (*Hsün-tzu*, 19, 248). Besides, a gentleman "broadens his heart by following Heaven as his way" (*Hsün-tzu*, 3,26).[44] The opening statement of the *Chung-yung* reads: "What Heaven has conferred is called the (human) nature" (1:1). Human nature is ordained by Heaven. Thus the perfection of humankind cannot depart from the revelation of heaven: "Being sincere is the way of Heaven; becoming sincere is the way of man" (*Chung-Yung*, 20:18).

Confucianism believes in the perfectibility of humans. This perfectibility entails an obligation that manifests the categorical imperative. People should sacrifice their lives for the sake of realizing the way of humankind, such as through benevolence and righteousness. This is to sanctify life by sacrificing life. The absolute obligation is not based on a closed immanence or an exclusive self-reliance. Rather, it is based on the faith in transcendence, an equivalent of heaven for Confucians. The original meaning of heaven is presented in the next section. For Confucianism, the realm of immanence is open to that of transcendence, and self-reliance is complemented by reliance on heaven.

Transcendence over Immanence

From the very beginning of Christian history transcendence has been clearly manifested. Transcendence appears in the form of a personal God, who communicates with people and leads them to believe that the universe has a purpose. History involves some destination, and human life is full of meanings to be realized. A religion like this is naturally inclined to emphasize reliance on God.

A typical example is Abraham's "justification through faith" in the Old Testament. However, since the time of Jesus, the New Testament has shown an ever-greater interest in emphasizing immanence. It is not difficult to discern three connecting foci in the New Testament:

1. *Focus on man.* In the Old Testament the Sabbath is the day of God and whoever does not observe it will be put to death. In the New Testament, we read, "The sabbath was made for man, and not man for the Sabbath" (Mark 2:28). Therefore, it is permitted to do good (to others) on the Sabbath day (Matthew 12:12).

2. *Focus on Love.* It is recorded in the Old Testament that "what I want is love, not sacrifice" (Hosea 6:6). But this ideal is realized in the New Testament. Jesus summarized what laws and prophets have taught in one sentence: People must love God and their neighbors (Matthew 22:37–39). Mere faith is no longer enough. Jesus said, "It is not those who say to me, 'Lord, Lord,' who will enter the kingdom of heaven, but the person who does the will of my Father in heaven" (Matthew 7:21). The will of God first of all consists of benevolent deeds. We hear, "In so far as you did this to one of the least of these brothers of mine, you did it to me" (Matthew 25:40). Charity thus becomes the hallmark of the Christian community: "By this love you have for one another, everyone will know that you are my disciples" (John 13:35).

3. *Focus on the Heart.* It has been mentioned in the Old Testament that the heart must also be circumcised. In the New Testament, the conversion of the heart is emphatically insisted. God's eyes see through a person's heart: "If a man looks at a woman lustfully, he has already committed adultery with her in his heart" (Matthew 5:28). The initial movement of the heart counts for much in judging a person. Jesus promised, "Happy are the pure in heart: they shall see God" (Matthew 5:18). This doctrine is in line with Confucian teaching: "If you wish to cultivate your persons, you first rectify your hearts. If you wish to rectify your hearts, you first sought to be sincere in your thoughts" (*Ta-Hsüeh*, 1:4). For Christians, this implies that transcendence and immanence are manifested simultaneously: "God is spirit, and those who worship must worship in spirit and truth" (John, 4:24).

The above three foci clearly indicate that Christianity as a religion does not merely preach reliance on God, it also stresses self-reliance. It never ignores immanence for the sake of transcendence. "Justification through faith" in the Old Testament must be complemented by "justification through love" in the New Testament.

To conclude this section, we can make the following observations. First, the transcendence of Christianity is embodied in the person of Jesus, and therefore he is able to preach a doctrine corresponding to the utmost demands of humankind. Teachings such as "love your enemy," "repay hatred by benevolence," and "do to others what you yourself desire" (Matthew 7:12) are unacceptable or even inconceivable for non-Christians.[45] Second, the transcendence of Confucianism signifies the decree of heaven that is manifested through the reflection of the heart as the innermost and spontaneous feeling of "intolerability" or "uneasiness." Thus Confucianism teaches, "Do not do to others what you yourself do not desire'' (*Analects,* 12:2); ''You repay an injury with straightness, but you repay a good turn with a good turn'' (*Analects,* 14:34). Third, the apparent distinction between the above two teachings is sometimes explained as resulting from the contrast between theism and humanism. This explanation, however, is superficial if viewed from what has been discussed in this section. We will suggest that the distinction here is one that comes from different emphases rather than different essences. Neither of these two systems of belief can be accused of one-sidedness in comprehending transcendence and immanence and in stressing reliance on God and self-reliance. The next step is to determine what transcendence signifies for Christianity and for Confucianism.

HEAVEN AND GOD

It is far beyond the scope of this chapter to deal with the necessary materials that this issue requires. All that we can do is to draw some fundamental ideas from relevant studies and try to indicate the convergent meaning of Chinese heaven and the Christian God.

The Cardinal Meaning of Heaven

The belief in heaven as transcendence is what Confucians inherited from the ancient Chinese. One of the significant achievements of early Confucianism is to offer a reasonable explication and demonstration as regards the connection between heaven (transcendence) and humans (immanence). No matter how profound and comprehensive the Confucian theory of human nature might be, it can never be complete without referring to the traditional belief in heaven. What, then, is the primordial sense of heaven? The answer to this question can be summarized as follows:

(1) According to the *Book of History* and the *Book of Odes,* the character of heaven can be described in terms of such aspects as Revealer, Creator, Sustainer, and Judge; (2) Heaven as Revealer is perceived from divination, the wisdom of the king, and the collective will of the people; (3) Heaven as Creator is first of all understood in the sense of the ultimate source of life rather than that of a creator creating *ex nihilo,* and along with the act of giving birth, Heaven bestows on man a moral sense; (4) Heaven as Sustainer appoints a qualified king as its representative on earth and thus leads the people to follow the right path and gain happiness; (5) Heaven as Judge is described such that it is itself the absolute judge and the king, the son of Heaven, the embodiment of the absolute justice.[46]

The last point in the passage quoted above can be elaborated to shed light on our discussion of heaven here. The ancient Chinese believed that the manifestation of heaven, the overall ruler, is manifold. Heaven is believed to be Creator, Sustainer, Revealer, and Judge. But heaven as Judge most directly influences people in their ordinary life. That is, the primary sense of heaven is to serve as a warrant for the realization of absolute justice. The king is called "the son of heaven" and thus becomes a parent of the people. The requirement for the king is first to embody absolute justice, which is described in the following way:

> Without deflection, without unevenness,
> Pursue the splendid righteousness;
> Without and selfish likings,
> Pursue the central way;
> Without any selfish dislikings,
> Pursue the middle path;
> Without deflection, without partiality,
> Broad and long is the middle path.
> Without partiality, without deflection,
> The middle path is level and easy;
> Without perversity, without one-sidedness,
> The middle path is right and straight,
> True to this perfect excellence,
> Turn to this perfect excellence. [47]

The term used in the original text is not "absolute justice" but "*huang-chi*," which means, literally, "the great center."

The great center, properly understood as absolute justice and perfect excellence, is actually the lesson that new kings learned from their predecessors in ancient China. What Yao passed on to Shun and Shun passed on to Yü was the same law: "Hold thou truly to the middle way (the center)."[48] T'ang, the founder of the Shang dynasty, was also advised, "Exert yourself, O King, to make your great virtue illustrious, and set up the pattern of the center before the people."[49] The faith behind this advice is that "when the great center is constructed, the mind of Heaven will be reached."[50] Therefore, we may affirm that the cardinal meaning of heaven is absolute justice. This is very probably true for the ancient Chinese before the time of Confucius. How Confucianism has transformed this characteristic of heaven is another interesting topic beyond the scope of this chapter. In any case, heaven still plays the role of transcendence for Confucians, and its revelation of justice supplies the basis for the categorical imperative of Confucianism.

The Essential Feature of God

The Christian God manifests his characteristic of justice in an unambiguous way. The gospel of love has indeed been spread over the world ever since the time of Jesus. However, the reason for Jesus' incarnation is to redeem the sin of humans and to indicate the way to heaven for all humankind. As the second Adam, Jesus earned back the grace lost by the first Adam. The underlying belief is that justice must be realized: Only the son of God can serve as compensation for the offense of humans against God. Besides, Jesus will embody the justice of God. He described the day of judgment in the following words: "Those who did good will rise again to life; and those who did evil, to condemnation. I can do nothing by myself; I can only judge as I am told to judge, and my judging is just, because my aim is to do not my own will, but the will of him who sent me" (John 5:29, 30). We should always keep this message in mind; otherwise the force of the Christian faith will be decreased if only the gospel of love is emphasized. In fact, the message that God is justice as expressed in the New Testament is a legitimate heir of the Old Testament.

In the Old Testament, what God does completely falls within the category of justice. God's justice cannot be separated from his power; that is, his activities are for the purpose of realizing his justice. Expressions like "Happy is the virtuous man, for he will feed on the fruit of his deeds; woe to the wicked, evil is on him, he will be treated as his actions deserve"(Isaiah 3:10, 11) can be found throughout the Scriptures. For the people of Israel, the function of God as judge is far more important than it is for other peoples. [51] The Old Testament firmly claims that judging is the business of God, that justice is the highest representative of God on earth and is also the primary qualification of kings and the Messiah. This conviction is very close to the ancient Chinese belief that the Son of heaven should embody the absolute justice.

To conclude, the difference between heaven and God is obvious in some respects, but our concern here is to seek the means of communicating these two concepts, that is, to figure out in what sense they can correspond to each other. The result is clear: Both heaven and God are names for transcendence and the common character they manifest is absolute justice. We may further suggest that human nature, be it tending toward goodness or toward evil, always in its distinguishing goodness from evil and commanding the choice of the good, exhibits a demand for justice. This demand is the most profound need and the most natural yearning of the realm of immanence and is thus the fundamental reason for transcendence to unfold itself primarily as absolute justice.

CONFUCIUS AND JESUS

Confucius and Jesus occupy a unique place in their respective contexts of history. We find striking similarities in their conceptions of their own status. The following three points are most obvious:

Sense of Mission

Confucius and Jesus both believed that they were the chosen person of their own tradition, be it a culture or faith tradition. That is, they claimed that people in their respective traditions must rely on them to enlighten themselves with regard to the meaning of life.

Confucius declared: "Heaven is author of the virtue that is in me. What can Huan Tui do to me?" (*Analects*, 7:23). "Virtue" here designates a special mission conferred on Confucius by heaven, that is, something that distinguishes Confucius from others; otherwise it is odd to proclaim: "What can Huan Tui do to me?" A more distinct passage reads: "With King Wen dead, is not culture invested here in me? If Heaven intends culture to be destroyed, those who come after me will not be able to have any part of it. If Heaven does not intend this culture to be destroyed, then what can the men of K'uang do to me?" (*Analects*, 9:5) This passage reveals Confucius' conviction that he is the chosen person on whom the continuity of his cultural tradition will be based.

On the side of Jesus, the sense of mission is spelled out in a more direct way. Jesus said, "I am the light of the world; anyone who follows me will not be walking in dark; he will have the light of life" (John 8:12). He is the one to come, the Saviour expected in the Judaic tradition. He made a further claim: "I am the way, the Truth and the Life. No one can come to the Father except through me" (John 14:6).

Connection with Transcendence

Confucius and Jesus both believed that they had a mutual understanding of transcendence. Confucius thought that no one understood him and expressed this feeling in the following words: "I do not complain against Heaven, nor do I blame Man. In my studies, I start from below and get through to what is up above. If I am understood at all, it is, perhaps, by Heaven" (*Analects*, 14:35). This passage, especially the last sentence, should be taken seriously, since Confucius described his own spiritual achievement at the age of fifty as "to understand the Decree of Heaven" (*Analects*, 2:4). We may thus infer that a close relation such as mutual understanding exists between Confucius and heaven. [52] Confucius insisted that the first thing a gentleman should be in awe of is "the Decree of Heaven" (*Analects*, 16:8). To this conviction his whole life serves as a good witness: "He works toward a goal the realization of which he knows to be hopeless" (*Analects*, 14:3). This is the consequence of his obeying the Decree of heaven to transmit the cultural tradition and to enlighten the way of humankind.

Jesus proclaimed: "Everything has been entrusted to me by my Father; and no one knows who the Son is except the Father, and who the Father is except the Son and those to whom the Son chooses to reveal him" (Luke 10:22). His whole life can also be described as "obeying the will of God." The mutual understanding of Jesus and God is taken for granted by Christian doctrine.

Final Appeal to Transcendence

Confucius and Jesus both make similar utterances in facing the critical situation of life. Confucius during the later years of his life took a journey to some clan-states but failed to win any feudal lord to carry out his ideal. He then set his heart on teaching in the hope that his disciples would take up his mission to fulfill the will of heaven. Therefore, the death of disciples is for Confucius the most serious attack. The following two instances will help clarify this point.

Being the favorite disciple of Confucius, Yen Yüan not only stands first among the ten well-established students but also is the only student praised by the master as "eager to learn." Confucius once told Yen Yüan, "Only you and I have the ability to go forward when employed and to stay out of sight when set aside" (*Analects*, 7:11). When Yen Yüan died, Confucius showed undue sorrow and cried, "Alas! Heaven has bereft me! Heaven has bereft me!" (*Analects*, 11:9). Another favorite disciple of Confucius was Tzu Lu. Tzu Lu was not so outstanding as Yen Yüan in some respects, but he had a good character filled with courage and strength to put what he believed into practice. Confucius once said, "If the Way should fail to prevail and I were to put to sea on a raft, the one who would follow me would no doubt be Yu (Tzu Lu)" (*Analects*, 5:7). On hearing the news of Tzu Lu's death, Confucius exclaimed, "Heaven has destroyed me!" The name of heaven is mentioned in both cases, exemplifying the criticalness of the situation in Confucius' life. Thus we may perceive that heaven is that to which Confucius made his final appeal.

Jesus preached the gospel of the heavenly kingdom, admonished the people to convert to God, and finally paid his life as the price of earning back eternal life for human beings. When his physical life was on the verge of extinction, still a tension between transcendence and immanence appeared. Having suffered all kinds of torture and humiliation, Jesus was hanged on the cross and uttered the following words: "My God, my God, why have you deserted me?" (Matthew 27:46).

Besides the above three points of similarity, in other cases Confucius and Jesus were treated by their contemporaries and later generations with similar respect and faith.

On the side of Confucius, the border official of Yi recognized that heaven is about to use Confucius as the wooden tongue for a bell (to rouse the empire) (*Analects*, 3:24). Tzu Kung believed that heaven set his Master on the path to sagehood (*Analects*, 9:6). The *Chung-yung* eulogized Confucius as the sage who is as great as heaven and earth (30:2). Mencius was convinced that "ever since man came into this world, there has never been another Confucius" (*Mencius*, II, A, 2). Viewed from the development of Chinese culture, it is understandable that Han Yü, a T'ang scholar, would claim, "The whole history would have been as in the dark night, had Confucius not been begotten by Heaven."

On the side of Jesus, the whole Old Testament anticipated his advent, and all of his words and deeds witnessed the beginning of a new age. In the New Testament, ever since Peter confessed to Jesus, "You are the Christ, the Son of the living God" (Matthew 16:16), similar recognitions appeared again and again. The prophesy of Isaiah was accepted by millions of people throughout human history; it reads: "The people that lived in darkness has seen a great light; on those who dwell in the land and shadow of death a light has dawned" (Matthew 4:16).

CONCLUSION

The above comparisons are made in accordance with profound similarities between Confucianism and Christianity. The purpose of this research is not to profess a pluralism that ignores the need for exchanging messages among different traditions. That is, it never contends that the Chinese people do not need the gospel of Christ. Rather, it wants to make clear that Christianity as a tradition of faith has a unique meaning for all humankind, whereas Confucianism as a tradition of culture has a unique meaning for the Chinese people. Consequently, as human beings the Chinese are capable of converting to Christianity, and as Chinese they are doomed to live with Confucianism. That is, the Chinese when accepting Confucianism must go beyond all derivative interpretations of later Confucians and look to early Confucians to appreciate their open mindedness toward transcendence. Once open to transcendence, they will naturally confront a series of questions: Is this transcendence manifest for me? Can it have a personal relationship with me? How does its demand correspond to the obligation of my heart? To answer these questions, they will find Christianity ready at hand for reference. As for the actual conversion, still many other conditions should be considered. Faith is in essence a choice made by each person as well as a gift offered by God. We may conclude that the communication between Confucianism and Christianity is not only possible but also promising.

NOTES

1. Pei-jung Fu, "On Religious Ideas of the Pre-Chou China," *Chinese Culture* (Taipei: Chinese Culture University), 26, no. 3 (September 1985): 24–25.

2. Pei-jung Fu, *Ju tao t'ien-lun fa-wei* (*Explication of the Doctrine of Heaven in Confucianism and Taoism*) (Taipei: Hsüeh-sheng, 1985), p. 40.

3. See Mou Tsung-san, *Chung-kuo che-hsüeh shih chiu chiang (Nineteen Lectures on Chinese Philosophy)* (Taipei: Hsüeh-sheng, 1983), pp. 62–63, 445–446.

4. For positive conclusions, see Julia Ching, *Confucianism and Christianity* (Tokyo: Kōdansha International, 1977). For negative conclusions, see Jacques Gernet, *China and the Christian Impact,* trans. Janet Lloyd (Cambridge: Cambridge University Press, 1985).

5. Pei-jung Fu, "Chinese Thought and Christianity," *Collectanea Theologica* (Taipei: Fu Jen Catholic University), no. 32 (Autumn 1977): 179-215; idem, "On the Communication of Chinese Thought and Christianity," *Chinese Culture Monthly* (Taichung: Tunghai University) (March 1980): 114–147.

6. This kind of question would be raised by scholars who concern themselves with the communication issue. Matteo Ricci served as an example of this. See Gernet, *China,* p. 150.

7. For an English translation of the *Analects,* I have followed D. C. Lau, *Confucius, The Analects* (New York: Penguin Classics, 1979).

8. Fu, *Ju tao t'ien-lun fa-wei,* pp. 30–35.

9. For an English translation of the *Mencius,* I have followed D. C. Lau, *Mencius* (New York: Penguin Classics, 1970).

10. Fu, *Ju tao t'ien-lun fa-wei,* pp. 131–152.

11. The numbers in parentheses refer to the chapter and the page of the edition of Wang Hsien-ch'ien's *Hsün-tzu chi-chieh* (reprint, Taipei: Shih-chieh, 1967). As for an English translation, I roughly followed Holmer Dubs, *The Works of Hsüntze* (London: Arthur Probsthain, 1928); and Burton Watson, *Hsün-tzu, Basic Writings* (New York: Columbia University Press, 1963).

12. See Donald Munro, *The Concept of Man in Early China* (Stanford, Calif.: Stanford University Press, 1969), p. 81.

13. For the text of the Bible, I followed *The Jerusalem Bible* (Garden City, N. Y.: Doubleday, 1966).

14. Daniel Rops, *Le Peuple de la Bible*, trans. into Chinese by Ignatius Chou (Tai-chung: Kuang-ch'i, 1957), p. 109.

15. F. R. Tennant, *The Fall Story* (n. p., 1905), p. 26.

16. Tennant, "Original Sin," in *Encyclopedia of Religion and Ethics*, vols. 9 and 10 (New York: Scribner's, 1928), p. 564.

17. F. R. Tennant, *Original Sin* (n. p., 1905), p. 32.

18. Ibid., p. 28.

19. Karl Rahner, *Foundations of Christian Faith*, trans. W. V. Dych (New York: Seabury Press, 1978), p. 110.

20. Karl Rahner, "Original Sin," in *Sacramentum Mundi* (New York: Herder and Herder, 1969), 4:332.

21. Rahner, *Foundations*, p. 106.

22. Rahner "Original Sin," p. 332.

23. Rahner, *Foundations*, p. 111.

24. Ibid.

25. Rahner, "Original Sin", p. 331.

26. Rahner, *Foundations*, p. 113.

27. Ibid., p. 126.

28. R. J. Pendergast, "The Supernatural Existential, Human Generation and Original Sin," *The Downside Review* (Exeter) 82, no. 266 (January 1964): 23.

29. Pei-jung Fu, "An Understanding of Original Sin—Through the Interpretations of Tennant, Rahner, and Ricoeur," *Philosophical Review* (Taipei: National Taiwan University), no. 7 (January 1984): 150–151.

30. Ibid.

31. Paul Ricoeur, *The Symbolism of Evil*, trans. E. Buchanan (Boston: Beacon Press, 1967), p. 5.

32. Ibid.

33. Ibid., p. 251.

34. Ibid., pp. 233–234.

35. Ibid., p. 312.

36. Paul Ricoeur, "Morality without Sin or Sin without Moralism," *Cross Currents* 5 (Fall 1955): 351.

37. Ibid., p. 346.

38. Paul Ricoeur, "The Image of God and the Epic of Man," *Cross Currents* 11 (Winter 1961): 41.

39. Ibid., p. 38.

40. Ibid., p. 46.

41. Ricoeur "Morality," p. 351.

42. Fu, *Ju tao t'ien-lun fa-wei*, pp. 109–112.

43. Ibid., pp. 145–147.

44. Ibid., pp. 164–165.

45. Lao-tzu expressed similar ideas but from practical consideration. He said, "Do good to him who has done you an injury" (Ch. 63). The reason is: "When peace is made between great enemies, some enmity is bound to remain undispelled. How can this be considered perfect?" (Ch. 79). See D. C. Lau, *Lao Tzu Tao Te Ching* (New York: Penguin Classics, 1963).

46. Fu, *Ju tao t'ien-lun fa-wei*, p. 40.

47. "Hung-fan," *Book of History*. For the English translation of this paragraph, see Thomé Fang, *Chinese Philosophy: Its Spirit and Its Development* (Taipei: Linking, 1980), p. 41.

48. See Lau, *Confucius, The Analects*, p. 158; "Ta-yü mo," *Book of History*.

49. "Chung-hui chih kao," *Book of History*.

50. Pan Ku, *Han Shu* (History of the Han Dynasty), chuan 85.

51. Jacob Edmond, *Theology of the Old Testament*, trans. into Chinese by Sung Ch'üan-sheng (Tainan: Tung-nan-ya shen-hsüeh-yüan, 1974), p. 109.

52. Benjamin Schwartz held a similar view. He maintained that in the *Analects* "we find considerable emphasis on his [Confucius'] own relationship to 'heaven' which is treated not simply as the immanent Tao of nature and society but as a transcendent conscious will interested in Confucius' redeeming mission." See Benjamin Schwartz, "Transcendence in Ancient China," *Daedalus*, Spring 1975, pp. 1–7.

SELECTED BIBLIOGRAPHY

Chan, Wing-tsit. *Religious Trends in Modern China*. New York: Columbia University Press, 1953.

Ching, Julia. *Confucianism and Christianity*. Tokyo: Kōdansha International, 1977.

Fang, Thomé. *Chinese Philosophy: Its Spirit and Its Development*. Taipei: Linking, 1981.

Fu, Charles Wei-hsün. *Che-hsüeh yü chung-chiao (Philosophy and Religion). Vol. 1: From Western Philosophy to Zen Buddhism; Vol. 2: Critical Inheritance and Creative Development*. Taipei: Tung-ta, 1986.

Fu, Pei-jung. "Chinese Thought and Christianity." *Collectanea Theologica* (Taipei: Fu Jen Catholic University), no. 32 (Autumn 1977): 179–215.

————. "On the Communication of Chinese Thought and Christianity." *Chinese Culture Monthly* (Taichung: Tunghai University), no. 5 (March 1980): 114–147.

————. *Ju tao t'ien-lun fa-wei (Explication of the Doctrine of Heaven in Confucianism and Taoism)*. Taipei: Hsüeh-sheng, 1985.

————. "On Religious Ideas of the Pre-Chou China." *Chinese Culture* (Taipei: Chinese Culture University), 26, no. 3 (September 1985): 23–39.

————. "An Understanding of Original Sin—Through the Interpretations of Tennant, Rahner, and Ricoeur." *Philosophical Review* (Taipei: National Taiwan University), no. 7 (January 1984): 141–161.

Gernet, Jacques. *China and the Christian Impact*. Translated into English by Janet Lloyd. Cambridge: Cambridge University Press, 1985.

Lau, D. C. *Confucius, The Analects*. New York: Penguin Classics, 1979.

————. *Lao Tzu Tao: Te Ching*. New York: Penguin Classics, 1963.

————. *Mencius*. New York: Penguin Classics, 1970.

Legge, James. *The Religions of China*. London, 1880.

Leibniz, Gottfried. *Discourse on the Natural Theology of the Chinese.* Translated into English by H. Rosemont and D. J. Cook. Hawaii: University of Hawaii Press, 1977.

Li, Tu. *Chung hsi che-hsüeh ssu-hsiang chung ti t'ien-tao yü shang-ti (Heaven-Tao and God in Chinese and Western Philosophy).* Taipei: Linking, 1978.

Liu, Shu-hsien. "The Confucian Approach to the Problem of Transcendence and Immanence." *Philosophy East and West* 22, no. 3 (1972): 45–52.

————. "The Religious Import of Confucian Philosophy: Its Traditional Outlook and Contemporary Significance." *Philosophy East and West* 21, no. 2 (1971): 157–175.

Mou, Tsung-san. *Chung-kuo che-hsüeh shih chiu chiang (Nineteen Lectures on Chinese Philosophy).* Taipei: Hsüeh-sheng, 1983.

Munro, Donald. *The Concept of Man in Early China.* Stanford, Calif.: Stanford University Press, 1969.

Rahner, Karl. *Foundations of Christian Faith.* Translated by W. V. Dych. New York: Seabury Press, 1978.

————. "Original Sin." In *Sacramentum Mundi.* New York: Herder and Herder, 1969.

Ricoeur, Paul. *The Symbolism of Evil.* Translated by E. Buchanan. Boston: Beacon Press, 1967.

Schwartz, Benjamin. "Transcendence in Ancient China." *Daedalus,* Spring 1975.

————. *The World of Thought in Ancient China.* Cambridge, Mass.: Harvard University Press, 1985.

Soothill, W. E. *The Three Religions of China.* London: Oxford University Press, 1929.

Tennant, F. R. *The Fall Story.* N.p., 1905.

————. *Original Sin.* N.p., 1905.

————. "Original Sin." In *Encyclopedia of Religion and Ethics.* New York: Scribner's, 1928.

Thompson, Laurence. *Chinese Religion,* Belmont, Calif.: Wadsworth, 1979.

Yang, Ch'ing-kun. *Chung-kuo ssu-hsiang yü chih-tu lun-chi (Essay on Chinese Thought and Institutions).* Taipei: Linking, 1976.

24

A Christian Response to Shu-hsien Liu and Pei-jung Fu

ROBERT CUMMINGS NEVILLE

Chapter 22 by Shu-hsien Liu and Chapter 23 by Pei-jung Fu are outstanding contributions to the developing dialogue between Confucians and Christians, and it is a pleasure to enter the discussion with them. We all share strong commitments to our respective background tradition, deep sympathy with the integrity and brilliance of the other tradition, sensitivity to the diversity within each tradition, and a longing for what Liu called a "religion beyond religion" that recognizes the particularities of its various sources. Although many of our colleagues may not join us in that last-mentioned longing, it is not an issue between us here.

For a Christian to be put on the defensive about the importance of history by Confucians is a gratifying surprise. Both of my colleagues take a historical approach to the study of religion, and Liu goes so far as to criticize Tillich's (and most Christians') claim that Christ is the center of history for being not historical enough. I shall return to the specific complaint about the pseudohistoricity of Christianity at the end of my response. At the outset I want to reinforce and formalize the historical approach to religion.

Although historical connections have many different structures, the historical development of traditions is fruitfully conceived according to the metaphor of sedimented layers. That is, the early strata of a culture's development are not so much left behind as covered over and carried along with new accretions in later developments. Fu has made excellent use of the work of Paul Ricoeur who has perfected the analytical technique of uncovering the earlier layers in the later cultural whole, giving a developmental dimension to historical understanding, explaining how earlier elements reappear in new guises and how the whole is richer for embodying the resonances, perhaps unconscious, of earlier strata.[1]

I suggest that we cannot compare or correlate Christianity and Confucianism without specifying the strata of historical development to which reference is being made. Therefore, it is helpful in understanding Liu to note that his point is to criticize a twentieth-century thinker with respect to the current viability of his ideas and to set this over against the views of Confucius, two and a half thousand years Tillich's senior. It is equally important to realize that Fu identified Confucianism and Christianity by the early texts of their canonical scriptures, not by their development to the present when in fact they meet in dialogue. My intent in this response is to clarify the dialogue between Christians and Confucians by locating the points raised by my colleagues in the respective historical strata of our traditions, relating them to the present religious and intellectual situation, and commenting on their validity for purposes of dialogue.

I

Confucianism and Christianity are farthest from one another in the assumptions about the nature of the self or person that obtained at the time of their classic founding writings. Those assumptions can be expressed philosophically as root metaphors, or models; these philosophic expressions are analytic abstractions made through archeological analysis of the early strata of the traditions' development. As assumption, they largely determined the early written documents, and they are carried along, with modifications, into the latest self-understanding. I call the Confucian assumptions bipolar and the Christian covenantal.

The Confucian assumptions are expressed in many contexts, but perhaps most clearly in the *Chung-Yung*. The self is a polar organization of activities running between two extremes. One extreme is the *chung,* the center, the pool of tranquil readiness to respond that is not yet responding. At the other is the *yung,* the ten thousand things of the world with which the self treats.[2] The self is neither of these extremes but the organization of activities connecting them. The more interior the self's behavior, the closer to the center of readiness to respond. The inner phenomena can be afferent, such as perceptions and impacts, or efferent, such as intentions, responses, or self-initiated movements. The afferent phenomena "stir" feelings into action; the efferent phenomena express the center's response. As Mencius argued in his remarks about the "Four Beginnings" (*Mencius* 2A: 6), the initial responses of the center are invariably appropriate, however they may be distorted subsequently as they percolate through the structures connecting the center with external things. The external things in themselves are not part of the self, but insofar as the self is the activities connecting the center to the things, they partially define the content of the self. The external things include the natural environment with which the Confucians, as much as the Taoists, insist on continuity. The ancient Confucians believed that the most central and ubiquitous external things that define an individual self are those marked out in the great relations, to parents, to siblings elder and younger, to social offices higher and lower than one's own, to spouse, to friends, and to strangers. There are other particularities of historical place and circumstance that also define the self's content.

As mentioned, the self is neither the *chung* or the *yung* in isolation but the mean, the personal, social, and physical structures connecting them, and the ancient Confucians knew that these structures require growth and cultivation. As to physical structures, one must learn to relate to things through one's body and to act effectively in the social and physical environment. As to social structures, one "treats with" external things only through the mediation of the institutions within which one lives and through the network of social arrangements. As to personal structures, there are psychological abilities and habits that must be formed to carry out activities. Since a person relates to many things at once, and does so over time, personal, social, and physical structures need to be integrated. Although one's initial "beginning" response might be appropriate to the object with which one is to treat, one's psychological, social, and physical structures must be adequate to carry out the appropriate response. Unlike the Western concept of self, which *contrasts* self with the world or environment, the Confucian takes the self to be the structured perspective of activities, relating to the world, formed from an individual's center. The boundary between self and world is fluid and is to be drawn only pragmatically. Since most of our activities are conjoint or social, much of daily life is not to be assigned to the experience of this person or that but to the overlapping influences on the network of public activities.

The goodness of actions, or of a person, requires not only the innately good "beginnings" but the properly developed, relevant, and effective structures of the self/society. When Hsun tze complained that human nature was evil, I don't think he meant to deny Mencius's theory of the Four Beginnings as far as it goes but rather to state that the Four Beginnings without a developed personal/social structure only leads to stupid conflict of primitive forces. Put paradoxically, for Hsun tze, what is innately human is not human; in addition, one needs conventional creations of learned personal and social structures as well as health and physical skills. Therefore, Hsun tze emphasized the positive importance of learning in order to make possible the human virtues.

Whether through neglect (Hsun tze) or malformation (Mencius), the personal, social, and sometimes physical structures are the source of evil. Where actions or habits are evil, it is because the structures distort or break the *chung-yung* connections. The importance of "sincerity" and "manifesting the clear character" is that the structures must be so ordered that the true nature and worth of the ten thousand things get conveyed sensitively to the center, and the normative responses initiating from the center carry through to the things appropriately. When the structures block, break, or distort, they constitute an interruption that the Confucians called selfishness. Attaining to the virtue of the worthy person or sage requires eliminating selfishness so that one is one body with the world. The *Ta Hsueh,* either in Chu Hsi's order or Wang Yang-ming's, shows how the perfection of the structures relating a person to the ten thousand things needs to begin with the innermost approach to the normative responsiveness of the center. In later neo-Confucian thought, the center was interpreted as

Principle, or heaven, universal in all things but diversified by the different positions things have and by the different structures things provide through which Principle is manifested.[3]

Although Confucius remarked that some people are virtuous easily, some virtuous with difficulty, and yet others find virtue impossible, the Confucians would agree with Christians that evil is a problem for all people, a problem in need of overcoming. As Fu pointed out, sin is original because any given person inherits much of his or her social and personal structure, as well as physical makeup. In contrast to the Taoists who advocated relaxing from effort, Confucians would agree with Christians that the overcoming of evil is a result of a process of sanctification or sage making: it doesn't happen naturally.

Most of the physical, personal, and social structures of the self, according to the ancient Confucians, are matters of conventional signs and are thus normed by propriety or ritual. From skills at adroit action through gestures, postures, and words, through the playing of roles in institutionalized social structures, the structural content is modified by, if not wholly formed by, conventional signs. The virtue of propriety has to do with mastering the signs necessary to constitute the finer human dimensions of life and with using them sincerely at the right time. On the one hand, the rules of propriety, indeed all signs, are conventional and differ from people to people. On the other hand, a body of people has to have some conventions to constitute the higher human levels of social and personal experience. The difference between the Chinese and the barbarians, from the former's standpoint, was not that the barbarians had the wrong conventions, the wrong rituals, but that they had insufficient rituals to be fully human or that their signs were in confusion, with the same result.

The reason that the Chinese trinity of heaven, earth, and humans does not reduce to the "natural" elements of heaven and earth is that those two by themselves do not produce the conventions so obviously constitutive of fulfilled human life. With respect to the sign-bearing structures of human existence, the human sphere is self-created, added to the mere conjunction of heaven and earth (or Principle and Material Force in later Confucian thought). Human beings are required to perfect heaven and earth because without the mediation of human conventions, the potential connections between heavenly readiness-to-respond-appropriately and earthly readiness-to-be-engaged remains merely potential at the level of human affairs. Human affairs would have no reality beyond procreation, minimal group self-protection, and competition for scarce resources, if they lack an elaborate set of conventional signs applied with propriety; this was the heart of Hsun tze's vision.

Definition of the Confucian self comes not from any intrinsic nature but from the structures by which the centered self engages the world. Mainly, these structures are social, and the most essential ones, particularly family structures, are those that most influence an individual's identity.

Despite the fact that the ancient Hebrew roots of Christianity embodied a strong kinship and generally social definition of personal identity, the Christian model of the self is entirely different from the Confucian and perhaps simply incommensurable with it. Although ancient Israel and Jews of Jesus' time obviously knew about different cultural customs, their understanding embodied a set of metaphors or model of its own. Contrary to the Confucian recognition of the conventionality of human-making signs, the ancient Hebrews regarded the essential signs as the direct expression of God, as the divine word. The primary metaphor in Hebrew thinking, laid down at the beginning of the identity of the culture, is the covenant or contract between God and the Hebrew people. Early on it was assumed that each people had its god and, therefore, had a unique or special way of life, ritual, and expression based on connections with that god. The Abrahamic covenant identified both the Hebrews and Yahweh in terms of the cult connecting them, separating both as a partnership from the other gods and tribes, especially those in Egypt. The Mosaic covenant began with Yahweh's admonition to "put no other gods before me" precisely because those other gods (and their cults) had to be segregated off to give identity to Israel. As the monotheistic inpulse developed in Israel, the divine word became associated with creation as such. The divine word was not a convention but ontologically constitutive of the world, more like heaven than the domain of humans. The relativity of customs was recognized, but those of Israel were assumed to have special status, by Second Isaiah, for instance, because they expressed the special covenant whereby Israel took up a world-redemptive role, thus functioning as an extension of the univeral God's creativity. As the understanding of the creative word of God took on Hellenistic connotations with the doctrine of Sophia, and by Jesus' time, the Logos, the ancient covenant was reinterpreted as participation in those senses of the divine word, and the adherance to Torah as particular cult was weakened among those attracted to Christianity. With the advent of Johannine and Pauline Christianity, the covenant defining Yahweh and his people was sharply redefined as participation in the word of God in Christ, or in the mind of Christ, and a new cult was formed to reinforce that covenantal participation. Whereas Confucians of the time understood the essential human reality to be an investment in the conventions of propriety, precisely as superadded to heavenly and earthly ontological elements, the Christians took the human-making signs not to be conventional but to be direct participation in the divine itself.

To understand this difference between Christianity and Confucianism we can look more deeply into the covenantal model of self. Whether as defining Israel as a society, or an individual as related to Yahweh through Israel's covenant, the covenant makes the relation to God to be constitutive of identity. Like the Confucians, the people of Israel had to make their way in the world, feeding, clothing, and securing themselves, coping with terrain and other peoples. Their identity, collectively and individually, did not consist precisely in how they structured their "way in the world." Rather, their identity consisted in being bound to God through the covenant, especially the Mosaic covenant. The covenant to a rather large degree specified how the Israelites were to make their way in the world, perhaps to as large a degree as the Confucian rules of propriety.

The fault in breaking the covenant is not merely in the wrongdoing but more importantly in the fact that the break contradicts the covenant itself. Since the people, and the individuals, are defined by the covenant, the break is a contradiction to the people and individuals themselves. Sinning is not merely immoral— indeed many cultic injunctions have no moral content—it leads to the people and its individuals contradicting themselves. They become alienated from themselves. Guilt in the sense deriving from the covenantal definition of the self is a kind of self-contradiction, a self-alienation; this is far more than being responsible for wrongdoing. Its repair requires not just making amends and mending one's way: repair requires a reconstitution of the people or the self by the reestablishment of the covenant. Because the human side is internally broken in the sin, the redemptive activity must come from the divine side.

By virtue of the fact that Christian guilt, unlike Confucian selfishness or impropriety, is an internal contradiction, the root metaphors for the self in the tradition of ancient Israel are inward turning. The self is defined in a bounded way, the boundaries being set by the contours of responsibility for breaking the covenant. Whereas Confucian personal identity bleeds off into the characteristics of the institutions structuring one's perceptions and actions, and even into the identities of other people with whom one participates, personal identity for the Sons of Israel is the moral identity one gives oneself that can be guilty. Although ancient Israel kept group and personal identity in balance, the interiority of guilt fostered a sense of individualism that came to extreme fruition in Christianity. For Jesus, rebirth into a new relation to God is an individual matter, and the covenant is with God who is father of us all. Jesus, however, was committed to the people of Israel, and took his own mission to be to them almost exclusively. Yet his understanding of the covenant focused not on group cultic practice but on the habits of the individual heart. For the early Christians, the group bound in the new covenant was not the historical kinship group that identified itself over–against other groups by the history of its allegiance to Yahweh but a voluntary group all of whose members had individually chosen the new covenant and symbolized this by participation in baptism, dying to their old kinship life and rising to a universal brotherhood and sisterhood, following Jesus as the "first born" of the children of God.

Christians from the beginning had families (although Paul had early on expected the end of the world and initially had advised against unnecessary human commitments). But their families, like their social and political life, were vehicles within which one lived out the new covenant with God. Whereas the Confucians regarded their family commitments and other engagements as the very stuff of life, and the arena in which humanity had the responsibility to fulfill heaven and earth, the early Christians took those commitments to be the tokens by which they played out a drama whose characters were almost accidentally in those circumstances.

With these extensive expository remarks about the ancient root models of self in Confucianism and Christianity, I want now to address in briefer but sharply focused ways some of the major points made by Pei-jung Fu and Shu-hsien Liu.

II

Fu's chapter has four major topics; I shall comment on the first here and the rest in conjunction with comments on Liu's chapter. Fu compared Confucianism and Christianity with regard to the nature of humans; according to his comparison, Confucianism holds that human nature tends toward goodness and Christianity holds that it tends toward evil. I thoroughly agree with Fu that Confucianism emphasizes the tendency of human nature toward the good and appreciate his citation of passages in which Confucius, Mencius, and Hsun tse (despite himself) affirm this. Beyond agreeing that the Confucians believed that human nature was good, I have tried above to give an explanation of why it would make sense for them to believe that, based on the analysis of the Four Beginnings.

Fu has emphasized *jen* in his exposition of goodness. Is it not the case that the doctrine of *jen* is in danger of romanticization and sentimentality if it is disconnected with the doctrine of *li* as ritual propriety? My own exposition has taken what I believe to be the hard case, the Confucian emphasis on the importance of convention as the means by which the self and social relations are structured so that the original impulse toward goodness can find functional expression.

Given that Confucius and his early followers believed that there is a natural and original impulse toward goodness, they also acknowledged that there is real personal, moral evil in the world. That evil, according to my account of ancient Confucianism, derives from the absence, insufficiency, or confusion of the structuring of the self by proper signs or semiotic propriety; more particularly, it derives from the malformation of those signific structures so that they take on a selfish form, clouding the sincere movement from *chung* to *yung* and vice versa. I believe that the Confucian theory of human goodness is incomplete without its theory of the nature and origin of evil. As to the statistical frequency with which completely good people are to be found, I have no reason to believe that Confucians, ancient or modern, believed that goodness unalloyed with evil occurs more often than Christians believe that moral perfection is obtained.

With regard to Fu's claim that Christianity believes human nature tends toward evil, I have some serious qualifications. Let us set aside for a moment his discussion of the twentieth-century Christian theologians, for they cannot be compared to the ancient Confucians without further mediation. Focusing rather on the New Testament understanding of human nature, Jesus, Paul, and the authors of the gospels agree with Confucius that there is a lot of evil in the world and that the worst of it proceeds from the heart of individuals. The New Testament writers believed that the cause of evil is not the divinely created human nature but rather the fact that the covenant with God has been broken. Their ancestors having broken the covenant, the children of Israel since that time have tended to reinforce that break, rebreaking the covenant each time. They do not do this by given nature but by virtue of their own responsible choices. The immoral and self-alienated nature resulting from the broken covenant is man-made.

Paul is a special case regarding the understanding of goodness and evil. Unlike other New Testament writers he operated less in the Jewish world of the Mosaic covenant than in the cosmopolitan world of the Roman Empire. He observed in the letter to the *Romans* that, although the Jews had the Torah, there is a kind of natural law, a Logos, that is available to all cultures; as Jews broke the Torah covenant, so Gentiles sinned against natural law. To assimilate this universal understanding to the story of God acting in history, Paul chose to use the legend of Adam, the father of all peoples, not only of the Jews. Paul assumed that Adam had been created naturally good, in the image of God. By deliberate sin, Adam fell, perverting the divine image and ruining people's naive goodness. From Adam to Jesus people tended inevitably to sin; this was not a natural condition but a historical one, not a divinely given condition but a contingent human failure. Paul called Jesus the "New Adam," and history after Jesus is significantly reversed. He did not suggest that "original sin" no longer would affect people. But he did argue that by participating in the mind of Christ through the grace of God in the Holy Spirit, there is no longer a historical necessity to sin. Sanctification is possible.

For the early Christians, the goodness of God's creation was taken for granted as a background condition for history. The moral content of history itself was thought to be historically particular. Original sin, as an inherited trait of society and human character, is a historical condition existing within the background of an originally good creation, a creation made according to the Divine Word itself. Given the grace of God in the Holy Spirit, that background goodness reasserts itself and repairs a portion of humankind as the image of God.

The Christian understanding of good and evil has evolved in many complex directions since the early days. F. R. Tennant's view is not particularly interesting. Karl Rahner's and Paul Ricoeur's views deserve some comment. Rahner did not differ from any Confucian in noting that the situation of human life is filled with evils that condition our activities. Where he differed is in his insistence on the connection between evil and freedom. Freedom in the Christian sense is a concept that makes sense only in a conception of self built upon the deep structure of covenant identity. Freedom does not mean lack of restraint or spontaneity (both of which Confucians understand plainly), but rather it means the capacity to exercise responsibility in a way that defines one's own identity. The Confucians understood responsibility for the moral content of actions, but they did not tie this to the constitution of an inward personal identity in terms of guilt and moral virtue.

The Dialectical view of sin that Fu found in Ricoeur and that derives from Georg Hegel treats sin as a God-given character through which human beings mature. We cannot be human unless we are free; we cannot be free unless we exercise our freedom; the exercise of freedom is not free unless sometimes it is rebellious, and hence we must sin to be human. This may well be true, but it is a far cry from early Christianity because it makes the development of human nature itself an evolutionary process.

Both the early Christian view of salvation history and the post-Hegelian view of the instrumental value of sin for freedom and human maturity give history a prominent place. I do not see that Confucianism has anything like this sense of the prominence of history. Fu said that Confucianism "is able to appreciate the potential perfectibility of human nature which can be described as tending toward goodness." But that "tending" is not historical; it is situational.

I am unpersuaded of Fu's claim that Confucians see the tendency toward goodness because they look from the human perspective and emphasize self-reliance, whereas Christians see the opposite tendency because they look from the divine perspective and await God's grace. Granted, the early Christians believed in a personal God (post-Hegelian theologians have greatly qualified that); nevertheless, Christians never thought they saw God or themselves except from the human perspective. Christ revealed "things divine" precisely in his human nature. As to the source of the action that leads to or back to goodness, Christians believe it comes from the presence of God in creation. Similarly, Confucians believe it comes from the heavenly principle that manifests itself in the Four Beginnings.

The distinction between early Confucians and early Christians comes rather in their different models of self. Confucians did not emphasize self-reliance in contrast to the divine principle; the divine principle is a constituent part of the self. Christians did not emphasize that people should sit passively while God works to sanctify them; rather, God's work consists in renewing the covenant, and that precisely entails that people live actively in the covenant. The "divine" functions in early Confucian thought according to the bipolar model of the self; the divine functions in early Christian thought according to the covenant or contract model. I do not see the point of the self-reliance/God-reliance distinction. Nor do I see that the models of self are close enough to compare.

Today, we can ask how contemporary-developed Confucianism and Christianity relate to the problem of goodness and evil. One of the most striking elements of contemporary thought about evil is that much of it is resident in the social structuring of situations, for instance, in oppressive political structures or exploitative economic ones, in slum conditions or in socially enforced ignorance. Because of the individuality and inwardness arising from the covenant model of the self, it is possible for Christians to imagine saying no to a whole situation, calling for personal dissociation from the social structures and, possibly, revolutionary action. Is this extreme capacity for negation possible for the Confucian? Granted, Confucians have often been reformers, and Mencius even justified rebellion against a regime that has lost the mandate of heaven. But does not the definition of the self in terms of the institutions and social relations in which one participates mean that for the Confucian, saying no means a tearing apart of oneself?

My own view is that Christian individualism is extreme and morally dangerous; I find it most tolerable when it is combined with a social or historical definition of the individual, as in Puritanism. The Confucian emphasis on the social-structure definition of the self is also morally dangerous because it does not easily sustain opposition to institutional evil. Perhaps we need a metaphysical model for the self that improves on both the Confucian and Christian roots.[4]

III

The issue of Christian transcendence is a deep concern for both Fu and Liu. I shall argue, as in the point above, that a new metaphysical model is required to make sense of the issue. First, consider a point about the history of the idea of transcendence. In both early China and the early Near East, the peoples believed in gods who constitute and manipulate human affairs from a heavenly realm. On the one hand, these accounts were legendary stories of genesis and historical beginnings; one thinks of the P'an Ku stories in China and the Babylonian Marduk myths.[5] On the other hand, these legends did not imagine a serious sense of transcendence because the world was simply many storied, with places for the gods, places for people, and sometimes places for the dead.

My contention is that the idea of transcendence becomes increasingly serious as a culture comes to appreciate the dialectical implications of its basic religious or world-forming stories, symbols, and conceptions. In the Judeo-Christian tradition there is a rough progression from a conception of God as a war leader of the Hebrews to a supreme being among the many gods of the pantheon to the only God who creates the entire world to a greatly transcendent God whose creation is mediated by Sophia or the Logos to the Trinity to a completely transcendent God understood as *Esse* or act of being; since St. Thomas, who developed the last notion in the thirteenth century, transcendence has received many variant interpretations, but none is more purely transcendent. A careful historical analysis of this progression would indicate that the following dialectical principle was at work: God must be conceived to be creator and Lord over the world, and as the conception of the boundary character of the world developed to be more general and inclusive, the conception of God changed accordingly. Early on, God could be conceived as managing Abraham's affairs; later, in *Second Isaiah,* God had to be conceived as the creator of all nature and Lord over all nations. With the subsequent incorporation of Greek neo-Platonic philosophy, nature came to be conceived as anything with determinate difference in it, as that which is unified by Plotinus's "Dyad," and hence God in *aseity* could not be determinate.

The dialectic is significant, however, only when God is conceived in connection with the world; hence God is not conceived in *aseity* (except trivially) and is rather conceived as the creator of all determinate being, creating relative to history as judge, redeemer, and so on. The general result of the Judeo-Christian dialectic is an intimate coimplication of transcendence and immanence. The mixture of determinate things constituting the world needs a creative ground outside itself: it exists as being created. God as the creative ground cannot be determinate in separation from creating: God, therefore, is not a transcendent principle (which would require a determinate transcendent character) but is rather the creating of the world. As Liu noted, Tillich clearly observed that God cannot be a thing without being a part of the world; not being a thing, God cannot be conceptualized except as the ground of being, or Being-itself.[6]

What is the history of transcendence in Chinese thought? To answer that, we must look at the history of the Chinese conception of the world. In ancient times, the world was taken to be a flowing mixture of affairs for which the hexagrams of the *I Ching* are emblematic. Although Confucius and his early followers were not much interested in dialectical questions of any sort, both the Taoists and Buddhists were, and the Confucians in turn reflected on the issue. The world of human affairs was conceived as the realm of the mixture of the influences of heaven and earth, as built upon and fulfilled by human inventiveness. Precisely because the world expressed these elements as mixed, heaven and earth *by themselves* were considered to be transcendent. Like the post-neo-Platonic creator God, they are determinate not in themselves but only in their contributions to the mixture. The neo-Confucianists transformed heaven and earth into the plainly ontological principles of Principle and Material Force. However one views the disputes between the Ch'eng-Chu school and the Lu-Wang school about the identity, separability, or priority of these ontological principles, there was agreement that they have determinate character only insofar as they are mixed in the world.

It is sometimes said that Chinese intellectual history pays little or no attention to concepts analogous to divine creativity. I admit that there is no analogue to the dialectic moving from warrior God to the ground of being. Yet the theme of ontological creativity has its own dialectical history in China. By ontological creativity I mean not the causation of one thing by its antecedents within time but the causation of the realm of nature, including its temporal flow, by that which is not within nature. A given event within the world, then, is involved in two senses of causation. There is its implication within the temporal causal patterns of the world, being caused by antecedents and causing its own effects; this can be called "cosmological causation." There is also its implication within "ontological causation" or, to use the Western terms, divine creativity. The *Tao Teh Ching* begins by contrasting the world as the nameable tao from the unnameable tao; in that very contrast it gives a relational name to the unnameable tao by suggesting that it is the ground of the worldly tao. The relation between the unnameable tao and the nameable one is that of ontological creation; they are not exactly two things precisely because the unnameable tao is nothing apart from grounding the nameable tao of worldly process. Wang Pi drew out these implications directly. Chou Tun-i, in the eleventh century, began his "Explanation of the Diagram of the Great Ultimate" with the "progression" from the Ultimate of Non-being to the Great Ultimate to yang to yin to the basic elements to the myriad things. Only with the myriad things is there production, reproduction, and unending transformation; that is, there is the temporal flow of the world only at the end of this "process" of ontological movement from nothingness to determinate being.[7] Within any part of natural process, there is an ontological depth reaching from universal yin-yang principles down to originary nothingness. I do not suggest that the unnameable tao or the Ultimate of Non-being is analogous to the theistic, historical Yahweh. Nevertheless, by the time the Judeo-Christian God is conceived as indeterminate in itself, determinate only in relation to the created world, as was the case with St. Thomas's theory of God as Esse, there is a functional equivalent between the ontologically creative Nothingnesses in both traditions. Furthermore, both traditions see the world as a complex of processes to be understood in terms of analytical elements expressive of ontological creativity, elements such as Logos and Prime Matter, Principle and Material Force, yin and yang; these elements are not themselves worldly processes but rather constituents that, when mixed, constitute the historical world.

For both traditions, the immanence of the mixed world implies the transcendence of an ontological ground, which is Nothing in itself; and for both, the character of the ground as creating implies the mixed world as created. For both traditions, there is an asymmetry in creative power and a symmetry in the mutual definition of character of the ground and world. Having noted these similarities I do not mean to minimize the differences between the Chinese and Western traditions. In the West the creative ground is often conceived theistically. God is talked about through metaphors of agency, mainly because ontological creativity even in Saint Thomas and Tillich is conceived as the creation of and within history. In China passage and change are rarely construed to have the overall contours of the action of a unifying agent. Nevertheless, associating immanence with China and transcendence with Christianity or the Western tradition is a misleading generalization.[8] Transcendence and immanence coimply each other, and both traditions have worked out elaborate and sophisticated conceptualities to make the point.

I am now in a position to comment on Liu's critique of Tillich's conception of God. As he pointed out, Tillich held that God is the ground of being, transcending the distinction between subject and object and all other distinctions. Tillich also called God being-itself; Liu perhaps would acknowledge that when Tillich explained this, being-itself turns out to be the ground or creator of determinate beings. Now, if literal statement means that one's proposition corresponds to structures in the world, there can be no literal statement about the creator of all determinateness. The question is rather whether statements can symbolize that which is the ground of all statement making. Tillich got himself into trouble by thinking, at one point in his career, as Liu remarked, that symbolism rests on at least one literal statement. He should have said that the symbolism rests on the dialectic of finding that which grounds the world, defining the ground over–against the definition of the world. The theological symbols thus do not refer to God as if God were the object of predication. Rather, they refer to the reality expressed in the dialectic of ontological thinking. As Tillich might put it, the symbols, based in the dialectic, lead us to participate in the appreciation of the ontological creativity involved in all cosmological creativity. The rest of Tillich's theology involves developing the particular historical character of ontological creativity. For instance, he argued that God completes the creation of human life in the life of Jesus as the Christ who heals the historical or existential breach between essential and actual humanity. The problem of symbols of that which grounds determinate being, including determinate symbols, is not unique to Tillich or Christianity. The unnameable tao, the Ultimate of Non-being, even Principle and Material Force, are symbols of things that are not things but rather the ontological causes of things.

Liu's most profound criticism of Tillich is not about the conception of God or Christ, however; it is about methodology. Liu dismissed speculative metaphysics or theology as transcending the limits of legitimate knowledge. By doing so he dismissed the significance of the entire dialectic on which I have based my argument, both historically and conceptually. He thus evaded the perennial problem in Western as well as Chinese thought of how to refer to that which is not an object over–against referers as subjects. The argument Liu gave for his large dismissal is that he prefers a Kantian limitation of knowledge to those things that conform to the structures of human knowing, and he prefers the Kantian limitation in the form of ontological phenomenology. I offer the following comments to suggest that Kantian transcendental philosophy and ontological phenomenology are large mistakes.

1. Kant's original argument begins with the premise that we have synthetic a priori knowledge in physics and mathematics. Subsequent developments in science and mathematics have overturned what he assumed was a priori true. Therefore, instead of being able to claim that the Kantian system is a necessary condition for certain knowledge, at best we can state that the system is a grand hypothesis making sense of lesser hypotheses in physics and mathematics. No hypothesis, however, ought to be believed that states that the subject matter cannot be understood; the formal nature of a hypothesis is to present an explanation. Therefore, one cannot legitimately accept a hypothesis that states that we cannot have knowledge of something. Kant (and Liu) would have to argue that there is no thing (God in this case) about which we might have knowledge.

2. If one likes the form of Kant's transcendental argument, it should be applied to theology as well as to physics. Relative to theology, it would run as follows. We know (in faith) that God exists; therefore, there must be a legitimate form of knowledge, of such and such a sort, that makes this possible. Rudolf Otto proposed such a transcendental deduction of mystical knowledge of God as ground of being, the *mysterium tremendum,* in *The Idea of the Holy.* This is a

dangerous kind of argument, however, since we similarly can give a transcendental deduction of witchcraft, astrology, and any claim to knowledge we want, simply by assuming it the way Kant assumed Newton's physics and Euclid's geometry.

3. Ontological phenomenology, in the hands of a master such as Martin Heidegger, escapes much of the dubious argumentation of Kantian transcendental philosophy, and it also provides provocative insights into human life. Yet it is utterly self-deceptive to think of it as a safe description. The terms with which one describes the existential categories of life are filled with one's own values. To describe the human situation using those values may be an aesthetic tour de force. But how do you justify using those value-terms rather than others? Liu appears to resonate with the categories expressing the values of nineteenth- and twentieth-century European existentialism. Why use those categories rather than those of Confucius or Chu Hsi, or Lao Tsu or Wang Pi, or Fa Tsang or Vasubandu? All of those thinkers provided descriptive categories for the essential elements of human existence, and they appear to be in competition. I submit that the way to adjudicate among them is to understand them as expressing models of nature and selfhood and then to engage in a dialectic concerning the adequacy of the various models. We would find, I suspect, that each model is able to appreciate some of what we know to be important but at the price of having to neglect much else, often the very values recognized by other models. Our own philosophic task is to provide a dialectically defensible and empirically applicable model that sustains the best in the historically available models and that eliminates the undesirable elements. My point is that ontological phenomenology is a mere dogmatic imposition of one's values in the guise of a pure description, unless it is implicated in a larger and more dialectical speculative metaphysics. Tillich understood this point in the necessary correlation he saw between theology and philosophy, as Liu noted.

IV

My final point concerns the historical character of Jesus, as discussed by Liu, and Fu's comparison of Jesus and Confucius. Fu aptly pointed out three similarities between Confucius and Jesus. Both had a strong sense of mission. Both felt a strong connection with transcendence. Both interpreted the significance of their life in terms of transcendence. To these three points I would add a fourth: despite being worldly failures, both changed history decisively. The life of Jesus provides the date for punctuating the European calendar. In China until recently, history before Confucius was history as Confucius saw it, and post-Confucian history was largely that of the affairs of Confucian civilization.

Liu led us to ask what the conception of history is that allows such a place for these figures. He had the splendid insight that Tillich's so-called existential theology makes Christ too eternal to be a genuine historical figure. I agree thoroughly with this criticism. Liu also suggested that a real philosophy of history would note that every moment is a center of history. Although there is a truth to the view that every present moment fixes the other moments as past and future relative to itself, it goes too far to state that every moment is a center of history. History is precisely the formation of the passage of time and the changes of affairs so as to have something of the form of an extended story, with a beginning, a middle, and at least a projected end. Events within history take their meaning not only from how they embody a past and influence a future. Their meaning also comes from the place they occupy in larger historical events.

Neither Christianity nor Confucianism offers an adequate notion of history. For traditional Christianity, history has to have an absolute beginning, an absolute end, and an absolutely decisive crisis in the middle to make the story. For traditional Confucianism, history is little more than a series of chronicles of events, like successive changes according to the emblems of the *I Ching*. History is in fact a cultural artifact, and on this reading history is a different thing in the Christian West from what it is in Confucian China. Yet the destinies of the two cultures are intertwined now, and our cultural coexistence is incomplete, ghostly, because we do not live in a common history. Liu seems to have adopted the sense of history supposed by Western scholarship, and Fu, in his advocacy of the combination of Confucianism and Christianity for Chinese people, seems to have adopted the Christian view that there is only one real form of history. Despite my own Christian background, I am slightly uneasy with this victory of the West.

I appreciate the opportunity to engage in such a serious dialogue between Christian and Confucian sources. Most likely, I am not alone in this conversation in feeling regret at the oversimplifications we have had to make concerning the representations of our traditions. Christianity is a great many things, and the representation I have made is just the one about which I have the most to say. Confucianism, too, is far more diverse than our conversation has acknowledged, and it cannot be abstracted from its relations with Taoism, Buddhism, shamanism, and more recently pragmatism and Marxism. Yet I believe we have found ways of epitomizing something of interest in both sides. The rest of the task is not to correct what we have left out but rather to get on with the discovery of new forms of culture and religion adequate to our most interesting time.

NOTES

1. See, for instance, Paul Ricoeur's early *Symbolism of Evil*, trans. Emerson Buchanan (Boston: Beacon Press, 1969).

2. I take it that *chung-yung* is a composite concept in Chinese thought, a polarity pointing in two directions. The directionality of *chung* is clearly toward the center of self-reception and action; *yung* is a more controversial notion. I construe its directionality to be opposite from *chung*, namely, toward the things with which the center needs to structure relations. Chu Hsi said that *yung* means the principle in worldly, perhaps ordinary, things; without reading back the neo-Confucian metaphysical interest in Principle, there surely is a sense in which *yung* refers to the constant or regular aspects of things. James Legge pointed out another connotation of *yung*, namely, "use"; I interpret

this to suggest both that external things are the object of *yung* insofar as they are working, active, or functioning, and that they are engaged by the self. Thus *chung-yung* is the mean connecting the pure readiness to respond with the things ready to be engaged.

3. For a more elaborate presentation of this view of the Confucian self, see Robert Cummings Neville, "The Scholar-Official as a Model for Ethics," *Journal of Chinese Philosophy* 13, no. 2 (June 1986): 185–201.

4. The further comparison of Western and Confucian elements, and the development of an appropriate integrating metaphysical model, is the aim in Robert Cummings Neville, *The Puritan Smile* (Albany: State University of New York Press, 1987).

5. For a sophisticated discussion of the earliest Chinese materials, see Norman Girardot's *Myth and Meaning in Early Taoism* (Berkeley: University of California Press, 1983).

6. Robert Cummings Neville, *God the Creator: On the Transcendence and Presence of God* (Chicago: University of Chicago Press, 1968), gives a detailed analysis of the notion of being-itself, arguing that only a nondeterminate creator of determinate being can be being-itself.

7. See Chou Tun-i's essay in Wing-tsit Chan, ed., *Source Book in Chinese Philosophy* (Princeton, N.J.: Princeton University Press, 1963), p. 463.

8. Thus I take issue with the major thesis of David Hall's and Roger Ames's *Thinking through Confucius* (Albany: State University of New York Press, 1987).

SELECTED BIBLIOGRAPHY

Chou, Tun-i. "Explanation of the Diagram of the Great Ultimate." In *Source Book in Chinese Philosophy*. Edited by Wing-tsit Chan. Princeton, N.J.: Princeton University Press, 1963.

Girardot, Norman. *Myth and Meaning in Early Taoism*. Berkeley: University of California Press, 1983.

Hall, David, and Roger Ames. *Thinking through Confucius*. Albany: State University of New York Press, 1987.

Neville, Robert Cummings. *God the Creator: On the Transcendence and Presence of God*. Chicago: University of Chicago Press, 1968.

————. *The Puritan Smile*. Albany: State University of New York Press, 1987.

————. "The Scholar-Official as a Model for Ethics." *Journal of Chinese Philosophy* 13, no. 2 (June 1986): 185–201.

Ricoeur, Paul. *Symbolism of Evil*. Translated by Emerson Buchanan. Boston: Beacon Press, 1969.

25

The Buddhist-Christian Dialogue Since 1946: The Christian Side

JOHN B. COBB, JR.

OVERVIEW

A Survey

Since World War II there has been an explosion of interest in Buddhism in the West and especially in North America. This has expressed itself in a significant growth of adherence to Buddhist denominations on the part of persons of European extraction, in great advances in the scholarly study of Buddhism in the context of the history of religions, in widespread unsystematic influence on the arts and psychiatry as well as in the counterculture, and to considerable popular interest in Buddhism on the part of persons who continue to identify themselves as Christians. The impact of Buddhism has also contributed to a large number of conferences and books seeking to understand the relation of East and West in general terms.

The effects of Buddhism on the leadership of Christian institutions and thought have been less. Nevertheless, the awareness of Buddhism has been one of the factors forcing the church to reevaluate its exclusivist rhetoric, and a significant number of Western Christian thinkers have shared in the turn to the East for challenge and inspiration.

It is important to recognize that as North American and European Christians seek encounter with Buddhism, they find that a significant amount of dialogue has already taken place in Asia. There have been two major centers of sustained dialogue with Buddhists in the period under review. One is in Sri Lanka and the other in Japan. The most important center in Sri Lanka, for many years directed by the late Lynn A. de Silva, is the Ecumenical Institute for Study and Dialogue in Colombo. This was formerly known as The Study Center for Religion and Society and was sponsored by the National Council of Churches. Today it has an independent board including Catholics. De Silva promoted dialogue with Theravada Buddhists and published, together with the Jesuit Aloysius Pieris, the periodical *Dialogue*. In Japan, Doi Masatoshi shaped the Christian Center for the Study of Japanese Religions in Kyoto into a place of dialogue especially with Mahāyāna Buddhists of the Kyoto school. This center is sponsored by the National Council of Churches in Japan. It has published *Japanese Religions* since 1959. Its contribution to theological dialogue is discussed further in the next section. Over the years Protestant theologians from the West have gone to these two centers to learn about Buddhism and to talk with Buddhist thinkers.

Since Vatican II, Roman Catholics have moved vigorously into theological dialogue in Asia. Indeed, in the past few years they have given leadership in Korea, Taiwan, Thailand, and Hong Kong. In Sri Lanka there is Yulana, Center for Research and Encounter, directed by Aloysius Pieris. But for Catholics the major center has been Japan. The Oriens Institute for Religious Research was founded in 1964 by Joseph Spae. It publishes the *Japan Missionary Bulletin*. In 1969 Heinrich Dumoulin founded the Institute of Oriental Religions at St. Sophia University. Since 1975 its work has been supplemented by the vigorous leadership of the Nanzan Institute for Religion and Culture in Nagoya under the direction of Jan van Bragt, with the assistance of James Heisig. The most important series of books in Christian-Buddhist dialogue is currently ''Nanzan Studies in Religion and Culture.'' Catholic and Protestant Centers are now organized into a Network of Christian Organizations for Interreligious Encounter in Eastern Asia. A newsletter, *Inter-religio,* is published, and representatives meet from time to time.

There has been serious reflection on Christianity and Buddhism in Japan periodically since their meeting in the sixteenth century. The most sustained discussion in the recent period on the part of Japanese Christians has been that of Takizawa Katsumi and Yagi Seiichi. Most of their writings are only in Japanese and are, therefore, not accessible to many Western readers. Takizawa's thought will be introduced in the next section.

As already noted, the theological response to Buddhism in the West is in the context of much wider Western interest. Some parts of this interest require particular notice. First, the work of historians of religion has done much to prepare the way. Although many in this field avoid the central issues of belief and engage instead in specialized historical studies, some have retained their Christian identity and work to draw other Christians into dialogue. In this respect the role of Frederick Streng has been particularly important. His book *Emptiness: A Study of Religious Meaning* has done much to make this central Buddhist idea accessible to Christian theologians and also a profound challenge to them. Other Buddhist scholars in the history of religions category, such as John Berthrong, Julia Ching, Paul Ingram, and Winston King, are also active supporters of, and participants in, dialogue. Such leaders of the discipline of the history of religions as Wilfred Cantwell Smith and Ninian Smart, while not primarily focused on

Buddhism, share with theologians the concern for reformulation of Christian claims in light of a global understanding of the religious traditions.

Second, much of the attention of Christian centers in Asia studying Buddhism is on the social reality of the countries in which they are located. The Interreligious Commission for Development in Thailand and The Christian Study Center on Chinese Religion and Culture in Hong Kong are good examples. The policies of the World Council of Churches encourage this emphasis. Given this focus, they often find the theoretical questions of theologians somewhat remote. Nevertheless, the sociocultural reality of Buddhism is not irrelevant to its more theoretical ideas. Since the question of social-ethical implications of ideas is always important to Christian thinkers, this context of encounter is theologically important.

Third, almost at the opposite extreme from these study centers are the grand visions of the role of religious traditions in world history. Arnold Toynbee and Karl Jaspers have given influential pictures of this sort that accentuate the importance of interaction among the great traditions. Aldous Huxley, Frithjof Schuon, and Houston Smith are among those who find in the mystical or esoteric traditions a unity that underlies all the great religions. This vision, too, has inspired a good deal of the dialogue.

Fourth, although the dominant view of philosophy in North America in the post–World War II period has not encouraged interest in Asian thought, there has still been considerable philosophical dialogue. Beginning in 1939 important "East-West Philosophers Conferences" have been held periodically in Honolulu, resulting in a number of publications. The journal *Philosophy East and West* has continued to promote work in comparative thought. Relevant papers have been produced for many international conferences.

Of special interest here are the more sustained efforts to relate Buddhist thought to particular philosophers of the Western tradition. Affinities between Heidegger and Buddhism were explored at a conference in 1969 on "Heidegger and Eastern Thought," sponsored by the Department of Philosophy of the University of Hawaii. A special issue of *Philosophy East and West* was devoted to these papers.[1] This interest has been developed further by Hans Waldenfels in his book *Absolute Nothingness*. Heinrich Ott has also contributed.[2]

In *Buddhism and American Thinkers*, a collection of essays edited by Kenneth K. Inada and Nolan P. Jacobson, a number of points of contact are discussed. Most of the essays belong to the tradition now called process philosophy, for which the conceptuality of Alfred North Whitehead is of central importance. The relationship to Buddhism (especially Nagarjuna) of Whitehead's thought inspired another conference in Hawaii in 1974, some of whose papers were published in a special issue of *Philosophy East and West*.[3] Interest in the comparison of Whitehead and Buddhism has led to articles by Thomas Altizer, Lewis Ford, David Griffin, Nolan Jacobson, Jay McDaniel, Robert Neville, and Nobuhara Tokiyuki, as well as a book by Steve Odin, *Process Metaphysics and*

Hua-Yen Buddhism.[4] A conference held in Claremont, California, in 1979 considered the fruitfulness of the use of Heidegger and Whitehead for Christian understanding and appropriation of Buddhist thought. Papers from this conference were published in *Japanese Religions*.[5]

There have been scattered comparisons of other Western philosophers to Buddhism. Chris Gŏdmunsen has published a book on the relation of Wittgenstein's philosophy to Buddhism. Yoel Hoffman has compared Buddhist thought to Hume.

Interest in Eastern philosophy among North American philosophers is growing. In the summer of 1984 the Institute for Comparative Philosophy was offered at the University of Hawaii designed to promote integration of Asian thought into standard courses in philosophy. There are signs that, in the future, departments of philosophy in North America may be less parochial in the understanding of their responsibility.

In regard to the response to Buddhism by Western Christians, consider that of missionaries. Most Protestant missionaries to Mahāyāna Buddhist countries saw Buddhism in terms of its popular practice. This appeared superstitious and even idolatrous. The missionaries were not impressed. Since many of the Orientals to whom they spoke also knew Buddhism only in these ways, most of the missionaries were not pushed to reflect seriously on Buddhist wisdom.

But there have long been exceptions. The most interesting is Karl Ludwig Reichelt, who addressed himself especially to serious Buddhists, offering them, first in China and later in Hong Kong, a place to study Christianity and to discuss what they found. Between the world wars his work was successful in drawing a number of Buddhist monks into the Christian faith without rupturing their relation to their Buddhist heritage. A small missionary society in Scandinavia composed of persons influenced by Nathan Sφderblom supported Reichelt and continues to support that kind of approach. Notto Thelle has worked with Doi Masatoshi under the auspices of this society.

In the years here under review the Southern Baptist missionary to Japan, Tucker Callaway, realized the importance of understanding Buddhism at its best. He published extensively on the relation of Buddhism and Christianity. He presented Buddhism appreciatively but nevertheless set it over–against Christianity in such a way as to display the meaning and importance of conversion to Christianity. William P. Woodard established the International Institute for the Study of Religions in Tokyo. In 1960 this institute began publication of *Contemporary Religions in Japan*. The institute continued this work in *Japanese Journal of Religious Studies* edited for a time by David Reid and now by the Nanzan Institute for Religion and Culture. More recent missionary contributors to the dialogue have included Richard Drummond in Japan and Paul Clasper in Hong Kong.

A number of Protestant missionaries in Theravada Buddhist countries have also contributed to the dialogue. Sinclair Thompson at the Protestant Theological Seminary at Chieng-mai was keenly interested in Buddhism. After his untimely death in 1960, a lecture series was established there to carry on his interests. Donald Swearer, who was a missionary in Thailand for several years, has given major leadership in the dialogue. The work of Lynn de Silva in Sri Lanka has already been mentioned.

Catholic missionaries together with monastic communities in the West have shown special interest in Buddhist religious practice. One area of interest has been in monasticism. In 1968 a conference was held on Buddhist and Catholic monasticism in Bangkok. In 1970 monasticism was discussed at a seminar at Oberlin College that included both Buddhist and Christian participants. In 1979 forty-seven Japanese religious practitioners spent about three weeks in European Catholic monasteries. Sponsors included the Nanzan Institute for Religion and Culture and the Institute for Oriental Religions at Sophia University. A book is in progress by Donald Swearer and Patrick Henry, *Betwixt and Between: An Interpretation of Buddhist and Christian Monasticism.*

Even more important for our purposes has been the interest of Catholics, many of them missionaries, in Zen meditation. This topic is treated in the third section, where the interpretations of a missionary, William Johnston, are given attention. Other missionaries who have written extensively on Buddhism, especially Zen, are Enomiya Lassalle, Heinrich Dumoulin, Joseph Spae, Yves Raguin.

Thus far, sustained interest in Buddhism has not been characteristic of the most influential Western Christian theologians. Nevertheless, it is worth noting that the global religious context for understanding Christianity, widely acknowledged in German nineteenth-century Protestant theology, has regained importance after a period of eclipse in the mainstream of Protestant twentieth-century theology. Since Vatican II it is especially prominent in Roman Catholic theology.

Although this concern to understand Christianity in a world-historical context often arises among theologians apart from detailed knowledge of Buddhism, one of the most dramatic moments did involve interaction with Buddhists. Very late in life Paul Tillich journeyed to Doi Masatoshi's Center in Kyoto for dialogue with leading Japanese Buddhists. On his return to the United States Tillich stated that if he had it to do over again, he would organize his whole theology in the context of the global religious situation.

Wolfhart Pannenberg has called for Christian theology to take the form of a universal theology of religions within which the Christian claim can be tested. Although this theological position was crafted in relation to Near Eastern and European history, its systematic intent to deal with the religious traditions of India and China has been clear from the first. Pannenberg has taken the time to visit Japan and to take certain Buddhist ideas seriously.[6]

Especially since Vatican II Hans Küng has also taken the global horizon of theology seriously. He has argued for the salvific effectiveness of traditions other than Christianity and denied that they are superseded by the coming of the church. Recently, he has sought out opportunities for dialogue with Buddhists.

An increasing number of other Western theologians have given sufficient attention to Buddhism in recent years to address features of its thought theologically. Fritz Buri, Heinrich Ott, Langdon Gilkey, George Rupp, Harvey Cox, and John Cobb are among those who have engaged Buddhism directly and seriously. A few have deeply internalized Buddhism without abandoning Christianity. Roger Corless wrote as one who is both Buddhist and Christian. Thomas J. J. Altizer throughout his career has internalized the challenge of Buddhism. His theological program has been extensively shaped thereby.

Whereas in Asia it has been Christians who have institutionalized the dialogue, within North America the leadership has often been with Buddhists. Zen Centers have sponsored dialogues and the Tibetan Buddhist Naropa Institute in Boulder, Colorado, has been particularly active. Among other things, beginning in the summer of 1981 it has hosted annual Conferences on Christian and Buddhist Meditation.

From the Western side the sponsorship of meetings of Buddhist and Christian thinkers has often been by universities. Most of these conferences have not led to permanent structural results. However, a conference in the summer of 1980, sponsored by the Department of Religion of the University of Hawaii, was different. Entitled "East-West Religions in Encounter: Buddhist-Christian Renewal and the Future of Humanity," it led to the establishment of the East-West Religions Project under the leadership of David Chappell, a project that has provided new visibility and status to Buddhist-Christian dialogue in North America. The project publishes *Buddhist-Christian Studies*. It also organized a second conference in January 1984. In conjunction with this second conference, for the first time, a significant group of leading North American systematic theologians engaged a group of Buddhist thinkers in dialogue. This dialogue will continue at subsequent meetings at Vancouver School of Theology in 1985 and at Purdue University in 1986.

Meanwhile, the Europeans have also been active. In June 1981 a conference was held in Austria that attracted leading Buddhists from Sri Lanka and Japan as well as major European theologians. Its theme was "Salvation in Christianity and Buddhism," and its proceedings were published as the third volume in the series "Contributions to the Theology of Religion," edited by Andreas Bsteh.

The Theological Discussion with Mahāyāna in Japan

The most important single stimulus to dialogue with Mahāyāna Buddhists has been the journal *Japanese Religions,* together with the other activities of its publisher, The Christian Center for the Study of Japanese Religions. In May 1961 this journal reported the important exchange between Paul Tillich and some Buddhist thinkers on the occasion of Tillich's visit to Japan. In 1963 it published a brilliant essay by the Zen Buddhist thinker, Abe Masao, on the relation of Buddhism and Christianity. This elicited widespread response. These responses were published in the same journal in 1964 and 1966, together with Abe's reply. This constitutes the first example of published dialogue in the period under review.

Abe Masao first called for a study of Buddhism and Christianity in terms of what they really mean for human life in our time. He sets them against the challenge of irreligion and especially the threat of nihilism. He proceeded to a remarkably sensitive and accurate account of the differences between the Christian understanding of total dependence on God as Absolute Being, known in Jesus Christ as self-giving love, on the one side, and the Buddhist realization of ordinary life in its as-it-is-ness. He shows that these differences can be understood as reflecting two views of nothingness. For Christians nothingness is the threat of nihility and death. For Buddhists Absolute Nothingness is beyond the distinction of such nihility and Being, and it is known in an experience of complete nondiscrimination. In his own evaluations, Abe found Christianity unable to embrace the nihilism associated with modern science, whereas he believed Buddhism can readily do this. On the other hand, he saw that Buddhism does not struggle seriously enough with specific ethical problems.

In subsequent issues of *Japanese Religions* fourteen responses to Abe's article were published, a number of them by Christians. Most of them were written personally to Abe without publication in view, and hence they are not comparable to his essay in scope, rigor, or depth. Nevertheless, they provide a preview of the ongoing dialogue for which they call.

Several of these replies object to Abe's characterizing all Christianity in such a Barthian way. *Creatio ex nihilo* is hardly to be found explicitly in the Bible, and the description of God as Wholly Other is an exaggeration, if not a distortion. Hence, Nels Ferré, for example, argued that the creation of the world is not, as Abe suggested, a self-negation of God but rather an expression of the divine character and intention. Also, Abe pictured science in terms of the mechanistic world view with its accompanying nihilistic implications, whereas many leading scientists are discarding this. Thus the Christian respondents are not willing to accept for themselves quite that formulation of the issues proposed by Abe.

One of the Christian respondents, Paul Wienpahl, sharply distinguished institutional from mystical or experiential Christianity. He objected to Abe's characterization of Christianity in terms of its official doctrines, which Wienpahl has long since rejected. He affirmed, instead, a mystical Christianity, that is in extensive agreement with Buddhism as Abe presented it.

Hans Waldenfels, who alone of the respondents composed his reply for publication, agreed as to the importance of Christian mysticism. But he saw this as integral to the orthodox tradition. He called for a probing of the Christian doctrine of Being, so that it might be freed from its association with beings and seen to direct attention to the same primal reality as that named by Buddhists as Absolute Nothingness. He suggested that, apart from revelation, Absolute Nothingness must indeed be the ultimate for human beings but that in revelation the ultimate manifests itself also as the personal God.

The reply of Winston King is especially well informed and pertinent in raising what continue to be key issues in the dialogue. Like other respondents he found that Abe, influenced by Barth's interpretation, overstated the otherness of God to human beings. King saw in the view of God as personal a relational emphasis, and he feared that the Suchness, to which the Buddhist transcendence of the personal leads, may be more Wholly Other to human beings than the personal God. King suspected that the Buddhist appeal to compatibility with modern science is a matter of superficial absence of conflict more than a profound congeniality with the interests and energies of science, which developed, after all, in Christian soil. He agreed that Buddhism has failed to motivate concern about specific ethical issues, and he doubted that this can be changed by minor adjustments in Buddhist formulations.

The first major conference of leading Buddhists and Christians was held at Oiso in 1967. Much of the credit for the occurrence of this event goes to the Quaker, Douglass Steere, who secured the support and sponsorship of the Friends World Committee for Consultation. The intention was to assemble a small group of Christians (Protestant and Catholic) and Zen Buddhists to live and talk together for five days. They were to share their personal experience and faith. They were not to represent their traditions or to argue for official positions.

This meeting fulfilled its intentions admirably. Without further support from the Friends, the participants decided to meet annually. In 1981 they published *Zen-Christian Pilgrimage: The Fruits of Ten Annual Colloquia in Japan, 1967– 1976*. Even after that, the meetings continued. There can be little doubt that this is the most sustained expression of Buddhist-Christian dialogue that has yet occurred and that it has created a genuine community of mutual understanding and trust.

Following its original guidelines, this dialogue has avoided confrontation and debate. Hence it has not sharpened the issues or worked for collective agreements. Each participant has grown in his (they have all been males) own spiritual understanding and appreciation of the others. There are no formalized "results."

The Japanese Christian who has done most to rethink the relation of Buddhism to Christianity in the period here under review is Takizawa Katsumi. Takizawa studied Western philosophy in Japan without finding there the key to fundamental understanding of the human situation. This he found for the first time in the writings of Nishida Kitarō, the Zen Buddhist philosopher. The key was the identity of the true self with the universal subject. Nishida commended him on his interpretation of Nishida's thought. Takizawa was going to Germany to continue his study of philosophy, but Nishida encouraged him to study theology there instead, specifically with Karl Barth. Takizawa did so and was profoundly moved. Years later he accepted baptism as a Christian without abandoning his basic insight derived from Nishida. Since then he has devoted much of his energy to clarifying the relation of the truth he found through Nishida in Zen and the truth he found through Barth in Christianity.

In Takizawa's view, in the actual human situation the true relation between the universal subject and the individual one is obscured and distorted. The relation is not thereby destroyed. There can be no individual subject that is not in its ultimate depths also the universal one. But the individual posits itself in such a way as falsely to render all else external to it. From this alienation and estrangement it must be rescued by discovery of its true condition. This point is made more clearly in Zen than in Christianity, although it can be found in Christianity as well.

But the restoration of the self to its true reality can only take place from the side of the universal subject. This point is obscured in Zen, which makes it appear that this restoration is an individual human being's attainment through special disciplines, whereas Christianity affirms clearly the priority of grace. Christ is the true unity of God with humanity at the base of all human existence.

Takizawa, accordingly, identified himself as a Christian. But he was critical of much Christian theology, including many who claim to follow Barth, for obscuring the universality of the presence of God in humankind and picturing Jesus not as the true man in whom the universal relation to God is fully realized but as one who held a relation to God peculiar to himself and unavailable to others except through him. Partially because of Takizawa's criticism of many conventional Christological formulations, he was only gradually accepted into the mainstream of Christian theology in Japan.

Since the death of Takizawa in 1984 the mantle of leadership of this radically Buddhized Christianity has fallen on Yagi Seiichi. Yagi studied New Testament at Tokyo University and in Germany, and his dissertation was published as a book that attracted widespread attention. Although this book did not show the influence of Zen Buddhism, Yagi encountered Zen seriously while in Germany and continued this interest on his return to Japan. Takizawa was one of the major critics of Yagi's work, and in the exchange between them Yagi accepted a pattern of thought much like Takizawa's, continuing to relate this to his New Testament studies.

The Catholic Response to Zen Practice

The deepest influence of Buddhism on Christianity thus far has been in the area of meditational practice. The use of Buddhist disciplines, taken especially from Zen, has been widespread in Western monasteries. It is even more developed in Catholic circles in Japan. The most famous locus is the Catholic Zen Center (Akikawa Shinmeikutsu) established by Father Enomiya-Lassalle north of Tokyo. Father K. Kadowaki is now the director. But in addition Catholic nuns are guided in Zen practice by Yamada Roshi in Kamakura and by Father Augustine Oshida in the Japanese Alps. At least one other group sits regularly in Kyoto. Overall the receptivity of Roman Catholics to Buddhist meditational practice is truly remarkable.

Although this phenomenon has no one cause, it cannot be doubted that the leadership of Thomas Merton has been especially important for Catholic openness. Merton is recognized as one of the greatest Christian contemplatives of this century. His study of Buddhism and adoption of Buddhist practice, therefore, legitimized this for many others.

Merton was deeply moved by his encounter with D. T. Suzuki. As a Christian he could not simply accept what Suzuki affirmed. But he recognized both the truth in Suzuki's position and the effectiveness of the Zen practice Suzuki promoted. There was no doubt in Merton's mind that this practice had profound and valuable spiritual consequences. At the same time, he saw that these consequences are not identical with the goal of Christian practice. This recognition of positive value combined with the acknowledgment of difference has set both the theoretical and the practical question for Roman Catholics.

Merton's own answer was to distinguish two phases or movements within Christian mystical experience. The first was the movement to Emptiness, the second, to God. Merton concluded that Buddhist meditation, especially in the form of Zen, was the method for the first of these movements. It is not merely permissible for Christians to appropriate Zen but highly desirable. Merton's seriousness about Buddhism expressed itself in the trip to Asia on which he died in an accident. But however fully Buddhist practice was appropriated, it remained essential, in his view, to remember that beyond the Emptying achieved by Zen there was another stage to be achieved only by the grace of Christ.

This pattern was more problematic for others, especially for those who were closer to the practice of Zen in Japanese Buddhism. Zen masters do not agree that one who has attained Enlightenment might then go on to another stage. Such an idea indicates clearly to them that the practitioner has not understood the true meaning of Enlightenment. They are glad for persons who are not Buddhists to practice Zen, and for the most part they hold that Zen is in principle something universal and not bound to Buddhist conceptuality and culture. But the results they expect from the practice are in conflict with orthodox Christian teaching. For example, the otherness of the Creator to the creature experientially disappears in Enlightenment. Worship, trust, and devotion cease to be appropriate.

Christians have responded in several ways. Aelred Graham, in *Zen Catholicism,* held that Zen is in fact neutral with respect to the structure of beliefs and attitudes. It is an aid to the deepening of faith and understanding in whatever context it is used. For him the use of Zen in Catholic spirituality is simply the adoption of helpful techniques for a meditation that is not otherwise affected.

Kadowaki Kakichi has had a much deeper experience of Zen as this is understood among Japanese Buddhists. There, for example, the bodily posture is extremely important, whereas for Merton this was incidental. Zen, Kadowaki taught, involves the whole body in a way that Western meditational disciplines have not. In this respect, it offers Christians a major advance in spirituality. On the other hand, Kadowaki did not believe that the outcome of Zen practice is unaffected by the unconscious beliefs and attitudes of the practitioner. The outcome among Buddhists does indeed confirm and strengthen Buddhist ways of understanding and experience. For Christians to practice Zen brings to the practice a different set of beliefs and attitudes. Kadowaki recommended strengthening these things by reading the Bible immediately before sitting. This reinforces the Christian content of the unconscious and thereby orients the effects of Zen practice.

Kadowaki thus took an intermediate position with respect to the neutrality of Zen. It can be adapted for use in diverse traditions and is in this respect neutral. But wherever it is used, it breaks through the dualism of mind and body. Also, the Zen experience gives one fresh insight not only into life but also into Christian Scriptures.

The person who has wrestled most extensively with these questions is William Johnston. He, too, has been deeply affected by his own Zen practice and is convinced that this practice with the specific techniques developed by its Buddhist masters has powerful effects that Christians need. In his book *Christian Zen* he strongly advocated the use of Zen by Christians.

In this book he dealt with the questions of God and Christ. He argued, however, that the deepest understanding of God and of Christ is not in conflict with the overcoming of dualism that is effected by Zen practice, and he appealed to the Christian mystics in support. Indeed, insofar as Zen enabled Christians to let go of their *concepts* of God and of Christ and their dualistic habits of mind, it strengthens their true faith.

On the other hand, Johnston did not suppose that the practice of Zen should replace all other forms of Christian spiritual life. Indeed, he himself testified to a powerfully transforming pentecostal experience in a meeting with Catholic charismatics. This, too, he saw as a form of Enlightenment, and he suggested that some combination of Zen sitting and charismatic activity may provide a way ahead for a church that has almost lost its ability to guide its people into the mystical life.

In his more recent writings Johnston's focus has been on mysticism as understood in the West, especially by St. John of the Cross. The emphasis is on love and the life of feeling. This has not turned Johnston away from Zen. First, he found that love mysticism is achieved in the East as well. Second, he continued to find in Zen practice a preparation for the mystical experience that is of great value to Christians. Zen offers methods for the control of the mind, the control of breathing, and the control of the body that are invaluable. But for Johnston the goal was that we be consumed by the flame of love of God.

The Christian Dialogue with Theravada

The vigor of the Christian dialogue with Mahāyāna has been due in part by the forcefulness of its dialogue partners. D. T. Suzuki spent many years as a pioneer missionary for Zen Buddhism in the United States. Through his lectures and writings he made an extraordinary impact. Japanese Buddhists, beginning with Nishida Kitarō, have dealt aggressively and thoroughly with the intellectual traditions of the West and have reformulated their own tradition so as to address the issues raised in the European one. Their readiness for systematic discussion cannot be questioned. Furthermore, the meditational disciplines, especially of Zen, have flourished in this century and have had an important appeal to Westerners. More recently, the considerable Zen mission in North America has been supplemented by a Tibetan one. In view of all this, a Christian response has been obviously needed.

There is nothing comparable to this with respect to Theravada Buddhists. There are some Theravada teachers now in North America, and some Theravada monks in south Asia have addressed themselves to the discussion with Christianity. Notable in this respect is the Thai monk Buddhadasa. But few have devoted themselves to the mastery of the Western traditions, and few seek dialogue. The initiative is more fully in the hands of Christians.

In addition to noting the writings of Donald Swearer and Lynn de Silva, who were mentioned in the first section, we will consider also the book of Sri Lankan monk Antony Fernando, who has done much to renew interest in Buddhism among Sri Lankan Catholics. Most of Fernando's book *Buddhism and Christianity: Their Inner Affinity* is written as an explanation of the Four Noble Truths for Christians. He presented them as a practical guide to human maturation, and he demonstrated the psychological wisdom that they embody. In his account the mysteriousness of Mahāyāna Emptiness or Absolute Nothingness plays no role. Instead, Nirvana becomes a way of identifying human maturity conceived as liberation from harmful passions. Similarly, the Buddha's teaching of no-self is not understood as a denial of separate and responsible individual selves but as the denial of the reality of that false self-image that plays so large a role in human psychology.

Fernando strongly recommended to Christians the wisdom of the Buddha's teaching. He noted that Christianity provides far less clarity about how people are to attain liberation from those attitudes and emotions that block maturation. But he is sure that this is the goal for Christian life as much as for Buddhist life.

In dealing with the problem of Buddha's rejection of belief in God, Fernando pointed out that both Buddha and Christ turned attention from speculative beliefs to practical matters. Both saw that what is truly needed is fullness of life. Fernando argued that the practical meaning of authentic belief in God for Christians is harmonious with the Buddha's teaching about the mature life.

Donald Swearer also presented Theravada ideas appreciatively and commended them to Christians. In his case, however, the recommendation is that Christians rethink and deepen traditional Christian beliefs in response to these ideas. For example, Christianity understands that this world will pass away. But the Buddhist teaching of impermanence and conditionality is far more rigorously developed. The encounter with this teaching can enable Christians to understand their own doctrines more profoundly.

Especially important is the Buddhist doctrine of *anatta,* or no-self. Swearer found three dimensions in this. First, it is a way of rejecting metaphysical interest in the self. Second, it undercuts attachment. Third, and most important, it points to a radical change in which the ordinary self is extinguished and something new comes into being. This can illuminate the Christian doctrine of new creation in Christ, of becoming truly a new self.

The pattern of de Silva's dialogue with Theravada is similar. He, too, believed that the nihility of the world in and by itself, implied by the Christian doctrine of *creatio ex nihilo,* is more powerfully expressed in the Buddhist teaching of *anicca, dukkha,* and *anatta* than in the usual Christian formulations. But he argued that when this nihility is fully understood, it follows that there can be no possibility from within it for salvific work. It is the Christian understanding of God's gift that is called for and that completes the Buddhist analysis of the nihility of the world. Thus both Buddhism and Christianity are enriched through their interaction.

To the doctrine of the self de Silva has devoted his most important book. There he pointed out that the biblical idea of the human being as constituted of *psyche* and *sarx* is much more like the Buddhist analysis of *nama-rupa* than like that of the immortal soul clothed with a mortal body that has become confused with it in Western Christianity. Hence the *anatta* idea is appropriate to the biblical understanding. But the Bible adds the idea of *pneuma,* which is not a possession of human beings but a gift of God. Through *pneuma* people are related to one another and to God and attain full personality. This supplements and completes the *anatta* doctrine but does not contradict it. Fuller incorporation of the Buddhist teaching within Christianity would help the latter avoid the false doctrine of the immortal soul, encourage an appropriate nonattachment to the things of the world, and help to overcome self-centeredness.

SYSTEMATIC REFLECTIONS

The Relation of Christianity to Buddhism

The discussion in the first part of this chapter has focused on those Christians who have been most open to dialogue with Buddhists and most involved in it. At times they have felt themselves to be straining at the limits of what their church's teachings have allowed. On the whole, however, resistance in the churches has declined, and dialogue is approved. But on the question of the rationale of dialogue, its purpose, and the implications for the understanding of the relation of Christianity to Buddhism, there is considerable diversity.

One function of dialogue can be to clarify issues so that the meaning and importance of conversion to Christianity can become clearer. However, this is not the primary viewpoint. More characteristic is the view that Christianity is the fulfillment of other traditions. In that case, it is only by understanding these traditions in their fullness that Christianity can be reformulated so as to present itself responsibly as their fulfillment. This was Reinelt's program in the 1930s. It is that of de Silva in recent years. Here there is genuine openness to learning from Buddhism and being transformed by that learning. The Christianity that would fulfil Buddhism must be different from that which has been inherited from the Western tradition. The value for Christians of this transformation is independent of its effectiveness in the conversion of Buddhists. It is especially important for the indigenization of Christianity in predominantly Buddhist countries. Sometimes the motive of conversion of the dialogue partner recedes far into the background.

The World Council of Churches has generally proposed a sharp separation of dialogue from interest in conversion. This is not merely a response to the resistance of representatives of other traditions to enter dialogue where the goal of their conversion is present. It is also because the dominant understanding of dialogue in the council is different. Its official statements have set dialogue in the context of common humanity and common concern for the world. It is not then an interaction about beliefs and religious practices. It is motivated by the urgency of cooperation in dealing with the needs of the entire community and of overcoming prejudices that conceal the humanity of those whose faith and practice differ. The official teaching of the council does not recognize that Christians have anything to learn about salvation from representatives of other traditions.

Traditional Protestant teaching encourages this reluctance on the part of the council. Even when it is admitted personally that the Christians involved in dialogue have learned something of spiritual importance from their partners, the inclination is to state that what has been learned was already present in the Christian tradition, only forgotten or obscured. The reason is that Protestants have long confessed the all-sufficiency of Scripture with respect to what has to do with salvation.

In view of this difficulty, many propose that Christians enter into dialogue without preconceptions of what is to be gained beyond the deepening of human ties. They encourage Christians to learn to worship with others as an expression of their common humanity. Through engagement they believe that a new situation will emerge, which is blocked when theological doctrines are placed at the center. Others, however, fear that this is the route to a syncretism that is incompatible with the Christian faith.

Wolfhart Pannenberg has proposed an understanding of the relations among the religious traditions that moves beyond these alternatives. The Christian Scriptures witness to the eschatological fullness that can be known now only in anticipation. John's gospel promises that the Spirit will lead Christians into new truth. Hence there are good scriptural reasons for arguing that Christians are especially faithful when they are open to what is new to them. Pannenberg has described Christian superiority to other traditions precisely in these terms. Christianity is uniquely able to assimilate the wisdom of other traditions because it is not bound to its past formulations.

Whether Christianity is indeed superior to all other traditions in this respect need not be determined now. But that the orientation of Christians to a future fullness is grounds for openness to all that can be learned today is sound Christian theology. It justifies and corresponds with the practice of those who give leadership today in dialogue with Buddhists.

This approach, which seems difficult for Protestants to accept fully, is much closer to official Catholic teaching. This helps to explain the remarkable openness among Catholics to the appropriation of meditational practices that are derived from Zen. Among Catholic thinkers the question is more whether it is necessary to assume the ultimate superiority of the Christian faith or whether dialogue can be pursued on a basis of full equality.

God and Emptying

As long as the topics on which learning from other traditions takes place do not go to the heart of the kerygma, or the creeds, Christians generally are not deeply disturbed. But most assume that there is a core or kernel or essence that cannot be altered without the abandonment of faith itself. Whether or not one accepts this essentialist view, there are certainly aspects of the Christian faith that are so overwhelmingly important to Christians today that their rejection would be a profound and unacceptable breach. At the heart of all this is belief in God. Hence the most disturbing feature of the meeting with Buddhism is the encounter with assertions that seem to deny the reality of the Christian God.

This is both the most complex and the most distinctive feature of the dialogue of Christians with Buddhists, especially with Mahāyāna Buddhists. In dialogues with Jews and Muslims there can be heated debates about the Incarnation and the Trinity, but the attack on these doctrines is based on the unity of the one God that Christians worship along with Jews and Muslims. In dealing with Hindus there are greater complexities, but most Hindus find the idea of God both meaningful and important. Even in Confucian tradition there are quasi-theistic notions with which the word *God* can be connected. But in most of Buddhism the Christian encounters a profoundly religious tradition whose practitioners declare themselves free from any idea of God and who celebrate that freedom as part of the final liberation.

The first inclination of Christian theologians in this encounter is to assure Buddhists that they do not subscribe to any of the anthropomorphic ideas of gods associated with popular piety in both East and West. Especially among Catholics, the appeal is to *esse,* the act of being, or Being Itself. God as Being Itself lies beyond all images and conceptualities associated with the deity in Scripture and tradition.

There is no doubt that this move brings the discussants closer together. But it does not solve the problem. As Buddhists listen to Christian explanations, they sense that Being stands out of and over–against a nothingness that Christians fear and seek to overcome. Although they do not want to identify Emptying with this dreaded annihilation, they are equally opposed to identifying it with Being. Emptying encompasses and transcends both Being and nothingness, and it is beyond the distinction between them. As long as Christians cling to Being, they are blocked from the enlightenment that comes through the realization that there is neither Being nor nothingness, only an Emptying that is at the same time always an Emptying of Emptying.

Christians are usually confused by this Buddhist radicalism. The move from beings to Being has seemed to them already the move to Ultimate Reality. They often feel that the effort to go beyond Being must be based on a misunderstanding of what they are saying, a confusion of Being with a being. Some respond by attempting to appropriate to Being the self-negation that the Buddhist requires. But in doing so they are in danger of cutting the last cord that connects Being Itself to the God of the Bible. Others respond by viewing Buddhism as really different—as focusing on Nothing instead of Being—and they reaffirm their Christian faith as an affirmation of the world rather than its negation. But dialogue with Buddhists makes it very difficult to retain the image of Buddhism as in any simple sense world negating.

Protestants are less accustomed than Catholics to identifying God with Being. This seems to many to threaten the personal character of God and God's relation to the world. Nevertheless, they, too, are prepared to recognize that God is far more than we can ever say or think. God is Ultimate Reality whereas all our language and thoughts are shaped in our experience of creatures. Hence Protestants can stress the radical transcendence of God over us and over all that we can know. On this basis they can prepare themselves to listen to what is learned of Ultimate Reality through the very different experience of Buddhists.

One way of conceptualizing this situation has been developed by John Hick. He proposed that we employ the distinction between noumenon and phenomenon. The noumenal reality of God is wholly beyond our grasp. But this God is present in and for human experience in many ways. To some, God appears personal; to others, impersonal. We could add that to some, God appears as Being; to some, as Emptying of Being. Hence in opening ourselves to the testimony of Buddhists, we learn more not of God's noumenal reality but of how God appears in and for human experience.

However, this approach also finds its severest challenge in the encounter with Buddhism. Although Buddhists agree that ordinary experience does not give us the true reality, this reality is not in principle beyond all human experience. Indeed, it *is* human experience when that experience is enlightened. Precisely when one realizes what is, as it is, namely as Emptying, one *is* "ultimate reality." This cannot be interpreted as one among many appearances of a noumenal reality that is beyond all experience.

Christians can dispute the Buddhist understanding of Buddhist experience. As they concede the relativity of their own experience, they feel they have the right to affirm the relativity of the Buddhist experience as well. But this does not lead to the common ground that is being sought in this way. Instead, it involves a flat denial of the heart of Buddhist self-understanding. This violates the intention of those who adopt this approach.

The frustration felt by Christians in their effort to conceptualize the relation of the Christian God and Buddhist Emptying leads some to urge that shared experience and not doctrine is the way ahead to mutual understanding. This approach is highly congenial to Buddhists. They gladly welcome Christians to share in their meditational disciplines. But the difficulties are not thereby resolved. Expectation and interpretation color experience. There is a connection between Buddhist meditation and Buddhist understanding that is not dissipated by the insistence that one need not reject one's Buddhist loyalties and beliefs in order to begin the practice.

God and Amida

The dialogue thus far has been primarily with Japanese Zen and secondarily with Theravada. In these movements the rejection of theism is clear. But much of popular Mahāyāna Buddhist practice and thought, especially in Japan, is shaped by the Pure Land tradition. Here the situation is different.

Pure Land Buddhism is often viewed as a concession to those who are incapable of pursuing the difficult disciplines of enlightenment. It is grounded in the conviction that the compassion of those who have attained Enlightenment extends to all—even to miserably lazy and sinful human beings. Since with Enlightenment there comes not only compassion but also great power, Buddhism developed legends of what these Buddhas have done to aid ordinary people. The usual form of these stories centers around the Buddha's vow not to enter Nirvana except as this becomes possible for all. This possibility is envisioned in terms of the creation of Pure Land or heaven. Whereas in our present world the attainment of Enlightenment is exceedingly difficult, in the Pure Land it is extremely easy. All that is required to be reborn after death is the meeting of the minimal conditions specified by the Buddha. Against this general background, there developed the legend that one Buddha, Dharmakara, had exceeded all others in such a way that the many vows, the many Pure Lands, and the many conditions were all superseded by his. This Buddha, known as Amitabha or, in Japan, as Amida has been the center of Pure Land Buddhist faith.

For the most part, both Buddhists and Christians have seen this as a pious myth. Even in the Pure Land tradition sophisticated scholars tend to depreciate it and reinterpret it in the direction of Zen. But another line of development is possible.

There is a long tradition in Buddhism of the three Buddha-bodies. There is the *Dharmakaya,* which is identified with Emptying, and which has been chiefly in view in the dialogue with Zen. There is the *Nirmanakaya,* which is the human body of an Enlightened One. There is also the *Sambhogakaya,* which is the cosmic Buddha body, characterized by wisdom and compassion. Amida has been identified with this. The Buddha's vow is then an embodiment of the wisdom and compassion that characterize the Sambhogakaya. It is this everlasting wisdom and compassion that ordinary mortals can and must trust for salvation, since apart from that they can contribute nothing at all. Along these lines, the thirteenth-century Japanese reformer Shinran developed Buddhism into an affirmation of justification by grace through faith alone.

Although the dominant pressure on Shinran's thoughtful followers has been to minimize the divergence of his thought from mainstream Buddhism, the presence of Pure Land within Buddhism provides an alternative point of contact for the Christian encounter. To bring Pure Land back into the Buddhist main-stream it has been customary to interpret faith or trust as itself a kind of practice associated with the *Nembutsu,* the calling on the name of Amida Buddha. The attainment of perfect sincerity in faith becomes analogous to the attainment of perfect Emptiness through meditation. It thus becomes very difficult and uncer-tain. But other scholars point out that this interpretation runs counter to Shinran's intentions, which are remarkable in their resemblance to those of Martin Luther three centuries later. For Shinran's intentions to be realized, the emphasis must be placed on the "other-power" and its gracious activity. This has, in Christian ears, a strongly theistic connotation. Hence there does seem to be an important strand of Buddhism in which what Christians mean by God is acknowledged and affirmed.

Here, too, there are differences. Amida is not understood as creator in any traditional Christian sense. One does not petition Amida to influence the course of history. Indeed, Amida is not thought of as hearing prayers. Belief in Amida is not associated with the coming of a New Age on earth. Nevertheless, the Christian cannot but recognize God in the one who works salvifically in the hearts of all and whose effectiveness both generates faith and is implemented by faith. The Christian and the believer in Amida can share their witness to grace, confident that it is one and the same Gracious One to whom they witness to grace, confident that it is one and the same Gracious One to whom they witness.

The doctrine of the Sambhogakaya is standard Mahāyāna Buddhism as is the attribution to this Buddha-body of wisdom and compassion. Hence a theistic element can be found throughout Mahāyāna Buddhism. But in Zen and some other traditions the Sambhogakaya is strongly subordinated to the Dharmakaya. This subordination entails that the experience of what-is as having the charac-teristics of wisdom and compassion is en route to the still deeper and truer experience of what-is as beyond all characteristics whatsoever. In this way the theistic experience is seen as less fundamental, less ultimate. Since Christians cannot accept the subordination of God to anything more ultimate, they have generally focused on the Dharmakaya rather than on the Sambhogakaya/Amida as the locus of "God" in Buddhism.

The alternative approach appears more promising. There are Buddhists who oppose the subordination of Amida to the Dharmakaya, that is, of God to pure Emptying. They do not deny reality to the Dharmakaya, but both theoretically and practically they deny to it a reality superior to that of the Sambhogakaya. Christians can enter the dialogue with Buddhists in support of this denial.

The claim of the superior reality of the Dharmakaya is based on the assumption that what is beyond all characteristics is more ultimate than what has character. This superiority is affirmed both experientially and metaphysically. Experientially, it means that the highest experience is one that realizes what-is, stripped of all characteristics whatsoever, even wisdom and compassion. To challenge this is to question whether in fact such experience ever occurs or whether, if it does, it is better than the experience of divine grace. Metaphysically, the argument for the superiority of the Dharmakaya is that it is more ultimate in its reality. But this may be countered by the question whether such a characterless reality is not an aspect or an element of a reality with character that is in fact the concrete actuality. One need not argue for the superior reality of the Sambhogakaya—only against the doctrine of its inferiority. In Christian terms, God is not subordinate to Godhead, and faith in God is not inferior to the mystical realization of Godhead.

NOTES

1. *Philosophy East and West* 20, no. 3 (July 1970): entire issue.
2. Heinrich Ott, "The Beginning Dialogue between Christianity and Buddhism, the Concept of 'Dialogical Theology,' and the Possible Contribution of Heideggerian Thought," *Japanese Religions* 11, nos. 2–3 (September 1980): 77–112. (Notes are provided only when the reference is not included in the bibliography.)
3. *Philosophy East and West* 25, no. 4 (October 1975): entire issue.
4. Jay McDaniel, "Mahayana Enlightenment in Process Perspective," in Kenneth Inada and Nolan P. Jacobson, eds., *Buddhism and American Thinkers* (Albany, N.Y.: SUNY Press, 1984), pp. 50–69; idem, "Christianity and Buddhism in Mutual Transformation," in G. W. Houston, ed., *Dharma and Gospel* (Delhi: Indian Book Center, 1984), pp. 70–90; Nobuhara Tokiyuki, "Whitehead and Nishida on Time," *Japanese Religions* 12, no. 2 (July 1982): 47–64; 12, no. 3 (December 1982): 41–50; idem, "A Christian Interpretation of the Four Noble Truths," in Houston, *Dharma and Gospel,* pp. 53–69.
5. *Japanese Religions* 11, nos. 2–3 (September 1980): enter issue.
6. Wolfhart Pannenberg, "Auf der Suche nach dem wahren Selbst," in Andreas Bsteh, ed., *Erlösung in Christentun und Buddhismus* Mödling, Austria: St. Gabriel, 1982), pp. 128–146.

SELECTED BIBLIOGRAPHY

Compiled by Sandra S. MacNevin and Jean L. Cobb

This bibliography is limited to books and articles in the European languages published since 1946. English-language translations are listed when available. It aims at thorough coverage of what has been written from the explicitly Christian perspective. It includes selected items that are neutrally comparative or relate Buddhism to Western philosophies instead of to Christian theology. Part I of this bibliography lists journals and collections of essays in book form; they contain scores of relevant articles. However, they are not included in the general bibliography that constitutes Part II. Bibliographies consulted in the compilation of this one were Joseph J. Spae's "A Buddhist-Christian Encounter Bibliography," in *Buddhist-Christian Empathy* (Chicago: The Chicago Institute of Theology and Culture, 1980), pp. 245–252; David G. Hackett's select bibliography "The Christian-Buddhist Encounter" (April 1979), Program for the Study of New Religious Movements in America, Graduate Theological Union, Berkeley, California; "A Bibliography of Books and Articles on Buddhism and Christianity," *The Northeast Asia Journal of Theology* 20–21 (March-September 1978): 94–110; a bibliography by Paul F. Knitter in Richard W. Rousseau, ed., *Christianity and the Religions of the East* (Scranton, Pa.: Ridge Row Press, 1982), pp. 108–110; Raymond Facelina's "Christianism and Religions" (International Bibliography, 1972–1974, in *RIC Supplement* 13 (Strasbourg: Cerdic Publications, 1974); and "Bibliography on World Mission and Evangelism," compiled by The Scottish Institute of Missionary Studies, *International Review of Missions*, 1972–July 1984. Spae refers to a bibliography of writings in Japanese and English by Mineshima Hideo, ed., in *Jōdokyō to Kirisutokyō* (Tokyo: Sankibobusshorin, 1977).

Part I

There are four journals extensively devoted to dialogue materials.

Dialogue, published thrice annually by the Ecumenical Institute for Study and Dialogue, Colombo, Sri Lanka.

Japanese Religions, published semiannually by the National Christian Council Center for the Study of Japanese Religions, Kyoto, Japan.

Philosophy East and West, published quarterly by the University of Hawaii, Honolulu, Hawaii.

Buddhist-Christian Studies, published annually by the East–West Project at the University of Hawaii, Honolulu, Hawaii.

In addition there are collections of relevant essays.

Bsteh, Andreas, ed. *Erlösung in Christentum und Buddhismus.* Mödling, Austria: St. Gabriel, 1982.

Geffré, Claude, and Mariasusa Dhavamony, eds. *Buddhism and Christianity.* New York: Seabury Press, 1979.

Gomez, Fausto, ed. *Asian Religious Traditions and Christianity.* Manila: The Faculty of Theology, University of Santo Tomas, 1983.

Houston, G. W., ed. *Dharma and Gospel.* Delhi: Indian Book Center, 1984.

Inada, Kenneth, and Nolan P. Jacobson, eds. *Buddhism and American Thinkers,* Albany, N.Y.: SUNY Press, 1984.

Ingram, Paul, and Frederick Streng, eds. *Buddhist-Christian Dialogue: Mutual Renewal and Transformation.* Honolulu: University of Hawaii Press, 1986.

Katz, Nathan, ed. *Buddhism and Western Philosophy.* Atlantic Highlands, N. J.: Humanities Press, 1981.

Pye, Michael, and Robert Morgan, eds. *The Cardinal Meaning: Essays in Comparative Hermeneutics: Buddhism and Christianity.* The Hague: Mouton, 1973.

Rousseau, Richard W., ed. *Christianity and the Religions of the East: Models for a Dynamic Relationship.* Scranton, Pa.: Ridge Row Press, 1982.

Samartha, Stanley J., ed. *Dialogue in Community: Statements and Reports of a Theological Consultation*. Geneva: World Council of Churches, April 18–27, 1977.

Samartha, Stanley J., and Lynn de Silva, eds. *Man in Nature: Guest or Engineer? A Preliminary Enquiry by Christians and Buddhists into the Religious Dimensions in Humanity's Relation to Nature*. Colombo: Ecumenical Institute for Study and Dialogue; with Geneva: World Council of Churches, 1979.

Slater, Peter, and Donald Wiebe, eds. *Traditions in Contact and Change*. Waterloo, Ont.: Wilfrid Laurier University Press, 1983.

Waldenfels, Hans, ed. *Begegnung mit dem Zen-Buddhismus*. Dusseldorf: Patmos, 1980.

Yagi, Seiichi, and Ulrich Luz, eds. *Gott in Japan*. Munich: Kaiser, 1973.

A Zen Christian Pilgrimmage: The Fruits of Ten Annual Colloquia in Japan, 1967–1976. Tokyo: The Zen-Christian Colloquium, 1981.

Part II

Abbott, Walter M., ed. *The Documents of Vatican II*. London: Chapman, 1966.

Abegg, Lily. *Ostasien denkt anders*. Zurich: Atlantis, 1949.

Aldwinkle, Russell F. "Jesus or Gotama?" In Russell F. Aldwinkle, ed., *More Than Man: A Study in Christology*. Grand Rapids, Mich.: Eerdmans, 1976, pp. 211–246.

Alles, Gregory D. " 'When Men Revile You and Persecute You': Advice, Conflict, and Grace in Shinran and Luther." *History of Religions* 25, no. 2 (1985): 148–162.

Altizer, Thomas, J. J. "Buddhist Ground of the Whiteheadian God." *Process Studies* 5 (Winter 1975): 227–236.

———. *Oriental Mysticism and Biblical Eschatology*. Philadelphia: Westminster Press, 1961.

———. "Stanley Romaine Hopper's 'The "Eclipse of God" and Existential Mistrust.' " *The Eastern Buddhist*, n.s. 4, no.1 (1971): 158–161.

Amore, Roy C. *Two Masters, One Message: The Lives and Teachings of Gautama and Jesus*. Nashville, Tenn.: Abingdon Press, 1978.

Amore, Roy C., and J. Elrod. "From Ignorance to Knowledge: A Study in the Kierkegaardian and Theravada Buddhist Notions of Freedom." *Union Seminary Quarterly Review* 26 (Fall 1970): 59–79.

Anatriello, Pasquale. "Buddismo ed origini del Cristianesimo." *Neue Zeitschrift für Missionswissenschaft* 31, no.4 (1975): 229–303.

Antes, Peter, Werner Rueck, and Bernhard Uhde. *Islam, Hinduismus, Buddhismus: Eine Herausforderung des Christentums*. Mainz: Matthias-Grünewald, 1973.

Appleton, George. "Challenge of Buddhism." *Modern Churchman*, n.s. 2 (October 1958): 84–95.

———. *The Christian Approach to the Buddhist*. London: Lutterworth Press, 1958.

———. *On the Eightfold Path: Christian Presence amid Buddhism*. London: SCM Press, 1961.

Ariga, T. "Christian-Buddhist Encounter." *Frontier* 4 (Spring 1961): 50–54.

Ashby, Philip H. *History and Future of Religious Thought: Christianity, Hinduism, Buddhism, Islam*. Englewood Cliffs, N.J.: Prentice-Hall, 1963.

Baker-Batsel, John D. "Western Interpretations of Eastern Religions, I: Buddhism," *American Theological Library Association Proceedings* 39 (1985): 171–189.

Bakker, J. W. N. "Interreligious Dialogue in Indonesia." *Bulletin Secretariatus pro Non-Christianis* 9, no. 1 (1974): 20–26.

Balasuriya, T. "Christian-Buddhist Dialogue in Ceylon." *Bulletin Secretariatus pro Non-Christianis* 11 (4,2) (1969): 130–135.

Balchand, Asandas. *The Salvific View of Non-Christian Religions according to Asian Christian Theologians Writing in Asian-Published Theological Journals, 1965–1970*. Manila: East Asian Pastoral Institute, 1973.

Barksdale, John O. "Yagi and Takizawa—Bultmann vs. Barth in Japan." *Japan Missionary Bulletin* 24 (1970): 38–43, 93–100, 193–200, 215–222.

Benz, Ernst, and M. Nambara. "L'idée de la paix dans le dialogue actuel entre Bouddhisme et Christianisme en Asie." *Le Monde Non-Chrétien* 79–80 (1966): 22–35.

Berrigan, Daniel, and Thich Nhat Hanh. *The Raft Is Not the Shore: Conversations toward a Buddhist-Christian Awareness*. Boston: Beacon Press, 1975.

Berthrong, John. "Trends in Contemporary Buddhist-Christian Dialogue." *Ecumenical Trends* 14, no. 9 (October 1985): 135–137.

Besnard, Albert-Marie. "Pratique du zen et foi chrétienne." *La Maison-Dieu* 109 (1972): 152–153.

Béthune, Pierre-François. "Two Patriarchs of Monasticism: Benedict and Bodhidharma." *Bulletin Secretariatus pro Non-Christianis* 16, no. 1 (1981): 23–39.

Bischoff, F. A. "Eine buddhistische Wiedergabe christlicher Brauche: Glanzvolles Manifest genanntes Sutra." *Monumenta Serica* 20 (1961): 282–310.

Bjørk, Anne-Brit. "Misjon blant buddhister-hvorfor det? Den nordiske Østasiamisjon i fortid og natid." *Norsk Tidsskrift for Misjon* 32, no. 1 (1978): 21–33.

Bloom, Alfred. "Biblical Faith as a Zen Koan." *Christian Century* 89 (July 19, 1972): 774–775.

Bocking, Brian. "Comparative Studies of Buddhism and Christianity." *Japanese Journal of Religious Studies* 10 (March 1983): 87–110.

Bond, George D. "History and Interpretation in Theravada Buddhism and Christianity." *Encounter* 39 (Autumn 1978): 405–434.

Bowker, John. *Problems of Suffering in Religions of the World*. London: Cambridge University Press, 1970.

Boyd, James W. "Buddhas and the Kalyana-mitta." *Studia Missionalia* 21 (1972): 57–76.

———. *Satan and Mara: Christian and Buddhist Symbols of Evil*. Leiden: Brill, 1975.

Braybrooke, M. *Faiths in Fellowship*. London: The World Congress of Faiths, 1976.

Brinton, Howard Haines. *The Religious Philosophy of Quakerism*. Wallingford, Pa.: Pendle Hill Publications, 1973.

Brunner, Emil. "Zwischen Buddhismus und Christentum: Wohin führt Japans Weg." *Christ und Welt* 9, no. 6 (1970).

Bruns, J. Edgar. "Ananda: The Fourth Evangelist's Model for the Disciple Whom Jesus Loved?" *Studies in Religion/Sciences Religieuses* 3 (1973–1974): 236–243.

———. *The Art and Thought of John*. New York: Herder and Herder, 1969.

———. *The Christian Buddhism of St. John: New Insights into the Fourth Gospel*. New York: Paulist Press, 1971.

Bu, Maung Hla. "Christian Encounter with Buddhism in Burma." *International Review of Missions* 47 (April 1958): 171–177.

"Buddismo e Cristianesimo. Un dialogo? Oltre i luoglie comuni." *La Missioni dei Servi di Maria* 56 (1983): 114–119.

Buri, Fritz. "The Concept of Grace in Paul, Shinran, and Luther." *The Eastern Buddhist* n.s. 9, no. 2 (October 1976): 21–42.

————. *Der Buddha-Christus als der Herr des Wahren Selbst: Die Religionsphilosophie der Kyoto-Schule und das Christentum*. Bern: P. Haupt, 1982.

————. "My Encounter with Buddhist Thought in Contemporary Japan." *The Northeast Asia Journal of Theology* 3 (September 1969): 38–53.

————. "The Void and the True Self in the Light of the Problems of Being and Meaning." *Scottish Journal of Religious Studies* 1, no. 2 (1980): 132–137.

Bürkle, Horst. "Hinduistische und Buddhistische Heilswege im Lichte der Christlichen Endzeithoffnung." In W. Strolz and Shizutera Ueda, eds., *Offenbarung als Heilserfahrung im Christentum, Hinduismus und Buddhismus*. Freiburg, W. Ger.: Herder, 1982, pp. 75–96.

Butschkus, Horst. *Luthers Religion und ihre Entsprechung im japanischen Amida-Buddhismus*. Emsdetten, West Germany: Lechte, 1940.

Callaway, Tucker N. *Japanese Buddhism and Christianity*. Tokyo: Shinkyō Shuppansha, 1957.

————. "Selflessness in Buddhism and Christianity." *Japanese Christian Quarterly* 31 (July-October 1965): 193–201, 272–277.

————. *Zen Way, Jesus Way*. Tokyo: Tuttle, 1976.

Camps, Arnulf. "Two Recent Studies on Buddhism and Christianity." In Nils Bloch-Hoell, ed., *Misjonskall og forskerglede*. Oslo: Universitetsforlaget, 1975, pp. 36–47.

Carmody, Denise Lardner, and John Carmody. *Religion: The Great Questions*. New York: Seabury Press, 1983.

Carretto, P. "Dialogue between Christians and Buddhists in Thailand." *Bulletin Secretariatus pro Non-Christianis* 27 (9, 3) (1974): 209–213.

Catholic Church. Secretariatus pro Non-Christianis. *Towards the Meeting with Buddhism*. 2 vols. Rome: Ancora, 1970.

Cheng, Hsueh-li. "Zen, Wittgenstein, and Neo-orthodox Theology: The Problem of Communicating Truth in Zen Buddhism." *Religious Studies* 18 (June 1982): 133–149.

Clasper, Paul D. "Buddhism and Christianity in the Light of God's Revelation in Christ." *South East Asia Journal of Theology* 3 (July 1961): 8–18.

————. *Eastern Paths and the Christian Way*. Maryknoll, N. Y.: Orbis Books, 1980.

————. *The Yogi, the Commissar, and the Third-World Church: Exploring a New Style of Christian Life*. Valley Forge, Pa.: Judson Press, 1972.

Clavier, H. "La Foi, le Merite et la Grace dans les religions d'Extreme-Orient et dans le Christianisme." *Revue d'Histoire et de Philosophie Religieuses* 42, no. 1 (1962): 1–16.

Cobb, John B., Jr. *Beyond Dialogue: Toward a Mutual Transformation of Christianity and Buddhism*. Philadelphia: Fortress Press, 1982.

————. "Buddhism and Christianity: A Dialogue between Drs. John Cobb, Jr., and Seiichi Yagi." *The Northeast Asia Journal of Theology* 20–21 (March-September 1978): 31–52.

————. "Buddhism and Christianity as Complementary." *The Northeast Asia Journal of Theology* 20–21 (March-September 1978): 19–31.

————. "The Buddhist-Christian Dialogue." *Ecumenical Trends* 16, no. 2 (February 1987): 17–19.

————. "Buddhist Emptiness and the Christian God." *Journal of the American Academy of Religion* 45 (March 1977): 11–25.

————. "The Buddhist Witness to God." In Axel D. Steuer and James W. McClendon, eds., *Is God God?* Nashville, Tenn.: Abingdon Press, 1981, pp. 268–286.

————. *Christ in a Pluralistic Age.* Philadelphia: Westminster Press, 1975.

————. "Christianity and Eastern Wisdom." *Japanese Journal of Religious Studies* 5, no. 4 (December 1978): 285–298.

————. "God and Buddhism." In David Tracy and John B. Cobb, Jr., *Talking about God.* New York: Seabury Press, 1983.

Copeland, E. L. "Buddhism and the Christian Faith." *Christianity Today* 4 (December 21, 1959): 14–16

Corless, Roger. *The Art of Christian Alchemy: Transfiguring the Ordinary through Holistic Meditation.* New York: Paulist Press, 1981.

————. *I Am Food: The Mass in Planetary Perspective.* New York: Crossroad, 1981.

Cornelis, Etienne. *Valeurs chretiennes des religions non-chretiennes: Histoire du salut et histoire des religions, Christianisme et Bouddhisme.* Paris: Cerf, 1965.

Cox, Charles H., and Jean W. Cox. "Mystical Experience: With an Emphasis on Wittgenstein and Zen." *Religious Studies* 12 (December 1976): 483–491.

Cox, Harvey. "Japan in Search of Its Soul: Again, the Chrysanthemum and the Sword." *Christianity and Crisis* 38 (October 2, 1978): 225–229.

————. *Turning East: The Promise and Peril of the New Orientalism.* New York: Simon and Schuster, 1977.

Cragg, Kenneth. "Buddhism and Baptism." *Theology* 82 (July 1979): 259–265.

Crowe, Drummond. "Towards Interreligious Dialogue in the Classroom." *East Asian Pastoral Review* 20, no. 2 (1983): 178–195.

Cuttat, Jacques-Albert. "Buddhistische und christliche Innerlichkeit in Guardinis Schau." In H. Kuhn, H. Kahlefeld, and K. Forster, eds. *Interpretation der Welt: Festschrift für Romano Guardini.* Wurzburg: Echter Verlag, 1965, pp. 445–471.

————. *Expérience chrétienne et spiritualité orientale.* Paris: Desclée de Brouwer, 1967.

————. "Fait bouddhique et fait chrétien selon l'oeuvre du Père de Lubac." In *L'Homme devant Dieu: Mélanges offerts au Père Henri de Lubac. Vol. 3: Perspectives d'aujourd'hui.* Paris: Aubier, 1963–1964, pp. 15–41.

————. "Östlicher Advent und gnostische Versuchung." *Kairos* 2 (1960): 145–163.

Cuvelier, André. *Comme une terre desséchée: De la méditation orientale à l'oraison chrétienne,* Paris: Apostolat des éditions, 1972.

Dale, Kenneth J. *Circle of Harmony: A Case Study in Popular Japanese Buddhism with Implications for Christian Mission.* Pasadena, Calif.: William Carey Library Publishers, 1975.

Damboriena, Prudencio. *La Salvación en las religiones no christianas.* Madrid: La Editorial Catolica, 1973.

Danielou, Jean. "Le problème théologique des religions non chrétiennes." *Archivo di filosophia* no. 1 (1956): 214–216.

Davis, Charles. *Christ and the World Religions.* New York: Hodder and Stoughton, 1970.

de Chardin, Teilhard. "L'Apport spirituel de l'Extreme Orient." *Monumenta Nipponica* 12 (1956): pp. 1–11.

de Lubac, Henri. *Amida.* Paris: Seuil, 1955.

————. *Aspects of Buddhism.* Translated by George Lamb. New York: Sheed and Ward, 1954.

————. "Faith and Devotion in Amidism." *Bulletin Secretariatus pro Non-Christianis* 19 (7, 1) (1972): 6–20.

————. *La Rencontre du Bouddhisme et de l'Occident*. Lyons: Aubier, 1952.

Deschâtelets, Léo. "Dialogue avec le bouddhisme lao." *Kerygma* 20 (1973): 68–71.

de Silva, Lynn A., ed., *Buddhism: Beliefs and Practices in Sri Lanka*. Colombo: The Study Center for Religion and Society, 1974.

————. "Buddhist-Christian Dialogue." In Herbert Jai Singh, ed., *Inter-Religious Dialogue: P. D. Devananden*. Bangalore: Christian Institute for the Study of Religion and Society, 1967, pp. 170–203.

————. *Consultation on Buddhist-Christian Encounter*. Colombo: Christian Institute of Buddhist Studies, 1963.

————. *Creation, Redemption, Consummation in Christian and Buddhist Thought*. Chiengmai, Thailand: Thailand Theological Seminary, 1964.

————. *The Problem of Self in Buddism and Christianity*. New York: Barnes and Noble, 1979.

————. "Reflections on Life in the Midst of Death." *Bulletin Secretariatus pro Non-Christianis* 17, no. 2 (1982): 220–229.

————. *Reincarnation in Buddhist and Christian Thought*. Colombo: Study Center for Religion and Society, 1964.

————. "Some Issues in the Buddhist-Christian Dialogue." In Stanley J. Samartha, ed., *Dialogue between Men of Living Faiths*. Geneva: World Council of Churches, 1971, pp. 47–58.

————. *Why Believe in God: The Christian Answer in Relation to Buddhism*. Colombo: Study Center for Religion and Society, 1970.

————. *Why Can't I Save Myself? The Christian Answers in Relation to Buddhist Thought*. Colombo: Study Center for Religion and Society, 1966.

Devananda, Yohan, and Fernando, Sarath. "Dialogue in the Context of Development: A Sri Lankan Experience." *Ecumenical Review* 37: (October 1985) 445–451.

Dhavamony, Mariasusai. *Evangelization, Dialogue, and Development*. Rome: Gregorian University, 1972.

Dialog der Weltreligionen: Begegnung Christentum und Buddhismus: tagung vom 12. bis 14. März 1976 in Bad Boll. Bad Boll, West Germany: Evangelische Akademie, 1976.

Doi, Masatoshi. "Dialogue between Living Faiths in Japan." In S. J. Samartha, ed., *Dialogue between Men of Living Faiths: Papers Presented at a Consultation Held at Ajaltoun, Lebanon, March 1970*. Geneva: World Council of Churches, 1971, pp. 32–46.

————. *Search for Meaning through Interfaith Dialogue*. Tokyo: Kyo Bun Kan, 1976.

————. "Vatican II and Ecumenism." *Japan Christian Quarterly* 33 (Fall 1968): 819–821.

Donnelly, Sally. "Marcel and Buddha: A Metaphysics of Enlightenment." *Journal of Religious Thought* 24, no. 1 (1967–1968): 51–81.

Drummond, Richard H. *Gautama the Buddha: An Essay in Religious Understanding*. Grand Rapids, Mich.: Eerdmans, 1974.

————. "Theological Table-talk: Reflections of a Repatriate." *Theology Today* 31 (1974): 132–139.

————. "Toward a Theological Understanding of Buddhism." *Journal of Ecumenical Studies* 7 (Winter 1970): 1–22.

Dumoulin, Heinrich. "Buddhismus und Christentum: Zu einigen Neuerscheinungen in

Japan." *Zeitschrift für Missionswissenschaft und Religionswissenschaft* 42, no. 3 (1958): 208–217.

———. "Buddhist Spirituality and Mysticism." *Bulletin Secretariatus pro Non-Christianis* 18 (6, 3) (1971): 136–148.

———. *Christianity Meets Buddhism.* Translated by John C. Maraldo. Lasalle, Ill.: Open Court, 1974.

———. *Christlicher Dialog mit Asien.* München: Hueber, 1970.

———. "The Consciousness of Sin and the Practice of Repentance in Japanese Buddhism." *Japan Missionary Bulletin* 29, no.2 (March 1975): 84–92.

———. "Dialog mit dem Buddhismus in Japan." *Die katholischen Missionen.* 90, no. 3 (1971): 76–80.

———. "Die religiose Geistigkeit des fernöstlichen Menschen in Gegenüber mit der westlichen Civilization." In Richard Schwarz, ed., *Menschliche Existenz und modern Welt.* Berlin: Walter de Gruyter, 1967, p. 355.

———. "En dialogue avec le Bouddhisme zen." *Concilium* (French ed.) 29 (1967): 131–147.

———. "The Encounter between Zen Buddhism and Christianity." *Journal of the China Society* 7 (1971): 533–563.

———. "Fragen an das Christentum aus buddhistischer Sicht." *Geist und Leben* 48 (1975): 50–62.

———. "Grace and Freedom in the Way of Salvation in Japanese Buddhism." In R. J. Werblowsky and C. J. Bleeker, eds., *Types of Redemption.* Leiden: Brill, 1970, pp. 98–104.

———. "Lebenswerte im Buddhismus: Wo Christen von Buddhisten lernen Können." *Geist und Leben* 47 (1974): 112–126.

———. *Östliche Meditation und Christliche Mystik.* Munich: Karl Alber, 1966.

———. "Theologische Aspekte des Christlichen Dialogs mit dem Buddhismus." *Zeitschrift für Missionswissenschaft und Religionswissenschaft* 55, no.3 (July 1971): 161–170.

———. "Understanding Other Religions: The Interreligious Dialogue between Buddhism and Christianity in Japan." *Japan Missionary Bulletin* 25, no.7 (1971): 367–376.

———. "The Western View of Zen." *Young East,* Summer 1978, pp. 11–19.

———. *Zen Enlightenment: Origins and Meaning.* New York: Weatherhill, 1979.

———. "Zehn Jahre buddhistisch-christliche Gespräch in Japan." In Manfred Plate, ed., *Engagierte Gelassenheit.* Freiburg, W. Ger.: Herder, 1978. pp. 145–147.

Dumoulin, Heinrich, and John C. Maraldo, eds. *Buddhism in the Modern World.* New York: Macmillan, 1976.

———. "Die Öffnung der Kirche zur Welt: Eine neue Sichtweise des Buddhismus." In Elmar Klinger and Klaus Wittstadt, eds., *Glaube im Prozess: Christsein nach dem II. Vatikanum: für Karl Rahner.* Freiburg, W. Ger.: Herder, 1984, pp. 703–712.

Dunne, Carrin. *Buddha and Jesus: Conversations.* Springfield, Ill.: Templegate Publishers, 1975.

Dunne, John S. *The Way of All Earth.* New York: Macmillan, 1972.

Durckheim, Karlfried Graf von. *The Grace of Zen: Zen Text for Meditation.* Selected and translated by John Griffiths. London: Search Press, 1977.

———. *Japan und die Kultur der Stille.* Munich: Barth, 1975.

Eakin, Paul A. *Buddhism and the Christian Approach to Buddhists in Thailand.* Bangkok: R. Hongladaromp, 1956.

Eck, Diana L. "What Do We Mean by 'Dialogue'? Part 3. Theological Dialogue." *Current Dialogue* 11 (December 1986): 10–11.

Edmunds, Albert J., and Anesaki Masaharu. *Buddhist and Christian Gospels.* Tokyo: Yokohan, 1905.

Edwards, Tilden H. "Criss-crossing the Christian-Buddhist Bridge." In Tarthang Tulku, ed., *Reflections of Mind: Western Psychology Meets Tibetan Buddhism.* Emeryville, Calif.: Dharma Publications, 1975, pp. 185–198.

Eilert, Hakan. *Boundlessness: Studies in Karl Ludvig Reichelt's Missionary Thinking with Special Regard to the Buddhist-Christian Encounter.* Aarhus: Aros, 1974.

Enomiya-Lassalle, Hugo M. *Meditation als Weg zur Gotteserfahrung.* Matthias Grünewald, 1980.

———. "The Mysticism of Carl Albrecht and Zen." In H. D. Lewis, ed., *Philosophy, East and West. Essays in Honour of Dr. T. M. P. Mahadevan.* Bombay: Blackie and Son, 1976.

———. "The Spiritual Exercises of St. Ignatius of Loyola and Zen." In T. M. Mahadevan, ed., *Spiritual Perspectives: Essays in Mysticism and Metaphysics.* New Delhi: Heinemann, 1975, pp. 197–211.

———. *Zen: Way to Enlightenment,* New York: Taplinger, 1968.

———. *Zen und Christliche Mystik.* 3d rev. ed. Freiburg im Breisgau, W. Ger.: Aurum-Verlag, 1986.

———. *Zen Meditation: Eine Einführung.* Zurich: Benziger, 1974.

———. *Zen Meditation for Christians.* Translated by John C. Maraldo. LaSalle, Ill.: Open Court, 1974.

Eusden, John Dykstra. "Zen Buddhist Insights for Christian Education." *Colloquy* (United Church Board for Homeland Ministries), 1, no. 7 (July-August 1968): 36–39.

———. *Zen and Christian: The Journey Between.* New York: Crossroad, 1981.

———. "Zen and Christianity." *Reports of the Society for Religion in Higher Education,* Fall 1971.

Evans, C. Stephen. "Kierkegaard on Subjective Truth: Is God an Ethical Fiction?" *International Journal for Philosophy of Religion* 7, no. 1 (1976): 288–299.

Fabilla, Virginia. *Asia's Struggle for Full Humanity.* Maryknoll, N. Y.: Orbis Books, 1980.

Fader, Larry A. "Zen in the West: Historical and Philosophical Implications of the 1893 Chicago World's Parliament of Religions." *The Eastern Buddhist,* n.s. 15 no. 1 (Spring 1982): 122–145.

Fefferman, Stanley, ed., *Awakened Heart: Buddhist-Christian Dialogue in Canada.* Toronto: Canadian Buddhist-Christian Dialogue, 1985.

Fenton, John Y. "Buddhist Meditation and Christian Practice." *Anglican Theological Review* 53, no. 4 (October 1971): 237–251.

———. "Experiential Transcendence in Hinduism and Buddhism." *IDOC/International Documentation* 71 (March-April 1976): 19–31.

———. "Mystical Experience as a Bridge for Cross-Cultural Philosophy of Religion: A Critique." *Journal of the American Academy of Religion* 49 (March 1981): 51–76.

Fernando, Antony. *Buddhism and Christianity: Their Inner Affinity.* Colombo. Ecumenical Institute for Study and Dialogue, 1981.

————. "Dialogue with Buddhism." In Joseph Pathrapankal, ed., *Service and Salvation: Nagpur Theological Conference on Evangelization*. Bangor: Theological Publications in India, 1973, pp. 331–347.

Fernando, Antony, and Leonard Swidler. *Buddhism: An Introduction for Westerners*. Maryknoll, N. Y.: Orbis Books, 1985.

Fernando, Charlie. "How Buddhists and Catholics of Sri Lanka See Each Other: A Factor Analytic Approach." *Social Compass* 20, 2 (1973): 321-322.

Fernando, Mervyn. "Self, Reality, and Salvation in Christianity and Buddhism." *International Philosophical Quarterly* 12, no. 3 (September 1972): 415–425.

Fidler, Paul. *Esprit et parole: nudité bouddhique, parure chrétienne*. Paris: Presses du temps present, 197?

Fingeston, Peter. *East Is East: Hinduism, Buddhism, Christianity: A Comparison*. Philadelphia: Muhlenberg Press, 1956.

Fittipaldi, Silvio E. "Freedom in Roman Catholicism and Zen Buddhism: A Study in Inter-religious Dialogue." In Thomas M. McFadden. *Liberation, Revolution and Freedom*. New York: Seabury Press, 1975, pp. 124–138.

————. "Zen-Mind, Christian-Mind, Empty-Mind." *Journal of Ecumenical Studies* 19 (Winter 1982): 62–84.

Ford, Lewis. "Whitehead's Appropriation of the Teachings of the Buddha." *Religion in Life* 45 (Summer 1976): 184–190.

Fox, Douglas A. "Being and Particularity." *Religion in Life* 35 (Autumn 1966): 587–602.

————. *Buddhism, Christianity, and the Future of Man*. Philadelphia: Westminster Press, 1972.

Franck, Frederick. *The Christ-Buddha*. Maryknoll, N. Y.: Orbis Books, 1974.

————. *Pilgrimmage to Now/here*. Maryknoll, N. Y.: Orbis Books, 1974.

————. "Sea Change: An Emerging Image of the Future." *The Eastern Buddhist*, n.s. 11, no. 1 (May 1978): 98–108.

Frank, L. "Dialogue with Other People of Faith—An Asia Forum." *Japan Missionary Bulletin* 37, no. 5 (1983): 243–247.

Friedli, Richard. "Der Grosse Tod und das Grosse Mitleid: Übersetzungsproblematik im Gespräch über Eckhart zwischen Christen und japanischen Buddhisten." In Alois M. Haas and Heinrich Stirnimann, eds., *Das "Eining Ein,"* Freiburg/Schweiz: Universitätsverlag, 1980, pp. 87–107.

————. "Dialoge mit Buddhistischen Menschen aus Thailand." *Zeitschrift für Missionswissenschaft und Religionswissenschaft* 59, no. 2 (April 1975): 81–93.

Gällmo, Gunnar. "Mission och dhammaduta ur dialogens perspektiv." *Svensk Missionstidskrift* 70, no. 4 (1982): 27–31.

Gilkey, Langdon. "Mystery of Being and Non-Being: An Experimental Project." *Journal of Religion*, 58 (January 1978): 1–12.

Glasenapp, Helmuth von. *Buddhism and Christianity*. Kandy: Buddhist Publication Society, 1963.

Glüer, Winfried. "The Encounter between Christianity and Chinese Buddhism during the Nineteenth Century and the First Half of the Twentieth Century." *Ching Feng* 11, no. 3 (1968): 39–57.

Godmunsen, Chris. "On the Mahayana and Wittgenstein." *Religion* 4 (Autumn 1974): 96–103.

————. *Wittgenstein and Buddhism*. New York: Barnes and Noble, 1977.

Gomane, Andre. "Missionar im buddhistischen Thailand." *Die Katholischen Missionen* 92 (1973): 162–166.

Gomis, O. "Dialogue with Buddhists in Sri Lanka." *Bulletin Secretariatus pro Non-Christianis* 27 (9, 3) (1974): 204–208.

Graham, Aelred. *Conversations: Christian and Buddhist*. New York: Harcourt Brace Jovanovich, 1968.

———. *Zen Catholicism: A Suggestion*. London: Collins, 1964.

Grether, H. G. "Cross and the Bodhi Tree." *Theology Today* 16 (January 1960): 446–458.

———. "When Faith Meets Faith." *South East Asia Journal of Theology* 10 (October 1968–January 1969): 141–147.

Griffin, David R. "Buddhist Thought and Whitehead's Philosophy." *International Philosophical Quarterly* 14, no. 3 (September 1974): 261–284.

Griffiths, Bede. *Return to the Center*. Springfield, Ill.: Templegate Publishers, 1977.

Guenther, Heinz. "Overtones of Japanese Religion in Japanese Theology: Kazoh Kitamori and Sciichi Yagi." *Studies in Religion/Sciences Religeuses* 6, no. 1 (1976–1977): 17–31.

———. "A View of the Challenge of Zen Buddhism to Christianity." *Japan Christian Quarterly* 31 (April 1965): 100–107.

Gulick, Sidney Lewis. *The East and the West: A Study of Their Psychic and Cultural Characteristics*. Tokyo: Tuttle, 1963.

Gunanand, M., and P. Silva. *Buddhism and Christianity*. Colombo: P.K.W. Siriwardhana, 1955.

Gunter-Jones, Roger. *Buddhism and the West: The Essex Hall Lecture for 1973*. London: The Lindsey Press, 1973.

Habito, Ruben L. F. "A Christian Reflects on His Zen Experience." *East Asian Pastoral Review* 20, no. 4 (1983): 351–352.

———. "On *Dharmakaya* as Ultimate Reality: Prolegomenon for a Buddhist-Christian Dialogue." *Japanese Journal of Religious Studies* 12, nos. 2–3 (1985): 233–252.

Hallencreutz, Carl F. "Korsets teologi-ett grundtema i japansk Kristendomstolking." *Svensk Missionstidskrift* 70, no. 4 (1982): 37–46.

Hamilton-Merritt, Jane. *A Meditator's Diary*. London: Souvenir Press, 1976.

Hartshorne, Charles. "Some Thoughts on 'Souls' and Neighborly Love." *Anglican Theological Review* 55 (1973): 144–147.

Hasumi, Toshimitsu. "Étude comparative de la théorie de la connaissance chez Saint Thomas d'Aquin, Kant, et de la pensée philosophique du Zen." In Jan P. Beckmann and Wolfgang Kluxen, eds., *Sprache und Erkenntnis im Mittelalter*. Vol. 2. Berlin: Walter de Gruyter, 1981, pp. 1094–1098.

———. "Über die Vereinbarkeit der Zen-Meditationsmethode mit dem Christentum." *Zeitschrift für Missionswissenschaft und Religionswissenschaft* 43, no. 4 (1959): 289–296.

Hecken, J. L. "Le problème du dialogue chrétien avec les bouddhistes du Japon." *Neue Zeitschrift für Missionswissenschaft* 1 (1967): 1–17; 2 (1967): 115–132.

Heiler, Friedrich. "Buddhism in Western Perspective." In Susumu Yamaguchi, ed., *Buddhism and Culture: Dedicated to D. T. Suzuki*. Kyoto: Nakano Press, 1960.

Heinrichs, Maurus. *Théologie catholique et pensée asiatique*. Tournai, Belg.: Casterman, 1965.

Heisig, James W. "Christian-Buddhist Encounter. Part I: The Mere Reality," *Spring Wind* 4, no. 4 (1985): 7–13.

———. "Facing Religious Pluralism in Asia." *Interreligio* 4 (Fall 1983): 34–65.

Hilliard, Frederick Hadaway. *The Buddha, The Prophet, and the Christ*. New York: Macmillan, 1956.

Hoffman, Yoel. *The Idea of the Self East and West: A Comparison between Buddhist Philosophy and the Philosophy of David Hume*. Calcutta: Firma KLM Private Ltd., 1980.

Hopper, Stanley Romaine. "The 'Eclipse of God' and Existential Mistrust." *The Eastern Buddhist*, n.s. 3, no. 2 (October 1970): 46–70.

Hossfield, Paul. "Jesus (der Christus) und Siddharta Gautama (der Buddha)." *Theologie und Glaube* 64 (1974): 366-389.

Houtart, Francois. *Religion and Theology in Sri Lanka*. Colombo: Hansa Publishers, 1974.

Hultberg, Thomas K. "Missionstanken i Theravābuddismen." *Svensk Missionstidskrift* 62, no. 4 (1974): 207–212.

Hungerleider, F., and S. Hohenberger. *Gespräch eines Buddhisten mit einem Christen: Zur Frage der Toleranz*. Oberbayern, W. Germany: O. W. Barth Verlag 1969.

Hunter, Louise H. *Buddhism in Hawaii: Its Impact on a Yankee Community*. Honolulu: University of Hawaii Press, 1971.

"In Memoriam, Dr. Lynn A. De Silva," *Current Dialogue* 4 (Winter 1982–1983): 18–19.

Ingram, Paul O. "To John Cobb: Questions to Gladden the Atman in an Age of Pluralism." *Journal of the American Academy of Religion* 45 (June 1977): 228.

———. "Shinran Shōnin and Martin Luther: A Soteriological Comparison." *Journal of the American Academy of Religion* 39 (December 1971): 430–447.

Italiaander, Rolf, ed. *Eine Religion für den Frieden. Die Rissho Kosei-kai: Japanische Buddhisten für die ökumene der Religionen*. Erlangen, W. Ger.: Verlag der Ev.-Luth. Mission, 1973.

Jacobson, Nolan P. "A Buddhist-Christian Probe of the Endangered Future." *The Eastern Buddhist*, n.s. 15, no. 1 (Spring 1982): 38–55.

———. "Creativity in Buddhist Perspective." *The Eastern Buddhist*, n.s. 9, no 2 (October 1976): 43–63.

———. "Whitehead and Buddhism on the Art of Living." *The Eastern Buddhist*, n.s. 8, no 2 (October 1975): 7–36.

Jaspers, Karl. *The Origin and Goal of History*. Translated by Michael Bullock. New Haven, Conn.: Yale University Press, 1953.

Johnston, William, "Buddhists and Christians Meet." *The Eastern Buddhist*, n.s. 3, no. 1 (June 1970): 139–146.

———. *Christian Mysticism Today*. New York: Harper and Row, 1984.

———. *Christian Zen*. New York: Harper and Row, 1971.

———. "Christianity in Dialogue with Zen." In Jacob Needleman and Dennis Lewis, eds., *Sacred Tradition and Present Need*. New York: Viking Press, 1977, pp. 20–38.

———. "Defining Mysticism: Suggestions from the Christian Encounter with Zen." *Theological Studies* 28 (March 1967): 94–110.

———. *The Inner Eye of Love: Mysticism and Religion*. New York: Harper and Row, 1978.

————. *The Mirror Mind: Spirituality and Transformation*. San Francisco: Harper and Row, 1981.

————. "Mystique orientale et prière chrétienne." In H. Balthasar, et al., eds., *Les Moines Chrétiens Face*. Vanves, Fr.: Secretariat AIM, 1973, pp. 157-161.

————. "Pure Land Buddhism and Nembutsu: The Meditation of Fatih." *Studia Missionalia* 25 (1976): 43–64.

————. *Silent Music: The Science of Meditation*. New York: Harper and Row, 1974.

————. *The Still Point: Reflections on Zen and Christian Mysticism*. New York: Fordham University Press, 1970.

Jung, Moses, Swami Nikhilananda, and Herbert Schneider, eds., *Relations among Religions Today*. Leiden: Brill, 1963.

Kadowaki Kakichi. *The Ignation Exercises and Zen: An Attempt at Synthesis*. Translated by William Johnston. Jersey City, N.J.: Program to Adapt the Spiritual Exercises, n.d.

————. "Introducing Zazen into Christian Spirituality." *The Eastern Buddhist*, n.s. 9, no. 1 (May 1976): 106–122.

————. "Ways of Knowing: A Buddhist-Thomist Dialogue." *International Philosophical Quarterly* 6, no. 4 (December 1966): 574–595.

————. *Zen and the Bible*. Translated by Joan Rieck. London: Routledge and Kegan Paul, 1980.

————. "Zen and Prayer." *Japan Missionary Bulletin* 30, no. 2 (March 1976): 97–101.

Kasper, Walter, ed. *Absolutheit des Christentums*. Freiburg, W. Ger.: Herder, 1977.

King, Marilyn, "It's a Bird, It's a Buddha, It's Jesus Christ, or Is It?" *Homiletic and Pastoral Review* 74, no. 5 (1974): 11–19.

King, Winston L. *Buddhism and Christianity*. Philadelphia: Westminster Press, 1962.

————. "East-West Religious Communication." *The Eastern Buddhist*, n.s. 1, no. 2 (September 1966): 91–110.

————. "Hua Yen Mutually Interpenetrative Identity and Whiteheadian Organic Relations." *Journal of Chinese Philosophy* (1979): 381–410.

————. "Some Buddhist and Christian Concepts Compared." *South East Asia Journal of Theology* 2 (April 1961): 59–62.

————. *A Thousand Lives Away*. Oxford: Cassirer, 1964.

————. "Zen and the Death of God." In John B. Cobb, Jr., ed., *The Theology of Altizer: Critique and Response*. Philadelphia: Westminster Press, 1970, pp. 207–226.

Kipps, W. CssR. "Some Characteristics of a Japanese Spirituality." *Japan Missionary Bulletin* 32, no. 12 (December 1978): 656–666.

Kishi, Augustin Hideshi. *Spiritual Consciousness in Zen from a Thomistic Theological Point of View*. Montreal: University of Montreal, 1966.

Kitamori, Kazo. "Christianity and Other Religions in Japan." *Japan Christian Quarterly* 26 (October 1968): 230-238.

Klimkeit, Hans J. "Christentum und Buddhismus in der innerasiatischen Religionsbewegung." *Zeitschrift für Religions-und Geistesgeschichte* 33, no. 3 (1981): 208–220.

Knitter, Paul F. "Horizons on Christianity's New Dialogue with Buddhism." *Horizons* 8 (Spring 1981): 40–61.

————. "Jesus-Buddha-Krishna: Still Present?" *Journal of Ecumenical Studies* 16 (Fall 1979): 651–671.

Kohler, Werner. "Christen und Buddhisten. Zu einer Dokumentation von U. Luz and
    S. Yagi." *Evangelische Missionszeitschrift* 31, no. 4 (1974): 190–194.
Kolp, Alan L. "Shinran and Martin Luther: Two Doctrines of Salvation by Faith Alone."
    International Philosophical Quarterly 16, no. 4 (December 1976): 341–357.
Koyama, K. "Wrath of God vs. Thai *theologia gloriae*" *South East Asia Journal of
    Theology* 5 (July 1963): 18–25.
Kraemer, Hendrik. *World Cultures and World Religions: The Coming Dialogue*. Phila-
    delphia: Westminster Press, 1960.
Kreeft, Peter. "Zen Buddhism and Christianity: An Experiment in Comparative Reli-
    gion." *Journal of Ecumenical Studies* 8 (Summer 1971): 513–538.
Kretser, Bryan de. *Man in Buddhism and Christianity*. Calcutta: YMCA Publishing
    House, 1954.
Kroehler, A. H. "Can Christ Fulfill Zen?" *Japan Christian Quarterly* 36 (Summer 1970):
    190–192.
Kumazawa, Yoshinobu. "The Absolute and the Relative in the Problem of God: An
    Attempt at an Asian Contribution." *The Northeast Asia Journal of Theology* 20–
    21 (March-September 1978): 80–93.
———. "Confessing Christ in the Context of Japanese Culture." *The Northeast Asia
    Journal of Theology*. 22–23 (March-September 1979): 1–14.
Küng, Hans. *On Being a Christian*. Translated by Edward Quinn. Garden City, N.Y.:
    Doubleday, 1976.
Küng, Hans, Josef van Ess, Heinrich von Stietencron, and Heinz Bechert, *Christianity
    and the World Religions*, Garden City, N.Y. Doubleday and Co., 1986.
Kunii, A. P. "Buddhism in Christian Perspective." *Thought* 40 (Autumn 1965): 390–
    414.
Kurz, W. "Das Denken des Fernen Ostens in der Sicht Teilhard de Chardins." *Per-
    spektiven der Zukunft* 1 (1967): 4–8.
Kuyama, Yasushi. "A Symposium: On Buddhist-Christian Encounter." *Japan Studies*
    15 (Autumn 1969): 1–19.
Lamotte, Etienne. "The Christian and the Buddhist Concepts of the Human Act." *Bulletin*
    22: (1973): 30–43.
———. "Dialogue avec le Bouddhisme." *Bulletin* 3 (1966): 123–133.
———. *Histoire du Bouddhisme indien*. Louvain, Belg.: Institut Orientaliste, 1958.
Lande, Aasulv. "Litteratur om Buddhistisk-kristen dialog." *Svensk Missionstidskrift* 70,
    no. 4 (1982): 47–53.
Laube, Johannes. "Der Glaubensakt bei Luther und bei Shinran." *Zeitschrift für Mis-
    sionswissenschaft und Religionswissenschaft* 67 (January 1983): 31–49.
Lausanne Committee for World Evangelization. *The Thailand Report on Buddhists: Re-
    port of the Consultation on World Evangelization. Mini-Consultation on Reaching
    Buddhists: Held in Pattaya, Thailand, from 16–27 June, 1980*. Wheaton, Ill.:
    Lausanne Committee for World Evangelization, 1980.
Law, Diana M. "Flight or Dialog: A Response to Book Reviews of W. Johnston's *The
    Inner Eye of Love* and *Christian Zen*." *The Eastern Buddhist*, n.s. 12, no. 2
    (October 1979): 150–152.
Lee, Agnes C. J. "Mahayana Teaching of No-Self and Christian Kenosis." *Ching Feng*
    28, nos. 2–3 (1985): 130–151.

Lee, Peter. "Opening Address to the Hong Kong Conference." *Interreligio* 4 (Fall 1983): 66–72.

Ling, Trevor. *Buddha, Marx and God*. London: Macmillan, 1966.

Lopez-Gay, Jesus. "Current Criticisms of the Theology and Practice of Dialogue." *Bulletin* 30 (1975): 328-339.

————. *La Mística del Budismo: Los monjes no cristianos del Oriente*. Madrid: Biblioteca de Autores Cristianos, 1974.

————. "Maitreya, futuro mediador de la ley, en la tradicion budista del extremo oriente." *Studia Missionalia* 21 (1972): 93–112.

Loth, Heinz-Jürgen, Michael Mildenberger, and Tworuschka Ubo. *Christentum im Spiegel der Weltreligionen*. Stuttgart: Quell, 1978.

Lotz, Johannes Bapt. "Der Koan als Meditationsweg für Christen." *Erbe und Auftrag* 49 (1973): 382–391.

Lucia of the Trinity. "Christian Zen and Franciscan Spirituality." *The Cord* 22, no. 6 (1972): 173–177.

Luz, U. "Zwischen Christentum und Buddhismus (Seiichi Yagi)." In Hans Waldenfels, ed., *Theologen der Dritten Welt*. Munich: C. H. Beck, 1982, pp. 161–178.

McDaniel, Jay B. "Faith without Foundations" *Quarterly Review* 5 (Spring 1985): 9–26.

MacCormack, C. "Zen Catholicism of Thomas Merton." *Journal of Ecumenical Studies* 9 (Fall 1972): 802–817.

Magliola, Robert. *Derrida on the Mend*. West Lafayette, Ind.: Purdue University Press, 1983.

Maraldo, John C. "The Hermeneutics of Practice in Dogen and Francis of Assisi: An Exercise in Buddhist-Christian Dialogue." *The Eastern Buddhist*, n.s. 14, no. 2 (Autumn 1981): 22–46.

Marrion, Malachy, "Unsullied Waters: The Buddha and Saint Benedict. A Comparison." *Studia Monastica* 28, no. 2 (1986): 265–296.

Martinson, Paul. "Wisdom and Love as the Basis for Preaching in Buddhism and Christianity." *Dialog* 17 (Summer 1978): 174–180.

Masson, Joseph. "Dialogue avec les bouddhistes." *Bulletin Secretariatus pro Non-Christianis* 19 (1972): 43–49.

————. "Dialogue with the Buddhists." *Bulletin Secretariatus pro Non-Christianis* 19 (7, 1) (1972): 38–44.

————. *Le Bouddhisme*. Paris: Desclee de Brouwer, 1975.

————. "Le chretien devant le Yoga et le Zen." *Nouvelle Revue Theologique* 94 (1972): 384–399.

————. "Positions et problems d'une 'morale' theravada." *Studia Missionalia* 27 (1978): 135–158.

Maung, Din Khin. "Some Problems and Possibilities for Burmese Christian Theology Today." *South East Asia Journal of Theology* 16, no. 2 (1975): 17–30.

May, John L. "Christian-Buddhist-Marxist Dialogue in Sri Lanka: A Model for Social Change in Asia?" *Journal of Ecumenical Studies* 19 (Fall 1982): 719–743.

————. " 'Making Sense of Death' in Christianity and Buddhism: 'Pragmasemenatic' Analysis of 1 Thess 4:13-5:11 and Sutta-Nipāta III, 8." *Zeitschrift für Missionswissenschaft und Religionswissenschaft* 65 (January 1981): 51–69.

————. "Vom Vergleich zur Verständigung Geschichte der Vergleiche zwischen Buddhismus und Christentum, 1880–1980.'' *Zeitschrift fur Missionwissenschaft und Religionswissenschaft* 66 (January 1982): 58–66.

Mensching, Gustav. *Buddha und Chrisus—ein Vergleich*. Stuttgart: Deutsche Verlags-Anstalt, 1978.

Merton, Thomas. *The Asian Journal of Thomas Merton*. London: Sheldon Press, 1974.

———. ''D. T. Suzuki: The Man and His Work.'' *The Eastern Buddhist*, n.s. 2, no. 1 (August 1967): 3–9.

———. *Mystics and Zen Masters*. New York: Farrar, Straus and Giroux, 1967.

———. *Zen and the Birds of Appetite*. New York: New Direction Books, 1968.

Mitchell, Donald William. ''A Buddhist Philosophy of Karma and Christian Spiritual Theology.'' Article followed by three responses: Ching Tat, ''Buddhist Transformation''; Ko Wing Siu, ''The Buddhist Concept of Karma''; Peter K. H. Lee, ''A Wesleyan Perspective.'' *Ching Feng* 29, no. 1 (1986): 5–19.

———. ''The Contemporary Relevance of Lay Spirituality in Buddhism and Christianity.'' *Nuovo Umanita* 19, no. 1 (January-February 1982): 47–60.

———. ''Faith in Zen Buddhism.'' *International Philosophical Quarterly* 20, no. 2 (June 1980): 183–197.

———. ''The 'Place' of Self in Christian Spirituality: A Response to the Buddhist-Christian Dialogue.'' *Nuovo Umanita,* 1985.

Moffitt, John, ed. *Journey to Gorakhpur: An Encounter with Christ Beyond Christianity*. New York: Holt, Rinehart and Winston, 1972.

———. *New Charter for Monasticism*. Notre Dame, Ind.: University of Notre Dame Press, 1970.

Mooney, Michael J. ''On Comparing Christian and Buddhist Traditions: A Response to Mervyn Fernando.'' *International Philosophical Quarterly* 13, no. 2 (June 1973): 267–270.

Morgan, Bruce. *Thai Buddhism and American Protestantism*. Chiengmai, Thailand: Thailand Theological Seminary, 1966.

Neuner, Joseph. *Christian Revelation and World Religions*. London: Burns and Oates, 1967.

Neville, Robert C. *Soldier, Sage, Saint*. New York: Fordham University Press, 1978.

———. *The Tao and the Daimon: Segments of a Religious Inquiry*. Albany, N.Y.: SUNY Press, 1982.

Nielsen, Niels C., Jr. ''Buddhism and Christianity: Advancing in Dialogue.'' *The Christian Century*, April 25, 1984, pp. 433–435.

Niles, D. T. *Buddhism and the Claims of Christ*. Richmond, Va.: John Knox, 1967.

Nishitani, Keiji, and Donald Mitchell, ''A Buddhist-Christian Colloquium in Japan. 'Compassionate Endurance: Mary and the Buddha.' '' *Bulletin Secretariatus pro Non-Christianis* 63 (21, 3) (1986): 296–300.

O'Connor, Patrick. *Buddhists Find Christ*. Tokyo: Tuttle, 1975.

Odin, Steve. *Process Metaphysics and Hua-Yen Buddhism*. Albany, N.Y.: SUNY Press, 1982.

O'Hanlon, Daniel J. ''Church and Buddhism.'' In *The New Catholic Encyclopedia*. Vol. 17. New York: McGraw-Hill, 1979, pp. 57–58.

———. ''Zen and the Spiritual Exercises.'' *Theological Studies* 39, no. 4 (December 1978): 737–768.

Okumura, Ichiro. ''The View of Nature and Religious Ethics Seen in Various Religions in the Cases of Buddhism and Christianity." *Bulletin Secretariatus pro Non-Christianis* 16, no. 2 (1981): 123–129.

Ostasien-Institut, ed. *Auf der Suche nach Ansatzpunkten für einen Christlichen Dialog mit Buddhisten.* Bonn, 1979.

Panikkar, Raimundo. "The Category of Growth in Comparative Religion: A Critical Self-Examination." *Harvard Theological Review* 66, no. 1 (January 1973): 113–140.

———. "Nirvana and the Awareness of the Absolute." In J. P. Whelen, ed., *The God Experience: Essays in Hope.* New York: Newman Press, 1971, pp. 81–99.

———. "Sūnyatā and Plērōma: The Buddhist and Christian Response to the Human Predicament." In James M. Robinson, ed., *Religion and the Humanizing of Man.* Waterloo, Ont.: Council on the Study of Religion, 1972, pp. 67–86.

Paul VI. "Allocution à des moines bouddhistes, 5.6.1972." *La Documentation Catholique* 69 (1972): 611–613.

Pennington, M. Basil. "Christian Zen Retreat." *Review for Religious* 31, no. 5 (1972): 710–713.

Perry, Edmund F. "Can Buddhists and Christians Live Together as Kalyāna-Mittā?" In S. Balasooriya et al., *Buddhist Studies in Honour of Walpola Rahula.* London: Gordon Fraser, 1980, pp. 201–212.

Peter, W. L. A., "I religiosi nel dialogo con il Buddhismo." *Studi Francescani* 69, no. 1 (1972): 49–71.

———. "Religious Life: Buddhist and Christian." *World Mission* 25, no. 2 (1974): 28–32.

Pezet, Edmond. "Le monachisme buddhique: Un défi séculaire aux traditions spirituelles de la chrétienté." *Irenikon* 48, no. 1 (1975): 5–40.

Pieris, Aloysius. "Contemporary Ecumenism and Asia's Search for Christ." *Teaching All Nations* (1976): 23–39.

———. "Mission of the Local Church in Relation to other Major Religious Traditions." *CTC Bulletin, Bulletin of the Commission on Third World Concerns* 4, no. 1 (1983): 30–43.

Pye, Michael. "Aufklärung und Religion in Europe und Japan." *Religious Studies* 9, no. 2 (1973): 201–217.

Pyun-Shin, Ock Hee, "Man in Wonhyo and Karl Jaspers." *Journal of Korean Cultural Research Institute* (1977): 289–312.

Quintos, Lily. *Buddhism in Dialogue.* Manila: Ateneo de Manila, 1977.

———. "Faith in the Milinda Panha from a Christian Perspective." *Ching Feng* 19, no. 1 (1976): 55–64.

Raguin, Yves. "The Art of Prayer." *Japan Missionary Bulletin* 28, no. 4 (April 1974): 219–226.

———. *Bouddhisme-Christianisme.* Paris: ēpi, 1973.

———. "Christianity and Zen." *East Asian Pastoral Review* 20, no. 4 (1983): 345–350.

———. *The Depth of God.* St. Meinrad, Ind.: Abbey Press, 1975.

———. "The Dialogue of Communities of Faith in Asia." *East Asian Pastoral Review* 20, no. 2 (1983): 167–169.

———. "How Buddhism Faces the Challenge of the Modern World." *Bulletin* 20 (1972): 10–29.

Raper, David. "L'interprétation des traditions hindoues et bouddhiques chez Simone

Weil.'' In G. Kahn, ed., *Simone Weil: Philosophe, Historienne et Mystique: Communications*. Paris: Aubier, 1978.

Ratschow, Carl H. ''Zu dem von Fritz Buri (*Der Buddha-Christus als der Herr des wahren Selbst*, Bern, 1982) vorgelegten religionsphilosophischen Gespräch.'' *Neue Zeitschrift für systematische Theologie und Religionsphilosophie* 27, no. 2 (1985): 195–221.

Reichelt, G. M. ''Chinese Religion and Christianity.'' *Review and Expositor* 58 (January 1961): 25–34.

Reldif-Fidlerski. *L'invité de l'inconnaissable: appel et réponse: les deux natures de l'hommes: Christianisme et Bouddhisme: incompatibles? complémentaires?* Paris: G. P. Fidler, 1977.

Ries, J. (Julien). *Salut et libération dans le Bouddhisme et théologies de la libération: cours problémes et méthodes en histoire des religions, 1978–1979*. Louvain-La-Neuve: Centre d'Histoire des Religions, 1979.

Robinson, John A. T. *Truth Is Two-Eyed*. Philadelphia: Westminster Press, 1979.

Röhr, Heinz. ''Buddha und Jesus in ihren Gleichnissen.'' *Neue Zeitschrift für Systematische Theologie und Religionsphilosophie* 15, no. 1 (1973): 65–86.

―――. ''Buddhismus und Christentum. Untersuchung zur Typologie zweier Weltreligionen.'' *Zeitschrift für Religions-und Geistesgeschichte* 25, no. 4 (1973): 289–303.

Rosenkranz, Gerhard. ''Die biblische Botschaft gegenüber dem Amida-Buddhismus.'' *Religion in Geschichte und Gegenwart* [3d ed.] 1 (1957): 323–325.

―――. *Evangelische Religionskunde*. Tübingen: J. C. B. Mohr, 1951.

Rossano, Pietro. ''Dialogue between Christian and Non-Christian Monks: The Possibilities and the Difficulties.'' *Bulletin Secretariatus pro Non-Christianis* 46 (16, 1) (1981): 52–62.

Ruiz, F. Perez. ''God Creator of All Things: A Philosophical-Christian Dialog with Buddhism.'' *Japan Missionary Bulletin* 25, no. 10 (November 1971): 601–608.

Rupp, George. *Beyond Existentialism and Zen: Religion in a Pluralistic World*. New York: Oxford University Press, 1979.

―――. *Christologies and Cultures: Toward a Typology of Religious Worldviews*. Hawthorne, N.Y.: Mouton, 1974.

Saad, Chaiwan, *The Christian Approach to Buddhists in Thailand*. Bangkok: Suriyaban Publishers, 1975.

Sang, Fr. -X. Nguyen-dinh. *Valeur salvifique du Bouddhisme à la lumière du Deuzième Concile du Vatican*. Rome: Université Pontificale Urbanienne, 1976.

Schmithausen, Lambert. ''Die vier 'Konzentrationen der Aufmerksamkeit.' '' *Zeitschrift für Missionswissenschaft und Religionswissenschaft* 60, no. 4 (1976): 241–266.

Scott, David. ''Christian Responses to Buddhism in Pre-Medieval Times.'' *Numen* 32, no. 1 (1985): 88–100.

Seeley, F. H. ''Thai Buddhism and the Christian Faith.'' *South East Asia Journal of Theology* 10 (October-January 1969): 132–140.

Sharpe, Eric J. *Karl Ludvig Reichelt, Missionary, Scholar, and Pilgrim*. Hong Kong: Tao Fong Shan Ecumenical Centre, 1984.

Shearburn, V. G. ''Spirituality: Buddhist and Christian.'' *The South East Asia Journal of Theology* 7, no.4 (April 1966): 6–14.

Shimizu, Masumi. ''Das māhāyana buddhistische 'Selbst' und die christliche 'Person':

zu einem Dialog zwischen Buddhismus und Christentum." *Zeitschrift für Religions-und Geistesgeschichte* 34, no. 2 (1982): 97–110.

————. *Das "Selbst" in Māhāyana-Buddhismus in Japanischen Sicht und die "Person" im Christentum im Licht der Neuen Testaments*. Leiden: Brill, 1981.

Siegmund, G. *Buddhism and Christianity: A Preface to Dialogue*. Translated by Mary Frances McCarthy. University: University of Alabama Press, 1980.

————. "Les bases du dialogue avec le Bouddhisme." *Concilium* (French ed.) 29 (1967): 115–117.

Singh, Herbert Jai. *Interreligious Dialogue*. Bangalore: Christian Institute for the Study of Religion and Society, 1967.

Smart, Ninian. *Beyond Ideology: Religion and the Future of Western Civilization*. San Francisco: Harper and Row, 1981.

————. *A Dialogue of Religions*. London: SCM Press, 1960.

————. "Learning from Others Faiths. II. Buddhism." *The Expository Times* 83 (1971–1972): 211–214.

————. "Numen, Nirvana and the Definition of Religion." *Church Quarterly Review* 160 (April-June 1959): 216–225.

————. "Work of the Buddha and the Work of Christ." In George F. Brandon, ed., *The Saviour God: Comparative Studies in the Concept of Salvation, Presented to Edwin Oliver James*. New York: Barnes and Noble, 1963, pp. 160–173.

Smith, Alex G. *The Gospel Facing Buddhist Cultures*. Taichung, Taiwan: Asia Theological Association, 1980.

Snellgrove, David. "Theological Reflection on the Buddhist Goal of Perfect Enlightenment." *Bulletin* 17 (1971): 76–98.

Song, Choan-Seng. "Love of God-and-Man in Action—Doing Theology with Asian Spirituality." In Choan-Seng Song, ed., *Doing Theology Today*. Madras: The Christian Literature Society, 1976, pp. 42–96.

Spae, Joseph J. *Buddhist-Christian Empathy*. Chicago: The Chicago Institute of Theology and Culture, 1980.

————. "The Buddhist-Christian Encounter: An Encouraging Reality." *Japan Missionary Bulletin* 31, no. 8 (1977): 477–483.

————. *Christian Corridors to Japan*. Tokyo: Oriens Institute for Religious Research, 1971.

————. *Christianity Encounters Japan*. Tokyo: Oriens Institute for Religious Research, 1968.

————. "Contents of the Christian-Buddhist Dialogue." *Zeitschrift für Missionswissenschaft und Religionswissenschaft* 57, no. 3 (1973): 187–201.

————. "Die Buddhistisch-christliche Begegnung: Ein ermutigende Tatsache." *Lebendiges Zeugnis* 32, no. 4 (1977): 35–44.

————. *Japanese Religiosity*. Tokyo: Oriens Institute for Religious Research, 1971.

————. "Marginal Notes on 'Absolute Nothingness.' " *Zeitschrift für Missionswissenschaft und Religionswissenschaft* 61, no. 4 (1977): 271–282.

————. "Sanctity in Buddhism." *Journal of Dharma* 8, no. 2 (1983): 182–191.

————. "Three Notes on the Christian-Buddhist Dialogue." *Zeitschrift für Missionswissenschaft und Religionswissenschaft* 59, no. 1 (1975): 20–29.

————. "Two Pillars of Buddhist Mysticism: Oneness and Compassion." *Studia Missionalia* 26 (1977): 191–214.

Spakovsky, Anatol von. *The Reflection of Buddhism in Arthur Schopenhauer, Albert*

Einstein, and Leo Tolstoy (and Its Perspectives in Its Confrontation with Christianity and Marxism). Huntsville, Ala.: Golden Rule Printing, 1980.

Sparks, I. A. "Buddha and Christ: A Functional Analysis. *Numen* 13 (October 1966): 190–204.

Srirangaraj, H. V. "Salvation in Buddhism." *Indian Missiological Review* 4, no. 4 (1982): 400–412.

Stambaugh, Joan. "Time-Being: East and West." *The Eastern Buddhist*, n.s. 9, no. 2 (October 1976): 107–114.

Steere, Douglas. "Religious Encounter." In Susumu Yamaguchi, ed., *Buddhism and Culture: Dedicated to D. T. Suzuki*. Kyoto: Nakano Press, 1960, pp. 170–180.

Steffney, John. "Compassion in Mahayana Buddhism and Meister Eckhart." *The Journal of Religious Thought* 31 (Fall-Winter 1974–1975): 64–77.

———. "Mind and Metaphysics in Heidegger and Zen Buddhism." *The Eastern Buddhist*, n.s. 14 no. 1 (Spring 1981): 61–74.

———. "Non-being-Being versus the Non-being of Being: Heidegger's Ontological Difference with Zen Buddhism." *The Eastern Buddhist* n.s. 10, no. 2 (October 1977): 65–75.

———. "Nothingness and Death in Heidegger and Zen Buddhism." *The Eastern Buddhist* 18, no. 1 (1985): 90–104.

Steindl-Rast, David. "Become What You Are: An Interview with Brother David Steindl-Rast [by John Loudon]." *Parabola* 7, no. 4 (1982): 60–67.

———. "Buddhist Insights for Christian Man." *Conversations* (Autumn 1973): 44–45.

———. "Christian Confrontation with Buddhism and Hinduism." *Monastic Studies* 8 (1972): 171–187.

Stowe, David M. *When Faith Meets Faith*. New York: Friendship Press, 1963.

Streng, Frederick. *Emptiness: A Study in Religious Meaning*. Nashville: Abingdon Press, 1967.

Suzuki, Daisetz T. and T. H. Callaway, "Dialogue: Christian and Buddhist." *The Eastern Buddhist*, n.s. 3, no. 1 (June 1970): 108–121.

Swain, Charles W. "Sharing a Language of Faith [Buddhists and Christians]. *Christian Century* 98 (December 9, 1981): 1282–1285.

Swearer, Donald K. "Appeal of Buddhism: a Christian Perspective." *Christian Century* 88 (November 3, 1971): 1289–1293.

———. *Buddhism in Transition*. Philadelphia: Westminster Press, 1970.

———. *Dialogue: The Key to Understanding Other Religions*. Philadelphia: Westminster Press, 1977.

———. *A Theology of Dialogue*. Bangkok: Church of Christ in Thailand, 1973.

Swyngedouw, Jan. "Partners for Dialogue: The Search for Discriminating Norms." *The Japan Missionary Bulletin* 40, no. 1 (Spring 1986): 39–44.

Tagawa, Kenzo. "The Yagi-Takizawa Debate." *The Northeast Asia Journal of Theology* 2 (March 1969): 41–59.

Takizawa, Katsumi. " 'Rechtfertigung' in Buddhismus und im Christentum." *Evangelische Theologie* 39 (May-June 1979): 182–195.

———. "Reflexionen über die universale Grundlage von Buddhismus und Christentum." *Studien zur interkulturellen Geschichte des Christentums* (Frankfurt am Main) (1980): 24.

———. "Zen Buddhism and Christianity in Contemporary Japan." *Northeast Asia Journal of Theology* 4 (March 1970): 106–121.

Tanaka, Franciscus-X. *L'Amidismo e l'unica salvezza in Cristo*. Rome: Institutum Spiritualitatis Teresianum, 1973.

Tawney, Joseph B. "The Failure of Mahayana Buddhism." *Eleventh International Conference for the Sociology of Religion*. Lille: Edition C.I.S.R., 1971, pp. 273–304.

Teahan, John F. "William Johnston's Writings on Mysticism: Analysis and Critique." *Studia Mystica* 4 (Summer 1981): 63–73.

Thabping, Joseph Ek. "Buddhist-Christian Dialogue in Thailand." *Bulletin Secretariatus pro Non-Christianis* 18, no. 1 (1983): 66–71.

———. *The Conversion of Thai Buddhists: Are Christianity and Thai Culture Irreconcilable?* Manila: Ateneo de Manila, 1974.

Than, U. K. "Man in Buddhism and Christianity." *South East Asia Journal of Theology* 3 (July 1961): 19–24.

Thelle, Notto. *Buddhism and Christianity in Japan: From Conflict to Dialogue, 1854–1899*. Honolulu: University of Hawaii Press, 1987.

———. "Buddhist-Christian Encounter: From Animosity to Dialogue." *Japan Christian Quarterly* 42 (Spring 1976): 96–104.

———. "Buddhistmisjonen 50 år." *Tidsskrift for Misjon* 26, no. 4 (1972): 193–204.

———. "Et buddistisk Romerbrev." *Norsk Tidsskrift for Misjon* 28, no. 3 (1974): 129–154.

———. "The Legacy of Karl Ludvig Reichelt." *International Bulletin of Missionary Research* 5 (April 1981): 65–70.

———. "Mahayana—troens oppvekkelse." *Norsk Tidsskrift tor Misjon* 31, no. 2 (1977): 110–113.

———. "Religion as a Force of Reconciliation: Overcoming the Abuse of Religion in Social and Political Conflicts." *Current Dialogue* 8 (June 1985): 14–18.

Thurston, Bonnie Bowman. "Buddhist-Christian Dialogue: A Report," *Mission Journal*, June 1984.

———. "The Conquered Self: Emptiness and God in a Buddhist-Christian Dialogue." *Japanese Journal of Religious Studies* 12 (December 1985): 343–353.

Tillich, Paul. *Christianity and the Encounter of the World Religions*. New York: Columbia University Press, 1963.

Tillich, Paul, and Hisamatsu Shin'ichi. "Dialogue East and West." *The Eastern Buddhist*, n.s. 4, no. 2 (October 1971): 89–107; 5, no. 2 (October 1972): 107–128; 6, no. 2 (October 1973): 87–114.

Tin, P. M. "Certain Factors in the Buddhist-Christian Encounter." *South East Asia Journal of Theology* 3 (October 1961): 27–33.

Titschack, Hans. *Christentum und Buddhismus. Ein Gegensatz*. Vienna: Octupus, 1980.

Tong, Paul K. K. "A Study of Thematic Differences between Eastern and Western Religious Thought." *Journal of Ecumenical Studies* 10 (Spring 1973): 337–360.

Toynbee, Arnold Joseph. *Christianity among the Religions of the World*. London: Oxford University Press, 1957.

Ueda, Shizutera. "Der Buddhismus und das Problem der Säkurlarisierung: Zur gegenwärtigen geistigen Situation Japans." In O. Schatz, ed., *Hat die Religion Zukunft?* Graz, Austria: Styria, 1971, pp. 255–275.

———. *Die Gottesgeburt in der Seele und der Durchbruch zur Gottheit: Die mystische Anthropologie Meister Eckharts und ihre Confrontation mit der Mystik des Zen-Buddhismus*. Gütersloh: Mohr, 1965.

Vachon, Robert. "Dying to Christ." *Revue Monchanin* 13, no. 1 (1980): 6–11.

Van Bragt, Jan. "Buddhism and Christianity." *Philippiniana Sacra* (Manila) 17, no. 50 (1983): 83–96.

———. "The Buddhist Challenge to Christian Theology." In *Asian Religious Traditions and Christianity*. Manila: University of Santo Tomás, 1983, pp. 23–28.

———. "Christ and Japanese Buddhism." *The Japan Missionary Bulletin* 33 (1979): 173–182.

———. "An East-West Spiritual Exchange." *The Eastern Buddhist*, n.s. 13, no. 1 (Spring 1980): 141–150.

———. "East-West Spiritual Exchange: A Project." *Nanzan Institute for Religion and Culture Bulletin* 3 (1979): 7–12.

———. "East-West Spiritual Exchange: A Report on a Project." *Nanzan Institute for Religion and Culture Bulletin* 4 (1980): 4–18.

———. "East-West Spiritual Exchange II, October 5 to November 5, 1983." *Nanzan Institute for Religion and Culture Bulletin* 8 (1984): 10–23.

———. "Historical Religion and Folk Religion: Shingon Buddhism and Christianity." *Nanzan Bulletin* 9 (1985): 11–23.

———. "Nuovo dialogo con il buddhismo in Giappone." *Concilium* (Brescia) 19, no. 1 (1983): 144–155.

———. "Zen and Christianity." *Zen Bunka* 78 (1983): 25–28.

Van Hecken, Joseph L. "Le problème du dialogue chrétien avec les bouddhistes du Japon." *Neue Zeitschrift für Missionswissenschaft* (1967): 1–17, 115–132.

Von Brück, Michael. "Advaita and Trinity: Reflections on the Vedantic and Christian Experience of God with Reference to Buddhist Non-Dualism." *Indian Theological Studies* 20, no. 1 (1983): 37–60.

———. "Christian-Buddhist Exchange Programme." *Gurukul Perspective* 23 (October 1983): 1–13.

Von Schweinitz, Helmut. *Buddhismus und Christentum*. Munich: E. Reinhardt, 1955.

Waldenfels, Hans. *Absolute Nothingness: Foundations for a Buddhist-Christian Dialogue*. Translated by James W. Heisig. Ramsey, N.J.: Paulist Press, 1980.

———. "Absolute Nothingness: Preliminary Considerations on a Central Notion in the Philosophy of Nishida Kitarō and the Kyoto School." *Monumenta Nipponica* 21 (1966): 354–391.

———. *Faszination des Buddhismus: Zum christlich-buddhistischen Dialog*. Mainz: Matthias-Grünewald, 1982.

———. "Gud-den stora frågeni en Kristen-Buddhistick dialog." *Svensk Missionstidskrift* 70, no. 4 (1982): 1–17.

———. "Im Gesprach mit Buddhisten: Die Frage nach dem persönlichen Gott." In Theo Sundermeier, ed., *Fides Pro Mundi Vita*. Gütersloh: Gütersloher Verlagshaus Gerd Mohn, 1980, pp. 184–196.

———. *Meditation—Ost und West*. Einsiedeln: Benziger, 1975.

Watanabe, Shōko. *Japanese Buddhism: A Critical Appraisal*. Tokyo: Kokusai Bunka Shinkōkai, 1968.

Wayman, Alexander. "Buddha as Saviour." *Studia Missionalia* 29 (1980): 191–207.

———. "Eschatology in Buddhism." *Studia Missionalia* 32 (1983): 71–94.

Wellbon, Guy Richard. *The Buddhist Nirvana and Its Western Interpreters*. Chicago: University of Chicago Press, 1968.

Wells, Kenneth E. *Theravada Buddhism and Protestant Christianity*. Chiengmai, Thailand: Thailand Theological Seminary, 1963.

Westerhoff, John H. III, and John Dykstra Eusden. *The Spiritual Life: Learning East and West*. New York: Seabury Press, 1982.

Whitson, Robley Edward. *The Coming Convergence of World Religions*. New York: Newman Press, 1971.

Wienpahl, Paul. "Eastern Buddhism and Wittgenstein's Philosophical Investigations." *The Eastern Buddhist*, n.s. 12, no. 2 (October 1979): 22–54.

Williams, J. G. *Yeshua Buddha*. Wheaton, Ill.: Theosophical Publishing House, 1978.

Yadav, Bibhuti S. "Protest against the Theology of Anonymous Christianity." *Religion and Society* 24 (December 1977): 69–81.

Yagi, Seiichi. "Buddhism and Christianity." *The Northeast Asia Journal of Theology* 20–21 (March-September 1978): 1–18.

———. "Weder persönlich noch generell—zum neutestamentlichen Denken anhand Rom VII." In M. Sekine and A. Satake, eds., *Annual of Japan Biblical Institute*. Vol. 2. Tokyo: Yamamoto Shoten, 1976, pp. 159–173.

Yonker, Nicholas. *God, Man, and the Planetary Age*. Corvallis, Oreg.: Oregon State University Press, 1978.

Young, David. "The Open Dialogue—Buddhist and Christian." In *Face to Face: Essays on Interfaith Dialogue*. London: Highway Press, 1971, pp. 48–58.

Zago, Marcello. *Buddhismo e Christianesimo in Dialogo*. Rome: Città Nuova Editrice, 1985.

———. "Evangelization to the Buddhists. Has the Gospel Re-echoed in Asia." *Omnis Terra* 17 (1983): 254–274.

———. "L'annonce du kérygma aux bouddhistes." *Kerygma* 24 (1975): 73–90.

———. "Le dialogue avec les Bouddhistes au Laos." *Bulletin Secretariatus pro Non-Christianis* 30 (10,2) (1975): 277–291.

———. "L'Équivalent de 'Dieu' dans le Bouddhisme." *Église et Théologie* 6 (January-May-October 1975): 25–49, 153–174, 297–317.

26

The Buddhist-Christian Dialogue in China

WHALEN LAI

The Buddhist-Christian encounter in China has not been as exciting or as fruitful as the one in neighboring Japan.[1] But China had a very different modern religious history. In Japan the Buddhist temples were and still are economically strong, having been part of the establishment during the Tokugawa period. Chinese temples never came as close. Japan, after Perry forced open its doors, was able to modernize itself without foreign harassment. China had its territories carved up by foreign powers, Japan included, and had a much shorter time in which to modernize. These events cannot but cast a shadow on its Buddhist response to Christianity.

The early nineteenth-century Protestant missionaries had little personal contact with Buddhist monks, and the monks gave little response to the challenge of the new faith. In the days of Matteo Ricci (1589–1610), Jesuit priests and Buddhist monks at least debated one another. But not so with the Protestant missionaries. Chinese Buddhism was not its old self, and the new Protestant missionaries cared little for monks. The Jesuits of old accommodated Chinese culture to Christ; the Protestants sought conquest of China for God. The Jesuits saw God in the Chinese cult of the Lord-on-High (*shang-ti*); the Protestants found nothing but pagan idols. But more than religion was involved. Nineteenth-century China was no longer the land of enlightened sages the West had once admired. The industrial revolution in Europe had turned Cathay now into a land of barbaric customs and pagan superstitions. One should not overstress this; the early Protestant missionaries were not champions of the progress of human civilization. To them, the world was mired hopelessly in sin, and science was suspect. They did not intend to bring the Enlightenment to China; they wanted only to save lost souls for the kingdom.[2]

Thus Robert Morrison, intent on bearing witness to the Bible, labored hard to translate the Bible into Chinese and had boxloads of the good book dumped off the coast—missionaries being then prohibited from entering China—in the hope that the Word of God would drift ashore into waiting hearts and hands. He studied Chinese, but he saw little good in what he learned. His biblical theology left little room for dialogue. Theologians then still entertained the idea of a Babylonian genesis of Chinese culture; some even thought that the Chinese were God's people dispersed eastward from the Tower of Babel. But if that sounds parochial, one should see how an informed Chinese like T'an Ssu-t'ung would similarly reduce European scientific ingenuity to the Chinese being somehow distant sons of Hsia, first of the Three (legendary) dynasties in ancient China known for their hard practicality. So far we have not mentioned Buddhist monks, but they were a cloistered group prohibited by imperial law from active contacts with lay society.

Before the century ended, though, that situation changed somewhat when missionary and classicist James Legge (1814–1897) became the first Sinologist, bringing together Buddhist and Christian idealism and internationalism. During the 1898 constitutional monarchy reform under New Text Confucianist K'ang Yu-wei (1858–1927), modernist Christians and modernist Buddhists crossed paths as they sought to rejuvenate China in both body and soul. The 1898 reform was soon cut short by the empress dowager, and China was being edged by conservatism toward more and more radical political solutions. In the first two decades of the twentieth century, liberal humanism gained a hearing in China. Within the missions, there were modernist elements and proponents of the American social gospel. The 1911 revolution that gave China a republican government was led by one such follower of modernist Christianity, Sun Yat-san. But this was also the time when modernist Buddhism learned to be critical of Christian theism. I will consider one revolutionary lay Buddhist and intellectual atheist later.

The 1911 revolution had support from all sectors of society. The new Constitution guaranteed the freedom of religion. For the decade of the 1910s, there was significant interreligious cooperation. When President Yüan Shih-k'ai attempted to declare Confucianism the state religion, Christians, Buddhists, and Muslims jointly opposed it and won. That was also the time when modernism finally impacted the monasteries. Reformist monk T'ai-hsü (1890–1949) urged renewed involvement with the world. Monks rebuilt their ties with laypersons inhibited since the Ming dynasty because of their potential for inspiring millenarian uprisings. Missionaries were building schools, spreading modern education in China as they had in Europe, and working among peasants deep in the countryside. But as in any modern, secular state, older religions tended to lose some ground to new ones. Land reforms always cut the monastic landholdings in the countryside while the missions in urban areas gained protection from the laws. The Buddhists lost many temples in 1912 when the government moved to confiscate their empty halls for use as schools. We will see that conflict between the old and the new surfaced in one bitter Buddhist-Christian exchange later.

The honeymoon between Christian humanism and secular humanism ended in the May Fourth movement of 1919. Young intellectuals at Peking University proclaimed a Renaissance and led an Enlightenment, crowned "Mr. Science and Mr. Democracy" as the new gods, and relegated religion to being excess baggage from a feudal past. It is ironic that just when the missionaries after Legge learned not to deprecate Chinese culture, a new generation of Chinese was ready to forsake the past. It is also tragic that just when Christians and Buddhists alike endorsed liberal ideals, the May Fourth anticlericalism would repudiate all things religious. Christianity then suffered the additional attack from the emerging Marxists who tied the missions to the imperialist enterprise. But even the many May Fourth debates were soon swallowed up by the national emergency of 1937. Japan's invasion of China had Christians leaving the church to help in the defense, and even Buddhist monks, encouraged by T'ai-hsü, endorsed such acts. Internationalist ideals faded (except among the Communists) as patriotic feelings ran high. Foreign missionaries soon began to leave a war-torn China in a world-torn world.

When the war ended in 1945, there was no peace—just more civil strife. By 1949 the Communists (PRC) controlled the mainland; the Kuomingtang (KMT) retrenched in Taiwan. Religious freedom was guaranteed by both republics, but religion was also closely supervised. In the PRC churches have to be native, and parasitic monks must rejoin the work force. Religion must serve the people and this material world and not be some idealist's opiate. To date, the People's Republic has not produced even any Marxist Buddhist or Christian Marxist of true renown (as India and Poland have). Taiwan has yet to hold any open and in-depth Buddhist-Christian conference. Instead, the Communist threat only fuels the Christian fundamentalist cause to do battle with this modern Satan. This fact, namely, that a quarter of the world's population remains to be converted, keeps the nineteenth-century missionary ideal alive. In that competition for hearts, sectarianism outpaced ecumenism. Even Christians and Buddhists are drawn no closer together by their common enemy. This makes it doubly difficult to report on the Buddhist-Christian dialogue in postwar China. There simply is not much going on, and some of the better examples have to come from an earlier time.

TWO CLASSIC POSITIONS: UNIVERSALISM VERSUS PARTICULARISM

At any time, there are people who sincerely believe that all religions are the same, but there are also people who as sincerely disagree. It is not hard to find such voices in modern China; what is hard to find are the truly great souls who could articulate the universalist and particularist positions. Two pre-1945 figures are chosen for examination below because they outshine more recent counterparts.

China has had a long tradition of considering Confucianism, Buddhism, and Taoism as one. But it was the young 1898 reformer T'an Ssu-t'ung (1866–1898) who applied this to Confucianism, Buddhism, and Christianity with a rare conviction. The trio preaches, said he, the unity of all beings: the selfless Love that flows from that cosmic oneness and the moral courage that is the imperative to heal fragmented reality. Such a vision had moved people before, but it had peculiar significance in China then because it came when China was still very much tied to tradition and the nations of the world still had internationalist dreams. It is true that T'an's vision was ultimately private. It was sanctioned by neither church nor Sangha. Yet it is also true that it was built on the faith of three other cosmopolitan souls torn between two worlds: a conservative Baptist missionary who became involved in modernist causes almost by chance, a Pure Land devotee at home in the world of bodhisattvic miracles who was the father of modern Chinese Buddhism, and a Confucian monarchist whose sagehood led him to seek a reform in the name of tradition itself. Into that circle, a young idealistic T'an wandered.

When T'an first went to join the budding reform movement in Peking in 1893, he was, reported fellow reformer Liang Ch'i-chao (1873–1929), full of Christian love—and blissfully ignorant of the utopian, Confucian humanism K'ang had discovered as well as the boundless compassion of Buddhism that Liang himself had made a study of. Through Liang, T'an was led first, in 1895, to a study of Western science under the missionary John Fryer in whose library he discovered a book on mental self-therapy. He also got to know Welsh Baptist Timothy Richard (1845–1919), a consultant during the Reform. T'an was then introduced to the learned layman Yang Wen-hui (Jen-shan, 1837–1911) with whom he studied Buddhism late in 1896. He must have been let into K'ang's yet-unpublished *ta-t'ung* (utopia) thesis; exactly when is still being debated. Of these teachers of T'an, Yang and Richard had their own religious dialogue, the first among Christians and Buddhists. Richard, back from the 1893 Parliament of Religions meeting in Chicago, visited Yang at his home in Nanking in 1894. He brought with him the founder of the Maha Bodhi Society, Ceylonese layman Anagarika Dharmapala.[3] Anagarika had dreams of spreading the Dharma to the whole world, and Yang was inspired by him. Soon after, Yang tutored Richard in Mahāyāna and agreed to help translate the *Awakening of Faith* and portions of the *Lotus Sūtra* into English.

Richard, however, had his own ideas. The first missionary to seriously try to bridge Buddhism and Christianity, Richard had accepted the idea that St. Thomas was responsible for changing atheistic Hinayana into devotional Mahāyāna. To him, the *Lotus Sūtra*'s declaration of Śākyamuni as eternal is Buddhism Christianized and the *Awakening of Faith*'s doctrine of the three Greatness of Suchness, a Trinitarianism of substance (Father), form (Son), and function (Holy Spirit). When Richard insisted on reading Suchness (*tathatā*) as God and the Suchness [in the sentient] Mind as God Immanuel [among men], Yang withdrew himself from the project and removed his name from the end product. Although this first Buddhist-Christian exchange ended unhappily, T'an, their mutual student, was able to put aside such differences. He followed the pious Yang in holding that China needed a spiritual reform and the active Richard in seeing that China needed more than the saving of souls. He fused their visions and then added something else that neither taught.

Neither Yang nor Richard identified science and religion. Yang considered science a mundane teaching and external to the deeper insights of the mind; Richard introduced science but then only as an expediency and not as an integral part of his mission. But T'an would declare an ultimate union of Matter (Ether) and Spirit (Love)—Ether being that immaterial medium that somehow unites all things as Christian Love, Confucian Jen, and Buddhist Compassion would. The science of magnetic force and of mental therapy demonstrated to T'an the power of the *citta* (mind) and the *pneuma* (soul). Endorsing Yogācara idealism, he envisaged a new world to come, the infinite world-spheres of Hua-yen, and embraced K'ang's revisionist view of Confucius as the model reformer. He mixed on his palate the conscience of the Lutheran Reformation and the liberties of the French Revolution. Believing either that no revolution can succeed without bloodshed or that no church can be founded without martyrs, or both, he offered to stay behind and face death when the empress dowager foiled the reform with her coup.[4]

The failure of the Reform ended China's hope to retain its ties with its past. Internationalism became a farce, with Europe soon embroiled in war. In the early twentieth century, we find a modern spokesman for the particularistic genius of Buddhism. Yang Wen-hui hardly wrote anything on Christianity; T'an was assured of its common cause with Buddhism; but the Old Text Confucian scholar Chang T'ai-yen (Ping-lin: 1868–1936) would champion Buddhist modernity. A supporter of the 1898 Reform despite his disagreement with K'ang's New Text scholarship, Chang now realized that the Manchu must go and join forces with Sun Yat-san. Jailed in 1904 for his subversive activities and possibly under torture, Chang discovered the strength of the Buddhist gospel. During his three years' imprisonment, he taught himself the Wei-shih, or Consciousness Only (Vijnaptimatrata, Yogacara), philosophy. This is a system of rational, mental, self-analysis that Yang had reimported from Japan, through his contact Nanjio Bunyu (whom he met through Max Müller during his stay in London as part of China's first diplomatic mission there). Chang became thereby the bodhisattva revolutionary ready to accept suffering and sacrifice for the good of all. He was the nihilist who wove concepts of no-soul, interdependence, and emptiness into a selfless devotion to democracy; the anarchist who looked forward to final peace in a stateless brotherhood; and the active pessimist who had no illusion about human progress, just a tragic sense of increasing karmic burden. A prolific writer and a brilliant scholar, Chang spoke of a classic, rational critique of the folly of the Christian faith in an essay titled "Wu-shen lun" ("On Atheism") (1908).[5]

There are, said Chang, only three basic types of religious philosophies: theism, materialism, and idealism—and India has the purer forms of them. Vedanta considers Brahman the sole reality and reduces all things to God. Visesika postulates nine elements—earth, water, fire, wind, ether, time, space, will, and consciousness—but reduces them all to Matter. Samkhya considers object–realities to be correlates of the subject–mind and reduces ultimately all of them to Idea. Christianity is an inferior form of Brahmanic theism; Consciousness Only is the most refined of idealism. The latter denies the existence of God or soul, but it employs the materialist critique only to demonstrate universal nonsubstantiality. It thus avoids both the fallacy of theism and the crudity of materialism.

Concerning theism, God is said to be eternal, almighty, omniscient, self-sufficient, and all-encompassing. But if God is without beginning, why speak of Creation? If endless, why Judgment? A God that creates and then destroys has already changed his mind. If God, omnipotent and omniscient, intended only the good for humankind, why did he knowingly create a human with the potential for evil? If sin is external and from Satan, why did God create Satan? If God created Satan to test humans, God did not intend the best for humans. If God did not create Satan, God would not be the creator of all. If Satan only fell into evil upon disobeying God, did God not create a flawed servant? If this is done to see if humans would choose good or evil, one wonders why an omniscient God would need a test to know the outcome. Why does a self-sufficient God need to create anything other than himself? If the created is not other than God, creation is coterminous with God. But if creation proceeded naturally from itself, why call it creation? There would be no time when the world was not, no time when things cannot appear at will, all at once, anywhere. If things appear in an instance as a result of a divine will, things should cease as God's will ceases. If so, divine providence is nothing more than a child's whim and not that different from the Buddhist idea of fleeting reality sustained by a blind impulse. But if creation is other than God and God only molded this preexisting substance into form, God is not the sole reality. If it is creation *ex nihilo,* there must be a deficiency on God's part to move him to create something out of nothing. If that something was good, that implies that God is insufficiently good because logically only those deficient in good would need to create some other good for their own edification. On these and other issues, theism contradicts itself.

Chang's critique of Christian theism and his judgment that the Wei-shih philosophy is the modern philosophy par excellence would be repeated by many. His Comtean positivism, though not his nihilism or pessimism, would endear him to leftists. Chang had boldly correlated religion and society in no uncertain terms. Polytheism goes with oligarchy, monotheism with monarchy, and atheism with democracy—and in that historical order. By that scheme, atheistic China should be ahead of the theistic Europe, and it would be too, said Chang, had China not been held back because it passed straight from primitive polytheism (Taoism) to radical atheism (Buddhism) without the benefit of a monotheistic purge of idols under its feudal monarchies. Pure Land devotion is one such theistic survival that blemished thorough atheism. The sooner China rids itself of Amitabha and the host of Buddhas and bodhisattvas, the better.

THE POLARIZATION OF BUDDHIST REASON VERSUS
CHRISTIAN FAITH

With this judgment came also a basic impasse in the Buddhist-Christian en-counter. The Buddhists, in keeping with the times, aligned themselves with rationality and modernity and joined others in finding Christianity prescientific and backward. But in so doing, they had to disown Pure Land and Ch'an, the two major traditions, one for its faith and the other for its anti-intellectualism. Ou-yang Ching-wu (1871–1944), a student of Yang Wen-hui and the authority on the Consciousness Only philosophy, reduced the belief in God to being a state of mind arrested at the seventh level of consciousness, *adana-vijñāna* (ego-grasping consciousness), a false self creating a false God. Only freedom from this egocentric consciousness, this psychic dependency or *paratanra,* can bring about the perfect enlightenment.

In a public lecture, Ou-yang dissociated Buddhism from being a religion like Christianity. Religion involves submitting oneself to God, to believing in the founder, to accepting infallible scriptures, but Buddhism knows only this: "Rely on truth, not on a person; on the meaning, not the word; on the complete teaching, not the incomplete one." The Buddha is no God, just an exemplar of the Way. Buddha-nature being within, one takes refuge ultimately in oneself. As to the words of the scriptures, they are expedient means, not some emotional faith in an Other but a wisdom uncovered through self-effort that liberates. So when Buddhists take refuge in the Buddha, the Dharma, and the Sangha, they mean by the Jewels, the One enlightened, the Reality most comprehensive, and the Fellowship of mind that the discipline of Yoga brings when the self like the Buddha is brought in line with Reality. A favorite argument of modern Buddhists from Sri Lanka to Japan, it turns the old Tertullian formula around: Athens not Jerusalem has the Truth. "Christianity assumes an inequality of the revered and the humbled, Buddhism the equality of all nondual realities; Christianity harbors a narrow set of beliefs, Buddhism a rational ideal conducive to freedom; Christianity restricts itself, unable to see the cause of it all, Buddhism is open, ready to verify in full; Christianity is timidly dependent on others, Buddhism is heroically striving forward by oneself."[6]

This singular emphasis of Wisdom over Grace, or Reason over Mystery, is no more open to their dialectics than Tertullian's. Limiting the Dharma to the Dharma of the Wei-shih philosophy is hardly doing justice to the full tradition.

A more realistic assessment of the situation was being offered by Norwegian Lutheran Karl Ludwig Reichelt (1877–1952). Yes, he believed that St. Thomas inspired Mahāyāna, that Nestorian missions influenced Shan-t'ao of the Pure Land school, and that survival of that Buddhist-Christian synthesis can still be found in his own days. Reichelt even adopted the Nestorian "cross on a lotus" as a symbol for his mission to convert monks to Christ on the premise of a *praeparatio evangelica* in the Lotus. There is a "seed of (the Johannine) Logos" present in all religions, and points of contact between the two religions should be explored. Tutored in Max Müller and Timothy Richard, Rudolf Otto and Nathan Soderblom, and keeping himself abreast of the Japanese discussions on Self-power, Other-power, Two Truths, and Emptiness, Reichelt combined the idea of the Holy (from Otto) present in all religions to the idea of God's universal revelation (from Soderblom), into seeing a boundless Godhead in Buddhism (Zen Emptiness) that encompasses instead of excludes personality (Pure Land faith). So just as this formless Dharmakāya should find fulfillment only in the Other Power of Sambhogakāya Buddha Amitābha's grace, so the latter should point the way to the full and special disclosure of God to human as human, as Christ Jesus in history.[7]

Reichelt's message still attracts some people today and can well engage some Japanese discussants. But it was lost to the rational Chinese Buddhists who did not know Schleiermacher or Otto and whose self-understanding involved little of the Two Truths or Emptiness. This divide between Buddhist reason and Christian faith was perceived as being so real that Reichelt converted few Buddhists to Christ, and T'ai-hsü on his European tour impressed few Europeans with his science. The situation became worse after the war. Europe had by then second thoughts about the promise of reason and progress, but the East is still pressing for their blessings. In theology, Karl Barth questioned all anthropocentric religion, and in missionology Heinrich Kramer was skeptical of "points of contact." Reichelt had to spend his final years defending himself, but the career of C. C. Wang, a Buddhist monk converted by Reichelt, can better tell of this change.

Wang wrote a Chinese book in 1945 called *A Look at Buddha and Christ*.[8] It tells the life and teaching of these two religious founders with no attempt to compare them. The view of Christ is strictly biblical as the view of the Buddha is strictly historical. So historical was it that Wang never got beyond primitive Buddhism, and no mention is made of Amitābha faith as *praeparatio evangelica*. Wang recalled in 1980 that he did write "another work (that) defended Buddhism against Christianity," but that was not published because "the new missionary did not agree with that." But all Wang did was to reinterpret some Buddhist teachings, such as the Ch'an idea of "one's original face." This idea of an innate Buddha-nature does not, Wang argued, contradict the Christian idea of original sin, since it refers to a nature before the Fall. It is a face no longer visible until and unless a person "confesses his sins."[9] This hardly seems that unorthodox as to require suppressing, but then between 1945 and 1963, Wang himself must have been won over to the new missionary view, for in a new 1963 edition of the book now retitled *Yeh Fo Ko-san (A Comparison of Jesus and Buddha)*, he mocked the same Ch'an metaphor by reading it now as a Buddhist denial of a soul. This version did cover the Pure Land teaching, but it cited eleven Buddhist criticisms of it to expose it as mere fiction. As a pastor, Wang then repeated the prevalent judgment of Buddhism as pessimistic and escapist, fatalistic and deprecative of the good earth God created and of humans to whom God had entrusted his creation.[10]

If Wang had so learned to criticize Buddhism, Buddhists, too, had learned to respond in kind. T'ai-hsü might not be an original thinker; his one real innovation was a schema using Wei-shih to reclassify the Buddhist schools. In substance or daring, he lagged behind the lay Buddhist intellectuals. But he had clerical authority, and he did reeducate his fellow monks, especially through popular, modern Buddhist magazines. Japanese and English debates on the relative merits and demerits of Buddhism and Christianity were being introduced. The Chinese now could catalogue their similarities: the ten precepts and the ten commandments, the ten good and the eight beatitudes, the ten schools and the ten churches, Buddhist compassion and Christian love, sons of Buddha and the baptismal new life, Buddha-name recitation and vocal prayer, Buddha land and God's kingdom, the bodhisattvic vow and the Lord's prayer. Or they could list the differences: theism versus atheism; divine omnipotence, human autonomy; original sin, a priori enlightenment; quality, equality; creation, causation; transcendence, internality; judgment after death, waking up in Pure Land, and so on.[11]

Building on such information, an obscure tract, *Yeh-chiao yü Fo-chiao* (*Christianity and Buddhism*), written in 1958 by a certain Chang Chüeh-i (n.d.) of Han Yang (Han-chou) turned Reichelt's thesis upside down. It is Buddhism that can best complete the Christian gospel. Chang had attended a missionary school, but after failing to receive divine guidance despite his incessant prayers, he turned at twenty-seven to Buddhism and, forty years later, came to this conclusion: Instead of Thomas Aquinas influencing Mahāyāna, it is Jesus going East to acquire wisdom. Returning to Palestine to leave home formally, Jesus took up the precepts, performed a series of Tantric miracles, and crowned it with a yogic resurrection. Jesus was a hidden Buddha who taught karma when he talked about trees bearing fruits; who hinted at rebirths, however incompletely, when talking about judgment after one life. The Holy Spirit is really Buddha-nature, and God along with his kingdom are truly within. Worship is an expediency; God in his pure form out there is just the mind purifying itself. As to Creation, God is Brahma at the beginning of a cosmic cycle who created the World with magical *mantras,* the world appearing "like images rising on the mirror of the mind." The Serpent is not Satan; it has become Tantric power. Evil is not external; it is what humans do. There is no original sin, just fundamental ignorance that rose suddenly, the result of the Buddha-mind being divided against itself. Karma being individual responsibility, Christ Jesus cannot remit sins. Faith is just preliminary trust in the truth of the teaching. In the end, everyone must bear one's own cross. Since all people are sons of God, Jesus represents only the Buddha-nature actualized. In Chang's hand, the Lord's prayer becomes a praise of the Dharmakāya ("Our Father in Heaven") from Buddha-sons who chant his name ("Hallowed Be Thy Name") waiting for the visitation of the heavenly host from the Pure Land ("Thy Kingdom Come"). At the very end, Chang offered this syncretistic prayer: "Christ Jesus our Lord, may your precious blood flow through our bodies, washing away our sins, that is, purifying our hearts such that we can see God and recognize our (true) selves, that we may leave the pain of rebirth and ascend with all sentient beings the stage of total freedom.''[12] In a curious way, he is being entirely sincere.

THE POLITICIZED DEBATES THAT GOT NOWHERE

Disagreements over religious ideas have a way of boiling over into politics, especially in changing times. We see a conflict emerging between the old-time religion and the new-time faith. The missionary schools in the cities had helped to bring up a new urban middle class, culturally Westernized. (We see this most in colonies like Hong Kong and Singapore.) In 1955 Dharma master Chu-yun gave a series of lectures in Tai-nan in which he criticized the tactics of the Christians. Missionaries did not just build churches next to temples or pass out pamphlets at temple gates; zealous evangelicals would disrupt Buddhist gatherings seeking to debate their gospel truth. Chu-yun compared such efforts to a new shop on the block aggressively advertising its untested merchandise with gimmicks. Buddhism he likened to the established, name-brand store confident that old customers would return for its genuine articles. Like most moderns, Chu-yun admired and envied the good work Christians did in education and charity. Monks could learn from that, but it was also time to ponder which of these two religions was better suited to the "Chinese national character."

Chu-yun spoke as a traditionalist. Śākyamuni to him was proven better than Jesus, because his past good karma had placed him into a royal home. The Buddha was a better teacher, too, since he had more than just twelve disciples. He taught more than one thin Bible. Chu-yun so believed in karmic justice that he was sure that when a certain Professor Wang tried to burn a Kuan-yin statue, he was duly stricken with a headache for three months. Insisting that karma is individualized, Chu-yun concluded that God cannot save people, nor can prayers remit sin. These lectures, later disseminated in a small book titled *Fo-chiao yü Chi-tu-chiao te pi-chiao (A Comparison of Buddhism and Christianity)*, aroused the ire of Pastor Wu yin-po.[13] Wu's rejoinder of a book has on its jacket a shining cross chasing away two pairs of foxes and snakes—crafty and poisonous bewitchers. A fundamentalist Christian, Wu cited chapter and verse to show how unforgivably the Dharma master misquoted the infallible Bible. There was much name calling, attacks *ad hominon,* and a baiting of anyone to prove him wrong with the reward of a thousand Taiwanese dollars.

All that need not detain us because the heart of the debate was not over religion but over *which* religion is in China's interest. By contrasting their histories in China, by pitting God against Buddha, master and pastor, the swastika and the cross, Chu-yun concluded that Buddhists are more loyal; more filial; more committed to liberty, equality, fraternity; more scientific and democratic, than Christians. He took the sinicized Buddhism of late imperial China as the norm, and he forgot how Buddhism had had its own un-Chinese beginning. When Wu tried to refute those charges, a certain Chang Chia-mi rallied more patriotic sons of China to Chu-yun's defense.[14] The tone became dangerously antiforeign, and

Wu apparently backed down from more politicized debates, but then he involved himself in another one in which he, in Hong Kong, alleged that his opponent in Taiwan was a Communist sympathizer, which amounts to treason in Taiwan.

The monk this time is Yin-shun (1906-), the most learned of T'ai-hsü's disciples. In a series of articles, "Does God Love the World?" Yin-shun condemned the "slave morality" of the biblical faith. Attracted to Christianity in his youth, Yin-shun ultimately abandoned it because he had difficulties with this faith. Granted that God reached out repeatedly to sinful people, why would he allow evil to exist in the first place? This is an old question. But Yin-shun went further. If faith requires a Job to submit in order to win back God's favor, he could consider that only as enslaving. The Christian faith seems to enjoy keeping people ignorant. Desiring after the knowledge of good and evil, did not Adam have to pay dearly? Was not God so jealous of human technological advances in the construction of the Tower of Babel that he scattered humankind? A religion of a Chosen People led naturally to bloodshed, and the Canaanites were slaughtered by the Israelites seeking a promised land. United under Yahweh, the tribes indeed soon saw the rise of kings. Yin-shun preferred the pacifism of the Buddha and took more to Jesus. As he said, his was not a Buddhist critique of Christianity, just a humanistic campaign against the Christian deprecation of humans.[15]

But Wu in his defense of faith minced no words. He called Yin-shun a "turncoat Christian," alleging Yin-shun had dined on "Christian rice" at Reichelt's mission at Tao Fong Shan in Hong Kong, a frequent stopover for monks fleeing the Communists. Yin-shun denied that complicity. He was not one who took that bribery. The monthly allowance of four dollars from the "Evil Wind Hill" was quite a sum in those days. The Christians, not he, were the Europhiles. Because of his sociological analysis, Yin-shun was called a leftist sympathizer; Yin-shun asked Wu to choose such politically charged words carefully. Other Christians tried to get Yin-shun to see the difference between voluntary submission to God and forced compliance to despots. But the monk could not see how freedom could possibly come of being "slaves to Christ." He also would not accept the oft-made argument that Luther's quest for liberty pointed ahead to the civil liberties of the French Revolution. Rather, he argued the Enlightenment did.

Yin-shun knew the Wei-shih philosophy but was a much broader scholar monk than that. There were signs that the Wei-shih philosophy that had drawn some keen minds had run its course. There were major defectors. Intellectuals such as Hsiung Shih-li (1882–1968) who fashioned a *Hsin Wei-shih* (New Idealism) of it had turned back to Confucianism. Liang Shu-ming (1893-) took a similar detour. His *Cultures of East and West and Their Philosophies* (1921) was a landmark in comparative religion. It reduces all cultures to the human will. The West is the product of an extrovert will manifested as pure intellect in a self set actively against the world. India represents introvert reflection fostering ascetic self-denial, mystical passivity, and profound insights into the mind. Yet even as the Consciousness Only philosophy provided him that analytical framework, in the end Liang, too, chose the middle path of Confucianism, valuing its Bergsonian intuition into change, its humanism and harmony with cosmos. It is this new Confucian tradition, not Buddhism, that holds now the promise of dialogue with the West.[16]

NEW DIRECTIONS: SPIRITUALISM AND EXISTENTIAL HORIZONS

Modern Buddhism assumes compatibility with science and democracy, but the spiritual dimension of Buddhism might have little or nothing to do with reason and modernity. Regarding traditional Buddhism, Catholics have shown more interest.[17] With H. M. Enomiya Lasalle drawing attention to the possibility of Catholic Zen in Japan, similar explorations were being attempted in Taiwan. Father Chang Chiung-shen sought out that bonus of Chinese spirituality for adoption. He spoke of the personal and transpersonal aspect of God, the former better covered by the extrovert, instrumental tradition of the West, the latter better covered by the introvert, expressive East. They complement each other.

The Christian prayer seeking communion with God can do with a Chinese sense of the transparency and nonabiding nature of all forms. One's spiritual flight upward premised on the dualism of body and soul can be balanced by the other's search for inner unity premised on integral Yoga. The nihilism of Buddhist no-self notwithstanding, in proper measures that radical self-analysis and autotheraphy may help in the purgation of the impure from within while looking to illumination from without. Less attached to externals, Buddhism can point to the transpersonal, the ineffable Godhead. It can better see the unity of the Three in love, even as Christian contemplation can better appreciate the distinct persona of the Trinity.[18]

But in reading Chang's East-West, Yin-Yang harmony, it seems almost too neat. He simplifies the Ch'an denial of Words and the Christian affirmation of Logos. His lectures somehow lack the experiential depth of Lasalle. Lasalle saw two self-sufficient systems of meditation with structural parallels, such as Thomas Aquinas' *ratio, intellectus,* and the Buddhist *byodo, sabetsu.* Questions of doctrinal differences Lasalle treated only later, but Chang began with the doctrinal differences, was reticent on techniques, and showed little knowledge of the subtleties of Mahāyāna dialectics, or the *kung-an(koan).* Unlike Japanese Buddhists who are able to engage Christians in their Zen practices or in their Jodo soteriology, Chinese Buddhists have yet to do this. Without that active cross-fertilization of Buddhism and Christianity, Chang repeated a lot of the Confucian criticism of Ch'an vacuity, but moralistic neo-Confucianism is not always the best authority on matters of the spirit. That moralism prevails in another book on this topic by another Catholic father, Chiu Pin-shih.[19] There, the mainstream of Chinese spiritual cultivation is traced through the Confucian and the Taoist tradition. Buddhism is notable by its absence.

A different spiritual journey is taken by a younger, contemporary Protestant thinker who moved beyond the formulaic to what such doctrines mean in real life. That existential excursion is told by Leung In-shing in his book *hui-ching shen-yao (A Spiritual Journey to Different Realms of Intellectual Experience)*.[20] Leung had acquired a Buddhist training from Fok Tou-hui, the leading Buddhologist in Hong Kong, and later discovered the Christian faith. In a mythical journey, Leung described his own passage from modern, Western rationalism through Taoist nonbeing and Buddhist emptiness to the moral universe of the Confucian, until he reached an impasse over the fallibility of humans that led to his encounter with Augustine and his experience of the Eternal Life in Christ. The whole journey is told in Kierkegaardian pathos but according to the Buddhist notion of realms—different levels of the same reality being unveiled through successively deeper perspectives.

Although the conclusion is Christian, Leung preserved well the insights from prior stages in that pilgrimage. Thus the Buddhist understanding of the (differentiating) consciousness clinging to an object prefigures the biblical Fall. This is because the eating of the fruit can be seen as the idolatry of attaching to an object the absoluteness that it does not have. In this way Leung read a Christian doctrine at a Buddhist level in Buddhist terms and overcame the obvious credal differences by locating the experiential core behind such doctrines. Even omnipresent Buddhahood can be tied to original sin for there is the facticity of Buddha-nature, the "*tathāgatagarbha* in bondage," being inexplicably polluted. In his participation in a Christian-Confucian discussion, begun between Tsai Jen-hou and Chou Luen-hua, Leung spoke of a need for a dehellenization of Christianity.[21] The difference between static Greek Being and dynamic Taoist Becoming has been noted before, but Leung used a new vocabulary first to unravel the Western presuppositions and then to reconstruct them according to an Oriental "relationism" and "perspectivism." Buddhism came into the discussion in that Leung sought a native theology of "perfect harmony" (a Sinitic Mahāyāna doctrine of the T'ien-t'ai school) to replace a theology of alienation dominant in the West.

Leung's spiritual pilgrimage recapitulates a major route many Chinese intellectuals since the nineteenth century have traveled. China was forced to confront Western rationalism. Some adopted that; others retreated into an Oriental mysticism. Still others tried to overcome both extremes by treading the Confucian middle path. Although Buddhism is not at the center of the China-Europe dialogue now, the Buddhist component in Chinese culture is too important to ignore. In any case, one must learn to go behind labels like atheistic Buddhists, theistic Christians, and agnostic Confucians. The three might agree among themselves more than those handy labels might suggest. The gods of nature of which the Buddha disapproved Moses also would have nothing to do with. But then, likewise, the God Moses knew is not exactly the Brahma that the Buddhists renounced. Both traditions outlived the old gods but in two different ways, and each then celebrated its break with the past with creeds to avoid any regression into that idolatrous past. In Christianity it is the dogma of creation *ex nihilo;* in Buddhism it could be the formula of the no-self, *anatman.*

These central creeds, created in that axial age against former enemies, have perpetuated themselves and are being used against more newly encountered religions. Christians are then mistaken by Buddhists as Brahma worshippers, and Buddhists are dismissed by Christians as godless heathens. Creation *ex nihilo* is confused with Vedantic *satkaryavada; anatman* is taken to imply soulless nihilism. Worse, cardinal doctrines meaningful in an earlier era might not even be relevant today. As a doctrine, creation *ex nihilo* removed, for the Greeks, any possibility of there being some prior substance, *hule,* that an Aristotelean God merely molded into intelligible form. It helped then to annihilate any idolatry of nature. But to apply that doctrine verbatim to Buddhism and to our time is hermeneutically unwise. Buddhism is not "nature mysticism"; it had totally desacralized nature. Modern humans also do not worship nature; they rape forests and destroy wildlife. So giving back to nature some of the sacredness it once had is hardly detrimental in our times. Likewise, the Buddhist idea of no-soul was meaningful only when the Hindu believed in a changeless soul. Most of us have no idea of or love for a changeless self, and Christians, who never took the spirit to mean simply such given eternity, should be less offended by the Buddhist denial of the same.

In short, a meaningful Buddhist-Christian dialogue must proceed with a radical deconstruction of its own metaphysical beliefs in order to uncover the real import of such doctrines for our times. We may find that creation *ex nihilo,* as that which affirms the sovereignty of God and the fallibility of humans, might well resonate with *anatman,* which removes the self-idolatry of the *atman* and recognizes the danger of the human will-to-be (*samskara*). Perhaps the whole point in the Buddha's insisting on the eventuality of good and evil action without insisting on the self is to locate the power of the good outside what St. Paul would see as the natural human. Only thus, and patiently step by step, may we be able to discover the structural similarities and differences between these two traditions. There is neither Jew nor Gentile in the church, but it is too early to state whether there will be neither Christian nor Buddhist in the new world Ecumene. Only through patient mutual solicitation may we approach, in fear and trembling, that unheard-of impossible possibility.

NOTES

1. See Chapter 25 by John Cobbs in this volume. On a prospectus of dialogue, see Peter Lee, "From Mission to Buddhists to Possibilities of Multi-faceted Religious Dialogue," *Ching Feng* 16, no. 3 (1978): 115–125. On the character of Chinese Christianity, see Ng Lee-ming, *Chi-tu-chiao yü Chung-kuo she-hui pien-ch'ien* (in Chinese) [*Christianity and Social Change in China*] (Hong Kong: Theological Educational Press, 1984), which covers the history of the indigenization of Christianity in China especially since the 1940s after the foreign missionaries left. Ng covered the five major modern Chinese

theologians, but none of the five figures concerned himself with the relatively minor contingent of Buddhists in China. For that reason, I have not included them in this survey.

2. See Winfried Gluer, "The Encounter between Christianity and Chinese Buddhism during the Nineteenth Century and the First Half of the Twentieth Century," *Ching Feng* 11, no. 3, pp. 39–57; Frederick P. Brandauer, "The Encounter of Christianity and Chinese Buddhism from the Fourteenth to the Seventeenth Century," *Ching Feng* 11, no. 3 (30–38). For general background, see Donald W. Treadgold, *The West in Russia and China: Religious and Secular Thoughts in Modern Times. Vol. 2: China, 1582–1949* (London: Cambridge University, 1973). See also John Young, "Comparing the Approaches of the Jesuit and the Protestant Missions in China," *Ching Feng* 22, no. 2 (1979): 107–115.

3. Anagarika Dharmapala was promised help by the monks of the Lung-hua Monastery, but then the monks, recalling fearfully the imperial interdict against monks forming associations, begged to be released from the promise. Richard was probably directed to approach Yang, the leading lay Buddhist active in Buddhist publication, as the person in a position to help.

4. On T'an's career, see Chan Sin-wei, *Buddhism in Late Ch'ing Political Thought* (Hong Kong: Chinese University of Hong Kong, 1985).

5. See Chang T'ai-yen, *Chang T'ai-yen hsüan-chi* (Shanghai: Jen-ming, 1980), pp. 322–352. The following is my paraphrase, from pp. 322–334.

6. Ou-yang Ching-wu, "Fo-chiao fei tsung-chiao" ("Buddhism Is Not a Religion"), from a public lecture c. 1912, in Fok Tou-hui, *Fo-hsüeh* (Hong Kong: Chinese University of Hong Kong, 1983), 2: 96–100. This rational reading of Buddhism, Theravada Buddhists, was and is being repeated in Mahāyāna China.

7. See Hakan Eihart, *Boundlessness: Studies in Karl Ludwig Reichelt's Missionary Thinking with Special Regard to the Buddhist Christian Encounter,* Studia Missionalia Upsaliensia 24 (Kobenhaaum: Aros Eksp., DBK, 1974), which sees Reichelt as a theologian and scholar of Mahāyāna philosophy. The picture drawn by Eric J. Sharpe in *Karl Ludwig Reichelt: Missionary, Scholar, and Pilgrim* (Hong Kong: The Tao Fong Shan Ecumenical Centre, 1984) is more modest. A Chinese lecture of Reichelt, "Buddhist Origin," issued from Tao Fong Shan (n.d.), is available at the library at Tao Fong Shan, Shatin, New Territories, Hong Kong. On the career of Tai-hsü, see Holmes Welch, *The Buddhist Revival* (Cambridge, Mass.: Harvard University Press, 1968).

8. Wang's 1945 treatise on Buddha and Christ has survived, probably as *Shih-chia yü Yeh-su* [*Śākyamuni and Jesus*] reprinted by Tao Fong Shan in Hong Kong in 1967. His life is told in "C. C. Wang," a mimeographed volume in the Midwest China Oral History and Archives Collection (1980).

9. On the incidents in 1945, see "C. C. Wang," pp. 21–22.

10. See *Yeh Fo Ko-san* issued from Tao Fong Shan in Hong Kong. Wang's criticism is of textbook Buddhism, doctrinally speaking, not untrue, but it is not based on the living religion. Look at how Chinese Buddhism is practiced in either cloisters or shrines, and although it might be magical, it is anything but "pessimistic and escapist, fatalistic and deprecative of world and man."

11. See articles from the *Hai-chao-yin* magazine now excerpted in the *Hai-chao-yin wen-fu* series, especially Division II on Chung-chiao jen-sheng (Religious Life), part 1, "Fo-chiao T'ung-lun (General Treatises)." See also the anthology of articles in Chang Man-tu, ed., *Ta-cheng wen-fu. Vol. 7: Fo-chiao yü yeh-chiao te pi-chiao (Mahāyāna Studies. Vol. 7: Comparing Buddhism and Christianity)* (Taipei: Ta-cheng wen-hua, 1971). The List above is taken from an essay by Chang Yu-chin, originally published in

Hai-chao-yin 15, no. 5, now included in Chang, *Ta-cheng wen-fu*, pp. 3–39, especially pp. 19–28. Often these comparative essays are very general, but this is a general magazine. There are a few exceptions.

12. Chang Chüeh-i's book is at the library at Tao Fong Shan, a gift from the University of Hong Kong, which thought it too insignificant to keep: *Yeh-chiao yü Fo-chiao* (*Christianity and Buddhism*) (Hang Yang?, 1958) privately issued, probably by Chang under a psuedonym, with no place given.

13. Chu-yun, *Fo-chiao yü Chi-tu-chiao te pi-chiao* (*A Comparison of Buddhism and Christianity*) (Taipei: Fo-chiao wen-hua fu-wu she, 1956). A comparison of Buddhism and Christianity.

14. Wu Yin-po, *Fo-chiao yü Chi-tu-chiao te pi-chiao kao* (Taipei: Sheng-wen she, 1956); Chang Chiun-sheng, *P'ing Fo-chiao yu Chi-tu-chiao te pi-chiao kao* (Taipei: Hing-fang Book Store, n.d.).

15. Yin-shun, "Shang-ti ai shih-jen?" ("God Loves Man?") and "Shang-ti ai shih-jen te tsai tu-lun" ("Again on Whether God Loves Man"), previously published in the *Hai-chao-yin* 44, nos. 7-8; 45, nos. 6-8; now included in Chang, *Ta-cheng wen-fu*, pp. 163–244.

16. Guy Alitto, *The Last Confucian: Liang Shu-ming and the Chinese Dilemma of Modernity* (Berkeley: University of California Press, 1979).

17. See, for example, Yyes Raguin, *Buddhism: Sixteen Lectures in Buddhism and Christianity* (Taipei: Mimeographed text from the Ricci Institute, 1974; permission to print, 1975). Given after Vatican II, it recognizes:

If we like to dialog with Buddhism, it is not enough to talk with Buddhists, we have to bring our own theology and philosophy in contact with Buddhist thought. The dialog has to start with us. . . . Surely there are similarities between Buddhism and Christianity. Some tend to see only the points on which we meet. . . . some may see only differences. We will try to understand where differences and similarities lie. This way it will be easier for us to see what is specific in Christian revelation. At the end it may become clear to us what differences it makes that Buddha pretended simply to "show the way to nirvana" while Christ said "I am the Way." The mysteries of the Incarnation, of the Trinity, of Salvation through Christ's death and resurrection will appear in a new light. (p. 3)

18. Chang Chiung-shen, *Chung-kuo ling-shu kan-i* (*Discussion on Chinese Spiritual Exercises*) (Tai-chung: Kuang-chi, 1978).

19. Chiu Pin-shih, *Ling-hsu hsüeh tsai Chung-kuo* (*The Art of Spiritual Exercises in China*) (Taipei: Hsing-ai, 1979).

20. Published in Taipei: Cosmic Light Press, 1982.

21. His participation in this Christian-Confucian discussion begun between Tsai Jen-hou and Chou Luen-hua now forms the second half of the published exchanges as *Hui-t'ung yü chuan-hua* (*Understanding and Transformation*) (Taipei: Yu-chiu, 1985).

SELECTED BIBLIOGRAPY

Some sources have been omitted from the discussion because of the nature of the presentation. They are as follows:

Several books of George Appleton (Anglican) on Christianity and Buddhism were translated into Chinese by the Christians. The Buddhists selected some works to translate, such as an exchange between the American Buddhist Frank Newton (aka Bhiksu Upaya, associated with the Harmony Buddhist Association, Clarksville, Arkansas) and the work of James D. Bales (professor of biblical literature at Harding College, Searcy, Arkansas). The title of the work in Chinese translates as "Is Buddhism a Higher Teaching Than Christianity?" (Hong Kong: Fo-shu t'ung-liao chu, n.d.).

In the *Catalogue of Chinese Buddhist Articles and Books Published in Taiwan during the Last Twenty Years (Erh-shih nen lai fo-chiao ching-shu lun-wen so-yin)*, published in Taipei in 1973 by the Chung-hua hsüeh-shu yuan (Chinese Academy), Research Department on Buddhist Culture (Fo-chiao yen-chiu sho), no Buddhist-Christian exchanges are even included. The omission is due to the distinction made—and the real gap that exists—between academic, often secular, "Buddhist studies" and the old, pious homilies in "Buddhist religion." In the collected articles of the modern Buddhist magazine founded by T'ai-hsu, *Hai-chao-yin wen-fu*, the only notable entry under Division II on Chung-chiao jen-sheng (Religious Life), Part 1, "Fo-chiao T'ung-lun" ("General Treatises on Buddhism"), is Master Hsu-ming's four-part piece on *shen fo chih feng* (the difference between God and Buddha) in Fascicle 3, pp. 619, 629, 660, 674. It addresses the topic of God's omniscience and omnipotence and in what limited and rational sense the Buddha by his self-effort and in his timely compassion is all-knowing and all-powerful. The Theological Educational Series sponsored by the Association of Theological Studies in South East Asia also has no book on Buddhism; under the heading of "World Religions" are included two translations from English of works by Joseph Kitagawa and Neill. In addition, Buddhism is not on the agenda of most native theological dissertations; *The Collection of Chinese Protestant Theological Essays (Chung-kuo chi-tu-chiao shen-hsüeh lun-shu* (Hong Kong, 1974) lists none.

Buddhist magazines are numerous. Most cover news items and almost none includes interfaith dialogues. Among these magazines are *Fa-yin (Dharmaghosa)* in Beijing, *Hsiang-Kang fo-chiao (Hong Kong Buddhism)*, and *Young Buddhist* in Singapore. There are two exceptions: *Ching Feng* from Tao Fong Shan and *Collectanla Theologica Universitaitis Fujen* from the Catholic Fujen University in Taipei. Peter Lee, the current director of the Christian Ecumenical Center at Tao Fong Shan, encouraged more open exchanges among faiths.

A high school text comparing various religious beliefs has been written by Lin Shih-min—*Pi-chiu tsung-chiao hsin-yang* (Taipei: T'ien-hua, 1981). The fourth chapter, "Comparative Religion" (pp. 30–53), contrasts Buddhism and Christianity while incorporating much of the old discussions.

Liang Shu-ning believed that China is ahead of its time, its spirit having been accidentally imprisoned by feudal structures. Laing's neo-traditionalism did not contribute anything new to the Buddhist-Christian dialogue. In fact, the West to him consists of ancient Greece, the Renaissance, and the Enlightenment. Under this interpretation, Christianity is a "Hebraic interlude." China for Laing is Confucianism, with Buddhism constituting another import. Liang's reconversion from Buddhism to Confucianism marked the end of the modern Chinese intellectual's interest in Buddhism.

Journals

Ching Feng, Tao Fong Shan Ecumenical Study Center, Hong Kong.
Collectanla Theologica Universitaitis Fujen, Fujen University (Catholic), Taipei.
Fa-yin (Dharmaghosa), Peking.
Hai-chao-yin, begun by Tai-hsu, China, Taiwan.
Hai-chao-yin wen-fu.

Hsiang-kang fo-chiao (Hong Kong Buddhism), Hong Kong.
Young Buddhist, Singapore.

Chinese Books

Chang, Chiung-shen. *Chung-kuo ling-shu kan-i (Discussion on Chinese Spiritual Exercises)*. Tai-chung: Kuang-chi, 1978.

————. *P'ing Fo-chiao yu Chi-tu-chiao te pi-chiao kao*. Taipei: Hing-fang Book Store, n.d.

Chang, Chueh-i. *Yeh-chiao yü Fo-chiao (Christianity and Buddhism)*. Han Yang?: Privately issued, 1958.

Chang, Man-tu, ed. *Ta-cheng wen-fu. Vol. 7: Fo-chiao yü yeh-chiao te pi-chiao (Mahāyāna Studies. Vol. 7: Comparing Buddhism and Christianity)*. Taipei: Ta-cheng wen-hua, 1971.

Chang, T'ai-yen. *Chang T'ai-yen hsüan-chi*. Shanghai: Jen-ming, 1980.

Chiu, Pin-shih. *Ling-hsu-hsüeh tsai Chung-kuo (The Art of Spiritual Exercises in China)*. Taipei: Hsing-ai, 1979.

Chu-yun. *Fo-chiao yu Chi-tu-chiao te pi-chiao (A Comparison of Buddhism and Christianity)*. Taipei: Fo-chiao wen-hua fu-wu she, 1956.

Fok, Tou-hui. *Fo-hsueh*. Vols. 1 and 2. Hong Kong: Chinese University of Hong Kong, 1983.

Leung, In-ching. *Hui-ching shen-yao*. Taipei: Cosmic Light Press, 1982.

Leung, In-ching, Tsai Jen-hou, and Chou Luen-hua, *Hui-t'ung yu chuan-hua (Understanding and Transformation)*. Taipei: Yu-chiu, 1985.

Lin, Shih-mien, *Pi-chiu tsung-chiao hsin-yang (Comparative Religious Beliefs)*. Taipei: T'ien-hua, 1981.

Ng, Lee-ming, *Chi-tu-chiao yu Chung-kuo she-hui pien-ch'ien (Christianity and Social Change in China)*. Hong Kong: Theological Educational Press, 1984.

Newton, Frank, American Buddhist, alias Bhiksu Upaya, associated with the Harmony Buddhist Association, Clarksville, Arkansas, and James D. Bales, professor of biblical literature at Harding College, Searcy, Arkansas. "Is Buddhism a Higher Teaching Than Christianity?" (in Chinese). Hong Kong: Fo-shu t'ung-liao chu, n.d.

Reichelt, Ludwig. *Fo-chiao ch'i-yuan (Buddhist Origins)*. Hong Kong: Tao Fong Shan, n.d.

Wang, C. C. *Shih-chia yü Yeh-su (Śākyamuni and Jesus)*. Hong Kong: Tao Fong Shan reprint, 1967.

————. *Yeh Fo Ko-san (A Comparison of Jesus and Buddha)*. Hong Kong: Tao Fong Shan, 1963.

Wu, Yin-po, *Fo-chiao yü Chi-tu-chiao te pi-chiao kao*. Taipei: Sheng-wen she, 1956.

Chinese Articles

Hsu-ming. "Shen fo chih feng" ("The Difference between God and Buddha") (in four parts). *Hai-chao-yin wen-fu*, Fascicle 3.

Ou-yang, Ching-wu. "Fo-chiao fei tsung-chiao" ("Buddhism Is Not a Religion") (from a public lecture c. 1912). In Fok Tou-hui, *Fo-hsüeh*. Vol. 2. Hong Kong: Chinese University of Hong Kong, 1983.

Yin-shun. "Shang-ti ai shih-jen?" ("God Loves Man?"), and "Shang-ti ai shih-jen te tsai tu-lun" ("Again on Whether God Loves Man"). In Chang, Man-tu, ed., *Ta-*

cheng wen-fu. Vol. 7: Fo-chiao yü yeh-chiao te pi-chiao (Mahāyāna Studies. Vol. 7: Comparing Buddhism and Christianity). Taipei: Ta-cheng wen-hua, 1971.

English Books

Alitto, Guy. *The Last Confucian: Liang Shu-ming and the Chinese Dilemma of Modernity.* Berkeley: University of California Press, 1979.

Chan, Sin-wei. *Buddhism in Late Ch'ing Political Thought.* Hong Kong: Chinese University of Hong Kong, 1985.

Eihart, Hakan. *Boundlessness: Studies in Karl Ludwig Reichelt's Missionary Thinking with Special Regard to the Buddhist Christian Encounter.* Studia Missionalia Upsaliensia 24. Wuppertal, West Germany: Verlag der Rheinischen Missions-Gesellschaft: Svenka Institutät für Missionsforschung, 1974.

Sharpe, Eric J. *Karl Ludwig Reichelt: Missionary, Scholar, and Pilgrim.* Hong Kong: The Tao Fong Shan Ecumenical Centre, 1984. This work is more modest.

Treadgold, Donald W. *The West in Russia and China: Religious and Secular Thoughts in Modern Times. Vol. 2: China, 1582-1949.* London: Cambridge University, 1973.

Welch, Holmes. *Buddhism under Mao.* Cambridge, Mass.: Harvard University Press, 1972.

————. *The Buddhist Revival.* Cambridge, Mass.: Harvard University Press, 1968.

————. *The Practice of Chinese Buddhism.* Cambridge, Mass: Harvard University Press, 1967.

English Articles

Brandauer, Frederick P. "The Encounter of Christianity and Chinese Buddhism from the Fourteenth to the Seventeenth Century." *Ching Feng* 11, no. 3.

Gluer, Winfried. "The Encounter between Christianity and Chinese Buddhism during the Nineteenth Century and the First Half of the Twentieth Century." *Ching Feng* 11, no. 3.

Lee, Peter. "From Mission to Buddhists to Possibilities of Multi-faceted Religious Dialogue." *Ching Feng* 21, no. 3 (1978).

Raguin, Yyes. "Buddhism: Sixteen Lectures in Buddhism and Christianity." Taipei: Ricci Institute, 1974; permission to print, 1975. Mimeographed.

Wang, C. C. "C. C. Wang." Mimeographed, 1980. Mid-West China Oral History and Archives Collection,

Young, John. "Comparing the Approaches of the Jesuit and the Protestant Missions in China." *Ching Feng* 22, no. 2 (1979).

Bibliography

Catalogue of Chinese Buddhist Articles (Erh-shih nen lai fo-chiao ching-shu lun-wen so-yin) and Books Published in Taiwan during the Last Twenty Years. Taipei: Chung-hua hsüeh-shu yuan, Research Department on Buddhist Culture, Fo-chiao yen-chiu sho, 1973.

Collection of Chinese Protestant Theological Essays (Chung-kuo chi-tu-chiao shen-hsueh lun-shu. Hong Kong: Chung-kuo chi-tu-chiao shen-hsueh "book-gift society," 1974.

27

Buddhism and the Japanese Tradition

KENNETH K. INADA

Japan today stands tall among the nations of the world, principally because of its economic prowess and power. It has unquestionably become the emulative symbol and goal of not only the developing nations but also those already developed. For a nation poorly endowed with natural resources, except perhaps with manpower, it is a success story unique in the annals of history, especially because it had to pick itself up by the bootstraps since the end of World War II. In consequence, since the mid-1960s many studies have been directed to probe and reveal this story, focusing naturally on its economic and industrial accomplishments, which peaked in a best-seller by Ezra F. Vogel, *Japan as Number One*.[1] The success, however, had a downside since the studies also revealed certain ungainful aspects that went along with those positive elements; that is, there were negative forces at play that minimized to some degree the nature of the success. These forces, for example, are the overregulated nature of society; the narrow, restrictive, and stultifying educational system, the over-exuberant work ethics; the tradition-bound nature of politics and management; and the group dependency psychology of the individual.[2]

Most of the studies are generally weighted in the direction of the ostensibly tangible and materialistic analysis of the success story and present only peripheral treatment of the deeper cultural aspects. Lately, however, the Japanese themselves have entered the scene to offer a somewhat balanced view by focusing on the historically oriented spiritual and cultural characteristics that were generally glossed over.[3] Even non-Japanese researchers with keen perception have contributed to correct the imbalanced view.[4]

We may conclude that these studies, though important in themselves, collectively still emphasize the merely observable and analyzable features without going into the more profound religio-philosophical elements nascent to the Japanese mind and behavior. These elements are part and parcel of the individual, societal, and national functions that cover the whole gamut of life, extending from the micro to the macro level of existence. Without understanding this feature, all discussions and analysis on the continuity and change in Japanese society would fall flat or would be superficial at best and incoherent at worst. This is equally true in considering the place of Buddhism within the Japanese tradition. The first priority, then, is to be clear about the kind of society one is dealing with and in what manner Buddhism or any other system of thought thrives in it. A careful examination of the situation would suggest a unique organismic society.

THE ORGANISMIC SOCIETY

A society is organismic in that, like an organism, there is total involvement and movement of all of its parts. Looked upon from another viewpoint, nothing is ineffective or fruitless within the total setting. This nature of society is full, a plenum if you will, where every element is accounted for, however small, weak, or insignificant it may seem. In fact, it is the nature of any society in the world, as it ought to be seen, interpreted, and encountered, but we are renegades in that we lose sight of our basic existential bearings by quickly moving on to indulge in whatever elements that attract and sustain our existence. In the case of Japan, the nature of a plenum of existence is more readily seen and felt than in other countries because of its cultural unity. It has had the good fortune of being blessed by a temperate climate and favorable geography to receive and cultivate the cultural characteristics from its continental neighbors.

Although the basic cultural heritage of Japan springs from both China and India, the cradles of Asiatic civilization, Japan nevertheless refined that heritage in innovative ways. In sizing up Japanese culture and the Japanese mind, it is mandatory that we sense the uniqueness in the whole rather than indulging in piecemeal comparative analysis of similar or dissimilar elements. This holistic understanding and perception of a nation and its people are most vital, yet most difficult, to achieve. But the challenge must be met and pursued.

In Japan the combination of Confucianism, Buddhism, and Shintoism has made the greatest cultural impact. Shintoism and Taoism are usually spoken of together, the former being an ideological extension of the latter. The former is more skewed toward the religious in tenor and spirit and the latter more philosophical and naturalistic. Because of its thoroughly naturalistic character, Taoism has given easy access to many areas of endeavor, the most facile of which are the resiliency and adaptability to accommodate every element of religion and culture. Thus Taoism and Shintoism retain their primitive roots, but they have grown separately in terms of their own peculiar characteristics as they germinate in different grounds.

Despite the similarity or difference, the most important character that runs through all three systems of thought is the notion of humanity within the context of an organismic society. This is not an exercise in metaphysics or a deep analysis of nature itself. Instead, it has to be considered to be the most penetrating adaptation of humans to the changing circumstances and conditions of the times. Humanity in this respect is the steady keel that has guided people of different persuasions to keep faith in humankind and to uphold it. It has been expressed in different ways, but it has always held attention by being the underpinning for common sense, integrity, and good causes. Thus humanity has been the key stabilizing element of existence.

Confucian humanity (*jen*) comes to mind as the most natural human trait and discipline, although for the most part we pay mere lip service to it. Confucius' great contribution is to make humanity the central force in humankind with an extensive universal quality. "To be a human is to be humane" is not only a truism but a veritable challenge. No better existential expression can be found in the world. Taoism generally followed this existential expression of humanity in promoting its own philosophy of nonaction or radical naturalism. In Buddhism, humanity is expressed in the *samādhi* exercise (meditative discipline) where the four components of loving kindness, compassion, sympathetic joy, and equanimity collapse into a unity to bring forth the purity of individual quest for true existence. The Mahāyāna Buddhist ideality of life as delineated by the Bodhisattva's life brings to clear focus every act of every person in a society but all of which are clearly couched within the organismic play of events. In brief, similar to Confucianism, Buddhism, too, is a thoroughly humanistic way of life, although critics tend to separate them into distinct systems. The manner in which Japanese civilization has brought the two systems together, particularly in the Edo Period, belies their separate treatment. Indeed, in contemporary Japan, their infrastructural nature, together with elements of Taoist-Shinto philosophy, including shamanistic tendencies, must be taken into account at all times. Therefore, in treating Buddhism in the Japanese tradition, a clear analysis of Buddhism is not only impossible but actually goes against the grain of the Japanese way of life.

As we peer into the nature of Japanese behavioral patterns, we are struck by the complexity of elements on the one hand and by the simplicity on the other hand. The complexity, in a word, is based on the manifestation of the plural strains of ideology, and the simplicity is based on the uncluttered unified manifestation of those strains. Concepts such as encounter, accommodation, synthesis, syncretism, and assimilation are all possible and cogent only within such a nature of reality, that is, where complexity and simplicity are two aspects of the same reality. To speak thus naturally confuses the neophyte, but there is actually no way out of this inevitable condition or paradoxical situation. To seek a simple answer to any facet of a society will not only disrupt the very nature of the society but will falsify it.

JAPANESE ATTITUDES

The cessation of hostilities in 1945 brought about a huge vacuum, a most devastating traumatic experience, to the Japanese nation. Not only was the so-called National Entity (*kokutai*) shattered but so also was the common spiritual foundation of the people. In fact, the former was relatively easy to recover from, for it was a concept engendered by the ultranationalists and military and thrust upon the people, although it cannot be denied that the concept was based on and manifested in the nature of an organismic society. The latter, however, would not heal readily and lingered for many years. The reason for this is that whereas the former was generally a mere facade in the life of the Japanese, temporary and expendable, the latter was a realistic element deeply rooted in and intimately related to the very nature of the Japanese organismic structure. Thus Joseph M. Kitagawa's indictment of postwar Japan as being rootless must be taken to be loose, shortsighted, simplistic, and shallow.[5] In truth, the Japanese cultural roots go far deeper, beyond mere surface observations, and touch the very wellspring of being, a being whose foundation rests on the basic organic mode of existence.

One of the surprises in Japanese behavior encountered by the Allied Forces in 1945 or even before the surrender in the combat zones of Asia was the fact that the Japanese exhibited remarkable traits of pliancy and flexibility in defeat and the willingness to adapt to a new situation and to implement a totally new point of view. That is, allegiance to the war effort on the one side could readily be shifted to allegiance to the other side or to the peace effort, or it could easily revert to a neutral state of affairs. How accommodating it must have been to the victor that the vanquished followed obediently. This is difficult to comprehend, much less accept, judging by our understanding of normal human behavior. How can we account for this seemingly enigmatic behavior? What do the Japanese say of themselves?

Yukawa Hideki, the first Nobel laureate of Japan, said simply, "The Japanese mentality is, in most cases, unfit for abstract thinking and takes interest merely in tangible things."[6] He concluded, "the abstract mode of thinking will continue to be foreign to the Japanese."[7] In this context, it will be seen that the concept of National Entity is indeed abstract and could never really take root. This trait of an antiabstract mode of thinking is confirmed from an early period. For example, Nakamura Hajime agreed that there is "an absence of theoretical or systematic thinking, along with an emphasis upon an aesthetic and intuitive and concrete, rather than a strictly logical, orientation."[8] This does not mean that the Japanese cannot think logically or rationally, which is not only absurd but ludicrous. Buddhist metaphysics imported from China and Korea had abundantly provided the Japanese with intricate analysis and understanding of reality, but it was not in their character to carry out systematic treatment of reality as such. Zen master Dōgen (1200–1253) is the paragon of an early Japanese thinker, but Nakamura said that he "was not the sort of thinker who developed a logically coherent system of thought. In spite of the fact that he cherished deep philosophical ideas which were gem-like in character, he was not inclined to elaborate the ethical thoughts he apprehended in a purely logical system. Probably he thought that a philosophical system set forth in a systematic way was useless or unnecessary."[9] This distaste for systematic philosophizing is detected early on in Japanese history. Nakamura recalled that Kakinomoto-no-Hitomaro had composed the following poem: "In our land covered with reed and rice-ears, / they have not argued since the time of the gods."[10]

Motoori Norinaga (1730–1801) expanded on this:

In ancient times in our land, even the "Way" was not talked about at all, and we had only ways directly leading to things themselves, while in foreign countries it is the custom to entertain and to talk about many different doctrines, about principles of things, this "Way" or that "Way." The Emperors' land in ancient times has no such theories or doctrines whatever, but we enjoyed peace and order then, and the descendants of the Sun Goddess have consecutively succeeded to the throne.[11]

The thrust of the argument here is that one should perceive things in their own nature or things as they are (*arinomama*). This again affirms the organismic nature where every element or thing, as it is, is always in proper proportion to the whole, and therefore, to manipulate or to cognize it in any isolated and systematic way is to disturb the original peaceful and harmonious nature of things. That is, although the organismic nature has no absolute center of being, every element, nevertheless, belongs in it in the most holistic and relativistic sense and thereby guarantees the nature of a thing as it is in an eternal or everlasting sense.[12]

Motoori's remark concerning the reticence of the Japanese in contrast to the foreigner's custom of talking about different doctrines strikes a responsive chord in contemporary Japan. Chie Nakane quoted a renowned Japanese physicist as follows: "Even when we were having a meal or enjoying a drink, the foreign physicist would immediately get into a discussion on physics; he would take out a pencil and a piece of paper, and jot down expressions. He would act as though he were possessed of something, and I found it very hard to keep up with him."[13] Nakane added her own experience with foreigners:

I can also recall a number of occasions when, before getting used to living abroad, I was bothered because my foreign colleagues would talk about matters that called for a great deal of brainwork, even at meals or in moments of pleasant relaxation. On the other hand, foreign intellectuals who come to Japan taste the loneliness of being left out of things because, they say, once their Japanese friends start drinking, they seem to go off to some distant spot beyond their reach.[14]

All of this shows a psychology of dependence (*amae*) framed within the larger holistic context of things, whether it is in reference to the head of the family, the president of a company, or the leader of the society at large. It is a keen relationship that broadens as well as deepens in its upward thrust or vertical connection. In such a relationship, it is easy to understand why differences no longer linger or become the central issue but are immediately submerged within the total realm of existence.

In early Japanese history, it is recalled that Buddhism and Shintoism were treated alike in regard to the pantheons of both that are capped with the famous doctrines of *shimbutsu-shūgō* (unification of Shinto gods and Buddhas) and *honji-suijaku* (manifestation of true reality). Certain scholars attribute these doctrines to the so-called Buddhist theory of assimilation, which dates from early Buddhism.[15] Now, that may be so, but we can easily carry the analysis a step further and assert that the theory itself could be possible or have substance only within the grounds of a selfsame reality, as stated earlier. In fact, conceptions such as identity, coexistence, self-sufficiency, self-realization, harmony, transformation, dialectic, mutuality, unity, and diversity take on meaning and significance as they function within an organismic mode of existence. Be that as it may, the fluidity of the situation found in Japan in 1945 and thereafter calls for patient observation of the interplay of elements within the total ambience. It would be extremely difficult to pinpoint anything within such an ambience where even notions such as change and continuity pale to indistinction. Yet the tendency to persist in simplicity, abstraction, or negligence of the total forces at play continues, but we must be wary of consequences that may arise. Understanding the Buddhist situation relative to the Japanese tradition is no exception.

THREE BUDDHIST TRENDS

In the past forty years or so, there occurred at least three prominent postwar Buddhist trends: (1) the rise and spread of lay Buddhism or so-called new religions, (2) the continuation and resurgence of traditional Buddhism, and (3) the rise of Buddhist scholarship centered in institutions of higher learning.

The trends have fairly well stabilized and are expected to continue more or less in the present forms. What is most interesting is that these trends are not isolated movements but invariably intersect with one another in many ways and on different levels, such as in the political, social, economic, and academic realms. The lay Buddhist organizations, for example, readily tap the talents and resources of Buddhist scholars from the ranks of universities and colleges in order to solidify their movements as well as to legitimize their mission with scholarly works. The scholars themselves willingly offer their expertise and services and, in extreme cases, even ghostwrite for the leaders. The activist character of some religions enable them to engage in broad social and political ventures. Again, it should be noted that the organismic structure of the society engenders a spirit of flexibility and accommodation that allows free functions that involve other sectors. Brushes with the law are infrequent, but should they arise, they are quietly resolved. This organismic society is not issue oriented.

These trends did not begin suddenly in 1945, since their rudiments can be traced to the Meiji era or even beyond. In early Meiji, however, the Buddhists were persecuted for a while, being victimized by the proponents of State Shinto, but the matter of freedom of religion was reinstated just before the promulgation of the Japanese Constitution in 1889. The initial frustration suffered by the

Buddhists, paradoxically, steeled them into a cohesive group and brought on an even greater dedication and zeal to understand their religion in a most objective (''scientific'') way. It was a fresh enthusiasm spawned by the exposure to things Western that had consumed the Japanese mind in Meiji Japan.

Authoritarian pressures during Japan's military ventures (1930–1945) suppressed all aspects of life and, most of all, the intellectual life of the individual. Marxists and leftists, as expected, were persecuted and incarcerated for the duration of the war. Moreover, those inimical to the spirit of National Entity were harshly treated and even imprisoned under flimsy pretext, some of whom were religious leaders, such as Makiguchi Tsunesaburō, the founder of Sōka Gakkai, and Toda Jōsei, his successor. Makiguchi died in prison.

The militarists undoubtedly had succeeded in slowing the democratic growth of modern Japan, but they were unable completely to stamp out the spirit of freedom and justice. Thus the protestant spirit was kept alive. Certainly, the imposition of a forced militaristic society, even in the name of National Entity, was not iron clad, for the cessation of hostilities immediately revealed the two faces of Japan, one militaristic and the other humanistic; yet curiously, both militarism and humanism function within the same society. It is a patent lesson in not adhering merely to the elements or characteristics of change but to focus on the basic nature of change itself that accommodates those very elements; put within the context of our central thesis, the organismic mode of existence is prior to any analysis on what particular elements change. For example, a nationalistic spirit should truly be a cosmological feel for things in toto that in turn absorbs everything in its wake.[16] Consider the famous speech made by the emperor renouncing his divinity to the Japanese people. It was a heroic act, a landmark decision, but upon close scrutiny of the whole situation, it will be seen that the decision made perfectly good sense within the total interrelationality of things. Furthermore, it is of little consequence within the scheme of things whether the emperor is a mere symbol or a divine creature. Japanese intellectuals have always taken the emperor system lightly.

The question of ancestor worship is a perennial puzzle to many, especially the Westerner, but to the Japanese it is a most common and welcome idea that gives their lives a distinctive feature. Actually, it is more than an idea since it is one of the most important elements that fosters continuity to their lives and to the nation as a whole. It gives a strong bond among the people by acting in the capacity of providing a discipline to ordinary day-to-day living. Technically, the relationship of the living to the dead, or spirits, can be said to be asymmetrical, that is, a relationship that takes the past as real in order to embody the present concretely. This feature, difficult to conceive as it is, is a necessary ingredient in bringing forth the nationalistic spirit and in firming up the holistic framework for united action. For the Japanese, then, there is a built-in bond that is activated as soon as the relationship is realized. This is another expression of the vertical (*tate*) relationship made famous by the social anthropologist Chie Nakane. Although Nakane did not use the term *asymmetric relationship* in the sense used here, there is strong indication and evidence in human relations that her vertical relationship assumes, to a large degree, the characteristic of asymmetry as a bond in the relations. In her case, the asymmetric nature is a two-way process, between superior and inferior or professor and student, as the case may be. Delving into religious matters, Nakane said:

In the Japanese mind, "kami" and "ancestors" can be conceived only in terms of the ties established by the vertical line, and one cannot find in Japanese culture any cognition of "kami" as an abstract being detached completely from the human world. One can go so far as to say that the Japanese cognition of "kami" starts from the direct contactual relations between individuals, which serve as the medium that enables them to apprehend "kami" as an extension of the vertical relationship.[17]

The concept of ancestor worship is one that brings Buddhist and Shinto consciousness together in quiet and implicit ways. It is a subject that the Japanese will not discuss openly, nor will they give any direct or explicit answer relative to it. Meanwhile, without fanfare and hesitation, they will visit Buddhist temples and Shinto shrines and actively participate in the respective functions and festivities.

Lay Buddhism (New Religions)

The period immediately following the war was not conducive to the perpetuation of religious activities or of any revival movement. State Shinto was abolished by an edict of the Allied Occupation Forces, and Buddhism suffered greatly. The mood of the people in defeat was general despair, disenchantment, apathy, resignation, and hopelessness.

In this national state of malaise, where Shinto and Buddhism were incapable of discharging their obligations fully, the lay Buddhist movements or new religions made their strong appearance. Within a few years' time, literally hundreds of these religions mushroomed across the nation to cater to the spiritless and helpless souls, but after the Korean War, with the mood of the people on an upswing, the number dwindled considerably to a point where it has stabilized by the grouping of smaller religious units or units joining stronger movements. The exact figures are not available because the official statistics no longer consider them in a separate category but count them as branches of the traditional Shinto and Buddhist organizations.[18]

These religions are actually not new in that most of the rudiments or fundamentals were in place before the end of the war. One of the strongest and most influential today is the Sōka Gakkai, which started a decade before World War II. Another is Tenrikyō, which began about a century and a half ago and was considered a new religious movement at that time. Both boast exceptionally strong following with impressive headquarters compounds in Tokyo and Nara, respectively.

It is not possible to discuss all of the new lay Buddhist movements and their activities.[19] But two representative types, Sōka Gakkai and Agon Shū, are described to give the reader an outline of these movements. The Agon Shū is relatively new and does not even appear in the 1972 survey conducted by the Japanese Agency for Cultural Affairs. Nevertheless, it is currently such a substantial movement with an auspicious future that it is included here.

The Sōka Gakkai, capitalizing on the spiritual vacuum created after the war, expanded its activities in a systematic way by propagandizing and using forceful means (*shakubuku*) to gain new converts. By 1955, a decade after the war, its membership had climbed to several million and now, more than forty years after the war, it boasts a general membership of over 16 million, according to its own reports. The number may be an exaggeration, which includes the total household members of the Nichiren Shōshū, the religious arm and umbrella of the Sōka Gakkai, but it is not a number that can be dismissed easily. The Nichiren Shōshū is what gives religious legitimacy to the Sōka Gakkai movement, but it is not recognized by the traditional Nichiren Sect, although the former claims direct line to the teachings of Saint Nichiren (1222–1282). Nichiren, it should be recalled, criticized all other religious sects of his time in a most derogatory way and declared the superiority of the teachings of the *Lotus Sūtra*. He used bold means like daring the shogunate to follow his lead or else suffer the consequences of doom in the degenerate age of the Buddhist Dharma. He predicted the invasion of Japan by the Mongols, which turned out to be true, only that the Mongols met their fate by the Divine Wind (*kamikaze*). He even resorted to forceful means (*shakubuku*) himself to win over converts, a means originated by him. Self-proclaimed as Viśistacārita Bodhisattva (Jōgyō Bosatsu), he sought to save the people and the nation in the dark days of the Dharma. He was banished from society several times for his scathing attacks on the rulers for their false faith in other teachings, but each time this charismatic figure returned miraculously to haunt them. If there ever was a colorful religious leader in Japanese history it was Nichiren.

The Sōka Gakkai is highly organized and effective, somewhat akin to a military establishment with various departments and divisions under a single administrative head. It has its own school system, including Sōka University established in 1971 with full curricula as found in any institution of higher learning. The Oriental Philosophy Institute was founded in 1962, now located adjacent to the university, to promote Oriental thought and culture as a means of fostering mutual understanding and to bring about peace throughout Asia and the world. The publication department prints literature in both Japanese and foreign languages, mainly English, and its international office publishes the monthly English organ *Sōka Gakkai News*, which is distributed among the members and foreign intellectuals free of charge. One of the great forces in Sōka Gakkai is the youth division, which is the veritable breeding ground for young aspirants of the movement. It is mainly responsible for the huge extravaganzas in the form of parades, exercises, and stadium spectacles that involve both spectator and participant.

Its immediate past president and current Sōka Gakkai International president, Ikeda Daisaku, has proved to be another charismatic leader, just as his predecessor. He now takes the role of an elder statesman and ventures in international affairs by courting world leaders on subjects such as nuclear war, peace movements, environmental problems, and world hunger. His many publications, including his maiden work, *Human Revolution,* have been translated into several languages and distributed widely throughout the world on a gratis basis.

Sōka Gakkai at one time ventured into politics by forming the Kōmeitō (Clean Government party) and garnered a substantial number of posts in selected wards of the government, but outside pressures forced it to cut formal ties with the party. Still, the party is supported mainly by its members and thrives to this day.

In the past decade Sōka Gakkai was troubled by all sorts of scandals in administrative, business, financial, and personal realms. Even Ikeda's personal life was subject to criticism. Despite all of the bad publicity and criticism, it seems to continue its mission with equal, if not stronger, force than ever before. There are no prospects of its destruction by internal dissension or from outside pressures; paradoxically, it seems to thrive better in the midst of such scandals and contending forces. It rides out such rough tides in great fashion. A great part of the success must be attributed to the bold charismatic leadership of Ikeda, who maintains a tight rein on the organization with a keen sense of perception and understanding. His power and influence, in this respect, are beyond dispute.

The future of Sōka Gakkai is bright as long as Ikeda's leadership is felt. After he is gone, the picture will necessarily change. There is no heir apparent at the moment, although his son is mentioned at times. But a massive highly organized institution has its own built-in sustaining power, and so it is unlikely that Sōka Gakkai's fate will be in question. Still, this highly controversial organization will be suspect for many observers of the religious scene.

The other strong lay Buddhist movement quickly spreading throughout Japan is so recent that very little attention is given to it, or written about it, especially in the West. Yet it has already demonstrated its great potential of becoming a great religious force. It is called the Agon Shū or, literally, the Āgama Sect, a sect that focuses on a return to the original teachings of the Buddha as compiled in the Āgamas. The Āgamas refers to the collection of early Buddhist sūtras that in the Theravāda Buddhist tradition are recorded in the Pāli texts known as *Dīgha-nikāya, Majjhima-nikāya, Saṃyutta-nikāya, Aṅguttara-nikāya,* and *Khuddaka-nikāya.*[20]

The Agon Shū's principal organ is aptly named *Āgama* ("going back" to the Buddha's words), which started publication in 1979. Each issue's inner page in part reads: "We here pledge to reaffirm our faith in the Āgama and attempt to extract a noble spirit and vigor from Śākyamuni's Sūtras for the revival of true Buddhism. We are convinced that our endeavor is the sole answer to the crisis of mankind and that it will definitely help us march on into the 21st century."[21]

The sect is undoubtedly revivalistic but with a different twist. Its main concern is with the understanding, propagation, and teaching of the true philosophy of Buddhism. With just over 300,000 members in 1985, it continues to grow steadily by mixing extremely well with the general populace. It is frank and unabashed about the fact that it is a postwar new religion. It claims that the whole of Japanese Buddhism is a series of new religions appearing in times of stresses and strains throughout history. For example, it points directly at the various sects that arose in the Kamakura Period as nothing but new religions. In many respects, the assertion is correct and enables one to have a balanced perception of the total religious dynamics of a nation without being caught up in any sectarian causes. Such established religions today as the Pure Land Sects of Hōnen and Shinran, the Zen Sects of Eisai and Dōgen, and the Nichiren Sect of Nichiren are therefore outcomes of the needs of the people coupled with the charismatic and dramatic leadership of the patriarchs. The Agon Shū, in consequence, is neither apologetic nor defensive concerning its role and mission. Its method is openly synthetic, such as to incorporate the esoteric ritual of Shingon Sect called *goma-hōyō*, where a huge bonfire is ceremoniously burned to cleanse the evils or defilements of individuals and groups.

The monthly journal *Āgama* is keyed to a layperson's understanding of the problems besetting the current world. One of the most interesting and valuable segments of the journal is the running translation of the Pāli *Nikāyas*. Outstanding scholars in the field have been marshaled to do systematic, easy-to-grasp translations of the original texts, with copious annotations, and Buddhist scholars are never in short supply. Each monthly installment, for example, carries a short section from the *Saṁyutta-nikāya* beautifully rendered by Nakamura Hajime.

The Agon Shū has the charismatic counterpart of Sōka Gakkai's Ikeda Daisaku in the figure of Kiriyama Yasuo, chief abbot. Like Ikeda, Kiriyama is a prolific writer whose works are in the same vein of awakening the minds of the masses to the wholesome and fruitful life awaiting them. One of his latest works and best-seller, *Buddhahood in This World,* brings to focus the need of relying on the Buddha's teachings for the realization of Buddhahood in this world.[22] He has recently ventured into the international scene by having an audience with the pope in the Vatican in 1985 to release a joint statement on peace in the world. In 1986 he went to Harbin, China, to conduct jointly an international fire ritual (*goma-hōyō*) under the auspices of the United Nations.

The success of the Agon Shū so far is an acknowledged fact, especially noteworthy in organizing the young and old to study Buddhism in the original. It has done exceptionally well in meshing the theoretical and practical components of a religious life. This is clearly a singular positive result in postwar Buddhist movements. Perhaps, Japan's recent affluence has some bearings on its success, but it certainly belies any "rootless" character of the Japanese, for they are certainly expanding and solidifying the roots by their own efforts.

Traditional Buddhism

In stark contrast to the opportunities opened up to the lay Buddhist movements in 1945, the various sects of traditional Buddhism (Pure Land Sects, Zen, Nichiren, Tendai, Shingon, and so on) practically had to close their doors. They had to lift themselves up by their own bootstraps to keep the temples open. The parishioners themselves were utterly stunned by the sudden negative turn of events and had to comply with the orders of the Allied Occupation Forces (1945–1952), suffering undue physical and emotional strains within a depressed economy. Their number understandably dwindled as they, like the clergy, had to busy themselves to make a living. The various sects acted on an individual basis in caring for the basic family needs, such as in the ministering of funeral services and marriage ceremonies, as they have been done traditionally. After the war, moreover, the landholdings of the Buddhist temples, the main source of sustenance, were ordered disbanded by a directive (Land Reform Act) of the Occupation Forces. It created an impossible situation that forced the priests to do manual labor and to supplement their meager income by taking up nonclerical jobs. Without the tax-sheltered revenues from the landholdings, the huge Buddhist populace could not be catered to in normal ways, but nevertheless, the temples endured the hardship.

As life under the Allied Occupation Forces improved, the parishioners cooperated admirably to repair and to build new temples. Yet the fact of the matter was that there was neither a central administrative organ nor a strong leadership in the Japan Buddhist Federation to mount a positive campaign of bringing all of the activities of the sects together in terms of projecting an identity to the traditional Buddhist movement. Perhaps it was an impossible task. At any rate, the lack of leadership should not be construed as anything negative or void, for, indeed, the spirit of the Japanese was gaining momentum as the occupation psychosis wore off gradually and the people bided time for a better ambience to arise. The moment came with the Korean Conflict in 1950, in which the Allied Forces operated from Japan proper and procured much needed material during and after the conflict. It had a rippling effect on the entire Japanese economy, which in turn gave its people the much-desired spiritual uplift.

The recovery of the nation came sooner than expected, and in the process, among other things, the demography shifted drastically from outlying districts to urban centers. Urban dwellers are not particularly noted for their religiosity, but in Japan they conventionally kept their traditional family religious bonds. The old rites, observances, and festivals that delighted young and old are back in full force, and, touched by affluence, they have become showpieces even in small hamlets. Bigger is not necessarily better, but if it is the outcome of the aspirations of a united effort, it may not be as incongruous to normal practice as one would think. Assuredly, Japanese traditional Buddhism is today riding the crest of the economic wave, alongside other Japanese cultural pursuits, and can be said to be firmly based and secure.[23]

As a sidelight to the Buddhist situation in Japan, the following question may be raised: Are the Japanese religious? Perhaps they are, but the question is ill-phrased since foreigners see much that is irreligious with the Japanese way of life. It is quickly pointed out that the Japanese are not regular temple-going people; they do not worship a single deity, and secularism has taken over much of their everyday lives. The young, in particular, are not imbued with any sense of loyalty to or faith in a particular religious symbol as their elders are, and their relationship with Buddhism is passive at best or a custom-oriented carryover from their ancestral past.

Secularism is a difficult term to apply in contrast to the nature of Japanese religiosity. It is problematic to analyze Japanese society into secular and non-secular segments. In many respects, secularism has nothing to do with Japanese religious behavior since the realm of religiosity is much larger than ordinary consciousness of religious matters; it encompasses a universal conscious mode in which all elements, religious as well as nonreligious, are involved. This is not pluralism but, as often expressed, diversity in unity and unity in diversity, which indicates a total organismic outlook to things. Indeed, this is how the Japanese look upon all religions of the world. As stated earlier, the Japanese mentality cannot readily cope with sharp lines of argumentation or with strict analysis or rationalization. The familiar Japanese term *gōrika* (literally, "rationalization"), for example, is not strictly a logical term, for it does not refer to a particular focus on a problem as such but to an overall insight into the total situation in which the problem resides. In a word, the problem must fit the situation and not the situation the problem. Likewise, the term *secular* is too narrow and limited in application to understanding Japanese religiosity or non-religiosity. It simply does not touch all of the bases of existence.

The Japanese mind may be relatively simple, nonabstract, and nonlogical seen from the outside, but from the inside it is at once unifying and totally involving. Similarly, traditional Buddhism always remains in the background and will manifest itself readily not in particularity but in terms of universal dimension. Such a dimension is vague and ambiguous, to be sure, especially to minds that are accustomed to sharp, precise perceptions. Yet the key to understanding Buddhist reality is that it is undisturbed by logic or perception since they are merely means or tools. So now when a concept such as transcendence is used, it may mean to go beyond logic and perception, but it may also have the more profound meaning of seeing through the functions of logic and perception in a total dimensional way. In this way, traditional Buddhism always has a staying power that sustains its own viable nature.[24]

Buddhist Scholarship

It may not be an exaggeration to state that Japan boasts the greatest number of Buddhist scholars, the highest concentration in Buddhist studies, and the largest production of Buddhist works in the world. The optimal conditions seem to be present in the right proportion to promote Buddhism in all of its aspects. Basically, Japan is a Buddhist country, although Shinto and other lesser religions, including folk religions, all interfuse to constitute the Japanese way of life.

Most major universities, including the prestigious national universities (Tokyo, Kyoto, Nagoya, Tōhoku, Kyūshū, and Hokkaidō) have departments in religious, philosophical, and comparative studies that carry out extensive research and instruction in Buddhism. In addition, there are many outstanding sectarian universities such as, Komazawa, Taishō, Tōyō, Risshō, Hanazono, Ōtani, Bukkyō, Ryūkoku, and Kōyasan, which naturally promote their respective research and dissemination of Buddhism. With several thousands of Buddhist scholars in residence throughout Japan, Buddhist scholarship is necessarily intense and highly competitive.

Even before the war, Japanese Buddhist scholarship was on the ascendancy, gaining force and recognition in the world. The printing of the *Chinese Tripitaka* in one hundred volumes, compiled and edited by Takakusu Junjirō and Watanabe Kaikyoku, was certainly a landmark publication.[25] Other scholars, such as, Wogihara Unrai, Anesaki Masaharu, Ui Hakuju and Daisetz T. Suzuki had paved the way and attained international recognition in their fields of endeavor, but it was not until after the war that Japanese Buddhist scholarship achieved full maturity and recognition.

The momentous event occurred in 1952 with the formation of the Japanese Association for Indian and Buddhist Studies, organized and led by the late Miyamoto Shōson. The association brought together scholars of diverse backgrounds and interests and instituted annual congresses at different institutions, alternately in the Tokyo and Kyoto areas. Its organ, the *Journal of Indian and Buddhist Studies* (office located in the University of Tokyo), publishes the proceedings of the congresses and is disseminated throughout the world. It contains some of the best individual research done in the wide spectrum of Buddhist studies, especially noted for the contributions by young aspiring scholars. Some articles are in English, and there is always an English table of contents.

Another important publication is the *Journal of Nippon Buddhist Research Association* (office located in Hanazono University, Kyoto), a nonsectarian periodical with papers selected from the annual conferences held at various institutions. The conference usually has a main theme on which all papers are addressed. The journal, started in 1934 but with strong united effort after the war, presents an excellent picture on the overall status of Japanese Buddhist scholarship.

The measure of contributions by Japanese Buddhist scholars can be seen readily by a recent work in English by Nakamura Hajime, *Indian Buddhism*.[26] Nakamura goes through the whole Indian Buddhist movement, from the time and rise of Buddhism through the Buddha and his disciplines, the scriptures of early Buddhism, Mahāyāna, and logicians to esoteric Buddhism. In each section, he has brought to bear the important works of Japanese scholars as well as non-Japanese scholars. One cannot help but be impressed by the extensive Japanese scholarship.

The vast amount of Buddhist literature is forbidding to all aspiring scholars, including the Japanese. As a way of alleviating the situation, the Japanese scholars have published a convenient work, *The Great Explanatory Dictionary of Buddhist Literature,* in twelve volumes.[27] It was published under the general editorship of Ono Gemmyō in collaboration with many experts in the various fields for separate entries. Each entry gives all available information on the work, whether extant or not, author, translator, date, *Chinese Tripitaka* volume and number, *Tibetan Tripitaka* number, and so on; best of all, it describes the content in general terms, although some descriptions are exhaustive. Several supplementary volumes have been added since 1945. The work focuses on Buddhist literature from Chinese and Japanese sources.

In addition to providing the above works, Japanese scholars have systematically improved or added supplementary volumes to existing dictionaries and encyclopedias of Buddhism. Besides governmental subsidies, sectarian aid is always available on these projects, which promote overall Buddhist scholarship.

Among the dictionaries, a crowning work by Nakamura Hajime ought to be mentioned. In 1975 his long-awaited, monumental, three-volume *Great Dictionary of Buddhist Terms* appeared.[28] This is a definitive work on all Buddhist terms in use in the Japanese language, with copious annotations. It includes the origin of each term, its meaning, and where it is cited in the Chinese, Japanese, Sanskrit, and Tibetan sources. It is perhaps the most practical and convenient dictionary of its kind in Japanese Buddhist scholarship.

Another momentous boon to Buddhist studies in general occurred when the Suzuki Research Foundation reprinted the Peking edition of the *Tibetan Tripitaka,* compiled and edited by Daisetz T. Suzuki and Yamaguchi Susumu, in 168 volumes.[29] It was followed by the popular one-volume *Catalogue and Index of the Tibetan Tripitaka.*[30] The Suzuki Research Foundation is continuing to reprint outstanding works.[31]

Several other significant works that give Japanese scholarship breadth and depth should also be mentioned. The first is by Mizuno Kōgen, *General Index of the Pali Tripitaka,* in three volumes.[32] Mizuno is regarded in Japan as the greatest scholar in early Buddhism. Another work of note is that of Hirakawa Akira and his associates *Index to the Abhidharmakośabhāṣya,* in two parts.[33] Hirakawa is an expert in the Vinaya (Buddhist discipline). His work has appeared in English.[34] Finally, two very convenient companion volumes have been authored by Yamada Ryūjō, *Introduction to the Development of Mahāyāna Buddhism* and *Various Literature on Sanskirt Buddhist Texts.*[35] The volumes give a textual analysis of all important Mahāyāna literature involved in the development of the different schools of thought.

Japanese scholars excel in textual studies and critiques. They do work in the original texts, emending and collating several versions, as necessary, of the text in question. They systematically translate Pali, Sanskrit, Tibetan, and Chinese works in order to understand all phases of Buddhism. Their work is a continuing and expanding phenomenon. In this sense, as a group, they are far ahead of any group of non-Japanese Buddhist scholars. In fact, many worthy Buddhist works by non-Japanese scholars are almost immediately translated into Japanese as a measure of their interest in and concern for the currency of Buddhist scholarship.

Thus literally hundreds of Buddhist books appear in print every year, ranging from the popular to the scholarly. Practically nothing is neglected in the areas of history, ideology, and practice of Buddhism. As the Japanese scholars approach their various fields of research with great enthusiasm, attention, and thoroughness, there will be no letup in their singular contributions, which should be felt increasingly and significantly throughout the world.

TWO RECENT ACADEMIC TRENDS

Within the current flourish of Buddhist activity by Japanese Buddhist scholars, there are two trends prominently appearing in Kyoto and Tokyo, respectively, as centers. They are (1) the activity relative to the so-called Kyoto School of philosophy and religion, which focuses on the philosophy of Nishida Kitarō (1870–1945), and (2) the activity relative to the Japanese Association of Comparative Philosophy, ably led by Nakamura Hajime (1912-). The activities of both centers are essentially Buddhistic.

Nishida's philosophy may be said to be comparative or even synthetic, but it is so in terms of seeking an accommodation with Buddhist thought, particularly Zen, since he was an ardent devotee of Zen discipline. His philosophy began with the maiden work *A Study of Good,* which expounds on the basic thought of "pure experience" (*junsui keiken*).[36] His subsequent works, even after retirement, pursued this thought by bringing into play the highly sophisticated analysis of immediate perception involving the logic of place (*basho no ronri*). A close examination of his works and his association with his boyhood friend Daisetz T. Suzuki reveal his genius of synthesizing deep philosophical Buddhist thought with Western ideas, such as those expounded by William James and Henri Bergson.

Fortunately for Nishida, he had a strong following at Kyoto University, and thus his philosophy, germinal in many respects, has been further developed in different dimensions by his able disciples. Today, we witness the second and third generation of Nishida scholars continuing his initial effort. Because of the synthetic nature, Nishida philosophy naturally has the comparative feature and an international flavor. In retrospect, it was the most probable path that any keen thinker could have taken and immersed into. A thinker may have international orientation and intensions, but it is extremely difficult for him to be an internationalist in the complete sense of the term. The yearnings and aspirations are present, but one cannot completely turn off one's own background or cultural heritage. Nishida then aspired for the universal element of experience, and he found it in his own back yard, in Zen experience. Subsequent writings by his followers attest to this fact. For example, see Nishitani Keiji's *Religion and Nothingness,* in which the Buddhist doctrine of nothingness or *śūnyatā (kū)* is principally employed and analyzed as central to all experiences.[37] Or take Abe Masao's recent *Zen and Western Thought,* which again emphasizes the doctrine of *śūnyatā* as a comparative basis for understanding experience and for excursions into other disciplines or other philosophies and religions.[38] Response to the Kyoto School has come early with a significant work by Hans Waldenfels, *Absolute Nothingness.*[39] This work is highly critical of Nishitani's book and is challenging not only to the Japanese Buddhists but to the whole enterprise of opening up dialogues.

The principal organ of the Kyoto School, though not designated as such by its followers, is the journal *Eastern Buddhist.* After a long hiatus, it resumed publication in 1965 as a new series based in Otani University, where D. T. Suzuki had originally started it. One of the most significant developments that has occurred in the new series is the opening up of a Buddhist-Christian dialogue. Nishitani's and Abe's writings, to be sure, already contained dialogic elements, but with their leadership, including those of Takeuchi Yoshinori and other followers, the journal as well as other independent publications began to amplify and focus on the dialogues. The journal, for example, contains an interesting series of dialogues between Hisamatsu Shin'ichi and Paul Tillich.[40] Out of this new trend, the dialogues have intensified to such a degree that they are now carried out with more frequency and even far beyond Kyoto, to the United States and Europe, principally in the form of conferences.

The *Eastern Buddhist* has also been responsible for the resurgence of two schools of thought, Dōgen studies and Pure Land Buddhist studies. The former is in reference to the works of Zen Master Dōgen (1200–1253) whose many selections from his major work *Shōbōgenzō (Eye-Treasury of the True Dharma)* have been ably translated and serially presented in the *Eastern Buddhist.* The latter refers principally to the writings of Shinran Shōnin (1173–1262), and essays relative to his thought have also appeared frequently in the journal. Daisetz T. Suzuki has capped his career by translating Shinran's *Kyōgyōshinshō (The True Teaching, Living, Faith, and Realizing of the Pure Land).*[41]

What is of major importance is that both Zen and Pure Land studies now figure prominently in the Buddhist-Christian dialogues. Thus in very direct ways the Japanese Buddhist impact in practice as well as in scholarship is being felt beyond Japanese shores.

The second prominent trend, the activity of the Japanese Association of Comparative Philosophy, is the brainchild of Nakamura Hajime. To know the nature of the association is really a reflection on the man Nakamura. Although his works reveal a phenomenal grasp of myriad aspects of Indian and Buddhist studies, he is basically a comparativist par excellence. It is fortunate that a person of his keen intelligence has gone to the sources in everything he has touched and has presented in simple, clear, and concise ways the subtle connections that exist in words and deeds. His *Collected Works,* though published ten years ago, are still in the making, since he continues unrelentingly to publish works of consequence. No scholar in Japan, to our recollection, has produced as much as he has in such a diversity of areas. His English publications already include the famous *Ways of Thinking of Eastern Peoples* and *Parallel Developments.*[42]

The association was organized in 1974 and conducts semiannual meetings in various parts of Japan. Its organ, *Studies in Comparative Philosophy* (office located in Taishō University, Tokyo) with an English table of contents, records the papers read at the meetings. The meetings are thematic. A recent symposium, for example, was "Knowledge and Wisdom—East and West," and the papers addressed the theme from the Greek, Indian, Chinese, Japanese, and contemporary Western standpoints. It amounted to a miniconference on East-West philosophy, but it also revealed at once the vigor, boldness, substance, and enthusiasm of the Japanese scholars to engage in East-West philosophical dialogues. Indeed, their enthusiasm spilled over in 1984 when a dozen members of the association made the trip to Hawaii to attend a conference on the theme "Interpreting across Boundaries," sponsored by the Society for Asian and Comparative Philosophy. Two of the group, Nakamura Hajime and Maeda Sengaku, were invited to present papers in the plenary sessions, and others presented individual papers in panel sessions and thereby made their presence felt.

Many works on comparative thought have already appeared, among which the following are worth mentioning: *Higashi-no-shisō Nishi-no-shisō* (*Eastern Thought and Western Thought*), an anthology, and *Hikaku-shisōron* (*Comparative Philosophy*), which has been revised and reprinted several times.[43]

A consistent and thoroughgoing attempt at comparative analysis was made by Saigusa Mitsuyoshi during the past thirty-five years. His writings have finally been collected into a convenient work in three volumes. The volumes are, respectively, *Hikaku-shisō-joron* (*An Introduction to Comparative Thought*), *Higashi-to-nishi-no-shisō* (*Eastern and Western Thought*), and *Bukkyō-to-seiyō-shisō* (*Buddhism and Western Thought*).[44] As the titles indicate, they are deliberations into East-West ideas and present an excellent view of how a Japanese scholar treats Western thought within the comparative framework. Saigusa, being a Buddhologist, has recently published a work on his lifelong interest in Madhyamaka philosophy, *Chūron-geju-sōran* (*Comprehensive View of the Verses of the Madhyamaka System*).[45] It is a definitive Japanese translation of the Sanskrit, Tibetan, and Chinese sources, some of which are in several versions and fully annotated. It shows again the thoroughness and excellent scholarship of the Japanese scholars.

The membership of the association is nearing the thousand mark and will soon go over it. It is a fast growing academic organization of its kind because of the appeal to the wide range of topics treated in the conferences. In this respect, their effort is totally in line with what the Kyoto School is doing and may well absorb the latter's activities. It would be interesting to observe what new developments in East-West intercourse are in store in the future as this group takes the lead.

CONCLUDING REMARKS

Whatever pessimism that seemed to have shadowed the Japanese way of life must now be cast aside. Although beset with all of the problems surrounding a highly developed nation, the Japanese are reasserting themselves by seeking their wellspring of being within the larger nature of things. In consequence, the alarm sounded by Kiyota Minoru need not be taken seriously. He concluded his article with the following words: "Sectarian indoctrination and exegesis will kill ideological responses as Japanese ideological interest gradually turns to parts outside their small island empire. Philosophical revival constitutes the only refuge from sectarian doctrine."[46]

As the assessment was made in the 1960s and, examined in the late 1980s, it is clearly overdrawn. Sectarian indoctrination and exegesis will continue as they have always been done by traditional or lay Buddhism. Japanese ideological interest must be distinguished from economic interest since the latter is apparent now, but the former is yet to be asserted. Moreover, the refuge sought from sectarian doctrine by philosophical revival is a *non sequitur* since no ideology or philosophy has ever been completely successful in curbing religion or religious matters, however noble, meaningful, or persuasive it may be. The Japanese did not have a set philosophy in the past, nor will they have one in the future; but assuredly, they do have a viable form of life that shows all of the signs of continuing in the future in wholesome ways. Much of their way of life has been the result of constant response-reaction to ideologies, both domestic and foreign. In different times, different sets of objects or ideas come to the fore, and at other times they recede into the background passively but are never destroyed or obliterated. This is the best and surest way to maintain the continuity of life without positively pointing at and adhering to certain elements in the process. In fact, the subtle nature of the continuity of life had been impressed on the Japanese mind by Buddhism with its profound doctrine of impermanence. Simply put, Buddhism taught the Japanese that impermanence is supreme over permanence, that letting go is the way of life rather than freezing it. This understanding may lead to the notion of a flimsy and delicate nature of life, but that does not mean that the Japanese way is fragile or lacks depth.

The spirit of the Japanese is many nuanced as the keen observer will perceive it in the cultural arts. The spirit is reflected in everything, and vice versa, everything reflects it. All of this is another way of exhibiting the essence of the organismic mode of existence that the Japanese way activates and reflects all of the time, unbeknownst to many. It is mainly Buddhism that gave the Japanese the larger holistic stand to take on everything, whether in matters of materialism or immaterialism.

As we conclude our discussion of Buddhism and the Japanese tradition, we cannot help but be optimistic concerning the future. The past forty years have shown a remarkable recovery and accommodation in the lives of the Japanese. Buddhism, too, has modified itself in many ways to suit the changing times, but the central teachings of tolerance, patience, humility, tranquillity, compassion, and wisdom have always stood fast to guide the course of events.

NOTES

1. Ezra F. Vogel, *Japan as Number One* (Cambridge, Mass.: Harvard University Press, 1979).

2. See, for example, Jon Woronoff, *Japan: The Coming Social Crisis* (Tokyo: Lotus Press, 1980); Frank Gibney, *Japan: The Fragile Superpower* (Tokyo: Tuttle, 1975).

3. See, for example, Masatsugu Mitsuyuki, *The Modern Samurai Society: Duty and Dependence in Contemporary Japan* (New York: American Management Association, 1982); Fukutake Tadashi, *The Japanese Social Structure,* trans. Ronald P. Dore (Tokyo: University of Tokyo Press, 1982); Morishima Michio, *Why Has Japan 'Succeeded'? Western Technology and the Japanese Ethos* (Cambridge: Cambridge University Press, 1982).

4. For example, Robert J. Smith, *Japanese Society* (Cambridge: Cambridge University Press, 1983).

5. Joseph M. Kitagawa, *Religion in Japanese History* (New York: Columbia University Press, 1966), p. 331.

6. Yukawa Hideki, "Modern Trend of Western Civilization and Cultural Peculiarities in Japan," in Charles A. Moore, ed., *The Japanese Mind* (Honolulu: University of Hawaii Press, 1967), p. 56.

7. Ibid., p. 57.

8. Nakamura Hajime, "Consciousness of the Individual and the Universal Among the Japanese," in Moore, *The Japanese Mind,* p. 179.

9. Ibid., p. 190.

10. Ibid., p. 189.

11. Ibid.

12. It seems odd indeed that a scholar of Robert J. Smith's stature in Japanese studies is puzzled or stymied by the Japanese unconcern for logical distinctions or the exclusivity of complementary alternatives. He concluded thus:

One plausible answer is that the claim is only a way of saying to foreigners that they will never understand the Japanese because they think differently. Viewed in this light, it serves as a powerful device for explaining away misconception and misunderstanding as inevitable outcomes of interaction between themselves and other peoples. Alternatively, it may be only one of the many ways in which the Japanese phrase their awful sense of isolation from the rest of the world, although the claim is not without an element of perverse pride. And finally—and even to suggest the possibility is to run the risk of rousing the ire of those who are repelled by the very thought—it is just conceivable that the authors are right. (Smith, *Japanese Society,* pp. 111–112)

Smith is clearly ambivalent, indecisive, and off the mark. He simply could not cast off his Western orientation in which logic and reason rule supreme over everything else and which prevents him from delving into the holistic organismic view of the Easterner, the Japanese in particular. The realm of reality is, after all, not always structured logically or rationally. It may be closer to an alogical nature, for example. Certainly, the authors (Yukawa and Nakamura, for example) are correct in their assertions. To cast doubt on their remarks only shows up the doubter's dogmatism and limited vision of things.

13. Chie Nakane, *Human Relations in Japan*, a summary translation of *Tateshakai-no-ningen-kankei* (*Personal Relations in a Vertical Society*) (Tokyo: Ministry of Foreign Affairs, 1972), pp. 84–85.

14. Ibid., p. 85.

15. See, in particular, Alicia Matsunaga, *The Buddhist Philosophy of Assimilation* (Rutland, Vt.: Tuttle, 1969).

16. Joseph M. Kitagawa properly characterized Shinto as a cosmic religion. See his *Religion in Japanese History*, pp. 11–19. It can further be analyzed that this cosmic consciousness, vague and mythical at the outset, will be refined and strengthened with a more positive basis for human existence by the Buddhist introduction and challenge. In fact, Buddhism aided Shinto in defining its own history. The rapprochement and accommodation of the two religions began early on and climaxed in the Heian Period (794–1185) with the concepts of *honji-suijaku* (manifestation of true reality) and *ryōbu Shinto* (Dual Shinto or Buddhist-Shinto accommodation). See Tsunoda Ryūsaku, Wm. Theodore de Bary, and Donald Keene, comp. and eds., *Sources of Japanese Tradition* (New York: Columbia University Press, 1958), pp. 268–272. See also Matsunaga Daigan and Alicia Matsunaga, *Foundations of Japanese Buddhism. Vol. 1: The Aristocratic Age* (Los Angeles and Tokyo: Buddhist Books International, 1974), pp. 238–241. In sum, the cosmic amalgation of Buddhist and Shinto doctrines worked on the Japanese mind for many centuries and continues to do so today in the life of the average Japanese. There is no clear-cut division of the two religions when it comes to the cosmic feeling and understanding of things. I have used the term *organismic* for *cosmic* to bring the highly metaphysical dimensions that the term *cosmic* implies to a more earthy organic level of human events in nature.

17. Nakane, *Human Relations in Japan*, p. 83.

18. For more detail on the lay movements with organizational statistics, see Adachi Kenji, Commissioner of the Agency for Cultural Affairs, Japan, *Japanese Religion: A Survey by the Agency for Cultural Affairs* (Tokyo and Palo Alto, Calif.: Kōdansha International Ltd., 1972). See especially the chapter on new religious movements, pp. 89–104.

19. See, for example, Clark B. Offner and Henry van Straelen, *Modern Japanese Religions: With Special Emphasis upon Their Doctrine of Healing* (Tokyo: Rupert Enderle, 1963), especially Ch. 5 on Nichiren-related Buddhist Religions; Henry Thomsen, *The New Religions of Japan* (Tokyo: Tuttle, 1963).

20. These texts belong to the Theravāda Canons known as *Sutta-Pitaka* ("Basket of Sutras" containing the teachings of the Buddha) and translated, respectively, as follow: *Dialogues of the Buddha, Middle Length Sayings, Kindred Sayings, Gradual Sayings*, and *Minor Anthologies*. They have been published for the Pali Text Society by Luzac & Company Ltd. in London. Various reprints are available, for example, 1957.

21. *Āgama* (Tokyo: Āgama Publications Office of the Agon Shū, 1983).

22. Kiriyama Yasuo, *Gense-jōbutsu* (Tokyo: Rikitomi Shobō, 1983).

23. The recovery of traditional Buddhism does not mean that it is absolved of all problems. As Shōkō Watanabe has rightly criticized the contemporary Buddhist scene, there are still many negative qualities carried over from the past that need serious addressing, for example, (1) subservience to the political authority and spirit of nationalism,

(2) prevalence of magical incantations and other superstitious beliefs and practices, (3) preoccupation with funeral rites and memorial services for the dead at the expense of providing spiritual guidance to the living, (4) lack of doctrinal integrity that leads to comprise with other religions and ideologies, and (5) stress on formalism without equal stress on inner spiritual disciplines. (Quoted in Kitagawa, *Religion in Japanese History* p. 296.)

24. This section did not discuss in detail the various traditional sects. Generally, the leading prewar sects have continued to dominate in the postwar period. The five dominant sects are, in order of importance, Pure Land, Shingon, Zen, Nichiren, and Tendai. If the Nichiren-related lay Buddhist sects were included, obviously the Nichiren Sect would be the most dominant.

25. Takakusu Junjirō and Watanabe Kaikyoku, eds., *Taishō-shinshū-daizōkyō* (*The Tripitaka in Chinese*), 100 vols. (Tokyo: Society for the Publication of the Taishō Edition of the Tripitaka, 1924–1929).

26. Nakamura Hajime, *Indian Buddhism: A Survey with Bibliographical Notes* (Tokyo: Sanseido Co., Ltd., 1980).

27. Ono Gemmyō, gen. ed., *Bussho-kaisetsu-daijiten* (*Great Explanatory Dictionary of Buddhist Literature*), 12 vols. (Tokyo: Daito Shuppan-sha, 1933).

28. Nakamura Hajime, *Bukkyō-go-daijiten* (*Great Dictionary of Buddhist Terms*), 3 vols. (Tokyo: Tokyo Shoseki, 1975).

29. Daisetz T. Suzuki and Yamaguchi Susumu, comp. and eds., *The Tibetan Tripitaka*, 168 vols., Peking ed. (Tokyo: Suzuki Research Foundation, 1955–1961.

30. Daisetz T. Suzuki, ed., *Catalogue and Index of the Tibetan Tripitaka* (Tokyo: Suzuki Research Foundation, 1960).

31. Other reprints of the Suzuki Research Foundation in Tokyo are *Dai-nihon-bukkyō-zensho* (*The Collected Works of Japanese Buddhism*), 100 vols. (1973); *Nihon Daizōkyō* (*Sacred Books of Japanese Buddhism*), 100 vols. (1973); Evgenii Obermiller, trans., *Buston: History of Buddhism* (*Chos-ḥbyung*) (1964); Yamaguchi Susumu, ed., *Madhyāntavibhāgatīkā de Ācārya Sthiramati* (1966); Nakamura Zuiryū, *A Study of the Ratnagotravibhāga Mahāyānottaratantra-Śāstra* (1967); Kitagawa Hidenori, *A Study of Indian Classical Logic—Dignāga's System* (1965); Tsuji Naoshirō, superviser, *Wogihara's Sanskrit-Chinese-Japanese Dictionary,* 16 vols. (1964–1974); Ui Hakuju, ed., *Index to the Bodhisattva-bhūmi,* Pts. I and II (1961); Daisetz T. Suzuki, comp., *An Index to the Laṅkāvatāra Sūtra* (1965); Gadjin M. Nagao, ed., *Madhyāntavibhāgo bhāṣya* (1964). The sole agent for all Suzuki Research Foundation publications is Kodansha Ltd., Tokyo, Japan.

32. Mizuno Kōgen, *Nanden-daizōkyō-sōsakuin* (*General Index of the Pali Tripitaka*), 3 vols. (Tokyo: Maruzen Co., Ltd., 1961).

33. Hirakawa Akira et al., *Index to the Abhidharmakośa bhāṣya,* Pt. I: Sanskrit-Tibetan-Chinese; Pt. II: Chinese-Sanskrit (Tokyo: Daizo Shuppan K.K., 1973, 1977).

34. Hirakawa Akira, *Monastic Discipline for the Buddhist Nuns.* An English translation of the Chinese Text of the Mahāsāṃghika-Bhikṣuṇī-Vinaya (Patna, India: Kashi Prasad Jayaswal Research Institute, 1982).

35. Yamada Ryūjō, *Daijō-bukkyō-seiritsuron-josetsu* (*Introduction to the Development of Mahāyāna Buddhism*). (Kyoto: Heiryakuji Shōten, 1959); *Bongo-butten-no-shobunken* (*Various Literature on Sanskrit Buddhist Texts*) (Kyoto: Heiryakuji Shōten, 1959).

36. Nishida Kitarō, *A Study of Good* (*Zen-no-kenkyū*), a Japanese Unesco publication, trans. V. H. Viglielmo (Japan: Ministry of Education, 1960).

37. Nishitani Keiji, *Religion and Nothingness (Shūkyō-towa-nanika?)*, trans. Jan van Bragt (Berkeley: University of California Press, 1982).

38. Abe Masao, *Zen and Western Thought*, ed. William R. LaFleur (Honolulu: University of Hawaii Press, 1985).

39. Hans Waldenfels, *Absolute Nothingness: Foundations for a Buddhist-Christian Dialogue*, trans. J. W. Heisig (New York: Paulist Press, 1980).

40. See "Dialogues, East and West," *Eastern Buddhist*, Pt. 1, vol. 4, no. 2 (1971): 89–107; Pt. 2, vol. 5, no. 2 (1972): 107–128; Pt. 3, vol. 6, no. 2 (1973): 87–114.

41. Shinran Gutoku Shaku, *The Kyōgyōshinshō (The True Teaching, Living, Faith, and Realizing of the Pure Land)*, trans. Suzuki Daisetz Teitaro, ed. The Eastern Buddhist Society (Kyoto: Shinshū Ōtaniha, 1973). A companion volume is Suzuki's own *Collected Writings on Shin Buddhism*, ed. The Eastern Buddhist Society (Kyoto: Shinshū Ōtaniha, 1973).

42. Nakamura Hajime, *Ways of Thinking of Eastern Peoples: India, China, Tibet, Japan,* ed. Philip P. Wiener (Honolulu: East-West Center Press, 1964); idem, *Parallel Developments: A Comparative History of Ideas* (Tokyo: Kōdansha, Ltd., 1975).

43. Kajiyoshi Mitsuyuki, ed., *Higashi-no-shisō Nishi-no-shisō (Eastern Thought and Western Thought)* (Tokyo: Sanshū-sha, 1973); Nakamura Hajime, *Hikaku-shisō-ron (Comparative Thought)* (Toyko: Iwanami Shōten, 1960).

44. Saigusa Mitsuyoshi, *Hikaku-shisō-joron (Introduction to Comparative Thought)*, vol. 1; *Higashi-to-nishi-no-shisō (Eastern and Western Thought),* vol. 2; *Bukkyō-to-sieyō-shisō (Buddhism and Western Thought,)* vol. 3 (Tokyo: Shunju-sha, 1982).

45. Saigusa Mitsuyoshi, *Chūron-geju-sōran (Comprehensive View on the Verses of the Madhyamaka System*; Nāgārjuna's *Mūlamadhyamakakārikā-s)*, Japanese translation of Chinese, Tibetan, and Sanskrit texts (Tokyo: Daisanbunmei-sha, 1985).

46. Kiyota Minoru, "Buddhism in Postwar Japan. A Critical Survey," *Monumenta Nipponica* 24, nos. 1–2 (1969): 136.

SELECTED BIBLIOGRAPHY

Abe, Masao. *Zen and Western Thought*. Edited by William R. LaFleur. Honolulu: University of Hawaii Press, 1985.

Adachi, Kenji. Commissioner of the Agency for Cultural Affairs, Japan. *Japanese Religion: A Survey by the Agency for Cultural Affairs*. Tokyo and Palo Alto, Calif: Kōdansha International, Ltd., 1972.

Āgama. Tokyo: Āgama Publications Office of the Agon Shū, 1983.

Dai-nihon-bukkyō-zensho (Collected Works of Japanese Buddhism). 100 vols. Tokyo: Suzuki Research Foundation, 1973.

Dator, James Allen. *Sōka Gakkai: Builders of the Third Civilization*. Seattle: University of Washington Press, 1969.

Earhart, H. Byron. *Japanese Religion: Unity and Diversity* 2d. ed. Encino and Belmont, Calif.: Dickenson, 1974.

———. *Religion in the Japanese Experience: Sources and Interpretations*. Belmont, Calif.: Wadsworth, 1974.

Fujiwara, Hirotatsu. *I Denounce Sāka Gakkai*. Translated by Worth C. Grant. Tokyo: Nisshin Hodo Co., 1970.

Fukutake, Tadashi. *The Japanese Social Structure: Its Evolution in the Modern Century*. Translated by Ronald P. Dore. Tokyo: University of Tokyo Press, 1982.

Gibney, Frank. *Japan: The Fragile Superpower*. Tokyo: Tuttle, 1975.

Hasegawa, Nyozekan. *The Japanese Character: A Cultural Profile*. Translated by John Bester. Tokyo: Kōdansha International Ltd., 1966.

Hirakawa, Akira, et al. *Index to the Abhidharmakośa bhāṣya*. Pt. 1: Sanskrit-Tibetan-Chinese; Pt. 2: Chinese-Sanskrit. Tokyo: Daizō Shuppan K. K., 1973, 1977.

———. *Monastic Discipline for the Buddhist Nuns*. An English translation of the Chinese text of the Mahāsāṃghika-Bhikṣuṇī-Vinaya. Patna, India: Kashi Prasad Jayaswal Research Institute, 1982.

Jansen, Marius B., ed. *Changing Japanese Attitudes Toward Modernization*. Princeton, N.J.: Princeton University Press, 1965.

Japanese Association for Religious Studies, ed. *Religious Studies in Japan*. Tokyo: Maruzen Company Ltd., 1959.

Kajiyoshi, Mitsuyoshi, ed. *Higashi-no-shisō Nishi-no-shisō (Eastern Thought and Western Thought)*. Tokyo: Sanshū-sha, 1973.

Kiriyama, Yasuo. *Gense-jōbutsu (Buddhahood in This World)*. Tokyo: Rikitomi Shobō, 1983.

Kishimoto, Hideo, ed. *Japanese Religion in the Meiji Era*. Translated and adapted by John F. Howes. Tokyo: The Tōyō Bunko, 1956.

Kitagawa, Hidenori. *A Study of Indian Classical Logic—Dignāga's System*. Tokyo: Suzuki Research Foundation, 1965.

Kitagawa, Joseph M. *Religion in Japanese History*. New York: Columbia University Press, 1966.

Masatsugu, Mitsuyuki. *The Modern Samurai Society: Duty and Dependence in Contemporary Japan*. New York: American Management Association, 1982.

Matsunaga, Alicia. *The Buddhist Philosophy of Assimilation*. Rutland, Vt.: Tuttle, 1969.

Matsunaga, Daigan, and Alicia Matsunaga. *Foundations of Japanese Buddhism. Vol. 1: The Aristocratic Age*. Los Angeles and Tokyo: Buddhist Books International, 1974.

Mizuno, Kōgen. *Nanden-daizōkyō-sōsakuin (General Index to the Pāli Tripiṭaka)*. 3 vols. Tokyo: Maruzen Co., Ltd., 1961.

Monumenta Nipponica. Tokyo: Sophia University Publications.

Moore, Charles A., ed. *The Japanese Mind*. Honolulu: University of Hawaii Press, 1967.

Morioka, Kiyomi. *Religion in Changing Japanese Society*. Tokyo: University of Tokyo Press, 1975.

Morioka, Kiyomi, and William H. Newell, eds. *The Sociology of Japanese Religion*. Leiden: E. J. Brill, 1968.

Morishima, Michio. *Why Has Japan 'Succeeded'? Western Technology and Japanese Ethos*. Cambridge: Cambridge University Press, 1982.

Murata, Kiyoaki. *Japan's New Buddhism: An Objective Account of Sōka Gakkai*. New York and Tokyo: Walker/Weatherhill, 1969.

Nagao, Gadjin M., ed. *Madhyāntavibhāga-bhāṣya*. Tokyo: Suzuki Research Foundation, 1964.

Nakamura, Hajime. *Bukkyō-go-daijiten (Great Dictionary of Buddhist Terms)*. 3 vols. Tokyo: Tokyo Shoseki, 1975.

———. *Hikaku-shisō-ron (Comparative Thought)*. Tokyo: Iwanami Shōten, 1960.

———. *Indian Buddhism: A Survey with Bibliographical Notes*. Tokyo: Sanseidō Co., Ltd., 1980.

————. *Parallel Developments: A Comparative History of Ideas.* Tokyo: Kōdansha, Ltd., 1975.

————. *Ways of Thinking of Eastern Peoples: India, China, Tibet, Japan.* Rev. ed. Edited by Philip P. Wiener. Honolulu: East-West Center Press, 1964.

Nakamura, Zuiryū. *A Study of the Ratnagotravibhāga Mahāyānottaratantra-Śāstra.* Tokyo: Suzuki Research Foundation, 1967.

Nakane, Chie. *Human Relations in Japan.* A summary translation of *Tateshakai-no-ningen-kankei (Personal Relations in a Vertical Society).* Tokyo: Ministry of Foreign Affairs, 1972.

————. *Japanese Society.* Berkeley: University of California Press, 1980.

Nihon Daizōkyō (Sacred Books of Japanese Buddhism). 100 vols. Tokyo: Suzuki Research Foundation, 1973.

Nishida, Kitarō. *A Study of Good (Zen-no-kenkyū).* Translated by V. H. Viglielmo. A Japanese Unesco Publication. Tokyo: Ministry of Education, 1960.

Nishitani, Keiji. *Religion and Nothingness (Shūkyō-towa-nanika?).* Translated by Jan van Bragt. Berkeley: University of California Press, 1982.

Obermiller, Evgenii, trans., *Bu-ston: History of Buddhism (Chos-ḥbyung).* Tokyo: Suzuki Research Foundation, 1964.

Offner, Clark B., and Henry van Straelen. *Modern Japanese Religions: With Special Emphasis upon Their Doctrines of Healing.* Tokyo: Rupert Enderle, 1963.

Ono, Gemmyō, general ed. *Bussho-kaisetsu-daijiten (Great Explanatory Dictionary of Buddhist Literature).* 12 vols. Tokyo: Daito Shuppan-sha, 1933.

Saigusa, Mitsuyoshi. *Chūron-geju-sōran (Comprehensive View on the Verses of the Madhyamaka System; Nāgārjuna's Mūlamadhyamakakārikā-s).* Japanese translation of Chinese, Tibetan and Sanskrit texts. Tokyo: Daisanbunmei-sha, 1985.

Saigusa, Mitsuyoshi. *Hikaku-shisō-joron (Introduction to Comparative Thought).* Vol. 1; *Higashi-to-nishi-no-shisō (Eastern and Western Thought).* Vol. 2; *Bukkyō-to-seiyō-shisō (Buddhism and Western Thought),* Vol. 3. Tokyo: Shunju-sha, 1982.

Shinran, Gutoku Shaku. *The Kyōgyōshinshō (The True Teaching, Living, Faith, and Realizing of the Pure Land).* Translated by Suzuki Daisetz Teitarō. Kyoto: Shinshū Ōtaniha, 1973.

Shively, Donald H., ed. *Tradition and Modernization in Japanese Culture.* Princeton, N.J.: Princeton University Press, 1971.

Smith, Robert J. *Japanese Society.* Cambridge: Cambridge University Press, 1983.

Sutta-piṭaka ("Basket of Sūtras" containing the teachings of the Buddha). Translated by various scholars for the Pāli Text Society. London: Luzac & Company Ltd., 1957. Translations: *Dialogues of the Buddha; Middle Length Sayings; Kindred Sayings; Gradual Sayings,* and *Minor Anthologies.*

Suzuki, Daisetz T. *Collected Writings on Shin Buddhism.* Kyoto: Shinshū Ōtaniha, 1973.

————, ed. *Catalogue and Index of the Tibetan Tripiṭaka.* Tokyo: Suzuki Research Foundation, 1960.

————, comp. *An Index to the Laṅkāvatāra Sūtra.* Tokyo: Suzuki Research Foundation, 1965.

Suzuki, Daisetz T., and Yamaguchi Susumu, comp. and ed. *The Tibetan Tripiṭaka.* 168 vols. Peking ed. Tokyo: Suzuki Research Foundation, 1955–1961.

Takakusu, Junjirō, and Watanabe Kaikyoku, eds. *Taishō-shinshū-daizōkyō (The Tripitaka in Chinese).* 100 vols. Tokyo: Society for the Publication of the Taisho Edition of the Tripitaka, 1924–1929.

Tamura, Yoshirō, with William P. Woodard. *Living Buddhism in Japan: Interviews with Ten Japanese Buddhist Leaders.* Tokyo: International Institute for the Study of Religions, 1960.

Thomsen, Harry. *The New Religions of Japan.* Tokyo: E. Tuttle, 1963.

Tsuji, Naoshirō, superviser. *Wogihara's Sanskrit-Chinese-Japanese Dictionary.* 16 vols. Tokyo: Suzuki Research Foundation, 1964-1974.

Tsunoda, Ryūsaku, Wm. Theodore de Bary, and Donald Keene, comp. and eds. *Sources of the Japanese Tradition.* New York: Columbia University Press, 1958.

Ui, Hakuju, ed. *Index to the Bodhisattva-bhūmi.* Pts. 1 and 2. Tokyo: Suzuki Research Foundation, 1961.

Vogel, Ezra F. *Japan as Number One.* Cambridge, Mass.: Harvard University Press, 1979.

Waldenfels, Hans. *Absolute Nothingness: Foundations for a Buddhist-Christian Dialogue.* Translated by J. W. Heisig. New York: Paulist Press, 1980.

Watanabe, Shōkō. *Japanese Buddhism: A Critical Appraisal.* Translated by Alfred Bloom. Tokyo: Kokusai Bunka Shinkōkai, 1968.

Woodard, William P. *The Allied Occupation of Japan, 1945-52, and Japanese Religions.* Leiden: E. J. Brill, 1972.

Woronoff, Jon, *Japan: The Coming Social Crisis.* Tokyo: Lotus Press, 1980.

Yamada, Ryūjō. *Bongo-butten-no-shobunken (Various Literature on Sanskrit Buddhist Texts).* Kyoto: Heiryakuji Shōten, 1959.

————. *Daijō-bukkyō-seiritsuron-josetsu (Introduction to the Development of Mahāyāna Buddhism).* Kyoto: Heiryakuji Shōten, 1959.

Yamaguchi, Susumu, ed., *Madhyāntavibhāgaṭīkā de Ācārya Sthiramati.* Tokyo: Suzuki Research Foundation, 1966.

Index

266; as a recent trend in scholarship, 648-49; and redemption, 253; and repentance, 252-53; and science, 255-56, 258-59, 261-62, 263, 271; and self-consciousness, 251; and self-criticism, 253; and self-identity, 252; and self-realization, 265; and social action, 250; and the temporal-historical foundations of culture, 252; and time, 252, 260-61; Tokyo School interchange with, 248-49, 268; and the Virgin Birth, 260; and Western thought, 245, 246, 249, 250, 251, 254-55, 256- 57, 258-59, 260, 261, 264, 265, 266, 267, 271; and world transcendence, 264-65. *See also* Buddhism in Japan; Zen Buddhism; *name of specific person or topic*

Lahbabi, Aziz, 211, 212
La Katos, Imre, 7
Lambert, Bernard, 441
Lao Tzu, 117, 284
Latin America: anticlericalism in, 187; and capitalism, 178- 79, 182, 364; Catholicism in, 177-89; and Christian Democratic party, 185-87; colonialism in, 178-81, 184, 188; and communism, 182, 188; communism in, 185-86, 188, 364; and conservatism, 185; "crusades" in, 183; dissent in, 180-81; and the distribution of wealth, 185-86, 364; Episcopalianism in, 364; and fascism, 182-83, 188; hierarchy in, 177-78, 184; liberation theology in, 133, 183, 185-86, 187, 188; and the middle class, 183, 186; minorities in, 180-82; modernization in, 177-89; Protestantism in, 179, 180-81; and social justice, 364; symbolism in, 183-84, 185, 187; tradition in, 177-89; and the United States, 188-89. *See also name of specific country*
Latourette, Kenneth Scott, 350
Lausanne Covenant (1977), 145
Lay Buddhism, 640-43
Lebanon, 231, 447, 448-49, 450
Lebret, L. J., 363
Lee, Mother Ann, 96

Legal system (Islam). See *Shariah*
Legge, James, 614
Lehman, Paul L., 133, 134, 163
Leo XIII (pope), 331
Lesbianism, 107
Leung In-shing, 625
Lvi-Strauss, Claude, 12
Lewis, Edwin, 130
Liang Ch'i-chao, 616
Liang Shu-ming, 277, 623-24
Liberalism: and American Protestantism, 124-25, 127-35, 136, 138, 140, 141, 142-43, 154; and the black churches, 141; and Catholicism, 136, 363; in China, 615; and the Christian humanists, 127, 128-29; and contextual theology, 134-35; definition of, 154; and ecumenicalism, 136; and ecumenism, 363; and the electronic pulpit, 142; and God is dead theology, 131-32; and humanism, 614; and Islam, 207, 210; and Judaism, 416; and liberation theology, 133- 34; as modernism, 126; and the new morality, 134-35; and the "new theology", 128-29; and "realistic theology", 129- 30; and "religionless Christianity", 132; and science, 130; and secular gospel/humanism, 131-32; and the social gospel, 124-25; and truth, 129; and World War I, 127
Liberation theology: and American Protestantism, 133-34, 140, 141, 154; and anticlericalism, 187; and the Bible, 167; and Catholicism, 133, 134, 171, 183, 364; and Christianity, 167-68; and covenantal theology, 168; definition of, 154, 185; and the distribution of wealth, 185-86; and ecumenism, 364; and evangelicalism, 134; and feminism, 100, 101, 108-12, 134, 167, 168; and history, 168; in Latin America, 133, 183, 185-86, 187, 188; and liberalism, 133-34; and liberation as a process, 108; and Marxism, 134, 167-68, 171, 185; and materialism, 168; and the moral majority, 141; and natural law, 168; and oppression, 108-10, 167; and Presbyterianism, 133-34; promi-

About the Contributors

GUSTAVO BENAVIDES is on the faculty of the Department of Religion, Villanova University. His works include chapters in *Buddhist and Western Philosophy* (1981), *Buddhist and Western Psychology* (1983), *Sein und Nichts in der abendlandischen Mystik* (1984), and *The Many Faces of Religion and Society* (1985).

JOHN B. COBB, JR., is Ingraham Professor of Theology in the School of Theology at Claremont, and Avery Professor of Religion, Claremont Graduate School. He is the founder and director of the Center for Process Studies, and publisher of *Process Studies*. His works include *A Christian Natural Theology, The Structure of Christian Existence, Christ in a Pluralistic Age, Process Theology as Political Theology,* and *Beyond Dialogue: Toward a Mutual Transformation of Christianity and Buddhism.*

DEMETRIOS J. CONSTANTELOS is Charles Cooper Townsend Distinguished Professor of History and Religious Studies, Stockton State College, Pomona, New Jersey. His publications include *Byzantine Philanthropy and Social Welfare* (1968), *Marriage, Sexuality, Celibacy: A Greek Orthodox Perspective* (1986), *Orthodox Theology and Diakonia: Trends and Prospects* (1981), *Understanding the Greek Orthodox Church* (1982), and *Poverty, Society, and Philanthropy in the Late Medieval Greek World* (1987). He is also associate editor of *The Journal of Ecumenical Studies.*

ARTHUR B. CRABTREE, an ordained Baptist minister, holds positions as Professor at the International Baptist Seminary, Zurich; the Eastern Baptist Seminary, Philadelphia, Pennsylvania; and Villanova University. His works include *The Restored Relationship,* a translation of Wilhelm Vischer's *The Witness of the OT to Christ* and articles in theological journals, including *The Journal of Ecumenical Studies*.

KHALID DURAN, Visiting Professor at Temple University, has been associated with the Islamic Research Institute at Islamabad University, the National Institute of Modern Languages in Pakistan, and the German Oriental Institute at Hamburg University. A leading scholar in Islamic studies, he has authored numerous articles as well as several books in German, including two volumes entitled *Das ist mein Islam* (1984–85) and *Islam und politische Extremismus* (1987).

JOHN L. ESPOSITO is Professor of Religious Studies and Director of the Center for International Studies at the College of the Holy Cross, Worcester, Massachusetts. His recent publications include *Islam and Politics*, 2d rev. ed., 1987, *Islam: The Straight Path* (1988), and *Islam in Aisa* (1987).

CHARLES WEI-HSUN FU is Professor of Buddhism and Far Eastern Thought at Temple University. He has authored numerous books and articles on Eastern and Western thought, among them, *Movements and Issues in World Religions,* 1987. He is editor of a series of volumes on Resources in Asian Philosophy and Religion for Greenwood Press, and editor of the Asian Thought and Culture Series.

PEI-JUNG FU is Professor of Philosophy at National Taiwan University. In 1986 he was Visiting Professor for "Chair Verbiest," Katholieke Universiteit, Leuven, Belgium. His works include *Explication of the Doctrine of Heaven in Confucianism and Taoism* (1985), *Beyond Absurdity—A Study of Albert Camus* (1985), and *The Way to Successful Life* (1985).

ASHOK K. GANGADEAN is Professor in the Department of Philosophy, Haverford College. An expert in logic, Western and Indian philosophy, he has many publications in these fields.

STEVEN HEINE is on the faculty of the Department of Religion, Villanova University, and served as a Fulbright senior researcher at Komazawa University, Tokyo. His publications include *Existential and Ontological Dimensions of Time in Heidegger and Dogen* and *A Blade of Grass: Japanese Poetry and Aesthetics in Dogen Zen*.

KENNETH K. INADA is Professor of Buddhism and Comparative Philosophy at the State University of New York at Buffalo. Among his works are *Nagarjuna, A Translation of His Mulamadhyamakakarika* (1970) and numerous articles in the *Journal of Chinese Philosophy* and *Philosophy East and West*. In addition, he has served as editor for the SUNY Series in Buddhist Studies as well as for

East-West Dialogues in Aesthetics, Guide to Buddhist Philosophy, and *Buddhism and American Thought.*

WHALEN LAI is Associate Professor in the Department of Religion at the University of California, Davis. He has authored numerous publications in the fields of Chinese and Japanese Buddhism, Confucianism, and interreligious dialogue.

SHU-HSIEN LIU is Professor and Chair of the Department of Chinese Philosophy at the Chinese University of Hong Kong. Among his many publications are *The Development and Completion of Chu Hsi's Philosophical Thought* (1982), *Harmony and Strife: Contemporary Perspectives East and West,* and articles in *Philosophy East and West, Inquiry, Journal of Chinese Philosophy,* and other professional journals.

JOSEPH MARGOLIS is Distinguished Professor in the Department of Philosophy, Temple University. An internationally known scholar in ontology, ethics, aesthetics, and other areas of Western philosophy, he has published many books and articles on these subjects.

ROBERT CUMMINGS NEVILLE, an ordained minister in the United Methodist Church, is Professor of Religion, Philosophy, and Theology, Boston University. Among his many publications are *The Puritan Smile, The Tao and the Daimon* and articles in *Philosophy East and West* and *The Journal of Chinese Philosophy.*

R. PANIKKAR is Professor Emeritus in the Department of Religion, the University of California, Santa Barbara. A world-renowned scholar, he has published innumerable books and articles in the fields of Hinduism, Catholicism, and interreligious dialogue.

ROSEMARY RADFORD RUETHER is Professor of Applied Theology at the Garrett-Evangelical Theological Seminary at Northwestern University. Her work in the area of feminism has achieved worldwide recognition. She has numerous publications in this and other fields, including *Religion and Sexism: Images of Women in Jewish and Christian Traditions* and *New Woman/New Earth: Sexist Ideologies and Human Liberation.*

NORBERT SAMUELSON is Professor of Judaica in the Department of Religion, Temple University. A well-known scholar on the philosophies of Spinoza and Maimonides, as well as medieval and modern Jewish thought, he has published extensively on these subjects. He also has edited several studies of Jewish philosophy.

ARVIND SHARMA is on the faculty of Philosophical Studies, McGill University, and was formerly Professor of Religious Studies at the University of Sydney. Among his books are *The Hindu Scriptural Value System and India's Economic Development* and *Religious Ferment in Modern India*. He is associate editor of *The Journal of South Asian Literature*.

TAMARA SONN was formerly Assistant Professor of Islamic Studies in the Department of Religion, Temple University. Previously she had been associated with the School of Religion, University of Iowa. She is the author of *Bandali al-Jawzi's History of Intellectual Movements in Islam*.

GERHARD E. SPIEGLER is President of Elizabethtown College, Elizabethtown, Pennsylvania. Previously he has served as Vice President for Academic Affairs at Temple University, and Professor and Chair of the Department of Religion. His publications include contributions to *The Eternal Covenant: Schleiermacher's Experiment in Cultural Theology, The Future of Empirical Theology,* and *Schleiermacher as Contemporary,* as well as articles in *The Christian Scholar, Religion and Life, Criterion,* and *Quest.*

F. ERNEST STOEFFLER is a minister in the United Methodist Church and Professor Emeritus in the Department of Religion, Temple University. Trained as a historian of Christianity, his personal inclination has led him into the history of ideas. He is a leading authority in the field of sixteenth- and seventeenth-century European Protestantism, with an emphasis on the Pietistic tradition (including Puritanism in England and Holland). He is the author of *The Rise of Evangelical Pietism,* along with numerous other books and articles.

LEONARD SWIDLER is Professor of Catholic Thought and Interreligious Dialogue in the Department of Religion, Temple University. He is the author of numerous books and articles in the fields of contemporary Catholicism and interreligious dialogue. He is editor of *The Journal of Ecumenical Studies*.

PAUL VAN BUREN, an ordained priest of the Episcopalian Church, was formerly Professor and Chair of the Department of Religion at Temple University. Among his publications are *The Secular Meaning of the Gospel, The Edges of Language,* and a two-volume text, *A Theology of the Jewish Christian Reality*.

SANDRA A. WAWRYTKO is currently on the faculty of the Department of Philosophy at San Diego State University. Her professional titles include Executive Director of the International Society for Philosophy and Psychotherapy (which she founded), and Secretary-Treasurer of the International Society for Chinese Philosophy. For four years she served as Secretary General of the World Congress of Logotherapy, for which she edited three volumes of conference proceedings. She is the author of *The Undercurrent of Feminine Philosophy in*

Eastern and Western Thought and of numerous articles in professional volumes and journals on comparative Chinese-Western philosophy and the philosophy of women. Presently she is completing a retrospective on feminism in the last twenty years, *Women in Transition: Beyond Liberation,* collaborating on a new series of translations of key Taoist philosophical texts from Chinese, and editing a ten-volume series in philosophy and psychotherapy. She is also editor-in-chief of *The International Journal of Philosophy and Psychotherapy: Hsin,* and co-author of the first six volumes in Chinese thought for Charles Wei-hsun Fu, ed., *Resources in Asian Philosophy and Religion Series* (Greenwood Press).

J. PHILIP WOGAMAN is Professor of Christian Social Ethics at the Wesley Theological Seminary in Washington, D.C. A leading authority in the fields of Christian social ethics, he has published extensively in this area.